ENCYCLOPEDIA OF SPORTS FILMS

K Edgington
Thomas L. Erskine
with
James M. Welsh

THE SCARECROW PRESS, INC.
Lanham • Toronto • Plymouth, UK
2011

Published by Scarecrow Press, Inc.
A wholly owned subsidiary of The Rowman & Littlefield Publishing Group, Inc.
4501 Forbes Boulevard, Suite 200, Lanham, Maryland 20706
http://www.scarecrowpress.com

Estover Road, Plymouth PL6 7PY, United Kingdom

British Library Cataloguing in Publication Information Available

All images from the *Literature/Film Quarterly* archives.

Library of Congress Cataloging-in-Publication Data

Edgington, K, 1946–
Encyclopedia of sports films / K Edgington, Thomas L. Erskine with James M. Welsh.
p. cm.
Includes bibliographical references and index.
ISBN 978-0-8108-7652-1 (hardback : alk. paper) — ISBN 978-0-8108-7653-8 (ebook)
1. Sports films—Catalogs. I. Erskine, Thomas L. II. Welsh, James Michael. III. Title.
PN1995.9.S67E34 2011
791.43'6579—dc22 2010030840

™ The paper used in this publication meets the minimum requirements of American National Standard for Information Sciences—Permanence of Paper for Printed Library Materials, ANSI/NISO Z39.48-1992.

Printed in the United States of America

CONTENTS

Acknowledgments
v
Introduction
vii
Films A to Z
1
Appendix A: Films by Sport
495
Appendix B: Chronological Title List
501
Appendix C: Movies Made for Television or Direct to Video
507
Appendix D: Movies Inspired by or Based upon Actual Events
511
Appendix E: Sports Documentaries
515
Appendix F: ESPY Awards for Best Sports Movie
517
Bibliography
519
Index
525
About the Authors
551

ACKNOWLEDGMENTS

K AND TOM would like to thank Jim Welsh for his assistance and support, not only in supplying some of the entries, but also for securing photos and working with Scarecrow Press. We would also like thank our editor at Scarecrow, Stephen Ryan, whose faith and patience enabled us to complete what turned out to be a much broader field than we had initially envisioned; Blackwell Library at Salisbury University, for allowing us access to the Literature/Film Archives, with its extensive collection of press kits; Wendy Samuels, for proofreading the manuscript; our student intern, Jeff Goldstein, for an excellent job of copyediting and fact checking; and Edna Quinn, who helped with the bibliography and supplied the perseverance necessary for what seemed at times to be a never-ending task, especially in light of the spate of sports films that have been produced in the last five years.

K is grateful to her Towson University colleagues Carl Behm, for arranging Jeff's internship; Margaret Benner, for assistance with esoteric grammar questions; and Professor Emerita Jo-Ann Pilardi, for her thoughtful comments and valued encouragement.

Tom would also like to express his appreciation to his grandchildren, Carly and Caleb Erskine, for providing a youthful perspective on films about gymnastics and skateboarding.

—K Edgington and Tom Erskine

I would also thank acquisitions editor Stephen H. Ryan, for working long and hard on personal time in order to design the book's appendices, and production editor Jessica McCleary, who is one of the very best in the business.

—Jim Welsh
Salisbury University Emeritus

INTRODUCTION

SPORTS AND FILM have been coupled since the early days of the motion picture, when filmed sports proved enormously popular. The first feature-length film, produced in 1894, was a staged boxing match between Michael Leonard and John Cushing, shot by the Edison Company with a single stationary camera. Later that year, Edison produced pieces on wrestling and body building. In France, the Lumiere Brothers followed suit. In America, where the motion picture industry would develop as entertainment for the masses rather than as an art form, "story films" featuring fans as well as athletes amused audiences. Perhaps the earliest of the sports story films is *Casey at the Bat* (1899), which takes its title from a poem; it shows a batter striking out and arguing with the umpire. In the first decade of the twentieth century, newsreels including sporting events appeared in Europe and the United States.

During the era of silent film, Harold Lloyd, Buster Keaton, and Charlie Chaplin all built comedies around sports, showcasing their athletic abilities. Sports comedies continued into the 1930s with the Marx Brothers and W. C. Fields, while boxing dramas attracted audiences who identified with working class heroes. During World War II, *Pride of the Yankees* (1942), the story of Lou Gehrig, was released with opening title cards connecting Gehrig's death with the heroic sacrifices of American soldiers. Following World War II, a gaggle of biopics was produced as well as screwball comedies, like *Pat and Mike* (1952) and *Rhubarb* (1951) and the musicals *Take Me Out to the Ballgame* (1949) and *Damned Yankees* (1958). In the sixties few sports films—comedy or drama—were being made, but in the bicentennial year, *The Bad News Bears* hit the silver screen, as did *Rocky*, which won an Academy Award for Best Picture, triggering a resurgence of sports films. Advances in technology have enabled moderately well-coordinated actors to look like professional athletes, thereby allowing studios to take even greater advantage of star appeal in casting.

The proliferation of sports films since the 1970s coincides with the emergence of African American studies, women's studies, and cultural studies as distinct academic disciplines, and not surprisingly, a growing body of scholarship has been devoted to sports films. Scholars, such as Aaron Baker, C. Richard King, David Leonard, and David Rowe, provide provocative readings of sports films and raise sometimes troubling questions about race, gender, sexuality, class, and cultural values. Academics generally agree that cinematographic representations of sports embody and reinforce cultural values in powerful ways, a power that derives in part from the realism with which athletic events are filmed.

Reel Sports

No matter what the sport and no matter whether slapstick comedy or gut-wrenching drama, sports films go to great lengths to present athletic action realistically. Athletes have been employed as actors in the roles of athletes from the very first. The argument has been made that boxer "Gentleman" Jim Corbett, whose staged bout against Peter Courtney was filmed in 1896, is the first movie star; following his retirement from the ring, he signed an exclusive film contract and played himself in scripted shorts before moving on to low-budget features. High school athlete Rob Brown (*Finding Forrester*, 2000; *Coach Carter*, 2005; *The Express*, 2008) had given no thought to a career in acting when he tried out for *Finding Forrester*—he was just hoping to earn some quick cash to pay his phone bill by landing a nonspeaking role. (Between his next films, he played football at Amherst College.)

Real athletes from Babe Ruth to Babe Didrikson have portrayed themselves, and real actors have trained with professional athletes to prepare for their parts, sometimes undergoing physical transformations. Production on *Raging Bull* came to a halt in order for Robert De Niro to add fifty pounds for scenes set after his character's retirement from the ring. Hilary Swank gained twenty pounds of muscle training for her role in *Million Dollar Baby* (2004). Will Smith put on thirty pounds during the year he spent learning to box for the role of Muhammad Ali. Executing Ali's famous "rope-a-dope" tactic against George Foreman, played by professional boxer Charles Shufford, Smith absorbed real punches. (Director Mann instructed Shufford to hit hard, but not knock Smith out.) Mickey Rourke, who took a sabbatical from acting to box professionally, needed to retrain for *The Wrestler* (2008). Although stunt doubles performed the high-risk moves, Rourke faced professional opponents from the ultraviolent Combat Zone Wrestling League, and scenes were filmed during a regular event at the New Alhambra Arena in New Jersey.

Cameos by sports figures and scenes featuring commentary by noted sportscasters contribute to the realism, as do settings, sometimes elaborately reconstructed: For *61** (2001), producer-director Billy Crystal's tribute to the home run duel between Yankees Roger Maris and Mickey Mantle, Crystal transformed Detroit's old Tiger Stadium into Yankee Stadium, even duplicating the color of paint on the seats and adding a digital skyline. Action scenes from the futuristic *Rollerball* (1975) were filmed in a refurbished stadium used for bicycle races during the Munich Olympics. Director Norman Jewison kept his film creepily within the realm of believability, avoiding the usual trappings of science fiction in terms of sets and costumes.

Camera work and editing reinforce verisimilitude as well. Camera operators have shot sequences on ice skates during hockey games and on roller skates during boxing matches. They've filmed on skis and on motorcycles; they've been strapped into race cars and dangled from platforms. Sometimes cranes are used and sometimes robots, but these are expensive. For capturing the action of sports like football, basketball, and soccer, directors often rely on television crews from Fox or ESPN, which use twenty cameras to capture live field action during regular broadcasts. Editing can place the viewer in the ring or behind the wheel—racing films are notorious for their realism, sometimes at the expense of plot since dialogue can't be heard over engine noises. James Taylor and Beach Boy costar Dennis Wilson barely open their mouths in *Two-Lane Blacktop* (1971), and the first forty minutes of Steve McQueen's *Le Mans* (1971) pass without a word of dialogue. Editing on *Le Mans* required two months to match engine noises to vehicles and another six months for carving up almost a hundred miles of footage.

Digital technology has expanded the director's toolkit, sometimes easing rather than taxing the budget. A single location can be used to shoot a season's worth—or a career's worth—of contests by digitally altering skylines and weather. Sellout crowds can be created with a relatively small group of extras and without relying on cardboard cutouts in the upper tiers. Clint Eastwood used two thousand extras to fill Ellis Park to its sixty-two-thousand capacity for the World Cup finals in *Invictus* (2009). Blue screen and green screen technologies allow actors to complete athletic movements—triple spins, slam dunks, leaping catches, diving saves—and digitalization can insert actors into footage of actual games (a common practice in soccer and American football movies). Actors portraying baseball players or tennis players need learn only the motions: the balls get added later.

While it has often been said that people don't go to sports films to watch sports, it is a truism that movie audiences expect to be entertained, and the artistry of action sequences carries a bundle of entertainment value. Audience enjoyment also comes from vicarious identification with underdogs, from come-from-behind victories, from the winning score at the end of the game. Not surprisingly, the plots of many sports films fall into patterns of predictability.

Plots and Themes: The Winning Formula

Winning isn't everything, but moviemakers almost always allow the underdogs to triumph after overcoming adversity. In the United States especially, the Protestant work ethic comes into play. Natural talent must be developed through effort for the individual to prevail, and an athlete who relies solely on talent is often portrayed as immoral, unethical, and/or merely unpleasant. In team sports, individual effort sometimes is carried through the figure of the coach. The training montage, often with dramatic or energetic musical accompaniment, and the inspirational locker room speech are staples in sports films, as is the soul-searching scene in the darkened arena or on the empty field, which conveys religious overtones and underscores the character-building aspect of athletics.

Athletes and coaches sometimes fall prey to greed and ambition, or they neglect family; at other times athletes are pushed too hard by coaches or family, or coaches are pressured by owners or fans. Most emerge better people for having faced adversity. Traditionally, sports films are uplifting and upbeat, even the ones like *Brian's Song* (1971) and *The Express* (2008) that end with an athlete's death.

The formulaic nature of mainstream sports films lends itself to parody, and a rich subgenre has emerged. *Blades of Glory* (2007) spoofs the romantic comedy *The Cutting Edge* (1992); Ben Stiller's farce about competition between male models, *Zoolander* (2001), incorporates a number of sports film clichés, as does *Dodgeball: A True Underdog Story* (2005), whose original ending—in which the underdogs lost—proved too unpopular during screenings and was altered to meet audience expectations. Woody Allen takes a swipe at *The Stratton Story* (1949) in *Radio Days* (1987) with a one-armed, one-legged, blind pitcher who continues his winning ways beyond the grave. Academy Award–winning documentarian Jessica Wu turned to table tennis (*Ping Pong Playa*, 2007) to poke fun at the immigrant experience. *Balls of Fury* (2007), another table tennis movie, satirizes the Bruce Lee classic *Enter the Dragon* (1973). *Kingpin* (1996), starring Woody Harrelson and Dennis Quaid, veterans of films in which sports are taken seriously, lampoons the pastoral sentimentality of *The Natural* (1984) and *Field of Dreams* (1989).

Of course, not all sports films follow the same script. Sometimes the aging veteran fails to save the day and secure the future. In *Pastime* (1991) the main character learns—on his first date with the woman he's fallen for—that he has been cut from the team. Instead of a traditional plot moving the character toward a coaching career and a loving relationship, *Pastime* has the protagonist drop dead, a broken and frustrated man. In *The Wrestler* (2008), Mickey Rourke's character faces a fading career with a literally broken heart. Hard work doesn't always lift the struggling rookie out of poverty and into the majors (*Sugar*, 2009); the underdogs lose the big game (*The Bad News Bears*, 1976, 2005); Casey does indeed strike out (*Casey at the Bat*, 1899).

Sidelined: Gender, Race, and Ethnicity

A year after Casey fanned on film, women were included in the Paris Olympics. By 1897 African Americans had formed a professional baseball league; black athletes joined white teams in the early years of professional football. Hispanic Americans introduced rodeo to the West, attracting Native Americans. Yet in Hollywood, sports film has been and remains a white male domain. Minority men and women of all races have been underrepresented and negatively stereotyped.

The majority of sports films with Native American and African American heroes are biopics. In *Jim Thorpe: All-American* (1951) and *Running Brave* (1983), Jim Thorpe and Billy Mills are played by Caucasian actors, Burt Lancaster and Robby Benson, respectively. Jackie Robinson played himself in *The Jackie Robinson Story* (1950). In *The Spirit of Youth* (1938), Joe Louis plays "Joe Thomas," whose life and career trajectory parallel his own. Both films, intended to help white audiences accept black athletes, reinforce individual effort and the American dream. Today, these films are recognized as blatantly patronizing.

Women and girls have rarely been portrayed as serious athletes on the silver screen and almost never in biopics. (A trio of made-for-television tearjerkers based on the lives of Maureen Connolly, Jill Kinmont, and Babe Didrikson have faded into obscurity.) In *National Velvet* (1944), Elizabeth Taylor rides her horse to victory in a steeplechase, but she is only twelve, has disguised herself as a male jockey, and faints from exhaustion immediately after crossing the finish. Not quite a decade later, in 1952, Katharine Hepburn competes in golf and tennis in the romantic comedy *Pat and Mike*, followed almost a quarter of a century later by Tatum O'Neal, who takes to the mound only because she seeks to reunite her mother and her coach (*The Bad News Bears*). Occasionally, a woman is cast as a villainous team owner or as a coach in a comedy, but for most of the twentieth century, women and girls portray minor characters appearing as wives, mothers, daughters, or girlfriends.

By the 1990s, sports films showed signs of catching up with the times. *White Men Can't Jump* (1992) foregrounds race and takes a different twist on the biracial buddy film. Spike Lee's *He Got Game* (1998) serves as an urban antidote to the white-dominated world of basketball and baseball films set in the Midwest. Penny Marshall's *A League of Their Own* (1992), although failing to meet feminist expectations, was a significant step for Hollywood. Sports films continue to move in a more inclusive direction. *Love and Basketball* (2000) and

Wimbledon (2004) feature women succeeding at the professional level while ironing out romantic conflicts with their less-successful male counterparts. *Million Dollar Baby* (2004) won four Oscars, including Best Actress for Hilary Swank as boxer Maggie Fitzgerald. *Sugar* (2008) examines baseball from the perspective of a Dominican immigrant. Foreign films, such as *Chak De! India* (2007) and Iran's *Offside* (2006) convey strong feminist messages.

However, the playing field can look level from one perspective and tilted from another, and underrepresentation means that any portrayal can be called upon to carry a burden of meaning. *The Blind Side* (2009) presents the adoptive mother of lineman Michael Oher as a strong and complex character, but in the process, neglects Oher, the ostensible subject of the film. Furthermore, *The Blind Side* fits into a pattern of films featuring minority athletes whose achievements are credited, at least partially, to white mentors. Because such films can be read from contrasting perspectives, they invite discussion and can be put to effective use in the classroom.

About *The Encyclopedia of Sports Films*

Ongoing debates about how sports film should be defined and whether sports films constitute a separate genre have not resulted in consensus, but have brought to light how widespread sports references are in movies. It is not our goal in the *Encyclopedia* to delimit or catalog the genre, but to present a representative sample of the range of films that have been classified as sports films. Time and space, the usual culprits, require that we set some boundaries. Therefore, we have excluded from our expanded entries

- documentaries, which deserve their own volume,
- films not readily available in VHS or DVD format at the time of publication,
- made-for-television movies, except for a handful of exceptional titles, and
- films about dog shows, spelling bees, crossword puzzle contests, chess tournaments, beauty pageants, and bullfighting.

We have included films from the silent era, films by prominent directors, films by independents, box office hits, and a few little-known gems. In addition to the expanded entries, we have also identified other sports films, providing credit information and a very brief summary. Readers are encouraged to look up these films on websites such as imdb.com or amazon.com to find additional information. We have also indicated if a film is or has been available on DVD and if not, its VHS availability. Of course, films are being released on a weekly basis, so for those films that do not indicate a DVD release, readers should check their status online.

A

ABOVE THE RIM (1994)

DIRECTOR: Jeff Pollack. SCREENPLAY: Barry Michael Cooper, Jeff Pollack. STORY: Benny Media, Jeff Pollack. PRODUCERS: Benny Media, Jeff Pollack. CINEMATOGRAPHY: Tom Priestly Jr. EDITING: James Mitchell, Michael Ripps. MUSIC: Marcus Miller. PRODUCTION DESIGN: Ina Mayhew. COSTUME DESIGN: Karen Perry.
CAST: Duane Martin (Kyle Watson), Leon Robinson (as Leon) (Shep), Tupac Shakur (Birdie), Tonya Pinkins (Mailika), Marlon Wayans (Bugaloo), Bernie Mac (Flip).
RUNNING TIME: 96 minutes. Color
DVD: New Line Home Video.

For talented point guard Kyle Watson (Duane Martin), basketball promises a ticket out of Harlem, but the cocky teenager is in danger of losing his passport. Fifteen years earlier Thomas "Shep" Shepard (Leon Robinson) surrendered his opportunity after the accidental death of a teammate, Nutso. Getting "above the rim" requires an inner strength that Kyle has yet to develop and that Shep has difficulty summoning. The two men become caught in an uneasy relationship when Coach Mike Rollins (David Bailey) arranges a job for Shep at the high school as a security guard. Shep begins dating Kyle's mother, Mailika (Tonya Pinkins), while Kyle begins hanging out with Shep's drug-dealing brother, Birdie (Tupac Shakur). Kyle needs a role model, but Shep is accustomed to running from responsibility. The plot is formulaic, the characters underdeveloped, but the on-court action is fast paced, and Tupac Shakur plays the villain with finesse.

The film opens with a nightmare that seems to reenact Nutso's accident: Shep has challenged Nutso to a contest to determine who can strike the backboard higher with his palm, but when Nutso takes a long running start and hits the lower corner, the backboard gives way, and his momentum propels him through a window to his death in the street below. Immediately after the accident, Shep's guilt, along with intense scrutiny from the press, interfered with his playing. The newspaper headline "Pure Talent, Fatal Flaw" predicted Shep's future; unable to secure the scholarship that had given him and his mother hope of a better life, he quit playing basketball and fled home, leaving behind his mother and Birdie. His mother's death has brought him back to his old Harlem neighborhood, where Birdie has become the local drug king. Rollins, who now coaches Kyle, hopes to lure Shep into coaching a team for the Rucker Park Shoot Out. Meanwhile, Birdie, who has bet heavily on his own team, plans to recruit Kyle to play for him.

The principal characters all appear at a basketball game where Kyle, intent on impressing a Georgetown University scout in the stands, hogs the ball, showboats,

Leon Robinson (right) and Darius Hawkins (left) in *Above the Rim*

and with the clock running out, misses a jump shot that would have won the game. As the players exit the floor, Shep prevents Mailika, who missed the game because of work, from catching up with Kyle; meanwhile, Birdie, who does see the game and anticipates the angry locker room response to Kyle's antics, instructs one of Kyle's old friends, Bugaloo (Marlon Wayans), to bring Kyle to Birdie's club afterward. In spite of a reprimand from Coach Rollins, Kyle tells Birdie he intends to honor his commitment to the coach's team; however, Kyle does not turn down Birdie's hospitality, which includes a willing young woman and the money to pay her.

That Kyle is headed for trouble becomes even more apparent the next day. After expressing to his mother his frustration that he has not heard from Georgetown, he leaves with Bugaloo, who has recently been released from prison and of whom Mailika disapproves. As soon as the boys are outside, Kyle announces he needs to relieve himself and proceeds to do so over a railing. This action prompts a verbal exchange that sets the tone for Kyle's subsequent conversations with the homeboys. Soon Kyle and Bugaloo are at a playground shooting hoops. When a derelict known as Flip (Bernie Mac) tries to compete against Kyle, the teenager first ridicules, then physically abuses the man until Shep happens by and intervenes. Kyle backs off, intimidated by Shep's size and no-nonsense attitude. Flip, who once played with Shep, recognizes him immediately and refers to their former glory as high school champions, but for Shep, of course, the past holds shame rather than pride.

The knowledge that Shep was once a local star increases Kyle's animosity. (For unexplained reasons, Kyle does not know that Shep and Birdie are siblings.) Shep is "old school," part of an adult world Kyle and the homeboys reject. Later that morning at the school gym, Kyle baits Shep, attempting to draw him into a competition, but Shep merely advises Kyle to snap his wrists more on his jump shot. Their encounter is interrupted by the coach, who has been waiting for Kyle. After Rollins reprimands him for playing selfishly and for jeopardizing his eligibility by approaching a recruiter, Kyle announces he is joining the Birdmen for the Shoot Out. Soon Kyle and Bugaloo are running with Birdie's lieutenant, Motaw (Wood Harris, who later played Avon Barksdale in *The Wire*), who roughs up two of Birdie's pushers to impress upon Kyle and Bugaloo that they are now soldiers who must carry out orders and maintain control of the streets. Kyle is too immature and arrogant to realize what he is getting into, and he naively believes he can walk away unscathed.

Meanwhile, Shep and Birdie have expressed their differences. They meet for the first time at their mother's grave on her birthday. Birdie embraces his older brother and welcomes him home, offering him an equal partnership in his business. Shep, who hesitated before returning his brother's hug, does not hesitate to turn down the business proposal. It is after this rejection that Birdie cites Shep's abandonment as the reason Birdie became a drug dealer. Birdie's resentment of their mother's admiration for Shep surfaces as he describes the poverty of his childhood. When next the brothers meet on the street, Birdie indicates that he is embarrassed by Shep's failure to succeed as an athlete and his rejection of the opportunity Birdie has offered.

Shep has rejected other offers as well. Coach Rollins has invited him to play for his team in the Shoot Out and is encouraging him to take over as the high school coach. He has also turned down a date with a waitress, but after running into Mailika again, he softens enough to go to a movie. Shep's interest in Mailika prompts him to reconsider assisting the coach, but Kyle, who has been warned by Birdie that Shep thinks only of himself, feels justified in his disapproval of his mother's dating Shep. Once again playing badly and in a foul mood because he spots Shep talking to his mother, Kyle draws a technical and is benched; then he throws a tantrum and must be escorted from the court. When Mailika and Shep enter the locker room, Kyle lunges at Shep, claiming he is protecting his mother. Mailika slaps Kyle and turns to Shep, expecting a supportive response, but Shep walks away. Coach Rollins finds him preparing to resign and leave town. The coach tries to persuade him to stay and help Kyle straighten out; however, Shep is not ready to take on the responsibility.

Before Shep leaves, Birdie seeks him out to say goodbye, and Shep again rejects him. The sight of two brothers shooting hoops nearby seems to take Shep into the past, yet he registers no affection for Birdie and remains silent. Birdie expresses resentment that he lacks Shep's skills, then remarks he has other talents and reveals a razor blade he keeps in his mouth. (Birdie's violent side was displayed earlier, when he sought out and murdered Flip over a minor flap.) After encountering Birdie, Shep tries to tell Mailika about his past, but she is not interested in his excuses. Explaining she has no time for "a runner," Mailika closes the door. Next Shep finds Kyle at the playground and challenges him to a game; the first to sink a basket gets to deliver "boonks" on the other's backside. Kyle is no match for Shep, but the older man declines to spank the younger. The episode seems an attempt at exorcizing the ghost of Nutso; Shep has now proven to himself that he can manage a court challenge without causing a fatality, and with that he walks away determined to leave town in the morning. The next day, however, he changes his mind and shows up at the Shoot Out.

The Shoot Out is aptly named. Even though it is a basketball tournament, it is a contest nearly without rules. The games consist of two twenty-minute halves during which the clock does not stop and no fouls appear to be called. Kyle returns the money and equipment Birdie has given him and announces that he will play for Coach Rollins's team, the Bombers. Predictably, the Bombers and the Birdmen face each other in the final round. A frustrated Birdie corners Kyle, who has just learned that Georgetown has made an offer, and threatens to reveal Kyle's missteps to the university unless Kyle throws the game. Kyle yields to Birdie's threats, but only until Shep appears and takes the court. Motaw flattens Shep a few times, prompting Shep to return the treatment. Shep calls on Kyle to work with him, and Kyle promptly switches his allegiance to the forces of good. Shep scores repeatedly to close the gap between the Bombers and the Birdmen, and he teams with Kyle for a game-winning alley-oop as the clock runs out. But Kyle has crossed Birdie, who provides Motaw with a gun and instructions to get rid of his betrayers. When Motaw sets his sights on Kyle, Shep reads the situation, pushes Kyle out of range, and takes the bullet himself in the process. Motaw is shot by an officer while Shep lies bleeding on the ground, surrounded by Kyle, Mailika, and Coach Rollins, who takes Shep's hand. Shep's fate is left hanging while the film skips to Birdie's club, where the previously dissed Bugaloo shoots and kills Birdie.

The final scene shows Kyle scoring the winning basket in a Georgetown game against Seton Hall. In a postgame interview, he tells announcer Bill Raftery (as himself) that he focused on snapping his wrists on the shot. The scene moves to a bar, where Coach Rollins and Mailika are watching the interview on television; then the camera takes in Shep, fully recovered, standing on the other side of Mailika.

Above the Rim, lensed by Tom Priestly (*Blue Chips*), contains some excellent basketball coverage, particularly of the high school games and practices; the Shoot Out, however, is frenetic and repetitious, showing more rough play and trash-talking than skillful maneuvering. Martin is convincing as the cocky athlete, but his character seems inexplicably lacking in street smarts. The script calls for Leon Robinson (*Cool Runnings*) to keep a stony silence for much of the film; as a result, the extent of his guilt over Nutso is never fully accounted for. At times the film borders on allegory; Birdie's club is illuminated in red, giving it a hellish glow, and on Kyle's first visit, Birdie is wearing a bandana with the points extending forward like horns. The scene suggests a morality play with Kyle caught between the forces of good and evil. Yet scenes between the brothers evoke sympathy for Birdie rather than for Shep. The result is a troubling inconsistency rather than a sense of depth and balance. The message that "pure talent" is not enough is clear, but it is unclear whether Kyle has overcome the "fatal flaw" or whether his self-destructive impulses, like Shep's, are being kept in check by a strong mother and a white coach.

ACROSS THE TRACKS (1991)

DIRECTOR: Sandy Tung. SCREENPLAY: Sandy Tung. PRODUCER: Dale Rosenbloom. CINEMATOGRAPHY: Michael Delahoussaye. EDITING: Farrel Levy. MUSIC: Joel Goldsmith. PRODUCTION DESIGN: Thomas Meleck. COSTUME DESIGN: Merrie Lawson.

CAST: Rick Schroder (Billy Maloney), Brad Pitt (Joe Maloney), Carrie Snodgress (Rosemary Maloney), David Anthony Marshall (Louie).

RUNNING TIME: 101 minutes.

DVD: First Look Pictures.

Teenage siblings with different priorities compete against each other on the high school track team.

AGAINST THE ROPES (2004)

Director: Charles S. Dutton. Screenplay: Cheryl Edwards. Producers: Robert W. Cort, David Madden. Cinematography: Jack N. Green. Editing: Eric L. Beason. Music: Michael Kamen. Production Design: Sandra Kybartas. Art Direction: Armando Sgrignuoli. Costume Design: Ruth E. Carter.

Cast: Meg Ryan (Jackie Kallen), Omar Epps (Luther Shaw), Charles S. Dutton (Felix Reynolds), Tony Shalhoub (Sam LaRocca), Tim Daly (Gavin Reese).

Running Time: 111 minutes.

DVD: Paramount Pictures.

Against the Ropes is an uneven boxing film very loosely based on the career of Jackie Kallen, one of only a few women to forge a successful career managing male fighters. Kallen, who worked as a publicist for Thomas Hearns, began promoting Bobby Hitz's career following his loss to George Foreman in 1988. Her next fighter, James Toney, was an established boxer when she became his manager; he went on to become a middleweight champion. Called the "First Lady of Boxing," Kallen has been widely respected in the field, and she reports experiencing little sexism in such a male-dominated arena. The film version of Kallen's early career paints a very different picture.

Meg Ryan plays Kallen, who in the film works as an administrative assistant for a promoter in Cleveland. Her nemesis is Sam LaRocca (Tony Shalhoub), a short-tempered, self-centered promoter who berates his fighters. Meg disagrees with Sam's style, believing that boxing is a "team sport." When Sam's fighter Devon Green (Tory Kittles) loses to Pedro Hernandez, the Pride of Puerto Rico (Juan Hernandez), Jackie blames Sam for failing to support Devon. Sam's response is to offer Devon's contract to her for a dollar, and Jackie allows journalist Gavin Reese (Tim Daly) to talk her into the deal.

Jackie recruits an African American coworker, Renee (Kerry Washington), to accompany her to Green's neighborhood in Cleveland's mean streets. The two women find themselves in a crack house, where a fight over a drug deal erupts. Enter Luther Shaw (Omar Epps), who takes on the thugs, decking Green in the process. When the police arrive, Luther is led off in handcuffs. Jackie, impressed by his natural ability, follows him to the police station and arranges his bail.

Jackie quickly overcomes Luther's resistance and signs him to a contract after engaging the services of Felix Reynolds (Charles S. Dutton), a retired trainer. The process of shaping Luther into a contender presents a number of predictable challenges. Jackie must pawn her jewelry to finance the endeavor. Luther, the product of a broken home and troubled friends, has anger management issues, and Jackie faces ridicule and discrimination at nearly every turn. When Luther is ready for his professional debut, Sam prevents Jackie from securing a match. Finally, Jackie travels to Buffalo, where she uses emotional blackmail to gain the cooperation of Crisco (Aidan Devine), a former fighter trained by her father and now a New York promoter. A fight is scheduled for Buffalo. Following Jackie's strategy, Luther knocks out his opponent, and his career moves forward smoothly—for a while.

At first, Luther and Jackie get along well. She engineers his move from the old 'hood into an upscale apartment and supervises his finances. But Jackie has allowed Luther's success to become her own. She opens a gym, named Kallen's, but spends little time there; instead, she works on publicity, signing autographs and preparing for an HBO special. As a result, she becomes increasingly distanced from the people who are most important to her: Renee, who has started dating Luther; Gavin, to whom Jackie has promised exclusive interviews; and Luther, whom Sam hopes to lure away from Jackie. Soon, only Felix remains emotionally in her corner.

Meanwhile, Sam is managing Pedro, now the title holder, and refuses to guarantee a fight with Luther. After the HBO special, which presents a harsh but accurate picture of Jackie, she relinquishes her contract with Luther in exchange for a championship fight. Then she takes a job with an insurance company, where she is just another administrative assistant in a cubicle.

Meanwhile, Sam has scheduled the championship bout in three weeks, not enough time for Luther to prepare. Although Jackie is concerned, she does not interfere until the last minute. While listening to the start of the fight on her car radio, she determines she must be by Luther's side. She rushes to the arena, circumvents locked entrances, and, in spite of being ticketless, reaches the rafters, where she is clearly visible to Gavin. Luther has taken a pounding and has been knocked down but not out; to make matters even more one-sided, Pedro is not fighting a clean fight. Suddenly, Jackie is in the ring apologizing to Luther and giving him a pep talk. Luther responds, knocking out Pedro and winning the championship.

After the fight, Jackie does not reenter the ring, but later that night, she appears at a celebration Sam is hosting. The crowd grows silent as Luther, the championship belt over his shoulder, walks up to Jackie. He begins a rhythmic applause that is joined by Felix and then taken up by the others, including, finally, Sam. Luther and Jackie embrace, and the film ends on this happy note.

In real life, Jackie Kallen did not discover a fighter and mold him into a champion. James Toney, her best-known fighter, was established professionally—as was Kallen—before they began working together. Their relationship was stormy, culminating in Toney's threatening Kallen after a defeat. Reportedly, they have since buried the hatchet. Toney portrayed Joe Frazier in *Ali.* Kallen became commissioner of the International Female Boxers Association.

Reviewers panned *Against the Ropes*, which was a box office flop as well. Ryan does not fit the role, nor does her character match her costumes, apparently inspired by Frederick's of Hollywood. Kelly Washington's character, the only supporting role lacking a surname, seems to exist only to steer the plot away from a romantic attraction between the leads.

AIR BUD (1997)

DIRECTOR: Charles Martin Smith. SCREENPLAY: Paul Tamasy. Aaron Mendelsohn. PRODUCERS: Robert Vince, William Vince. CINEMATOGRAPHY: Mike Southon. EDITING: Alison Grace. MUSIC: Brahm Wenger. PRODUCTION DESIGN: Elizabeth Wilcox. ART DIRECTION: Eric Fraser. COSTUME DESIGN: Jana Stern.

CAST: Michael Jeter (Norm Snively), Kevin Zegers (Josh Framm), Wendy Makkena (Jackie Framm), Bill Cobbs (Arthur Chaney).

RUNNING TIME: 98 minutes.

DVD: Walt Disney Home Entertainment.

In the dubious tradition of *Gus* (1976) and *Ed* (1996), an animal becomes a sports star, this time a golden retriever succeeds on the basketball court. Followed by several sequels, most direct to video, each one focusing on a different sport.

AIR BUD: GOLDEN RECEIVER (1998)

DIRECTOR: Richard Martin. SCREENPLAY: Paul Tamasy, Aaron Mendelsohn. PRODUCER: Robert Vince. CINEMATOGRAPHY: Mike Southon. EDITING: Melinda Seabrook, Bruce Lange. MUSIC: Brahm Wenger. PRODUCTION DESIGN: Rex Raglan. ART DIRECTION: Art Norlin. COSTUME DESIGN: Patricia Hargreaves.

CAST: Kevin Zegers (Josh Framm), Gregory Harrison (Dr. Patrick Sullivan), Shayn Sholberg (Tom), Cynthia Stevenson (Jackie Framm), Nora Dunn (Natalya), Tim Conway (Fred Davis), Dick Martin (Phil Phil).

RUNNING TIME: 90 minutes.

DVD: Walt Disney Studios Home Entertainment.

Sequel to *Air Bud* (1997), but instead of shooting hoops, the golden retriever and his owner join a football team. More direct-to-video sequels followed, each showcasing a different sport.

THE AIR UP THERE (1994)

DIRECTOR: Paul Michael Glaser. SCREENPLAY: Max Apple. PRODUCERS: Robert W. Cort, Ted Field, Rosalie Swedlin. CINEMATOGRAPHY: Dick Pope. EDITING: Tom McMurtry, Michael E. Polakow. MUSIC: David Newman. PRODUCTION DESIGN: Roger Hall, Brent Thomas. ART DIRECTION: Alicia Keywan. COSTUME DESIGN: Hope Hanafin.

CAST: Kevin Bacon (Jimmy Dolan), Charles Gitonga Maina (Saleh), Yolanda Vazquez (Sister Susan), Winston Ntshona (Urudu).

RUNNING TIME: 107 minutes.

VHS: Hollywood Pictures Home Video.

A college basketball coach travels to Africa in search of a player who will help him advance his career.

ALI (2001)

DIRECTOR: Michael Mann. SCREENPLAY: Stephen J. Rivele, Christopher Wilkinson, Eric Roth, Michael Mann. STORY: Gregory Alan Howard. PRODUCERS: Paul Ardaji, A. Kitman Ho, James Lassiter, Michael Mann, Jon Peters. CINEMATOGRAPHY: Emmanuel Lubezki. EDITING: William Goldenberg, Lynzee Klingman, Stephen Rivkin, Stuart Waks. MUSIC: Pieter Bourke, Lisa Gerrard. PRODUCTION DESIGN: John Myhre. ART DIRECTION: Jonathan Lee, Bill Rea, Tomas Voth. COSTUME DESIGN: Marlene Stewart.

CAST: Will Smith (Muhammad Ali), Jamie Foxx (Drew "Bundini" Brown), Jon Voight (Howard Cosell), Mario Van Peebles (Malcolm X), Ron Silver (Angelo Dundee), Jeffrey Wright (Howard Bingham), Jada Pinkettt Smith (Sonji), Mykelti Williamson (Don King).

RUNNING TIME: 165 minutes (director's cut).

ACADEMY AWARD NOMINATIONS: Best Actor (Smith), Best Supporting Actor (Voight).

DVD: Sony Pictures.

Four directors tried to develop this biopic: Oliver Stone (*Any Given Sunday*, 1999), Spike Lee (*He Got Game*, 1998), Norman Jewison (*Rollerball*, 1975), and finally, Michael Mann, who with Eric Roth rewrote the script originally developed by Gregory Allen Howard, Stephen J. Rivele, and Christopher Wilkinson.

Mann follows Muhammad Ali's boxing career between 1964 and 1974, opening with the Sonny Liston match and closing with the "Rumble in the Jungle" against George Foreman. He also focuses on Ali's involvement with Malcolm X and the Nation of Islam. (Herbert Muhammad, son of Elijah Muhammad, the founder of the Nation of Islam, became Ali's manager following his conversion.) However, Ali's refusal to be inducted into the U.S. Army is treated not as a decision

Will Smith as Muhammad Ali

based on religious belief but as a reaction to racism in America.

The film opens with a stunning montage that runs for several minutes, establishing the sociopolitical context that shaped young Cassius Clay, as he was then known, and that framed his celebrity. The montage intercuts Sam Cooke (David Elliott) singing "Bring It on Home," Clay (Will Smith) working out, flashbacks to Clay growing up during the civil rights movement, and segments of Malcolm X speaking.

Following the montage, *Ali* jumps to the weigh-in for the Liston fight, where Clay taunts Liston (Michael Bentt) with a poem. Swarming reporters show more interest in Clay's relationship with Malcolm X than in his rivalry with Liston and suggest that Malcolm has left town to divert publicity from Clay's involvement with the Nation of Islam. At the fight Malcolm (Mario Van Peebles) has a ringside seat. The fight sequence portrays Liston as an angry man whose attempts to intimidate Clay fail to penetrate the confidence Clay has in his speed and agility. Clay dominates until Liston resorts to foul play, having his corner man rub an irritant on his gloves that blurs Clay's vision. In spite of his difficulty, Clay is able to avoid Liston until his eyes clear; then he begins once again to wear down the champ. When the bell sounds for round seven, Liston remains in his corner, unable to continue.

After winning the championship, Clay tells Malcolm that he wants to be known as Cassius X because "Clay" is the name of slave owners. A short time later Elijah Muhammad (Albert Hall) gives him the name "Muhammad Ali"—and cautions him not to go to Africa with Malcolm, who, after quarreling with Elijah, has been suspended indefinitely from the Nation of Islam organization. Ali travels to Africa on his own, where he gently reprimands Malcolm for the disagreement. Meanwhile, the

FBI has begun monitoring Ali's telephone calls and keeping him under surveillance, a relatively easy task given his high profile.

The film returns to the United States, where Ali has just met Sonji (Jada Pinkett Smith), whom he wants to marry in spite of the opposition of his advisers. Sonji is not Muslim, and her refusal to conform to Muslim traditions soon sours the relationship. Ali learns of Malcolm's assassination over the radio, and the film cuts to the Liston rematch, which ends in the first round as Liston falls to the canvas after an apparent knockout and Ali is declared the winner. Skipping over the controversial "phantom punch" that concluded the actual fight, the film jumps to the topic of Ali's draft eligibility, which has been reclassified after changes to the qualifying exam he had earlier failed. When Ali refuses to step forward and be inducted, he is arrested and faces a series of setbacks. Although he is able to avoid prison while the case is appealed, his boxing license is suspended, and he is stripped of his title. He soon learns that his corner man, Drew "Bundini" Brown (Jamie Foxx), has sold his championship belt and spent the money on drugs. Not even the Nation of Islam stands behind him, as Elijah Muhammad suspends Ali for "loving sport too much." The only bright spot is that Ali has married Belinda (Nona Gaye), a Muslim. At this point the sportscaster Howard Cosell (Jon Voight) is one of his few supporters and arranges an interview that presents Ali in a positive light.

During a private meeting with Joe Frazier (James Toney), Ali tries to arrange a fight in Georgia, the only state without a boxing commission. Frazier offers him money and finally agrees to a match, but first Ali must meet Jerry Quarry (Robert Sale), whom he defeats in three rounds after a cut opens over Quarry's eye; the match is called, and the two fighters embrace. Ali's wife has become suspicious of Herbert Muhammad and wants him replaced, but Ali refuses, in spite of his rift with the Nation of Islam. Soon after, Cosell calls Ali to inform him that the Supreme Court has given him a unanimous decision, and Ali is cleared for a title fight against Frazier. Ali, now slower and not as powerful, loses to Frazier, but before a rematch can be scheduled, Frazier loses the title to George Foreman (Charles Shufford).

Foreman agrees to fight Ali in Zaire, the so-called Rumble in the Jungle, but there are numerous delays. Belinda, who is still unhappy that Ali retains Herbert, returns to America, and Ali soon takes up with another woman, Veronica Porche (Michael Michele); Belinda comes back to confront Ali about the relationship, but there is no reconciliation. Finally, the fight takes place, with Foreman favored to win. Against the advice of his trainer, Angelo Dundee (Ron Silver), Ali spends much of his time with his back against the ropes absorbing punches; however, this is all part of the "rope-a-dope" strategy Ali has decided on—protecting his head from a knockout punch and letting Foreman wear himself out. The strategy works, and in the eighth round Ali lands a series of blows, knocking Foreman out. The film ends with his moment of triumph.

Technically the film is superb, and Emmanuel Lubezki's photography makes the film visually pleasing, although one scene in Zaire, as Ali walks through the city, resembles a Bollywood production. Will Smith spent a year training for the part and actually absorbed real punches from ring veteran Charles Shufford during filming of the Rumble. Jon Voight's portrayal of the legendary sportscaster Howard Cosell is remarkable. Voight and Smith were nominated for Oscars, Golden Globes, and the

Critics Choice Awards; the film received an ESPY nomination.

In spite of excellent acting and high production values, the film received lukewarm reviews for presenting Ali as a reticent figure and for downplaying his womanizing and his relationship with trainer Angelo Dundee.

ALIBI IKE (1935)

DIRECTOR: Ray Enright. SCREENPLAY: William Wister Haines, based on the short stories by Ring Lardner. PRODUCER: Edward Chodorov. CINEMATOGRAPHY: Arthur L. Todd. EDITING: Thomas Pratt. ART DIRECTION: Esdras Hartley.
CAST: Joe E. Brown (Frank "Ike" Farrell), Olivia De Havilland (Dolly Stevens), Ruth Donnelly (Bess), Roscoe Karns (Carey), William Frawley (Cap).
RUNNING TIME: 72 minutes.
DVD: Warner Archives.

Alibi Ike is the third film in a baseball trilogy featuring comedian Joe E. Brown. It is preceded by *Fireman, Save My Child* (1932) and *Elmer, the Great* (1933).

. . . ALL THE MARBLES (1981)

DIRECTOR: Robert Aldrich. SCREENPLAY: Mel Frohman. PRODUCER: William Aldrich. CINEMATOGRAPHY: Joseph Biroc. EDITING: Richard Lane, Irving C. Rosenblum. MUSIC: Frank De Vol. PRODUCTION DESIGN: Carl Anderson. ART DIRECTION: Beala Neel. COSTUME DESIGN: Bob Mackie.
CAST: Peter Falk (Harry Sears), Vicki Frederick (Iris), Laurene Landon (Molly), Burt Young (Eddie Cisco), Tracy Reed (Diane).
RUNNING TIME: 113 minutes.
DVD: Warner Bros. Archives.

This film is a comedy about a pair of female wrestlers and their manager.

ALL THE RIGHT MOVES (1983)

DIRECTOR: Michael Chapman. SCREENPLAY: Michael Kane, based on an article by Pat Jordan. PRODUCER: Stephen Deutsch. CINEMATOGRAPHY: Jan DeBont. EDITING: David Garfield. MUSIC: David Richard Campbell. ART DIRECTION: Mary Ann Biddle.
CAST: Tom Cruise (Stefen Djordjevic), Craig T. Nelson (Coach Nickerson), Lea Thompson (Lisa), Charles Cioffi (Pop), Chris Penn (Brian), Gary Graham (Greg).
RUNNING TIME: 91 minutes.
DVD: 20th Century Fox.

Football is the way out of Ampipe, Pennsylvania, a town named for American Pipe and Steel. The company dominates the town, and its iron gates seem like an ominous maw through which workers pass to be consumed in corporate America. Stefen Djordjevic (Tom Cruise), a cornerback on Ampipe's football team, plans on parlaying his football skills into an athletic scholarship to a school with a good engineering program. Nickerson (Craig T. Nelson), his coach, is equally determined to leave high school coaching for a football job at a college or university. Unfortunately, both men are accustomed to having their own way, and conflict between the two seems inevitable. Adding to the mix is yet another person intent on leaving Ampipe to pursue a career in music education, Stefen's girlfriend, Lisa (Lea Thompson).

Things come to a head at practice when Stefen tackles a receiver rather than going for the ball. Coach Nickerson is irate, telling Stefen that his action will result in a penalty. When Stefen responds that he made the play, Nickerson states, "It's my way or the highway" and assigns him ten laps around the track rather than the five the rest of the team does. After the practice, Nickerson makes two points to the team:

the team represents not just the school but the community, including the steelworkers; and there are no "quitters" on a team that is "together."

At the next game the opposing Knights, undefeated against Ampipe, score first. Then Ampipe rallies to tie the game before the Knights kick a field goal to lead 10–7 at the half. In the second half Stefen intercepts a pass and runs it back for a touchdown and a 14–10 lead. Ampipe's defense stiffens and forces the Knights to pass. As in practice, Stefen goes for the receiver rather than the ball and gets an interference penalty, putting the ball just short of the goal line. On fourth down Ampipe stops the Knights and regains the ball with seconds remaining. Common sense dictates that the Ampipe quarterback should either "take a knee" or allow the Knights to get a safety, bringing the score to 14–12 and giving Ampipe the ball to kick to the opposition, by which time the clock would have run out. Instead, Nickerson calls for a running play, but Salvucci (Paul Carafotes) fumbles the handoff, and the Knights recover the ball in the end zone, winning 17–14.

After the game Nickerson verbally attacks Salvucci, who is in tears, and calls him a quitter who lost the game. Stefen stands up to his coach and insists that what happened was a fluke. When Nickerson turns on Stefen and blames him for the interference penalty, Stefen points out that if the quarterback had held the ball, there would not have been a fumble; he goes on to say that Nickerson was the one who "quit." Irate at having his authority challenged, Nickerson tells Stefen that he is off the team and then makes things worse by not allowing Stefen on the team bus, suggesting that he travel with the cheerleaders instead.

Stefen's problems are compounded when he accepts a ride home with Bosko (James A. Baffico), an alum who criticizes the coach and offers Stefen some beer. Bosko stops his car at Nickerson's house, and he and his buddies spray paint the house. Stefen, who kicks over a garbage can, sees how far Bosko and his friends have gone and tries unsuccessfully to persuade them to stop. When Nickerson comes to the door, Bosko's bunch take off, leaving Stefen behind. As Stefen runs off, Nickerson sees him. Trashing the coach's house prevents Stefen from salvaging the situation with his coach, who admitted to his wife after the game that he made the mistake. Stefen apologizes to the coach the next day at practice, but Nickerson, furious that his family has also been victimized by the vandalism, tells him that he's played his last football game. An angry and frustrated Stefen retorts, "You're fucked," to which Nickerson answers, "No, you are," and backs up the threat by blackballing Stefen during recruiting, leaving him with no chance of getting to college.

Stefen attempts to convince Bosko to confess to the coach about the house trashing, but he is insulted and beaten by Bosko's pals. He then apologizes to Mrs. Nickerson in a restaurant; however, the incident ends with both Nickerson and Stefen angry. Although Nickerson is concerned about Stefen, he doesn't know how to admit his mistakes. His literal question, "Where are you going?" is answered by Stefen's metaphorical "Nowhere." Nickerson's concern stems from his wife, who had talked with Lisa and showed some sympathy. Certain that he has no future, Stefen goes to work with his brother demolishing one of the machines at the factory that has "demolished" so many of the workers. One day a repentant Nickerson appears at the factory and offers Stefen a full scholarship to Cal Poly, where he has been hired. The film ends with the two men thanking each other.

Although there is a happy ending, *All the Right Moves* demonstrates how even a young man with the "right moves," who does the right thing in defending a teammate from an unjustified attack, can have his future ruined by a coach who assumes a God-like role in deciding who does or does not get a scholarship. It also shows the disparity in scholarship offers between males and females. As Lisa points out to Stefen, she cannot get a music scholarship and is "stuck" in Ampipe. Lisa knows that she will lose Stefen if he gets a scholarship and leaves Ampipe, but she talks with Mrs. Nickerson, brings Nickerson to the factory, and accepts her lot because she loves Stefen. Stefen's friend Brian (Chris Penn), another star player, has a scholarship offer from the University of Southern California, but his girlfriend, Tracy (Paige Lyn Price), is pregnant, and Brian gives up his chances at college and marries her. At a party, Brian maintains that he got what he wanted, but he is also aware of what he has lost. He asks Stefen, "What happens to our dreams?" The film suggests that the dreams are fragile.

ALL YOU'VE GOT (2006)

DIRECTOR: Neema Barnette. SCREENPLAY: K. A. Hoeffner. PRODUCERS: Leslie Belzberg, Patrick Faulstich, Karen Firestone, Max Wong. CINEMATOGRAPHY: Chuck Cohen. EDITING: David Beatty. MUSIC: Kenn Michael. PRODUCTION DESIGN: Cecil Gentry. COSTUME DESIGN: Mynka Draper.
CAST: Adrienne Bailon (Gabby Espinoza), Sarah Wright (Lauren McDonald), Ciara Harris (Becca Watley), Jennifer Peña (Lettie)
RUNNING TIME: 92 minutes.
DVD: Paramount.

After their high school is damaged by a fire, three female volleyball players are transferred to the school of their rivals.

THE AMATEUR (1999)

DIRECTOR: Juan Bautista Stagnaro. SCREENPLAY: Juan Bautista Stagnaro, based on the novel by Mauricio Dayub. PRODUCERS: Bruno Stagnaro, Juan Bautista Stagnaro. CINEMATOGRAPHY: Víctor González. EDITING: Miguel Perez. MUSIC: Jamie Roos. ART DIRECTION: Evelyn Bendjeskov. COSTUME DESIGN: Evelyn Bendjeskov.
CAST: Mauricio Dayub (Alfonso "Pájaro" Romero), Pedro Heredia (Ramón), Vando Villamil (Lopecito), Arturo Goetz (Concejal).
RUNNING TIME: 94 minutes.

In order to be enshrined in the *Guinness Book of World Records*, an Argentine man sets out to break the record for the longest bike ride.

AMAZING GRACE AND CHUCK (1987)

DIRECTOR: Mike Newell. SCREENPLAY: David Field. PRODUCER: David Field. CINEMATOGRAPHY: Robert Elswit. EDITING: Peter Hollywood. MUSIC: Elmer Bernstein. PRODUCTION DESIGN: Dena Roth. ART DIRECTION: John Myhre. COSTUME DESIGN: Jack Buehler.
CAST: Jamie Lee Curtis (Lynn Taylor), Joshua Zuehlke (Chuck Murdock), Alex English (Amazing Grace Smith), William Peterson (Russell), Gregory Peck (the President).
RUNNING TIME: 114 minutes.
VHS: Warner Home Video.

A Little League player who refuses to play baseball until the world agrees to nuclear disarmament inspires professional athletes to follow his lead.

AMERICAN ANTHEM (1986)

DIRECTOR: Albert Magnoli. SCREENPLAY: Evan Archerd, Jeff Benjamin, Susan Williams. PRODUCERS: Doug Chapin, Robert

Schaffel. CINEMATOGRAPHY: Donald E. Thorin. EDITING: James Oliver. MUSIC: Alan Silvestri. PRODUCTION DESIGN: Ward Preston. COSTUME DESIGN: Jodie Lynn Tillen.
CAST: Mitch Gaylord (Steve Tevere), Janet Jones (Julie Lloyd), Michelle Phillips (Linda Tevere), R. J. Williams (Mikey Tevere).
RUNNING TIME: 102 minutes.
DVD: Warner Bros. Archives.

A gymnast who had given up his Olympic hopes for his family returns to the gym for one last shot at glory.

AMERICAN FLYERS (1985)

DIRECTOR: John Badham. SCREENPLAY: Steve Tesich. PRODUCERS: Paula Weinstein, Gareth Wigan. CINEMATOGRAPHY: Donald Peterman. EDITING: Jeff Jones, Frank Morriss, Dallas Puett. MUSIC: Greg Mathieson, Lee Ritenour. PRODUCTION DESIGN: Lawrence Paull. COSTUME DESIGN: Marianna Elliott.
CAST: Kevin Costner (Marcus Sommers), David Grant (David Sommers), Rae Dawn Chong (Sarah), Alexandra Paul (Becky), Janice Rule (Mrs. Sommers), Robert Townsend (Jerome), John Amos (Dr. Conrad), Jennifer Grey (Leslie).
RUNNING TIME: 113 minutes.
DVD: Warner Home Video.

Steve Tesich, who won an Oscar for his screenplay for *Breaking Away* (1979), teamed with director John Badham (*Bingo Long and the Traveling All-Stars and Motor Kings*, 1976) on this cycling drama, but their combined talents, even with Kevin Costner in a starring role, couldn't prevent the film from falling flat. The central conflict is never fully explained, and the film is too slender to support the subplots.

Twenty-year-old David Sommers (David Grant), a college dropout, lives at home with his widowed mother (Janice Rule), who worries about David's health because his father died of a brain aneurysm. (The cause of his father's death is only hinted at by a quick shot of a book open to an article about aneurysms.) David spends his time riding his bicycle around St. Louis, fantasizing about beating his older brother, Marcus (Costner), in a race, and watching martial arts movies. A surprise visit from Marcus reveals deeper family tension stemming from Mrs. Sommers's inability to cope with the death of the boys' father. Marcus, now a physician at a sports medicine institute in Madison, Wisconsin, left home in anger immediately after the father's death. Both his mother and his brother have felt abandoned. The old wounds are reopened quickly. Marcus, who explains he has returned because he is concerned about his brother's lack of direction, complains that "could've" is the family motto, that they are all quitters. How Marcus has become a quitter remains unclear; he appears to be overreacting to placing second in a bicycle race.

In spite of the tension, Mrs. Sommers agrees that David should go to Wisconsin and have Marcus supervise some tests at the institute. When they arrive at Marcus's apartment, Marcus points David toward the couch and gulps a few swallows of juice from the container. Just as David is pulling off his jeans, Marcus's live-in girlfriend, Sarah (Rae Dawn Chong), appears from the bedroom. Marcus has not mentioned her to David, and, enjoying his younger brother's discomfort, he announces that there will be sounds of passion coming from the next room. The following day, the tension between the brothers abates as they go for a ride together. Marcus deliberately chooses a route that takes them on a road past a bicycle-chasing dog to which David loses a shoe, but he enjoys the joke. Their camaraderie dissipates later at dinner when it turns out that Marcus has invited a young woman from the institute who had earlier exchanged smiles with David. However, David, upset that Marcus has provided him with a dinner partner, creates a scene, first embarrassing his date (Jennifer Grey, in a brief appearance), then returning to the subject of their father's death and Marcus's departure from St. Louis. The Jennifer Grey character flees in tears, never to be seen or mentioned again.

The next day at the institute, David undergoes the director's "torture test," which requires the subject to remain on a treadmill as the speed and incline increase until the subject reaches the point of oxygen depletion where he or she keels over. Marcus holds the institute's record of fourteen minutes and eleven seconds, which David is determined to break. He does, and as the others cheer, Marcus shouts for him to keep going. When David collapses, Marcus catches him in his arms. Soon after, David undergoes a brain scan, then falls asleep. When he wakes up, he finds folded over his chest an institute T-shirt with a Latin motto that translates, roughly, "Once you've got it up, keep it up." He makes his way quietly into Marcus's office and finding no one at the desk, is about to read his file, but he overhears Marcus debating with the director, Dr. Conrad (John Amos), whether to "tell" David. Marcus says that he loves his brother too much to tell him and that he wants the two of them to participate in the upcoming Hell of the Wheels race. What Marcus isn't telling David isn't clear, but David assumes that he is a walking time bomb, having inherited the faulty blood vessels that killed his father. Marcus finds David outside, assures him that his test results are all excellent, and approaches the topic of the race. David accepts the offer before Marcus has a chance to make it. The rift between the brothers is now mended, but Marcus's relationship with his mother remains painful: when he phones with David's report, her thankful, but thoughtless, response is, "Davie is all I've got."

As the reconciled brothers prepare for the race, Marcus shows David a tape of an earlier contest that he lost to archrival "Cannibal" Muzzin (Luca Bercovici), who was once married to Sarah. Marcus stops the tape at the point where he "quit," meaning, apparently, where he mentally began to doubt himself. Soon Sarah and the brothers begin their journey to Colorado. At a burger place David meets a hippie hitchhiker (Alexandra Paul as Becky) who has abandoned her vegetarian companions. David offers her a ride in Marcus's van and has fallen in love by the time he's finished his fries. That evening, the two trade T-shirts and sing the national anthem together.

The first stage of the race is the Morgul-Bismarck circuit in Boulder. Marcus wins, but David barely qualifies; having crashed near the finish, he carries his bike over the line, just making the cut. In spite of the mishap, he's less than two-and-a-half minutes behind Marcus. That evening they check into a hotel, and Becky signals to David that she will share his room. Upstairs, Marcus has some difficulty inserting the key in the lock and nearly collapses. Then the scene shifts to Becky and David, who have just kissed. David confesses that he thinks he's going to die, but Becky assumes he's speaking metaphorically and echoes his feelings. Fireworks appear on the television screen as the national anthem begins to play. "Our song," remarks Becky. On the television, a rocket launch is pictured as the anthem reaches its end. The heavy-handedness of this symbolism is in keeping with the clumsiness with which sexual references are inserted into the script.

The next morning, Marcus wakes early with a headache, and Sarah notifies

Dr. Conrad that "it" is beginning. Conrad is stricken by the news, but the dramatic moment is interrupted by the appearance of Conrad's overweight, unathletic son, Randolph (Doi Johnson), who wants to take up bowling because it is a sport in which blacks are underrepresented.

Marcus remains determined to ride in the second stage of the race, the "Tour of the Moon," so named for both its altitude and its lunar-like landscape. He has devised a scheme for David to make up two minutes by being the first to pass strategically placed flags along the course; the first rider to reach each flag gains an additional thirty seconds. Since David is a rookie rider whose phenomenal stamina is unknown to the others, Marcus has advised him to break early and maintain a lead. Following Marcus's plan, David surges ahead, gains his two minutes, and although he finishes third behind the Cannibal and a Russian Olympic medalist, he is only eleven seconds back going into the third stage.

Marcus, however, has not made the third stage. Shortly after David's breakaway, Marcus suffers a nosebleed, then disorientation, and unable to control his bike, he careens downhill while Sarah and Becky attempt to snatch him from the bike and pull him into the van. After several misses, they succeed in holding onto Marcus long enough that he can free himself from the bicycle. He tumbles from the van as it slows, but whether he has been injured is not revealed. Later, at the hotel, Marcus tells David that there's nothing that can be done to help him because his condition is inoperable. He refuses hospitalization and insists David finish the race, returning to the old argument about the Sommers family being quitters. David repeats to Marcus the words "I love you too much" and agrees to compete in the final stage.

Marcus rides in the van for stage 3, now wearing the cowboy hat that David has worn throughout most of the film. Mrs. Sommers appears along the race route, having been contacted by Dr. Conrad. She demonstrates her love for her older son by running across the road without first pausing to look both ways, but she is not struck by the oncoming vehicles. She wraps her arms around Marcus; then mother and son direct their attention to the progress of the race. David and the Cannibal have pulled away from the Russian, and the Cannibal expects David to cooperate in keeping a steady pace without allowing the Russian to gain; however, David sprints ahead, causing the Cannibal to resort to aggressive—and dangerous—bumping and shoving. David holds his own and finishes significantly ahead of the Cannibal for an overall victory. The brothers embrace; then Marcus motions for their mother to join them. The film ends with the happy trio being photographed, and the credits roll across the framed black-and-white photo.

American Flyers is no *Breaking Away*, which takes place against a background of socioeconomic tensions, moves smoothly between comic and dramatic moments, and develops characters who are both likeable and believable. In *Flyers* the central conflict is ill-defined; the nature of the fatal hereditary condition is not clarified; and the Sommers family seems to toss aside old hurts that have had years to fester without ever discussing them. Characterizations are flat and inconsistent, and the Sommers appear too self-absorbed to draw much sympathy. The title comes from a photo of the brothers as children. Marcus, on a bicycle, is pulling David, on an American Flyer sled.

Racing scenes were shot at the Coors Classic cycling race. One extra escaped serious injury during filming at Colorado National Monument. His bicycle went off the road at a point with a thousand-foot drop, but his rig became snagged in the undergrowth, preventing him from plummeting the height of the cliff. Five-time winner of the Tour de France, Eddy Merckx (nicknamed "The Cannibal"), appears onscreen long enough for his name to be mentioned.

AMERICAN PASTIME (2007)

DIRECTOR: Desmond Nakano. SCREENPLAY: Desmond Nakano, Tony Kayden. PRODUCERS: Tom Gorai, Barry Rosenbush, Terry Spazek. CINEMATOGRAPHY: Matthew Williams. EDITING: Mark Yoshikawa. MUSIC: Joseph Conlan. PRODUCTION DESIGN: Christopher Demuri. COSTUME DESIGN: Lawane Boltz.

CAST: Aaron Yoo (Lyle Nomura), Olesya Rulin (Cathy Reyes), Carlton Bluford (Lester Johnson), Sami Roe (Jimmy Gorney).

RUNNING TIME: 105 minutes.

DVD: Warner Home Video

Asian Americans sent to interment camp during World War II start up a baseball team and challenge local minor league players to a game.

ANGELS IN THE OUTFIELD (1951)

DIRECTOR: Clarence Brown. SCREENPLAY: Dorothy Kinsgley, George Wells. STORY: Richard Conlin. PRODUCER: Clarence Brown. CINEMATOGRAPHY: Paul C. Vogel. EDITING: Robert J. Kern. MUSIC: Daniele Amfitheatrof. ART DIRECTION: Edward Carfagno, Cedric Gibbons.

CAST: Paul Douglas (Guffy McGovern), Janet Leigh (Jennifer Paiger), Keenan Wynn (Fred Bayles), Lewis Stone (Arnold Hapgood), Spring Byington (Sister Edwitha), Donna Corcoran (Bridget).

RUNNING TIME: 99 minutes. B&W.

DVD: Warner Home Video.

Divine intervention is required to snap the Pittsburgh Pirates' losing streak in this 1951 comedy directed by Clarence Brown (*National Velvet*, 1944; *Intruder in the Dust*, 1949) and featuring Paul Douglas as the team's irascible manager, Guffy McGovern, and Janet Leigh as naïve reporter Jennifer Paige.

Jennifer, who has been assigned by her newspaper to write about "What's Wrong with the Pirates," determines after witnessing an outburst from Guffy that the problem is the manager. Her editor assigns her to continue writing about Guffy, so she sets off to observe more of the manager in action. Accompanied by the paper's obituary writer, Jennifer confronts Guffy at a steak house, where she introduces herself and quotes part of her article; Guffy seems unfazed by her criticism and responds by scrawling "Boo" on a napkin. However, when he encounters caustic sportscaster Fred Bayles (Keenan Wynn) a few minutes later, it takes little provocation for Guffy to throw a punch that leaves Fred on the floor of the men's room.

In spite of Jennifer's articles and Fred's critical commentary (for which Guffy gets him fired), Guffy makes no attempt to moderate his behavior. He speaks harshly to his players and colorfully to umpires (the latter language being cleverly garbled in the sound track) and is more likely to start a brawl than to intercede. Then, one night while Guffy's searching the outfield for a lucky charm he lost during a skirmish, the voice of an angel tells him that he's "fed up" with the manager's antics and has appeared because someone has been praying for the team. The angel offers a deal: if Guffy cleans up his act, the Pirates will start winning. To convince the skeptical Guffy that this is not some sort of trick, the angel promises a miracle in the third inning of the next day's game. Sure enough, the third-inning miracle occurs—the Pirates get three straight outs on excellent fielding, then hit away in the bottom half; one ball flies so high that it disappears from view.

Soon the Pirates are on a winning streak. Guffy suffers a brief relapse, which prompts a second visit from the angel. This time, the angel explains how the miracles work. Since so many good players are in heaven, they've formed their own team, the Heavenly Choir Nine. The angelic Nine stand behind the Pirates and assist on plays. The angel assures Guffy that he knows many of the players but refuses to reveal their identities. The angel also warns that few managers make it through the pearly gates. Perhaps concerned about the warning, Guffy appears not only to have abandoned his bad habits but also to have acquired some good ones. He compliments players on their performance, takes up reading Shakespeare, and doesn't rise to the bait when tested by the team.

At a home game following the successful road trip, a little girl sitting with a group of nuns exclaims that she sees angels. The nuns, figuring the child has been in the sun too long, take her from the bleachers. However, word of the girl's vision gets passed on to Jennifer, who writes an article about the orphan—Bridget (Donna Corcoran)—who has been praying to the Archangel Gabriel for the Pirates. The article draws Guffy to the orphanage, where his statement that he is "looking for a little girl" is misinterpreted by the sisters, who think he wants to adopt; but Guffy is there to learn the identity of the angels and presses Bridget for details about their uniforms. Their discussion is interrupted by the arrival of an aggressive group of reporters intent on pursuing the story. When one of the reporters asks to take Bridget to a game, the mother superior agrees, thinking that the outing will put an end to speculation in the press. This tactic backfires, however, when Bridget spots the angels again, and the story is further sensationalized.

Meanwhile, the friction between Jennifer and Guffy has dissipated. Jennifer, appalled by the behavior of her fellow journalists, has traipsed through the rain to the manager's apartment to apologize. Guffy, obviously pleased, makes every attempt to be hospitable, placing Jennifer's sopping wet shoes in the oven, where they burn. Guffy gets the now barefoot reporter home by sweeping her up in his arms in the manner of a bridegroom and carrying her out to a waiting cab. From this point on, the two conduct themselves like a couple, although neither openly indicates there is a romantic aspect to their relationship. When Bridget gets sick from eating too much at the ballpark, Jennifer and Guffy promise to visit her every day. The image of the three as a family is established in a scene celebrating Guffy's birthday. Jennifer and Bridget have cleaned his apartment and cooked a surprise dinner, which proves inedible since Jennifer has mistaken Guffy's glove oil for olive oil. They continue the celebration at the restaurant where Jennifer first met Guffy, and a series of parallel scenes unfolds, underscoring the change in Guffy and strengthening expectations that the rookie reporter, the crabby manager, and the orphaned child are made for one another. Thus, once again Guffy encounters Fred outside of the men's room, but this time refuses to take a swing, getting slugged himself instead. Later that evening, Guffy carries the sleepy Bridget into the orphanage and after tucking her in, hints to the mother superior that he is interested in adoption. The mother superior's response that children are not usually awarded to unmarried people prompts an awkward goodnight between Guffy and Jennifer.

As the baseball season draws to a close, Fred stirs up more trouble, making a case that Guffy is emotionally unstable. After Fred interviews a groundskeeper who witnessed Guffy alone in the outfield at night, apparently talking to himself, the commissioner of baseball agrees to investigate. What follows is a hilarious scene staged as a formal hearing. To save his career, Guffy must demonstrate not only that angels exist but also that mortals can talk to them. In his defense, Guffy calls a rabbi, a priest, and a minister—all Pirates fans—to testify. This trio, usually populating the rowboats of bad jokes, provide interdenominational testimony that invokes a sense of community and strengthens the sense of baseball as a locus of nonsectarian belief. However, the commissioner still wants concrete evidence, so Bridget is called as an eyewitness. When Fred's hostility proves too trying for Guffy, Guffy once again takes a swing at the announcer, causing a disapproving thunderclap from the heavens to shock the room. As a feather floats down before the commissioner's eyes, he declares the case dismissed. Guffy's job is safe, but he's in trouble with the angel, who says the fight negates their agreement. There will be no angels in the outfield when the Pirates play their decisive game.

The last game proceeds along standard plotlines. The Pirates, having improved under the leadership of a kinder, gentler Guffy, carry a slim lead into the ninth inning. Guffy has used Saul Hellman (Bruce Bennett) as his starting pitcher because he has learned from the angel that Saul will be in heaven next season. Although Saul gets into trouble, loading the bases with two outs, Guffy keeps him in, and he strikes out the last batter with three pitches. The angel, in a final bit of mischief, makes his presence known to Fred by telling him to shut up; Guffy leaves the stadium with Jennifer and Bridget, soon to become a lawfully sanctioned family, and the film ends with the sounds of a baseball game drifting up from an empty field.

The film balances fantasy and realism cleverly. The angels never appear onscreen, and aside from a couple of thunderclaps and the odd feather, there are no special effects to indicate their presence; even James Whitmore, who does the voice of the Archangel Gabriel, is not listed in the credits. A sequence of interviews with contemporary celebrities, including Ty Cobb and Pirates' part owner Bing Crosby, on the existence of angels is inserted as newsreel footage. Many of the baseball scenes were filmed at Forbes Stadium with real Pirates in action. Winning performances by Douglas, Leigh, and eight-year-old Donna Corcoran make this an enjoyable film, one that spawned a 1994 remake.

ANGELS IN THE OUTFIELD (1994)

Director: William Dear. Screenplay: Dorothy Kinsgley, George Wells, Holly Goldberg Sloan. Story: Richard Conlin. Producers: Roger Birnbaum, Joe Roth, Irby Smith. Cinematography: Matthew F. Leonetti. Editing: Bruce Green, Paul Dixon. Music: Randy Edelman. Production Design: J. Dennis Washington. Art Direction: Carlos Arguello, Tom Targownik. Costume Design: Rosanna Norton.

Cast: Danny Glover (George Knox), Joseph Gordon-Levitt (Roger), Tony Danza (Mel Clark), Brenda Fricker (Maggie Nelson), Christopher Lloyd (Al), Ben Johnson (Hank Murphy), Jay O. Saunders (Ranch Wilder).

Running Time: 102 minutes.

DVD: Walt Disney Video.

The original *Angels in the Outfield* (1951) was a romantic comedy that reaffirmed conventional values of the day, celebrating religion, family, and baseball as pillars of the nation. The Disney remake reflects a shift from post–World War II community-centered thinking and national pride to a more personalized concern with individual freedom and responsibility, while complex social issues, such as racism, are simplified by reversing stereotypes and deproblematizing diversity.

Unlike the 1951 film, in which the evolving relationship of the cantankerous manager and a female reporter was predominant and the child whose prayers are answered is an orphaned girl in a supporting role, Disney's version eliminates the love story and makes the child, a boy abandoned by his father, the central figure. It is his fate and his relationship with the manager that drive the story.

As the Disney film opens, Roger (Joseph Gordon-Levitt) and his best friend, J.P. (Milton Davis Jr.), both in foster care with the pragmatic and loving Maggie Nelson (Brenda Fricker), are riding their bikes around Anaheim Stadium and wondering if J.P.'s deceased father and Roger's deceased mother are best friends in heaven. When they reach Maggie's, Roger finds his father (Dermot Mulroney) waiting for him; his dad rides a motorcycle and, as is characteristic of many bad guys in films from the 1990s, smokes cigarettes. He has come to say he's moving. To Roger's question of when they will be a family again, his dad responds, sarcastically, "when the Angels win the pennant." But the Angels are in last place, on a fourteen-game losing streak, so Roger prays for help.

Angels' owner Hank Murphy (Ben Johnson) has brought in manager George Knox (Danny Glover), who had a winning record with Cincinnati, to replace Ranch Wilder (Jay O. Sanders), who is now the "Voice of the Angels" and one of George Knox's harshest critics. George, frustrated by the lack of talent and teamwork on the Angels' roster, has trouble controlling his temper. During one game, which Roger and J.P. watch from a tree, George attacks his own pitcher, causing a bench-clearing brawl and providing Ranch (another smoker) with more evidence of George's unsuitability for the job. After the game George overturns a food table in the locker room, hurls a rack of bats, and then slugs Ranch on camera.

The following day Roger and J.P. get to sit in the stadium to watch the Angels because it's Kids' Day, and during the game Roger sees "shiny people" helping the Angels. Suddenly, Al, the "Boss" (Christopher Lloyd), appears in the stands and explains he's here to help, but cautions that no one else can see or hear him or the other angels. Al dematerializes, and Roger and J.P. win a photo op with George, giving Roger the opportunity to explain how the team pulled off several miraculous plays. Although George doesn't believe in the celestial intervention, he does interview the players who were affected. Each player reports experiencing something unusual, a sense of being guided or transported. George is still skeptical, but he senses that Roger has some sort of gift and delivers the photograph in person, along with passes for the next game. From Maggie he learns that the boys are in a temporary foster home.

At the next game Roger sees the angels again and advises George to put in an unlikely pinch hitter because an angel has been massaging his shoulders. The batter scores a game-winning, inside-the-park home run, thanks to Al and company. When aging pitcher Mel Clark (Tony Danza), who has been on injured reserve with a blown arm, throws a shutout, George begins to believe Roger really does see angels. Soon George and Roger have worked out a system of signals to indicate when the angels appear, and the earthbound Angels go on a winning streak. The streak ends when Roger misses a game for a hearing during which his dad signs him over for "permanent placement." Roger's disappointment challenges his faith, but only temporarily. He has developed a close bond with George, who has become a surrogate father for both Roger and J.P.

Meanwhile, J.P., who attended the game alone, tells Ranch about the angels, and a story appears in the paper, causing the team owner to demand an explanation. If George wants to keep his job, Hank declares, he must issue a statement renouncing the story. George calls a press conference, attended by Roger, J.P., and Maggie, whose presence give George the boost he needs to challenge Hank. George says he has no logical explanation for events, but whether faith or angels, something extraordinary has occurred. Then Maggie speaks up in defense of believing in angels, and Mel, who has carried a grudge against George, leads the rest of the team in insisting George be kept on as manager. Hank agrees, and the team heads for the championship game. Mel is the starting pitcher, and the fans are wearing angel wings.

There is one last twist: The heavenly angels can't load the dice in a championship game, so the Angels are going to be on their own. Furthermore, George learns, via Al, that Mel, another smoker, is headed for the great roster in the sky. George decides not to mention the absence of the angels to the team, and when Mel tires in the ninth inning and gets into trouble, George keeps him in. Roger and J.P. lead the fans in flapping their arms—the team's sign that the angels are present—and Mel fields a line drive to end the inning and save the game. George adopts both Roger and J.P., who finally sees an angel, too.

Although Disney owned interest in the Anaheim Angels, filming was done at the Oakland Athletics' park while the L.A. Rams were in Anaheim. Several Oakland players appear in the film, and former third baseman Carney Lansford ran a training camp for the actors. Tony Danza's athletic ability contributed greatly to the quality of play, especially near the end of the film, when the Disney angels and the studio's special effects had been benched.

ANNAPOLIS (2006)

Director: Justin Lin. Screenplay: David Collard. Producers: Damien Saccani, Mark Vahradian. Cinematography: Phil Abraham. Editing: Fred Raskin. Music: Brian Tyler. Production Design: Patti Podesta. Art Direction: Christopher Tandon. Costume Design: Gloria Gresham.

Cast: James Franco (Jake Huard), Jordana Brewster (Ali), Tyrese Gibson (Cole), Donnie Wahlberg, (Lt. Burton), Vicellous Shannon (Twins).

Running Time: 108 minutes.

DVD: Buena Vista Home Entertainment.

A young man joins the academy and must prove himself as a cadet and in the boxing ring.

ANY GIVEN SUNDAY (1999)

Director: Oliver Stone. Screenplay: John Logan, Oliver Stone, Daniel Pyne. Producers: Dan Halsted, Lauren Shuler Donner, Clayton Townsend. Cinematography: Salvatore Totino. Editing: Stuart Levy, Tom Nordberg, Keith Salmon, Stuart Waks. Music: Richard Horowitz, Paul Kelly. Production Design: Victor Kempster. Art Direction: Derek Hill, Stella Vaccaro. Costume Design: Mary Zophres.

Cast: Al Pacino (Tony D'Amato), Cameron Diaz (Christina Pagniacci), Dennis Quaid (Cap Rooney), James Woods (Dr. Harvey Mandrake), Jamie Foxx (Willie Beamen), LL Cool J (Julian Washington), Matthew Modine (Ollie Powers), Ann-Margaret (Margaret).

Running Time: 156 minutes (director's cut).

DVD: Warner Home Video.

Oliver Stone assembled this classic football drama from three scripts: the Daniel Pyne screenplay *Playing Hurt*, John Logan's *On Any Given Sunday*, and former professional player Jamie Williams's *Monday Night*;

Stone also drew on *You're Okay, It's Just a Bruise* by former Oakland Raiders' intern doctor Robert Huizenga. The result is a film that covers a number of themes common to the genre: aging athletes who know nothing but the sport, the rookie who is corrupted by success, the coach pressured to turn around a struggling team, owners driven by greed, journalists driven by ratings rather than facts, gold-digging women, and come-from-behind victories. The film is bracketed by extended game sequences using varied film speed and rapid cutting to simulate the point of view of the players on the field.

In the opening scene, the Miami Sharks, coached by veteran Tony D'Amato (Al Pacino), are trying to break a three-game losing streak. When both the starting quarterback, Cap Rooney (Dennis Quaid), and his backup are injured, Tony is forced to send in the third-stringer, Willie Beamen (Jamie Foxx). Willie distinguishes himself by upchucking in the huddle, a moment that will be frequently repeated on televised sports highlights, before throwing an interception. Although Tony manages to settle Willie down in the second half and he completes a pass for a touchdown, the Sharks still lose. In a postgame prayer session, the team chaplain reminds the players that "rain falls on the just and the unjust" and that "there are no atheists in fox holes." As the team joins the chaplain in reciting "The Lord's Prayer," rock music pounds and the scene jump cuts to the hospital, where Cap is writhing in pain and demanding his medication be increased.

Tony spends the evening lubricating his postgame letdown in a bar. Caricatures of him and other key sports figures are prominently displayed, indicating the bar is a regular Sharks' hangout; it is a place also frequented by groupies and high-end prostitutes, one of whom leaves Tony with her number for future reference. Stone employs complex editing in this scene as well, cutting between faces and caricatures and Tony's drink being replenished to suggest a blurred perspective and to connect hard drinking with the game.

Tony has given up his wife and children, now grown, for his coaching, but his career is winding down. The Sharks' owner, Christina Pagniacci (Cameron Diaz), who has inherited the team from her father, disagrees with Tony's coaching strategies. She is ready to trade Cap and veteran defensive player Luther Lavay (former pro Lawrence Taylor) for draft picks and has hired a computer-savvy offensive coordinator, Nick Crozier (Aaron Eckhart). Christina does not intend to renew Tony's contract at the end of the season, and she has been secretly negotiating a deal to move the team to Los Angeles in an attempt to force the mayor of Miami to bankroll a new stadium.

During the next game, Tony puts in Willie, who, after a repeat performance of his debut attack of nerves, throws one touchdown pass and scores another to clinch the game. Although the Sharks win thanks to Willie's efforts, he alienates the team by calling his own shots rather than following the coach's instructions. Willie passed to a favored receiver rather than to the designated back, Julian Washington (LL Cool J), who is on track to set a record and benefit financially, and his taking the ball into the end zone on an apparently broken play is seen as selfish. Willie's sudden success goes quickly to his head, costing him a good relationship with a sensible woman, Vanessa Struthers (Lela Rochon).

As Willie continues to quarterback the team to victories, he makes a rap video, rakes in endorsements, and grows increasingly arrogant. When Tony tries to talk reasonably with him about his responsibilities as a team leader, Willie resorts to the race card, claiming that the coach is "disrespecting" his experience. However, other African American Sharks are becoming exasperated with Willie's self-centeredness. To illustrate the unhappiness among the defensive squad, Luther takes an electric saw to the top of Willie's new Chevy Suburban, cutting it in half. The tension on the team grows so intense that Willie's line refuses to block for him, allowing him to be repeatedly sacked during the last regular season game. Willie loses the football, the game, and ultimately home field advantage for the playoffs, a result that displeases the ambitious Christina immensely. A very angry Tony pushes a reporter out of his way, prompting an uproar from the press.

The film does not show much football during the winning streak, focusing on plotlines instead. Meanwhile, Cap, recovering from his injuries, reveals to his wife his fears of returning to the game; she responds by slapping him. As the playoffs near, the team's orthopedist, Dr. Harvey Mandrake (James Woods), and intern physician, Ollie Powers (Matthew Modine), quarrel over Luther's fitness. After Dr. Mandrake agrees to do additional tests, it is revealed that Luther has a potentially life-threatening neck injury and that the doctor has withheld results from both Luther and Tony. Dr. Mandrake defends himself by asking rhetorically, "Who am I to tell these men they cannot live their dream?" Tony fires Mandrake, but Luther insists on playing because football is all he knows and because he is close to earning a million-dollar bonus. Tony has been bending the ear of Christina's alcoholic mother, Margaret (Ann-Margret), to try to rein in Christina's ambitions; with Christina within earshot, Margaret tells Tony that Christina's father wanted a son "more than anything else in the world." In spite of Christina's protests, by game day Tony has decided to start Cap rather than Willie.

After a pregame press conference during which Tony apologizes for shoving the reporter, he gives an impassioned locker room speech about teamwork and learning from his own mistakes. Life and football are both about inches, he tells the team, and the "inches we need are everywhere around us." As Tony speaks, Willie moves forward, becoming physically more a part of the group, and appears to be taking to heart the coach's words.

The playoff game, which consumes just over thirty minutes, is shot in the same manner as the opening game sequence, using tricky camera work and avoiding almost entirely the point of view provided by standard network coverage; as a result, it is difficult to follow the progress of the game much beyond the opening kickoff, which the Dallas Knights return for a touchdown. Cap manages a score on a broken play, but is hit hard. With Dallas leading at the half, Tony decides to put in Willie, who has undergone a sudden ego adjustment, aided in part, it is suggested, by his renewed relationship with Vanessa. He apologizes in the huddle for his "swelled head" and demonstrates that he can function as both team player and team leader. On the sidelines he confers with Cap, listening intently to the veteran's advice; in the huddle, he no longer changes plays, and he passes frequently to Julian. Near the end of the fourth quarter, Miami trails, and Dallas has decided to go for a first down on fourth and one. Luther sacks the quarterback, giving Miami the ball, but reinjures his neck on the play and lies on the field unconscious. Then, as Tony bends over him, a ray of light appears in the sky, and Luther opens his eyes. Tony promises Luther his bonus, and as he is stretchered off the field, Luther tells his bearers to be careful because he's worth a million, then wiggles his fingers toward the crowd, a reassuring gesture that he is not paralyzed. Meanwhile, in the owner's box, Christina has been informed by the commissioner (Charlton Heston) that she is being called before the commission to face possible disciplinary action for rules violations; crushed, she turns to her mother for solace, and the two put aside past differences and embrace. Then they both watch the final plays of the game.

It is a dramatic finish, with Tony allowing Willie to call the plays in the huddle. Willie opts for a running play that will eat up precious seconds; Julian takes the ball down the sideline, but instead of attempting a high-risk dive for the end zone, goes out of bounds, allowing time for one last play. Willie keeps the ball and finds the necessary inches for the winning score. After the game, Tony encounters Willie on the empty field, and Willie marvels at how much he learned from Cap. Tony reveals he will be leaving Miami and offers a parting anecdote about a retired quarterback who missed the unity of the men in the huddle more than anything else about the game.

Stone superimposes the closing credits over the film's resolution. The scene is a press conference at which Tony officially announces that he is leaving Miami to coach an expansion team in New Mexico and that the offensive coordinator will replace him. His great coup is that he has signed Willie to quarterback the new franchise. The Sharks have not won the championship after all, but the semifinal and final are not shown.

Any Given Sunday was well received, although most reviewers found the dizzying camerawork and editing—over three thousand cuts—overwhelming. The dramatic tensions developed throughout most of the film are undermined in the fourth quarter by the contrived endings that erase conflict without resolving larger issues introduced earlier. Harvey Mandrake's rationalization of his own breech of ethics raises but never answers the question of how responsible athletes are for the conditions under which they play. The issue of racism is expressed in a context that makes Willie look manipulative, and the real problems are never addressed. The film leaves unchallenged Tony's assumption that some ideal character-building form of the sport has been ruined by television. By substituting a package of fortunate outcomes for a more realistic conclusion, Stone seems to dismiss the serious matters at the heart of the film.

THE ARSENAL STADIUM MYSTERY (1939)

DIRECTOR: Thorold Dickinson. SCREENPLAY: Donald Bull, Patrick Kirwan, Thorold Dickinson, Alan Hyman; based on the short story by Leonard Gribble. PRODUCER: Josef Somlo. CINEMATOGRAPHY: Desmond Dickinson. EDITING: Sidney Stone. ART DIRECTION: Ralph Brinton.

CAST: Leslie Banks (Inspector Slade), Greta Gynt (Gwen Lee), Ian McLean (Sergeant Clinton), Liane Linden (Inga Larson).

RUNNING TIME: 84 minutes.

DVD: Network (UK: PAL).

A member of an amateur football (soccer) team dies during a charity match with a professional team, leading to a murder investigation.

AUSTRALIAN RULES (2002)

DIRECTOR: Paul Goldman. SCREENPLAY: Paul Goldman, Phillip Gwynne; based on the novel *Deadly, Unna?* by Phillip Gwynne. PRODUCER: Mark Lazarus. CINEMATOGRAPHY: Mandy Walker. EDITING: Stephen Evans. MUSIC: Mick Harvey. PRODUCTION DESIGN: Steven Jones-Evans. ART DIRECTION: Nell Hanson. COSTUME DESIGN: Ruth De La Lande.

CAST: Nathan Phillips (Gary "Blacky" Black), Luke Carroll (Dumby Red), Lisa Flanagan (Clarence), Tom Budge (Pickles), Simon Westaway (Bob Black).

RUNNING TIME: 95 minutes.

DVD: Beyond Entertainment Limited.

This film is a drama about two teenage friends on an Australian rules football team, one white, the other an Aboriginal, whose expectations of glory are thwarted by racism.

B

THE BABE (1992)

DIRECTOR: Arthur Hiller. SCREENPLAY: John Fusco. PRODUCER: John Fusco. CINEMATOGRAPHY: Haskell Wexler. EDITING: Robert C. Jones. MUSIC: Elmer Bernstein. PRODUCTION DESIGN: James D. Vance. ART DIRECTION: Gary Baugh. COSTUME DESIGN: April Ferry.

CAST: John Goodman (Babe Ruth), Kelly McGillis (Claire Hodgson), Trini Alvarado (Helen Woodford), James Cromwell (Brother Matthias), Bruce Boxleitner (Joe Dugan), Peter Donat (Harry Frazee), Richard Tyson (Guy Bush).

RUNNING TIME: 115 minutes.

DVD: Universal Studios.

Arthur Hiller, whose early credits include the antiwar film *The Americanization of Emily* (1964) and the box office gold mine *Love Story* (1970), directed this biopic starring John Goodman as the Sultan of Swat. While the film shows aspects of Babe Ruth's coarser side, it also allows the audience to view his flaws as the result of a painful childhood, resulting in a generally sympathetic portrait.

The film opens in Baltimore in 1902, with the Babe's father leaving the seven-year-old Jidge, as he was called, in the hands of the priests at St. Mary's Industrial School for Boys, a reform school that puts its wards to work in a clothing factory. Jidge, whose father has labeled him "incorrigible," does not see him again. At St. Mary's he is taunted by the other boys because he receives no visitors, is overweight, and, a left-hander, has difficulty using scissors. His fortünes improve, however, when one of the priests, Brother Matthias (James Cromwell), recognizes Jidge's talent with a baseball bat. Twelve years later, Jack Dunn (J. C. Quinn) of the Baltimore Orioles and Brother Matthias arrange for Jidge to be "paroled" to the O's. Two years later, Jidge is playing for Boston and has become "the Babe."

In spite of growing up in an institution run by the Catholic Church, the Babe has developed neither social skills nor a sense of moderation. At an owner's party he tells an offensive joke and behaves inappropriately. He eats and drinks to excess on a regular basis, once showing up drunk at the ballpark, yet still managing to knock a ball out of Fenway Park. The Babe is also excessively generous and well-meaning. He is especially kind to children, hauling them around by the carload or buying them ballpark treats by the cartload. The film recounts Babe's promise to hit, in this version of the tale, two home runs for Johnny Sylvester, a hospitalized child.

When he is courting a waitress, Helen Woodford (Trini Alvarado), who has mentioned being fond of farm animals, Babe buys her a farm before he proposes.

John Goodman calls his shot in *The Babe*

Six months later they are married, but Babe is bored with the countryside. He wants to "go upstairs" when Helen would rather catch lightning bugs; he wants to go to town for a steak dinner and drinks when Helen wants a quiet evening at home. A night on the town—resulting in a minor traffic accident with an inebriated Babe at the wheel and a strange woman beside him—leads to headlines and scandal. To demonstrate his remorse to Helen, the Babe buys her horses. After he is sold to the New York Yankees, Babe plunges into the raucous night life of the Big Apple and begins an affair with Claire Hodgson (Kelly McGillis), a high-spirited former Ziegfeld dancer. After a particularly wild party at Babe's suite, Helen returns to the farm in disgust. This time Babe presents her with a baby girl he has adopted. The marriage, however, is beyond redemption. During one of their quarrels Helen calls Babe "incorrigible," setting off a furniture-smashing rage. Helen leaves permanently, and the Babe goes into a batting slump, during which he attacks hecklers in the stands and throws a tantrum on top of the dugout.

The Babe is rescued from himself by his long-time friend and fellow ballplayer, Joe Dugan (Bruce Boxleitner), and by Claire, who understands the Babe's child-like behavior and is able to convince him to back off a bit. After the two marry, Babe stays sober, loses weight, and lets Claire manage the money. The Babe goes on a streak and, motivated by rivalry with Lou Gehrig, hits sixty home runs in the season. He begins to believe he can realize a dream to become a manager.

The following year, Helen's death in a fire sends Babe into another slump, and determined to manage, he signs with the Boston Braves. Claire distrusts the deal, correctly believing it to be a publicity stunt rather than a sincere trial as an assistant manager. The Babe overhears talk that he's merely "a sideshow" now. In his next at bat, at Forbes Field, he hits his famous "called shot" home run, followed by two others. After the game, as he leaves the stadium, Johnny Sylvester shows up to return the ball Babe gave him years earlier. The Babe tells Johnny he's retiring.

Director Hiller played fast and loose with chronology, making Ruth's slumps appear to be a direct result of his divorce and, later, the death of his ex-wife. Hiller also reordered Ruth's on-field accomplishments to manipulate the dramatic elements. *The Babe* was neither a box office nor a critical success.

THE BABE RUTH STORY (1948)

DIRECTOR: Roy Del Ruth. SCREENPLAY: George Callahan, Bob Considine, based on the book by Babe Ruth and Bob Considine. PRODUCER: Roy Del Ruth. CINEMATOGRAPHY: Philip Tanura. EDITING: Richard Heermance. MUSIC: Edward Ward. ART DIRECTION: Richard Heermance. COSTUME DESIGN: Lorraine MacLean.

CAST: William Bendix (Babe Ruth), Claire Trevor (Claire Ruth), Charles Bickford (Brother Matthias), Sam Levene (Phil Conrad), William Frawley (Jack Dunn), Bobby Ellis (young Babe Ruth).

RUNNING TIME: 106 minutes.

DVD: Warner Bros. Archives

A weak biographical film about one of the game's greatest players.

THE BAD NEWS BEARS (1976)

DIRECTOR: Michael Ritchie. SCREENPLAY: Bill Lancaster. PRODUCER: Stanley R. Jaffe. CINEMATOGRAPHY: John A. Alonzo. EDITING: Richard A. Harris. MUSIC: Jerry Fielding. PRODUCTION DESIGN: Polly Platt.

CAST: Walter Matthau (Morris Buttermaker), Tatum O'Neal (Amanda Whurlitzer), Vic Morrow (Roy Turner), Jackie Earle Haley (Kelly Leak), Chris Barnes (Tanner Boyle), Joyce Van Patten (Cleveland).

RUNNING TIME: 102 minutes.

DVD: Paramount.

This tween comedy about an inept junior league baseball team and their grumpy coach was a box office hit that drew in audiences with an unlikely crew of characters—a girl pitching for a boys' baseball team, a beer-guzzling curmudgeon for a coach, and a diverse roster of trash-talking kids. Much of the humor rests on the incongruity between audience expectations and the earthiness of the coach and the salty language of the team, but there's a serious subtext to the film as well that exposes adults who have lost sight of the purpose of the game. Screenwriter William Lancaster won a Writer's Guild award for the script, although director Michael Ritchie (*Downhill Racer*, 1969) did some extensive rewriting. Stars Walter Matthau, as the coach, and Tatum O'Neal, as the Bears' pitcher, turn in excellent performances, as do Vic Morrow (rival coach Roy Turner) and Joyce Van Patten in a minor role as a league official.

Morris Buttermaker (Matthau), a mercenary drunk who cleans swimming pools for a living, is hired by lawyer Bob Whitewood (Ben Piazza) to coach his son's baseball team, the Bears. Buttermaker arrives at the ballpark in a battered convertible with a cooler full of beer on the seat and a bottle of Jack Daniels in the glove compartment. He mixes a Jack-and-brew and pulls out a cigar before leaving the car to meet with the lawyer. Buttermaker shows more interest in his check than in what Whitewood has to say about the team, which is such a miserable group that the lawyer filed a class action suit to get them admitted to the league. Buttermaker pays little attention to the players, whom the cherubic-looking infielder, Tanner Boyle (Chris Barnes), describes as "a Jew, a spick, a nigger, a pansy, and a booger-eating moron." Mike Engelberg (Gary Lee Cavagnaro), who is overweight, bears the brunt of jokes about his size, but he gives as good as he gets.

Mini-militant Ahmad Abdul Rahim (Erin Blunt) calls Buttermaker a "honky"; the Mexican brothers, Jose (Jaime Escobedo) and Miguel Agilar (George Gonzales), speak no English. The other less vocal Bears are either nerdy, Albert Ogilvie (Alfred W. Lutter), or timid—Whitewood's shy son, Toby (David Stambaugh), and Timmy Lupus (Quinn Smith).

The Bears' first practice ends with a wild throw shattering the windshield of Buttermaker's car. Soon Buttermaker has the Bears cleaning pools while Tanner mixes him drinks. The coach regales the boys with tales from his time in the major leagues and eventually passes out on the pitcher's mound during practice. By opening day Buttermaker has managed to secure a team sponsor—Chico's Bail Bonds—but has done nothing to organize the team. Following a miserable loss to the Yankees, who rack up a 26–0 lead in the first inning, the Yankees' coach, Roy Turner, begs Buttermaker to drop the team from the league; Whitewood is ready to disband the team entirely, and the players, ridiculed the next day at school, vote to quit. However, the scrappy Tanner, who has taken on the entire seventh grade defending the Bears' honor, refuses to throw in the towel, and Buttermaker, not willing to relinquish the easy money, talks the boys into staying. He begins to do some actual coaching, and to beef up the bullpen, he tries to recruit Amanda Whurlitzer (O'Neal), the twelve-year-old daughter of a former girlfriend. Amanda wants nothing to do with Buttermaker, whom she sees as deserting her and her mother. It takes a couple of tries and the promise of ballet lessons and French designer jeans, but Buttermaker convinces Amanda to join the Bears, whose performance improves remarkably in their next outing, even though they lose by a run.

The Bears still lack a good power hitter and skilled fielder. Their best prospect, Kelly Leak (Jackie Earle Haley), is a rebellious thirteen-year-old who smokes, drives a motorcycle (albeit illegally), hangs out at pool halls, and gets into minor mischief. Buttermaker sends Amanda to recruit Kelly. When he claims to be uninterested, she bets she can beat him at air hockey: if she wins, he plays; if he wins, he gets whatever he wants from Amanda. Kelly wins the bet, and the "whatever" is a date to a Rolling Stones concert, but Kelly still shows up to play the next game. Soon the team begins to jell. When Lupus is bullied by a pair of Yankees, Tanner stands up for him, and the two become best friends. Amanda's pitching, Kelly's hitting, and Buttermaker's coaching send the team on a winning streak.

The Bears' harmony is short-lived as winning gains overriding importance for Buttermaker, who is locked into competition with the Yankees' coach. In order to assure a key win that will put the Bears into a championship game, Buttermaker instructs Kelly to assume control in the field. Kelly runs into the others' territory to make plays, offending his teammates in the process. Then Kelly ignores Buttermaker's instructions at the plate; although Kelly produces a solid hit, he and the coach quarrel. Amanda isn't too happy either. Her arm is sore. More importantly, she has invited her mother to the game, hoping for a reunion with Buttermaker, but he is not interested in a relationship that carries family responsibilities.

By the day of the championship game, team morale is low, and Buttermaker is fixated on winning, as is the Yankee coach, who places enormous pressure on his son, Joey (Brandon Cruz), who is pitching. When Joey intentionally throws at Ogilvie, Roy runs to the mound and strikes his son. Joey then delivers a weak pitch that Ogilvie grounds back to the mound. Joey fields the ball, but holds onto it as the runner rounds the bases and the other Yankees fight for the ball. After Ogilvie scores, tying the game, Joey walks off the field. His pain and frustration register with both coaches. Buttermaker decides to put in the worst of the Bad News Bears, including Lupus, in spite of objections by Whitewood. Lupus makes a serendipitous catch that astounds everyone and thrills the Bears, but the Yankees still score in their at bat. In the final inning, with the bases loaded, Kelly comes to the plate, and, surprisingly, strikes out. Although the Bears have lost the championship, they've proven something to themselves and to the adults associated with the sport. Buttermaker passes around beers for everyone. At the trophy presentation, Tanner cuts off an insincere speech about sportsmanship by the other team with "shove it," and the Bears celebrate by pouring beer over one another's heads.

The success of *The Bad News Bears* led to two sequels. A remake of the original, starring Billy Bob Thornton in the Matthau role, was released in 2005 to a much less enthusiastic reception.

THE BAD NEWS BEARS (2005)

DIRECTOR: Richard Linklater. SCREENPLAY: Bill Lancaster, Glenn Ficarra, John Recqua. PRODUCERS: Geyer Kosinski, Richard Linklater. CINEMATOGRAPHY: Rogier Stoffers. EDITING: Sandra Adair. MUSIC: Ed Shearmur. PRODUCTION DESIGN: Bruce Curtis. ART DIRECTION: David Lazan. COSTUME DESIGN: Karen Patch.

CAST: Billy Bob Thornton (Morris Buttermaker), Marcia Gay Harden (Liz), Greg Kinnear (Roy Bullock), Sammi Kane Kraft (Amanda Whurlitzer).

RUNNING TIME: 113 minutes.

DVD: Paramount.

Rick Linklater (*School of Rock*, 2003) directed this remake of the 1976 *The Bad News Bears*. Linklater's version, which writer Glenn Ficarra calls more a "remix," sticks close to the plot of the original. Billy Bob Thornton plays Coach Buttermaker as a randy drunk untouched by political correctness. Lawyer Bob Whitewood (1976) is replaced by a woman, Liz (Marcia Gay Harden), allowing for a romantic subplot. Although scrubbed of the most offensive racial epithets, the 2005 version takes the language several notches higher on the obscenity meter. The result is a much darker comedy.

The opening scene establishes Buttermaker's character—and distinguishes Thornton's interpretation from Matthau's—by showing Buttermaker performing his regular job as an exterminator. As rats run amok through a house, Buttermaker informs the terrified home owner that it's quitting time for him and that she should call the company to schedule a follow-up appointment. In the next scene at the ballpark, Buttermaker ogles a girls' softball team; then, after looking over the ethnically diverse Bears, he displays both cynicism and insensitivity. He describes their batting practice as "Helen Keller at a piñata party," purposely hits the players with pitched balls, puts them to work spreading poison in crawl spaces, and gets a strip club to sponsor the team and provide uniforms. When the Bears fail to make it out of the first inning and rival coach Roy Bullock (Greg Kinnear) approaches Buttermaker about calling the game and ending the rout, Buttermaker responds, "Who are you, Shoeless Joe walking out of the holy cornfield?" When the kids decide to quit, Buttermaker declares, "This is not a democracy. This is a dictatorship, and I'm Hitler."

The remake reincarnates most of the Bears' roster, while adding an Armenian (Aman Johal as Prem) and a paraplegic (the able-bodied Troy Gentile as Hooper). Mike Engelberg (Brandon Craggs) is foul-tempered and overweight; Toby Whitewood

(Ridge Canipe) suffers from his mother's overprotectiveness; the new Ahmad (K. C. Harris) admires Mark McGwire rather than Muhammad Ali; the Aligar brothers (Carlos and Emmanuel Estrada) speak no English; Lupus (Tyler Patrick Jones) is harassed by bullies; and Tanner (Timmy Deters) turns the air blue when he speaks, usually at the top of his lungs. Amanda (Sammi Kane Kraft), the daughter of one of Buttermaker's old girlfriends, injects sexual references into her speech with a tone of understanding beyond her twelve years; when she recruits the talented hooligan Kelly Leak (Jeffrey Davies) to play for the Bears by offering herself in a bet, she purrs with innuendo. (Buttermaker insists on going along on their date to a Blood Farts concert, where he gets caught in the mosh pit). Like the earlier team, these Bears do a good job at playing baseball badly, but with the exception of Timmy Deters, the acting is lackluster.

The remake repeats the tension between Buttermaker, who resists commitment, and Amanda, who is angry with Buttermaker for walking out on her mother. It also replicates the competitiveness between coaches and the overinvolvement of parents in children's athletics. *Bears* 2005 concludes like the 1976 version with Buttermaker's realization that he has lost track of the point of Little League. He lets all of the kids play, even wheelchair-bound Hooper, who makes a catch. The Bears lose the game and interrupt the canned speeches about sportsmanship. Buttermaker expresses his intention to spend more time with Amanda, and a flag waves over the field as the closing credits appear.

THE BAD NEWS BEARS GO TO JAPAN (1978)

DIRECTOR: John Berry. SCREENPLAY: Bill Lancaster. PRODUCER: Michael Ritchie. CINEMATOGRAPHY: Kozo Okazaki. EDITING: Richard A. Harris, Dennis Virkler. MUSIC: Paul Chihara. PRODUCTION DESIGN: Walter Scott Herndon. COSTUME DESIGN: Tommy Welsh.

CAST: Tony Curtis (Marvin Lazar), Jackie Earle Haley (Kelly Leak), George Wyner (the network director), Erin Blunt (Ahmad Abdul Rahim), Tomisaburo Wakayama (Coach Schimizu), Antonio Inoki (himself), Hatsune Ishihara (Arika).

RUNNING TIME: 91 minutes.

DVD: Paramount.

Tony Curtis plays a fast-talking promoter who plans to exploit the Bears for his own financial gain in the sequel to *The Bad News Bears in Breaking Training* (1977). William Lancaster wrote the script and coproduced it with Michael Ritchie, who directed the original *Bears* in 1976. The result is a film with a bit more substance than *Breaking Training*, but with an unnecessarily complex plot, and baseball takes a back seat to the separate adventures of stars Curtis and Jackie Earle Haley (Kelly Leak), still a Little Leaguer, but one more interested in chasing girls than in supporting his team.

When the film opens, it appears that the Bears won't be traveling to Japan to play against the Japanese all-star team after all. The Japanese team is so good that the Bears' backers are afraid of being embarrassed. However, after Tanner Boyle (Chris Barnes) watches a World War II movie about the war in the South Pacific, he decides that national honor is at stake. Soon he's taken his message to the public through a television interview. While watching the interview, promoter Marvin Lazar (Curtis), who is close to broke, sees an enormous potential for profit from television coverage and sells himself as the Bears' agent with the assurance that he has the money to bankroll the team's trip.

Lazar, predictably, is lying about his solvency, and much of the story derives from his attempts to keep ahead of the rapidly mounting expenses long enough to score a windfall. As Lazar's attempts to secure a television contract for the all-star game fail, he resorts to publicity stunts that include participating in a professional wrestling match and getting the Bears and the Japanese team onto a talent show, where the All-Stars sing "Take Me Out to the Ballgame" in Japanese. Lazar's misadventures are intercut with scenes of Kelly Leak's pursuit of a geisha, whom he follows about, trying to make a date; finally, a Japanese man in a UCLA shirt translates Kelly's compliments, facilitating the courtship. While the unfolding of this romance slows the film and adds little to the humor, it does provide some attractive footage.

The film relies on cultural differences for some of its gags—Lazar frequently hits his head going through doorways and has difficulty with greeting rituals—but it resists cheap jokes at the expense of the Japanese. One of the film's few virtues is the warm relationship that grows between the two teams even as Lazar tries to enflame national rivalry to publicize the upcoming contest.

The conclusion is spurred along when Lazar consorts with Las Vegas gamblers who plan to bet heavily on the Bears and to assure a win by importing three ringers. After one of the imposters heaves a pitch at a Japanese batter, a brawl breaks out that includes both coaches as well as fans, resulting in the game being cancelled. The Japanese coach is fired, but Lazar consoles him with plans for another matchup the following year in Cuba, a location that ensures a fourth sequel is not forthcoming. Meanwhile, both teams are enjoying themselves in a sandlot game, and *The Bad News Bears Go to Japan* closes on a note reminiscent of the original movie, in which adult interference threatens to undermine the wholesomeness of the kids' game.

THE BAD NEWS BEARS IN BREAKING TRAINING (1977)

DIRECTOR: Michael Pressman. SCREENPLAY: Paul Brickman. PRODUCER: Leonard Goldberg. CINEMATOGRAPHY: Fred J. Koenekamp. EDITING: John W. Wheeler. MUSIC: Craig Safan. ART DIRECTION: Stephen Berger. COSTUME DESIGN: Jack Martell.

CAST: William Devane (Mike Leak), Clifton James (Sy Orlansky), Chris Barnes (Tanner Boyle), Jackie Earle Haley (Kelly Leak), Jimmy Baio (Carmen Ronzonni), Erin Blunt (Ahmad Abdul Rahim).

RUNNING TIME: 100 minutes.

DVD: Paramount.

Neither Walter Matthau, who played Coach Buttermaker, nor Tatum O'Neal, who starred as the Bears' starting pitcher, returned for the sequel to *The Bad News Bears* (1976), and their characters are dropped, but a number of young actors retained their original roles. Jackie Earle Haley is back as the rebellious motorcyclist Kelly Leak, still with long hair and a nicotine habit; Chris Barnes continues as the race-baiting, potty-mouthed infielder Tanner Boyle; Erin Blunt (Ahmad Abdul Rahim), Jaime Escobedo (Jose Agilar), George Gonzales (Miguel Agilar), and Alfred W. Lutter (Albert Ogilvie) reprise their roles; David Stambaugh returns as Toby Whitewood, now a born-again Christian; and Quinn Smith (Timmy Lupus) puts in a brief appearance. The character of Mike Engelberg is now played by Jeffrey Louis Starr. Although Tanner has grown close to Lupus and is determined to "win one for the Looper," the friendship between the two does not figure into the story except superficially as Tanner's postcards to Lupus fill in information for the viewer, allowing the film to short-circuit some of its plotlines.

The movie begins with the Bears confronting a new coach who has the demeanor of a Marine sergeant. It appears that the Bears are in for bad news, indeed, but Kelly comes to the rescue, running the coach off the field with his bike; however, this leaves the team without a coach and with a playoff game on the horizon. The team is also without a pitcher because Lupus (who has moved from the outfield to the mound since the original version) has a broken leg. Kelly has a solution to both problems. He imports a leather-jacketed delinquent, Carmen Ronzonni (Jimmy Baio), to pitch and transforms Lester (Fred Stuthman), a mentally retarded groundskeeper, into a coach.

The Bears are scheduled to meet a Texas team, the Houston Toros, at the Astrodome for a four-inning contest held between games of a major league doubleheader. The players assure their parents that their new coach has "been with Parks and Services for years," and ask for money to cover their expenses. Meanwhile, Kelly and Carmen teach Lester to shake hands and say "Hello. How are you?" On the day the team departs, Lester performs flawlessly as he greets the parents. Carmen has provided a van—which turns out to be stolen—and the Bears take off with Kelly, still unlicensed, behind the wheel and Lester left behind. The Bears' road trip is an extended journey into juvenile humor with crude toilet jokes and a pillow fight. Perhaps the most interesting scene in this segment is a pickup game against a group of Native Americans. Although the local boys lack equipment, they easily defeat the Bears, who are undisciplined and out of shape, and whose new pitcher has only two pitches: wild and lollypop.

Once the Bears arrive in Houston, they check into a cheap hotel that has the markings of a brothel and stupidly park the van in a tow-away zone. After the police run the van's tag number, they begin to ask questions and want to meet the Bears' coach. Again, Kelly produces a coach, his estranged father, Mike (William Devane), who happens to work nearby; although the possibility that Kelly has an ulterior motive for getting the team to Houston has been hinted at, he has kept information about his father's whereabouts from the rest of the Bears. Having satisfied the police, at least for the moment, the team moves ahead to the next obstacle—because the Bears failed to arrive on schedule, the Toros' coach has brought in a team from El Paso to replace the Bears; however, Mike convinces the Toros' sponsor, a Budweiser distributor, to send the replacements packing. The sponsor, whose largesse extends beyond his own players, puts the Bears up in ritzy digs at the brewery's expense.

Leading up to the big game, there are few surprises. The opposing team conducts practice drills with military precision while the Bears' first practice ends with them fighting one another. Under Mike's guidance, the team begins to show improvement, and Mike even gets Carmen to abandon his posturing and settle into his role. Kelly turns sullen and resentful, unable to handle the anger he still feels because his father abandoned the family. After a quarrel Kelly runs off, apparently unwilling to continue playing for the Bears now that his father has been embraced by the team. However, just before the Bears take the field for the big game, he shows up in uniform.

The Bears get off to a slow start, allowing the Texas team to gain an early lead. In a plot twist to the usual come-from-behind scenario, the game is suddenly called after the second inning because the latter half of the Astros' doubleheader is scheduled to begin. Tanner, characteristically, refuses to leave the field and leads the umpires on a merry chase. Soon several Astros shout, "Let the kids play," and Mike takes up the cheer, waving a towel and firing up the fans. Kelly joins his father; then the Toros' sponsor throws his considerable weight behind the cause, and play resumes. Carmen gets to score the winning run with an in-the-park homer, and the Bears win a trip to Japan (sequel alert!).

Kelly and Mike leave the Astrodome with their arms around each other's shoulders, but the film ends where it began, with Lester on his tractor, mowing the outfield of the Bears' home field and Kelly on his bike. The father-son angle is not adequately explored within *Breaking Training*, and the status of Kelly and Mike's relationship remains open to conjecture at the film's end.

BALLS OF FURY (2007)

Director: Robert Ben Garant. Screenplay: Thomas Lennon, Robert Ben Garant. Producers: Gary Barber, Roger Birnbaum, Jonathan Glickman, Thomas Lennon. Cinematography: Thomas E. Ackerman. Editing: John Refoua. Music: Randy Edelman. Production Design: Jeff Knipp. Art Direction: Steve Arnold. Costume Design: Maryann Bozek.

Cast: Dan Fogler (Randy Daytona), Christopher Walken (Master Feng), George Lopez (Agent Ernie Rodriguez), Terry Crews (Freddy), Maggie Q (Maggie), James Hong (Master Wong), Robert Patrick (Pete Daytona), Aisha Tyler (Mahogany).

Running Time: 90 minutes.

DVD: Universal Studios.

Balls of Fury, one of the few sports films to feature Ping-Pong (table tennis), parodies Bruce Lee's *Enter the Dragon* (1973). Like the martial arts classic, *Balls of Fury* contains a great deal of action footage, along with a government plot to capture a criminal mastermind, in this case Master Feng, played with incredible panache by Christopher Walken. The FBI must depend on the assistance of Randy Daytona (Dan Fogler), a Ping-Pong prodigy until his defeat at the Seoul 1988 Olympics. Now a washed-up entertainer performing in a second-rate Las Vegas bar, Randy loses even that job when he accidentally causes a customer to die of a heart attack. Initially reluctant to accept the assignment from Agent Ernie Rodriguez (George Lopez), Randy finally agrees once he is told that his past makes him uniquely qualified for the task.

At the 1988 Olympics the young Randy (Brett DelBuono), who has several lucrative sponsorships lined up, is slated to play Karl Wolfschtagg (Thomas Lennon), the East German champion, in the semifinals, but Randy loses his composure when he learns that his father, a compulsive gambler, has bet heavily on him. In the course of one long point featuring high, deep lobs, Randy backs up too far, falls, and is too dazed to continue. Actually, he does manage to blurt out to the television cameras, "I'm going to Disneyland," a remark that follows him throughout his life. As a result of this defeat, Randy's father, who can't pay his debt, is killed by Mr. Feng's thugs. If Randy can recover enough ability to qualify for Feng's invitational Ping-Pong tournament, Randy will be able to get close to Feng and discover his next criminal move. When Randy is routed 11–3 in a regional tournament by the Hammer (Patton Oswalt), an overweight player with an inhaler, Agent Rodriquez gets him a coach, Master Wong (James Hong), whose blindness causes him to bump into obstacles and tumble down an elevator shaft. However, Wong's lovely niece, Maggie (Maggie Q), is a skilled Ping-Pong player who improves Randy's game. She falls for Randy, but his experiences with her uncle are unfortunate: he accidentally kills Wong's lucky cricket, and Wong, no doubt to improve Randy's strokes, locks him in a room with a swarm of bees.

Because Master Wong is teaching Randy, who is not Chinese, he has violated the Chinatown rules created by the "Triad," and his instructional facility is trashed. Agent Rodriquez then turns to plan B, which consists of having Randy battle the "Dragon" (Na Shi La) in a Ping-Pong match. Wong leads Randy into what he calls the "underbelly of Ping-Pong," and Maggie gives him her father's paddle and a kiss to prepare him for the contest against an opponent who turns out to be a young girl with a supposedly unreturnable serve. Randy smashes her first two serves for winners, and the Dragon collapses into tears. After Randy wins the match, the audience hoists him onto their shoulders, but what seems like adulation becomes a short trip to a dumpster, where he is unceremoniously dumped. All is not lost because a large Chinese man and Mahogany (Aisha Tyler), Master Feng's henchwoman, appear to give Randy an invitation to Feng's tournament.

The tournament is held "somewhere in Central America," where Feng has his stronghold. At a lavish party Feng graciously offers Randy a selection of sexual slaves, all of whom are male, and bids Randy, Agent Rodriquez, Maggie, and Wong "toodles." After an all-night board game with the sex slave Mahogany selected for him, Randy enters the first day of the single-elimination tournament. His opponent is the Canadian champion, who tries to intimidate him with a "stare down" and menacing looks and rhetoric right out of professional wrestling. Randy wins the match, and Mahogany kills Randy's opponent with a blow gun. In response to Randy's surprise and horror, Feng asks, "What part of 'sudden elimination' didn't you understand?" Impressed by Randy's skill, Feng offers him employment and reveals that he deals in guns that can pass unnoticed through metal detectors. Randy declines and tells Agent Rodriquez his news, but the FBI man is caught before he can transmit the information to allies outside Feng's stronghold. Karl, the East German who had beaten him in Seoul, is to be Randy's next opponent, but Feng alters the schedule, pitting Randy against Maggie, who is ready to lose and die to save her man. Randy, however, succeeds in killing the murderous Mahogany, and in the ensuing fracas, Randy frees the grateful male sex slaves and takes on Feng in a match in which each is wired to an apparatus that will automatically fry the loser. The Ping-Pong final, which is played without a net, continues out of Feng's stronghold onto a wooden bridge, where Randy imitates Indiana Jones as he pulls himself up from a dangling rail to defeat and electrocute Feng, thereby avenging his father's death. The FBI forces outside, who have received Rodriquez's message from a plan C extra transmitter, demolish Feng's men and then his building.

Two months later Wong has established a Ping-Pong school, which Maggie and Randy will operate. To celebrate the occasion, Randy gives his mentor a replacement lucky cricket in a gift box. Wong, of course, excitedly shakes the box and kills the cricket. To complete the absurdity, the Dragon reappears, telling Randy, "It ain't over yet, Whitey," and aiming a furious strike at his gonads. The film concludes (mercifully) with Wong falling into an empty elevator shaft.

No one in the film exhibits the level of table tennis skills demonstrated by Forrest Gump, as played by Tom Hanks in the 1994 film.

BANG THE DRUM SLOWLY (1973)

DIRECTOR: John D. Hancock. SCREENPLAY: Mark Harris, based on his novel. PRODUCERS: Lois Rosenfield, Maurice

Rosenfield. CINEMATOGRAPHY: Richard Shore. EDITING: Richard Marks. MUSIC: Stephen Lawrence. PRODUCTION DESIGN: Robert Gundlach. COSTUME DESIGN: Domingo Rodriguez.
CAST: Michael Moriarty (Henry "Author" Wiggen), Robert De Niro (Bruce Pearson), Vincent Gardenia (Dutch Schnell), Phil Foster (Joe Jaros), Ann Wedgeworth (Katie).
RUNNING TIME: 96 minutes.
ACADEMY AWARD NOMINATIONS: Best Supporting Actor (Gardenia)
DVD: Paramount.

Based on the novel of the same title by Mark Harris, who also wrote the screenplay, *Bang the Drum Slowly* is a baseball film that focuses on the relationship between a successful pitcher, Henry "Author" Wiggen (Michael Moriarty), and his mediocre catcher, Bruce Pearson (Robert De Niro), who is terminally ill. It is an offbeat film combining gentle humor and convincing dialogue in a story that strays from conventional plotlines and characterizations.

Before spring training begins, Henry accompanies Bruce to the Mayo Clinic in Minneapolis, where Bruce is diagnosed with Hodgkin's disease. Since Bruce has never lived up to his athletic potential and his future with the New York Mammoths is in doubt, the two men decide to keep the diagnosis to themselves, and in order to assure security for Bruce, Henry insists that his contract include Bruce in a package deal. The team manager, Dutch Schnell (Vincent Gardenia), suspects something is up, but his attempts to elicit information about their trip to Minnesota yield conflicting stories. Henry claims they went fishing, Bruce that they went hunting. Then Henry states that Bruce has been dating a flight attendant. Dutch becomes so frustrated that he hires a detective to investigate.

The other team members are also perplexed by Henry's loyalty to his catcher. Off the field, the two seem to have little in common. Henry, who is both smart and articulate, has published a book and is writing another; his teammates have nicknamed him "Author," but Bruce, an inarticulate, poorly educated farm boy from rural Georgia, calls him "Arthur." Henry is a happily married man; Bruce has fallen for a prostitute who has promised to marry him if he makes her the beneficiary of his life insurance policy. Bruce is frequently the butt of locker room jokes that only thinly disguise the team's growing resentment that Bruce's place on the roster is protected even though his performance has been spotty.

Eventually, word of Bruce's condition circulates among the players. First, Henry takes another pitcher into his confidence to get the man to ease up on riding Bruce. Then, one night Bruce suddenly feels sick, and Henry enlists the aid of two other players in getting him to the hospital. Afterward, the teasing stops, and the players keep their knowledge from Dutch. When Dutch learns from his detective of the hospital visit, Henry hints that Bruce has contracted syphilis, an untruth that results in what in military terms is known as a "short arm inspection."

As the season continues, Bruce breaks from his slump and begins hitting steadily. He is now included in more team activities, playing cards in the hotel room on road trips, even appearing on television with the "Singing Mammoths," in spite of the fact that he sings badly and is out of step. Bruce's father attends a game and has difficulty understanding how Bruce can be terminally ill, yet play better than in the previous season. The team has improved as well and, although getting off to a slow start, is headed for the playoffs.

Until the playoffs, the film pays little attention to the team's record, focusing more on their interactions off the field. The first base coach, Joe Jaros (Phil Foster), has invented a card game with ever-changing rules designed to fleece outsiders; Joe and Henry often play in hotel lobbies, hoping to attract innocent bystanders, but Bruce, who is not mentally sharp, is never included. Only snatches of the baseball games are shown, and although the Mammoths win the pennant, the World Series is skipped over completely. The manager's requisite locker room speech to fire up the team comes early in the season, not before a big game, and consists of a bizarre metaphor about catching flies—the common household pests, not balls hit into the outfield; Dutch speaks none-too-eloquently about how the fingers must all work together to form a fist in order to entrap the insect. During the playoffs Bruce is feeling "dipsy," but he manages a couple of good hits. The Mammoths win the pennant with the victory coming quietly on a pop fly caught by Goose Williams (Tom Signorelli), a minor character.

Following the pennant win, the scene shifts to a hospital where Henry, Joe, and another player are visiting Bruce, who says he'll be back in the spring. A brief time later, he is boarding an airplane for home, struggling to manage his suitcase as he walks across the tarmac. He has asked Henry to send him a scorecard from the World Series, but Henry's voiceover narration informs the viewer that he never did. Bruce dies in December. Henry serves as a pallbearer, but no one else from the club attends. Henry's closing words, "From here on in, I rag nobody," indicate that Bruce's friendship has reminded him of the importance of respect for one's fellow humans, a major theme of the film.

The film's title comes from the song "Streets of Laredo," a lament for a dying cowboy that one of the players, Piney Woods (Tom Ligon), sings in the locker room during a rain delay. Piney, having only recently joined the team, does not realize the meaning that the lyrics hold for Bruce and the others, who listen in silence while the camera records Bruce's somber, resigned expression. This was a breakthrough role for De Niro, who prepared intensely, traveling to rural Georgia to study accents and pouring over baseball games to learn about catching.

In 1956, an abbreviated adaptation of Harris's novel was broadcast live on the *U.S. Steel Hour*, starring Paul Newman as Henry and, in a minor role, George Peppard as Piney Woods. This early version shifts the spotlight from Bruce Pearson (Albert Salmi) to Henry Wiggen and his decision to protect Bruce through his contract negotiation. The telecast was made available on DVD in 2008 as part of a series *Paul Newman: Remembering the Legend.*

BASE*KETBALL* (1998)

DIRECTOR: David Zucker.

SCREENPLAY: David Zucker, Robert LoCash, Lewis Friedman, Jeff Wright. PRODUCERS: Robert LoCash, Gil Netter, David Zucker. CINEMATOGRAPHY: Steve Mason. EDITING: Jeffrey Reiner. MUSIC: Ira Newborn. PRODUCTION DESIGN: Steven Jordan. ART DIRECTION: Bill Hiney. COSTUME DESIGN: Catherine Adair.

CAST: Trey Parker (Joe Cooper), Matt Stone (Doug Reemer), Yasmine Bleeth (Jenna Reed), Jenny McCarthy (Yvette Denslow), Robert Vaughn (Baxter Cain), Ernest Borgnine (Ted Denslow).

RUNNING TIME: 103 minutes.

DVD: Universal Studios.

This film is a broad comedy about a pair of friends who invent a new sport with some outrageous rules. Several sports broadcasters appear as themselves, including Bob Costas, Al Michaels, Dan Patrick, and Kenny Mayne.

BASKETBALL DIARIES (1995)

DIRECTOR: Scott Kalvert. SCREENPLAY: Bryan Goluboff, based on the novel by Jim Carroll. PRODUCERS: Liz Heller, John Bard Manulis. CINEMATOGRAPHY: David Phillips. EDITING: Dana Congdon. MUSIC: Graeme Revell. PRODUCTION DESIGN: Christopher Nowak. COSTUME DESIGN: David C. Robinson.

CAST: Leonardo DiCaprio (Jim Carroll), Lorraine Bracco (Jim's mother), Bruno Kirby (Swifty), Mark Wahlberg (Mickey), Marilyn Sokol (chanting woman).

RUNNING TIME: 102 minutes.

DVD: Palm Pictures.

The film adaptation of Jim Carroll's autobiographical novel, *Basketball Diaries*, catapulted Leonardo DiCaprio into starring roles in other films and became a cult favorite. Although the title suggests that basketball is the focus, the film is really about a young man's descent into drug addiction and his triumph over his habit, all chronicled by the voice-over narration of Carroll (DiCaprio), who reads from the pages of his published diary.

Jim moves from being interested in doing drugs and playing basketball to just doing drugs. He is initially presented as an outstanding member of the St. Vitus basketball team; he is also a rebellious, troubled youth who chafes at his single mother's nagging and his priest/teacher's chastising. His outlet, in addition to breaking rules, skipping school, sniffing dope, and humiliating Diane (Juliette Lewis), a junkie/whore, is basketball, both on the court and on the playground, where he and Reggie (Ernie Hudson) daily duel. Jim and his gang share the loot that another gang member, Pedro (James Madio), steals from an opposing team's lockers, fight the opposing team outside a fast-food place, and then split up. Jim visits Bobby (Michael Imperioli), a team member who is dying of leukemia, and in a well-intentioned effort to cheer his buddy up, takes him from the hospital to a strip club, where he hopes Bobby will be aroused. Weak from the drugs he has been taking, Bobby fails to get an erection, feels frustrated, and demands to be returned to the hospital. Jim callously asks Bobby if they can wait until the stripper finishes her act. Jim is a complex, almost contradictory character who can be sensitive—as his poetry indicates—and insensitive and cruel. How does one interpret the line from Jim's diary that Bobby reads: "I just want to be pure" ?

Throughout the film good and evil are juxtaposed. Scenes of Jim reciting poetry as he lies naked on a rooftop under the stars are followed by the gang mooning Circle Line passengers from their perch high above the Hudson and by a torrid sex scene in an up-scale condominium, featuring Jim, Mickey (Mark Wahlberg), and Winkie and Blinkie, who are sisters (played by twins Brittany and Cynthia Daniel). After Bobby's funeral (the scene is shot first as a dream but soon becomes reality), the gang discuss Bobby, and Jim becomes angry at them (and at himself). They then begin to play basketball during a thunderstorm, and at one point Jim hangs onto the rim in a Christ-like pose. Confrontations with his mother and the priest follow; after he confesses his sins to the bored priest, an incredulous Jim receives ten Hail Marys and five Our Fathers as his penance.

A basketball game serves as a kind of "wake-up call." Before the game Swifty (Bruno Kirby), the coach, finds Jim in the shower doing drugs and asks him for sex. Jim rejects the offer and returns to the court, where his performance culminates with a missed foul shot and his collapse to the floor. He and Mickey are suspended from school for two weeks and are kicked off the team. His mother also throws him and a small basketball trophy out of her place; then the petty crimes to support the drug habit begin. These are included in a lengthy recitation about his growing dependence on drugs and follow a shocking dream that eerily anticipates the Columbine High School shootings. In the dream sequence Jim, dressed in a floor-length coat and carrying a rifle, enters a classroom and begins gunning down students and then threatening the priest/teacher. The dream ends in the classroom with the teacher tapping the sleeping Jim on the shoulder.

A real-life drama follows in which Pedro, Mickey, and Jim break into a bar, hoping to find some cash. Instead, Mickey finds a gun, which he waves around before he threatens Pedro with it. When the police arrive, Mickey pistol whips Pedro and leaves him on the floor. Pedro is arrested, and Mickey and Jim escape to another bar, where they see Neutron, a former teammate, being interviewed on television. Neutron mentions getting a basketball scholarship to St. John's and says hello to his mother. Jim now understands that if he had not used drugs, he could have earned a basketball scholarship and he would still have a relationship with his own mother.

Jim then revisits Winkie and Blinkie, but this time is confronted by their father, who has him escorted out. Next he is chased down and beaten up by the irate boyfriend of a young woman to whom he had sold bad dope. In the dream that follows, Jim is shot dead and is sprawled Christ-like on the floor of a gym. He is actually on the snow-covered playground basketball court, where Reggie picks him up and carries him to his apartment. Reggie, who has been where Jim is now, forces him to go through a painful withdrawal from drugs, but as soon as he survives the withdrawal, the ungrateful Jim steals Reggie's money and leaves in search of a dealer. What goes around comes around as Jim meets Diane, whom he had earlier humiliated and who now taunts him about his appearance, asking him, "Who's the whore now?" Jim is, since he has sex with a man in a toilet booth and perhaps sees Swifty. (It's not clear if Swifty is also there or Jim imagines him laughing at him.) The action runs downhill from there as Mickey joins Jim, and the two buy what turns out to be bad dope from a Latino, whom Mickey pursues until the Latino falls off a roof and dies. (The audience later learns that Mickey gets a five-to-fifteen-year sentence for the crime.) When Jim finally turns to his mother for help, she will not let him in. In perhaps the most effective scene in the film, Jim promises to "be a good boy" as his mother, torn between wanting to help him and knowing that he needs more than money, holds the cash in one hand and the telephone—to call the police—in the other.

Sentenced to six months at Rikers Island, Jim continues to write his diaries, and when he has served his time, he meets Pedro, who offers him some drugs. Jim turns down the gift and walks through a "Stage Door." In the ending sequence Jim is seated on the floor in a Yoga pose and reciting material from his diaries. When he concludes, he receives the applause of the small audience.

The last scene suggests that Jim's new outlet will be his writing and performing. The "afterword" informs the audience that Jim has gone on to become a novelist, performer, and poet. *Basketball Diaries* is not as much about basketball as it is about addiction and the role that writing can play in helping a young man work his way through adolescent issues.

The real Jim Carroll published two volumes of poetry while still a teenager. He became a fixture in the Manhattan avant-garde, befriending painters Andy Warhol and Larry Rivers. Singer Patti Smith encouraged him to pursue music; his band caught the attention of Keith Richards, who helped him secure recording contracts. Carroll continued to publish poetry throughout the late twentieth century. He died in September 2009.

BATTLING BUTLER (1926)

DIRECTOR: Buster Keaton. SCREENPLAY: Al Boasberg, Lex Neal, Charles H. Smith, Paul Gerard Smith. PRODUCER: Buster Keaton. CINEMATOGRAPHY: Bert Haines, J. D. (Devereaux) Jennings.
CAST: Buster Keaton (Alfred Butler), Sally O'Neil (mountain girl), Walter James (girl's father), Budd Fine (girl's brother), Francis McDonald (Alfred "Battling" Butler).
RUNNING TIME: 71 minutes.
DVD: Kino Video.

Buster Keaton directed and starred in this silent-era comedy based on a Broadway musical. Keaton plays Alfred Butler, a pampered young man who impersonates a boxer in order to win favor with the family of his beloved.

When the film opens, Alfred's father has decided that the young man needs to be toughened up, so he sends Alfred on a camping trip into the mountains. Alfred leaves for the wilderness in a touring car laden with supplies and driven by his valet (Snitz Edwards). The valet sets up an elaborate tent for Alfred, complete with brass bed and portable bath tub. Alfred takes his breakfast in bed, and a boy on a bicycle delivers the morning paper. On the first hunting expedition, the valet serves as a caddy, carrying the guns, a wise arrangement since Alfred doesn't know one end of a shotgun from the other. As the camera zooms in on a menagerie of forest creatures and one stray chicken, Alfred laments the lack of game. While holding a gun awkwardly with the barrel pointing behind him, he somehow discharges the weapon, sending a load of buckshot very near a mountain girl (Sally O'Neil). She confronts Alfred, who is captivated by her beauty. But then his gun goes off again, putting a stop to further conversation.

The scene shifts to a mountain stream in which Alfred is attempting to fish from a chair he has positioned in the shallow water. He quickly abandons his efforts and moves to a boat, which he rows next to a duck. Alfred seizes the shotgun and with the end of the barrel inches from the fowl, squeezes the trigger, but he has neglected to load the gun; his attempts to do so while standing in the boat cause him to capsize. As he stands in water up to his armpits, the mountain girl paddles by, and he tips his hat. Charmed, the girl offers him a ride; the scene ends with Alfred still in the water, hanging on to the stern as the girl tows him off.

When the pair arrive at the campsite, Alfred invites the girl to stay for dinner. The valet sets a formal table and prepares an elegant meal while Alfred dresses in black tie and tux. As Alfred serves, the girl's father (Walter James) and brother (Budd Fine), both large men, arrive and stare at the setup. After they leave, the title cards inform us that Alfred asks the girl whether she has any more brothers or fathers at home. At nightfall, Alfred walks the girl home, but then she must lead him back to his campsite.

The next morning Alfred relaxes with a hot bath and the morning paper, where he reads about a boxer, Alfred "Battling" Butler, who is scheduled to take on the lightweight champion. Alfred shows the valet the article, then turns to a more serious subject: he wants to marry the mountain girl. Alfred sends the valet to deliver the proposal. The mountain girl is thrilled, but her father and brother are concerned that Alfred is too much of a weakling to take care of her. To enhance his employer's chances, the valet produces the newspaper article and indicates that his employer

Alfred Butler and Alfred "Battling" Butler are one and the same. When the father and brother appear at the camp to congratulate Alfred on his engagement, he is too intimidated to tell the truth. He and the valet hurry off to the championship fight while the mountain family stay at home to listen on the radio. Alfred assumes that Battling Butler, the underdog, will lose, bringing a speedy retirement from the ring and an end to the publicity. Unfortunately for Alfred, Battling Butler (Francis McDonald) KO's the champ, and Alfred returns to a hero's welcome. A brass band marches him straight to the mountain cabin, where the family is gathered for the wedding. The ceremony goes off without a hitch, but Alfred learns that he is expected to leave immediately to prepare for his next match against a fighter known as the Alabama Murderer.

After forbidding his wife to join him, using the excuse that he doesn't want her to know him as the vicious fighter he becomes in the ring, Alfred, along with his valet, heads for Battling Butler's training camp in order to post letters from there. The boxer arrives before Alfred does and registers at the hotel with his wife (Mary O'Brien), who receives some scrutiny from the desk clerk because she has neglected to put on a wedding ring. After checking into their room, Mrs. Battling Butler goes for a walk in her pumps. Soon she is limping, but gets a ride back to the hotel with Alfred and the valet. Alfred signs in at the desk as "Alfred Butler and man" just beneath "Alfred Battling Butler and wife." The camera lingers on the signatures, inviting comparison and suggesting that Alfred is not yet "a man," for he has had no opportunity to consummate his marriage.

Later Alfred encounters Mrs. B. Butler at the training camp. When he asks about her heel, she responds, "He's fine," another example of the verbal humor in this silent film. Battling watches the exchange and glares at the two, simultaneously knocking out his sparring partner. Alfred is about to leave the training camp when he learns his own wife is approaching. He darts back inside, where Battling is preparing to go for a run. Alfred suits up and follows the boxer and his trainer. When his wife catches his attention, Alfred pauses long enough to thank her for coming and to tell her to go back home. That evening, Mrs. B. Butler asks Alfred to fix a light in her room. Battling, who sees Alfred enter the room, rushes in after. Alfred escapes unharmed, but it is clear that Battling is angry. The next day, the two Mrs. Butlers are sitting outside with a table between them when a waiter brings over a box of chocolates, compliments of "Mr. Butler." The women begin to argue over the candy as Alfred and Battling appear. Alfred takes Battling aside and quickly explains his dilemma. The boxer agrees to go along with the deception. Although he has seemed good-natured, his pleasant humor is only a façade; he intends to get even with Alfred by forcing him to face the Alabama Murderer.

The next segment of the film follows Alfred's training. On his first attempt to climb into the ring, he becomes hopelessly caught up in the ropes; then he puts his gloves on backward. When he finally begins to spar, he watches the trainer instead of his partner and receives a pummeling. The regimen of diet and exercise leaves him hungry and exhausted, yet still unprepared to take on the Murderer.

On the night of the fight, Alfred arrives dressed for a funeral. An ambulance waits just outside. Although Alfred has attempted to persuade his wife to stay at the hotel, she arrives at the dressing room, announcing that her father and brother have bet all of their savings on him. Alfred asks the valet to find her a seat; instead he locks her in an adjacent storage room. Meanwhile, the Alabama Murderer has knocked his sparring partner for a literal loop. During the preliminary bout, Alfred can barely watch, but as he peeks through the shutter separating him from a view of the ring, he realizes that the main event is underway with the real Battling Butler fighting the Murderer. It is a brief fight. Battling retains his championship easily, and for a moment, Alfred is relieved. However, Battling's intent was to defend his championship and claim his winnings, not to save Alfred's hide. In fact, Battling is now determined to deliver Alfred a beating. Alfred ducks and dodges to no avail. Just when it seems Alfred's about to go down for the count, his wife gets out of the closet. The sight of her spurs Alfred to lash back at Battling, and soon Alfred has defeated both the boxer and the trainer. He turns to Mrs. A. Butler and confesses that he's not a real fighter, to which she responds, "I'm glad." The film ends with Alfred in top hat and boxing trunks strolling arm and arm with the mountain girl.

Like Keaton's later film, *College* (1928), *Battling Butler* equates physical prowess with manliness. In both films the Keaton character must prove himself athletically in order to secure a marriage, but in neither case does the woman reject the "weak" man. In *College*, the bookish Ronald is admired by Mary until he uses his valedictory address to attack school athletics and belittle athletes. In *Battling Butler*, the mountain girl agrees to marriage even though she knows Alfred is inept in the great outdoors; it is her father and brother who insist she wed a manly man. Keaton, a talented athlete who performed nearly all of his own stunts, manages to poke fun at conventional masculinity while excelling in the skills associated with it.

THE BEAR **(1984)**

DIRECTOR: Richard C. Sarafian. SCREENPLAY: Michael Kane. PRODUCER: Larry G. Spangler. CINEMATOGRAPHY: Laszlo George. EDITING: Robert Florio. MUSIC: Bill Conti. PRODUCTION DESIGN: George Costello. ART DIRECTION: Mario Rebman Caso. COSTUME DESIGN: Ron Talsky.

CAST: Gary Busey (Paul W. Bryant), Cynthia Leake (Mary Harmon Bryant), Harry Dean Stanton (Coach Thomas), Jon-Erik Hexum (Pat Trammell).

RUNNING TIME: 112 minutes.

The Bear is a biographical film about Alabama football coach Paul "Bear" Bryant.

BEER LEAGUE **(2006)**

DIRECTOR: Frank Sebastiano. SCREENPLAY: Frank Sebastiano, Artie Lange. PRODUCERS: Artie Lange, Anthony Mastromauro. CINEMATOGRAPHY: David Phillips. EDITING: Peter Fandetti. MUSIC: B. C. Smith. PRODUCTION DESIGN: Kelly McGehee. COSTUME DESIGN: Nancy Brous.

CAST: Artie Lange (Artie DeVanzo), Ralph Macchio (Maz), Anthony DeSando (Dennis Mangenelli), Cara Buono (Linda Salvo), Seymour Cassel (Dirt).

RUNNING TIME: 86 minutes.

DVD: Echo Bridge Home Entertainment.

Slackers on a New Jersey softball team try to transform themselves into winners.

THE BENCHWARMERS **(2006)**

DIRECTOR: Dennis Dugan. SCREENPLAY: Allen Covert, Nick Swarson. PRODUCERS: Jack Giarraputo, Adam Sandler. CINEMATOGRAPHY: Thomas E. Ackerman. EDITING: Peck Prior, Sandy Solowitz. MUSIC: Waddy Wachtel. PRODUCTION DESIGN: Perry Andelin Blake. ART DIRECTION: Alan Au, Jeffrey Mossa. COSTUME DESIGN: Mary Jane Fort.

CAST: Rob Schneider (Gus), David Spade (Richie), Jon Heder (Clark), Jon Lovitz (Mel), Tim Meadows (Wayne), Craig Kilborn (Jerry), James Earl Jones (Darth Vader voice).

RUNNING TIME: 80 minutes.
DVD: Sony Pictures.

Adult nerds compete against Little Leaguers in this unfunny comedy.

BEND IT LIKE BECKHAM (2002)

DIRECTOR: Gurinder Chadha. SCREENPLAY: Gurinder Chadha, Guljit Bindra, Paul Mayeda Berges. PRODUCERS: Gurinder Chadha, Deepak Nayar. CINEMATOGRAPHY: Jong Lin. EDITING: Justin Krish. MUSIC: Craig Pruess. PRODUCTION DESIGN: Nick Ellis. ART DIRECTION: Mark Scruton. COSTUME DESIGN: Ralph Holes.
CAST: Parminder Nagra (Jesminder "Jess" Bhamra), Keira Knightley (Juliette "Jules" Paxton), Jonathan Rhys Meyers (Joe), Anupam Kher (Mr. Bhamra), Archie Panjabi (Pinky), Juliet Stevenson (Mrs. Paxton), Frank Harper (Mr. Paxton).
RUNNING TIME: 112 minutes.
DVD: 20th Century Fox.

Director Gurinder Chadha calls *Bend It Like Beckham* an autobiographical film because, like her main character, she grew up in an orthodox Sikh family in west London and was constrained by traditional expectations. Unlike her main character, she was not a soccer player, but she did want to follow a career path. Her inspiration for the film came when she noticed the diversity of soccer fans at her local pub, and she determined "to make a film combining the English passion for football with the Indian passion for marriage." Chadha introduces a number of plot threads: generational conflict, prejudices of all sorts, and a romantic triangle. While many of the issues addressed are serious, the film never strays far from comedy.

Jesminder Bhamra (Parminder Nagra), known as Jess, has taken her A-levels, and her parents plan for her to attend university, become a solicitor, and marry an Indian man. Jess wants to play soccer. In her room, decorated with posters of David Beckham, she fantasizes scoring the winning goal in a professional match; in her spare time she plays soccer in the park with boys her age. Some of them tease her, but they respect her skill. Jess's father (Anupam Kher), bitter that he was not allowed to play cricket at an English club in Nairobi, repeatedly suggests Jess get rid of her posters and give up sports. Her mother (Shaheen Khan) wants Jess to perfect her domestic skills and take more interest in her appearance.

Jess's life changes when she meets Juliette Paxton (Keira Knightley), a white English girl. Like Jess, "Jules" is devoted to playing soccer but faces pressure from her mother, who, fearful that Jules will fail to attract a suitable mate, persists in steering her toward more "feminine" interests. As Mrs. Paxton (Juliet Stevenson) puts it, "There's a reason Sporty Spice is the only one without a fellow." Trouble begins when Jules, who plays with the Hounslow Harriers in a girls' soccer league, persuades Jess to try out. In order to join the Harriers, she must deceive her parents. Misunderstandings abound, complicating Jess's friendship with Jules and disrupting both the Paxton and the Bhamra families.

Because Jess's parents are preoccupied with plans for her sister's (Archie Panjabi as Pinky) upcoming wedding, they have not been keeping close watch over Jess's actions and believe that she has a summer job; of course, she is playing soccer instead. Twice she is spotted by Pinky's future mother-in-law, who misinterprets friendly contact with her soccer mates for promiscuity. As a result, the wedding is called off, and Pinky tells on Jess, who is forbidden to play in an upcoming match in Germany, where there will be scouts from universities in the United States. But Pinky and Jess make up quickly and scheme to escape their parents' home by saying they are visiting cousins for a few days. Pinky slips away with her fiancé, Teetu (Kulvinder Ghir), while Jess travels to Germany with the team.

In Germany, Jess and the Harriers' coach, Joe (Jonathan Rhys Meyers), become close. Joe, whose career was cut short by a knee injury, is an Irishman estranged from his demanding father. He understands Jess's problems and tries to encourage her to establish her own goals and stick to them. He also finds her attractive. But Jules has been hiding a crush on Joe and becomes jealous when she sees Joe and Jess about to kiss. Jess's parents, having read about the soccer match in the paper, learn of her trip, and Jules's mother, overhearing part of an argument between the girls, thinks they have had a lovers' quarrel.

On the bright side, the wedding plans are proceeding once again, the soccer scouts have been impressed by both Jess and Jules, Mrs. Paxton is determined to learn the game and support her daughter, Jess has done well on her A-levels, and Joe has spoken with Jess's father about her potential. Joe also talks with Jess again, encouraging her not to give up and telling her she is fortunate that her family cares so much about her. Although Jess is determined to play in a tournament match where the scouts will be watching closely, her hopes are dashed when Pinky's wedding is scheduled for the day of the tournament.

The film crosscuts between preparations for the tournament and the wedding, continuing through the first half of play, on the one hand, and the wedding reception on the other. The Harriers are down 1–0, and Jess is looking beautiful but absolutely miserable in her sari. Her cousin Tony (Ameet Chana) suggests he take her to the match for the second half, and to Jess's surprise, her father insists that the three of them go. Jess and Jules patch up their friendship on the pitch and play together well. Jess scores the winning goal, a penalty kick, by "bending" the ball around a wall of defenders, and the scouts offer both girls full scholarships to a university in California. Knowing that she has played her best because she now has her father's support and has not had to lie to her family, Jess returns to the reception. Jules arrives, driven by her mother, who becomes upset and calls Jess a lesbian. This alarms Jess's mother and aunts, who think she has been called "Lebanese," but the scene serves the purpose of convincing Mrs. Paxton that she has been wrong about her daughter. Jess's father decides to allow her to attend the American university because he has seen how happy she is. He does not want her to repeat his mistake when he gave up cricket. Joe is offered a position with the boys' team, but declines it, electing instead to continue coaching the girls and turn the Harriers into a professional team; he has even called his father to share the news. Joe appears at the airport just before Jules and Jess depart, and his affectionate goodbye to Jess draws no indication of jealousy from Jules nor any sign of shock from the Bhamras. During the closing credits, Mr. Bhamra and Joe are playing cricket.

Bend It Like Beckham has been an extraordinarily popular film. In the United States it won an ESPY for Best Sports Movie (2003), and in England it earned a Best Comedy Award (2002); Keira Knightley took the London Film Critics Circle Award for Britain's Best Newcomer. The film has been well received in India as well, and Gurinda Chadha has been highly praised for her lighthearted but honest portrayal of how the British and the Indian people have been affected by exposure to each other's cultures.

THE BEST OF TIMES (1986)

DIRECTOR: Roger Spottiswoode. SCREENPLAY: Ron Shelton. PRODUCER: Gordon

Carroll. CINEMATOGRAPHY: Charles F. Wheeler. EDITING: Garth Craven. MUSIC: Arthur B. Rubenstein. SET DECORATION: Marc E. Meyer Jr. COSTUME DESIGN: Patricia Norris.
CAST: Robin Williams (Jack Dundee), Kurt Russell (Reno Hightower), Pamela Reed (Gigi Hightower), Holly Palance (Elly Dundee), Donald Moffat (the Colonel), Margaret Whitton (Darla), M. Emmet Walsh (Charlie).
RUNNING TIME: 104 minutes.
DVD: Lions Gate.

This football comedy pokes fun at much of the standard fare of sports films—grown men trying to relive their high school sports experience, the triumph of the underdogs, the winning score as the clock runs out, and, above all, the connection between athletics and community. *The Best of Times*, echoing Dickens, is a tale of two cities, Bakersfield, California, and neighboring Taft, a small town whose fate seems linked to its miserable record against Bakersfield.

The film begins with pseudo-documentary footage of Taft's misfortunes. Torrential rains and flooding followed a 1911 loss. Two years later, local boxing hero Kid Lester was knocked out by a heavyweight contender, and Taft fell to Bakersfield's Tigers by an even larger margin. Then came an invasion of mice, more rain, and an 82–6 defeat. Even the oil boom seemed a bust. But in 1972, Taft quarterback Reno Hightower (Kurt Russell) spirited the Taft Rockets to a winning season. With seconds remaining in a scoreless game against the Tigers, Reno dropped back to pass, sending a beautiful spiral into the hands of an open receiver, Jack Dundee (Robin Williams), who dropped the ball. Reno was sacked on the play, suffering a career-ending injury, and Jack has been haunted ever since. Following suit, the town of Taft has "slipped into oblivion."

Thirteen years later, Jack sequesters himself in his office and replays film of his disastrous drop in the end zone. When his wife, Elly (Holly Palance), arrives, he asks her if she is happy, a question she's heard an alarming number of times. Before they can discuss their happiness, Elly's father, the Colonel (Donald Moffatt), comes in with a portrait of himself done "in the style of Velasquez," whom he believes is Mexican. The Colonel, a Bakersfield man, owns ten banks, including the one where Jack serves as vice president. The Colonel considers his son-in-law a dolt and takes every opportunity to remind him of the pass he failed to catch back in the 1970s.

Similarly, Reno has not been completely happy since his glory days of high school. His garage, where he paints vans, is losing money, and his wife, Gigi (Pamela Reed), wants to leave Taft to pursue a singing career. She turns up at the garage to tell him she wants a divorce and is moving to the Top Hat Motel. Then Jack comes in, as he does every week, to complain about how his car is running and to borrow a loaner. Reno suggests that all of this is a ploy so that Jack can visit Darla (Margaret Whitton), the local masseuse, without anyone recognizing his automobile. Of course, Jack denies the accusation; then he drives to Darla's, where he pays her to listen to him whine about the old football game.

Darla, like Elly, is tired of hearing about the past. She advises him to replay the game in order to put the incident behind him once and for all. Although initially hesitant, Jack leaves Darla's convinced that restaging the game will allow him to redeem his reputation and will revitalize the town. He hurries to Reno's to share his idea. As he speaks of "raising Taft out of lethargy," the camera pans the main street with its rundown shops and closed theater. Reno does not embrace his enthusiasm.

Top: Robin Williams (left) and Kurt Russell (right) have a team workout in *The Best of Times*; bottom: Williams and Russell on the night of the big game

Jack approaches the Colonel with the idea, claiming that he represents the whole town. To his surprise, the Colonel readily accepts the challenge because it provides an opportunity to reinforce the "natural order," a system in which the underdogs always lose because of their natural inferiority. At dinner Jack can garner no support from Elly, who anticipates community-wide humiliation. As they quarrel, their intensity turns to passion, but just as they are about to make love, Elly demands Jack choose between her and football. The film cuts to the Top Hat Motel, where Jack has just rented a room.

Driven from the motel by noise from next door and two mice, Jack walks to Reno's, where the former quarterback is painting a version of *Starry Night* on a vehicle dubbed a "Van Go." Jack once again tries to sell Reno on his plan, this time offering to refinance his business loan at a lower rate if Reno will use his influence at the next meeting of the Caribou Club, where Jack hopes to win community support from Taft alumni.

Jack fails to persuade the Caribou to participate, and to make matters worse, the Colonel has easily recruited the old Bakersfield players. Jack resorts to skullduggery. Wearing a tiger suit, he vandalizes the Caribou Club, plasters graffiti on public surfaces, and storms the Safari Bar and Grill while Darla is performing and throws a bucket of orange paint at the stage. The attack on Darla and her backup singers motivates the Caribou to action: they will replay the game in defense of their womenfolk. The original linemen return to Taft, and the hard work of getting in shape begins. Their pathetic efforts are presented in a montage, intercut with scenes of the Bakersfield group, which has a playbook containing two hundred plays. Back in Taft, Reno is scrawling plays in the dirt with a twig. Meanwhile, the entire town is cleaning itself up, and the movie theater is scheduled to reopen.

Gigi and Elly are ready to forgive their husbands and invite them to a romantic dinner. The catch is that the men can't talk about football. Unfortunately, it's Monday night, and the guys can't resist the allure of Monday Night Football. Jack turns on a television in the next room so that he and Reno can catch snatches of the game during trips to the bathroom, but when the game gets interesting—and their wives are beginning to wonder about their husbands' bladders—Jack pushes the TV within view. Gigi and Elly, who have their backs to the set, are primed for postdinner passion until, inevitably, they discover the television and kick the guys out. Reno and Jack spend the rest of the evening drinking, and after a midnight visit to Bakersfield, where their team is still practicing, Jack fears he has set the entire town up for irreparable damage.

The night before the big game, Taft holds a dance. Gigi and Elly retreat to the ladies' room to discuss whether to dance with Reno and Jack, who are playing the role of mournful wallflowers. Gigi determines that they should take advantage of the moment because the next day will be disastrous. When Gigi leaves, Jack slips inside the ladies' room and pours his heart out, speaking directly to a closed stall door. His sincerity draws Elly out of the stall, and the pair waltz in front of a row of sinks. Meanwhile, Reno has left the dance, but Gigi finds him at the garage, where he is repairing her Volkswagen, a task he's been promising to undertake but has put off for way too long. Soon they are waltzing too.

The big game starts off as anticipated. The out-of-shape Rockets are no match for the Tigers, whose star running back, Johnny "O" (Jeff Severson), scores on the opening kickoff. Reno has entered the game dispirited by the realization that actually returning to the sport will undermine his status as a local hero. As the first half draws to a close, Reno has been sacked repeatedly, Jack has been unable to shake the defensive end, and Johnny "O" has scored his fifth touchdown. Then the Rockets' luck turns as Johnny "O" is injured by a teammate on the sidelines and leaves the field on a stretcher. The Taft coach offers an inspiring locker room speech, but Reno has lost what little drive he had. Fortunately, Jack has anticipated that extreme action may be required to get Reno fired up. After the others have taken the field, Jack leaves his duffel bag, with the tiger head fully visible. When Reno discovers the tiger head, he realizes it was Jack who attacked the Caribou Club. Reno flies into a rage, but Jack provokes him further, declaring he is not a quarterback and not a leader, just a "van specialist." Reno vows to prove Jack wrong. He changes into his treasured white shoes, which earlier he had not bothered to wear, chews out a running back who has ducked inside for a smoke, and breaks Jack's glasses.

A rainstorm that began at the half has turned the field to a mud wallow, but as Reno strides purposefully into the muck, all of Taft notices the white shoes, and their spirits lift. Reno takes the team into the end zone on the first possession; then Taft's defense scores, and the pattern continues until Taft has narrowed the Bakersfield lead to under six points. With less than a minute left, Taft forces a fumble and regains the ball on its own five-yard line. Reno, his self confidence restored, allows Jack into the game. As the final seconds tick away, Jack eludes coverage using his "Jack Aquarius" dance move, and manages to hang onto Reno's pass, scoring as the buzzer sounds. The defeated Colonel vows revenge, but quickly changes his tune, boasting that Jack is his son-in-law. The film closes with the revelation that a mysterious elderly fan who has watched the game intently—and who had the foresight to carry an umbrella—is none other than Kid Lester, Taft's great white hope from 1913.

BIG FAN (2009)

DIRECTOR: Robert D. Siegel. SCREENPLAY: Robert D. Siegel. PRODUCERS: Jean Kouremetis, Elan Bogarin. CINEMATOGRAPHY: Michael Simmonds. EDITING: Joshua Trank. MUSIC: Philip Nashel-Watts. PRODUCTION DESIGN: Sharoz Makarechi. COSTUME DESIGN: Vera Chow.

CAST: Patton Oswalt (Paul Aufiero), Kevin Corrigan (Sal), Michael Rappaport (Philadelphia Phil), Marcia Jean Kurtz (Paul's mom), Matt Servitto (Detective Velarde).

RUNNING TIME: 86 minutes.

DVD: Vivendi Entertainment.

A fan of the New Yorks Giants football team is humiliated by his favorite player.

THE BIG GREEN (1995)

DIRECTOR: Holly Goldberg Sloan. SCREENPLAY: Holly Goldberg Sloan. PRODUCER: Roger Birnbaum. CINEMATOGRAPHY: Ralf Bode. EDITING: John F. Link. MUSIC: Randy Edelman. PRODUCTION DESIGN: Evelyn Sakash. ART DIRECTION: Harry Darrow. COSTUME DESIGN: Rondi Hillstrom Davis.

CAST: Steve Guttenberg (Sheriff Tom Palmer), Olivia d'Abo (Anna Mongomery), Jay O. Sanders (Coach Jay Huffer), John Terry (Edwin V. Douglas).

RUNNING TIME: 100 minutes.

DVD: Walt Disney Video.

In the tradition of *The Mighty Ducks*, soccer gets the Disney treatment.

THE BIG LEBOWSKI (1998)

DIRECTOR: Joel Coen. SCREENPLAY: Ethan Coen, Joel Coen. PRODUCER: Ethan Coen. CINEMATOGRAPHY: Roger Deakins. EDITING: Roderick Jaynes, Joel Coen, Ethan Coen, Tricia Cooke. MUSIC: Carter Burwell. PRODUCTION DESIGN:

Rick Heinrichs. ART DIRECTION: John Dexter. COSTUME DESIGN: Mary Zophres.
CAST: Jeff Bridges (Jeffrey Lebowski), John Goodman (Walter Sobchak), Steve Buscemi (Donny Kerabatsos), Julianne Moore (Maude), David Huddleston (the "Big" Lebowski), John Turturro (Jesus Quintana), Philip Seymour Hoffman (Brandt), Tara Reid (Bunny).
RUNNING TIME: 117 minutes.
DVD: Universal Studios.

In this Coen brothers' cult classic, a bowling team becomes enmeshed in a kidnapping on the eve of a tournament. The Coens based their plot on Raymond Chandler's *The Big Sleep*, which is episodic in structure and notorious for its loose ends. Jeff Bridges stars as Jeffrey Lebowski, a stuck-in-the-sixties pothead who likes to be called "The Dude." His best friend, Walter Sobchak (John Goodman), is a Vietnam veteran who goes through life heavily armed and potentially dangerous. The third member of the team, Donny Kerabatsos (Steve Buscemi), bowls strikes and rarely gets to speak, an ironic twist on his motor-mouthed character from *Fargo*, another Coen brothers' product.

The film takes place in Los Angeles during the Persian Gulf War of 1990–1991. As the camera follows a tumbleweed blowing across the desert, through downtown Los Angeles and on to the Pacific Ocean, the gravelly, Western-accented voice of a character known only as The Stranger (Sam Elliott) proclaims The Dude to be a "man for his time and place." The camera shifts to The Dude's apartment, where he is being dunked in his toilet by two thugs who claim his wife, Bunny (Tara Reid), owes money to their boss, Jackie Treehorn (Ben Gazzara). However, The Dude isn't married, and after the thugs look around the apartment, they realize they've found the wrong Jeffrey Lebowski; the man they are looking for is a multimillionaire married to a shopaholic former porn star. But before the thugs leave, one of them micturates on the carpet, causing The Dude great distress. As Walter puts it, "That rug really tied the room together."

After discussing the matter at the bowling alley with Donny and Walter, The Dude decides he's owed compensation from the other Lebowski and sets off for the mansion, where he's greeted by Lebowski's assistant, Brandt (Philip Seymour Hoffman). The "Big" Lebowski (David Huddleston) is a Korean War veteran confined to a wheelchair. He declares The Dude an opportunistic bum before dismissing him compensationless; however, The Dude tells Brandt that Mr. Lebowski has given him his choice of any rug in the house. As The Dude, Brandt, and a pricey Persian carpet leave the mansion, they pass Bunny, who is painting her toenails green to match her bikini. She asks The Dude to blow on her toes, then offers him her services—for a thousand dollars. Brandt makes a weak joke about Bunny's sense of humor and hustles The Dude off the property.

Back at the bowling alley, Walter has brought his ex-wife's Yorkshire terrier, which he refers to as a Pomeranian; his dogsitting indicates the degree to which he has been influenced by his ex, Cynthia. Later it is learned that Walter adheres strictly to the rules of Shabbos even though it is Cynthia who is Jewish. When another bowler inadvertently steps over the foul line, Walter pulls a gun, an action that typifies his response to minor confrontations.

When The Dude returns to his apartment, he finds a message from Brandt that his assistance is needed. Bunny has been kidnapped, and Mr. Lebowski wants The Dude to deliver the ransom so that he can determine whether the kidnappers are the same thugs who peed on his carpet. The Dude agrees, assuming that Bunny has kidnapped herself in order to pay off her debts and keep the change for future expenses.

The scene returns to the bowling alley, where a rival bowler, the villainous pedophile Jesus Quintana (John Turturro), taunts Donny and Walter. Quintana, clad from head to toe in purple, caresses the bowling ball with the tip of his tongue before rolling a strike, and then performs a suggestive dance. The Dude's team has made the semifinals and is scheduled to meet Quintana on an upcoming Saturday, a date that, of course, conflicts with Walter's observation of Shabbos.

The Dude, having returned to his apartment, is lounging on the Persian carpet while a tape of the Venice Beach League Players 1987 tournament plays on his Walkman. He drifts off to sleep to the sound of tenpins tumbling, only to be awakened by another pair of thugs and a female accomplice. A fist strikes his jaw, followed by an explosion of stars that rearrange themselves as the lights of Los Angeles, over which the hallucinating Dude finds himself flying while attached to a bowling ball. When the ball pulls him down to earth, he lands on his own, now rugless, floor.

The next day, sent off to meet the kidnappers with a portable telephone and a serious-looking briefcase stuffed with the million-dollar ransom, The Dude stops for Walter, who has brought a "ringer," a less elegant briefcase stuffed with Walter's dirty underwear. He has also brought an Uzi with which he nearly destroys The Dude's car, an aging Ford, during the drop. In spite of The Dude's efforts to get the money to Bunny and collect his fee from Mr. Lebowski, Walter manages to throw the ringer from the car. Then they go bowling and practice for the semifinals while the portable phone rings away. When the two leave the bowling alley, they discover that The Dude's car has been stolen and with it, the briefcase containing the ransom. After filing a stolen vehicle report, The Dude returns home to a message from Mr. Lebowski's daughter, Maude (Julianne Moore), who explains she has the Persian carpet and is sending a limo to pick him up.

The Dude finds himself in Maude's studio, where she is producing a work of art about female form by swinging naked on a trapeze. Maude apologizes for hitting The Dude and refers him to a physician. She refuses to relinquish the carpet, which has sentimental value to her, but she offers The Dude 10 percent of the ransom if he will recover it from the kidnappers. Maude shows The Dude a portion of a video, *Logjammin'*, featuring her stepmother, of whom Maude is not fond. As Maude's limo pulls up at his place, The Dude is jerked into Mr. Lebowski's limo, spilling part of the white Russian cocktail he's brought from Maude's. Brandt and Mr. Lebowski accuse The Dude of stealing the ransom and demand its return. The Dude denies that he failed to make the delivery and shares his theory of Bunny's self-kidnapping, concluding she just wants more money. However, Mr. Lebowski has received a second note, this one containing a severed toe with green nail polish.

In the next scene, Walter and The Dude are having coffee at a diner. The Dude now feels responsible for endangering Bunny, but Walter insists it isn't her toe. Walter's frequent use of obscenities results in an altercation with the waitress, and The Dude exits, leaving Walter to finish his coffee while exercising his first amendment rights.

The Dude retreats to his bathtub, where, surrounded by candles, he is getting stoned. His mellow state is interrupted by three German nihilists (Peter Stormare, Torsten Voges, and Flea of the Red Hot Chili Peppers) and an "aquatic mammal" that The Dude calls a marmot (an uncredited ferret, actually). The nihilists demand the ransom and drop the animal into the tub (special effects were used so that the ferret was not mistreated during filming). At the bowling alley The Dude shares his latest adventure with Donny and Walter, who regards nihilists as worse than Nazis: "Say what you will about National Socialism, at least it's an ethos." The Dude retreats to the bar for another white Russian. The Bob Nolan song "Tumbling Tumbleweeds" plays in the background, and The Stranger makes his first physical appearance, ordering a sarsaparilla. He offers The Dude a bit of wisdom: "Sometimes you eat the 'bar,' and sometimes the 'bar' eats you." Given the Stranger's accent, "bar" translates as "bear."

The plot grows more complex in the following scenes. The Dude visits Maude again and recognizes one of the nihilists from an Autobahn album cover; he discovers he's being followed by someone in a blue Volkswagen; and the police recover his car, but not the briefcase. The Dude does find a homework paper in the back seat, and Walter tracks down the student, the son of a famous science fiction writer confined to an iron lung in the living room of the family home. The boy refuses to say a word when confronted. A new Corvette parked in front of the boy's house convinces Walter that the kid has the money, and in a rage, Walter begins smashing it with a golf club. The car, unfortunately, belongs to a neighbor who retaliates by bashing The Dude's Ford. Next, Jackie Treehorn's thugs reappear and take The Dude to Jackie's. The Dude explains Bunny's kidnapping, but is slipped a mickey, and after an elaborate Busby Berkeley-esque hallucination featuring a chorus line wearing headdresses of fanned bowling pins, he awakes on a road in Malibu and is temporarily detained in police custody. He returns to find his apartment has been ransacked, but Maude is waiting for him because she wants to conceive a child. During the pillow talk The Dude learns that the ransom money is not Mr. Lebowski's but belongs to a charitable foundation established by Maude's mother; Mr. Lebowski is broke.

Suddenly, all of the pieces of the puzzle come together for The Dude, who realizes that Mr. Lebowski set up the whole thing when Bunny conveniently went AWOL. There was no money in the briefcase, ever. Walter and The Dude confront Mr. Lebowski (even though it's Saturday); they leave the mansion after Walter dumps Mr. Lebowski out of his wheelchair, under the mistaken impression that the veteran is faking his paralysis. Then the two head for the bowling alley, where they encounter, first, the trash-talking Quintana, and then the nihilists, who have set the Ford ablaze, still believing there is money. A fight ensues, led by Walter, who uses his bowling ball rather than a gun to take out the nihilists. The battle is brief, and the nihilists beat a hasty retreat, but Donny suffers a fatal heart attack.

The Dude and Walter retrieve Donny's ashes from the funeral home in a Folger's coffee container. On a cliff overlooking the Pacific, Walter offers a eulogy that segues into his memories of Vietnam, and when he scatters the ashes, a breeze blows them back into The Dude's face. At the bowling alley, The Stranger has returned to close the film, hinting "there's a Little Lebowski on the way" and hoping The Dude makes the finals of the tournament.

Although the Coens wrote characters specifically for Goodman, Turturro, Buscemi, Gazzaro, and Elliott, The Dude is based on two friends who assisted in the distribution of the brothers' first film, *Blood Simple* (1984). Some events in the film are also taken from the experiences of Coen acquaintances, and there are a number of self-referential touches. For example, many of The Dude's lines consist of variations on the lines of other characters. The unexpected death of Donny continues a Coen tradition of killing off Buscemi's character in each of their films. *The Big Lebowski* opened to critical acclaim and has engendered a cottage industry of scholarship devoted to tracking down sources and allusions. The DVD features a spoof, "The Making of *The Big Lebowski*," narrated by one Mortimer Young of the Forever Young Film Preservation Company.

BIG WEDNESDAY (1978)

DIRECTOR: John Milius. SCREENPLAY: John Milius, Dennis Aaberg. PRODUCERS: Buzz Feitshans, Greg MacGillivray. CINEMATOGRAPHY: Bruce Surtees. EDITING: Tim O'Meara, Robert L. Wolfe. MUSIC: Basil Poledouris. PRODUCTION DESIGN: Charles Rosen. ART DIRECTION: Dean Mitzner.
CAST: Jan-Michael Vincent (Matt Johnson), William Katt (Jack Barlow), Gary Busey (Leroy Smith), Patti D'Arbanville (Sally Jacobson), Lee Purcell (Peggy).
RUNNING TIME: 120 minutes.
DVD: Warner Home Video.

Big Wednesday, written and directed by John Milius and loosely based on his own experience, is a beautifully filmed surfing movie. It traces the progression of friendship between three young men over the course of a dozen years. The film is sectioned into four seasons with corresponding compass points, beginning with the South Swell in the summer of 1962 and concluding with the Great Swell in the spring of 1974; Big Wednesday refers to the day the waves peak.

In the opening scene it is dawn in Malibu, and the surfing community is coming to life. Many surfers have slept on the beach or in their cars. Two surfers, Jack Barlow (William Katt) and Leroy Smith (Gary Busey), arrive supporting their buddy, Matt Johnson (Jan-Michael Vincent), between them. They demand that Matt, still drunk from the night before, negotiate the steps on his own. He staggers down, borrows a battered board from a youngster, and paddles out behind his friends, complaining he's going to drown. Then in a flash he's "in the tube" and "walking the board" to the admiration of the crowd. Later that morning, they visit Bear (Sam Melville), a former surfer who waxes boards on a dilapidated pier and offers bits of wisdom, such as "never depend on anyone," which reflect his bitterness that his own surfing days are past.

Being young is of ultimate importance in the surf culture of Southern California, as recently arrived Chicagoan Sally Jacobson (Patti D'Arbanville) observes. Sally works at a beachside café, where the three friends are notorious. Soon after they are served, Matt and Leroy begin a food fight. Although Jack, who is the most mature of the trio, does not participate, he is tossed out with the other two, but not before inviting Sally to a party at his mother's house. The party is a predictable display of teen excess—alcohol in abundance, property damage, uninhibited sexual activity, and the crasher-inspired brawl. What is unusual about this scene is that, throughout, Jack's mother (Barbara Hale, William Katt's real mother) is upstairs reading *Catch-22* and maintaining a complacent expression. One suspects she's on valium.

While the party is developed as comedy, the next adventure, a trip to Mexico, takes a serious turn. As they approach the border, Leroy is brandishing an air rifle; Matt and his girl, Peggy (Lee Purcell), are rolling around in the back of the station wagon; and Sally is wedged in the front seat between Jack and Leroy. They park on the outskirts of Tijuana and resume drinking. Peggy announces that she is pregnant and intends to keep the baby. Later that evening, Leroy heads off on his own, and the two couples go to a strip club, where Matt takes a swing at a guy who has made a suggestive remark about Peggy. A fight breaks out in the bar, but unlike the brawl at Jack's party, this one is no laughing matter. The locals are armed with switchblades, and someone fires a gun. The Americans escape unharmed, but find their car has been trashed. Just as the two couples are ready to leave, Leroy appears with a Mexican woman he claims is his new bride; he abandons her on the spot to rejoin the others, who are intent on fleeing the country immediately. Back in Malibu, the pier where Bear plied his trade has been condemned. Drunk amid the ruins, he claims he is doomed to live out his life like an inlander.

In the next section—West Swell, fall of 1965—the sun has set on the youth of summer. Leroy and Jack, now a lifeguard, have received induction notices. In his official capacity as a rule enforcer, Jack clashes with Matt, who, unable to accept family responsibility, stumbles through life in an alcoholic haze. After playing matador with oncoming traffic and causing an accident, he staggers into Bear's thriving surf shop. Bear has been manufacturing signature boards and paying Matt endorsement fees, but Matt has grown uncomfortable with celebrity. Bear, who is soon to be married, offers friendship and advice. At the wedding, Bear assumes the role of peacemaker and gets Jack to join the others in toasting their friendship.

The scene shifts to the induction center. Jack, conventionally dressed, is standing in line outside when Leroy, Matt, and Waxer (Darrell Fetty), another surfer, drive past. They also have received draft notices, but they have plans to dodge induction. Waxer, in tight tangerine-colored pants and a slinky, fringed shirt, tries to pass himself off as gay, but ends up a Marine. Leroy, posing as a madman, and Matt, sporting an elaborate leg brace, are rejected. The irony here is that the masochistic Leroy really does freak out during his interview, and Matt is genuinely crippled, albeit not physically. Jack has enlisted in the army. He goes surfing by himself one last time. His farewell party is a subdued contrast to the fling three years earlier. Many of the same people attend, but they sit quietly while a black-and-white television in the background chronicles the Watts riots occurring a few miles away. Sally is the first to leave, tearfully and wordlessly. Matt's parting words are "Come back." Jack says, "Take care of these people."

The North Swell section takes place in the winter of 1968 and opens at Waxer's funeral. Matt is the only surfer who appears. He seems not to know that Waxer's first name was Jim. When he introduces himself to Waxer's family as an old friend from the beach, they do not respond to him. After the funeral, Matt meets Peggy at the beach café, now the Cosmic Café, which is run by hippies and which now serves vegetarian fare. Matt grouses at the owner to turn off the Eastern-influenced music and douses the table incense burner. That evening, Matt, Peggy, and their daughter attend the screening of a surfing film that features footage of Matt in his heyday but dwells on surfing's current star, Gerry Lopez. This glimpse into his past makes Matt uncomfortable. He's a family man now, running a swimming pool business, and he doesn't surf much anymore. However, in the next scene, he's at the beach, where his daughter is building a sandcastle and Peggy is reading. A pair of boots in the sand marks the return of Jack. In a flash, he's out of uniform and paddling out to Matt, who's just lying on his board, but soon they are both up on their feet. Matt brings Jack up to date: Leroy is in Hawaii, surfing the Pipeline. Bear has lost everything, including his wife, and has reverted to being an alcoholic drifter. Matt asks if Jack has seen Sally yet (he hasn't) and fails to mention that Sally is now married. When Jack does look her up, her husband answers the door, and Jack leaves. Apparently, he hasn't kept in touch. Matt, Leroy, and Jack visit the cemetery searching for Waxer's grave and hold their own memorial to "a good surfer" with a "nice cutback." Then the three seem headed along separate paths—Jack to a job, maybe up north; Leroy in search of the next wave; Matt to his ordinary life. The screen fades to black.

The Great Swell occurs in the spring of 1974. Matt visits Mrs. Barlow in search of Jack, who is a forest ranger on a tower somewhere in the Pacific Northwest. He says that Bear has asked him to round up the guys because the Great Swell is on its way and remarks that he hasn't seen Leroy in three years. After apologizing for his role in trashing her home when he was younger, Matt drives to the collapsed pier to meet Bear, who seems to live among the pilings. Bear gives Matt his prized surfboard and talks about how much he cared for the three boys. Matt tries to get Bear to come home with him, but Bear refuses. The next morning, Matt leaves with the board to surf Big Wednesday.

Towering waves are breaking on the beach, where lifeguards are trying to keep surfers out of the water. Rescue boats and helicopters fish people from the waves as pieces of broken boards wash ashore. On a cliff overlooking the water, a line of surfers stands surveying the scene and very much resembling Indians about to mount an attack in a B-grade Western. Matt spots Gerry (Gerry Lopez playing himself), who, ignoring the warnings, is striding toward the waves. Matt is not far behind. His path takes him down the decrepit beach stairs from the opening scene, and as in the opening, Jack and Leroy are waiting at the bottom. They maneuver their way through powerful waves and begin the most incredible ride of their lives. Leroy and Jack are in good form, but it is Matt who outshines everyone else in the ocean. Even Gerry watches in obvious appreciation. Matt's ride ends in a spiraling crush of water that pulls him down into a rip tide, but Jack and Leroy, who have been taking in the spectacle from the shore, race to his rescue.

As Matt limps between his two friends—another reference to the film's opening—a young admirer rushes up to return Matt's board. Matt caresses the board, then gives it to the young man. Bear observes the scene from a distance, approving of Matt's action. When someone asks Bear if he surfs, he says, "No, I'm just a garbage man." Meanwhile, Matt looks back to the water, where Gerry is still lounging on his board. Matt proclaims Gerry is as good as his reputation, to which Leroy responds, "So were we." Leroy and Jack walk off in separate directions, and Matt, boardless and alone, takes one last look at the waves before limping off.

Big Wednesday contains some stunning photography, and the action sequences take the audience inside the waves. However, critics panned the movie, finding it shallow and uneven, and audiences stayed away in droves in spite of the star-appeal of Jan-Michael Vincent. However, the film is interesting for its portrayal of Southern California during the 1960s and early 1970s. Milius's treatment captures a sense of the social isolation of surf culture, which evolved into the skateboard culture of the latter part of the twentieth century. The surfers have no political interests. The Watts riots draw no response from them. With the exception of Jack, they treat the draft as a carnival; they express no opposition to or support for the conflict in Vietnam; they honor Waxer as a decent surfer, not as a soldier who died in combat. Matt's outburst at the Cosmic Café, during which he expresses his disdain for hippies, signifies divisions among the self-styled counterculture. Without connection to the larger society, the surfers face a future without direction or meaning.

THE BIG WHEEL (1949)

DIRECTOR: Edward Ludwig. SCREENPLAY: Robert Smith. PRODUCERS: Mort Briskin, Samuel H. Stiefel. CINEMATOGRAPHY: Ernest Laszlo. EDITING: Walter Thompson. MUSIC: Gerard Carbonera, Nat W. Finston, John Leipold. PRODUCTION DESIGN: Rudi Feld. COSTUME DESIGN: Maria Donovan.

CAST: Mickey Rooney (Billy Coy), Thomas Mitchell (Arthur "Red" Stanley), Mary Hatcher (Louise Riley), Spring Byington (Mary Coy).

RUNNING TIME: 92 minutes.

DVD: Good Times Video.

Rooney plays a racetrack driver who dreams of success in Indianapolis, where his father was killed.

THE BINGO LONG TRAVELLING ALL-STARS AND MOTOR KINGS (1976)

DIRECTOR: John Badham. SCREENPLAY: Hal Barwood, Matthew Robbins, based on the novel by William Brashler. PRODUCER: Rob Cohen. CINEMATOGRAPHY: Bill Butler. EDITING: David Rawlins. MUSIC: William Goldstein. PRODUCTION DESIGN: Lawrence G. Paull. COSTUME DESIGN: Bernard Johnson.

CAST: Billy Dee Williams (Bingo Long), James Earl Jones (Leon Carter), Richard Pryor (Charlie Snow), Rico Dawson (Willie Lee Shively), Otis Day (Rainbow Miles), Sam Brison (Louis Keystone), Jophery C. Brown (Emory "Champ" Chambers), Stan Shaw ("Esquire Joe"), Ted Ross (Salison "Sallie" Potter), Mabel King (Bertha Dewitt).

RUNNING TIME: 110 minutes.

DVD: Universal Studios.

Based on the William Brashler novel (1973), *The Bingo Long Travelling All-Stars and Motor Kings* is a crossover film intended to attract black viewers while appealing to a white mainstream audience. It features leading African American actors of the time—Billy Dee Williams, James Earl Jones, Richard Pryor—as well as several members of the original Broadway cast of *The Wiz,* including Mabel King and Ted Ross as owners of Negro League baseball teams. Like the novel, the film is set in 1939 and follows the exploits of a group of players from the Negro baseball leagues who become disgruntled because of the owners' greed and form a breakaway all-star team that tours the Midwest, playing any games they can arrange. Unlike the novel, the film develops the comedic aspects of the story at the expense of characterization, but it does preserve much of the historical detail while tightening the plot.

To set the time period and create an historical context, the film opens with newsreel footage. Clips of Hitler's invasion of Czechoslovakia and of a man who chews razor blades and extinguishes cigarettes on his tongue reflect the juxtaposition of serious events and novelty stories characteristic of early newsreels shown in theaters. These vignettes, which have no immediate relevance to the film, are followed without comment by footage of the Negro League playing at Yankee Stadium; the original soundtrack has been replaced to allow the introduction of the fictitious characters Bingo Long and Leon Carter, along with their real-life counterparts, Satchel Paige and Josh Gibson.

As the screen changes from black and white to sepia to color, the opening credits roll, and the camera moves into a small stadium where two Negro League teams are playing. In the fashion of the legendary Paige, Bingo (Billy Dee Williams) throws an "invite pitch" to the first batter while the fielders stand on the sidelines. This crowd-pleasing stunt assured that even a ground ball or a pop up over the pitcher's head would produce an in-the-park home run, but it also had the advantage of enticing teams to put their strongest batter up first. Bingo succeeds with his first pitch against the opposing catcher, slugger Leon Carter (James Earl Jones), but Leon is able to distract Bingo with his banter and burns him for a run on the second pitch. The game itself is not important, and the script moves quickly to introduce the conflict between owners and players that will carry the plot. Appropriately, a hearse arrives at the ballpark, transporting funeral parlor and team owner Salison "Sallie" Potter (Ted Ross), who in short succession evicts from the park a former pennant-winning pitcher reduced to juggling for donations before games; fires Rainbow Miles (DeWayne Jessie, also known as Otis Day), who has just been injured by a pitched ball; and announces he is docking the team's salaries to cover travel expenses.

Later that evening, Bingo tells Leon about Rainbow's firing and describes the team owners as masters on a plantation. Leon, who is the more intellectual of the two, quotes W. E. B. DuBois and a bit of Marxist doctrine, inspiring Bingo to envision a revolt against the owners. Although Leon is skeptical, Bingo convinces him that they should form their own barnstorming team to travel the countryside, playing local black teams. With a hatful of change, Bingo sets up his recruiting station at a phone booth and soon puts together the All-Stars, the most high-profile being Charlie Snow aka Carlos Nevada (Richard Pryor), who is scheming to break into the white league by masquerading as a Cuban. Soon the group takes to the road with Leon leading the two-car motorcade on his motorcycle and Rainbow serving as accountant. At their first stop on the circuit, the All-Stars arrive at a general store in a black neighborhood of a small town. The store owner, who booked the game, instructs them to enter the town via Main Street and to put on a show by doing a cakewalk. Leon objects, asking whether they are "a ballclub or a circus," but he yields when the owner insists that the team needs to attract attention. After a few false starts, the team masters the dance steps, an offscreen orchestra strikes up, and residents from the neighborhood rush from their homes and yards to join in. Once the parade reaches Main Street, the white townspeople scowl at the display, but they show up for the game, and the future looks prosperous for Bingo's team.

Meanwhile, back at Sallie's funeral home, the Negro National League owners meet to determine how to get their players back. This scene introduces an ongoing rivalry between Sallie and Bertha Dewitt (Mabel King), who has inherited a team from her late husband. When Bertha bursts into the room, Sallie lets loose with a tirade of epithets, most directed at Bertha's large size. Bertha's suggestions are ignored, and Sallie insists on going forward with his own agenda, one that suggests foul play.

The film shifts back to the All-Stars, who are on the road again, tossing balls back and forth between their vehicles and thoroughly enjoying themselves. Their tour continues to be successful, and they have added to their roster an amazingly talented youngster whom they nickname "Esquire Joe" (Stan Shaw). Soon, however, Sallie's schemes put an end to this good fortune, for he has pressured all of the local Negro teams into cancelling games with the All-Stars. After a brief period of frustration, Bingo hits on a solution that he expresses in one of the film's few direct statements on race: "What do we never run out of in this country? White folks!" White team owners are immune to threats from Sallie and his ilk, and so once again the All-Stars are on their merry way.

Playing against white teams is profitable but difficult. The first game, ironically taking place on Independence Day, opens with the All-Stars looking grim as a high school band churns out "The Star Spangled Banner" and an inept majorette bobbles her baton. White children hurl firecrackers into the dugout; white adults hurl epithets and demand to be entertained. Bingo, who has anticipated a potentially hostile reception, is prepared to sacrifice dignity for getting out of town safely. He relieves the opposing pitcher in order to throw a firecracker instead of the ball to an unsuspecting Leon. Charlie/Carlos slides into second base, then turns around to reveal "torn" pants and polka-dot underwear. At later engagements, players bat facing the wrong way, and Bingo even pitches wearing a gorilla suit.

Before long, misfortune catches up with the team. First, Rainbow, who is in charge of the cashbox, is mugged by two of Sallie's goons, and Bingo must use all of the day's gate receipts, including his and Leon's shares, to pay the players. Then Charlie/Carlos, still pretending to be Cuban, gets chased after soliciting a white hooker. At the next game, played against the House of David, a team composed of Orthodox Jews, Charlie is cornered by the two thugs from his misadventure at the brothel. Here, the film takes a sudden turn from the comedic as Charlie is knifed. Although he survives, his medical bill at the local hospital takes all of the team's money. Flat broke, the All-Stars attempt to sneak out of their hotel since they can't pay the bill, but they are caught by the owner, who confiscates Bingo's car. Stranded, the team stoops—literally—to picking potatoes for a white farmer; then they are paid less than promised.

To recoup their losses, Bingo steals back his car, an act that Leon cannot sanction. Consequently, Leon leaves. The team continues without him, but their game has become even more of a circus act, complete with a one-armed player and a midget catcher. Just as the plot seems to have reached a dead end, Sallie Potter appears, announces he has fixed the problem of Bingo's car theft, and offers a deal: Bingo's All-Stars will play an all-star team put together by the owners. If Bingo's team wins, it can join the Negro League, but if the team loses, the players must return to their former teams. Certain he can persuade Leon to rejoin his All-Stars, Bingo accepts.

Sallie, still up to his old tricks, has his goons kidnap Leon and lock him in the funeral home. Leon escapes by switching places with the recently deceased occupant of one of the caskets, arriving at the field just in time to hit a game-winning home run, and the film moves quickly to tie up remaining loose ends. A furious Sallie is informed by Bertha that Bingo's team will replace Sallie's in the league. Esquire Joe is offered a contract with the white Brooklyn Dodgers, just as Charlie/Carlos arrives sporting a Mohawk and claiming to be a Native American. As the film closes, Leon anticipates that integration will mean the end of black baseball, but Bingo remains upbeat: "We can't never lose, never."

There's not much baseball in *The Bingo Long Travelling All-Stars and Motor Kings*; in fact, posters for the film gave no indication it was about baseball. Although the cast includes professional players, game coverage focuses on stunts and clowning. The film has been criticized for presenting Negro baseball as a minstrel show rather than as a serious sport and for the stereotyping that results from the comic drive of the script. However, it is important to note that the Negro teams did incorporate clowning in their games to maintain favor with white audiences, and some of the stunts—such as batting backward—were understood by African American fans as reflecting negatively on the quality of players on white opposing teams. Director John Badham, working on such a low budget that he staged one scene of an owners' meeting in a sauna to save money on costumes, chose not to invest in on-field scenes that would run up expenses.

Badham tried to balance the film by including the comic Jewish teams (several House of David groups played throughout the Midwest in the 1930s) and by exaggerating the Swedish accents of Minnesotans from the town where the All-Stars find themselves reduced to picking potatoes. Badham also had to battle studio heads who wanted to avoid social commentary; he did succeed in including an ironic billboard celebrating the American Dream in a background shot, and he used close-ups of extras drawn from the Macon, Georgia, area, people whose expressions of disgust at the All-Stars reflect what Badham has described as genuine racism. His next film, *Saturday Night Fever* (1977), also has been criticized for superficial treatment of racism.

THE BLACK STALLION (1979)

Director: Carroll Ballard. Screenplay: Melissa Mathison, Jeanne Rosenberg, William D. Wittliff, based on the novel by Walter Farley. Producers: Fred Roos, Tom Sternberg. Cinematography: Caleb Deschanel. Editing: Robert Dalva. Music: Carmine Coppola. Art Direction: Aurelio Crugnola, Earl Preston.

Cast: Kelly Reno (Alec Ramsey), Mickey Rooney (Henry Dailey), Teri Garr (Alec's mother), Clarence Muse (Mr. Snoe).

Running Time: 118 minutes.

Academy Award: Special Achievement Award, Sound (Alan Splet). Nominations: Best Supporting Actor (Rooney), Best Editing.

DVD: MGM.

Based on a 1961 novel by Walter Farley, *The Black Stallion* is about the relationship between a young boy, Alec Ramsey (Kelly Reno), and a wild black stallion.

The film begins off the coast of Africa in 1946. Alec and his father (Hoyt Axton) are on a ship that catches fire and sinks near a deserted island. Before the disaster, Alec has become intrigued by the stallion, known as Black. Although the animal is hard to handle, Alec leaves sugar cubes for him, establishing a thread of trust. Their relationship is linked to that of Alexander the Great and his horse, Bucephalus, when Alec's father tells him the legend. After a night of gambling, Mr. Ramsey has won a pocketknife and a figurine he identifies as Bucephalus. According to legend, Alexander the Great won the wild horse because he alone could ride it. By tying Alec to Alexander the Great, the film introduces a mythic element.

When the ship sinks, Alec alone survives; he grasps the ropes tied to Black, and together they are washed up on shore. Using an impressive assortment of skills (starting a fire, catching fish) Alec manages to survive, but, overcome by fatigue and the intense heat, he collapses. He awakes to find himself threatened by a large cobra within striking range. Black, who has avoided Alec's earlier overtures, suddenly appears and stomps the snake to death, again saving the boy's life. The bond between Alec and Black is strengthened when Alec feeds Black, this time with seaweed.

After this experience, the two frolic together on the beach, even playing a kind of tag. Their play, which consumes much film time, is captured by the lyrical photography of Caleb Deschanel. Their idyllic relationship, reminiscent of that between Robinson Crusoe and Friday, is threatened, however, when some fishermen appear near the island. Alec swims to the boat and is overjoyed to be rescued until he realizes the fishermen do not intend to save Black. He pleads with them to let him go back or to save the horse. Meanwhile, Black swims out to the boat and is hoisted aboard.

Alec and Black are eventually taken to Alec's mother (Teri Garr) in America. Black, confined to the family backyard, is startled by a trash collector and runs away. Alec searches unsuccessfully for Black until he is helped by Mr. Snoe (Clarence Muse) and his horse, Napoleon. Following Snoe's directions, Alec comes to a large farm and enters a dilapidated barn. He then falls through the flooring to a lower level, where he finds Black. His passage through his fall suggests that Alec is entering another world, that of horse racing.

Henry Dailey (Mickey Rooney), the owner of the farm and a former jockey, appears and does not contest the boy's ownership of the horse. Moreover, Henry becomes Alec's guide and mentor as the two recognize Black's racing potential. Henry not only advises Alec about being a jockey, but also arranges a match race between Black and two racing champions. At first, Henry has difficulty getting Black included because he is unknown. Henry is assisted in his efforts by a sportswriter, Neville (Michael Higgins), whose articles force the other owners to allow Black to run. (The match race, unlike regular races, does not require "papers" detailing the horse's pedigree. Black's lack of papers is an indication of his mysterious identity.) In the prerace newspaper coverage, Black is referred to as a mystery horse, and Alec is described as the mystery rider.

Unfortunately, Black's time trial and track experience have not included other horses or a starting gate. When the match race begins, Black's inexperience with the starting gates causes a minor injury and he immediately falls behind the two other horses. Black recovers quickly and sets off to overcome his bad start, but Alec, having noticed blood on the horse's leg, tries in vain to pull him up. Accepting that Black's natural competitiveness has kicked in, Alec tosses off his mask-like livery and rides bareheaded.

The film does not devote much time to Black's remarkable comeback and viewers do not see Black actually winning the race. Postrace coverage is also kept to a minimum. The focus becomes not Black's victory, but footage showing Alec riding Black on the beach at the deserted island. Thus, the film is less about a racing triumph than it is about the bond between Alec and Black. In effect, viewers see a modern Bucephalus and Alexander. Alec emerges as a talented jockey, and Black the fastest horse in the world.

The film became a classic for children. Although it has been described as an adventure tale, *The Black Stallion* contains few dangerous scenes, aside from the shipwreck and the cobra. Other potential threats—the injury to the horse, Snoe's ominous statement that perhaps Black should remain a wild horse rather than compete as a race horse—fail to develop into suspenseful situations.

The Black Stallion was a box office and critical success. Rooney was nominated for an Oscar, and Robert Dalva received another Oscar nomination for Best Editing. So popular was the film that a sequel, *The Black Stallion Returns*, appeared in 1983.

THE BLACK STALLION RETURNS (1983)

DIRECTOR: Robert Dalva. SCREENPLAY: Jerome Krass, Richard Kletter, based on the novel by Walter Farley. PRODUCER: Doug Claybourne, Fred Roos, Tom Sternberg. CINEMATOGRAPHY: Carlo Di Palma. EDITING: Paul Hirsch. MUSIC: Georges Delerue. ART DIRECTION: Aurelio Crugnola. COSTUME DESIGN: Danda Ortona.

CAST: Kelly Reno (Alec Ramsey), Vincent Spano (Raj), Allen Garfield (Kurr), Woody Strode (Meslar), Terri Garr (Alec's mother).
RUNNING TIME: 103 minutes.
DVD: MGM.

A sequel to the 1979 film, this film follows the young hero as he seeks to retrieve his beloved horse.

BLACK SUNDAY (1977)

DIRECTOR: John Frankenheimer. SCREENPLAY: Ernest Lehman, Ivan Moffat, Kenneth Ross, based on the novel by Thomas Harris. PRODUCER: Robert Evans. CINEMATOGRAPHY: John A. Alonzo. EDITING: Tom Rolf. MUSIC: John Williams. ART DIRECTION: Walter Tyler. COSTUME DESIGN: Ray Summers.
CAST: Robert Shaw (Kabakov), Bruce Dern (Lander), Marthe Keller (Dahlia), Fritz Weaver (Corley), Steven Keats (Moshevsky).
RUNNING TIME: 143 minutes.
DVD: Paramount.

Terrorists plot an attack that will culminate at the Super Bowl in Miami.

BLADES OF GLORY (2007)

DIRECTORS: Josh Gordon, Will Speck. SCREENPLAY: Jeff Cox, Craig Cox, John Altschuler, Dave Krinsky, Busy Philipps. PRODUCERS: Stuart Cornfeld, John Jacobs, Ben Stiller. CINEMATOGRAPHY: Stefan Czapsky. EDITING: Richard Pearson. MUSIC: Theodore Shapiro. PRODUCTION DESIGN: Stephen J. Lineweaver. ART DIRECTION: Seth Reed. COSTUME DESIGN: Julie Weiss.
CAST: Will Ferrell (Chazz Michael Michaels), Jon Heder (Jimmy MacElroy), Amy Poehler (Fairchild Van Waldenberg), Will Arnett (Stranz Van Waldenberg), Jenna Fischer (Katie Van Waldenberg), Craig T. Nelson (Jimmy's coach), Romany Malco (Jesse).
RUNNING TIME: 93 minutes.
DVD: DreamWorks Video.

Directed by Josh Gordon and Will Speck (known for the Geico caveman commercials), *Blades of Glory* spoofs ice skating and films like *The Cutting Edge* (1992). Will Ferrell and Jon Heder (*Napoleon Dynamite*) star as rival skaters who team up after getting banned for life from singles competition.

Chazz Michael Michaels (Ferrell), who honed his skills practicing underground sewer skating in his hometown of Detroit, imitates the athletic style of Elvis Stojko and refers to himself as "Sex on Ice." Archrival Jimmy MacElroy (Heder), an orphan with a gift for skating, was adopted by wealthy Darren MacElroy (William Fichtner), whose sole intent was to develop an Olympic gold medalist. Jimmy's training has incorporated state-of-the-art technology. He has been molded into a graceful skater known for his signature arm-flapping glide, the Galloping Peacock. His sequined costume, complete with tail feathers, parodies the swan outfit worn by Johnny Weir for the 2006 Winter Olympics. When Chazz and Jimmy tie for the gold at the Winter Games, the two begin fighting on the podium during the awards ceremony, a brawl that leads to their being barred from future competition. Millionaire MacElroy is so disturbed by the tie that he disowns Jimmy, saying if he wanted Jimmy to win half a medal he "would have bought [him] a brother." MacElroy boots Jimmy from his limo, leaving him on the side of a snowy road. Jimmy ends up working in a sporting goods store. Chazz lands a job skating the part of an evil wizard in a children's ice show.

Three and a half years pass. Jimmy has been demoted to stockroom boy, and

Chazz has been fired for drunken antics in front of the audience. Their fates seem bleak until Jimmy's stalker, Hector (Nick Swardson), finds a loophole in the regulations: Jimmy and Chazz have been banned from *singles* competition; they can still skate in pairs competition. When Jimmy's former coach (Craig T. Nelson) shows no interest in helping Jimmy get his career back on track, Jimmy visits "Grublets on Ice" in search of a partner. There, he encounters Chazz, and the two pick up where they left off, exchanging punches. A magnificent fight ensues, landing them in jail and making the news. As Jimmy's old coach watches footage of Chazz hefting Jimmy overhead and spinning him around before tossing him to the floor, he sees an amazing future for them all. Soon the coach has posted bail, and the two athletes register for the Winter Games tryouts as a pair, making the news once again.

The next segments are devoted largely to the evolution of the skaters' relationship as they overcome their hostilities and learn to skate together as a couple, with Jimmy taking the feminine position for dance moves. The storyline invites gay jokes, but the dialogue does not dwell on sexuality. The action, however, tells a different story; when the pair make their first appearance in competition, the camera targets the proximity of skater's groin to partner's face or hands. A subplot introduces competitors, an incestuous pair of siblings, Stranz (Will Arnett) and Fairchild (Amy Poehler) Van Waldenberg. This evil duo maintains control over a younger, virtuous sister, Katie (Jenna Fischer), whom they force to spy on Jimmy and Chazz. Katie and Jimmy are attracted to one another, a plot twist that reinforces Jimmy's heterosexuality and allows Chazz and Jimmy to become closer. Following Chazz and Jimmy's successful performance, Chazz coaches Jimmy in asking Katie on a date. The young couple go out for snow cones, and Katie confesses that she is supposed to spy, an admission that does not dampen Jimmy's affection.

Meanwhile, the coach is concerned that without a spectacular move, Chazz and Jimmy won't be able to defeat the Van Waldenbergs, so he has his skaters view a tape of the Iron Lotus, a North Korean move that has never been executed without the female skater being decapitated. (The Iron Lotus parodies the Pamchenko from *The Cutting Edge*. It is based on a spin called a "headbanger" and is illegal in Olympic competition.) Chazz practices with dummies, holding each by the ankles and spinning while lowering the head inches from the ice; the real danger comes with the conclusion of the move, in which Chazz flings the dummy and goes into a jump. The blades of his skates are supposed to pass his partner's head, but Chazz has been unable to perfect his role, and the rink is littered with dummy heads.

Just before the opening of the Montreal World Wintersport Games, Stranz and Fairchild threaten Katie that they will harm Jimmy unless she seduces Chazz in order to create discord between the two men. Katie follows Chazz to a support group for sex addicts and arranges to meet him at her room just before midnight so that they can resist temptation together. When Jimmy arrives at midnight with a bunch of balloons, he discovers Chazz and Katie in a compromising position. Brokenhearted, Jimmy runs from the room. Katie explains her siblings' threats to Chazz, who then attempts to set things straight, but Jimmy won't answer the phone. The Van Waldenbergs, realizing that Katie has revealed their treachery, determine to prevent Jimmy and Chazz from performing. They handcuff Jimmy to a toilet at the arena, and Stranz, disguised as a cabbie, kidnaps Chazz. Chazz is able to escape from the cab and get to a frozen stretch of river. He laces up his skates and takes off, with Stranz, now on skates, right behind him. As the chase continues, the men keep their skates on, climbing steps, getting on escalators, and making their way across pavement. Then, because Stranz and Fairchild are scheduled to perform ahead of Chazz and Jimmy, Stranz must reverse himself and race back.

The Van Waldenbergs, dressed as Marilyn Monroe and JFK, complete their act only to discover that Jimmy has managed to free himself. Jimmy takes center ice alone, and after a dramatic pause, Chazz appears in the rafters and slides down a cable with the aid of a jock strap. In a last desperate attempt to sabotage the pair, Fairchild casts her pearls in front of Chazz, who stumbles, breaking his ankle. In order to defeat the Van Waldenbergs, Jimmy and Chazz must do the Iron Lotus, but Chazz cannot complete the spin and jump with his fracture. Jimmy insists they switch places, a decision that requires the smaller, lighter Jimmy assume the power position, holding Chazz by the ankles in the spin. Both skaters complete their twists with Jimmy's skates coming within a literal whisker of Chazz's neck. Katie and Jimmy kiss and make up; the Van Waldenbergs are arrested; Chazz and Jimmy take the gold, and the two leave the arena via rockets; Hector the stalker plays with a pair of Jimmy and Chazz action figures.

A number of former Olympic skaters make cameo appearances, including Peggy Fleming, Dorothy Hamill, Nancy Kerrigan, Scott Hamilton, and Sasha Cohen. Heder and Ferrell worked with Sarah Hawahara, Michelle Kwan's coach, to prepare for their roles and did some of their own skating and stunts with the aid of blue screen and wire work; stunt doubles were used as well.

THE BLIND SIDE (2009)

DIRECTOR: John Lee Hancock. SCREENPLAY: John Lee Hancock, based on the book by Michael Lewis. PRODUCERS: Broderick Johnson, Andrew A. Kosove, Gil Netter. CINEMATOGRAPHY: Alar Kivilo. EDITING: Mark Livolsi. MUSIC: Carter Burwell. PRODUCTION DESIGN: Michael Corenblith. ART DIRECTION: Thomas Minton. COSTUME DESIGN: Daniel Orlandi.

CAST: Sandra Bullock (Leigh Anne Tuohy), Tim McGraw (Sean Tuohy), Quinton Aaron (Michael Oher), Kathy Bates (Miss Sue), Kim Dickens (Mrs. Boswell).

RUNNING TIME: 129 minutes.

ACADEMY AWARDS: Best Actress (Bullock). NOMINATIONS: Best Picture.

DVD: New Line Home Video.

The Blind Side is the film adaptation of Michael Lewis's 2006 biography of Michael Oher, who was the Baltimore Ravens' first-round pick in the 2009 NFL draft. One of thirteen children, Oher spent much of his childhood in foster care; his mother was an addict, and his father had abandoned the family. When Oher was sixteen, his athletic ability and the efforts of an acquaintance resulted in his being admitted to Briarcrest Christian School in Memphis. Being literally homeless, he lived with several families before becoming a permanent member of the Tuohy family. With their support, he raised his grade point average from a .6 to a 2.5+ and was aggressively pursued by college recruiters. He accepted a scholarship to the University of Mississippi, the alma mater of his adoptive parents, and played on Ole Miss's offensive line.

In the hands of director John Lee Hancock, Oher's adoptive mother, Leigh Anne Tuohy, played by Sandra Bullock, becomes the central character. The film opens with Leigh Anne providing a voiceover. As footage of the flea-flicker play that ended Redskins' quarterback Joe Theismann's professional career is shown, Leigh Anne explains that Lawrence Taylor, the New York Giant who tackled Theismann, changed the game, making the left tackle, whose job it is to protect a right-handed quarterback's "blind side," the second-most valuable and second-highest paid member of a squad. This scene, reminiscent of Annie Savoy's opening monologue in *Bull Durham,* follows Lewis's biography, but in the book, it is Lewis, not Leigh Anne, presenting views on the importance of the position. (At the time the film was released, Oher was starting at left tackle for the Baltimore Ravens; however, he can handle both the left and right side of the line and started at right guard in college.)

The scene shifts to the massive Michael Oher, played by Quinton Aaron (who slimmed down for the role), lumbering through his Hurt Village neighborhood, an aptly named project in Memphis, Tennessee. Then the film flashes ahead two years to an office building, where Michael faces hard questioning from an unidentified "investigator" (Sharon Morris as Granger) about a situation that remains a mystery for the audience until late in the story.

When the film moves back to the narrative present, Michael is riding in the backseat of a car as it passes through rundown neighborhoods marked by graffiti and trash into an affluent white area with manicured lawns, a pristine church, children on bicycles, a mother pushing a baby carriage. The car stops at the Wingate Christian School. Tony Hamilton (Omar Dorsey) has brought his son, Steven (Paul Amadi), and Michael in hopes of getting the two boys admitted. As the boys shoot basketballs outside, Tony explains to Coach Cotton (Ray McKinnon) that Steven is a good student and a talented athlete and that Tony can pay his fees; he also explains that Michael, the son of a crack-addicted mother and a missing father, is virtually homeless. As the coach watches Michael sinking baskets and moving gracefully and quickly on the court, he murmurs, "Mother of God." Soon the coach is arguing before the school's officers for Michael's admission, in spite of a .6 GPA and an 80 IQ. Wingate is, he reminds the committee, a Christian school.

Once classes begin, Michael suffers silently in what is for him an alien environment. (Both Steven and his father have disappeared from the script.) He is a weak reader who has never done homework before and who, as his teachers suspect, has trouble comprehending what's going on in the classroom. The other students shun him, except for the young, outgoing S.J. Tuohy (Jae Head), who greets him warmly when they pass. After a volleyball game in which S.J.'s sister, Collins (Lily Collins), is playing, Sean Tuohy (Tim McGraw) notices Michael picking through the popcorn containers left behind by the fans. The camera follows Michael to a Laundromat, where he rinses out some clothing in a sink, stalling until a paying customer leaves; then he tosses his items in with her load.

One drizzly November evening as the Tuohys are driving home, they pass Michael, and Leigh Anne asks who he is. "Stop the car," she commands, and soon she has ordered Michael into the backseat. At the Tuohys' he sleeps on the couch because the guest room is full of samples—Leigh Anne is a designer. Upstairs, she tells Sean she may have made a mistake and wonders if the family will be robbed. However, in the morning, when she discovers Michael missing (but nothing else) and the bedclothes neatly folded on the couch, she dashes out to look for him. Finding him not yet at the end of the driveway, she orders him back inside. It is Thanksgiving Day, and Michael has no where else to go.

Leigh Anne ventures out to purchase a festive dinner which is traditionally consumed in front of a pair of televisions tuned to football games. When she realizes that Michael is sitting alone in the dining room, she seizes the remotes and commands everyone to table. The next morning, she takes Michael out to shop for clothes. At first he resists, claiming he has clothing at his mother's. Leigh Anne makes her first trip to Hurt Village and waits in the car; on a nearby stoop, a group of young men close to Michael's age stare menacingly at Leigh Anne as Michael walks to his mother's apartment and discovers an eviction notice on the padlocked door. Back in the car he tells Leigh Anne his mother has moved. The two drive to a big-and-tall store in the neighborhood, where Leigh Anne, uncharacteristically, asks Michael if she will be safe on the street. He replies, "I've got your back." Michael becomes a fixture in the household, and Leigh Anne learns from the school counselor that on an aptitude test he scored in the 98th percentile in "protectiveness." Michael's protectiveness is illustrated later in the film, when he and S.J. are in a minor vehicle accident. Michael, who is driving, is able to throw his arm across S.J., who is too small to be sitting in the passenger's seat, before the airbag can deploy.

As the school year progresses, Michael becomes more comfortable with his new family, and they with him. Leigh Ann tracks down Michael's mother, whose crack addiction prevents her from reestablishing a relationship with her son. The Tuohys begin the process that will lead to adoption; at the same time, they help Michael improve his academic skills so that he will be eligible to train with the football team. To this end, they hire a tutor, Miss Sue (Kathy Bates), even though she is a Democrat and a nonbeliever. With her assistance, Michael's grades improve steadily, and soon he is in uniform. Meanwhile, S.J. assumes the role of personal trainer to help Michael get in shape.

In spite of his size and skill, Michael lacks aggression, and he has little sense of how the game is played. Coach Cotton grows increasingly frustrated. Then Leigh Ann takes charge, marching onto the field and dragging players around by their chin guards as she explains the team is like Michael's family, which Michael needs to protect. Once Michael views his position as one of ensuring the safety and well-being of the quarterback, his protectiveness instinct kicks in.

Michael quickly catches on and begins blocking in earnest, at one point taking an obnoxious opponent completely off the field. S.J., acting as his agent, prepares a video of highlights which he then distributes. Soon a procession of college coaches lands on the Tuohy doorstep: Nick Saban of Alabama, Tommy Tuberville of Auburn, Phillip Fulmer of Tennessee, and Houston Nutt and Ed Orgeron of Ole Miss (all playing themselves). Although Michael likes Tennessee, Sean, Leigh Anne, and Miss Sue want him to choose Ole Miss, their alma mater. And he finally does, but his selection triggers an NCAA investigation, and the scene shifts to Granger's interrogation, which began early in the film.

The NCAA is suspicious that the Tuohys took Michael into their home and treated him like a son, legally adopting him, as part of a recruitment scheme. When Granger suggests this to Michael, he rushes from her office. Outside, he asks Leigh Anne if this is true, but he is afraid to hear her answer and takes off. Back in his old neighborhood, he is welcomed by streetwise acquaintances who are now immersed in the drug trade. Michael is hesitant to accept their offers of hospitality, and when one makes lewd comments about Leigh Anne and Collins, he storms out, knocking a few heads together in the process. A bit later, Leigh Anne drives into the neighborhood looking for him. When one of the toughs tries to intimidate her, she lashes back with her own threats. Michael calls soon after, and the two are reunited. Leigh Anne apologizes for being pushy and offers him the reassurance that he needs.

Michael returns to Ms. Granger's office and apologizes for his abrupt departure. He points out that she had never simply asked him why he had chosen Ole Miss. When she does, he answers that he wants to attend the school his parents graduated from. It is a touching moment, and Ms. Granger ends her questioning. The closing scenes show Michael's graduation, Leigh Anne thumbing through clippings revealing the violent deaths of several young men from Hurt Village, and footage of the NFL draft.

Sandra Bullock has been highly praised for her performance, yet critics have been near unanimous in faulting the film for making her character the focus of the story. Reviewers have also noted that *The Blind Side* fits a pattern in sports films in which a black athlete's success is attributed to the intervention of whites. A *New York Times* essay by A. O. Scott, "Two Films, Two Routes from Poverty" (November 22, 2009), contrasts *The Blind Side* with *Precious*, identifying a conservative ideology at work in the former. In interviews immediately following the film's release, Oher stated he enjoyed the film, but expressed disappointment at being portrayed as a high school student without a working knowledge of football.

BLUE CHIPS (1994)

DIRECTOR: William Friedkin. SCREENPLAY: Ron Shelton. PRODUCER: Michele Rappaport. CINEMATOGRAPHY: Tom Priestley Jr. EDITING: Robert K. Lambert, David Rosenbloom. MUSIC: Jeff Beck, Jed Leiber, Nile Rodgers. PRODUCTION DESIGN: James Bissell. ART DIRECTION: Ed Verreaux. COSTUME DESIGN: Bernie Pollack.

CAST: Nick Nolte (Pete Bell), Mary McDonnell (Jenny Bell), J. T. Walsh (Happy), Ed O'Neill (Ed Axel), Alfre Woodard (Butch's mother), Bob Cousy (Western athletic director), Shaquille O'Neal (Neon), Robert Wuhl (Marty).

RUNNING TIME: 108 minutes.

DVD: Paramount.

Many basketball sports films contain relatively little actual basketball footage, and even when they do, it is sometimes poor in quality. *Blue Chips*, which includes such outstanding basketball players as Penny Hardaway and Shaquille O'Neal, is the exception. Since the film also features cameo appearances by college coaches Bobby Knight, Jim Boeheim, Rick Pitino, and Jerry Tarkanian, it seems "real." While the film concerns the plight of a specific coach, Pete Bell (Nick Nolte), of Western University, it is also the story of "Everycoach," who is torn between the will to succeed and the desire to act ethically. *Blue Chips* is another *Dr. Faustus* story about a man's pact with the Devil and his discovery that the price of success is too high.

After winning two national championships and a collection of conference titles, Coach Bell has several mediocre seasons before experiencing his first losing season. At the press conference following a loss to Pitino's Texas Western team, Ed Axel (Ed O'Neill), a local sportswriter, asks Bell if a recent recruiting scandal at Western has hurt Bell's recruiting efforts. Bell, who is proud of having run a clean program, angrily replies that the scandal was never proved and stomps out of the room. When he gets to his apartment, he hears a local television sportswriter tell his audience that it is time to "tell Pete Bell to take a hike." When he talks to the Western athletic director (Bob Cousy), he says that he needs some "thoroughbreds," the "blue chips" of the film's title. Marty (Roert Wuhl), a college talent scout, meets with Bell and his staff and identifies two players who could make an immediate impact on his program.

Bell takes to the road to recruit. He first stops in Chicago, where he contacts Butch McRae's (Penny Hardaway) coach and gets invited to Butch's home; he then travels to Indiana to see Ricky Roe (Matt Nover) and his parents. The parents of both players know the value of their sons' basketball skills and are unconcerned about the legality of under-the-table payoffs.

Butch's mother (Alfre Woodard) tells Bell, "A foul is not a foul unless the whistle is blown," and Ricky's father (Jim Beaver) assures Bell, "I'm not bothered about bending rules, especially if they're not mine." Butch's mother wants a house with a lawn, and Ricky's father wants a new tractor. As mercenary as the parents are, Bell's behavior is not above reproach. When he thinks Mrs. McRae is Catholic, so then is he; when he correctly guesses that the Roes are First Baptists, he automatically converts. Slick (Cylk Cozart), a recruiter, then suggests that Bell visit a seven-foot-four prospect who lives in Algiers, Louisiana, which is accessible only by railroad, boat, and then wading. Neon (O'Neal) had scored only five hundred on the SATs, making him academically ineligible—he needs seven hundred. Bell convinces all three to visit Western, but he fails to get commitments from them. When Ricky tells him that he needs the tractor and thirty thousand dollars cash in a gym bag, Bell throws him out.

Bell approaches the athletic director, who says that he wants "no part of this" and adds that "I know nothing." Next, Bell stops to see Happy (J.T. Walsh), who heads the Friends of the Program, a group of boosters who provide money and gifts for players but whose contributions are carefully laundered. Although he despises Happy and what he represents, Bell agrees to do business with him. The tractor, house, and gym bag stuffed with money follow quickly. Neon, who has received SAT tutoring from Bell's ex-wife, Jenny (Mary McDonnell), is also given a Lexus, which he turns down.

With these three freshmen in the program, success is guaranteed, but Bell begins to discover the extent of power the Friends of the Program command. When Bell tries to prevent Happy from hanging around the players, an argument ensues during which Happy proclaims that he "owns" both Bell and the team and then reveals that Tony (Anthony C. Hall), one of Bell's best players, shaved points in a game. As Bell reviews the tape of the game, he realizes that Happy's assertion is true; a reluctant confession from Tony provides final confirmation. Bell's words to Tony, "You corrupted the purest thing in your life," apply to the coach as well.

After he reminds his team that it's not what you do but how you do it, Bell leads the team out to play their first opponent, Bobby Knight's Indiana Hoosiers, ranked number one in the country. Following commentary by the always enthusiastic Dick Vitale, the game begins and features excellent basketball footage. (Duke's Bobby Hurley plays for Knight.) The game finally ends with a one-point victory for Western, but Bell does not act like the winning coach. At the press conference, Bell confesses that he has broken the rules and says, "I can't win like this." In response to Ed's query about Neon's Lexus, Bell goes on to discuss the tractor, house, and bags of cash and concludes, "It's about money." He admits that he "bought into it," and when Happy warns him about his words, threatening to see to it that he never coaches again, he declares, "I've become what I despise."

As he walks home from the stadium, he sees some youngsters playing basketball on the playground. Intrigued, he watches, then decides to show them how to play, especially how to master the jump shot. This is Bell at his finest, and the scene reminds viewers of the great amount of footage the film devotes to showing Bell instructing his players on the court and counseling them off the court. Before the credits come up, the screen reveals information about what happened after his resignation: Western was banned from postseason competition for four years; Ricky injured his knee and went back to farming; Tony played pro basketball in Europe; Butch and Neon dropped out of school and are playing in the NBA; and Bell is coaching at a small high school in the Midwest.

BLUE CRUSH (2002)

DIRECTOR: John Stockwell. SCREENPLAY: Lizzie Weiss, John Stockwell. PRODUCERS: Brian Grazer, Karen Kehela. CINEMATOGRAPHY: David Hennings. EDITING: Emma E. Hickox. MUSIC: Paul Haslinger. PRODUCTION DESIGN: Tom Meyer. ART DIRECTION: Denise Hudson. COSTUME DESIGN: Susan Matheson.

CAST: Kate Bosworth (Anne Marie Chadwick), Matthew Davis (Matt Tollman), Michelle Rodriguez (Eden), Sanoe Lake (Lena), Mika Boorem (Penny Chadwick).

RUNNING TIME: 104 minutes.

DVD: Universal Studios.

A young woman's dreams of competing in a surfing event are complicated by a romantic entanglement.

BLUE IN THE FACE (1995)

DIRECTORS: Paul Auster, Wayne Wang. PRODUCER: Greg Johnson, Peter Newman, Diana Phillips. CINEMATOGRAPHY: Adam Holender. EDITING: Christopher Tellefsen. PRODUCTION DESIGN: Kalina Ivanov. COSTUME DESIGN: Claudia Brown.

CAST: Harvey Keitel (Auggie), Mira Sorvino, Lou Reed (man with strange glasses), Michael J. Fox (Pete Maloney), Roseanne (Dot), Jim Jarmusch (Bob), Lily Tomlin (waffle eater), Giancarlo Esposito (Tommy Finelli), Jared Harris, Malik Yoba (watch man), Madonna (singing telegram).

RUNNING TIME: 83 minutes.

DVD: Miramax Home Entertainment.

Blue in the Face is a sequel, of sorts, to *Smoke*, a film directed by Wayne Wang and based on writer Paul Auster's "Auggie Wren's Christmas Story," which appeared in the *New York Times* in 1990. Auster also wrote the script. *Smoke* is structured as a series of vignettes featuring the patrons of the Brooklyn Cigar Company. Auggie, the proprietor, photographs the store every day from across the street, yet each photograph is subtly different, and each small difference is emblematic of the potential each moment holds for dramatic change. In spite of inevitable and often unexpected events, the lives of Auster's characters overlap and intertwine, strengthening the social fabric. At the heart of the film is a strong sense of connection that is represented by the Brooklyn Cigar Company, which serves as both a neighborhood hangout and a crossroads where strangers meet. One point of common interest that facilitates the inclusion of outsiders into the network is baseball. Brooklyn continues to mourn the Dodgers by reminiscing about the old team and by rooting for whoever is playing the present-day Yankees.

While filming *Smoke*, Wang and Auster decided to follow up immediately with a loosely structured sequel in order to develop more of the characters from the original. Whereas *Smoke* was fully scripted, *Blue in the Face* presents the actors with scenarios and encourages them to ad lib, talking until they are "blue in the face." These improvisational sketches are staged in or near the Brooklyn Cigar Shop, feature a number of well-known performers, and are intercut with videotaped interviews of Brooklyn natives. Michael J. Fox portrays a survey-taker whose questions become invasively personal. Lily Tomlin, disguised as an apparently homeless man, searches for a nonexistent address and talks about Belgian waffles. Director Jim Jarmusch muses about smoking his last cigarette. A man who invented a device for removing plastic bags from tree branches demonstrates how it works. Madonna delivers a singing telegram. A group of statisticians provide demographics.

As with *Smoke*, the Brooklyn Dodgers provide a common element, but since the plotlines, such as they are, do not intersect, the baseball references serve as a unifying element that is as central to the structure as the cigar shop itself. Singer Lou Reed discusses why he can't be a Yankees or a Mets fan. Old time residents recall the closing of Ebbetts Field. Archival footage documents the ceremonious prying of home plate from the ground as former Dodger catcher Roy Campanella looks on; then film of the actual demolition is shown. Auggie (Harvey Keitel) articulates the link between the cigar shop and the Dodgers when the store owner, Vinnie (Victor Argo), decides to sell the business. Auggie predicts that another piece of Brooklyn will die, just like when the Dodgers left.

Alone in the store, contemplating his decision and Auggie's reaction, Vinnie experiences a visitation from none other than Jackie Robinson (Keith David), who broke the color line in baseball in 1945, when the Dodgers' general manager, Branch Rickey, signed him. Jackie describes himself as "the man who changed baseball," and adds, "It takes its toll, being a martyr." The two men talk about how Brooklyn has changed. Jackie misses the old neighborhood and is happy to learn that it has retained many of its treasures. He wanders off in search of a Belgian waffle.

This bizarre vignette seems to parody *Field of Dreams* with its pastoral sentimentality. The urban version of nostalgia in *Blue in the Face* has a postmodernist edge. Auggie and company don't want to return to a romanticized past, but they want to preserve those places and institutions that lend vitality to their community. Vinnie decides not to sell the store. A spontaneous celebration pours into the street and gathers momentum. RuPaul appears to lead the neighborhood in a dance called the Brooklyn Cha Cha. A year later, Auggie and his girlfriend, Violet (Mel Gorham) have a baby boy named Jackie, whom they dress in a baseball uniform. Inside the cigar store, the patrons talk about baseball.

This experimental piece was not as well received as *Smoke*, but it is interesting in the contrast it presents between the countercultural characters and their conventional love of America's pastime.

BLUE SKIES AGAIN **(1983)**

DIRECTOR: Richard Michaels. SCREENPLAY: Kevin Sellers. PRODUCERS: Arlene Sellers, Alex Winitsky. CINEMATOGRAPHY: Donald McAlpine. MUSIC: John Kander.
CAST: Harry Hamlin (Sandy), Mimi Rogers (Liz), Kenneth McMillan (Dirk), Robyn Barto (Paula), Dana Elcar (Lou).
RUNNING TIME: 96 minutes.
VHS: Warner Home Video.

A female baseball player tries to join a minor league men's team.

BMX BANDITS **(1983)**

DIRECTOR: Brian Trenchard-Smith. SCREENPLAY: Patrick Edgeworth, Russell Hagg.
PRODUCERS: Tom Broadbridge, Paul F. Davies. CINEMATOGRAPHY: John Seale. EDITING: Alan Lake. MUSIC: Colin Stead, Frank Strangio. PRODUCTION DESIGN: Ross Major. COSTUME DESIGN: Lesley McLennan.
CAST: Nicole Kidman (Judy), Davide Argue (Whitey), Angelo D'Angelo (P.J.), John Ley (Moustache), James Lugton (Goose), Bryan Marshall (the Boss).
RUNNING TIME: 88 minutes.
DVD: Miracle Pictures.

This is an Australian film about teenage bikers who encounter bank robbers.

BOBBY DEERFIELD (1977)

DIRECTOR: Sydney Pollack. SCREENPLAY: Alvin Sargent, based on the novel *Heaven Has No Favorites* by Erich Maria Remarque. PRODUCER: Sydney Pollack. CINEMATOGRAPHY: Henri Decaë. EDITING: Fredric Steinkamp. MUSIC: Dave Grusin. PRODUCTION DESIGN: Stephen Grimes. ART DIRECTION: Mark Frederix.
CAST: Al Pacino (Bobby Deerfield), Marthe Keller (Lillian), Anny Duperey (Lydia).
RUNNING TIME: 124 minutes.
DVD: Sony Pictures.

Pacino is a Grand Prix race car driver who falls in love with a dying woman.

BOBBY JONES: STROKES OF GENIUS (2004)

DIRECTOR: Rowdy Herrington. SCREENPLAY: Rowdy Herrington, Bill Pryor, Tony De Paul (Story: Rowdy Herrington, Kim Dawson). PRODUCERS: Kim Dawson, Tim Moore, John Shepherd. CINEMATOGRAPHY: Tom Stern. EDITING: Pasquale Buba. MUSIC: James Horner. PRODUCTION DESIGN: Bruce Alan Miller. ART DIRECTION: Tom Minton. COSTUME DESIGN: Beverly Safier.
CAST: James Caviezel (Bobby Jones), Claire Forlani (Mary Malone Jones), Jeremy Northam (Walter Hagen), Malcolm McDowell (O. B. Keeler), Aidan Quinn (Harry Vardon).
RUNNING TIME: 120 minutes.
DVD: Sony Pictures.

Bobby Jones is a biography of a 1920s golf hero who was determined to remain an amateur despite pressure to go professional.

BODY AND SOUL (1947)

DIRECTOR: Robert Rossen. SCREENPLAY: Abraham Polonsky. PRODUCER: Bob Roberts. CINEMATOGRAPHY: James Wong Howe. EDITING: Francis D. Lyon, Robert Parrish. MUSIC: Hugo Friedhofer. ART DIRECTION: Nathan Juran.
CAST: John Garfield (Charlie Davis), Lilli Palmer (Peg Born), Hazel Brooks (Alice), Anne Revere (Charlie's mother), William Conrad (Quinn), Joseph Pevney (Shorty), Canada Lee (Ben Chaplin).
RUNNING TIME: 104 minutes.
ACADEMY AWARDS: Best Editing. NOMINATIONS: Best Actor (Garfield), Best Original Screenplay.
DVD: Republic Pictures.

Directed by Robert Rossen, who later directed *The Hustler* (1961), *Body and Soul* is a noir picture about an ambitious young man who is drawn into a boxing career to make money, becomes corrupted by his success, sells out to a seedy gambler, and then achieves redemption. The film begins with Charlie Davis (John Garfield) waking from a nightmare the day before his title defense against Jack Marlowe (Artie Dorrell). After getting into a scuffle at the weigh-in, Charlie flashes back to how he arrived in his current position—alienated from his mother and the girlfriend who really loved him and manipulated by a mobster.

After winning his first amateur fight, Charlie and his pal, Shorty (Joseph Pevney), meet Peg Born (Lilli Palmer), a Greenwich Village artist who invites them to her apartment, where she paints Charlie. She admires his build, or "symmetry," and quotes from William Blake's "The Tyger." However, the tyger's symmetry is "fearful" as well as beautiful, signaling that Charlie represents a dangerous liaison. Later the camera reveals that Peg has given Charlie horns, reflecting his attraction to Peg and foreshadowing the selling of his soul. However, the still-naïve Charlie tells Peg, "I just want to be a success," not understanding what he will lose in order to succeed.

Shorty, who recognizes Charlie's potential as a fighter, persuades a promoter, Quinn (William Conrad), to manage Charlie's career. Initially, Charlie is reluctant to become a professional fighter, but when his father, who runs a mom-and-pop candy store, is killed during the bombing of a speakeasy adjacent to his store, Charlie and his mother (Anne Revere) are left without adequate income. His mother applies to social services for help, but the social worker's visit turns humiliating, and Charlie orders her to leave. In spite of his mother's objections, he determines to box professionally.

Quinn lines up a series of fights on the road, all of which Charlie wins. Meanwhile, Shorty, who has been sending money from Charlie's winnings to Mrs. Davis without Charlie's knowledge, realizes that Charlie has become obsessed with getting rich and living well. Shorty advises Peg to marry him soon and tells her that her only rival is "money." However, Quinn's mercenary girlfriend, Alice (Hazel Brooks), is about to become another rival.

Quinn has not been able to secure a championship match for Charlie, but when title-holder Ben Chaplin (Canada Lee) develops a blood clot, Roberts (Lloyd Goff), a New York gambler who runs a boxing racket, is ready to give Charlie a shot. Roberts works out a deal with Chaplin's manager, Arnold (James Burke), to have Chaplin throw the fight with Charlie winning a decision. Roberts then approaches Charlie with his terms: a fifty-fifty split between Charlie and Roberts, with each of them giving Quinn 5 percent. Roberts advises Charlie to fire Shorty and postpone the wedding. Charlie accepts the deal and delays marrying Peg, who is willing to wait, but he is hesitant to fire Shorty and determines to pay him a percentage of his take.

On the night of the fight, Roberts double-crosses Arnold, instructing Charlie to go for the knockout. Charlie succeeds, injuring Ben in the process, but Roberts, who has bet on Charlie to win with a knockout, has profited. Shorty learns of Roberts's treachery and later that night, as Charlie and Peg celebrate, tells them the fight was fixed. Wanting nothing to do with Roberts and his underhanded dealings, Shorty quits. Roberts's henchman follows Shorty from the bar and beats him. Peg, who has followed Shorty, alerts Charlie, who comes to Shorty's defense. However, Shorty, dazed from the savage attack, stumbles into the path of a car and is killed. Peg announces an ultimatum: give up boxing or give up their relationship. Charlie chooses boxing and soon begins an affair with Alice.

When Ben has sufficiently recovered from the knockout, Charlie hires him as his trainer and continues to box and reel in cash. Then it is Charlie's turn to throw a fight, giving up his championship to Jack Marlowe, Roberts's latest money machine. Roberts gives Charlie sixty thousand dollars in advance to bet against himself, but Charlie is uneasy about the fix. As he usually does when he is troubled, Charlie visits Peg, who asks him, "Why are you here? What do you want?" He confesses that he is scared and admits that he wants her back. He also tells her about the money, and while he sleeps, she deposits it in the bank. Irate, Charlie leaves but is stopped by an old acquaintance from whom he learns his former neighbors have all placed bets on him to win.

At the training camp, Ben questions Charlie about the upcoming match, and Charlie admits he is throwing the fight. Ben insists that he could easily defeat Jack Marlowe. Roberts, who has been lurking in the shadows, overhears their conversation and orders Ben off the premises. Ben responds by throwing air punches and proclaiming, "I'm the champ." He then collapses and dies.

The title fight is a farce: there is no action; the crowd boos the boxers; and the referee upbraids them for not boxing. In the thirteenth round Jack staggers Charlie, who is knocked down three times and realizes that he, like Ben, has been double-crossed by Roberts, who has bet on Jack winning by a knockout. In the next round Charlie makes a comeback and has Jack on the ropes. Before round fifteen begins, Quinn asks Charlie if he knows what he's doing. After he knocks out Jack in the fifteenth round, Charlie brushes off Alice and finds Peg. When Roberts sees him, Charlie says, "What you going to do? Kill me?" He then adds, "Everybody dies," words Roberts callously used in reference to Ben after his championship loss. The film ends with Charlie and Peg embracing.

Body and Soul is widely considered one of the best fight films of all time. The acting is excellent throughout, and former middleweight boxer Canada Lee turns in an exceptional performance. Cinematographer James Wong Howe filmed portions of the fight scenes in the ring on roller skates, creating incredibly convincing—and dizzying—point-of-view shots. He was nominated for an Academy Award, as was screenwriter Abraham Polonsky.

BODY SLAM (1986)

DIRECTOR: Hal Needham. SCREENPLAY: Steve Burkow, Shel Lytton. PRODUCERS: Mike Curb, Shel Lytton. CINEMATOGRAPHY: Michael Shea. EDITING: Randy D. Thornton.

MUSIC: John D'Andrea, Michael Lloyd. ART DIRECTION: Pamela B. Warner. COSTUME DESIGN: Jerry R. Allen.

CAST: Dirk Benedict (M. Harry Smilac), Tanya Roberts (Candace Vandervagen), Roddy Piper (Quick Rick Roberts), Lou Albano (Lou Murano), Charles Nelson Reilly (Vic Carson), Billy Barty (Tim McClusky).

RUNNING TIME: 89 minutes.

VHS: Nelson Entertainment.

In this comedy, a music promoter hires wrestlers to join his band's concert tour.

BOOTS MALONE (1952)

DIRECTOR: William Dieterle. SCREENPLAY: Milton Holmes, Harold Buchman. PRODUCER: Milton Holmes. CINEMATOGRAPHY: Charles Lawton Jr. EDITING: Al Clark. MUSIC: Elmer Bernstein. ART DIRECTION: Cary Odell.

CAST: William Holden (Boots Malone), Johnny Stewart (Thomas Gibson Jr.), Ed Begley (Howard Whitehead), Harry Morgan (Quarter Horse Henry).

RUNNING TIME: 102 minutes.

VHS: Goodtimes Home Video.

A shady agent for horse jockeys is reformed when he takes one jockey under his wing.

THE BOXER (1997)

DIRECTOR: Jim Sheridan. SCREENPLAY: Jim Sheridan, Terry George. PRODUCERS: Arthur Lappin, Jim Sheridan. CINEMATOGRAPHY: Chris Menges. EDITING: Clive Barrett, Gerry Hambling. MUSIC: Gavin Friday, Maurice Seezer. PRODUCTION DESIGN: Brian Morris. ART DIRECTION: Fiona Daly, Richard Earl. COSTUME DESIGN: Joan Bergin.

CAST: Daniel Day-Lewis (Danny Flynn), Emily Watson (Maggie), Brian Cox (Joe Hamill), Ken Stott (Ike Weir), Gerald McSorley (Harry).

RUNNING TIME: 113 minutes.

DVD: Universal Studios.

According to writer-director Jim Sheridan, *The Boxer* is based upon the life of the Irish world featherweight champion Barry McGuigan. McGuigan was captain of the Irish Olympic Boxing Team at the 1980 Moscow Olympic Games. As a professional boxer he won both the British and European titles in 1983, and in 1985 he was named World Boxing Association (WBA) world featherweight champion and received the WBA Boxer of the Year award. McGuigan was on board as boxing consultant for Jim Sheridan's film and trained Daniel Day-Lewis for his role for over two years. That's a larger dose of authenticity than many filmmakers might be willing to invest, and it helps to make the film convincing.

Danny Flynn is the name of the boxer played by Daniel Day-Lewis. The film picks him up shadow-boxing in a hooded sweatshirt in a British prison yard on the day of his scheduled release. He has been in prison for fourteen years because of his connections with the Irish Republican Army (IRA). He refused to associate with other IRA prisoners, but he never betrayed them or the cause. He just wants to go home to his old neighborhood in Belfast to become a professional boxer and to train youngsters interested in boxing. But since Danny is now thirty-two, his former trainer, Ike Weir (Ken Stott), has doubts about Danny's ability. Nonetheless, Ike arranges a match for Danny with a fighter from Scotland.

A further complication involves Maggie (Emily Watson), the girl Danny left behind when he went to prison. While Danny was serving his time, Maggie married another IRA member, and she now has a son, Liam (fourteen-year-old Ciaran Fitzgerald). Meanwhile, Maggie's husband, whom she no longer loves, is himself serving a prison term for political terrorism. The neighborhood code requires Maggie to be faithful, regardless of her feelings toward Danny, who obviously loves her. Maggie's father, IRA leader Joe Hamill (Brian Cox), believes in the code, but he is not as willing to enforce it strictly as is one of his lieutenants, Harry (Gerard McSorley), who hates Danny for other reasons.

While Joe Hamill has negotiated a cease-fire with the British and wants to work toward a peaceful settlement on the condition that the British will release all political prisoners, Harry wants to continue the bombings. Danny alienates Harry further when he finds a satchel of explosives hidden in the gym where he works out and pitches it into the river. Danny is also bringing Protestants and Catholics together through their common interest in boxing. While Danny boxes the Scot on the Protestant side of Belfast, Harry rigs a car bomb that explodes a British police car, killing an officer and violating the truce.

Meanwhile, young Liam has seen Danny visiting his mother and fears Danny will take his mother away from him; so Liam and his friends burn down Danny's gym. Maggie asks Danny to leave, and defeated, he goes to England to box. Danny is successful in London, but when pitted against a Nigerian who is clearly no match for him, Danny refuses to finish the fight—he does not want to kill his opponent. Watching this fight back in Northern Ireland on television, Harry claims Danny is a quitter, but the audience knows better. When Ike stands up to Harry and accuses him of being a coward, Harry simply puts a bullet in Ike's head. Young Liam is devastated by Ike's death, and Danny is enraged when he learns about it. By this time Liam has accepted Danny, and Danny goes to Maggie's father to declare his intentions. Harry, of course, wants Danny executed, and the power struggle between Harry and his chief yields interesting and surprising results.

The film never strikes a false note, even when it seems headed toward pure blar-

Daniel Day-Lewis and Emily Watson in *The Boxer*

ney, as when "Danny Boy" is sung before one of Danny's boxing matches. Interestingly, *New York Times* sports columnist Ira Berkow (in a piece dated January 4, 1998) questioned the way Danny stopped fighting the battered Nigerian in his London bout: "A true pro would know how to continue and win the fight without seriously damaging his opponent." However, it should be noted that Danny does not have enough experience to qualify as a "true pro" at that point of his career. At the heart of this film is a nonpolitical fighter who abhors violence but is made to survive in terribly violent circumstances. Even Joe Hamill, wonderfully played by Brian Cox, is weary of the killing and wants to put an end to it.

The title is both metaphorical and ironic. The "boxer" of the title is ultimately a peaceful man, opposed to political violence and terrorism. Of course, Sheridan's film is primarily about politics and the IRA and the "troubles" in Northern Ireland; in fact, the writer-director has described *The Boxer* as the third increment of his Irish trilogy, including *My Left Foot* (1989), which also starred Daniel Day-Lewis, who earned a Best Actor Academy Award for his performance, and *In The Name of the Father* (1993), another "true story" about a man unjustly imprisoned for fifteen years. Even so, the Day-Lewis character of *The Boxer* certainly defines himself through his dedication to sport as well as to peace. It's not the first time a filmmaker has used the sport to make a parallel point about society at large. The film was praised for its moderate stance and for its innately likable principals. Jim Sheridan told *New York Times* reporter Bernard Weintraub that he wanted to tell a universal, human story "that cuts through politics," as his love story of forbidden romance does accomplish. Though the picture does not trade in false hope or false emotion, it does end on an optimistic note, as did the actual filming, which wrapped in Dublin on the same day a cease-fire was declared, one that would ultimately lead to a resolution of a conflict that goes back to at least the Easter Rebellion of 1916.

THE BREAK (1995)

DIRECTOR: Lee H. Katzin. SCREENPLAY: Vincent Van Patten, Stephanie Warren. STORY: Van Patten, Tom Caffrey. PRODUCERS: Christopher J. Brough, Vincent Van Patten. CINEMATOGRAPHY: Frank P. Flynn. EDITING: David Campling, Douglas Ibold. MUSIC: Kim Bullard. PRODUCTION DESIGN: Tim Duffy. ART DIRECTION: William Tabor. COSTUME DESIGN: Denise Walsh.
CAST: Vincent Van Patten (Nick Irons), Ben Jorgensen (Joel Robbins), Martin Sheen (Gil Robbins), Rae Dawn Chong (Jennifer Hudson), Valerie Perrine (Delores Smith).
RUNNING TIME: 104 minutes.
DVD: Platinum Disc.

Vincent Van Patten, a former top-thirty tennis pro (in Tokyo in 1981, he beat John McEnroe in the semifinals en route to his only title), cowrote and starred in this film about a disgraced player who is asked to coach a young player. The film features appearances by some notable names of the sport including Fred Stolle, Cliff Drysdale, and Vitas Gerulaitis.

BREAKING AWAY (1979)

DIRECTOR: Peter Yates. SCREENPLAY: Steve Tesich. PRODUCER: Peter Yates. CINEMATOGRAPHY: Matthew F. Leonetti. EDITING: Cynthia Scheider. MUSIC: Patrick Williams. PRODUCTION DESIGN: Patrizia Von Brandenstein. COSTUME DESIGN: Betsy Cox.
CAST: Dennis Christopher (Dave Stoller), Dennis Quaid (Mike), Jackie Earle Haley (Mooch), Daniel Stern (Cyril), Barbara Barrie (Dave's mother), Paul Dooley ("Papa" Ray).
RUNNING TIME: 101 minutes.
ACADEMY AWARDS: Best Original Screenplay. NOMINATIONS: Best Picture, Best Director, Best Supporting Actress (Barrie), Best Score.
DVD: 20th Century Fox.

Trailers for this Peter Yates cycling film describe it as a story of four recent high school graduates taking "a detour on the road to adulthood." But it is also about father-son relationships, class conflict, and the changing structure of American society. The film is set in Bloomington, Indiana, home of Indiana University and one of the world's largest suppliers of limestone. In the 1960s the limestone industry experienced a dramatic slump because of the vulnerability of limestone to acid rain and the increasing popularity of the international style of architecture, characterized by glass walls rather than stone facings. The slump continued into the early 1970s. Quarries that had provided employment for generations of local workers downsized or went out of business. (The Bloomington Limestone Company reinvented itself as a golf cart dealership during this time.)

The four young men at the center of this film are sons of former quarry workers. They have fashioned their own never-never-land, where they can stay boys and avoid an adult world that appears unpromising. All four resent the Indiana University students, among whom they are known as "cutters," a derogatory reference to the locals. Mike (Dennis Quaid), who quarterbacked the high school football team, is bitter that his glory days are over, and he feels pressured by his older brother, a police officer, to straighten up and do something constructive with his life. Cyril (Daniel Stern), a sharp, witty teen, suffers from an overly critical father who sees only his potential for failure. Mooch's father has moved to Chicago to look for work, leaving Mooch (Jackie Earl Haley) behind in a house that's up for sale. Dave Stoller (Dennis Christopher), who has acquired an Italian bike, is the only one of the group possessing the determination and imagination to break away.

A sickly child until he took up biking, Dave now trains every spare moment, riding fifty miles at a stretch and keeping pace with the highway traffic. He has also embraced Italian culture, wearing a crucifix and crossing himself, although he's not Catholic. He listens to opera, studies Italian, and even affects an Italian accent when he speaks English. "Papa" Ray (Paul Dooley) is not amused. The elder Stoller's aversion to all things "Eytie," while suggesting Midwestern xenophobia, represents a larger fear of losing Dave to a world his father cannot enter, a world of culture, privilege, and opportunity represented by the college students.

In cycling, a breakaway is a group of riders who move ahead of the pack, or peloton, establishing a faster pace for themselves. Through his devotion to cycling, Dave is figuratively breaking away from the ennui that entraps his friends, but riding in the metaphorical slipstream produces risks as well. Dave sets himself up for trouble when a coed, Kathy/"Katarina" (Robyn Douglass), mistakes him for an exchange student, and Dave, who is immediately attracted, does not encourage her to think otherwise. Soon he is serenading her in Italian and regaling her with tales of his warm Italian family. But Kathy has been going out with Rod (Hart Bochner), a fraternity boy who is a star athlete and who has had a few run-ins with the Cutters. When Mike, Mooch, and Cyril decide to wander through the campus, they run into Rod and a few of his frat brothers, and a brawl ensues. Dave, still masquerading as an exchange student, is sitting with Kathy

Dennis Christopher in *Breaking Away*

when the trouble starts, but he escapes unscathed and with his persona intact.

The aftermath of the brouhaha poses a dilemma for Dave. The university administration, upset by the inhospitable behavior of its students, invites a local team to participate in the "Little 500," an annual campus bicycle race held on the school's athletic track. The four Cutters are confident that they can win if Dave does most of the riding, but Dave can't participate without revealing to Kathy that he's just a local guy. Besides, at his parents' insistence, he is now employed as a car washer at his father's used car lot. The time spent away from the other Cutters threatens the group's interdependence, especially once Dave becomes preoccupied with another upcoming race, one in which an Italian team will participate. Just before this race, Dave's father collapses after an altercation with a college student demanding a refund on the car he's purchased. Dave, who sided with the student and insisted that a money-back guarantee must be honored, is hesitant to enter the race while his father is sedated; his mother (Barbara Barrie) shows him her never-used passport and convinces him he must not pass up this opportunity to display his ability.

Dave does indeed impress the Italian team, catching up with their breakaway and shouting greetings to them in their native language as they labor up a hill. While Dave is busy trying to engage the team in conversation, one member reaches over and flips the gear lever on Dave's bike, causing him to fall behind. When he once again reaches the breakaway, apparently unaware of the earlier sabotage, the Italians take more drastic action, this time resulting in a crash that damages his bicycle. Although Dave is not injured, he has neither the vehicle nor the heart to finish the race. When he returns home, he apologizes to his father for the disagreement at the car lot: "Everybody cheats. I just didn't know." He throws his arms around his father and bursts into tears, and Ray's awkward embrace of his son signals a change in their relationship. Dave now calls his father Dad instead of Papa, and he finalizes his divorce from his Italian persona by confessing his true identity to Kathy—who promptly slaps him.

Dave's disenchantment leaves him still unwilling to ride for the Cutters in the Little 500, but two experiences change his mind. First, he and his father go for a walk after his father has found him removing the Italian cycling posters from his bedroom walls. As they sit on a bench in front of a campus building, Ray talks about cutting the stone for the buildings. He and his friends—fathers of the other boys—were proud of their work, but afterward they were uncomfortable on campus, "as if the buildings were too good for [the builders]." Next, the Cutters, still trying to persuade Dave to enter the race, bring him a used bike. Dave calls it a piece of junk, but when Mike admits, using language similar to Ray's, that he thinks maybe the college guys are better, Dave begins fine-tuning the bicycle.

At this point, things begin falling into place. Kathy approaches Dave to say that she's travelling to Italy on vacation and that she has confidence he'll be going somewhere soon, a remark that carries meaning beyond geographic destinations. Dave learns that he is to become an older brother—his parents are expecting and delighted to be bringing a child into a world that suddenly seems brighter and a family that has regained its closeness. Dave's mother presents Dave with T-shirts for the race that say "Cutters." The T-shirts are a reminder that the Cutters are a team. In order for each member to feel validated, the race must be a team effort. Not surprisingly, then, the plan for Dave to ride the entire fifty-mile race himself gets derailed.

After Dave has opened up an impressive lead and is lapping the peloton, he is bumped by another cyclist and injures himself in the resulting spill.

At first the other Cutters stand by in confusion as Dave limps off the track, his left leg bleeding. Then Mooch, the smallest of the group, jumps on the bike and rejoins the race until he's too fatigued to keep up. Next, Cyril takes over. Mike, who is a better rider than either Mooch or Cyril, has convinced himself that the team hasn't a chance without Dave and has resisted participating. He changes his mind when the race leader taunts him in passing. Cheered on by the others, including his brother, Mike begins to close the gap. By the time Mike has moved into fourth place, he's tiring, and Dave realizes Mike won't be able to overtake the leader, so he calls him in. With his feet taped to the pedals, Dave finishes the last fifteen laps, winning the race for the hometown as well as for the team. Even the college students applaud.

The Cutters are now ready to grow up. Mike, the most vulnerable of the four, has reconciled with his brother and proven something to himself. Dave goes on to college, where he meets a female French exchange student and is back to calling his dad "Papa," this time with a French accent.

Writer Steve Tesich, who immigrated to Indiana from Yugoslavia when he was fourteen, attended Indiana University and rode in the Little 500. His story was inspired by his 1962 Phi Kappa Psi team and cyclist Dave Blase, who did most of the riding for the team. (Blase appears in the film as the announcer.) Shooting was done entirely on location in Bloomington, adding to the film's sense of authenticity. Yates makes good use of the setting to establish the ongoing conflict between the locals and the college students. Tesich won an Oscar for his screenplay; his later writing credits include the 1985 cycling film *American Flyers*, starring Kevin Costner. *Breaking Away* received Oscar nominations for Best Picture, Best Director, and Best Actress in a Supporting Role. It ranks number eight on the American Film Institute's list of Best Sports Films.

BREWSTER'S MILLIONS (1983)

DIRECTOR: Walter Hill. SCREENPLAY: Herschel Weingrod, Timothy Harris, based on the novel by George Barr McCutcheon. PRODUCERS: Lawrence Gordon, Joel Silver. CINEMATOGRAPHY: Ric Waite. EDITING: Freeman Davies, Michael Ripps. MUSIC: Ry Cooder. PRODUCTION DESIGN: John Vallone. ART DIRECTION: William Hiney. COSTUME DESIGN: Marilyn Vance.

CAST: Richard Pryor (Montgomery Brewster), John Candy (Spike Nolan), Lonette McKee (Angela Drake), Stephen Collins (Warren Cox), Jerry Orbach (Charley Pegler).

RUNNING TIME: 97 minutes.

DVD: Universal Studios.

This is a frequently filmed story about a man who must spend a fortune in order to collect many more millions in return. In this version, Brewster is a minor league baseball player.

BRIAN'S SONG (1971)

DIRECTOR: Buzz Kulik. SCREENPLAY: William Blinn, based on the book *I Am Third* by Gale Sayers and Al Silverman. PRODUCER: Paul Junger Witt. CINEMATOGRAPHY: Joseph F. Biroc. EDITING: Bud S. Isaacs. MUSIC: Michel Legrand. ART DIRECTION: Ross Bellah.

CAST: James Caan (Brain Piccolo), Billy Dee Williams (Gale Sayers), Jack Warden (George Halas), Bernie Casey, Shelley Fabares, Judy Pace, David Huddleston.

RUNNING TIME: 73 minutes.

EMMY AWARDS: Outstanding Single Program, Drama or Comedy, Outstanding

Writing Achievement-Adaptation, Outstanding Supporting Actor-Drama (Warden). NOMINATIONS: Outstanding Directorial Achievement, Single Program-Drama, Outstanding Single Performance by an Actor in a Leading Role (Caan), Outstanding Single Performance by an Actor in a Leading Role (Williams), Outstanding Achievement in Music Composition for a Special Program.
DVD: Sony Pictures.

Brian's Song, based on *I Am Third* (1971) by Gale Sayers and Al Silverman, appeared first on television, where it won three Emmys and had the highest rating, 33.2, of any television movie up to that time. The film is about the close relationship between Brian Piccolo (James Caan) and Gale Sayers (Billy Dee Williams), players for the Chicago Bears. Narrated by George Halas (Jack Warden), the Bears' coach, the film begins in training camp and ends a few years later with Piccolo's death from cancer. Although the film is about the closeness of the two men, it also concerns courage and racism: they were the first interracial roommates on the Bears' team and received hate mail.

Piccolo and Sayers, a consensus All-American, are rookies competing for the running back position for the Bears. Their relationship begins with Piccolo playing a joke on Sayers; he tells him that Halas is deaf in one ear, so Sayers jumps from one spot to another to get on Halas's "good side," confusing Halas, who does not have a hearing problem. To retaliate, while Piccolo is standing at the lunch table singing the Wake Forest fight song, Sayers places a plate of mashed potatoes and gravy on the chair Piccolo will sit in. The two continue with pranks and good-natured banter that pull them together, and the extroverted Piccolo draws the introverted Sayers out. When he receives the Rookie of the Year Award, Sayers gets Piccolo to help him with his acceptance speech, but he is unable to say much more than "Thank you." When he later receives the George Halas Award for Courage, Sayers delivers an articulate, moving testimony to Piccolo's courage, saying "It [the award] is mine tonight and Brian Piccolo's tomorrow." When both players learn that they have made the team, they call their wives and go out to eat together. During one of their dinners Sayers makes a joke, and Piccolo calls attention to it because Sayers is usually more sedate.

In their second season Sayers is severely injured, and it is Piccolo who helps him recover physically and mentally by challenging him. When Sayers returns to his home, he finds Piccolo in the basement with exercise equipment. Although frustrated and irritated by his lack of progress, Sayers responds to the challenge: Piccolo says he doesn't want to be number one "by default," that he wants to beat Sayers when he is at his best. The two train together, racing until Sayers can finally beat Piccolo. When Piccolo tells him that he owes him a beer, Sayers answers, "I owe you a lot more than that."

In the third season Halas switches Piccolo from second-string running back to first-team fullback, and Piccolo's blocking and running produce touchdowns for both players. During the season Piccolo begins to lose weight, slows down, and develops a cough (almost always fatal in a movie) and is sent back to Chicago for tests. Halas tells Sayers that Piccolo has cancer and will have to have part of his right lung removed; Sayers relays that information to the rest of the team. Piccolo keeps up a good front, calls the cancer a "detour," and jokes about becoming a kicker, a less physically demanding position, but Joy (Shelley Fabares), Piccolo's wife, asks Sayers to be there when the doctor informs him that he will have to have another operation. Seeing that Piccolo is not ready to handle the bad news,

Sayers convinces the doctor to postpone conveying the information. After the surgery Piccolo tells Sayers that he will "get" him at the next training camp and adds that he needs some sleep.

Halas concludes his narration by stating that Piccolo died at age twenty-six and then urges his audience to remember Piccolo not as he died, but as he lived. Brian's "song" was not the Wake Forest fight song, but his life. The film is memorable not because of the footage of Caan and Williams running for touchdowns—the only football footage consists of black-and-white shots of the real Sayers and Piccolo—but because of the footage off the field, in training camps and in the hospital, where two courageous young men demonstrate their compassion and caring.

BRING IT ON (2000)

DIRECTOR: Peyton Reed. SCREENPLAY: Jessica Bendinger. PRODUCERS: Marc Abraham, Thomas A. Bliss. CINEMATOGRAPHY: Shawn Maurer. EDITING: Larry Bock. MUSIC: Christophe Beck. PRODUCTION DESIGN: Sharon Lomofsky. COSTUME DESIGN: Mary Jane Fort.

CAST: Kirsten Dunst (Torrance Shipman), Eliza Dushku (Missy Pantone), Gabrielle Union (Isis), Jesse Bradford (Cliff Pantone), Clare Kramer (Courtney), Nicole Bilderback (Whitney).

RUNNING TIME: 98 minutes.

DVD: Universal Studios.

Bring It On sounds like an unlikely title for a film about cheerleading, a sport that includes dancing and gymnastics, but the title succeeds in reflecting the intensity of the competition within a sport that, at college and high school levels, demands participants execute complex and sometimes high-risk gymnastic maneuvers. *Bring It On* concerns the rivalry between two cheerleading squads, one safely ensconced in privileged WASP America and the other located in a low-income black neighborhood in Los Angeles. The film also addresses the nature of winning and the role of responsible leadership.

Jessica Bendinger, who wrote the script, later wrote *Stick It* (2006), a similarly "edged" film about gymnastics. *Bring It On* begins with a rosy portrait of Rancho Carne (which translates to "Meat Ranch") High School's cheerleading squad as the cheerleaders jockey for election as team captain. Bouncy Torrance (Kirsten Dunst) is elected, partly through the intervention of Big Red (Lindsay Stone), the outgoing captain who has been instrumental in Rancho Carne's past five national championships. In her exuberance, Torrance proposes that the team form one of the most dangerous cheerleading pyramids, and one of the cheerleaders is severely injured. Torrance's decision is important for two reasons: it undermines her competency as captain, and it creates the need for a replacement cheerleader.

The ensuing tryouts, like those for *American Idol*, are both pathetic and amusing until the entrance of Missy Pantone (Eliza Dushku), a transfer student and gymnastics whiz who can easily perform the most challenging routines. For Missy, cheerleading is the closest thing to gymnastics that Rancho Carne has to offer. Her enthusiasm dims, however, when she sees the squad perform the routine they will use in competition. She tells the incredulous Torrance that the routine was ripped off from the East Compton Clovers squad in Los Angeles. The two young women drive to Los Angeles, where they are greeted with a lot of hostility, especially from the head cheerleader, Isis (Gabrielle Union), who describes Big Red photographing their routines. Torrance pleads ignorance, saving herself and Missy from probable violence, but now that she knows her school has cheated, she has a big problem.

Big Red feels no guilt about cheating, and she's not worried about getting caught because she knows the Clovers lack the financial backing to participate in the national championships. For Torrance, however, winning by cheating is not the answer. Her feelings are reinforced when Isis and some other Clovers attend a Rancho Carne football game and taunt Torrance's squad by doing "their" routine before the football audience. Despite the opposition of a few squad members, Torrance convinces the squad to acquire a new routine, one courtesy of Sparky Polastri (Ian Roberts), a choreographer recommended by her boyfriend, Aaron (Richard Hillman). When the squad sees another school execute Sparky's two-thousand-dollar "spirit fingers," they discover that their choreographer has peddled the same act to six other schools, and the cheerleading officials threaten to disqualify Torrance's team. Since this is her second error in judgment, Torrance begins to believe that she has been cursed for dropping a cheerleading baton at an earlier competition. Cliff (Jesse Bradford), Missy's brother, has fallen for Torrance and believes in her, but Aaron tells her she may not have the "stuff" to be a captain.

Using a videotape Cliff has made for her, Torrance gets some ideas of her own and creates an eclectic routine, drawing on dance, mime, and hip-hop. When it finally seems as if winning is within the squad's grasp, she learns that the East Compton Clovers, who have qualified for the Nationals, cannot go because of finances; she realizes that unless her squad beats East Compton, it will not be a satisfactory victory. Torrance gets her father's company to sponsor Compton and presents the check to Isis, who tears it up and accuses Torrance of pulling a liberal "feel-good" tactic—which is partly true. The Clovers get their funds with the help of the black community and a talk-show host.

At the Daytona Beach Nationals, Isis and Torrance meet again, and Isis tells her, "Bring it on." Torrance's squad comes in second, barely trailing the Clovers, who are ranked number one. When asked how she feels, Torrance replies, "Second feels like first." Considering what she has been through, she has a better understanding of what winning is all about. During the postproduction credits at the end of the film, the two squads do routines together, providing more evidence of bonding.

The bonding seems to have been restricted to the young women. Although Rancho Carne's squad has males, they are not treated very sympathetically. The football players (their team is terrible) joke about male cheerleaders' sexuality, and the male squad members show themselves as insensitive louts. Reviewers have noted the unevenness of the film, which swerves from crude teen comedy to sensitive consideration of race, class, and sexuality. Roger Ebert in the *Chicago Sun-Tribune* has speculated that the film was conceived as satire, then edited to assure a PG rating.

BULL DURHAM (1988)

DIRECTOR: Ron Shelton. SCREENPLAY: Ron Shelton. PRODUCERS: Mark Burg, Thom Mount. CINEMATOGRAPHY: Bobby Byrne. EDITING: Robert Leighton, Adam Weiss. MUSIC: Michael Convertino. PRODUCTION DESIGN: Armin Ganz. ART DIRECTION: David Lubin. COSTUME DESIGN: Louise Frogley.

CAST: Kevin Costner (Crash Davis), Susan Sarandon (Annie Savoy), Tim Robbins (Ebby "Nuke" LaLoosh), Trey Wilson (Joe Riggins), Robert Wuhl (Larry Hockett), William O'Leary (Jimmy).

RUNNING TIME: 108 minutes.

ACADEMY AWARD NOMINATIONS: Best Original Screenplay.

DVD: MGM.

Considered one of the all-time great sports films, *Bull Durham* is a romantic comedy noted for its realistic portrayal of minor league baseball and for its variations on plot conventions. The script is grounded in the experience of writer/director Ron Shelton, a former minor leaguer who left a Baltimore Orioles' farm team after five years to study sculpture and write stories and screenplays. While working as a script doctor for *Under Fire* (1983), Shelton came to the attention of director Robert Spottiswoode, who later assigned him to direct the sports sequences of *The Best of Times* (1986). Shelton's achievement paved the way for him to turn one of his early stories, "A Player to Be Named Later," into *Bull Durham*. The script eschews dramatic come-from-behind wins, inspired locker room speeches, and heroic big plays, and in an original twist places a female groupie as the film's primary narrator rather than as a marginalized sex object.

Annie Savoy (Susan Sarandon) is a literary dominatrix who every season selects one player, usually young, to "coach" for the season. One of her favorite tactics is to tie the man to her bed and read poetry to him; as she explains, "a guy will listen to anything if he thinks it's foreplay." In the opening voiceover, Annie establishes her belief, based in part on there being 108 beads on a rosary and the same number of stitches on a ball, that baseball is a religion. She even keeps a shrine to Thurman Munson in her house. As the film gets under way, her home team, the Carolina League Durham Bulls, is off to a slow start, and she has yet to choose her annual trainee. The two leading candidates are rookie pitcher Ebby LaLoosh (Tim Robbins) and veteran catcher Crash Davis (Kevin Costner). Crash, whose career is in its waning years, has been called to Durham to help tame Ebby, who is considered major league potential but is wild both on and off the field.

Kevin Costner as Crash Davis; Tim Robbins as "Nuke" LaLoosh in *Bull Durham*

Annie, Ebby, and Crash meet at a bar where the team has congregated after a game. Annie is sitting with Max Patkin (as himself), the team clown, when Crash sends over drinks in an obvious ploy to get himself introduced to Annie. The ploy succeeds, but Crash has little time to work his charm, for Ebby intrudes, asking Annie to dance. Crash insists she's dancing with him—although he's just told Annie he doesn't dance. Ebby and Crash end up outside in the alley. Crash says he doesn't fight and goads Ebby into throwing a fastball at his head; the pitch goes wild, breaking a window; Ebby slugs Crash, who introduces himself as the new catcher; and the two bond immediately, returning inside for a drink. Annie, who has had her sights on Ebby but is intrigued by Crash, invites both men to her place. Both accept the invitation, but Crash isn't willing to play by Annie's ground rules. After reeling off a litany of beliefs that comically reveal that he is highly intelligent and well-read (if a bit harsh in his assessment of Susan Sontag's fiction), Crash stomps out. Ebby determines that the conquest is his and begins pulling off his clothes; however, Annie stops him and makes him start over, undressing slowly. She assumes complete control, producing a length of rope from the nightstand and, having secured the willing and expectant Ebby to the bed frame, entertains him with Whitman's "Leaves of Grass." Even though Annie has begun her ritual with Ebby, she still desires Crash, and Crash is clearly suffering from what his inner voice describes as "broad in the head." The result is an unlikely triangle with both Annie and Crash continuing Ebby's education. Annie has him breathing through his eyelids "like a lava lizard" and encourages him to wear a garter belt to keep him slightly off center; at the same time, Crash offers instruction on handling interviews and avoiding foot fungus.

Ebby, who has decided upon "Nuke" as a nickname, is not always cooperative. He doesn't wear the garters at first, and he shakes off Crash's signals, insisting on hurling fastballs. Annie chastises him about the garters, and Crash gets even with him by telling a batter that the next pitch will be a fastball. Once Ebby dons the garter belt and heeds the signals, his pitching improves, but Crash is able to convince the superstitious Ebby that having sex will interfere with his winning streak. Annie's frustration is complicated by Crash's refusal to yield to her advances.

The dynamics shift after Ebby gets called up to "the Show," but Ebby's promotion means Crash is no longer of much use to the Bulls since his sole responsibility was to settle the rookie. Crash gets drunk and hurls a glass at Ebby, who throws a punch in return, but Crash resumes his role of mentor and advises, "Don't hit a drunk with your pitching hand." Their final fight is over as quickly as their first, with their camaraderie restored. After Annie and Ebby part tenderly, Crash visits Annie, and the two engage in marathon sex with interludes during which they dance and Crash paints Annie's toenails; no one reads Whitman or discusses Sontag. Crash leaves to check out an opening with another team and continues to play long enough to hit his 247th minor league home run, a record that says more about how much time he's spent in the minors than about how well he hits. Crash returns to Annie and says he's thinking of managing. Annie, in accepting Crash, is giving up her seasonal training session. Both have grown, yet both retain their love of baseball.

Shelton received an Oscar nomination for his script, which is both witty and believable. The film's authentic feel comes in part from his behind-the-scenes knowledge—for example, the drunken attempt to produce a "rainout" by turning on the sprinkler system and flooding the infield is based on an actual prank. Shelton insisted that his actors be able to play ball. Cast members spent several weeks in a baseball camp led by a former semipro player, and minor leaguers were recruited for some of the parts. Costner, a talented switch hitter, proved his mettle by reportedly homering twice during filming. Producer Thom Mount, a part owner of the real Durham Bulls, was able to arrange for baseball sequences to be shot at the Bulls' home field, where the snorting "bull board," originally a prop, still stands.

Well-drawn characters and strong performances contribute to the film's popularity. Robbins is convincing as the rookie whose ego has developed more quickly than his talent, and Sarandon combines earnestness with extravagance in a manner that avoids stereotypes. (Robbins and Sarandon began their real-life romance during shooting.) *Bull Durham* is at or near the top of every list of best sports films and, like *The Natural* and *Field of Dreams*, has retained its popularity.

BY THE SWORD (1991)

DIRECTOR: Jeremy Kagan. SCREENPLAY: James Donadio, John McDonald. PRODUCERS: Marlon Staggs, Peter E. Strauss. CINEMATOGRAPHY: Arthur Albert. EDITING: David Holden, Martha Huntley. MUSIC: Bill Conti. PRODUCTION DESIGN: Gary Frutkoff. ART DIRECTION: Kim Rees. COSTUME DESIGN: Susan Nininger.

CAST: F. Murray Abraham (Maximilian Suba), Eric Roberts (Alexander Villard), Mia Sara (Erin Clavelli), Christopher Rydell (Jim Trebor), Elaine Kagan (Rachel).

RUNNING TIME: 91 minutes.

VHS: Sony Pictures.

A man who runs a fencing academy reluctantly hires a mysterious stranger to work for him, not knowing that the two have something dark in common.

C

CADDYSHACK (1980)

DIRECTOR: Harold Ramis. SCREENPLAY: Brian-Doyle Murray, Harold Ramis, Douglas Kenney. PRODUCER: Douglas Kenney. CINEMATOGRAPHY: Stevan Larner. EDITING: William Carruth. MUSIC: Johnny Mandel. PRODUCTION DESIGN: Stan Jolley. ART DIRECTION: George Szeptycki.
CAST: Chevy Chase (Ty Webb), Rodney Dangerfield (Al Czervik), Ted Knight (Judge Smails), Michael O'Keefe (Danny), Bill Murray (Carl Spackler).
RUNNING TIME: 98 minutes.
DVD: Warner Home Video.

Caddyshack is a loosely structured comedy frequently compared to *Animal House*. Writer Brian Doyle-Murray, one of Bill Murray's brothers, and writer/director Harold Ramis drew on their experiences caddying in their teens in putting together the script. However, much of the film is improvised. The plotlines include a caddy's attempt to win a college scholarship, a boorish real estate developer's plan to acquire the club, and a groundskeeper's attempts to exterminate a rodent.

The film opens at the home of the Noonan family, which is teeming with children. Son Danny (Michael O'Keefe) caddies at the exclusive Bushwood Country Club, but he doesn't earn enough for college and fears he will end up working in a lumberyard. At the club, he carries for Ty Webb (Chevy Chase), a Zen-like golfer who sometimes plays blindfolded. Webb is the mellow son and heir of the club's cofounder; he roams through the film only tangentially involved with the plotlines until late in the script. Back at the caddyshack, where the manager, Lou Loomis (Doyle-Murray), places bets with his bookie and overcharges the caddies for snacks, Danny learns that a caddy scholarship is available.

In order to receive the scholarship, Danny must court favor with Judge Smails (Ted Knight), the club's president. To this end, Danny begins to caddy for Smails, an arrogant snob, dishonest sportsman, and poor tipper. When a club Smails has hurled after missing a putt strikes another member, Danny assumes responsibility, earning brownie points. Later, after Danny and Smails's niece, Lacey Underall (Cindy Morgan), are caught in flagrante delicto, Smails offers Danny the scholarship as a bribe for keeping quiet about Lacey's promiscuity.

Judge Smails has larger concerns than Lacey's reputation. A nouveau riche developer, Al Czervik (Rodney Dangerfield) has designs on Bushwood. Al has offended Smails with his loud behavior and equally loud wardrobe, thrown Smails off his golf game, and thrown an anchor through the hull of Smails's sailboat. The exasperated Smails agrees to a challenge match and a twenty-thousand-dollar wager, which will increase to eighty thousand dollars by the final hole. Judge Smails has expected Ty to team with him; however, Ty elects to play with Al, leaving Smails to partner with Dr. Beeper (Dan Resin), another prominent club member. Al, a terrible player to begin with, has a worse-than-usual day, and soon he and Ty are trailing. When one of his drives ricochets and strikes his arm, Al claims that he is unable to continue. Unwilling to call off the match, Smails insists someone substitute for Al. It is Danny who steps forward and who must save the day by sinking a long putt on the last hole. The ball rolls to a halt at the edge of the cup and remains there until explosions rack the course—Carl the groundskeeper (Bill Murray) has planted plastic explosives in the gopher holes—and the aftershocks cause Danny's ball to drop.

Caddyshack's reputation rests on its comic sketches rather than on its plot. One set piece, a spoof of *Jaws* featuring a Baby Ruth candy bar in a swimming pool, has become a classic. Most of the other well-known scenes were almost entirely improvised: Carl's "Cinderalla story," a riff on how a humble groundskeeper wins a pro tournament, was Murray's inspiration, and the single scene between Murray and Chase, who did not get along, was unscripted. Dangerfield, a standup comedian by trade, ad-libbed much of his running commentary on the Bushwood club and its members. The original script called for Knight and Scott Colomby, who plays the chain-smoking caddy Tony D'Annunzio, to have much larger roles, but Knight's part was modified to make Chase the central character, and Colomby ended up with a minor supporting role.

Reviewers in the mainstream press gave the film a lukewarm reception, finding the humor sophomoric and noting numerous breaks in continuity. It is especially apparent that the footage of the gopher (a puppet known as Chuck Rodent) and his tunnels—filmed later in a well-equipped soundstage—is of much higher quality than that of the rest of the movie, which was shot on location. However, *Caddyshack* has always been popular with audiences, and today it graces a number of top-film lists, including Bravo's and the American Film Institute's 100 funniest movies.

CADDYSHACK II (1988)

DIRECTOR: Allan Arkush. SCREENPLAY: Harold Ramis, Peter Torokvei. PRODUCERS: Neil Canton, Peter Guber, Jon Peters. CINEMATOGRAPHY: Harry Stradling. EDITING: Bernard Gribble. MUSIC: Ira Newborn. PRODUCTION DESIGN: William F. Matthews. ART DIRECTION: Joseph P. Lucky. COSTUME DESIGN: May Routh.

CAST: Jackie Mason (Jack Hartounian), Dyan Cannon (Elizabeth Pearce), Robert Stack (Chandler Young), Dina Merrill (Cynthia Young), Chevy Chase (Ty Webb), Dan Aykroyd (Capt. Tom Everett).

RUNNING TIME: 98 minutes.

DVD: Warner Home Video.

In this semisequel to the hit film (Chevy Chase, the only star from the original, appears briefly), a self-made millionaire takes on country club snobs.

CARMAN: THE CHAMPION (2001)

DIRECTOR: Lee Stanley. SCREENPLAY: Lee Stanley, Carman, Tony Cinciripini, Tadd Callies. PRODUCERS: Tadd Callies, Tony Cinciripini, Richard J. Crook, Matthew Crouch, Lawrence Mortorff. CINEMATOGRAPHY: Steve Adcock. EDITING: Shane Stanley. MUSIC: Harry Manfredini. PRODUCTION DESIGN: Nanci Roberts. COSTUME DESIGN: Jyl Moder.

CAST: Carman (Orlando Leone), Michael Nouri (Freddie), Patricia Manterola (Allia), Jeremy Williams (Keshon Banks).

RUNNING TIME: 82 minutes.

DVD: Good Times Video.

Christian music recording artist Carman cowrote this mediocre film about a retired boxer who returns to the ring to raise money for a youth ministry.

CARS (2006)

DIRECTORS: John Lasseter, Joe Ranft. SCREENPLAY: John Lasseter, Joe Ranft, Jorgen Klubian, Dan Fogelman, Kiel Murray, Phil Lorin. PRODUCER: Darla K. Anderson. CINEMATOGRAPHY: Jeremy Lasky. EDITING: Ken Schretzmann. MUSIC: Randy Newman. PRODUCTION DESIGN: William Cone, Bob Pauley.

CAST (VOICES): Owen Wilson (Lightning McQueen), Paul Newman (Doc Hudson), Bonnie Hunt (Sally Carerra), Cheech Marin (Ramone), Tony Shalhoub (Luigi).

RUNNING TIME: 117 minutes. Animated.

ACADEMY AWARD NOMINATIONS: Best Animated Feature, Best Original Song ("Our Town").

DVD: Walt Disney Video.

In this animated film, a race car winds up in a small town and learns important lessons from the others cars.

CELTIC PRIDE (1996)

DIRECTOR: Tom DeCerchio. SCREENPLAY: Judd Apatow. STORY: Judd Apatow, Colin Quinn. PRODUCER: Roger Birnbaum. CINEMATOGRAPHY: Oliver Wood. EDITING: Hubert De La Bouillerie. MUSIC: Basil Poledouris. PRODUCTION DESIGN: Stephen Marsh. ART DIRECTION: Dina Lipton. COSTUME DESIGN: Mary Claire Hannan.

CAST: Damon Wayans (Lewis Scott), Daniel Stern (Mike O'Hara), Dan Akyroyd (Jimmy Flaherty), Gail O'Grady (Carol O'Hara), Christopher McDonald (Chris McCarthy), Paul Guilfoyle (Officer Kevin O'Grady), Darrell Hammond (Coach Kimball).

RUNNING TIME: 91 minutes.

DVD: Walt Disney Video.

Two Bostonians of Irish descent come up with a harebrained scheme to help their beloved Celtics win an NBA championship in this heavy-handed comedy scripted by Judd Apatow and Colin Quinn and directed by Tom DeCerchio. Daniel Stern stars as Mike O'Hara, a former high school basketball player whose fanaticism about the Celtics threatens his marriage. His sidekick, plumber Jimmy Flaherty (Dan Aykroyd), lives in a bachelor's pad filled with sports memorabilia. Both men spend much of their lives watching sports on television, and they have season tickets for the Celtics. When the film opens, the Celtics hold a three-to-two lead over the Utah Jazz going into game 6. This may well be the last game played in the Boston Garden, which is scheduled for demolition.

Mike, who now teaches physical education, is so caught up in Celtic fever that he raves at his class of elementary school children about the upcoming game and barely reacts when his wife, Carol (Gail O'Grady), waves divorce papers under his nose. Carol complains that she's tired of his moods shifting with the fate of the basketball team and identifies the source of his obsession with his failure to succeed at the sport after high school. Mike lights a cigarette and accuses Carol—and her therapist—of "twisting things around."

The film cuts to a grey-tone Nike commercial featuring Utah Jazz star Lewis Scott (Damon Wayans), who proclaims, "I am not a hero" and "I don't want to raise your kids" while showing off his court skills. Lewis's ego is as great as his talent. He has a reputation for missing practices, hogging the ball, and blaming his teammates when there's a problem.

For game 6 Mike and Jimmy arrive at the Garden decked out in Celtic jerseys and waving pennants. When they take their seats, they are warmly greeted by similarly dressed fans. A hotdog vendor, Suzy (Con-

Dan Aykroyd, Damon Wayans, and Daniel Stern in *Celtic Pride*; Wayans on the bench

nie Perry), presents Jimmy with a complimentary sandwich. Her interest in him is obvious, but Jimmy is too excited about the game to pay her much attention. During the first half the Celtics play well, taking a substantial lead into the locker room, but in the second half, Lewis gets hot and begins to close the gap with a series of baskets. At Mike's instigation, the highly superstitious fans begin switching seats in an attempt to reverse the Celtics' sudden cold streak. It doesn't work, and the Jazz pull ahead as the buzzer sounds.

Troubled by the loss, Mike and Jimmy reinforce each other's fears that if Lewis continues to play well, the Celtics have no chance to win the title. When they learn from a bartending buddy that Lewis is celebrating at the Roxy, a local club, they hit upon the idea of getting Lewis drunk so that he will be too hung over to function during the next game. In order to befriend Lewis, they pretend to be admirers and avid supporters of the Jazz. When a Boston fan berates Lewis, they come to his defense, proclaiming him the greatest player in the history of the game. At just that moment, Larry Bird (as himself), legendary retired Celtic forward, walks up, much to the chagrin of Mike and Jimmy, but they manage to hide their true feelings and succeed in winning over Lewis. Long after the Roxy has closed, the three continue to party. Lewis, who is black, is amused to have two white Irish Bostonians as fans.

In the morning, Mike, who is staying at Jimmy's, awakens to discover not only that he is sharing a futon with Lewis but also that Lewis's hands and feet are bound with duct tape. Neither Mike nor Jimmy can remember exactly what happened after they left the Roxy, supporting Lewis between them, but it is apparent that at some point they determined to kidnap him. Before deciding what to do with their captive, the pair dress him in a Celtics' jersey for a photo op; then they decide to have breakfast. Jimmy performs guard duty armed with a Russian biathlon rifle (an Olympic souvenir) while Mike makes a coffee run. On the way Mike encounters another friend, Officer Kevin O'Grady (Paul Guilfoyle), to whom he suggests—hypothetically, of course—kidnapping

Lewis. Kevin indicates he would support such a plan and advises that the hypothetical kidnappers should detain Lewis until after the game. "Kidnapping is kidnapping," Kevin explains, no matter how long the captive is held.

While Mike has been on his errand, Lewis has been trying to turn Jimmy against Mike, pointing out that Mike tells Jimmy what to do. Lewis also makes fun of Jimmy's collection of sports memorabilia. He notes that Jimmy's identification with "other people's accomplishments" is not reciprocal and utters one of the film's few memorable lines: "Do you think Larry Bird has a picture of you with your hand down a toilet?" When Mike returns, Lewis shows equal insight into Mike's sports obsession, identifying him as a wannabe who likes to criticize the pros in order to perpetuate the illusion that he could do a better job. The appearance at the apartment of Carol and son Tommy (Adam Henershott), who is lugging a box of Mike's high school trophies, seems to confirm Lewis's appraisal. Tommy recognizes Lewis immediately, but Carol has no idea who he is. Mike expects sympathy from Lewis and Jimmy at Carol's ignorance. When Carol realizes what Mike and Jimmy are up to, she hurries out with Tommy and threatens to call the police, a threat that is of little concern to Mike. Later that evening, Lewis convinces his captors to let him go to the bathroom. At this point, Jimmy's landlord arrives demanding the rent, and Lewis takes advantage of the interruption to escape.

Lewis doesn't get far. He flags down a taxi, only to be kicked out by the driver, a Celtics fan. Then, with Mike and Jimmy in pursuit, he runs toward a police officer, screaming for help. The officer is Kevin, who allows Mike and Jimmy to drive off with Lewis in the plumbing van. When Kevin swings into action, it is to arrange a money-making venture; he orders twenty thousand T-shirts boasting the Celtics' championship victory. Meanwhile, Mike and Lewis continue their verbal sparring. Mike criticizes Lewis's attitude; Lewis defends himself on the basis of his natural talent. Tempers flare, and Mike challenges Lewis to a game of one-on-one. As Jimmy pretends to call the play-by-play, using the rifle barrel as a microphone, Lewis dribbles circles around Mike. After he has worn Mike out and left him face down on the court gasping for air, Lewis beans Jimmy with a pass and snatches the gun. Before he drives off in Jimmy's van, Lewis offers his abductors a deal: he won't report them to the police, but they must cheer for him at the game and start wearing purple.

Wearing purple, Mike and Jimmy take their seats among the Celtic fans and avoid being assaulted by explaining they think that they have brought misfortune to the Celtics and now seek to infect the Jazz with their bad luck. On the floor, Lewis has failed to appear, and Mike and Jimmy begin to worry that the van has broken down. If Lewis misses the game, he won't know they've kept their end of the bargain. Just as the game is about to begin, Lewis arrives, and Mike and Jimmy welcome him with applause and shouts of encouragement. However, Lewis is missing his shots, and his teammates, irate over his skipping practice and turning up at the last minute, do not have their hearts in the game. As the Celtics run up a fifteen-point lead, Mike and Jimmy fear that Lewis will turn them in. Their fears and humiliation mount during the half. Jimmy holds the winning ticket in a $100,000 promotion and is called onto the court in all of his Jazz finery. Although he sinks a basket and is awarded the money, his only thought is that at least he and Mike can afford a lawyer. As the two contemplate prison terms, they grow sincere in their support of the Jazz. When Utah returns to the court, Mike begins shouting at Lewis to pass the ball and work with his team, advice that Lewis has heard repeatedly from his coach, his teammates, and the press. However, he heeds Mike's words and starts feeding the ball to his teammates. In a repeat of game 6, the Jazz pull to within a point and score the winning goal at the buzzer. Mike and Jimmy celebrate amid the astounded Celtic fans, and the camera cuts to Carol and Tommy, who have also been cheering on Lewis and the Jazz from their living room. When Kevin, now stuck with twenty thousand worthless championship tees, asks Lewis to press charges, Lewis declares Mike and Jimmy are his friends and bumps chests with them.

Seven months later, Mike and Jimmy are tiptoeing down a hotel corridor in the middle of the night. They sneak into a room where Deion Sanders is sleeping, awaken him, and flash a roll of duct tape.

Writing for the *New York Times*, Stephen Holden termed Apatow's two main characters, "cretinous," and most reviews, though not as harsh as Holden's, found the film uneven at best. The plot leaves too many loose ends and fails to work effectively with secondary characters. Some scenes seem meaningless. The totally unexpected appearance of Jimmy's landlord facilitates Lewis's first escape, but the fact that Jimmy is behind on his rent and broke is neither accounted for nor elaborated on.

Another odd scene injects the "Rainbow Man" into the final game. Just before the half, as Jimmy tells Mike he's going to become a born-again Christian in jail to avoid becoming someone's "bitch," a man wearing a multi-colored afro wig and carrying a sign that reads "John 3:16" walks by. Jimmy attacks the man, raging about religious fanatics. It seems a throw-away gag inserted to extend the film's running time, but the actual Rainbow Man, Rollen Stewart, who spent much of the 1980s attending televised sporting events and waving his sign at the cameras, staged a bizarre kidnapping in 1992; he was sentenced to three concurrent life sentences and has been denied parole. However, the film provides no clue to the thematic significance of Rainbow Man's appearance; it is a reference many viewers will not catch.

At the end of the credits, the film includes a staged sequence of Boston Garden being demolished (the actual demolition occurred in 1997), but as *Variety* writer Joe Leydon (April 19, 1996) notes, this expensive scene occurs at a time when few viewers will still be watching.

CHAK DE! INDIA (2007)

DIRECTOR: Shimit Amin. SCREENPLAY: Jaideep Sahni. PRODUCER: Aditya Chopra, Yash Chopra. CINEMATOGRAPHY: Sudeep Chatterjee. EDITING: Amitabh Shukla. MUSIC: Salim Merchant, Suleiman Merchant. ART DIRECTION: Sukant Panigrahy. COSTUME DESIGN: Mandira Shukla.

CAST: Shahrukh Khan (Kabir Khan), Vidya Malvade (Vidya Sharma), Tanya Abrol (Balbir Kaur), Chitrashi Rawat (Komal Chautala), Arya Menon (Gul Iqbal).

RUNNING TIME: 153 minutes.

In 2002 India's national women's field hockey team won the gold medal at the Commonwealth Games held in Manchester, England. One of the team's coaches, Mir Ranjan Negi, goalkeeper for India's men's team in the early 1980s, had been accused of accepting a bribe to throw the 1982 Asian games, which India lost to Pakistan 1–7. Negi was called a traitor in the press and driven from the sport. Twenty years later, his assistance in preparing the women's team and their victories over Australia in the semifinals and England in the final helped him redeem his reputation. The team's performance also drew the attention of screenwriter Jaideep Sahni, who began work on the script that became

Chak De! India. Although claiming he was not aware of the extent of Negi's difficulties at the time of writing, Sahwi created a character, Kabir Khan, who endured a similar experience. Reportedly, Negi was concerned about the resemblance when he first learned of the script; however, he was so reassured after meeting Sahwi and the director, Shimit Amin, that he became a technical consultant, working for six months with the actors to help them develop their hockey skills. *Chak De! India* (which translates to a rallying cry, "Go! India") is an ensemble film that concentrates on the sport, but it is also a political film that draws on the country's history under English rule and partition and carries a strong feminist theme.

Bollywood star Shahrukh Khan plays Kabir Khan, who is captain of the Indian field hockey team and who misses a penalty stroke in a world championship match against Pakistan. Kabir is tried and found guilty in the press and is soon officially denounced following a committee investigation. He is burned in effigy in the streets, and even his neighbors turn against him, forcing him and his mother (Jayshree Arora) to abandon their ancestral home. After seven years of exile, Kabir returns to coach the women's field hockey team, which exists as a "formality" rather than a "reality." The team has received little funding or support from the committee overseeing the national field hockey teams, and the sport is considered greatly inferior to cricket, which gained popularity under the British Raj.

Kabir's team, selected by the committee, consists of sixteen of India's best players. Tension among the young women is immediately evident. They are strongly identified with their states rather than with their country. Two players from the far northeast are made to feel like foreigners; two from a jungle village in Jharkhand are also regarded with disdain—that one does not speak Hindi illustrates the extent of her cultural alienation. When the players introduce themselves, adding their states' names, Kabir, in a scene quite like one from *Miracle* (2004), dismisses each until one catches on and identifies herself as a player for India.

Kabir realizes that his greatest challenge is to get the women to work together as a team, and he achieves this by making himself unpopular (again, mirroring the plot of *Miracle*). He threatens to throw the goalie, Vidya Sharma (Vidya Malvade), off the team because she arrived a few minutes late. He benches his most experienced player, Bindia Naik (Shilpa Shukla), because she doesn't want to move to center forward. She is joined by another forward, Komal Chautala (Chitrashi Rawat), who wants to play center and refuses to pass, and by the team's hothead, Balbir Kaur (Tanya Abrol). After the punished players apologize, Kabir puts the entire team through strenuous training that soon has Bindia organizing a petition to have him replaced. When the team confronts Kabir with their request, he agrees to resign, explaining that he had wanted to resolve the questions about his past, but now he has lost, not the team, but his country. The next day Kabir tells the team he is taking the staff out to lunch and invites them to join. At a McDonald's he sits with the staff while the players separate into the small groups they have established in spite of his efforts to prevent their cultural-political segregation. Trouble begins when the two northeasterners, who are light-skinned, are harassed by a pair of young men. Balbir, never one to back away from a disagreement, comes to her teammates' defense, and soon the Indian women's field hockey team is whipping the male patrons. Kabir intervenes only to prevent a diner from clubbing one of his players with a cricket bat. Once the melee is over, he tells the women that they have finally demonstrated team spirit and that practice will resume the next morning at 5 a.m.

The film continues, following an intermission, with a training montage and shots of locker room high jinks, but before the team can move on to the World Cup, the Indian Field Hockey Association decides it cannot afford to support both a women's and a men's team. Kabir, who has expressed support for equal opportunity for women in the larger culture, gives an impassioned speech that results in a challenge match between the men's and women's team. When the women doubt their ability to compete, Kabir tells them that they are playing for a larger principle—women's rights. Kabir's enthusiasm fails to lift the team's spirit for the first period of the contest. The men play aggressively, and the officials neglect to call fouls. Trailing by three goals, the women are dispirited until riled by the criticism of an association member. In the second period they outplay the men, but score only twice; however, their performance is strong enough to win the respect of the men's team and the association. They will travel to Melbourne, Australia, for the World Cup after all.

The Melbourne trip brings out the women's unresolved personal problems. Vidya, who is married, faces pressure from her husband and father-in-law to return to her family responsibilities. Preety's fiancé, a star cricket player, wants to schedule the wedding during the time of the tournament. In order to prove to him that she can achieve success as a field hockey player, she reverts to selfishness during the game, refusing to pass to the other forward, Komal; in turn, Komal, whose father does not approve of her passion for the sport, feels she must prove herself by being the team's highest scorer. As a result, the opposing teams realize that the Indian forwards won't pass. Bindia, jealous that Vidya is the team captain, tries to seduce Kabir, who not only rejects her offer but also removes her from the starting lineup. With the team spirit eroding, Balbir's anger management issues reappear, drawing penalties and further demoralizing the women. India loses its opening match to Australia in the double-elimination tournament.

In order to stay in the tournament, the Indians must win all of their remaining contests. Kabir calls on Bindia to play against Korea, which uses man-to-man marking. Recognizing that the coach respects her talents, she rejoins the group and plays brilliantly. Balbir reels in her temper, but Komal and Preety continue their hostilities. Their rivalry has not hurt the team during its lower-bracket matches, but Kabir knows that the team cannot win the final, a rematch with Australia, unless the forwards shelve their personal agendas. Although he gives them a stern lecture about their larger responsibilities, their conflict remains unresolved and seems destined to interfere with the team's chances for success. However, in the closing seconds of regular play, Koma drives down the field and at the very last opportunity passes to Preety, who scores the tying goal, forcing a tie-breaker. The Australians score on their first two penalty strokes, while the Indians fail, requiring the Indian team to function perfectly, not missing any shots nor giving up another score. When the game comes down to the final stroke, it is Preety's turn, but she insists that Komal take her stroke. Komal scores, India wins, and the film ends with Komal's father now expressing his pride in her skill, with Vidya earning the respect of her father-in-law, with Preety refusing to marry the cricket star—who has staged a media event to present her with a ring—and with Kabir and his mother welcomed back to the ancestral home by the neighbors.

Chak De! India is the most successful of several sports films released in India within a short time frame. Strong performances by the cast, the use of field hockey as metaphor for national unity, and the feminist sensibility account for the film's international popularity.

THE CHAMP (1932)

DIRECTOR: King Vidor. SCREENPLAY: Frances Marion, Leonard Praskins, Wanda Tuchock. STORY: Frances Marion. PRODUCER: King Vidor. CINEMATOGRAPHY: Gordon Avil. EDITING: Hugh Wynn. ART DIRECTION: Cedric Gibbons.
CAST: Wallace Beery (Andy, the Champ), Jackie Cooper (Dink), Irene Rich (Linda), Roscoe Ates (Sponge), Edward Brophy (Tim), Hale Hamilton (Tony Carleton).
RUNNING TIME: 86 minutes. B&W.
ACADEMY AWARDS: Best Actor (Beery; tied with Fredric March), Best Original Story. NOMINATIONS: Best Picture, Best Director.
DVD: Warner Home Video.

Without much boxing footage but with plenty of sentiment, *The Champ* has more in common with *Stella Dallas* and other "weepies" than it does with the likes of *Raging Bull* (1980) and *Rocky* (1976). Despite the elevated handkerchief index, the film, directed by veteran King Vidor, was popular with the Academy, garnering Oscars for Best Actor (Wallace Beery as Andy, the Champ) and for Frances Marion's screenplay. Jackie Cooper plays Dink, the Champ's son, in the first of three Beery-Cooper screen collaborations.

The Champ, as Dink calls his father, is doing some roadwork to prepare for a comeback fight after losing the heavyweight championship because he was drunk. Unfortunately, the bar is not far enough away, and Dink has to put his inebriated father to bed. In spite of his drinking problem, Andy is a kind and well-intentioned father. Dink's mother, Linda (Irene Rich), who had given up custody of Dink in order to get Andy to agree to a divorce, is becoming concerned about the atmosphere her son is growing up in. Now remarried to the affluent Tony Carleton (Hale Hamilton), Linda asks her husband to talk to Andy about allowing Dink to live with them, but Andy will not agree. Nor will he agree to a plan for Dink to attend an exclusive boarding school. He will, however, let Linda see Dink, as long as he is paid two hundred dollars. His mother's intentions hold little attraction for Dink, whose behavior toward her is cool and aloof.

Andy promptly gambles away both the two hundred dollars and a horse, Little Champ, that he had obtained for Dink. Promising to win back the horse, Andy secures another deal with Linda and Tony; in exchange for more cash, he will permit Dink to choose between his parents. Dink elects to remain with his father. However, Andy, drinking again, loses the money, fails to get back Little Champ, and is arrested for starting a fight.

In jail the Champ realizes that his son would be better off with the Carletons, but in order to get Dink to go with them, he has to tell his son he doesn't love him. When even that fails, he actually hits Dink. Tony pays Andy's bail and then leaves for New York with Linda and Dink, but Dink manages to slip away from them and make his way off the train and back to his father.

Determined to redeem himself, the Champ begins to train for an upcoming fight in which he is the decided underdog. Early in the fight the Champ takes a terrible beating, but he refuses to quit. Once he is even saved by the bell. In a most improbable ending the Champ stages a comeback and knocks out his opponent. The victory is pyrrhic, however, since the out-of-shape Champ dies of a heart attack after the bout. The last scene with the dead Champ, the distraught and sobbing Dink, and the weeping mother is one of the most sentimental in sports films and one of the most criticized by hard-boiled boxing fans. Moviegoers may have been accustomed to *Stella Dallas*–like sacrifice, but father-son bonding and caring (usually expressed by shrugs or physical action, not words) was difficult to come to terms with. Since *The Champ*, however, many sports films have featured father-son bonding, surrogate fathers, and even cases, such as in *Hoosiers* (1986), in which the son acts as caregiver to his father.

The film includes only brief boxing footage, but that is overshadowed by scenes displaying the chemistry between Beery and Cooper. Interestingly enough, the film does not portray Dink's mother in a very favorable light. She gave up custody of her son, and when she gets him back, it is to send him to boarding school instead of renewing their relationship. This Depression-era film clearly places its sympathies with the downtrodden fighter, whose love and determination allow him, finally, to overcome his weaknesses and achieve his goals. In *Out of Bounds*, scholar Aaron Baker offers a skeptical reading of the film, describing *The Champ* as "a last-ditch effort to endorse the old myth of individual self-reliance, essentially discounting any notion that social or economic forces might put limits on the rise to success out of bounds."

The plot of *The Champ* was later used in *The Clown* (1952), featuring Red Skelton, who plays a fading comedian rather than a boxer. *The Champ* was remade in 1979.

THE CHAMP (1979)

DIRECTOR: Franco Zeffirelli. SCREENPLAY: Walter Newman. STORY: Frances Marion. PRODUCER: Dyson Lovell. CINEMATOGRAPHY: Fred J. Koenekamp. EDITING: Michael J. Sheridan. MUSIC: Dave Grusin. PRODUCTION DESIGN: Herman A. Blumenthal. COSTUME DESIGN: Theoni V. Aldredge.

CAST: Jon Voight (Billy), Faye Dunaway (Annie), Rick Schroder (T.J.), Jack Warden (Jackie), Arthur Hill (Mike), Joan Blondell (Dolly Kenyon).

RUNNING TIME: 121 minutes.

ACADEMY AWARD NOMINATIONS: Best Original Score.

DVD: Warner Home Video.

In this remake of the 1931 classic, Jon Voight and Rick Schroder take on the roles made famous by Wallace Beery and Jackie Cooper.

CHAMPION (1949)

DIRECTOR: Mark Robson. SCREENPLAY: Carl Foreman. STORY: Ring Lardner. PRODUCER: Stanley Kramer. CINEMATOGRAPHY: Franz Planer. EDITING: Harry Gerstad. MUSIC: Dimitri Tiomkin. PRODUCTION DESIGN: Rudolph Sternad. COSTUME DESIGN: Joe King, Adele Parmenter.

CAST: Kirk Douglas (Midge Kelly), Marilyn Maxwell (Grace), Arthur Kennedy (Connie), Ruth Roman (Emma), Paul Stewart (Tom Haley), Lola Albright (Palmer Harris).

RUNNING TIME: 99 minutes. B&W.

ACADEMY AWARDS: Best Editing. NOMINATIONS: Best Actor (Douglas), Best Supporting Actor (Kennedy), Best Original Screenplay, Best Cinematography, Best Scoring of a Dramatic or Comedy Picture.

DVD: Republic Pictures.

Like *Body and Soul* (1947) and *The Set-Up* (1949), *Champion* is a noir film set in the boxing world, but unlike the two other films, in which the fighter comes to his senses, *Champion* reveals a man who is irredeemably corrupted by greed and ambition. It is based on a similarly bleak story by Ring Lardner.

Champion opens with champion Midge Kelly (Kirk Douglas) entering the ring to defend his title against a former contender, Johnny Dunne (John Day). Midge is the crowd favorite, and as a radio announcer puts it, the fans cheer for a "story of a boy who rose from the depths of poverty to become champion of the world." The film continues as a flashback, but the varnished story the announcer has begun turns into a sinister account of a man who stoops to the depths of depravity in his quest to become someone who will be called "mister."

The flashback begins with Midge and his brother, Connie (Arthur Kennedy), who walks with a cane, riding in a boxcar; they are mugged by three hoboes and thrown off the train, but Midge puts up a good fight defending himself and his brother. The two are on their way to Los Angeles, where they have purchased part interest in a diner from one of Midge's former navy buddies. As they hitchhike, they are picked up by boxer Johnny Dunne and his girlfriend, Grace (Marilyn Maxwell), who regards them with disdain. Johnny suggests the brothers pick up some cash selling sodas at the boxing match, but at the venue, Midge loses his temper, and his fit of pique results in several cases of beverages being smashed. Now in debt to the management, he agrees to replace a minor boxer in a preliminary bout. Midge lasts the requisite four rounds and collects his money; a Los Angeles–based promoter, Tom Haley (Paul Stewart), who watched the match and was impressed by Midge's ability to take a beating, offers to manage him. Midge declines, but Tom keeps the offer open and leaves him with the name of a gym.

Midge and Connie make their way to Los Angeles, once again riding the rails, only to discover that the navy buddy never owned the diner—he was merely employed there and was fired. The real owner, Lew Bryce (Harry Shannon), has little sympathy for the brothers but puts them to work washing dishes and bussing tables. Both Midge and Connie are attracted to Lew's daughter, Emma (Ruth Roman). Although at first Emma rejects Midge's overtures, finding him too cynical about life, she sympathizes with the hardships he endured as a child—being sent to an orphanage because his mother couldn't afford to keep both of her children after his father deserted the family, going hungry and cold; she is also unable to resist his sheer animal magnetism. After yielding to Midge, Emma assumes they are to be married, an assumption Midge does not share. As soon as he expresses that he's not ready for marriage, Lew barges into the room wielding a handgun and insists an immediate wedding is the only way for his daughter to retain her reputation. Midge has no choice but to go through with the wedding, but believing he has been set up, he deserts his wife immediately after the ceremony, and a reluctant Connie follows.

Reminded of Tom Haley's offer, Midge ventures to the gym, where he finds Tom retired, having grown weary of the blood lust and corruption. Still, he allows Midge to strong-arm him into training him for a professional career. Connie does not approved of Midge's career move and wants Midge to leave the ring as soon as he has proven himself by winning a match and earning some money. Connie explains that Midge is transformed into someone alien as he releases pent up anger against his opponents. But having tasted the spoils of success, Midge is hungry for more; he continues to fight, reveling in the cheers of the crowd and the luxuries he can now afford. He continues winning and is able to provide a comfortable apartment in Chicago for his mother, but he cannot get a crack at the title, now held by Johnny Dunne.

After three years Tom arranges a title match; the catch is that Midge must agree to throw the fight, or the deal is off. However, Midge is too arrogant—not too ethical—to go through with the fix and knocks out Johnny in the first round. Before he is rushed from the arena, he manages to slip his phone number to Grace, who has been sitting ringside. As a result of Midge's betrayal of the gangsters, he, Connie, and Tom are all beaten, but none is seriously injured, and Midge has become a media darling for standing up to the crooks. And Grace calls. Over drinks at her place, she tells Midge that Johnny is in the hospital and will never fight again. She's in the market for a new man to support her expensive tastes, and she has connections that will get Midge off the hook with the mob.

Grace's conditions include replacing Tom with businessman Jerome Harris (Luis Van Rooten) from whom he can borrow $130,000 to buy off the gambling interests he has offended. When Connie hears of the arrangements to which Midge has agreed, the two argue and Connie leaves. He traces Emma, who has never divorced Midge, and after confessing his love, asks her to come to Chicago to live with his and Midge's mother, who is growing old and needs a companion. Emma tells Connie that she still has feelings for Midge, but agrees to move to Chicago.

Meanwhile, Midge has successfully defended his title under Harris's management and at a nightclub with Grace, meets Palmer Harris (Lola Albright), Jerome's attractive young wife. Palmer, who sculpts, invites Midge to pose for her. The modeling scene ends in a passionate kiss that leaves the viewer to imagine what happens next. Grace, who has become suspicious, demands that Midge marry her, but, of course, he can't since he is still legally married to Emma. After accusing Grace of being mercenary, Midge dumps her unceremoniously and continues to meet Palmer.

Back in Chicago, as Mrs. Kelly, Connie, and Emma listen to the radio, Midge is awarded Athlete of the Year, and Mrs. Kelly, now ill, expresses her desire to see her famous son. Later that evening, Emma reveals to Connie that she no longer loves Midge; the two embrace and soon are planning a divorce/wedding. Meanwhile, Jerome confronts Palmer about Midge. Palmer declares that she wants a divorce in order to marry Midge, but Jerome determines to prove that Midge does not love her. In her presence, Jerome offers Midge a deal: he will forgive the debt Midge still owes and will arrange a title bout with Johnny Dunne, who has recovered from his injuries years ago and has been seeking a rematch; in exchange, Midge will give up Palmer. Midge does not hesitate to accept the deal. Jerome warns Midge to train for the fight because Johnny is in the best shape of his career.

Midge visits Tom to pay back money he borrowed years earlier and to beg Tom to prepare him for the upcoming match. Tom accepts, but only after demanding a third of Midge's purse. Midge's next stop is Chicago, where his mother is dying, but he arrives too late. When he learns of Connie's engagement to Emma, he asks them to wait until after the fight and asks Connie to help with his training as well. Midge's efforts to reconcile with Connie appear merely a ploy to seduce Emma, something she seems to realize but cannot prevent. After Midge reminds Emma that she is still his wife, she yields to his conjugal demands, then disappears. Just before the Johnny Dunne match, Connie confronts Midge in the locker room, calling him "corrupt." In a shot reminiscent of the first appearance of the brothers together, when Connie is roughly pushed into a corner of the boxcar by the hoboes, Midge shoves his brother, leaving him on the locker room floor.

The film has come full circle, arriving at the announcer repeating that "this is a story of a boy . . . a story that could only happen in the fight game." The fight is presented in great detail, complete with an announcer who contributes to the verisimilitude. The Harrises are at ringside, as is Grace, now back with Johnny. Midge knocks Johnny down in the first round, but he is up quickly and soon takes control of the match. A cut opens over Midge's left eye, leaving him vulnerable. In spite of knockdowns in the tenth and eleventh rounds, the referee fails to call the fight, and Midge refuses to let Tom throw in the towel. In the last round, as he looks into the audience and sees Grace and the Harrises, now staring back at him with contempt, Midge snaps. His face distorted with rage, he delivers savage blows before knocking out Johnny to retain the championship.

As Midge leaves the ring, Tom calls for a doctor. Back in the locker room, Midge is talking to himself, muttering that people cheer for him and that he doesn't need to hitchhike anymore; then he collapses and is pronounced dead of a brain hemorrhage. Outside, a reporter asks Connie for a statement. After a pause during which Connie visibly softens, he calls his late brother "champion."

Producer Stanley Kramer, who served as second unit director, filming and editing the fight scenes and training montages, and director Mark Robson, brought the film in under budget and ahead of schedule, shooting half the average footage. *Champion* cost half a million dollars to make and earned 18 million. It made Kirk Douglas a star, earning him his first Oscar nomination. The film garnered four other nominations and a win for editor Harry Gerstad.

***CHARIOTS OF FIRE* (1981)**

DIRECTOR: Hugh Hudson. SCREENPLAY: Colin Welland. PRODUCER: David Puttnam. CINEMATOGRAPHY: David Watkin. EDITING: Terry Rawlings. MUSIC: Vangelis Papathanassiou. ART DIRECTION: Jonathan Amberston, Len Huntingford, Anne Ridley, Andrew Sanders. COSTUME DESIGN: Milena Canonero.

CAST: Ben Cross (Harold Abrahams), Ian Charleson (Eric Liddell), Nigel Havers (Lord Andrew Lindsay), Nicholas Farrell (Aubrey Montague), Alice Krige (Sybil Gordon), Ian Holm (Sam Mussabini), John Gielgud (master of the college), Dennis Christopher (Charles Paddock), Brad Davis (Jackson Scholz).

RUNNING TIME: 124 minutes.

ACADEMY AWARDS: Best Picture, Best Adapted Screenplay, Best Original Score, Best Costume Design. NOMINATIONS: Best Director, Best Supporting Actor (Holm), Best Editing.

DVD: Warner Home Video.

Set in Britain and France in the 1920s, *Chariots of Fire* is loosely based on the athletic careers of two runners, Harold Abrahams and Eric Liddell, who competed in the 1924 Olympic Games. Abrahams, the son of a Lithuanian Jew, was an outstanding jumper and runner who hired Sam Mussabini to train him for the Paris Olympics. Abrahams's athletic career ended in 1925 after he fractured his leg; he took up law and later became a sports journalist. Eric Liddell, the son of a missionary, was born in Tientsin in northern China and educated in Scotland, completing his course of studies at the University of Edinburgh. In 1925, after competing in the Olympic Games, Liddell returned to China as a missionary. He died there in 1945, a Japanese prisoner of war in Shantung Province. The film portrays both men as marginalized from the mainstream of English society. Like *This Sporting Life* (1963), directed by Lindsay Anderson (who has a cameo in *Chariots of Fire*) and *Match Point* (2005), directed by Woody Allen and set in England, this film examines sport as a means of transcending class. It is equally concerned with individualism, patriotism, religion, and character. The title comes from William Blake's "Preface to Milton."

The film's structure is complex. It is doubly framed by scenes set in 1978 of a memorial service for Abrahams (Ben Cross) and by the iconic scene of the main characters running along the beach while the theme song plays. One member of the Olympic team, Cambridge student Aubrey Montague (Nicholas Farrell), narrates parts of the story through letters written to his parents and fills in background information. Abrahams's arrival and settling in at Cambridge are presented in counterpoint to Liddell's (Ian Charleson) running and practicing his religion in Scotland.

Major themes appear in quick succession. At the train station two young disabled World War I veterans heft the baggage of the Cambridge-bound students for tips, and one remarks that this is what they fought to protect. Later, at the freshmen dinner, tribute is paid to the war dead among Cambridge alumni whose names appear embossed on the wall. The contrast between the respect for the "flower of a generation" who "died for all England stands for" and the plight of the working-class veterans reveals continuing inequities of class and provides an ironic comment on patriotism by invoking "all" that England values. Liddell reveals his Scottish loyalty as readily as he does his "muscular Christianity"; his speeches compare faith to running, mention unemployment and hardship, and express pride in his country. Anti-Semitism is indicated when Abrahams checks in at Cambridge. The masters of the college (Sir John

Ian Charleson (left) and Ben Cross (right) in *Chariots of Fire*

Gielgud and Lindsay Anderson) regard him as arrogant. A snide remark that Abrahams won't be joining the chapel choir underscores his outsider status, but it turns out he has a fine voice and, in another ironic touch, ends up singing center stage "I Am an Englishman" in a campus production of *The Pirates of Penzance.*

Abrahams demonstrates his running ability shortly after his arrival at Cambridge, taking up the Trinity Challenge to circle the yard before the clock strikes twelve times, a seemingly impossible task. Abrahams succeeds. Finishing close behind him is Lord Andrew Lindsay (Nigel Havers), an old-school aristocrat who trains for the hurdles by having his butler balance glasses of champagne atop each barrier. When Abrahams observes Liddell win a race even after being tripped, he determines to race against him; Abrahams takes the controversial step of approaching a professional trainer, Sam Mussabini (Ian Holm), to assist him. Mussabini agrees to watch Abrahams run against Liddell in London, a contest Liddell wins. Nonetheless, the trainer is highly impressed and begins working with Abrahams. In keeping with the sports film genre, a training montage shifts from Liddell running in his native land to Abrahams working out on a track and on paved roads. In between, Lindsay leaps over shallow-bowled glasses of bubbly.

Abrahams's employment of Mussabini draws criticism from the masters of the college, who believe he is violating the spirit, if not the letter, of the amateur code under which the Olympic Games operated at the time. The masters question Abrahams's loyalty, indicating he has lost sight of the larger purpose of the games by placing personal ambition above esprit de corps. Abrahams, who defends his patriotism, regards this opposition as bigotry intensified by Mussabini's Arab-Italian heritage.

Liddell, too, finds his patriotism questioned when he refuses to compete in a qualifying 100-meter heat because it is scheduled for a Sunday. Although pressured by both the Olympic committee and the Prince of Wales (David Yelland), Liddell chooses moral principle over national pride; he will not run on the Sabbath. The conflict is resolved when Lindsay, who has already medaled in the long hurdles, offers his position in the 400-meter race to Liddell. This shift places Liddell at a disadvantage: not only must he run against the highly favored American, Jackson Scholz (Brad Davis), but he must also do so without having trained for the event. (In actuality, Liddell knew of the qualifying schedule months in advance and was able to prepare adequately for the longer run; neither the fictitious Lord Lindsay nor the real Prince of Wales was involved.)

Both Abrahams and Liddell win gold medals. After finishing well behind the American winners, Scholz and Charles Paddock (Dennis Christopher), in the 200 meters, Abrahams is victorious in the 100-meter race. Mussabini, who cannot watch in person without jeopardizing Abrahams's amateur standing, learns the outcome when from his hotel room he hears the English anthem played. Briefly, he stands at attention, holding his hat over his heart. That night, he and Abrahams close down a café, celebrating by themselves. The next day Liddell overcomes both the odds and the Americans. The scene jumps from his triumph to the team's arrival in London. The flag-draped car that awaits the athletes looks fleetingly like a coffin, reflecting the framing scene of Abrahams's memorial service. Abrahams does not join the others in the vehicle, having waited in the train. He is met at the station by his girl, Sybil Gordon (Alice Kriege), who has played a small, but significant role in his success. As they leave the station, they pass a small hand-lettered sign welcoming him home from Paris in language that reminds one of World War I and the veterans from the earlier station scene. A choir provides a musical transition from the train station in 1924 to the funeral service and into the closing credits superimposed on the long shot of the athletes running on the beach.

The music, composed, arranged, and performed by Vangelis Papathanassiou, won an Academy Award for Best Original Score. The film also brought in Oscars for Best Original Screenplay, Best Costume Design, and Best Picture. Ian Holm was nominated for Best Supporting Actor. Film editor Terry Rawlings and director Hugh Hudson were also nominated. *Chariots of Fire* was Hudson's first feature film.

CHASING 3000 (2010)

DIRECTOR: Gregory J. Lanesey. SCREENPLAY: Bill Mikita, Cris D'Annunzio, Gregory J. Lanesey. PRODUCERS: Ryan R. Johnson, Bill Mikita. CINEMATOGRAPHY: Denis Maloney. EDITING: Shannon Mitchell. MUSIC: Lawrence Shragge. PRODUCTION DESIGN: Kenn Coplan. COSTUME DESIGN: Marianne Parker.

CAST: Trevor Morgan (Mickey), Rory Culkin (Roger), Ray Liotta (Mickey as an adult), Lauren Holly (Marilyn), Seymour Cassel (Poppy).

RUNNING TIME: 98 minutes.

This film is based on a true story about two brothers transplanted to Los Angeles who travel back home to Pittsburgh, so they can witness baseball great Roberto Clemente reach his 3,000th hit.

CINDERELLA MAN (2005)

DIRECTOR: Ron Howard. SCREENPLAY: Cliff Hollinsworth, Akiva Goldsman. PRODUCERS: Brian Grazer, Ron Howard, Penny Marshall. CINEMATOGRAPHY: Salvatore Totino. EDITING: Daniel Hanley, Mile Hill. MUSIC: Thomas Newman. PRODUCTION DESIGN: Wynn Thomas. ART DIRECTION: Peter Grundy, Dan Yarhi. COSTUME DESIGN: Daniel Orlandi.

CAST: Russell Crowe (Jim Braddock), Renée Zellweger (Mae Braddock), Paul Giamatti (Joe Gould), Craig Bierko (Max Baer), Paddy Considine (Mike Wilson), Bruce McGill (Jimmy Johnston).

RUNNING TIME: 144 minutes.

ACADEMY AWARD NOMINATIONS: Best Supporting Actor (Giamatti), Best Editing, Best Makeup.

DVD: Universal Studios.

Ron Howard and Russell Crowe, whose *A Beautiful Mind* (2001) earned a Best Actor nomination for Crowe and four Oscars, including Best Director for Howard, teamed up once again on another screen adaptation, this time of Jeremy Schaap's *Cinderella Man: James Braddock, Max Baer, and the Greatest Upset in Boxing History.* Like *Seabiscuit* (2003), it is set against the Depression and features an underdog whose determination reflects the American Dream and inspires the downtrodden.

The film opens in 1928, the year before the stock market crash, to reveal Jim (Crowe) as a successful fighter who has provided a comfortable, although not ostentatious, home for his wife, Mae (Renée Zellweger), and their three children. The screen fades to dark, and the scene shifts to 1933. The Braddocks are now living in a dark, cramped basement apartment. When Jim's daughter, Rosie (Ariel Waller), requests a second slice of fried bologna at breakfast, Jim gives her his thin portion, claiming he dreamt he ate a big dinner and is no longer hungry. Then Jim spends the day walking the streets in a futile search for work. He returns home to discover his son Jay (Connor Price) has stolen a salami after learning that a friend was sent to live with relatives because his parents didn't have enough food for the family. Jim lectures his son about honesty and returns the salami, but he also promises Jay he will never break up the family.

Although Jim had injured his right hand in 1929, he appeals to his old manager, Joe Gould (Paul Giamatti), to arrange a fight for him. In spite of Mae's objections—she detests boxing and cannot bear to watch her husband in action—Jim returns to the ring and promptly breaks his hand. He refuses to let Joe throw in the towel, but the referee calls the match, and the promoter, Jimmy Johnston (Bruce McGill), thinking Jim has quit, terminates their contract, effectively ending Jim's career.

Jim joins a group of men who seek employment at the docks. He is chosen and paired with a former stockbroker, Mike Wilson (Paddy Considine). When Mike sees that Jim cannot use his right hand, he fears that they will fail to keep up the expected pace, but Jim proves equal to the task. Mike comes to his defense when their boss also notices Jim's injury. Jim retains his job at the docks, but he doesn't earn enough to cover his utility bills and must scavenge for scrap lumber to burn. Soon his son Howard (Patrick Louis) becomes ill. While Jim is out working, Mae sends the children to stay with family members, breaking Jim's promise never to farm the children out to relatives. Swallowing his pride, he applies for public assistance and is recognized at the relief office. The money he is given is not enough to cover his overdue bills, so Jim goes to Madison Square Garden, where he passes the hat among the promoters and managers of the boxing world. In an awkward moment, he approaches Joe, who contributes to the cause. Jim succeeds in having power restored to the apartment, and the children return home. Howard is now healthy, and it is a happy reunion.

In the spring Joe convinces Jimmy Johnston to allow Jim to box. Jim turns up in borrowed gear, including a robe that says "Fred." He hasn't eaten before the match because the soup kitchen ran out of food. Joe manages to locate a bowl of hash for him, but no cutlery. Jim sinks his face into the meal just as a reporter, Sporty Lewis (Nicholas Campbell), walks by and predicts Jim will be flat on the canvas soon after the opening bell. Sporty is right. Jim goes down in the first round, but he gets back up and wins the match. Back in the locker room, he finishes the hash. At home the Braddocks enjoy a bologna feast.

Now that Jim has demonstrated his fitness, Joe believes his license can be restored and offers to front him $175 for training and fees. Mae is opposed to the idea and appears at Joe's apartment to confront him privately. Joe is not home, but Mrs. Gould (Linda Kash) invites her in to tea. Mae discovers that the beautiful rooms are empty: the Goulds have hocked their furniture to get Jim's career back on track. Soon Jim is winning bouts and earning money. His year of slinging cargo have strengthened his left arm and given him a lethal hook. His next trip to the relief office, where he is again recognized, is to repay the money he received earlier.

One day Mike's wife visits Jim because her husband is missing. He had gone to a Hooverville in Central Park as a labor organizer. Jim searches for Mike in the park, but when he finds him, Mike is dying from injuries incurred in a suspicious accident. Mike's function in the film is to advance political subplots. Earlier, hardship and poverty had led him to drink, and although he was never physically abusive, he began quarreling with his wife. However, after listening to one of Jim's bouts, Mike turned his life around, becoming an activist intent on helping others regain control over their lives. Mike's death and his wife's grief further serve to intensify Mae's fears for Jim's well-being, for Jim is scheduled to meet champion Max

Baer (Craig Bierko), who has, according to the film, killed two men in the ring.

Max is portrayed as a coarse bully who taunts Jim when they are introduced at a restaurant and makes suggestive comments about taking care of Mae after Jim's demise. Mae pleads with Jim to cancel the fight, but to no avail. Still unable to watch, she leaves him at the arena and goes to church, where she finds the entire congregation is there to pray for him as well. The priest has set up a radio near the altar. After leaving the church, Mae joins the children at her sister's house. They have been forbidden to listen to the match but have sneaked a radio into a closet. By the late rounds, Mae joins them. Jim is holding his own against Max, who has neglected his training. In contrast, Jim has carefully studied Max's films, particularly footage of his lethal blows. Jim succeeds in avoiding potentially fatal punches and scores a unanimous decision. Two years later, the film explains, Jim lost his title to Joe Louis. After serving in World War II, he became a heavy equipment operator and moved his family to a modest house in New Jersey.

Cinderella Man opened to mixed reviews and did poorly at the box office. Critics found Howard's treatment heavy-handed, resembling the idealized biopics of the 1940s and 1950s. Howard's Braddock is an uncomplicated man without fault, while his Max is monstrous. Max's relatives objected strongly to Howard's portrayal of Max as a fighter with lethal intent. Max's distress over the death of opponent Frankie Campbell is well documented, and the death of boxer Ernie Schaaf came in a bout against Primo Camero, five months after Schaaf had lost to Max.

CITY FOR CONQUEST (1940)

DIRECTOR: Anatole Litvak. SCREENPLAY: John Wexley, based on the novel by Aben Kandel. PRODUCER: Anatole Litvak. CINEMATOGRAPHY: James Wong Howe, Sol Polito. EDITING: William Holmes. MUSIC: Max Steiner. ART DIRECTION: Robert Haas. COSTUME DESIGN: Howard Shoup.

CAST: James Cagney (Danny Kenny), Ann Sheridan (Peggy), Frank Craven (old man), Donald Crisp (Scotty McPherson), Frank McHugh (Mitt), Arthur Kennedy (Eddie Kenny), Elia Kazan (Googi Zucco), Anthony Quinn (Murray Burns).

RUNNING TIME: 104 minutes.

DVD: Warner Home Video.

The city of the title is New York, and the would-be conquerors are three young people from the Lower East Side. Danny Kenny (James Cagney) is a truck driver with boxing skills; Peggy (Ann Sheridan), his girlfriend, is a talented dancer; and Eddie Kenny (Arthur Kennedy), Danny's brother, is a serious musician who wants to write a symphony about New York City. The film employs a narrator, an old man (Frank Craven), who comments on the action as he had for Thornton Wilder's *Our Town*. Although this film is a sports film, it is the musician rather than the fighter who conquers New York.

As the film begins, Murray Burns (Anthony Quinn), a talented, smooth, but despicable character, recognizes Peggy's ability. He persuades her to become his partner, and the pair win several dance contests. Blinded by applause and determined to make it to the top, Peggy has little time for Danny. It becomes apparent that she is more ambitious than he is, and they discover that they want different things. For a while, both Peggy and Danny meet with modest success. Murray, who always gets top billing and who handles all the money, succeeds in landing good tours. Danny's boxing career is also making progress. At one point the marquees in some cities feature the fighter as well as the dancers.

Meanwhile, Eddie continues with his symphony, and Danny helps him financially and even arranges a gig at a swanky cocktail party. However, the guests largely ignore Eddie's classical music and prefer when he plays swing. Some Broadway producers ask Eddie to write a show for them, but Danny encourages him to stay with his own music.

Danny finally gets a chance at a championship bout against Cannonball Wales (Joe Gray). The match goes well for Danny, so well that the champ's manager, Cobb (Ben Welden), puts resin on Cannonball's gloves and encourages him to rub it in Danny's eyes. By the fourteenth round Danny is almost blind, and the champ wins. When Googi Zucco (Elia Kazan), an East End pal of Danny's, discovers what has happened, he takes the crooked manager for a ride and shoots him. He then is killed by the manager's henchman. The point seems to be that the East End past is never that far away and is always a threat to those attempting to escape from it.

Danny is through as a fighter, but his spirit remains unbroken. His manager, Scotty McPherson (Donald Crisp), finances a street corner newspaper stand for Danny so he can mix with people. He says, "I can now see better." When Eddie's symphony debuts at Carnegie Hall, Peggy is in attendance, and Danny is listening to the radio at his newsstand. The symphony, which captures the sounds and the feel of the city, earns a standing ovation. To emphasize Danny's role in Eddie's success, the film superimposes Danny's photo over the orchestra. Eddie dedicates the symphony to Danny, who doesn't "know" music, but has it in his heart. Peggy rushes to the newsstand, where she and Danny are reunited. Although he lost his championship fight, he has won back the woman he loves. All three of the principals have conquered what they have needed to. At the newsstand, Danny says to Peggy, "I can see what I want to see" and repeats his standard line, "Always my girl." Danny, who lost in the title fight, has a bigger "conquest" than would have been possible to achieve with his fists.

CITY LIGHTS (1931)

DIRECTOR: Charles Chaplin. SCREENPLAY: Charles Chaplin. PRODUCER: Charles Chaplin. CINEMATOGRAPHY: Gordon Pollock, Rolland Totheroh. EDITING: Charles Chaplin, Willard Nico. MUSIC: Charles Chaplin. SET DECORATION: Charles D. Hall.
CAST: Charlie Chaplin (the Little Tramp), Virginia Cherrill (blind girl), Florence Lee (the girl's grandmother), Harry Myers (an eccentric millionaire), Allan Garcia (the butler), Hank Mann (a prizefighter).
RUNNING TIME: 83 minutes. B&W.
DVD: Warner Home Video.

Written and directed by Charlie Chaplin, *City Lights* is his last silent film. By 1931, audiences wanted sound, but Chaplin, whose character the Little Tramp had made him internationally famous, believed that allowing the Little Tramp to speak would destroy his charm and cost him his European following. The film, then, is self-consciously "silent," relying on title cards rather than dialogue and incorporating sound—including a score Chaplin composed himself—to emphasize silence as choice. Ironically, a key figure is a blind girl who relies heavily on sound to interpret her surroundings, but it is a misinterpretation of sound that causes her to mistake the Little Tramp for a wealthy gentleman. As the story progresses, the Little Tramp attempts to earn enough money for an operation to restore the girl's sight. One of his endeavors, a boxing match, is a classic Chaplin routine.

The opening scene takes place at a monument dedication. Speeches by dignitaries are garbled to the point of unintelligibility, while title cards announce that the monument celebrates peace and prosperity (during the early years of the Great Depression). When the sculpture is unveiled, the Little Tramp is revealed asleep in the lap of one of the figures. He scurries down via a sword, ripping his pants in the process, and escapes arrest when a band strikes up the national anthem and the police officers snap to attention.

Later that afternoon, the Little Tramp crosses a gridlocked street by going through the vehicles, the last being a limousine parked at the curb. He pauses to buy a flower from a young woman (Virginia Cherrill) and realizes she is blind. Just as he turns to leave, the limousine passenger returns, and the flower girl turns in the direction of the car as it pulls away, assuming her customer is the man with the limousine. Later that night, the Little Tramp meets a drunken millionaire who has decided to kill himself because his wife has left him. The tramp prevents the suicide and is invited to accompany the millionaire back to his mansion after a night on the town. Remembering the blind girl, the tramp suggests buying some flowers. The millionaire provides a fistful of cash and the keys to his Rolls Royce. After purchasing the contents of the girl's basket, the Little Tramp drives her home, initiating a courtship.

Complications arise because the millionaire, when sober and hung over, does not recall what has occurred the previous evening. It is only when he is intoxicated that he recognizes his new friend. When the millionaire leaves for Europe, the Little Tramp is left to his poverty. At the same time, the flower girl has become ill, and her grandmother goes out each day to sell the flowers, but without much success. Soon their rent is overdue and they face eviction. To raise money, the Little Tramp strikes a deal to enter a boxing match, lose quickly without getting hurt, and split the fifty dollars the winner will receive; however, the fighter with whom the tramp has bargained is replaced at the last minute, and the new boxer is not willing to split the winnings.

The boxing segment of *City Lights* is a refinement of Chaplin's earlier short film, *The Champion* (1915). In *The Champion* the Little Tramp, having found a horseshoe beneath a sign advertising for sparring partners, signs on to fight. Not knowing what to do with the horseshoe, he stuffs it in his glove, subsequently knocking out everyone he hits. Soon he is booked for a championship fight against a substantially larger and stronger opponent. Much of Chaplin's physical humor is staged in the corner before the match and between rounds; his boxing routine includes windmilling his arms and well-timed ducking. The main gag involves the referee trying to count out the fighters. Before he can get to ten, the presumed winner takes a bow and gets knocked down, causing the referee to switch the count from one fighter to the other. *The Champion* ends chaotically with the tramp's bulldog entering the fray, and the tramp emerging the winner.

By *City Lights*, Chaplin has refined this routine into a much more sophisticated piece of choreography. The Little Tramp positions himself behind the referee and duplicates his moves as he tries to step from between the boxers. At the start of each round, the three men two-step around the ring. The segment repeats the count gag with both boxers on the mat, but the routine is tightened and does not dominate the scene. Without the intervention of dog, horseshoe, or fate, the Little Tramp cannot prevail, and the match ends with his defeat.

After the fight, the Little Tramp wanders the streets forlornly, but his fortunes improve when he once again encounters the millionaire, just returning from abroad and in celebratory mode. He embraces the tramp and continues his revelry. When they return to the mansion, the Little Tramp explains his predicament, and the millionaire gives him a generous roll of bills to pay for an operation to cure the flower girl's blindness as well as to cover her overdue rent. But unbeknownst to either the millionaire or the tramp, burglars have entered the house. In the melee that follows, the police are summoned, the burglars escape, and the millionaire is hit on the head and doesn't recognize the tramp when he regains consciousness. The Little Tramp is assumed to have stolen the millionaire's cash, and once again the police chase the tramp, who escapes being caught just long enough to present the flower girl with the money and say goodbye.

By autumn the Little Tramp has been released from prison, and the flower girl, no longer blind, has opened her own shop. When the tramp, looking badly disheveled, discovers the shop, he stares through the window at the girl, who comes outside to offer him a coin and a flower. He tries to refuse, but she touches his hand and realizes who he is. The film ends with her realization, and the viewer is left to imagine a happy ending.

City Lights is critically acclaimed for the cleverness of the comedy routines and for the integration of story line and slapstick. Chaplin and Cherrill reportedly did not like working together. Cherrill, a complete novice, had little patience for the number of takes Chaplin required—over three hundred for the brief scene in which the two meet for the first time; Chaplin had little patience for her lack of dedication. In spite of the friction, Chaplin was able to coax a convincing portrayal from Cherrill and in the end was pleased with both their performances.

THE CLUB (1980)

DIRECTOR: Bruce Beresford. SCREENPLAY: David Williamson, based on his play. PRODUCER: Matt Carroll. CINEMATOGRAPHY: Donal McAlpine. EDITING: William M. Anderson, David Wu. MUSIC: Mike Brady. PRODUCTION DESIGN: David Copping. COSTUME DESIGN: Ruth De La Lande.
CAST: Jack Thompson (Laurie Holden), Graham Kennedy (Ted Parker), Frank Wilson (Jock Riley), Harold Hopkins (Danny Rowe), John Howard (Geoff Hayward).
RUNNING TIME: 96 minutes.

The Club presents a season in the life of an Australian football team, mostly focused on the coach and the political maneuverings by board members to oust him.

COACH (1978)

DIRECTOR: Bud Townsend. SCREENPLAY: Nancy Larson, Stephen Bruce Rose. PRODUCER: Mark Tenser. CINEMATOGRAPHY: Michael D. Murphy. EDITING: Robert Gordon. MUSIC: Anthony Harris. ART DIRECTION: Kenneth Herzenroder. COSTUME DESIGN: Patty Koehnen.
CAST: Cathy Lee Crosby (Randy Rawlings), Michael Biehn (Jack Ripley), Keenan Wynn (Fenton Granger), Channing Clarkson (Bradley Granger).
RUNNING TIME: 100 minutes.
DVD: Rhino Theatrical.

In *Coach*, a female Olympic medalist is hired to coach a boys high school basketball team.

COACH CARTER (2005)

DIRECTOR: Thomas Carter. SCREENPLAY: Mark Schwahn, John Gatins. PRODUCER: David Gale, Brian Robbins, Michael Tollin. CINEMATOGRAPHY: Sharone Meir. EDITING: Peter Berger. MUSIC: Trevor Rabin. PRODUCTION DESIGN: Carlos Barbosa. ART DIRECTION: Tim Beach. COSTUME DESIGN: Debrae Little.

CAST: Samuel L. Jackson (Ken Carter), Rob Brown (Kenyon Stone), Robert Ri'chard (Damien), Rick Gonzalez (Timo Cruz), Nana Gbewonyo (Junior Battle), Channing Tatum (Jason Lyle), Ashanti (Kyra), Debbi Morgan (Tonya).
RUNNING TIME: 136 minutes.
DVD: Paramount.

Coach Carter is about high school basketball, but it is not like *Hoosiers* (1986), a film about the triumph of an underdog against all odds; instead, it is about the transition of boys to men and of athletes to students. Set in Richmond, California, where only half the high school students graduate and only 6 percent of the graduates go to college, the film, based on a true story, demonstrates how the efforts of a determined coach/mentor can help five of the seniors on his team get scholarships to attend college. Ken Carter (Samuel L. Jackson) sets high academic standards for his players, and they, despite the opposition of other teachers, the principal, and the community, meet those standards and become "winners."

By crosscutting between Carter closing up his athletic goods store and the Richmond High School game with St. Francis, a prestigious high school with an affluent student body, the film suggests that Carter will become involved with the Richmond team. Carter, who had attended Richmond and who holds all the scoring records there, goes to the game for two reasons: his son, Damien (Robert Ri'chard), is a freshman on the St. Francis team, and the Richmond coach, unable to control his players, has asked Carter to replace him as coach. After the game, which is called off because the trash-talking leads to a bench-clearing brawl between the two teams, Carter tells the coach that he hasn't yet made up his mind. He recites to his wife all the reasons he shouldn't take on the job, but she knows he will. Damien, who has always wanted to play for his father, is upset but leaves St. Francis for Richmond. (At the end of the film the audience learns that Damien has broken his father's records and has been accepted at West Point.)

At the first practice Coach Carter sets the tone. All players and their parents must sign a contract: the players will maintain a 2.3 grade point average (Damien will have to get a 3.7), attend all classes, sit in the front row, and wear coats and ties on game days. Carter wants the players to respect themselves and others and insists on their using "Sir" just as he uses it to address them. Timo Cruz (Rick Gonzalez), who will not abide by the rules, challenges Carter and leaves the gym shouting, "This ain't over."

Intent on getting his players into top physical shape, Coach Carter has them doing "suicides" (short sprints up and down the court) and push ups. Since they are a team, any player's failure means punishment not just for him, but for the whole team. Using the names of his fictitious sisters, he also installs "Diane," a man-to-man defense; "Delilah," a trap defense; and "Linda," the pick and roll. Things go well at first, and the parents understand that the rules are designed to help their sons earn the grades they need to get into college. Even Cruz, who is into drugs with his cousin Randall, finally comes around and asks what he has to do to rejoin the team. When he cannot physically do the number of push-ups and suicides that Carter requires, the other team members offer to complete part of the assignment for him. Carter realizes then that he has a team. More victories follow, but the team members showboat and taunt their opponents, behavior Carter insists will have to stop. When he discovers that Junior Battle (Nana Gbewonyo) is not attending one of his classes, Carter suspends him until he makes up the work. At first Junior quits the team, but his mother asks Carter to let him play. Junior apologizes, makes promises, and rejoins the team so a junior-college recruiter can observe him in action.

Because they are undefeated, the team is invited to the Bay Hill Invitational Tournament, which they win, in part because of Damien's outstanding play. But the problems begin after the final game, when a white girl invites the team to a party in the wealthy suburbs. Drinking, dancing, jumping in the swimming pool in their underwear, and having sex—the players are enjoying themselves until Carter and the girl's parents arrive and find Worm (Antwon Turner) with their daughter in an upstairs bedroom. To add to their problems, the teachers' progress reports on the players indicate that the team is academically failing to live up to the terms of their contracts. When Carter locks the gymnasium, takes his team to the library for study hall, and tells them there will be no games until the academic scores are up to par, there is a firestorm of protest by the parents, teachers, and Principal Garrison (Denise Dowse). She tells Carter his standards are too high and that basketball is all his players have. When she comments that "this season will be the highlight of their lives," Carter answers, "That's the problem." A series of forfeits gains national media coverage, and one commentator suggests that Carter's actions show that somebody cares about "student athletes." At a school board meeting the community votes to take down the chains on the door and let the team play. Coach Carter resigns in protest. When he picks up the broken chains, those chains acquire symbolic value, for they suggest the bonds that keep his players in Richmond tied to dead-end lives. When he enters the gym, however, he sees his players studying, intent on "finishing what [he] started." Cruz, whose life has been threatened through his association with Randall, himself the victim of gang violence, speaks for the team, thanking Carter for saving his life.

The players attain the required grades and are invited to the state tournament, where they will play St. Francis. If this were *Hoosiers*, Richmond would win, but the team loses a heartbreaker by one point. Afterward, Carter's speech, a variant of the "it's not whether you won or lost, it's how you played the game," pays tribute to the progress the team has made academically and to the maturity they have displayed. Considering their situation, their previous losing seasons, the loss of good players who couldn't accept the responsibility of the contract, the rampant drug culture, the low expectations of their families, their teachers, and their principal, these players were winners. Reviews of the film were mixed. Most found the script clichéd and the message heavy-handed; however Jackson's performance earned praise.

COBB (1994)

DIRECTOR: Ron Shelton. SCREENPLAY: Ron Shelton, based on the writings of Al Stump. PRODUCER: David V. Lester. CINEMATOGRAPHY: Russell Boyd. EDITING: Kimberly Ray, Paul Seydor. MUSIC: Elliot Goldenthal. PRODUCTION DESIGN: Armin Ganz, Scott Ritenour. ART DIRECTION: Charles Butcher, Troy Sizemore. COSTUME DESIGN: Ruth E. Carter.

CAST: Tommy Lee Jones (Ty Cobb), Robert Wuhl (Al Stump), Lolita Davidovich (Ramona), Ned Bellamy (Ray), Scott Burkholder (Jimmy).

RUNNING TIME: 128 minutes.

DVD: Warner Home Video.

In 1961 sportswriter Al Stump was the ghostwriter for Ty Cobb's *My Life in Baseball: The True Record*, a sanitized and hardly accurate account of the life of baseball's highly gifted and equally despised player. Stump and Cobb, who met only a few times to discuss the book, split the six thousand dollars they received from Doubleday, the publisher. In 1994 Stump described the book as a cover-up and said he "felt very bad about it." The relationship between the two was not close: Stump twice quit the project and once was dismissed by Cobb. Much of the book derives not from Cobb himself, but from Stump's use of other sources: H. G. Salsinger's biographical sketch in the *Sporting News*, Cobb's 1952 articles in *Life* magazine, and a book that Cobb wrote with John D. McCallum. After the autobiography was published, which was shortly after Cobb's death, Stump wrote an article for *True* magazine entitled "Ty Cobb's Wild 10-Month Fight to Live," which presented a much *truer* record of the psychotic personality who revolutionized the game of baseball; however, the article falsely implied that he and Cobb had been constant companions during those ten months. Almost thirty years later Stump mailed the *True* article and another chapter to Algonquin Books, who commissioned the completion of *Cobb: A Biography*, which was published in 1994; Stump died late in 1995.

The film's credits state it is "based on the book by Al Stump [*Cobb*]," but director Ron Shelton also drew, albeit to a lesser extent, on Stump's 1961 book. Despite relying on Stump's two books, Shelton presents his own version not only of Cobb (Tommy Lee Jones) but also of Stump himself.

Stump began his biography with a brief account of the hazardous journey he and Cobb made from Cobb's Lake Tahoe lodge through a blizzard to Reno, Nevada, where Cobb admitted his sexual impotence, got into a brawl in a casino, and eventually won three thousand dollars gambling. The rest of Stump's book is primarily about Cobb's baseball career, but Stump also discusses Cobb's wealth, his two marriages, his pistol-whipping a man to death in Detroit, and the killing of his father by his mother. What Stump does not discuss is his relationship with Cobb. This becomes one of Shelton's themes.

Shelton's *Cobb* begins in *Citizen Kane*–fashion with a black-and-white "Cavalcade of Heroes," which presents a capsule version of Cobb's life, including childhood photos, snapshots with his children, and baseball commissioner Landis exonerating Cobb from charges of fixing games. In a sense, this part of the film is the first Stump book, the one on which Cobb had the final say. The second Stump book is the source for the portion of the film when Cobb views the same footage at a Cooperstown testimonial. Shelton interposes color shots of Cobb's "real" behavior: his beating of his wives, his savage attack on an armless heckler, his parties with women and booze, and shots of the pistol-whipping. Macbeth-like, Cobb is the only one at the dinner to see the ghosts of his past. The "Cavalcade of Heroes" footage ends again, this time ironically, with "What a ballplayer!"

After a brief sequence at a bar where the sportswriters hang out, Shelton takes Stump to Lake Tahoe, where he embellishes the events that occurred in Reno. He adds a scene involving a cigarette girl whom Cobb terrifies before giving her one thousand dollars to tell everyone he was the greatest lover she'd ever had, and then another scene where the woman is with Brownie, the black cook Cobb had earlier fired. Their appearance together prompts Cobb to shoot a few rounds from his ever-present Luger. The major change, however, involves Shelton's development of the passage in which Stump summarizes what he did for Cobb during those last ten months. The film becomes a kind of "buddy" movie about two guys on the road.

Initially, the relationship is based on mutual need. Feeling he has been misunderstood, Cobb wants Stump to tell the

Tommy Lee Jones as Ty Cobb

real story of his life, a story that begins with the words Cobb wants for his epitaph: "A prince and a great man has fallen today." From Cobb's point of view, Stump needs Cobb, the subject whose story will make him more than a "hopeless romantic and moderate success." Cobb's boast that "I'm your meal ticket" ultimately proves to be true when Stump writes his second Cobb book, which was critically acclaimed.

To accomplish this role reversal, Shelton alters Stump's character. In his book Stump never mentions his marital situation, and in fact he and his wife, Jo Mosher, never divorced. In the film, Stump's marriage is on the rocks; Cobb knows about Stump's relationship with a "little brunette," and Stump makes a pass at the Reno cigarette girl. Late in the film, when an inebriated Stump is served with divorce papers, he pulls a "Cobb" and, using his gun, fires away, barely missing the process server, whom he then hits with the gun. Stump collapses, and Cobb puts him to bed and consoles him with stories of his own two divorces. Stump's response to Cobb's is "You're my friend, Ty." This comment is one of several similar remarks made by the two men, who become increasingly intimate with each other. As is often the case in buddy films, there is a homosexual subtext. Early in the film Stump, who does his share of sniveling and whining, protests that Cobb "treats him like a stenographer" and later complains to Cobb, "You give me nothing." Cobb assures Stump, "You're the only friend I have left, the only one I can trust."

The "film Cobb" trusts Stump much more than the "biography Cobb," and that trust is misplaced. Not content with showing the "real Cobb," Shelton attempts to reveal the reason for Cobb's psychotic behavior. In the book Cobb tells Stump that his father, whom he feared and respected, was killed by a family member; but in the film, Cobb twice recounts the story of his father's death. In the first version, his mother kills his father, whom she mistakes for an intruder; in the second version it is his mother's lover who kills his father. Shelton again repeats footage but adds additional footage to alter the final result. By asserting the importance of Cobb's father's death, Shelton implies that the "missing piece" of evidence, the cause of Cobb's psychosis, is in this pivotal scene. Cobb even asks Stump, "Was my father inadequate? Was my mother a tramp?"

In the film the paranoid Cobb terms Stump a "predatory little bastard," an apt description of a writer, who like a mob accountant, keeps two sets of books. Stump is writing the book Cobb wants written, *My Life in Baseball*, which he allows Cobb to read, but he is also writing another book, the one that becomes *Cobb*. As the film progresses, Stump wrestles with his conscience: should he tell the truth, or should he abide by the terms of his contract and publish the book Cobb wants? At one point Stump declares, "I'll write the story I want if you die first." Once Cobb dies, Stump will be free to act as he chooses. In effect, there is a kind of race between Stump's writing and Cobb's living. After Stump attacks the process server and passes out, Cobb discovers Stump's hidden notes and reads them all—in effect, he has a chance to read Stump's second biography some thirty years before it is published! Cobb declares Stump not worth killing because he "doesn't have a point of view." This literary critique applies to Stump's ambivalent feelings about Cobb, which are visualized in the film but missing from the book. When Stump comes to, he finds a predictably ambivalent note from Cobb: "Al Stump, you lying son of a bitch, your friend, Ty."

Shelton also adds a scene at the hospital where Stump visits Cobb, who fires his Luger and terrifies the staff. After Stump tells him, "I don't know which version I'll publish," Cobb says, "Print it all. You won." The additional dialogue implies that Cobb has given his blessing not only to the two biographies but also to Shelton's biopic, which contains "it all." Stump decides to finish the manuscript after Cobb passes away, but the audience does not know which biography he will publish. Stump ironically comments, "We know writers never lie." In the last scene in the film, Stump returns to his sportswriter cronies at their favorite bar. Just as we see two murders and see two newsreel clips, we see two scenes at the bar, where the discussion has not changed—one of the writers echoes his earlier comment when he lamely admits that he has yet to begin his Great American Novel. When queried about the "truth" about Cobb, Stump repeats Cobb's earlier words: "A prince and a great man has fallen today."

Stump, the writer who never lies, admits he lies and explains his reasons: "I didn't lie for kids to have heroes. I lied for myself. I needed him to be a hero." Perhaps Cobb was right when he called Stump a "hopeless romantic," and in Stump's justification there is the nostalgia that Shelton used so effectively in *Bull Durham*. However, since the end is so at odds with the realism, sexism, racism, and sadism of the rest of the film, it is tempting to apply Cobb's description of Stump as a person-without-a-point-of-view to Shelton.

Cobb is not an entertaining film; it is the portrait of a sexist, racist psychotic who turned the game of baseball into a battle and, consequently, had his admirers but no real friends. Only three baseball players attended his funeral. Shelton isolates Cobb, who twice has doors shut in his face—once by his daughter and once by players who won't admit him to their posttestimonial party after he has just been honored at Cooperstown. (Mickey Cochrane [Stephen

Mendillo], whom Cobb financially supported, is, significantly, the doorman.) And there is little to invoke sympathy for Cobb, who in truth built a hospital for his hometown, created scholarships for needy students, and was largely responsible for the establishment of free agency. Shelton creates a monster, albeit a tormented one. He also alters Stump's character, just as Stump had exaggerated his ties to Cobb, and focuses his biopic, not on baseball (there is almost no baseball footage), but on the relationship between Cobb and Stump.

COLLEGE (1927)

DIRECTORS: James W. Horne, Buster Keaton. SCREENPLAY: Brian Foy, Carl Harbaugh. PRODUCER: Joseph M. Schenck. CINEMATOGRAPHY: Bert Haines, Devereaux Jennings. EDITING: Sherman Kell.
CAST: Buster Keaton (Ronald), Ann Cornwall (Mary Haynes), Flora Bramley (Mary's friend), Harold Goodwin (Jeff Brown), Snitz Edwards (Dean Edwards).
RUNNING TIME: 66 minutes. B&W.
DVD: Kino Video.

In this silent comedy, Buster Keaton plays a bookish teenager, Ronald, who must embrace sports in order to win over his high school sweetheart. A predictable plot is developed through a series of vignettes featuring sight gags and pratfalls. *College* is classic slapstick.

Ronald's troubles begin at his high school graduation. En route to the ceremony, he has gotten soaked in the rain, and once he is inside the school and sitting near a radiator, his new suit begins to shrink. When he steps onstage to receive a medal for academic achievement, his classmates, led by the school's star athlete, Jeff Brown (Harold Goodwin), begin to ridicule him. Only Ronald's girlfriend, Mary Haynes (Anne Cornwall), and his mother applaud. But when Ronald delivers his valedictory address on "The Curse of Athletics," Mary becomes disenchanted and informs him that he must change his attitude in order to regain her affection. As a result, Ronald decides to follow Mary to Clayton College, take up sports, and work to pay his expenses.

At Clayton, Ronald finds securing employment harder than he anticipated. His first position as a soda jerk requires him not just to concoct ice cream treats, but to do so with flourish. He creates a fine mess trying to juggle ingredients and slide glasses along the countertop, managing to avoid getting axed only long enough to be spotted by Mary and Jeff, who is now an obvious rival for Mary's affection. Ronald's next job is at a restaurant that has advertised for a "colored waiter." In a scene modern viewers may find disquieting, Keaton appears in blackface. Ronald "passes," fooling customers and kitchen staff alike until he smears half of his makeup taking a spectacular spill while carrying a bowl of soup, which he amazingly does not spill. Of course, this mishap is also witnessed by Mary and Jeff.

Ronald's athletic endeavors meet with similar disaster. Although he has come armed with "how-to" booklets from Spalding, the sports equipment company, he has failed to absorb the basics. On the baseball diamond he takes third base wearing catcher's gear, makes a number of fielding errors, and creates general havoc at the plate. On the track he orchestrates his own decathlon of misadventures, tossing himself instead of the hammer, knocking down hurdles, burying himself headfirst in the sand completing a high jump, and running well behind the field in the races.

To make matters even worse, Ronald is failing academically. Called into a conference with the dean, he confesses that he has ignored his schoolwork for love. The dean, who once was in the same predicament but chose academics over the girl, comes to Ronald's aid by forcing the crew coach to name Ronald coxswain. By this time, Mary has been impressed by Ronald's spirit and effort, causing Jeff to take drastic measures: on the day of the big boat race, Jeff locks Mary and himself in her dorm room, knowing that she will be expelled as soon as they are discovered. Meanwhile, the crew coach has attempted to keep Ronald out of the race by placing sleeping powders in his coffee; however, Ronald inadvertently drinks from the wrong cup, and the regular coxswain is the one who is drugged.

After sinking the first boat when he jumps in, Ronald finally gets his crew off and rowing, but the rudder breaks off, causing a near collision. Ronald saves the day by strapping the rudder onto his body and directing the crew from the tip of the scull. Clayton wins the race, and a celebration ensues. Unable to locate Mary among the crowd, Ronald returns alone to the locker room, where he receives a call for help from his beloved, who has managed to sneak to her phone. In an extraordinary sequence, Ronald completes all of the athletic feats at which he previously had failed—running interference through a crowd at incredible speed, hurdling over hedges, broad jumping over obstacles, pole vaulting into Mary's room, tackling Jeff, and fending him off by throwing an assortment of furnishings at him. Jeff flees, the dean arrives, and before anyone can be expelled, Mary announces that she and Ronald are getting married. They do so immediately. The film ends with three still shots depicting the couple's future as they appear first sitting with their children, then by themselves in a similar pose in old age, and finally in their graves, still side by side. These shots contrast sharply with the dynamic nature of the courtship and can be read as a subversion of conventional happily-ever-after endings.

College is not as well-known as Keaton's other films. Reviewers generally regarded the film as a vehicle for displaying Keaton's versatile skills—except for the pole vault, executed by Olympic champ Lee Barnes, Keaton performed all of his own stunts—and criticized the apparent lack of structure to the plot. However, *College* was highly regarded by European surrealists. Both Luis Brunel and Salvador Dali found a kindred mind in Keaton's work, particularly in his blank expression and "transformational" use of objects in the climactic scene. (See, for example, Paul Hammond's *The Shadow and Its Silence: Surrealist Writing on the Cinema.*) Keaton described *College* as one of his favorite films.

THE COLOR OF MONEY (1986)

Director: Martin Scorsese. Screenplay: Richard Price, based on the novel by Walter Tevis. Producers: Irving Axelrad, Barbara De Fina. Cinematography: Michael Ballhaus. Editing: Thelma Schoonmaker. Production Design: Boris Leven. Set Decoration: Karen O'Hara. Costume Design: Richard Bruno.

Cast: Paul Newman (Eddie Felson), Tom Cruise (Vincent "Vinnie" Lauria), Mary Elizabeth Mastrantonio (Carmen), Helen Shaver (Janelle), John Turturro (Julian), Bill Cobbs (Orvis).

Running Time: 119 minutes.

Academy Awards: Best Actor (Newman). Nominations: Best Supporting Actress (Mastrantonio), Best Adapted Screenplay, Best Art Direction/Set Decoration.

DVD: Walt Disney Video.

Directed by Martin Scorsese, *The Color of Money* picks up the story of "Fast" Eddie Felson a quarter of a century after he soundly defeated Minnesota Fats (Jackie Gleason) in *The Hustler* (1961) and learned about "character" in the process. Like the earlier film, *The Color of Money* is based on a novel by Walter Tevis; however, this adaptation deviates sharply from the book, in which Eddie owns a pool hall and faces

Minnesota Fats once again. In the film version neither Fats nor Gleason makes an appearance; Paul Newman returns as Eddie, now a liquor salesman who no longer plays but who bankrolls younger prospects. Scorsese's Eddie is more likeable than the earlier version, yet in the role of stake horse, Eddie resembles Bert Gordon (George C. Scott), his old nemesis from *The Hustler*.

Scorsese opens his film with the camera focused on a cigarette burning in an ashtray while in an uncredited voiceover he explains the game of nine ball and adds that luck, which can play a large role in the game, is itself an art form. Eddie's "art" is in reading people and in understanding human nature, skills he uses to manipulate outcomes. The title of the film, which refers to the color of the baize used to cover the tops of pool tables, accentuates the connection between the sport and wagering; in fact, the game of pool derives its name from "pool" in the sense of collective betting.

The action begins in a poolroom where Eddie's player, Julian (John Turturro), points out a brash unknown talent, Vincent "Vinnie" Lauria (Tom Cruise), who has what Eddie calls a "sledgehammer" break. Eddie gives Julian twenty dollars and looks on as Vinnie, who twirls his cue like a Ninja wielding a bow staff, quickly wins the money. Knowing he's outclassed, Julian declines another game.

Vinnie wants to continue playing but can find no takers. His girlfriend, Carmen (Mary Elizabeth Mastrantonio), with whom Eddie has been making eye contact, asks if Eddie wants to go against Vinnie. When Eddie suggests a wager of five hundred dollars a rack, Carmen turns him down. Eddie tells her she's just lost five hundred dollars; then he repeats the offer, which she again refuses. Realizing that the young couple do not know how to use Vinnie's talent to their advantage, Eddie decides to show them the path to "the big time" and to the riches along the way. To illustrate how he works, Eddie bets Vinnie a dollar that a guy at the bar will not make any headway with the woman he's talking to. As soon as Eddie has won the first bet, he makes a second one that he can get the woman to leave with him. Eddie wins again because the woman is his girlfriend, Janelle (Helen Shaver).

Carmen has more street smarts than Vinnie. In fact, she met him when her former boyfriend was robbing the Lauria house. Carmen wears a ring from the robbery; when Vinnie noticed it, he remarked that his mother had one just like it. It is Carmen who figures out that Eddie set them up with the bets at the bar, and it is she who takes the initiative in forming a partnership with Eddie.

Eddie's plan is to take Vinnie on the road for six weeks before a championship tournament in Atlantic City. During the trip, Eddie will instruct Vinnie in the fine art of the hustle. To persuade Vinnie to leave his day job and hit the road, Eddie maintains that Carmen is getting bored; he gives Vinnie his cue stick, a Balabushka (pool's equivalent to a Stradivarius), as a sign of his confidence in Vinnie. Although hesitant at first, Vinnie yields, and his education begins. However, in committing to train Vinnie, Eddie is abandoning his sponsorship of Julian and is backing out of a promise to take Janelle on a Caribbean vacation. Neither Julian nor Janelle is pleased.

Eddie sets the terms of the deal with Vinnie: in exchange for a 60 percent commission, Eddie will cover expenses and stake money. Soon he discovers that his protégé is hard to handle. Vinnie balks at reining in his talent and complains about leaving the Balabushka behind and using a house stick for hustling. He doesn't like to lose, and he's reluctant to con less highly skilled players. When Vinnie refuses to take any more money from an old-timer with a tracheotomy scar, Eddie slips out, leaving Vinnie without any cash to pay up after he lets the old guy win back his money. The other men in the pool hall surround Vinnie, but Eddie, pretending to be his irate father, reappears and drags him out before he suffers much damage.

Their next stop is Chalkies, a pool hall in a rough neighborhood. The manager, Orvis (Bill Cobbs), remembers Eddie from the old days and offers to make some "arrangements" on Eddie's behalf. The plan is for Vinnie to play Eddie, demonstrating just enough skill to attract the attention of a patron who has deep pockets and who is generally willing to bet five thousand dollars when he thinks he has a decent chance against an opponent. However, Vinnie wants to challenge the best man in the parlor, Moselle (Bruce Young). Instead of holding back, Vinnie shows off to impress Moselle, and Eddie walks out, disgusted.

In the morning, muttering about "child care," Eddie knocks on Vinnie and Carmen's motel door. Carmen answers wearing bikini underwear and tells Eddie that Vinnie has gone out. Comparing Vinnie to a race horse, Eddie scolds Carmen about flirting. Then he notices that the Balabushka is missing. Back at Chalkies, Vinnie is ready to take on Moselle. He performs his Ninja routine and runs the table, dancing between shots and howling along with the song "Werewolves of London," which plays throughout the scene. Eddie is furious because, by revealing his talent, Vinnie has blown his chance of cleaning up at Chalkies. Vinnie, who has won $150 from Moselle, stomps off in a huff, but Eddie eventually calms him down. He also makes Vinnie fork over the 60 percent commission.

Another falling out occurs after they pull off a scam known as "two brothers and a stranger." For this hustle, Eddie and Carmen snuggle at a bar and pretend not to know Vinnie. As Vinnie plays a local shark, Eddie keeps up a running commentary and Vinnie acts as if it's getting under his skin. What is actually upsetting Vinnie is that Eddie has his hands on Carmen, but he does his job, which is to drop a game to the local. Then Eddie says he'll bet five hundred dollars on Vinnie's opponent, and the bartender announces he's in for one thousand dollars. Afterward, Eddie and Carmen insist that they are just acting, like in the movies.

A montage documents a series of successful hustles over the next two weeks, but Vinnie continues to struggle with holding back. When top money winner Grady Seasons (Keith McCready) crosses their path, Eddie sees an opportunity for Vinnie to assure he'll be a "nobody" at the tournament; all he needs to do is play poorly against Grady. Vinnie manages to keep his cool until Grady begins taunting him. As Eddie and Carmen grow increasingly concerned, Vinnie settles into a serious game. It takes a threat from Carmen for Vinnie to get back into character.

After a brief celebration, Eddie retrieves the Balabushka, announcing he's decided to check out the action himself. He wins a few games and has a few drinks, keeping his eye on another player, Amos (Forrest Whitaker), whom Eddie has pegged for a sucker. However, Eddie has missed his mark in several senses of the word. As Vinnie and Carmen look on, Eddie drops a bundle. Humiliated, he tells the young couple he has nothing left to teach them. Vinnie, who has grown genuinely fond of his mentor, begs Eddie to stay, but he refuses. Vinnie hurls the Balabushka (fortunately, secure in its case), and Carmen accepts the travel money Eddie has tried to press on Vinnie.

Determined to redeem his dignity, Eddie prepares himself to compete in

Atlantic City: he swims; he practices shots; he even has his eyes tested and starts wearing prescription lenses. To measure his progress, he challenges Moselle, losing in their first meeting, but winning decisively in their next. When he first arrives in Atlantic City, Eddie visits the deserted tournament poolroom, where the camera pans from the ornate vaulted ceiling to the austere rows of empty tables. This shot references the scene from *The Hustler* when Eddie and his partner Charlie arrive at the Ames pool hall in New York. Eddie likens the place to a cathedral, but Charlie says it's more like a morgue. Both scenes reflect the oppositional forces of the game and foreshadow Eddie's potential for self-enlightenment and for self-destruction.

Once the tournament begins, Eddie makes quick work of his first opponent. Later that evening, he notices Carmen and Vinnie hustling a guy at the bar; after the man leaves, Vinnie chides Carmen for settling on too low a wager. When Vinnie realizes Eddie is watching, he and Carmen pause at his table. Eddie shakes hands with Vinnie and remarks on how well they are doing without his guidance. He seems sad as they leave. The next day at the tournament, Eddie defeats a bitter Julian, and Vinnie exacts revenge against Grady Seasons, repeating the older man's taunts and beating him easily. Later, Eddie calls Janelle and invites her to Atlantic City with promises of the Bahamas trip and a tentative suggestion she move into his apartment to save money. She rejoins him quickly and presents him with a silver cue chalk holder.

In the next round Eddie faces Vinnie. Both men play with confidence. The match is presented through a montage of fast shots with no attempt to indicate the score until the camera settles on Vinnie just missing the pocket. Eddie takes over the table and clears the remaining balls to win. Afterward, Carmen and Vinnie stop by Eddie's hotel room to drop off an envelope full of cash. Vinnie reveals that he "dogged" several shots to ensure Eddie's victory; Vinnie, of course, had placed a large bet on Eddie. Eddie feels dishonored on two fronts: he has not really beaten Vinnie, and he has been conned.

At the beginning of the next round of the tournament, as he stares at his face reflected in the cue ball, Eddie decides to forfeit; on his way past the spectators, he returns the envelope to Vinnie. Janelle tells Eddie she admires character—an ironic reference to the subject of *The Hustler*—and adds that she's cancelled her lease and is ready to move in with him once they return from the Bahamas. Then Carmen appears, trying to return the envelope. Eddie once again refuses the money, but sends word back to Vinnie that he "wants his best game." A bit later, Vinnie shows up in the practice room, where Eddie is waiting. Vinnie whines that Eddie has used him, but he agrees to play. The film ends with the beginning of the game and with Eddie's announcement, "I'm back."

For viewers familiar with *The Hustler*, Eddie's final words suggest not just that he has revived his skills but that he has recovered the sense of character he developed a quarter of a century earlier when he walked out on Bert.

THE COMEBACKS (2007)

Director: Tom Brady. Screenplay: Ed Yeager, Joey Gutierrez. Story: John Aboud, Michael Colton, Adam Jay Epstein, Andrew Jacobson. Producers: Peter Abrams, Robert L. Levy, Andrew Panay. Cinematography: Anthony B. Richmond. Editing: Alan Edward Bell. Music: Christopher Lennertz. Production Design: Marc Fisichella. Art Direction: Douglas Cumming. Costume Design: Salvador Pérez Jr.

Cast: David Koechner (Lambeau "Coach" Fields), Carl Weathers (Freddie Wiseman), Melora Hardin (Barb Fields), Matthew Lawrence (Lance Truman).
Running Time: 84 minutes.
DVD: 20th Century Fox.

A crude satirical film in the vein of *Scary Movie*, this one takes shots at all the typical clichés in other sports films.

COOL RUNNINGS (1993)

Director: Jon Turtletaub. Screenplay: Lynn Seifert, Tommy Swerdlow, Michael Goldberg. Story: Lynn Siefert, Michael Ritchie. Producer: Dawn Steel. Cinematography: Phedon Papamichael. Editing: Bruce Green. Music: Jimmy Cliff, Nick Glennie-Smith, Hans Zimmer. Production Design: Stephen Marsh. Art Direction: Gary Kosko, Rick Roberts. Costume Design: Grania Preston.
Cast: John Candy (Irving Blitzer), Leon Robinson (Dernice Bannock), Doug E. Doug (Sanka Coffie), Malik Yoba (Yul Brenner), Rawle D. Lewis (Junior Bevil), Raymond J. Barry (Kurt Hemphill).
Running Time: 98 minutes.
DVD: Walt Disney Video.

While in Jamaica in the 1980s, two Americans, George Fitch and William Maloney, attended a pushcart derby and noted the similarity between the pushcart race and a bobsled race. Soon they were speculating that Jamaica, which has produced a good number of world-class runners, could field a competitive bobsled team relying on the speed and stamina of Jamaican sprinters. Although the two men were not successful in recruiting sprinters for the Winter Games, they found a number of interested athletes in the Jamaican military, including Deron Harris, who became a member of the original four-man Olympic team (1988), which was eliminated from competition after a dramatic crash, and of the 1992 team, which finished fourteenth, outranking both the United States and France.

Cool Runnings is a sports comedy loosely based on Jamaica's first Olympic bobsled team. The action begins with an annual pushcart derby where the defending champion, Sanka Coffie (Doug E. Doug), wins decisively in spite of crashing at the finish line. Sanka's friend Dernice Bannock (Leon Robinson) is a school teacher who hopes to make the Olympic track team; the other two runners with the best chances are a wealthy young man, Junior Bevil (Rawle D. Lewis), and a bald, muscular athlete who calls himself Yul Brenner (Malik Yoba) after the Roma actor who kept his head shaved long before bare scalps were fashionable. At the qualifying meet, Dernice is holding a slight lead over Yul Brenner, with Junior a step behind. As the trio near the finish, Junior stumbles and falls between the other two, causing both to trip.

Disappointed, Dernice appeals to the head of the Jamaican Olympic Committee, but to no avail. Before leaving the commissioner's office, however, he pauses at a photo of his father, an Olympic medalist, standing beside a white man whom Dernice does not recognize. The commissioner explains that the man is Irving Blitzer, once a member of the United States bobsled team. Blitzer had a theory about using runners to push a bobsled and had approached Dernice's father with his plan. However, Blitzer's career ended in disgrace, and his theory was long forgotten. Dernice tracks down Blitzer (John Candy) and eventually persuades him to coach. Blitzer's reluctance is evident at the town meeting called to recruit athletes; he informs the group that bones don't break in bobsledding accidents, "they shatter." Nonetheless, Sanka and the two other runners sign on, Yul for a chance to leave the island, Junior to avoid a job his father has arranged for him in a Miami brokerage house. Although Junior is not a welcome member, having ruined Dernice's and Yul's chances of making the Olympic track team, no other Jamaican steps forward, and the event requires four men.

The team begins training on the island, without a bobsled, and most definitely without snow, by pushing a cart down the mountainsides. To prepare for colder weather, they try to expose themselves to the cold—Sanka freezes his dreadlocks in an ice cream truck. Their fund-raising efforts include a kissing booth and an arm wrestling contest. Neither project succeeds, but Junior sells his sports car and donates the proceeds to the common cause.

Once the Jamaicans arrive in Calgary, they face a number of obstacles: adjusting to the cold, obtaining a sled, and registering. The team's experiences with snow and ice are exploited for laughs, and at first they are ridiculed and snubbed by teams from other countries. Coach Blitzer, however, is able to obtain a practice sled from the U.S. team, and he also comes through when the Olympic committee wants to prevent the team from competing because it has not participated in an international race. After Blitzer barges in on a meeting of the officials and delivers an impassioned speech, the Jamaicans receive permission to race.

Meanwhile, the team is starting to shape up, transforming themselves from clowns, who lose the sled on their first push start and wipe out on their first run, into accomplished bobsledders. A training montage shows Blitzer putting them through the paces, even using a bathtub to teach them how to lean into turns. When a rivalry develops with the East Germans, who are especially cruel in their comments, the effect is to draw the Jamaicans closer. Junior and Yul become inseparable, and Yul encourages Junior to stand up to his controlling father, who has turned up in Calgary to retrieve him.

By the time the race begins, the Jamaicans are ready. Blitzer has had the sled painted and produces uniforms, all in Jamaica's national colors. After their first run, however, the team is in last place, providing an opportunity for Sanka to pep up his teammates with a talk about Jamaican cultural identity and national pride. After their second run, the team moves up to eighth place. In their final run, they get off to a fine start, but an equipment failure causes a breathtaking crash. There are a few tense moments as the rescue team arrives; then the film cuts to the Jamaicans, emerging from a turn, proudly carrying their damaged sled on their shoulders to the applause of fans and fellow athletes.

"Cool runnings" means "peace be the journey," but the journey of *Cool Runnings* was anything but. The idea for the film was conceived immediately after the 1988 Olympics, and development began at Columbia Studios. When the film finally came out, three directors later, it was a Disney production, and the Jamaican bobsled team had finished in fourteenth place, ahead of both the United States and France, in the 1992 Olympics at Lillehammer. Budget cuts required some revisionist history: the real 1988 team competed in Austria before the Olympics, and faced no difficulty meeting eligibility requirements. It was the two-man sled, excluded entirely from the film version, that crashed at Calgary, while the four-man sled finished in twenty-eighth place. The team received financial support from the Jamaican Tourist Board and a local rum company. Perhaps the most significant change is the portrayal of other countries' teams as hostile to the Jamaicans. In reality, athletes from other nations welcomed and assisted the Jamaicans. The film is often compared to *The Gods Must Be Crazy* (1980) and analyzed for its portrayal of minorities and its treatment of culture shock.

CROSSOVER (2006)

DIRECTOR: Preston A. Whitmore II. SCREENPLAY: Preston A. Whitmore II. PRODUCER: Frank Mancuso Jr. CINEMATOGRAPHY: Christian Sebaldt. EDITING: Stuart Archer, Anthony Adler. MUSIC: Matthias Weber. PRODUCTION DESIGN: Dawn Snyder. COSTUME DESIGN: Okera Banks.
CAST: Anthony Mackie (Tech), Wesley Jonathan (Noah Cruise), Wayne Brady (Vaughn), Kristen Wilson (Nikki), Eva Pigford (Vanessa).
RUNNING TIME: 95 minutes.
DVD: Sony Pictures.

Detroit street-ball players looking for a better life are tempted by a former agent-turned-promoter.

THE CROWD ROARS (1932)

DIRECTOR: Howard Hawks. SCREENPLAY: John Bright, Niven Busch, Kubec Glasmon. Story: Howard Hawks, Seton I. Miller. CINEMATOGRAPHY: Sidney Hickox, John Stumar. EDITING: Thomas Pratt. MUSIC: Bernhard Kaun. ART DIRECTION: Jack Okey.
CAST: James Cagney (Joe Greer), Joan Blondell (Anne Scott), Eric Linden (Eddie Greer), Ann Dvorak (Lee Merrick), Guy Kibbee (Pop Greer), Frank McHugh (Spud Connors).
RUNNING TIME: 70 minutes.

This drama stars Cagney as an arrogant race-car driver whose relationship with his brother becomes strained when the younger sibling aims to become a driver himself.

THE CROWD ROARS (1938)

DIRECTOR: Richard Thorpe. SCREENPLAY: Thomas Lennon, George Bruce, George Oppenheimer. PRODUCER: Sam Zimbalist. CINEMATOGRAPHY: John Seitz. EDITING: Conrad A. Nervig. MUSIC: Edward Ward. ART DIRECTION: Cedric Gibbons.
CAST: Robert Taylor (Tommy "Killer" McCoy), Maureen O'Sullivan (Sheila Carson), Frank Morgan (Brian McCoy), Edward Arnold (Jim Cain).
RUNNING TIME: 90 minutes.
DVD: Warner Bros. Archives

"Killer" McCoy's father sells his son's contract to a gangster, whose daughter takes a liking to the young boxer.

THE CUTTING EDGE (1992)

DIRECTOR: Paul Michael Glaser. SCREENPLAY: Tony Gilroy. PRODUCERS: Robert W. Cort, Ted Field, Karen Murphy. CINEMATOGRAPHY: Elliot Davis. EDITING: Michael E. Polakow. MUSIC: Patrick Williams. PRODUCTION DESIGN: David Gropman. ART DIRECTION: Dan Davis. COSTUME DESIGN: William Ivey Long.
CAST: D. B. Sweeney (Doug Dorsey), Moira Kelly (Kate Moseley), Roy Dotrice (Anton Pamchenko), Terry O'Quinn (Kate's father), Dwier Brown (Kate's fiancé), Chris Benson (Walter Dorsey).
RUNNING TIME: 101 minutes.
DVD: MGM.

Directed by Paul Michael Glaser, *The Cutting Edge* was released shortly after the Winter Olympics in Albertville, France, and enjoyed moderate success in spite of a formulaic plot and clichéd script. The story follows an unlikely duo's progress toward an Olympic berth as a figure skating pair; en route, they fall in love in spite of themselves. Doug Dorsey (D. B. Sweeney), known as the Minnesota Machine, is a talented hockey player whose dreams of a professional career are shattered when an injury leaves him with impaired peripheral vision in one eye. Similarly, Kate Moseley's (Moira Kelly) chance for Olympic gold is dashed when she and her soon-to-be-ex husband flub a lift, and she ends up sprawled on the ice. Doug, having returned to Duluth and his working-class roots, clings to the hope that he can attract the attention of a hockey coach. Back at her father's mansion in Connecticut, Kate throws tantrums and alienates a string of potential partners. Inevitably, Kate's coach thinks of Doug and lures him to Connecticut for a tryout.

The bulk of the film concentrates on the relationship between the primary characters. In the tradition of Hepburn and Tracy, Kelly and Sweeney maintain a romantic tension that sustains the film. The spoiled rich girl holds hockey players in contempt, regarding them as testosterone-driven, semi-literate louts. The blue-collar hockey player espouses a disdain for figure skaters and the refinement they represent. But both athletes are highly competitive and determined to out-skate one another. Glaser relies heavily on montage to reveal the couple's progress both on and off the ice. As their practice and training sessions grow more rigorous, Kate and Doug begin to enjoy themselves, yet neither is able to admit attraction to the other. Obstacles to their relationship include Kate's fiancé (Dwier Brown), who makes cameo appearances whenever Doug and Kate are getting along well, and Doug's penchant for casual sexual encounters. The skaters reach an apparent turning point after qualifying for the Olympics. To celebrate, the pair go out dancing, and Kate uncharacteristically downs several shots of tequila, tells Doug she has broken off her engagement, and invites him to spend the night. But Kate is drunk, and Doug is a gentleman, something Kate is in no shape to appreciate. While Kate sleeps it off, Doug spends a lonely night in his own room with just the mini bar for company—until another skater whom he met earlier in an elevator knocks on his door. The next morning, a badly hung-over Kate locks herself out of her room and makes her way to Doug's, only to be greeted by the rival skater. Doug, clutching a towel, pursues Kate through the hotel, to no avail.

It seems that the two will be unable to repair the damage, and just when it appears things can't get worse, Anton Pamchenko (Roy Dotrice), the coach, informs them that the Russian pair is unbeatable; the Americans' only chance to bring home the gold is to perform a dangerous move he has devised. Of course, Kate and Doug are too competitive to resist the challenge and immediately engross themselves in mastering the "Pamchenko," a maneuver based on a spin known as a "headbanger" and illegal in real-life competition because it requires the male skater to grip his partner by the ankles and spin rapidly, dipping her so that her head nearly skims the ice. But headbangers have not been outlawed in the celluloid Olympics, and Kate and Doug perform the move flawlessly only moments after declaring their love for one another. At the end of their performance, they kiss passionately, and the credits roll.

Although the film introduces a number of standard themes—the parent who pushes the child too hard, the brothers who grow apart, competition between athletes, jilted lovers—there is no follow through. Kate's father (Terry O'Quinn) keeps an empty medal case in his study, which is lined with photos of his late wife, Kate's mother, a figure skater as well; however, it is only near the end of the movie that Kate indicates she's felt pressured by her father. When she announces that she will retire after she and Doug perform, her actions seem an impulsive response to her disappointment in love rather than the result of insight or careful consideration.

Family conflict crops up in Doug's life, first when his brother presses him to relinquish his dream of becoming a pro hockey player and later when the brother learns Doug has taken up figure skating. But the brothers' disagreements require only two short scenes, and the resolution—the brother's presence in the audience during Doug and Kate's final performance—is easily missed. Kate's marriage to her first partner is an unnecessary element, even after it is revealed late in the film that Kate was to blame for their dramatic fall in the previous Olympics. There's no discussion of the divorce, and nothing is made of the fact that the ex-husband, now skating with a new partner, is also competing to make the U.S. team.

Technically, *The Cutting Edge* is superb. Since neither Sweeney nor Kelly is a skater, stunt doubles were used for all of the skating sequences, requiring extensive editing. The result is a slickly cut film with smooth transitions. The success of *The Cutting Edge* prompted a made-for-television sequel, *The Cutting Edge: Going for the Gold* (2006), which repeats the original plot, this time featuring Doug and Kate's figure-skating daughter and an in-line skater dude who becomes her partner. In spite of green screen special effects, the sequel has little to offer. As with the original, the couple's success, both on and off the ice, is predictable; in the sequel, however, the dialogue is tepid and the actors lack the spark of their predecessors.

D

THE DAMNED UNITED (2009)

Director: Tom Hooper. Screenplay: Peter Morgan, based on the novel by David Peace. Producers: Andy Harries, Grainne Marmion. Cinematography: Ben Smithard. Editing: Melanie Oliver. Music: Robert Lane. Production Design: Eve Stewart. Art Direction: Andrew Holden-Stokes, Leon McCarthy. Costume Design: Mike O'Neill.
Cast: Michael Sheen (Brian Clough), Timothy Spall (Peter Taylor), Colm Meaney (Don Revie), Jim Broadbent (Sam Longson).
Running Time: 98 minutes.
DVD: Sony Pictures.

Writer Peter Morgan and actor Michael Sheen have created impressive portrayals of former prime minister Tony Blair (*The Queen*, 2006) and the British television personality David Frost (*Frost/Nixon*, 2008). In *The Damned United* they team up once again for a portrait of notorious football (soccer) manager Brian Clough. The film draws on David Peace's novel, *The Damned Utd* (2006), which is based on Clough's career. Like the novel, the film intercuts scenes from 1974, when Clough became manager of Leeds United, and the 1960s, during which Clough, with his assistant Peter Taylor, built a winning record with lower division clubs. However, the film provides a more positive picture of the egomaniacal Clough than does the novel, and Sheen invests the character with an irresistible exuberance.

The Damned United opens in 1974 with Leeds's popular, successful manager Don Revie (Colm Meaney) announcing that he is resigning in order to helm England's national team. His replacement, Brian Clough (Sheen), has throughout his career voiced criticism of Leeds and Don, so the offer from Leeds's directors and Brian's acceptance are extraordinary news. Brian, whose skillful management of the media has helped establish his fame, schedules a television interview immediately upon his arrival in Leeds, during which he refers to his new team as "champions, but not good champions" because of their rough play. Don, watching the interview, is not pleased. By the time Brian meets with the directors, Don has telephoned to express his outrage.

The film cuts to 1968, when Brian and Peter Taylor (Timothy Spall) were managing the second division Derby club. Derby has just drawn the first division Leeds club in the Football Association Challenge Cup, a single-elimination event. Although Derby stands little chance of winning, there will be a sellout crowd come to see the Leeds players, and the Derby club chairman, Sam Longson (Jim Broadbent), is delighted. Brian does his best to spiff up the visitors' locker room, placing oranges and ashtrays on the benches and polishing the brass on the doors. In anticipation of meeting Don for the first time, Brian has brought out an expensive bottle and the fine crystal. Like Don, Brian played for the Sunderland and England clubs, and they grew up in the same part of Yorkshire. Consequently, Brian anticipates that the two will form an instant bond.

When Leeds arrives, their coach (the British term for "bus") does not drive up to the entrance, parking instead a block away so that the players can parade down the street. Outside the stadium, Brian extends his hand toward Don, but his introduction is drowned out in the crush, either unnoticed or ignored by Don. For Brian, this is an unforgivable slight, made even more painful by Don's failure to stop by the office for a postmatch drink. Derby has lost, but Leeds has not been sporting. An unnecessarily rough tackle early in the contest injured Derby's best player, and Leeds's captain, Billy Bremner (Stephen Graham), has "taken a dive," faked being tripped, to draw a penalty shot. Brian vows revenge. Peter reminds him that Derby will need to reach division one in order to deliver the goods. To accomplish all of this, Peter sets off to obtain the talent while Brian figures how to finance new players.

With Peter's strategy and Brian's combination of charm and bravado, a solid team is assembled, led by Dave Mackay (Brian McCardie), a clever veteran lured from the brink of retirement. Derby steadily improves, taking the title and advancing to the first division. In the same season, Leeds once again wins the first division championship, and Don is named manager of the year. Brian's resentment of Don is balanced by his warm friendship with Peter. Throughout the film, the Brian-Peter relationship is portrayed as an ideal marriage of opposites; at one point, celebrating a title, the pair dance to the song, "Love and Marriage," much to the delight of their families and the Derby players.

When the film returns to the narrative present, it is Brian's first day on the job at Leeds, and he is for the first time working without Peter, with whom he has quarreled. Brian deliberately offends the players, saying their past accomplishments are worthless because they have not competed fairly. He singles out key players—Jimmy Giles (Peter McDonald) and Billy Bremner—for unsportsmanlike conduct, orders the team to complete drills not required by Don, and forbids them from referring to their old coach.

The scene reverts to the 1969 season. When Derby loses to Leeds, the game is not shown, but Don's television interview is. Peter searches for new prospects, and Brian signs them on, at great expense to the owners, who have lost money in the past season. When next Derby plays Leeds, Don has the coach drive up to the players' entrance. Brian is too wired to watch the game; the camera stays with him in his office as he tries to interpret the cheers from outside. Derby wins this contest 2–1. Thus vindicated, Brian goes on to generate so much publicity that in the United States, Muhammad Ali notices and accuses him of talking too much.

In 1974, Brian prepares Leeds for a major cup match, the Charity Shield, by demanding fair play and a new attitude. The players respond by drawing penalties and starting a row that results in Billy Bremner being fined and suspended for six weeks. That Leeds has lost is less of an embarrassment than the team's conduct. Brian drinks to excess and rings up Peter for advice, but Peter, alluding to their troubled split, refuses to assist.

The scene shifts once again to Derby, where the chairman insists Brian start his weaker players against Leeds because Derby has made it to the semifinals of the

European cup the next week. Brian ignores the instructions and puts in his first squad, but Leeds plays with vicious intent, injuring several Derby men. As he leaves the pitch at the end of the match, Billy wishes Brian "good luck in Europe." Sam Longson is furious with Brian, and Peter suffers a heart attack. Visiting Peter in the hospital, Brian declares that his strategy is for them both to resign in order to force Sam to bankroll new players. Peter wisely points out that it is Don and Brian's ambition that is the problem, not the chairman. However, Brian has already delivered the letter, and to his astonishment (but not Peter's), the resignations are accepted. Dave Mackay has been named the new manager.

In 1974, Leeds has now lost its first two matches, and Brian has brought in two players from Derby, a move that only increases hostilities among the other players. Realizing that Leeds is still Don's team, he once again overindulges and rings up his nemesis.

Then the time frame reverses to 1973 and the seaside resort of Brighton, whose team is at the bottom of the third division. The chairman there is offering Brian and Peter enormous salaries to manage the Brighton and Hove Albion club. Brian, reluctant to move south and take on a weak team, remains confident that Derby will rehire them; Peter insists that they won't. It is the salary offer that sways Brian, who insists on a holiday before going to work.

The Cloughs and Taylors are enjoying the beach at Majorca when it is announced that Don is leaving Leeds to manage England. The secretary of Leeds United tracks down Brian with an offer. Peter warns that Leeds will remain Don's team, even if they have an excellent season; he also refuses to break his word to Brighton. The two men have a bitter fight during which Brian delivers an egomaniacal rant. Afterward, he is shown looking very small against a large sky that fills the screen.

At Leeds United, the fans are chanting the praises of Don and screeching obscenities directed toward Brian. In the players' lounge, Billy asks Brian to wait outside; the team's complaints can be heard through the door. The directors determine that he should not have been hired without Peter. Relieved of his duties, Brian grants a television interview, but much to his surprise Don is also there. Brian, speaking of Don's slight six years earlier, sounds pitiful. At the end of the interview, he remains alone on the set. Don exits, laughing with the interviewer.

With his children in the back seat of his car—in a shot that mirrors the film's opening—Brian tells them he is a "bloody fool" and suggests they visit "Uncle Pete," Peter. At first Peter is hesitant to make up, but Brian drops to his knees and recites the apology Peter dictates. The men hug warmly, the children pour out of the car, and everyone goes inside the Taylors' cottage.

As the film concludes, the audience is informed that after failing as England's manager, Don went to the United Arab Emirates, where his career ended ingloriously amidst allegations of financial irregularity. Film footage shows the real Brian Clough and Peter Taylor together and refers to Clough's career record, including European Cups in 1978 and 1979, and deeming him "the greatest manager England never had."

David Peace's novel was published after the deaths of Clough, Taylor, Revie, and Bremner. In spite of its popular success, it displeased the Clough family, who denounced the book, and Jimmy Giles, who brought a successful suit against Peace. The Cloughs refused to view the film because it is based on the novel. Dave Mackay, upset by his portrayal, won a settlement against Lions Gate Studios. However, the film received positive reviews in both the United

States and United Kingdom. Nicholas Barber of the *Independent* called it "an upbeat alternative to the humourless Hollywood model of an inspirational sports biopic" (March 29, 2009).

DAMN YANKEES (1958)

DIRECTORS: George Abbott, Stanley Donen. SCREENPLAY: George Abbott, Douglass Wallop, based on the book *The Year the Yankees Lost the Pennant* by Wallop. PRODUCER: Stanley Donen. CINEMATOGRAPHY: Harold Lipstein. EDITING: Frank Bracht. MUSIC: Ray Heindorf. PRODUCTION DESIGN: Jean Eckart, William Eckart. ART DIRECTION: Stanley Fleischer.
CAST: Tab Hunter (Joe Hardy), Gwen Verdon (Lola), Ray Walston (Mr. Applegate), Russ Brown (Benny Van Buren), Shannon Bolin (Meg Boyd), Nathaniel Frey (Smokey), Jean Stapleton (Sister Miller).
RUNNING TIME: 111 minutes.
ACADEMY AWARD NOMINATIONS: Best Scoring of a Musical Picture.
DVD: Warner Home Video.

Damn Yankees is the screen version of the Broadway play based on Douglass Wallop's novel *The Year the Yankees Lost the Pennant.* Both the play and the film were directed by George Abbott and choreographed by Bob Fosse. The principal players reprised their stage roles for the film, with the exception of Stephen Douglass, who was replaced by Tab Hunter. As a song-and-dance man, Hunter is outclassed, but he is convincing in the role of a modest, but extraordinarily talented baseball player. (Hunter played Red Sox outfielder Jimmy Pearsall in the television version of *Fear Strikes Out.*)

Joe Boyd (Robert Shafer), a middle-aged real estate agent and devoted Washington Senators' fan, like Vernon Simpson from *It Happens Every Spring* (1949), undergoes a transformation every year when baseball season starts. For the next six months, his wife, Meg (Shannon Bolin), is a baseball widow. The film opens on a typical summer evening. As Meg sits by a window, complaining about the heat, Joe remains oblivious to all but the game on television, which the Senators are losing to those "Damn Yankees." Later that night, after Meg has gone upstairs, Joe wanders out on the front porch and thinks aloud that he would trade his soul for one Senator slugger. Suddenly, a man who calls himself Mr. Applegate, a person of "historical significance," appears on the porch; it doesn't take long for Joe to figure out who Applegate really is—he lights a cigarette by producing fire from his hand, and he wears red socks.

In exchange for Joe's soul, Applegate offers to turn him into his alter ego, twenty-two-year-old Joe Hardy, a long-ball hitter and ace fielder. Because Joe is reluctant to leave Meg (Applegate credits wives with creating more problems for him than the Methodist Church), he insists on an escape clause: he has until midnight of September 24 to change his mind. The Devil is reluctant to enter a deal with a catch, but he thinks he is clever enough to prevent Joe from using the clause. Joe leaves a note for Meg that he will be away for a few months, and while he sits at the desk with his back to the camera, Boyd becomes Hardy (Tab Hunter).

Applegate arranges a tryout during which Senators' manager Benny Van Buren (Russ Brown) and a handful of players watch from the bench. The camera follows their craning necks at each crack of the bat, a clever theatrical device that simplifies the technical aspects of the scene. Joe makes the team in spite of the fact that he has had to borrow a pair of shoes; however, a savvy reporter, Gloria Thorpe (Rae Allen), suspects a rat since such a talented player seems to have come from nowhere and neither Applegate nor Joe volunteers any history. When pressed, Joe finally claims that he's from Hannibal, Missouri, his wife's hometown. Gloria, intent on a big story, dubs the rookie "Shoeless Joe from Hannibal, MO," a handle that cues a song-and-dance number. Benny, delighted with the team's new prospect, willingly defends Joe from prying reporters; when the manager confidently predicts that by the last game, on September 25, the Senators will have clinched the pennant, Joe insists that the feat will be accomplished by the 24th.

Alerted that Joe fully intends to activate the escape clause, Applegate enlists the aid of the seductress Lola (Gwen Verdon), a 170-year-old witch who sold her soul for beauty. But before Lola can get to Joe, he has rented a room from Meg, who, of course, adores the young man. Gwen Verdon's classic "Whatever Lola Wants" fails to work its magic, and Joe returns home to his new landlady. To compensate, Applegate enacts plan B, spreading rumors in the Boyds' suburban neighborhood about the Boyd-Hardy living arrangements. To preserve Meg's reputation, Joe moves into a hotel. His anger at the Devil causes him to "crack up" during a game, throwing a ball into the stands (aimed at Applegate) rather than to the relay man.

Lola, instead of feeling spurned by Joe, has developed a genuine fondness for him and has started a fan club. The furious Applegate circulates another rumor, that Joe is really a ballplayer named Shifty McCoy, who took a bribe in Mexico. The story hits the papers, with help from Gloria, who has been unable to confirm Joe's claim to be from Hannibal. The commissioner calls a hearing for September 24, the deadline for Joe to escape the clutches of the Devil. Gloria has introduced witnesses from Hannibal, but Meg and her friends, Sister and Doris Miller (Jean Stapleton and Elizabeth Howell), decide to testify on Joe's behalf. Meg and her coconspirators elbow their way through the crowd, greet Gloria's witnesses, whom they know as former friends and neighbors, and convince the commissioner that Joe is indeed Shoeless Joe from Hannibal, MO, not Shifty. However, the hearing has continued late into the night, and as the clock begins to strike twelve, Joe cannot extract himself from the talkative Meg in time to reach Applegate and cancel the contract. Applegate is now ready to move forward with the second part of his scheme, crushing the hopes of Senators' fans by orchestrating a key loss to the Yankees: the Yanks will win the pennant, and Washington fans will defenestrate.

Now a condemned man, Joe kisses Lola, whom Applegate has sent to prevent him from playing in the deciding game. Lola, seeming to cooperate with the Devil, takes Joe out on the town, drinking and dancing into the wee hours. However, Lola decides to betray Applegate by slipping him sleeping pills so that he will miss the game and not be able to sabotage Joe's playing. Lola carries out her plan and even tries to prolong Applegate's sleep by singing a lullaby every time he stirs; nevertheless, he awakens and realizes what has transpired. Hastening to the ballpark with Lola in tow, he arrives in the last inning. As punishment for Lola's treachery, he changes her back into an old hag. Then, as Joe is in position to make a game-winning catch, he transforms Joe Hardy back to Joe Boyd. But Joe Boyd makes the running catch and keeps running through a door in the outfield fence. The Senators secure the pennant, and foul play is suspected in Joe Hardy's disappearance. Joe Boyd returns to Meg, and Applegate, frustrated that he's been cheated out of a soul, throws a spectacular tantrum.

Damn Yankees received favorable reviews and was chosen as one of the year's ten best films by the *New York Times*; however, it received only one Oscar nomination, Best Score, unlike the play, for which

Walston, Verdon, and Fosse won Tony Awards. A remake is in the workings, produced by Craig Zaden and Neil Meron, who brought *Chicago* and *Hairspray* to the screen, and starring Jake Gyllenhaal and Jim Carrey.

DANS LES CORDES [*ON THE ROPES*] (2007)

DIRECTOR: Magaly Richard-Serrano. SCREENPLAY: Pierre Chosson, Gaëlle Macé, Magaly Richard-Serrano. PRODUCER: Nathalie Mesuret. CINEMATOGRAPHY: Isabelle Razavet. EDITING: Yann Dedet. MUSIC: Jérôme Bensoussan. PRODUCTION DESIGN: Benoît Pfauvadel. COSTUME DESIGN: Catherine Rigault.

CAST: Richard Anconina (Joseph), Maria de Madeiros (Térésa), Louise Szpindel (Angie), Stéphanie Sokolinski (Sandra), Bruno Putzulu (Billy), Jean-Pierre Kalfon (Henri).

RUNNING TIME: 93 minutes.

Dans les Cordes (in French with English subtitles) is a boxing film in which the brutality of the ring reflects the psychological turmoil of the fighters, two girls raised like sisters. Director Magaly Richard-Serrano, a former boxer, combines stark realism with dreamlike sequences to convey the thoughts and moods of her largely reticent characters.

Joseph (Richard Anconina) runs a gym and trains his daughter, Angie (Louise Szpindel), and his niece, Sandra (Stéphanie Sokolinski), both talented kickboxers. When the film opens, the two girls are preparing for the national championships. Angie, a bantamweight, and Sandra, a featherweight, run with Joseph every morning, breathing and punching the air in unison. Hours before the fight, Sandra weighs in twenty ounces over her weight limit and must sweat out the excess by jumping rope while swathed in a hooded raincoat; then, having made her weight, she panics when she cannot find her socks. In contrast, Angie remains calm. The two girls braid each other's hair and enact a ritual of kissing their good luck charms, tiny gold gloves on neck chains. A hint of trouble occurs with the appearance of a former neighbor, Vickie (Ninon Bretecher), now grown up and running a company that provides dancers and pompom girls for events. She has entered the locker room to wish the girls luck and to promote her business, but her attention is focused on Joe, and her demeanor suggests she is making herself available. After Vickie leaves, the girls feel jinxed, and, although Joe claims he doesn't even remember Vickie, his wife, Térésa (Maria De Medeiros), appears skeptical.

In spite of her nervousness, Sandra wins the championship in her division. Angie, however, seems to freeze in the ring, backing away from her opponent, Vera, and refusing to fight. After receiving a warning for her passivity, she allows herself to be badly beaten, offering little defense. Her father refuses to throw in the towel until she is being counted out. Her mother, who has remained outside of the building during Angie's match, is furious that Joe allowed her to absorb so much punishment. She drives Angie home while Joe and Sandra celebrate with the other members of the boxing club. When Sandra returns, she tries to console Angie, insisting that the two are as one, sharing both victory and defeat. Sandra promises they will avenge Angie's loss, but Angie remains unresponsive.

Térésa tries to cheer Angie by telling a romantic story, prompted by a song on the radio, about an early period in her marriage to Joseph, when he was still boxing. However, the marriage has chilled, as becomes readily apparent that evening when Térésa denies Joseph access to her bedroom. He responds by calling on Vickie, who is eager for his company; the encounter quickly becomes a sexual one. Meanwhile, Sandra has reached out to Angie again, this time with a copy of Joyce Carol Oates's *On Boxing*. The passage from the book stating that boxing is "a quiet rage transformed to art" takes on significance as Angie's silence dominates her character. She has not spoken since losing the championship, and, in fact, had no memorable lines earlier in the film. She listens to music, almost obsessively, allowing the sound to isolate her from her family and from the boxer, Jamel (Chems Dahmani), who would like to be close to her.

Sandra continues the morning workouts with Joseph while Angie recuperates. On one of their runs, they go through the cemetery where Sandra's mother is buried, and she touches the grave as she passes. Later, while Joseph picks roses from a private garden, Sandra steals potatoes. Sandra tells Joseph that she plans to lose weight in order to fight in Vera's division. Although Angie is also in the division, Sandra believes that Angie will not return to the ring. That evening, when Sandra decides to skip dinner, Térésa becomes angry with her.

Tension builds in the family. Angie resumes training while Sandra continues to diet. Térésa finds Vickie's card in Joseph's pocket. Later, spying on the girls with binoculars, Térésa spots them with Adbou (Diouc Koma), who has been seeing Sandra, and Jamel; she confronts the girls and slaps Sandra. As the days pass, Teresa's animosity toward Sandra increases and is finally explained when Térésa calls a talk radio show and shares her story, revealing that Joseph is Sandra's father. Angie hears the broadcast and recognizes both her mother's voice and the situation being described. Soon after, Térésa moves out, leaving Joseph and the two girls.

Whatever resentment Angie has held toward Sandra intensifies, and the plot moves toward an inevitable confrontation in the ring. During a sparring session, Angie becomes aggressive, turning the exercise into a real fight during which she fractures Sandra's ankle with apparent intent. As a result, Angie secures a rematch with Vera. Before the fight she breaks the necklace that represents the bond between the two girls. Sandra, too, appears to have gone her own way, leaving Joseph's establishment for the National Institute.

Whether the fight against Vera takes place is difficult to determine, as the film cuts from fight scenes that may occur in Angie's head to Joseph searching for Angie as the match is about to begin, to Angie running from the arena and tearing off her gloves. For the first time in the film, she appears happy.

Dans les Cordes differs from other films about women boxers, such as *Girlfight* (2000) and *Million Dollar Baby* (2004), in that the young women are accepted as serious athletes by their male peers at the gym and by their father, who trains them and takes pride in their accomplishments. However, as in *Girlfight*, boxing provides a therapeutic outlet for a young woman's anger.

A DAY AT THE RACES (1937)

DIRECTOR: Sam Wood. SCREENPLAY: Robert Pirosh, George Seaton, George Oppenheimer. PRODUCER: Sam Wood. CINEMATOGRAPHY: Joseph Ruttenberg. EDITING: Frank E. Hull. MUSIC: Walter Jurmann, Bronislau Kaper. ART DIRECTION: Cedric Gibbons.

CAST: Groucho Marx (Dr. Hugo Hackenbush), Chico Marx (Tony), Harpo Marx (Stuffy), Allan Jones (Gil), Maureen O'Sullivan (Judy Standish), Margaret Dumont (Mrs. Emily Upjohn), Sig Ruman (Dr. Steinberg).

RUNNING TIME: 111 minutes. B&W.

ACADEMY AWARD NOMINATIONS: Best Dance Direction.

DVD: Warner Home Video.

A Day at the Races is the second Marx Brothers comedy produced by Irving Thalberg for MGM. As with the earlier film, *A Night at the Opera* (1935), Thalberg used director Sam Wood and tied the comic routines to a plotline that includes a love story. Big-budget musical production numbers were added to attract more women viewers.

Much of the film is set at a financially troubled sanatorium. (Sanatoria of the era resembled resorts for members of the fashionable set in need of a rest.) The owner, Judy Standish (Maureen O'Sullivan), has only a month before she loses her business to the villainous Morgan (Douglass Dumbrille), who also owns a nearby race track and wants to convert the sanatorium into a casino. Judy's fiancé, Gil (Allan Jones), in an attempt to raise the funds, has invested all of their savings in a race horse, but instead of showing gratitude, Judy is outraged. To make matters worse, her wealthiest client, Mrs. Emily Upjohn (Margaret Dumont), a demanding hypochondriac, is checking out because she's been proclaimed perfectly healthy by one of the physicians. She announces her intentions to return to the care of one Dr. Hugo Hackenbush (Groucho Marx) from Florida. Judy's friend Tony (Chico Marx) overhears Mrs. Upjohn and short-circuits her departure by announcing that Dr. Hackenbush has joined the staff; then he wires the doctor, who turns out to be a veterinarian who has in the past posed as a medical doctor.

As Hackenbush arrives at the sanatorium and is questioned by Morgan's skeptical business manager, Gil is encountering difficulty from the sheriff (Robert Middlemass) because he owes stable fees for Hi-Hat, his horse. Tony's friend, a mute jockey known as "Stuffy" (Harpo Marx), has also gotten himself in hot water for winning a race he was supposed to lose. Tony and Stuffy happen upon Gil and the sheriff and help Gil by offering some cash. In a slapstick routine, Stuffy removes a five-dollar bill from the sheriff's pocket and slips it to Tony, who, after some fumbling with his own pockets, hands the bill to the sheriff, who stuffs the money in his pocket, and the cycle continues until the sheriff puts the bill in his vest pocket instead of his trouser pocket. After the sheriff leaves, Tony suggests betting on a horse, Sun Up, in the next race. Since no one has any money, Tony goes off in search of a "sucker."

The first sucker to cross Tony's path is Dr. Hackenbush, who is about to place a bet on Sun Up. Tony, pushing an ice cream wagon and calling out in an Italian accent "Tootsie Frootsie Ice Cream," interrupts Hackenbush before he can put down his bet and offers to sell him a tip. Hackenbush takes the bait, only to discover the tip is in code and he must also purchase a code book that is also written in code, requiring the purchase of yet another book, and so on. Although Hackenbush realizes he is being conned, he plays along. Once Tony has collected six dollars, he quickly places his bet, then continues his scam. Claiming not to have change for a ten, Tony gives Hackenbush nine more books. While Hackenbush juggles the books and his cigar, the window closes. Sun Up wins, and Hackenbush is left with the ice cream cart, which he pushes off, shouting "Tootsie Frootsie Ice Cream," apparently ready to repeat the con and recoup his losses at the expense of another sucker.

The next comic routine features Dr. Hackenbush doing a number of voices as he pretends to be a switchboard operator and an official from the Florida State Medical Board, whom Judy's business manager, Whitmore (Leonard Ceeley), has attempted to contact to establish Hackenbush's credentials. Hackenbush is able to frustrate Whitmore, but the manager, who is in cahoots with Morgan, persists in his attempts to discredit Hackenbush.

Tony and Stuffy also suspect Hackenbush is a fraud, so Tony brings Stuffy in for an examination during which Stuffy eats a thermometer and tries to wash it down with a bottle of poison. Hackenbush catches him just in time, admonishing Stuffy that the substance is expensive and not to be wasted. The sequence ends with Tony and Stuffy discovering that Hackenbush is a horse doctor, but enlisting his aid in saving the sanitarium by cultivating Mrs. Upjohn's affection.

The scene shifts to a water carnival and several musical numbers, including a song by Gil, after which he and Judy make up. As a dance band plays and couples take the floor, Hackenbush, shuffling Mrs. Upjohn about, catches the eye of a seductive blonde and keeps waltzing off into her arms, only to be retrieved by Mrs. Upjohn. While peering over Mrs. Upjohn's shoulder to maintain eye contact with the mysterious woman, he cleverly arranges a rendezvous in his room later that night. Another musical interlude showcases Chico's skills at the piano and Harpo's on the harp, which he fashions from the innards of the piano Chico has just played.

The appearance of the sheriff sends Tony and Stuffy running off. Hiding in a thicket, Stuffy overhears the mystery woman plotting with Whitmore to trap Hackenbush and spoil his good standing with Mrs. Upjohn. Stuffy mimes this message to Tony, and the pair set off to interrupt the liaison. They pose as house detectives and as paper hangers, wallpapering over Hackenbush while he manages to hide the blonde woman under the couch cushions. Mrs. Upjohn is convinced that Hackenbush has been faithful and begs forgiveness, promising to cosign a note for Judy. Morgan has not given up on proving Hackenbush a fraud and brings to the sanatorium a Viennese physician, Dr. Steinberg (Sig Ruman). Steinberg proposes an examination of Mrs. Upjohn, but Hackenbush has no idea how to conduct a physical on a person, so he stalls with a hand-washing routine that includes Tony and Stuffy posing as assistants. After some high jinks with adjusting the examination table, Hi-Hat, who has been stabled in Hackenbush's room to avoid the sheriff, trots in, and the scene ends in chaos.

Hackenbush, Tony, Stuffy, Gil, Judy, and Hi-Hat all end up at the stable, still on the lam. Judy is trying to keep her spirits up, but she still fears losing the sanatorium. Her sadness prompts Gil to croon "Tomorrow Is Another Day." Stuffy begins to play the flute and is followed, Pied Piper–like, by a group of African American children who live near the stables. An energetic production number ensues with gospel music, jazz, and swing dancing. Dorothy Dandridge makes her film debut, and the Duke Ellington Orchestra (uncredited) plays "All God's Chillun Got Rhythm." The party is broken up by the arrival of Morgan and the sheriff. Hi-Hat, who rears every time he hears or sees Morgan, takes off, followed by the rest. After watching Hi-Hat clear a few hurdles during the escape, Gil realizes that his horse is a jumper, trained to run in steeplechases rather than track races. Conveniently, there is a steeplechase the very next day, and a win would provide the security Judy needs.

Gil and Judy attempt to smuggle Hi-Hat to the race in the back of an ambulance, but the horse hears Morgan and begins to rear and whinny. The sheriff takes Gil and Hi-Hat off in the ambulance while Tony, Stuffy, and Hackenbush scheme to delay the start of the race. First they put soap on the saddles so that the jockeys fall off; next, they blow hats onto the track. Their most elaborate bit of chicanery is to direct traffic onto the track with the promise of free parking. Meanwhile, Judy has cleverly staged an accident along the route the ambulance is taking. She pretends to be unconscious so that Hi-Hat is removed from the vehicle; then she and Gil leap from the back of the ambulance as it takes off and return to the track with the horse. Stuffy makes a grand entrance driving a fire wagon, causing a false start to the race and giving him enough time to enter with Hi-Hat.

Once the race begins, Stuffy shoves a photo of Morgan in front of the horse to get him over the first jump, but he loses the photo. Hackenbush, Tony, and Judy conspire to get Morgan to shout over the track's loudspeaker by liberating a microphone and creating annoyances every time Hi-Hat approaches a jump. As Hi-Hat runs neck and neck with a horse Morgan owns, Stuffy and the other jockey struggle, and both men fall into a mud puddle. They emerge coated in grime, remount, and take off for the home stretch. Stuffy finishes a nose behind the other jockey, and it appears all is lost until Morgan approaches the winning horse, which turns out to be a mud-covered Hi-Hat. Gil's horse is declared the winner, the sanatorium is saved, and Hackenbush proposes to Mrs. Upjohn, promising he'll never look at another horse if she will marry him.

Like *A Night at the Opera*, *A Day at the Races* was a box office success and is considered one of the Marx Brothers' best films. Thalberg was able to translate the Marxes' vaudeville-style comedy to film by trying the routines out on live audiences and timing their laughter, then placing pauses in the film to allow for the response of moviegoers. (These pauses, however, slow down the film for television and DVD viewers, whose laughter subsides more quickly in a small space with a small audience.) Thalberg died two weeks into the filming, and his successors were less able to maintain control over the antics of the Marx Brothers, who are commonly described as "anarchic" in their work habits. Groucho frequently ad-libbed, tossing off one-liners that sometimes left his costars uncertain how to respond. Director Woods insisted on retakes, sometimes twenty or thirty for a simple scene, and a number of scenes appear to have been deleted entirely from the finished product. The result is numerous breaks in the continuity of the plot, but the lively humor overshadows the flaws in the storyline. Racing sequences were shot at Santa Anita. Harpo Marx began doing his own riding, but was injured, although not seriously, during filming; a stunt double was used for part of the racing sequence.

DAYS OF THUNDER (1990)

Director: Tony Scott. Screenplay: Robert Towne. Story: Robert Towne, Tom Cruise. Producers: Jerry Bruckheimer, Don Simpson. Cinematography: Ward Russell. Editing: Robert C. Jones, Chris Lebenzon, Bert Lovitt, Michael Tronick, Stuart Waks, Billy Weber. Music: Hans Zimmer. Art Direction: Benjamin Fernandez, Thomas E. Sanders. Costume Design: Susan Becker.

Cast: Tom Cruise (Cole Trickle), Robert Duvall (Harry Hogge), Nicole Kidman (Dr. Claire Lewicki), Randy Quaid (Tim Daland), Cary Elwes (Russ Wheeler), Michael Rooker (Rowdy Burns), Fred Dalton Thompson (Big John), John C. Reilly (Buck Bretherton).

Running Time: 107 minutes.

Academy Award Nomination: Best Sound.

DVD: Paramount.

Director Tony Scott and star Tom Cruise, who teamed up for *Top Gun* in 1986, are together again in *Days of Thunder*, a stock-car racing film that bears a resemblance to the earlier film, featuring a rule breaker who bonds with a veteran, pursues a rivalry that results in an accident and a crisis of courage, and emerges victorious.

Veteran race car builder Harry Hogge (Robert Duvall) lives on a farm near

Charlotte, North Carolina, where he has taken an extended sabbatical from the racing business. Harry, who harbors guilt feelings over the death of a friend in one of his cars, is reluctant to build a machine for Tim Daland (Randy Quaid), a used car dealer who has pinned his hopes on a newly discovered talent, Cole Trickle (Cruise). To lure Harry off his tractor, Tim arranges for him to observe an "audition," driving a car belonging to Rowdy Burns (Michael Rooker), another driver. When Cole arrives—on a motorcycle—and the others learn that his racing experience is all with open-wheel cars (the type used in the Indianapolis 500), Rowdy nearly backs out of the deal, and Harry is more skeptical than ever. Finally Rowdy gives in, sensing a challenge in Cole's confidence, and Cole turns in a time faster than Rowdy's run while ignoring Rowdy's instructions about the vehicle. Harry is won over and agrees to build a car; Rowdy murmurs something about seeing how well Cole will perform "in traffic."

At first Cole has trouble finishing races. He is accustomed to lightweight, speedy cars whose design allows for greater maneuverability and braking power than that of the bulkier, fendered stock car. And since wheel contact can flip an open-wheel vehicle, Cole isn't prepared for the "rubbing" that Rowdy subjects him to in every race; as soon as Cole's car is bumped from the rear or sideswiped, he panics and starts to lose control. If he doesn't spin out as a result of rubbing, he burns up his tires. Cole and Harry are both frustrated. Cole doesn't follow the radioed instructions he receives through his headphones during a race, in part, because he doesn't know much about how cars run. Once he admits that he lacks the vocabulary to benefit from Harry's advice, the two men arrive at a working agreement. By the end of the season, Cole is still winless, and Tim has yet to secure a sponsor; however, when the next season begins, Cole wins the opening race, and the future starts to brighten.

Several victories later, Harry arranges an elaborate joke to reward Cole for his success. The van in which Harry, Cole, and the pit crew are traveling is pulled over by state troopers who claim the group is breaking a number of laws by drinking in the back of the van. The officer who frisks Cole turns out to be a female escort hired to entertain him, an incident that takes on greater significance later in the film. The ongoing rivalry between Cole and Rowdy involves them in a serious crash that sends both of them to the hospital with head injuries. When Cole, who has suffered a concussion, regains consciousness and meets his neurosurgeon, Dr. Claire Lewicki (Nicole Kidman), he assumes that Harry and the pit crew have hired another escort to cheer him up. Eager to prove he's fine, Harry grabs the doctor's hand and places it on his crotch. Once Cole has realized his mistake, he is embarrassed. Both he and Harry explain the misunderstanding, but Claire appears neither pleased nor moved; she has low expectations of men who devote their lives to racing cars.

Cole and Rowdy reinforce Claire's misgivings about drivers as they continue their competition in the hospital, racing in their wheelchairs down the hospital corridors. After a joint conference with Claire, Harry, and Tim, the drivers are warned by the track owner that they face suspension if they continue their dangerous bumping. To end the rivalry, the owner insists both men join him and other officials at dinner. They are to come together in a single car; instead, they rent two cars and take off on a wild race through town. In the process of damaging the rental cars and resisting the authority of the officials, Cole and Rowdy bond. They show up late for dinner, but they have their stories straight.

Cole continues his pursuit of Claire, having her apartment filled with flowers and balloons, then trying to kiss her during an examination. Claire resists his advances while she's fulfilling her professional role, but as soon as the exam is over, she pins him to the wall in a passionate embrace. Despite her attraction to Cole, Claire has difficulty understanding why he has no goals beyond racing, especially given the risks. Soon, it becomes apparent that Rowdy's injuries are more serious than they first appeared and that he will not be able to resume his career. Meanwhile, Russ Wheeler (Cary Elwes), the driver whom Tim hired to replace Cole during his recuperation, has been winning races. When Cole returns to the track, he learns that Tim is now running a second team but is having trouble finding sponsors for Cole. While Rowdy puts off seeing a neurosurgeon, Cole struggles to regain his confidence on the track. Russ, determined to undermine Cole, rams him from behind, forces him against the wall, and during a pit stop, blocks his exit. When Russ wins, Cole drives back onto the track during the victory lap, ramming into Russ and destroying both of Tim's cars. Later, with Claire in the passenger seat of a private vehicle, his road rage reemerges when an impatient cabbie taps his rear bumper. Cole reverses into the cab, then tries to run the driver off the road. Another accident is avoided only when Claire, who has insisted he let her out, opens the door of the moving vehicle. Cole stops, and Claire calls him, among other things, an egomaniac.

The fight with Claire causes Cole to reexamine his behavior. He visits Rowdy, whom he has been avoiding, and convinces him to go to the hospital for tests. Rowdy is diagnosed with a damaged blood vessel in his brain and must undergo surgery. His driving days are over, but he still owns a car and needs an income. Cole agrees to drive for him in the Daytona 500, but without Harry's help, he doubts that he can make a good showing. After a confrontation at the farm, both Harry and Cole admit their fears, and Harry agrees to get Rowdy's car ready for the race.

At the eleventh hour, the car requires a new engine—supplied by Tim, who has always believed in Cole; Claire arrives to wish him good luck and decides to watch with Harry and the crew. An accident on the track creates a hazard similar to the one that resulted in Rowdy and Cole's collision, but this time Cole steers a clear path through the debris, thus regaining his confidence. In spite of a sticking accelerator, he outmaneuvers Russ in the final lap to win the 500. After a quick kiss from Claire, Cole joins Harry, and the two men race on foot to Victory Lane.

Cruise's character was loosely based on driver Tim Richmond, whose short career as a stock-car driver followed a similar trajectory; Duvall's character bears a strong resemblance to crew chief Harry Hyde. To maintain a realistic tone, segments of the film were shot at the 1990 Daytona 500 using two movie cars that completed 100 laps. ESPN announcers Bob Jenkins and Jerry Pinch provide commentary, and a handful of real drivers are "interviewed" about Cole's comeback. Driver Greg Sacks doubled for Cruise during staged segments of races. Members of the racing community were displeased with the portrayal of rubbing and bumping as common, intentional practices. The critical reception was mediocre, and Nicole Kidman, twenty-three at the time of filming, was generally viewed as badly miscast.

DEATH RACE (2008)

DIRECTOR: Paul W. S. Anderson. SCREENPLAY: Paul W. S. Anderson, based on the screenplay by Robert Thom and

Charles Griffith and story by Ib Melchior. PRODUCERS: Paul W. S. Anderson, Jeremy Bolt, Paula Wagner. CINEMATOGRAPHY: Scott Kevan. EDITING: Niven Howie. MUSIC: Paul Haslinger. PRODUCTION DESIGN: Paul D. Austerberry. ART DIRECTION: Nigel Churcher, Michel Laliberte. COSTUME DESIGN: Gregory Mah.
CAST: Jason Statham (Jensen Ames), Joan Allen (Hennessey), Ian McShane (Coach), Tyrese Gibson (Machine Gun Joe), Natalie Martinez (Case), Max Ryan (Pachenko).
RUNNING TIME: 111 minutes.
DVD: Universal Studios.

This remake of the 1975 film features Jason Statham as a wrongfully imprisoned driver who competes in a brutal car race rigged by warden Joan Allen.

DEATH RACE 2000 (1975)

DIRECTOR: Paul Bartel. SCREENPLAY: Robert Thom, Charles Griffith. STORY: Ib Melchior. PRODUCER: Robert Corman. CINEMATOGRAPHY: Tak Fujimoto. EDITING: Tina Hirsch. MUSIC: Paul Chihara. ART DIRECTION: B. B. Neel, Robinson Royce. COSTUME DESIGN: Jane Ruhm.
CAST: David Carradine (Frankenstein), Simone Griffeth (Annie Smith), Sylvester Stallone (Machine Gun Joe Viterbo), Mary Woronov (Calamity Jane).
RUNNING TIME: 84 minutes.
DVD: New Concorde.

"In the year 2000, hit and run is no longer a crime. It's the national sport!"

THE DERBY STALLION (2005)

DIRECTOR: Craig Clyde. SCREENPLAY: Kimberly Gough. PRODUCERS: Kevin Summerfield, Tonja Walker. CINEMATOGRAPHY: John Gunselman. MUSIC: Billy Preston. PRODUCTION DESIGN: Margaret M. Miles. ART DIRECTION: Jaclyn Marshall.
CAST: Zac Efron (Patrick McCardle), Bill Cobbs (Houston Jones), Crystal Hunt (Jill Overton), William R. Moses (Jim McCardle), Tonja Walker (Linda McCardle).
RUNNING TIME: 98 minutes.
DVD: Echo Bridge Home Entertainment.

A teenager prepares to enter a horse racing competition, despite the disapproval of his father, a former baseball player.

DIGGSTOWN (1992)

DIRECTOR: Michael Ritchie. SCREENPLAY: Steven McKay, based on the novel by Leonard Wise. PRODUCER: Robert Schaffel. CINEMATOGRAPHY: Gerry Fisher. EDITING: Don Zimmerman. MUSIC: James Newton Howard. PRODUCTION DESIGN: Steve Hendrickson. ART DIRECTION: Michael Okowita. COSTUME DESIGN: Wayne A. Finkelman.
CAST: James Woods (Gabriel Caine), Louis Gossett Jr. ("Honey" Roy Palmer), Bruce Dern (John Gillon), Oliver Platt (Fitz), Heather Graham (Emily Forrester).
RUNNING TIME: 98 minutes.
DVD: MGM.

A con man makes a bet that he can find a boxer to take down ten other boxers in twenty-four hours. His best prospect is an aging boxer who hasn't had a professional bout in years.

DODGEBALL (1995)

DIRECTOR: Art Jones. SCREENPLAY: Art Jones. PRODUCER: Art Jones. EDITING: May Liao.
CAST: John Wolfe (Coach Clifford Butz), Tom Oppenheim (Joey Pro), Gregory Wolfe (Buddy Steinmetz), Molly O'Donnell (Nora Blakey), Jenny Lumet (Claudette Mitty).
RUNNING TIME: 81 minutes.

In flashbacks, former grade school students recall how the game of dodgeball had an impact on their lives.

DODGEBALL: A TRUE UNDERDOG STORY (2004)

DIRECTOR: Rawson Marshall Thurber. SCREENPLAY: Rawson Marshall Thurber. PRODUCERS: Stuart Cornfeld, Ben Stiller. CINEMATOGRAPHY: Jerzy Zielinski. EDITING: Alan Baumgarten, Peter Teschner. MUSIC: Theodore Shapiro. PRODUCTION DESIGN: Maher Ahmad. ART DIRECTION: Andrew Max Cahn. COSTUME DESIGN: Carol Ramsey.

CAST: Vince Vaughn (Peter La Fleur), Ben Stiller (White Goodman), Christine Taylor (Kate Veatch), Justin Long (Justin), Rip Torn (Patches O'Houlihan), Stephen Root (Gordon), Alan Tudyk (Steve), Hank Azaria (young Patches O'Houlihan), Jason Bateman (Pepper Brooks), Gary Cole (Cotton McKnight).

RUNNING TIME: 92 minutes.

DVD: 20th Century Fox.

This comedy revolves around a sport that is rarely the subject of films, but the activity is quite familiar to many viewers who remember it from their elementary school days, though some not fondly. A staple in some PE classes, where many were forced to participate, dodgeball rarely saw play beyond the school gymnasium or blacktop. To some extent, however, *Dodgeball: A True Underdog Story* revived interest in the sport, an influence on athletic culture that few other films can claim. And with wider acceptance, the sport has even established an organization to oversee its regulations. For adults who have painful memories—both physical and emotional—concerns about injuries seem to have been addressed. According to the National Amateur Dodgeball Association website (www.dodgeballusa.com), "Dodgeball is now safe and more enjoyable with rubber coated foam balls, safety conscious rules, and a festive tournament atmosphere."

Peter La Fleur (Vince Vaughn) owns a rundown gym named Average Joe's, whose staff and patrons are a motley assortment of misfits, including Gordon (Stephen Root), a portly nerd who regularly reads *Obscure Sports Quarterly* magazine; Steve (Alan Tudyk), a man who fancies himself a pirate; and Justin (Justin Long), a high school student who wants to join the cheerleading team to prove to Amber, a girl on the squad he has feelings for, that he's not a loser.

While auditing Peter's books, Kate Veatch (Christine Taylor), a real estate and tax lawyer, informs La Fleur that unless he pays off the fifty-thousand-dollar balance on his mortgage in thirty days, he will lose the gym. Meanwhile Peter's nemesis, White Goodman (Ben Stiller), the founder and owner of Globo Gym America Corp., a chain of fitness centers, plans to buy Peter's gym so he can erect a parking garage in its place.

Peter brainstorms with Gordon, Justin, Steve, Dwight (Chris Williams), and Owen (Joel David Moore) for some money-generating ideas. After the first idea, an all-male car wash, actually puts them further in debt, Gordon suggests another possibility: an international dodgeball tournament being held in Las Vegas. Open to any team that wins a regional qualifying match, the tournament boasts a first prize of fifty thousand dollars.

In the meantime, White has begun to show an interest in Kate, who is handling his pending acquisition of Average Joe's. Though Kate rebuffs him, White has other prey on his mind. In order to spy on Peter, White has sent to Average Joe's a cardboard cutout of himself with a hidden camera inside. When he learns of Peter's plans to drum up cash, White puts another scheme into motion.

Justin brings in a film shown in his physical education class the year before.

Produced by Über-American Instruction Films ("Teaching America's Youth since 1938"), the film explains that dodgeball was invented in the fifteenth century by drug-addicted Chinese who played with human heads. The film then describes how the current game is played: two teams with six players each throw balls at each other. Once all the players on one side are knocked out, the other team wins. The highlight of the film occurs when seven-time American Dodgeball Association all-star Patches O'Houlihan (Hank Azaria) appears to explain some of the finer points of the sport to Timmy and the viewers: If a player catches a ball thrown by an opponent, the thrower is knocked out and the team that caught the ball gets to reinstate one of their players. Patches also advises Timmy to pick the biggest and strongest players, because "dodgeball is a sport of violence, exclusion, and degradation." Finally, he also elaborates on the five Ds of the sport: Dodge, Duck, Dip, Dive, and . . . Dodge.

Gordon announces that he has signed the team up for the regional qualifiers. Only one other team shows up, so to make it to Las Vegas, the Average Joe's just have to beat a Girl Scout troop. One by one, the preteens pummel all of Peter's teammates, while Kate arrives just in time to witness the slaughter. Peter delivers his first blow to a girl who immediately questions why he would hit a girl. He is aghast just long enough for another troop member to deliver the final blow, eliminating Average Joe's chances. However, just as Troop 417 is to be declared the winners, it is announced that one of the girls has tested positive for three steroids. Average Joe's Gym wins by default.

Later, celebrating at the Dirty Sanchez bar, the team is taunted by White Goodman, who announces that his Globo Gym Purple Cobras have qualified for the tournament as well, via a friend of White's, the dodgeball chancellor. White introduces the beefed-up jocks on his squad: Blade, Lazer, Blazer, Me'Shell, and last but not least, Fran Stalinovakovichdaviddivichski (Missi Pyle), a woman from Romanovia, whose national sport is dodgeball. A grotesque-looking woman with one eyebrow, a facial wart, and jagged, wayward teeth, she nonetheless charms Owen.

Out in the parking lot, an older patron who had witnessed the confrontation approaches Pete and introduces himself as Average Joe's new coach. He's Patches O'Houlihan (Rip Torn), decades after his heyday and now confined to a wheelchair. He shows up the next morning, barking at the intimidated crew. Patches proclaims, "If you master the five Ds, no amount of balls on earth can hit you." For his first lesson, he hurls a wrench at Justin, who falls to the ground in agony. During practice, Patches tosses more wrenches at the team. Another unconventional training tactic involves dodging traffic. Gordon is hit twice.

Kate, who shows up at the gym during one of the practice sessions, demonstrates an unexpected skill at the game, whipping an underhand dodgeball that knocks off the cardboard head of White's poster. However, she declines the team's offer to join them, since it would represent a conflict of interest. Meanwhile, White's second in command, Me'Shell (Jamal Duff), reports the latest hidden camera results to White: the team is getting better and Kate can throw. This news prompts White to more actively pursue Kate. He shows up at her front door and gleefully announces that since he lied to her bank that she's been drinking on the job and stealing, she's been fired from his account, which leaves them free to date. Before he can make further advances, Peter arrives, and White leaves. Over drinks, Kate agrees to join Peter's team.

It's game time. Announcing for ESPN 8—"The Ocho,"televising "seldom seen sports from around the globe since

1999"—are Cotton McKnight (Gary Cole) and Pepper Brooks (Jason Bateman), who explain the tournament's elimination setup: thirty-two teams from around the world have qualified, and the winning team must defeat five opponents to claim the fifty-thousand-dollar prize. In the locker room, Average Joe's team stares in disbelief at the extremes the other teams undergo to prepare for battle. Owen surprises his teammates with a box full of new uniforms—only to discover they have received the wrong box: theirs contains leather garments meant for one of the other teams, a squad of sadomasochist fetishists. Knowing that they must either wear matching uniforms or be disqualified, the Average Joe's don the outfits and take on their first opponent, Blitzkrieg from Germany.

Gordon is knocked out first, followed by Peter, Steve, and Dwight. Then one of the Blitzkrieg team steps over the line and is called out. Justin knocks out one opponent before getting struck. As the remaining team member standing, Kate strikes out one of the Germans and then catches the ball from another, bringing Peter back into the game. The duo whip their balls at the last German defender, eliminating Blitzkrieg from the competition.

That evening, Justin runs into Amber, whose school is in the finals of the National Cheerleading Championships.

Day 2 arrives, and Patches gives the team his usual "pep talk" of taunts before the team takes on the Lumberjacks. Justin is knocked out first, but Peter and Dwight quickly take out one of the Lumberjacks, and Kate follows that with a kill as well. Peter then cuts down another opponent, and before long, Average Joe's has won again. Meanwhile, White Goodman's Purple Cobras eliminate the Kamikazes from Osaka, Japan, to make it to the semifinals.

Average Joe's then takes on Skillz That Killz, an inner-city team that breakdances its way to defeat. Then White's team takes out the Las Vegas Police Department members, who have worn sunglasses on the court. The victory sends the Purple Cobras to the finals. To join them the Average Joe's must get past the Flying Cougars, but one by one their players go down until only Gordon remains standing, a solitary defender against all five of the Cougars. Calling a timeout, the team huddles up, and Patches tells a nodding Gordon that his only chance is to get angry. Back on the court, Gordon looks around him for inspiration until he spots his wife flirting with a stranger. This is the spark Gordon needs. At the resumption of the game, he growls, picks up a ball, deflects three balls thrown at him, and retaliates with five kills in a row.

In a celebratory mood after the match, the team follows Patches into a bar, where a sign reading "The Luck of the Irish" falls from the ceiling and crushes Patches to death. Peter goes up to his hotel room, where White and Me'Shell are waiting for him. White offers Peter $100,000 for the deed to his gym. Back at the bar, a guilty-looking Peter deflects the team's entreaties for guidance as they anticipate the finals. He tells them that they're likely to lose and walks away. Near the exit, he runs into Steve and shoves him against a door, telling him he is not a pirate. As the others also depart, Owen spies Fran at the bar and tells her she's the most beautiful woman he's ever seen. Steve wanders the streets of Las Vegas, where he is abused by other tourists for his pirate costume.

The next morning, a couple of hours before the championship, Kate discovers that Peter has checked out of the hotel. Meanwhile, Amber locates Justin and asks him to replace an injured member on her cheerleading team. In the locker room, the team learns about Peter's disappearance, and Steve is a no-show as well. Owen, the team manager, must take his place. After Justin helps Amber's team he plants an unexpected but not unwelcome kiss on her, then runs off to join his dodgeball teammates.

Waiting at the Las Vegas airport bar, Peter is recognized by Tour de France legend Lance Armstrong, who has been rooting for the Average Joe's team. After Peter admits that he quit the team, Lance recalls a time when he was tempted to quit himself—soon after he was diagnosed with lung, brain, and testicular cancer, all at once. But he's sure Peter has his own good reason to quit. Without Peter or Steve, the team is one player short and must forfeit. Before the Cobras are announced the winners, however, Peter appears on the court, and the dodgeball committee members agree to overturn the forfeit.

In the absence of Patches, it's Peter's turn to provide the team with a pep talk. He reminds them of their team motto: Aim low.

At the start of the match, White and Blazer fling their balls at Kate, sending her to the sidelines. Peter hurls a ball that hits White in the face, but it bounces in the air and Me'Shell dives to catch it. Peter is out. Dwight leaps in the air to dodge a ball, then strikes out Me'Shell. White hits Dwight on the back, sending him packing. Gordon's ball is deflected by Fran, who races to the middle line, where she stops in front of Owen. They smile at each other before both get hit and are eliminated. Gordon and Justin knock out another Cobra, but Gordon's next throw is caught by White, bringing Me'Shell back in the game. Justin is the lone Joe standing against four Cobras. After a series of balletic dodges, he catches one of the balls, bringing Kate back in, who immediately catches another ball, allowing Peter into the game as well. But when Justin is distracted by Amber in the stands, White takes advantage and hits him in the face with a ball.

An awkward dodge sends Peter to the floor, and just as White's ball is about to strike, Kate leaps into the air and takes the hit instead. As she walks off the court, White sees the affection the two share and strikes Kate in the face with a ball. Though given a warning, White is still allowed to play. Kate's sacrifice has left Peter alone against White and Me'Shell. After dodging Me'Shell's throw, Peter's throw knocks his opponent down. But scant seconds later, White hurls a ball at the distracted Peter. White is overcome with jubilation, but his glee is short-lived: The referee declares he stepped over the line as he threw, a double fault. The referee cites "88-a continuation rule 113-d": sudden death!

The referee explains the sudden death rules: Catching the ball is of no consequence. Only striking a player wins the game. As each man walks away from the center line, Peter withdraws from his shorts the scarf Patches O'Houliahn gave him a couple of nights before and seeks inspiration from it. Standing next to his ball, which has been stenciled with a skull and crossbones, Peter blindfolds himself with the scarf. With sensei-like awareness, Peter leans out of the way from White's ball, then picks his own up and hurls against Goodman. His ball connects, and the Average Joe's team is victorious.

After the team receives the fifty-thousand-dollar check from the dodgeball chancellor (William Shatner), Peter admits he sold Average Joe's to White the night before. Before White can gloat too long, Peter also discloses that he bet all of the $100,000 on his team, 50–1 underdogs, which brings him a $5 million payoff. He announces that he will invest the money in a controlling stake of White's publicly traded gym, which saves Average Joe's.

During the ending credits, the White Goodman character, now morbidly obese, speaks to the audience. Wallowing in greasy food that rests upon his ample stomach and surrounded by mounds of empty packages, he expresses his disgust with the movie's happy ending. It's a result of American cinema lacking complexity, he proclaims, so that the good guy wins and the bad guy loses. Viewers don't want to think, just be entertained, he laments. Perhaps. But like most sports films, comedy or not, *Dodgeball* delivers on its promise to entertain. It also delivers on its subtitle's premise: the triumph of the underdog. And this is just one of several tropes of sports films that the movie generates, along with winning requires teamwork, winners never quit, and cheaters get their comeuppance. But the film features tropes found in other film genres as well, particularly romances: love is blind and love conquers all. Perhaps the only twist on any of these clichés is the final interaction between Peter and Kate, who the others have assumed is a lesbian. When her girlfriend shows up at the finale and the two kiss passionately, this seems to confirm their assumptions. But when Kate reveals that she's actually bisexual, then delivers another passionate kiss on Peter as her girlfriend watches, the film suggests that Peter has not only triumphed financially and on the playing field but also in the bedroom.

DOWNHILL RACER (1969)

DIRECTOR: Michael Ritchie. SCREENPLAY: James Salter, based on the novel by Oakley Hall. PRODUCER: Richard Gregson. CINEMATOGRAPHY: Brian Probyn. EDITING: Richard Harris. MUSIC: Kenyon Hopkins. ART DIRECTION: Ian Whittaker.
CAST: Robert Redford (Dave Chappellet), Gene Hackman (Eugene Claire), Camilla Sparv (Carole), Karl Michael Vogler (Machet), Jim McMullan (John Creech), Dabney Coleman (Mayo).
RUNNING TIME: 101 minutes.
DVD: Criterion.

Michael Ritchie's feature debut is a portrait of a self-absorbed skier whose success on the slopes provides him only fleeting satisfaction. The film mixes dramatic footage of downhill racing, some of it shot with a camera mounted on a skier's helmet, with an excellent performance by Robert Redford as a truly unpleasant young man. In spite of the climactic race at the end, *Downhill Racer* avoids standard Hollywood formulae. An absence of background information and dialogue marked by awkward silences give the film a cinema verité feel. Skiing scenes were filmed on location in France, Austria, and Switzerland.

After an opening montage of landscape, equipment, spectators, and athletes, the film juxtaposes a downhill run with the credits in freeze frames until the skier wipes out, suffering serious fractures. The accident creates an opening on the U.S. team, and coach Eugene Claire (Gene Hackman) invites Colorado native Dave Chappellet (Redford) and an East Coast skier, D.K. (Kenneth Kirk), to race with the team in Europe. From the first, Dave's behavior ranges from arrogant to surly. Arriving in Europe, he is rude to an airport employee who directs him to a telephone, and he snaps at the operator who connects his call. He and D.K., with whom he rooms, have little to say to each other. Dave scowls when he learns that D.K. and another team member, Mayo (Dabney Coleman), attended Dartmouth. Dave is perhaps insecure because he comes from a rural background and feels uncomfortable in the presence of more experienced travelers. He doesn't understand French or German and has no idea what a bidet is—although he denies this to his roommate.

In a trial run, Dave impresses the coach with his speed, but because he is a newcomer, he receives a high number for his first race and is scheduled to start in the sixth grouping. After complaining that the snow will be too deeply rutted from the previous skiers for him to achieve any speed, he refuses to race. Coach Claire does not punish him, letting the incident pass with only a barbed comment when Dave receives a slightly lower start for his second race. In spite of his position, he finishes fourth and indicates the coach should see that his next grouping is in the top ten. Claire tells Dave he must earn his place, a point one might think Dave should have realized. Still, his earlier success places him in the second group for his next race. However, he loses his balance when he hits a bumpy section of the run. Afterward, he blames his fall on his position behind the first group, but Claire dismisses his excuses, telling Dave that he's simply not strong enough to compete against world-class racers. Dave responds sarcastically about working out during the summer, but training is exactly what the coach has in mind. Dave, with the rest of the team, spends the off-season in Oregon, running laps in the high altitude.

During a break in training, Dave visits his father (Walter Stroud) at the family farm in Colorado. Their relationship is obviously strained, and the elder Chappellet's reticence creates some sympathy for Dave, who seems to be making an attempt to diminish the distance between them. When Dave puts on a denim jacket and goes outside where his father has been working, it seems at first that he's going to help with the farm chores; instead, after remarking that his father's old car looks as if it's in good shape, he suggests his father quit work and the two go into town for a beer. His father responds that the keys are in the car, "if that's what you want." And perhaps use of the car is all Dave wants. Nothing in his demeanor indicates frustration or disappointment as he cruises into town in search of a former girlfriend. Although the girlfriend claims to be angry, she readily agrees to go for a ride, which ends with the couple in the backseat. Once they've repositioned themselves in the front seats, the young woman begins talking about an opportunity to train as a dental hygienist; she obviously wants Dave to offer comment on the decisions she faces about her future, but he ignores her while she talks, then asks her for a piece of chewing gum.

The scene returns to the farmhouse, where Dave and his father engage in a halting exchange punctuated by silences. Dave mentions that he's on the U.S. ski team, and his father asks if he's won any money. His father doesn't understand why Dave races, and Dave's response that he wants to become a famous champion prompts his father's reply, "World's full of 'em." The scene jumps to the ski season in Europe, and the story resumes without further reference to Dave's family or his unnamed girlfriend.

In Austria Dave sets his eye on another woman whom he spots sitting at a table with Claire, rival American skier John Creech (James McMullan), and a third man. Dave contrives to pass by their table and finagle an introduction. The unknown man is Machet (Karl Michael Vogler), a ski manufacturer eager to equip potential Olympic medalists, but Dave is not interested in cultivating a sponsor, only in meeting Carole (Camilla Sparv), who works for Machet. The next day Dave and Carole (whose name is mentioned only once) do some leisurely skiing, and Dave drives her Porsche skillfully but dangerously fast. Back at the hotel Dave encounters a female reporter who has been dining with Coach Claire and some of the team; however, she abandons them when she spots Dave, who has been attracting media attention. Her opening question, whether he "practices self-denial," indicates that his growing popularity is connected to his good looks as well as his skill. Dave answers "sometimes," but his next encounter with Carole indicates that his denial refers only to consumption of alcoholic beverages.

Success does nothing to improve Dave's personality. After winning a race, he spits out the ceremonial drink of milk and tosses the remainder over his shoulder, splattering a bystander. With the other skiers he is cocky. He baits John, challenging him to a risky contest that gets both in trouble with Claire. He is rude to Machet when he visits the office looking for Carole. His relationship with her doesn't survive the Christmas holidays, which she spends with family rather than with him. His final scene with her parallels that with his Colorado girlfriend. The two sit in Carole's Porsche, where he has just opened her Christmas gift to him, a pair of gloves that he clearly finds inadequate. Carole, perhaps a bit uncomfortable with the situation, chatters on about how wonderful her holidays were. Dave, unable to ignore this conversation, slams his hand on the car horn. She walks off, leaving him behind in the parking lot, where he puts on the gloves and shrugs. There is no attempt at reconciliation, no indication that the relationship had any meaning for either of them.

Two weeks before the Olympics, John breaks his leg. Dave visits him in the hospital and twice tries to say something, but is interrupted first by a nurse, then by the arrival of Coach Claire. John talks bitterly about the sacrifices one makes, and Dave leaves without responding. At the Olympics the athletes pass a restless night, eat breakfast, and prepare for the downhill in silence. Tension mounts as the race begins and an Austrian has a magnificent run, followed by a Frenchman who moves into second place. Dave, whose inconsistency has been troubling, is able to maintain both speed and balance, beating the Austrian's time and securing first place; however, amid the jubilation at the finish, a final skier begins his run and is moving at a pace to beat Dave's time. Just as it appears the gold is going to slip away, the skier slips in the last turn, failing to finish the course. Dave wins the gold and is mobbed by reporters. As Claire shouts into a microphone, Dave turns toward the losing skier, a handsome, fair-haired young man looking very much like a slightly younger version of Dave, right down to his expression.

Redford, an avid skier, conceived of the project himself and prepared for his role by spending time with professional skiers. In a *Sports Illustrated* interview, he stated that he based his portrayal on U.S. alpine skiers Billy Kidd and Spider Sabich; however, the film includes a disclaimer in the opening credits. Both Redford and Ritchie intended to expose the pressure of competition and the stress of celebrity in the film, but since its focus remains fixed on Redford's character, the theme is revealed only in subtle moments, and it is easy to view Chappellet simply as an unlikeable person rather than as an athlete unable to handle the limelight.

DREAMER (1979)

DIRECTOR: Noel Nosseck. SCREENPLAY: Larry Bischof, James Proctor. PRODUCER: Mike Lobell. CINEMATOGRAPHY: Bruce Surtees. EDITING: Fred A. Chulack. MUSIC: Bill Conti. ART DIRECTION: Archie Sharp. COSTUME DESIGN: Guy C. Verhille.

CAST: Tim Matheson (Dreamer), Susan Blakely (Karen), Jack Warden (Harry), Richard B. Schull (Taylor), Matt Clark (Spider).

RUNNING TIME: 90 minutes.

VHS: Magnetic Video.

This is a predictable film about a small town dreamer's desire for success in the bowling alley.

DREAMER: INSPIRED BY A TRUE STORY (2005)

DIRECTOR: John Gatins. SCREENPLAY: John Gatins. PRODUCERS: Brian Robbins,

Michael Tollin. CINEMATOGRAPHY: Fred Murphy. EDITING: David Rosenbloom. MUSIC: John Debney. PRODUCTION DESIGN: Brent Thomas. ART DIRECTION: Scott Plauche. COSTUME DESIGN: Judy Ruskin.
CAST: Kurt Russell (Ben Crane), Dakota Fanning (Cale Crane), Kris Kristofferson (Pop Crane), Elisabeth Shue (Lily), David Morse (Palmer), Freddy Rodríguez (Manolin).
RUNNING TIME: 106 minutes.
DVD: Dreamworks Video.

A young girl and her father rehabilitate a racehorse with a broken leg, believing the mare still has a chance to compete.

DRIBBLES (2007)

DIRECTOR: Thomas Tosi. SCREENPLAY: Thomas Tosi. PRODUCERS: Heidi Tosi, Thomas Tosi. CINEMATOGRAPHY: David Hjelm. EDITING: Heidi Tosi, Lincoln Tosi, Thomas Tosi. MUSIC: John Sharpley. ART DIRECTION: Heidi Tosi.
CAST: Joe Orrigo (David McNeil), Robert Shea (Dribbles), Eliza Rose Fichter (Mary Todd), Harmony Stempel (Sarah McNeil).
RUNNING TIME: 100 minutes.
DVD: Tosi Productions.

This is a low-budget film about a mentally challenged high school janitor and an arts-minded basketball player with something to prove to his father.

DRIVEN (2000)

DIRECTOR: Renny Harlin. SCREENPLAY: Sylvester Stallone. STORY: Jan Skrentny, Neal Tabachnick. PRODUCERS: Renny Harlin, Elie Samaha, Sylvester Stallone. CINEMATOGRAPHY: Mauro Fiore. EDITING: Steve Gilson, Stuart Levy. MUSIC: BT. PRODUCTION DESIGN: Charles Wood. ART DIRECTION: Nigel Churcher, Chris Cornwell. COSTUME DESIGN: Mary McLeod.
CAST: Sylvester Stallone (Joe Tanto), Burt Reynolds (Carl Henry), Kip Pardue (Jimmy Bly), Estella Warren (Sophia Simone), Gina Gershon (Cathy Heguy), Robert Sean Leonard (DeMille Bly).
RUNNING TIME: 116 minutes.
DVD: Warner Home Video.

A rookie race car driver is mentored by a former champion who still suffers from the physical and emotional scars of a crash years earlier.

D2: THE MIGHTY DUCKS (1994)

DIRECTOR: Sam Weisman. SCREENPLAY: Steven Brill. PRODUCERS: Jon Avnet, Jordan Kerner. CINEMATOGRAPHY: Mark Irwin. EDITING: John F. Link, Eric Sears. MUSIC: J. A. C. Redford. PRODUCTION DESIGN: Gary Frutkoff. ART DIRECTION: Dawn Snyder. COSTUME DESIGN: Grania Preston.
CAST: Emilio Estevez (Gordon Bombay), Kathryn Erbe (Michele MacKay), Michael Tucker (Tibbles), Jan Rubes (Jan), Joshua Jackson (Charlie Conway).
RUNNING TIME: 106 minutes.
DVD: Walt Disney Video.

Heady with his success, the coach of the Ducks takes on a new opportunity that will bring him further fame.

D3: THE MIGHTY DUCKS (1996)

DIRECTOR: Robert Lieberman. SCREENPLAY: Steven Brill, Jim Burnstein, Kenneth Johnson. PRODUCERS: Jon Avnet, Jordan Kerner. CINEMATOGRAPHY: David Hennings. EDITING: Colleen Halsey, Patrick Lussier. MUSIC: J. A. C. Redford. PRODUCTION DESIGN: Stephen Storer. ART DIRECTION: Harry Darrow. COSTUME DESIGN: Kimberly A. Tillman.
CAST: Emilio Estevez (Gordon Bombay), Jeffrey Nordling (Ted Orion), Joshua Jackson (Charlie Conway), David Selby (Dean Buckley), Heidi Kling (Casey Conway).
RUNNING TIME: 104 minutes.
DVD: Walt Disney Video.

The team heads off to a new school and a new coach.

E

ED (1996)

DIRECTOR: Bill Couturié. SCREENPLAY: David M. Evans. STORY: Ken Richards, Janus Cercone. PRODUCER: Rosalie Swedlin. CINEMATOGRAPHY: Alan Caso. EDITING: Robert K. Lambert, Todd E. Miller. MUSIC: Stephen Endelman. PRODUCTION DESIGN: Curtis A. Schnell. ART DIRECTION: Michael L. Fox. COSTUME DESIGN: Robin Lewis-West.
CAST: Matt LeBlanc (Jack "Deuce" Cooper), Jayne Brook (Lydia), Bill Cobbs (Tipton), Jack Warden (Chubb), Gene Ross (Red), Paul Hewitt (Bucky).
RUNNING TIME: 94 minutes.
DVD: Universal Studios.

Unfunny comedy about a minor league baseball player who's forced to share his room with a chimpanzee who also plays on the team.

EDDIE (1996)

DIRECTOR: Steve Rash. SCREENPLAY: Steve Zacharias, Jeff Buhai, Jon Connelly, David Loucka, Eric Champnella, Keith Mitchell. PRODUCERS: Mark Burg, David Permut. CINEMATOGRAPHY: Victor Kemper. EDITING: Richard Halsey. MUSIC: Stanley Clarke. PRODUCTION DESIGN: Dan Davis. ART DIRECTION: Robert K. Shaw Jr. COSTUME DESIGN: Molly Maginnis.
CAST: Whoopi Goldberg (Edwina "Eddie" Franklin), Frank Langella ("Wild Bill" Burgess), Dennis Farina (John Bailey), Richard Jenkins (Carl Zimmer), Lisa Ann Walter (Claudine), John Salley (Nate Wilson), Rick Fox (Terry Hastings).
RUNNING TIME: 100 minutes.
DVD: Walt Disney Video.

This simple-minded comedy is a basketball fantasy that trots out cliché after cliché in a plot that moves so quickly the bad guys have trouble maintaining their villainy. Whoopi Goldberg plays Edwina (Eddie) Franklin, a widow who drives for a limousine company and fills her spare time coaching a youth basketball team and rooting for the New York Knicks from the nosebleed seats at Madison Square Garden.

The plot veers into fairytale land when Eddie, while on the job, calls in to a radio show with advice for the Knicks' new owner, only to discover that her passenger *is* the Knicks' new owner, "Wild Bill" Burgess (Frank Langella). Wild Bill is a self-made millionaire whose interest in basketball is commercial; he's more concerned with increasing box office receipts than with winning. When, from the owner's box, he spots Eddie giving the Knicks' coach, John Bailey (Dennis Farina), a rough time, he arranges for her to sit on the bench with Bailey as an honorary coach. A dispute with

Coach Bailey gets her kicked off the bench, but Bill realizes that Eddie is a crowd pleaser and insists she return as guest coach for the next game. This is too much for Bailey, who resigns, and Bill appoints Eddie to replace him.

Eddie knows exactly what's wrong with the Knicks: they aren't playing together as a team, and individually, they've lost focus. Superstar Stacy Patton (Malik Sealy, who died in an automobile accident in 2000) is so enmeshed in a celestial ego trip that he refers to himself in the third person and refuses to pass the ball. Terry Hastings (Rick Fox), preoccupied with divorce proceedings, doesn't shoot when he's open. Russian Ivan Radovadovich (Dwayne Schintzius) can speak only three words of English—"Ivan make basket." The players are too busy shooting ads and music videos and granting interviews to practice.

At first, none of the players takes Eddie seriously, and several have reservations about being coached by a woman, but they all make too much money to carry out a protest and quickly quit complaining. Fan objections to a woman at the helm are typified by a construction worker who tells an interviewer he's giving his tickets to "the little woman," a decision he later regrets. However, the film glides over gender issues. During a literally steamy shower scene, Eddie mocks the ordinary endowments of the prize athletes; because the camera stays on Eddie rather than on the men, the reversal of sexual objectification is incomplete. Throughout, Eddie refers to the players as "girls" and "ladies," indicating a lack of feminist consciousness on her part. The role of the coach was originally written for a man and went to Goldberg after Billy Crystal turned it down. It appears little modification was done to accommodate the change in the character's sex. It is the veteran, Nate Wilson (John Salley), sidelined with bad knees, who advises Eddie to demonstrate more concern for the players as complete individuals, not just highly paid athletes. As a result of their talk, she counsels Terry on winning back his wife, learns enough Russian to coach Ivan effectively, and takes a hit showing him how to defend against a charge. She benches Stacy temporarily for hogging the ball and enlists his mother to help contain his ego.

The result of Eddie's efforts is a winning streak that puts the Knicks on track for the playoffs. Throughout, Wild Bill has supported Eddie, and on the eve of the deciding game against the Charlotte Hornets, now coached by Bailey, Bill gives Eddie the key to her own penthouse and a million-dollar contract, but there's one catch: the penthouse is in St. Louis—Bill has arranged to sell the team, contingent on their final victory. When Eddie objects that the team belongs in New York, her challenge to Bill's authority transforms him from a good-natured, flamboyant businessman into a vicious tyrant. After claiming that he owns not only the team but also the coach, he sneers that in the Knicks he purchased a circus and that she is his clown.

At the deciding game, Eddie shows up just before it starts. Bailey has instructed the Hornets to go after Nate, and they do, taking him out of the game in the second half. Eddie puts in Stacy, who is ready to play well with the others, and with ten seconds left, the Knicks have a single point lead. Eddie signals for a time out, seizes a microphone, and moves to the center of the court, where she discloses Bill's plan to sell the team and announces she isn't moving. She's quickly joined by her assistant coach, the players, led by Stacy, and the Hornets, including Bailey, who doesn't want to win by a disqualification. A security guard joins the protest, followed by droves of fans. Bill descends from the owner's box to deny publicly that he's selling the team and to admit privately to Eddie that she's outsmarted him. In the remaining seconds of the game, Ivan holds his ground against a charge up the lane, and the Knicks win.

The film's apparent theme is that commercialization and self-promotion pose a threat to professional basketball, but the film itself is an obviously commercial venture that features product placement and celebrity cameos. In addition to the NBA players in credited roles—Sealy, Salley, Fox, Schintzius—and the players playing themselves on opposing teams, there are appearances by Fabio, Donald Trump, and the mayors Koch and Giuliani. Goldberg was nominated for a RAZZIE Award (Worst Actress) but lost out to Demi Moore for her performance in *The Juror.*

EIGHT MEN OUT (1988)

DIRECTOR: John Sayles. SCREENPLAY: John Sayles, based on the book *Eight Men Out* by Eliot Asinof. PRODUCERS: Sarah Pilsbury, Midge Sanford. CINEMATOGRAPHY: Robert Richardson. EDITING: John Tintori. MUSIC: Mason Daring. PRODUCTION DESIGN: Nora Chavooshian. ART DIRECTION: Dan Bishop. COSTUME DESIGN: Cynthia Flint.

CAST: John Cusack (Buck Weaver), Clifton James (Charles Comiskey), Michael Lerner (Arnold Rothstein), Christopher Lloyd ("Sleepy" Bill Burns), John Mahoney (Kid Gleason), Charlie Sheen (Hap Felsch), David Strathairn (Eddie Cicotte), D. B. Sweeney (Shoeless Joe Jackson), Michael Rooker (Chick Gandil), James Read (Claude "Lefty" Williams).

RUNNING TIME: 119 minutes.

DVD: MGM.

In 1919, Chicago White Sox first baseman "Chick" Gandil devised a scheme to throw the World Series, allowing a gambling syndicate to profit by betting on Chicago's underdog opponents, the Cincinnati Reds. Because of animosity between Chicago players and team owner Charles Comiskey, Gandil was able to involve a number of key players in the fix. However, early betting created rumors among sportswriters who kept a close eye on plays and players, and the following year a grand jury was convened. When the dust had settled, eight players were banned from baseball for life, including the illiterate Shoeless Joe Jackson, who accepted money but played well in the series, and third baseman Buck Weaver, who did not participate in the fix but knew about it and failed to report it. *Eight Men Out,* the story of the "Black Sox" scandal, is based on Eliot Asinof's book. The film, directed and scripted by John Sayles, does not condone the players' actions, but it clearly sympathizes with the men and demonstrates why a players' union became necessary to protect athletes from unscrupulous owners.

One of the challenges of this type of film is developing depth when presenting a large number of primary characters. Sayles employs a shifting focus to reveal the complexity of the scandal and its effects. Some reviewers found Sayles's treatment too destabilizing, particularly for audiences not familiar with the story. Roger Ebert, writing for the *Chicago Sun-Times* (September 2, 1988), described the film as "unfocused" and criticized Sayles for failing to individualize his characters. Rita Kempley, in the *Washington Post* (September 23, 1988), identified similar weaknesses and derisively called the picture "'Matewan' at Comiskey Park," a reference to Sayles's 1987 film about attempts to unionize West Virginia miners. In the *New York Times* (September 2, 1988), Janet Muslin also cited *Matewan,* but made a favorable comparison; in contrast to Ebert and Kempley, she praised Sayles's approach for avoiding "pious oversimplification."

The opening scene establishes parallels between baseball and traditional American values as two boys hawk newspapers to earn money for bleacher seats to the game that will send the White Sox to the World Series. The boys' enthusiasm for the sport foreshadows the immortalized "Say it ain't so" plea of a young fan to Shoeless Joe Jackson after the scandal. At the stadium the film jumps between the stands, the press box, the locker room, and the playing field while presenting the major characters in the drama. Before the game, the manager, Kid Gleason (John Mahoney), stresses the importance of individual sacrifice for the good of the team; the players squabble among themselves. During the game, gamblers scout the players to determine which are essential to their scheme and which are most likely to cooperate. When the victorious Sox return to the locker room, they discover, in lieu of bonuses, owner Charles Comiskey (Clifton James) has rewarded them with flat champagne.

Almost from the beginning it is clear that Charles is so miserly that several players are ready and willing to throw the Series. When pitcher Eddie Cicotte (David Strathairn) won his twenty-ninth game, Charles had him benched so that he could not collect a ten-thousand-dollar bonus for a thirty-game season. Realizing how frustrated their teammates are, Chick Gandil (Michael Rooker) and Swede Risberg (Don Harvey) discuss the possibility of pulling off a fix. Chick approaches the shady Sport Sullivan (Kevin Tighe), who has connections to big-time gambler Arnold Rothstein (Michael Lerner). After Chick recruits Eddie, who is worried that his arm won't hold up for another season, two other players commit themselves to the conspiracy—starting pitcher Claude "Lefty" Williams (James Read) and outfielder Hap Felsch (Charlie Sheen). Joe Jackson (D. B. Sweeney) yields to peer pressure without apparently understanding what he has involved himself in. Buck Weaver (John Cusack) is portrayed as an ethical man who is opposed to the plan but who chooses loyalty to his teammates over fidelity to the sport. The eighth man, Fred McMullin (Perry Lang),

The "Black Sox" of *Eight Men Out*

blackmails the others for a cut when he learns of the plan, but like Buck, he doesn't contribute to the fix.

On game day Eddie has been instructed to hit the first batter if the fix is in. He fires his first pitch across the plate, but the second strikes the batter, and the gamblers know to place their bets. Although some of the players are concerned about looking bad and Joe doesn't want to play at all, they follow through on their commitment, and Cincinnati takes the opener 9–1. Suspicions mount quickly. During the second game, a plane drops a dummy in a White Sox uniform on the field. Kid, who doubts that Lefty has his heart in the game, stares down at the dummy and quips, "Ask if it can pitch." Some of the fielding, base running, and hitting lapses are so obvious that journalists Ring Lardner (John Sayles) and Hugh Fullerton (Studs Terkel) begin tallying them. It seems as if everyone knows that the Sox are on the take. On the train Lardner sings "I'm Forever Blowing Ballgames" to the tune of "I'm Forever Blowing Bubbles." Eddie is even asked if the rumors are true.

Meanwhile, the players' anxiety mounts. The gamblers have made only a partial payment to the men, claiming that their backer's money is reinvested in additional bets. Slowly, the players realize they will never receive the balance promised them; they have no legal recourse. Their attempt to apply pressure on the gamblers by winning a game results only in threats of violence to which the players easily yield. In turn, the gamblers are intimidated by Arnold Rothstein, who has manipulated the fix so that he has never been directly involved. When news of the scandal breaks, he is immune to prosecution and leaves for Europe until the scandal is resolved.

When the newspapers print stories about the World Series being rigged, pressure is brought to bear on Charles, who promises an investigation and offers a ten-thousand-dollar reward for any evidence. With a trial looming, the leagues select Judge Kenesaw Mountain Landis (John Anderson) as the baseball commissioner; he is appointed for life and granted absolute authority. Judge Landis attends the trial of the players, some of whom have signed confessions, but those confessions have, as they say, "gone missing." The trial, which contains some comic moments, ends with a "not guilty" verdict, despite all the evidence to the contrary. However, Chicagoans do not want their heroes sullied. Landis's letter banning the eight from baseball is read as the players celebrate after their exoneration.

Years later Buck is in the stands watching a semipro baseball game and sees an older player in shallow center field. As the man sprints to catch a fly, Buck knows it is Shoeless Joe. When another fan thinks he recognizes Joe, Buck says Joe was the best, but the player on the field is not him. He adds that those guys are all gone now. Another fan describes the Black Sox as "bums from Chicago." When Joe catches Buck's eye, he tips his hat to him.

The film includes quite a bit of footage from the Series. Sayles had his actors train with former pro Ken Berry and watch newsreels of games from the time period. He also commissioned replicas of vintage equipment. Sweeney and Sheen are particularly convincing as big-league ballplayers. Editing by John Tintori is first rate.

8 SECONDS (1994)

Director: John G. Avildsen. Screenplay: Monte Merrick. Producer: Michael Shamberg. Cinematography: Victor Hammer. Editing: J. Douglas Seelig. Music: Bill Conti. Production Design: William J. Cassidy. Art Direction: John Frick. Costume Design: Deena Appel.

CAST: Luke Perry (Lane Frost), Stephen Baldwin (Tuff Hedeman), Cynthia Geary (Kellie Frost), James Rebhorn (Clyde Frost), Carrie Snodgrass (Elsie Frost).
RUNNING TIME: 105 minutes.
DVD: New Line Home Video.

The film is based on the life of Lane Frost, a professional bull rider whose life was cut short.

ELMER, THE GREAT (1933)

DIRECTOR: Mervyn LeRoy. SCREENPLAY: Thomas J. Geraghty, based on the play by Ring Lardner and George M. Cohan. CINEMATOGRAPHY: Arthur Todd. EDITING: Thomas Pratt. ART DIRECTION: Robert M. Haas. COSTUME DESIGN: Orry-Kelly.
CAST: Joe E. Brown (Elmer Kane), Patricia Ellis (Nellie Poole), Frank McHugh (Healy High-Hips), Claire Dodd (Evelyn Corey), Preston S. Foster (Dave Walker).
RUNNING TIME: 74 minutes.

This is the second film in a baseball trilogy featuring comedian Joe E. Brown, preceded by *Fireman, Save My Child* (1932) and followed by *Alibi Ike* (1935).

ENTER THE DRAGON (1973)

DIRECTOR: Robert Clouse. SCREENPLAY: Michael Allin. PRODUCERS: Paul Heller, Bruce Lee, Fred Weintraub. CINEMATOGRAPHY: Gilbert Hubbs. EDITING: Yao Chung Chang, Kurt Hirschler, George Watters. MUSIC: Lalo Schifrin. COSTUME DESIGN: Louis Sheng.
CAST: Bruce Lee (Lee), John Saxon (Roper), Kien Shih (Han), Ahna Capri (the hostess), Angela Mao Ying (Su Lin), Jim Kelly (Williams).
RUNNING TIME: 98 minutes.
DVD: Warner Home Video.

Enter the Dragon is the last film Bruce Lee completed before his death at age thirty-two. The film was added to the Library of Congress National Film Registry in 2004 and is generally considered a classic martial arts picture distinguished by expertly choreographed action scenes.

Lee plays a Shaolin student (named Lee) sent by his teacher to deal with a rogue former student, Han (Kien Shih), who has disgraced the temple and who was responsible for the death of Lee's sister. An international intelligence agency is also eager to dispose of Han, who is engaged in the white slave trade and drug trafficking. Han lives on an island near Hong Kong but outside of its jurisdiction, preventing authorities from executing searches there. He operates a martial arts school at his compound, where he is hosting a competition to which Lee has been invited. Also included are two Americans: Williams (Jim Kelly), an African American who has run afoul of the Los Angeles Police Department, and Roper (John Saxon), a gambler who has accrued a good bit of debt with a bad sort of organization.

The athletes are treated to a lavish banquet where acrobats, wrestlers, and clowns perform. When a gong announces Han's arrival, the performers freeze in position, and the vast dining hall falls silent. Han conducts a demonstration in which he throws apples to the athletes, each pierced in midflight by a dart hurled by a female attendant. Lee's apple has been skewered by an undercover agent, Mei Ling (Betty Chung), allowing the two to communicate. Later that evening, the hostess (Ahna Capri) brings to each of the men a selection of women. Lee picks Mei Ling from the group in order to conduct a formal debriefing. Williams, unable to make up his mind, opts for the company of the entire selection. Roper shrewdly requests the hostess herself.

The next evening, acting on Mei Ling's information, Lee slips outside and locates a secret entrance to an underground facility where drugs are processed and where kidnapped women are imprisoned awaiting purchase and transport. When he returns to the surface, Lee is spotted by the guards but escapes without being identified. Williams, who has ventured into the garden, is recognized by a guard.

In the morning, Han warns the contestants that they are not to roam the grounds at night. Because the guards have not carried out their responsibilities, they are required to prove themselves against one of Han's assassins, Bolo (Bolo Young), who systematically breaks the necks of each. Next, Lee faces Han's bodyguard, O'Harra (Robert Wall), who was instrumental in the death of Lee's sister. Lee makes quick work of O'Harra, who in a fatal attempt to eliminate Lee, attacks him with a broken bottle.

By this point, both Roper and Williams have realized that this is no ordinary martial arts tournament; however, before they can extract themselves, Han confronts Williams. Although Williams dispatches Han's guards, he cannot defeat Han, who has a metal hand. Next, Han attempts to recruit Roper as his representative in the United States. Han gives Roper a tour of his operation during which they pass Williams's body. Roper stalls when asked for a commitment; Han, generously, does not have him murdered on the spot. Meanwhile, Lee has once again entered the facility and a spectacular fight sequence ensues as he fights off dozens of Han's henchmen—including Jackie Chan in one of his early roles. Finally, Lee is entrapped in a well.

The next morning, the competition is to continue. Han tries to pit Roper against Lee, but Roper refuses to fight; as an alternative, he must face the sadistic Bolo. Meanwhile, Mei Ling has been busy—she has freed the prisoners and contacted another agent, Braithwaite (Geoffrey Weeks). Roper's fight against Bolo has just gotten underway when chaos erupts. The freed prisoners converge upon the guards, and helicopters sent by Braithwaite descend upon the compound. Lee, who has been keeping an eye on Han, notices that he has now armed himself with a claw attached to his iron hand. Lee pursues Han through the palace.

Han exchanges the claw for a razor-edged set of fingers with which he is able to slash Lee, but the wounds are superficial. The battle between the two moves through the palace and into a hall of mirrors, where Lee must distinguish between his opponent and multiple reflections. Finally, Lee smashes the correct mirror and defeats Han. Back on the lawn, Lee finds Roper sitting on a lawn chair while the released captives polish off the last of Han's minions. The helicopters arrive, and the movie ends.

Enter the Dragon is Hollywood's first martial arts film, a joint venture between Warner Brothers, Golden Harvest, and Lee's production company. Its plot and characters resemble those of the James Bond 007 movies of the sixties; it has often been compared to *Dr. No* (1962).

EVERYBODY'S ALL-AMERICAN (1988)

DIRECTOR: Taylor Hackford. SCREENPLAY: Thomas Rickman, based on the novel by Frank Deford. PRODUCERS: Taylor Hackford, Ian Sander, Laura Ziskin. CINEMATOGRAPHY: Stephen Goldblatt. EDITING: Don Zimmerman. MUSIC: James Newton Howard. PRODUCTION DESIGN: Joe Alves. ART DIRECTION: George Jenson. COSTUME DESIGN: Theadora Van Runkle.

CAST: Dennis Quaid (Gavin Grey), Jessica Lange (Babs Rogers), Timothy Hutton (Donnie), John Goodman (Edward Lawrence), Carl Lumbly (Narvel Blue), Ray Baker (Bolling Kiely), Patricia Clarkson (Leslie Stone), Wayne Knight (fraternity pisser).

RUNNING TIME: 127 minutes.

DVD: Warner Home Video.

Everybody's All-American begins with a black-and-white newsreel about the "Gridiron Game of the Week," which features the football ability of LSU's (Louisiana State University) Gavin Grey—the Grey Ghost. The rest of the film focuses on the difference between what seems to be and what is—the real person behind the public persona. Gavin (Dennis Quaid), despite the adulation, is from the beginning uneasy about the fact that people think he is special. He realizes that "when [he] stop[s] making touchdowns, it's over." However, as time passes, he seems unable to shed his past and revels in retelling stories about his time in the spotlight. In contrast, his friend Donnie (Timothy Hutton) accepts change; Donnie becomes a history professor who has written about another Southern legend, Jefferson Davis.

Gavin's college days are filled with success. He carries his 1956 team to a national championship; marries Babs Rogers (Jessica Lange), the head cheerleader and homecoming queen; and is drafted in the first round by the Washington Redskins. Hangers-on want to use his name and benefit from his success, and one of them, Edward Lawrence (John Goodman), a coarse racist, is responsible for Gavin's financial problems. (He had persuaded Gavin to invest in a bar, which failed because of Edward's gambling debts. He had also tried unsuccessfully to get Gavin to alter the outcome of some of the football games.)

Edward introduces Gavin to Narvel Blue (Carl Lumbly), an outstanding black football player who never had the opportunity to play either in college or in the Canadian Football League. Narvel and Gavin compete in an impromptu 100-yard dash, which Gavin barely wins. Narvel is content with his life and rejects Gavin's offer of getting him a tryout with the Redskins. Instead, Narvel devotes himself to making substantial change by participating in the civil rights movement. Both Edward and Gavin reveal their own racism and seem

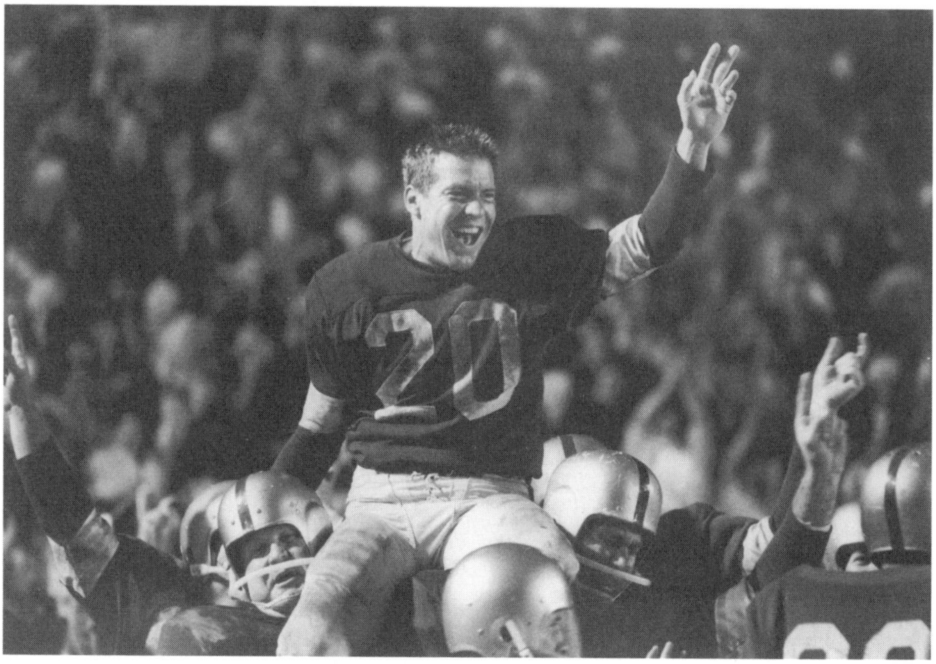

Dennis Quaid as the Grey Ghost in *Everybody's All-American*

almost unperturbed by the political unrest in the rest of the country.

Babs is an interesting figure in the film. Although she declares that she is majoring in Gavin, she is not content with being just a player's wife. When Edward's gambling almost ruins them, she goes to work for Bolling Kiely (Ray Baker), Gavin's partner in the resurrected bar/restaurant Edward mismanaged, but she is clearly responsible for the restaurant's success. Gavin, meanwhile, retires from football and becomes a pitchman for Terra Turf. When the American Football League beckons, however, he decides to quit working for Terra Turf and signs with the fledgling Denver Broncos. Babs elects not to go with him and asks Narvel, now a successful businessman and legislative candidate, for a job. While Gavin's football debut with the Broncos is marked by mediocrity (he watches as his substitute scores the winning touchdown in an important game), Babs proves herself to be an effective executive who can wheel and deal. Gavin is predictably upset by the role reversal. He accepts a job as an assistant golf pro and tries to persuade Donnie to ghostwrite his football memoirs. Donnie, too, has his problems. Devoted to Gavin, but constantly thrust by Gavin into Babs's company, he falls in love with her. Although they sleep together once, Donnie is unwilling to further betray Gavin and encourages Babs to "stand by her man." Edward is the film's most colorful character. Unfortunately, he is killed off early.

The film ends at LSU, where the school is celebrating the twenty-fifth anniversary of its national championship, and Gavin is the featured speaker. As Babs looks on, Gavin saves his marriage and himself with his speech. He declares that he played football because he loved it and goes on, Lou Gehrig–style, to call himself "the luckiest man alive," mainly because of Babs. Gavin is a basically decent man. He turns down Bolling's illegal offer of a car while he is at LSU and ignores Edward's talk of fixing football games, but he cannot give up his past and is prone to peer pressure. Gavin stands up Babs to go out with his teammates the night he retires, and Babs knows he and his teammates party with groupies. At the twenty-fifth reunion he leaves the stadium to visit the LSU mascot, a caged tiger. The tiger and Gavin are similar in that both are mascots, icons for fans, but they are also imprisoned, although Gavin is partly responsible for his own entrapment.

EVERYONE'S HERO (2006)

DIRECTORS: Colin Brady, Christopher Reeve, Dan St. Pierre. SCREENPLAY: Robert Kurtz, Jeff Hand. STORY: Howard Jonas. PRODUCERS: Igor Khait, Ron Tippe. CINEMATOGRAPHY: Jan Carlee, Andy Wang. EDITING: John Bryant. MUSIC: John Debney. PRODUCTION DESIGN: Dan St. Pierre.

CAST (VOICES): William H. Macy (Lefty Maginnis), Rob Reiner (Screwie), Brian Dennehy (Babe Ruth), Raven Symoné (Marti Brewster), Robert Wagner (Mr. Robinson), Richard Kind (Hobo Andy), Mandy Patinkin (Stanley Irving), Forest Whitaker (Lonnie Brewster), Whoopi Goldberg (Darlin').

RUNNING TIME: 88 minutes. Animated.

DVD: 20th Century Fox.

Everyone's Hero is an animated film produced by Christopher Reeve, who also conceived the story and worked out many of the scenes with his wife, Dana. The theme, most appropriately, is "never give up."

"Yankee" Irving, whose father is a maintenance worker for the 1932 Yankees, idolizes Babe Ruth and would love to be able to slug the ball, but he just can't connect. Even though he is so small that he offers "no strike zone" and could easily draw walks, he insists on swinging away, much to the dismay of the other boys on his team. On his way home after losing another game, the dejected Yankee spots a baseball under an abandoned car. The scruffy ball, which can talk, explains that he was in the majors once and dreamt of becoming a home run ball; instead he was fouled away and left outside to rot. "Screwie," as Yankee calls the ball, proves cranky and disagreeable—all he wants is to return to the abandoned car in the vacant lot where he can disintegrate in peace. Yankee is almost as depressed as Screwie. He tears down the baseball poster in his bedroom and is ready to give up his own dreams of someday playing in "the Bigs."

To cheer him up, his mother sends him to the stadium with his father's dinner, and his dad shows him Babe Ruth's locker. While his father goes back to work, Yankee stays behind, gazing at Darlin', Babe Ruth's lucky bat, until he's chased out by the scheming Cubs pitcher, Lefty Maginnis, disguised as a security guard. Lefty has been dispatched by the unscrupulous owner of the Cubs to steal Darlin' in hopes of sending the Babe into a slump that will help secure a Cubs' victory in the World Series. Lefty makes off with Darlin', and as a result, Yankee's dad is fired. It's up to Yankee to rescue Darlin', save the World Series, and clear the family name.

When Yankee recognizes Lefty from a baseball card, he figures the pitcher is intent on rejoining the team, which is en route to Chicago. Yankee, toting the reluctant Screwie, sets off in pursuit. Sure enough, he spots Lefty at Penn Station and manages to gain possession of Darlin', but not in time to board the train carrying the Yankees. The chase is on as Yankee heads west to catch up with the Babe, while Lefty is not far behind. There are numerous close encounters, but Yankee always escapes, aided by a group of hoboes, by a Negro League team from whom he receives coaching to improve his hitting, and by a reformed Screwie and the even more talkative Darlin'. Meanwhile, Yankee's parents have called the police and, with the help of the daughter of one of the Negro League players, are hot on the trail.

Just before the last game of the World Series, Yankee catches up with the Babe in a hotel restaurant, but Lefty snatches Darlin', and the team owner snatches Yankee, locking him in the owner's box during the game. As the Yankees fall behind, Yankee Irving is ready to concede defeat; however, Screwie provides a pep talk and helps him escape by breaking through the glass of the box. Yankee runs onto the field, chased by security until the Babe recognizes him and talks the manager into putting Yankee in to bat against Lefty. Wielding Darlin' and encouraged by Screwie, who has also gotten into the game, Yankee whacks Screwie out of the park, securing both of their dreams.

Everyone's Hero features an all-star cast doing the voices (William H. Macy as Lefty Maginnis, Rob Reiner as Screwie, Whoopi Goldberg as Darlin', Robin Williams as Mr. Cross) and some lively animation, but the story itself suffers from a number of gaps. Screwie and Darlin' are the only articulate inanimate objects, and their powers of speech are never explained. In order to remain faithful to the premise that individual effort is paramount, the script has Darlin' revealing, and Babe Ruth confirming, that Darlin' has nothing to do with performance: "It's the batter, not the bat." While the Babe's pronouncement places responsibility squarely on Yankee's shoulders when the boy goes to the plate, it doesn't explain why the theft of Darlin' sent the Babe into a slump, which in turn so demoralized the team that only Yankee Irving stands a chance at saving the day.

The film is also puzzling in that it establishes an historical setting that it fails to contextualize. The Depression is hinted at by the presence of friendly hoboes at a railroad yard, but there is no indication that the country is in the throes of an economic crisis and that the firing of Yankee's father could have dire consequences for the family. More disconcerting is that the film treats the Negro League as if it exists in a separate-but-equal universe into which Yankee has stumbled. The effect is to present racial segregation as unproblematic. Anachronisms throughout may create some humor for adult viewers, but their incorporation as normal parts of everyday life in the 1930s provides but another opportunity for misunderstanding by young viewers.

Christopher Reeve died before the film was completed, and his wife succumbed to lung cancer before it was released. The film did not do well at the box office, and reviews were, at best, lukewarm.

THE EXPRESS (2008)

DIRECTOR: Gary Fleder. SCREENPLAY: Charles Leavitt, based on the book by Robert Gallagher. PRODUCER: John Davis. CINEMATOGRAPHY: Kramer Morgenthau. EDITING: Padraic McKinley, William Steinkamp. MUSIC: Mark Isham. PRODUCTION DESIGN: Nelson Coates. ART DIRECTION: Seth Reed. COSTUME DESIGN: Abigail Murray.

CAST: Rob Brown (Ernie Davis), Dennis Quaid (Ben Schwartzwalder), Darrin Dewitt Henson (Jim Brown), Omar Benson Miller (Jack Buckley), Nelsan Ellis (Will Davis Jr.), Charles S. Dutton (Willie "Pops" Davis), Clancy Brown (Roy Simmons).

RUNNING TIME: 130 minutes.

DVD: Universal Studios.

Ernie Davis was the first African American to win the coveted Heisman Trophy, presented yearly to the best collegiate football player in America. *The Express* is based on Robert Gallagher's book, *The Express: The Ernie Davis Story* (1983). While the film, which was highly promoted, played to a mixed critical response, it features a good script by Charles Leavitt and solid performances by the lead actors, Rob Brown as Davis and Dennis Quaid as Syracuse University coach Ben Schwartzwalder. Brown, whose first acting role was as the basketball player/aspiring writer in *Finding Forrester* (2000), played football while he was a student at Amherst College between pictures.

In the beginning of the film "lines" are identified as the theme. Lines are dividers, not only on highways, but with regard to class, geography, and race. The first sequence, shot in black and white to provide an historical context, features young Ernie (Justin Martin) and his cousin Will (Justin Jones) walking the railroad tracks and picking up bottles to return for cash. They are then confronted by a gang of young white toughs who believe that the blacks have crossed the line, invading their territory. When the white boys demand the bottles, Will runs away, but Ernie, who has the bottles, runs forward, staying on the wrong side of the line. He breaks attempted tackles and sprints, football player-like, away from his pursuers. Like Forrest Gump, his running leads directly to his success on the football field.

The action soon switches from South Salem, a poverty-stricken western Pennsylvania mining town where he has lived with his grandparents, to Elmira, New York, where his mother, who is separated from her husband, moves him. While the family lived in Pennsylvania with "Pops" Davis, his grandfather, Ernie acquired solid values; in New York, he plays football, first in middle school, where he and another young black player are the only ones not to get regular uniforms, and then in high school, where his achievements draw many recruiters, including Coach Schwartzwalder. In order to convince Ernie to come to Syracuse, Schwartzwalder gets Jim Brown (Darrin Dewitt Henson), an All-American lacrosse and football player at Syracuse and then an outstanding professional football player with the Cleveland Browns, to help him recruit Ernie. Jim, who did not always observe the lines and consequently encountered some trouble with the coach, nevertheless glosses over the racism at Syracuse and grudgingly admits that Schwartzwalder is a good coach.

When Ernie arrives in Syracuse and walks the streets on his way to the campus, his greeting to a white storeowner is met with contemptuous coldness, and the situation is little better on campus. There are few black students, and Ernie and his new football player pal, Jack Buckley (Omar Benson Miller), do not see any black coeds, whom Jack describes as being as rare as "white buffalos." On the practice field the reception is hostile, and one linebacker who is criticized for not tackling Ernie, hits him after a play is over. Schwartzwalder does not sympathize with Ernie, who was not at fault for the ensuing fight, and observes to his assistants that Ernie will have to learn to deal with more than a late hit. After one practice Ernie smiles at a white cheerleader, who reciprocates, but Ernie has crossed another line, as his coach explains to him. When Ernie finds Jim Brown's number 44 football jersey in his locker and is taunted by teammates who compare him to Jim, he goes to the coach, who tells him that he has assigned that number to Ernie. Whether or not he likes it, he is the new Jim Brown, and expectations are high.

The Jim-Ernie relationship is important to the story because initially the two men are opposites: Jim carries a chip on his shoulder and offends white authorities; the shy and good-natured Ernie seems indifferent to the racial conflict dividing the country. As the film progresses, however, Ernie, thanks in part to his cousin Will's prodding, acquires a bit of an "edge," confronts his coach, and becomes involved in the civil rights movement.

Ernie stars on the field, and in 1959 Syracuse is contending for the national championship. One of the roadblocks is the University of West Virginia, whose fans are depicted as racist bigots. In the course of the game Ernie successfully runs the ball to the West Virginia three yard line, but there is a problem. The coach replaces Ernie with another running back who scores on the next play. Why was Ernie replaced? The coach explains that he does not want Ernie to cross the goal line, ostensibly because it would offend the West Virginia fans. The explanation upsets Ernie, who has never been replaced except for an injury, and he asks the coach if the lines are his, not the opponents'.

After going undefeated, the team must decide which bowl game to play in. The players opt to face second-ranked Texas and travel to the Cotton Bowl. The racist atmosphere in Houston is highly charged. When the Syracuse players arrive at their hotel, they discover that blacks are not allowed. Finally, Ernie and Buckley are housed in a decrepit room. During the game, which consumes about twenty minutes of screen time, the Texas coach encourages his two outstanding defensive tackles to take Ernie out. After several late hits and flagrant fouls, none of which the referees apparently notice, Ernie is hurt and subsequently benched. He does not take the field for the second half, but Jim Brown's visit to the locker room inspires him to return to the game, where Texas has erased the Syracuse lead. Of course, Ernie's reappearance rejuvenates Syracuse, which wins with Ernie crossing the goal line to secure the victory. He is carried off the field on his teammates' shoulders and is voted the game's Most Valuable Player. However, the championship trophies are scheduled to be awarded at a country club that does not admit blacks, so Syracuse chooses not to attend the presentation and has its own celebration in Houston. The trophies are brought to the team later at the hotel.

Ever since Ernie's arrival at Syracuse, where photos of the Heisman winners are on display in the sports building, the question of who will win the trophy has been before the audience, and the next important scene is at the Heisman presentation, where Ernie receives the award. Following the season, Ernie is selected first in the draft by the Washington Redskins, who quickly trade him to the Cleveland Browns. The Browns want to have Ernie in the same backfield as Jim Brown, whose college rushing records Ernie has broken.

Ernie's career comes to an abrupt end when, after collapsing during practice, he is diagnosed with leukemia. Before Ernie dies, he helps Schwartzwalder recruit another number 44, Floyd Little, who went on to star at Syracuse and to play professional football. In a scene reminiscent of the earlier one with Jim and Ernie, Ernie tells Floyd essentially what Jim had told him: Schwartzwalder is a good coach. The "mantle" thus passes from Jim to Ernie to Floyd.

While reviewers generally found Davis's story inspiring, the film has been criticized for its depiction of racist behavior at the University of West Virginia and at the Cotton Bowl. The *Charleston Daily Mail* (October 8, 2008) pointed out that in 1959, the West Virginia Mountaineers played at Syracuse, not at home; furthermore Schwartzwalder, a native West Virginian and former high school coach, was highly respected in his home state, and Mountaineer fans did not taunt his Syracuse teams. Some former players have claimed that the hostility of Texans at the Cotton Bowl has also been exaggerated. Writing for the *Chicago Sun-Times* (October 8, 2008), Roger Ebert states that the team boycott of the Cotton Bowl awards ceremony was not unanimous, evidence that the Syracuse Orangemen had not achieved the solidarity the film suggests.

F

FACING THE GIANTS (2006)

DIRECTOR: Alex Kendrick. SCREENPLAY: Alex Kendrick, Stephen Kendrick. PRODUCERS: Alex Kendrick, Stephen Kendrick. CINEMATOGRAPHY: Bob Scott. EDITING: Ryan Hensley. MUSIC: Alex Kendrick, Mark Willard. COSTUME DESIGN: Terri Catt.

CAST: Alex Kendrick (Grant Taylor), Shannen Fields (Brooke Taylor), Tracy Goode (Brady Owens), Chris Willis (J. T. Hawkins Jr.), Bailey Cave (David Childers).

RUNNING TIME: 111 minutes.

DVD: Sony Pictures.

This low-budget, Christian-themed film is about a losing high school football coach whose team resorts to prayer.

THE FAN (1996)

DIRECTOR: Tony Scott. SCREENPLAY: Phoef Sutton, based on the novel by Peter Abrahams. PRODUCER: Wendy Finerman. CINEMATOGRAPHY: Dariusz Wolski. EDITING: Claire Simpson, Christian Wagner. MUSIC: Hans Zimmer. PRODUCTION DESIGN: Ida Random. ART DIRECTION: Mayne Berke, Adam Lustig. COSTUME DESIGN: Daniel Orlandi, Rita Ryack.

CAST: Robert De Niro (Gil Renard), Wesley Snipes (Bobby Rayburn), Ellen Barkin (Jewel Stern), John Leguizamo (Manny), Benicio Del Toro (Juan Primo), Patti D'Arbanville (Ellen Renard), Chris Mulkey (Tim).

RUNNING TIME: 116 minutes.

DVD: Sony Pictures.

Tony Scott's adaptation of Peter Abrahams's baseball novel, *The Fan*, turns a story about a slumping hitter and an obsessed fan into a B-grade thriller displaying the usual excesses of the slasher flicks it so closely resembles. In spite of top-notch performances by Robert De Niro, Wesley Snipes, Ellen Barkin, and John Leguizamo, the film was panned by critics and performed miserably at the box office.

The Fan opens with a photo montage and voice-over of Gil Renard (De Niro) reciting a dreadful poem, presumably his own, about a baseball game and memories of being carried off the field in triumph. The scene jumps abruptly to Gil in his van on the phone with radio journalist Jewel Stern (Barkin). He is on the air live, defending the San Francisco Giants' decision to award slugger Bobby Rayburn a $40 million contract. Jewel, who has prearranged a call-in interview with Bobby (Snipes), allows Gil to speak directly to the player, who appreciates Gil's defense of his salary.

Having established a direct contact between fan and athlete, Scott cuts back and forth between locker room and boardroom. Bobby has discovered that his agent,

Manny (Leguizamo), has failed to negotiate his uniform number as part of the trade because Giant Juan Primo (Benicio Del Toro) already wears number 11 and isn't willing to surrender it. Simultaneously, on the other side of town, Gil is watching his boss demonstrating Renard Knives' latest product: a cheap, foreign-made dagger. Gil, whose father founded the company, complains about the poor quality of material and craft, but his boss counters that cheap and replaceable goods are what people want. Parallel editing helps establish Gil's identification with the ballplayer as does Gil's belief that people should expect well-made knives to be expensive—just like home run–producing outfielders.

The parallels continue as the camera follows both men "on the job." Gil's sales have been slipping; he's losing old accounts and failing to secure new ones. His forced patter as he demonstrates his wares to a potential client readily gives way to angry outbursts. Bobby is having similar difficulty sticking to an acceptable public relations script as Jewel presses him about personal topics, such as his divorce, and other reporters are poised to exploit any resentment they sense among the lesser-paid Giants. Bobby explodes at Manny just after a photo op with a hospitalized child who requests Bobby hit a home run for him. The boy, who, like Bobby's son, is named Sean, is dying. As with the Babe Ruth/Johnny Sylvester story, Bobby homers, but the gravely ill Sean has slipped into a coma and dies without ever knowing Bobby has fulfilled the request.

When Gil takes his son, Richie (Andrew J. Ferchland), a little leaguer, to opening day, it becomes apparent that Gil is using the boy only to relive his own youth and to mask his obsession. He scolds Richie for watching the team mascot instead of the game and drills him on baseball dos and don'ts. "Baseball is better than life," Gil claims. "It's fair." As an example, he cites the sacrifice fly, which not only is a noble deed but also doesn't count against the batter's average. In spite of the nobility he attributes to the sport, Gil behaves badly as a fan, yelling at others in the stands and stomping on Richie's foot in an attempt to catch a foul ball. During the middle innings, Gil abandons Richie at the stadium while he rushes to an appointment with a client. It turns out that the client is at the ballgame, compliments of another Renard sales rep. By the time Gil makes his way back to the stadium, his son has been taken home by an older couple who had been sitting nearby.

Soon Gil loses his job and his visitation rights. Meanwhile, Bobby has gone into a slump, and Juan, still wearing number 11, is on a streak. Gil, who seems to think his own problems can be resolved through Bobby, begins stalking him. At a bar frequented by the players, Gil tries to talk to Bobby but is ignored. When Bobby and Juan go into the restroom, Gil follows and ducks into a stall, where he overhears the two arguing about the uniform number, which Bobby has offered to buy from Juan. Gil calls Jewel's radio program to offer his theory that Bobby's poor performance at the plate is due to Juan's not surrendering the number. A few days later, Gil follows Juan into a sauna and insists he give up the number for the good of the team. Juan's response is to turn and show Gil an "11" tattooed on his bicep. Gil pulls out one of his knives and expertly slashes Juan's femoral artery, fatally wounding him.

When the Giants play their next game, all wear Juan's number on their sleeves, and Bobby, batting cleanup in Juan's old position, starts hitting. Gil watches televised interviews and listens to Jewel's program, eager to hear Bobby credit his success at the plate to Juan's murder. But Bobby expresses only sadness at his team-

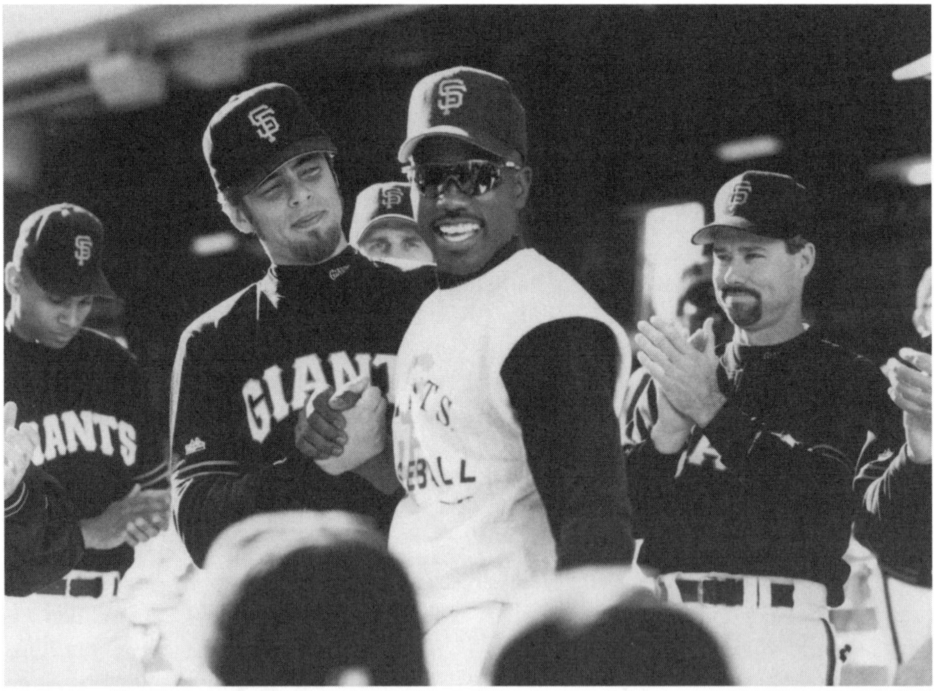

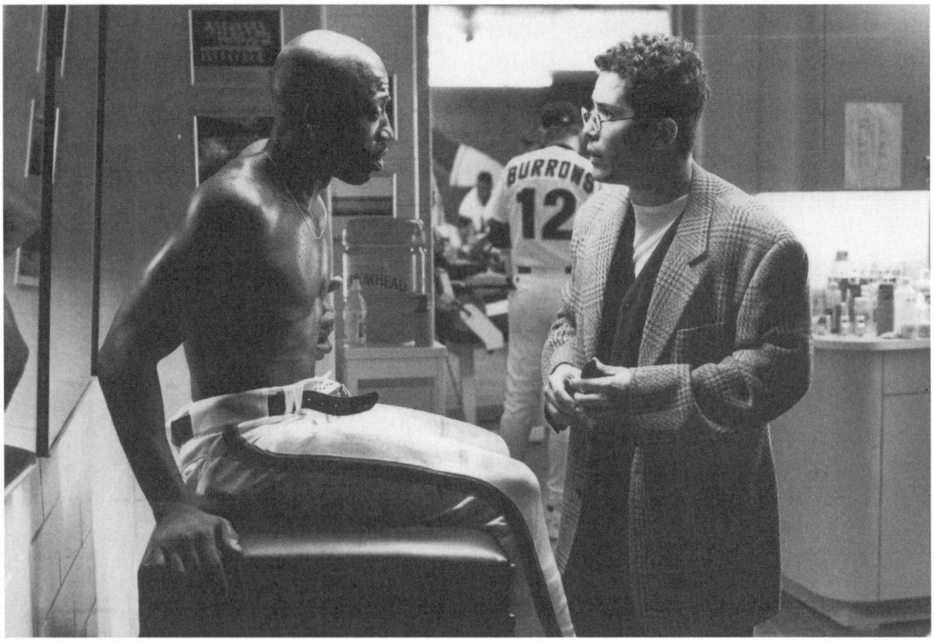

Top: Wesley Snipes (center) and Benicio Del Toro (center left) are rival teammates in *The Fan*; bottom: Snipes and John Leguizamo

mate's death. Gil, who has gone completely around the bend, expects to be thanked. He sets out to obtain Bobby's gratitude, and from here on, the plot's logic breaks down as Gil turns into a comic book villain able to defy the usual laws of time and space.

Watching Bobby's house through binoculars, Gil spots Bobby's son, Sean (Brandon Hammond), playing on a surfboard in the shallow water. When the family puppy upsets the board, Gil is the first to reach the beach and pull the frightened child from the water. Bobby insists Gil come inside to dry off. In Bobby's closet, Gil finds an old uniform with the number 11, which he puts on, then tops with a warm-up jacket. After asking if Bobby is Barry Bonds, Gil introduces himself as "Curly" and says he follows the game but gives no indication of his obsession. The casual attitude Gil feigns prompts Bobby to remark that he considers "die-hard" fans losers. When Bobby again thanks Gil and offers a return favor—a cue that it's time for Gil to leave—Gil responds by asking to throw him a few pitches.

Outside, Gil asks Bobby about his hitting streak and Juan's death. To Gil's dismay, Bobby reiterates his sorrow and says that he is now hitting well because he no longer cares. He refuses to concur with Gil's idealized view of baseball. Before throwing his last pitch, Gil removes the jacket and turns slowly so that Bobby can see the number 11 on the uniform. Realizing something is not right about Gil, Bobby calls it a night and starts moving toward the house. Gil shouts at the retreating figure to look in his freezer.

In the freezer Bobby finds Juan's tattoo. Then he runs upstairs to Sean's room, but his son is not there. The scene shifts to Bobby's SUV. Gil is behind the wheel, and Sean sits in the passenger seat playing with a switchblade, a scene that echoes Gil and Richie's trip to the stadium on opening day. Gil drives to a rail yard where his childhood friend and little league teammate, Coop (Charles Hallahan), is the night watchman. Gil persuades Coop to take Polaroids of him and Sean holding knives in their teeth. Then Gil insists they all play ball. As he fires a pitch inside to Sean, Coop realizes Gil is a tad crazed and tries to help Sean escape. However, Gil kills Coop and recaptures Sean. Next, Gil calls Bobby and demands that at the upcoming game he dedicate a home run "to Gil—a true fan."

Meanwhile, Bobby has contacted the authorities, and Jewel, who has learned of the situation from Manny, realizes her frequent caller is the kidnapper. A detective examining the Renard knife used in Juan's murder solves the rest of the puzzle. After interviewing Richie, the police mobilize, headed for the abandoned park where Gil played Little League and where they are certain Sean is hidden. At Giant Stadium, Bobby is not having a good day at the plate, and the weather is threatening to put an early end to the game. As the raindrops begin, Bobby steps up for his last at bat only to discover the pitcher intends to walk him. The call is two balls and no strikes when the umpire decides to delay the game.

When play resumes, it is still raining. The opposing team has apparently not been told of Gil's threats, but the pitcher does aim for the plate. Down two strikes, Bobby connects, but the well-hit ball bounces off the top of the wall. By this time the rain is pouring, and the field has turned into a morass. Bobby goes for an in-the-park home run, and slides into the plate well ahead of the ball. To everyone's surprise, he is called out—because Gil is the man in the umpire's suit! Armed with another knife, Gil holds the two teams and a bevy of armed officers at bay until it becomes apparent he is going to throw the knife at Bobby. The officers open fire, riddling Gil with bullets, but his chest protector allows him a dying monologue, unrepentant and unrevealing.

The entire post-rain-delay scene and Gil's death are intercut with shots showing the progress of the rescue team that has been dispatched to the abandoned ballpark where Sean is believed to be. Strangely, it is Bobby who arrives in time to save his son, who is bewildered but unharmed. In closing, the camera pans the bizarre baseball shrine Gil has set up there—bobble heads, souvenirs, his Little League trophies, and clippings of both his and Bobby's achievements.

The Fan leaves the viewer trying to negotiate the plot holes rather than contemplating the nature of hero worship and its effects on both heroes and worshippers. De Niro prepared for his role by reviewing audio tapes of convicted celebrity stalker and murderer Robert John Bordo. Snipes and Leguizamo, who costarred in *To Wong Foo Thanks for Everything, Julie Newmar* (1995), recapture their old chemistry. Former Baltimore Oriole Cal Ripken Jr. worked as a technical consultant on the film.

FAST BREAK (1979)

Director: Jack Smight. Screenplay: Marc Kaplan, Sandor Stern. Producer: Stephen Friedman. Cinematography: Charles Correll. Editing: Frank J. Urioste. Music: David Shire, James DiPasquale. Production Design: John Barry. Art Direction: Norm Baron.

Cast: Gabe Kaplan (David Greene), Harold Sylvester (D.C.), Michael Warren (Tommy "Preacher" White), Bernard King (Hustler), Reb Brown (Bull), Bert Remsen (Bo Winnegar).

Running Time: 107 minutes.

VHS: Vidmark/Trimark.

This comedy is about a New York City basketball coach who moves to a college in the Midwest, along with some street players.

FAT CITY (1972)

Director: John Huston. Screenplay: Leonard Gardner, based on his novel. Producers: John Huston, Ray Stark. Cinematography: Conrad L. Hall. Editing: Walter Thompson. Production Design: Richard Sylbert. Costume Design: Dorothy Jeakins.

Cast: Stacy Keach (Tully), Jeff Bridges (Ernie), Susan Tyrrell (Oma), Candy Clark (Faye), Nicholas Colasanto (Ruben).

Running Time: 100 minutes.

Academy Award Nominations: Best Supporting Actress (Tyrrell).

DVD: Sony Pictures.

An alcoholic fighter on the decline crosses paths with a young up-and-comer.

FEAR STRIKES OUT (1957)

Director: Robert Mulligan. Screenplay: Ted Berkman, Raphael Blau, based on the story by Jimmy Piersall, Albert S. Hirshberg. Producer: Alan J. Pakula. Cinematography: Haskell Boggs. Editing: Aaron Stell. Music: Elmer Bernstein. Art Direction: Hilyard Brown, Hal Pereira. Costume Design: Edith Head.

Cast: Anthony Perkins (Jim Piersall), Karl Malden (John Piersall), Norma Moore (Mary), Adam Williams (Dr. Brown), Perry Wilson (Mrs. John Piersall), Peter J. Votrian (young Jim Piersall).

Running Time: 100 minutes.

DVD: Paramount.

Anthony Perkins stars as the troubled Boston Red Sox outfielder Jim Piersall in this biopic based on Piersall's memoir of the same title. The film follows Piersall from his teens through his first year in the major leagues and subsequent hospitalization as a result of a breakdown. The real Jim Piersall later criticized the film for portraying his father as the source of all of his mental problems, noting that his mother spent much of his childhood institutionalized. In the film Piersall's mother plays a very minor role; however, she is presented as supportive in contrast to his hypercritical father, and her own mental illness is alluded to only briefly as a time that she was away. As media historian Hal Erickson suggests in *The Baseball Filmography*, the film's treatment of the elder Piersalls is in keeping with conventions of the time that idealized motherhood while often demonizing fathers.

The film establishes the significance of John Piersall (Karl Malden) by opening with a scene of him losing his job after an altercation with his foreman. In spite of the fact that he has just been fired and his wife is not feeling well, he goes outside to practice ball with Jimmy (Peter Votrian as young Jimmy), insisting that Jimmy will grow up to play for the Red Sox. John hurls ball after ball with as much force as he can; even though the pitches sting Jimmy's hand and he appears fatigued, the boy doesn't complain. The film cuts ahead to Jimmy as a teenager pitching his high school team to a state championship. Afterward, John criticizes Jimmy for small lapses before telling him that the Red Sox are going to scout him next year when he is a senior. John keeps the pressure on his son to prepare for the future, not allowing him time to socialize. The only time Jimmy sneaks away, to go ice skating with friends, he breaks his ankle, sending his father into near cardiac arrest. While John undergoes an electrocardiogram, Jimmy lies on his bed as shadows from the bedrail fall across him like bars on a cage, signifying the emotional prison in which he is trapped.

By spring both father and son have recovered physically, but their relationship remains unchanged. When the scouts from the Red Sox appear, John demands Jimmy get a hit but warns him not to slide. Jimmy reaches base, and in defiance of his father, slides not once, but twice. His actions earn praise from the scouts, deflecting criticism from his father; they also suggest Jimmy's subconscious desire to resist his father and to escape from his father's dreams by injuring himself. Jimmy is offered a contract to join the Red Sox farm team in Scranton, Pennsylvania, prompting his father to raise the bar, now demanding that Jimmy work his way onto the major league team by the end of the year.

In Scranton Jim applies himself as if his father were still monitoring him. Finally, at the urging of a teammate, he asks out Mary (Norma Moore), a nurse whom he had encountered after a practice. The two fall quickly in love, and when the minor league season ends, Jim is reluctant to return home. Although he tells Mary he's too insecure about his future to get married, in the next instant, he declares his love and proposes. While waiting in his hotel room for Mary to phone him about wedding arrangements, Jim overhears a radio broadcast during which the sportscaster expresses doubts about whether Jim is ready to move up to the majors. Angered, Jim begins to lose control, first shouting for someone to turn down the radio, then pounding on the wall.

In the next scene, the newlyweds are living with Jim's parents and are already expecting when Jim learns from his father that the Red Sox are sending him to their Louisville farm team. John offers no encouragement, instead predicting that Jim will "rot in the minors." At Louisville Jim's hitting improves, and by the time the baby is born, he is confident he will be called up for next season and talks of building a bigger house for the whole family. Back in Waterbury, however, his confidence abandons him, his mood shifts, and he wants to scrap plans to move into the larger house.

Shortly after, Jim is summoned to the head office of the Red Sox, where the general manager, Joe Cronin (Bart Burns), offers him a position with the team at shortstop rather than in the outfield, where he is accustomed to playing. Jim talks to his father before accepting the offer, then visits Fenway Park, where, alone, he experiences an auditory hallucination. His mental condition continues to deteriorate, and once he returns home, he tells Mary that Boston is putting him at shortstop in order to get rid of him. Then he runs to a nearby baseball field and cowers under the bleachers until his father arrives and scolds him as if he were a child misbehaving.

At the Red Sox spring training camp, Jim overworks. At the beginning of the season he plays well but does not get along with his teammates, who he believes do not put enough effort into the sport. Labeled a "problem boy" by the press, he is first benched and then suspended for fighting. John intervenes with Joe Cronin on his son's behalf, asking that Joe put Jim back in the outfield, where he is more comfortable. Joe agrees, but in the next game, Jim goes berserk after hitting a home run and must be restrained by the police. This violent outburst lands him in a mental hospital, where he undergoes electroshock therapy and intense sessions with a psychiatrist, Dr. Brown (Adam Williams).

Jim makes slow progress. The largest obstacle is his inability to admit to himself his anger with his father. When Dr. Brown confronts him about the harsh criticism and the pressure, Jim defends his father, proclaiming without a trace of irony that he wouldn't be where he is today without his father pushing him. Soon afterward, John, who has not been allowed to visit, sneaks into Jim's room and berates his son for feeling sorry for himself. This unauthorized visit proves a turning point that puts Jim in touch with his anger. Jim understands that his father loves him, but he fears he can never see him again and that he will never return to professional baseball. Dr. Brown, unlike John, provides encouragement to which Jim readily responds.

When Jim is ready to see his father again, John finds him bouncing a ball against a wall. Jim states that he wants to return to the Red Sox and tosses the ball to John. The two men play catch, gently, in contrast to the movie's first scene of young Jimmy practicing with his dad. The film ends with Jim's return to the Red Sox. Although nervous, he walks from the locker room toward the light of the ballpark as the final credits roll.

Fear Strikes Out is the first feature film of Robert Mulligan, who in 1963 was nominated for an Academy Award for *To Kill a Mockingbird.* In spite of some trite conventions, such as themed music to indicate Jim's mood shifts, and a melodramatic script, *Fear Strikes Out* is cinematographically interesting. Like Hitchcock in *Strangers on a Train* (1951), Mulligan uses shadows to cage young Jim, and his interior shots reinforce the unhappy ballplayer's growing sense of imprisonment. The closing shot of Jim poised at the end of the tunnel leading from the locker room to the ball field parallels so closely shots of the corridor of the mental hospital that any optimistic response to Jim's return is visually undermined. In contrast to sports biopics of the forties, like *Pride of the Yankees* (1942) and *The Stratton Story* (1949), this film does not present baseball as an arena for success, and the hero's brave return is not marked by memorable speeches, accomplishment through hard work, and cheering crowds. The real Jim Piersall, however, was back playing for Boston by the time the film was released.

FEVER PITCH (1996)

DIRECTOR: David Evans. SCREENPLAY: Nick Hornby, based on his memoir. PRODUCER: Amanda Posey. CINEMATOGRAPHY: Chris Seager. EDITING: Scott Thomas. MUSIC: Bob Hewerdine, Neil MacColl. PRODUCTION DESIGN: Michael Carlin. ART DIRECTION: Karen Wakefield. COSTUME DESIGN: Mary-Jane Reyner.
CAST: Colin Firth (Paul Ashworth), Ruth Gemmell (Ms. Sarah Hughes), Neil Pearson (Paul's father), Lorraine Ashburn (Paul's mother), Mark Strong (Steve).
RUNNING TIME: 102 minutes.
DVD: Lions Gate.

Nick Hornby's memoir, *Fever Pitch*, has been twice adapted for the silver screen. He wrote the screenplay for the 1997 U.K. version, which, like the memoir, is set in England and traces the making of an Arsenal football (soccer) fan and the effects of his obsession on his adult relationships. The U.S. version (2005), directed by the Farrelly brothers and starring Jimmy Fallon, converts the main character to a fanatical Boston Red Sox supporter who undergoes a radical personality shift each baseball season.

In *Fever Pitch* (U.K., 1997) Colin Firth plays Paul Ashworth, a popular teacher and soccer coach at a small London school. His obsession with the sport and with the Arsenal team began when he was a boy struggling with his parents' divorce. A trip to a match with his father, whose visits had become widely spaced and horridly stilted, resulted in young Paul bonding with Arsenal rather than with his father. A series of flashbacks connects the adult fan who allows the sport to undermine his personal life with the lad for whom soccer provided a sense of belonging.

Paul's life is complicated by the arrival at his school of a new teacher, Ms. Sarah Hughes (Ruth Gemmell), whose reserved and polished manner clash with Paul's raucous teaching and casual style. The two dislike one another immediately. Paul's friend Steve (Mark Strong) and Sarah's flatmate, Jo (Holly Aird), accurately predict a romance will blossom in the near future. In short order, Paul offers Sarah a ride home from school on a rainy evening; Sarah invites Paul in for coffee. After telling him he can't smoke in the flat, she adds that he is welcome to spend the night.

The relationship starts off smoothly. Sarah is amused by Paul's attachment to Arsenal and admits to Jo that she is taking a bit of an interest in the sport. Six months later, she attends a match with Paul, but is greatly put off by the press of the crowd and the jostling as people make their way through the stadium; when she learns of fans being trampled, her horror prevents her from comprehending how Paul can contemplate ever attending another match. They quarrel, and Sarah leaves.

The rift is a short one. Paul intuits that Sarah is pregnant, seeks a reconciliation, and vows to become a responsible husband and father. He applies for a promotion that earlier had not interested him, and the couple begin searching for a place to live. However, their reconciliation is also brief. They cannot agree on a flat, especially after Paul finds rooms literally within the shadow of Arsenal Stadium. Sarah grows weary of Paul's moods shifting with the football team's fortunes. His promotion is doubtful since Sarah's pregnancy has embarrassed school officials. When word arrives that Paul has been turned down for the position, Sarah arrives with condolences to find Paul terribly upset, not about the job, but about Arsenal's recent loss. So absorbed is he in the team that he thinks Sarah is talking about Arsenal rather than his job. Once more, they separate. At school, Paul ignores

Sarah, who appears to regret their split. He speaks with her only to announce he has taken a position with another school, where he can more comfortably carry out the role of the "absent father."

As the school term draws to a close, Sarah attends a party for graduating students and is surprised to find herself treated warmly by several girls who have brought her a present. However, her attention strays to the television. Arsenal is playing Liverpool in an important match. Impulsively, she leaves the party for Paul's. Meanwhile, Paul is reacting emotionally to each turn in the game. When Liverpool scores, he is ready to leave for a pub, but as Arsenal's game picks up, he is once again enthralled, so much so that he shouts "fuck off" when Sarah buzzes repeatedly at the door. Too late, he realizes it is Sarah. He runs downstairs, but instead of pursuing her, he hurries back to the telly, arriving just as Arsenal scores.

With Arsenal's win the street becomes alive, and Sarah is caught up in the celebration, she kisses an elderly man and dances with a group of children. Sitting on the bonnet of an automobile, she spies Paul in the crowd and watches as he picks up a baby. She calls to him; he approaches. They kiss, and a voice-over explains that their relationship improves, Paul having learned to distance himself from Arsenal.

Reviewers' responses were lukewarm. While acknowledging the performances of the leads and the thoughtful analysis given to fan obsession, most critics were troubled by the gap between the social role of sports for observers and the love story.

FEVER PITCH (2005)

DIRECTORS: Bobby Farrelly, Peter Farrelly. SCREENPLAY: Lowell Ganz, Babaloo Mandel, based on the memoir by Nick Hornby. PRODUCERS: Drew Barrymore, Alan Greenspan, Nancy Juvonen, Gil Netter, Amanda Posey, Bradley Thomas. CINEMATOGRAPHY: Matthew F. Leonetti. EDITING: Alan Baumgarten. MUSIC: Craig Armstrong. PRODUCTION DESIGN: Maher Ahmad. ART DIRECTION: Brandt Gordon. COSTUME DESIGN: Sophie de Rakoff.

CAST: Jimmy Fallon (Ben Wrightman), Drew Barrymore (Lindsey Meeks), James B. Sikking (Doug Meeks), JoBeth Williams (Maureen Meeks), Lenny Clarke (Uncle Carl), Willie Garson (Kevin), Ione Skye (Molly).

RUNNING TIME: 103 minutes.

DVD: 20th Century Fox.

In 1919, Boston Red Sox owner Harry Frazee sold Babe Ruth to the New York Yankees for $125,000 in order to finance a Broadway play. The play flopped, the Yankees went on to dominate the sport, and the Curse of the Bambino fell upon Fenway Park, assuring that the Sox would never win a World Series. When Bobby and Peter Farrelly began filming *Fever Pitch*, a romantic comedy about an obsessed Sox fan, the Boston team was ten games out of first place, and the curse seemed to be working as usual. Perhaps it was the script, based loosely on Nick Hornby's memoir of soccer fandom in England, that broke the curse, causing the Farrelly brothers to rework the ending to match the baseball history unfolding in the early autumn of 2004.

Ben Wrightman, played with a characteristic mix of charm and immaturity by Jimmy Fallon, is a high school teacher in his early thirties who has been a member of the Red Sox Nation for twenty-three years. He attended his first game with his Uncle Carl, who held season tickets for two box seats behind home plate. Uncle Carl willed the tickets to Ben, who has never missed a game. From October through March, Ben behaves like a responsible adult; then, like his cinematic predecessor, Vernon Simpson from *It Happens Every Spring*, he undergoes a dramatic change as he becomes preoccupied with the new baseball season.

The film first introduces "Winter Guy," the adult version of Ben, taking a group of students on a field trip to interview an up-and-coming professional who has turned her math skills into a lucrative career with a prestigious firm. The up-and-comer, Lindsey Meeks (Drew Barrymore), is anything but mild, and Ben returns without the students to ask her out. At first she turns him down, but after she realizes she's being snobbish about his profession, she calls to ask if the offer is still open. Their first date is a disaster because Lindsey has food poisoning, but Ben proves gallant and attentive, tucking her in bed, cleaning the bathroom, and attending to the dog. Once Lindsey recovers, the two begin spending more time together, and she invites him to a party, where he is scrutinized by her friends. Ben earns immediate acceptance by the men, whose conversation is focused on the Red Sox, but in another part of the house, the women are worried: Ben seems such a good catch that something must be wrong with him that he is still single. The extent of his character flaw becomes apparent as the scene cuts to Ben's apartment, which is filled with baseball souvenirs—Bo-Sox sheets and towels and Yankee toilet paper, bobble heads, pennants, and a complete Red Sox wardrobe.

Although Lindsey compares his apartment to a gift shop, it takes her a while to recognize the full force of his obsession. She is understanding when he turns down an invitation to meet her parents because he has planned to spend his spring break at the Red Sox training camp. Since Lindsey is up for promotion and working hard to impress the corporate bigwigs, the time Ben will spend attending games with his friends won't interfere with their relationship. However, she does accept an offer to join him on opening day when he presents her ticket in a ring box. Soon she begins accompanying him more frequently, even though she spends much of the time working on her laptop, to the dismay of the hardcore fans surrounding her.

This arrangement doesn't last. Between working every spare moment and post-game passion, Lindsey is exhausted; she has started to fall asleep at her desk. At one game she is hit by a foul ball, but Ben, caught up in the excitement of trying to grab the ball, doesn't realize she's been knocked out. A news clip of Ben and another fan exchanging high fives over Lindsey's unconscious body runs on the local stations. Lindsey decides she'll work late at the office instead of going to the games. As her promotion looks more certain, her office sends her to Paris on a short business trip. Lindsey wants Ben to come along, but he refuses because the Yankees will be in Boston that weekend. She reveals that her menstrual period is late, an announcement that does not elicit an immediate display of joy from Ben. Although this is a false alarm, the relationship has been damaged. Convinced that the Red Sox are more important to Ben than she is, she is ready to call off the romance.

Ben is crushed. In spite of his nervousness about parenthood, he's already purchased Red Sox infant apparel. After seeking advice from a student, who points out that the Red Sox don't reciprocate his affection, Ben tries to patch things up by skipping a game to take Lindsey to a costume party one of her friends is throwing. The two enjoy themselves immensely, and later that evening, Ben tells Lindsey it has been one of the best times of his life. But then the phone rings, and he learns from his friends that Boston, after an amazing comeback in the bottom of the ninth inning, has won, keeping their playoff hopes alive. Suddenly Ben is inconsolable because he's missed the game of a lifetime. Lindsey leaves, apparently for good. Ben slips into a depression, but after he spots a trio of Red Sox players relaxing over dinner following a loss, he realizes how far overboard he has gone. He rushes to Lindsey's apartment, where another man answers the door. Lindsey claims his presence is work-related, but it doesn't matter. She's too hurt to reconnect with Ben.

In a desperate act of self-punishment, Ben decides to sell his tickets to the husband of one of Lindsey's friends. Lindsey learns of this just before she receives word that she has been promoted. She is at the office in mid-champagne toast when she realizes that Ben is selling the tickets because of her. She rushes to the game to prevent him from going through with the sale, finally running across the playing field to reach him just in time. The film ends happily, with the couple reunited and an elderly fan who provided exposition at the beginning of the film narrating the details of the Red Sox breaking the Curse of the Bambino.

Fever Pitch captures the fever of Redsoxmania. It was filmed at a number of ballparks and includes footage from several games; the crowd scenes are composed of actual fans responding to real play, and numbers of fans kept their seats during postgame shooting. The final scene was shot during the fourth and final game of the 2004 World Series in St. Louis. Actors were permitted to join players on the field immediately following the Boston victory. Because the decision to travel to St. Louis was made at the last minute, the directors took only the stars and a few key crew members. Fallon and Barrymore got into costume in the plane and applied their own makeup. The Farrellys borrowed a camera from Fox News to capture the spontaneous reactions of fans and players and the unrehearsed exuberance of the actors.

Hornby wrote the screenplay for the 1997 British film, *Fever Pitch*, which more closely follows his memoir, and which is about soccer, not baseball. The themes are similar, but the comedy is more subtle, and the main character's observations about why sports matter to fans are quite serious.

FIELD OF DREAMS (1989)

DIRECTOR: Phil Alden Robinson. SCREENPLAY: Phil Alden Robinson, based on the novel *Shoeless Joe* by W. P. Kinsella. PRODUCERS: Charles Gordon, Lawrence Gordon. CINEMATOGRAPHY: John Lindley. EDITING: Ian Crafford. MUSIC: James Horner. PRODUCTION DESIGN: Dennis Gassner. ART DIRECTION: Leslie McDonald. COSTUME DESIGN: Linda Bass.

CAST: Kevin Costner (Ray Kinsella), Amy Madigan (Annie), Ray Liotta (Shoeless Joe Jackson), Timothy Busfield (Mark), Gaby Hoffmann (Karin), James Earl Jones (Terence Mann), Burt Lancaster (Doc Graham), Frank Whaley (Archie Graham).

RUNNING TIME: 107 minutes.

ACADEMY AWARD NOMINATIONS: Best Picture, Best Adapted Screenplay, Best Original Score.

DVD: Universal Studios.

Field of Dreams, an adaptation of W. P. Kinsella's novel *Shoeless Joe*, is a mystical film that elevates baseball to the level of religion. Kevin Costner, having completed the baseball film *Bull Durham* the previous year, stars as Ray Kinsella (a name author Kinsella borrowed from a J. D. Salinger short story), a former-hippie-turned-Iowa-farmer.

In a voice-over, Ray narrates a condensed family biography accompanied by a photo montage. His mother died when he was three, and his father, John, once a minor league player, raised him with the dream that he would become a ballplayer. As a rebellious teenager, Ray refused to continue playing ball, and, as he came to regret, refused even to play catch with his father. He elected to go to Berkeley for college because it was far away from home. On the West Coast, Ray became caught up in the antiwar movement and the acid scene. He married his college girlfriend, Annie (Amy Madigan), with whom he has a daughter, Karin (Gaby Hoffmann). His father died shortly after the wedding without ever meeting Annie and before Karin was born. Annie talked him into buying the Iowa farm, which he says is "the only crazy thing I've ever done." Ray is a risk-taker, and unlike his late father, is willing to act spontaneously. Although Ray is content on the farm, he is still troubled by the resentment he felt over what he saw as his father's lack of spirit. Now that he is older, Ray realizes that he is angry with his father for failing to follow his own dreams and for dying before he and Ray were reconciled.

When the film's action begins, Ray is walking through his lush, shoulder-high corn crop. Then a voice (uncredited) whispers from the stalks: "If you build it, he will come." Since Annie and Karin, who are sitting nearby on the porch swing, hear nothing, Ray begins to think he has experienced a sort of mirage from spending too much time alone on the acreage. Annie thinks he may be having an acid flashback. The next day, Ray turns off the television while Karin is watching *Harvey*, a Jimmy Stewart movie about a man who "sees" a giant, invisible rabbit. At the feed store, Ray asks some of the other farmers if they ever hear voices in their fields; they don't.

Back in his cornfield as he puzzles over the meaning of the message, Ray has a vision of a baseball diamond. He tells Annie that if he plows under his crop and builds a baseball field, Shoeless Joe Jackson, one of eight players banned from the sport for life as part of the 1919 "Black Sox" scandal, will return to play. Ray explains to Annie that his father considered Jackson the best hitter in the game and believed in Jackson's innocence. Understanding Ray's need to pursue this phantasm and drawn to its inexplicability, Annie lends her support. The next day Ray plows down the corn. As Karin rides on the tractor with him, he tells her about how well Jackson performed in the 1919 World Series, even though he had accepted money from gamblers to fix the games. The Kinsellas' astounded neighbors line the road to watch Ray destroy his cash crop.

Ray exhausts the family savings constructing the field, complete with stadium lights and bleachers, but no one comes. At Christmas the completed field lies snow covered and empty. In the spring as Annie and Ray pour over their finances, trying to determine how to make ends meet, Karin interrupts to say that there is a man outside. It's Shoeless Joe (Ray Liotta) in his

Kevin Costner as Ray Kinsella in *Field of Dreams*

White Sox uniform, ready to field a few balls. Ray pitches to Joe while Annie and Karin watch. When Joe introduces himself, Karin asks if he is a ghost, but Joe does not reply. He knows he cannot venture beyond the perimeter of the field. But before he disappears into the corn beyond the outfield, he asks Ray if he's in heaven. Ray answers that Joe is in Iowa.

The next day Annie's brother, Mark (Timothy Busfield), and her mother (Fern Persons) visit, concerned that they will lose the farm unless they plow the baseball diamond and replant. When Karin calls to the adults that play is about to begin, the Kinsellas discover that they are the only ones who can see or hear the athletes, yet all eight of the banned players are now on the field.

While the Black Sox enjoy themselves, Ray's troubles are mounting, for he has heard the voice again, commanding, "Ease his pain." While Ray ponders the meaning of the message, Annie drags him off to a PTA meeting, where an irate parent wants to ban a book by Terence Mann (James Earl Jones), an influential author and activist from the sixties who has retreated from the public eye. As Annie delivers an impassioned speech about freedom and Stalinist-style censorship, Ray realizes that his latest message refers to Terence. To decipher the meaning, he researches the author and learns that Terence wrote an early story about a baseball player named John Kinsella—Ray's father's name—and that in his last interview Terence discussed his love of baseball and dream of playing on a team with Jackie Robinson. Then Ray has a dream about taking Terence to a game at Fenway Park. When Annie realizes she and Ray have had the same dream, she encourages Ray to drive to Boston to find Terence, even though the Kinsellas are nearly broke and behind in their mortgage payments.

Ray has little difficulty tracking down the reclusive writer, but gaining an audience proves more challenging. The curmudgeonly Terence keeps an old-fashioned insecticide pump handy to send admirers "back to the sixties." In desperation, Ray pretends to have a gun, but Terence reaches for a crowbar and is ready to apply it to Ray's skull until Ray reminds him that he's a pacifist. Somehow, Ray persuades Terence to attend the game, where Ray finds a message on the scoreboard about "Moonlight" Graham, a minor leaguer who made it to the big leagues for a single inning. When the voice says, "Go the distance," Ray believes he should locate Graham. Ray is ready to leave Terence in peace, but Terence reveals that he too has seen the message.

Their search for Graham takes them to Chisholm, Minnesota, where a helpful librarian assembles clippings about Moonlight. After playing for half an inning in the majors, Graham left baseball for medicine and became a small-town doctor. Although Graham died in 1972, a number of residents remember him fondly, and Terence collects their stories of the good doctor and his wife, Alicia. Uncertain about his next step, Ray goes out for a walk and finds he has stepped into a time warp: it is 1972 and *The Godfather* is playing at the local cinema. Soon Ray meets Doc Graham (Burt Lancaster), who speaks of his unfulfilled wish to bat in the major leagues. Ray invites Graham to come to Iowa, but he refuses, saying his wife is expecting him home. Later that evening, Terence remarks that "a single inning can change the world," meaning that had Graham had the opportunity to display his talent during his inning, he may have remained in baseball, and Chisholm would have lost its doctor.

Ray and Terence start on the road back to Iowa. Annie has called saying they must sell the farm to her brother to avoid foreclosure. En route, Ray stops for a hitchhiker, a young man named Archie Graham, who is looking for a place to play baseball. It is night when they arrive at the farm. By this time there are enough players on the field for an actual game. Joe shouts, "Welcome back." Archie joins the game as a pinch hitter, and his long fly ball brings in a run.

The next morning, Mark demands that Ray sign over the property. Karin, who is sitting atop the bleachers, announces they don't need to sell because "people will come" and pay to watch. Inspired, Terence delivers a short speech on baseball as the singular constant good in American history. Ray refuses to sign, but in the course of a heated exchange with Mark, Karin falls from the bleachers. As she lies inert on the ground, Ray looks across the diamond to Graham, who runs toward the bleachers. When he crosses the boundary, he is transformed into old Doc Graham. He revives Karin, whose breathing passage was clogged by a chunk of hot dog. Having left the field of dreams, Graham cannot return to his ball playing youth; however, he is content with the brief experience and eager to get back to Alicia. Mark, who has witnessed Doc Graham's appearance, suddenly notices the men on the field and advises, "Don't sell the farm, Ray."

Joe tells Ray the players are finished for the day. He invites Terence to join them. At first Ray is disappointed and angry that he has not been included, but Joe explains there is a reason Terence was chosen and there is a reason Ray needs to stay. Terence realizes his purpose is to write about whatever lies beyond the outfield, and he follows Joe with a renewed sense of excitement about writing. Then Ray discovers why he needs to remain behind: the catcher, who is just removing his equipment, is his father, young John Kinsella (Dwier Brown). Repeating Joe's earlier question, John asks Ray, "Is this heaven?" and Ray responds, again, "It's Iowa." Then Ray asks John about heaven, and John answers, "It's a place where dreams come true." Ray glances back at his house, where Annie and Karin are on the porch, and concludes perhaps he has found heaven. Ray realizes that the messages referred not to Shoeless Joe or Terence Mann or Moonlight Graham, but to his father. Ray calls John "Dad" and asks him to play catch. Annie turns on the lights, and the two men toss a ball back and forth. The camera zooms out to reveal a line of cars stretching to the horizon, their headlights twinkling as darkness falls.

Field of Dreams, a box office success, generally received favorable reviews, and Costner, Jones, and Liotta were widely praised for making the fantasy seem believable. It was frequently termed "Capra-esque" and compared to *The Natural* (1984), with which it shares mystical elements—a pastoral ideal, significant father-son relationships, and the theme of redemption. However, *Field of Dreams* has been criticized for its romanticized, unproblematic vision. Although, as Ray explains to Karin, Shoeless Joe played well in the 1919 World Series, Ray never addresses the issue of why Joe accepted money from the gamblers backing the fix. Joe and the other Black Sox are granted redemption, but never held accountable for their misdeeds. And the more recently deceased, scandal-free players who Joe mentions will join his teammates are all white. Strangely enough, activist Terence Mann (who dreamed of playing with Jackie Robinson) fails to notice that baseball has become resegregated, and his redemption is presented as an apolitical one. As scholar Vivian Sobchack wryly notes, the movie "literally consume[s] a black radical in its corn" ("Baseball in the Post-American Cinema, or Life in the Minor Leagues," 186).

The film fails to examine the loss of idealism that troubles Terence, Ray, and Annie, and it overlooks the civil rights and feminist movements. Annie feels empowered at the PTA meeting when she calls another woman a "Nazi cow," but Annie spends much of the film in the kitchen. She and Karin retreat to the house or the porch swing for the dramatic moments. Neither enters the playing field, and Ray never invites his daughter to "have a catch." Scholars such as Andrew Britton ("Blissing Out: The Politics of Reaganite Entertainment") and Alan Nadal (*Flatlining on the Field of Dreams*) have discussed the film as a conservative response to the social reforms of the sixties and seventies that, in leveling the playing field through affirmative action, created a "crisis in white masculinity" as white men feared losing power and economic advancement to members of marginalized groups.

THE FINAL SEASON (2007)

Director: David M. Evans. Screenplay: Art D'Alessandro, James Grayford. Producers: Steven Schott, Michael Wasserman, Herschel Weingrod, D. Parker Widemire Jr., Tony Wilson. Cinematography: Daniel Stoloff. Editing: Harry Keramidas. Music: Nathan Wang. Production Design: Chester Kaczenski. Art Direction: Barry Gelber. Costume Design: Lynn Brannelly-Newman.

Cast: Sean Astin (Kent Stock), Rachael Leigh Cook (Polly Hudson), Powers Boothe (Jim Van Scoyoc), Michael Angarano (Mitch Akers), Mackenzie Astin (Chip Dolan), Tom Arnold (Mitch's father).

Running Time: 119 minutes.

DVD: Sony Pictures.

Sean Astin, who played the title character in the underdog sports film *Rudy* (1993), stars in *The Final Season*, a different kind of underdog film. Based on a true story, it concerns Norway High School (101 students), which has won nineteen Iowa high school baseball championships, but its quest for a twentieth is threatened when it loses its legendary coach, Jim Van Scoyoc (Powers Boothe). He has been transferred to Madison High School by Harvey Makepeace (Marshall Bell), the ironically named school superintendent intent on closing Norway and merging it with Madison. When Norway residents—all 586 of them—object to the merger, Harvey knows that they are partially motivated by the school's baseball success. He reluctantly agrees to keep the school open one more year, but he wants to ensure that the last season is a losing one. To achieve that goal, he decides to hire the worst coach he can find. He thinks he has located the perfect failure in Kent Stock (Astin), who once served as Van Scoyoc's assistant for two months and whose only head coaching experience is of a girls' volleyball team.

In addition to the baseball season, the film focuses on school consolidation. The state of Iowa, represented by Polly Hudson (Rachel Leigh Cook), maintains that financial savings can be realized through school mergers that eliminate duplicate courses and that require less staffing. However, small schools have their advantages, and from an athletic standpoint, students have a better opportunity to participate in team sports. Kent, who opposes Polly in the town meeting, also states that small towns affected by mergers die when the schools are closed. He challenges her to visit some of those towns and see the effects of merger firsthand. Kent says, "You don't know what you're killing."

Another theme is the relationship between father and son. After the death of his mother, Mitch Akers (Michael Angarano) and his father (Tom Arnold) are not getting along, so his father takes Mitch to visit his grandparents, Jared (James Gannon) and Anne (Angela Paton) Akers, in Norway. At dinner Mitch's father comes to the table late, misses the prayer, and then reprimands Mitch for not saying "ma'am." The grandfather states that Mitch is "supposed to learn that stuff from you." Instead, Mitch will learn from his grandparents and from Kent, who teaches him that "we don't do late."

After his father leaves, Mitch learns that his grandparents do not tolerate bad behavior. When he takes the pickup truck without permission, the police catch him, and, upon his return, his grandfather has some chores waiting. From his grandmother he learns that it is important to find something to do that he can put his heart into. That something is baseball, but his initial encounters with his classmates do not go well. A potential friend, Patrick Iverson (Brett Claywell), rebukes him for talking about drugs in the presence of Patrick's younger brother. When Mitch and Patrick play in a pickup game, Mitch acts like an angry loser. But Mitch does love the sport and approaches Jim about joining the team. Jim refers him to Kent, but he also adds a story about a player who didn't follow instructions and succeeded only in being benched. The player was Mitch's father.

After Kent watches Mitch hit in the batting cage, he wants Mitch to join the team, not as a catcher, which is his regular position, but as an outfielder. Instead of being upset, a normal reaction for him, Mitch accepts the assignment for the good of the team. Just as Mitch is being tested, Kent is challenged by his players, who don't believe that the ex-volleyball coach has the experience and skill to lead them. When he gets to the practice field, Kent finds the dugout full of volleyballs. Determined to demonstrate his competence, Kent tells Kevin Stewart (Nick Livingston), their top pitcher, to throw his best three pitches and Kent will hit one of them over the fence. To the players' surprise, he does and then structures his practice session the Jim Van Scoyoc way. After practice, Kent verbally spars with Roger Dempsey (Larry Miller), the sports reporter for the Madison paper, who seems ready to give Kent a chance.

Using Jim's tactics, Kent's team wins the first three games, but when the team goes on a losing streak, Kent's confidence in his coaching is shaken. Polly provides moral support. Then, following an injury to the starting catcher, Mitch takes over the position. Soon Norway resumes its winning ways and accrues a 17–12 record, enough to get the team into the sectional playoffs. In the final home game Mitch hits a triple and scores the winning run on a squeeze play called by Kent. Before the state finals, everything is going well for the main characters: Kent and Polly affirm their relationship with a moonlight game of catch; Mitch demonstrates to his father, who has returned to Norway to stay, how much he has matured by shaking hands and voluntarily helping with the luggage.

Before the Norway players board the bus for the finals, they each pick up some dirt from the Norway infield, which they later sprinkle on the playing field, symbolically making it their home turf. A caravan sets out as well, leaving the town deserted. Even the post office is closed. Prospects for a Norway win are dim because South Clay, their opponent, has Reed Ellis (Josh Merino), who throws a 95 mph fastball and is recruited by big league scouts. South Clay takes a 2–1 lead, but Patrick hits a home run, infuriating Reed, who berates his teammates for their lack of hitting support. Sammy, who is pitching for Norway, is timid at the plate, but he is determined to get on base, crowding the plate and almost daring Reed to throw inside. Sammy is hit by the next pitch and takes first base with the score tied at four. Mitch is at the plate, and, given the situation, is expected to bunt, just as his father had been instructed to do years earlier. When the South Clay infield pulls in, Mitch fakes a bunt and swings away, driving in Sammy with the winning run.

As the game ends, Kent and Jim exchange a tip of the hat, signifying the continuation of the tradition. After the game, one of Harvey's friends calls to tell him about the Norway victory. When Harvey says that it won't change anything, his friend answers, "But it will change the way you'll be remembered." Norway High School closes, but a postscript reveals that Kent continued coaching and then became a high school principal. Fourteen Norway players played professional baseball. Norway pre-high school teams won twenty state championships, and, most notably, Madison High School never won a state championship. The film ends with a father-son reconciliation, the growth and maturity of both Kent and Mitch, and affirmation of the idea that baseball, when played the right way, builds character and solidifies community spirit.

THE FINAL TEST (1953)

DIRECTOR: Anthony Asquith. SCREENPLAY: Terrence Rattigan. PRODUCER: R. J. Minney. CINEMATOGRAPHY: William McLeod. EDITING: Helga Cranston. MUSIC: Benjamin Frankel. ART DIRECTION: R. Holmes-Paul.

CAST: Jack Warner (Sam Palmer), Robert Morley (Alexander Whitehead), Jim Laker (cricket player), Dennis Compton (cricket player).

RUNNING TIME: 84 minutes.

DVD: Odeon Entertainment (U.K.: PAL).

Acclaimed playwright Terrence Rattigan wrote this comedy about an aging cricketer who worries that his teenage son won't attend his final appearance in a test between England and Australia.

FINDING FORRESTER (2000)

DIRECTOR: Gus Van Sant. SCREENPLAY: Mike Rich. PRODUCERS: Sean Connery, Laurence Mark, Rhonda Tollefson. CINEMATOGRAPHY: Harris Savides. EDITING: Valdis Óskarsdóttir. PRODUCTION DESIGN: Jane Musky. ART DIRECTION: Robert Guera, Darrell L. Keister. COSTUME DESIGN: Ann Roth.

CAST: Sean Connery (Forrester), Rob Brown (Jamal), F. Murray Abraham (Professor Crawford), Anna Paquin (Claire Spence), Busta Rhymes (Jamal's brother), April Grace (Ms. Joyce), Michael Pitt (John Coleridge), Michael Nouri (Dr. Spence).

RUNNING TIME: 136 minutes.

DVD: Sony Pictures.

Finding Forrester is an underrated basketball film (strangely omitted from Randy Williams's book on best one hundred sports films) with a literate, tight script and fine performances by Sean Connery, Rob Brown, and F. Murray Abraham. Jamal (Brown) is an underachieving inner-city teenager who excels in basketball, earning him street respect. He also excels in writing, a talent he cautiously hides from his peers. Forrester (Connery) is a Pulitzer Prize–winning novelist who never published a second book and who, using the name "Mr. Johansen," lives in J. D. Salinger–like seclusion in an apartment near Jamal. From his window he observes Jamal and his friends playing basketball; they, in turn, speculate about Forrester. On a dare, Jamal climbs the fire escape up to Forrester's apartment, picks up a knife and a book, and, when Forrester surprises him, flees. In his haste he leaves behind his backpack, which contains his notebooks, but the next day Forrester throws the backpack, complete with corrections and comments, down to Jamal. Thus begins a deep friendship that few people can comprehend.

The mentor-apprentice relationship starts with Jamal writing five thousand words about why he shouldn't have broken into Forrester's apartment. The relationship intensifies after Jamal is offered a scholarship to the Mailor School, a Manhattan prep school. Although Jamal has ostensibly been approached because of his outstanding test scores (his grades are mediocre), Mailor expects him to play basketball.

Jamal finds the atmosphere at Mailor chilly. The only other African American student, also a basketball player, resents Jamal's presence and does not want to be associated with him. His English instructor, Professor Crawford (Abraham), is a pompous man who belittles students and pesters them for answers he knows they don't have. Crawford, a failed creative writer, has published one book of literary criticism, an analysis of Forrester's novel, *Avalon*. Crawford requires his students to read *Avalon*, and by the next time Jamal sees Forrester, Jamal has discovered his real identity.

Rob Brown as Jamal Wallace in *Finding Forrester*

Forrester agrees to take on Jamal as a student, but he has rules: no questions about him, his family, or why he wrote just one book; whatever work Jamal completes at the apartment must remain there. Forrester is willing to answer questions about the soup he serves, but will answer only "soup" questions in the future. At one point Jamal asks what it's like to write a book like his, and Forrester says, "Maybe you'll find out." To get Jamal started, Forrester gives him the manuscript of one of his own stories and tells him to type the title and first paragraph and then take off on his own.

At school Jamal is proving himself both academically and athletically. Following a game in which Jamal scores twenty-six points, there is a social event at which many alumni offer him their business cards and assurances of help should he need it. He dances with Claire Spence (Anna Paquin), who has become his closest friend at the school. Later, as he shows her how to defend against an opponent by touching her back, Claire's father, Dr. Spence (Michael Nouri), intervenes, temporarily disrupting the progress of their relationship. Jamal is not intimidated by Dr. Spence, even though he is a school trustee. After seeking advice from Forrester, Jamal presents Claire with an autographed copy of *Avalon*.

For Forrester's birthday, Jamal invites the reclusive author to a basketball game at Madison Square Garden, but the two become separated, and Forrester has an apparent attack of agoraphobia. Jamal finds him slumped on the floor. On their way home, he takes Forrester to Yankee Stadium, where he has arranged for his brother (Busta Rhymes), who works as a parking attendant there, to have the lights in the empty stadium turned on. The scene prompts Forrester to discuss the brother he attended Yankee games with and the fatal night he let his inebriated brother drive home by himself. Forrester's guilt over his brother's death lies behind his seclusion and his failure to publish a second book.

While Jamal has gained Forrester's trust, he has aroused only suspicion in Crawford, who is convinced that Jamal is plagiarizing. When Crawford insists he write his next paper under supervision, Jamal freezes under the pressure and is unable to perform. His problems with Crawford are compounded when Jamal submits for the school's writing competition the first paper that he had written at Forrester's. However, he failed to acknowledge that the title and first paragraph were copied from Forrester's work. Crawford recognizes Forrester's writing—the piece had been published years earlier—and demands that Jamal write a letter of apology to the class for his dishonesty. Even Forrester agrees that he should apologize to prevent more trouble from Crawford. Then Claire's father tells Jamal that if Mailor wins the championship game, the whole incident can be forgotten.

With the game on the line and Jamal shooting two foul shots, victory for Mailor seems inevitable, since Jamal had earlier made fifty straight foul shots in practice. However, he misses both shots, and Mailor loses. Jamal seems doomed. When he visits the playground, the camera photographs him through the fence, suggesting that he cannot return to his pre-Mailor life, yet he seems to have sealed his fate at the school.

The writing competition is held before the student body and the school officials. After the first competitor reads his paper, Forrester enters the classroom, is introduced by the obsequious Crawford, and proceeds to read a paper which is greeted with resounding applause. Forrester then informs the audience that the paper is not his, but Jamal's, and that Jamal is his friend. He adds that Jamal has given him what he had wished for, the gift of friendship. Jamal is judged the winner of the writing contest. As Forrester and Jamal leave the classroom, Forrester, who had seen the missed foul shots on television, asks Jamal if he missed them on purpose. Jamal responds that this is a "non-soup" question. When Forrester tells him that he plans to visit Scotland, Jamal says, "Be sure to write."

A year later Forrester's lawyer notifies Jamal that Forrester has died of cancer in Scotland and that he has left his estate to Jamal. When he and his family go to Forrester's apartment, Jamal finds the knife, which Forrester used as a letter opener, and a letter informing him that he has completed another novel for which he wants Jamal to write an introduction. The book suggests Forrester has rediscovered himself after expunging his guilt and reentering the world outside his window, while Jamal has found the writer within himself.

Director Gus Van Sant won an award at the Berlin International Film Festival, and Rob Brown, a high school athlete with no prior acting experience, won a Young Artist Award. Brown later played Ernie Davis in *The Express* (2008).

FIREBALL 500 **(1966)**

Director: William Asher. Screenplay: William Asher, Leo Townsend. Producers: Samuel Z. Arkoff, James H. Nicholson. Cinematography: Floyd Crosby. Editing: Fred Feitshans, Eve Newman. Music: Les Baxter. Art Direction: Daniel Haller. Costume Design: Richard Bruno.

Cast: Frankie Avalon (Dave), Annette Funicello (Jane), Fabian (Leander), Chill Wills (Big Jaw), Harvey Lembeck (Charlie Bigg).

Running Time: 92 minutes.

DVD: MGM.

Beach blankets take a back seat to this Funicello-Avalon vehicle in which Frankie plays a stock-car driver.

FIRED UP! (2009)

DIRECTOR: Will Gluck. SCREENPLAY: Freedom Jones. PRODUCERS: Matthew Gross, Peter Jaysen, Charles Weinstock. CINEMATOGRAPHY: Thomas Ackerman. EDITING: Tracey Wamore-Smith. MUSIC: Richard Gibbs. PRODUCTION DESIGN: Marcia Hinds. ART DIRECTION: Bo Johnson. COSTUME DESIGN: Mynka Draper.

CAST: Eric Christian Olsen (Nick Brady), Nicholas D'Agosto (Shawn Colfax), Sarah Roemer (Carly Barkley), Molly Sims (Diora), Philip Baker Hall (Coach Byrnes), John Michael Higgins (Coach Keith).

RUNNING TIME: 90 minutes.

DVD: Sony Pictures.

Two football players in search of new female conquests attend a summer cheerleading camp.

FIREMAN, SAVE MY CHILD (1932)

DIRECTOR: Lloyd Bacon. SCREENPLAY: Ray Enright, Robert Lord, Arthur Caesar. CINEMATOGRAPHY: Sol Polito. EDITING: George Marks. ART DIRECTION: Esdras Hartley.

CAST: Joe E. Brown ("Smokey" Joe Grant), Evalyn Knapp (Sally Toby), Lillian Bond (June Farnum), Guy Kibbee (Pop Devlin).

RUNNING TIME: 67 minutes.

This is the first film in a baseball trilogy featuring comedian Joe E. Brown, followed by *Elmer, the Great* (1933) and *Alibi Ike* (1935).

THE FISH THAT SAVED PITTSBURGH (1977)

DIRECTOR: Gilbert Moses. SCREENPLAY: Jaison Starkes, Edmond Stevens. STORY: David Dashev, Gary Stromberg. PRODUCERS: David Dashev, Gary Stromberg. CINEMATOGRAPHY: Frank Stanley. EDITING: Frank Mazzola, Peter Zinner. MUSIC: Thom Bell.

CAST: Julius Erving (Moses Guthrie), James Bond III (Tyrone Millman), Stockard Channing (Mona Mondieu), Jonathan Winters (Harvey Tilson), Meadowlark Lemon (Reverend Grady Jackson), Jack Kehoe (Setshot).

RUNNING TIME: 102 minutes.

DVD: Warner Bros. Archives.

A basketball team turns to an astrologer to help it turn around its losing ways. The film features many real-life players, including Kareem Abdul-Jabbar.

THE FLYING SCOTSMAN (2007)

DIRECTOR: Douglas Mackinnon. SCREENPLAY: Jon Brown, Simon Rose, Declan Hughes. PRODUCERS: Peter Broughan, Claire Chapman, Peter Gallagher, Sara Giles, Damita Nikapota. CINEMATOGRAPHY: Gavin Finney. EDITING: Colin Monie. MUSIC: Martin Phipps. PRODUCTION DESIGN: Mike Gunn. ART DIRECTION: Ursula Cleary. COSTUME DESIGN: Alexandra Caulfield.

CAST: Jonny Lee Miller (Graeme Obree), Billy Boyd (Malky), Laura Fraser (Anne), Morven Christie (Katie), Steven Berkoff (Ernst Hagemann), Brian Cox (Douglas Baxter).

RUNNING TIME: 96 minutes.

DVD: MGM.

The Flying Scotsman is based on the life of Scottish cyclist Graeme Obree, who twice broke the world's one-hour record riding a bicycle he designed and built himself. However, Obree faced ongoing opposition from Hein Verbroggen, the head of the World Cycling Federation, who repeatedly changed rules in attempts to disqualify the young Scotsman. He also struggled with inner demons that he attributes to abuse at the hands of his peers when he and his brother were children. Obree was later diagnosed with bipolar disorder. His autobiography, *The Flying Scotsman: Cycling to Triumph through My Darkest Hours*, was published in Scotland in 2003.

The film opens with Graeme (Jonny Lee Miller)—although his face is not shown—carrying a bicycle through a wooded area bordering a bike trail. He drops his bicycle and tosses a length of rope over a tree branch; the scene ends with the camera focused on his shoes as he stands on a stump beneath the tree. The film then flashes back to Graeme's youth. It is the holiday season, and the school children are singing religious carols, but this harmonious moment dissolves into a violent one in the schoolyard as a pack of bullies lays into Graeme for no apparent reason. At home he faces his father, who advises Graeme to stand up for himself. Then his father brings out his Christmas present: a new bicycle.

The next scene jumps forward to Glasgow, 1993. Graeme is now married, working part-time as a bicycle courier, and operating a small bicycle shop, albeit one that is going out of business. He has also raced successfully, holding his own against England's Chris Boardman (Adrian Smith), who medaled in the Olympics the previous year. Graeme not only wants to challenge Boardman, but also has designs on the world's hour record, held since 1984 by the Italian Francesco Moser. The hour race is an individual time trial, run on a circular indoor track called a velodrome, usually in high altitudes to improve aerodynamics. The cyclist travels alone on the track while officials from Union Cycliste Internationale (UCI) record the distance traveled in sixty minutes. A gun is fired if the cyclist breaks the existing record, and a bell signals the end of the time period.

Graeme meets two people who will figure significantly in his plan to go for the record: a fellow courier, Malky (Billy Boyd), and a local priest, Douglas Baxter (Brian Cox). Douglas has come to the shop in need of a new crank; while he is there, Graeme challenges a customer—actually a rival shop owner—to a race, with Graeme cycling and the customer driving. At stake: the price of the bicycle the man has purchased. Douglas rides shotgun and holds the money. The customer wins, but only by causing Graeme to take a spill. Several nights later, Graeme and Malky pay a quiet visit to the customer's storage yard and emerge with a few key components of a disassembled bicycle. When they are spotted by a witness, they flee, but the witness turns out to be Douglas, who brings them the items they've dropped in their haste. Douglas and Malky join forces to support Graeme's drive to break the record. Douglas provides a workshop well stocked with tools and a collection of junk that can be mined for parts; Malky takes over the business end, soliciting sponsors and managing the finances.

Graeme works out on a stationary bike and concentrates on how to improve bicycle design. First, he reverses the handlebars to allow the rider to lean farther forward, mimicking the position of a skier taking off. Next, while lying on his back and pedaling in the air, he observes that the body's natural pedaling position keeps the feet closer together than an ordinary cycle allows, so he reduces the distance between pedals on his model. Then, after staring at a front-loading washing machine during a spin cycle, he cannibalizes the machine to remove its bearings and their housing. Fortunately, his wife, Anne (Laura Fraser), is a good sport. Meanwhile, Malky has located a sole sponsor who has contributed enough money for Team Obree to book a velodrome in Norway for twenty-four hours.

In Norway, Malky surprises Graeme with a bicycle he had engaged a world-class builder to make, based on Graeme's specs. The wheel manufacturer has agreed to sponsor Graeme for a year if he breaks the record. Although the new bike is slightly heavier, Graeme decides to use it. When officials from the World Cycling Federation (WCF) arrive, they raise questions about his odd-looking machine, but it passes their inspection, and Graeme is permitted to make an official run at the record. Although his first effort falls short of Moser's distance, Graeme refuses to give up. Since he has rented the space until the next afternoon, he determines to go for the record again the next morning. In order to keep his legs from cramping, he awakens every two hours to rehydrate. He avoids cramps but oversleeps, as does Malky, who has stayed up very late replacing the wheels on "Old Faithful" with the new set. In spite of their late start, they arrive at the velodrome in time for Graeme to race, and on this try, he succeeds. Afterward, as Anne and Malky celebrate, Graeme wanders off by himself, apparently unable to savor his victory.

Graeme's record doesn't stand for long. On the day that Boardman outdistances him by seven hundred meters in the sixty minutes, Graeme is unable to watch on television and instead goes riding. A bad tire forces him to alter his route, and he ends up in what he calls "the Valley of the Damned," the village where he grew up. Outside a pub where he has stopped to phone home, he is confronted by several of his former classmates. Once again, they harangue him. In the car with Malky, he determines to challenge Boardman in a four-kilometer pursuit race only a few weeks away. Graeme defeats his English rival in the semifinals, although Boardman is riding a carbon-fiber machine that cost half a million dollars. For the final, Boardman lends Graeme his helmet, and Graeme wins, setting a new record. Again, he suffers from a postvictory let down.

His triumph leads to an exhibition tour through France, but while he is enjoying the fruits of victory, Ernst Hagemann (Stephen Berkoff), chairman of the WCF, has called a meeting to tweak the rules in order to disqualify Graeme from future competition. Because he is setting records with a homemade bicycle, he poses a threat to future sponsorship: if a high-performance machine can be constructed in a garage, the officials reason, cyclists will not be readily persuaded to purchase expensive models. Ernst concludes that Old Faithful is unsafe and before the 1994 World Championships, begins a series of challenges. Graeme adds a pair of training wheels to prevent spills, unveiling his modification to the press and making the WCF a laughingstock. The next rule change specifies a longer distance between the post and the saddle. When Graeme takes a hacksaw to the tip of the seat, he's told he's now in violation of the "spirit" of the rule. He resolves this issue by using a saddle from a child's mountain bike. The final straw is a regulation that riders must maintain a gap between their hands and their chests. Since Graeme is the only cyclist who rides with his chest resting on his hands, the new rule is clearly intended to disadvantage him. Malky wants to use a tribar instead of Graeme's standard handlebar, but Graeme refuses. His race ends with a disqualification and a spill.

Back in Glasgow, Graeme slips into a depression, avoiding Malky and Douglas. One day, while Anne is at work, one of the bullies from his childhood shows up at his house. Graeme refuses to answer the door, hiding around the corner, but the ruffian peers through the letter slot and ridicules Graeme for his loss, intensifying his sense of worthlessness. Graeme takes off on his bike with a rope. The scene returns to the beginning of the film, but this time the feet push away from the stump. However, he's spotted by a passing cyclist and rescued before suffering any physical harm. After the suicide attempt Graeme begins to get himself back on track. He has a long talk with Douglas, whose wife, he learns, committed suicide; he also reconnects with Malky and soon is back in the saddle, in a new position inspired by his son's lunchbox. Riding in the "superman" position, Graeme wins the 1995 World Championships. The film closes on a note of uncertainty with a close-up that zooms in on Graeme's eyes until they fill the screen. The effect is chilling, suggesting he is in a manic phase soon to be followed by a crash.

Although the film portrays the head of the WCF as pursuing a personal vendetta against Obree and acting to protect commercial interests, in the real world of cycling, the UCI was concerned that technological innovation was damaging the integrity of the records, and other cyclists, including Chris Boardman, whose machine was designed and built by Lotus, also faced challenges from officials. Shortly after Obree's 1995 victory, the superman position was banned, as were disc wheels and tear-shaped time trial helmets. Since 2000, the hour race has required the use of traditional racing bikes.

FOLLOW THE SUN (1951)

DIRECTOR: Sidney Lanfield. SCREENPLAY: Frederick Hazlitt Brennan. PRODUCER: Samuel G. Engel. CINEMATOGRAPHY: Leo Tover. EDITING: Barbara McLean. MUSIC: Cyril Mockridge. ART DIRECTION: Richard Irvine, Lyle Wheeler. COSTUME DESIGN: Renie.

CAST: Glenn Ford (Ben Hogan), Anne Baxter (Valerie Hogan), Dennis O'Keefe (Chuck Williams), June Havoc (Norma), Larry Keating (Jay Dexter).

RUNNING TIME: 93 minutes.

VHS: 20th Century Fox.

Follow the Sun is a biography of Ben Hogan, a golfing great who retired twenty years after this film was produced.

FOR LOVE OF THE GAME (1999)

DIRECTOR: Sam Raimi. SCREENPLAY: Dana Stevens, based on the book by Michael Shaara. PRODUCER: Armryan Bernstein, Amy Robinson. CINEMATOGRAPHY: John Bailey. EDITING: Eric L. Beason, Arthur Coburn. MUSIC: Basil Poledouris. PRODUCTION DESIGN: Neil Spisak. ART DIRECTION: Steve Arnold, James C. Feng. COSTUME DESIGN: Judianna Makovsky.

CAST: Kevin Costner (Billy Chapel), Kelly Preston (Jane Aubrey), John C. Reilly (Gus Sinski), Jena Malone (Heather), Brian Cox (Gary Wheeler), J. K. Simmons (Frank Perry), Vin Scully (himself).

RUNNING TIME: 137 minutes.

DVD: Universal Studios.

Based on the novella by Michael Shaara, *For Love of the Game* is part baseball drama, part love story. While pitching what may be the last game of his career, veteran Billy Chapel (Kevin Costner) contemplates his on-again-off-again relationship with writer Jane Aubrey (Kelly Preston). The film opens with a montage of family snapshots (including photos from Costner's family albums), home movies, and newspaper clippings that establish the significance of baseball from Billy's toddlerhood through his professional career with the Detroit Tigers.

When the story begins, the last-place Tigers are headed for New York and their final game of the season. Although he has a sore arm, Billy, now forty, is scheduled to start the next day in what his catcher, Gus Sinski (John C. Reilly), calls a "throw away game." Billy points out that it is an important contest for the Boston Red Sox since New York has not yet clinched the division title. It's also an important game for Billy as he soon learns that the Tigers' owner, Gary Wheeler (Brian Cox), has grown frustrated with the sport and is selling the team; Billy will be traded as part of the deal, and Gary has advised him to retire. For Billy, who has spent his entire career with Detroit, playing for another team is almost as unthinkable as not playing at all. To make matters worse, he's been stood up by Jane, with whom he had hopes of rekindling a romance. On game day he wakes up with an apparent hangover and a hospitality mint stuck to his face. Jane has left a message to meet her in the lobby, but she hasn't waited. When Billy finally locates her in Central Park, he learns she has accepted a new job in London and is leaving on a six o'clock flight that very day. After five years she has discovered that he really doesn't need her; she has just come to say goodbye.

At Yankee Stadium, Billy meets a young player, Ken Strout (Carmine Giovinazzo), whose father once played with Billy. Ken has just been called up to the majors by the Yankees and will figure later in the film. At this point he serves as a reminder of how long Billy has been playing. In the locker room, when he thinks no one is looking, Billy pinches his love handles in disgust; however, he is observed by Gary's nephew, who has been sent to learn Billy's decision about announcing his retirement. The Detroit manager, Frank Perry (J. K. Simmons), after complaining that Billy is late, tells him Gus won't be his catcher. Billy dismisses the complaint and delivers an ultimatum: Gus catches, or Billy doesn't pitch. Period. From here on, the film cuts between Yankee Stadium, where Billy reviews his relationship with Jane in a series of flashbacks, and the airport, where Jane's flight has been delayed and where she cannot avoid the game, which is being telecast throughout the facility.

During his warm up, Billy reveals to Gus that he is going to throw harder than usual. "You and me, one more time," is Gus's reply. In the first inning Billy faces his old nemesis, Sam Tuttle (Michael Papajohn), whom he fans with a combination of fastballs and curves. After retiring the side, Billy pulls his cap over his face and lets his mind wander to when he first met Jane. Her car, a cheap rental, had broken down, and he had stopped to help. After some slight awkwardness, he explains he's on his way to the ballpark and invites her along. Seated in the friends' box, Jane overhears a player's wife refer to her as "the blonde of the week." In spite of this warning about Billy's reputation and her own distaste for one-night stands, she is so captivated by Billy's charm that she says "yes" before he has a chance to finish the question. However, the next morning she regrets her impulsiveness. Even though Billy has already checked his calendar and set up their next date, a month away, she hesitates, fearing he won't show.

Billy does appear at the agreed upon date and time, but Jane is nowhere to be seen. As he leaves the bar where they were to meet, he sees Jane hurrying toward him. She tells him that she's not a groupie and isn't comfortable hooking up with strangers, but she does like him. As she tries to explain her ambivalence, gawkers and autograph seekers interrupt. For Jane, Billy's celebrity status is a drawback. Finally, the two go for a walk, and Billy tells her about his parents, both deceased, and his love of baseball. When they reach her doorstep, Jane suggests ground rules that indicate she is not ready to make a commitment and holds no claim over him.

The following spring Billy calls her from spring training camp in Lakeland, Florida, and invites her down for the weekend. Jane

Top: Kevin Costner takes the mound as Billy Chapel in *For Love of the Game*; bottom: Costner with costar Kelly Preston

refuses to be persuaded, claiming she has work to complete, and they have their first disagreement. Then Jane changes her mind and arrives, without prior warning, on his doorstep. Alas, she discovers that Billy is not alone. Jane leaves in tears, now insisting that she was lying about her own ground rules. When next he hears from her, he is playing in Boston. She calls to say that she has a teenaged daughter, Heather (Jena Malone), who has run away from home to her father, a useless pothead now living in Boston. Billy talks the manager into a detour with the team bus to retrieve Heather, and she flies with the Tigers to New York. Heather tells Billy she and her mother fought because Jane, who was sixteen when Heather was born, fears her daughter will make the same mistake. According to Heather, Jane "never had a love story" and now "doesn't believe" in love.

At Jane's apartment, Heather hugs her mother and conveniently retires, allowing Jane and Billy to reconcile. Billy envisions a future that includes the three of them. A montage of family scenes shows a fun-filled holiday season. Jane's insecurities are still on display as she questions Billy, "Would you love me if . . . ?" The scene shifts to Billy's winter place, where he badly injures his hand using a table saw. Jane rushes him to the closest medical facility and shrieks to get him immediate attention. As Billy is medevaced out, he asks her to call his trainer. She is upset that there is not room for her in the helicopter and that the trainer has suddenly replaced her as the most important person in Billy's life. When he grows frustrated that his rehabilitation is progressing slowly, he takes his anger out on her. Jane leaves once again. When Billy next contacts her, it is not clear how long they have been out of touch, but she has begun dating her boss and expresses no interest in seeing him again. More time passes, and Billy runs into Heather in California. She is a student at the University of Southern California and reports only briefly that she and her mother are fine before scampering off with her friends.

At this point, the flashbacks have come full circle, repeating an early scene of Billy making the dinner date before his last game, the date that Jane doesn't keep. In the narrative present, Billy, who has alternated between pitching "in the zone" and reliving the past, realizes that he is well on his way to hurling a no-hitter, and thanks to a double and a gutsy slide by Gus, the Tigers hold a 1-0 lead. Meanwhile, Jane, unable to escape the ubiquitous television coverage at Kennedy International, has become engrossed in the game and missed her flight. Surrounded by vocal Yankee fans, she roots for Billy.

Back on the mound, Billy's arm is sore, and he can no longer rely on his curve ball. Gus offers encouragement, advising him to trust the rest of the team, which has become energized by his performance. Billy offers a prayer and an apology to God for involving him in a ballgame. Before the ninth inning Billy sends Gary a note, written on a baseball, confirming that he's retiring. Then he takes the mound to face the top of the Yankee lineup. An outfielder snags a well-hit pitch at the wall, and Gus catches a pop foul. With one out to go, young Ken Strout is sent in to pinch hit in his first major league appearance. Billy delivers the heat, what's left of it. The best the kid can do is send a chopper past the mound, and the infield manages the final out.

Later that night, after he has tucked a very inebriated Gus into bed, Billy returns to his room alone and cries. The next morning he is at the airport, where he finds Jane, who is waiting on the next plane for London. Billy is also headed for London. Jane struggles with her emotions, but finally takes Billy's hand. He tells her, at last, that he loves her, and the credits roll.

The love story is much less compelling than the baseball story. The ambivalence of the Jane Aubrey character grows tiresome quickly, and the flashbacks fail to convince that there's much to the relationship. Although Billy is drawn to the sense of home he experiences when he takes Heather back to Jane's apartment, the film strays away from the newly formed family, and Heather disappears almost immediately. Billy's friendship with Gus is more interesting than his shaky romance, and it is disappointing that the film does not do more with the relationships Billy has established with teammates over the years. In this, his third baseball movie, following *Bull Durham* (1988) and *Field of Dreams* (1989), Costner turns in another effective performance. He does much of his own pitching and looks comfortable on the mound. The baseball footage incorporates telecasts, diamond vision, and instant replays, and announcers Vin Scully and Steve Lyons provide a running commentary that contributes to the film's verisimilitude.

FOREVER STRONG (2008)

DIRECTOR: Ryan Little. SCREENPLAY: David Pliler. PRODUCERS: Adam Abel, Ryan Little. CINEMATOGRAPHY: T. C. Christensen. EDITING: John Lyde. MUSIC: J Bateman, Bart Hendrickson. PRODUCTION DESIGN: Gary Sivertsen. COSTUME DESIGN: Anna K. Findlay.

CAST: Sean Faris (Rick Penning), Penn Badgley (Lars), Sean Astin (Marcus Tate), Gary Cole (Larry Gelwix), Neal McDonough (Richard Penning).

RUNNING TIME: 112 minutes.

DVD: Crane Movie Company.

After a young rugby player runs afoul of the law, he joins his former rivals and squares off against his father.

FORGET PARIS (1995)

DIRECTOR: Billy Crystal. SCREENPLAY: Billy Crystal, Lowell Ganz, Babaloo Mandel. PRODUCER: Billy Crystal. CINEMATOGRAPHY: Don Burgess. EDITING: Kent Beyda. MUSIC: Marc Shaiman. PRODUCTION DESIGN: Terence Marsh. ART DIRECTION: William Cruse. COSTUME DESIGN: Judy Ruskin.

CAST: Billy Crystal (Mickey Gordon), Debra Winger (Ellen Andrews Gordon), Joe Mantegna (Andy), Cynthia Stevenson (Liz), Julie Kavner (Lucy), Richard Masur (Craig).

RUNNING TIME: 101 minutes.

DVD: Turner Home Entertainment.

In this film, an NBA referee must decide between his career and the woman he loves. Crystal is shown interacting with several basketball greats, including Patrick Ewing, Reggie Miller, and Kareem Abdul-Jabbar.

THE FRESHMAN (1925)

DIRECTORS: Fred C. Newmeyer, Sam Taylor. SCREENPLAY: Sam Taylor, Ted Wilde. PRODUCER: Harold Lloyd. CINEMATOGRAPHY: Walter Lundin. EDITING: Allen McNeil. ART DIRECTION: Liell K. Vedder.

CAST: Harold Lloyd (Harold Lamb), Jobyna Ralston (Peggy), Brooks Benedict (the College Cad), James Anderson (Chet), Hazel Keener (the belle), Joseph Harrington (the tailor), Pat Harmon (the coach).

RUNNING TIME: 76 minutes.

DVD: New Line Home Video.

This silent film is a slapstick comedy about a teenager who tries out for the college football team in order to win social acceptance from his peers. Harold Lloyd, a successful comic whose films were even more profitable than those of Charlie Chaplin and Buster Keaton, produced and starred in

The Freshman, even though he was thirty-one when it was made.

Harold Lamb (Lloyd) is an ordinary middle-class high school graduate who, through industriousness and thrift, has earned a spot at Tate University, which the title cards describe as "a large football stadium with a college attached." To prepare himself for college, he has learned cheers, read books on grooming, and memorized parts of a movie about a college hero, including a complex jig that the hero does every time he is introduced to someone. Harold's goal is to replace Chet (James Anderson) as the most popular fellow on campus.

The requisite love interest appears on the train en route to the campus when Harold is seated in the dining car next to Peggy (Jobyna Ralston), whose mother runs a boarding house near Tate. Peggy is working a crossword puzzle while she eats, and Harold directs his attention to the puzzle as well. When he suggests that "sweetheart" may be the answer to "a term for the one you love," the two exchange a number of words of endearment. A busybody at the next table, overhearing, assumes the two are a couple and comments to that effect, prompting Harold to flee in embarrassment, colliding with a waiter as he does so.

When the train pulls into the college town's station, a group of Tate upperclassmen, observing Harold's jig, immediately recognize that he is a freshman and begin a series of practical jokes. They tell Harold that a chauffeur-driven automobile parked nearby is his transportation to the school, but it is really the dean's private car. While the driver is distracted, Harold hops aboard, and it is not until the car stops at the side entrance of the Tate auditorium that the driver realizes his mistake and rushes back to the train station to fetch the dean. Harold finds himself backstage, where a kitten has climbed to the top of the curtain. He rescues the kitten just as the curtain goes up. Stuffing the kitten under his sweater, he tries to run into the wings, but is urged back to center stage by the College Cad (Brooks Benedict), who insists it is customary for new students to introduce themselves to the student body. There are a number of mishaps with his luggage and the kitten that leave the audience in stitches; then Harold delivers a monologue from the college movie in which he introduces himself as "Speedy." Exiting, he hears cheers, although it is clear the others are laughing at his expense. Harold invites the Cad and his friends for ice cream (prohibition was still in effect in the mid-1920s), but the entire audience tags along, making quite a dent in Harold's bank account.

Needing to reduce his living expenses, Harold takes a room in the boarding house operated, he later discovers to his delight, by Peggy's mother. Harold is attempting to sew a button onto the shirt he is wearing when he spots Peggy in a mirror she has come to finish cleaning. Peggy takes over the repair, and while she is looking elsewhere, Harold sabotages the buttons on his coat sleeve. It is obvious that the two are quite taken with each other. Peggy is happy with Harold as he is but understands his desire for popularity. When the school paper publishes his photo with a caption calling him "Speedy the Spender," she snips off the caption and saves the photo.

In spite of his generosity, Harold cannot match Chet's popularity, so he decides to join the football team. Harold's first day at football practice is a sequence of gags, during which he absorbs an enormous amount of physical punishment. After accidentally tackling the coach (Pat Harmon) and breaking the tackling dummy, Harold is called upon to substitute for the dummy. Hours pass as the coach drills his team on their defensive skills, and Harold is taken down time after time after time. Finally, he is so exhausted that he has to return to the boarding house in a cab. However, the coach has been impressed by Harold's spirit and, at Chet's suggestion, allows him to stay on as water boy while letting him think he is a substitute. This deception fools only Harold; the other students know he is just the water boy and ridicule him behind his back. When Peggy overhears the Cad making fun of Harold, she defends him; later when Harold tells Peggy he has made the team, she does not reveal the truth.

His position with the team having failed to enhance his status on campus, Harold decides to host a fall gala at the hotel where Peggy works. In preparation, he engages a tailor (Joseph Harrington) to make him a tuxedo, but the tailor is a tippler and suffers from frequent "dizzy spells" that require medicinal doses of spirits. Consequently, on the night of the gala, the tux is only basted together, and the tailor accompanies Harold in case his services are needed. At the hotel Harold presents Peggy with a bouquet—she is working at the coat check—before joining the others. As host, he is expected to dance with a number of the young women present, but each time he is dragged onto the floor, another part of his suit gives way. The gags in this sequence are classics. At one point, Harold, having lost a sleeve, stands by a curtain concealing the tailor, who is reattaching the sleeve. When someone comes up to Harold to shake hands, Harold does his jig, and the tailor's hand emerges from behind the curtain; when someone asks Harold to lend him money, the tailor's hand reaches into Harold's pocket and offers up the cash, and then, with the tailor's hand still visible, Harold's hand retrieves his cash. With the aid of the curtain, the tailor is able to stitch Harold's pants while Harold appears to be sitting at a table. The gags continue as the suit fails, the tailor requires alcohol, and Harold attempts to communicate with Peggy while dancing with others. Then, the gags end abruptly when the College Cad makes a pass at Peggy, and Harold comes to her rescue. Soon after, he discovers that the others have been making fun of him all along. Peggy tries to comfort him by saying he should just be himself. Still, Harold believes he has something to prove and determines that he must become the hero of the upcoming football game. He has yet to realize that he's only the water boy.

At the game Tate is trailing Union State by three points in the fourth quarter. As injuries pile up, Harold waits on the bench. At one point the coach calls him over, but only to give his jersey (number zero) to a player whose uniform has been ripped. Finally, with no substitutes left, the coach reluctantly allows Harold to play. (Because he has given his jersey to another, for the remainder of the sequence he is the only player on the field without the full uniform, so is easily identifiable in all of the shots. After being tackled for the first time, he is knocked out and placed on a stretcher, but he comes to as he's being carted off and jumps off the stretcher, returning to the huddle. He sees double, mistakes a hat thrown in the air for a football, and when he does run with the ball, keeps getting up and running again after being tackled. The official explains that the whistle means the play is over; on his next carry, Harold is about to score when a nearby factory whistle sounds, causing him to stop in his tracks just shy of the goal line. (Lloyd uses a sound gag earlier, as well; clever theater managers supplied the proper effects.) Several stunts later, Harold recovers a fumble and makes a triumphant run for the winning score with Peggy cheering him on. Harold becomes the college hero, and even his coach imitates his jig. In the midst of the postgame hullabaloo, he slips away to read a love note from Peggy.

The Freshman has a stronger plot than most of Lloyd's films. Although he generally staged the comic sequences first and then filled in scenes to connect the dots, he discovered that this method of operating did not work well with *The Freshman.* Lloyd had begun shooting the final football sequence first, but was displeased with the results, so started over, filming scenes in chronological order to establish a stronger sense of character and motivation. Crowd scenes of the football game were lensed at the Rose Bowl, but action sequences were shot at USC during half time of an East-West championship game. Members of the USC team portrayed the football players in the film. Lloyd performed all of his own stunts and was actually tackled repeatedly by the college athletes during the practice sequence. Technically, the film is sophisticated, making good use of point of view and reveal shots, and the acting is strong enough that the title cards, while clever in their own right, are not necessary to explain the story.

FRIDAY NIGHT LIGHTS (2004)

DIRECTORS: Peter Berg, Josh Tate. SCREENPLAY: David Aaron Cohen, Peter Berg, based on the book by Buzz Bissinger. PRODUCER: Brian Grazer. CINEMATOGRAPHY: Tobias Schliessler. EDITING: Colby Parker, Jr., David Rosenbloom, Gabrielle Fasulo. MUSIC: Brian Reitzell, Explosions in the Sky, David Tom. PRODUCTION DESIGN: Sharon Seymour. ART DIRECTION: Peter Borck. COSTUME DESIGN: Susan Matheson.

CAST: Billy Bob Thornton (Gary Gaines), Lucas Black (Mike Winchell), Garrett Hedlund (Don Billingsley), Derek Luke (Boobie Miles), Jay Hernandez (Brian Chavez), Lee Jackson (Ivory Christian), Tim McGraw (Don's father), Connie Britton (Sharon Gaines).

RUNNING TIME: 118 minutes.

DVD: Universal Studios.

Friday Night Lights, adapted from H. G. Bissinger's book of the same name (1990), depicts the 1988 Permian Panthers' run for the 1988 Texas 5A high school championship in football. The film grossed over $60 million, won the Best Film Award from the American Film Institute, spawned the NBC television series *Friday Night Lights* (premiered October 3, 2006), and is widely regarded as the best film about high school football. Its popularity stems from its themes: conflicts between fathers and sons and between the coach and boosters, and the athletes' struggles with self-esteem and their unrealistic expectations about professional careers.

Don Billingsley (Garrett Hedlund), the fullback who blocks for Boobie Miles (Derek Luke), the team's star, has a tendency to fumble on the rare occasions when he carries the ball. Don's father (Tim McGraw), who had been on a championship Permian team, has become an alcoholic who cannot stop criticizing his son. At one point he physically attacks Don on the football field, and he humiliates him by duct-taping his hands to the football in front of his girlfriend. In true sports-film fashion, Don loves his father and seeks his approval, even though he is embarrassed by his father's atrocious behavior. (The relationship closely parallels the father-son relationship in *Hoosiers* [1986], a film *Friday Night Lights* resembles in a number of ways.) In the championship game, however, Don, who has a separated shoulder, has his shoulder pulled back into place and goes back in the game. Dragging several opposing players with him, he comes close to scoring a winning touchdown. His father finally recognizes Don's grit and comes down onto the field, where he embraces his son and gives him his championship ring.

Gary Gaines (Billy Bob Thornton) is the new coach of the Permian squad, which the Odessa townspeople expect to win their fifth championship. He receives a lot of advice, all unsolicited, from the team's supporters, who turn against him after Boobie is injured and the team loses a game. That injury occurred in a game when Permian held a substantial lead and the reserves should have been playing. When the coach returns home, his yard is full of "For Sale" signs. The criticism is relentless, especially on the sports radio programs; even a dinner party is filled with veiled threats. Although the fans come around when the team makes the playoffs, Coach Gaines receives a win-or-else threat from one of the boosters.

Boobie has his troubles, too. A talented running back who believes that he can safely neglect his studies because of his athletic ability, he is staking his future on sports. He even jokes about football being the only subject he does well in. Before the season starts, Boobie is being recruited by several Division I teams; but after his injury, their enthusiasm wanes. After his second injury, Boobie's career is over. One telling shot occurs while he is sitting on his porch and watching two garbage men at work. It is as if he sees his future since he believes that football is the only thing that he can do.

In the championship, Permian faces Dallas Carter, whose larger, more powerful athletes are known for their hard hitting; furthermore, without Boobie, Permian has lost its offensive edge. In an "underdog" film like this, the coach often becomes a kind of father figure, a dispenser of good counsel to his players. Since Mike Winchell (Lucas Black), the quarterback, has an absentee father and a sick mother, Coach Gaines becomes Mike's surrogate father. In a conversation between the two coming back from a game, Gaines tells Mike, who has little confidence and a feeling of impending doom, that the "curses" he feels heaped on him are really self-imposed ones. He adds that Mike needs to take responsibility for himself and for others as he assumes a leadership role. At halftime of the Carter game, Gaines talks about the nature of success, which he defines as being true to family, friends, and one's self. His beliefs contrast with those of Don's father, for whom success means winning, something that can be represented by an object, like a trophy or a ring. He does not understand, however, that his ring and the memories it holds have hardly sustained him in his own life.

The memories the seniors take with them are not of victory, but of Gaines's philosophy. They have been true to teammates, family, friends, and community. What Odessa has is oil and football, and precious little else. Because the landscape is so bleak and arid, the town seems a bit like a fortress under siege by the sophisticated, metropolitan world outside, here suggested by the Dallas school. The procession of cars going to the big games resembles a caravan setting out across the prairie, and the "gone to the game" signs on storefronts suggest that life stops in town when the football team is away. At the end of the film three players toss the football around outside the stadium and say their goodbyes. Mike then throws a long pass to a group of kids playing football. The pass and catch signify the continuation of a tradition.

FULL-COURT MIRACLE (2003)

DIRECTOR: Stuart Gillard. SCREENPLAY: Joel Silverman, Joel Kauffmann, Donald C. Yost. PRODUCER: Jacqueline George. CINEMATOGRAPHY: Thomas Burstyn. EDITING: Anthony Redman. MUSIC: Christopher Brady. PRODUCTION DESIGN: Michael Joy. COSTUME DESIGN: Julie Whitfield.

CAST: Richard T. Jones (Lamont Carr), Alex D. Linz (Alex Schlotsky), R. H. Thompson (Rabbi Lewis), Sean Marquette (Big Ben Swartz), Jase Blankfort (Stick Goldstein), Erik Knudsen (T.J. Murphy).

RUNNING TIME: 90 minutes.

This Disney telepic is a Hanukkah story very loosely based on the career of Lamont Carr, who in 1976 became the first African American basketball player to graduate from the University of Virginia. Carr did not play professional basketball; eventually, he took up dart throwing and has become the sport's leading promoter. *Full-Court Miracle*, however, focuses on the segment of Carr's career when, in the mid-1990s, he began coaching basketball at a Jewish school in Boca Raton, Florida.

The Disney story is set in Philadelphia (although filmed in Toronto) at Philadelphia Hebrew Academy, a yeshiva—a Jewish day school—that has yet to win a basketball game. The team's point guard, Alex Schlotsky (Alex D. Linz), approaches Rabbi Lewis (R. H. Thomson) about replacing the coach, the school math teacher who is ill suited for athletic coaching. The rabbi, referring to his lessons on the history of Hanukkah, tells Alex that the team needs a Judah Maccabee, a reference to the Jewish military hero whose successful revolt against the Greek-Syrians in the second century BCE is celebrated on Hanukkah. The rabbi can't tell Alex where to find a modern-day Judah, but assures Alex that this Judah will be identifiable.

Shortly after their talk, Alex thinks he recognizes his Judah at the neighborhood basketball court, but the tall African American with the killer jump shot wants nothing to do with Alex and refuses to reveal his name. But as "Judah" drives off, Alex notes the special tags on the van indicate the owner is a University of Virginia (UVA) alum. Alex uses his home computer to examine photos of former UVA Cavaliers, identifies Lamont Carr (played by Richard T. Jones), and becomes convinced Lamont is Judah because of some shared biographical information, including the nickname "Hammer."

Lamont has left his family in Virginia while he tries to renew his career with the 76ers following a knee injury. He is living in his van and is uninterested in coaching a sorry-looking group of boys, but Alex offers to pay, and Lamont needs money. The boys pool their allowances and hawk lattes after borrowing the Schlotsky family's espresso maker to finance their endeavor; Alex even sells a prized basketball card. When his parents (Linda Kash and Jason Blicker) realize what he is up to, Alex faces the difficult task of convincing his mother-the-doctor that basketball is a worthwhile pursuit. Dr. Schlotsky, however, has her heart set on Alex's following in her footsteps—quite literally in a "shadow program" at her hospital that allows students to follow a physician, the goal being to stimulate interest in the profession. Alex's father, Marshall, is much more sympathetic, but has limited authority in this instance; besides, he's preoccupied trying to keep up with his own career as a real estate agent. Objections also come from Mrs. Klein (Sheila McCarthy), the school principal, who is skeptical about the academy team practicing at a neighborhood playground with a coach who isn't affiliated with the school.

In spite of the obstacles, the boys continue to practice and learn the importance of teamwork. Alex, having sent his friend Julie (Cassie Steele) in his place at the hospital's shadow program, learns of Lamont's living arrangements and of his longing for his wife and children. When the van requires expensive repairs, Alex meets with Rabbi Lewis, who proposes the school hire Lamont as a temporary coach, an arrangement that allows Lamont to leave if he gets called up by the 76ers. Neither Dr. Schlotsky nor Mrs. Klein is happy with the plan, both women being skeptical about the impact of athletics on academics. Mrs. Klein is also suspicious that the address Alex has provided for

Lamont doesn't exist, so she decides to follow Lamont after practice. Fortunately, Alex has discovered her intentions, and he contrives for Lamont to meet him at the vacant condo unit Marshall still hasn't sold. Mrs. Klein is deceived by the ploy, and Lamont ends up living in the unit in exchange for completing some painting and minor repairs. For a while, all runs smoothly, and the Lions begin to win. When Alex's grades slip and he's benched, the other players help him study and retain his eligibility.

The Lions qualify for a tournament, but shortly before the final against their archrivals, the Warriors, Lamont is summoned by the 76ers and joins the team on the road. Gloom settles over the team; the boys sit listlessly in class as Rabbi Lewis continues his lesson on the history of Hanukkah and the spiritual darkness of the Maccabees when they found themselves lacking enough oil to purify the Temple of Jerusalem. The rabbi completes the story of the miracle of the lamp, which burned for eight days, long enough for the Maccabees to obtain enough oil to complete their obligation, and he encourages the boys to have faith. Still, during the game, the Lions fall behind at the half, and when a storm knocks out the power, it appears the Warriors will be declared the winners. Of course, all is not lost, and, in the interim, the remaining plot threads have been coming together. Dr. Schlotsky has caught up with Lamont after a game and asked him to help her understand Alex's passion for basketball. Lamont, having learned in his brief time with the Philadelphia team that his knees cannot tolerate the stress of professional-level competition, is ready to retire and reconnect with his family. In a flurry of activity, Dr. Schlotsky arranges for Lamont's family to fly to Philadelphia, for Lamont to secure a full-time coaching position at the Hebrew Academy, and for everyone—including Julie, who is shadowing Dr. Schlotsky—to arrive at the game before it ends.

On the basketball court, play has resumed with the agreement that the game will end officially when the generator, now powering the lights in the gymnasium, runs out of fuel. But there is not much gasoline left, and the Lions' coach has determined the teams have only minutes to play. Nonetheless, the Lions have made a valiant comeback, pulling within a point. Even though the Warriors have attempted to run out the generator with timeouts, the lights have continued to burn way longer than physically possible, providing just enough electricity for Alex to set up the winning shot. Even Mrs. Klein is ecstatic. Astute viewers will note parallels between the performance of the generator and the Miracle of the Lamp. *Full-Court Miracle* is a corny but endearing feel-good film imbued with a multicultural holiday spirit. Viewers unfamiliar with the story of Hanukkah will find it instructive, as well.

FULL RIDE (2002)

DIRECTOR: Mark Hoeger. SCREENPLAY: George Mills, Don Winslow. PRODUCERS: Andy Anderson, Peter Heller, Mark Hoeger. CINEMATOGRAPHY: Andy Anderson. EDITING: Mike Hill. MUSIC: Peter Buffett. PRODUCTION DESIGN: Michael De Silva. ART DIRECTION: Michael De Silva. COSTUME DESIGN: Deborah Fiscus.

CAST: Meredith Monroe (Amy Lear), Riley Smith (Matt Sabo), Bob Cady (Coach Perry), Jonathan Wayne Wilson (Coach Neuberger).

RUNNING TIME: 95 minutes.

DVD: Allumination.

With the help of a pretty young woman, a belligerent high school football player comes to realize how the sport can help him.

G

THE GALLOPING MAJOR (1951)

DIRECTOR: Henry Cornelius. SCREENPLAY: Henry Cornelius, Monja Danischewsky. STORY: Basil Radford. PRODUCER: Monja Danischewsky. CINEMATOGRAPHY: Stanley Pavey. EDITING: Geoffrey Foot. MUSIC: Georges Auric. ART DIRECTION: Norman Arnold. COSTUME DESIGN: Joan Ellacott.
CAST: Basil Radford (Major Arthur Hill), Jimmy Hanley (Bill Collins), Joyce Grenfall (Maggie), Hugh Griffith (Harold Temple).
RUNNING TIME: 80 minutes.

An unsuccessful racehorse is conditioned to become a jumper.

THE GAME PLAN (2007)

DIRECTOR: Andy Fickman. SCREENPLAY: Nichole Millard, Kathryn Price, Audrey Wells. PRODUCERS: Mark Ciardi, Gordon Gray. CINEMATOGRAPHY: Greg Gardiner. EDITING: Michael Jablow. MUSIC: Nathan Wang. PRODUCTION DESIGN: David J. Bomba. ART DIRECTION: John R. Jensen. COSTUME DESIGN: Genevieve Tyrrell.
CAST: Dwayne Johnson (Joe Kingman), Kyra Sedgwick (Stella Peck), Madison Pettis (Peyton Kelly), Roselyn Sanchez (Monique Vasquez).
RUNNING TIME: 110 minutes.
DVD: Walt Disney Video.

In this Disney comedy, a professional football player is forced to take care of the young daughter he never knew existed.

GAME 6 (2006)

DIRECTOR: Michael Hoffmann. SCREENPLAY: Don DeLillo. PRODUCERS: Griffin Dunne, Amy Robinson, Leslie Urdang. CINEMATOGRAPHY: David M. Dunlap. EDITING: Camilla Toniolo. MUSIC: Yo La Tengo. PRODUCTION DESIGN: Bill Groom. ART DIRECTION: Kate Aronsson Brown. COSTUME DESIGN: Renée Ehrlich Kalfus, Elizabeth Shelton.
CAST: Michael Keaton (Nicky Rogan), Robert Downey Jr. (Steven Schwimmer), Ari Graynor (Laurel Rogan), Bebe Neuwirth (Joanna Bourne), Griffin Dunne (Elliott Litvak).
RUNNING TIME: 87 minutes.
DVD: Arts Alliance America.

Acclaimed novelist Don DeLillo wrote the screenplay for this film about a playwright whose beloved Boston Red Sox are competing in the 1986 World Series.

GENEVIEVE (1953)

DIRECTOR: Henry Cornelius. SCREENPLAY: William Rose. PRODUCER: Henry Cornelius. CINEMATOGRAPHY: Christopher

Challis. EDITING: Clive Donner. MUSIC: Larry Adler. ART DIRECTION: Michael Stringer. COSTUME DESIGN: Marjory Cornelius.
CAST: Dinah Sheridan (Wendy McKim), John Gregson (Alan McKim), Kay Kendall (Rosalind Peters), Kenneth More (Ambrose Claverhouse).
RUNNING TIME: 86 minutes.
ACADEMY AWARD NOMINATIONS: Best Story and Screenplay, Best Scoring of a Dramatic or Comedy Picture.

In this British film, two couples participate in a cross-country race featuring antique roadsters.

GENTLEMAN JIM (1942)

DIRECTOR: Raoul Walsh. SCREENPLAY: Vincent Lawrence, Horace McCoy, based on the memoir *The Roar of the Crowd* by James J. Corbett. PRODUCER: Robert Buckner. CINEMATOGRAPHY: Sidney Hickox. EDITING: Jack Killifer. MUSIC: Heinz Roemheld. ART DIRECTION: Ted Smith. COSTUME DESIGN: Milo Anderson.
CAST: Errol Flynn (Jim Corbett), Alexis Smith (Vicky Ware), Jack Carson (Walter Lowrie), Alan Hale (Jim's father), John Loder (Carlton De Witt), William Frawley (Bill Delaney), Ward Bond (John L. Sullivan).
RUNNING TIME: 104 minutes. B&W.
DVD: Warner Home Video.

Set in San Francisco in 1887, *Gentleman Jim* is based on the career of James J. Corbett, who succeeded John L. Sullivan as the heavyweight champion of the world. By the late nineteenth century, prize fighting had progressed from bare-knuckle fights—conducted without rules and staged where the law could not interfere—to a more orderly sport governed by the Marquis of Queensbury rules. Fighters, thus, had the opportunity to become "gentlemen." Jim Corbett (Errol Flynn) is one of the battling, brawling Corbett clan whose family fisticuffs are heralded throughout the film by the cry, "The Corbetts are at it again." The Corbetts live on the south side of San Francisco, far from Nob Hill, whose wealthy families belong to the prestigious Olympic Club.

While watching an illegal fight, Jim and his friend Walter (Jack Carson) are apprehended by the police, who have also nabbed Judge Geary (Wallis Clark), a member of the board at the bank where Jim and Walter work as tellers. Thanks to Jim's quick thinking and ingenious lies, all are released, and Jim is given a raise. Later Jim finagles a visit to the Olympic Club, accompanying a bank customer, Vicky Ware (Alexis Smith), on an errand. The Olympic Club has recently engaged a boxing instructor, Harry Watson (Rhys Williams), in the interest of bringing respectability to the sport. Jim demonstrates his skills sparring with Harry and is immediately invited to join the club. However, his cockiness annoys Vicky and eventually aggravates the club members. When they meet Jack Burke, a former British boxing champ and a friend of the boxing instructor, the club members recognize the chance to put Jim in his place and ensure that he gets a "good drubbing." Much to their dismay (inflated by the loss of one thousand dollars), Jim knocks out Jack. The Corbetts, led by Jim's boisterous father (Alan Hale), make a lot of money on side bets. Unfortunately, at the postfight party at the Olympic Club, Walter gets drunk, and because of his boorish behavior, is asked to leave. Jim, insulted by Walter's treatment, which he interprets as class motivated, leaves with his friend. After visiting several bars, the pair find themselves in Salt Lake City.

After a few more successful bouts and a theatrical production about himself, Jim has enough money to buy a bar for his brothers and a home on Nob Hill for the family. The move from one side of the tracks to the other is itself a source of comedy. Tied behind the wagon that contains the family's belongings are two goats, which are not likely to make a good impression on their new neighbors. Although there are some references to class in the film, Jim's upward social mobility is treated humorously rather than seriously.

Champion John L. Sullivan (Ward Bond) has his own show, *The Honest Woodsman*, which Jim attends. He goes backstage and goads John into agreeing to fight him for the title. The catch is that John wants a side bet of ten thousand dollars, which Jim doesn't have. He needs a sponsor, and the unlikely donor is Vicky, who has maintained her disdain for Jim throughout the film. She reveals her true feelings, however, when she sees Jim with Anna Held (Madeleine Lebeau) and hears that people believe that Anna has provided Jim with the necessary ten thousand dollars.

At the training camp, the champ alternates between knocking down his sparring partners and swigging beer. Before the fight Jim learns that the superstitious John always enters the ring after his opponent, so he tricks the champion into entering first, thus demonstrating his skill at head games as well as footwork. Once the fight begins, John is no match for Jim's speed and conditioning. John swings wildly, gets turned around, and is even uncertain where Jim is. As America listens to news about the fight, Jim's punches begin to take their toll, and John is knocked out in the twenty-first round. Unable to mask her true feelings, Vicky shouts, "Hooray, Jim!" However, at the postfight party, Vicky again plays games, giving Jim an outsized hat, implying that he has a swelled head. Jim accepts the hat with grace and makes a joke at his own expense.

John's entrance at the party hushes the crowd. Like a true gentleman, John gives Jim his championship belt, and as the two shake hands, John tells Jim, "You're bringing something new to the fighting game," a statement that signals a real transition in boxing from the days of bare-knuckled brawlers to the future with boxers who rely on speed, footwork, and finesse rather than brute strength. Vicky is touched by Jim's "gentlemanly" behavior and his sympathy for the former champion, and she is embarrassed by her own misreading of Jim. She follows Jim out of the club and tries to articulate her feelings. However, the couple have been at each other's throats for too long, and the reconciliation that should occur produces another verbal gaffe, this time by Jim. He saves the situation like a real man by embracing her and telling her, "You're going to make a wonderful Corbett." This scene is followed by one featuring a brawl between the Corbett brothers, and Walter's words to the camera, "The Corbetts are at it again," imply all manner of sparks will continue to fly between Jim and Vicky.

A GENTLEMAN'S GAME (2002)

DIRECTOR: J. Mills Goodloe. SCREENPLAY: Tom Coyne, J. Mills Goodloe, based on the novel by Tom Coyne. PRODUCER: Kimberly Braswell. CINEMATOGRAPHY: Conrad W. Hall. EDITING: Tia Nolan. MUSIC: Jeff Beal. PRODUCTION DESIGN: Tim Galvin.
CAST: Mason Gamble (Timmy Price), Gary Sinise (Foster Pearse), Philip Baker Hall (Charlie Logan), Dylan Baker (Mr. Price).
RUNNING TIME: 112 minutes.
DVD: First Look Pictures.

A teen golfer who shows promise is mentored by a former champion who teaches him important lessons beyond the course.

GIRLFIGHT (2000)

DIRECTOR: Karyn Kusama. SCREENPLAY: Karyn Kusama. PRODUCERS: Sarah Green, Martha Griffin, Maggie Renzi.

CINEMATOGRAPHY: Patrick Cady. EDITING: Plummy Tucker. MUSIC: Gene McDaniels, Theodore Shapiro. PRODUCTION DESIGN: Stephen Beatrice. ART DIRECTION: Miguel Fernandez. COSTUME DESIGN: Marco Cattoretti, Luca Mosca.
CAST: Michelle Rodriguez (Diana Guzman), Santiago Douglas (Adrian Sturges), Jaime Tirelli (Hector Soto), Paul Calderon (Sandro Guzman), Ray Santiago (Tiny Guzman), Victor Sierra (Ray Cortez).
RUNNING TIME: 110 minutes.
DVD: Sony Pictures.

Written and directed by Karyn Kusama and executive produced by John Sayles, this Sundance winner presents boxing as a constructive way of channeling anger, a familiar theme but with a twist—the angry young person is a teenaged girl who, at the slightest provocation, reacts violently. Michelle Rodriguez turns in a dazzling performance as Diana Guzman, who lives in the Red Hook housing projects in Brooklyn with her gentle brother, Tiny (Ray Santiago), and her abusive father, Sandro (Paul Calderon), whom Diana holds responsible for her mother's suicide.

The film opens in the crowded corridor of a high school with the camera trained on the midsections of passing students. Then the camera pans to Diana, her back literally against the wall, her head lowered; when she looks up, her eyes smolder. It comes as no surprise in the next scene that she attacks a girl who has apparently slept with the boyfriend of Diana's best friend, Marisol (Elisa Bocanegra). It's the fourth fight of the semester for Diana, and she's in deep trouble with the principal. Her home life is rife with tension, as well. Sandro expects his children to assume traditional gender roles. Although Tiny wants to go to art school, his father insists he learn to box so that he can take care of himself; Sandro treats Diana as if her sole function is to prepare meals, tidy up, and fetch him beer. When he sends her to the gym with money for Tiny's trainer, Hector (Jaime Tirelli), she slugs Tiny's sparring partner, Ray (Victor Sierra), for delivering an unsporting blow to her brother.

A short time later, after serving another tense meal at home and a detention at school, Diana shows up at Hector's office, saying she wants to be a boxer. At first Hector and his friends are skeptical, but Diana silences them with her terse replies and her piercing glare. When Hector mentions the cost, he is able to postpone the inevitable, but not for long. Diana steals some of her father's cash after he has turned down her request for an allowance, adding that she ought to "wear a skirt once in a while." The next day after detention, she appears at the gym ready to work. Hector expresses a few weak objections before giving in. Tiny is not pleased, but Hector puts an end to his complaints by declaring the first rule of the gym: no personal business. Diana sets up shop with a janitor's closet for a locker room and begins to work.

At first, she has trouble getting into the rhythm of training and soon discovers, with Hector's assistance, that power alone will not make her a good boxer, that she needs both technique and endurance to compete. She begins road work, rising early to run before school. Hector is quickly becoming both a mentor and a father figure, not someone with all the answers, but someone who is trustworthy. A former fighter who knows that the young men he trains have more dream than talent, he nevertheless understands the importance of goals and drive. As her talent develops, Diana has befriended another boxer, Adrian Sturges (Santiago Douglas), who also lives in the projects and offers her a ride home one evening. Adrian works at his father's garage and dreams of becoming a professional fighter. His parents seem not to expect much from him; just graduating from high school was accomplishment enough to bring his mother to tears. After watching a professional match for which Hector has obtained discounted tickets, Adrian and Diana go out to eat. To keep within his weight classification, Adrian orders soup and salad, while Diana chows down on a deluxe burger platter; the two are almost the same size. When Adrian asks Diana how she became interested in boxing, she replies, "I didn't make the cheerleading squad" in a tone that ends that line of questioning. In spite of some awkwardness—and the fact that Adrian has a girlfriend, one who wears makeup and high heels—the two exchange a sweet first kiss, launching them into a romance. (Adrian's name is perhaps a reference to Rocky Balboa's beloved wife, Adrian.)

When Sandro spots Diana with Adrian, he confronts her about both the missing money and her boyfriend—whom he assumes has hit her since she has a bruise from practice. Diana does not deny the theft, stating simply she will repay the money, but when her father suggests that she is dating a batterer, she explodes, reminding him of his treatment of her mother. She stomps out and goes straight to Adrian, who sneaks her into his room, where they sleep side by side, Adrian being reluctant to spend his strength on sex with an important bout coming up. When Diana returns home, Tiny offers her the money his father provides for his training with Hector. Now that Tiny has accepted how much boxing means to Diana, it seems that her life has taken a turn for the better. In school she has avoided getting into trouble and has astounded her physical education teacher with her performance on a Presidential Fitness Test. Although she has little time now to spend with Marisol, the girls are still close.

Disruption to all of this harmony comes at Hector's birthday party, where Adrian shows up with his "sometime girlfriend," Karina (Belqui Ortiz). Diana, visibly crushed, leaves the party. When they next meet at the gym, Hector pits Diana against Adrian in a sparring match. Diana is aggressive, but Adrian keeps dancing away, refusing to engage her. Finally, in a clinch, Diana tells Adrian she loves him, then hurries to the locker room; Adrian calls for her to wait, insisting that he won't run after her. But Diana doesn't stop, and Adrian won't go to her; their quarrel remains unresolved.

The next complication occurs at a scheduled match at the gym. Neither Diana's opponent nor Ray's has shown up, so Hector announces they will fight each other, a solution made possible by recent legislation in New York State permitting contests between members of the opposite sex. This matchup also foreshadows a later contest with Adrian. Hector is convinced that Diana is the better fighter, but she is distracted when Sandro shows up at the gym. Ray scores a knockdown, but is disqualified in the second round for illegal punches. When Diana returns home, her father is in the kitchen, drinking. He calls her a loser; she responds that she learned from him, and the argument escalates to a physical confrontation. But Diana is now strong enough and agile enough to gain the upper hand, and she asserts, convincingly, that she is capable of breaking his neck; fortunately Tiny intervenes before she acts on her threat. Diana leaves her father on the floor with a reminder that she has inherited his violent temper and his coldness. After this fight she is goes to Hector, not Adrian.

Soon Diana's life seems to improve. Regretting his behavior and realizing how important she has become to him, Adrian appears at the school, where Marisol convinces Diana to talk with him. After apologizing, he tells her that she is "someone" to him. Next, Hector arranges a bout for

Diana to fight another woman in a tournament. A training montage shows her working to achieve versatility and to manage her strength. Tiny, Marisol, and Adrian attend Diana's fight, which she wins by a point in a split decision. But her progress places her in the finals against Adrian, who says he doesn't want to fight "a girl." Diana thinks he's afraid that he'll lose. And he does. In spite of fighting in earnest, Adrian gets knocked down and loses in a unanimous decision. "Satisfied?" he asks at the decision. Although Hector tells Diana how proud he is, the scene ends with Diana alone in the locker room, crying.

Later, Diana goes to the garage where Adrian works, but he slides under a car without acknowledging her. At the gym Diana is packing her gear, apparently ready to give up boxing, when Adrian appears. He tells her she has a "deadly hook." Diana offers him a compliment on his right cross as well, and both admit that they fought as hard as they could. For Diana, this means that Adrian respects her as a fellow athlete, and she is once again willing to forgive him for his earlier behavior. Adrian laments the bellicose nature of their relationship, to which Diana replies, "Maybe life is just war." The film ends with Diana kissing Adrian.

Girlfight is a realistic film in its portrayal of ring action, its gritty setting, and its emotion. Kusama captures a fighter's point of view with punches aimed directly at the camera. On the walls of Hector's gym are taped hand-lettered signs with clichéd messages, such as "Champions are made, not born." Before the tournament, a wizened man sings the national anthem a cappella. Although portions of the plot seem obviously contrived, the standard devices of the come-from-behind win and the big play are not present. Diana never knocks anyone out; her victories come via disqualification and decision. In the tournament final, who wins is less significant than how the loser will respond. The concluding scene promises that the future will contain its own conflicts. Diana has not reconciled with her father, and her relationship with Adrian may not survive his dream of becoming a professional fighter. But Diana has gained enough confidence in herself that she can envision a future, and, importantly, she has allowed herself to love.

GLADIATOR (1992)

DIRECTOR: Rowdy Herrington. SCREENPLAY: Lyle Kessler, Robert Kamen. STORY: Djordje Milicevic, Robert Kamen. PRODUCERS: Frank Price, Stephen J. Roth. CINEMATOGRAPHY: Tak Fujimoto. EDITING: Harry B. Miller III, Peter Zinner. MUSIC: Brad Fiedel. PRODUCTION DESIGN: Gregg Fonseca. ART DIRECTION: Bruce Miller. COSTUME DESIGN: Donfeld.
CAST: James Marshall (Tommy Riley), Cuba Gooding Jr. (Abraham Lincoln Haines), Brian Dennehy (Jimmy Horn), Robert Loggia (Pappy Jack), T. E. Russell (Spits).
RUNNING TIME: 101 minutes.
DVD: Sony Pictures.

This film is about two teen friends who compete in illegal underground boxing and are inevitably forced to fight each other in the ring.

GLEAMING THE CUBE (1989)

DIRECTOR: Graeme Clifford. SCREENPLAY: Michael Tolkin. PRODUCERS: David Foster, Bruce McNall, Lawrence Turman. CINEMATOGRAPHY: Reed Smoot. EDITING: John Wright. PRODUCTION DESIGN: John Muto. ART DIRECTION: Dan Webster. COSTUME DESIGN: Ann Somers Major.
CAST: Christian Slater (Brian Kelly), Steven Bauer (Al Lucero), Ed Lauter (Mr. Kelly), Richard Herd (Ed Lawndale).
RUNNING TIME: 105 minutes.
DVD: Geneon.

In *Gleaming the Cube*, a skateboarder must find his brother's killers.

GLORY ROAD (2006)

DIRECTOR: James Gartner. SCREENPLAY: Chris Cleveland, Bettina Gilois. PRODUCER: Jerry Bruckheimer. CINEMATOGRAPHY: Jeffrey L. Kimball, John Wright. EDITING: Jason Hellmann, John Wright. MUSIC: Trevor Rabin. PRODUCTION DESIGN: Geoffrey Kirkland. ART DIRECTION: Kevin Constant. COSTUME DESIGN: Alix Friedberg.

CAST: Josh Lucas (Don Haskins), Derek Luke (Bobby Joe Hill), Austin Nichols (Jerry Armstrong), Jon Voight (Adolph Rupp), Evan Jones (Moe Iba), Schin A. S. Kerr (David Lattin), Alphonso McAuley (Orsten Artis).

RUNNING TIME: 118 minutes.

DVD: Buena Vista Home Entertainment.

The 1966 NCAA championship game between the University of Kentucky and Texas Western University is perhaps the most significant event in the history of college basketball. In going for his first title, the Texas Western coach, Don Haskins, played only his black athletes. Texas Western's victory demolished contemporary myths about the abilities of African American athletes to work together as a team exhibiting discipline and executing complex strategies; the game effectively integrated college basketball throughout the nation. *Glory Road* is based on the early years of Coach Haskins's career leading to his team's historic victory.

Director James Gartner establishes the social context of the film with an opening montage of black-and-white video clips from 1965. Basketball footage is intercut with shots of the Beatles, Martin Luther King Jr., a missile launch, and civil rights demonstrations. Throughout the film television screens appear in background shots, reminding the audience of the national milieu.

Glory Road introduces Haskins (Josh Lucas) coaching a high school game, shouting at his team, "You're playing like girls." A closer shot reveals that the team is a girls' team, but Haskins is unaware of the irony of his remarks. His sideline taunts reflect an unexamined set of assumptions. He is a man focused on winning, not on promoting equality. When he accepts a position at Texas Western, a "football school," his decision to recruit black athletes—something just not done at that time in the South—is motivated by a very limited budget and an intense desire to win rather than a determination to integrate the sport. In fact, the first high school players he attempts to recruit are white, but they are not interested in signing with a school that has a losing record.

It is after watching a highly talented black player who has spent much of a game warming the bench that Coach Haskins realizes he will need to recruit his players from northern schools and factories and playground courts. When the team trainer, Ross Moore (Red West), realizes what Haskins is up to, he claims there are "no coloreds playing Division I in the South," but Ross remains loyal to Haskins and the goal of putting together a roster capable of a victorious season. The final group of seven blacks and five whites raises complaints from the team's largest financial supporter, an El Paso furniture store owner, and, consequently, concerns from the school's administration. However, since basketball is not a popular sport at Texas Western, Haskins is able to continue developing his team with little interference.

There are predictable tensions between the black and white players. Their initial meeting in the cafeteria turns into a trashball showdown, but before it can erupt in violence, the trainer intervenes. Once practice begins, the team's attention is diverted from their racial differences to their coach's rigorous expectations. Haskins and his point guard, Bobby Hill (Derek Luke), spar over Haskins' demands for discipline off the court and strict fundamental defense on the court. Haskins punishes Bobby harshly when he catches the young man out with a girl, a flagrant violation of the coach's policy. Soon after, Bobby and Haskins quarrel over strategy in a game against an undefeated Iowa team. Even though Haskins's zone defense and offensive setups clearly aren't working, Haskins refuses to allow the black players to "play their own game," a game marked by fast breaks and slam dunks. Finally, with the Texas Miners trailing by a sizeable margin, Coach Haskins agrees to a compromise of fast offense and man-to-man defense. The Miners win by a single point and continue undefeated until the final game of the season.

As the victories mount, so does controversy over the integration of the team. Players are pelted with trash as they enter the court. On a road trip one of the black players is badly beaten in the restroom of a diner, and just before the final regular season game, the players' hotel rooms are vandalized and racial slurs are scrawled on the walls. Frightened and angered by the intensity of the white hatred they have experienced, the black players respond by withdrawing from their white teammates. The Miners lose their last game as a result of failing to work together. The loss, however, has the effect of demonstrating the essential importance of teamwork, and by the time the NCAA tournament begins, the Miners are reunited.

On the eve of the championship game against legendary Adolf Rupp's (Jon Voight) all-white University of Kentucky team, Coach Haskins calls his players to meet in the empty stadium. After beginning a speech that reiterates the racial stereotypes heard from announcers, other coaches, and reporters, Haskins reveals his decision to play only the black athletes. The white players are deeply disappointed at being benched but express support for their "brothers." The Miners take home the championship, and the film ends with the homecoming. As the players emerge from the plane, subtitles divulge the fate of actual team members, and the closing image is a photo of the real 1966 NCAA champions.

Although *Glory Road* does little with character development, there are some fine performances. Jon Voight is memorable as Adolf Rupp. Al Shearer and Schin A. S. Kerr are believable in their roles as the future NBA players Nevil Shed and David Lattin. USC coach Tim Floyd, a former assistant to Haskins, served as technical adviser, and Haskins himself put the actors through a practice session. This preparation, combined with skillful editing, makes the action sequences convincing.

Ultimately, the film is a tribute to Don Haskins, portraying him as a pioneer who, in the end, acted intentionally to promote integration and racial equality. Haskins himself maintains that he simply started his best players in the game now known as the Emancipation Proclamation of 1966.

GOAL! THE DREAM BEGINS (2005)

DIRECTOR: Danny Cannon. SCREENPLAY: Dick Clement, Ian Le Frenais. STORY: Mike Jefferies, Adrian Butchart. PRODUCERS: Matt Barrelle, Mark Huffam, Mike Jefferies. CINEMATOGRAPHY: Michael Barrett. EDITING: Chris Dickens. MUSIC: Graeme Revell. PRODUCTION DESIGN: Laurence Dorman. ART DIRECTION: Stuart Rose. COSTUME DESIGN: Lindsay Pugh.

CAST: Kuno Becker (Santiago Munez), Alessandro Nivola (Gavin Harris), Anna Friel (Roz Harmison), Leonardo Guerra (young Santiago), Stephen Dillane (Glen Foy), Sean Pertwee (Barry Rankin).

RUNNING TIME: 118 minutes.

DVD: Buena Vista Pictures.

As the title indicates, this is a soccer film built on the theme of achieving success through a combination of natural talent and hard work. The plot follows the usual route of struggle, success, setback, struggle, success, setback, concluding with the game-winning goal and resolution of a central conflict. The major twist is that the main character, Santiago Muñez (Kuno Becker), is an illegal Mexican immigrant who must travel from Los Angeles to London in order to realize the American Dream.

The film opens with the Muñez family crossing into the United States. As the border patrol closes in, young Santiago drops his soccer ball at the fence, and it rolls several yards back into Mexico. His father, Herman (Tony Plana), orders him to leave the ball behind and hurry through the aperture in the barrier, foreshadowing a tension between Santiago's devotion to the sport and his father's practicality. When next seen, Santiago, now a young man, is floating on a raft in the pool of a gated mansion, but he is only one of the gardening crew. He abandons the raft for a seat in the bed of an old pickup that spirits him from the trappings of wealth and deposits him at a soccer match, where he uses pieces of cardboard from a trashcan as shin guards. At home, where he is asked to speak Spanish instead of English, his father believes soccer is a waste of time. Señor Muñez, perhaps bitter because his wife abandoned the family, has accepted a deterministic worldview; even Santiago's younger brother, Julio (Alfredo Rodriguez), defines the American Dream as winning a lottery. At his night job as a busboy in a Chinese restaurant, Santiago can't get promoted to waiter because he isn't Chinese—and lacks a green card. Santiago's response, "This is America," although expressed with good humor, serves to remind the viewer of the mythology of America as a melting pot and the reality of distinct ethnic cultures that reject hyphenization and assimilation.

Santiago's first break comes when a part-time scout for Newcastle United, Glen Foy (Stephen Dillane), visiting his daughter in California, observes one of Santiago's matches. After some negotiating with Newcastle's manager, Erik Dornhelm (Marcel Iures), Glen secures a promise that Santiago will be granted a trial if he can make his way to England. Before Santiago lands at Heathrow, he must earn enough money to finance the trip; once he has adequate savings, however, his father uses the cash to purchase a new truck for his landscaping business. Although Santiago's grandmother (Miriam Colon) provides him with a plane ticket bought with her own secret savings, the relationship between father and son has suffered a seemingly irreparable breech. Santiago leaves home—flying to London via Mexico City because he has no U.S. passport—without saying goodbye to his father.

In England, Santiago faces a number of barriers to his career. In spite of how far he has come, he seems incapable of standing up for himself and must rely on others to take up his case. When Dornhelm, preoccupied with the antics of recently signed bad boy Gavin Harris (Alessandro Nivola), is unwilling to let Santiago try out, Santiago is ready to walk off the field without protest. It is Glen, the scout, who speaks on his behalf. After a bad showing in the pouring rain on an impossibly muddy pitch, Santiago slumps away. Although he can be credited for making no excuses for his poor performance, it is once again left to Glen to salvage his chance. Through Glen's intervention, Dornhelm agrees to give Santiago a month to make the reserve squad. Santiago distinguishes himself during the trial period, but once he advances to the reserves, he jeopardizes his future by failing to pass the ball to open teammates and, more significantly, by lying during his physical: even though he has asthma and sometimes uses an inhaler before a match, he states on his medical forms that he has no respiratory problems. When another player, perhaps motivated by Santiago's ball hogging, intentionally crushes his inhaler just before a game, Santiago is unable to keep up and is taken out of the match. Questioned by his coach, he refuses to offer any explanation and is consequently dismissed from United on the assumption that he lacks the stamina to compete in the English game. Santiago abandons his dream and decides to return to his family, but first he goes to say goodbye to Roz (Anna Friel), the team nurse he has been dating.

Fate intervenes in a highly contrived coincidence: the taxi transporting Santiago to the train station gets sidetracked by the dispatcher because Gavin Harris, finding himself late for practice and without wheels after a night of debauchery, requires immediate service. So Santiago's taxi picks up Gavin; Santiago tells Gavin his story; Gavin speaks to Dornhelm about Santiago's talent and explains the asthma. Dornhelm, impressed by Gavin's doing "a decent thing" in standing up for a teammate, rehires Santiago and sends him to see a doctor for proper medication. Soon Santiago has moved up from the reserves and in with Gavin, who exposes him to the fast lane. Santiago is not drawn to the disco scene; however, when Gavin drags him to a party and a misleading photo hits the tabloids, Santiago refuses to incriminate Gavin in the misadventure. He avoids punishment from Dornhelm, but Roz is more difficult to convince of his innocence. Her father was a rock musician who was unable to manage his bit of stardom, deserting the family when Roz was a child; consequently, she distrusts athletes exposed to the limelight.

After the dust settles, Santiago lectures Gavin about his responsibilities to the team and to young fans, advice that Gavin does not accept graciously. However his anger dissipates quickly, having no effect on his or Santiago's play. Santiago earns the respect of his teammates, the manager, and, unknown to him, his father. Although Señor Muñez has refused to speak with his son on the phone, he slips out to an L.A. sports bar to watch him play and announces to the patrons, "That's my son," when Santiago is introduced. A few days later Señor Muñez collapses on the job and dies of a heart attack. Santiago, who still has no idea his father has seen him play, at first feels he should return home, but he changes his mind, telling Roz, who has forgiven him for the earlier misunderstanding, that he doesn't know where home is. Roz says his home is on the soccer pitch, reinforcing his decision to remain in England and play in the final match against Liverpool. Gavin, too, has made peace with Santiago, acknowledged his responsibility for the bad publicity to Dornhelm, and mended his ways. Santiago starts in the final match and passes the ball brilliantly to Gavin, who scores. In the last seconds Santiago is given the chance to make a tie-breaking penalty kick. With his grandmother and younger brother watching from the L.A. sports bar, Santiago makes the goal. In a telephone call to his family, he learns about his father's earlier visits to the bar to watch him play. By the film's end, Gavin has reformed, United has won, and Santiago, with a promising career ahead of him, has resolved his emotional insecurities, made up with his girl, and signed Glen as his agent.

Goal! The Dream Begins received mixed reviews. Critics lamented the idealized vision of professional soccer and its fans presented in the film, but the acting of Nivola and Becker drew wide recognition.

Becker, a star in Mexican telenovelas, spent much of his youth studying violin and attributes his understanding of his character's devotion to soccer to his own musical training. Becker's experience as a soccer player, however, was limited to schoolyard contests. He spent several weeks training with a professional, suffering stress fractures to both ankles in the process. Yet he developed enough skill to imitate proper athletic form, and blue screen technology and digitalization allowed the filmmakers to insert the actors into footage of actual matches. International soccer stars David Beckham, Zinedine Zidane, and Ronaldinho make cameo appearances.

Goal! The Dream Begins was conceived as a trilogy. *Goal! Living the Dream*, released in 2008, follows Santiago's progress as he joins the Real Madrid team but manages his success badly. *Goal! III* was released straight to DVD in the United Kingdom.

GOAL! II: LIVING THE DREAM (2008)

DIRECTOR: Jaume Collet-Serra. SCREENPLAY: Mike Jefferies, Adrian Butchart, Terry Loane. PRODUCERS: Matt Barrelle, Mark Huffam, Mike Jefferies. CINEMATOGRAPHY: Flavio Martinez Labiano. EDITING: Niven Howie. MUSIC: Stephen Warbeck. PRODUCTION DESIGN: Joel Collins. ART DIRECTION: Antonio Calvo-Dominguez, Daniel May, Robin Paiba. COSTUME DESIGN: Nancy Collini, Lindsay Pugh.

CAST: Kuno Becker (Santiago Muñez), Stephen Dillane (Glen Foy), Anna Friel (Roz Harmison), Leonor Varela (Jordana Garcia), Elizabeth Peña (Rosa Maria), Carmelo Gómez (Burruchaga).

RUNNING TIME: 115 minutes.

DVD: Genius Products.

In this sequel, Santiago Muñez is traded to Real Madrid and achieves glory, but at what price?

GOAL! III (2009)

DIRECTOR: Andrew Morahan. SCREENPLAY: Mike Jefferies, Piers Ashworth. PRODUCERS: Matt Barrelle, Peter Heslop, Mike Jefferies. CINEMATOGRAPHY: George Tiffin. EDITING: Giles Bury. MUSIC: Mark Thomas. PRODUCTION DESIGN: Russell De Rozario. ART DIRECTION: Joe Howard. COSTUME DESIGN: Cressida Lewis.

CAST: J. J. Field (Liam Adams), Leo Gregory (Charlie Braithwaite), Kuno Becker (Santiago Muñez), Tamer Hassan (Ronnie), Nick Moran (Nick Ashworth).

RUNNING TIME: 92 minutes.

DVD: Metrodome (UK: PAL).

In the final film of the soccer trilogy, Santiago Muñez's former teammates compete against him for FIFA glory.

THE GOALIE'S ANXIETY AT THE PENALTY KICK (1971)

DIRECTOR: Wim Wenders. SCREENPLAY: Peter Handke, Wim Wenders, based on Handke's novel. PRODUCERS: Peter Genée, Thomas Schamoni. CINEMATOGRAPHY: Robby Müller. EDITING: Peter Przygodda. MUSIC: Jürgen Knieper. PRODUCTION DESIGN: Burghard Schlicht, R. Schneider Manns-Au.

CAST: Arthur Brauss (Joseph Bloch), Erika Pluhar (Gloria), Kai Fischer (Hertha Gabler), Libgart Schwarz (Maid), Maria Bardischewski (Kellnerin).

RUNNING TIME: 101 minutes.

VHS: Pacific Arts Video.

A goalie is ejected from a game, and his despair leads him to even greater darkness.

GOLDEN BOY (1939)

DIRECTOR: Rouben Mamoulian. SCREENPLAY: Lewis Meltzer, Daniel Taradash, Sarah Y. Mason, Victor Heerman, based on

the play by Clifford Odets. PRODUCERS: Rouben Mamoulian, William Perlberg. CINEMATOGRAPHY: Karl Freund, Nicholas Musuraca. EDITING: Otto Meyer. MUSIC: Victor Young. ART DIRECTION: Lionel Banks. COSTUME DESIGN: Robert Kalloch.
CAST: Barbara Stanwyck (Lorna Moon), William Holden (Joe Bonaparte), Adolphe Menjou (Tom Moody), Lee J. Cobb (Joe's father), Joseph Calleia (Eddie Fuseli), Sam Levene (Siggie), Edward Brody (Roxy Lewis).
RUNNING TIME: 99 minutes. B&W.
ACADEMY AWARD NOMINATIONS: Best Original Score.
DVD: Sony Pictures.

Rouben Mamoulian's film *Golden Boy*, adapted from Clifford Odets's 1937 play, focuses on Joe Bonaparte (William Holden), who must choose between being a violinist and becoming a boxer. The film suggests that the two careers are incompatible and that his choice will determine his identity and his true "home." Like many boxing films, *Golden Boy* details the triumph of an underdog, but it also questions the nature of boxing success and portrays the callousness and brutality of all concerned, including the managers, promoters, and spectators.

Joe, who has studied the violin and won a scholarship to a music school, discovers that his hands are also adept at boxing. In his tough New York City neighborhood, he has been ridiculed by his peers for his "sissy" interest in music, and he is concerned about his economic future as a violinist. When he substitutes for a fighter whose hand he has broken while sparring in the gym, he wins the fight; gains a manager in Tom Moody (Adolphe Menjou); meets Lorna Moon (Barbara Stanwyck), Tom's mistress; and earns some money. When he returns home, his father (Lee J. Cobb) is distraught that Joe has fought and does not show him the fifteen-hundred-dollar violin he purchased for Joe's twenty-first birthday. This scene establishes the conflict between boxing and music, money and culture, and head and heart. Balanced against a fistful of dollars is the portrait of Madonna and child, which is on the wall behind Joe's father. Joe declares on his birthday that he is changing his life and that, Western style, "I gotta do what I gotta do."

However, when he later discovers the violin, he plays it and is heard by his father; his sister Anna (Beatrice Blinn); her husband, Siggie (Sam Levene); and Mr. Karp (William H. Strauss), a family friend. When Anna accompanies Joe on the piano, the rest break into song, establishing the Bonaparte home as a haven for culture, harmony, fellowship, and love. Joe and his violin are photographed in a close-up to signify his real commitment to music. Realizing that he must protect his hands, Joe boxes defensively and barely wins his next few bouts. Tom Moody and Roxy Lewis (Edward Brophy), who owns 10 percent of Joe's contract, wonder about Joe's tactics and, taking Lorna with them, go to the Bonaparte home. After they confront Joe, he determines to quit the ring; however, Lorna uses her feminine charms to persuade Joe to change his mind.

When Joe subsequently leaves home for a series of out-of-town bouts, he tells his father that he "doesn't have room" (literally and figuratively) for his violin. His disappointed father refuses to give Joe his blessing, and he also refuses to take the money Joe wins fighting. Without the support of family, Joe soon faces temptation from a gangster/promoter, Eddie Fuseli (Joseph Calleia), who wants to buy part of his contract, and Joe must decide how important his desire is to, Napoleon-like, "conquer the world." Lorna, fearing that Joe will sell his soul, warns him about Eddie. When she and Joe return to his father's home, they reenact the earlier family musical interlude, enjoy a communal meal, and reestablish the Bonaparte home as the place where Joe truly belongs. Unfortunately, Joe's attempt at playing Brahm's "Cradle Song," which he performed successfully at the age of twelve, fails miserably, emphasizing how his musical skills have deteriorated. Joe has learned that boxing and music do not mix, but he has forgotten his earlier speech about boxing being an "insult to a man's soul."

Lorna's feelings for Joe change as a result of hearing him play the violin, attending an outdoor concert with him, and experiencing the wholesome atmosphere of the Bonaparte home. She tells Joe that his "heart" is in his music but he has become "hard shelled and tough." Joe has been "homeless" away from his father's house and not "at home" in the boxing world. In fact, Tom pointedly tells Joe, who has been spending time with Lorna at Tom's Boxing Enterprises office, that his office is not Joe's home. Although five weeks elapse after Joe returns from his out-of-town matches, Joe does not return to his father's. The film indicates this period of homelessness by not showing Joe inside an apartment, hotel, or house.

It appears that Joe has heeded Lorna's advice about staying away from Eddie Fuseli, but after he misinterprets a meeting between Lorna and Tom as a romantic tryst, Joe angrily accepts Eddie's offer to get him a bout at Madison Square Garden. Thinking that Joe is lost, Lorna states her love for Tom. Until the end of the film, Eddie replaces both Joe's father and Lorna in Joe's life. In fact, some of Eddie's comments about Joe suggest a homoerotic subtext not uncommon in boxing films.

When Joe accepts Eddie's offer of a Madison Square Garden bout against a fighter known as "Chocolate Drop" (James "Cannonball" Green), he changes his personality and appearance. Lorna says he is not "the boy I cared about—you murdered him" and adds that Joe is a bad imitation of his gangster friend. When Eddie later offers him a new silk shirt, Joe begins to see the truth, that he has been bought and sold to be used "like a gun." The evening of the fight the violent talk continues as Eddie tells Joe to "go out and kill that Chocolate Drop," to "send him to the cemetery." Balancing Eddie's sadistic advice is Joe's father, who sits like Joe's conscience in the dressing room. Joe's father, acknowledging that it's too late for music, gives Joe his blessing; but Joe knows that he has broken his father's heart. Full of self-pity and sobbing on the table while his sympathetic trainer gives him a rubdown, Joe seems like a little boy motivated by despair and hate. That hatred enables him to knock out his African American opponent in the second round. (During the fight Mamoulian suggests through close-ups that the fans are more crazed and barbaric than the fighters.) Joe's victory, however, is a pyrrhic one: he has killed Chocolate Drop.

After the fight Joe's culpability is the issue. A boxing official enters his dressing room, inspects Joe's gloves and hands (one has been broken in the fight), and states, "Your hands are clean," a reference to Pontius Pilate's hand washing. This religious theme extends to Joe's receiving absolution from Chocolate Drop's father, who advises him to "carry your burden." Lorna, who has learned of Chocolate Drop's death, knows Joe needs her, tells Tom she loves Joe, and goes to Joe. Joe's redemption takes place not in the ring, but out of it; the climax occurs when he confronts Eddie and, after rejecting the prize money, quits fighting. Joe utters the "naked truth" when he tells Eddie, "You made a killer out of me." Eddie responds by slapping Joe, an ambiguous action, and stating that Joe is off his list. When Lorna tells Joe, "You're free," the words sound like the breaking of a contract between a demonic figure and his regenerate pawn.

Faced with a mob of boxing fans, Lorna and Joe leave by an exit that takes them past the ring, where Chocolate Drop died. Joe passes the test but worries that with his broken hand he has no future. When Lorna assures him that the hand will heal, she implies that the healing process is emotional as well as physical. She is no longer just "a dame from Newark," and he, like the Prodigal Son, has returned "home" to his father. The last shots of the film feature Joe and his father embracing with the Madonna and child in the background. Lorna, as much mother and nurturer as lover, joins them in the embrace.

GRACIE (2007)

DIRECTOR: Davis Guggenheim. SCREENPLAY: Lisa Marie Petersen, Karen Janszen. STORY: Andrew Shue, Ken Himmelman, Davis Guggenheim. PRODUCERS: Davis Guggenheim, Andrew Shue, Elisabeth Shue, Lemore Syvan. CINEMATOGRAPHY: Chris Manley.

EDITING: Elizabeth Kling. MUSIC: Mark Isham. PRODUCTION DESIGN: Dina Goldman. ART DIRECTION: Jennifer Dehghan. COSTUME DESIGN: Elizabeth Caitlin Ward)

CAST: Carly Schroeder (Gracie Bowen), Elisabeth Shue (Lindsay Bowen), Dermot Mulroney (Bryan Bowen), Andrew Shue (Coach Clark).

RUNNING TIME: 95 minutes.

DVD: New Line Home Video.

Loosely based on Elisabeth Shue's early years, this film focuses on a young girl's attempt to replace her brother on a high school soccer team after his death in a car accident.

GRAND PRIX (1966)

DIRECTOR: John Frankenheimer. SCREENPLAY: Robert Alan Arthur, William Hanley. PRODUCER: Edward Lewis. CINEMATOGRAPHY: Lionel Lindon. EDITING: Henry Berman, Stu Linder, Frank Santillo. MUSIC: Maurice Jarre. PRODUCTION DESIGN: Richard Sylbert.

CAST: James Garner (Pete Aron), Eva Marie Saint (Louise Frederickson), Yves Montand (Jean-Pierre Sarti), Toshirô Mifune (Izo Yamura), Brian Bedford (Scott Stoddard), Jessica Walter (Pat Stoddard), Antonio Sabato (Nino Barlini).

RUNNING TIME: 176 minutes.

ACADEMY AWARDS: Best Editing, Best Sound, Best Sound Effects.

DVD: MGM.

Grand Prix is a grand tour of the European Formula One racing circuit in the days before race cars were equipped with seatbelts. There's enough of a plot to keep viewers on track for the three hours of viewing time, but the movie is primarily a celebration of speed and skill.

The film's quest for verisimilitude begins with the opening montage, which juxtaposes last-minute preparations of real drivers, rather than actors, minutes before the start of the first race at Monaco. The main characters are introduced briefly, and then the race begins. Filmed in Super Panavision 70 for Cinerama, widescreen projection that creates three-dimensional illusion, *Grand Prix* shifts point of view, sometimes placing the audience in the car with the driver, sometimes using dramatic aerial shots, as well as splitting the screen and tiling with multiple frames.

The film begins at the Monaco Grand Prix, a twisting course of hairpin turns and a range of elevations. Veteran driver Pete Aron (James Garner) is having difficulty with a sticking gear, but is reluctant to allow a British driver and fellow team member, Scott Stoddard (Brian Bedford), to pass. After being given a warning flag, Pete finally signals Scott to go around, but what follows is a spectacular crash that sends Pete's car into the Monte Carlo harbor. Pete is uninjured; however it seems his racing days are over because he is held responsible for the crash. Scott survives, and in spite of the severity of his injuries, is determined to return to the sport. Scott's wife, Pat (Jessica Walter), recognizes that Scott is mentally competing against his dead brother Roger, who was a more successful driver, and she fears that Scott, too, will die in a crash. Unable to handle the tension, she turns her attention to Pete, who has been hired by a network to cover the circuit. Another journalist on the scene, Louise Frederickson (Eva Marie Saint), has begun spending time with a French driver, Jean-Pierre Sarti (Yves Montand), whose marriage has devolved into a business partnership. After Jean-Pierre and Louise fall in love and after his car loses a wheel and goes off the road, killing two young boys in the Belgian Grand Prix, Jean-Pierre decides he will retire at the end of the season, effectively ending his business relationship and his marriage.

Pete does not remain a broadcast journalist for long. Japanese owner Izo Yamura (Toshiro Mifune) recognizes Pete's skill and engages him to drive for the remainder of the season. Although Mr. Yamura was a fighter pilot in World War II and shot down seventeen U.S. planes, both he and Pete have left the past behind and are able to maintain a comfortable working relationship. Pete's return to driving dampens Pat's interest in him, and when Scott takes the initiative to repair the marriage, she agrees, even though Scott also intends to resume driving. Scott wins in the Netherlands but is forced to retire from the British Grand Prix at Brands Hatch when his pain medication affects his concentration. Pete's car begins blowing fuel in the last lap, and he finishes the race with his car in flames, narrowly escaping injury.

The final race takes place in Monza, Italy, on a six-and-a-quarter-mile circuit, half public road and half banked track. Jean-Pierre's wife arrives to say she's not divorcing him no matter what and causes a delay in the delivery of his car. Louise has decided not to watch the race, having grown disillusioned by the dangers of the sport; instead, she goes to a restaurant, but the race is being televised there. Jean-Pierre's car stalls at the start, costing him valuable time. Once he is underway, he steadily increases his speed to catch up. He is making progress when a car ahead of him loses a chunk of metal. Jean-Pierre is unable to avoid the debris and maintain control; his car flies off the road, and he is killed. Louise, who learns of the accident from the television, rushes to the site, but it is Jean-Pierre's wife who gets into the ambulance with his body, leaving Louise behind. Louise extends her hands, smeared with Jean-Pierre's blood, toward the gathered crowd and shrieks, "Is this what you want?" Ferrari displays its black flag to call in the other drivers of the team in a gesture of respect. With the Ferrari team sidelined, Scott and Pete battle for the lead. Pete edges ahead at the finish, a win that puts him in first place for the season. On the winner's stand he invites Scott to join him in celebration. They are drinking champagne from the trophy when Jean-Pierre's death is announced. The scene dissolves to Pete alone on the deserted track, staring at the starting marks and hearing the roar of the engines. Earlier, Pete explained to Mr. Yamura that he drives to feel "more intensely alive," but the closing scene suggests that the degree of intensity is relative to one's sense of mortality.

Director John Frankenheimer, a lifelong racing enthusiast, faced a number of obstacles in completing the project. When first approached, Ferrari refused to cooperate but after agreeing to preview some staged footage, gave filmmakers access to all of its facilities. Similarly, the drivers did not initially welcome the idea of camera crews and actors in their midst, but were soon caught up in the excitement and novelty. In Monaco, local shopkeepers, upset that streets were closed off during filming, staged protests that interrupted the crew and prevented Garner from leaving the scene after his dip in the harbor. Shooting the staged race at Monte Carlo began an hour before the actual race, requiring the filmmakers to work under strict time constraints. Rain during the Belgium race made it necessary to rework staged scenes. Because of an existing contract, Frankenheimer could not use footage shot in Germany. Originally, Frankenheimer had wanted Steve McQueen for the role of Pete Aron, but McQueen was under contract with Warner Brothers, and Frankenheimer was making the film for MGM. McQueen, who was filming *The Sand Pebbles* in Taiwan, had plans of his own for a film, *Day of the Champion* with director John Sturgis. Because *Grand Prix* had gotten off to a sufficient head start in production, Warner Brothers scrapped the project. McQueen later made *Le Mans* (1971) with Lee Katzin as director. McQueen's neighbor and occasional costar, James Garner, also a racing buff, proved a good second choice for the starring role, earning high praise from former driver Bob Bonderant, who trained Garner to handle the Formula One cars. Garner did his own driving in the film, but the other stars required doubles—John Sartees for Yves Montand and Jackie Stewart for Brian Bedford.

THE GREATEST (1977)

DIRECTORS: Tom Gries, Monte Hellman.
SCREENPLAY: Ring Lardner Jr. based on the book *The Greatest: My Own Story* by Muhammad Ali with Richard Durham.
PRODUCER: John Marshall. CINEMATOGRAPHY: Harry Stradling Jr. EDITING: Byron Brandt. MUSIC: Michael Masser. PRODUCTION DESIGN: Robert S. Smith. COSTUME DESIGN: Eric Seelig, Sandra Stewart.
CAST: Muhammad Ali (himself), Ernest Borgnine (Angelo Dundee), John Marley (Dr. Ferdie Pacheco), Robert Duvall (Bill McDonald), James Earl Jones (Malcolm X), Roger E. Mosely (Sonny Liston), Lloyd Haynes (Herbert Muhammad), Ben Johnson (Hollis), Paul Winfield (lawyer).
RUNNING TIME: 101 minutes.
DVD: Sony Pictures.

Muhammad Ali plays himself with the ease of a professional actor in this biopic. The script, based on Ali's autobiography (written with Richard Durham), reveals him as a man with a clear sense of direction, very much in charge of his career and his image.

The film opens with young Cassius Clay (Chip McAllister), as he was then known, being awarded a gold medal at the 1960 Olympics in Rome. Although the American flag forms a backdrop for the scene and the national anthem plays, the pomp and glory of the medal presentation is missing from the shot, which has so little spectacle that the scene could be taking place in a high school gymnasium. The shot anticipates the alienation Cassius experiences in pre–civil rights America.

Upon his return from Italy, Clay greets the local press with a poem, attends church with his parents, entertains several children, and reports for work on the estate of a wealthy white family, where he is called "boy" and scolded for befriending the guard dogs because "it will confuse them in a crisis." He soon quits the job.

Another wealthy white has organized a group of sponsors who will underwrite

Clay's preparation for a professional career. He is invited to an exclusive club to meet them, but he draws stares and glares when a young woman at the table invites him to order a beverage and join the group. Sensing the tension in the room, Clay asks that a friend who has accompanied him to the club be allowed inside as well. His request is obliquely denied. Later, crossing a bridge with the friend, he stops and pitches his Olympic medal into the water below.

The film cuts to a gym, where Clay (now played by Muhammad Ali) has connected with Angelo Dundee (Ernest Borgnine). He correctly predicts the round during which he will take out his more experienced opponent, Lamar Clark, and regales the press with rhyme. The story jumps ahead from this early victory to Clay's growing interest in and eventual conversion to Islam. First, he is shown listening to Malcolm X (James Earl Jones) describing Christianity as a white religion, whereby the "white devil" resides in a heaven on earth while selling black people on the notion of eternal heaven in the hereafter.

Clay's growing attraction to Islam is intercut with his attempts to lure Sonny Liston into the ring. Clay drives a flashy bus to Las Vegas, where he confronts Liston in a casino, prompting Liston to pull out a pistol and fire into the air. Next Clay calls a news desk and, disguising his voice, claims that Cassius Clay has parked outside of Liston's house and is causing trouble. Then he causes trouble, taunting Liston and tossing a bear trap near the front door as he departs. Faced with so much publicity, Liston consents to a title match.

While jogging in preparation for the Liston fight, Clay flirts with a young woman, Ruby Sanderson (Mira Waters), and makes a date. He has also become personally acquainted with Malcolm X, a relationship that concerns the fight promoters. Faced with insistence that he renounce Islam or risk cancelation of the bout, Clay remains firm, promising only to refrain from announcing his faith until after the fight.

At the weigh-in for the Liston bout, Cassius arrives fired up and motormouthing, a tactic he employs to make Liston believe he is mentally and physically unsound—his blood pressure and pulse rate are incredibly high. Moments later, once the press has gone, his vital signs are normal. The fight itself is anticlimactic. A brief section of footage shows Liston being battered, then unable to leave his corner. At the postmatch press conference, Muhammad Ali announces his new name. He ridicules a reporter who asks if he is a black Muslim, as if religions were as racially segregated as America in 1964. He also announces that Herbert Muhammad, son of Elijah Muhammad, will take over as his manager and advisor.

Ali's religious conversion creates conflict in his relationship with Ruby (who is his first wife, although the film skips that information). When she wears a short, tight dress (a dress that Ali has bought for her) to a party, he is upset that she is appearing so uncovered in public. In a scene that does not show Ali in a positive light, he strong-arms her up the stairs and rips the dress in an effort to lengthen the hem. The film skirts the breakup with Ruby and moves to a scene in which Herbert advises Ali to eliminate middlemen who are cutting into his profit. Herbert reminds Ali that black fighters have a history of being exploited financially. The story then shifts to Ali's draft reclassification. Although he failed an eligibility exam, standards have been lowered, making him eligible for the draft.

Following an interview during which he expresses that he has nothing against the Viet Cong, Ali enters a bakery, where he has noticed an attractive Muslim woman.

Ali has already introduced himself to her parents and acquired their permission to take her out. The film jumps to an induction center. Outside, there are antiwar protests. Inside, Ali refuses to step forward and accept induction into the military. He is taken aside by an officer who tries to persuade him that declaring conscientious objector status will not wash because there are Muslims in the armed services. A major then lays out a scenario in which Ali will be kept out of combat, and, like Sergeant Joe Louis from an earlier era, be assigned to fight exhibition matches and boost morale. Once again, Ali demonstrates that he possesses the courage of his convictions and refuses the offer. He appeals a mandatory jail sentence and is permitted bail, but he is stripped of his title, and his boxing license and passport are revoked. In the midst of this, Ali marries Belinda. Joe Frazier becomes heavyweight champion.

Ali's attempts to meet Frazier in Toronto are squashed by the government, which will not permit him to travel outside of the country. Lester Maddox, governor of Georgia, allows Ali to fight there, but he is pitted against Jerry Quarry rather than Frazier. Ali wins the bout, but his stay in Georgia is marked by repeated racial incidents.

Finally, in 1971, the Supreme Court decides in his favor, and Ali is able to return to the boxing circuit. After a disappointing loss to Frazier, he embarks on a comeback, but that is cut short when Ken Norton fractures Ali's jaw and wins a decision. After the fight, Belinda, unable to cope with the punishment Ali has absorbed, experiences a breakdown.

The film skips over rematches with both Frazier and Norton, decisions which went to Ali, and picks up with Ali preparing to meet George Foreman, who had won the heavyweight title from Frazier. Foreman is a powerful fighter with a long reach and is heavily favored to win. Angelo Dundee's advice is to avoid getting hit and to stay off the ropes, but Ali has devised his own "rope-a-dope" strategy. For seven rounds, Ali absorbs hundreds of body punches from Foreman, exhausting the younger fighter. Then, in the eighth, Ali decks Foreman and regains the title. The knockout is shown in slow motion, and then the credits run.

Although the film ignores Ali's womanizing and his marriage troubles, it does not gloss over his controversial criticisms of Christianity, the government, and institutionalized racism. Still, Muhammad Ali comes across as a likeable, sincere, and admirable man.

THE GREATEST GAME EVER PLAYED (2005)

DIRECTOR: Bill Paxton. SCREENPLAY: Mark Frost, based on his book. PRODUCERS: David Blocker, Larry Brezner, Mark Frost. CINEMATOGRAPHY: Shane Hurlbut. EDITING: Elliot Graham. MUSIC: Brian Tyler. PRODUCTION DESIGN: François Séguin. ART DIRECTION: Martin Gendron, Pierre Perrault. COSTUME DESIGN: Renée April.

CAST: Shia LaBeouf (Francis Ouimet), Stephen Dillane (Harry Vardon), Elias Koteas (Arthur Ouimet), James Paxton (young Harry Vardon).

RUNNING TIME: 120 minutes.

DVD: Buena Vista Home Entertainment.

Walt Disney Films has produced inspiring films about dramatic events in sports history: *Miracle* (2004), the story of the American hockey team's surprising triumph at the 1980 Olympics and *Remember the Titans* (2000), about the successful integration of a Virginia high school football team. *The Greatest Game Ever Played* also captures an historic moment in sports history. It is perhaps the best golf movie ever shot, in part because it contains a good deal of golf footage, but also because it depicts a turning point in the history of golf. Mark Frost wrote the screenplay, which he adapted from his book of the same title. In the course of the film the game of golf changes considerably. Played in private clubs by "gentlemen" and in tournaments by professionals, golf at the U.S. Open tournament provides the opportunity to break down the class barriers that existed not only in England but also in the United States. The two principals, Harry Vardon and Francis Ouimet, are rivals, but they are remarkably similar in their roles as "outsiders" who seek admittance and acceptance into the "genteel" world of golf.

Director Bill Paxton incorporates black-and-white footage in the opening sequence to establish the authenticity of the story being told. It begins on the Isle of Jersey in 1879, when young Harry Vardon (James Paxton, Bill Paxton's son) awakes to find that the thatched-roof cottage in which his family live is being razed to make room for a golf club. The four black-clad figures who haunt the adult Harry's life explain that the club is "not for the likes of you" because the sport is "played by gentlemen." Flipping Harry a dismissive coin, they leave, but the coin continues to flip on the screen until it seems to land in Brookline, Massachusetts, where the Ouimet family lives adjacent to another golf club. Both Francis Ouimet and Harry are people close to "the club" but not belonging to that world. The moral quality of that world is demonstrated when a club member kicks his found ball into a better lie, thereby cheating. Francis (played by Matthew Knight), who finds the member's ball, also finds a Harry Vardon ball, which becomes an icon for him. At night he religiously reads Vardon's *The Stylist* while holding the ball in his other hand. His mother (Marnie McPhail), knowing that Francis also practices putting in his room at night, takes her son to an exhibition in Boston, where he meets Harry. Under Harry's tutelage, Francis learns to grip and hit the ball correctly.

Francis's father (Elias Koteas), Arthur, however, is not as supportive of Francis's desire to play golf, which he believes is "not for the likes of us." He, too, has had dreams, but he has learned to accept things as they are. For Arthur, "a man knows his place," and he wants to protect Francis from failure and disappointment. He insists, "We're not those kind of people." Finally, Arthur extracts a promise from Francis to quit playing if he fails to qualify for the tournament.

In the meantime, Harry faces his own class barriers. Upon his return to England, he and Lord Northcliffe (Peter Firth) discuss the upcoming U.S. Open, which Northcliffe is determined to have in English hands. For him, it is an extension of the empire on which the sun never sets, and he wants Harry to bring the trophy home so that the Brits dominate golf as well as cricket and the other "gentlemanly" sports. To enlist Harry's help, he mentions the possibility of an "honorary" membership, not a real membership, in the club. Harry agrees to play but will need financing and another strong player. Although Northcliffe suggests Wilfred Reid, a top British amateur, as a partner, Harry has someone else in mind, Ted Ray (Stephen Marcus), a burly Jersey man like himself. When he introduces Northcliffe to Ted, the meeting is at a sleazy bar, where Northcliffe is out of his element. Ted mentions "ruling class masters" and facetiously kisses Northcliffe's hand.

Back in Massachusetts, Francis (now Shia LaBeouf), having been exposed to the good life, sees young Sarah Wallis (Amanda Tillson) in riding habit and becomes acquainted with some of the members in the club across the street (the street his father said he would never be allowed to cross) who are more democratic than their English counterparts. Francis wins the Massachusetts high school golf championship and begins playing with a man who eventually becomes the sponsor he needs to play in the qualifying round for the U.S. Open. Mr. Campbell (Luke Askew), who runs the club, becomes Francis's early morning golf tutor and helps him improve. After he is approved for the qualifying round, a matter of social acceptability, Francis is invited to the club for the pretournament party, where he meets the older Sarah (Peyton List), who is with her snobbish brother and father. Determined to fit in, Francis lies about the whereabouts of his tuxedo, invents a family in Philadelphia, and avoids mentioning college by telling Sarah he is "considering his options." The pose is ruined by her brother (Max Kasch), who calls him "Caddie Boy," and her father, who tells him, "You may have been invited, but don't get the idea you belong here."

Francis does well in the qualifying round, but under pressure on the last hole, he looks up, sees his father, and misses the putt, failing to qualify by one stroke. He returns home, packs up his golf mementos, and resigns himself to learning a trade, bringing home some money, and forgetting his dream. The last shot of his father shows him reading an edition of *L'Etoile*, a French newspaper that ties him to the Old World and its notions of class. Francis's job is with a sporting goods store, where he is physically close to the golf equipment he has pledged not to use. One night he accompanies his mother to a vaudeville show where he sees Sarah and her family sitting in posh seats. Francis feels a connection to the opera singer, who says that she channels the words through her body. He wants to feel the same sensation when he plays golf. The next day a U.S. Open official visits Francis at the store and tells him the Open is looking for a local to compete in the tournament. Honoring his promise, Francis rejects the offer to play, but after seeing Sarah again and talking with Harry, he changes his mind. Once again he must play in a qualifying round. This time he makes up six shots with six birdies to join the tournament field.

A setback occurs the next day when Billy, his caddy, opts to take a better offer from another golfer, but Billy's undersized brother Eddie (Josh Flitter) volunteers to caddy for Francis. Eddie has the golf patter down, knows the course, and acts as moral support for Francis, who stays in contention. Meanwhile, John McDermott (Michael Weaver), the reigning American champ, is playing with Harry, who at one point sees in the gallery the four men from his childhood—he seems unable to shake them from his memory. Francis has his own problems when he lets the sight of President Taft break his concentration and hits into the woods. However, Eddie gets him back on course. Sarah gives Eddie a pendant to give to Francis as a kind of good-luck charm.

That night, after two rounds have been completed, two dinners take place that keep the class issue before the audience. Wilfred Reid, who has been playing well, enters the club dining room and joins Ted Ray and Harry. Wilfred tells Ted that he should feel right at home in America with "your kind of people," where "you're a working-class hero." Ted knocks him out of his chair. At the Ouimet home Francis's father asks Francis about "pay" and "work," warning him that the rich will only use him. In round three, Wilfred's game falters, as does John McDermott's, so that Francis is the only American hope left, trailing Ted and Harry by one stroke.

In the final round Harry can't shake the four men from his past, Francis dons Sarah's "token," Lord Northcliffe calls Eddie a "pygmy," and Ted and Harry seem headed for an all-English playoff the next day. As the Brits stage a premature celebration in the clubhouse, during which Northcliffe dismisses Francis as a "peasant," "common clay, not a gentleman," Francis comes back to tie Ted and Harry. Harry intervenes on Francis's behalf and demands respect for him.

The morning of the playoff, termed a battle of "one David and two Goliaths" by the sportswriters, the Brookline Club officials attempt to replace Eddie with another caddie, but Francis defends him and tells them, Harry-like, not to talk to his caddie again. During the round Ted tries to replicate a shot through the trees he had made earlier but misses, taking him out of contention. Likewise, Harry flies the trees on a dogleg, encouraging Francis to follow his lead, but Eddie wisely warns him against the shot. Harry is in a sand trap rather than on the green. Francis wins, as Ted applauds. Since he is an amateur, Francis cannot take any of the money he's offered, but he sees that the hat is passed for Eddie—even his father, who has come to the course, contributes. A postscript explains that Francis won two American amateur championships and that he and Eddie, who became a millionaire, were lifelong friends.

The film, which addresses the relationship between sports and class and which demonstrates the parallels between Vardon and Ouimet, was nominated for an ESPN Best Sports Movie Award in 2006, and Josh Flitter's performance as Eddie won him a nomination from ESPN for Best Performance in a Supporting Role.

THE GREAT GAME (1930)

Director: Jack Raymond. Screenplay: Ralph Gilbert Bettison, W. P. Lipscomb. Story: William Hunter, John Lees. Producer: L'Estrange Fawcett. Cinematography: Basil Emmott.

Cast: John Batten (Dicky Brown), Renee Clama (Peggy Jackson), Jack Cock (Jim Blake), Randle Ayrton (Henderson), Rex Harrison (George).

Running Time: 79 minutes.

This early British sound film is about a young football (soccer) player who dreams of joining the local club as they pursue cup glory.

THE GREAT GAME (1953)

Director: Maurice Elvey. Screenplay: Wolfgang Wilhelm, based on the play *Shooting Star* by Basil Thomas. Producer: David Dent. Cinematography: Phil Grindrod. Editing: Lito Carruthers. Music: W. L. Trytel. Art Direction: George Haslam.

Cast: James Hayter (Joe Lawson), Thora Hird (Miss Rawlings), Diana Dors (Lulu Smith), Sheila Shand Gibbs (Mavis Pink), John Laurie ("Mac" Wells).

Running Time: 80 minutes.

Scandal erupts after a football (soccer) club tries to recruit a player from a rival club.

THE GREAT MATCH (2006)

Director: Gerardo Olivares. Screenplay: Gerardo Olivares, Chema Rodríguez. Producers: José María Morales, Andre Sikojev, Sophokles Tasioulis. Cinematography: Gerardo Olivares. Editing: Rosario Sainz de Rozas. Music: Martin Meissonnier.

Cast: Atibou Aboubacar (Hasan), Adalberto Jr. (missionary), Ahmed Alansar (Aboubacar), Tano Alansar (Hamidou), Abu Aldanish (Aldanish).

Running Time: 88 minutes.

DVD: Film Movement.

Directed by Gerardo Olivares, a documentary filmmaker for the Discovery

Channel, *The Great Match* is a visually pleasing comedy about soccer fans in remote parts of the world. Using "nonactors," Olivares tracks the efforts of three unlikely groups to watch the televised 2002 World Cup match between Germany and Brazil. The film alternates among locations—the Mongolian steppe, the Tenere region of the Sahara, and the Brazilian rainforest—as it follows the progress of the various tribes.

The Mongolian nomads are introduced first on the snow-covered Altai Mountains, hunting on horseback with eagles. After catching a fox, they begin their journey home to the communal yurt, which is set up near a power line on the steppe. Although they are successful in tapping the line, a security force arrives and issues the nomads a citation for unauthorized use of electricity. But when the officers realize the World Cup is soon to be played, they accept the nomads' offer to stay for tea. While waiting for the match to begin, the officers and the nomads play their own game of soccer. A policeman who misses a penalty kick is assigned to stand guard outside of the yurt during the match. (The Mongolian women think the men's obsession with soccer is foolish.)

In the Saharan desert a Tuareg caravan is making its way toward a "tree," the remnant of a military installation that they plan to use as an antenna. A truck overloaded with passengers and baggage is headed in the opposite direction toward the nearest city, where the male passengers hope to watch the game. Since both sets of fans fear they are too far from their destinations to arrive in time for the match, they quickly reach a deal: the truck driver will transport the Tuareg and their television to the "tree," while one unfortunate nomad stays behind to watch the camels. Using the truck battery for power, the Saharan group obtains a clear picture—in color no less. (The Arab women passengers do not share the men's enthusiasm for the sport and would rather be continuing toward their destination than sitting in the middle of the desert waiting for the match to end.)

In Brazil, a group of Amazon Indians is unsuccessfully hunting monkeys in the Brazilian jungle. The leader wears a soccer jersey that he claims is a Nike original rather than a knockoff. As they return to camp, the men weigh their options for watching the game, deciding to power up their own telly with a hand-cranked generator rather than venturing to the mission or a nearby sawmill. One of the men climbs a tree, where he positions a satellite dish on his head, producing a blurred, rolling picture. When the member of the tribe cranking the generator becomes exasperated, the men head off first to the mission, where they are rebuffed, and finally, to the sawmill, where they are able to watch with the white mill operators. (The Amazon women have sabotaged the men's original plan—to run a stolen cable from the mission—by slicing up the wire and making jewelry, an act that the men believe must result from the women's stupidity rather than a clever plot.)

Much of the humor in the film derives from the juxtaposition of tribal customs and contemporary Western culture, but in each segment, the nomadic tribes find common ground with those representing more modern societies. While the film reflects an idealized view of sports as promoting harmony, the portrayal of the ethnic groups is uneven. The Mongolians, who open the film, are shown as skilled horsemen and hunters; the family elders are revered eccentrics—the grandmother's utterances are dutifully recorded as ancient wisdom whether they make sense or not, and the grandfather's collection of rubber ducks, acquired while he worked in Russia, is prominently displayed in the yurt. The humor here relies on incongruity more than disparagement. When the scene shifts to the desert, however, the comedy acquires more bite. The Tuareg are shown as comfortable in their environment, but their leader, who demands to be treated as royalty—carried about in his lawn chair and given the choice seat for the match—is presented satirically as a petty tyrant whose power erodes as the film progresses. The Amazon Indians are portrayed as clowns from the very start, outwitted by the monkeys they hunt. They are the only group who fail in their efforts to power up their television, and they are the only people who must rely on whites for access to the broadcast. This imbalance works against the film's central theme of transcending racial and ethnic boundaries and reinforces rather than satirizes stereotypes of jungle dwellers.

THE GREAT RACE (1965)

DIRECTOR: Blake Edwards. SCREENPLAY: Arthur A. Ross, Blake Edwards. PRODUCER: Martin Jurow. CINEMATOGRAPHY: Russell Harlan. EDITING: Ralph E. Winters. MUSIC: Henry Mancini. PRODUCTION DESIGN: Fernando Carrere. COSTUME DESIGN: Don Feld

CAST: Tony Curtis (The Great Leslie), Jack Lemmon (Professor Fate), Natalie Wood (Maggie Dubois), Peter Falk (Max), Keenan Wynn (Hezekiah), Arthur O'Connell (Henry Goodbody), Vivian Vance (Hester Goodbody).

RUNNING TIME: 160 minutes.

ACADEMY AWARDS: Best Sound Effects (Treg Brown). NOMINATIONS: Best Cinematography (Color), Best Film Editing, Best Original Song ("The Sweetheart Tree"; music by Henry Mancini, lyrics by Johnny Mercer), Best Sound (George Groves).

DVD: Warner Home Video.

This comedy, set in 1908, is about a New York-to-Paris car race and features Jack Lemmon as the villain.

THE GREAT WHITE HOPE (1970)

DIRECTOR: Martin Ritt. SCREENPLAY: Howard Sackler, based on his play. PRODUCER: Lawrence Turman. CINEMATOGRAPHY: Burnett Guffey. EDITING: William Reynolds. PRODUCTION DESIGN: John De Cuir. ART DIRECTION: Jack Martin Smith. COSTUME DESIGN: Irene Sharaff.

CAST: James Earl Jones (Jack Jefferson), Jane Alexander (Eleanor Backman), Lou Gilbert (Goldie), Joel Fluellen (Tick), Chester Morris (Pop Weaver), Robert Webber (Dixon), Hal Holbrook (Al Cameron), Beah Richards (Mama Tiny), Moses Gunn (Scipio).

RUNNING TIME: 103 minutes.

ACADEMY AWARD NOMINATIONS: Best Actor (Jones), Best Actress (Alexander).

DVD: 20th Century Fox.

The Great White Hope begins with the written statement "Much of what follows is true," and to America's shame this story of white complicity to destroy the boxing career of Jack Jefferson (a thinly disguised Jack Johnson) and preserve the myth of white supremacy is right on target. The source of the film is a Pulitzer Prize–winning play by Howard Sackler, who also wrote the screenplay, which won him a nomination from the Writer's Guild of America for Best Drama Adapted from Another Medium. James Earl Jones (Jack Jefferson) and Jane Alexander (Eleanor Backman) reprised their Broadway roles, and both were nominated for Oscars. The story begins with Jefferson's triumph in Sydney, Australia, and ends with his defeat.

The first fight footage is restricted to shots of the legs of two boxers, one black and one white, and then the prone body of the white fighter on the mat. It is that sight that prompts bigoted white promoters to plead with Frank Brady (Larry Pennell), the retired white champion, to return to the ring and restore racial pride. The promoters schedule the title bout for Reno, Nevada, "white man's country," which will prove more inaccessible to black fans, who also are unable to buy tickets for the bout. In Reno there are flags, parades, a black effigy, and trainloads of whites who jeer at Jack at the official weigh-in.

Before the bout Jack and his manager, Goldie (Lou Gilbert), are in the gymnasium awaiting the arrival of reporters. Jack's white girlfriend, Eleanor, who is also there, presents a problem for Goldie, who does not want to give the reporters a story that could inflame racial tension. The reporters yield to Goldie's request that they not write about Eleanor and Jack, but then Clara (Marlene Warfield), Jack's former lover, appears, calling herself his common-law wife and calling Eleanor "grey meat." Jack reminds her that she left him for a pimp and has her taken out of the gym, but she reappears later in the film.

Although they are greatly outnumbered, many black fans support Jack, hoping he will "win for us colored." Jack's response disappoints. He says he is fighting for himself and that he is "just a black ugly fist" to his fans. The minister who accompanies the crowd tells him, "You ain't thinking colored," a quotation that resurfaces when he travels back to Chicago in triumph after the fight. There, a black man takes Jack to task for "hustling for the white man," asking him, "How white you want to be?" At this point Jack is certainly aware of racial problems, but he does not want to be a black leader or to engage in political action.

Others, including black leaders like Booker T. Washington, who favored accommodation, and federal agents who feared the northern migration of southern blacks and the influence of successful men like Jack, saw him as a political activist and were intent on discrediting him. Agent Dixon (Robert Webber) and the Chicago district attorney go so far as to interview Eleanor about her association with Jack. The questions are initially innocuous, but soon the word *unnatural* reveals the exact nature of the questions. Eleanor calls them "slimy, no-dick money grabbers" and leaves. While the district attorney is doubtful about pinning something on Jack, Dixon intends to pursue him for violating the Mann Act, legislation intended to outlaw trafficking in prostitution. When Jack and Eleanor cross the Illinois state line, their vacation is interrupted by Dixon and state troopers. Jack is arrested and subsequently convicted of violating the Mann Act, fined, and sentenced to three years in jail.

Free on bail, Jack visits his mother, family, and friends, including the Detroit Blue Jays, a black baseball team. By wearing the uniform of one of the players, he escapes, fleeing to Canada, where Eleanor joins him. When Clara learns he is intent on escape, she tries to stop him, but fails. He then goes to England, where he plans to box; however, the American government uses its influence and, citing his "immorality," prevents him from fighting there. In France he fares no better. Showered with boos, taunts, and vegetables after administering a savage beating to a French fighter, Jack tries Germany, where he is reduced to playing Uncle Tom in a stage version of *Uncle Tom's Cabin*—Eleanor and Tick (Joel Fluellen), his trainer, also perform in the play. He manages to keep his infuriating grin until he sings "I See a Band of Spirits Bright" and breaks into a shuffling stint that includes acting like a monkey.

Pop Weaver (Chester Morris), a promoter, has been talking with Goldie and offers Jack a deal. Pop advises him to go back to America, visit his ailing mother, and throw a fight for the championship, all in return for $100,000. Jack declines. After Pop and Goldie leave, Jack and Eleanor go to Mexico, where they live in squalor as Jack trains for fights that will never take place. Frustrated and angry, he verbally abuses her; when she refuses to leave him, he beats her with a towel. Dixon and a Mexican official notify Jack that the Mexicans have caved to American pressure and he will be sent to prison unless he fights—and loses—in Havana against the Kid (Jim Beattie), the white contender, for the championship. At that point Eleanor's body is brought in—she has thrown herself down a well and broken her neck.

The Havana travesty contains more boxing footage than any of Jack's other fights, and it features his terrible beating at the hands of an inferior fighter, thereby stressing what the government has subjected him to. As Agent Dixon, Pop, and thousands of the Kid's supporters watch, Jack is repeatedly knocked down, but he does make a comeback, demonstrating what he could have done to the challenger. In the twelfth round, however, Jack lets himself be knocked out, and Frank Brady triumphantly holds the championship belt aloft. The belt is safely in the hands of the "family" again. (It would be 1937 before Joe Louis would win the title from the white boxer Jim Braddock.) In response to a question about whether or not he "really" lost, Jack answers, "I ain't got those 'reallies'" and disappears through a narrow walkway that serves to emphasize his entrapment and powerlessness.

Such was the bigotry and fear of blacks in the early twentieth century that the U.S. Congress in 1912 voted to prohibit transporting movies of boxing matches over state lines. The government believed that films of Johnson's victories would incite blacks and encourage political activism. *The Great White Hope* is not, of course, a reference to Johnson/Jefferson, who is the protagonist in the story. Rather it is about the determined effort to replace him with a white fighter.

The Great White Hope fared as well as a film as it did as a drama. Jones received an Oscar nomination for Best Actor and won the Golden Globe Award for Most Promising Newcomer; Alexander also was nominated for an Oscar as Best Actress and for a Golden Globe for Most Promising Newcomer.

GREAT WHITE HYPE (1996)

DIRECTOR: Reginald Hudlin. SCREENPLAY: Ron Shelton, Tony Hendra. PRODUCERS: Fred Berner, Joshua Donen. CINEMATOGRAPHY: Ron Garcia. EDITING: Earl Watson. MUSIC: Marcus Miller. PRODUCTION DESIGN: Charles Rosen. ART DIRECTION: Scott Ritenour. COSTUME DESIGN: Ruth E. Carter.

CAST: Samuel L. Jackson (Reverend Fred Sultan), Jeff Goldblum (Mitchell Kane), Damon Wayans (James "The Grim Reaper" Roper), Peter Berg (Terry Conklin), Corbin Bernsen (Peter Prince), Jon Lovitz (Sol), Cheech Marin (Julio Escobar), John Rhys-Davies (Johnny Windsor), Jamie Foxx (Hassan El Ruk'n).

RUNNING TIME: 91 minutes.

DVD: 20th Century Fox.

Tony Hendra, the founding editor of *National Lampoon*, originally developed this screenplay in 1990 for director Ron Shelton. Hendra described the project for *Entertainment Weekly* as a satire about racism and the way the "black boxing establishment handpicks white contenders." But the project ended up with director Reginald Hudlin, whose biggest hit was *House Party* (1990). The result of this change was an unfortunate "cynical inversion" of *Rocky* (1976), as one reviewer described it. Hudlin directs with a heavier hand than Shelton might have used.

Samuel L. Jackson plays the Reverend Fred Sultan, a flamboyant fight promoter patterned after the notorious Don King. Reverend Sultan handles heavyweight

Samuel L. Jackson, Damon Wayans, and Corbin Bernsen in *Great White Hype*

champion James "The Grim Reaper" Roper (Damon Wayans). Another black boxer, Marvin Shabazz (Michael Jace) and his manager Hassan El Ruk'n (Jamie Foxx) want to challenge the champ, but Sultan is worried about the gate and pay-for-view television sales, which are down. Apparently fans have tired of the black-on-black boxing scene, and something needs to be done to get the fans excited.

A groupie named Bambi (Salli Richardson) hits upon a solution that the men are not clever enough to think of. As a professional, Reaper is undefeated, but Bambi remembers that while James was still an amateur, he was defeated by a white boxer named Terry Conklin (played by Peter Berg of the television series *Chicago Hope*), who has since become a punk rocker in Cleveland and the leader of a band called Massive Head Wound. Sultan goes to Cleveland and manages to cut a deal with Terry, who now claims to be a nonviolent Buddhist devoted to a cause—helping the homeless. Terry gets over his nonviolent reservations after Sultan promises him $10 million to help the homeless. Conklin acquires a "clean-cut white-boy" haircut and goes into training, but James isn't worried. He smokes cigarettes, gains over twenty pounds, and for inspiration watches the blaxploitation cult film *Dolemite* (1975). "My blackness will beat that kid," he claims.

Meanwhile, a parallel plot kicks in involving Mitchell Kane (Jeff Goldblum), an investigative journalist and documentary filmmaker who has photographic evidence showing Reverend Sultan in compromising positions with a number of women. Sultan easily buys him off by hir-

Corbin Bernsen and Samuel L. Jackson in *Great White Hype*

ing Mitchell to replace his public relations officer, Sol (Jon Lovitz). Mitchell turns out to be an overreacher who actually believes that Terry might beat the champ and therefore shifts his allegiance away from Sultan in order to become Terry's manager; this betrayal comes just before the fight, which will end with a first-round knockout by James. Terry's trainer, Johnny Windsor (John Rhys-Davies), has anticipated the outcome, but he understands boxing. His job is merely to train Terry to *look* like a professional boxer.

For the fight, Terry is called "Irish Terry," even though he is not really Irish. His trainer explains that in boxing, "if you're white, you're Irish." So when Irish Terry shows up for the fight, he is wearing a modified kilt, and his fans are wearing the green. Paul Newman's Buffalo Bill Cody said it best in Robert Altman's *Buffalo Bill and the Indians* (1976): "The Truth is whatever gets the loudest applause." The "hype" of the title is amusingly developed, leading up to the so-called Fight of the Millennium. An entourage of midgets dressed as leprechauns and playing bagpipes lead Irish Terry into the ring. Reaper Roper is robed as a hip Grim Reaper, a hooded specter who makes his entrance accompanied by the Reaper Roper Rappers.

The real challenge here is to satirize the professional boxing scene, which has been so obviously corrupted by greed and manipulation and the antics of real-life promoters like Don King. It seems beyond the pale of mere satire. *Variety* claimed that at times the satire was "dead on," despite the "thin, uneven scripting and unfocused direction," in the words of reviewer Godfrey Cheshire (May 6–12, 1996). Sultan is a caricature, and so is Cheech Marin's Hispanic president of the World Boxing Association and Jon Lovitz's Jewish publicist. Of course the film is not without some comic moments, but the reviews tended to be as cliché ridden as the characters. Janet Maslin's *New York Times* review (May 3, 1996) was entitled "Float Like a Butterball, Hit Like a Flea." *Washington Post* reviewer Rita Kempley found "more laughs in the Tyson-McNeeley bout" than in this "cynical inversion" of *Rocky*.

GREGORY'S GIRL (1981)

DIRECTOR: Bill Forsyth. SCREENPLAY: Bill Forsyth. PRODUCERS: Davina Belling, Clive Parsons. CINEMATOGRAPHY: Michael Coulter. EDITING: John Gow. MUSIC: Colin Tully. ART DIRECTION: Adrienne Atkinson.
CAST: John Gordon Sinclair (Gregory), Dee Hepburn (Dorothy), Jake D'Arcy (Phil Menzies), Clare Grogan (Susan), Robert Buchanan (Andy), William Greenlees (Steve).
RUNNING TIME: 91 minutes.
DVD: MGM.

Gregory's Girl, written and directed by Bill Forsyth, was a success with audiences and critics. Forsyth won the British Academy Award for Best Screenplay and was nominated for Best Director, and John Gordon Sinclair, who played Gregory, was nominated for Best Newcomer. The film was also a nominee for Best Film. Considering that *Chariots of Fire* was among the competition, this low-budget coming-of-age film did very well. Although Gregory and Dorothy (Dee Hepburn), his "girl," are both soccer players, there is little soccer footage. Most of the on-field action is of the practice variety; in some scenes Dorothy peppers shots past Gregory, an inept goalie more intent on watching her than on blocking her shots.

In the opening sequence Gregory and his pals stand behind a clump of trees and watch a young woman undress. Their adolescent reactions are mocked by a group of younger boys who dismiss the action as childish, but the film focuses on the awakening sexual interest of inexperienced youth who are fascinated and mystified by the actions of their more sophisticated and physically mature female classmates. In the next sequence young boys play soccer as Dorothy runs in the distance, a shot unifying the boys' interests.

Phil Menzies (Jake D'Arcy), Gregory's soccer coach, informs Gregory that he intends to make some changes in the team's lineup since the team has lost eight straight games. Gregory, who seems blissfully unaware of any implications for him, states that soccer is "only a game," a comment that hardly impresses Phil. In response to Phil's comments about his lackluster play, Gregory admits that "it's a tricky time for me" since he has grown four inches in the past year, but he does not realize just how "tricky" his situation is. Phil announces a tryout for new players, and the few who appear are simply awful.

Although Dorothy is late and is a girl, Phil decides to let her try out. She outruns the boys, dribbles the ball skillfully, and shoots accurately; however, Phil must consult with the headmaster before she can join the team. The headmaster, perhaps aware of the gathering storm of women's rights, gives his permission. After Phil assigns her to Gregory's position, Gregory is moved to goalie, displacing his dimwitted friend Andy (Robert Buchanan), who tells Gregory, "Girls weren't made to play football [soccer]." But Gregory is so infatuated with Dorothy that her mere mention of spending time in Italy makes him want to enroll in Italian classes. When she asks him to practice with her at lunchtime, he eagerly agrees and watches her score at will against him. After she is interviewed by a reporter for the school newspaper, he finally gets enough nerve to ask her for a date, and she accepts, much to his disbelief.

For his date Gregory is coached by his younger sister, Madeline (Allison Forster), a precocious ten-year-old who is more knowledgeable than Gregory. In fact, most of Gregory's peers seem as sexually clueless as he. Billy (Douglas Sannachan) brags about his voyeuristic exploits as a window washer, but has not had any sexual experience. Andy and Charley (Graham Thompson) prove to be conversational duds when they attempt to join two girls at lunch. Gregory, despite his borrowed coat and new shoes, is hardly prepared for the game that begins when he waits for Dorothy to meet him by the clock in town.

Gregory is posed before a large clock, which ticks ominously, and when he thinks he's been stood up, Carol (Caroline Guthrie) appears and tells him that Dorothy is not coming because "something turned up" (she was receiving coaching that turned into dancing with Phil). Gregory has been passed from Dorothy to Carol, who goes for a snack with Gregory before making a phone call and passing him on to Margot, who walks with him, makes a phone call, and passes him on to Susan (Clare Grogan), who has had a crush on him. The two go for a walk in the park (Andy and Charley are impressed since they've seen him with three girls), where they dance, lie on the grass, stare at the sky, and talk. The camera photographs them as they lie on their backs, then tilts so that they appear to be upright facing each other, increasing the intimacy. After Susan walks him home and kisses him good night, she has "scored," thanks to the deft passes from her teammates/fellow conspirators.

GRIDIRON GANG (2006)

Director: Phil Joanou. Screenplay: Jeff Maguire, Jac Flanders. Producers: Neal H. Moritz, Lee Stanley. Cinematography: Jeff Cutter. Editing: Joel Negron. Music: Trevor Rabin. Production Design: Floyd Albee. Costume Design: Sanja Milkovic Hays.

Cast: Dwayne Johnson (Sean Porter), Xzibit (Malcolm Moore), L. Scott Caldwell (Bobbi Porter), Leon Rippy (Paul Higa), Kevin Dunn (Ted Dexter).

Running Time: 125 minutes.

DVD: Sony Pictures.

Gridiron Gang is based on a true story, Sean Porter's successful efforts to create a football team at Camp Kilpatrick, a juvenile detention center in California; Porter's accomplishments were also chronicled in an Emmy Award–winning documentary in 1993. The movie's plot may seem familiar because the idea of molding a bunch of criminals into an effective team has a cinematic history. *The Dirty Dozen* (1967) may have been the seed of this plot, but the success of *The Longest Yard* (1974, with a 2005 remake featuring Adam Sandler) suggests that the story is an appealing one for sports fans, especially those who cling to the idea that sports develop character.

In *Gridiron Gang*, Sean Porter (Dwayne "The Rock" Johnson) is exposed to the street life of the young men at Kilpatrick and wants to find something to fill the void in their lives. After watching a high school football game, he seeks permission from his reluctant supervisor to start a team. Even Sean's aging and ill mother supports Sean's idea.

Sean acquires equipment and uniforms, but setting up a schedule proves to be more difficult: most schools are reluctant to face a squad of young hoodlums. The resourceful Sean quotes the Bible to the coach of a private Christian school and secures his first game; the other teams in that league also agree to play the Kilpatrick Mustangs.

From the start Sean makes two points: the team plays his way, and the Mustangs have to shed the "loser" image and see themselves as winners. As in *The Longest Yard*, some of the inmates are skeptical and suspicious and won't play; one cannot accept the discipline and quits. The squad Sean does have is a collection of misfits, some of whom have real talent. Sean's aim is to keep his team from returning to the street life that constantly threatens them.

Willie Weathers (Jade Yorker), whose cousin Roger was gunned down on the streets, becomes a test case for keeping inmates from reverting to gang behavior. Kelvin (David V. Thomas), an inmate who belongs to a rival gang, wants to retain his gang identity, and Willie and he do not get along. Kelvin doesn't want to block for Willie initially, but the two begin to respect each other's abilities, and they bond. In fact, Kelvin is wounded when he takes a bullet meant for Willie. Willie's growth is also revealed by his developing relationship with Danielle, who is at first repelled by Willie's anger, but his letters to her and his changed behavior convince her and her father that he is not the same young man as he was when he began his sentence at Kilpatrick. The audience later learns that Willie received a scholarship to a private boarding school after he "graduated" from Kilpatrick.

Junior Palaita (Seter Taase) is another test case. His size, speed, and athletic ability make him the best player on the team, but he is hurt badly in a scrimmage and is unable to play anymore. He stays with the team, however, and becomes their inspirational leader. In the final game, despite the risk of permanent injury, Junior dons a uniform and leads the Mustangs to victory. (This part of the plot also occurs in both versions of *The Longest Yard.*)

Kenny Bates (Trever O'Brien), one of the few white players on the team, presents another plus for the program. Undersized and insecure, Kenny is a wide receiver who cannot catch a pass. His self-esteem problems stem from a troubled relationship with his mother. As the season progresses, Kenny writes to his mother, and his play improves. In the final game he comes through and finally wins his mother's respect and love. Like Junior and Willie, Kenny sees himself as a winner.

Despite the team's ultimate success, the season has its highs and lows. In addition to financial and scheduling difficulties, the team is initially plagued with internal dissension because of gang loyalties and is subjected to racial discrimination. Stevens (Barry Tolli), one of the Barrington linemen, spews racial taunts at Kilpatrick players, but the winning touchdown appropriately goes right through him.

It's not just the players who develop, but also Sean, the coach, who has unresolved issues with his father. He can encourage Willie to reconcile with his father, but resists when Willie offers him the same advice, though he finally resolves to forgive his father.

At the end of the film, the audience learns that only five players went back to jail, though the team manager was killed in a drive-by shooting. There are also updates on some of the players, including Willie Weathers. The interviews with the real Sean Porter and Kenny Bates reinforce the message of the film, that commitment and loyalty to worthwhile causes enable people to become "winners," and give the film credibility.

GRUNT! THE WRESTLING MOVIE (1985)

DIRECTOR: Allan Holzman. SCREENPLAY: Roger D. Manning. STORY: Allan Holzman, Anthony Randel, Lisa Tomei, Barry Zetlin. PRODUCERS: Don Zormann, Anthony Randel. CINEMATOGRAPHY: Eddie Van Der Enden. EDITING: Allan Holzman, Barry Zetlin. MUSIC: Susan Justin. ART DIRECTION: Lynda Burbank, J. Rae Fox. COSTUME DESIGN: Merril Greene.

CAST: Magic Schwarz (Mad Dog DeCurso), Steven Cepello (The Mask), Bill Grant (Captain Carnage), Jeff Dial (Lesley Uggams), Wally George (himself).

RUNNING TIME: 91 minutes.

VHS: Starmaker Video.

This comedy is about a pro wrestler who may or may not have committed suicide after killing his opponent in a match.

GUS (1976)

Director: Vincent McEveety. Screenplay: Arthur Alsberg, Don Nelson (Story: Ted Key). Producer: Ron Miller. Cinematography: Frank Phillips. Editing: Robert Stafford. Music: Robert F. Brunner. Art Direction: John B. Mansbridge, Al Roelofs.

Cast: Edward Asner (Hank Cooper), Don Knotts (Coach Venner), Gary Grimes (Andy Petrovic), Tim Conway (Crankcase), Dick Van Patten (Cal Wilson).

Running Time: 96 minutes.

DVD: Disney Home Entertainment.

This film is Disney family fare about a hapless football team that starts winning with the help of a mule.

H

THE HAMMER (2007)

DIRECTOR: Charles Herman-Wurmfeld. SCREENPLAY: Kevin Hench. STORY: Adam Carolla. PRODUCERS: Eric Ganz, Heather Juergensen, Eden Wurmfeld. CINEMATOGRAPHY: Marco Fargnoli. EDITING: Rich Fox. MUSIC: Matt Mariano, John Swihart. PRODUCTION DESIGN: Mickey Siggins. ART DIRECTION: Kelley Sean Crawford. COSTUME DESIGN: Abigail Nieto.
CAST: Adam Carolla (Jerry Ferro), Oswaldo Castillo (Oswaldo Sanchez), Heather Juergensen (Lindsay Pratt), Harold House Moore (Robert Brown), Tom Quinn (Coach Bell).
RUNNING TIME: 88 minutes.
DVD: Weinstein Company.

A former fighter is given the chance to join the Olympic boxing team—or so he believes.

HAPPY GILMORE (1996)

DIRECTOR: Dennis Dugan. SCREENPLAY: Adam Sandler, Tim Herlihy. PRODUCER: Robert Simonds. CINEMATOGRAPHY: Arthur Albert. EDITING: Jeff Gourson, Steve R. Moore. MUSIC: Mark Mothersbaugh. PRODUCTION DESIGN: Perry Andelin Blake. ART DIRECTION: Richard Harrison. COSTUME DESIGN: Tish Monaghan.
CAST: Adam Sandler (Happy Gilmore), Christopher McDonald (Shooter McGavin), Julie Bowen (Virginia Venit), Frances Bay (Grandma), Carl Weathers (Chubbs), Robert Smigel (IRS agent), Bob Barker (himself).
RUNNING TIME: 92 minutes.
DVD: Universal Studios.

Happy Gilmore begins with voice-over narration by Happy (Adam Sandler) and clips from home movies of him as a youngster attempting to play hockey. Although blessed with a vicious slap shot, he is neither a good skater nor an adequate puck handler. When his father, a rabid hockey fan, is killed by an errant puck at a hockey game, Happy moves in with his grandmother (Frances Bay); his mother, who despised hockey, had earlier moved to Egypt. His two most outstanding hockey achievements in high school are serving the most time in the penalty box and trying to cut someone with his skate. Unable to catch on at any level with a professional hockey team, he takes a variety of jobs, most of which end in disaster.

After his girlfriend tells him that he is "going nowhere" and leaves, he returns to his grandmother's house and discovers not only that she is being evicted for failing to pay taxes, but also that her furniture is being repossessed. Happy tosses an IRS agent out the door after learning that he will need $270,000 to eliminate the debt. While workers remove the furniture, Happy places a bet on who can hit a golf ball farthest. Using his slap-shot technique, he wins the bet, but also breaks a window four hundred yards away—in subsequent shots he hits the homeowner and his wife. Armed with the knowledge of his ability, Happy hustles bets on local driving ranges. Chubbs (Carl Weathers), the golf pro, encourages him to learn the game of golf. At first, Happy rejects the offered lessons. However, when he realizes how much he can win playing professionally, he decides to enter the Waterbury Open, where his rival both in the tournament and for the heart of Virginia Venit (Julie Bowen), the tour's public relations director, is Shooter McGavin (Christopher McDonald).

To enter the tournament, Happy plays a qualifying round with mixed results. Thanks to his long drives and a hole-in-one, he wins, thus qualifying for the tour, but he lacks any knowledge of golf etiquette—he attacks his caddy, punches a heckler, and dives into a water hazard to retrieve his ball. Before the AT&T tournament in six weeks, he works with Chubbs on his game. Chubbs, who had lost part of his hand to an alligator in a Florida tournament, wears a prosthesis, which Happy accidentally destroys. When Happy retrieves his own ball in the water, he confronts the same alligator and decides he will exterminate the 'gator to atone for breaking the prosthesis. (Much later, when Happy presents Chubbs with a gift box containing the alligator's head, the terrified Chubbs staggers backward, falling through a window to his death.)

At the AT&T tournament, where Shooter is the favorite, Happy is duped into a bogus meeting on the course when the sprinklers are turned on. After he is told he will need a caddie, he hires a windshield-cleaning hustler (Allen Covert) who knows less than Happy about golf. Happy's inappropriate antics, which include signing autographs on women's chests, delight the fans, much to Shooter's disgust. When he tries to get Happy thrown off the tour, Shooter is told that Happy has become a "working-class hero" and that the Dallas tournament is sold out because of him. Even though Happy does not win, he does well enough to make progress on the $270,000 owed to the IRS. In the meantime, Happy and Virginia, who had earlier told him she doesn't date golfers, become romantically involved, skating to "Endless Love" as a Zamboni operator waits patiently for the song to end.

At the next tournament Shooter hires a heckler to taunt Happy into losing his temper and risking suspension from the tour. In the Pro-Am part of the tournament, Happy is paired with game-show host Bob Barker of *The Price Is Right*. Although the heckler is annoying, Happy restrains himself—until he finally turns his anger on Barker, who is grousing about Happy's poor play. Eventually the partners begin to fight before the television cameras, with Barker the surprising victor. (The fight won the 1996 Best Fight Award from MTV.) Happy receives a suspension and a twenty-five-thousand-dollar fine, which he pays by doing commercials. Thinking he has enough money to regain his grandmother's home, Happy discovers that the house will instead be sold to the highest bidder, Shooter, who vows to burn down the house and urinate on it.

Happy then challenges Shooter: if Happy wins, he gets the house; if Shooter wins, Happy quits the tour. To prepare for the tournament after his suspension, Happy returns to Chubbs for help, but in his effusive handshake with his mentor, he destroys another of Chubb's prosthetic hands. Knowing that much of golf is mental, Chubbs instructs Happy to stay focused by "going to a happy place" in his mind:

for Happy, this place is an idyllic spot with Virginia looking seductive and offering him a drink while his grandmother wins on slot machines. It works, but a visit to a miniature golf course does not seem to be as beneficial. After destroying some of the obstacles, Happy hits a ball that bounces off a wall, travels a circuitous route, and rolls into the hole.

After the first round at the tournament, Happy leads by one stroke, so the unscrupulous Shooter hires the heckler again. On the final round he uses a Volkswagen to run down Happy, who injures his shoulder. After this, Happy's attempt to return to his happy place fails because now Shooter is in the dream, coming on to Virginia and embracing Happy's grandmother. Fortunately, his grandmother appears at the tournament and tells him not to worry about the house. The happy place is transformed to its original state, but this time it includes Chubbs, with yet another restored hand, playing the piano and singing "We've Only Just Begun."

With the score tied going into the last hole, Shooter is first off the tee and hits into the woods, where his ball comes to rest atop the shoe of Mr. Larsen (Richard Kiel, the hulking brute with metal teeth who was one of James Bond's most formidable opponents), whom Happy had earlier wounded in the head with a nail gun. Fortunately, even Mr. Larsen has become one of Happy's "working-class fans." When informed that he must "play it as it lies," Shooter somehow hits onto the green. Happy, who reached the green with his tee shot, needs only to sink his putt to win. At this point, the tower that the Volkswagen hit collapses onto the green between Happy's ball and the hole. Shooter insists that Happy play it as it lies; and recalling his miniature-golf-course shot, Happy banks his ball off an unoccupied portable toilet, knocking the ball onto a similarly circuitous route over the tower, and the ball falls safely into the hole for the victory.

The frustrated and incensed Shooter tears the coveted championship jacket away from Happy and flees, with Mr. Larsen in hot pursuit, while Happy, Virginia, and Granny Gilmore offer a champagne toast to Chubbs. Sandler's performance received mixed reviews. He managed to win both the MTV Best Comedic Performance Award and a RAZZIE Award for Worst Performance.

HARDBALL (2001)

Director: Brian Robbins. Screenplay: John Gatins, based on the book *Hardball: A Season in the Projects* by Daniel Coyle. Producers: Tina Nides, Brian Robbins, Michael Tollin. Cinematography: Tom Richmond. Editing: Ned Bastille. Music: Mark Isham. Production Design: Jaymes Hinkle. Costume Design: Francine Jamison-Tanchuck.
Cast: Keanu Reeves (Conor O'Neill), Diane Lane (Elizabeth Wilkes), John Hawkes (Ticky Tobin), Bryan Hearne (Andrre Ray Peetes), Julian Griffith (Jefferson Albert Tibbs).
Running Time: 106 minutes.
DVD: Paramount.

Based on true events, this film is about a gambling addict who reluctantly agrees to coach a ragtag group of young baseball players from the projects.

THE HARDER THEY FALL (1956)

Director: Mark Robson. Screenplay: Philip Yordan, based on the novel by Budd Schulberg. Producer: Philip Yordan. Cinematography: Burnett Guffey. Editing: Jerome Thoms. Music: Hugo Friedhofer. Art Direction: William Flannery.
Cast: Humphrey Bogart (Eddie Willis), Rod Steiger (Nick Benko), Jan Ster-

ling (Beth Willis), Mike Lane (Toro Moreno), Max Baer (Buddy Brannen).
RUNNING TIME: 109 minutes.
ACADEMY AWARD NOMINATION: Best Cinematography, Black-and-White.
DVD: Sony Pictures.

A sportswriter is recruited to promote a boxer from Argentina but learns the hard way how such athletes are exploited.

HARD TIMES (1975)

DIRECTOR: Walter Hill. SCREENPLAY: Walter Hill, Bryan Gindoff, Bruce Henstell. PRODUCER: Lawrence Gordon. CINEMATOGRAPHY: Philip H. Lathrop. EDITING: Roger Spottiswoode. MUSIC: Barry De Vorzon. ART DIRECTION: Trevor Williams. COSTUME DESIGN: Jack Bear.
CAST: Charles Bronson (Chaney), James Coburn (Speed), Jill Ireland (Lucy Simpson), Strother Martin (Poe), Margaret Blye (Gayleen Schoonover), Michael McGuire (Gandil), Bruce Glover (Doty).
RUNNING TIME: 93 minutes.
DVD: Sony Pictures.

Hard Times, which takes place in New Orleans in 1933, is a sports film about street fighting, the bare knuckles, fight-to-the-finish brawl, with no rules except one against hitting or kicking an opponent when he is down. Unlike boxing films that focus on how fighters are manipulated by crooked promoters and managers, *Hard Times* features a protagonist who dictates the terms of his deal with his manager, turns down a contract with another manager, and decides whether or not he will fight an opponent. Chaney (Charles Bronson) is an outsider who arrives in town to do a job, reveals little about his past, avoids commitments, speaks only when necessary, and then leaves the community without a backward glance. Speed (James Coburn), his manager, is all flash without substance—a pawn, rather than a player.

Chaney arrives in a boxcar, breakfasts at a diner, and follows a group of men into a building where Speed is making bets on his "hitter," who is pitted against Jim Henry (Robert Tessier). Jim Henry's manager, Gandil (Michael McGuire), controls the street-fighting scene in New Orleans. After his fighter loses, Speed pays off Gandil (this is not the first time Speed has lost money to him) and goes to a diner, where Chaney joins him. Chaney, who has six dollars, convinces Speed to get him a fight, which he wins by knocking his opponent out with one punch. Regarding Chaney as "money on the hoof," Speed takes him to New Orleans, where he attempts to become Chaney's manager. After checking out New Orleans, Chaney visits Speed, dictates the financial arrangement, and goes with Speed to see Jim Henry batter his opponent with punches, kicks, and head butts. Intent on getting even with Gandil, Speed tries to arrange a match between Chaney and Jim Henry, but Gandil insists on Speed producing the three thousand dollars before he will agree to a fight.

Speed's efforts to raise the money include borrowing from a tough loan shark, Doty (Bruce Gover), and pitting Chaney against an opponent from the bayou. After Chaney quickly knocks out his opponent, LeBeau (Felice Orlandi), the other manager refuses to pay off his bet to Speed. When Speed protests, LeBeau pulls out a gun. Chaney convinces Speed to leave without making any more trouble; but that night Chaney, Speed, Mr. Poe (Strother Martin), and Gayleen Schoonover (Margaret Blye), Speed's fiancée, return to LeBeau's tavern, where Chaney repossesses the gun and, after encountering some of LeBeau's thugs, demands the money. He gets it, but only after savagely pistol-whipping LeBeau. With the money in hand, Speed seals the deal with Gandil.

The battle, which takes place in a metal cage, is brutal. Jim Henry, overconfident and intent on killing Chaney, is beaten, and Speed wins his bet and his revenge. In a crap game that night, Speed loses the money he was to use to repay Doty, and Doty's thugs destroy his car and threaten him. Ironically, it is Gandil who offers a solution to Speed's financial problems: he will pay Speed five thousand dollars for half rights to Chaney. Chaney, however, turns down the offer, saying Gandil will have to deal with him, not Speed, and that he will not be owned by anyone. Gandil, who fears losing his reputation, then brings in Street (Nick Dimitri), a street fighter from Chicago, and offers Speed and Chaney five thousand dollars if Chaney will fight his import. However, Chaney, who told Speed that he was fighting to put together some money, has acquired enough cash and does not want the match. Gandil and Doty collaborate to collect the debt and to restore Gandil's reputation, and when Chaney refuses to fight, their thugs kidnap Speed. If Chaney does not show up for the bout, Jim Henry will dispose of him.

Though Speed has maintained that Chaney "owes" him, Chaney states that he doesn't "owe" anyone, including Lucy (Jill Ireland), the woman he has been sleeping with. Chaney has his own flophouse room, to which he returns every night, and his only outside connection is to a cat he brings home and feeds. Chaney's indifference irritates Lucy, who complains, "You never answer any questions." Later she declares that all he cares about is money; he responds by walking away. Shortly before the fight with Street is scheduled, Chaney goes to her place, where she is entertaining someone else, a person who has made her a "better offer." When he fails to comment, she asks, "Is that all you have to say?" His silence says it all.

Poe, the trainer and cut man, appeals to Chaney to save Speed's life and apparently reaches him, for Chaney shows up to take on Street, who proves to be a less dangerous adversary than Jim Henry. Street, however, is like Chaney in observing an unwritten code of honor for street fighters, for when Gandil offers his almost-beaten fighter brass knuckles, he contemptuously pushes them aside and takes his beating.

In the last scene Chaney, who has displayed only mercenary motives, gives quite a bit of money to Poe, whom he wants to feed the cat, and to Speed, whom he wants to take care of Poe. Poe and Speed are also reluctant to express their gratitude in words. Speed can only utter, "We ought to say something." After Poe offers, "He sure was something," Speed cuts off any further emotionalizing by commenting, "Let's go get the cat."

Hard Times was director Walter Hill's first feature film. Although the script was considered weak, the director's debut garnered praise from reviewers, as did performances by Martin, Ireland, Bronson, and Coburn.

HEART LIKE A WHEEL (1983)

DIRECTOR: Jonathan Kaplan. SCREENPLAY: Ken Friedman, David E. Peckinpah. PRODUCER: Charles Roven. CINEMATOGRAPHY: Tak Fujimoto. EDITING: O. Nicholas Brown. MUSIC: Laurence Rosenthal. PRODUCTION DESIGN: James William Newport. COSTUME DESIGN: William Ware Theiss.

CAST: Bonnie Bedelia (Shirley Muldowney), Beau Bridges (Conrad "Connie" Kalitta), Bruce Barlow (bass player), Leo Rossi (Jack Muldowney), Anthony Edwards (John Muldowney), Hoyt Axton (Tex Roque), Paul Bartel (Chef Paul).

RUNNING TIME: 113 minutes.

ACADEMY AWARD NOMINATION: Best Costume Design.

DVD: Starz/Anchor Bay

Heart Like a Wheel is a biopic about Shirley Muldowney, a drag racer who won thirty-one titles in her thirty-year career, including three National Hot Rod Association Top Fuel championships.

The film opens with a black-and-white scene of Shirley as a preschooler sitting on her father's lap and steering the family sedan as it speeds along a country road. Then color begins to emerge, and the scene shifts to the narrative present. Teenaged Shirley (Bonnie Bedelia) works in a Schenectady diner by day and attends drag races with her high school sweetheart, Jack Muldowney (Leo Rossi), by night. In a challenge race against Sonny Rigotti (Dean Paul Martin), Jack chokes, and Shirley loses a twenty-five-dollar bet.

In spite of Jack's lack of prowess behind the wheel, he is a top mechanic, and Shirley loves him. When Jack asks Shirley's father, Roque (Hoyt Axton), for permission to marry her, Roque leaves his poker game to talk with his daughter. He expresses his concern that Jack is too young and that Shirley has not finished high school. He wants her to have the ability to support herself and gives his consent on condition she graduate.

The film jumps to the wedding. When the newlyweds drive off, Shirley is behind the wheel. They park at an abandoned service station where Jack describes his dream of owning a garage. Later, at the drag strip, Sonny challenges Jack again, but Jack declines, fearing he will choke. However, Shirley is confident she can win and scoots behind the wheel at the starting line, to the surprise and amusement of Sonny's crowd. Shirley leaves him in a cloud of exhaust, collecting one hundred dollars for her efforts and exhilarated by the speed and competition.

A few years later, Jack is a mechanic at Buddy's Texaco, and Shirley, now a mother, still works at the diner and races for grocery money. In the local papers she is known as "Curvette." As a spectator at a National Hot Rod Association meet, she encounters a nationally known racer, Big Daddy (Bill McKinney), who is showing off his dragster, a promotional freebie from the Detroit manufacturers. Shirley wants one, too, and, in spite of discouragement from Jack, she journeys to Detroit in a futile effort to obtain a complimentary vehicle. However, when she returns, Jack has sold Buddy (Tim Kimber) on the idea of building Shirley a car.

In 1966 at Englishtown, New Jersey, Shirley attempts to register as a driver but meets opposition until Big Daddy and Conrad "Connie" Kalitta (Beau Bridges) intervene. In the lead-up to her qualifying run, the track announcer dwells on the unlikelihood of a female driver safely completing a run. To the amazement of everyone except Jack, Shirley sets a new track record. Shirley's success intensifies her competitiveness but begins to take a toll on her marriage. For Jack, racing has been a hobby, not an obsession. Although Jack is a top mechanic, he does not share the limelight. He begins to drink heavily, and he grows increasingly jealous of Connie, who has befriended both Shirley and son John. After another race at Englishtown, Connie encourages Shirley to continue on the circuit, traveling in the South where the sport is more popular, the sponsors more prestigious, and the purses much larger. Shirley and Jack quarrel again, and he drives off without her. Connie takes her home, where Shirley discovers that Jack has destroyed the race car. The quarrel resumes, becoming physical, and Shirley leaves Jack, John, and Schenectady.

By 1972, Shirley is racing on the West Coast. She is now known as "Cha Cha" and poses for publicity photos in fringed gogo boots and hot pants. She drives

Connie's car, and the two have begun an affair, although Connie is still married. The following year, Shirley is badly burned when a new engine blower catches fire, igniting the entire vehicle. In her hospital room Shirley watches the much-hyped "Battle of the Sexes" tennis match between Billie Jean King and Bobby Riggs. When she looks outside, she sees Connie arriving with a young woman who remains in the automobile while he drops by with flowers. She speaks with John on the telephone to assure him the accident was not a result of her driving. Later, John tries to persuade Jack to phone Shirley, but he refuses.

Once Shirley is on her feet, she is ready to race again. When Connie receives a suspension following an altercation, Shirley suggests that he become her crew chief, making them a team both on and off the track. Over drinks, as Shirley divulges her plan, Connie listens, but his eyes are following the movements of an attractive cocktail waitress. Connie appears uninterested in Shirley's offer until Sonny Rigotti walks into the lounge, spots Shirley, and greets her affectionately. Connie immediately announces he will be "the best crew chief in the whole world." And for a while, he is. Cha Cha wins a national event and moves into the top fifteen; she makes appearances on local television programs and tries to convince reporters to call her Shirley. In spite of being a good crew chief, Connie is still a philanderer. When Shirley discovers he has been seeing another woman, she is unforgiving. The breach in their personal relationship expands when Connie is featured on the cover of *Hot Rod* magazine and is credited with making Shirley a top driver. In a radio interview, Shirley announces that she and Connie are splitting and that she has a new crew chief. A confrontation between the two turns vicious. John, now a mechanic on the crew, intervenes and absorbs the brunt of Connie's wrath.

Three years later, Shirley is pitted against Connie in a contest for a world title. Jack, who manages a struggling service station, watches on television. The announcer proclaims that Shirley is no longer regarded as a novelty, but simply as a competitor. Shirley defeats Connie for the title. Afterward, she seeks him out, and the two hug. The film ends with a list of Shirley's achievements, including an unprecedented three world titles.

Like most biopics, *Heart Like a Wheel* rearranges and distorts the facts. Shirley Muldowney was injured in a crash in 1984, after—not before—winning her major titles. Her real-life return to racing was anticlimactic. Like her cinematic representation, she faced discrimination, but unlike celluloid Shirley, she did not have major sponsors. Her relationship with Kalitta was stormy. Muldowney married mechanic Rahn Tobler, whom Kalitta hired in 1976, and two years later, Muldowney and Tobler left Kalitta, the split marked by animosity. Muldowney was not pleased with the film and took a personal dislike to Bonnie Bedelia, whose portrayal Kalitta characterized as not "feisty" enough. However, reviewers praised both the movie and Bedelia's acting, and she was nominated for a Golden Globe Award.

HEAVEN CAN WAIT (1978)

DIRECTORS: Warren Beatty, Buck Henry. SCREENPLAY: Elaine May, Warren Beatty, based on the play by Harry Segall. PRODUCER: Warren Beatty. CINEMATOGRAPHY: William A. Fraker. EDITING: Robert C. Jones, Don Zimmerman. MUSIC: Dave Grusin. PRODUCTION DESIGN: Paul Sylbert. ART DIRECTION: Edwin O'Donovan. SET DECORATION: George Gaines. COSTUME DESIGN: Richard Bruno.

CAST: Warren Beatty (Joe Pendleton), Julie Christie (Betty Logan), James Mason

(Mr. Jordan), Dyan Cannon (Julia Farnsworth), Jack Warden (Max Corkle), Charles Grodin (Tony Abbott), Buck Henry (the escort), Vincent Gardenia (Krim), Joseph Maher (Sisk).
RUNNING TIME: 101 minutes.
ACADEMY AWARDS: Best Art Direction/Set Decoration. NOMINATIONS: Best Picture, Best Director, Best Actor (Beatty), Best Supporting Actor (Warden), Best Supporting Actress (Cannon), Best Adapted Screenplay, Best Cinematography, Best Original Score.
DVD: Paramount.

Warren Beatty, Julie Christie, and James Mason star in this remake of *Here Comes Mr. Jordan* (1941). As with the earlier film, *Heaven Can Wait* extols the virtues of hard work and practicality, qualities embodied in the disembodied spirit of an athlete mistakenly spirited off before his time.

During the opening credits the camera follows Rams quarterback Joe Pendleton (Beatty) pursuing a regimen of exercise and diet. At practice he impresses the coaches, who discuss starting him in the upcoming game. The audience learns that Joe has been rehabilitating an injured knee, eschewing both surgery and pain killers. That evening, Joe's trainer, Max Corkle (Jack Warden), visits, bringing a birthday cake and the news that he is to start Sunday's game. Before Max leaves, Joe insists on gripping Max in a therapeutic headlock and cracking his neck. In the morning, Joe resumes training, pedaling his bicycle along a nearly deserted road. Just as he approaches a tunnel, a car enters from the opposite direction; there is a squeal of brakes, and the screen goes black.

When light reappears, Joe is striding through clouds as his escort (Buck Henry) struggles to keep up. Joe, carrying his lucky clarinet, believes he is dreaming and argues with the escort. They come to an airplane, where Joe encounters a Mr. Jordan (James Mason), who explains to Joe that he is dead and the plane is bound for heaven. However, Joe refuses to board, insisting there has been some mistake. And there has indeed. Mr. Jordan learns that Joe isn't scheduled for transport for another half century. The escort, a rookie, explains that he removed Joe from the tunnel just before the collision in order to spare him the pain of the accident. The escort's kindheartedness has interfered with fate, for Joe would have avoided the accident and emerged unscathed.

Mr. Jordan sends Joe and the escort back to earth so that Joe can reclaim his body and continue with his mortal life, but the two arrive too late: Joe's remains have been cremated. Since Joe is determined to play in the Dallas game the coming Sunday, he requires a suitable body, but locating a doomed athlete with the right skill set is difficult—an aerialist is too short to see over the offensive line, and a German race car driver doesn't speak English. Finally, Joe is offered Leo Farnsworth, a wealthy and powerful businessman who is about to be murdered by his wife, Julia (Dyan Cannon), and his secretary, Tony Abbott (Charles Grodin), with whom Julia is having an affair. Joe is about to refuse Leo's body as well, but then Miss Betty Logan (Julie Christie) appears. She represents a group of English villagers about to be evicted from their homes because of one of Leo's business schemes. Joe is so taken with Betty that he agrees to become Leo temporarily in order to assist her.

Mr. Jordan engineers the switch immediately after Leo has been drugged by his wife and drowned in his bathtub by his secretary. Joe/Leo emerges from the tub, dresses, and goes downstairs, where he encounters his astounded murderers, who now believe he is trying to drive them insane, and where he listens to Betty's pleas. Later that night, Joe studies for the upcoming board meeting to which he has invited Betty and a throng of reporters. Using football metaphors, Joe relies on his natural leadership ability to convince the board to cancel the toxic-producing manufacturing project that would have destroyed Betty's village.

That evening, Betty calls at the mansion to thank Joe, who takes her out for dinner. They sit at a drive-in, parked in his limousine because Joe doesn't think she would want to be seen in public with him, given his reputation for ruthlessness in his business deals. However, Betty sees something special when she looks into his eyes. When Joe drops her off, he tells her he is divorcing his wife.

Now that Joe has fallen for Betty, he decides to remain in Leo's body and get into shape, a task for which he hires Max. After Joe cracks Max's neck and plays his clarinet, Max realizes that Leo and Joe are one and the same. Joe begins training, recruiting his domestic staff to assist in practice sessions. When Max points out that scrimmaging with butlers won't get him onto the Rams for the Super Bowl, Joe purchases the team.

Meanwhile, Tony and Julia, concerned that a divorce will leave Julia penniless, continue in their attempts to murder him. As Joe is walking with Betty, he spots his escort, who warns him that he must relinquish Leo's body. Realizing that trouble lies ahead, Joe asks Betty to memorize his eyes and predicts she will see the same spirit in someone else in the future. After a brief embrace, Betty leaves, and a shot rings out. Joe/Leo topples into a well, mortally wounded. Joe Pendleton, clutching his clarinet, emerges and wanders off into the future with Mr. Jordan, who reassures him that there is a plan.

At the Farnsworth mansion, a detective has gathered Julia, Tony, and the household staff in the drawing room, where the game is on television. At the Super Bowl, quarterback Tom Jarrett lies inert on the field after being sacked. The film cuts between the mansion, where Leo's body is being hauled from the well, and the stadium, where Jarrett is about to be stretchered off the field. Mr. Jordan explains to Joe that his destiny is to become Tom Jarrett. Joe will remember nothing of his past as Joe Pendleton or Leo Farnsworth. With their revived quarterback at the helm, the Rams win their game.

Afterward, Max, having realized all that has transpired, is sad that Joe has no memory of who he was. However, when Betty arrives in search of Max, she meets Tom, and the two click. Seeming to comprehend the incomprehensible, Betty accepts Tom's invitation to coffee, and the two walk back across the field toward the goal posts as the closing credits roll.

Heaven Can Wait received mixed reviews, although critics generally agreed that Cannon and Grodin turned in excellent performances, and the film earned an Oscar for Best Art Direction–Set Decoration and nominations for Best Picture, Best Director, Best Cinematography, Best Writing, Best Actor in a Leading Role, Best Actor in a Supporting Role, and Best Actress in a Supporting Role.

HE GOT GAME (1998)

DIRECTOR: Spike Lee. SCREENPLAY: Spike Lee. PRODUCERS: Jon Kilik, Spike Lee. CINEMATOGRAPHY: Ellen Kuras, Malik Hassan Sayeed. EDITING: Barry Alexander Brown. PRODUCTION DESIGN: Wynn Thomas. ART DIRECTION: David Stein. COSTUME DESIGN: Sandra Hernandez.

CAST: Denzel Washington (Jake Shuttlesworth), Milla Jovovich (Dakota Burns), Ray Allen (Jesus Shuttlesworth), Rosario Dawson (Lala Bonilla), Hill Harper (Coleman "Booger" Sykes), Zelda Har-

ris (Mary Shuttlesworth), Ned Beatty (Warden Wyatt), Jim Brown (Spivey), Bill Nunn (Uncle Bubba).
RUNNING TIME: 136 minutes.
DVD: Walt Disney Video.

Spike Lee's *He Got Game* focuses on the struggles of the country's most highly rated high school basketball player to maintain his balance as the people closest to him regard him as a commodity. Jesus Shuttlesworth, played by NBA star Ray Allen, views an athletic scholarship as a ticket to a good education, but his coach, his girlfriend, and his family have their own agendas.

Although set in New York City, the film opens with footage of America's heartland and of a boy shooting baskets near a barn. The sequence may be a reference to *Hoosiers* (1986), a film Lee has denounced as a racist response to the dominance of black players in the NBA and NCAA. The opening cuts from pastoral imagery to shots of pickup games being played on city courts. This juxtaposition of rural and urban signals that Lee is taking the genre to another level, one that rejects the nostalgia of *Hoosiers.*

Lee repeats parallel sequences to introduce the central conflict of the film, that between Jesus and his father, Jake (Denzel Washington), who is serving time at Attica for the death of Jesus's mother—an accident for which Jesus holds Jake responsible. Scenes of Jesus shooting baskets at Coney Island's street court are intercut with scenes of Jake taking jump shots fed to him by a fellow inmate under the watchful eye of a prison guard.

Jake has come to the attention of the warden (Ned Beatty) because the governor is an avid supporter of the Big State basketball team. The warden offers Jake a reduced sentence if he can convince Jesus to sign with Big State. The warden expresses little interest in Jake beyond his ability to "deliver" his son for the governor; however, the meeting between the warden and Jake allows Lee to introduce discussion of the contrasting experiences of suburban and urban athletes.

Wearing an electronic ankle bracelet, Jake is released a week before the deadline for players to submit their declarations of intent. He first meets with his daughter, Mary (Zelda Harris), who greets him warmly, but his reunion with Jesus triggers the son's anger over his mother's death, over the pressure Jake placed on Jesus to develop his skills, and over Jesus's resentment that classmates teased him about his name. (The tension between the two that developed throughout Jesus's childhood is revealed through flashbacks. At one point, Jesus became so frustrated at his father's expectations that he hurled a basketball over the playground fence and refused to continue practicing with his father. It was this act of rebellion that led to an argument between his parents, resulting in his mother's death.)

Meanwhile, Jesus is discovering that a number of people he should be able to trust are eager to exploit him. Coach Cincota (Arthur Nascarella) claims to treat his players like his own children, but he, too, hopes to influence Jesus's choice of school and receive a kickback from the institution. Since his father's incarceration, Jesus has been accepting financial assistance from the coach to cover the rent. However, when Cincota offers ten thousand dollars, Jesus recognizes the implications and has the scruples to refuse. Jesus's legal guardian, Uncle Bubba (Bill Nunns), demands "compensation." Jesus's girlfriend, Lala Bonilla (Rosario Dawson), pressures him to meet a "friend of the family," a go-between for sports agent Dom Pagnotti (Al Palagonia), who hopes to sign him with a professional team.

A meeting with Dom and a campus visit to Tech U illustrate the temptations to which a talented athlete is exposed. Dom offers bling and flashy cars. Tech's coach, Billy Sunday (John Turturro), produces willing women and an inspired speech. Although Jesus is tempted by the glitz, he tells Dom that when he's ready to turn pro, he'll sign with a black agent, and even though he does not resist the sexual favors of Sunday's "assistant coaches," he refuses to commit to Tech.

Back at Coney Island, Jesus encounters Jake once again. As the two walk along the boardwalk, Jake reveals that he named his son after the legendary guard Earl "the Pearl" Monroe, whose lesser-known nickname was Jesus because with his graceful ball-handling and spinning he brought "the truth" to the game. Jake then confesses the real reason behind his temporary release. Although Jake is pursuing self-interest, he is more concerned with his son's future and fears Jesus's anger will land him behind bars as well.

With the deadline nearing, Jake challenges Jesus to a game of one-on-one. If Jake wins, Jesus will declare his intention to attend Big State; if Jesus wins, he will make his own choice. It is a hard-fought contest. Jesus wins and refuses to sign the letter. The police cuff his father, but before they put him in the squad car, Jesus stares deeply into his father's eyes and hears his mother calling him in from the playground.

Jesus undergoes a change of heart and calls a press conference at which he reads a letter of intent announcing his decision to attend Big State. The letter also contains a prayer for his father and his sister. In spite of Jesus's decision, the warden claims that, technically, Jake failed in his mission. Jake's fate remains unsettled. He writes a letter to his son acknowledging his mistakes and accepting his punishment; then he goes outside and shoots baskets in the prison yard. In a repeat of his son's earlier action, he throws the ball over the fence, but it keeps sailing until it bounces onto the court at Big State, where Jesus is practicing. Jesus drops his ball and takes his father's, indicating that the two are reconciled and that both have grown: Jake can let go of the game and Jesus can let go of his anger.

Lee cast several NBA players and personalities, as well as other pro athletes, to add to the realism and mystique of the film. Reportedly, Kobe Bryant turned down Lee's request to play Jesus, but the older and less flashy Allen surprised critics with his acting skills. Allen's performance was convincing enough for T-shirt vendors to sell Shuttlesworth jerseys to fans of the fictional character. Casting other NBA players in the roles of teammates, including New York Knicks Walter McCarty (as Mance) and John Wallace (as Lonnie) and Indiana Pacers' guard Travis Best (as Sip), allowed Lee to shoot some first-rate basketball footage; however there is comparatively little footage of high school games. More time is devoted to one-on-one contests, especially the final one between father and son. In addition, Lee enlisted several college coaches—Roy Williams, Rick Pitino, Jim Boeheim, John Thompson, and Nolan Richardson—for cameos. Other NBA players appear as well, including Shaquille O'Neal, Charles Barkley, and Reggie Miller. NFL legend-turned-actor Jim Brown portrays Jake's unsympathetic parole officer. Earl Monroe served as a technical advisor.

The depth of Lee's knowledge about basketball, particularly basketball in Coney Island, also contributes to the movie. In his autobiography, *Best Seat in the House*, Lee devotes thirteen pages to a discussion of Coney Island basketball stars Stephon Marbury and his older brothers. Ironically, Marbury was traded for Allen on the evening of the 1996 NBA draft after Marbury refused to sign with Milwaukee. The film contains a reference to Marbury.

He Got Game was a critical success, in spite of a widely panned, misguided subplot involving Jake and a neighborhood prostitute. The acting is superb. Washington and Allen are convincing in their portrayals of troubled father and son, and Harris and Turturro turn in memorable performances in minor roles. Lee heightens his drama with music drawn from the unlikely pairing of Aaron Copland and Chuck D and Public Enemy.

HELL ON WHEELS (1967)

DIRECTOR: Will Zens. SCREENPLAY: Wesley Cox. PRODUCER: Robert Patrick. CINEMATOGRAPHY: Leif Rise. EDITING: Michael David. ART DIRECTION: Dallas Thomas.
CAST: Marty Robbins (himself), John Ashley (Del Robbins), Gigi Perreau (Sue Robbins), Robert Dornan (Steve Robbins), Frank Gerstle (Ben).
RUNNING TIME: 97 minutes.
DVD: Rhino Theatrical.

Three brothers—a stock car driver, a mechanic, and a revenue agent—tangle with each other and moonshiners in this low-budget film starring country singer Marty Robbins.

HER BEST MOVE (2007)

DIRECTOR: Norm Hunter. SCREENPLAY: Norm Hunter, Tony Vidal. PRODUCER: Norm Hunter. CINEMATOGRAPHY: Paul Ryan. EDITING: Mitchel Stanley. MUSIC: Didier Rachou. PRODUCTION DESIGN: Dwane Platt. ART DIRECTION: Molly Hunter.
CAST: Leah Pipes (Sara Davis), Scott Patterson (Gil), Lisa Darr (Julia), Drew Bell (Josh), Lalaine (Tutti), Daryl Sabara (Doogie).
RUNNING TIME: 101 minutes.
DVD: MGM.

A teen phenom hopes to become the youngest member of the U.S. national soccer team.

HERBIE: FULLY LOADED (2005)

DIRECTOR: Angela Robinson. SCREENPLAY: Thomas Lennon, Robert Ben Garant PRODUCER: Robert Simonds. CINEMATOGRAPHY: George Gardiner. EDITING: Wendy Greene Bricmont. MUSIC: Mark Mothersbaugh. PRODUCTION DESIGN: Daniel Bradford.
ART DIRECTION: David S. Lazan. COSTUME DESIGN: Frank Helmer.
CAST: Lindsay Lohan (Maggie Peyton), Michael Keaton (Ray Peyton Sr.), Matt Dillon (Trip Murphy), Breckin Meyer (Ray Peyton Jr.), Justin Long (Kevin), Cheryl Hines (Sally).
RUNNING TIME: 101 minutes.
DVD: Walt Disney Home Entertainment.

Disney's 1969 film *The Love Bug* gets updated in the new century as Lindsay Lohan and Herbie take on a NASCAR driver.

HERBIE GOES BANANAS (1980)

DIRECTOR: Vincent McEveety. SCREENPLAY: Don Tait. PRODUCER: Ron Miller. CINEMATOGRAPHY: Frank Phillips. EDITING: Gordon D. Brenner. MUSIC: Frank De Vol. ART DIRECTION: John D. Mansbridge, Rodger Maus.
CAST: Charles Martin Smith (D.J.), Steven W. Burns (Pete), Cloris Leachman (Aunt Louise), John Vernon (Prindle), Harvey Korman (Captain Blythe).
RUNNING TIME: 100 minutes.
DVD: Walt Disney Video.

The third sequel to *The Love Bug* finds Herbie and his driver competing in a car race in Brazil.

HERBIE GOES TO MONTE CARLO (1977)

DIRECTOR: Vincent McEveety. SCREENPLAY: Arthur Alsberg, Don Nelson. PRODUCER: Ron Miller. CINEMATOGRAPHY: Leonard J. South. EDITING: Cotton Warburton. MUSIC: Frank De Vol. ART DIRECTION:

Peggy Ferguson, John B. Mansbridge.
CAST: Dean Jones (Jim Douglas), Don Knotts (Wheely Applegate), Julie Sommars (Diane Darcy), Jacques Marin (Inspector Bouchet), Roy Kinnear (Quincey), Bernard Fox (Max).
RUNNING TIME: 105 minutes.
DVD: Walt Disney Video.

In this second sequel to *The Love Bug*, the Volkswagen competes in Europe and his owner tangles with spies.

HERBIE RIDES AGAIN (1974)

DIRECTOR: Robert Stevenson. SCREENPLAY: Bill Walsh. STORY: Gordon Buford. PRODUCER: Bill Walsh. CINEMATOGRAPHY: Frank Phillips. EDITING: Cotton Warburton. MUSIC: George Bruns. ART DIRECTION: John Mansbridge, Walter Tyler.
CAST: Helen Hayes (Mrs. Steinmetz), Ken Berry (Willoughby Whitfield), Stefanie Powers (Nicole), John McIntire (Mr. Judson), Keenan Wynn (Alonzo Hawk), Huntz Hall (Judge).
RUNNING TIME: 88 minutes.
DVD: Walt Disney Video.

In this sequel to the Disney hit, the anthropomorphic Volkswagen helps Mrs. Steinmetz (Helen Hayes) fend off an unscrupulous developer who wants to raze her home.

HERE COMES MR. JORDAN (1941)

DIRECTOR: Alexander Hall. SCREENPLAY: Sidney Buchman, Seton I. Miller, based on the play *Heaven Can Wait* by Harry Segall. PRODUCER: Everett Riskin. CINEMATOGRAPHY: Joseph Walker. EDITING: Viola Lawrence. MUSIC: Friedrich Hollaendar. ART DIRECTION: Lionel Banks. COSTUME DESIGN: Edith Head.
CAST: Robert Montgomery (Joe Pendleton), Claude Rains (Mr. Jordan), Evelyn Keyes (Bette Logan), James Gleason (Max Corkle), Edward Everett Horton (Messenger 7013), Rita Johnson (Julia Farnsworth), John Emory (Tony Abbott).
RUNNING TIME: 94 minutes. B&W.
ACADEMY AWARDS: Best Original Story, Best Screenplay. NOMINATIONS: Best Picture, Best Director, Best Actor (Montgomery), Best Supporting Actor (Gleason), Best Cinematography, Black-and-White.
DVD: Sony Pictures.

Based on the play *Heaven Can Wait* by Harry Segall, this fantasy film stars Robert Montgomery as boxer Joe Pendleton, a wholesome young man mistakenly transported to heaven before his time. It's up to Mr. Jordan (Claude Rains), a management-level angel, to rectify the situation so that Joe can fulfill his destiny. *Here Comes Mr. Jordan*, like many light comedies of this era, carries a heavy dose of moral instruction.

The film opens at Pendleton's training camp, which is located in the midst of a highly idealized pastoral setting. The contrast between nature's tranquility and man's "ferocity" is exaggerated to draw laughter rather than to comment on blood sport. The film shows very little ring action and makes clear distinctions between "clean" fighters who abide by the rules of the ring and who are incorruptible and those who throw low blows and the occasional fight. Joe belongs among the former group of honest, hardworking citizens.

Joe has been training for a match with another clean fighter, Ralph Murdoch. The winner will earn a title shot against Lou Gilbert (Joe Hickey). As the training camp crew prepares to leave for New York, Joe's manager, Max Corkle (James Gleason), pleads with him to travel by train with the others instead of piloting his small plane. But Joe loves to fly and soon is cruising among the clouds, tootling inexpertly on his lucky saxophone. The scene cuts between

Joe in the cockpit wailing away and a fraying cable between wing and fuselage. Suddenly the plane nosedives, crashing into a clump of trees. However, Joe is still among the clouds, now walking with Messenger 7013 (Edward Everett Horton). The two are engaged in a heated conversation: 7013 insists that Joe was killed in the crash and must now board a plane for heaven; Joe insists he's still alive in spite of the fact that he's walking on air. When they arrive at the transport to heaven, Joe's name isn't on the passenger list, and a brief investigation reveals that he isn't scheduled to depart for another fifty years. The angel in charge, Mr. Jordan, learns that 7013 intervened, removing Joe's spirit from his airplane before it crashed, a well-intentioned, but ill-timed move, for had Joe not been spirited off, he would have regained control of the plane and landed safely.

To rectify the damage, 7013 whisks Joe back to the crash site so that he can reinhabit his body, but they are too late. Max has not only had Joe's body removed, but also had it cremated. It is now up to Mr. Jordan to locate a suitable body for Joe, who is determined to resume his boxing career. After 130 visits, Mr. Jordan has failed to locate an about-to-be-dead person with a physique that meets Joe's standards. They return to New York, where Mr. Jordan escorts Joe to the mansion of a wealthy but corrupt financier, Bruce Farnsworth, who is about to be murdered by his wife, Julia (Rita Johnson), and his secretary, Tony Abbott (John Emery).

Joe wants nothing to do with Bruce's wealth, his homicidal wife, his treacherous secretary, or his dishonest business practices. Then Bette Logan (Evelyn Keyes) arrives asking to see Bruce, who has sold worthless securities under her father's name. Now her father has been arrested. Although Joe does not want to involve himself in the squalid affairs of the Farnsworths, he believes he must come to the assistance of the lovely Bette. He negotiates a quick deal with Mr. Jordan: He will occupy Bruce Farnsworth's body temporarily—long enough to resolve Bette's problems—and then he'll be transported to another body, one with which he can resume his professional boxing career.

Joe and Mr. Jordan reach their agreement just as Tony is drowning Bruce, who has been drugged, in his bathtub. Moments later, the butler (Halliwell Hobbes as Sisk) knocks on Bruce's door to inform him that Bette wishes to speak with him. Tony and Julia expect that the butler will discover Bruce's body; instead, the butler finds Joe, who looks and sounds—to everyone except the viewing audience—like Bruce Farnsworth.

With encouragement from Mr. Jordan, Joe assumes the identity of the murdered financier and goes downstairs, greeting his wife, who faints, and Tony, who is taken aback. Joe/Bruce offers Bette tea and assistance; however, Bette interprets his honest desire to save her father as a cruel joke. Complicating matters, Mr. Jordan leaves Joe on his own to learn about stocks, advising him to follow his heart. When Sisk discovers the saxophone in the bathroom, Joe cheers up and decides to repurchase the bad securities, sending the press and the board members of his company into a frenzy.

The immediate effect of Joe's action is that Bruce's stock drops dramatically, but Joe is more concerned about a report that Ralph Murdoch is to fight Lou Gilbert for the championship. Mr. Jordan reappears with news that he has located a doomed Australian who is quite fit and assures Joe that he is destined to become the next champion. Then a visit from Bette alters Joe's plan. After Bette stares into Joe's eyes and sees something very special, Joe determines to remain Bruce and get his body into shape. Joe summons Max to the mansion to direct the training, and Max agrees after hearing Joe play the saxophone and realizing that Joe has indeed returned to life in Bruce's body.

As Joe prepares his return to the ring, he takes care of business by informing the board of directors that he plans to keep his interests focused on one product. He tells Bette that he cares for her but cannot go out with her because he is a married man. Meanwhile, Julia and Tony are worried that the Farnsworth fortune will suffer as a result of Joe's recent actions, and Julia insists that he be murdered (again).

Bette returns to the mansion to see Joe, but their visit is interrupted by 7013, who warns him that he cannot continue to inhabit Bruce's body. Realizing something is about to happen, Joe tries to prepare Bette for the future by reminding her of the special qualities she recognizes in his eyes and predicting that she will experience the same thing with someone else if anything happens to him. Joe kisses Bette goodbye, then finds Mr. Jordan waiting for him. Mr. Jordan has come to announce that Joe's time as Bruce Farnsworth is nearly over and repeats that the course of destiny cannot be altered. Julia shoots Joe and with Tony's assistance hides the body in a basement refrigerator. When Max arrives for the training session, the butler explains that Bruce has disappeared, while Tony claims that the financier has decided against fighting Ralph. Max suspects foul play, as do the authorities.

The night of the Murdoch-Gilbert match finds Joe and Mr. Jordan ringside, albeit invisible now that Joe is bodiless. Joe, realizing he doesn't have his sax, returns to the Farnsworths', where Inspector Williams (Donald MacBride) has gathered the usual suspects, including Max, Julia, Tony, and the butler, in the drawing room. Max, who has noticed the sax on the piano, suspects Joe is nearby. Joe sends a telepathic message to Max to turn on the radio so that they can listen to the progress of the fight. As the police continue their investigation, another murder takes place: Ralph, who has refused to throw the fight, is shot while still in the ring. Mr. Jordan notifies Joe that he has just enough time to fulfill his destiny. The two transport themselves to the arena, where Joe occupies Ralph's body and Mr. Jordan makes it appear that Ralph has been sent to the canvas by Lou. Joe/Ralph recovers before the ten count and defeats Lou. At the mansion Max, who has been listening to the fight on the radio, sees that the saxophone is no longer on the piano, realizes that Joe has departed, and heads for the arena.

In the dressing room Joe tells Mr. Jordan that he is happy to fulfill his destiny as Ralph, for like Joe, he was a clean fighter. However, Ralph's manager, Lefty, is not to be trusted, so Joe fires him. When Max enters, he spots the saxophone Joe is holding and faints but recovers quickly. Joe tells Max where Bruce's body is hidden; Max relays the information to the police, and Julia and Tony are arrested. Then Mr. Jordan reveals to Joe that he will live his life from this point on as Ralph Murdoch and that he will forget he was ever Joe. Max returns to discover that Joe remembers nothing of his past—as Joe Pendleton or as Bruce Farnsworth. But Max also understands that Joe's spirit lives inside Ralph's body and accepts his offer to serve as his manager.

Finally, Bette appears as Joe is leaving the dressing room. She knows that Bruce has been murdered and is searching for Max, but when she sees Joe/Ralph, something passes between the two. Joe tries to explain that he thinks he remembers her voice, and as Mr. Jordan, invisible now to Joe as well as to Bette, looks on, the couple leave the arena together and move into their future lives.

The film underplays the unpleasant side of the sport, which is so often the subject of boxing films from that era. Although Ralph at first appears to have been gravely injured by Lou in their bout, the film skips over the dangers of the sport. The ring is presented as an arena where hard work is rewarded, not as a stage for revealing the dark rages of contenders. Corruption, whether the result of greedy promoters and gamblers or greedy industrialists and investors, is overcome by clean-living, honest men like Joe, who makes a point of denouncing those who indulge in wine and women, and who resolves business problems by following his heart rather than by studying the bottom line.

Here Comes Mr. Jordan won Oscars for Harry Segall (Best Original Story) and writers Sidney Buchman and Seton Miller (Best Screenplay). The Academy also nominated Montgomery and Gleason for acting, Alexander Hall for directing, and Joseph Walker for cinematography. The success of the film spawned a 1947 sequel, *Down to Earth*, and remakes, *Heaven Can Wait* (1978) and *Down to Earth* (2001).

HOME OF THE GIANTS (2007)

DIRECTOR: Rusty Gorman. SCREENPLAY: Rusty Gorman. PRODUCERS: William R. Greenblatt, L. Charles Grimes, Eugene Osment, Dan Schalk. CINEMATOGRAPHY: Rodney Taylor. EDITING: Dan Schalk. MUSIC: Michael Suby. PRODUCTION DESIGN: Julie Briggs. ART DIRECTION: Jennifer O'Kelly. COSTUME DESIGN: Lisa Norcia.

CAST: Haley Joel Osment (Robert "Gar" Gartland), Ryan Merriman (Matt Morrison), Danielle Panabaker (Bridgette Bachman), Kenneth Mitchell (Keith Morrison).

RUNNING TIME: 101 minutes.

DVD: Screen Media.

A high school basketball player is asked to throw a game by a local drug dealer, while the player's best friend covers the story for the school paper.

HOMETOWN LEGEND (2002)

DIRECTOR: James Anderson. SCREENPLAY: Michael Patwin, Shawn Hoffman. PRODUCER: Dallas Jenkins. CINEMATOGRAPHY: Mark Peterson. EDITING: Daniel Cahn. MUSIC: Dan Haseltine, Joe Hogue. PRODUCTION DESIGN: Alice Baker. ART DIRECTION: Kristin Bicksler. COSTUME DESIGN: Liz Staub.

CAST: Terry O'Quinn (Buster Schuler), Lacey Chabert (Rachel Sawyer), Nick Cornish (Elvis Jackson), Kirk B.R. Woller (Cal Sawyer), Ian Bohen (Brian Schuler).

RUNNING TIME: 108 minutes.

DVD: Warner Home Video.

This Christian-themed film is about a successful high school football coach who returns to the field many years after a family tragedy.

HOOSIERS (1986)

DIRECTOR: David Anspaugh. SCREENPLAY: Angelo Pizzo. PRODUCERS: Carter De Haven, Angelo Pizzo. CINEMATOGRAPHY: Fred Murphy. EDITING: Carroll Timothy O'Meara. MUSIC: Jerry Goldsmith. PRODUCTION DESIGN: David Nichols. ART DIRECTION: David Lubin. COSTUME DESIGN: Jane Anderson.

CAST: Gene Hackman (Norman Dale), Barbara Hershey (Myra Fleener), Dennis Hopper (Shooter), Sheb Wooley (Cletus), Fern Persons (Opal Fleener), Chelcie Ross (George).

RUNNING TIME: 114 minutes.

ACADEMY AWARD NOMINATIONS: Best Supporting Actor (Hopper), Best Original Score.

DVD: MGM.

Hoosiers, the story of the high school basketball team from Milan, Indiana, that won the 1954 state championship, is the quintessential underdog sports film. In the film, the entire school, which is called Hickory, has only sixty-four boys, while South Bend, its opponent in the state final, has more than 3,400 students in its high school. The Indiana newspapers point out that Hickory is the smallest school ever to appear in the finals and describe it as a Cinderella team. Before the game a school official reads to the team the biblical text about David and Goliath, perhaps suggesting that God is on their side. The most success that Hickory achieved prior to 1951, the year the film takes place, was reaching—and losing—the sectionals in a game the townsfolk cannot forget.

In *Sports Cinema 100 Movies*, Randy Williams quotes Angelo Pizzo, the Indiana native who wrote the script, as stating that the film is about "redemption. About individuals succeeding through the help of each other." The theme is stated a bit differently by the Hickory players before the final when discussing to whom the game should be dedicated: all the small schools that never had the chance to be here; Coach Norman Dale (Gene Hackman); and Shooter (Dennis Hopper), who assists the team. Norman, who was suspended from coaching by the NCAA for hitting one of his players at Ithaca College, knows he has to succeed this time or his career is over; and Shooter, who is the town drunk yet possesses the best basketball mind in Hickory, almost dies before he is hospitalized and reconciles with his son, Everett (David Neidorf).

Early in the film the audience learns that Norman holds the coaching job because of his long friendship with Cletus (Sheb Wooley), the Hickory principal, but many of the local townspeople and the school's English teacher, Myra Fleener (Barbara Hershey), disapprove of the choice. Myra has become the protector and adviser of the best player in Hickory, Jimmy Chitwood (Maris Vanainis), who has decided not to rejoin the team. When Norman meets several of the local men in the barbershop, they give him unsolicited advice about not changing things, employing a zone defense, and seeking their help. Norman's "Good night" does not endear him to them. At the first practice, when Norman tells the former coach, George (Chelcie Ross), that his coaching days are over, George is irate and utters veiled threats. Then Norman dismisses a crowd of onlookers, telling them that he conducts closed practices.

Even the players give him trouble. When one of them won't keep quiet, Norman kicks him off the team, and another player leaves with him. The players, who are accustomed to shooting during practice, have to get used to the conditioning and defensive drills Norman puts them through. He makes it clear that they are in "his army" and will follow his orders. In the first game, when Rade (Steve Hollar), defies Norman's rule that the ball must be passed four times before anyone shoots, Norm benches him, and when another player fouls out, he chooses to play with four men and lose rather than reinsert Rade into the lineup.

Before the Cedar Knob game, Shooter provides Norman with information about the team and the gymnasium. Then Norman visits Myra and her mother; but Myra is still aloof, suspecting that he wants to convince Jimmy to play. At the game Cedar Knob plays roughly; however, the referees don't call fouls. After a blatant violation, Rade punches a Cedar Knob player, Norman gets involved, and both are thrown out of the game. Cletus, who has been assisting Norman, takes over as coach, but the strain is too much for him, and he has

Gene Hackman as Coach Dale in *Hoosiers*

to relinquish his duties as principal and assistant coach, leaving Norman on his own. Before the next game Norman visits Shooter and asks him to be his assistant coach on the condition that he clean himself up and stay sober. He adds that Shooter is embarrassing his son. Although he rejects the offer, Shooter does appear at the next game, much to the anger of the men critical of Norman. Norman is again ejected from the game for protesting calls.

Myra, who has been appointed interim principal, informs Norman that she has a newspaper clipping about his past and that there will be a meeting to consider removing him as coach. Although he has been advised not to appear, he attends the meeting and tells the crowd that he has nothing to apologize for and that he is pleased with the results of his coaching. When Myra asks to speak, she does not mention the clipping and recommends that he be given a chance. The vote is being taken when Jimmy enters the room and announces to the crowd he's ready to play basketball, but only if Norman is kept as coach. (Jimmy has been surreptitiously watching the practices and games and likes Norman's coaching; he also respects Norman for not pressuring him to join the team.) The town votes to keep Norman as coach.

Norman's efforts to rehabilitate Shooter are initially so successful that he invites a referee to eject him from a game so that Shooter can assume coaching duties. At first Shooter seems panicked, but he gains some confidence and actually calls the winning play, "the picket fence," in the game. After the game Everett tells his father, "You did real good, Pop." However, when the team gets to the sectionals, Shooter shows up late and so drunk that he has to be removed from the floor, incurring a technical for his behavior. After another brawl Hickory wins the sectionals, but Everett and Norman, who have been looking for Shooter, find him half-dead and have him hospitalized.

In the regional finals Norman demonstrates how much he has changed since the Ithaca incident. Earlier in the film Norman had told Jimmy that years ago he would have stopped at nothing to win, but he didn't try to recruit Jimmy to the team; and in the Linton game he has to decide whether or not to have the injured Rade return to the floor. As Myra watches apprehensively from the stands, Norman takes Rade out. When another of his players fouls out, he has to substitute the undersized Ollie (Wade Schenck), who is fouled by the savvy opposition. Ollie comes through, using the long-outmoded underhand free throw, winning the game. Afterward, Norman and Myra go for a walk that ends with the inevitable embrace.

Before the final game, Everett visits his father and tells him, "I love you," completing their reconciliation. (Hopper's performance is so outstanding that he received a Best Supporting Oscar nomination for his role.) In the locker room Norm also tells his players that he loves them and is proud of them. Despite having to play against a much taller front line and an All-American player, Hickory comes back after trailing early, thanks primarily to Jimmy, who goes on a scoring binge. Behind by one with seconds to go, the team rejects Norman's plan to use Jimmy as a decoy, and Jimmy takes the last winning shot. After the game Norman and Myra exchange significant looks, but the film is not really about their romance. The last shots are of the fields, then the gymnasium where a little boy is shooting baskets as the camera focuses on a photograph of the actual Milan team that won the championship. On the sound track are snippets of significant dialogue taken from earlier in the film.

Sports films sometimes provide information about what happens to the characters or team after the season is completed, but *Hoosiers* does not. Did Jimmy win a scholarship to go to Wabash? Did Myra and Norman marry? Did Shooter stay sober? The film is concerned only with one improbable season in Indiana basketball.

HORSE FEATHERS (1932)

Four Marx brothers are featured in this screwball comedy from the early 1930s.

> DIRECTOR: Norman Z. McLeod. SCREENPLAY: Bert Kalmar, Harry Ruby, S.J. Perelman, Will B. Johnstone. PRODUCER: Herman J. Mankiewicz. CINEMATOGRAPHY: Ray June. MUSIC: John Leipold.
> CAST: Groucho Marx (Professor Quincy Adams Wagstaff), Chico Marx (Baravelli), Harpo Marx (Pinky), Zeppo Marx (Frank Wagstaff), Thelma Todd (Connie Bailey), David Landau (Jennings).
> RUNNING TIME: 68 minutes. B&W.
> DVD: Universal Studios.

Groucho plays a college president who, after noting a correlation between the succession of school presidents and the success of the football team, plans to beef up the team with mercenaries. College athletics, however, is not the subject of the film; rather it is one of several plot hooks on which to hang a relentless series of gags. Much of the humor is risqué, and every mention of a woman or appearance of a female character triggers, at the very least, innuendo. Within such a context, even the name of Groucho Marx's character—Professor Quincy Adams Wagstaff—is suspect, the quince representing fertility in classical art.

The film opens with the arrival of Wagstaff, Huxley College's new president. As the welcoming ceremony begins, Wagstaff is at the side of the stage shaving and smoking a cigar, which he refuses to relinquish or extinguish in spite of college policy. His inaugural address is a nonsensical parody of academic speeches that expands by free association and puns; at one point Wagstaff bursts into song and leads the faculty in a soft shoe. His address concludes with an auction. Then he announces that he came to Huxley in order to extract his son, who has been attending the school for twelve years, spending most of his time attending to a "college widow"—an older woman who specializes in educating college boys outside of the classroom. In a private conversation, Wagstaff tells Frank (Zeppo Marx) that he is a disgrace to the family, for President Wagstaff managed three colleges and three college widows in the same amount of time. Frank and his father then discuss the importance of football to the presidency. Huxley's rival, Darwin College, headed by the unethical Mr. Jennings (David Landau), hires professionals who frequent a local speakeasy. Wagstaff determines to locate his own professionals as well.

At the speakeasy, Jennings has already purchased the services of footballers Mullen (James Pierce) and McHardie (Nat Pendleton) for the upcoming game against Huxley. The speakeasy's doorman is the Italian immigrant Baravelli (Chico Marx), who has been instructed not to admit anyone without the password, "swordfish." Baravelli's silent friend, Pinky (Harpo Marx), soon arrives and produces a fish impaled on a sword from under his coat. Inside the bar, Pinky pours an entire bottle of scotch into a seemingly bottomless glass, hits the jackpot on a slot machine using a button from his coat, and collects another bonanza from a pay phone. When Wagstaff appears at the speakeasy, Baravelli offers him a hint about the password and gives him three tries. Wagstaff fails to guess the word, so Baravelli reveals the answer, and then lets him try again. Wagstaff gains entry, but locks Baravelli out and changes the password, which he promptly forgets, and so joins Baravelli outside; the two sneak in when another customer says "swordfish." Wagstaff, having learned that Mullen and McHardie can generally be found at the speakeasy, mistakes Pinky and Baravelli for football players and signs them on to play.

Wagstaff enrolls the two as students and escorts them to their first class. The scene that follows offers up another parody of academia as Wagstaff takes over an anatomy lecture that moves from corpuscles to the Alps and prompts Wagstaff to remark, "The Lord Alps those who Alp themselves." Pinky changes the professor's charts, substituting one of a horse, then one of a scantily clad woman; Baravelli volunteers answers based on his mangling of English—thus he identifies a corpuscle as a military rank. The scene, like many of their routines, ends in chaos.

Wagstaff's mission to wean his son from the college widow, Connie Bailey (Thelma Todd), and his plan to defeat Darwin in football become intertwined because Connie has been recruited by Jennings to talk Frank into giving her the signals for the game. Wagstaff telephones Connie to ask her to his office, but quickly volunteers to go to her "office" after learning she's still in bed. At Connie's, all of the main male characters appear in succession, producing a great deal of activity. First, Jennings drops by to tell Connie that he has bet heavily on Darwin and that she must pump Frank for information about Huxley's strategy. Soon after Jennings departs, Frank appears. When Frank leaves the room to fetch drinks, his father shows up wearing galoshes and carrying an umbrella. A knock on the door, which turns out to be Pinky delivering ice, sends Wagstaff scurrying to put on his boots and hide. Connie disposes of the ice out the window, Pinky leaves, and Wagstaff has jumped onto Connie's lap by the time Frank returns with the drinks. Wagstaff escorts Frank out the door, but before he can make much progress in his attempt to seduce Connie, there's another knock. Wagstaff repeats a set of antics with the galoshes and umbrella, which constitute a bawdy pun, and hides again. This time it is Baravelli returning the ice that Connie "dropped." He wastes no time putting the moves on Connie, only to be interrupted by Pinky, who dashes in with the ice and throws it back out the window. The next knock is Jennings. Baravelli pretends to be giving Connie a music lesson; Wagstaff, tired of hiding, emerges and claims to be the plumber. As Baravelli plays the piano and sings "Everyone Says I Love You" (which Frank had earlier sung to Connie), Wagstaff addresses the audience directly, stating that he has to stay, but the moviegoers are free to go into the lobby until the musical interlude is over. The scene in Connie's living room ends abruptly, perhaps because of censorship. Later, the plot, such as it is, screeches to a halt so that Pinky can serenade Connie by playing "Everyone Says I Love You" on his harp.

As the game day approaches, Wagstaff learns that Baravelli and Pinky are not footballers, so he tells Baravelli he must kidnap Mullen and McHardie. Outside the locker room Baravelli meets Jennings, who offers to buy the signals for the game. Baravelli readily agrees and hands over the information, but he has sold Jennings the Darwin signals. Baravelli leaves three hundred dollars richer; however, he accidentally reveals the plan to kidnap the real players. Jennings alerts his coconspirators, who spring into action. Connie tries to charm Wagstaff into handing over the signals by taking him on a romantic canoe ride. Wagstaff alludes to *An American Tragedy*, Theodore Dreiser's naturalistic novel in which the main character lures his pregnant girlfriend into a canoe, then causes it to capsize, leaving her to drown. After Wagstaff sings "Everyone Says I Love You" and tosses the guitar into the lake, he drops a copy of the signals in the water. Connie tries using baby talk to get Wagstaff to produce his extra copy, but her posturing irritates him. She loses her balance and falls into the lake. Wagstaff throws her a candy lifesaver from a roll in his pocket, and a duck that has been following the couple flaps into the canoe.

Meanwhile, Mullen and McHardie lock Baravelli and Pinky in a room. After some clowning and punning, Baravelli and Pinky saw a hole through the floor and fall through, only to encounter Mullen and McHardie once again. This time the footballers make their captives strip to their Skivvies before locking them up. But Baravelli and Pinky magically produce another pair of saws and repeat their escape, landing among a group of ladies, whom they startle. While Baravelli seizes a bicycle and pedals off, Pinky takes the reins of a garbage truck and gallops off in the manner of Ben-Hur. They arrive at the football stadium to learn that Huxley is trailing. Wagstaff, wearing a helmet and professorial frock coat, takes the field occasionally—once interrupting a flirtation on the sidelines to tackle the Darwin ball carrier; another time to announce a play, unfortunately to the wrong huddle. Baravelli and Pinky carry on a game of cards, oblivious to the contest in which they are supposed to be participating. In the second half, the duo come to Huxley's aid. They attach a bungee cord to the ball, resulting in one touchdown, litter the field with banana peels to foil Darwin, and in spite of Baravelli's rhyming signals that broadcast the upcoming plays to the defense, manage to score the winning touchdown(s) by driving the garbage cart, now full of footballs, over the goal line. The film ends with Frank, Baravelli, Pinky, and Wagstaff all marrying Connie. At the end of the ceremony, pandemonium ensues as all of the grooms attempt to kiss the bride.

For all of its nonsense, *Horse Feathers* offers up a stinging satire of academia and the role of sports within it. In one of the most well-known passages from the film, Wagstaff addresses two professors: "Where would this college be without football? Have we got a stadium?" The answer is yes, so Wagstaff continues, "Have we got a college?" When the professors answer yes once more, the president proclaims, "Well, we can't support both. Tomorrow we start tearing down the college." In response, the professors ask where the students will sleep, and Wagstaff replies, "Where they always sleep. In the classroom." The flagrant rule breaking during the game, largely ignored by officials and accepted by the fans, serves as a comment on the unethical practices of the college administrations in acquiring their players.

THE HURRICANE (1999)

DIRECTOR: Norman Jewison. SCREENPLAY: Armyan Bernstein, Dan Gordon, based on the books *The 16th Round* by Rubin "Hurricane" Carter and *Lazarus and the Hurricane* by Sam Chaiton and Terry Swinton. PRODUCERS: Armyan Bernstein, Norman Jewison, John Ketcham. CINEMATOGRAPHY: Roger Deakins. EDITING: Stephen Rivkin. MUSIC: Christopher Young. PRODUCTION DESIGN: Philip Rosenberg. ART DIRECTION: Dennis Davenport. COSTUME DESIGN: Aggie Guerard Rodgers.

CAST: Denzel Washington (Rubin "Hurricane" Carter), Vicellous Reon Shannon (Lesra Martin), Deborah Kara Unge (Lisa Peters), Live Schreiber (Sam Chaiton), John Hannah (Terry Swinton), Dan Hedaya (Det. Sgt. Della Pesca), Clancy Brown (Lt. Jimmy Williams), Rod Steiger (Judge Sarokin).

RUNNING TIME: 146 minutes.

ACADEMY AWARD NOMINATION: Best Actor (Washington).

DVD: Universal Studios.

Hurricane is about Rubin "Hurricane" Carter, a prizefighter who was wrongfully convicted of murder, and the efforts to exonerate him.

THE HUSTLER (1961)

DIRECTOR: Robert Rossen. SCREENPLAY: Sidney Carroll, Robert Rossen, based on the novel by Walter Tevis. PRODUCER: Robert Rossen. CINEMATOGRAPHY: Eugen Schüfftan. EDITING: Dede Allen. MUSIC: Kenyon Hopkins. PRODUCTION DESIGN: Harry Horner. SET DECORATION: Gene Callahan. COSTUME DESIGN: Ruth Morley.

CAST: Paul Newman ("Fast" Eddie Felson), Jackie Gleason (Minnesota Fats), Piper Laurie (Sarah Packard), George C. Scott (Bert Gordon), Myron McCormick (Charlie Burns), Murray Hamilton (James Findley), Michael Constantine (Big John), Jake La Motta (bartender), Vincent Gardenia (bartender).

RUNNING TIME: 134 minutes.

ACADEMY AWARDS: Best Art Direction/Set Decoration, Black-and-White; Best Cinematography, Black-and-White. NOMINATIONS: Best Picture, Best Director, Best Actor (Newman), Best Supporting Actor (Gleason), Best Supporting Actor (Scott), Best Supporting Actress (Laurie), Best Adapted Screenplay.

DVD: 20th Century Fox.

The Hustler is a drama based on Walter Tevis's 1959 novel about a small-time pool shark, "Fast" Eddie Felson, who sets out to beat the best player in the country, Minnesota Fats. (The pool player Rudolph Walderone used the name Minnesota Fats after the film was released, claiming that he was the inspiration for the character. Walter Tevis denied this claim, insisting that Minnesota Fats is a fictional character and that any resemblance to Walderone, who never won a major tournament, was coincidental.) The film's focus is on character rather than plot, and the pool games provide insight into Eddie's personality rather than suspenseful contests. The story gets off quickly as Eddie (Paul Newman) and his partner Charlie Burns (Myron McCormick) pull their first con before the opening credits roll. At a crossroads bar Eddie, pretending to be a successful salesman who has had too much to drink, challenges Charlie to a few games of pool. When Charlie declares he's won enough of Eddie's money and refuses to bet on a tricky shot, several locals step forward to place their own bets. Before pocketing his winnings, Eddie berates the locals for trying to take advantage of someone who is drunk. This opening scene demonstrates that Eddie rationalizes his own behavior while indicating that deeper moral questions lie at the heart of the film.

In the following scene Eddie and Charlie arrive at the Ames Pool Hall, which Eddie likens to a cathedral, but Charlie sees as a morgue. Charlie's pessimism foreshadows Eddie's self-destructiveness, which becomes readily apparent as the action moves quickly to Eddie's contest with Minnesota Fats (Jackie Gleason). Although the Fat Man opens with a strong run, once Eddie takes over, he seems unstoppable. After eight hours of play, Eddie is ahead and offers to increase the stakes from two hundred to a thousand dollars a game. Minnesota agrees, but first sends out for a bottle of whiskey and a glass; Eddie requests bourbon, without a glass.

The scene shifts to a backroom poker game, where one of the players, Bert Gordon (George C. Scott), receives a message from a member of Minnesota's entourage. By the time play resumes at the Ames, Bert Gordon has taken a seat beside Minnesota. Eddie's streak continues, but, although he is ahead eighteen thousand dollars after twenty-five hours, he is looking increasingly drunk and disheveled. Charlie insists that Eddie quit; however, Eddie is determined to continue until Minnesota is ready to stop. Minnesota, meanwhile, has taken a short break to wash up so that he returns to the game looking fresh. In contrast, Eddie looks slovenly, and a corresponding sloppiness enters his game. He even falls asleep while Minnesota is shooting. Finally, when Eddie is down to two hundred dollars, Minnesota says the game is over. Eddie passes out on the floor, and everyone leaves while Charlie tries to get Eddie literally back up on his feet. The following morning Eddie slips out of the hotel room he shares with Charlie, leaving the car keys and a cut of what remains of the money.

At the local bus station Eddie meets Sarah (Piper Laurie), who tells him that she attends college on Tuesdays and Thursdays and on the other days she drinks. Although Sarah struggles to maintain her dignity, her alcoholism clouds her judgment. She can, in fact, be bought for a bottle, and soon she and Eddie begin an affair. Sarah recognizes that the relationship is doomed because both are deeply troubled people whose problems are compounded by their drinking; nonetheless, she does not break from Eddie.

Every scene of this romantic interlude ends with foreboding. An evening of domesticity with a home-cooked dinner is cut short by the appearance of Charlie, who has held back some of Eddie's winnings from the game with Minnesota Fats. Although Charlie has acted protectively and has sought out Eddie in hopes of getting him back on the road, Eddie is enraged, claiming he could have beaten Minnesota had Charlie allowed him to bet the money. Eddie has no sense of loyalty toward his friend and dismisses him so harshly that Sarah bursts into tears. Later, on one of her drinking days, Sarah starts writing a story based on their relationship, which she terms "a contract with depravity." The quarrel that follows ends with Eddie slapping Sarah and Sarah calling him a "poolroom bum."

After the fight Eddie goes to a bar and joins a backroom poker game, where he loses, then orders a drink. Bert, who has witnessed Eddie's unsuccessful run at the poker table, tells Eddie that he loses because of his character; however, Bert offers to bankroll Eddie, demanding 75 percent of the take. Eddie turns him down and moves on to work his next scam on his own. He out-hustles a local hustler, but the other bar patrons—thugs whom Bert has hired—break Eddie's thumbs. Having nowhere else to go, Eddie returns to Sarah. While he recovers, Sarah writes and stays sober. Eddie talks about winning in terms of the feeling of satisfaction one gets when one does something well. Sarah tells him that she loves him. Once his casts are removed, Eddie takes up the cue again and agrees to work for Bert. Eddie and Sarah go to the Parisien, a restaurant they walked past en route to a liquor store on the day they met. Their celebration is short-lived because Eddie tells her he is leaving with Bert for a while. Sarah confesses that she has lied to him about her past: her limp is from a childhood bout of polio, not a dramatic car crash, and the rich old man who pays her living expenses is her father, not a former lover. She also admits that she has invented Eddie as well, creating a reliable, steady mate from the selfish hustler.

Eddie decides to bring Sarah with him, although Bert, who expressed doubts about Eddie's abilities, is not pleased that she has been included. They arrive in Louisville, Kentucky, during derby week, and Bert introduces Eddie to James Findley (Murray Hamilton), a wealthy Kentuckian who likes to gamble. James invites them to a party, where Sarah gets drunk and passes out upstairs. Eddie, who has not been drinking, goes with James and Bert to shoot billiards. After losing two hundred dollars, Bert is ready for Eddie to quit, but Eddie insists on continuing, using money he has won on the ponies at Churchill Downs. He loses this too and again asks Eddie to put up the cash. By this time, Sarah has joined them and objects to Eddie's "begging." Her objections prompt Bert not only to stake Eddie but also to up the stakes to a thousand dollars a game. James loses twelve thousand dollars, and Eddie gets his 25 percent. Eddie decides to walk back to the hotel rather than take a cab with Bert. As a result, Bert arrives at their adjoining suites well ahead of Eddie and makes a pass at Sarah. Although she doesn't immediately respond to his advances, after he leaves, she follows, essentially taking control of her own destruction. Eddie reaches the hotel just as a police photographer is leaving. Sarah has scrawled a message on the bathroom mirror, "Perverted Twisted Crippled," and killed herself. Bert tells Eddie that he and Sarah "had drinks." The scene ends with Eddie attacking Bert.

The next scene returns to the Ames pool hall, where Minnesota Fats is reading and Bert is lurking. Eddie walks in and challenges Minnesota to play for three thousand dollars a game, all that Eddie has. As Eddie runs the table, playing "fast and loose," he tells Bert that he acquired "character" in Louisville. Minnesota, unable to compete with Eddie, concedes defeat. Bert demands his take from Eddie's winnings. Eddie refuses, and the two men exchange threats. Eddie now confesses that he loved Sarah, admitting that he "traded her in on a pool game." Bert gives Eddie a final warning, indicating that he has lost any chance of playing "big-time pool" again. Ignoring Bert, Eddie praises Minnesota for his game, and Minnesota returns the compliment. The film ends with Eddie walking out of the Ames into an uncertain future, but seemingly a better person than he was at the beginning of the film. A sequel, *The Color of Money* (1986), also based on a novel by Tevis and starring Newman, suggests that Fast Eddie has not in the closing scene of *The Hustler* hustled anyone.

The film was nominated for nine Oscars, including four for acting, as well as for Best Picture, Best Director, and Best Screenplay. It won for Best Cinematography and Best Art Direction. Newman was coached by veteran pool player Willie Mosconi (who holds the money in the first meeting between Minnesota and Eddie). Mosconi completed Newman's more difficult shots. Gleason, who worked a successful hustle against Newman during filming, made his own shots. Many consider *The Hustler* Newman's best performance.

I

ICE CASTLES (1978)

DIRECTOR: Donald Wrye. SCREENPLAY: Gary L. Baim, Donald Wrye. PRODUCER: John Kemeny. CINEMATOGRAPHY: Bill Butler. EDITING: Michael Kahn, Melvin Shapiro, Maury Winetrobe. MUSIC: Marvin Hamlisch. PRODUCTION DESIGN: Joel Schiller. COSTUME DESIGN: Richard Bruno.

CAST: Lynn-Holly Johnson (Alexis "Lexie" Winston), Robby Benson (Nick Peterson), Colleen Dewhurst (Beulah Smith), Tom Skerritt (Marcus Winston), Jennifer Warren (Deborah Machland), David Huffman (Brian Dockett), Diane Reilly (Sandy).

RUNNING TIME: 108 minutes.

ACADEMY AWARD NOMINATION: Best Original Song ("Theme from Ice Castles: Through the Eyes of Love"; music by Marvin Hamlisch, lyrics by Carole Bayer Sager).

DVD: Sony Pictures.

Ice Castles combines a love story with some good figure skating in this family favorite. Professional skater Lynn-Holly Johnson makes her acting debut in the role of an Olympic hopeful. Robby Benson, who took skating lessons for the part, portrays her hockey-playing boyfriend. Although the plot is hokey, the acting is sound, with good supporting performances by Colleen Dewhurst and Jennifer Warren.

Alexis Winston (Johnson), a sixteen-year-old from a small town, has a natural talent for skating that she's developed with the help of a former regional champion, Beulah Smith (Dewhurst), who now operates the local bowling alley/hockey rink, The Ice Castle. Lexie wants to participate in the regionals herself, even though her age is a hindrance—she'll be older than most of the other skaters. Her father, Marcus (Tom Skerritt), objects, fearing that she will be outclassed by the younger girls, who have been groomed for competition with years of expensive training. Beulah supports Lexie, realizing that this is Lexie's last chance to test her skills. Lexie also receives encouragement from her boyfriend, Nick (Benson), who has dropped out of college to pursue his dream of playing professional hockey.

Marcus, an overly protective parent since the death of Lexie's mother years earlier, is reluctant to extend his blessing. As Lexie says goodbye, Marcus doesn't interrupt his work to give her a hug or wish her luck. At the arena Lexie, clad in an old costume of Beulah's with a Peter Pan collar, draws stares from the younger girls in spangly togs, causing her to run down the corridor to join Beulah and Nick. This moment of insecurity passes once the skating begins and Lexie's love of the sport kicks in. She appreciates the skill of the others without being intimidated. Feeling she has nothing to lose, she skates with crowd-pleasing abandon and impressive athleticism. During her routine, the audience responds enthusiastically, and a well-known trainer watches intently. The judges, who are bound by tradition and a set of scoring guidelines, assign Lexie's performance a low rating, drawing a protest from the crowd. Lexie acknowledges the fans by circling the ice, and they toss roses at her feet in a scene that foreshadows the film's end.

Soon after the competition, the trainer, Deborah Machland (Warren), makes her way to The Ice Castle, where she asks Beulah about Lexie's background. Deborah starts to leave when she learns Lexie's age, but Beulah points out that in the Olympics compulsory figures, which demand perfection, make up only 30 percent of a skater's score. (Figures—in which skaters make circles and figure-eights with their blades—were dropped from Olympic competition in 1990.) Beulah convinces Deborah to take on Lexie, but dealing with Marcus requires extensive negotiation. When Beulah argues that Lexie has an opportunity "to be something," Marcus counters that she "is something." Their discussion introduces the question of whether one should be satisfied with who one is or pursue becoming someone at the risk of losing connections with one's roots. This question is never adequately explored, and later in the film, Marcus seems to express a different point of view. However, for Nick the answer seems obvious. He tells Lexie that he doesn't want to do what is expected of him—to attend college and settle down to marriage and a family. He has landed a tryout with a professional hockey team and envisions a fabulous career ahead. Lexie listens without speaking as Nick outlines his plan, which obviously has not taken her feelings into account. Perhaps it is Nick's determination to follow his dream that prompts Lexie to follow hers.

As the two young people head off on parallel paths, the film follows their progress, switching back and forth. Lexie faces an uphill battle in acquiring the precision she will need to move up through the ranks. When she shows off by completing a triple spin, Deborah threatens to send her packing because of the unnecessary risk she has taken performing a dangerous stunt. Lexie sheds a few tears during the scolding, but she doesn't quit. Nick plays well enough in his tryout to make the farm team, but his coach questions why he's dropped out of college and a pre-med program. Perhaps Nick asks himself that question too, because in short measure he finds minor league hockey isn't fun; the sport is grueling, and his chances of achieving success are slim. Meanwhile, Lexie is becoming a media darling. Deborah and journalist Brian Dockett (David Huffman) have launched a series of television news features on Lexie's quest for an Olympic berth. Nick, frustrated by his failure to make comparable progress and jealous of the publicity Lexie has received, quits the farm team, turns down Lexie's invitation to visit her during the holidays, and hangs up the phone without responding to her "I love you."

Lexie faces pressure as well, and she sees how someone can crack under the glare of the limelight when a leading skater loses her composure in a televised event. In Nick's absence, Lexie grows closer to Brian, who helps her understand her newly acquired celebrity status. By the regionals, Lexie has regained her confidence and places first. Nick, who has watched from the stands, hurries to the floor, arriving just in time to witness a kiss between Lexie and Brian. Now jealous of her success *and* faced with a rival, Nick stomps off.

At an arena party that evening, Lexie wanders through the gathering looking uncomfortable while Deborah and Brian are caught up with other people. After staring at the rink below, Lexie decides to skate. Soon the guests are all watching. As Lexie gains speed, Deborah's expression reflects concern. Lexie does indeed show off again, executing a triple spin, and although she lands cleanly, she is tripped up by a chain near the edge of the rink and strikes her head. At the hospital, the doctor explains to Beulah and Marcus that Lexie has lost most of her vision as a result of the injury to her brain. The camera shifts to her point of view, revealing a murky world of grey shadows.

Lexie sinks into depression, with an occasional angry outburst. Her father takes her to the pond where she learned to skate, but the outing only increases her sense of helplessness. When Beulah visits, the two sit in front of the television. One day Beulah finds Lexie in the attic wearing her mother's sweater. A struggle ensues as Beulah tries to extract Lexie from the sweater and from the cocoon of self-pity she has wrapped around herself. The confrontation proves cathartic as Lexie rages and cries, until, exhausted, she collapses in Beulah's arms.

In the very next scene, Lexie is on the pond with Marcus, both wearing skates. Lexie is hesitant to let go at first, and soon falls; however, it is Nick who extends a hand to help her up, and Marcus slips off. Nick continues to work with Lexie, pushing her to challenge after challenge. How long they practice at the pond is unclear, whether a single session or several. At times Nick appears to be trying to build up Lexie's confidence; at other times he seems cold and demanding, not unlike Deborah. Later, Nick confesses to Marcus that he wanted to hurt Lexie. Marcus does not respond directly, saying that Nick needs to decide what he's going to do with his life and warns him he could end up like Marcus. It is never explained what Marcus means here; he has given no previous indication that he is discontent with his life. He does recognize that Nick has lost his sense of direction; so too, it appears, has the script.

When next seen, Nick is back on the ice with Lexie, and they kiss and make up. Nick convinces the others that Lexie should skate in the upcoming regionals; she agrees, providing that no one knows of her blindness. So, a year after her accident, she returns, wearing the same little blue dress from her first competition. With a few cues from Nick, she conceals her blindness from a skater she knows, but when Brian follows her to the dressing room, he realizes that she can't see. Lexie and Brian part amicably, and Brian agrees to keep her secret. Lexie takes the ice for her long program and once again stuns the crowd. All seems well until, as she skates toward the exit, fans begin throwing roses onto the ice, and she falls. Lexie remains on her hands and knees, trying to get her bearings while silence hangs over the arena. Then Nick walks out to her and leads her to the center of the ice amid thundering applause. The film ends on this high note and avoids any hint of what lies ahead for the principal characters.

ICE PRINCESS (2005)

DIRECTOR: Tim Fywell. SCREENPLAY: Hadley Davis, Meg Cabot. PRODUCER: Bridget Johnson. CINEMATOGRAPHY: David Hennings. EDITING: Janice Hampton. MUSIC: Christophe Beck. PRODUCTION DESIGN: Lester Cohen. ART DIRECTION: Dennis Davenport, Aleksandra Marinkovich. COSTUME DESIGN: Michael Dennison.

CAST: Michelle Trachtenberg (Casey Carlyle), Kim Cattrall (Tina Harwood), Trevor Blumas (Teddy Harwood), Joan Cusack (Joan Carlyle), Amy Stewart (Ann), Hayden Panettiere (Gen Harwood), Steve Ross (Mr. Bast).

RUNNING TIME: 98 minutes.

DVD: Walt Disney Home Entertainment.

Ice Princess is a chickette flick from Disney Studios that revisits the pursue-your-dreams theme. Michelle Trachtenberg, of

Buffy the Vampire Slayer renown, stars as Casey Carlyle, an introverted physics-whiz-turned-figure-skater who sacrifices a shot at attending Harvard for a chance at earning an Olympic berth. Her decision, however, alienates her from her domineering mother, Joan (Joan Cusack), who has been grooming her for the Ivy Leagues. Although parental conflict over career decisions is a staple of the sports film genre, *Ice Princess* fails to develop major plot elements, undermining the film's credibility but playing into the fantasies of young viewers. The most glaring weakness is that neither Casey's passion for figure skating nor her skill on ice seems genuine.

The film opens with Casey skating in lazy circles on a pond, where she appears more lost in thought than dreaming of Olympic gold and cheering crowds, and there is nothing in her movement to suggest natural athleticism. A few days later, as she watches a figure skating program on television with an equally nerdy friend, it is an idea for a science project rather than an urge to take up the sport that leads her to the local rink. There she encounters Tina Harwood (Kim Cattrall), former skater and mother of Gen (Hayden Panettiere), a typical "mean girl" at Casey's school. Tina, who coaches and gives lessons, agrees to allow Casey to videotape her students while they practice so that Casey can determine the aerodynamic formulae required to execute difficult maneuvers. The resulting project is scientifically sound, but dry. Acting on the advice of her science teacher to make the project more personal, Casey enrolls in a beginners' class taught by Tina so that she can apply her research to her own progress.

Towering over her elementary school–age classmates, Casey masters the basics, but shows little interest beyond her science project until, just before a recital, she lands a jump and decides to participate in the children's program. Her mother expresses misgivings about Casey's new-found interest, singling out the skimpy costumes worn by female skaters as being particularly offensive. Of course, Casey has no costume at all and must borrow one from her coach—a flimsy scarlet number with black beading. After a remarkably good showing at the recital (which her mother fails to attend), Casey decides to continue lessons, this time in a class with Gen and other teens from her school.

To finance the coaching and rink time, she uses her computer skills to help her fellow skaters improve their jumps; however, there's no indication that her own rapid progress is a result of applied physics. Tina attributes Casey's success to natural ability and desire. Digital analysis fades into the background as Casey morphs into a polished athlete. Trachtenberg, who spent eight months preparing for the part, does some of her own skating, but she looks amateurish in the presence of the real skaters in supporting roles. Performances by Kirsten Olson as Nikki-the-Jumping-Shrimp and Juliana Cannarozzo as punk troublemaker Zoey Bloch are filmed to suggest television coverage of figure skating events. When Trachtenberg is on the ice, her face and feet seldom appear in the same frame, drawing attention to the editing.

Unevenness and contradiction mar character and story line. None of the characters shows much depth. Gen is introduced as a snobby "type A" teen, but loses her attitude and befriends Casey without explanation. Similarly, Zoey Bloch, who starts off as a scheming competitor, turns into a reliable source of straightforward information. Casey herself exhibits little capacity for self-reflection, and she makes major decisions about her future without apparent consideration and certainly without consulting adults. Grownups do not come off well in *Ice Princess.* Tina has pushed Gen into figure skating even though

Gen is only modestly talented at the sport. When it appears that Casey will beat out Gen for a qualifying spot, Tina sabotages Casey's performance in the long program, an act for which the coach is unabashedly unapologetic. Joan Carlyle, Casey's mother, is presented as a strident, humorless feminist who, while not ruthless, is certainly relentless in attempting to mold her daughter in her own image. Neither Casey's nor Gen's father is on the scene. Tina's son, Teddy (Trevor Blumas), provides the obligatory love interest, but his role is minor—he drives the Zamboni at the practice rink—and by the end of the movie, it seems that Tina has forgotten he is actually her son. An obvious blunder is that Joan, who tells Casey she has always regretted not going to college, is shown near the end of the film teaching what appears to be a roomful of college students.

By the end of the film, Casey has landed two triple jumps, gained her mother's support, determined to apply herself to making the Olympic team with Tina as her coach, and kissed Teddy. As the final credits begin, the two mothers are negotiating how Casey will spend her time, indicating that neither mother has changed in her determination to control. Nor is there any indication that Tina has acquired a code of ethics. In pursuing her dreams, Casey has sacrificed her chance of attending Harvard and placed her figure skating career in the hands of a woman who values winning above everything.

INDIANAPOLIS SPEEDWAY (1939)

DIRECTOR: Lloyd Bacon. SCREENPLAY: Sid Herzig, Wally Kline. STORY: Howard Hawks, William Hawks. PRODUCER: Hal B. Wallis. CINEMATOGRAPHY: Sid Hickox. EDITING: William Holmes. MUSIC: Adolph Deutsch. ART DIRECTION: Esdras Hartley. COSTUME DESIGN: Orry-Kelly.

CAST: Pat O'Brien (Joe Greer), Ann Sheridan (Frankie Merrick), John Payne (Eddie Greer), Frank McHugh ("Spud" Connors).

RUNNING TIME: 85 minutes.

In this remake of the 1932 Howard Hawks film *The Crowd Roars*, Pat O'Brien and John Payne take over the roles of car-racing brothers.

IN GOD'S HANDS (1998)

DIRECTOR: Zalman King. SCREENPLAY: Zalman King, Matt George. PRODUCER: Tom Stern. CINEMATOGRAPHY: John Aronson. EDITING: James Gavin Bedford, Joe Shugart. MUSIC: Paradise. PRODUCTION DESIGN: Marc Greville-Mason, Paul Holt. ART DIRECTION: Jacqueline R. Masson. COSTUME DESIGN: Jolie Anna Andreatta.

CAST: Matt George (Mickey), Matty Liu (Keoni), Patrick Shane Dorian (Shane), Shaun Tomson (Wyatt), Maylin Pultar (Serena).

RUNNING TIME: 96 minutes.

DVD: Sony Pictures.

Surfers travel the world in search of the biggest waves.

INTERNATIONAL VELVET (1978)

DIRECTOR: Bryan Forbes. SCREENPLAY: Bryan Forbes, based on the novel by Enid Bagnold. PRODUCER: Bryan Forbes. CINEMATOGRAPHY: Tony Imi. EDITING: Timothy Gee. MUSIC: Francis Lai. PRODUCTION DESIGN: Keith Wilson. COSTUME DESIGN: John Furness.

CAST: Tatum O'Neal (Sarah Brown), Christopher Plummer (John Seaton), Anthony Hopkins (Captain Johnson), Nanette Newman (Velvet Brown).

RUNNING TIME: 127 minutes.

VHS: MGM.

More than thirty years after *National Velvet* comes this sequel about Velvet's niece, who wants to compete in the Olympics.

INVICTUS (2009)

DIRECTOR: Clint Eastwood. SCREENPLAY: Anthony Peckham, based on the book *Playing the Enemy: Nelson Mandela and the Game That Made a Nation* by John Carlin. PRODUCERS: Clint Eastwood, Robert Lorenz, Lori McCreary, Mace Neufeld. CINEMATOGRAPHY: Tom Stern. EDITING: Joel Cox, Gary D. Roach. MUSIC: Kyle Eastwood, Michael Stevens. PRODUCTION DESIGN: James J. Murakami. ART DIRECTION: Tom Hannam, Jonathan Hely-Hutchinson. COSTUME DESIGN: Deborah Hopper, Daryl Matthee.

CAST: Morgan Freeman (Nelson Mandela), Matt Damon (François Pienaar), Tony Kgoroge (Jason Tshabalala), Patrick Mofokeng (Linga Moonsamy), Matt Stern (Hendrick Booyens), Julian Lewis Jones (Etienne Feyder), Adjoa Andoh (Brenda Mazibuko).

RUNNING TIME: 133 minutes.

ACADEMY AWARD NOMINATIONS: Best Actor (Freeman), Best Supporting Actor (Damon).

DVD: Warner Home Video.

In 1994 the African National Congress (ANC) won South Africa's general election, the first held under universal suffrage, and Nelson Mandela assumed the presidency of a country deeply divided along racial lines. As part of his effort to unify the nation, Mandela began to promote acceptance among blacks of South Africa's white-supported rugby team, the Springboks. After being banned from international play because of its policy of apartheid, the national team had been readmitted to World Cup competition in 1992, and the 1995 World Cup was scheduled to be held in South Africa. Mandela's plan to generate black enthusiasm for the sport and to prod the team to victory is the subject of Clint Eastwood's *Invictus.*

The film opens in February 1990, with Mandela's release from prison after serving twenty-seven years of a life sentence for "treason"—his efforts to bring democratic government to the nation. As his motorcade travels from the jail, it passes a group of black children kicking a soccer ball behind a chain link fence and, on the opposite side of the road, uniformed white youngsters playing rugby behind a high, spiked wrought iron fence. Footage of violence in the streets is mixed with scenes of small gatherings of whites expressing fears of retaliation now that a black majority has assumed power.

The scene moves quickly to the newly elected president's first day on the job. Observing that the mostly white staff members of the previous administration are packing their belongings, Mandela (Morgan Freeman) calls an impromptu meeting at which he encourages the office employees to stay because they are needed by their government. His decision to retain white workers extends to the security force, which will include members of the Special Branch, whose forces often clashed with the ANC. When Hendrick Booyens (Matt Stern) and Etienne Feyder (Julian Lewis Jones), formerly of the Special Branch, report to work, Mandela's security heads, Jason Tshabalala (Tony Kgorogo) and Linga Moonsamy (Patrick Mofokeng), fear the white men have come to arrest them. Later, when Jason protests working with the Special Branch, Mandela responds, "Reconciliation starts here."

Shortly after the election, Mandela attends the Springbok-England rugby match, where the blacks cheer for England, which wins handily. When South Africa is chosen to host the 1995 World Cup, the all-black National Sports Council votes to have the team's name eliminated. In spite of objections from his chief of staff, Brenda Mazibuko (Adjoa Andoh), Mandela addresses the group, urging them to allow the team to retain its name and its gold and green colors. Then, he continues his efforts by inviting the Springboks' captain, François Pienaar (Matt Damon), to tea, where the two men address the question "How do we inspire everyone to greatness?" François leaves the meeting realizing that the Springboks are "more than a rugby team," and he encourages his teammates to cooperate in Mandela's plan to conduct rugby clinics in impoverished black neighborhoods around the country. Although the players grumble at first, they are soon enjoying themselves. The presence on the team of one black player, Chester Williams (McNeil Hendricks), facilitates their acceptance.

By the time the World Cup begins, François has gotten the team in shape, but South Africa is a decided underdog, and some of the players still reject the idea of the Springboks as ambassadors. François provides them with copies of "Nkosi Sikelele Afrika," the anthem of the black resistance movement, now sung alongside the existing national anthem; however, most players wad up their copies and toss them aside. In a parallel sequence, Mandela writes out the words to William Ernest Henley's poem "Invictus," which is delivered to François before the final contest against New Zealand. François, moved by the gesture, takes the 'Boks on a field trip to the Robben Island prison, now deserted, and they visit the sparse, narrow cell Mandela inhabited.

Eastwood has worked several plotlines into the story, and these are resolved during the sequence of the championship match. François, whose parents (Patrick Lyster and Penny Downie) have been portrayed as insensitive whites, presents their black housekeeper, Eunice (Sibongile Nojila), with a ticket to the match, where she sits with the family. The tension between the white and black security guards has been abating as the blacks have become more interested in rugby, eventually tossing a ball about on the president's lawn. Concern for Mandela's safety—a recurrent theme—is heightened by the ominous presence of a man in dark glasses casing Ellis Park Stadium. The film cuts from the packed stadium just before the opening ceremony to a 747, where the mysterious stranger is revealed to be the copilot. He takes control of the aircraft, steering the plane low over the stadium and creating alarm among the security forces. On the underside of the wings is painted the message "Good Luck Bokke [Boks]." During the national anthems, the camera lingers on the players, all of whom sing.

The New Zealand team, featuring the seemingly unstoppable Johan Lomu (Zak Feaunati), is heavily favored, but against all odds, the match remains close as the teams exchange goals. Eastwood devotes eighteen minutes to the action on the pitch. The film cuts several times to a scene outside the stadium, where a black boy gathering bottles from the gutter hovers near a police car where two white officers are listening to the match on the radio. As the match progresses, the boy moves closer until he is sitting on the automobile. When the 'Boks win in overtime, the officers dance in the street, one holding the boy on his shoulder. François's mother and Eunice embrace, as do Mandela's security guards. Even Brenda is jumping for joy.

Morgan Freeman, who won an Oscar for his role in Eastwood's *Million Dollar Baby*, had, with Mandela's approval, undertaken to develop a film adaptation of his autobiography, *Long Walk to Freedom*, but found the project overwhelming. *Invictus* is based on John Carlin's book, *Playing the Enemy*. South African native Tony Peckham began working on the script before the book was published, relying on Carlin's notes and research. Peckham reports, in an article in *Script* magazine (November/December, 2009), that although the rugby provided a structure and an ending to the story, he found it difficult to determine where to begin. Peckham also needed to explain the basics of rugby for American audiences and to capture a sense of South Africa's troubled history for viewers who did not grow up learning about apartheid. Most challenging was how to present so remarkable a figure as Mandela. By including references to Mandela's family and a brief scene with his daughter, Peckham humanizes his portrayal of a man who seems much larger than life. The writer incorporates lines from Mandela's writings into the dialogue to illustrate his subject's philosophy. The effect is that the character speaks aphoristically, but Freeman manages to sound thoughtful and modest.

Eastwood adhered closely to the original script. Reviewer A. O. Scott, writing for the *New York Times* (December 11, 2009), refers to *Invictus* as Eastwood's "latest exploration of revenge, the defining theme of his career." While Mandela represents forgiveness, the flip side of revenge, the coin of South African hatred seems poised on edge through much of the film. Eastwood maintains tension by intercutting footage of past rioting and by making Mandela's safety a central concern. In an early scene, as Mandela, flanked by bodyguards, takes his predawn walk, a battered van nears the trio. When their paths intersect at a corner, a loud noise alarms the men (not to mention the audience), but the source of the sound is a stack of newspapers being dropped on the pavement. The van's driver is a deliveryman, not a would-be assassin. Eastwood departs from fact in developing the sequence with the 747. In actuality, the 1995 buzzing of Ellis Park was a planned stunt approved by the proper authorities. (These twists, in which the anticipated act of violence proves otherwise, are reminiscent of the climax of Eastwood's 2008 *Gran Torino.*) Eastwood also uses color and verticals to reinforce the sense of racial tension. As Mandela prepares to shave on his first day in power, he stares in the mirror at his dark face, half-coated in white foam. When he enters his office, white furniture gleams in the dimly illuminated room. Throughout the film, fences, shadows, and the zebra stripes of crosswalks and referees' uniforms remind the viewer of Mandela's years of incarceration and of South Africa's decades of apartheid.

The acting in the film is superb. Freeman studied tapes of Mandela's speeches to capture his accent, posture, and mannerisms. Damon also worked diligently on the accent, although it is perhaps fortunate that his character is a man of few words. Chester Williams coached Damon and served as technical director. The rugby games were shot at Ellis Park Stadium with two thousand extras. Motion-capture techniques were employed to fill the stadium to its sixty-two-thousand-seat capacity.

INVINCIBLE (2006)

DIRECTOR: Ericson Core. SCREENPLAY: Brad Gann. PRODUCERS: Mark Ciardi, Gordon Gray, Ken Mok. CINEMATOGRAPHY: Ericson Core. EDITING: Gerald B. Greenberg. MUSIC: Mark Isham. PRODUCTION DESIGN: Sarah Knowles. ART DIRECTION: Charley Beal. COSTUME DESIGN: Susan Lyall.

CAST: Mark Wahlberg (Vince Papale), Greg Kinnear (Dick Vermeil), Elizabeth Banks (Janet Cantrell), Kevin Conway (Frank Papale), Michael Rispoli (Max Cantrell), Kirk Acevedo (Tommy).

RUNNING TIME: 105 minutes.

DVD: Buena Vista Home Entertainment.

Invincible is based on the life of Vince Papale, a thirty-year-old substitute teacher and part-time barkeeper who tried out for the Philadelphia Eagles and made the squad. Like *Rocky* (1976), it features an underdog South Philadelphia hero. While not nearly as successful as *Rocky*, *Invincible* did well, garnering a nomination from the ESPY Awards for Best Sports Movie of the Year.

The film is solidly grounded in South Philadelphia, where the fans and neighborhood are tied to the fate of the Eagles. As the film begins, a group of children is playing football in a vacant lot near a factory that is closing. Jim Croce's "I've Got a Name" is featured on the sound track, signaling that identity is one of the themes of the film. (Throughout, Papale's name is often mispronounced and misspelled.) Then the scene shifts to a snow-covered Eagles Stadium, where the Eagles are being thrashed by the Cincinnati Bengals. The fate of the Eagles is again tied to that of their fans when one says, "See you on the unemployment line."

Vince (Mark Wahlberg), hardly "invincible" at this time, is shown starring in a rough touch football game between teams sponsored by local bars. After the game he returns to his apartment, where his wife, Sharon (Lola Glaudini), confronts him about their desperate financial situation. He leaves in a huff, goes to his friend Max's (Michael Rispoli) bar, and learns that Dick Vermeil (Greg Kinnear), the newly appointed Eagles' coach, is conducting a tryout for walk-ons. His pals urge him to go out for the team. When he returns home, Sharon is gone, along with most of their possessions. Since he has also been informed that he will not get the summer teaching assignment he had counted on, he is reduced to asking his father, Frank (Kevin Conway), for money.

When his father offers little comfort, stating, "A man can only take so much failure," Vince determines to attend the tryout. He has also met Janet Cantrell (Elizabeth Banks), Max's cousin and an avid New York Giants fan. She and Vince verbally spar about the merits of their teams and compete about football knowledge. Eventually they marry.

The tryouts, which are covered by the local media, are amusing because of the motley group of nonathletes who show up. Vince, who runs the 40-yard dash in 4.5 seconds and who can catch passes, is the only one who is invited to the training camp. Coach Vermeil informs him of this while Vince is trying to start his old car in the parking lot. Both the car and Vince need a jump start. That night at Max's the crowd learns that Vince has made training camp, and a television announcer comes to the bar to interview him. The scene ends with Vince walking Janet home.

While he is at training camp at Widener College, Vince takes some hard knocks and is mentally prepared to be cut before the season opens; but he perseveres, learns a few tricks from a veteran, and makes the team, mainly because Vermeil believes in him. Of course, he is helped by the Giants' sweatshirt that Janet sends him. Vince's second talk with his father also lifts his spirits. Frank, who has always remembered Steve Van Buren's winning touchdown run, declares that that one touchdown "got me through thirty years at the factory." Then, he adds, "Van Buren has nothing on you." Unfortunately, the Eagles lose their preseason games, and their losses parallel the losses the neighborhood workers are experiencing at the Westinghouse plant. The striking workers, however, "always have the Eagles."

Vince and Vermeil also have much in common. Both are unproven newcomers who must produce before fans so tough that they "threw snowballs at Santa Claus." Before the opening game against Dallas, the two even vomit together. On the opening kickoff Vince, who is poised to tackle the runner, acts like the proverbial deer in the headlights and is leveled by a Dallas blocker. Vermeil and Vince are both criticized by the press, and Leonard Tose (Michael Nouri), the Eagles' owner, pressures both of them. The two are redeemed in the Giants game, when Vince not only completes key tackles, but also causes a fumble, picks it up, and scores a touchdown. Back at Max's, Max tells Frank, "That's your boy!"

When the action ends, the audience learns that Vince spent three years with the Eagles before suffering a career-ending shoulder injury, that he married Janet, and that they and their children live in New Jersey. This information would suggest that Disney has presented a factual account, but there are some "improvements," especially ones that make Vince even more of an underdog than he was. While Vince did play only one year of high school football because of his size, he grew to be six foot two, weighed 185 pounds, and played for two seasons with the Philadelphia Bell in the World Football League. The Eagles invited him, along with other former Bells, to the tryouts. Despite the embellishments, the story is essentially accurate, has *Rocky* elements in its South Philadelphia location, and demonstrates how the fate of a team can affect the morale of a community.

THE IRON LADIES (2000)

DIRECTOR: Yongyoot Thongkongtoon. SCREENPLAY: Visuttchai Boonyakarnjawa, Jiri Maligool, Yongyoot Thongkongtoon. CINEMATOGRAPHY: Jiri Maligool. EDITING: Sunji Asavinikul. COSTUME DESIGN: Ekasith Meeprasertsakul.

CAST: Jesdaporn Pholdee (Chai), Sahaphap Tor (Mon), Ekachai Buranapanit (Wit), Giorgio Maiocchi (Nong).

RUNNING TIME: 104 minutes.

DVD: Strand Releasing.

This Thai film is based on the true story of a volleyball team comprised of gay and transgender players who achieved success at the Thailand national championships in 1996.

THE IRON LADIES 2 (2003)

DIRECTOR: Yongyoot Thongkongtoon. SCREENPLAY: Yongyoot Thongkongtoon. PRODUCERS: Jiri Maligool, Prasert Vivattanananpong. CINEMATOGRAPHY: Jiri Maligool, Sayombhu Mukdeeprom. EDITING: Sunji Asavinikul. MUSIC: Amornbhong Methakunavudh. COSTUME DESIGN: Ekasith Meeprasertsakul.

CAST: Sujira Arunpipat (Muk), Kokkorn Benjathikoon (Pia), Anucha Chatkaew (June).

RUNNING TIME: 100 minutes.

DVD: Strand Releasing.

A prequel and sequel to *The Iron Ladies*, this film shows how the players met and reunited after their success at the Thailand volleyball championships in 1996.

IT HAPPENS EVERY SPRING (1949)

DIRECTOR: Lloyd Bacon. SCREENPLAY: Valentine Davies. STORY: Valentine Davies, Shirley W. Smith. PRODUCER: William Perlberg. CINEMATOGRAPHY: Joseph MacDonald. EDITING: Bruce Pierce, Dorothy Spencer. MUSIC: Leigh Harline. ART DIRECTION: J. Russell Spencer, Lyle Wheeler. COSTUME DESIGN: Bonnie Chashin.

CAST: Ray Milland (Vernon Simpson), Jean Peters (Debbie Grreenleaf), Paul Douglas (Monk Lanigan), Ed Begley (Edgar Stone), Ray Collins (Alfred Greenleaf), Jessie Royce Landis (Mrs. Greenleaf), Alan Hale Jr (Schmidt).

RUNNING TIME: 87 minutes. B&W.

ACADEMY AWARD NOMINATION: Best Motion Picture Story.

VHS: 20th Century Fox.

What happens every spring is that chemistry professor Vernon Simpson (Ray Milland) gets baseball fever, which leaves him unable to focus on his research between April and October. As a result, Vernon hasn't completed his doctoral dissertation, and his career is in jeopardy. Unless he can make more progress on developing a "biophobic" formula that will cause trees to repel insects, he hasn't a hope of securing an income adequate for marrying his sweetheart, Debbie Greenleaf (Jean Peters), who is also the daughter of the university president. Vernon has been plagued by bad luck, and true to fashion, he runs afoul of fate just as he is perfecting his formula: an errant baseball crashes through the window of his laboratory, bringing down a complex network of beakers and tubes. The ball ends up in a lab tray with what's left of the biophobe.

Although the lab equipment is easily replaced, replicating the formula will require months and months, possibly years. It appears Vernon's worst fears are about to become reality, but then he discovers that the baseball exposed to the formula swerves away from wood. After trying out the baseball on a pair of unsuspecting college athletes who are unable to connect with Vernon's pitches, he develops a plan to win enough money to marry Debbie. He acquires a leave of absence from the university, ostensibly to continue his research, and travels to St. Louis, where the team is looking for one more pitcher to round out its roster. He talks his way into a tryout and manages to deliver his special pitch by concealing in his glove a pad moistened with the formula.

Vernon makes the team, playing under the name of Kelly, but suspicion surrounds him. Team manager Jimmy Dolan (Ted de Corsia) thinks he's a crackpot and assigns his catcher, Monk Lanigan (Paul Douglas), to spy on him. Meanwhile, Vernon discovers that he has been reported missing. In order to have a police search called off, Vernon sends Debbie an engagement ring with a vaguely worded note that leads her father to believe Vernon has become involved with criminals. This misconception is reinforced when Debbie's mother spots Vernon with several team members at the St. Louis train station and overhears snatches of conversation about stealing (bases) and knocking someone around (getting hits from a pitcher).

As Kelly's exploits on the mound draw press attention, Vernon is hard pressed to keep his photo out of the papers and his true identity secret. He has a close call during one game when he spots Dr. Greenleaf, a man who finds sports antithetic to academics, sitting with the owner, Mr. Stone, a potential donor to the university. Debbie, thinking she has recognized Kelly from a published photo, pours over the newspaper with a magnifying glass and shows up at a game with binoculars. Meanwhile, Monk recognizes Debbie from the picture Vernon keeps on his nightstand; inevitably, he seeks her out to introduce himself. Once Debbie learns of Vernon's dual identity, she tells her mother, and word soon spreads on campus.

The source of Vernon's pitching skill remains a secret, but trouble is brewing there as well. When Monk is injured by a foul tip, the team doctor puts a wooden splint on his finger, and Monk returns to the game; when he tries to extract a pitched ball from his mitt, it scoots away. The puzzled catcher is removed from the game before it becomes obvious the ball is juiced, and Vernon escapes detection. However, unknown to Vernon, the supply of biophobe is dwindling. Vernon has told Monk that the vial of formula is hair tonic, so Monk has been helping himself on the sly. His hair crackles and misbehaves every time he leans too close to the frame of a mirror or tries to use a wooden-handled brush, but he's convinced his hair is thicker, if less manageable. Monk then passes the vial on to another player; Vernon finally tracks it down just before the deciding game of the series, but he spills most of what remains.

When Vernon takes the mound against New York, he must rely on his own pitching. At first he has trouble settling in. New York jumps to a two-run lead, but Monk reminds him that there are "seven men behind you," and the fielders come through. St. Louis takes a one-run lead into the ninth. With two out in the bottom of the ninth, New York's "Blockbuster" Marx hits a potentially game-winning line drive, but Vernon makes a diving, barehanded catch, injuring his pitching hand in the process. Monk breaks the news that Vernon has suffered a career-ending injury, and Vernon confides that he's in too much trouble to get his old job back. Feeling very much a failure, he takes the train back home, expecting rejection from his fiancée and her father. Instead, he is greeted by a brass band and a throng of fans, including Dr. Greenleaf, who reveals that Mr. Stone has agreed to fund the university lab on the condition that Vernon be named director.

This highly improbable story proved popular with audiences and won an Oscar nomination for screenwriter Valentine Davies (*Miracle on 34th Street*). Delightful special effects, from biophobic baseballs to literal hair raising, were created by Fred Sersen.

J

THE JACKIE ROBINSON STORY (1950)

DIRECTOR: Alfred E. Green. SCREENPLAY: Arthur Mann, Louis Pollock. PRODUCER: Mort Briskin. CINEMATOGRAPHY: Ernest Laszlo. EDITING: Arthur H. Nadel. MUSIC: Herschel Burke Gilbert. PRODUCTION DESIGN: Boris Leven. COSTUME DESIGN: Maria Donovan.

CAST: Jackie Robinson (himself), Ruby Dee (Rae Robinson), Minor Watson (Branch Rickey), Louise Beavers (Jackie's mother), Richard Lane (Clay Hopper), Harry Shannon (Frank Shaughnessy), Bernie Hamilton (Ernie).

RUNNING TIME: 76 minutes. B&W.

DVD: MGM.

Jackie Robinson plays himself in this low-budget, cold war–era docudrama. The movie portrays Robinson as an iconic figure while promoting an optimistic view of America, one in which equal opportunity prevails and bigoted whites are quick to see the error of their ways. The film opens in 1928 with a young black boy walking down an open road leading past a row of run-down buildings. A voice-over tells the audience that this is not just a story of a boy's dreams, but a story of a uniquely American dream. The film reinforces the Protestant work ethic through a montage in which Jackie is shown shining shoes and delivering newspapers, usually with a baseball glove jammed in his rear pocket. After he is awarded a scholarship to UCLA through the efforts of a white coach, Jackie breaks track records and excels at football as well as baseball. However, in the early 1940s racial discrimination still limited opportunities for even talented and well-educated black men. Jackie's older brother, Mack (Joel Fluellen), an Olympic medalist with a college degree, can find steady employment only as a street sweeper for the city of Pasadena. Jackie, too, seems unable to put his education and skills to use. He receives rejection after rejection when he applies for teaching and coaching positions. Finally a job offer arrives that he can't refuse—a draft notice from the U.S. Army.

After completing his service, Jackie begins playing baseball with the Negro Leagues, where he quickly distinguishes himself. However, life in the Negro Leagues is presented as hard: the pay is low, and the team must spend much of its time traveling on a rickety bus. On the road racial discrimination makes obtaining food, lodging, and access to restroom facilities an ongoing challenge. Jackie, who would like to marry his sweetheart, Rae (Ruby Dee), realizes that the travel schedule and paltry salary make marriage and starting a family impractical. But Jackie's life is about to change. The general manager of the Brooklyn Dodgers, Branch Rickey (Minor Watson), has been scouting the Negro Leagues for promising young players to add to his aging roster. Jackie possesses the skills Branch is looking for, but more importantly, the character to withstand the pressure, what Branch calls "the guts *not* to fight back."

At spring training, Jackie faces blatant racism from his teammates, who ostracize him, and from his manager, who questions whether Jackie is even a human being. Once the regular season begins in the minor leagues, Jackie is greeted with boos when he steps up to bat, pitchers aim at his head, thugs threaten him. Rae, now his wife, is afraid to leave the house. When Branch moves Jackie up to the majors, the pressure continues. Several Dodgers sign a petition trying to keep Jackie off the team; in the locker room, he hangs his clothes on a hook behind a door because he doesn't have a locker. Opposing teams wave shoeshine boxes, display watermelons, and jeer. Fans boo and throw trash onto the field when Jackie steps into the on-deck circle.

Through all of these painful displays of prejudice and acts of discrimination, Jackie remains calm and stoic, while others—whites—come to his defense. Throughout, the film counterbalances white bigotry with white support and acceptance and suggests that integration will overcome prejudice as white people come to appreciate the abilities of black people. This point is introduced early in the first reel when young Jackie asks two white men hitting balls to a group of children if he can play. "Watch this," says the batter to the other adult and then hits a hard grounder right at Jackie. After Jackie has skillfully handled two tough balls, the man calls him over, asks whether his hands sting, and gives him a torn glove to keep. This scene introduces a pattern: Jackie's manager, his teammates, even a particularly rude fan are all won over by both his talent and his attitude. He acknowledges kindness, ignores taunts, and backs away from confrontations with apparent ease. The film provides no indication that Jackie's passive response to hostility may have been difficult for him. In fact, the film glosses over his fiery temper, which made itself evident once he had established his position with the Dodgers and once the fear that he might trigger a race riot by reacting to abuse had passed. It also omits his outspokenness and activism: as an army lieutenant, he faced court martial for refusing to sit in the back of a transport bus during World War II. When he finally speaks for himself at the end of the film, his message is a scripted one, a reenactment of his appearance before the House Un-American Activities Committee, which was a rebuttal to the African American actor Paul Robeson's statement that blacks would not support a war against communism. As Jackie speaks, a shot of the Statue of Liberty is superimposed on his image, and his voice gives way to the voice-over claiming that in America *every* child has the opportunity to become president or play for the Brooklyn Dodgers.

The twenty-first-century viewer may find much to criticize in *The Jackie Robinson Story*. Its portrayal of the Negro Leagues is distorted, overlooking the success and popularity of the league games. Branch repeatedly calls Jackie "boy" while referring to the white players as "men." The paternalism of white characters and their naïve integrationist strategies are unacceptable by today's standards. But for its time, *The Jackie Robinson Story* makes a remarkably strong statement about civil rights.

JERRY MAGUIRE (1996)

DIRECTOR: Cameron Crowe. SCREENPLAY: Cameron Crowe. PRODUCERS: James L. Brooks, Cameron Crowe, Laurence Mark, Richard Sakai. CINEMATOGRAPHY: Janusz Kaminski. EDITING: Joe Hutshing. PRODUCTION DESIGN: Stephen

Lineweaver. Art Direction: Clayton Hartley, Virginia Randolph. Costume Design: Betsy Heimann.
Cast: Tom Cruise (Jerry Maguire), Cuba Gooding Jr. (Rod Tidwell), Renée Zellweger (Dorothy Boyd), Regina King (Marcee Tidwell), Bonnie Hunt (Laurel Boyd), Jay Mohr (Bob Sugar), Jerry O'Connell (Frank "Cush" Cushman), Jonathan Lipnicki (Ray Boyd), Kelly Preston (Avery Bishop).
Running Time: 139 minutes.
Academy Awards: Best Supporting Actor (Gooding Jr.). Nominations: Best Picture, Best Actor (Cruise), Best Original Screenplay, Best Editing.
DVD: Sony Pictures.

Nominated for a Best Picture Academy Award and ranked by the American Film Institute among the top ten sports films ever made, *Jerry Maguire* is both a satire of the commercial aspect of professional sports and a touching love story. Writer/director Cameron Crowe spent several years researching and writing the script about a sports agent, Jerry Maguire (Tom Cruise), who tries to work and live according to a set of ethical principles that he had abandoned in the course of becoming successful.

The film opens with Jerry doing a harsh self-assessment. He has become, in his own words, "just another shark in a suit." Several incidents have caused him to question his professional ethics. First, a client is arrested; then another refuses to sign an "unauthorized" baseball card for a young fan. Finally, a hockey player suffers his fourth concussion, and the man's son begs Jerry to persuade his father to retire. One night, troubled by nightmares, Jerry writes a mission statement for his company, Sports Management International (SMI), calling for a closer relationship between agent and client, an improvement that will require handling fewer athletes and will result in the company's earning less in commissions. After the statement is distributed to other SMI employees, Jerry receives a unanimous show of approval, but behind his back, the others anticipate he won't last more than two weeks. In fact, he's quickly fired, unceremoniously, in a crowded restaurant.

Temporarily abandoning his ethical stance, Jerry responds to SMI by trying to take his existing clients with him. He and a rival agent, Bob Sugar (Jay Mahr), square off on their phones in a frantic competition to secure agreements. Jerry loses the duel, retaining only one athlete, mediocre wide receiver Rod Tillman (Cuba Gooding Jr.), who, in one of the best known scenes of the film, demands Jerry shout repeatedly "Show me the money!" Afterward, Jerry makes a dramatic exit during which he challenges other employees to defect. He leaves, taking with him the goldfish

Tom Cruise is a frustrated sports agent in *Jerry Maguire*

from the company aquarium and a lone employee, Dorothy Boyd (Renée Zellweger), a young widow and single parent who admires his courage and values loyalty.

Jerry soon finds both his professional and his personal life in trouble. His relationship with his fiancée, Avery (Kelly Preston), has been cooling since the engagement party, where Jerry watches a video of testimonials by former girlfriends that reveals a pattern—his involvements with women have been fairly superficial, having little to do with intimacy and much to do with Jerry's fear of being alone. His financial security and the future of his new business depend on top college draft pick "Cush" Cushman (Jerry O'Connell), whose father has given Jerry his sworn word that they have a deal. Then Jerry loses Cush to the unscrupulous Bob Sugar after the elder Cushman spots Jerry networking with Rod. In quick succession, Jerry breaks up with Avery, gets drunk, and ends up at Dorothy's.

The growing romance between Jerry and Dorothy is by turns poignant and lighthearted, with a number of comic moments. Jerry is charmed by Dorothy's six-year-old son, Ray (Jonathan Lipnicki); Ray clearly adores Jerry, and Dorothy's attraction to Jerry is enhanced by the affection the other two show for each other. In spite of warnings from her sister, Laurel (Bonnie Hunt), who hosts weekly support sessions for a group of divorced women, Dorothy embarks on a subtle yet steady mission to attract Jerry. For his part, Jerry is attracted, but he's also trying very hard to be a model employer. When he kisses Dorothy during his drunken visit, he immediately feels guilty, comparing himself to Clarence Thomas (who, before gaining Senate approval for his appointment to the Supreme Court, was accused of harassing a female coworker). The next morning, Jerry repeats his apology and reiterates the appropriate boundaries of their working relationship. Dorothy expresses agreement, but cleverly repeats the word "alone," having learned the previous evening of Jerry's weakness. As she heads out the door to give him some "alone" time to think about their business strategy, Jerry asks her out to dinner.

At the restaurant he tries to keep a professional distance, waving away the mariachi with the explanation that Dorothy is a business associate. But Dorothy looks particularly fetching, and when she excuses herself from the table to call the nanny, she sends the musicians back to the table. Inevitably, Jerry spends the night, exchanges fake smiles the next morning with Laurel, and chows down on Apple Jacks with a delighted Ray as Dorothy beams in the background.

Jerry's other significant relationship is with Rod, who carries his resentment about his lack of endorsements and his relatively low salary onto the playing field. Although Rod is a difficult client, he is a dedicated family man deeply in love with his wife, Marcee (Regina King), and determined to make whatever adjustments are required to obtain financial security for the future. As the friendship between the two men deepens, they are able to help one another. Rod, dissatisfied with the Cardinals' contract offer, decides to opt for free agency in the coming year, and with Jerry's advice and support, he begins to play with more feeling for the game. Jerry, having overheard Dorothy tell her sister that she loves him, confesses to Rod his confusion about his own feelings.

Rod encourages him to be upfront with Dorothy. But when Dorothy packs up Ray and a rental truck to move to San Diego, where there's a job with a much-needed benefits package, Jerry proposes marriage, which will save them money on health care insurance. Although his proposal is sincere, he is acting from the head rather than from the heart. Soon, the marriage seems little more than an extension of the business partnership. It is Dorothy who articulates the unhappiness that has settled over them, but later that evening it is Jerry, watching Ray sleep, who cries. When Jerry leaves on his next road trip with Rod, Dorothy and Ray move back with her sister, and Jerry concentrates on keeping his client in good form. Rod, who has been playing well, has the game of his career, reeling in difficult catches, breaking tackles, and finding the end zone. But he's also taken some punishing hits, and when he's brought down hard after a touchdown catch, he lies on the ground unconscious. Jerry hurries to the field, and as the trainers kneel over Rod, calls Marcee on his cell phone. After a tense moment, Rod recovers, realizes he's scored, and puts on a wild display of antics, turning back flips, dancing, and dangling from the stands. Then he makes his way through a clutch of reporters to Jerry and the cell phone. As Jerry listens, yet again, to Rod telling his wife how much he loves her, something finally clicks inside him, and he returns with due haste to Dorothy, proclaiming, "I'm not ready for you to get rid of me." The film ends with Rod landing a multiyear, multimillion dollar contract and Jerry, once again a successful agent, strolling happily through the park with Dorothy and Ray—who he's just discovered has a really good arm.

Jerry Maguire grossed over $140 million in its first year, thanks to an excellent script and strong performances. There's a fine balance between comedy and drama, which makes the story both compelling and believable. Avery's ambition, the male nanny's defensiveness, and the bitterness of Laurel's women's group situate Jerry's problems in a cultural context while contributing to the film's humor. Periodically, the narrative is interrupted for an appearance by Jerry's mentor, who offers conventional wisdom from behind his desk. Tom Cruise, who was nominated for an Oscar, showed he was capable of handling a complex dramatic role, while Cuba Gooding Jr., best known for serious roles, such as Tre Styles in *Boyz n the Hood* (1991), won the Oscar for Best Supporting Actor. For Renée Zellweger, whose earlier credits include *The Return of the Texas Chainsaw Massacre* (1994) and who was not yet using a diacritical mark in her first name, Dorothy Boyd was a breakthrough role. The film earned Oscar nominations for Best Writing and for Best Editing as well as Best Picture.

Ironically, *Jerry Maguire* contains nearly two-dozen product placements, which brought in millions of corporate dollars. Reebok, the athletic apparel company against which Rod holds a particular grudge, filed a multimillion dollar suit against the producers in a dispute over the film's ending. Reebok shot and paid for an authentic commercial starring Rod Tillman with the agreement that the ad would figure largely in the movie's conclusion. The producers and director argued that the agreement did not guarantee that the commercial would be included, and it landed, subsequently, on the cutting room floor. Terms of the out-of-court settlement are confidential, but the television version of *Jerry Maguire* aired on HBO has been reedited to include the Reebok ad, which also appears as a "special feature" on the DVD.

JIM THORPE: ALL AMERICAN (1951)

DIRECTOR: Michael Curtiz. SCREENPLAY: Everett Freeman, Douglas Morrow, Vincent X. Flaherty, Frank Davis, based on the biography by Jim Thorpe II and Russell Birdwell. PRODUCER: Everett Freeman. CINEMATOGRAPHY: Ernest Haller. EDITING: Folmar Blangsted. MUSIC: Max Steiner. ART DIRECTION: Edward Carrere. COSTUME DESIGN: Milo Anderson.

CAST: Burt Lancaster (Jim Thorpe), Charles Bickford (Glenn S. "Pop" Warner),

Steve Cochran (Peter Allendine), Phyllis Thaxter (Margaret Miller), Dick Wesson (Ed Guyac).
RUNNING TIME: 107 minutes. B&W.
DVD: Warner Home Video.

Based in part on a book by Russell Birdwell and Jim Thorpe II, this biopic of Native American track star Jim Thorpe follows a pattern of rise, fall, and redemption. The film focuses on the first two phases of Thorpe's illustrious and tumultuous career.

From the start Jim (Burt Lancaster) demonstrates an independent streak that plagues him throughout his life. Unwillingly taken to school by his father, he runs twelve miles home, arriving as his father pulls up on his buckboard. Although his mother hands her husband a belt, his father, knowing that force will not break his son's spirit, counsels Jim into seeing beyond the boy's world of the reservation to the future, where he can make something of himself by using what is in the schoolbooks. Jim promises to attend the Carlisle Indian School, but he doesn't really fit in at first. At the school only English is spoken; however, the film omits some of the other more onerous rules that imposed stiff penalties for failure to assimilate to the white culture.

Jim finds the confinement and discipline of school in conflict with the freedom of the out-of-doors. Outside, he can run, an activity that he resorts to when school becomes too stressful. One day as he is running, he accidentally enters a race and sprints by all the competition, much to the amazement of Coach Pop Warner (Charles Bickford), who enlists him in the track team. Ultimately, Carlisle's team consists of Jim, who handles all the events except the long races, and one other runner. Even with just a two-man team, the Carlisle Indians win the Pennsylvania Collegiate Track and Field Championship.

Jim also competes against a football player, Peter Allendine (Steve Cochran), for the affections of Margaret Miller (Phyllis Thaxter). Unfortunately, track doesn't have the star appeal of football, so in order to win over Margaret, Jim joins the football team. Coach Warner, however, keeps Jim on the bench until he has run out of healthy players. At last, Jim enters the Harvard game with instructions to kick a field goal to tie the score. When he runs for a touchdown instead, Carlisle wins 11–10. Jim decides that he wants to become a coach like Warner and also decides that he will marry Margaret after the summer vacation is over. Warner suggests that he at least talk to Margaret about his plans. Jim gives her a football bracelet as an engagement gift and tells her that they belong together because they have the "same blood, same background." Then he leaves to work on a farm. During that summer he plays third base for the Rocky Mount, North Carolina, baseball team, totally unaware that he is jeopardizing his amateur standing by taking expense money.

When Jim looks for Margaret at school in the fall, he discovers that she is not there and that she is not a Native American as he had supposed. He turns his disappointment into anger and has a terrific football season, winning All-American status. Warner, who has become a surrogate father, knows Jim is suffering. He takes him to the infirmary, where he has found a job for Margaret, and the couple are reunited after they resolve the misunderstanding about "blood and background."

As the Carlisle-Penn game approaches, Jim and Tom Ashenbrunner (Hubie Kerns) of Penn State are the top candidates for a coaching position at Allegheny College. Although Carlisle ekes out a 14–13 win, Tom gets the Allegheny post. Jim is furious, suspecting that he was passed over because he is a Native

American. Warner counsels that coaching is more than winning; it's also about leading, and Warner reminds Jim that he kept Little Boy, his blocker, in the game despite knowing that he was injured. This is another instance of Jim's determination to excel, perhaps at a cost to others.

That determination leads him to prepare for the Olympics in Stockholm, Sweden, where he wins not only the pentathlon, but also the decathlon, and is called the "best athlete in the world" by the king of Sweden. Upon his return to the United States, Jim receives a letter from President Taft, enjoys a parade in New York City, and is offered a coaching job at the University of Virginia, where he and Margaret get married. However, his good fortune dissolves when news of his summer baseball stint for Rocky Mount surfaces. Despite a vigorous defense by Warner and Jim's protestations, the Olympic Committee strips him of his medals. And he loses the Virginia coaching position.

Jim's only course of action is to turn professional. He signs to play baseball with the Giants under manager John McGraw (Roy Gordon, uncredited), who seems determined to show Jim who is boss. After failing to bunt as ordered, Jim gets the winning hit, but McGraw fines him fifty dollars. Jim then quits and signs to play professional football, where he becomes a star. When he and Margaret have a son, Jim devotes himself to making the little boy a successful athlete and often misses practices to work out with the boy. His behavior seems driven by the idea that his son can somehow get back the records that had been taken away from him. Jim's teammates and coach are frustrated by his lack of team spirit.

After an away game, Jim receives a letter from Margaret informing him that they have lost their son, and the coach picks the wrong time to criticize Jim's play. Jim attacks him, and his slide begins. He moves from one team to another, drinks heavily, and is crushed by sportswriters whose columns describe his deteriorating athletic skills. Not even a visit from his Carlisle chums can pick up his spirits, especially since all three have gone on to successful careers. Unwilling to blame himself, he turns on Margaret, who finally leaves him. After he is caught from behind in a semipro game, his career is over, except for a stint where, dressed in Native American costume, he's the announcer at a dance marathon, and he fails even at that.

Warner, who is now coaching at Stanford University, again intervenes, offering Jim tickets to the 1932 Olympics, where he tells Jim that the vice president of the United States, Charles Curtis, whose mother was Native American, is opening the games. Long after the crowds have left, Jim sits alone in the stands, remembering what he has been told by his father and by Warner, who is trying to get Jim to take responsibility for his own behavior. The turning point occurs soon after when Jim accidentally runs over a football some kids have been playing with. The next day he presents them with a new football, gives them some instructions, and is asked to help them with their next opponent. One kid's "OK, Coach," seems to have enabled Jim to find himself and to return to the "Bright Path" that was his childhood Indian name.

The frame for the film is an awards banquet in Oklahoma, where Jim is being honored not for just his records on the field, but for his off-field achievements. Pop Warner narrates the film before introducing Jim, who is posed beside his mentor. As a biopic, the film describes, without soft-pedaling, the rise and, especially, the fall of a hero. Thorpe died in 1953 in near poverty. His medals were returned to the Thorpe family in 1982.

JOHNNY BE GOOD (1988)

DIRECTOR: Bud S. Smith. SCREENPLAY: Steve Zacharias, Jeff Buhai, David Obst. PRODUCER: Adam Fields. CINEMATOGRAPHY: Robert D. Yeoman. EDITING: Scott Smith. MUSIC: Jay Ferguson. PRODUCTION DESIGN: Gregg Fonseca. ART DIRECTION: Sharon Seymour. COSTUME DESIGN: Dorree Cooper.

CAST: Anthony Michael Hall (Johnny Walker), Robert Downey Jr. (Leo Wiggins), Paul Gleason (Wayne Hisler), Uma Thurman (Georgia Elkans), Steve James (Coach Sanders).

RUNNING TIME: 91 minutes.

DVD: MGM.

This crude comedy is about a high school football superstar who is being wooed by various colleges.

JUNIOR BONNER (1972)

DIRECTOR: Sam Peckinpah. SCREENPLAY: Jeb Rosebrook. PRODUCER: Joe Wizan. CINEMATOGRAPHY: Lucien Ballard. EDITING: Frank Santillo, Robert L. Wolfe. MUSIC: Jerry Fielding. ART DIRECTION: Ted Haworth.

CAST: Steve McQueen (Junior Bonner), Robert Preston (Ace Bonner), Ida Lupino (Elvira "Ellie" Bonner), Ben Johnson (Buck Roan).

RUNNING TIME: 100 minutes.

DVD: MGM.

Sam Peckinpah's rodeo classic reflects a number of signature elements from his Westerns, particularly his reverence for the values associated with the Old West—individualism and independence. Steve McQueen stars as the title character, a rodeo star whose fading career reflects the receding of a nobler past. Robert Preston plays his father, Ace, an irrepressible free spirit who, like Junior, was once a rodeo star. Ida Lupino, who had turned to directing in the 1950s, accepted the role of Ace's wife, Ellie. Joe Don Baker rounds out the family as Junior's younger brother, Curly, a local entrepreneur trying to keep his father under control, but profiting in the process.

The film opens with a flashback using split screens as Junior relives an attempt to ride Sunshine, a bull that no one has been able to stay on for the requisite eight seconds. In the narrative present, Junior is pulling a horse trailer behind a once-flashy Cadillac convertible, now dinged and dirty. At a roadside gas station, he buys oil for the car and a bag of apples to share with his horse. Back on the road, he's passed by a more prosperous group in a newer Cadillac; one of the women in the backseat tosses him a beer as they cruise by. When Junior arrives at the family ranch outside of Prescott, Arizona, the house is abandoned, and a menacing bulldozer idles nearby. As Junior watches, the dozer plows under the mailbox and crushes the house. Since Junior shows no sign of leaving, the driver of the dozer scoops up a load of rock and aims for the Caddy. Junior skedaddles.

In the next scene Curly is visiting Ace, who has totaled his truck while under the influence and is recovering at the local hospital. The two men do not get along, and when a television ad appears featuring Curly plugging his Trading Post, Ace hurls a glass at the screen. The film cuts to the rodeo grounds, where preparations are underway for Prescott's annual Frontier Days Celebration. Junior has another flashback of the bull; then he registers for events, putting himself and his father down for bulldogging and wild cow milking. At the bar of the Palace Hotel, Junior approaches Buck Roan (Ben Johnson), Sunshine's owner. Junior is willing to pass along a few bills to assure that he will draw Sunshine, but Buck turns him down, reminding him that he's not as good as he used to be.

Next, Junior visits his mother, who has been living in town and taking in boarders for the past year. She tells him that Curly bought the ranch and is starting a mobile home development on the acreage. Before venturing out to Curly's Trading Post, Junior stops at the hospital, but Ace is asleep. At the Trading Post the camera pans Curly's "zoo," a row of caged wildlife symbolizing the replacement of freedom with confinement. From an outdoor stage, Curly is making a sales pitch to a busload of recently arrived potential customers. He interrupts the promotion when he sees Junior, whom he welcomes warmly. Junior does not seem equally joyous. That night at dinner Curly explains that he bought the ranch and put his father on an allowance to prevent him from squandering money on foolish schemes; then he offers Junior a job selling lots. Junior steps outside, and when Curly comes out as well, Junior knocks him backward through a window.

The next morning Ace leaves the hospital against doctor's orders, while his nurse, Arlis (Sandra Deel), with whom he has been flirting, watches with disapproval. A short while later Junior arrives at the hospital with a bottle and a bouquet; realizing that his father has checked himself out, he presents the flowers to the nurse and returns to his horse trailer, where he discovers his father has taken off with his horse. Junior interrupts his search for his father long enough to attend the draw for the bull-riding event. He is matched with Sunshine. (Whether Buck had a hand in the outcome of the drawing is not revealed.) Once the parade begins, Junior finds his father riding in the midst of it. Ace invites Junior aboard, then spurs the horse, and they bolt down a side street. Their wild ride comes to an end when they encounter a clothesline.

At the deserted train station, Ace and Junior share the bottle. Ace asks about some of the riders still on the circuit, and Junior tells him one is dead and another retired. Ace shares with his son his plan to go to Australia and prospect for gold. He invites Junior along, but asks him to grubstake the venture. When Junior says he's broke, Ace knocks his son's hat off and walks across the tracks. A train passes between the two, underscoring the tense moment; however, Ace's irritation has dissolved by the time the track is clear, and he retrieves Junior's hat.

When the rodeo kicks off, Junior performs well, but not quite well enough, coming in second behind his friend Red (Bill McKinney) at saddle bronc riding and bulldogging. He and Ace would have won the wild cow milking contest had they not fought over who would run with the milk bottle. During the interval the entire Bonner family meets up at the Palace Hotel bar. In spite of Ellie's presence, Arlis asks Ace to dance. After a brief standoff, Ace leaves with Ellie. Curly, still angry with Junior for slugging him the night before, decks Junior with a single punch. The score settled, the brothers have a beer, and Curly explains that he's just trying to keep the family together. Curly still wants Junior to work for him and suggests that it's time Junior leave the circuit and start making money.

Throughout the day Junior has been exchanging glances with an attractive woman whom he now notices watching him from a nearby booth. Although she is clearly with another man, he asks her to dance, and she agrees over the objections of her date. Red tries to cut in, but Junior good-naturedly tells him to find his own partner. The woman, a rodeo groupie named Charmagne (Barbara Leigh), lets Junior know she's attracted to him. When the next song begins, Junior and she resume dancing. As her angry date heads in their direction, Junior nudges Red, they trade partners, and Red takes the brunt of the jilted date's wrath. Charmagne turns back to Junior, and they continue to waltz as the brawl spreads around them. Junior steers her toward a phone booth, removes his hat, and places it over the glass door to provide them some privacy. The band begins to play the national anthem, and the brawlers snap to attention. At the bar Ace is trying to charm Ellie into getting back together. Unhappy about Ace's latest scheme, Ellie declares, "You can go to hell or to Australia, but not with me." Ace retorts, "They're both down under." Ellie is won over, and they disappear up the stairs. Although Ace's restless need for adventure disrupts the marriage, the relationship is passionate, in contrast to the sterile, emotionless connection between Junior and Charmagne.

The second portion of the rodeo gets underway. Junior stays on Sunshine for more than eight seconds and dismounts gracefully, earning $950 in prize money. The next day, he delivers Charmagne to the airport before stopping to say goodbye to his mother. She won't let him in, knowing that he'll use the prize money to stake Ace's Australia trip, but she does wave from the window. On the street, Junior walks past Ace without acknowledging him. Still, he uses most of his winnings to buy his father a first-class ticket, which he has delivered to the Palace Bar. Then Junior drives off to the next rodeo.

For Peckinpah, the passing of the Old West and all it stands for in American mythology is a national tragedy. He employs a number of techniques in the film to keep the passage of time in check. Flashbacks and split-screen montage remove events from conventional chronological representation, while slow-motion shots of bulls and bulldozers suspend the falling of man and homestead (albeit not eternally, like Thelma and Louise hanging in midair over the Grand Canyon). While the editing and camera work remind viewers that they are watching a movie, the film achieves realism through use of actual settings. For example, in the scene where Junior registers for events, Peckinpah used the real registration for the Frontier Days events. No sets were constructed for the film and background action was not staged. The result is a complex film, underrated at the time of its release but now considered among Peckinpah's and McQueen's best.

JUST MY LUCK (1957)

Director: John Paddy Carstairs. Screenplay: Alfred Shaughnessy, Peter Blackmore. Producer: Hugh Stewart. Cinematography: Jack Cox. Editing: Roger Cherrill. Music: Philip Green. Art Direction: Ernest Archer. Costume Design: Yvonne Caffin.

Cast: Norman Wisdom (Norman Hackett), Margaret Rutherford (Mrs. Dooley), Jill Dixon (Anne), Leslie Phillips (Richard Lumb), Joan Sims (Phoebe).

Running Time: 86 minutes.

DVD: ITV Studios Home Entertainment (PAL).

A man places bets with a bookie who may not be able to pay off the winnings.

JUWANNA MANN (2002)

Director: Jesse Vaughan. Screenplay: Bradley Allenstein. Producers: Bill Gerber, James G. Robinson. Cinematography: Reynaldo Villalobos. Editing: Seth Flaum. Music: Lisa Coleman, Wendy Melvoin. Production Design: Eve Cauley. Art Direction: Jennifer O'Kelly. Costume Design: Peggy Farrell, Richard Owings.

Cast: Miguel A. Núñez Jr. (Jamal Jefferies), Vivica A. Fox (Michelle Langford), Kevin Pollak (Lorne Daniels), Tommy Davidson (Puff Smokey Smoke), Kim Wayans (Latisha Jansen).

Running Time: 91 minutes.

DVD: Warner Home Video.

In this predictable comedy, a player disguises himself as a woman to join the WNBA after getting kicked out of the men's league.

K

KANSAS CITY BOMBER (1972)

DIRECTOR: Jerrold Freedman. SCREENPLAY: Calvin Clements Sr., Thomas Rickman. STORY: Barry Sandler. PRODUCERS: Martin Elfand, Arthur Gardner, Jules V. Levy. CINEMATOGRAPHY: Fred J. Koenekamp. EDITING: David Berlatsky. MUSIC: Don Ellis. PRODUCTION DESIGN, ART DIRECTION: Joseph R. Jennnings. COSTUME DESIGN: Ron Talsky.

CAST: Raquel Welch (K.C.), Kevin McCarthy (Burt Henry), Helena Kallianiotes (Jackie Burdette), Jodie Foster (Rita).

RUNNING TIME: 99 minutes.

DVD: Warner Home Video.

Kansas City Bomber is a drama set in the world of coed roller derby, a sport that enjoyed a run of popularity in the early 1970s before the resurgence of professional wrestling. The two sports have much in common: scripted feuds, performers/athletes who assume roles, staged violence, and unpunished rule breaking. Raquel Welch, a sex symbol of the time, plays a divorced mother who has turned her skating talent into a career that is profitable but that keeps her away from her children for too long.

When the film opens, K.C. (Welch), the star of the Kansas City Bombers, has been challenged to a race by a rival teammate. The loser must leave the Kansas City team. The challenge race is merely a cover story, for K.C. has agreed to be traded to the Portland Loggers, where she will be closer to her children, who live with her mother. K.C.'s mother disapproves of her chosen career, and her withdrawn son resents her absences, but her daughter, played by ten-year-old Jodie Foster, is an adoring child ready to roll in her mother's tracks.

The move to Portland generates a series of complications. The new team owner, Burt Henry (Kevin McCarthy), has designs on K.C. and soon maneuvers her into a romantic relationship. He also intends to manipulate her career by first building up her following, then using her popularity to establish yet another team in Chicago. However, he keeps K.C. in the dark about his plans for her. When she first arrives in Portland, K.C. is assigned to skate with a different team, a plot element whose only purpose seems to be to underscore the control that team owners hold over their skaters. Shortly after K.C. arrives, Burt transfers her roommate, a popular Logger, because he finds K.C.'s having a roommate inconvenient. Burt also becomes jealous of her friendship with "Horrible Hank" (Norman Alden), a slow-witted Logger who plays a villain, although he is by nature gentle. Burt takes advantage of Hank's trust, encouraging him to enrage fans and opponents to the point of unprecedented violence; as a result, Hank is severely injured and his skating career ended.

On the team, K.C. must deal with a bitter rival, the aging Loggers' star Jackie Burdett (Helena Kallianiotes in an excellent performance). Jackie, whose career is fading, begins drinking and slides into a depression. Her performance suffers and K.C.'s efforts to cover for her only increase Jackie's rage. Not even when K.C. saves her life by pulling her from the path of a train does Jackie accept K.C.'s attempts at friendship.

After Burt finalizes his Chicago deal, he arranges a challenge race between Jackie and K.C. As with the race in Kansas City that brought K.C. to Portland, the loser will be forced to leave. Burt anticipates that K.C. will cooperate by losing the race in order to move to Chicago with him. But K.C., who wants to remain near her family, realizes that Burt is greedy and untrustworthy. In the challenge race, which Jackie is intent on winning, K.C. battles her way across the finish line ahead of her opponent.

Although the lead characters are two-dimensional, Welch was praised for her performance. She completed many of her own stunts, breaking a wrist during filming. Kallianotes received a Golden Globe nomination for her portrayal of the troubled Jackie.

THE KARATE KID (1984)

DIRECTOR: John G. Avildsen. SCREENPLAY: Robert Mark Kamen. PRODUCER: Jerry Weintraub. CINEMATOGRAPHY: James Crabe. EDITING: John G. Avildsen, Walt Mulconery, Bud Smith. MUSIC: Bill Conti. PRODUCTION DESIGN: William J. Cassidy. COSTUME DESIGN: Richard Bruno, Aida Swenson.

CAST: Ralph Macchio (Daniel LaRusso), Pat Morita (Mr. Miyagi), Elisabeth Shue (Ali Mills), Martin Kove (John Kreese), Randee Heller (Lucille LaRusso), William Zabka (Johnny Lawrence), Chad McQueen (Dutch), Larry B. Scott (Jerry).

RUNNING TIME: 126 minutes.

ACADEMY AWARD NOMINATION: Best Supporting Actor (Morita).

DVD: Sony Pictures.

The Karate Kid is a popular coming-of-age film that won critical praise for its director John G. Avildsen (*Rocky*, 1976) and for its acting: Pat Morita, who played the Okinawan martial-arts teacher, Mr. Miyagi, won Oscar and Golden Globe nominations; Elisabeth Shue (Ali Mills) won a Young Artist Award for Best Supporting Actress; and William Zabka (Johnny Lawrence) was nominated for a Young Artist Award for Best Supporting Actor. The film, which concerns the nature of the sport, not just position and technique, contrasts the philosophies of Mr. Miyagi and John Kreese (Martin Kove), who runs the Cobra Kai Karate School. A second conflict, between the rich students and the poorer ones in the high school, is played out in the competition between Daniel LaRusso (Ralph Macchio) and Johnny Lawrence for Ali's attention.

When his optimistic, palm-tree loving mother (Randee Heller) uproots him from Newark, New Jersey, and moves to California, Daniel is thrown into a new culture, one for which he doesn't know the rules. At first he does well. He meets Ali, who seems to like him, and he enjoys himself at the beach before Johnny and his karate pals arrive and harass him. Daniel, who has been studying karate from a book, is no match for Johnny and his friends, who also conspire to make him look bad on the soccer field. When they catch him after a Halloween dance and Johnny savagely beats him, Mr. Miyagi suddenly appears and takes down all five of the bullies. Miyagi becomes a surrogate father to the boy and exposes him to new ideas and customs.

For Miyagi, there are no bad students, only bad teachers, and Kreese is one of them. When Daniel enters his school, Kreese has his students shouting "no mercy, no fear, no defeat," and he tells one of them to "finish off" his downed opponent. Kreese's emphasis is on using karate to fight, rather than to avoid the fight; his followers are portrayed as sneering, hate-filled, vicious hoodlums who do as they please. When Daniel asks Miyagi to teach him karate, his teacher cautions that revenge is not a good reason to learn the martial art. Karate, he explains, operates from the heart and the brain, and "balance," both physical and mental, is the key. To spare Daniel from any more beatings, Miyagi takes him to the Cobra Kai School, where the two instructors make a deal: Daniel will fight pupils of the Cobra Kai School at the upcoming All-Valley Karate Tournament, but Kreese's boys will leave him alone to train.

Daniel wants to learn how to punch, but Miyagi's training saves punching for last. First, Daniel sands, paints, waxes, and polishes Miyagi's decks, fences, and cars, all the while learning how to breathe and how to perfect the defensive hand motions he will require to ward off blows. The second lesson involves balance, first on the bow of a boat, then on poles sticking out of the sand. When Daniel becomes impatient with what seems pointless work, Miyagi demonstrates how it all fits together. He also offers a few instructions. In the course of learning karate, Daniel learns a great deal more: about Miyagi's wife, who died in childbirth; Miyagi's outstanding war record; and the internment of Japanese Americans during World War II. When he leaves the inebriated Miyagi, who has been "celebrating" his wedding anniversary, Daniel bows in respect to his mentor. Miyagi even stages a birthday party for Daniel and gives him two presents—a classic American convertible and the robe that his wife had sown for him. When Daniel expresses his gratitude, Miyagi repeats his advice to "find the balance."

Part of the balance is his relationship with Ali, whose parents and friends are snobs. The distance between Rosita, Daniel's neighborhood, and Encino, Ali's, seems almost impossible to negotiate. Misunderstandings occur, but the young couple are reconciled, and Ali supports Daniel at the tournament, where she supposedly serves as Miyagi's interpreter.

Although neither he nor Miyagi knows the formal rules for karate, Daniel manages to win his first few bouts, and Kreese and his boys are concerned. So determined is Kreese to hurt Daniel that he actually tells one of his boys to "put him out," even though the illegal blow will result in disqualification. The boy reluctantly complies, and Daniel, who is badly hurt, has only fifteen minutes to get back to the mat for the finals against Johnny. Insisting he needs balance, Daniel persuades Miyagi to use his healing powers to help him. Still in pain and limping badly, Daniel takes on Johnny and gains a two-point lead. During a break Kreese advises Johnny to go for Daniel's leg and hit him illegally. With the score knotted at two and with one more point deciding the match, Daniel uses his balance to maintain himself like a crane and deliver the winning kick. Even Johnny congratulates Daniel. The film ends at this point—no romantic kiss from Ali, no afterword, no look at the crushed Kreese. The film is about learning and obtaining balance in one's entire life.

THE KARATE KID (2010)

DIRECTOR: Harald Zwart. SCREENPLAY: Christopher Murphey. STORY: Robert Mark Kamen. PRODUCERS: James Lassiter, Jada Pinkett Smith, Will Smith, Ken Stovitz, Jerry Weintraub. CINEMATOGRAPHY: Roger Pratt. EDITING: Joel Negron. MUSIC: James

Horner. PRODUCTION DESIGN: François Seguin. ART DIRECTION: Second Chan. COSTUME DESIGN: Han Feng.
CAST: Jaden Smith (Dre Parker), Jackie Chan (Mr. Han), Taraji P. Henson (Sherry Parker), Wenwen Han (Mei Ying).
RUNNING TIME: 140 minutes.
DVD: Columbia.

In this very successful remake of the iconic 1984 film, Jaden Smith (son of producers Will Smith and Jada Pinkett Smith) takes over for Ralph Macchio, and Jackie Chan assumes the role of his martial arts mentor.

THE KARATE KID II (1986)

DIRECTOR: John G. Avildsen. SCREENPLAY: Robert Mark Kamen. PRODUCER: Jerry Weintraub. CINEMATOGRAPHY: James Crabe. EDITING: John G. Avildsen, David Garfield, Jane Kurson. MUSIC: Bill Conti. PRODUCTION DESIGN: William J. Cassidy. ART DIRECTION: William F. Matthews. COSTUME DESIGN: Mary Malin.
CAST: Ralph Macchio (Daniel LaRusso), Pat Morita (Mr. Miyagi), Nobu McCarthy (Yukie), Danny Kamekona (Sato), Tamlyn Tomita (Kumiko), Martin Kove (John Kreese).
RUNNING TIME: 113 minutes.
ACADEMY AWARD NOMINATION: Best Song ("Glory of Love" by Peter Cetera, David Foster, and Diane Nini).
DVD: Sony Pictures.

This sequel to the 1984 hit has Daniel and Mr. Miyagi traveling to Japan, where they take on more foes.

THE KARATE KID, PART III (1989)

DIRECTOR: John G. Avildsen. SCREENPLAY: Robert Mark Kamen. PRODUCER: Jerry Weintraub. CINEMATOGRAPHY: Stephen Yaconelli. EDITING: John G. Avildsen, John Carter. MUSIC: Bill Conti. PRODUCTION DESIGN: William F. Matthews. ART DIRECTION: Christopher Burian-Mohr.
CAST: Ralph Macchio (Daniel LaRusso), Pat Morita (Mr. Miyagi), Robyn Lively (Jessica Andrews), Thomas Ian Griffith (Terry Silver), Martin Kove (John Kreese).
RUNNING TIME: 112 minutes.
DVD: Sony Pictures.

Daniel again appeals to his mentor, Mr. Miyagi, but is rebuffed, so he looks elsewhere with disastrous results.

KICKING & SCREAMING (2005)

DIRECTOR: Jesse Dylan. SCREENPLAY: Leo Benvenuti, Steve Rudnick. PRODUCER: Jimmy Miller. CINEMATOGRAPHY: Lloyd Ahern II. EDITING: Stuart H. Pappé, Peter Teschner. MUSIC: Mark Isham. PRODUCTION DESIGN: Clayton R. Hartley. ART DIRECTION: Virginia Randolph-Weaver. COSTUME DESIGN: Pamela Withers-Chilton.
CAST: Will Ferrell (Phil Weston), Robert Duvall (Buck Weston), Josh Hutcherson (Bucky Weston), Mike Ditka (himself).
RUNNING TIME: 95 minutes.
DVD: Universal Pictures.

The son of a soccer coach agrees to lead a team after his son is cut from the grandfather's squad.

THE KID FROM LEFT FIELD (1953)

DIRECTOR: Harmon Jones. SCREENPLAY: Jack Sher. PRODUCER: Leonard Goldstein. CINEMATOGRAPHY: Harry Jackson. EDITING: William Reynolds. MUSIC: Lionel Newman. ART DIRECTION: Addison Hehr, Lyle R. Wheeler. COSTUME DESIGN: Dorothy Jeakins.
CAST: Dan Dailey (Larry "Pop" Cooper), Anne Bancroft (Marian Foley), Billy Chapin (Christie Cooper), Lloyd Bridges (Pete Haines), Ray Collins (Fred F. Whacker), Fess Parker (McDougal).
RUNNING TIME: 80 minutes.

The son of an ex-baseball-player-turned-peanut-vendor ingratiates himself with the local team and soon gets promoted to manager.

KILL THE UMPIRE (1950)

DIRECTOR: Lloyd Bacon. SCREENPLAY: Frank Tashlin. PRODUCER: John Beck. CINEMATOGRAPHY: Charles Lawton Jr. EDITING: Charles Nelson. MUSIC: Heinz Roemheld. ART DIRECTION: Perry Smith. COSTUME DESIGN: Jean Louis.
CAST: William Bendix (Bill "Two Call" Johnson), Una Merkel (Betty Johnson), Ray Collins (Jonah Evans), Gloria Henry (Lucy Johnson), William Frawley (Jimmy O'Brien).
RUNNING TIME: 78 minutes.
DVD: Sony Pictures.

An ex-baseball player becomes an umpire and learns how difficult and important the job is.

KINGPIN (1996)

DIRECTORS: Bobby Farrelly, Peter Farrelly. SCREENPLAY: Barry Fanaro, Mort Nathan. PRODUCERS: Brad Krevoy, Steven Stabler, Bradley Thomas. CINEMATOGRAPHY: Mark Irwin. EDITING: Christopher Greenbury. MUSIC: Freedy Johnston. PRODUCTION DESIGN: Sidney Bartholomew Jr. ART DIRECTION: Arlan Jay Vetter. COSTUME DESIGN: Mary Zophres.
CAST: Woody Harrelson (Roy Munson), Randy Quaid (Ishmael), Bill Murray (Ernie McCracken), Vanessa Angel (Claudia), Chris Elliott (the Gambler), William Jordan (Mr. Boorg), Richard Tyson (Owner of Stiffy's).
RUNNING TIME: 113 minutes.
DVD: MGM.

Woody Harrelson, who has appeared in more sports films than Kevin Costner, stars as Roy Munson in *Kingpin*, a film about professional bowling; however, Munson's character development is the focus of the story. The film, which begins in 1969, looks like a baseball film with father and son playing catch, but Roy's father has set up an outdoor bowling alley where he teaches Roy to bowl and advises him about applying bowling lessons to life. Ten years later, when Roy wins a big tournament, his father gives him a watch, which later proves to be significant.

Roy has the misfortune to encounter Ernie McCracken (Bill Murray), a seasoned pro and ruthless con artist who includes Roy in his scheme, but their hustle results in Ernie leaving Roy to take on some roughnecks led by a fake priest, who is himself a hustler. In the ensuing scuffle, the thugs jam Roy's hand into the ball-return machine, bringing an abrupt halt to his career. Roy now wears a rubber prosthesis that comes off at inopportune times, leaving his hook exposed. While attempting to peddle goods to bowling alleys in Scranton, Pennsylvania, Roy hears the sound of a strike being thrown by Ishmael (Randy Quaid), an Amish farmer who has real bowling talent but knows his parents and community would not approve of his bowling.

Because Roy is in financial trouble—he is behind on his rent to a lecherous landlady (Lin Shaye)—he has sunk very low. He actually steals a baby's bottle to use the milk for his coffee, and then he and a pal stage a fake robbery so he can be a hero with his landlady, who then forgives the rent. When she realizes that she has been scammed, she offers Roy a choice: either she can call the police, or Roy can take her to bed. As he clings pathetically to the toilet after executing the latter, he spots an ad about a million-dollar bowling tournament in Reno. He dons an Amish disguise, poses as Hezekiah, and visits Ishmael; but his Amish pose is not entirely successful: he "milks" a bull; abandons the wall he

Top: Woody Harrelson, Vanessa Angel, and Randy Quaid in *Kingpin*; bottom: Quaid being coached by Angel and Harrelson

is supporting at a barn raising, leading to the collapse of the barn; and cannot identify a quotation from the Bible. He finally succeeds in getting "Ish" to go with him because the Amish community must raise a half million dollars (presumably Ish's share of the winnings) to prevent the bank from foreclosing on the community.

En route to Reno, Roy persuades Ish to smoke, drink coffee, and participate in a hustle similar to the earlier one with Ernie. In this hustle Roy meets Stanley Osmanski (Rob Moran), a rich jerk who loves to bowl, and Miss Claudia (Vanessa Angel), his mistress. After Ish defeats Stanley, things get rough. Stanley beats up Claudia, and Roy is threatened. Claudia, who has stake money, helps Roy and Ish escape unscathed. When Roy attempts to leave Claudia, she attacks him and says she feels she has been "munsoned," a coinage universally equated with being a loser. (Even Ish uses the word appropriately.) On their way to Reno they stop at Roy's hometown, where he finds things have changed radically. He tells Claudia about his dreams, remarks that his father's watch stopped when he left to pursue his bowling ambitions, and then talks with her about starting over together.

Meanwhile, Ish, who had seen the couple fighting, is on the road by himself and soon in trouble. His naïveté about lap dancing results in his being forced to dance as a transvestite in a bar, but Roy and Claudia rescue him. When they get to Reno, Ernie is there as the favorite to win the tournament. Bill Murray is superb as the over-the-top showoff masquerading as a nice guy. Stanley also resurfaces, threatening to hurt Ish and Roy if Claudia doesn't return to him. She goes with Stanley, taking the money the trio have collected on the trip. In a confrontation Ish swings at Ernie, breaking his hand. Since Ish cannot compete, Roy must replace him in the tournament.

Roy is the underdog, but he makes it to the finals, where Ernie is his opponent. In the final frame, Roy leaves the seven and ten pins standing. Although he converts the spare, Ernie bowls three consecutive strikes to win by a pin. After the tournament Stanley is looking for Claudia, who has left him. In a rare moment of insight, Roy blames himself for his injured hand.

A week later Claudia appears at Roy's place with the money and declares that she is now betting on Roy. Roy, however, also has some money, a $500,000 check from Trojan in exchange for his endorsement of their products. By the time that Ish and his brother Thomas (Zen Gesner), who has been sent to retrieve Ish, return to their family, Roy and Claudia are already there, having informed Ish's parents that he saved the souls of Roy and Claudia (whom they refer to as the "whore"). Roy also has prevented the community foreclosure by giving the bank his Trojan money. Ish's father is proud of him; Roy tells Ish, "You saved me," and Claudia has succeeded in getting Roy's father's watch to work (she simply wound it), thereby setting time in motion again and giving new meaning to starting over. At the end of the film Roy and Claudia drive off as the Amish shout, "Bye, bye, Brother Munson; bye, bye, whore." To indicate that the cultural clash has not resulted in a one-sided victory for the Amish, the Amish Blues Travelers band, with Ish leading the dancing, loosens up the Amish crowd with their music.

KNUTE ROCKNE: ALL AMERICAN (1940)

DIRECTOR: Lloyd Bacon. SCREENPLAY: Robert Buckner. PRODUCER: Hal B. Wallis. CINEMATOGRAPHY: Tony Gaudio. EDITING: Ralph Dawson. MUSIC: Heinz Roemheld. ART DIRECTION: Robert M. Haas. COSTUME DESIGN: Milo Anderson.

Cast: Pat O'Brien (Knute Rockne), Gale Page (Bonnie Skiles Rockne), Ronald Reagan (George Gipp), Donald Crisp (Father Callahan), Albert Basserman (Father Nieuwland), John Litel (committee chairman), John Qualen (Lars Knutson Rockne).
Running Time: 98 minutes. B&W.
DVD: Warner Home Video.

Knute Rockne's fame rests not on his athletic prowess but on the innovations he made to the game of football while he played for and coached the University of Notre Dame's Fighting Irish. The son of an ambitious Norwegian immigrant, Rockne demonstrated his athletic abilities as a child playing football with older youngsters. As a young man, in what the film's narrator describes as the "melting pot of Chicago," he adapted, worked hard at the Post Office for six years after high school graduation, and entered Notre Dame, where he soon came under the influence of Father Callahan (played by Donald Crisp).

At Notre Dame, Knute (Pat O'Brien) excels at chemistry and attracts the attention of Father Nieuwland (Albert Basserman), who encourages him to pursue a science career. He even offers him a summer job working on a project to develop synthetic rubber, but Knute's first love is football, and he and his friend Gus Dorias (Owen Davis Jr.) plan to spend the summer as lifeguards while they practice football. During one of their workouts, they pass the ball, and Knute becomes convinced that passing will open up what has been essentially a running game dominated by power.

When Notre Dame plays heavily favored Army, the Fighting Irish are outmanned and trail 13–0, but when Knute prevails upon the coach to try passing, Knute and Gus connect on several plays and upset Army 35–13. The newspapers declare that Notre Dame has revolutionized football, and the team goes on to win games. After graduation Knute is at a crossroads: he must choose between chemistry or coaching. After Knute and his wife, Bonnie Skiles Rockne (Gale Page), have their first child, Knute informs Father Callahan that he has decided on coaching.

During tryouts Knute encounters George Gipp (Ronald Reagan), a talented walk-on who can both kick and run fullback. After being given a chance, George storms through the opposition and comments laconically, "I guess the boys are just tired." George leads the Irish to a string of victories over highly rated opponents. Although comparatively little screen time is devoted to the Knute-George relationship, it is a close one. George is reserved and generally keeps a distance between himself and others, but there is a chair at the Knute's where he often sits and talks with his coach, who comes to regard George as a son. When George is stricken with a sore throat (nearly always a death sentence in films of this time), Knute takes him to the hospital, where they learn that his season is over. George is named to Walter Camp's All-American team, but he dies soon after. Before his death the most famous locker-room speech of all time is set up: George tells Knute, "Someday when the team's up against it, tell them to win one for the Gipper."

Knute's next football innovation is a backfield shift inspired by his viewing of a Rockettes' dance routine. While his players are enjoying the show, Knute makes notes and diagrams, which he incorporates during the next season. He even uses piano music at practice so the players can make the right moves. To him, "this shift is music." With the legendary "four horsemen" in the lineup, the Irish use the new shift to win national championships. The only defeat during one season is the Army game, which Knute is overconfident about winning. Unable to face what he expects will be criticism, he and his family take the later train into South Bend, only to be met with scores of Notre Dame fans who only want to know, "Do we still have you, Rock?" He answers, "I'll never leave Notre Dame."

The years take their toll on Knute, who becomes stricken with phlebitis and ordered not to get out of bed, but the canny Knute has his bed brought to the practice field, where he can continue to give instructions. The crucial Army game is next, and it presents him with the opportunity to use the Gipper speech, which results in a 7–6 win.

Knute's last important contribution occurs when he is asked to represent the football coaches before Congress. Questions are raised about the huge sums of money and attention devoted to football, and there is the possibility that there may be a "football purge." Knute defends the sport, claiming that man's competitive spirit can be expended in sport, not war, and that education cannot be limited to libraries and labs. Warning against the dangers of becoming "soft inside and out" (this film was made during World War II), he points out the challenge of "working the flaccid philosophy out of men" and making them good citizens. He adds that rather than being judged in college, players should be evaluated five years later to see what they have become. His argument succeeds in winning over Congress.

Years later, while vacationing in Florida, he agrees to fly to California for an important meeting, and during a severe storm his plane goes down. At his funeral mass, Knute is described as Notre Dame's "true son," and letters are read from the president and the king of Norway. His legacy was to "right living" and to "his boys," a list of whom is intoned at the end of this unabashedly sentimental biopic.

L

LADYBUGS (1992)

DIRECTOR: Sidney J. Furie. SCREENPLAY: Curtis Burch. PRODUCERS: Andre Morgan, Albert S. Ruddy. CINEMATOGRAPHY: Dan Burstall. EDITING: Tim Board, John W. Wheeler. MUSIC: Richard Gibbs, Michael Jay, D. A. Young. PRODUCTION DESIGN: Robb Wilson King. COSTUME DESIGN: Isis Mussenden.
CAST: Rodney Dangerfield (Chester Lee), Jackée Harry (Julie Benson), Jonathan Brandis (Matthew), Ilene Graff (Bess), Tommy Lasorda (Coach Cannoli).
RUNNING TIME: 90 minutes.
DVD: Lions Gate.

Lowbrow comedy about a man forced to coach a girls' soccer team, which also includes his girlfriend's son in drag.

LAGAAN: ONCE UPON A TIME IN INDIA (2001)

DIRECTOR: Ashutosh Gowariker. SCREENPLAY: Ashutosh Gowariker, Kumar Dave, Sanjay Dayma, K. P. Saxena. PRODUCER: Aamir Khan. CINEMATOGRAPHY: Anil Mehta. EDITING: Ballu Saluja. MUSIC: A. R. Rahman. PRODUCTION DESIGN: Nitin Chandrakant Desai. COSTUME DESIGN: Bhanu Athaiya.
CAST: Aamir Khan (Bhuvan), Gracy Singh (Gauri), Rachel Shelley (Elizabeth Russell), Paul Blackthorne (Captain Russell), Suhasini Mulay (Yashodamai), Kulbhushan Kharbanda (Rajah Puran Singh).
RUNNING TIME: 224 minutes.
ACADEMY AWARD NOMINATION: Best Foreign Language Film.
DVD: Sony Pictures.

The title of this film means "land tax" and refers to assessments paid by villagers during the period of British rule in India. *Lagaan* takes place in the late nineteenth century in a rural village of central India, where an egotistical officer abuses his power by humiliating the local ruler, increasing the *lagaan* in spite of a drought, and eventually challenging a villager to establish a cricket team to play against the British for triple *lagaan* or nothing. Like typical Bollywood productions, the film incorporates musical numbers into the plot, stretching the running time to over three and a half hours. More than an hour of footage is devoted to the cricket match, which extends over a three-day period. While the film is overtly critical of British rule, it presents a fantasy of Indian unity that functions as a commentary on religious, ethnic, and class divisions that have persisted into the twenty-first century.

The film establishes major plot elements within the first few minutes. There is conflict among the inhabitants of Champaner, a small rural village entering the second year of drought. Bhura (Rhaghuvir Yadav), who raises chickens, quarrels with Goli (Daya Shankar Pandey), whose sons disturb the coop. Lakha (Yashpal Sharma), the woodcutter, is hopelessly in love with Gauri (Gracy Singh), who has eyes only for Bhuvan (Aamir Khan), who pretends not to notice. However, all of the villagers agree that the local British soldiers are "sons of unmarried jackals." The commanding officer of the cantonment, Captain Russell (Paul Blackthorne), is an unpleasant, egotistical man who abuses his power. Antagonism develops between Russell and Bhuvan when the villager interferes with the captain's deer hunting by startling the animals. After Bhuvan is discovered, Russell threatens him and then proceeds with his senseless slaughter of wildlife. Russell's cruelty becomes even more apparent in a meeting with the local ruler, Rajah Puran Singh (Kulbhushan Kharbanda), a vegetarian. Russell demands the rajah eat meat or else the *lagaan* will be doubled. The rajah refuses to violate his religious principles, and Russell refuses to back down. Meanwhile, at Champaner, dark clouds begin to form, signaling the beginning of the monsoon season and the first musical number; as the villagers sing and dance in anticipation of the coming rain, Gauri flirts with Bhuvan; the celebration halts abruptly as the clouds break up. Rain fails to arrive, but the rajah's messengers do.

When the villagers learn of the new tax, Bhuvan persuades the Champaner leader that a group should go to the palace to plead with the rajah for understanding. Near the palace the group pauses to watch British soldiers playing cricket. Bhuvan ridicules the game, comparing it to the Indian children's game *gilli-danda* and ignores orders not to touch a ball that has rolled toward him. Once again Bhuvan finds himself in contention with Russell, who challenges him to a cricket match with the land taxes for the entire province at stake—triple *lagaan* or nothing. Although Bhuvan has no authority to make decisions for Champaner, let alone the entire province, Russell insists that Bhuvan alone must chose. Bhuvan accepts the challenge, reasoning that the current double *lagaan* is impossible to meet, so there is nothing to lose; however, the villagers are horrified and interpret his decision as motivated by bravado rather than by concern for the welfare of the community.

Bhuvan has three months to assemble a team and train them to play a game whose rules are quite literally foreign in spite of superficial resemblances to *gilli-danda.* At first the villagers are reluctant to participate. Only Bagha (Amin Hajee), the mute drummer, Guran (Rajesh Vivek), a soothsayer of little renown, and a few children demonstrate interest in playing. Gauri seizes the opportunity to express her confidence in Bhuvan, but before their relationship advances, an unexpected rival for Bhuvan's attention arrives on the scene: Russell's sister, Elizabeth (Rachael Shelley). Acting at first from a sense of fair play, Elizabeth, with the aid of her Indian translator—she does not understand Hindi, nor does Bhuvan know English—offers to teach the villagers the rules of cricket. As her instruction progresses, so does her attraction to Bhuvan, and although he gives no indication that he is aware of her feelings, Gauri has caught on immediately. She interrupts the lessons, insisting the players take breaks and nourishment. Later, her jealousy becomes more pronounced as Elizabeth attends a celebration of Prince Krishna's birthday at the temple, and Gauri persistently attempts to distract Bhuran from his guest.

While Elizabeth's presence unsettles Gauri, it draws more favorable support from the community, and soon more people are stepping forward: Bhura, whose skill chasing chickens translates into fielding; Goli, whose ability with a slingshot makes him a strong bowler; Gauri's father; and Deva, a Sikh from a neighboring village. However, Lakha, still desirous of Gauri, betrays the village by sneaking off to the cantonment and informing Russell of Elizabeth's assistance. Russell enlists Lakha as a spy and tells him to join the Indian team. Lakha finds himself valued because his hard hands, calloused from years of woodcutting, make him well-suited for catching fly balls, but some of the men distrust him; it is Bhuvan who insists he be allowed to join.

For Russell the cricket match has become much more than a macho ego trip; he is in trouble with his superiors for overstepping the boundaries of his authority. One of his superior officers imagines Indian villages all over the country demanding to play cricket matches to get out of paying taxes. Russell is informed that if the English team loses, he will be transferred to a post in the heart of Africa.

After Russell confronts Elizabeth and forbids her from leaving the cantonment, she sneaks off to Champaner on horseback to meet privately with Bhuvan. Without her translator present, she speaks in Hindi, which she has now mastered, saying she has trouble getting out of the compound. She continues to tell him that his friendship is important to her, then confesses her love in English, which Bhuvan does not understand. Gauri, although not present, understands only too well, and has gone off by herself. Bhuvan finds her weeping, and she reveals her anger that Bhuvan "flutters around Elizabeth like a pigeon." Bhuvan replies that he knows she is jealous and indicates that—as Guran has predicted—he is destined to marry Gauri. They begin to sing and dance; back at the compound, Elizabeth fantasizes about waltzing with Bhuvan, but is interrupted by her brother, who announces he is sending her off.

As the match nears, the Englishmen are in top form, but the villagers still need an eleventh player. They discover their last man when Kachra, an untouchable, is asked to retrieve a ball and returns it with his crippled hand, producing a wicked spin, known in cricket as a leg break. Despite initial objection from the others, Bhuvan gains their approval with a speech denouncing the Indian caste system, and Kachra is added to the roster. A training montage cuts between the villagers and the English, and there is a face off between Russell, on horseback, and Bhuvan, shirtless.

Finally, cricket day arrives, and the camera pans each side, the British spectators sitting at shaded tables, the Indians sitting on the dusty earth under the full sun; the British team wear red blazers and caps, the Indians their standard peasant garb. Rajah Singh makes a grand entrance on an elephant and offers a ritual blessing. The Brits win the coin toss, choose to bat first, and accumulate 182 runs on the first day. Lakha has intentionally dropped several balls, Kachra has lost his spin, and the Brits have discovered that Goli, whose windup copies his slingshot movement, grunts before he releases the ball. That night, Elizabeth observes Lakha sneaking across the compound and sneaks out herself to warn Bhuvan. The villagers are intent on revenge; but Bhuvan comes to Lakha's defense, and he is given a chance to redeem himself.

When play resumes the next day, Lakha demonstrates his loyalty by making difficult catches. Kachra's spin returns, and even Guran bowls well. At last, the English turn at bat is over, but the villagers must score 323 runs with only six good batters on the team. By day's end, they have scored only ninety-nine runs, but Bhuvan is still batting. The villagers gather in the temple, and their prayers introduce another musical number.

On the final day, Bhuvan and Ishwar, Gauri's father, are the batsmen. They play well at first, but Ishwar does not have the stamina to continue to run between wickets. Finally, Kachra must replace him as batsman. The match comes down to the last bowl on Kachra's turn, and it appears the game is lost when the official calls a no-ball, the equivalent of a foot fault, and Bhuvan is once again the batsman. He hits a long high ball, which Russell, playing near the boundary, is able to catch; however, he has caught the ball outside of the boundary, giving the villagers an automatic six runs, just enough to win.

In the rejoicing that follows, Elizabeth stands alone, witnessing the embrace of Bhuvan and Gauri. Her stricken expression reveals that she can no longer deny that his heart belongs to the woman from his village and that in spite of her efforts to absorb the language and customs of the Indians, she remains an outsider. Elizabeth bids a sad farewell to Champaner and returns to London. The narrator finishes the story: Elizabeth never married, but Gauri and Bhuvan did; Russell was required to pay the lost *lagaan* for the province himself and was also sent to the African desert. Bhuvan's name is not remembered, making him emblematic of an ideal Indian everyman rather than an individual hero, thus reinforcing the film's vision of unproblematic national unity.

Lagaan was shot in the ancient village of Bhuj, where the climate is dry and there are no power lines or other signs of modern technology. The residents built authentic houses and a temple to Lord Krishna and provided many of the props. After the filming, when the village was severely damaged in an earthquake and its residents displaced, cast and crew members established a relief fund. The film has won a number of awards at international festivals and was nominated for an Oscar for Best Foreign Language Film.

THE LAST AMERICAN HERO (1971)

DIRECTOR: Lamont Johnston. SCREENPLAY: William Roberts, based on articles by Tom Wolfe. PRODUCER: John Cutts, William Roberts. CINEMATOGRAPHY: George Silano. EDITING: Robbe Roberts, Tom Rolf. MUSIC: Charles Fox. ART DIRECTION: Lawrence G. Paull.

CAST: Jeff Bridges (Junior Jackson), Valerie Perrine (Marge Dennison), Geraldine Fitzgerald (Mrs. Jackson), Ned Beatty (Hackel), Gary Busey (Wayne Jackson), Ed Lauter (Burton Colt), William Smith (Kyle Kingman).

RUNNING TIME: 95 minutes.

DVD: 20th Century Fox.

In 1965 *Esquire* published "The Last American Hero," an article by Tom Wolfe profiling stock car driver Junior Johnson. Johnson, a product of rural North Carolina, honed his racing skills while a teenager running moonshine for his father. Johnson learned to throw his car into a 180 degree spin to elude authorities. He was never nabbed behind the wheel of a vehicle loaded with contraband, but he was arrested at his father's still. Johnson served ten months of a two-year sentence in a federal penitentiary before continuing his racing career. (President Reagan granted him a pardon in 1986.) On the track, he was known for his ingenuity as well as his risk taking. Off the track, he married his high school sweetheart, bought his own farm, and raised chickens.

The 1973 film *The Last American Hero* draws on Wolfe's article, but the movie's hero, Junior Jackson (Jeff Bridges) is a somewhat different hero. In her *New Yorker* review (October 1, 1973), Pauline Kael classifies him as a Vietnam-era protagonist, one who realizes that compromising one's values is necessary for survival in a world ruled by corruption and greed. The trick of selling out is to not sell oneself short. According to Kael, the real Johnson rather than the fictional Jackson fits the title in that traditional American heroes have been portrayed as fiercely independent men who buck the system, exposing its weaknesses and somehow leaving it stronger without becoming a part of it. Jackson's story doesn't follow this familiar path, but it's a believable story and one that fared well with reviewers, including Kael.

The film introduces Junior Jackson making a run using all of the tricks for which Johnson was notorious, tracking police activity on his own radio, attaching a bubble light and siren to his car, executing the 180 reverse. Although Junior's father, Roy (Art Lund), cautions Junior to show respect to Collins, the local law enforcement agent, Junior's encounter leaves Collins's car stuck at an uncomfortable angle on an embankment. Shortly thereafter, Roy's still is raided, and Roy is arrested. His lawyer advises him to renounce his evil ways at the trial to receive a reduced sentence, but Roy has his principles—he makes a high-quality product, one that is consumed by most of the local upstanding citizens, and he is proud of his business. Roy receives a one-year sentence.

Although the family lawyer indicates he will accept whiskey as a portion of his fees, the Jacksons still need cash. Junior decides to earn money by entering a demolition derby. He outfits his car with illegal equipment—a pointed chunk of railroad iron—that he uses to disable other vehicles, but the promoter, Hackle (Ned Beatty) does not disqualify him. He recognizes Junior as a talented driver and a crowd-pleaser and allows him to race the following week in a stock-car event, which Junior wins after threading his way through an accident. Junior acquires a string of victories, but after a fistfight with another driver, Hackle dismisses him.

In racing, Junior has found his vocation, and his track experience has shown him that he has the talent to reach the top of the field. However, to move to the next level, he requires a better car, and a better car requires money. Junior begins running liquor again, this time by the tank load. When Roy learns of his son's new enterprise, he is horrified that Junior is transporting an inferior product, but he understands his son's motivation.

With a previously owned but never crashed car, Junior sets out to qualify at a track in Wilkesboro. After some difficulty with the promoter, he is granted a time trial and turns in a respectable run on his first lap. Afterward, he flirts with the promoter's secretary, Marge (Valerie Perrine), who has helped him register and who has arranged a discounted motel room for him. (Director Lamont Johnson plays the desk clerk at the motel.) Although she turns down a date, claiming a previous engagement, she changes her mind and attends a promotional affair with him. Then she dances with driver Kyle Kingman (William Smith), the season's top moneymaker. While Marge is with Kyle, Junior overhears another driver arguing with car owner Burton Colt (Ed Lauter), who micromanages his drivers. When Burton moves on, the driver complains to Junior, who is unsympathetic; at this point, Junior believes that a driver who lacks the initiative to finance his own operation gets what he deserves. Marge returns and drags Junior from the party, but she doesn't invite him in and leaves him with a quick peck on the cheek. Later, Junior phones her, but Kyle answers and says Marge is busy. The two are in bed.

On the day of the race, Junior makes his way through the pack to take the lead from

Kyle, but his engine blows and he spins out. Kyle wins and Marge applauds wildly.

Burton, whose driver has failed to complete the race, suggests that Junior drive for him, but Junior wants nothing to do with Burton. Meanwhile, Marge is hanging onto Kyle; however, Kyle's wife has made an appearance, so Marge locates Junior and asks for a ride home. Soon Marge is in bed with Junior.

Without a vehicle, Junior returns home, where he and his brother, Wayne (Gary Busey), rebuild the still, this time placing it underground. When Roy is released from prison, he has mixed emotions about the still and about Junior's racing. Junior needs a source of income to repair the car, but Roy fears another bust and another jail term, and he wants his sons to avoid following a path that leads inevitably to the slammer.

To finance his return, Junior seeks out Burton, and they strike a deal: Junior will drive in the Old Dominion 500 race using Burton's car and crew, keeping 30 percent of the prize money. It's less than Junior wants, but more than Burton originally offered. Burton has Junior wear a helmet with a headphone so that he can communicate instructions. Once the race is underway, Junior rips out the headphone and drives his own race, following a strategy counter to Burton's. It is a close contest with Junior, Kyle, and handsome Davie Baer (Ernie Orsotti) in contention. Junior emerges the victor as Marge and his brother and original crew cheer from the stands.

After the race Marge congratulates Junior affectionately, even though she is clearly with Davie. Junior has learned that Marge is a racing groupie faithful to no one, and he registers neither disappointment nor surprise that she has taken up with yet another driver. Before the postrace press conference, Junior negotiates a partnership with Burton, one that will include his crew and increase his percentage; he will no longer be his own man, but he has not relinquished complete control. At the doorway leading to the press conference, he spots his old crew gathered across the road. He holds the trophy aloft and shouts, "Hey, we won." The credits roll without a reaction shot to indicate how Junior's crew respond or if they have even heard him.

THE LAST BOY SCOUT (1991)

DIRECTOR: Tony Scott. SCREENPLAY: Shane Black, Greg Hicks. PRODUCERS: Michael Levy, Joel Silver. CINEMATOGRAPHY: Ward Russell. EDITING: Stuart Baird, Mark Goldblatt, Mark Helfrich. MUSIC: Michael Kamen. PRODUCTION DESIGN: Brian Morris. ART DIRECTION: Christiaan Wagener. COSTUME DESIGN: Marilyn Vance-Straker.
CAST: Bruce Willis (Joe Hallenbeck), Damon Wayans (Jimmy Dix), Chelsea Field (Sarah Hallenbeck), Noble Willingham (Sheldon Marcone), Halle Berry (Cory).
RUNNING TIME: 105 minutes.
DVD: Warner Home Video.

In this slick, violent film, a former secret service agent and ex-quarterback expose a football team owner's nasty plans. The film features cameos by such NFL greats as Lynn Swann and Dick Butkus.

A LEAGUE OF THEIR OWN (1992)

DIRECTOR: Penny Marshall. SCREENPLAY: Lowell Ganz, Babloo Mandel. STORY: Kim Wilson, Kelly Candaele. PRODUCERS: Elliot Abbott, Robert Greenhut. CINEMATOGRAPHY: Miroslav Ondricek. EDITING: Adam Bernardi, George Bowers. MUSIC: Hans Zimmer. PRODUCTION DESIGN: Bill Groom. ART DIRECTION: Tim Galvin. COSTUME DESIGN: Cynthia Flint.
CAST: Tom Hanks (Jimmy Dugan), Geena Davis (Dottie Hinson), Lori Petty (Kit Keller), Madonna (Mae Mordabito),

Rosie O'Donnell (Doris Murphy), Jon Lovitz (Ernie Capadino), David Strathairn (Ira Lowestein), Garry Marshall (Walter Harvey), Bill Pullman (Bob Hinson), Bitty Schram (Evelyn Gardner), Ann Cusack (Shirley Baker).
RUNNING TIME: 128 minutes.
DVD: Sony Pictures.

In 1942, Chicago Cubs owner Philip Wrigley, concerned that professional baseball would be closed down for the duration of World War II by the enlistment of male athletes, established the All-American Girls Professional Baseball League (AAGBL). He recruited players from women's softball leagues and launched a successful publicity campaign promoting the sport as a display of patriotism. By 1944, Wrigley was ready to abandon the AAGBL in spite of its popularity; he sold the enterprise to his assistant, Arthur Meyerhoff, who expanded the number of teams. The league's popularity increased in the immediate postwar period, but by the early 1950s it began to lose money and was disbanded in 1954.

A League of Their Own is director Penny Marshall's fictionalized account of the league's conception and first year. Marshall frames the film with scenes from the 1988 ceremony dedicating a new wing of the Cooperstown Baseball Museum to Women in Baseball. Recently widowed Dottie Hinson (Lynn Cartwright), a former AAGBL star, is reluctant to attend the ceremony. She claims it isn't really important, but her daughter comprehends the significance of the AAGBL and of its recognition. The scene shifts to Cooperstown, where members of the original teams are playing ball. Faux newsreel footage shows candy bar mogul Walter Harvey (Garry Marshall) meeting with team owners to contemplate the future of baseball during the war. Harvey leaves the dilemma to his assistant, Ira Lowenstein (David Strathairn), to resolve.

The film cuts to a women's softball game, where the twenty-something Dottie (now played by Geena Davis) is advising her kid sister, Kit (Lori Petty), to lay off the high fastballs. Kit ignores the advice and strikes out. Dottie then slugs a game-winning homer, and Kit sulks, a response that typifies her resentment of her older sister's skill and success. The tension between the sisters increases with the arrival at the family farm of Ernie Capadino (Jon Lovitz), a scout for the newly formed AAGBL. Ernie, a tactless, obnoxious man, makes it clear that he wants Dottie, but not Kit—he is looking for players who are "dollies." However, after he feels Kit's arm muscles—she is a hard-throwing pitcher—he agrees to take Kit if Dottie will join up as well. Dottie, whose husband is overseas in combat, agrees to the deal because it is important to Kit. The trio head for Chicago, with a stop along the way to look at another player, Marla Hooch (Megan Cavanagh). Marla is a power hitter, but she does not measure up to Ernie's standards of attractiveness; however, when Kit and Dottie refuse to continue without Marla, Ernie gives in. As the train pulls out with all three players, a flag waves at the station, and the image is reflected in the train window, a not-so-subtle reminder of the patriotic wash laid over the founding of the women's league.

At Harvey Field, dozens of players have gathered for tryouts, including "All-the-Way" Mae Mordabito (Madonna) and the trash-talking New Yorker, Doris Murphy (Rosie O'Donnell). As the women go through demanding workouts, a radio program laments the "masculinization" of women, foreshadowing the league's emphasis on the femininity of the players. The women selected for teams are informed they will wear uniforms with short skirts and attend charm school. There is to be no drinking, smoking, or seeing men. The earlier training montage is mirrored in shots of the athletes learning to cross their legs at the ankle, sip tea, apply makeup, and balance books on their heads as they walk.

Dottie, Kit, Mae, Doris, and Marla have joined the Rockford Peaches, which include a mother with child care problems (Bitty Schram as Evelyn Gardner) and a beauty queen, Ellen Sue Gotlander (Freddie Simpson). The team's coach, Jimmy Dugan (Tom Hanks), is a former athlete with a marquee name and a drinking problem. At the first game he shows up at the locker room very drunk. Ignoring the women, he staggers to the bathroom and urinates for an exceptionally long time (Mae takes out a stopwatch). After stepping from the dugout to acknowledge the sparse crowd, he dozes off, and Dottie assumes the coaching responsibilities.

A road trip develops several comic episodes. Evelyn must bring her bratty son along on the bus, and he behaves so badly that the team driver quits and Jimmy must take over the wheel. When they stop for the night, Mae poisons their chaperone, the prim Miss Cuthbert (Pauline Brailsford), and the team skips out to a roadhouse, where Mae puts on quite a display on the dance floor. Meanwhile, an inebriated Marla has shed her inhibitions and is singing on stage; although she sings badly, she has enchanted a bar patron, assuring romance in her future. Dottie arrives to extract her teammates before they are caught breaking the rules. As the team continues to travel, the bus ride reveals their closeness. Mae teaches an illiterate player, Shirley Baker (Ann Cusack), to read, albeit using erotic literature. Doris talks about her boyfriends being losers and then rips up a photo of her current ne'er-do-well.

On the field, conflicts develop. When Jimmy decides to step in and do some coaching, Dottie is unwilling to yield authority. Later, he yells at Evelyn for miss-

Rockford Peaches (left to right) Ann Cusack, Anne Elizabeth Ramsay, Madonna, and Rosie O'Donnell in *A League of Their Own*

ing a play. As she begins to cry, the exasperated coach screams the memorable line, "There is no crying in baseball." The most intense tension develops because of Kit's jealousy of Dottie, who has become the star of the team and a media darling. Her acrobatic defensive moves have helped promote the league, and the teams now play to full audiences. When Kit is pulled because her arm is tiring, she loses her temper at Doris, who has made a wisecrack about Kit's not finishing the game. Jimmy wrestles Kit into the shower to cool her off, but afterward she lashes out at Dottie, who she believes holds her back. Dottie, who does not plan to continue playing once her husband returns from the war, tells Ira she wants to quit. When Ira suggests a trade to separate the sisters, Dottie agrees, but it is Kit, not Dottie, who is traded.

After Kit begins playing for the Racine Belles, Dottie's husband is shipped home, and true to her word, Dottie abandons the Peaches just before the World Series, in which the Peaches will face the Belles. Dottie's leaving saddens Jimmy, who has grown quite fond of her, but in her absence, he proves a worthy coach. Before the last game of the series, he leads the Peaches in a prayer that is only moderately sacrilegious, and he later demonstrates patience with Evelyn. To Jimmy's surprise, but not to the audience's, Dottie turns up in her catcher's equipment ready to play. When she comes to bat against Kit, she cracks a line drive straight back to the mound, nearly taking out her sister. By the last inning, the Belles are trailing. Kit, batting with two outs, represents the winning run. The unforgiving Dottie tells her pitcher about Kit's weakness for high fastballs. Quickly, the count is two balls, no strikes. Then Kit connects for a hit that she tries to stretch into a game-winning, inside-the-park home run. She slides hard into Dottie, well behind the throw, but Dottie drops the ball in a move that looks intentional.

Following the game, Dottie and Kit reconcile. Jimmy, after meeting Dottie's husband, announces that he has rejected an offer to coach in the minors in order to stay with the AAGBL. As the team bus pulls off, the scene dissolves to Cooperstown, where the older Dottie discovers many of her former teammates, but Jimmy has died a few years earlier. Ira presides at the induction. As Dottie wanders through the museum exhibit, she encounters Kit with a bevy of children, and they share a warm embrace. The credits are superimposed on footage of members of the original league playing ball.

A League of Their Own was a great success, helped along by the enormous popularity of *Thelma and Louise*, released the previous year and also starring Geena Davis. It has been credited for bringing to light the story of the AAGBL and discredited for directing attention to Tom Hanks's character. (In fact, the script had originally called for Dottie and Jimmy to have a brief fling. The affair was scrapped, but the story's attention was not deflected from the growing relationship between the two.) The film has also been criticized for focusing on a main character who did not consider participation in the AAGBL particularly significant and for its deliberate emphasis on the heterosexuality of the athletes. However, there is general agreement that the major characters performed well in action. Rosie O'Donnell brought ball-playing experience to the film, while Madonna and Davis practiced hard to develop convincing skills. *Sports Illustrated* conceded that none of the cast "throws like a girl."

LEATHERHEADS (2008)

DIRECTOR: George Clooney. SCREENPLAY: Duncan Bradley, Rick Reilly. PRODUCERS: George Clooney, Grant Heslov, Casey Silver. CINEMATOGRAPHY: Newton Thomas Sigel. EDITING: Stephen Mirri-

one. Music: Randy Newman. Production Design: James D. Bissell. Art Direction: Christa Munro, Scott Ritenour. Costume Design: Louise Frogley.
Cast: George Clooney (Dodge Connolly), Renée Zellweger (Lexie Littleton), John Krasinski (Carter Rutherford), Jonathan Pryce (C.C. Frazier), Peter Gerety (Pete Harkin), Jack Thompson (Harvey), Stephen Root (Suds).
Running Time: 114 minutes.
DVD: Universal Studios.

Director George Clooney has made his *Leatherheads* a screwball comedy in the manner of 1940s films like *His Girl Friday* (1940), directed by Howard Hawks and starring Cary Grant, an actor to whom Clooney has been compared. Instead of the fast-talking, wise-cracking Rosalind Russell, the more-than-competent match for the cynical, opportunistic Grant, the audience watches Lexie Littleton (Renée Zellweger) spar verbally with Dodge Connolly (Clooney). While some of the action takes place in a newsroom full of male reporters, the setting is on the football field, and the subject is the creation of the modern professional football league.

In 1925, when the story begins, it is college football, not professional football, that is drawing big crowds. Clooney underscores the difference between the two by cutting from a Princeton University game with a huge crowd and a swarm of sportswriters to a professional game played in a cow pasture (complete with a cow) before few fans and with the reporting done by Dodge, a team captain, who dictates an article to Suds (Stephen Root), a besotted reporter who doesn't take notes. Carter "Bullet" Rutherford (John Krasinski), the star Princeton player, chats with reporters about his future, and when one of the reporters suggests professional football, Carter and the others break up in laughter. Meanwhile, Dodge is having his problems with getting a decent blocker on his pro team—he finally finds one in an out-sized high school student named Gus (Keith Loneker)—and with winning a game. When the team's only football is stolen, he has to forfeit. The team learns that several other teams have folded, a fate that happens to Dodge's Duluth team after another loss.

While it seems inevitable that professional football will die, events unfold in Chicago that will bring new life to the sport. Lexie, a reporter for the *Chicago Tribune*, is summoned to her boss's office and assigned to write an article about Carter, whose war-service story of single-handedly capturing thirty German soldiers seems to have been grossly exaggerated. If Lexie can uncover the truth about Carter's war exploits, she is promised an assistant editor's desk.

Lexie and Dodge meet at the Ambassador Hotel in Chicago, where she is waiting for Carter and his agent, the sleazy C.C. Frazier (Jonathan Pryce). Dodge is immediately attracted to Lexie, who is decidedly underwhelmed. Dodge, however, does get a chance to talk with C.C. about a plan to resurrect pro football by persuading Carter to sign with Duluth to increase attendance at the games—Carter would receive five thousand dollars a game. With the deal closed, Dodge calls his old teammates, and then he hears Lexie on the phone, telling her boss that she will uncover the story and expose Carter as a fraud.

On the train headed for the first game, Dodge and Lexie share a room in screwball fashion. Double entendre repartee follows with Dodge in the upper berth, Lexie in the lower, and their curtains opening and closing as they exchange wisecracks. When Dodge arrives at the stadium (the venue having been changed from the cow pasture because of the crowd), he is greeted with "Welcome to show business." There are blocking sleds; several footballs; new shoes (in the right sizes); new plays, which Carter describes as "like your [Dodge's] plays except more effective"—even ads and a press box, where Lexie is the only woman. Her stories, which herald "the new era in professional football," describe the team's victories, but her editor is still intent on getting the exposé.

Finally, Carter tells Lexie what happened at the Argonne, where he was left behind in a trench occupied by Germans. When he awoke, he saw the Germans, raised his hands, and shouted "I surrender" in German, and the Germans followed his lead, much to the delight of the advancing American soldiers. Everyone involved agreed on the enhanced story in order to increase morale and establish a war hero. The disillusioned Lexie, who still sympathizes with Carter, goes to a speakeasy, where she meets Dodge, who, in the company of a young woman, is violating curfew (a newly instituted rule). Lexie remarks, "It must be quiet at the Adirondack without you," a putdown probably lost on most of the movie audience, but one Grant and Russell fans will enjoy. When the police raid the speakeasy, Lexie and Dodge flee, but they have to don cop uniforms to mislead their pursuers. The resulting sequence is reminiscent of Charlie Chaplin and of the Keystone Cops.

Confrontations follow. C.C. learns that Lexie is going to expose Carter and threatens to see her fired. Dodge and Carter, who realizes that Dodge and Lexie are romantically involved, have a strange kind of fight (because of previous injuries they can only hit each other's face) outside the hotel, and despite several heavy blows, there is no blood. When the story breaks, Carter signs on with the Chicago team, which is scheduled to play Duluth. At a press conference Lexie is under pressure to renounce her story. Pete Harkin (Peter Gerety), who has been appointed the commissioner of football, vows to get to the "bottom of this." Lexie's editor wants her to retract her story and apologize, and Dodge advises her to "punt," to give up and marry him since she "can't make it in a man's world."

Lexie won't give in, even though she can't get eyewitnesses to tell the truth about Carter because C.C. has paid them off. In an unlikely turn of events, Dodge comes up with a solution to her problem. At another speakeasy Dodge meets an old army buddy and his friends, and after a friendly brawl between Chicago fans and the Duluth team, the combatants sing army songs together. The next day at the hearing with the commissioner, Dodge has the soldiers outside in a truck. When the hearing goes badly and the commissioner wants the retraction, Dodge tells the commissioner that the soldiers outside were with Carter at the Argonne and now want to say hello to him. Anticipating that the men will tell the truth, Carter confesses, and Lexie and her boss leave. Of course, the soldiers outside do not know Carter and could not have refuted his testimony, but Carter doesn't know that. Commissioner Harkin then informs C.C. that he is through in professional football since he will be unable to obtain a license from the commissioner's office. Dodge also gets unwelcome news: Harkin tells him now that pro football "has come of age," there will be rules prohibiting current procedures, such as the "Crusty Bob" and "the pig in a poke." Harkin concludes by suggesting Carter retire.

At the Duluth-Chicago game the new regulations are in effect, including no swearing by the announcers, a tough habit to break. On the field before the kickoff, the referees are uncertain about the rules involved in tossing the coin, and while the game goes on, Dodge holds Carter so he can't receive a pass. The "whole new game," however, is regarded as "boring without the usual tricks." The game is close, and when it begins to pour, the field turns into a quagmire. (In fact, after one play is over, a mud-covered player emerges from the ground where he has been buried.) Trailing by three points, Duluth has a chance to tie the game with a field goal, but the players want to win. Even though he realizes that his trick play, the "Sergeant York," is illegal and that he will certainly be thrown out of the league for using it, Dodge decides to go for the win and succeeds.

Later, when Dodge and Lexie meet, she hops on his motorcycle and asks him to get on behind her. He adds that certain jobs are for men, and she responds, "You mean manly men?" He gets on, but falls off, giving her the last laugh on the gender issue. As they ride off, Dodge asks, "Lexie, what will become of us?" She says, "Call me Miss Littleton." Four photographs at the end of the film sum up the action: a wedding photo of Lexie and Dodge; a graduation photo of Gus; a newspaper photo of Carter, still the hero fans want, donating a big check to the American Legion; and one of C.C. posing as the agent for Lou Gehrig and Babe Ruth of the New York Yankees.

Leatherheads is a successful screwball comedy with its struggle between the sexes, its witty lines, and lots of physical comedy. It is also a wonderful commentary on what happens when rules govern a game that is played by boys who don't want to grow up.

THE LEGEND OF BAGGER VANCE (2000)

DIRECTOR: Robert Redford. SCREENPLAY: Jeremy Leven, based on the novel by Steven Pressfield. PRODUCERS: Jake Eberts, Michael Nozik, Robert Redford. CINEMATOGRAPHY: Michael Ballhaus. EDITING: Hank Corwin. MUSIC: Rachel Portman. PRODUCTION DESIGN: Stuart Craig. ART DIRECTION: Angelo P. Graham, W. Steven Graham. COSTUME DESIGN: Judianna Makovsky.

CAST: Will Smith (Bagger Vance), Matt Damon (Rannulph Junuh), Charlize Theron (Adele Invergordon), Bruce McGill (Walter Hagen), Joel Gretsch (Bobby Jones), Lane Smith (Grantland Rice).

RUNNING TIME: 126 minutes.

DVD: Dreamworks Video.

Steven Pressfield's novel *The Legend of Bagger Vance: A Novel of Golf and the Game of Life* (1995) is loosely based on a seven-hundred-verse spiritual poem, *Bhagavad-gita*, in which Bhagavan Sri Krishna, disguised as a charioteer, guides the troubled warrior Arjuna toward self discovery. In director Robert Redford's screen adaptation, the Krishna figure (Will Smith as Bagger Vance), disguised as a caddy, assists a troubled World War I veteran (Matt Damon as Rannulph Junuh) in resuming his golf career and regaining his swing. The film, narrated by elderly golfer Hardy Greaves (Jack Lemmon in his last role, uncredited), is a straightforward account of how a young man with seemingly unlimited potential loses his way (his "swing," his "groove," his "mojo") during World War I and returns home to Savannah, Georgia, to "forget and be forgotten" and then recovers that which he had lost.

As he strolls along the course with his clubs, the Hardy Greaves/Jack Lemmon character reflects on a "little bit of magic time" associated with the course, where he has already suffered five heart attacks. After another spell he begins to recount the story that took place on the venerable golf course when he was the young Hardy J. Greaves (played by J. Michael Moncrief).

Before World War I, Bobby Jones (Joel Gretsch) and Walter Hagen (Bruce McGill) were the preeminent golfers in the United States, but Savannah had its own Rannulph Junuh, who was "on track to be the best." He courts and wins Adele Invergordon (Charlize Theron), whose father's dream is to build the Krewe Island Golf Club. Unfortunately, before the course can be completed and Rannulph can realize his golf ambitions, World War I begins. Though it was "to be his [Rannulph's] crowning glory," the war instead leaves Rannulph confused and broken. After the war he avoids Adele, whose father completes building his dream course. Within a few years, however, the Great Depression begins, and the Savannah economy bottoms out.

When her despondent father commits suicide, Adele finds herself in financial straits and is besieged by opportunistic local businessmen who try to pressure her to sell the course to them for ten cents on the dollar. To avert financial ruin, she concocts an exhibition golf match between Bobby Jones and Walter Hagen to be played at her course, thereby making money and helping the Savannah economy. In spite of skepticism, she uses her conning ability and womanly wiles, especially with Walter, to get the two golfers to compete. When the financial backers insist on including a local golfer in the field, Adele seems stymied, but young Hardy reminds them about Rannulph.

Hardy finds his hero among some revelers drinking and playing cards, but Rannulph does not want to enter the tournament. When Hardy asks him what has happened, Rannulph describes how alcohol affects the cells, first the sadness ones, then the quiet ones, then the stupid cells, but it cannot destroy the memory cells—and that's Rannulph's problem. Even when the townsfolk beg him to reconsider, he turns them down. However, when Adele offers sexual favors in exchange for his playing, he agrees.

In order to find his lost swing, he takes his clubs outside and by lamplight hits a few balls. At this point he hears Bagger and asks his identity. Bagger's "Just me" is enigmatic, suggesting that Rannulph might have once known him. Bagger tells him that

Matt Damon (as Rannulph Junuh) and Will Smith (as Bagger Vance) in *The Legend of Bagger Vance*

Will Smith caddying for Matt Damon in *The Legend of Bagger Vance*

he is here "to find your swing," the swing Rannulph had in 1916. Self-doubt, however, plagues Junah, and he is ready to leave Savannah, but before he can get his pickup truck out of town, he is mobbed by townspeople of all races and ages.

Young Hardy approaches Bagger, and the two become close as they measure the golf course, fixing in their minds yardage markers and observing how the grass on the greens follows the sun, thus changing the line the ball will follow. For Bagger, victory comes on the green, not off the tee, and Rannulph will have to find his "authentic swing," which he can remember if he can shed his "inner demons."

The first round goes badly for Rannulph, who trails both Bobby and Walter by twelve strokes. Using some reverse psychology, Bagger suggests that Rannulph quit, putting himself out of his misery; but Rannulph can't quit and Bagger knows it. When a reporter asks him about Rannulph, Bagger answers, "He is and he ain't Rannulph Junuh," a statement that captures the golfer's situation. Bagger also adds an anecdote about a man named Rufus who lost, successively, his arms and his teeth, but kept adjusting to his adversities. Bagger admits that Rannulph will never fully regain his skills but cautions Rannulph about losing his soul and being alone. Some of Bagger's advice reaches Rannulph, who talks with Hardy about his father, who has lost his job and is working on the street for the city of Savannah. He tells Hardy, who is embarrassed by his father's fate, "Your dad looked adversity in the eye." Rannulph's comments, of course, apply to his own situation.

Thanks to more philosophical intervention by Bagger, Rannulph does well in the second round. He takes time to see the field, feels the focus, lets the shot choose him, and realizes that his "hands are wiser than his head." When he "goes to his soul," the course shrinks in perspective, allowing him to make up six shots on the last eight holes. Walter is so impressed that he proposes that after he quits playing tournaments, he and Rannulph should put on exhibitions with Walter taking a 70-30 cut of the profits. In the next round Rannulph hears from Bobby, who is retiring from golf to focus on his law practice and his family. He praises Rannulph and reminds him, "It's just a game."

In the final round the three golfers are even, but one of Rannulph's shots lands in the woods, bringing on memories of his war experiences, including the sounds of battles and explosives. Bagger reassures him, "You ain't alone," and adds almost religiously, "I been here all along." Rannulph makes his shot. Meanwhile, it is getting dark, and when the golfers declare that they want to play the eighteenth hole, people drive their cars to the course and park them with their lights on. Walter makes a miraculous recovery from a sand bar in a water hazard; Rannulph, who hit into the woods again, moves his ball accidentally, incurring a stroke penalty that everyone is willing to overlook. However, this is truth time for Rannulph, who takes the penalty. He still hits onto the green, but Bagger is leaving. Telling Hardy, "This man is yours, Hardy. Take him in," Bagger walks into the darkness.

Walter and Bobby both miss their putts. Remembering the advice about the ball following the sun, Rannulph focuses, seeing the route that his putt must follow to fall in the cup. It does and the match ends in a three-way tie. Bagger, who is now on the beach, hears the cheers and disappears. The Hardy/Lemmon character reappears to inform the audience that Adele and Rannulph, who liked to dance together, were reconciled, that Bobby quit golf, and that Walter played only exhibitions. "And me? I play on, looking for my place in the field." Bagger Vance continues to beckon him on.

Unfortunately, the film did not receive the critical or financial success that it deserved. Perhaps audiences were expecting slapstick or screwball comedy; perhaps, not understanding the basis for the characters, they did not know how to respond. The difficulty of finding a niche for the film is reflected in Will Smith's being nominated for a Saturn Award for Best Supporting Actor from the Academy of Science Fiction, Fantasy, and Horror Films. Whatever the reason, the film, which cost over $60 million to produce, bombed at the box office, bringing less than $40 million in ticket sales.

LE MANS (1971)

Director: Lee H. Katzin. Screenplay: Harry Kleiner. Producer: Jack N. Reddish. Cinematography: René Guissart Jr., Robert B. Hauser. Editing: Ghislaine Desjonquères, Donald W. Ernst, John Woodcock. Music: Michel Legrand. Production Design: Phil Abramson. Costume Design: Phil Abramson, Ray Summers.

Cast: Steve McQueen (Michael Delaney), Siegfried Rauch (Erich Stahler), Elga Andersen (Lisa Belgetti), Ronald Leigh-Hunt (David Townsend), Fred Haltiner (Johann Ritter), Luc Merenda (Claude Aurac).

Running Time: 106 minutes.

DVD: Paramount.

The title says it all. *Le Mans* is about the annual sports car endurance race in which drivers work in alternate shifts over a twenty-four-hour period. It is run on a circuit over public roads near Le Mans, France. Shot on location, the film has the look of a documentary with extensive footage taken from inside a vehicle during the actual 1970 race. Tension arose between star Steve McQueen and the original director, John Sturgis, over the script and led to costly production delays. Sturgis, who had begun filming before the script was finished, envisioned a love story with a race in the background. McQueen, a racing enthusiast who had placed second in an earlier event at Sebring and who did much of his own driving in the staged sequences, saw the project as a film about the race that would showcase his driving skills. Although McQueen and Sturgis had worked together comfortably on *The Great Escape* (1963) and *The Magnificent Seven* (1960), they were not able to come to an agreement on how to proceed with *Le Mans*. Sturgis was eventually replaced by Lee Katzin, and McQueen's ideas dominated the final product.

The plot is very simple: driver Michael Delaney (McQueen) returns to Le Mans the year after an accident that killed a close friend and for which he may have been responsible. He is drawn to his friend's widow, Lisa (Elga Andersen), and looks for her when he's on break from driving for the Gulf-Porsche team. After he wrecks the number one Porsche, he replaces the driver of the number three Porsche and jockeys with rival Erich Stahler (Siegfried Rauch) for position behind the lead car, the number two Porsche. In the final laps Michael edges out Erich's Ferrari, but instead of trying to gain the lead, he keeps Erich trapped behind the two Porsches. Michael's strategy assures Gulf-Porsche of a one-two finish ahead of Ferrari, but Michael must settle for second place. There is no intelligible dialogue during the first half hour of the movie and no sustained conversation for the remainder of the film. The most telling exchange between Lisa and Michael is only a few lines long: following his accident, Michael calls racing "a professional blood sport"; Lisa wonders aloud why driving faster than someone else is so important, to which he replies, "racing is life . . . everything that happens before or after is just waiting." In *Le Mans* the love story just fills the breaks between racing scenes. It is so peripheral to the action that Elga Andersen was not cast until six weeks into the shooting.

The real story is the verisimilitude of the racing sequences. Filming was done on location. Since the structure at Le Mans is used only for the race, the studio was able to rent the facility afterward and set up a prefabricated village on site to house offices and store equipment. Staged sequences were intercut with footage from the actual race, which was shot from a race car equipped with cameras. For staged sequences, a camera car was used as well. To reproduce the field, duplicate cars were leased or replicated. Facsimiles of the Ferrari 512 and the Porsche 917 that are destroyed in the film were created using less expensive Lolas. These cars were operated by remote control for the crash scenes. Rainy weather during the race meant that subsequent filming had to be done on cloudy days and the track had to be kept wet. Because a concrete barrier wall had been constructed between the pit and the grandstand after the 1969 race, footage shot inside the track from previous years could not be incorporated. Actors and crew were frequently at risk. The weight of camera equipment affected the handling of the camera car, making it more susceptible to skidding. On the first attempt to film a crash, the remote-controlled vehicle suddenly reversed itself and headed directly for the platform on which the controller was standing. One stunt driver, David Piper, lost a leg as a result of an accident during a shot.

The film went over budget, and at one point the project was almost scrapped. Nearly half a million feet of film had been shot, and editing took half a year. Because the sound was recorded separately, the editors needed to match engine noises to vehicles, a process that took another two months to complete. When *Le Mans* was released in 1971, it received tepid reviews because of its plotlessness, but it has since become a cult favorite among racing aficionados.

LES BOYS (1997)

Director: Louis Saïa. Screenplay: Christian Fournier, Louis Saïa. Producers: Richard Goudreau, Jeffrey Tinnell. Cinematography: Sylvain Brault. Editing: Yvann Thibaudeau. Music: Normand Corbeil. Production Design: Claude Paré. Costume Design: Suzanne Harel.
Cast: Marc Messier (Bob), Rémy Girard (Stan), Patrick Huard (Ti-Guy), Michel Barrette (Francois), Paul Houde (Fernand).
Running Time: 107 minutes.
DVD: Lions Gate.

This film is a comedy about a team of amateur hockey players in Quebec.

LET'S DO IT AGAIN (1975)

Director: Sidney Poitier. Screenplay: Richard Wesley. Story: Timothy March. Producer: Melville Tucker. Cinematography: Donald M. Morgan. Editing: Pembroke J. Herring. Music: Curtis Mayfield. Production Design: Alfred Sweeney.
Cast: Sidney Poitier (Clyde Williams), Bill Cosby (Billy Foster), Calvin Lockhart (Biggie Smalls), John Amos (Kansas City Mack), Jimmie Walker (Bootney Farnsworth).
Running Time: 110 minutes.
DVD: Warner Home Video.

By hypnotizing a scrawny man into winning a boxing match, a pair of friends win a bet that earns them riches—and some unhappy gangsters wanting their money back.

LIGHTNING, THE WHITE STALLION (1986)

Director: William A. Levey. Screenplay: Harry Alan Towers (Story: Peter Welbeck). Producer: Harry Alan Towers. Cinematography: Steven Shaw. Editing: Ken Bornstein. Music: Maurizio Albeni, Annakarin Klockar. Art Direction: Hector B. Lopez. Costume Design: Richard Abramson.
Cast: Mickey Rooney (Barney Ingram), Isabel García Lorca (Stephanie Ward), Susan George (Madame Rene), Billy Wesley (Lucas Mitchell).
Running Time: 95 minutes.
DVD: MGM.

A stolen stallion ends up in the care of a young girl who grooms the horse for show-jumping competition.

LIKE MIKE (2002)

Director: John Schultz. Screenplay: Michael Elliott, Jordan Moffett. Producers: Peter Heller, Barry Josephson. Cinematography: Shawn Maurer. Editing: Peter Berger, John Pace. Music: Richard Gibbs. Production Design: Arlan Jay Vetter. Art Direction: John R. Zachary. Costume Design: Mary Jane Fort.
Cast: Bow Wow (Calvin Cambridge), Jonathan Lipnicki (Murph), Morris Chestnut (Tracey Reynolds), Robert Forster (Coach Wagner), Eugene Levy (Frank Bernard), Brenda Song (Reg Stevens), Crispin Glover (Stan Bittleman).
Running Time: 99 minutes.
DVD: 20th Century Fox.

In this family film, a young teenager joins the NBA after finding a pair of shoes that may have belonged to Michael Jordan.

LITTLE BIG LEAGUE (1994)

DIRECTOR: Andrew Scheinman. SCREENPLAY: Gregory K. Pincus, Andrew Scheinman. PRODUCER: Mike Lobell. CINEMATOGRAPHY: Donald E. Thorin. EDITING: Michael Jablow. MUSIC: Stanley Clarke. PRODUCTION DESIGN: Jeffrey Howard. COSTUME DESIGN: Erica Edell Phillips.
CAST: Luke Edwards (Billy Heywood), Timothy Busfield (Lou Collins), John Ashton (Mac Macnally), Ashley Crow (Jenny Heywood), Kevin Dunn (Arthur Goslin), Jason Robards (Thomas Heywood).
RUNNING TIME: 119 minutes.
DVD: Turner Home Entertainment.

With echoes of *The Kid from Left Field* (1953), a preteen inherits a baseball team and decides to manage it himself.

LITTLE GIANTS (1994)

DIRECTOR: Duwayne Dunham. SCREENPLAY: James Ferguson, Robert Shallcross, Tommy Swerdlow, Michael Goldberg. PRODUCER: Arne L. Schmidt. CINEMATOGRAPHY: Janusz Kaminski. EDITING: Donn Cambern, Jonathan Shaw. MUSIC: John Debney. PRODUCTION DESIGN: Bill Kenney. ART DIRECTION: William Ladd Skinner. COSTUME DESIGN: April Ferry.
CAST: Rick Moranis (Danny O'Shea), Ed O'Neill (Kevin O'Shea), Shawna Waldron (Becky "Icebox" O'Shea), Devon Sawa (Junior Floyd).
RUNNING TIME: 107 minutes.
DVD: Warner Home Video.

Sibling rivalry extends to the football field, when two brothers coach competing teams.

THE LONELINESS OF THE LONG-DISTANCE RUNNER (1962)

DIRECTOR: Tony Richardson. SCREENPLAY: Alan Sillitoe, based on his short story. PRODUCER: Tony Richardson. CINEMATOGRAPHY: Walter Lassally. EDITING: Antony Gibbs. MUSIC: John Addison. PRODUCTION DESIGN: Ralph Brinton. ART DIRECTION: Ted Marshall. COSTUME DESIGN: Sophie Devine.
CAST: Tom Courtenay (Colin Smith), Michael Redgrave (Borstal governor), Avis Bunnage (Mrs. Smith), Alec McCowen (Brown), James Bolam (Mike), Joe Robinson (Roach), James Fox (Willy Gunthrope).
RUNNING TIME: 104 minutes.
DVD: Warner Home Video.

Director Tony Richardson adapted *The Loneliness of the Long-Distance Runner* from a short story by Alan Sillitoe, who also wrote the screenplay. Richardson, like Lindsay Anderson, whose *This Sporting Life* came out in 1963, is considered part of the generation of "angry young men" associated with playwright John Osborne, whose *Look Back in Anger* Richardson had adapted to film in 1958. While *The Loneliness of the Long-Distance Runner* is not as nihilistic and cynical as its source, Richardson's film criticizes the British establishment, assails what passes for social work and justice, and satirizes the notion that England's battles are won on the playing fields of Eton. The film features a track meet between the Borstal (reform school) where Colin Smith (Tom Courtenay) is incarcerated and a nearby public (what Americans call "private") school, but the focus is on the cross-country event in which Colin competes.

Colin is certainly an alienated youth. While his father dies a slow death from cancer incurred through his work at a factory, his mother (Avis Bunnage) begins seeing a "fancy man," Gordon (Ramon Dyer), who moves in after Colin's father dies. The struggle between Colin and Gordon to be the "governor" assumes Oedipal dimensions that are later revealed in Colin's interview with the prison psychologist. After a scuffle between Colin and Gordon, Colin's mother tells her son to leave and not come back until he gets some money. Unfortunately, Colin then meets Mike (James Bolam), a young hoodlum with whom he breaks into a baker's business and steals a large sum of money. The detective who investigates the case (Dervis Ward) has little sympathy for young lawbreakers and finally acquires evidence against Colin, who is sent to the Borstal.

There he meets the Borstal governor (Michael Redgrave), who aspires to a headmaster's position at a public school. He would also like to redeem himself for his youthful athletic mediocrity ("I was a bit of a plodder," he admits) by having one of his "boys" excel in cross country. For the governor, sport makes men, builds character, channels their aggressions, and strengthens Great Britain. He sees the experience at the Borstal as a kind of game: "If you play ball with us, we'll play ball with you." Stacy (Philip Martin), another inmate, is presently the governor's favorite to win the race and the coveted cup that goes with it; when Colin outruns him, Stacy fears losing his privileges and provokes a fight with Colin. After he is punished and demoted from his position of authority at the Borstal, Stacy escapes from the prison, and Colin becomes the governor's head boy.

The governor gives him the freedom to run unsupervised in the morning, and these dawn excursions, with an upbeat musical accompaniment, provide a temporary sense of exhilaration and freedom. Despite the governor's suggestion that he might someday represent England in the Olympics, Colin is plagued by recurring thoughts about his past, especially domestic problems, his encounters with the detective, and his relationship with Audrey (Topsy Jane). His past is revealed in a series of flashbacks, during which he runs in a variety of styles: he runs in fast motion and in a comic style; he runs wild with Audrey on the beach at Skegness, where the couple spend a weekend that provides only a brief respite from their problems. As Audrey suggests, however, he runs but doesn't seem to make any real progress. All of the running brings him back to his present condition.

Colin remains alienated from his society. He rejects a job and the working conditions at the factory where his father was employed; he and Mike, the "telly boys," watch a Tory politician and then turn off the volume—mute or not, his comments are unintelligible to them. There is a general failure to communicate in the film. The Borstal psychologist's bumbling attempts to administer a Rorschach test to Colin result in failure; the governor's evening of entertainment features a bird imitator and an aging duo singing classical music and doing it badly; and there are cuts between the Borstal boys singing "Jerusalem," a patriotic anthem, and shots of Stacy being beaten after his escape fails. Richardson seems to find risible the idea of there being a new Jerusalem in the England he depicts. ("Jerusalem" is used quite differently in *Chariots of Fire.*)

Before the cross-country race Mike appears at the Borstal, and when he hears about Colin's privileged treatment and work for the governor, he asks Colin whose side he's on. Mike's comment, as well as memories of the detective, Audrey, his mother, and Gordon, haunts Colin as he runs the race. He also sees his dying father, the "blood money" Colin burns when his mother offers him some of the insurance settlement, and the championship cup. In the race he takes the lead, easily passing his chief competitor, and nears the finish line. Considering himself the governor's "bloody racehorse," he recalls the governor's earlier admonition: "Always remember who has the whip hand." He stops, despite the pleading from his mates and the governor, and as the next runner passes him, he gives him a sardonic bow, believing that he has shown he could have won the race and yet depriving the governor of the coveted cup. His action naturally provokes the governor, but it also alienates him from the other boys. In the last shot of the film, he is back where he started, dismantling gas masks. Colin may have made his point, but he has made no progress. (Sillitoe's short-story ending is even bleaker: the fact that people are reading Colin's story means that he is again in prison.)

This is a sports film in which a gifted athlete chooses not to use his skills to escape the poverty and despair he lives in; Richardson and Sillitoe apparently do not see sports as character building and do not regard the society they describe as worth joining.

THE LONGEST YARD (1974)

DIRECTOR: Robert Aldrich. SCREENPLAY: Tracy Keenan Wynn. STORY: Albert S. Ruddy. PRODUCER: Albert S. Ruddy. CINEMATOGRAPHY: Joseph F. Biroc. EDITING: Michael Luciano. MUSIC: Frank De Vol. PRODUCTION DESIGN: James Dowell Vance.

CAST: Burt Reynolds (Paul Crewe), Eddie Albert (Warden Hazen), Ed Lauter (Captain Knauer), Michael Conrad (Nate Scarboro), James Hampton (Caretaker), Bernadette Peters (Miss Toot).

RUNNING TIME: 121 minutes.

ACADEMY AWARD NOMINATION: Best Editing.

DVD: Paramount.

Following a blowup with the woman (Anitra Ford) who is keeping him, Paul Crewe (Burt Reynolds) steals her Maserati, leads the police in a chase scene similar to ones in the Smokey and the Bandit flicks, is arrested, and is taken to Citrus State Prison, where he is sentenced to serve two to five years. Shortly after his arrival, he learns that Warden Hazen (Eddie Albert) has pulled strings to get him placed at Citrus so that he can coach the prison football team to a semipro championship. Paul, who wants only to do his time and get out, declines the offer, infuriating the warden. In the past Paul had been caught shaving points, an act that brought him disgrace and the end of his promising football career. (The motive behind his action is a question that puzzles the warden and inmates alike.)

Soon after he is assigned to the chain gang and shackled to Granville (Harry Caesar), a black inmate who also has played football, Paul is prodded into a fight with another prisoner. After hitting Captain Knauer (Ed Lauter), the leader of the guards' football team, he is put in the "box" as punishment. There is another meeting between Paul and the warden, who informs him that because he hit the guard his sentence will be extended. Paul is ready to coach the warden's team, but he unintentionally gives the warden the idea of using an inmates' team in a tune-up game before their season begins. In exchange for Paul's coaching and quarterbacking the inmates, plus a few concessions for the inmates who make the team, the warden will grant Paul an early parole. In the four weeks Paul is given to select and train his team (nicknamed the "Mean Machine"), he recruits, with the aid of former professional football player Nate Scarborough (Michael Conrad) and manager Caretaker (James Hampton), a collection of high-security prisoners who resemble Lee Marvin's crew in *The Dirty Dozen* (also directed by Robert Aldrich); chief among them is Samson (Richard Kiel), who was the toothy adversary of 007 in *The Spy Who Loved Me* (1977). Caretaker is the scrounger who gains access to prisoner files, medical records, and even films of the guards' past football games, all in exchange for Paul rendering "personal service" to the warden's beehived secretary (Bernadette Peters).

For Paul, the matchup between the inmates and guards is "just a game," something to get him out of prison; but he quickly learns that it is more than that to the warden, for whom it is about *power*, about showing the inmates that he has absolute control. In addition to problems Paul has in recruiting his team (black inmates join the team only after the guards humiliate Granville), he has to deal with Unger (Charles Tyner), an unsavory murderer who informs Knauer about Paul's progress with the team. Meanwhile, while drinking with Caretaker, Paul reluctantly reveals why he shaved the points: to get enough money to take care of his father for the rest of his life. While the audience knows Paul is being truthful, both he and Caretaker, unwilling to deal with sincerity and compassion, laugh and pretend that Paul was joking.

Concerned that Paul's team of misfits may actually be talented, Knauer persuades Unger to eliminate Paul. Unger rigs a booby trap, but Caretaker, not Paul, is killed. The game takes place shortly after Caretaker's funeral and features three transvestites imitating the Supremes and a squad of transvestite cheerleaders. Although the guards get an early lead, the inmates come back to narrow the lead to 8–7. The warden, concerned about a possible upset, threatens Paul again, saying that he will have him charged for the murder of Caretaker unless Paul agrees to let the guards build a twenty-one-point lead, after which he promises to have the guards ease up on their dirty play. Paul's fumble and two intercepted passes enable the guards to achieve the required lead, but the inmates accuse Paul of selling them out. When the warden reneges on his promise to have the guards ease up and Knauer's team deliberately injures Nate and Granville, Paul reenters the game. After his teammates allow him to get mauled, Paul leads the Mean Machine to a victory and obtains redemption for himself and a sense of dignity for the inmates. Before the game ends, Bogdanski (Ray Nitschke, one of the former professional football players in the film), who was responsible for Nate's and Granville's injuries, is injured when Paul deliberately throws the ball into his groin. Violence abounds, heightened effectively by the editing of Michael Luciano, who was nominated for an Oscar.

After the game one of the guards grudgingly admits to an inmate, "You guys ain't half bad," but the real turnaround involves Knauer. When the vindictive warden sees Paul walking toward the exit, he orders Knauer to shoot him to prevent his escape. Instead of shooting, Knauer calls out to Paul, who ends his walk by reaching down to pick up the game ball, which he gives to the warden with the words, "Stick this in your trophy case." (Aldrich had filmed another ending in which Paul is shot, but it was rejected because it was too much of a "downer.") By defying the warden, Paul knows that he will experience the same fate as Pop (John Steadman), whose punching of the warden led to his lifelong incarceration at Citrus. For both Paul and Pop, who walk off the field together, the rebellious act was worth it.

The Longest Yard was a huge financial success, in part because the on-field action was authentic: Reynolds had played at Florida State University; several college and professional football players appeared in the film; and the game was filmed in the same way as regular Sunday afternoon football games—it is one of the few football films that includes a great deal of actual football footage. The film was shot at a prison, and a field was built for the game. It was also influential in that it led to other sports films, including those about misfits who triumph over more talented, better financed teams. An English version, featuring soccer instead of football, was *The*

Mean Machine (2001), and Al Ruddy, the film's producer, envisioned a sequel featuring Burt Reynolds as a released prisoner who joins the NFL. While that film was not made, a remake of *The Longest Yard* starring Adam Sandler appeared in 2005.

THE LONGEST YARD (2005)

DIRECTOR: Peter Segal. SCREENPLAY: Sheldon Turner, from the original 1974 screenplay by Tracy Keenan Wynn. STORY: Albert S. Ruddy. PRODUCER: Jack Giarraputo. CINEMATOGRAPHY: Dean Semler. EDITING: Jeff Gourson. MUSIC: Teddy Castellucci. PRODUCTION DESIGN: Perry Andelin Blake. ART DIRECTION: Alan Au, Domenic Silvestri. COSTUME DESIGN: Ellen Lutter.

CAST: Adam Sandler (Paul Crewe), Chris Rock (Caretaker), Burt Reynolds (Coach Nate Scarborough), Nelly (Megget), Terry Crews (Cheeseburger Eddy), Nicholas Turturro (Brucie).

RUNNING TIME: 113 minutes.

DVD: Paramount.

In this remake of the 1974 film, Adam Sandler takes over for Burt Reynolds, while the latter is cast in the role of a former pro-player turned inmate-coach.

THE LONGSHOTS (2008)

DIRECTOR: Fred Durst. SCREENPLAY: Nick Santora. PRODUCERS: Matt Alvarez, Ice Cube, Nick Santora. CINEMATOGRAPHY: Conrad W. Hall. EDITING: Jeffrey Wolf. MUSIC: Teddy Castellucci. PRODUCTION DESIGN: Charles Breen. ART DIRECTION: Brian Stultz.

CAST: Ice Cube (Curtis Plummer), Keke Palmer (Jasmine), Tasha Smith (Claire Plummer), Jill Marie Jones (Ronnie Macer), Dash Mihok (Cyrus), Matt Craven (Coach Fisher), Glenn Plummer (Winston), Garrett Morris (Reverend Pratt).

RUNNING TIME: 94 minutes.

DVD: Weinstein Company.

The Longshots is an underdog film in which a ragtag football team represents a struggling town. Minden, Illinois, the setting of the film, is a small city in America's Rust Belt, where factories close, stores go out of business, and massive unemployment affects both blacks and whites. The film is about a weak Pop Warner football team; an unemployed black man whose promising athletic career was cut short by a serious knee injury; his niece, a shy young woman with a strong throwing arm and a hope that her absentee father will return; and a city that is reborn. *The Longshots* lacks the sorts of themes one usually finds in this type of sports film: there is no racial tension; there are no pushy parents to criticize the coach; there is relatively little sexism; the player who loses his starting spot to the girl is neither bitter nor vindictive; and there is no conflict between the star and the rest of the team.

Ice Cube, who produced and starred in the film, plays Curtis, a former high school football star who drinks beer, saves money for his "Escape from Minden" fund, avoids dealing with his past, and tries to dodge responsibility and commitment, as does his brother, Roy, who has abandoned his wife and daughter. When Ray's wife, Claire (Tasha Smith), asks him to watch her daughter, Jasmine (Keke Palmer), after school so that she can work another shift at the diner, he is unenthusiastic. Nor is Jasmine impressed with Curtis, who dresses like a bum and needs a shower. They do not "need" each other, but that will change. Curtis, who always carries a football around with him, sees Jasmine throw the ball and encourages her. After he teaches her pass routes, the correct grip, and the right throwing motion, he thinks she is ready for

Pop Warner (middle school) football and asks Coach Fisher (Matt Craven) to give her a chance. She is reluctant but makes a deal with Curtis: she will go out for the team if he asks her teacher, Miss Macer (Jill Marie Jones), for a date. When the coach sees her complete a long pass to Curtis, he lets her join the team and assigns her a separate "dressing room" in a janitor's closet. She finally succeeds in getting on the uniform, having a problem only with what she finds in her helmet—a large jock strap, which she discards in disgust.

At her first practice the center expresses indignation that Jasmine will touch his "ding dongs" when she puts her hands under him. The coach suggests that "ping pongs" might be more appropriate and tells the center to get over it. Predictably, the line fails to block for her, and she gets sacked by a defensive lineman. She proves herself when she gets up and continues to play. After the starting quarterback fails to throw a decent pass, the coach yields to Curtis's insistence that he give Jasmine a chance. She succeeds, but it is not until the team trails in the first game that she plays again, throwing a touchdown pass. She basks in her teammates' approval and finds the self-confidence she had lacked.

At the beginning of the season, attendance at games is low, but as Jasmine leads her team to one victory after another, the town rallies, and the stands are filled. With two crucial games to go, the coach has a heart attack and is unable to continue in his role. He asks his assistant to take over, but the assistant persuades Curtis to assume the coach's job. Under Curtis's leadership the team improves even more, and they win the two games, gaining a spot in the Pop Warner championship game in Miami. Jasmine, meanwhile, has been attracting media attention and putting Minden on the map. Her success prompts the return of her father, Roy (Malcolm Goodwin), whose watch Jasmine has been wearing since he left. (She has it taped over so she can wear it during the games.) Jasmine and her father go out to celebrate with sundaes as Curtis and Claire, who know what Roy is like, look on skeptically. Roy promises he will be in Miami to watch her play.

There is some question about whether the team will be able to afford to travel to Florida; however, the minister of the church responds by trying to raise money, and in a scene reminiscent of *It's a Wonderful Life* (1946), the townspeople gather to donate their money and possessions to finance the Miami trip. One contributes his wining lottery ticket; one gives his prize "football" (a soccer ball); and Curtis sacrifices his "escape Minden" money. The townspeople also gather to clean up Main Street so that the town will look better on television.

The opposition in Miami consists of last year's champions from a more prosperous city with hundreds of fans in attendance. Few fans are there from Minden—Roy is among the missing, much to Jasmine's disappointment. When Minden trails at the half, Curtis talks to Jasmine, telling her that he will never leave her and that it's time to move on. Jasmine does, sparking a comeback that just falls short of victory. After the game Curtis is offered a job coaching in Miami, but he later turns the job down because he wants to be "home." Despite the loss, the Minden folks greet the returning school bus as if the team had won. Roy shows up as Curtis, Claire, and Jasmine are hugging each other and offers a pathetic excuse about his absence. This time Jasmine doesn't fall for it and removes his watch—it is time to do that—and takes Curtis's hand rather than her father's. Like so many sports films, this one is about parent-child relationships, only this time a surrogate father steps forward to help a young girl. As Claire points out, the town, which has been reborn in its support of the team, has won. The film, based on a true story, celebrates small-town America, the American belief in the underdog, and the idea that one can succeed without winning.

LOOKING FOR ERIC (2009)

DIRECTOR: Ken Loach. SCREENPLAY: Paul Laverty. PRODUCER: Rebecca O'Brien. CINEMATOGRAPHY: Barry Ackroyd. EDITING: Jonathan Morris. MUSIC: George Fenton. PRODUCTION DESIGN: Fergus Clegg. ART DIRECTION: Julie Ann Horan. COSTUME DESIGN: Sarah Ryan.
CAST: Steve Evets (Eric Bishop), Eric Cantona (Eric), John Henshaw (Meatballs), Stephanie Bishop (Lily), Gerard Kearns (Ryan).
RUNNING TIME: 116 minutes.
DVD: Icon Home Entertainment (UK: PAL)

A downtrodden football (soccer) fanatic looks for counsel from a poster of his idol, Manchester United's Eric Cantona, who then appears to him in hallucinations.

LORDS OF DOGTOWN (2005)

DIRECTOR: Catherine Hardwicke. SCREENPLAY: Stacy Peralta. PRODUCER: John Linson. CINEMATOGRAPHY: Elliot Davis. EDITING: Nancy Richardson. MUSIC: Mark Mothersbaugh. PRODUCTION DESIGN: Chris Gorak. ART DIRECTION: Seth Reed. COSTUME DESIGN: Cindy Evans.
CAST: Emile Hirsch (Jay), Victor Rasuk (Tony), John Robinson (Stacy), Michael Angarano (Sid), Nikki Reed (Kathy), Rebecca De Mornay (Philane), Johnny Knoxville (Topper Burks), Heath Ledger (Skip Engblom).
RUNNING TIME: 107 minutes.
DVD: Sony Pictures.

Former skateboarder Stacy Peralta won a directing award at the Sundance Festival for his documentary *Dogtown and Z-Boys* (2001), chronicling the Zephyr Club skaters who turned skateboarding into an extreme sport, becoming internationally known in the process. Following the success of the documentary, Peralta wrote a script for a feature film based on the same material.

Lords of Dogtown opens in 1975 with the principal players gathering at Venice Beach to surf. The Zephyr crew includes Skip Engblom (Heath Ledger), owner of the Zephyr surf shop; his pal Chino (Vincent Laresca); and three younger teens, Jay Adams (Emile Hirsch), Tony Alva (Victor Rasuk), and Stacy Peralta (John Robinson). The older guys call the shots, determining who gets to surf and who draws shore patrol, keeping a lookout for "Vals," residents of the San Fernando Valley who "invade" Zephyr surf. The scene anticipates the importance of group allegiance in the surf culture.

The surfers hang out at the Zephyr, where Skip mixes business and pitchers of drinks. His workshop employees choose their own hours, leaving when the ocean calls. Sid (Michael Angarano), a young teen with an inner ear problem that affects his balance, works for Skip in order to be part of the gang. One afternoon, a cool dude (Mitch Hedberg) comes in to show Skip a set of urethane skateboard wheels, which he says will greatly increase maneuverability. Skip attaches a set to one of his boards and takes it to a park for the teens to try out. Tony, Jay, and Stacy show off their stuff, and Tony's sister, Kathy (Nikki Reed), flirts with Stacy. In comparison to the others, Stacy is a straight arrow; he holds down a job, wears a watch, turns his nose up when offered a beer, and practices his skateboard technique alone at night. Skip says of him, "He's not one of us."

Skip realizes the new wheels can revolutionize skateboarding—and that he can profit from shifting the focus of his manufacturing from surfboards to skateboards, especially since decent swells are less plentiful than concrete surfaces in Southern California. He summons a dozen teens to a meeting at his shop and presents them each with a new board and a Zephyr T-shirt. Jay asks if there's a board for Stacy, who has gone to work rather than to the meeting, but Skip doesn't respond. Skip instructs the group that they are to practice every day for the next month to prepare for competition. The newly formed team hurries out into the street, and within seconds the sound of shattering glass is heard. As Skip rushes to close the iron grille at the front of the shop to prevent the team from dashing back inside, he remarks that the Zephyr Club is "supposed to keep them out of trouble." In his own pot-smoking, alcohol-guzzling way, Skip is a mentor for the teens, and his shop provides them with a sense of stability and belonging that is lacking in their lives. Jay's mother, Philaine (Rebecca De Mornay), has not outgrown the sex–drugs–rock 'n' roll phase of her youth. Her factory job doesn't cover the bills, and Jay is often scrounging groceries and cash for beer and dope to keep Philaine in party mode. Tony's father works nights and grouses that his good-for-nothing son is going to end up a ditch digger. Stacy's parents seem to care enough about him that he has to sneak out his bedroom window to surf at daybreak, but the brief glimpse into his home life reflects tension as his father sits drinking in front of a television. Sid, who is from a wealthy family, longs to be cool, so acts as Skip's gofer and lets the others take advantage of him in order to secure acceptance.

At the tournament the Zephyrs find the course is a "tabletop," a flat surface that cramps their style. Nonetheless, they put on an impressive show. Jay, who is first up, stuns the crowd with his freestyle tricks, but the judges, noting that he has performed none of the compulsory moves, give him low scores. Tony's routine combines power glides and walking spinners with low, driving turns, earning top marks. Stacy, who has entered as an independent, ties Tony's scores, but one of the officials wants to disqualify him for touching the ground. Tony comes to Stacy's defense, and fists fly, costing Tony his trophy. As the Zephyrs leave the tournament, Skip invites Stacy to have dinner with them. At the restaurant Skip awards Stacy a T-shirt, making him an official team member. A food fight ensues.

Later in the week, the Zephyrs descend on the home of a girl whose parents are away and whose pool, like many in Southern California, is empty because of the drought. The Zephyrs begin skating the bowl of the pool, riding higher on the sides as they get the hang of it. Soon they are roaming the Valley in search of empty pools and absent homeowners, perfecting their skills and avoiding arrest. Meanwhile, Skip is trying to keep pace with the orders flooding in for skateboards with urethane wheels.

One night when their father is out, Tony and Kathy throw a party. Kathy, who has been dating Stacy, is in a romantic mood, but Stacy needs more privacy. He leaves the party, saying he just wanted to be alone with her. Jay, who has observed the exchange, quickly moves in, dancing around her seductively. By the time Mr. Alva returns home, Kathy and Jay are in bed together, and Tony is entertaining a girl on the other side of their narrow room. They barely avoid discovery.

By the 1976 Ocean Front Festival, Jay, Tony, and Stacy are becoming well-known and are beginning to see one another as rivals. Meanwhile, Skip, who has been profiting from the Zephyrs' popularity, faces competition from other manufacturers and promoters seeking to recruit the top skaters to endorse their products. Soon the Zephyr team makes the cover of a glossy 'zine. Skip holds an open house at the surf shop to celebrate, but the key players aren't too happy.

Promoter Topper Burks (Johnny Knoxville) crashes the party and courts Tony with promises of big money. Jay and Stacy resist when Tony talks with them about leaving Skip for greener pastures. Although the team has been like family, Tony feels increased competition from Stacy, and Stacy has just learned that Kathy is sleeping with Jay. Then Chino's girlfriend flirts with Jay, and the two fight. Tony talks with Topper again, and Skip, who is totally wasted, climbs on the roof of the shop and hurls boards into the street. Then he straddles the cornice and looks as if he may fall or jump, but only a bottle topples, shattering on the street and bringing the festivities to a close.

Morning finds Tony riding in a convertible with Topper and trying to persuade Jay to join them. He brushes them off gently. Jay's mother is partying with a houseful of people, including a man from an advertising agency who wants Jay to do a Slinky commercial. Jay refuses, but it seems only a matter of time before he accepts an offer that will help support his mother.

Soon Stacy is the only member of the Zephyr team still with Skip, and he is ready to move on. Skip rambles on about plans to change how he is running the business to increase production. He makes Stacy an offer, but Stacy doesn't reply. When next seen, Stacy has a new sponsor and has edged out Tony and Jay in competition and in fame. He makes a guest appearance on an episode of *Charlie's Angels*, a popular television show at the time; travels; and does photo shoots. Tony expresses frustration at coming in second once again by breaking a trophy. Jay flies off the old pier with his skateboard, alone.

At the 1977 Long Beach championships, when Tony arrives in a very long limo, Jay remarks that Tony is "competing with the sun for the center of the universe." Stacy has recently returned from Australia and has a new girlfriend, whom he introduces to Kathy. Jay has signed with a new sponsor; however, his signature board is not ready, and he is unhappy with the prototype. Jay's performance mirrors his first one for the Zephyr team. He executes a breathtaking aerial move no one has ever seen before and receives low marks from the judges, who don't know how to respond to his originality. Jay walks out, handing his board to a spectator as he leaves. As the final heat begins, Tony collides with another skater, and the two begin to fight. Tony's eye is severely injured, and he is stretchered out. His injury requires several surgeries, and he fears that his career is over.

While Tony is recovering, Pacific Ocean Park burns. Jay sits among the charred ruins, where he is discovered by Skip. Jay apologizes for leaving the Zephyr group, but Skip doesn't hold a grudge, even though he has fallen on hard times; he no longer owns the shop and now works for the new owner, crafting boards. He offers Jay a drink and leaves him with the bottle. Back at home, Jay shaves his head, obliterating the surfer look that appealed to sponsors and fans. One evening Stacy and his girlfriend are cornered by a gang of punks, but one of them turns out to be Jay, who calls off his compatriots. Later, Stacy learns from Kathy that Sid has a brain tumor. Jay wants to organize a get together, but Stacy says he's committed to a competition in Florida.

Jay, who has a zipper tattooed down the center of his skull, visits Sid, who is now confined to a wheelchair, but is in good spirits, partially because he has been prescribed medical marijuana. Jay has barely had a chance to apologize for Stacy and Tony's absences, when Stacy appears. He explains he is starting his own company and is no longer obligated to his former sponsors. Stacy seems to feel uncomfortable about his good fortune and is soon ready to leave, but Sid insists they "check out the pool." Sid has two surprises: his father has agreed to drain the pool, and the "Mexican" by the pool "ain't cleanin' it." It's Tony, and he's brought extra skateboards. The three skate the bowl, just like old times, and Jay still astounds with his aerials. Then they lower Sid and his chair for a couple of low-speed circuits. The film ends with the four re-experiencing the joy of the sport and the feeling of camaraderie they had enjoyed as Skip's "grommets." Viewers learn that Tony also formed his own company, that Jay served a jail sentence for a drug conviction but is credited as pioneering extreme sports, and that Sid died of brain cancer.

The real Skip Engblom, Tony Alva, and Jay Adams served as consultants and appeared in minor roles, as did writer Stacy Peralta. Peralta received some criticism for his script because his own character is portrayed as nearly faultless while his treatments of Tony and Jay illuminate their insecurities. Yet, in showing more of their struggles, Peralta gives their characters a depth that his Stacy lacks. In interviews, Alva and Adams have highly praised Peralta's work and seem pleased with both their representations and involvement in the production, as does Engblom, who was delighted to be portrayed by Heath Ledger.

LOVE AND BASKETBALL (2000)

DIRECTOR: Gina Prince-Bythewood. SCREENPLAY: Gina Prince-Bythewood. PRODUCERS: Sam Kitt, Spike Lee. CINEMATOGRAPHY: Reynaldo Villalobos. EDITING: Terilyn A. Shropshire. MUSIC: Terence Blanchard. PRODUCTION DESIGN: Jeffrey Howard. ART DIRECTION: Sue Chan. COSTUME DESIGN: Ruth E. Carter.

CAST: Sanaa Lathan (Monica Wright), Omar Epps (Quincy McCall), Alfre Woodard (Camille Wright), Dennis Haysbert (Zeke McCall), Debbi Morgan (Nona McCall), Harry Lennix (Nathan Wright), Glenndon Chatman (young Quincy), Kyla Pratt (young Monica).

RUNNING TIME: 124 minutes.

DVD: New Line Home Video.

Gina Prince-Bythewood, who wrote and directed *Love and Basketball*, is no stranger to sports, having run track at UCLA, where she received her degree in film studies. Her movie is a sports film with a lot of basketball footage, but it is also a love story about two young black students in an upper-middle-class neighborhood. Although they clearly have been in love since childhood, theirs is a volatile relationship featuring jealousy, miscommunication, and the denial of feelings. The plot is divided, high school–basketball style, into four quarters separated by time and location.

In the first quarter the audience is introduced to Quincy McCall (Glenndon Chatman) and Monica Wright (Kyla Pratt). Quincy and two friends are playing HORSE when Monica, whose family has just moved in next door, asks if she can play with them. It is only when she takes off her cap that the boys realize that she's a girl and tell her that girls can't play basketball. The gender bias she experiences is normal, but her response, beating them in the game, is not. After she bests Quincy, he angrily pushes her into some shrubbery, giving her some bloody scratches. He rides off but returns to look at her through his window. (Their windows, which are directly opposite each other, are symbolic "thresholds"; they later enter each other's bedrooms through the window, signaling changes in their relationship.) The next morning Quincy asks if she wants to be his "girl." After learning that not much is required of her, she agrees, and they exchange a five-second kiss. When she refuses to ride on his bike, however, the two end up in a wrestling match on the lawn. What happens in the first quarter—romantic sparks followed by other sorts of sparks—is repeated throughout the film.

The second quarter focuses on their relationship during their senior year in high school. Both star on their basketball teams and unconvincingly pretend not to be interested in each other. Monica (now played by Sanaa Lathan) is jealous of Shawnee (Gabrielle Union), one of several girls ("hos" according to Quincy's mother) that he is sleeping with; and Quincy (now played by Omar Epps) attends all of Monica's games and knows her basketball statistics. Both want basketball scholarships to the University of Southern California, but Quincy's Father, Zeke (Dennis Haysbert), who plays in the NBA, wants Quincy to consider Princeton. Quincy, like Monica, wants to play professionally and knows he will draw more media attention at USC. Zeke and his wife, Nona (Debbie Morgan), argue constantly about the amount of time Zeke is away and the fact that he has never completed his undergraduate degree. The arguing gets to Quincy, who sees Monica, asks if he can come in, and spends the night sleeping beside her bed. The climactic point in the second quarter occurs when Monica's loss of temper leads to a loss of game. Quincy suggests that her anger is the reason she hasn't received a scholarship offer from USC.

For the Spring Dance, which follows the game, Monica's sister has arranged a date for her. The date is a dud, and at the same time, Quincy finds he's not enjoying Shawnee's company. Monica and Quincy commiserate with each other outside their windows; then Monica asks him to open her letter from USC, which contains a scholarship offer. (Quincy already has his USC offer.) The evening ends with Monica inviting Quincy into her bedroom, where they make love.

The third quarter focuses on their years at USC, where Monica contends with Sidra O'Neal (Erika Ringor), a veteran, for the point guard position. Her coach rides her, criticizing Monica for posing after making a successful shot, thereby preventing her from getting back on defense in time; but when Sidra is injured, Monica replaces her and goes on to become the star of the team. Quincy starts at point guard as a freshman and also becomes a star for USC. One of the highlights of this section is a game of "strip basketball," which Quincy allows Monica to win. Soon after this, Zeke tells Quincy about a paternity suit that has been filed against him. Although Zeke denies the charges, Quincy discovers photos of Zeke with another woman. Angered at his father, Quincy loses his on-court concentration, and his game quickly derails. He tries to talk with Monica about his problems, but she has to obey her team's curfew, so she leaves before Quincy can unburden himself. Feeling rejected, he turns to another young woman, Kerry (Monica Calhoun), who "had time for [him]." He and Monica break up.

About five years later Monica, after having earned first-team All-American honors, is playing for the Barcelona team in the European women's championship, where she encounters Sidra, point guard for the Parma, Italy, team. Barcelona wins, and Monica and Sidra have dinner together after the game. While Sidra enjoys the recognition, money, and Italian men, Monica is unhappy, admitting to Sidra that basketball isn't fun for her anymore. Meanwhile, Quincy, who has been used mainly as a reserve by his NBA team, is injured after entering a game in "junk time." While he is in the hospital, he is visited by a contrite father, a mother with a new boyfriend, and Monica, who brings him flowers. Unfortunately, Quincy has a new girlfriend, Kyra (Tyra Banks), a gorgeous airline attendant. The disheartened Monica talks with her mother (Regina Hall), with whom she has had a troubled relationship.

In a conversation with Quincy, Monica learns that Kyra is out of town, that the couple plan to marry in two weeks, and that he is considering going back to school because he, too, no longer finds basketball enjoyable. Since he hasn't talked with Kyra about his plans to leave the NBA and return to college, Monica senses that she may still have a chance with Quincy. At night she goes to his bedroom window and asks him to come out for a talk. She confesses that she has loved him since she was eleven, but Quincy is standoffish until she challenges him to another game of one-on-one with his heart as the prize. Knowing that he let her win before, she hopes that he will let her win again. He defeats her, however, 5–4; but when he proposes that they play another game double or nothing, she knows that he loves her. (Apparently, he had to defeat her just to prove his superiority in the sport.) The last sequence in the film shows Quincy and their child in the stands as Monica goes out on the court to play for her team in the newly formed Women's Basketball Association.

Love and Basketball is a rarity in sports films in that it has a feminist message. It demonstrates the sexist attitude that exists in sports and shows how aggressiveness is prized when displayed by male athletes but is seen as being "unfeminine" for women. And like *Wimbledon* (2004) it concludes with a scene depicting the female athlete continuing in a successful career while her husband minds the children.

THE LOVE BUG (1968)

DIRECTOR: Robert Stevenson. SCREENPLAY: Bill Walsh, Don DaGradi, based on the story "Car-Boy-Girl" by Gordon Buford. PRODUCER: Bill Walsh. CINEMATOGRAPHY: Edward Colman. EDITING: Cotton Warburton. MUSIC: George Bruns. ART DIRECTION: Carroll Clark, John Mansbridge. COSTUME DESIGN: Bill Thomas.

CAST: Dean Jones (Jim Douglas), Michele Lee (Carol Bennett), David Tomlinson (Peter Thorndyke), Buddy Hackett (Tennessee Steinmetz), Joe Flynn (Havershaw).

RUNNING TIME: 108 minutes.

DVD: Walt Disney Home Entertainment.

This Disney comedy is about a Volkswagen named Herbie that teams up with a hapless race-car driver who mistakes his skills for the real star of the track: number 53.

THE LOVE GURU (2008)

DIRECTOR: Marco Schnabel. SCREENPLAY: Mike Myers, Graham Gordy. PRODUCERS: Mike Myers, Michael De Luca. CINEMATOGRAPHY: Peter Deming. EDITING: Lee Haxall, Gregory Perler, Billy Weber. MUSIC: George S. Clinton. PRODUCTION DESIGN: Charles Wood. ART DIRECTION: Dennis Davenport, David G. Fremlin. COSTUME DESIGN: Karen Patch.

CAST: Mike Myers (Guru Pitka), Jessica Alba (Jane Bullard), Romany Malco (Darren Roanoke), Justin Timberlake (Jacque Grand), Ben Kingsley (Guru Tugginmypuddha).

RUNNING TIME: 87 minutes.

DVD: Paramount.

In this comedy, a guru is hired to provide guidance to a Toronto Maple Leafs hockey player.

LUCAS (1986)

DIRECTOR: David Seltzer. SCREENPLAY: David Seltzer. PRODUCER: David Nicksay. CINEMATOGRAPHY: Reynaldo Villalobos. EDITING: Priscilla Nedd. MUSIC: Dave Grusin. ART DIRECTION: James Murakami. COSTUME DESIGN: Molly Maginnis.

CAST: Corey Haim (Lucas), Kerri Green (Maggie), Charlie Sheen (Cappie), Courtney Thorne-Smith (Alise), Winona Ryder (Rina).

RUNNING TIME: 100 minutes.

DVD: 20th Century Fox.

In *Lucas*, a nerdish teenager befriended by a high school football star forms a crush on the new cheerleader, who only has eyes for the quarterback.

M

THE MAIN EVENT (1979)

DIRECTOR: Howard Zieff. SCREENPLAY: Gail Parent, Andrew Smith. PRODUCERS: Jon Peters, Barbra Streisand. CINEMATOGRAPHY: Mario Tosi. EDITING: Edward Warschilka. MUSIC: Michael Melvoin. PRODUCTION DESIGN: Charles Rosen. COSTUME DESIGN: Ruth Myers.
CAST: Barbra Streisand (Hillary Kramer), Ryan O'Neal (Eddie "Kid Natural" Scanlon), Paul Sand (David), Whitman Mayo (Percy), Patti D'Arbanville (Donna).
RUNNING TIME: 112 minutes.
DVD: Warner Home Video.

The Main Event, a boxing film hidden inside a 1930s-style screwball comedy, features Barbra Streisand and Ryan O'Neal, both of whom also starred in Peter Bogdanovich's *What's Up, Doc?* (1972)—a film made in homage to Howard Hawks's *Bringing Up Baby* (1938). The producers hoped to cash in on the popularity of the Streisand-O'Neal pairing, and while *The Main Event* was not a critical success, it did well at the box office.

The film begins in a perfume company owned by Hillary Kramer (Streisand), who soon learns from her ex-husband/lawyer, David (Paul Sand), that her business manager has absconded to South America with all her funds. The only paper that separates her from destitution is the contract she owns on boxer Eddie "Kid Natural" Scanlon (O'Neal). What she doesn't know is that the contract is merely a tax write-off, another of her business manager's schemes.

After Hillary completes the sale of her once-lucrative business, she attempts to find her boxer at the 31st Street Gym. Unfortunately, the Kid has not fought in four years, despite continuing to take her money for salary and living expenses. She wants him to fight or to refund her money. The Kid, however, has invested everything in his Knockout Driving School (which is housed in a boxing glove-shaped building), and he doesn't want to fight anymore.

Hillary points out that since he has not fought, he is in breach of contract and owes her over sixty thousand dollars. The Kid and his manager, Percy (Whitman Mayo), try to con Hillary with a hard-luck story about the Kid not being able to box since he accidentally killed his best friend in a bout. Hillary doesn't buy the story and insists that Percy line up some fights. Percy arranges one with the "Bakersfield Bleeder" hoping to turn her off with the sight of blood, but Hillary is undeterred and directs her attention to training the Kid and acquiring some investors. As this action continues, the two do more sparring outside the ring than in it. There is an obvious physical attraction between them, which must be masked as mutual dislike in true screwball tradition.

A fund-raising event begins badly, but after the Kid punches an obnoxious karate master in the solar plexus, things get better, not worse. Nobody likes the karate boor, and several of Hillary's friends offer to invest. On the beach after the party, the Kid tries to become romantic with Hillary, but she rebuffs him, leaving him pouting and calling her "boss."

Trying for the big payday, Hillary approaches a prominent boxing promoter, Gough (James Gregory), who tells her the Kid has "no right hand" and dismisses her. She persists, however, and lines up a fight for the Kid with the "Gorilla," an oversized beast who has "been away for ten years." Somehow, the Kid manages to do well, but before he can finish off his opponent, Hillary brings the Kid's stool into the ring, getting the Kid disqualified. To promote interest in her fighter, she also arranges for their training ground to be included on a Hollywood bus tour; Hillary and the Kid appear in the ring together and put on a verbal match for the entertainment of the crowd. Not done with Gough, she sees him again, mentions the press, and tries to interest him in staging "the fight that never was," a bout scheduled against Hector Mantilla (Richard Lawson) four years earlier but cancelled when the combatants clobbered one another outside of their dressing rooms just before the match. Since Hector has gone on to be a contender and the Kid is now a driving instructor, Gough insists that the Kid beat someone to give him some credibility. At this preliminary fight Hillary barks orders from ringside. The Kid struggles and looks doomed until she pours ice water down the front of his trunks. This energizes the Kid, amuses the fans, including Gough, and results in the Kid's victory.

Before the fight with Hector, Gough arranges for the Kid and his entourage to train in a forest retreat away from Las Vegas. There the Kid occupies the only private cabin; the sparring partners, manager, and Hillary sleep in the bunkhouse, where her presence disrupts the male camaraderie and makes her very uneasy. Meanwhile, the Kid reveals a softer side, spends time talking with Hillary, and eventually and inevitably, allows her to sleep in his cabin the night before the fight. When they climb into bed together, it is Hillary who makes the romantic overtures. The next morning, however, the sparring resumes when the couple revert to stereotypical roles: she maintains he still owes her money; he believes he should control the winnings from the fight. Then the roles are reversed for comic purposes. The Kid objects to being treated like an object and resents that he has been used for a one-night stand. Hillary figures that she has received precious little return for her sixty thousand dollars and wants to compute the cost of the sex by the minute. The Kid determines that if he can win and pay her off, he never wants to see her again.

Still angry, the Kid does well and is on his way to victory over Hector when Hillary realizes that his victory will end his financial obligation and with it, the relationship. What to do? She asks Percy for advice, and then she tosses in the towel, which seems to float interminably above the ring as the Kid pummels Hector to the canvas. The Kid loses, but he and Hillary win, embracing and concluding that the only thing they can do is to keep fighting.

Although it lacks the chemistry and "punch" of *What's Up, Doc? The Main Event* has some entertaining dialogue. O'Neal endured 150 rounds during his training for the role. Fight scenes were shot at the Olympic Auditorium in Los Angeles, and the boxing-glove shaped structure was erected in an L.A. residential area.

MAJOR LEAGUE (1989)

DIRECTOR: David S. Ward. SCREENPLAY: David S. Ward. PRODUCERS: Chris Chesser, Irby Smith. CINEMATOGRAPHY: Reynaldo Villalobos. EDITING: Dennis M. Hill. MUSIC: James Newton Howard. PRODUCTION DESIGN: Jeffrey Howard. ART DIRECTION: John Krenz Reinhart Jr. COSTUME DESIGN: Erica Edell Phillips.

CAST: Tom Berenger (Jake Taylor), Charlie Sheen (Rick Vaughn), Corbin Bernsen (Roger Dorn), Margaret Whitton (Rachel Phelps), Rene Russo (Lynn Wells), Wesley Snipes (Willie Mays Hayes), Dennis Haysbert (Pedro Cerrano), Bob Uecker (Harry Doyle).

RUNNING TIME: 107 minutes.

DVD: Paramount.

This comedy by David Ward, who wrote the screenplay for *The Sting* (1973), works almost exclusively through humor as it follows the antics of a group of misfit ballplayers recruited by the Cleveland Indians. The main plot is simple: former showgirl Rachel Phelps (Margaret Whitton) has inherited the Indians from her late husband and plans to move the team to Miami, where she's been promised a bevy of perks, including membership in an exclusive country club.

In order to secure the Miami deal, she must first wriggle out of her stadium lease in Cleveland, something she can do if attendance for the season falls below eight hundred thousand. To drive down attendance, she has assembled a roster guaranteed to continue the Indians' losing record. Power hitter Pedro Cerrano (Dennis Haysbert) is a Cuban who has come to America to enjoy religious freedom. He practices voodoo and sets up a shrine in his locker to cure his "sick" bat; Pedro, it turns out, cannot hit a curveball. Manager Lou Brown (James Gammon) has been running a tire dealership. Free agent Roger Dorn (Corbin Bernsen) believes in avoiding injury at all cost, so has a tendency not to field anything hit in his direction. Ace pitcher Rick "Wild Thing" Vaughn (Charlie Sheen) has a rocket of a fastball but little control; he's serving out a sentence for car theft. Willie Mays Hayes (Wesley Snipes), who can run like the wind, dreams of setting records for base stealing—if only he can get on base. Veteran catcher Jake Taylor (Tom Berenger) is a mediocre player with bad knees; when first seen, he's sleeping off a drinking binge somewhere in Mexico. Jake assumes a leadership role, helping rookies Rick and Willie adjust and diffusing tensions that arise between Rick and Roger. In his spare time, he attempts to rekindle a romance with an Olympic-athlete-turned-librarian.

Training camp is disastrous, and the season's opener against the New York Yankees is literally a comedy of errors. Slapstick prevails as players collide with one another, drop balls, and strike out. The Indians' radio announcer, Harry Doyle (Bob Uecker), offers creative commentary often at odds with the activity on the field. In spite of their deficiencies, however, the team gradually improves. After Lou discovers that Rick needs glasses, the young pitcher finds his range, and soon his nickname reflects his punk haircut and tattoos rather than his efforts on the mound. Willie manages to beat out a few weak hits; Pedro pounds a few fastballs, and Roger fields the occasional grounder.

Midway through the season, Lou learns of the owner's plan to relocate the franchise. He calls a team meeting and announces his own plan: through sheer determination, they will win thirty-two of their remaining games and take the pennant. To inspire the team, he has rigged

Corbin Bernsen (top), Tom Berenger (middle), and Charlie Sheen (bottom) in *Major League*

a cardboard cutout of Rachel Phelps clad in a thirty-two-piece leopard print outfit; for each victory, he will remove a section. Soon the team is on a winning streak, and the league championship comes down to the final two games against the Yankees. Possible difficulty arises when Roger's wife, getting even for an apparent indiscretion, seduces an unwitting Rick; however, the effect is to put an end to the tension between Roger and Rick, and Rick wins the game by striking out the Yankee's best hitter, a man who had burned Rick for two home runs in their previous matchups.

The final game is tied with two outs in the ninth when Willie reaches first on a poorly hit ball, bringing up Jake. Imitating Babe Ruth, Jake points toward the left-field stands before he takes his stance. He swings, missing intentionally, to allow Willie to steal second. Before the next pitch, Jake again points to the stands, then lays down a perfect bunt. In spite of his knees, he beats the throw to first, and Willie slides home safely to win the pennant. As the fans swarm onto the field, Rachel Phelps admits defeat, and Jake finds his old girlfriend, no longer engaged, waiting to embrace him.

Neither plot nor character development figures prominently in *Major League*. The story line does not lead up to the turning point in the film, when the team learns of the owner's scheme. The manager simply hears about the plan, and the team seemingly acquires the necessary skill to win overnight. Little emphasis is given to individual motivation. Jake Taylor decides to pursue his old girlfriend after three years following a chance encounter, although she clearly has established a new life for herself with a successful and fulfilling career and a new man. Jake's two subsequent attempts to woo her are played for comic effect. After Jake follows her from work, driving the dugout cart to her fiancé's penthouse apartment and crashing a small party, he seems to give up; the film offers no explanation for why Lynn ditches her fiancé and shows up for the finale. There's little sign of personal growth or change in any of the characters, and there's nothing to account for the bonding among the team members. It is the comedy that carries the film, which was a hit at the box office and led to two sequels.

MAJOR LEAGUE: BACK TO THE MINORS (1998)

DIRECTOR: John Warren. SCREENPLAY: John Warren. PRODUCER: James G. Robinson. CINEMATOGRAPHY: Tim Suhrstedt. EDITING: O. Nicholas Brown, Bryan H. Carroll. MUSIC: Robert Folk. PRODUCTION DESIGN: David Crank. COSTUME DESIGN: Mary McLeod.

CAST: Scott Bakula (Gus Cantrell), Corbin Bernsen (Roger Dorn), Dennis Haysbert (Pedro Cerrano), Ted McGinley (Leonard Huff), Bob Uecker (Harry Doyle).

RUNNING TIME: 100 minutes.

DVD: Warner Home Video.

This final and least successful film in the series retains only a few links to its predecessors. A mellower Roger Dorn (Corbin Bernsen) now owns the Minnesota Twins, but over-the-hill Jake has disappeared without a trace. In his stead, aging minor leaguer Gus Cantrell (Scott Bakula) accepts an offer from Roger to manage his triple-A farm team, the Littletown Buzz. Gus's roster includes a twenty-year veteran first baseman, Pops Morgan (Thom Barry); a philosophizing pitcher, Doc Windgate (Peter Mackenzie), who throws the world's slowest fastball; identical twin infielders, who are both named Juan Lopez (Tim, Tom, and Ted DiFilippo) and who are locked in a vicious sibling rivalry; arrogant hitter Downtown Anderson (Walton Goggins), who doesn't realize he's not quite ready for the big leagues; and a ballet dancer, Lance Peré (Kenneth Johnson), who pirouettes about in the outfield. Rube Baker (Eric Bruskotter), the hapless catcher from *Major League II*, is behind the plate once again, and Gus tracks down Samurai outfielder Isuro Tanaka (Takaaki Ishibashi), who has been operating a miniature golf course. Tanaka's buddy, slugger Pedro Cerrano (Dennis Haysbert), now a born-again Christian, rounds out the starting lineup. A sober Harry Doyle (Bob Uecker) is the voice of the Littletown Buzz.

The plot turns on a disagreement between Gus and the Twins' unpleasant manager, Leonard Huff (Ted McGinley), whose players are not performing well. Roger decides to schedule an exhibition game between the Buzz and the Twins. When Downtown ties the game in the late innings, Huff cuts the lights so that the game ends in a tie. However, Huff decides to call Downtown up in order to weaken Gus's team. Without their power hitter, the dispirited Buzz begin to doubt themselves, but Gus gives an inspiring speech, stating "baseball is not about one player." The team returns to its winning ways, and soon after, Downtown rejoins them.

Dennis Haysbert (top row, center) returns as Pedro Cerrano in *Major League: Back to the Minors*

Gus challenges Huff to a rematch, which ends predictably. Downtown gets to hit the winning homer in the bottom of the ninth, and Roger offers Huff's job to Gus. Gus opts to stay on with the Buzz and exits for a honeymoon with Maggie Reynolds (Jensen Daggett), the supportive love interest who has been plunked into the story in a minor role. In spite of some impressive baseball action, the film didn't last long in theaters.

MAJOR LEAGUE II (1994)

DIRECTOR: David S. Ward. SCREENPLAY: R. J. Stewart, Tom S. Parker, Jim Jennewein. PRODUCERS: James G. Robinson, David S. Ward. CINEMATOGRAPHY: Victor Hammer. EDITING: Donn Cambern, Kimberly Ray, Paul Seydor, Frederick Wardell. MUSIC: Michel Colombier. PRODUCTION DESIGN: Stephen Hendrickson. ART DIRECTION: Gary Diamond. COSTUME DESIGN: Bobbie Read.

CAST: Tom Berenger (Jake Taylor), Charlie Sheen (Rick Vaughn), Corbin Bernsen (Roger Dorn), Dennis Haysbert (Pedro Cerrano), James Gammon (Lou Brown), Omar Epps (Willie Mays Hayes), David Keith (Jack Parkman), Bob Uecker (Harry Doyle).

RUNNING TIME: 105 minutes.

DVD: Warner Home Video.

This sequel picks up the story of *Major League* a year later, continuing the gags of the original and following a parallel plotline. The task of providing back story falls to Bob Uecker, who returns in the role of sportscaster Harry Doyle. Harry reports that after winning the American League East Division, the Indians were defeated by the Chicago White Sox. Roger Dorn (Corbin Bernsen), a player more interested in his investments than in his fielding, has purchased the Cleveland Indians from the villainous Rachel Phelps, who in *Major League* had assembled what she hoped would be a losing team in order to break her stadium contract and relocate the Indians to Florida. Roger has signed the hard-hitting Jack Parkman (David Keith), an unlikeable bad boy, to beef up the roster, and at the start of the season, the Indians are favored to win the pennant.

However, the players have not handled their previous success well, and the season doesn't look too promising. "Wild Thing" Rick Vaughn (Charlie Sheen), under the influence of a new agent, Rebecca Flannery (Alison Doody), has moved out of the fast lane off field and has lost his fastball on. Willie Mays Hayes (now played by Omar Epps) has capitalized on his fame by starring in action films and acquiring an entourage. The voodoo practitioner Pedro Cerrano (Dennis Haysbert) has shifted his system of beliefs to Buddhism, and his newly achieved state of bliss has made him much too gentle to perform as an aggressive slugger. In contrast to Pedro, Isuro Tanaka (Takaaki Ishibashi), recently acquired in a trade, adheres to the Samurai Code with often disastrous results. Now retired, Jake Taylor (Tom Berenger) works as a coach under manager Lou Brown (James Gammon) and, prior to the signing of Jack Parkman, called up Rube Baker (Eric Bruskotter), a catcher who has a phenomenal throw to second base but who has difficulty getting the ball back to the pitcher.

Roger soon runs into financial difficulty. In spite of selling ad space to anyone who will part with the cash, he is forced to sign the team over to Rachel Phelps (Margaret Whitton), who resumes her plot to ruin the Indians' chances for success. The stress contributes to Lou's having a heart attack, and Jake takes over managing in his absence.

Under Jake's leadership, the team resumes its winning ways. Jake solves Rube's problem by instructing him not to think about throwing to the mound; instead, Rube memorizes statistics from *Playboy* and Victoria's Secret catalogs. Later, Rube provides an inspiring locker-room speech. Pedro and Isuro meld their belief systems into a joint ritual that restores both men's skills. Meanwhile, Rick's former girlfriend, Nikki Reese (Michelle Burke), returns, complicating his life but jarring him out of his funk in time to pitch against Jack, who has been traded back to the White Sox, in the deciding game of the pennant race.

As Lou, still hospitalized, follows the game on a forbidden radio while pretending to watch PBS, the Indians secure the pennant. Once again Rachel Phelps is foiled, and once again, the season's final outcome remains unknown as the film ends before the World Series begins.

A MAN AND A WOMAN (1967)

DIRECTOR: Claude Lelouch. SCREENPLAY: Pierre Uytterhoeven, Claude Lelouch. PRODUCER: Claude Lelouch. CINEMATOGRAPHY: Claude Lelouch. EDITING: Claude Barrois, Claude Lelouch. MUSIC: Francis Lai. PRODUCTION DESIGN: Robert Luchaire. COSTUME DESIGN: Richard Marvil.

CAST: Jean-Louis Trintignant (Jean-Louis Duroc), Anouk Aimée (Anne Gautier), Pierre Barouh (Pierre Gautier), Valérie Lagrange (Valerie Duroc).

RUNNING TIME: 102 minutes.

ACADEMY AWARDS: Best Foreign Language Film, Best Original Screenplay. NOMINATIONS: Best Director, Best Actress (Aimée).

DVD: Warner Home Video

This French romance features Trintignant as a race car driver who falls in love with a widow.

THE MAN WITH THE PERFECT SWING (1995)

DIRECTOR: Michael Hovis. SCREENPLAY: Michael Hovis. PRODUCER: Angela Sembera Hovis. CINEMATOGRAPHY: Jim Bar-

ham. EDITING: Michael Hovis. ART DIRECTION: Christopher Stull.
CAST: James Monroe Black (Anthony "Babe" Lombardo), Suzanne Savoy (Susan Lombardo), Marco Perella (Chuck Carter), James Belcher (Lou Gallo).
RUNNING TIME: 95 minutes.
DVD: Monarch Home Video.

In this comedy/drama, a man with little ambition finds purpose in life after developing a golf swing that will transform the game.

MATCH POINT (2005)

DIRECTOR: Woody Allen. SCREENPLAY: Woody Allen. PRODUCER: Letty Aronson, Lucy Darwin, Gareth Wiley. CINEMATOGRAPHY: Remi Adefarasin. EDITING: Alisa Lepselter. PRODUCTION DESIGN: Jim Clay. ART DIRECTION: Diane Dancklefsen, Jan Spoczynski. COSTUME DESIGN: Jill Taylor.
CAST: Jonathan Rhys Meyers (Chris Wilton), Scarlett Johansson (Nola Rice), Emily Mortimer (Chloe Hewett), Matthew Goode (Tom Hewett), Brian Cox (Alec Hewett).
RUNNING TIME: 124 minutes.
ACADEMY AWARD NOMINATIONS: Best Original Screenplay.
DVD: Dreamworks Video.

Written and directed by Woody Allen, this thriller presents tennis as a vehicle for socioeconomic advancement in a world where luck often trumps skill. The film opens with a voice-over musing Machiavellian on the role of luck as a tennis ball strikes the net cord and bounces vertically, poised to roll down one side of the net. Or the other. The voice belongs to Chris Wilton (Jonathan Rhys Meyers), an Irishman who is leaving the pro tour for a position at an exclusive tennis club in London.

Chris is an ambitious and not particularly likeable chap who spends his evenings perusing the *Oxford Companion to Dostoevsky* in order to impress the upper classes with his determination to improve himself. Although Chris presents himself well by saying the correct things, his voice is without conviction, and he appears simply to be repeating what is expected of him rather than expressing his true feelings. Nonetheless, he is successful in winning over the wealthy Hewett family, first befriending son Tom (Matthew Goode); then Tom's sister, Chloe (Emily Mortimer); and finally the parents (Brian Cox and Penelope Wilton). Tom's father is impressed by how Chris has managed to "pull himself up" and offers him a job in his company. Chris promptly refuses, then allows himself to be talked into accepting. Soon he is engaged to Chloe, but his real attraction is to Tom's girlfriend, Nola (Scarlett Johansson), an aspiring thespian from the United States. Like Chris, Nola is an ambitious outsider who has come to London to establish a career. But unlike Chris, Nola lacks confidence in her abilities and repeatedly fails at auditions. Although Chris is able to conceal his attraction from the Hewetts, he is barely able to contain his passion, and he pursues an affair even after his marriage to Chloe and in spite of the risks of discovery. Their affair is interrupted when Tom dumps Nola, whom the Hewetts find entirely unsuitable, for another woman, and Nola returns to America without telling Chris that she is leaving.

Boredom sets in for Chris. Married life has become routine. Chloe, intent on becoming pregnant, gears their sex life toward procreation rather than desire. He finds his office claustrophobic. Then, at the Tate Museum, he spots Nola, recently returned to London. He is able to secure her number, and they resume their affair with even more intensity. Consequently, Chris leads a frantic life, trying to spend as much time as possible in bed with Nola while concealing his infidelities. Eventually, he tells Nola that he is considering leaving Chloe, even though such a move will cost him his career and significantly impact his lifestyle.

A few months later, Nola discovers she's pregnant and informs Chris she intends to have his child. Chris agrees to tell Chloe everything, but when the opportunity arises, Chris denies his involvement with anyone else and attributes his unhappiness to his dependence on his father-in-law and to his inability to impregnate Chloe. It seems that Chris is simply deceiving his wife in order to buy himself time to find a way of appeasing Nola without sacrificing his wealth and status; however, Chris unexpectedly calls on an old friend from his tennis-playing days and explains his dilemma. After articulating his feelings, he concludes that he truly loves Chloe and that his relationship with Nola is purely lust.

Although Chris has decided to stay with his wife, he refuses to deal honestly with either woman, keeping his affair secret from Chloe while reassuring Nola that he's going to tell his wife everything and ask for a divorce. As Nola grows increasingly demanding and threatens to confront Chloe herself, Chris formulates a plan to murder Nola. After sneaking one of his father-in-law's shotguns from the estate in his tennis bag, he arranges to meet his wife at the theater that evening and then scurries off to Nola's building. There, he shoots an elderly neighbor and pockets her prescription medications and jewelry; this murder leaves him shaken, but he goes through with the second part of his plan and kills Nola as she steps out of the lift. In a cab en route to the theater, he begins to cry but quickly pulls himself together. He meets Chloe, checks his tennis bag at the theater, and watches Andrew Lloyd Webber's *The Woman in White*.

The next morning Chloe reads of Nola's murder, and Chris appears convincingly surprised. Because there had been several burglaries in the neighborhood, the police believe that the crimes have been committed by drug addicts interrupted during a theft.

Chris's luck seems to be holding up, and it is not long before Chloe announces she is pregnant. But Chris's fortunes reverse when the police discover that Nola kept a diary in which she detailed the affair. On his way to an interview with the detectives, Chris disposes of the jewelry and medications by tossing everything in the Thames; however, in a sequence paralleling the opening footage, the neighbor's wedding ring strikes a railing, bounces up, and falls on the pavement rather than into the water. Chris, who has turned and hurried off, does not see that the ring has failed to clear the railing. At the police station he admits to the affair and begs the officers to be discreet. The officers agree that there is no need to reveal anything about Chris's personal life, provided, of course, he is innocent, and Chris is allowed to leave after finishing his statement. That night Chris falls asleep at his laptop and dreams that Nola and her neighbor pay him a visit. "You can learn to push guilt under the rug," he claims. But whether Chris feels guilty, it seems inevitable that he will be found guilty. A jump cut to the bedroom of one of the detectives has the man bolting upright from a dream and announcing he knows how Chris committed the murders.

Luck intercedes once again. Before the detective can resume his investigation, another shotgun shooting occurs, and the victim, a junkie, has the wedding ring in his pocket. The film ends with a family celebration as Chloe and Chris return home with their newborn. A champagne toast is offered, and Tom, referring to the baby, declares, "I don't care if he's great. I just hope he's lucky."

MEAN MACHINE (2001)

DIRECTOR: Barry Skolnick. SCREENPLAY: Charlie Fletcher, Chris Baker, Andrew Day, based on the original screenplay *The Longest Yard* by Tracy Keenan Wynn. PRODUCER: Matthew Vaughn. CINEMATOGRAPHY: Alex Barber. EDITING: Eddie Hamilton, Dayn Williams. MUSIC: Marilyn Mason, John Murphy. PRODUCTION DESIGN: Russell De Rozario. ART DIRECTION: Tom Wales. COSTUME DESIGN: Stephanie Collie.

CAST: Vinnie Jones (Danny Meehan), Jason Statham (Monk), David Hemmings (the governor), David Kelly (Doc), Vas Blackwood (Massive).

RUNNING TIME: 99 minutes.

DVD: Paramount.

Directed by Barry Skolnick, *Mean Machine* is a British remake of the American football movie *The Longest Yard* (1974), which was scripted by Tracy Keenan Wynn and directed by Robert Aldrich. The game in *Mean Machine* is soccer, yet the overall subject and the themes remain much the same. Vinnie Jones, a British soccer star with a handful of film credits, takes on the Burt Reynolds role. Jones lacks Reynolds's boyishness and humor, but his hard edge is in keeping with the grittiness of the film. Although *Mean Machine*, featuring law enforcement officers and convicts, is not a comedy, it has its comedic touches. Like its predecessor, the film begins with the protagonist being jailed for drunken driving and assault on a police officer, being transferred to a jail at the request of the warden ("governor" [David Hemmings] in this film), then being asked to coach the prison guards' team. Again, the inmate refuses, but this time for a different reason. The chief guard, Mr. Burton (Ralph Brown), already has the coaching job and tells Danny Meehan (Vinnie Jones) to turn down the offer. The plot is complicated by the governor's gambling addiction and by Sykes (John Forgeham), a crime boss who runs the prison and who has introduced the governor to betting. After two convicts goad Danny into a fight, Danny is put into solitary, and when he is released, he again turns down the governor's offer, despite learning that his one-year sentence has been increased to three. Back in solitary, Danny finds out from Massive (Vas Blackwood), a black ally who becomes the convict team's manager, that one way to get out of solitary is to convince the governor to agree to a soccer game between the cops and the cons.

The problem is recruiting good players. With the aid of Massive and Doc (David Kelly), an elderly inmate who acts as Danny's advisor, Danny finds talent in unlikely places. Danny's overweight Iranian cellmate (Omid Djalili) and Trojan (Robbie Gee), a dreadlocked convict, are the only players who display soccer skills, but they are aided by Monk (Jason Stratham), a sociopath who has reportedly killed twenty-three people with his bare hands—before he learned martial arts. Monk is the goalkeeper. Help comes from an unexpected source (only to those who are not familiar with *The Longest Yard* and who ignore the early exchange of meaningful glances between Danny and the governor's secretary). Tracey, the governor's secretary, furnishes Danny with films of the guards' games; Tracey is also ready for some action with Danny.

Danny's efforts are undermined by a double-crossing convict who works in the kitchen and who wants to exchange information about the convict team for a transfer to a better prison. If he can kill Danny, he expects his transfer, but the bomb he plants kills Doc, not Danny; and his reward is a transfer, not to a better prison, but to an insane asylum. The guards have double-crossed him. Without Sykes's men, some of whom are talented soccer players, Danny's team hasn't a chance, so Danny approaches Sykes for help. If Danny will fight one of Sykes's men, Sykes will agree to let his men play for Danny. The fight is a brutal one; seated across from each other, each with a hand chained to the table, the two exchange blows with their free hands. Sykes substitutes a ringer for Danny's announced opponent, but Danny somehow wins the battle.

Sykes pressures Danny to ensure the cons will defeat the cops, but the governor, who has bet heavily on the guards, is counting on a large profit. As a result, Danny is between the proverbial rock and a hard place. At this point the film cuts between the cons and the guards: the governor tells his players that each of them is playing for his job; Danny appeals to his players to win for themselves and their self-respect. The head guard declares that the game is about "character."

The game is in many ways similar to the one in *The Longest Yard*. The cons wear new uniforms stolen from the guards. The game has announcers, but Bob and Bob (Jake Abraham and Jason Flemyng) are more comedic and profane than their predecessors. The soccer action is interspersed by undetected fouls, and the cons take an early lead. There are, however, no cheerleaders, and the convicts are not released from their cells to watch the game. At the half the governor tells Danny that he has been implicated in Doc's death and that he faces thirty years in prison if the guards lose. Danny is reluctant to give in, but he agrees after being reminded that he's "done it before." In the second half Danny plays so badly that his teammates know he's throwing the game, and he finally fakes an injury and sits on the bench. The guards take the lead 2–1 before Danny returns to the game. At this point Sykes, who has told the officials that he is the team's owner and is sitting on the bench, talks to Danny about winning the game. Soon the cons have tied the score, and as time runs out, Danny breaks free and heads for the opponent's goal, stopping only to kick the ball in front of Billy, who scores the winning goal off Danny's assist.

After the game there is an explosion (the governor's Saab has been blown up), and the governor threatens Danny. Mr. Burton, who has come to respect Danny as a player and a man, shakes hands with Danny and defies orders from the governor, who is left standing by himself as the former adversaries walk away from him. Although Danny's life is not in danger in the film, *Mean Machine* is a more violent, less comedic, more realistic film about prison life and society than its source. Unfortunately, it is also less entertaining.

MEN WITH BROOMS (2002)

DIRECTOR: Paul Gross. SCREENPLAY: Paul Gross, John Kriznac, Paul Quarrington. PRODUCER: Robert Lantos. CINEMATOGRAPHY: Thom Best. EDITING: Susan Maggi. MUSIC: Paul Gross, Jack Lenz. PRODUCTION DESIGN: Paul D. Austerberry. ART DIRECTION: Nigel Churcher. COSTUME DESIGN: Noreen Landry.

CAST: Paul Gross (Chris Cutter), Molly Parker (Amy Folley), Leslie Nielsen (Gordon Cutter), James Allodi (Neil Bucyk), Jed Rees (Eddie Strombeck), Peter Outerbridge (James Lennox).

RUNNING TIME: 102 minutes.

DVD: Artisan Entertainment.

Men with Brooms is an English-Canadian comedy about curling, a sport often described as shuffleboard on ice. Unlike ice hockey, curling is a slow-paced, noncontact sport in which teams of four alternate sliding ("throwing") forty-two-pound granite ovals ("stones") across a sheet of ice toward a target zone. After the stone is thrown, its direction and speed can be controlled by sweepers, who smooth the ice with brooms just ahead of the stone. If a sweeper touches ("burns") a stone, it is his or her responsibility to call the foul. Honorable conduct is expected in curling, and the game is often played without referees.

Writer, director, and star Paul Gross draws on the curling code of honor to set up his story. His character, Chris Cutter, having failed to call a burnt stone on his team, is so guilt ridden that he cannot face the people he loves. Consequently, he strands his fiancée—his coach's older daughter, Julie (Michelle Nolden)—at the altar, hurls the team stones in a lake, and skips town. With the subsequent demise of the team, the remaining members have found happiness illusive. Neil Bucyk (James Allodi) is dissatisfied with his social-climbing wife and with the undertaking business that he has acquired from his father-in-law. Unlike Neil, Eddie Strombeck (Jed Rees) is absolutely blissful about his marriage, but he suffers from a low sperm count and feels his life is incomplete because of his inability to start a family. James Lennox (Peter Outerbridge) has become a small-time drug dealer in trouble over a debt to his supplier.

The film begins ten years later with the death of Coach Foley (James B. Douglas), who collapses while retrieving the curling stones from the lake. A codicil in his will requests that his ashes be placed in the stones and that the team reunite to win the Golden Broom competition by placing "his" stone in the center of the target. But carrying out the coach's final wishes requires each of the curlin' men to confront his own problems. For Chris, this means confessing his breech of code to his former teammates, renewing his relationship with his estranged father, and facing Julie, now an astronaut. The first two tasks are relatively simple. Chris's teammates offer immediate forgiveness, and Chris finds a good reason to approach his father when it becomes apparent that the rusty team is in desperate need of a coach. Making up with Julie proves more difficult since she was both hurt and humiliated by his abandonment. Although he is able to admit that he did love her, he is confused about his current feelings, which are complicated by his affection for Julie's younger sister, Amy (Molly Parker), a single parent and recovering alcoholic who has fallen in love with him.

While the love triangle is painful for all of the parties involved, the tone of the film remains light. The presence of Coach Foley, whose ashes Chris totes around in the curling stone, is played for laughs; occasionally the coach narrates from beyond the grave. Much of the humor is specifically Canadian. Beavers appear almost mystically, at one point blocking the road and forcing the team to stop Neil's hearse, which they are using for transportation. Their attempt to urge the beavers along using curling brooms fails when a beaver chomps on a broom, sending the team a message. The film also pokes fun at the leisurely pace of the sport, and in their first contest the reestablished team is walloped by a group of octogenarians, one of whom plays using a walker.

It is after this defeat that Chris calls upon his father, Gordon (Leslie Nielsen), a retired player who now raises hallucinogenic mushrooms (the fertilization of which fuels another set of jokes). Gordon subjects the curlers to a rigorous training program, interrupted at frequent intervals by Eddie's wife, whose fertility cycles determine when they will attempt to conceive. By the time tournament day arrives, the team has improved, but they must play against a "rink" that includes Alexander Yount (Greg Bryk), an Olympic medalist. (Curling became an Olympic sport in 1998.) The match stays close, tension mounts, and Chris, troubled by his complex relationships with Julie and Amy, once again fails to call a burnt rock. This time, Chris's lapse demoralizes the team and reopens the breach with his father. Chris faces the situation he's created by taking Coach Foley's remains to a local bar, where, after he pays for his beer, he asks the price of the glass and the television, plunks the money on the bar, and throws the glass at the television. In the context of the film, this is the Canadian version of drunk and disorderly conduct. Before he can create more trouble, Amy appears. She has had a heart-to-heart talk with her sister, who is about to be launched into outer space by the Americans. Julie accepts that Amy loves Chris; Chris just needs to acknowledge that he loves Amy. In order to pull himself together, Chris visits his mother's grave only to find his father there. The two men touch hands, and Gordon advises his son "Amy is the one" for him.

As the tournament continues, now with Gordon replacing Neil, who has caved in to pressure from his wife and quit, the team manages to make it to the finals, where once again they meet up with Alexander Yount. The match proceeds with predictable tension, and the outcome rests, not surprisingly, on Chris making an impossible throw. He executes a perfect shot, but one of the sweepers burns a stone, a foul only Chris witnesses. This time, Chris calls the burnt stone, demonstrating that he has rejoined the ranks of respectability among both curlers and citizens. But the tournament doesn't end here. The Olympian Alexander demonstrates his sportspersonship by allowing Chris's team to replay the throw. On his final throw, Chris hurls the stone containing Coach Foley with enough force to clear the target of the opposing team's stones and leave the coach's remains in the center, in accordance with his last wishes.

The movie uses a celebration to tie up the plotlines in the manner of a Shakespearean comedy with all of the characters properly paired off. Eddie's wife has conceived, and the drug dealer who has been after Lennox turns out to be a curlin' man himself and forgives the debt. As the film closes, a colony of beavers cross the road, an unseen hand hurls the curling stones back into the lake, and as the credits continue, outtakes are shown, reminding the viewer—in case there was ever any doubt—of the fictitious nature of *Men with Brooms.*

MICKEY (2004)

DIRECTOR: Hugh Wilson. SCREENPLAY: John Grisham. PRODUCER: John Grisham. MUSIC: Guy Moon. COSTUME DESIGN: Johnetta Boone.
CAST: Shawn Salinas (Mickey), Harry Connick Jr. (Glen), Michelle Johnson (Patty), Mike Starr (Tony), Gill Baker (Peggy), Danny Bell (Griff).
RUNNING TIME: 90 minutes.
DVD: Starz/Anchor Bay Entertainment.

Assuming a new identity, a man on the run from the IRS signs his son up for the local Little League, but the team's success brings unwanted attention.

THE MIGHTY DUCKS (1992)

DIRECTOR: Stephen Herek. SCREENPLAY: Steven Brill. PRODUCERS: Jon Avnet, Jordan Kerner. CINEMATOGRAPHY: Thomas Del Ruth. EDITING: Larry Bock, John F. Link. MUSIC: David Newman. PRODUCTION DESIGN: Randy Ser. ART DIRECTION: Tony Fanning. COSTUME DESIGN: Grania Preston.
CAST: Emilio Estevez (Gordon Bombay), Joss Ackland (Hans), Lane Smith (Jack Reilly), Joshua Jackson (Charlie Conway), Elden Henson (Fulton Reed), Heidi Kling (Casey Conway).
RUNNING TIME: 100 minutes.
DVD: Walt Disney Video.

The Mighty Ducks, the first in a series of family-oriented Disney films, bears a strong resemblance to *The Bad News Bears* (1976)—a reluctant and cranky coach takes over a ragtag team of kids and turns them into winners who have lessons to teach the adults in their lives. The sport is ice hockey rather than baseball, and the coach is a young never-was who drinks (Emilio Estevez) instead of an old has-been who drinks (Walter Mathau).

In 1973, young Gordon Bombay (Estevez), a promising hockey player still grieving over the death of his father, blew a penalty shot that would have clinched the championship for his team and his harsh coach, Jack Reilly (Lane Smith). The ridicule and criticism he receives cause him to hang up his skates. He grows up to become a lawyer obsessed with winning. After a particularly satisfying victory in court, Gordon is cautioned by his boss, Mr. Ducksworth, to exercise restraint, advice Gordon ignores. He is arrested for driving while intoxicated and faces a judge with whom he has clashed in the past. Mr. Ducksworth intervenes and arranges a deal. He will grant Gordon a leave of absence to complete community service—coaching an ice hockey team.

Gordon arrives at the first practice in a limousine and orders the driver to pull right onto the ice. He announces that he "hates kids" and "hates hockey." The children, who have surrounded the limo, begin to rock it. Then they pile inside, and Gordon instructs the chauffeur to drive them across the ice. This bit of foolishness is witnessed by a parent, who shrieks that he has endangered the children's lives, and Gordon declares that practice is over.

Gordon's players are undisciplined and poorly equipped. He does little to prepare them for their first game, which is against his former team, the Hawks. Reilly is still the coach and is still angry about the 1973 loss, the only blot on his record.

Gordon's team plays badly, and Reilly lets his boys run up the score. At the next practice, Gordon shows the boys how to take a fall and fake an injury in order to draw penalties. However, one boy—Charlie

Emilio Estevez (right) as Gordon Bombay, meeting his team in *The Mighty Ducks*

Emilio Estevez coaching his team in *The Mighty Ducks*

Conway (Joshua Jackson)—refuses to cheat, and those who do ham it up, drawing criticism from officials, opponents, and parents.

After the team's second loss, Gordon visits his former mentor, Hans (Joss Ackland), who owns a sporting goods store. The walls are lined with framed clippings and photos of young Gordon with his father. Hans encourages Gordon to teach his team to have fun and gives him a pair of skates. That night, Gordon skates, remembering himself as a boy and the sheer pleasure of playing hockey while his father watched. Then he visits Charlie to apologize. Charlie invites Gordon to stay for dinner. Charlie's mother, Casey (Heidi Kling), is a single parent, and a romantic subplot ensues.

Gordon directs his energies toward improving the team. He persuades Mr. Ducksworth to support the team by suggesting the name Mighty Ducks. With fifteen thousand dollars of the firm's money, Gordon takes his players to Hans's store, and soon the team is fully outfitted. At practice, Gordon helps the youngsters overcome their fears and develop their skills. He adds to the roster a figure skater, Tammy (Jane Plank), who is the sister of another player, and a youngster with a killer slap shot (Elden Henson as Fulton Reed) who can't skate. Soon the Ducks are flocking together and have a good chance of making the playoffs.

Conflict arises when Hans informs Gordon that because of redistricting, the Hawks' star, Adam Banks (Vincent Larusso), should be a Duck. Now that Gordon is insistent on playing by the rules, he demands that Adam play for the Ducks or not at all. Gordon files an official protest that displeases nearly everyone: Adam's father, a friend of Ducksworth, wants Adam to remain a Hawk, as does Coach Reilly. Adam is not particularly keen on playing against the Hawks, and the Ducks don't want Adam playing for them. The Ducks rebel. All but Fulton and Charlie refuse to play, and the team forfeits a game. Gordon decides to resign as coach, a decision that upsets Charlie. But when

Ducksworth pressures Gordon to drop his protest and allow Adam to remain a Hawk, Gordon refuses. Ducksworth fires him on the spot, prompting Gordon to quack on his way out. Meanwhile, at the school the Ducks attend, the players have quarreled about the forfeited match, but the principal's intervention has led to a quackfest on the part of the team. When Gordon arrives at the school, hoping to rally the players, he finds them in detention for quacking at the principal. The reunited team accepts Adam after some initial reluctance, and the team moves closer to a showdown against the Hawks.

The championship match pits Ducks and Hawks in a predictable contest. Reilly encourages his team to take cheap shots and "finish off" Adam, who is intentionally slammed into a goal post. Adam's injury requires that he leave the game, so it's up to the original players to salvage the championship. Tammy executes a distracting spin, Fulton scores with his terrifying slap shot, and the "flying V" play leads to a penalty shot that can win the tournament. Charlie is now in the same position Gordon was in as a boy, but with support and encouragement, rather than unbearable pressure, from coach and team, Charlie makes the shot.

In the closing scene, the Ducks are seeing Charlie off—he is trying out for a minor league team, but he has promised to return to coach the Ducks and presumably to continue his relationship with Charlie's mother.

Although *The Mighty Ducks* was panned by reviewers, it was a profitable and popular film, spawning two sequels and an animation. When the Disney-owned ice hockey team joined the National Hockey League in 1993 as an expansion team, it was named the Mighty Ducks of Anaheim. The name was later changed to the Anaheim Ducks. Disney sold the team in 2005.

MIKE BASSETT: ENGLAND MANAGER (2001)

DIRECTOR: Steve Barron. SCREENPLAY: John R. Smith, Rob Sprackling. PRODUCERS: Steve Barron, Neil Peplow. CINEMATOGRAPHY: Mike Eley. EDITING: Colin Green. MUSIC: Antony Glen, Duncan Mackay, Mike Neary. PRODUCTION DESIGN: John Reid. ART DIRECTION: Ged Boyan, Ged Bryan, Marcos Flaksman. COSTUME DESIGN: Siobhan Barron.

CAST: Ricky Tomlinson (Mike Bassett), Bradley Walsh (Dave Dodds), Amanda Redman (Karine Bassett), Philip Jackson (Lonnie Urquart), Pelé (himself), Ronaldo (himself).

RUNNING TIME: 89 minutes.

DVD: Entertainment in Video (UK: PAL).

This British mockumentary is about an obnoxious and inept manager who takes over the national football (soccer) team.

MILLION DOLLAR BABY (2004)

DIRECTOR: Clint Eastwood. SCREENPLAY: Paul Haggis, based on the stories of F. X. Toole. PRODUCERS: Clint Eastwood, Paul Haggis, Tom Rosenberg, Albert S. Ruddy. CINEMATOGRAPHY: Tom Stern. EDITING: Joel Cox. MUSIC: Clint Eastwood. PRODUCTION DESIGN: Henry Bumstead. ART DIRECTION: Jack G. Taylor Jr. COSTUME DESIGN: Deborah Hopper.

CAST: Clint Eastwood (Frankie Dunn), Hilary Swank (Maggie Fitzgerald), Morgan Freeman (Eddie "Scrap" Dupris), Brian O'Byrne (Father Horvak), Michael Peña (Omar), Anthony Mackie (Shawrelle Berry), Jay Baruchel (Danger Barch).

RUNNING TIME: 132 minutes.

ACADEMY AWARDS: Best Picture, Best Director, Best Actress (Swank), Best Supporting Actor (Freeman). NOMINATIONS: Best Actor (Eastwood), Best Adapted Screenplay, Best Editing.

DVD: Warner Home Video.

Million Dollar Baby, directed by Clint Eastwood—who also plays the male lead, Frankie, a gym owner and trainer—was a commercial and critical success, grossing over $200 million internationally and providing Eastwood (Best Director), Hilary Swank (Best Actress), and Morgan Freeman (Best Supporting Actor) with Oscars. The film resonated with audiences who could identify with the themes: failed family relationships, individualism, and perseverance. Like most successful boxing films, *Million Dollar Baby* uses the sport as a means of exploring human relationships and current social/political issues, in this case, euthanasia. Freeman's voice-over narration describes and comments on events, but not until the end of the film does the audience learn that the narration is to be contained in a letter to Frankie's estranged daughter, who has been returning unopened her father's many letters.

As a manager, Frankie attempts to protect his fighters, postponing their chances for title bouts until he thinks they are "ready," a state they never achieve under his tutelage; consequently, other managers step in, sign them to contracts, and promote matches that take them to the top. Willie (Mike Colter), whom Frankie has treated as a son, even lending him money during tough times, is a case in point; he signs with Mickey Mack (Bruce MacVittie), gets a shot at the title, and wins. Scrap (Morgan Freeman), Frankie's assistant, tells Frankie that in protecting Willie he was also giving Willie the impression that he didn't believe in him.

This scenario is nearly repeated with Frankie and Maggie (Hilary Swank), a thirty-eight-year-old woman who wants Frankie to train and manage her. When she first approaches Frankie, he says, "I don't train girls," but she is persistent, working out for long hours on the heavy bag and winning the approval of Scrap, who shows her how to use the bag correctly and lends her Frankie's speed bag. By scrimping and by eating orts from the diner where she waitresses, Maggie saves enough to buy her own speed bag. Frankie notices her hard work but tries to discourage her by saying she is "too old" to fight and describing women's boxing as "the latest freak show." He finally relents, providing that she stop calling him "boss," and shows her how to breathe properly when she is working on the speed bag. Explaining that she has nothing except for boxing, Maggie describes her dysfunctional family, and she later tells Frankie that he is all she has. Frankie's family situation is similar. Although he writes unanswered letters to his daughter and prays for her nightly, she does not seek reconciliation with him. His daily attendance at mass doesn't seem to help, and the priest, who tells him that his attendance indicates a person who cannot forgive himself, calls him a "fucking pagan."

Still unwilling to commit to Maggie, Frankie turns her over to Sally Mendoza (Ned Eisenberg), who sets up her first fight. However, when the fight goes badly, Frankie steps in and calls her "my fighter," and she wins the bout. Her question, "You going to leave me again?" reflects the interdependence she and Frankie have. She has become his surrogate daughter, another daughter who would be hurt by his leaving. Other victories, mostly by knockouts, follow in rapid succession, but Frankie is reluctant to arrange fights with more challenging competition. Scrap, afraid that Frankie will let his desire to protect Maggie prevent her from getting a title bout, warns her that Frankie may not be the one to take her to the title and introduces her to Mickey Mack, who had led Willie to a championship, but Maggie refuses to leave Frankie. Frankie then arranges a fight for Maggie in England; after telling her that her opponent is younger, stronger, and more experienced, he asks, "What are you going to do about it?" Maggie wins.

After more victories, Maggie has enough money to buy her mother a home, but this well-intentioned act of generosity backfires. Her mother (Margo Martindale) wants money instead. After claiming that people are laughing at Maggie's boxing career, Mrs. Fitzgerald advises her to "live proper" and "find a man." The homecoming visit, however, is not without its benefits. Maggie's memory of an incident from her childhood foreshadows events at the end of the film. She recalls her father taking his beloved but aging dog out into the woods to put the animal out of his misery. She and Frankie also visit Ira and Rosalie's Place, which Maggie claims makes the world's best lemon pie. At the end of the film, the audience sees the diner in flashback and remembers Frankie's off-hand question about the place being for sale. More foreshadowing is provided in the scene at the gym when Maggie says she wants to fly to Las Vegas for her title shot and then to drive back home. She does travel by vehicle on her way home, but it is in a specially equipped ambulance. What happens to her is also foreshadowed by what happens to Danger, an ironically named kid who aspires to greatness but is totally without talent and who is badly beaten by a skilled, mean-spirited boxer.

In Las Vegas Maggie is beating the Blue Bear (Lucia Rijker, a professional boxer and title holder), the champion, but at the end of a round, forgetting Frankie's oft-repeated admonition to always "protect yourself," Maggie turns away from the champ at the bell, gets hit, and falls, hitting her head on the stool Frankie has just put in her corner. When she awakens, she is a quadriplegic in a hospital bed, blaming herself for what happened. Frankie is similarly beset by guilt, believing he shouldn't have trained her. The arrival of Maggie's family, intent on forcing her to sign papers giving them all her possessions, only makes matters worse. For the next year and a half she suffers from bed sores, bites off her own tongue, has a leg amputated, and asks Frankie to do what her father did for his dog. She explains that she had it all and doesn't want to lose it. Frankie, however, is reluctant to let go. He reads to her at her bedside and suggests she could attend college. When she asks him the meaning of the Gaelic "Mo cuishle" on her boxing robe, she learns that it is "my darling, my blood." Finally, Frankie enters her room, disconnects the oxygen, and gives her a shot to stay asleep while she passes away. Scrap has the last words, as he reveals that the narration is intended to be a letter to Frankie's estranged daughter. However, since the film never identifies the source of conflict between Frankie and his daughter, the letter seems more a dramatic device allowing Scrap to narrate than an attempt to bring about a reconciliation. The viewer is left to wonder if Frankie purchases the diner famous for its lemon pie.

MILLION DOLLAR LEGS (1932)

DIRECTOR: Edward F. Cline. SCREENPLAY: Joseph Mankiewicz, Henry Myers, Ben Hecht, Nicholas T. Barrows. PRODUCER: Herman J. Mankiewicz. CINEMATOGRAPHY: Arthur L. Todd.

CAST: W. C. Fields (the President), Jack Oakie (Migg Tweeny), Andy Clyde (the Major-Domo), Susan Fleming (Angela), Ben Turpin (mysterious man), Dickie Moore (Willie).

RUNNING TIME: 64 minutes. B&W.

VHS: Universal Studios.

This zany comedy from the era of the Great Depression lampoons politics, love stories, and the Olympics. Based on a screen story by Joseph Mankiewicz, the plot includes an attempted coup in the fictitious country

Klopstokia, a romance between an American brush salesman and the daughter of Klopstokia's president, and the efforts of the Klopstokian Olympic team to save the country from bankruptcy, thus preventing the overthrow of the President and enabling the marriage of his daughter and the American to take place.

Klopstokia, population roughly eighty-one thousand, is known for its goats and nuts. All of the men are named George; all of the women, Angela; and the President (W. C. Fields) maintains power because he is physically the strongest man in the country. When the film opens, Migg Tweeny (Jack Oakie), the brush salesman, is hurrying to meet the owner of the brush company, Mr. Baldwin (George Barbier), at the dock where their ship is about to disembark. In his haste Migg knocks down a young woman (Susan Fleming) and falls immediately in love. After he brushes her off with his wares, he hails a passing carriage, which he mistakes for a taxi. The carriage is transporting the President and stops because the Angela with whom Migg has fallen in love is the President's daughter. Migg is tossed out, but manages to get to the ship. Mr. Baldwin is in a hurry to leave Klopstokia because he is an avid sports fan and doesn't want to miss the Olympic tryouts. Migg decides to stay behind and goes off in search of Angela.

The scene shifts to the President's office, where the cabinet is planning to take control of the government. This overthrow hinges on the country's debt and the President's wrestling ability. If the President fails to produce eight million dollars and/or if the Secretary of the Treasury can beat him at arm wrestling or Indian wrestling, the coup will succeed. The cabinet meeting is brief: first the President wins the arm wrestling contest and then orders the assembled group to find a way to produce income; the cabinet demands power, resulting in an Indian wrestling contest that the President also wins. Meanwhile, Migg and Angela have been reunited; Migg has proposed, and Angela has revealed that her father is the President and may respond violently to Migg's proposal. Instead of injuring "Sweetheart," as Migg is called, the President orders him shot. Angela and her father then begin a discussion worthy of Shakespeare as she talks of her love and her father ponders his fiscal problems. Outside, Sweetheart appears to be demonstrating his brushes to the soldiers assigned to execute him. The President concludes that he needs a wizard, and Angela, believing Sweetheart is one, given his persuasive powers, recommends his services. Sweetheart and the President strike a deal: if Sweetheart can raise $8 million, he can marry Angela. After witnessing the President's great strength—he literally tosses a row of soldiers from his office in a fit of pique—Sweetheart suggests the country enter the Olympics. If the President can win a gold medal in weightlifting, Sweetheart reasons, Mr. Baldwin will bail out Klopstokia.

When the cabinet members hear of the plan, they meet secretly in an underground chamber and scheme to destroy the morale of the athletes by enlisting Mata Machree (Lyda Roberti, parodying Greta Garbo's performance in the 1932 film, *Mata Hari*), the world's most irresistible woman. However, Angela and Sweetheart have stumbled onto the lift that provides access to the secret chamber and overhear the plan. Back at government headquarters, the President sends his Major-Domo (Andy Clyde), disguised as a goat, to find Angela. When he locates her with Sweetheart, they are frightened by his costume and flee first on horseback, then by car and by boat, but the Major-Domo is able to keep up with them; once they recognize him, he is recruited for the track team. A bit later Angela gives Sweetheart a copy of a traditional love song, which she says he must sing to her to seal their engagement, but she startles him with the information that the hide on which the song is inscribed is that of her late grandfather. Sweetheart drops the hide, which falls over the rail of a high bridge into the water below. Angela executes a perfect swan dive and rescues her late grandfather without missing a beat. Sweetheart discovers that nearly all of the Georges and Angelas are gifted athletes, and soon the Klopstokian Olympic team, the corrupt cabinet, and the seductive Mata Machree sail for the United States.

During the voyage, Sweetheart attempts to serenade Angela with the traditional love song (actually, the title song with Kloptokian lyrics from the Maurice Chevalier-Jeanette MacDonald romantic comedy *One Night with You*), but each time he is interrupted and must rescue one of the Georges from Mata's clutches; each time Angela appears just as Mata has turned her charms on Sweetheart. By the time the group has boarded a train for Los Angeles, Angela is unhappy with Sweetheart because of Mata, and the conspirators are unhappy with Mata about her apparent failure; however Mata has a plan. On the eve of the games, she arranges to meet each athlete, to whom she has privately professed her love, at a club. The men are not pleased to discover the presence of the others, and they begin to fight. The next day, the Georges are demoralized—and injured. While Sweetheart attempts a pep talk, Angela, having realized that he can resist Mata, takes matters into her own hands. She confronts Mata, who runs off, and the chase takes both women into the diving competition, which Angela wins while pursuing Mata. Mata surrenders and confesses to the athletes that she was flirting with them as part of the conspiracy to overthrow the President.

Now determined to do their part to save Klopstokia, the Georges go off to compete, and Angela and Sweetheart urge them on. The final event, in which the President is participating, is weight lifting. Klopstokia needs just one more gold medal to finish in first place, but the Secretary of the Treasury has entered the contest as an independent and has persuaded Mata to "inspire" him. Each time the Secretary must lift a weight to keep up with the President, Mata dances. As the weights get heavier, the dance becomes more animated. With the contest even and the weights at half a ton, the Secretary and Mata are too exhausted to continue. It appears the President has also run out of energy until Sweetheart steps on his foot to anger him. The trick works, and the raging President not only lifts the weight, but also hurls it at Sweetheart with such force that it sails beyond its target. The fleeing Sweetheart trips over the weight; the President wins gold medals for both weight lifting *and* shot put; Mr. Baldwin offers to bankroll the President; and Angela and Sweetheart are now free to marry.

Million Dollar Legs was released a few weeks before the opening ceremony of the 1932 Olympics in Los Angeles, so it was able both to profit from excitement about the upcoming event and to contribute to that excitement. The film was well received, and the Olympics set attendance records. These celluloid games bear little resemblance to the real thing. Some of the jumps and dives were performed by stunt doubles, and to simulate extraordinary athletic feats, film was reversed and run at slower or faster speeds. For the most part, the camera remains stationary and the comedy is performed as if on stage.

The title, like much of the film, is tangential to the plot. Susan Fleming, a former Ziegfeld Follies dancer, became known as "the girl with the million dollar legs" after the release of the film, although the honorific was transferred to Betty Grable, who made an entirely different film with the same title in 1939. Fleming retired from film after marrying Harpo Marx in 1936.

MIRACLE (2004)

DIRECTOR: Gavin O'Connor. SCREENPLAY: Eric Guggenheim. PRODUCERS: Marc Ciardi, Gordon Gray. CINEMATOGRAPHY: Dan Stoloff. EDITING: John Gilroy, Daric Loo. MUSIC: Mark Isham. PRODUCTION DESIGN: John Willett. ART DIRECTION: Ross Dempster, Martina Javorova. COSTUME DESIGN: Tom Bronson.

CAST: Kurt Russell (Herb Brooks), Patricia Clarkson (Patty Brooks), Noah Emmerich (Craig Patrick), Patrick Dempsey (Mike Eruzione), Nathan West (Rob McClanahan).

RUNNING TIME: 135 minutes.

DVD: Walt Disney Video.

Miracle is based on the 1980 U.S. Olympic ice hockey team's gold medal run. Director Gavin O'Connor places the team's achievement in a historical setting to spotlight the role of sports in revitalizing national pride, but the story itself focuses on Coach Herb Brooks's role in assembling and training the team.

The film opens with newsreel footage reflecting events of the 1960s that divided Americans and from the 1970s that dampened the national spirit, from the Soviet Union's defeating the United States and winning the gold medal in basketball in 1972, through Watergate, the fall of Saigon, the Three Mile Island nuclear accident, the toxic waste disaster of Love Canal, the Iranian hostage crisis, and gas shortages. Then the scene shifts to Colorado Springs in early 1979, where Herb Brooks (Kurt Russell), hockey coach at the University of Minnesota, is meeting with officials from the National Hockey Federation. Brooks wants to adopt a hybrid style of Canadian and Russian play in order to defeat Eastern bloc teams. The United States has fared badly in previous contests because of rules barring professionals from Olympic play. Communist countries, which did not allow privately owned professional teams, claimed amateur status for their state-supported athletes. In the United States the most talented amateurs turned pro early; consequently, the Americans fielded teams of college all-stars, which, according to Brooks, "fail because they rely solely on the individual's talent."

Back in St. Paul, Brooks tells his wife, Patty (Patricia Clarkson), he doesn't think he'll get the job, but later that evening, as the Brookses host a costume party about which Herb is unenthusiastic, the phone rings, and he's offered the position. Brooks returns to Colorado Springs, where the amateur ice hockey association is holding tryouts. Committee members have assumed that the tryouts will continue for at least a week and that they will have a say in which players are selected. However, Herb needs only a day to winnow the bunch to twenty-six young men, mostly players from Minnesota and Boston. In spite of complaints from the would-be advisors that he has eliminated some of the best players, Herb's decision stands after he reiterates that the best players have not in the past produced winning teams.

With seven months to train, Herb establishes himself as a hard-nosed, demanding coach. His strategy for building unity on a team rife with conflict is to make himself unpopular by enforcing strict rules and pushing the players well beyond their comfort levels. Still, regional rivalries and personal grudges threaten to undermine the team's progress. The East Coast players and the Northwesterners regard each other with disdain, while two key figures, Jack "O.C." O'Callahan (Michael Mantenuto) and Rob "Mack" McClanahan (Nathan West), continue a quarrel over a cheap shot from a college game three years earlier. After the two slug it out during practice,

Brooks has the players introduce themselves, but he cuts off the introductions when the youngsters identify themselves with reference to their college affiliations.

Herb also faces conflict at home. He is too busy preparing for the Olympics to undertake any family responsibility. When he is not overseeing training, he is viewing tapes and taking notes. Angry that she was excluded from his decision to apply for and then accept the job, Patty confronts Herb about his motives. Herb was the final man cut from the roster of the 1960 team, the last U.S. hockey team to take the gold from the Russians. Patty fears that Herb will continue with this obsession every four years. Herb needs only a bit of time to himself to contemplate the past, represented through the standard photo album tucked away in a drawer. After a short detour down memory lane, Herb joins his wife in bed, where he apologizes and asks for her support; Patty, of course, agrees.

His domestic difficulties resolved, Herb once again concentrates his energies on his team, which still hasn't jelled. During an exhibition match against Norway, he observes the players on the bench ogling the women in the stands rather than focusing on the game. When the match ends in a tie, Herb keeps the team on the ice. Announcing that if they won't work during the game, they'll work after, he puts them through drills skating from one end of the rink to the other. The drills continue into the night after the custodian has cut off the lights. Most of the players are too exhausted to stand, and many are vomiting. The assistant coach, Craig Patrick (Noah Emmerich), and the team physician, Doc Nagobads (Kenneth Welsh), think Herb has worked the players too hard, but Herb calls on Craig to blow the whistle yet again for another run. Then, the team captain, Mike Eruzione (Patrick Demsey), calls out his name, introducing himself not by his college team, but as a player for the United States of America. Herb declares the practice is over.

The athletes, having absorbed the lesson, begin to work together more effectively, but Herb is still not completely happy with their performance. To test them once again, he brings in a talented outsider, Tim Harrer (Adam Knight), and allows him to replace Eruzione, who has not been scoring. Later, a group of players, including O.C. and Mack, tell Herb they think it is wrong to bring in Tim in spite of his skills because the original group is now "family." Herb agrees to dismiss Tim.

As the holidays approach, there are still uncertainties. The powerful Soviet team has soundly defeated a U.S. all-star team, and Herb has faced criticism for scheduling an exhibition game against the Soviets just days before the opening ceremony at Lake Placid. However, Soviet participation in the Winter Olympics is questionable because President Carter, in response to the Soviet invasion of Afghanistan, has called a boycott of the summer games in Moscow. As the coach drives home from a team Christmas party (at which he's been given a bullwhip), he listens to snatches of a Carter speech in which the president addresses the "erosion of confidence in our future." As the speech continues to extol the virtues of working together, the camera cuts to the team tossing a football in the snow.

After the announcement from the Kremlin that the entire Eastern bloc will compete at Lake Placid, Herb must make some key decisions about his roster. He cuts the twenty-first man, Ralph Cox (Kenneth Mitchell), who accepts his fate stoically. Then O.C. is injured in the exhibition match against the Russians, who win 10–3, and Herb must decide whether to replace him. Herb also threatens to remove goalie Jim Craig, who hasn't played his best. When Mack sustains a painful contusion during the first round against Sweden, Herb, after learning from Doc that Mack will not complicate the injury by continuing, orders Mack to get his gear back on. Sweden has taken a 2–1 lead, but the Americans stage a dramatic comeback. With Mack on the ice, they tie the score in the final seconds.

The film scurries past the games leading to the medal round, barely mentioning the stunning 7–3 upset over the Czechoslovakians, instead turning to postmatch press conferences, where Herb comes under fire for not allowing journalists access to individual players. When he is accused of hogging the spotlight, his response is to send Craig to meet the press in his place.

The film devotes over twenty minutes to the United States–Soviet Union contest and incorporates portions of the actual play-by-play featuring Al Michaels, Ken Dryden, and Jim McKay. O'Connor recreated many of the plays and stuck to reality, but there was no need to embellish the script. The United States ties the game just at the end of the first period, and is able to take the lead when the Soviets draw a slashing penalty. Jim Craig protects the goal with save after remarkable save, and the Americans hold off the Russians until the clock runs out. As the fans and the players celebrate, Herb finds a deserted corridor and takes a quiet moment to relish the victory without publically displaying the intensity of his feelings.

The "Miracle Match" was not the final Olympic contest for the United States, which met and defeated Finland a few days later for the gold. But that match is summed up in a voice-over by Herb, acknowledging the national significance of the victory over the Russians. The film ends with the medal ceremony.

O'Connor and crew succeeded in putting together a dramatic film with convincing action. For the most part, he chose hockey players rather than actors for his cast. Plays were choreographed to reconstruct portions of the real Soviet match, and O'Connor actually put his cast through the grueling postmatch drills that create a turning point in the plot. Edmonton Oiler Bill Ranford doubled for Eddie Cahill as goalie, a switch facilitated by the mask. Cahill's character, Jim Craig, is the only player given a back story, but his role is not highly developed. By not individualizing the players, O'Connor reinforces Brooks's emphasis on teamwork rather than personal ability.

THE MIRACLE OF BERN (2003)

DIRECTOR: Sönke Wortmann. SCREENPLAY: Rochus Hahn, Sönke Wortmann. PRODUCERS: Hanno Huth, Tom Spiess, Sönke Wortmann. CINEMATOGRAPHY: Tom Fährmann. EDITING: Ueli Christen. MUSIC: Marcel Barsotti. PRODUCTION DESIGN: Uli Hanisch. COSTUME DESIGN: Ursula Welter.

CAST: Louis Klamroth (Matthias Lubanski), Peter Lohmeyer (Richard Lubanski), Johanna Gastdorf (Christa Lubanski), Mirko Lang (Bruno Lubanski).

RUNNING TIME: 118 minutes.

This German family drama revolves around the 1954 FIFA World Cup when a father and son attend the final.

MOVIE MOVIE (1978)

DIRECTOR: Stanley Donen. SCREENPLAY: Larry Gelbart, Sheldon Keller. PRODUCER: Stanley Donen. CINEMATOGRAPHY: Charles Rosher Jr., Bruce Surtees. EDITING: George Hively. MUSIC: Ralph Burns. ART DIRECTION: Jack Fisk. COSTUME DESIGN: Patricia Norris.

CAST: George C. Scott (Gloves Malloy/Spats Baxter), Trish Van Devere (Betsy McGuire/Isobel Stuart), Eli Wallach (Vince Marlow/Pop), Red Buttons (Pea-

nuts/Jinks Murphy), Harry Hamlin (Joey Popchik).
RUNNING TIME: 105 minutes.
VHS: Magnetic Video.

This comedy spoofs two genres of classic Hollywood—musicals and sports films. Divided into a double bill of separate stories, much of the cast plays a role in each film. In the sports segment, "Dynamite Hands" Harry Hamlin plays an up-and-coming boxer.

MR. BASEBALL (1992)

DIRECTOR: Fred Schipisi. SCREENPLAY: Gary Ross, Kevin Wade, Monte Merrick. STORY: Theo Pelletier, John Junkerman. PRODUCERS: Doug Claybourne, Robert Newmyer, Fred Schipisi. CINEMATOGRAPHY: Ian Baker. EDITING: Peter Honess. MUSIC: Jerry Goldsmith. PRODUCTION DESIGN: Ted Haworth. ART DIRECTION: Kenneth J. Creber, Katsumi Kaneda, Russell J. Smith. COSTUME DESIGN: Bruce Finlayson.
CAST: Tom Selleck (Jack Elliot), Ken Takakura (Uchiyama), Dennis Haysbert (Max Dubois), Toshi Shioya (Yoji Nishimura), Aya Takanashi (Hiroko Uchiyama).
RUNNING TIME: 108 minutes.
DVD: Universal Studios.

Tom Selleck stars as Jack Elliot, an aging baseball player whose extended slump and off-the-field antics have led to his being sold to the Chunichi Dragons. From the time he deplanes in Tokyo, Jack plays the part of the ugly American. He makes ethnic jokes about the Japanese, ridicules their culture, and shows no respect toward his Japanese teammates. His translator, Yoji Nishimura (Toshi Shioya), has the awkward job of trying to cover up for Jack's boorishness. When Jack discovers a fellow American, Max Dubois (Dennis Haysbert), on the team, he expects Max to share his disdain for their hosts. Although Max is eager to return to the United States, he has adapted to the etiquette of Japanese baseball and has learned enough of the language to communicate with the other Dragons. However, Jack neither follows Max's example nor seeks his advice on the local customs.

Jack alienates the team manager, Uchiyama (Ken Takakura), who requires rigorous workouts and strict discipline from his players. Uchiyama is also cautious and discourages the sort of aggressive, risk-taking play that can result in "loss of face" if it fails. When Jack refuses to cooperate with Uchiyama's training regimen, the Dragons, in the interest of harmony, communicate through Yoji that they will all do Jack's exercises. In keeping with his contemptuous attitude, Jack leads the team in a series of face stretches, mooning practice, and a version of the hokey pokey. During batting practice, he ignores Uchiyama's observation that he has "a hole in his swing," even when he fans on three pitches in a row. He spits on the field, ignoring Max's warning that the action is considered disrespectful. In the locker room he bypasses the washing up and plunges directly into a tub for a hot soak, again failing to heed local custom.

When the team's public relations representative, Hiroko Uchiyama (Aya Takanashi), suggests a meeting, Jack responds with a lewd comment, not realizing that she speaks English. He also fails to realize—and not even his translator informs him—that she is the manager's daughter. At a restaurant with Hiroko, Jack complains that he doesn't "eat bait," apparently not noticing that they are in a French restaurant and also apparently unfamiliar with the existence of Japanese steakhouses and Kobe beef. Hiroko seems unfazed by Jack's rudeness and quietly explains more about her culture and the importance of its

Tom Selleck (center) as Jack Elliot, an American playing for a Japanese team in *Mr. Baseball*

customs and rituals. Jack becomes a bit more cooperative until he learns that his contract requires him to do commercials and that he has no say in the matter. He stomps out of the restaurant, but must return because he has no idea where he lives.

At first Jack plays well, and the Japanese press dubs him "Mr. Baseball." However, he is not happy that Yoji has been editing his remarks to reporters, and Uchiyama's conservative style is frustrating him to no end. Against the rival Giants, who hold a winning record over the Dragons, Jack swings away when instructed to bunt and throws a tantrum over being fined. Soon he is in a slump, which only worsens his mood; his behavior deteriorates even more. Eventually, Jack apologizes to Hiroko and asks her to explain the difference between a shrine and a temple. He is willing to try the "Zen thing" to improve his batting average, which has sunk to .200. She, in turn, realizes that Jack is on the make. In the end it is she, not Jack, who initiates sex.

In spite of having mellowed off the field, on the baseball diamond Jack continues to behave badly. He complains excessively about calls, pulls a prank on the Dragon's captain, and when a pitched ball comes too close, attacks the pitcher, although the man has indicated by tipping his hat that the throw was unintentional. As a result of this round of antics, the Dragons' owners tell Uchiyama to suspend Jack, and they warn that his own job is in jeopardy.

Hiroko insists that Jack accompany her to visit her family. Still unaware of her relationship to Uchiyama, Jack agrees to the trip. Of course, he is ready to leave once he discovers he's been set up, but Uchiyama, who has also been caught unawares, requests (speaking English for the first time) that he stay since his mother has prepared a meal. At dinner Jack goes out of his way to insult the others, mimicking their manners in a rudely exaggerated fashion and deliberately breaking taboos. Hiroko, unhappy with both her father and Jack, makes an abrupt exit, which the manager then assures Jack has been planned. Finally, the two men get down to talking business. Uchiyama reveals that he had taken a risk in signing Jack against the wishes of the owners, who preferred another player. Now both men will lose their jobs unless Jack starts hitting.

Jack agrees to individual fitness training, rising before dawn to get himself back in shape, all under the watchful eye of the chief. As his training continues at the field, the Dragons join him in the workouts. With some assistance from Yoji, Jack apologizes to his teammates in Japanese for having been discourteous and bows to them. Uchiyama says that now Jack is ready to start hitting, and he does. He also makes amends with Hiroko, offering her flowers and champagne and good intentions. She accepts.

At the next game—the season has seemed to be on hold while Jack was getting back in shape—Jack homers. Later he visits Uchiyama, bottle in hand, saying he's heard that according to custom, if a player is drunk and speaks frankly to a manager, the player's words cannot be held against him. As the two men drink, Jack elaborates on what he has found to be frustrating about Uchiyama's managing style. He says the younger ones are intimidated by his strictness and recommends he allow the players more latitude on the field. Jack's comments are sincere, and Uchiyama takes them to heart.

In the climactic game, the Dragons once again face the Giants, and Uchiyama is again pressured by the team's owners. Adding to the excitement, Jack is on the verge of breaking the national record for home runs in consecutive games, a record held by the manager. Then, Jack's agent in the United States calls to say the Dodgers need to pick up a power hitter and are sending scouts to Japan, providing more incentive for Jack to continue his streak. Unfortunately, the Giants have decided to walk Jack. As the score seesaws from inning to inning, the action scenes focus on the changes Uchiyama has made, allowing his pitcher to work his way out of trouble, permitting runners to go for extra bases, and joining the team in cheering one another on. At Jack's last at bat, with two outs in the bottom of the ninth and runners in scoring position, Uchiyama signals him to swing away, knowing that a home run will break his record. Instead, Jack lays down a bunt, and the Dragons win.

After the victory, the plotlines all fall into place. Max earns a spot with the Dodgers and rejoins his family. Uchiyama visits Hiroko, who has been miffed that Jack wants to return to the States and whose relationship with her father has remained strained. Father and daughter reconcile, and the next scene, in Lakeland, Florida, reveals that Jack and Hiroko have made up. While Jack coaches, she watches from the stands between phone calls—she is able to continue her career, as well.

Two years before *Mr. Baseball* was released, the Japanese firm Matsushita Electric Industrial Company acquired MCA, the parent company of Universal. *Mr. Baseball* was the first Japanese-themed film produced after the acquisition, and according to the *New York Times* (November 20, 1991) the script was revised to eliminate jokes about World War II and to make Jack Elliot's success a result of his cultural assimilation and his acceptance of Uchiyama's training strategy. In spite of the studio's efforts to improve the film, the comedy falls flat most of the time.

MR. DESTINY (1990)

DIRECTOR: James Orr. SCREENPLAY: James Orr, Jim Cruickshank. PRODUCER: Jim Cruickshank, James Orr. CINEMATOGRAPHY: Alex Thomson. EDITING: Michael R. Miller. MUSIC: David Newman. PRODUCTION DESIGN: Michael Seymour. ART

DIRECTION: Catherine Hardwicke. COSTUME DESIGN: Jane Greenwood.
CAST: James Belushi (Larry Burrows), Linda Hamilton (Ellen Burrows), Michael Caine (Mike), Jon Lovitz (Chip Metzler), Hart Bochner (Niles Pender).
RUNNING TIME: 110 minutes.
DVD: Walt Disney Video.

In this fantasy film, a grown man relives a high school baseball game whose new outcome changes his life in unexpected ways.

MR. 3000 (2004)

DIRECTOR: Charles Stone III. SCREENPLAY: Eric Champnella, Keith Mitchell, Howard Michael Gould. PRODUCERS: Gary Barber, Roger Birnbaum, Maggie Wilde. CINEMATOGRAPHY: Shane Hurlbut. EDITING: Bill Pankow. MUSIC: John Powell. PRODUCTION DESIGN: Maher Ahmad. COSTUME DESIGN: Salvador Pérez Jr.
CAST: Bernie Mac (Stan Ross), Angela Bassett (Mo Simmons), Paul Sorvino (Gus Panas), Chris Noth (Schiembri), Michael Rispoli (Boca), Brian J. White (T-Rex Pennebaker).
RUNNING TIME: 104 minutes.
DVD: Buena Vista Home Entertainment.

Years after retiring, an egotistical baseball player must return to the game to make up for a statistical error that deprived him of his three thousandth hit.

MVP: MOST VALUABLE PRIMATE (2000)

DIRECTOR: Robert Vince. SCREENPLAY: Anne Vince, Robert Vince. PRODUCER: Ian Fodie. CINEMATOGRAPHY: Glen Winter. EDITING: Kelly Herron. MUSIC: Brahm Wenger. PRODUCTION DESIGN: Brian Davie. ART DIRECTION: Elizabeth Shelton. COSTUME DESIGN: Cali Newcomen.
CAST: Kevin Zegers (Steven Westover), Jamie Renee Smith (Tara Westover), Rick Duccomen (Coach Marlowe), Russell Ferrier (Darren).
RUNNING TIME: 93 minutes.
DVD: Warner Home Video.

From the people who produced *Air Bud* comes another kids comedy about a sport-playing animal, this time a hockey star monkey.

MVP 2: MOST VERTICAL PRIMATE (2001)

DIRECTOR: Robert Vince. SCREENPLAY: Anne Vince, Robert Vince, Elan Mastai. PRODUCERS: Anna McRoberts, Robert Vince. CINEMATOGRAPHY: Glen Winter. EDITING: Kelly Herron. MUSIC: Brahm Wenger. PRODUCTION DESIGN: Peter Andringa. ART DIRECTION: Emma Faroh. COSTUME DESIGN: Maria Livingstone.
CAST: Cameron Bancroft (Rob Poirier), Richard Karn (Ollie Plant), Robert Costanzo (cop), Oliver Muirhead (Raheja).
RUNNING TIME: 87 minutes.
DVD: Warner Home Video.

In this film, the chimpanzee who scored on the ice turns to skateboarding.

MYSTERY, ALASKA (1999)

DIRECTOR: Jay Roach. SCREENPLAY: David E. Kelley, Sean O'Byrne. PRODUCERS: Howard Baldwin, David E. Kelley. CINEMATOGRAPHY: Peter Deming. EDITING: Jon Poll. MUSIC: Carter Burwell. PRODUCTION DESIGN: Rusty Smith. ART DIRECTION: Denise Hudson, Andrew Neskoromny. COSTUME DESIGN: Deena Appel.
CAST: Russell Crowe (John Biebe), Burt Reynolds (Judge Burns), Hank Azaria (Charlie Danner), Mary McCormack (Donna Biebe), Ron Eldard (Skank Marden).
RUNNING TIME: 119 minutes.
DVD: Walt Disney Video.

At its core *Mystery, Alaska* is a film about small-town hockey, but the script is heavily freighted with characters, backstories, and subplots. As reviewers have noted, the movie resembles a pilot for a television series more than a feature film, perhaps a reflection of screenwriter and producer David E. Kelley's television experience as creator of *Ally McBeal* and writer for *LA Law*.

The entire town is caught up in Saturday hockey matches played between teams of local skaters. Council members determine the makeup of the teams. Sheriff John Biebe (Russell Crowe) has been a team member for thirteen years, but he has slowed in the past year and hasn't scored well. John knows that soon he will be replaced to make room on the roster for a talented teenager, Stevie Weeks (Ryan Northcuit). Mystery is about to receive national attention because a former resident, Charlie Danner (Hank Azaria), has written an article about the hockey players for *Sports Illustrated.* Charlie is also trying to arrange an exhibition game between Mystery and the New York Rangers of the National Hockey League. Because Charlie left his hometown to pursue a career—on the East Coast, no less—he is regarded with suspicion; he is also a shameless self-promoter. When Charlie makes a grand return via helicopter, one of the Mystery residents remarks that the 'copter "looks Russian," a reference to America's enemy during the cold war, not a jab aimed at Sarah Palin, who at the time of filming was little known outside of Wasilla, where she was mayor.

The residents distrust Charlie and are skeptical of his plan. At a town meeting, strong opposition comes from Judge Walter Burns (Burt Reynolds), who fears the locals are no match for a professional team and that the nationally televised event will make Mystery the object of ridicule. However, Charlie points out that the game will be played on a pond, not in a rink. John, agreeing with both Judge Burns and Charlie, claims that the Mystery men can outskate anyone. The players begin to testify as to their skills and readiness. The match is on.

Of course there are complications. The team's best scorer, Connor Banks (Michael Buie), a grocery clerk, must stand trial for shooting in the foot a representative of a Walmart-like operation interested in opening a store in Mystery. Connor's attorney, Bailey Pruitt (Maury Chaykin), sways the jury by quoting insults uttered by the sales rep after he was wounded. Connor is found not guilty, but Judge Burns is embarrassed by the miscarriage of justice. The judge is embittered because, in spite of playing hockey at Princeton, he was not talented enough to make the grade in Mystery. Although he is a skilled coach, he refuses to prepare Mystery for their match with the Rangers. His relationship with his own children, a daughter who is dating Stevie Weeks and a son who is on the team, is strained. Mayor Scott Pitcher (Colm Meaney) discovers that player Skank Marden (Ron Eldard), a notorious fornicator, is having an affair with his wife, Mary Jane (Lolita Davidovich). Bailey, who is overweight, has developed a bad cough and apparently suffers from a weakened heart. And adding to John's unhappiness about being bumped from the team, his wife, Donna (Mary McCormack), and Charlie were high school sweethearts. John fears Donna finds the more worldly Charlie attractive. And the Rangers don't want to travel to Mystery, Alaska, for the exhibition.

Judge Burns, experiencing an unexplained change of heart, asks Bailey to go to New York to represent Mystery at a hearing to determine whether the Rangers' contract requires them to compete in the exhibition. Bailey speaks emotionally, interrupted by coughing. At the conclusion of his speech, he proclaims that the match is "not about money: it's about . . ." Bailey clutches his chest and, unable to get out the word *heart*, collapses and dies. It is a tacky scene.

At his graveside, John offers a community-themed tribute. Later that night, John returns to the grave, where Judge Burns has just offered Bailey a final toast from his silver flask. The judge tells John that Bailey won his last case and that the game is back on. John asks the judge to coach, and the judge asks John to captain the team.

The press and network personnel have descended on the town. They regard Mystery as the edge of civilization, invoke predictable stereotypes, and speak in clichés. In yet another complication, the nature of the game has changed from pond hockey to a rink match. Charlie has produced an ancient Zamboni to groom the ice, and boards are being erected to form a rink. These enhancements provide an advantage for the Rangers. But the Mystery men remain confident as the judge directs their practices.

When the Rangers arrive, they are arrogant and ignore the locals who have gathered to welcome them to Mystery. Only one Ranger signs an autograph. On the eve of the match, Skank visits the mayor to apologize and to promise to sacrifice his all to make certain Mystery is not disgraced on the ice. The mayor assists the town's fortunes by convincing Little Richard (himself), the celebrity imported by the networks to perform the National Anthem, not only to stretch out the song as long as possible, but also to sing "O, Canada." The result is that the Rangers, unaccustomed to the cold, must stand for several minutes in the frigid air. They get off to a slow start, and after the first period, Mystery leads 2–0.

In the second period, the Rangers devise a strategy of allowing one platoon of players to return to the warmth of the locker room while the others are on the ice so that one group of players is always, literally, warmed up. New York scores five unanswered goals. The atmosphere in the Mystery locker room is funereal before the third period. Judge Burns suggests a plan designed not to win but to prevent the Rangers from running the score up. Burns's recommendation has the intended effect of riling up John, who is not ready to give up hope of winning. He offers up an inspirational speech similar to the one he delivered at the town hall meeting early in the film, and the Mystery men return to the ice determined to win. They hold the Rangers scoreless and with time running out come within an eyelash of tying the score.

The screen falls silent, and the film slows as Mystery copes with its painful defeat. Then, the judge begins to applaud slowly. Gradually, the people in the stands catch on and begin to applaud. The Rangers tap their sticks on the ice. The mayor rises, followed by the townspeople. Judge Burns hugs his son. The next day Stevie and Connor leave with the Rangers to try out for their minor league team. John is certain that they will succeed and that they will return. Much leave-taking follows, differences are resolved, and the film concludes with John visiting Bailey's grave.

N

NACHO LIBRE (2006)

Director: Jared Hess. Screenplay: Jared Hess, Jerusha Hess, Mike White. Producers: Jack Black, David Klawans, Julia Pistor, Mike White. Cinematography: Xavier Pérez Grobet. Editing: Billy Weber. Music: Danny Elfman. Production Design: Gideon Ponte. Art Direction: Hania Robledo. Costume Design: Graciela Mazón.
Cast: Jack Black (Nacho), Ana de la Reguera (Sister Encarnación), Héctor Jiménez (Esqueleto), Peter Stormare (Emperor).
Running Time: 92 minutes.
DVD: Paramount.

Loosely based on an actual person, a Mexican monk earns money for an orphanage by wrestling in disguise.

NATIONAL VELVET (1944)

Director: Clarence Brown. Screenplay: Theodore Reeves, Helen Deutsch, based on the novel by Enid Bagnold. Producer: Pandro S. Berman. Cinematography: Leonard Smith. Editing: Robert Kern. Music: Herbert Stothart. Art Direction: Cedric Gibbons, Urie McCleary. Costume Design: Irene (women), Valles (men).
Cast: Elizabeth Taylor (Velvet Brown), Mickey Rooney (Mi Taylor), Donald Crisp (Mr. Brown), Anne Revere (Mrs. Brown), Angela Lansbury (Edwina Brown), Jackie Jenkins (Donald Brown), Arthur Treacher (race patron).
Running Time: 123 minutes.
Academy Awards: Best Supporting Actress (Revere), Best Editing. Nominations: Best Director, Best Cinematography, Best Art Direction/Interior Decoration.
DVD: MGM.

Based on the Enid Bagnold novel, *National Velvet* tells a delightful story of a girl determined to fulfill her dreams by winning the Grand National Steeplechase. The film premiered in December 1944 and opened in theaters in 1945. It received Oscar nominations for directing (Clarence Brown), color cinematography (Leonard Smith), and interior art decoration (Cedric Gibbons et al.). Academy Awards went to Robert Kern for editing and Anne Revere for her portrayal of Velvet Brown's mother. Velvet was Elizabeth Taylor's first major role, and she became a star overnight once the film was released.

National Velvet is set in England during the 1920s. It opens with the camera following a teenaged boy, Mi Taylor (Mickey Rooney), walking along the coastal road toward the village of Sewels in Sussex in search of the Brown family because he has found Mrs. Brown's name and address among the possessions of his late father.

Mi stops to rest, and the scene shifts to a small schoolhouse on the last day of classes before the summer break, where the three Brown sisters are saying goodbye to their teacher. The oldest girl, Edwina (Angela Lansbury), is preoccupied with plans to meet a boy later in the afternoon. Malvolia (Juanita Quigley) has her mind on sweets. Eleven-year-old Velvet (Elizabeth Taylor) is a daydreamer who pretends to be riding a horse and gallops off on her own. As she approaches the place where Mi is resting, he calls "Whoa," and she stops to talk, learning that Mi is an orphan who doesn't want people to feel sorry for him. Their conversation is interrupted by a man chasing a horse (King Charles, grandson of Man o' War). When the horse jumps a fence and runs into the road, Velvet dashes in front of the animal, which comes to a halt. The man, Mr. Ede (Reginald Owen), plans to sell the horse because it is terribly rambunctious. Mi, who has demonstrated an impressive knowledge of horses, is impressed by the animal's jump. Velvet has fallen in love—with the horse, which she dubs "Pie" and dreams of owning.

Velvet invites Mi home, and at dinner the family dynamics are on display. Mr. Brown (Donald Crisp), a butcher, is only the nominal head of household. Everyone ignores his instructions not to feed the dog (Jacob) when he begs; in fact, Mr. Brown also sneaks the dog treats from his plate. Mr. Brown's stuffiness dissolves quickly in the presence of his family, and he yields final decisions to Mrs. Brown (Anne Revere), who is quick-witted, charming, and wise. The atmosphere is warm, problems are easily resolved, and lapses forgiven. Edwina fibs to cover her newfound romance, but her parents respond good-naturedly, letting her know that they know but trying not to embarrass her. The youngest child, Donald (Jackie Jenkins), tells wild stories that the Browns take in stride while upholding rules about bedtimes. Velvet removes a dental plate at every opportunity, receiving only firm but gentle rebukes. When Velvet suggests her father offer Mi some summer work, Mrs. Brown insists Mi spend the night in a room in the stable and later convinces Mr. Brown to hire him full time at a good wage.

After settling the day's receipts, Mrs. Brown, observed by Mi through the window, places the cash in a coffee pot on a shelf, then goes upstairs. Velvet, who has not been able to fall asleep, asks her mother if she knew Mi's father and learns that he had helped Mrs. Brown to train for a Channel swim, which she completed successfully, becoming the first woman to do so. (In the real world, it was Gertrude Ederle in 1926.) Mrs. Brown explains to Velvet that she will tell Mi about his father when the proper time comes; however, Velvet may inform him of Mr. Brown's offer of employment, room, and board.

When Velvet reaches Mi's room, he has just finished counting the money he has removed from the coffee pot, but after he learns of the Browns' generosity, he makes an excuse to go to the kitchen and replace the cash before anyone realizes it was taken. The next day, Velvet accompanies Mi on a delivery in order to pass by Mr. Ede's farm to catch a glimpse of Pie. Mi, who has expressed a dislike for horses, admits to Velvet that he had a bad fall once, but he does not provide details, and Velvet does not press him for more information. When they reach the farm, Jacob chases after Pie, who makes another spectacular jump and takes off down the road toward the village. Mi stops to measure the jump and tells Velvet the horse has cleared a distance equivalent to that of a major jump in the annual Grand National Steeplechase. Meanwhile, Jacob has gotten into the meat Velvet and Mi were to deliver, and Pie has created a bit of damage to a garden in the village. The local constable holds Mr. Ede accountable for the repairs, an irritation that prompts Ede to raffle off the horse.

Although Mr. Brown has refused to purchase raffle tickets, Mi buys enough for all of the Brown children. Velvet is convinced that she will win, and, of course, she does. Soon Velvet is riding Pie and dreaming of winning the race. Without telling anyone, she obtains an entry form and set of instructions. Mi tries to talk her out of her plan because of the expense and the amount of hard work, but her mother not only encourages her to go forward, but produces the necessary cash—her prize money for swimming the Channel. Mrs. Brown believes that Velvet and she are alike in their spirit and determination. She also tells Velvet that one moves on from one adventure to the next; for Mrs. Brown, raising a family has been the next adventure, suggesting that eventually Velvet's passion for her horse will be transformed into romantic love and the challenges of adulthood.

Mi is sent to London with the entry fee and a half crown for his "entertainment." Mr. Brown indicates Mi should enjoy himself in the city, but after Mi departs, Mr. Brown expresses his reservations to Mrs. Brown. In fact, Mi has packed all of his belongings and is contemplating running off with the money. However, Mrs. Brown is confident that whatever bit of wickedness Mi has in him will be overcome by her trust. In a London pub, where Mi has met with two former associates, it appears that he is about to yield to temptation. They ply him with drinks and try to convince him to throw his lot and the cash in with them. Even though he is quite drunk, Mi refuses because, he explains, of the Browns' trust. Mi returns to Sewels with a receipt, five pounds in change, and a very bad hangover.

Mi's London experience is a turning point for him. He devotes himself to training Pie for the race, and when the horse suddenly becomes sick, asks Velvet to trust him to care for the animal. Under Mi's ministrations, which rely heavily on an equine version of a hot toddy, Pie recovers and resumes his exercises with Velvet aboard. Although Mi has grown fond of the horse, he remains saddle-shy because of his earlier accident, which he still cannot discuss. Consequently, Mi must find a rider for the race. Velvet cannot enter because, even if she were not an inexperienced amateur, she is a girl. On the eve of the race, Mi produces a jockey, but when he and Velvet meet the man, they are distressed by his negative attitude. When he expresses no interest in seeing the horse before the race, Velvet fires him. Afterward, Mi explains to Velvet that he was once a jockey, but in a race he caused an accident that killed another rider and has not been on a horse since. Velvet offers understanding and does not pressure Mi to ride in the race, but later that night, Mi saddles Pie and mounts up. After circling the paddock, Mi takes Pie over the fence and determines to ride him the next day; however, when he goes to tell Velvet, he finds her wearing the silks, convinced that she is destined to win the National herself. Mi does not mention his decision, just concurs with hers.

Before the race, Mi leads Velvet through the preparations, telling others she is Latvian and doesn't speak English. She experiences some last minute jitters, but Mi calms her and sends her off on the ride of her life. It is a long race of four and a half miles, thirty jumps, and a field of thirty-two horses. Tension mounts as spill after spill occurs, but Velvet and Pie persevere, and in the final stretch, overtake the leader to win the race.

After crossing the finish line, the exhausted Velvet faints and slips from the saddle. She is taken off to the first aid building on a stretcher, where the doctor quickly discovers she is a girl. Meanwhile, an objection has been raised because the rules state that the jockey must not dismount before reaching the enclosure. Pie is disqualified, but the officials do not press charges against Velvet or Mi, and they return home triumphant. In spite of the disqualification, Velvet is heralded as a national hero in the press and offers pour in. Faced with the opportunity to go on tour with Pie in America, Velvet turns it down, reasoning that it would not be good for the horse. She has learned from her mother that it is time to move on to whatever is next, not to exploit her previous exploits.

Mi, too, is ready to move on. He has overcome his demons. Before leaving, he confesses to Mr. Brown that he had not intended to return from his London trip. Mi elects not to wait to say goodbye to Velvet, but once she discovers he has gone, Velvet consults with her mother, then rides off to catch up with him. It is time for Mi to hear about his father.

Following filming, MGM arranged for Elizabeth Taylor to keep King Charles.

THE NATURAL (1984)

DIRECTOR: Barry Levinson. SCREENPLAY: Roger Towne, Phil Dusenberry, based on the novel by Bernard Malamud. PRODUCER: Mark Johnson. CINEMATOGRAPHY: Caleb Deschanel. EDITING: Christopher Holmes, Stu Linder. MUSIC: Randy Newman. PRODUCTION DESIGN: Mel Bourne, Angelo Graham. SET DECORATION: Bruce Weintraub. COSTUME DESIGN: Gloria Gresham, Bernie Pollack.

CAST: Robert Redford (Roy Hobbs), Glenn Close (Iris Gaines), Barbara Hershey (Harriet Bird), Wilford Brimley (Pop Fisher), Robert Duvall (Max Mercy), Richard Farnsworth (Red Blow).

RUNNING TIME: 134 minutes.

ACADEMY AWARD NOMINATIONS: Best Supporting Actress (Close), Best Cinematography, Best Original Score, Best Art Direction/Set Decoration.

DVD: Sony Pictures.

Director Barry Levinson's adaptation of the 1952 novel transforms Bernard Malamud's dark narrative into a sentimental film. Levinson retains Malamud's allegorical elements but alters the themes, giving his film strong religious overtones. It is often compared with *Field of Dreams* (1989).

The Natural opens in the 1930s with thirty-something Roy Hobbs (forty-six-year-old Robert Redford) waiting for a train that will take him to the New York Knights and a second chance at a baseball career. That trouble lies ahead is foreshadowed by literal shadows from a window blind that fall across Roy's face. Throughout the film, Levinson employs light and shade symbolically.

A flashback to Roy's childhood fills in key events from his youth and establishes the film's central message. First, Roy (Paul Sullivan Jr.) is shown as a boy playing catch in a brightly illuminated wheat field with his father while a little girl, Iris (Rachel Hall), looks on. Roy's father advises him that having natural talent is "not enough" and warns of failure if he relies too heavily on his "gift." Not long after dispensing this wisdom, the senior Hobbs suffers a fatal heart attack, dying under a tree that is then struck by lightning, emitting a shower of sparks resembling fireworks. Roy makes a baseball bat from the trunk, carving into the wood a lightning bolt and the name "Wonderboy."

Still in the flashback, the scene shifts to the nineteen-year-old Roy throwing stones at Iris's (now played by Glenn Close) window. She joins him outside, and he explains he has a tryout in Chicago. The screen turns black, indicating a sexual encounter between the two.

In the next scene, it is still 1923, and Roy is on a train bound for Chicago, accompanied by Sam Simpson (John Finnegan), a scout who introduces him to reporter Max Mercy (Robert Duvall) and the Babe Ruth–like "Whammer" (Joe Don

Baker). A woman in black, Harriet Bird (Barbara Hershey), observes the men with interest. During a stop the passengers take in a carnival, where Roy has attracted some attention by knocking over bottles at a pitching booth. Sam bets Max that Roy can strike out Whammer. Roy fires three strikes (the final one filmed in slow motion), and Harriet shifts her attention from Whammer to Roy. In the dining car, when Harriet asks Roy about his goals and ambitions, all he can respond is that he wants to be famous. She presses him to expand, citing Homer and Arthurian legend, but Roy, unfamiliar with the references and uninterested in learning more, can only add that he wants to be "known as the best there ever was, that's all." The scene invites the viewer to recall the warnings of Roy's father about relying only on one's talent. Roy is eager to have fame bestowed upon him because of his gift, but he has not thought of his gift as requiring anything from him.

Soon after Roy arrives at his hotel, Harriet invites him to her room. Anticipating a romantic tryst, Roy accepts the invitation. The camera records his short trip through a blurred corridor and into an elevator, where he disappears into blackness as the doors close. Harriet greets him dressed in her usual black and wearing a hat with a veil. She repeats her question and Roy repeats his response, which disappoints Harriet. She produces a small gun and shoots him in the stomach, after which she disappears from the frame as the camera cuts to a pair of white curtains fluttering in the breeze from her open balcony. (It is later revealed that she jumped to her death, resulting in a small, but quickly forgotten scandal.)

Once again the screen turns black, bringing to an end the first section of the story, which resumes sixteen years later in New York. The New York Knights are in last place, and manager Pop Fisher (Wilford Brimley) is lamenting that he did

Robert Redford as Roy Hobbs in *The Natural*

not become a farmer. Pop has been sent a new right fielder, who turns out to be Roy Hobbs. Although Roy has a contract, Pop is not happy to receive an over-the-hill player with an incredibly slender résumé. Roy has spent two weeks with a minor league team; he tells Pop he played in high school and has "knocked around" in the intervening years. When Pop tries to learn more about Roy over dinner, Roy ignores his questions, focusing instead on Pop's niece, Memo Paris (Kim Basinger), who is sitting nearby.

The Knights continue their losing streak, documented by a montage of newspaper articles, yet Pop refuses to play Roy. Finally, Roy expresses his exasperation by walking out of a therapeutic team session with a psychologist Pop has brought in. After a confrontation during which Pop threatens to send Roy down to the minors, Pop decides to let Roy take batting practice. To the astonishment of the team, Roy, using Wonderboy, hits a series of pitches into the far stands. When he finally gets to the plate in a game, as storm clouds form, he literally knocks the cover off of the ball. Lightning strikes, and Roy becomes a person of interest to the press and to the Judge (Robert Prosky), an evil figure who owns a large share of the Knights.

When the Knights' starting right fielder is killed in a freak accident, Roy's position is secured. The baseball commissioner has examined Wonderboy and declared it legal; the team members now wear lightning bolt patches on their sleeves. Roy has befriended the batboy, Bobby Savoy (George Wilkosz), and promises to show him how to make his own bat. Meanwhile, Iris has seen Roy's photo in a newspaper. As Iris continues to follow Roy's progress through newsreels, Roy's fame spreads, and a montage chronicles his success.

Roy learns that Pop has been forced to sell part of his shares to the Judge, but can reclaim the shares if the Knights win the pennant; however, if they lose, the Judge can buy Pop out. Soon Roy is called to the Judge's office, which the Judge likes to keep darkened. The Judge tries to bribe Roy, but Roy refuses and turns on the lights as he exits. Roy's next offer of money comes from Max, who has finally remembered meeting Roy with Sam. Max wants exclusive rights to the true story, but again Roy turns down the cash.

Later, at a club, he encounters Memo sitting with a gambler, Gus Sands (Darren McGavin, uncredited), who has lost money betting against Roy. After Gus illustrates his cleverness by guessing how much cash Roy has in his pockets, Roy counters with a magic trick, pulling coins from Memo's hair. Memo dances with Roy, and they leave together. Although Pop tries to warn Roy, saying Memo is "bad luck," Roy ignores the advice. The parallels with Harriet are foregrounded when Roy, in bed with Memo, awakens from a nightmare about the shooting. The relationship with Memo sends him into a slump.

Back in Chicago, Iris has read about Roy and attends a game at Wrigley field. Roy has struck out in his previous at bats, but in the ninth inning, Iris, wearing a white dress, stands up. Backlit, she glows like an angel. Roy recognizes her and hits a home run that breaks the scoreboard clock, a symbolic stopping of time. She sends a note to the dugout, and the two meet at a soda fountain. It is as if, in Iris's presence, Roy returns to the innocence of his youth. As Roy continues to meet with Iris, his hitting improves. One day, he visits her apartment, where he learns that she still owns the farm and that she has a sixteen-year-old son whose existence is marked by a ball glove on the couch. Iris tells Roy that his father "lives in New York." After Roy leaves, he is shown in the dining car of a train clowning with the batboy. The Knights continue their streak, led by Roy, on their road trip. Meanwhile, the Judge, Gus, and Memo meet to debate their next move.

Yet another elevator delivers Roy to a party, where Memo, now dressed in white, greets him. Gus takes him aside to warn that he could lose Memo if he doesn't have enough money; he adds that he has already bet against Roy. As before, Roy is not tempted by money, and whether from overconfidence or waning interest, he appears unmoved by the idea that Memo will leave him. In fact, she betrays him, feeding him a poisoned canapé. In the hospital, where, interestingly, he is being kept in the maternity ward, he learns that the lining of his stomach has been deteriorating because of a previous injury. The doctor has found a silver bullet in his stomach. If he plays in the pennant-clinching game, the results could be fatal. When Memo visits, dressed in black, Roy tells her he will play this last game.

Roy's next visitor is the Judge, who has obtained photos of Roy lying in the doorway of Harriet's hotel room after being shot and of Harriet's scantily clad body in the street below. The next morning, the Knights visit, followed shortly by Iris. But before Iris reaches the room, Max stops her, shows her the photos, and asks for information about what happened. Iris returns the pictures without a word and enters Roy's room, where he tells her, "Some mistakes you never quit paying for." He expresses regret that he has not become "the best there ever was." Iris offers her belief that everyone has "two lives," one "we learn with" and the other "we live with after." She reminds him that he has influenced young boys who admire him. When she tells him she will attend the game, he asks if her son is coming. He is.

Before the game Roy visits the Judge's office, where he finds Memo and Gus. Roy is returning the envelope of cash the Judge left at the hospital. Memo pulls a gun from the Judge's desk and shoots, apparently intending to hit Roy, but missing badly. Roy seizes the gun. Gus then repeats Mr. Hobbs's admonition that talent is not enough. Gus proclaims Roy a loser. Roy tosses the gun aside and leaves. When he shows up at the locker room, Pop is once again talking about farming. Roy speaks of the joys of rural life, and Pop tells him to suit up. Max puts in an appearance and claims his function is to protect the game by what he chooses to write about Roy. Roy notes that Max has never played.

The game moves into the fateful ninth inning. Roy has not been able to hit, and Iris has sent him a note, presumably revealing that he is the father of her son, who is in the stands with her. Roy's first swing is a foul ball that smashes the press box in front of Max's face. Lightning strikes as Roy's second foul shatters Wonderboy. Undaunted, Roy asks the batboy to "pick a winner." Bobby produces the bat they made together, the "Savoy Special." As the storm builds and lightning continues, a splotch of blood appears on Roy's abdomen. Nevertheless, in the slow motion that signals triumph, Roy connects, and the ball strikes the stadium lights, showering sparks onto the field. The ball, still traveling as Roy rounds the bases, turns into a ball being tossed in a wheat field. The film has come full circle as Roy plays catch with his and Iris's son.

The Natural is visually attractive, but reviewers found Levinson's symbolism heavy-handed, particularly the halo-like glowing of Redford's hair and Close's angel-like appearance in the stands. The film was popular with viewers, grossing over $48 million. It was nominated for four Academy Awards: Best Supporting Actress (Close), Best Cinematography (Caleb Deschanel), Best Original Score (Randy Newman), and Best Art Direction (Angelo Graham, Mel Bourne, and Bruce Weintraub).

NECESSARY ROUGHNESS (1991)

DIRECTOR: Stan Dragoti. SCREENPLAY: Rick Natkin, David Fuller. PRODUCERS: Mace Neufeld, Robert Rehme. CINEMATOGRAPHY: Peter Stein. EDITING: Steve Mirkovich, John Wright. MUSIC: Bill Conti. PRODUCTION DESIGN: Paul Peters. COSTUME DESIGN: Dan Moore.

CAST: Scott Bakula (Paul Blake), Robert Loggia (Coach Wally Rig), Hector Elizondo (Coach Ed Gennero), Harley Jane Kozak (Dr. Suzanne Carter), Larry Miller (Dean Elias), Sinbad (Andre Krimm).

RUNNING TIME: 108 minutes.

DVD: Paramount.

A university coach lures his former high school star, now in his thirties, back to the game in order to preserve the college's football program.

THE NEXT KARATE KID (1994)

DIRECTOR: Christopher Cain. SCREENPLAY: Mark Lee. PRODUCER: Jerry Weintraub. CINEMATOGRAPHY: Laszlo Kovacs. EDITING:

Ronald Roose. MUSIC: Bill Conti. PRODUCTION DESIGN: Walter P. Martishius.
CAST: Pat Morita (Mr. Miyagi), Hilary Swank (Julie Pierce), Michael Ironside (Colonel Dugan), Constance Towers (Louisa Pierce), Chris Conrad (Eric McGowen).
RUNNING TIME: 107 minutes.
DVD: Sony Pictures.

This time Mr. Miyagi teaches martial arts to a young girl who needs help with her self-esteem.

NIGHT AND THE CITY (1950)

DIRECTOR: Jules Dassin. SCREENPLAY: Jo Eisinger, based on the novel by Gerald Kersh. PRODUCER: Samuel G. Engel. CINEMATOGRAPHY: Mutz Greenbaum. EDITING: Nick De Maggio, Sidney Stone. MUSIC: Franz Waxman (American release); Benjamin Frankel (British release). ART DIRECTION: C.P. Norman. COSTUME DESIGN: Oleg Cassini, Margaret Furse, Ivy Baker.
CAST: Richard Widmark (Harry Fabian), Gene Tierney (Mary Bristol), Googie Withers (Helen Nosseross), Mike Mazurki (the Strangler).
RUNNING TIME: 101 minutes.
DVD: Criterion.

Night and the City, based on Gerald Kersh's novel of the same name (1938), is about Harry Fabian (Richard Widmark), a scheming, amoral hustler with grandiose dreams of rising to the top of the game in London. Although he is a figure of ridicule to those who know him, he is also manipulative and charming enough to make most people like him. The film focuses on his attempt to con his way into gaining control of professional wrestling in the city. There is little wrestling in the film, with the exception of the match between the Strangler (Mike Mazurki), an "entertainment wrestler," and Gregorius (Stanislaus Zbyszko), the embodiment of classical Greco-Roman wrestling.

As the film opens, Harry is fleeing for his life, just as he does at the end of the movie. He goes to see his girlfriend, Mary (Gene Tierney), to get money to pay off his pursuers. Thinking that she is not at home, he rifles through her purse, and she catches him at the attempted theft. When she asks him why he needs money, he describes yet another get-rich-quick scheme but finally admits that he needs five pounds to pay off a debt. She observes that he is always running, urges him to "grow up," and tells him she wants to get married and live like "nice people." After Harry leaves with the money, Mary goes to see Adam (Hugh Marlowe), a neighbor who cares for her but is the antithesis of Harry. As he gives her three pounds, he describes Harry as "an artist without an art."

Harry's chance occurs when he overhears an argument between Gregorius and his son, Kristo (Herbert Lom), over the wrestling matches the son is staging in London. Calling Kristo's bouts "fake," Gregorius leaves the arena with his young friend Nikolas (Ken Richmond), another Greco-Roman wrestler. Claiming to be a fan of Greco-Roman wrestling, Harry cons Gregorius into sponsoring his plans for a renewal of classical wrestling. Harry needs money to promote his scheme and approaches his boss, Philip Nosseross (Francis Sullivan), who employs Harry as a tout to get wealthy foreigners into his nightclub to rip them off. Philip laughs at the scheme but promises to give him two hundred pounds if he can raise the other two hundred pounds. After some of his associates turn him down, Harry asks Philip's wife, Helen (Googie Withers), a former lover, for the money. She agrees, but only if Harry secures a nightclub license for her so she can leave Philip and run her own club. Harry obtains a phony license from one of his crooked friends. When Philip notices that Helen's new silver fox fur coat is missing from her closet, he is convinced that she sold the coat and gave money to Harry and swears revenge. He tells Harry that he will put up the money if Harry can set up a match between Nikolas and the Strangler. Because Gregorius disapproves of fake wrestlers, Harry must find a way of getting Gregorius to agree to the match. He doesn't know that Philip and Kristo are in league with each other.

Since he has bought nameplates and fancy clothes to promote his image, Harry needs money to stage the first match and goes to Mary's apartment to steal cash. Thanks to Adam, Mary returns to confront Harry again. After Mary laments, "You're killing me and yourself," Harry takes the money and returns to the gym. Meanwhile, the Strangler, who has heard Harry's lies about Nikolas insulting him, also goes to the gym, where in a struggle Nikolas breaks his wrist. This provokes Gregorius, who takes on the Strangler in a clash between two kinds of wrestling, the "brains and the guts," the Greco-Roman and the modern. Gregorius abides by the rules, and the Strangler punches. Eventually, Gregorius's bear hug earns him the victory, but it is Pyrrhic since Gregorius has a heart attack and dies from the exertion. Kristo arrives before his father dies and blames Harry for his father's death. Since the Strangler believes that he may well be held responsible for the death, he also wants to get Harry.

Kristo offers a one-thousand-pound reward for Harry, and in a montage sequence the audience sees the word passing from one place to another. The Strangler goes to the Silver Fox Club, where Philip and Helen are arguing. Helen tells Philip she's leaving with Harry, and Philip predicts that she'll return to him, adding ruefully after she leaves, "And I'll want to take you back." Meanwhile, Harry is on the run, twice narrowly escaping from his pursuers. He first goes to Figler (James Hayter), "king of the fake beggars," who promises him safety, but then calls Kristo; Harry then goes to Anna O'Leary's (Maureen Delaney), who hides him, although she believes he is beyond hope. The ever-loyal Mary finds him, but it's too late since Kristo's men also know where he is. In a last-minute, well-intentioned gesture, Harry tries to convince Kristo's people that Mary has betrayed him, has turned him in, and wants the one-thousand-pound reward; but, like his other schemes, it doesn't work. The Strangler kills Harry and throws his body off a bridge into the Thames. Back at the Silver Fox Club, things have not gone well for Helen. The police have discovered that her license is a forgery and closed her place. When she returns to Philip, he seems immune to her entreaties. Then, she discovers that rather than turning his back on her, Philip is dead in his chair. Molly, a down-and-out denizen of the place, reveals that Philip's will left all his property to her, not to Helen. On the glimmer-of-hope side, Adam is seen comforting Mary at the end of the film.

In director Jules Dassin's film noir, with its darkness, shadows, and bars of light, cinematographer Max Greene paints a grainy, seamy, portrait of a London underground. *Night and the City* is not so much about wrestling as it is about how a man's unrealistic dreams blind him to a woman's love and result in his self-destruction.

NIGHT GAME (1989)

DIRECTOR: Peter Masterson. SCREENPLAY: Spencer Eastman. PRODUCER: George Litto. CINEMATOGRAPHY: Fred Murphy. EDITING: Robert Barrere, King Wilder. MUSIC: Pino Donaggio. PRODUCTION DESIGN: Neil Spisak. COSTUME DESIGN: Vicki Sánchez.

CAST: Roy Scheider (Mike Seaver), Karen Young (Roxy), Lane Smith (Witty), Richard Bradford (Nelson), Paul Gleason (Broussard).
RUNNING TIME: 95 minutes.
VHS: Warner Home Video.

A serial killer strikes each time a particular baseball pitcher wins a game.

NOBODY'S PERFECT (1990)

DIRECTOR: Robert Kaylor. SCREENPLAY: Joel Block, Annie Korzen. STORY: Steven Ader. PRODUCER: Benni Korzen. CINEMATOGRAPHY: Claus Loof. EDITING: Robert Gordon. MUSIC: Robert Randles. PRODUCTION DESIGN: Gilbert Wong. ART DIRECTION: Don Maskovich. COSTUME DESIGN: Lennie Barin.
CAST: Chad Lowe (Stephen), Gail O'Grady (Shelly), Patrick Breen (Andy), Kim Flowers (Jackie).
RUNNING TIME: 90 minutes.
DVD: MGM.

A shy college tennis player dresses like a woman to get closer to the girl he yearns for.

NO HOLDS BARRED (1989)

DIRECTOR: Thomas J, Wright. SCREENPLAY: Dennis Hackin. PRODUCERS: Vincent Kennedy McMahon Jr., Michael Rachmil. CINEMATOGRAPHY: Frank Beascoechea. EDITING: Tom Pryor. MUSIC: Jim Johnston. PRODUCTION DESIGN: James Shanahan.
CAST: Hulk Hogan (Rip), Joan Severance (Samantha Moore), Kurt Fuller (Brell), Tommy "Tiny" Lister (Zeus), Jesse Ventura (himself).
RUNNING TIME: 93 minutes.
VHS: Sony Pictures.

In *No Holds Barred* a television executive tries to lure a TV wrestler from his network.

NORTH DALLAS FORTY (1979)

DIRECTOR: Ted Kotcheff. SCREENPLAY: Peter Gent, Ted Kotcheff, Frank Yablans, based on the novel by Peter Gent. PRODUCER: Frank Yablans. CINEMATOGRAPHY: Paul Lohmann. EDITING: Jay Kamen. MUSIC: John Scott. PRODUCTION DESIGN: Alfred Sweeney. COSTUME DESIGN: Dorothy Jeakins.
CAST: Nick Nolte (Phillip Elliott), Mac Davis (Seth Maxwell), Charles Durning (Coach Johnson), Bo Svenson (Jo Bob Priddy), Dayle Haddon (Charlotte Caulder), Dabney Coleman (Emmett Hunter), Steve Forrest (Conrad Hunter).
RUNNING TIME: 119 minutes.
DVD: Paramount.

Nick Nolte stars as Phillip Elliott, a burned-out professional NFL wide receiver with "great hands" who is past his prime but soldiering on in a broken body, limping on weak knees that are constantly painful. Consequently, Phillip is addicted to pain-killing medications, but that is also true for most of his teammates, who are constantly popping pills or shooting up. The story derives from the novel by Peter

Nick Nolte in *North Dallas Forty*

Gent, who played for the Dallas Cowboys and worked with director Ted Kotcheff and producer Frank Yablans on the screenplay. Mac Davis made his film debut playing Phillip's presumed friend, the team quarterback, Seth Maxwell. Their friendship is established early on, but fizzles out in the last few minutes of the film.

The film is not as well plotted as it needs to be. Phillip has an attitude problem that the coaching staff and the owners have recognized and seem to resent, claiming it affects team morale. The team is headed toward a championship game in Chicago—but even that climactic match is not shown in the film in its entirety, since the film is ultimately not about gridiron action. Instead, the viewer is treated to far too many snarling practice sessions and rather too many howling locker-room antics and practical jokes. Meanwhile, Phillip has bought twenty acres of farmland and speaks of settling down to train horses once he is finished with football; the problem is that he can't seem to imagine himself ever finished with football.

The irony is that Phillip is not really in control of either his body or his career. When the defining Chicago game draws near, Seth tells Phillip that he should prepare himself to be in the game; but, Phillip later discovers, this is done mainly to motivate another player, Delma Huddle (Tommy Reamon), who has the same problem as Phillip but has so far resisted taking shots to deaden the pain. The prospect of being replaced by an older pro makes Delma rethink his options. At the last minute he agrees to take the shots and becomes the starter, leaving Phillip on the bench. But when Delma collapses on the field late in the game, with the team trailing by a touchdown, Phillip is taken off the bench. With seconds to go, in what seems to be the film's only exciting football moment, he catches a touchdown pass that should have won the game; however, the kicker misses the extra point, and the team loses.

So what happens, then, back in Dallas (without sufficient exposition, it might be added)? Phillip is called into the owner's office and confronted with evidence that he has smoked marijuana and is probably addicted to pain-killing drugs and steroids. He soon realizes he is being set up, and before he can be put on probation and suspended without pay, a huge argument ensues (since, as Phillip points out, nearly *everyone* on the team smokes pot and is addicted), so that he is able to quit in the film's dramatic moment. What is especially peculiar about this plot twist is that the coach would want to be rid of the receiver with the best hands in the game who all but won the championship for them. Phillip is able to see through the game's hypocrisy and corruption, but as the team owner informs him at the end, "seeing through the game is not the same as winning." After he leaves this meeting, Seth is waiting for him on the street below, and Phillip senses that his friend has betrayed him.

North Dallas Forty has been regarded as one of the best football movies ever made, no doubt on the strength of Nolte's bravura performance and the grit and pain it attempts to show of the game's seamier side. Add to this the vulgarity and banality suggested by the antics of Bo Svenson, who plays linebacker Jo Bob Priddy, and other helmeted yahoos, and it is clear that the game is not being glamorized. The film has been praised for its "realistic" and "hard-hitting" exposé of pro football. But its treatment is over the top, and, in fact, there is very little emphasis here on the game itself. Most of the players seem to be cartoonish oafs addicted to alcohol and drugs and obsessed with sex. The opening party scene, intended to establish the Nolte character as someone potentially more sensitive than his goonish teammates, is painfully embarrassing. The corruption of the team owners and coaching staff is both transparent and ultimately unconvincing—perhaps because the film seems rather obviously dated, thirty years past its release date. *North Dallas Forty* apparently wants to be about relationships, but doesn't quite know how to achieve that goal. Though it seems at first to be character driven, the only characters with any depth are Nolte and his lady friend, Charlotte Caulder (Dayle Haddon), who seems to understand horses and broken-down athletes, but is left lurking in the background for most of the film.

NORTH SHORE (1987)

DIRECTOR: William Phelps. SCREENPLAY: Tim McCanlies, William Phelps. STORY: Randal Kleiser. PRODUCER: Bill Finnegan. CINEMATOGRAPHY: Peter Smokler. EDITING: Robert Gordon. MUSIC: Richard Stone.
CAST: Matt Adler (Rick Kane), Nia Peeples (Kiani), John Philbin (Turtle), Gerry Lopez (Vince), Gregory Harrison (Chandler).
RUNNING TIME: 96 minutes.
DVD: Universal Studios.

An Arizona teenager who has only surfed artificial waves travels to Hawaii to experience the real thing.

O

O (2001)

DIRECTOR: Tim Blake Nelson.
SCREENPLAY: Brad Kaaya, based on the play *Othello* by William Shakespeare. PRODUCERS: Daniel L. Fried, Eric Gitter, Anthony Rhulen. CINEMATOGRAPHY: Russell Lee Fine. EDITING: Kate Sanford. MUSIC: Jeff Danna. PRODUCTION DESIGN: Dina Goldman. ART DIRECTION: Jack Balance. COSTUME DESIGN: Jill Ohanneson.
CAST: Mekhi Phifer (Odin James), Julia Stiles (Desi Brable), Josh Hartnett (Hugo Goulding), Andrew Keegan (Michael Cassio), Rain Phoenix (Emily), Martin Sheen (Coach "Duke" Goulding).
RUNNING TIME: 95 minutes.
DVD: Lion's Gate.

William Shakespeare's tragedies have been bowdlerized to soften their tragic import and have often been altered in production to make them more modern (for example, *Julius Caesar* performed in contemporary dress); they have even been "adapted" to fiction (Jane Smiley's *A Thousand Acres* as a Midwestern *Lear*). Countless film adaptations have also been made with varying degrees of success. Baz Luhrman, for example, modernized *Romeo and Juliet* into the teen tragedy *Romeo + Juliet* (1996) to relate it to younger audiences, so perhaps it is not surprising that filmmakers should try their hands at giving the Bard's plays a "sports twist." *She's the Man* (2006), for example, is a reworking of Shakespeare's *Twelfth Night*, in which the complications resulting from gender confusion are transformed to a soccer field. Brad Kaaya's screenplay for *O*, a reworking of *Othello*, is a similar kind of effort.

The scene is set in the South at the Palmetto Grove Academy, a prestigious private school that prides itself on its academics and on its athletics, particularly basketball. Odin James (Mekhi Phifer), the film's Othello, is the star of the basketball team and the lone African American in the school; Desi Brable (Julia Stiles), or "Dee," serves as Desdemona; Hugo Goulding (Josh Hartnett) plays Iago; Michael Cassio (Andrew Keegan) is Cassio; Roger Rodriquez (Elden Henson) is Roderigo; "Duke" Goulding (Martin Sheen) is the basketball coach and Hugo's father; Emily (Rain Phoenix), Hugo's girlfriend, is Emilia; Dean Brable (John Heard), Dee's father, serves as the duped Brabantio; and Brandy (Rachel Shumate) is Bianca. The essentials of the plot are retained with some substitutions (a scarf for the stolen handkerchief, the "ocular proof" of Desdemona's betrayal, for example) and some additions (Hugo's use of cocaine and steroids, which alters his behavior). Hugo's sense of "injured merit" derives from Duke's fatherly love for Odin as well as from Odin's decision to recognize Michael, rather than Hugo, as the person who really deserves to share the Most Valuable Player Award.

Using Roger, who seeks popularity and Dee's affection, as his "gull," Hugo plots to ruin the love between Odin, ostensibly his best friend, and Dee by suggesting that Dee and Michael are secretly having an affair. When his first scheme (informing Dean Brable that Odin has forced himself on Dee) fails, he uses Dee's independence and defiance of her father to suggest that she may not be the girl Odin believes her to be. Hugo then instigates a fight between Roger and Michael that results in the latter's suspension from the team. When Michael consults him about getting the suspension lifted, Hugo recommends that he work through his friendship with Dee to persuade her to intervene on his behalf with Odin. Since Michael and she are already close friends, their increased togetherness and her appeal on his behalf help convince Odin that they are lovers. Hugo adds to Odin's suspicions when he warns him that white girls are "snaky sexy," especially since Dee has already told Odin that she wants him to do whatever he wants with her. When they are next together, Odin ignores Dee's "no." She later tells her roommate Emily he "didn't really rape me."

A scarf Odin had given Dee convinces him of her infidelity. At Hugo's instigation, Emily takes and passes it on to Hugo, who in turn gives it to Michael, suggesting he present it to Brandy in order to win her favor. When Hugo has Odin eavesdrop on a conversation between Michael and Hugo, Odin believes that Michael is discussing Dee rather than Brandy and is enraged.

Back on the court, the Palmetto Grove Hawks have finished their regular season and have gained the home-court advantage throughout the playoffs, but Odin's play begins to deteriorate, partly because of his jealousy and partly because of the drugs that Hugo encourages him to take. At the slam dunk competition that precedes the championship game, Odin makes a thunderous dunk, smashing the glass backboard, receiving a perfect score from the judges and an ovation from the crowd. When a little boy approaches him, asking for the ball, Odin pushes the boy down, throws the ball through what remains of the backboard, glares at the crowd, and drops the basketball rim on the court. From the periphery, where he frequently lurks, Hugo asks bitterly, "Who's your favorite now, Dad?"

After supplying Odin with more drugs and informing him that Dee and Michael refer to him as "the nigger," Hugo convinces an unscrupulous pawn-shop dealer to swap one of Roger's expensive watches for a gun and then concocts a murder plot that will result in the deaths of Dee, Odin, Michael, and Roger, who will be blamed for Michael's death. After Roger fails to do as he is told, Hugo kills him and Michael; back in the dormitory Odin strangles Dee but is confronted by Emily, who has begun to suspect Hugo's treachery. Hugo, however, arrives and shoots her, too.

In this part of the film, there is a lot of cross-cutting between the dormitory, the car scene involving Michael's and Roger's murder, and the basketball court, where recruiters from major universities want to talk with the missing Odin. As Duke, who has sent people out looking for Odin and Hugo, talks to the recruiters, it becomes clear that he is not only ensuring that Odin gets a scholarship, but he is also interested in having his own coaching talents recognized, perhaps enough to get himself a job at one of the universities. Duke's obsession with winning and furthering himself, even at the expense of his family, seems almost as reprehensible as Hugo's jealousy.

When the police arrive, Odin stands with the gun in his hand and delivers what passes for a paraphrased soliloquy. He says that his life is over, that he was not a product of poverty, not into drugs and gangs, but was simply "played" by a "white prep school motherfucker." Then, as in the source, he kills himself. When asked about his motives, Hugo responds, "I say nothing," consistent with Iago's "motiveless malignity," even though it is clear that his motives are jealousy and ambition. As Desdemona's aria from Verdi's *Otello* wafts over the set, Hugo comments on the significance of the hawk, the Palmetto Grove mascot. Odin was the hawk, but the hawk can't fit in with the pigeons (birds that are featured both at the beginning and end of the film). The hawk wants attention, and, Hugo says, "I'm going to fly, too."

Although basketball exploits hardly seem as important as military ones involving the fates of countries and Palmetto Grove is no Venice, the *Othello* story here seems very powerful. Race and sex were significant in Shakespeare's play, but the *O* screenplay emphasizes them even more, partly because it deals with teenagers and American racial and sexual stereotypes.

OFFSIDE (2006)

Director: Jafar Panahi. Screenplay: Jafar Panahi, Shadmehr Rastin. Producer: Jafar Panahi. Cinematography: Rami Agami, Mahmoud Kalari. Editing: Jafar Panahi. Music: Yuval Barazani, Korosh Bozorgpour. Production Design: Iraj Raminfar.

Cast: Sima Mobarak-Shahi (First Girl), Shayesteh Irani (Smoking Girl), Ayda Sadeqi (Soccer Girl), Golnaz Farmani (Girl with Tchador), Mahnaz Zabihi (Girl Disguised as Soldier).

Running Time: 93 minutes. In Persian with English subtitles.

DVD: Sony Pictures.

In Iran, where it is illegal for women to attend soccer matches, female fans sometimes disguise themselves as males in order to gain admittance to games. When director Jafar Panahi discovered his daughter had successfully crashed a World Cup qualifying match, he decided to make a film based on this form of resistance to the stringent restrictions placed on Iranian women and girls. *Offside* features an ensemble cast of nonactors, and the women constructed their own male disguises. The characters are unnamed.

The film opens with a man in a taxi chasing a bus filled with soccer fans. He has learned that his daughter did not go to school that day, and her friends believe she is on her way to the stadium to attend the World Cup qualifying match between Iran and Bahrain. She is, in fact, en route to the match, but she is not on the bus that her father is following. The scene shifts to a minibus filled with male fans and First Girl (Sima Mobarak-Shahi), whose getup isn't fooling the other riders. Two boys who have spotted her worry that she will be arrested. When another bus pulls alongside, the boys notice two of its passengers are also girls, but this pair have more expertly concealed their identities. The boys conclude that First Girl is a "first timer" and offer to help her in spite of their doubts that she can elude detection. First Girl declines their assistance.

Outside of the stadium First Girl purchases a ticket from a scalper who immediately recognizes that she is female and charges her twice the going price and forces her to buy a poster as well. As she approaches the entrance, she observes that soldiers are frisking many of the ticket holders. She has not anticipated this possibility and moves out of line, debating what to do. When she observes another girl with glasses and a cane slip past the guards without difficulty, she summons her courage and returns to the line. However, once she has surrendered her ticket, First Girl cannot bluff her way past the guard who wants to search her. Although she tries to flee, she is quickly apprehended and turned over to the Soldier from Azerbaijan, a lieutenant (Safdar Samandar).

First Girl pleads with the lieutenant to allow her to call her father, but he is supposed to confiscate her cell phone. He agrees to take just the battery; then he asks her permission to use the phone to call his girlfriend, who is unhappy that his leave has been cancelled because of the game. After the phone call, he takes First Girl to a holding pen at the top level of the stadium, where she joins the other prisoners. In all, the guards have caught half a dozen offenders: Smoking Girl (Shayesteh Irani), whose cigarettes indicate that her rebellion against state prohibitions extends beyond attending sporting events; Soccer Girl (Ayda Sadeqi), a devoted fan who plays on an all-girl team at events males are not permitted to attend; Girl with Tchador (Golnaz Farmani), who dons the traditional black *tchador* after she is captured and her father shows up; Girl Disguised as Soldier (Mahnaz Zabihi), who not only wears a military uniform but also tries to sit in a section of the stadium reserved for officers; Young Girl (Nazanin Sediq-zadeh), who has become separated from her uncle; and, of course, First Girl. Several of the prisoners have friends inside who have escaped detection. Outside, a hundred women protesters wear white scarves. Later, it is learned that several have been admitted because of the presence of Western journalists.

The soldiers who stand guard over the holding pen alternate between concern for the young women, who face discipline, and frustration at their requests to make phone calls and to watch the match from a nearby passageway; one needs to use the bathroom. The soldiers, under obligation to enforce the law, face punishment themselves if they are caught being lenient, yet they find the law harsh and unjust; besides, they too would rather be watching the game. Exasperated, the lieutenant laments that his captives represent everything that is wrong with Tehrani women, but he relents. First, he allows one soldier to stand in the passageway overlooking the soccer field and provide a play-by-play for the others. Then he permits a soldier to escort Soccer Girl to the men's room (there being no women's facilities in the arena).

The farcical scene that follows underscores the absurdity of the situation. Wearing a mask that the soldier has fashioned from a poster and his shoelaces, Soccer Girl stumbles after the man, who, after verifying that the facility is vacant, instructs her not to read any graffiti. After she enters a stall, the soldier bars others from entering the restroom. He faces resistance from the rowdy men, but cheers from outside indicating a goal create a temporary distraction. Suddenly, the group of fans return just as Soccer Girl is exiting, and the men, who have suspected all along that a girl was on the premises, part to let her run, then block the soldier's pursuit.

Back at the holding pen, Smoking Girl asks the lieutenant why Japanese women were allowed into the stadium for the Japan-Iran game the previous week. Samandar replies that the Japanese do not understand Farsi and therefore would not comprehend the Iranian men's insults and obscenities. The lieutenant does not refer to the deaths that occurred at that match when fans stampeded, a matter of later significance. When the soldier-escort returns without Soccer Girl, the other girls, while happy one of their group has escaped and hopeful she secures a seat, express concern that the soldiers will be penalized. In return, the soldiers fear that the girls will be treated harshly, for they are to be taken to the vice squad. As the game continues unobserved by the principal characters, two men visit the holding pen. The first is a father searching for his daughter, who is not among the detainees; he is advised to wait for her at home. The second is Girl with Tchador's father. When he raises his hand to strike her, the soldiers intervene; however, she extracts her *tchador* from her backpack and obediently dons it. After a while, Soccer Girl returns voluntarily, explaining that she feels sorry for the cattle on Samandar's family's farm, which will suffer if he is punished for losing a prisoner. To pass the time, the girls decide to act out a play one of them saw, and they assign roles, including the soldiers in their casting.

As the game nears its end, a soldier returns to the opening and reports the on-field action until an official vehicle arrives. The girls are herded into a van along with a teenage boy who has been arrested for carrying sparklers. When he refers to the girls with the Farsi equivalent of "chicks," Soccer Girl head-butts him. Girl Disguised as a Soldier begins to cry, fearing she may be in serious trouble over the uniform. In the van, the soldiers try to catch the final minutes of the match on the radio, but the antenna is broken.

One of the girls complains that she is thirsty, and a soldier volunteers to get drinks for everyone. Since the van is caught in gridlock, he can easily slip out long enough to make the purchase and seek out a nearby television. When he returns with the refreshments, there are three minutes left and the score is tied. After fiddling with the antenna, he locates a position that permits reception, and everyone is able to hear Iran score the winning goal. Fireworks go off in the van, but the soldiers do not mind; they are ready to celebrate.

First Girl begins to cry, revealing that one of her friends was killed at the earlier match against Japan. She had intended to attend the qualifying round as a memorial for the friend. Now, she decides to make the celebration her memorial and asks the teenage boy for seven sparklers, which she distributes to the others, including the soldier. A vendor with a snack tray appears at the window. The treats are passed around, and the soldier is asked to dance. He willingly joins the celebrants outside and remains oblivious as the girls exit the van and dance off into the evening holding their sparklers aloft.

Offside manages to criticize the treatment of women in Iranian society while presenting the Iranian people in a positive light. The soccer fans, both male and female, wear the colors of the Iranian flag—and sometimes the flag itself—proudly, and the sport, while taking place off stage, offers the potential for a constructive nationalism.

Although the Iranian government denied Panahi permission to film *Offside*, he was able to do so under the pretense of shooting a different script. The movie has been banned in Iran but has been well received in the West, earning a Silver Bear Award at the Berlin International Film Festival. *Salon* reports that the George W. Bush administration denied Panahi a visa to attend screenings at U.S. festivals.

ON A CLEAR DAY (2005)

Director: Gaby Dellal. Screenplay: Alex Rose. Producers: Dorothy Berwin, Sarah Curtis. Cinematography: David Johnson. Editing: Robin Sales. Music: Stephen Warbeck. Production Design: Mark Leese. Art Direction: Caroline Grebbell. Costume Design: Kate Hawley.
Cast: Peter Mullan (Frank), Brenda Blethyn (Joan), Jamie Sives (Rob), Billy Boyd (Danny), Sean McGinley (Eddie).
Running Time: 98 minutes.
DVD: Universal Studios.

An unemployed, middle-aged shipyard worker decides he wants to swim the English Channel.

ONE ON ONE (1977)

DIRECTOR: Lamont Johnson. SCREENPLAY: Robby Benson, Jerry Segal. PRODUCER: Martin Hornstein. CINEMATOGRAPHY: Donald M. Morgan. EDITING: Robbe Roberts. MUSIC: Charles Fox. ART DIRECTION: Sherman Loudermilk.
CAST: Robby Benson (Henry Steele), Annette O'Toole (Janet Hays), G. D. Spradlin (Coach Smith), Gail Strickland (B.J. Rudolph), Melanie Griffith (hitchhiker).
RUNNING TIME: 98 minutes.
DVD: Warner Bros. Archives.

A small-town basketball player gets a rude awakening in college, as he is burdened by high expectations and a sadistic coach.

OUT COLD (2001)

DIRECTORS: Brendan Malloy, Emmett Malloy. SCREENPLAY: Jon Zack. PRODUCERS: Michael Aguilar, Jonathan Glickman, Lee R. Mayes. CINEMATOGRAPHY: Richard Crudo. EDITING: Jeffrey Wolf. MUSIC: Michael Andrews. PRODUCTION DESIGN: Michael Bolton. ART DIRECTION: James Steuart. COSTUME DESIGN: Carla Hetland.
CAST: Jason London (Rick Rambis), Lee Majors (John Majors), A. J. Cook (Jenny), Willie Garson (Ted Muntz), Zack Galifianakis (Luke).
RUNNING TIME: 89 minutes.
DVD: Walt Disney Video.

Snowboarders must prevent a land developer from tearing down their ski resort.

OVER THE TOP (1987)

DIRECTOR: Menahem Golan. SCREENPLAY: Stirling Silliphant, Sylvester Stallone. STORY: Gary Conway, David Engelbach. PRODUCERS: Yoram Globus, Menahem Golan. CINEMATOGRAPHY: David Gurfinkel. EDITING: James Symons, Don Zimmerman. MUSIC: Giorgio Moroder. PRODUCTION DESIGN: James Schoppe. ART DIRECTION: William Ladd Skinner. COSTUME DESIGN: Tom Bronson.
CAST: Sylvester Stallone (Lincoln "Linc" Hawk), Robert Loggia (Jason Cutler), Susan Blakely (Christina Hawk), Rick Zumwalt (Bob "Bull" Hurley), David Mendenhall (Mike).
RUNNING TIME: 93 minutes.
DVD: Warner Home Video.

Sylvester Stallone, whose *Rocky* (1976) is the epitome of the underdog sports film, plays Lincoln "Linc" Hawk in yet another underdog film, this time one about arm wrestling, a sport closely related in its colorful participants to professional wrestling. As in Stallone's *Rocky* films, there is also a story about a father-son relationship that goes sour and then has to be restored. In *Over the Top*, Linc is an on-the-road truck driver who had left his wife (Susan Blakely) and son, Mike (David Mendenhall), ten years ago and returns to keep his promise to his dying wife, who wants to see father and son reunited. Complicating matters is Mike's grandfather, Jason Cutler (Robert Loggia), a wealthy patriarch who had been responsible for Linc's leaving and who is now intent on living vicariously through his grandson.

The film begins at the graduation ceremonies of a military school, where Jason has a great deal of influence. Linc, who has driven his aging semi and who is casually dressed, stands in marked contrast to the other parents, whose expensive clothing and luxury cars indicate their wealth. A limousine ordered by Jason waits for Mike, but the school commandant, acting on instructions from Mike's mother, tells him to go with Linc, who will take him to the hospital where his mother is soon to undergo surgery. When he learns that Mike has left with his father, Jason rebukes the commandant and orders his subordinates to find Mike and bring him back.

At first, the journey to the hospital does not go well because Mike's anger about his father's absence and lack of communication prompt him to try to run away. However, the two begin to bond when Linc shows him how to drive the semi. At a diner Linc is challenged to an arm-wrestling contest by a man called Smasher. After defeating Smasher, Linc sets up a match between Mike and an aggressive older teen who insults Mike and beats him in the first of a best-of-three contest; then, with some encouragement from his father, Mike betters his opponent to win the last two challenges. As father and son leave the diner, three men employed by Jason attempt to seize Mike, but Linc dispatches them in quick measure, and he and Mike continue toward their destination.

When they arrive at the hospital, they learn that Mike's mother has died during surgery. Mike's anger returns and is directed at Linc: had Linc not become caught up in the arm wrestling, they might have reached the hospital before the operation began. Mike returns to his grandfather's house. Linc follows. After being turned away at the iron gates to the Cutler mansion, he rams his semi through the gates and into the front door of the house. Linc is arrested and faces enormous legal fees; however, Jason agrees to drop all charges if Linc will relinquish custody of Mike. Reluctantly, Linc agrees.

Linc drives to Las Vegas, for the World Arm-Wrestling Championships. He sells his truck in order to bet on himself to win. (Since the winner's prize includes a new semi as well as $500,000, Linc's selling the truck seems a bit "over the top.") Linc differs from the contestants: he doesn't dress like a thug or use a moniker like Smasher or Blaster, and he refrains from threatening his opponents and grunting loudly during his bouts. Although a newcomer, he makes it to the finals of the double elimination tournament. Meanwhile, Mike has found dozens of letters from Linc that Jason had hidden. Mike takes Jason's pickup and, pursued by Jason and his henchmen, speeds toward Las Vegas.

When Mike finds his father, Linc has just lost a round, but Mike's presence restores his spirits. Linc enters the last match an underdog against Bull Hurley (Rick Zumwalt). It is a long and grueling match, with the advantage alternating from one man to the other. Finally, Mike instructs his father to go "over the top," and Linc manages to win, thus clinching the championship. (The plot skips over the double elimination.) In a scene reminiscent of the *Rocky* films, the victorious Linc holds Mike and the trophy aloft as the music swells. Jason, who has been watching the action, finally understands that Linc and Mike belong together and disappears into the crowd. Mike's mother's dream has been realized.

Perhaps because of the subject matter, *Over the Top* did not fare well with the critics. In fact, the RAZZIE Awards for Worst Supporting Actor and Worst New Star went to Mendenhall, while Stallone was nominated for, but did not win, the RAZZIE for Worst Actor.

***OXFORD BLUES* (1984)**

DIRECTOR: Robert Boris. SCREENPLAY: Robert Boris. PRODUCERS: Cassian Elwes, Elliott Kastner. CINEMATOGRAPHY: John Stanier. EDITING: Patrick Moore. MUSIC: John Du Prez. PRODUCTION DESIGN: Terry Pritchard. COSTUME DESIGN: Pip Newbery.
CAST: Rob Lowe (Nick De Angelo), Ally Sheedy (Rona), Julian Sands (Colin Gilchrist Fisher), Amanda Pays (Victoria Wingate), Michael Gough (Doctor Ambrose).
RUNNING TIME: 97 minutes.
DVD: Warner Archives.

An American enrolls in Oxford and joins the rowing team to impress a girl.

P

PAPER LION (1968)

DIRECTOR: Alex March. SCREENPLAY: Lawrence Roman, based on the book by George Plimpton. PRODUCER: Stuart Millar. CINEMATOGRAPHY: Louis San Andres. MUSIC: Roger Kellaway.
CAST: Alan Alda (George Plimpton), Lauren Hutton (Kate), Joe Schmidt (himself), Alex Karras (himself), Frank Gifford (himself), Vince Lombardi (himself).
RUNNING TIME: 107 minutes.
VHS: Weston Woods.

This film is based on George's Plimpton's nonfiction book about joining the Detroit Lions as an honorary member and actually taking the field.

PARADISE ALLEY (1978)

DIRECTOR: Sylvester Stallone. SCREENPLAY: Sylvester Stallone. PRODUCERS: John F. Roach, Ronald A. Suppa, Jeff Wald. CINEMATOGRAPHY: László Kovács. EDITING: Eve Newman. MUSIC: Bill Conti. PRODUCTION DESIGN: John W. Corso. ART DIRECTION: Deborah Beaudet
CAST: Sylvester Stallone (Cosmo Carboni), Lee Canalito (Victor Carboni), Armand Assante (Lenny Carboni), Anne Archer (Annie).
RUNNING TIME: 107 minutes.
DVD: Universal Studios.

This film depicts the story of three brothers in the 1940s, one of whom wants to be a professional wrestler.

PASTIME (1991)

DIRECTOR: Robin B. Armstrong. SCREENPLAY: David Eyre Jr. PRODUCERS: Robin B. Armstrong, Eric Tynan Young. CINEMATOGRAPHY: Tom Richmond. EDITING: Mark S. Westmore. MUSIC: Lee Holdridge. PRODUCTION DESIGN: David W. Ford. COSTUME DESIGN: Kristine Brown.
CAST: William Russ (Roy Dean Bream), Scott Plank (Randy Keever), Noble Willingham (Clyde Bigby), Glenn Plummer (Tyrone Debray), Jeffrey Tambor (Peter DePorte).
RUNNING TIME: 94 minutes.
DVD: Miramax.

Pastime is a dramatic story about an aging minor league pitcher who mentors a seventeen-year-old rookie, the only African American on the team. Roy Dean Bream (William Russ), now forty-one, has made just one major league appearance, giving up a grand slam to Stan Musial, but being a baseball player has been a consuming passion for all of his adult life. When the film opens, it is 1957, and Roy Dean is holding down the bench in the bullpen of the Tri-City Steamers, a Central California team that is losing money for its owner, who sometimes fills in for the hotdog vendor.

For Roy Dean, whom the owner refers to as "Methuselah," just staying in shape is a full-time job. During the opening credits the camera pans Roy Dean's living quarters, where every surface is littered with ointments, Ace bandages, and prescription medications. Even though he jogs each morning, he can't keep up with his younger teammates, some of whom smoke during practice. The owner is ready to send Roy Dean into retirement now that the new youngster has been added to the roster, but the Steamers' manager, Clyde (Noble Willingham), who values Roy Dean for his experience and his love of the game, is reluctant to let him go.

For the most part, the younger players neither share Roy Dean's enthusiasm nor appreciate his expertise. A Steamers' starting pitcher, Randy Keever (Scott Plank), is particularly resentful of Roy Dean's advice, rejecting suggestions that could both improve his pitching and reduce risk of injury to his throwing arm. After the Steamers lose their opening game, Randy's bad mood infects the locker room, and none of the other players accept Roy Dean's invitation to discuss the game over a beer.

At a nearby tavern Roy Dean is sitting by himself when an argument breaks out between a young pool player and an elderly drunk who has palmed the young man's quarter. Roy Dean intervenes to protect the old man and finds himself quickly knocked to his knees. After staggering to his feet, he seizes the cue ball from the pool table and cocks his arm, but then drops the ball onto the table and walks out. The bartender, an attractive young woman who has been impressed by Roy's composure, checks to make certain he is not hurt. Although Roy Dean rejects her offer of ice for his bruised head, the ice between the two has been broken.

A short while later Roy Dean passes the rookie, Tyrone Debray (Glenn Plummer), on the street and, as an afterthought, invites him to have a soda. Conversation is awkward. Roy Dean's attempt to compliment Tyrone on his skills by calling him "a credit to his race" articulates a tension that earlier in the film has been conveyed primarily through silence—other players ignore Tyrone, and he avoids eye contact. Roy Dean, however, persists in his efforts to engage the rookie and finally gains his interest by talking about the major leagues. Then he tells Tyrone his dream of staying in the game long enough to set a minor league iron man record.

The next morning Roy Dean takes Tyrone to the diner where many team members have breakfast. Although Tyrone is served without incident, the racism of the other players surfaces as Randy, sitting nearby, calls several times for salt and pepper while his teammates laugh and nudge one another. Roy Dean's advice to Tyrone is to ignore the taunts and focus on developing his talent. Soon, Roy Dean begins coaching Tyrone and shows him his signature pitch.

Before an away game in which Tyrone is to make his debut, Randy intimates to the manager that the others on the team are suspicious about the nature of bonding between Roy Dean and Tyrone, a transparent attempt to eliminate competition from the rookie. But Clyde is not deceived and reprimands Randy, albeit gently. During the game a fight breaks out, and Tyrone is one of the players ejected. Randy takes over, but the game stretches to seventeen innings. Then, with the bases loaded, Roy Dean is sent to relieve Randy. Roy Dean throws his signature pitch for a strike against the strongest hitter; however, when he tries to repeat the tactic, the pitch sails wild, scoring the winning run. As a result the Steamers' owner determines that Roy Dean must go.

On the return trip the bus breaks down, requiring the team to take turns pushing. Roy insists on shouldering his share of the load, but the effort shows as he huffs beside his younger teammates. During a break the coach mentions a retired player who has started a successful business and suggests Roy Dean give him a call. Later, Tyrone asks if he has considered coaching. Roy Dean, however, fails to hear the message. It isn't until a party at the owner's house, when Randy disingenuously wishes him well, that Roy Dean realizes his fate. Instead of waiting for the very intoxicated owner to summon the courage to fire him, Roy Dean tells the owner that he's leaving the team to pursue an opportunity that has suddenly arisen. Then he rejoins Tyrone and Inez (Deirdre O'Connell), the bartender whom he has finally asked out, and tells them he's no longer a baseball player. The three go to Inez's house, but Roy Dean says he needs some time to himself, so he drives off, leaving Inez and Tyrone to wait for his return.

Roy Dean goes to the baseball field; instead of clearing out his locker, he dons his uniform, turns on the stadium lights, and takes a duffel bag of balls out to the mound, where he begins pitching. Suddenly he stops, smiles, and collapses, dead from a stroke. Tyrone, who has left Inez's to look for Roy Dean, notices the field lights and discovers the body. He, Inez, the coach, and three members of the Veterans of Foreign Wars attend the funeral. Immediately afterward, Tyrone and the manager leave for a game that had started thirty minutes earlier.

At the field Clyde pulls Randy and sends in Tyrone. When Randy loses his temper and makes a disrespectful remark about Roy Dean, Tyrone throws a punch, but it is Randy who gets thrown off the team. At this point the other players seem to have accepted Tyrone, although in a particularly fifties' way; one even rubs his head. On the mound Tyrone fires two strikes. As he prepares to deliver Roy Dean's special pitch, the scene changes and suddenly Tyrone is wearing a White Sox uniform before a packed, cheering crowd. The film ends here on an ambiguous note. Perhaps Tyrone has achieved success in the majors; perhaps, like Roy Dean, he will blow his one chance to make it big; perhaps he's just dreaming.

Pastime breaks from the usual patterns for baseball films. The main character is unheroic: he doesn't win the big game, and he's waited too long to win the woman; if he's learned a great lesson in life, it's nothing he shares in a dramatic moment. His death, alone, throwing baseballs at nothing, reflects the futility of his career, if one measures success by personal achievement. However, Roy Dean seems to have been content just being a ballplayer, if only a mediocre one. More importantly, he is a decent guy. Without being aggressive, he is someone who looks out for those weaker than he. He overcomes his discomfort about race enough to befriend Tyrone. The film has been criticized for Roy Dean's patronization of Tyrone, but Roy Dean is well meaning and, for the time in which the film is set, progressive.

PAT AND MIKE (1952)

DIRECTOR: George Cukor. SCREENPLAY: Ruth Gordon, Garson Kanin. PRODUCER: Lawrence Weingarten. CINEMATOGRAPHY: William Daniels. EDITING: George Boemler. MUSIC: David Raksin. ART DIRECTION: Cedric Gibbons, Urie McCleary. COSTUME DESIGN: Orry-Kelly.

CAST: Spencer Tracy (Mike Conovan), Katharine Hepburn (Pat Pemberton), Aldo Ray (Davie Hucko), Jim Backus (Charles Berry), William Ching (Collier Weld).

Running Time: 95 minutes. B&W.
Academy Award Nomination: Best Original Screenplay.
DVD: Warner Home Video.

Katharine Hepburn's athleticism inspired this romantic comedy about the relationship between a talented athlete and her less-than-virtuous promoter, played by Spencer Tracy. The film was directed by George Cukor and written by Ruth Gordon and Garson Kanin, the same team that created *Adam's Rib*, which, like *Pat and Mike*, explores issues of equality between the sexes. Although by today's standards the Hepburn character seems overly dependent on the men in her life, the film challenged conventions of the time. It also showcased some of the best-known female athletes of the late 1940s and early 1950s, all of whom portrayed themselves.

When the film opens, Pat Pemberton (Hepburn) is a college athletic instructor engaged to Collier Weld (William Ching), the administrative vice president at the college. That Collier is an unsuitable fiancé becomes readily apparent during a round of golf with one of the school's benefactors and his wife, an ardent golfer. Collier is counting on Pat to play well so that the benefactor can win a bet with his wife, but Collier's presence unnerves Pat, and she fails to perform adequately. Angered by the power Collier seems to hold over her and determined to prove herself, she quits her job and decides to enter the Women's National Tournament. In Collier's absence she qualifies easily and is set to compete against the likes of Betty Hicks, Helen Dettweiler, and the legendary Babe Didrikson Zaharias.

On the eve of the tournament, sports promoter Mike Conovan (Spencer Tracy) and his assistant sneak into Pat's room, hoping to persuade her to throw the match and profit in the process. Pat refuses, but Mike is smitten and leaves his card with her, offering to promote her career. He tells his assistant that her honesty is "the only disgusting thing about her." Mike bets on Pat and seems certain to come out ahead as Pat moves through the field. In the final round she maintains a one-stroke lead over Babe Didrikson Zaharias—until she spots Collier in the crowd and overshoots the green. On the final hole, with the two tied, Pat again notices Collier and blows the putt, losing the tournament.

After the tournament Collier and Pat board a train together, and Collier suggests that they marry soon; however, Pat fears that Collier wants to rescue her after her disappointing loss and expects her to assume the role of "little woman." She tosses her bags out the window and leaps from the train as it is pulling out of the station, determined to pursue an athletic career and regain confidence in herself.

The scene shifts to Mike's office in New York, where he is lecturing Davie Hucko (Aldo Ray), a not-too-bright boxer who is a pound over his weight limit, when Pat knocks on the door, seeking Mike's assistance. They quickly agree to a fifty-fifty deal, and Mike becomes Pat's manager, trainer, and constant companion. He enforces a strict set of rules—no alcohol, no cigarettes, no men—and Pat follows with little protest. Soon her professional career is underway. First, she excels in tennis, winning at mixed doubles with Frank Parker over Don Budge and Alice Marble. Then, in a singles competition in California against Gussie Moran, Collier appears in a courtside box, and Pat blows a one-set, single-game lead. In the locker room after the loss, Mike and Collier argue about which man owns Pat, who dismisses them both, albeit tearfully. Yet, she is soon back in training. Mike tries to convince her that Collier is a jinx, but Pat attributes his effect on her to love. However, Pat doesn't sound too convinced, and her relationship with Mike continues to warm.

One evening after Mike has broken up a card game between Pat, Davie, and the assistant, which has gone past the 9:00 p.m. curfew, he walks Pat to her room and suggests coming in. She rebuffs him good-naturedly with his own rules, but as she gazes at the bedside photo of herself with Collier, Collier's face is replaced with Mike's. Meanwhile, Mike, visiting his prize horse, Little Nell, begins to see Pat's face instead of the horse's.

As the attraction between Pat and Mike intensifies, Pat shows increasing self-confidence while Mike demonstrates he's become an honest promoter. When his East Coast "business partners" pressure him to "assure" the outcome of Pat's next golf tournament, Mike refuses to cooperate, even though Pat is willing to do whatever is necessary to protect him. Later that evening Pat has her chance when the thuggish partners interrupt their dinner and take Mike outside. Pat follows and, before the partners can throw a punch, levels them both; she then reenacts the scene at the local police station. Embarrassed at being rescued, Mike tells Pat he's created a Mrs. Frankenstein. Their argument over proper gender behavior is broken off abruptly when they encounter Collier at the hotel. A literal tug of war ensues as each man tries to pull Pat way from the other. Pat frees herself and marches off, leaving the two men to discuss Collier's effect on Pat's athletic performance.

That night Pat is restless, and neither Mike nor Collier can sleep. Mike, who has a key to Pat's room, enters quietly to check the windows and pull up the covers. Just as he is about to tiptoe out, he sneezes, Pat wakes up, and Collier arrives. Assuming the worst, Collier barges into the room. Frightened by the intrusion, Pat screams for Mike and, after Collier stomps off, tells Mike that she trusts him to take care of her. As they lean toward each other and a kiss seems inevitable, Mike retreats, offering a handshake instead. At the tournament the next day, Collier shows up in the crowd, deliberately trying to catch Pat's eye. Although she notices him, he cannot break her concentration, indicating that whatever power he once held over her has dissolved, and she can now move confidently into a relationship with Mike based on mutual respect and shared responsibility.

PEACEFUL WARRIOR (2006)

DIRECTOR: Victor Salva. SCREENPLAY: Kevin Bernhardt, based on the book *Way of the Peaceful Warrior* by Dan Millman. PRODUCERS: Mark Amin, Robin Schorr, David Welch, Cami Winikoff. CINEMATOGRAPHY: Sharone Meir. EDITING: Ed Marx. MUSIC: Bennett Salvay. PRODUCTION DESIGN: Bernt Capra. ART DIRECTION: Anthony Tremblay. COSTUME DESIGN: Lynette Meyer.

CAST: Scott Mechlowicz (Dan Millman), Amy Smart (Joy), Nick Nolte (Socrates), Ray Wise (Doctor Hayden).

RUNNING TIME: 121 minutes.

DVD: Universal Studios.

A gymnast with Olympic hopes encounters both psychological and physical obstacles to his dreams.

PENITENTIARY (1979)

DIRECTOR: Jamaa Fanaka. SCREENPLAY: Jamaa Fanaka. PRODUCER: Jamaa Fanaka. CINEMATOGRAPHY: Marty Ollstein. EDITING: Betsy Blankett. MUSIC: William Anderson, Andre Douglas, Frankie Gaye. ART DIRECTION: Adel Mazen.

CAST: Leon Isaac Kennedy (Martel "Too Sweet" Gordone), Thommy Pollard (Eugene T. Lawson), Hazel Spears (Linda), Donovan Womack (Jesse Amos).

RUNNING TIME: 99 minutes.

DVD: Xenon.

After being convicted for murder, a young man joins the prison's boxing team.

PENITENTIARY II (1982)

DIRECTOR: Jamaa Fanaka. SCREENPLAY: Jamaa Fanaka. PRODUCER: Jamaa Fanaka. CINEMATOGRAPHY: Stephen L. Posey. MUSIC: Jack Wheaton. ART DIRECTION: Adel Mazen. COSTUME DESIGN: Katherine Dover.
CAST: Leon Isaac Kennedy (Martel "Too Sweet" Gordone), Ernie Hudson ("Half Dead"), Glynn Turnman (Charles), Peggy Blow (Ellen), Mr. T (himself).
RUNNING TIME: 108 minutes.
DVD: Xenon.

In this sequel to the 1979 film, the young boxer is back in prison and fighting for his life once again.

PENITENTIARY III (1987)

DIRECTOR: Jamaa Fanaka. SCREENPLAY: Jamaa Fanaka. PRODUCERS: Jamaa Fanaka, Leon Isaac Kennedy. CINEMATOGRAPHY: Marty Ollstein. EDITING: Alain Jakubowicz. MUSIC: Garry Schyman. ART DIRECTION: Craig Freitag. COSTUME DESIGN: Marie Burrell Fanaka.
CAST: Leon Isaac Kennedy (Martel "Too Sweet" Gordone), Anthony Geary (Serenghetti), Steven Antin (Roscoe), Ric Mancini (The Warden).
RUNNING TIME: 90 minutes.
VHS: Warner Home Video.

For the third time, a fighter finds himself wrongfully accused, back in prison, and back in the boxing ring.

PERSONAL BEST (1982)

DIRECTOR: Robert Towne. SCREENPLAY: Robert Towne. PRODUCER: Robert Towne. CINEMATOGRAPHY: Michael Chapman. EDITING: Jacqueline Cambas, Jere Huggins, Ned Humphreys, Walt Mulconery, Bud Smith. MUSIC: Jill Fraser, Jack Nitzche. PRODUCTION DESIGN: Ron Hobbs. COSTUME DESIGN: Ron Heilman, Linda Henrikson.
CAST: Mariel Hemingway (Chris Cahill), Patrice Donnelly (Tory Skinner), Scott Glenn (Terry Tingloff), Kenny Moore (Denny Stites), Jim Moody (Roscoe Travis).
RUNNING TIME: 124 minutes.
DVD: Warner Home Video.

Personal Best is a drama about two athletes who become romantically involved while training to make the U.S. women's track and field team. The U.S. boycott of the 1980 Moscow Olympics, which occurred while the film was in production, required script changes affecting the nature of competition between the main characters, Chris Cahill (Mariel Hemingway) and Tory Skinner (pentathlon athlete Patrice Donnelly). *Personal Best* is one of the first Hollywood productions to present a lesbian relationship in which the principal participants are unburdened by personal guilt and social condemnation, yet the movie has remained controversial.

The film opens at a track meet in 1976, where hurdler Chris Cahill has not performed well and has been chastised by her father. That evening she drinks too much at a bar where the athletes are relaxing and is driven home by another athlete, Tory Skinner. In the car, Chris breaks down and cries on Tory's shoulder. Tory, who competes in the pentathlon, admires Chris's flexibility and technique and tries to boost her courage. Chris cheers up, and the two smoke marijuana, drink, arm wrestle, and kiss. An erotic love scene follows, filmed in a children's room that, according to director Robert Towne, was intended to convey a sense of innocence. With apparent immediacy, the two set up housekeeping, and Tory convinces her coach (Scott Glenn as Terry Tingloff) to work with Chris. He regards Chris as a second-rate athlete, but concedes, sighing about "young love."

At first Terry ignores Chris as she trains with the other athletes, but with some prodding from Tory, he gives her a trial. Chris slips coming off the block but doesn't give up and finishes with the rest of the pack, impressing both the coach and the other hurdlers. Chris is included on the team when it travels to Colombia for the 1978 World Student Games. The day before the meet, she buys fruit from a street vendor and becomes violently ill. Tory sits up all night with her; even after the worst has passed, the weepy Chris does not want to be left alone. The next day Tory fails in her events, provoking anger from Terry. When Chris tries to take the blame, he complains to her, "You're sick, and she can't perform. What is this shit?" Following this exchange, Chris wins her event. That evening as the team celebrates, it is Tory who has too much to drink. She appears jealous that Chris is talking to a guy and enjoying herself. When Tory is ready to leave, Chris isn't.

The growing tension in the relationship is highlighted in the next scene, in which Chris has gone off by herself and is relaxing on a blanket under a tree. As she starts stretching her legs, Terry drives up and walks over. He tells her to continue her stretches; she immediately develops a cramp, and Terry massages her thigh while he tells her he wants her to train for the pentathlon, a move that places her in direct competition with Tory for a spot on the Olympic team. The two women now train together under Terry's scrutiny, and when Tory offers Chris some advice, Terry plants seeds of distrust, privately telling Chris that Tory may be trying to sabotage Chris's progress. As Terry pays more attention to Chris, Tory's distress deepens. During a discussion with Chris about their relationship, Chris repeatedly uses the word "friend," indicating that she and Tory have

Patrice Donnelly (left), Jodi Anderson (center), and Mariel Hemingway (right) in *Personal Best*

very different views of both their present situation and their future. There is reconciliation, but it lasts only until, following Tory's suggestion, Chris changes her mark for the high jump and as a result, injures her knee. Once again, Chris dissolves in tears, but this time it is Terry, not Tory, who assumes the role of caretaker. He takes her to his place, where he refuses to let her talk to Tory on the telephone. After ranting about Chris and Tory and the complications of coaching women, he kisses her.

The next morning Chris returns to the apartment she and Tory have been sharing and announces that she wants her own place. Chris quickly moves on to a new relationship, this time with a man, water polo player Denny Stites (Kenny Moore). Meanwhile, Terry is trying to control Chris and to keep her away from Tory, but Chris is becoming more independent. When the coach says he doesn't want the two women on the practice field at the same time, Chris insists that she practice with the whole team or not at all. Later, at the field trials that would have determined the Olympic team, Chris approaches Tory to wish her luck.

Although the American athletes will not participate in the 1980 Olympics, qualifying is still important to them. There are only two slots for the pentathlon and competition is stiff. After the first day, Chris has a chance of placing first among the contenders, but Tory is in trouble; she needs to finish well in the last event, the 800-meter run, an event at which Chris excels. Instead of running her own race and finishing with a kick, Chris sets a fast pace in order to challenge the runner Tory needs to beat. Chris's strategy is successful, exhausting both lead runners and allowing Tory to place first in the race and qualify for the team. The two women stand together to receive their awards, and Tory acknowledges Chris's relationship with Denny, saying, "He's cute. For a guy."

The film was daring for its time in presenting a lesbian relationship without condemnation, but its subject drew criticism. Some felt the movie stereotyped female athletes as homosexual. Others thought the movie failed to acknowledge true lesbian sexuality because the Hemingway character moves so easily into a heterosexual relationship. Still others objected to the nudity—in addition to the love scene, there are two scenes set in a sauna and featuring a number of naked women athletes, and a bathroom scene with Moore and Hemingway that does little to advance plot or develop character. In general those associated with the production have defended its photography of the women as a celebration of female athleticism—and there is some good footage of track and field events—but a number of point-of-view shots indicate otherwise.

PHAR LAP (1983)

Director: Simon Wincer. Screenplay: David Williamson. Producer: John Sexton. Cinematography: Russell Boyd. Editing: Tony Paterson. Music: Bruce Rowland. Production Design: Lawrence Eastwood. Costume Design: Anna Senior.
Cast: Tom Burlinson (Tommy Woodcock), Martin Vaughan (Harry Telford), Judy Morris (Bea Davis), Ron Leibman (Dave Davis), Celia De Burgh (Vi Telford).
Running Time: 107 minutes.
VHS: 20th Century Fox.

This is an Australian film about real-life legend Phar Lap (Thai for "lightning"), a racehorse champion in the early years of the Depression, who died under mysterious circumstances.

PING PONG PLAYA (2007)

Director: Jessica Yu. Screenplay: Jimmy Tsai, Jessica Yu. Producer: Anne Clements, Joan Huang. Cinematography: Frank G.

DeMarco. EDITING: Zene Baker. MUSIC: Jeff Beal. PRODUCTION DESIGN: Denise Hudson. ART DIRECTION: Gabor Norman. COSTUME DESIGN: Jessica Flaherty.
CAST: Jimmy Tsai (Christopher "C-Dub" Wang), Roger Fan (Michael Wang), Shelley Malil (D. B. Reddy), Stephnie Weir (Cheryl Davis).
RUNNING TIME: 96 minutes.
DVD: Image Entertainment.

In her first feature film, documentary filmmaker Jessica Yu, who won an Academy Award for *Breathing Lessons* in 1997, moves in a radically new direction with a hip-hop comedy based on a mock commercial made by a studio accountant to promote his fledgling clothing line. Jimmy Tsai, in addition to designing Venom sportswear, producing his own commercial, and holding down a day job, trained for weeks to portray Christopher "C-Dub" Wang, a Chinese slacker who blames genetics for his failure to realize his dream of becoming the first Chinese player in the NBA. This film is definitely a change of pace for Yu, whose documentary subjects have been obscure artists living in unusual circumstances—poet Mark O'Brien (*Breathing Lessons*) was confined to an iron lung for forty of his fifty years; writer/artist Henry Darger (*In the Realms of the Unreal*, 2004) worked as a janitor and died in a charitable facility, leaving behind a disturbing fifteen-thousand-page illustrated manuscript about enslaved children; six mentally ill artists from the Creedmoor Psychiatric Center in Queens were interviewed in *The Living Museum* (1998).

Ping Pong Playa opens in documentary style with a mock interview between Ron Howard look-alike Jon Howard (Sir Jonathan Oliver), and C-Dub, who is explaining his theory of biological determination and its relation to Chinese athletes. C-Dub refers to Yao Ming as a statistical anomaly. The scene shifts to C-Dub on the basketball court, outplaying a group of younger children as he talks trash, the obscenities cleverly synchronized with his dribbling. As a result of his playground antics, he is late for work and loses yet another mall job. Parallel editing of C-Dub's confrontation with his boss and his account of the incident to his friend, J.P. Money (Khary Payton), illustrate C-Dub's penchant for revisionism.

While C-Dub affects gangsta style, the rest of his family remains traditional. They run a Ping-Pong school and sporting goods store specializing in table tennis equipment. Their older son, Michael (Roger Fan), is a champion player whose success is vital to the family business. However, complications arise when a minor car accident injures Michael and his mother (Elizabeth Sung); Michael will be unable to compete in the upcoming Golden Cock Tournament, and Mrs. Wang cannot continue to conduct lessons. The Wangs turn to C-Dub, who at the time is wearing a T-shirt that reads "I speak English."

The ethnic-identity humor continues as C-Dub drops by a Chinese language class, where, among the first generation Chinese-American children, sits J.P., who is African American. The image reverses that of C-Dub on the basketball court challenging black youngsters half his size. At the Ping-Pong school are two Caucasian players who, buoyed by Michael's withdrawal from competition, hope to win the tournament and open a rival school, luring away the Wangs' students.

C-Dub has taken over his mother's classes, but he doesn't do much instructing. When he realizes one of the boys, Felix (Andrew Vo), receives a fat allowance, he devises ways to appropriate major sums and in the process teaches the boys about gambling. Soon his irresponsibility creates friction. Michael berates him for having no aspirations and calls him a "yellow Fonzie," a reference to a character in the television series *Happy Days* (which starred Ron Howard). A young woman who has attracted C-Dub's attention turns out to be Felix's sister, Jennifer (Smith Cho), a graduate student; she regards C-Dub as a total loser. When his parents learn about the gambling at their school, his father (Jim Lau) threatens C-Dub with a Ping-Pong paddle. Chris seeks asylum in a tree house, where his mother finds him and offers another lecture on responsibility. J.P. arranges a pickup basketball game with some adult players in an attempt to show C-Dub how out of line with reality his hoops dreams are.

Between his mother's lecture and his friend's straight talk, C-Dub sees the light and, with the help of his students and his father, begins training in earnest for the table tennis tournament. A montage follows. On tournament day, Mr. Wang presents his son with the "official" Wang family Ping-Pong uniform—a pair of tiny, snug-fitting shorts that C-Dub calls "Daisy Dukes."

As the Golden Cock progresses, the Chinese community, once skeptical about C-Dub, gradually comes to believe in him. They are helped along by J.P., who speaks with the adults in Chinese, extolling his friend's virtues, such as they are. There is a setback when C-Dub loses a match and throws a tantrum. (Fortunately, this is a double elimination contest.) Mr. Wang confronts him about his temper and his self-destructive habit of making excuses. When play resumes, C-Dub has regained his composure. Montage and split screen speed the elimination round along.

The championship match is a showdown between C-Dub and Gerald (Peter Paige), one of the white players planning to open a rival school. Just before play begins, one of C-Dub's students, Prabakar (Javin Reid), appears with a pair of athletic shoes he has modified for the competition and with the news that there are no regulations about uniforms. C-Dub changes into his baggy basketball shorts and a Yao Ming jersey. Gerald wins the first game, but C-Dub takes the second. However, C-Dub has been trash talking between points, and Gerald insists he has violated the code by making racial slurs. The judges decide that C-Dub must remain silent throughout the final game or withdraw. The last game is marked by C-Dub's struggle to keep quiet, an injury, and a come-from-behind win for the hero.

All turns out well. The Wang school is thriving. J.P.'s and Prabakar's fathers have gone into business together manufacturing athletic shoes, and C-Dub seems to have won the heart of Felix's sister, Jennifer.

In interviews, Yu has described *Ping Pong Playa* as "healthy self-mockery of our generation's navigation of the ethnic American experience." She is also using a conventional sports film plot to poke fun at race-card playing and documentary film making. C-Dub maintains a page on MySpace as C Dub, a professional Ping-Pong player (not to be confused with the rap artist also known as C-Dub).

PISTOL: THE BIRTH OF A LEGEND (1991)

Director: Frank C. Schroeder. Screenplay: Darrel Campbell. Producers: Samuel Benedict, Darrel Campbell. Cinematography: Randy Walsh. Music: Brent Havens. Production Design: John Sperry Wade. Costume Design: Deanna Doran.

Cast: Adam Guier (Pete Maravich), Millie Perkins (Helen Maravich), Nick Benedict (Press Maravich), Murrell Garland (Coach Pendleton), Tom Lester (Pete as an adult).

Running Time: 90 minutes.

DVD: VCI Video.

This is a low-budget biography of basketball Hall of Famer Pete Maravich, who died at the age of forty.

PLAYERS (1979)

DIRECTOR: Anthony Harvey. SCREENPLAY: Arnold Schulman. PRODUCER: Robert Evans. CINEMATOGRAPHY: James Crabe. EDITING: Randy Roberts. MUSIC: Jerry Goldsmith. PRODUCTION DESIGN: Richard Sylbert. COSTUME DESIGN: Richard Bruno.
CAST: Ali MacGraw (Nicole Boucher), Dean Paul Martin (Chris), Maximilian Schell (Marco), Steve Guttenberg (Rusty), Pancho González (himself).
RUNNING TIME: 120 minutes.
VHS: Paramount.

In this romantic drama, a tennis player gets involved with an older woman. In addition to Pancho González, the film features several other tennis greats including John McEnroe, Ion Tiriac, Guillermo Vilas, Ilie Nastase, and Vijay Amritraj.

PLAYING AWAY (1987)

DIRECTOR: Horace Ové. SCREENPLAY: Caryl Phillips. PRODUCERS: Vijay Amarnani, Brian Skilton. CINEMATOGRAPHY: Nicholas D. Knowland. EDITING: Graham Whitlock. MUSIC: Simon Webb. ART DIRECTION: Pip Gardner. COSTUME DESIGN: Alyson Ritchie.
CAST: Norman Beaton (Willie Boy), Robert Urquhart (Godfrey), Helen Lindsay (Marjorie), Nicholas Farrell (Derek).
RUNNING TIME: 100 minutes.
VHS: Nelson Entertainment.

In this comedy, a British team from Suffolk and a group of West Indians from London engage in a cricket test match.

PLAY IT TO THE BONE (1999)

DIRECTOR: Ron Shelton. SCREENPLAY: Ron Shelton. PRODUCER: Stephen Chin. CINEMATOGRAPHY: Mark Vargo. EDITING: Patrick Flannery, Paul Seydor. MUSIC: Alex Wurman. PRODUCTION DESIGN: Claire Jenora Brown. ART DIRECTION: Mary Saisselin COSTUME DESIGN: Kathryn Morrison.
CAST: Woody Harrelson (Vince Boudreau), Antonio Banderas (Cesar Dominguez), Lolita Davidovich (Grace Pasic), Tom Sizemore (Joe Domino), Lucy Liu (Lia).
RUNNING TIME: 124 minutes.
DVD: Walt Disney Video.

Two boxers are called upon at the last minute to fight in Las Vegas, and they hit the road with a woman both of them have been involved with.

POINT BREAK (1991)

DIRECTOR: Kathryn Bigelow. SCREENPLAY: W. Peter Iliff. STORY: W. Peter Iliff, Rick King. PRODUCERS: Peter Abrams, Robert L. Levy. CINEMATOGRAPHY: Donald Peterman. EDITING: Howard Smith. MUSIC: Mark Isham. PRODUCTION DESIGN: Peter Jamison. ART DIRECTION: Pamela Marcotte.
CAST: Patrick Swayze (Bodhi), Keanu Reeves (Johnny Utah), Gary Busey (Pappas), Lori Petty (Tyler), John C. McGinley (Ben Harp).
RUNNING TIME: 120 minutes.
DVD: 20th Century Fox.

An FBI agent looking for bank robbers tracks his suspects among California surfers.

POOLHALL JUNKIES (2002)

DIRECTOR: Mars Callahan. SCREENPLAY: Mars Callahan, Chris Corso. PRODUCER: Karen Beninati, David Kronemeyer, Vincent Newman, David Peters, Tucker Tooley. CINEMATOGRAPHY: Robert Morris. EDITING: James Tooley. MUSIC: Richard Glasser. PRODUCTION DESIGN: Robert La Liberte. ART DIRECTION: Nicole Lee. COSTUME DESIGN: Kristin Persson.
CAST: Chazz Palminteri (Joe), Rick Schroder (Brad), Rod Steiger (Nick), Michael

Rosenbaum (Danny), Mars Callahan (Johnny), Alison Eastwood (Tara).
RUNNING TIME: 99 minutes.
DVD: HBO Home Video.

A pool hustler must return to the game he abandoned in order to save his younger brother and redeem himself.

THE POWER OF ONE (1992)

DIRECTOR: John G. Avildsen. SCREENPLAY: Robert Mark Kamen, based on the novel by Bryce Courtenay. PRODUCER: Arnon Milchan. CINEMATOGRAPHY: Dean Semler. EDITING: John G. Avildsen, Trevor Jolly. MUSIC: Hans Zimmer. PRODUCTION DESIGN: Roger Hall. ART DIRECTION: Martin Hitchcock, Kevin Phipps, Leslie Tomkins. COSTUME DESIGN: Tom Rand.
CAST: Stephen Dorff (P.K. at age eighteen), Armin Mueller-Stahl (Doc), Morgan Freeman (Geel Piet), John Gielgud (St. John).
RUNNING TIME: 127 minutes.
DVD: Warner Home Video.

The Power of One is part political saga, part boxing film based on the novel by Bryce Courtenay and directed by John Avildsen (*Rocky*, 1976; *Rocky V*, 1990; *The Karate Kid*, 1984). Set in South Africa, the film opens in 1930, before the country's policy of apartheid, or legalized racial segregation, and follows the story of an orphan of English descent.

His father having been trampled to death by an elephant, seven-year-old P.K. (Guy Witcher) has been raised on a small farm by his widowed mother and a Zulu nanny (Nomadlozi Kubheka). After their cattle are struck by disease, P.K.'s mother (Tracy Brooks Swope) suffers a breakdown, and P.K. is sent to the closest affordable boarding school, an Afrikaner school, where he is the only English boy and is mercilessly bullied by the Afrikaners, people of German and Dutch descent, who have inherited a nationalistic hatred of the British as a result of the Boer Wars. The Afrikaners call him "Pisskopf" and urinate on him; soon P.K. begins wetting his bed.

P.K. returns to the farm briefly for his mother's funeral. Reunited with his nanny, he tells her of the bed wetting. She engages the services of a Zulu holy man, Dabula Manzi (Jeremiah Mnisi), who helps P.K. envision his greatest fear, a charging elephant. In a lovely fantasy sequence, P.K. stands his ground before an elephant and reaches out to touch its trunk. Thus cured, P.K. returns to the boarding school, taking with him a pet chicken, a gift from the holy man.

At the school P.K. enjoys only a brief respite from harassment. The leader of the bullies, Jaapie Botha (Robbie Bulloch), has organized a Hitler youth group. One night they seize P.K. and drag him into a rally where Jaapie kills the chicken. Enraged, P.K. pushes Jaapie, who falls onto a sharpened stick. The injury to Jaapie's pride is worse than the puncture wound, and he retaliates by calling on the already-frenzied group to hang P.K. The timely arrival of a schoolmaster saves P.K.'s life.

P.K. is sent to live in Barberton with his grandfather (Paul Tingay), who is kind but has little interest in the boy. However, the grandfather prevails upon an acquaintance, a German-born botanist and pianist (Armin Mueller-Stahl) to tutor P.K. "Doc," as P.K. calls his tutor, believes that all answers can be found in nature if one learns to look closely enough. During an idyllic interlude, teacher and pupil bond, but World War II intervenes: because he has failed to register as an alien, Doc is placed under arrest and moved, along with his piano, to Barberton Prison, where he is treated with respect and lives in relative comfort. However, conditions for the other internees, all black

African and Cape Coloured, are brutal. One guard, Sergeant Bormann (Clive Russell), is particularly harsh.

P.K. visits Doc every day, taking him plants for a succulent garden and receiving a piano lesson. But now that P.K. is attending school again, he is suffering at the hands of classmates who beat him because he is both English and intelligent. Doc enlists one of the prisoners, Geel Piet (Morgan Freeman), to teach P.K. to box. Four years later, twelve-year-old P.K. (now played by Simon Fenton) has become a skilled boxer. He is also admired by the prisoners because he smuggles in tobacco and writes letters for them; the prisoners begin to call him "Rainmaker," after a legendary figure.

As the end of World War II approaches, Doc is asked to give a concert to honor visiting officials. He and P.K. devise a plan to have the prisoners form a chorus and sing African music with subversive lyrics that the Afrikaners will not understand. In a ludicrous scene, P.K. directs the chorus, then, realizing Geel is missing, abandons the stage in search of his friend. Geel has been cornered by Sergeant Bormann and forced to translate the lyrics. When P.K. finally locates him, Geel is near death from Bormann's brutality; Geel dies at peace, however, because P.K. has united all of the tribes, now singing in one voice.

When the war ends, Doc returns to Germany, and the film skips to Johannesburg in 1948. By this time the National Party has gained power and racial segregation has been legalized. P.K. (now played by Stephen Dorff), now a student at the Prince of Wales School, has applied to Oxford, supported by Professor St. John (Sir John Gielgud), a left-leaning intellectual who opposes apartheid.

P.K. has continued to box and wins a school tournament. His victory is observed by Maria Marais (Fay Masterson), daughter of a leading member of the National Party, and by a large number of blacks who have gathered outside, chanting, "Rainmaker." P.K. pursues, simultaneously, a relationship with Maria—to which her father is adamantly opposed—and a boxing career.

A triumphant P.K. (Stephen Dorff) gets a lift in *The Power of One*

With his friend Morrie Gilbert (Dominic Walker) posing as his manager, P.K. gains a trainer, Hoppie Gruenewald (Ian Roberts), who operates an integrated gym. There, P.K. meets a black fighter, Gideon Duma (Alois Moyo), who arranges a fight in Alexandra, a restricted area. Morrie and Maria accompany Hoppie and P.K. After P. K. wins the match, Gideon proclaims him the Rainmaker. Soon P.K. and Maria join Gideon and his girlfriend in a clandestine project to teach blacks to read. Professor St. John allows them use of a classroom.

Meanwhile, Maria has announced to her father that she has visited Alexandra, and he has ordered police officers to keep P.K. under surveillance. When Marais learns of the activities at the Prince of Wales School, he sends officers to order Professor St. John to close the building to the Africans. One of the officers, identifiable by a crude swastika tattoo on his bicep, is Jaapie Botha (now played by Daniel Craig). Gideon and P.K. locate a church in which to continue their school, but it is raided by the police (led by Jaapie). In the ensuing melee, Maria is killed.

The grief-stricken P.K. feels defeated. As with the prison concert that resulted in Geel's death, P.K. feels that in doing the right thing, he has succeeded only in destroying the people he has loved. The police have raided Hoppie's gym and set it on fire, and their presence in the community is ominous. However, P.K.'s spirits lift once more when Gideon takes him back to Alexandra, where the school is flourishing in small groups throughout the area: those who have learned to read are now teaching others.

This glimpse of a hopeful future vanishes quickly as the police raid the area, beating anyone in their reach, burning homes, and opening fire on frightened people trying to flee. Jaapie leads the search for P.K., which ends in a bare-knuckle fight that one would think P.K. would win easily. After a prolonged struggle, P.K. knocks Jaapie out, but only temporarily. As P.K. turns to aid a fallen friend, Jaapie recovers and is about to shoot when Gideon emerges from the darkness with a two-by-four and bludgeons Jaapie with lethal force. The film ends with Gideon and P.K., having eluded the police, walking to Pretoria, where they plan to continue their efforts to empower black Africans and end apartheid.

The film was generally panned by critics, who found its scope too broad to do justice to its serious themes. Writing for the *Washington Post* (March 27, 1992) Rita Kempley declared, "Though rife with worthy intentions and great notions, this populist safari manages to be both patronizing and manipulative." Roger Ebert in the *Chicago Sun-Times* (March 27, 1992) was equally critical: "You can almost feel the film slipping out of the hands of its director, John G. Avildsen, as the South African reality is upstaged by the standard clichés of a fight picture."

PREFONTAINE (1997)

DIRECTOR: Steve James. SCREENPLAY: Steve James, Eugene Corr. PRODUCERS: Mark Doonan, Peter Gilbert, Jon Lutz, Irby Smith. CINEMATOGRAPHY: Peter Gilbert. EDITING: Peter Frank. MUSIC: Mason Daring. PRODUCTION DESIGN: Carol Winstead Wood. ART DIRECTION: Gregory A. Weimerskirch. COSTUME DESIGN: Tom Bronson.

CAST: Jared Leto (Steve Prefontaine), R. Lee Ermey (Bill Bowerman), Ed O'Neill (Bill Dellinger), Amy Locane (Nancy Alleman), Linsday Crouse (Elfriede Prefontaine), Kurtwood Smith (Curtis Cunnigham).

RUNNING TIME: 106 minutes.

DVD: Walt Disney Video.

Prefontaine is a biopic starring Jared Leto as Steve Prefontaine, an American runner who dominated long-distance events in the 1970s. It incorporates documentary footage of Prefontaine in action as well as interviews with a former coach and a former girlfriend. The film presents Prefontaine as a risk taker with a determined and often defiant attitude. His relationship with his coach, Bill Bowerman (R. Lee Ermey), is depicted as tumultuous—he is embroiled in a bitter conflict with Bowerman at the University of Oregon. He also quarrels with the AAU, the body that at the time controlled amateur athletes in track and field.

Although the film begins with black-and-white footage of Steve breaking the NCAA record in the 5,000-meter race, it quickly shifts to the past. As a boy, Steve demonstrates his reluctance to accept limits by jumping from a bridge, an act that anticipates his recklessness behind the wheel and foreshadows his death. In high school Steve fails to make the starting lineups in football and baseball because of his size. Determined to excel in sports, he begins running, often at night and always by himself. His drive leads him to set state long-distance records in Oregon. After watching famed miler Jim Ryun on television, Steve decides he wants to make the Olympic team for the Munich games. Despite his family's belief that Munich is only a dream, Steve intends to run track at the University of Oregon, where Bill Bowerman is coach. Steve's high school success has bred an outsized ego, and he expects a personal visit from Bowerman. Instead, he receives a form letter from the coach.

Coach Bowerman sees Steve as a three-miler since the team already has an excellent mile runner in Thomas Becker (Adam Fitzhugh). Although Steve outruns his rival in their first mile race, he loses the rematch, and Bowerman advises him to make the three-mile race his own. At that distance Steve proves unbeatable, breaking the NCAA record despite running with twelve stitches in his foot, the result of another ill-advised leap into the water.

Steve's self-centeredness is evident in his lack of interest in campus activism—war protests are being held on campus—and in his relationships. He alienates teammates by grandstanding. He ditches his high school sweetheart for Nancy Alleman (Amy Locane), another runner. He continues to ignore traffic rules. However, he does attempt to win the respect of Bowerman, who is portrayed as preoccupied with developing a new running shoe with the use of his wife's waffle iron.

Bowerman is named track coach for the 1972 Olympics. At the trials Steve wins the 5,000-meter race at which a hostile crowd wear T-shirts that read "Stop Pre." He dons a shirt for his victory lap and predicts that in Munich he will run the last mile in under four minutes.

At the Olympics Mark Spitz's seven gold medals in swimming and the contested Russian gold medal in basketball make headlines, but those stories are eclipsed by the murder of eleven Israeli athletes by the Islamic militant group Black September. Steve, who had watched Lasse Viren's record-breaking performance in the 10,000-meter race, seems more affected than his competitors by the massacre and spends the night before the race in Bowerman's apartment. The 5,000—which had never been won by a twenty-one-year-old—seems designed for older, more experienced runners, and Steve, who finishes fourth, discovers that it takes more than "pure guts" to win the race. Although Steve's father praises his effort, Steve considers himself a "fucking loser." Bowerman observes that Steve ran to win when he could have come in second or third with a different strategy.

After the Olympics, Steve returns to Oregon, where he resumes his winning ways, but something seems to be missing. The AAU, however, wants to control his athletic future by attempting to force him to compete in Russia, when Steve simply wants a rematch with Viren. Steve comments,

"I can't beat Viren if I can't race him." He takes on the AAU, which finally sanctions a track meet between Oregon and a Finnish team, but Viren does not compete, further frustrating Steve, who had turned down a $200,000 offer to go professional.

At the meet Steve wins his race, declaring, "Today was what I thought Munich would be." At a party following the meet, his teammates honor him for standing up to the AAU, but when he drives home, Prefontaine is killed in a car crash, an accident that has seemed inevitable. At Hayward Stadium, Steve is honored at a memorial service. Bowerman's comment "He ran every race as if it were his last" describes Steve's determination and helps explain why he was so concerned with having athletes, not organizations like the AAU, control their own futures.

When the film was made, Steve held every American record between 2,000 and 10,000 meters. Bowerman, who had written a best-selling book called *Jogging* (1967), eventually succeeded in using the waffle iron design to create the Nike shoe.

PRIDE (2007)

DIRECTOR: Sunu Gonera. SCREENPLAY: Kevin Michael Smith, Michael Gozzard, J. Mills Goodloe, Norman Vance Jr. PRODUCERS: Brett Forbes, Paul Hall, Michael Ohoven, Patrick Rizzotti, Adam Rosenfelt. CINEMATOGRAPHY: Matthew F. Leonetti. EDITING: Billy Fox. MUSIC: Aaron Zigman. PRODUCTION DESIGN: Steve Saklad. ART DIRECTION: Monroe Kelly. COSTUME DESIGN: Paul Simmons.

CAST: Terrence Howard (Jim Ellis), Bernie Mac (Elston), Kimberly Elise (Sue Davis), Tom Arnold (Bink), Brandon Fobbs (Puddin Head).

RUNNING TIME: 104 minutes.

DVD: Lion's Gate.

Based on the true story of Jim Ellis, who founded PDR, a black swimming team in Philadelphia, *Pride* is a sports film that focuses on practice sessions and meets and includes a romantic subplot. Although the film begins in 1964, the action in Salisbury, North Carolina, serves as a prelude to the rest of the film, which takes place ten years later in Philadelphia. As the only black on the Cheney University swim team, Jim (Terrence Howard) is subjected to boos and racial taunts by the white audience, still irate about mandated integration. When he dives into the pool in his first race, none of the white swimmers enter the water, presumably because it has been contaminated. Angered by his treatment, Jim confronts the swimming officials; white police officers who utter racial slurs provoke Jim. As a result of the ensuing melee, Jim is charged with and convicted of a felony. His criminal record becomes a problem as he seeks employment.

Ten years later Jim travels to Philadelphia, where he interviews for a job at the prestigious, all-white Main Line Academy, which is noted for its academic and athletic programs. After he sees that Jim is black, Main Line's athletic director, Bink (Tom Arnold), who practices his putting during their interview, ends their conversation by telling Jim, "A person like you can't communicate with our students." At a subsequent interview at an employment agency, the black interviewer laughs at the idea of Jim being hired at the Main Line Academy and finally offers him a position at the Foster Recreation Center, which is scheduled for closure. His job will be to pack things up.

When he arrives at the decrepit recreation center, it is deserted except for Elston (Bernie Mac), who is hostile and angry after he learns that the center, where he has worked for years, is going to be closed. In addition to having to cope with Elston, Jim encounters Frank, a local gang leader who believes that the kids belong to him. When Reggie (Evan Ross), a neighborhood youth who stutters and lacks confidence, accidentally breaks Frank's boom box, Frank threatens him and demands to be paid for the radio. In the course of the film Jim and Frank will battle over the teenagers in the community.

As he cleans up the center, Jim discovers it includes a swimming pool in disrepair. Jim restores the pool and resumes his swimming. He is able to lure some of the neighborhood youngsters into the center when the city removes the basketball hoops. Jim gives one of the teens, Andre (Kevin Phillips), unwelcome advice about cupping his hands when he swims; Andre challenges him to a race and bets him twenty dollars on the outcome. After Jim wins handily, he has the kids' respect, and they begin taking instructions from him. Encouraged by their progress, Reggie suggests that they become a team and compete against others. However, Jim, who is concerned that they are underprepared for competition, is reluctant to agree. Nevertheless, Elston files the necessary paperwork, and the team is sanctioned.

Their first meet is with Main Line Academy, coached by Bink. As Jim's team, which has added a young woman, travels through the wealthy, white suburbs, they are overconfident. When they arrive, they are greeted by suspicious stares and comments about the possibility of a demonstration. Bink, unaware of Jim's extensive experience, is patronizing as he offers to help Jim with the rules and format of the meet. Jim's swimmers, who had regarded his swimming suit as fruity, will not wear their uniforms and choose to swim in their cutoffs. One of the boys loses his cutoffs during a race, much to the amusement of the white crowd. The rec center team loses race after race to Main Line. When Andre, who swims competitively in the last race, is kicked by a Main Liner, the foul is not called; after Jim's protest is rejected, a fight breaks out.

After the trip home, Jim scolds the boys because they didn't take the meet seriously and because on the return trip, they were boisterous, behaving as if they had won. He and Elston then imitate their street talk and high fives, trying to get them to recognize the inappropriateness of their bravado in the wake of a crushing defeat. Jim tells them to forget about having a team, but at 6:00 a.m. the next morning he finds them in the pool swimming laps in their team uniforms. "This is our house," one of the boys proclaims. After this turning point, the team put themselves through strenuous workouts.

Although Elston has come on board, Sue Davis (Kimberly Elise), a local politician and the sister of Hakim (Nate Parker), one of the swimmers, has not. She is concerned about her brother's grades and fears that his swimming will detract from his study time. Initially, she was in favor of closing the unused center, but is softened by Elston and a box of chocolates, as well as by Jim's responsible behavior. After Jim promises her that he will insist on Hakim doing his schoolwork, she agrees that if he stays in school, he can stay in the pool.

At this point Frank resurfaces. Demanding some form of payment for his broken radio, he makes Reggie get in his car, and Andre, trying to protect the weaker Reggie, joins them. Jim and Sue are in a restaurant together when Jim sees "his boys" in Frank's car. He intervenes, gets Andre and Reggie out of the car, and tells Frank to leave his guys alone. Frank responds with, "These are my kids," and mutters that Jim is a "dead man walking."

The team solidifies but faces racism in its next encounter with Main Line. Elston has received approval from the Philadelphia Department of Recreation (PDR) to hold a meet, which is scheduled against Bink's team. Thanks to Elston's networking with the local preacher, there is a large audience, but when the opposing team appears, Bink comes up with a bogus claim that his swimmers have the flu; he insists the meet be rescheduled at a "more appropriate location," presumably not in a black neighborhood. Disheartened, Jim remarks, "Some things don't change"; however, his team members take their starting positions and swim despite the lack of competition and much to the delight of the cheering audience. As the season progresses, the team, now known as PDR, wins several meets, gets favorable press, and is cited for their contributions to the community.

Before the championship meet Frank and his gang trash the rec center, but Jim and his team catch them before they can flee. In the fight that follows, Jim loses control, and only Andre's intervention prevents him from drowning Frank. Jim is arrested and criminal charges are threatened. When Sue, who has learned about Jim's felony conviction ten years ago, meets Jim, she is upset, maintaining that he conned the team, her, and the community. Yet, in a telling moment she reveals her own love for him. Later at her home, when she sees Hakim pick up a book and read it, she realizes the positive influence that Jim has had on her brother.

Before the last meet, Jim confesses about his past, apologizes for his behavior, and suspends himself from coaching. He then redefines PDR as representing "pride, determination, resistance." While he stands outside the University of Baltimore's Aquatic Center, where the meet is staged, Elston is coaching the team. After losing the first two races, the team scores when Andre wins his event; and by the time the individual races have been completed, PDR is in second place behind Main Line Academy. The winner of the relay event will be champions. Andre decides to swim first and names Reggie to be the anchor. The race ends in a photo finish. Before the outcome is decided Sue and Elston join Jim outside. PDR emerges with the trophy, and Bink even shakes hands with Jim.

In a postscript the audience learns that Jim continued to coach for many years (we actually see the real Jim Ellis at work) and that many of his swimmers went on to the Olympic trials and to college scholarships. The film is an inspiring account of how one person can make a difference.

THE PRIDE OF ST. LOUIS (1952)

DIRECTOR: Harmon Jones. SCREENPLAY: Herman J. Mankiewicz. STORY: Guy Trosper. PRODUCER: Jules Schermer. CINEMATOGRAPHY: Leo Tover. EDITING: Robert Simpson. MUSIC: Arthur Lange. ART DIRECTION: Addison Hehr, Lyle R. Wheeler. COSTUME DESIGN: Travilla.

CAST: Dan Dailey (Jerome Hanna "Dizzy" Dean), Joanne Dru (Patricia Nash Dean), Richard Hyton (Johnny Kendall), Richard Crenna (Paul Dean), Hugh Sanders (Horst).

RUNNING TIME: 93 minutes.

ACADEMY AWARD NOMINATIONS: Best Motion Picture Story (Trosper).

VHS: 20th Century Fox.

This is a biographical film about Dizzy Dean, a major league pitcher for the St. Louis Cardinals and the Chicago Cubs.

PRIDE OF THE YANKEES (1942)

DIRECTOR: Sam Wood. SCREENPLAY: Jo Swerling, Herman J. Mankiewicz. STORY: Paul Gallico. PRODUCER: Samuel Goldwyn. CINEMATOGRAPHY: Rudolph Maté. EDITING: Daniel Mandell. MUSIC: Leigh Harline. PRODUCTION DESIGN: William Cameron Menzies. ART DIRECTION: Perry Ferguson. COSTUME DESIGN: René Hubert.

CAST: Gary Cooper (Lou Gehrig), Teresa Wright (Eleanor Twitchell), Walter Brennan (Sam Blake), Babe Ruth (himself), Dan Duryea (Hank Hanneman).

RUNNING TIME: 128 minutes. B&W.

ACADEMY AWARDS: Best Editing. NOMINATIONS: Best Picture; Best Director; Best Actor (Cooper); Best Actress (Wright); Best Original Motion Picture Story; Best Screenplay; Best Cinematography, Black-and-White; Best Scoring of a Dramatic or Comedy Picture; Best Art Direction, Black-and-White; Best Sound Recording; Best Special Effects.
DVD: MGM.

Gary Cooper stars in this World War II era biopic about Lou Gehrig, a Yankee slugger who died in 1941 of ALS (amyotrophic lateral sclerosis) after establishing the "iron man" record for most consecutive games played. (The record of 2,130 games stood until 1995, when it was surpassed by Baltimore Orioles infielder Cal Ripken Jr.) The film was well received, garnering eleven Academy Award nominations and an Oscar for editing. The American Film Institute ranks it as the third all-time best sports film.

The opening scene establishes young Lou's early talent and passion for baseball as well as his mother's opposition to the sport. In a sandlot game Lou has walloped a ball, smashing a shop window. The irate shopkeeper and a police officer escort him home, where Mr. Gehrig (Ludwig Stossel) tells the officer they all must wait for his wife to return from work. Once Mrs. Gehrig (Elsa Janssen) arrives, it becomes apparent that she dominates the household and controls the finances. Baseball she considers a waste of time—and now money. Her desire is for Lou to become an engineer like his Uncle Otto, whose portrait is prominently displayed in the dining room. For Ma Gehrig, America is a land of opportunity, and she works as a cook at Columbia University so that eventually Lou can attend there. And in the very next scene, he's a college student.

Although he must wait tables at Columbia, he is accepted into a fraternity. Lou excels in sports, yet remains modest and shy, qualities that make him a target of jokes by his frat brothers, who tease him about his awkwardness around women. One bit of razzing prompts Lou to knock a brother out of his chair in his singular display of anger in the film. The matter is soon swept aside with the arrival of sportswriter Sam Blake (Walter Brennan). Sam has recognized Lou's hitting talent and tries to convince both Lou and the university football coach that Lou should consider signing with the New York Yankees. However, Lou is still intent on following his mother's wishes and studying engineering. He changes his mind only when she becomes ill and requires hospitalization. Unwilling to place her in a charity ward, Lou joins the Yankees and uses his cash advance to pay for a private hospital. Both Lou and his father keep this arrangement hidden from Mrs. Gehrig, who believes she's being treated like royalty in a public institution. When Lou learns he must report to a farm team in Hartford, he must finally confess to his mother that he is playing ball. However, Mrs. Gehrig thinks Lou has said "Harvard," and he does nothing to disabuse her of this illusion. It is not until the story that Lou is being called up from the minors hits the New York papers and the neighbors pour in with congratulations that Mrs. Gehrig learns the truth. She is not happy, but allows herself to be persuaded to attend Lou's first game.

Lou sits on the bench for much of the season, observing the first baseman. When he finally gets a chance to hit, he stumbles over a row of bats, and a young woman in the stands calls out "Tanglefoot," momentarily distracting him. Later, he encounters the young woman in a restaurant. Sam introduces them. She is Eleanor Twitchell (Teresa Wright), daughter of a Chicago businessman. With Sam's help, the two begin dating. At the end of the season Lou proposes and takes Eleanor home to meet his parents, who have planned a surprise party for Lou. Mrs. Gehrig has mixed emotions about her son's engagement and tries to control their household by imposing her tastes on the furnishings of the new apartment. Lou intervenes, finally finding the courage to confront his mother directly, yet gently. Eleanor's choice in wallpaper prevails, and the couple are married in their unfinished apartment with the senior Gehrigs, Sam, and a host of workmen as witnesses.

Until Lou's illness reaches a point that his play is affected, there's very little conflict in the film. Mrs. Gehrig's desire to control her son's career and to manage his marriage fails to prevent him from attaining success and happiness. She quickly makes the transition to baseball enthusiast, losing her admiration for Uncle Otto, the successful engineer. Once Lou establishes boundaries between his new home with Eleanor and his childhood home, his mother ceases her interference and fades into the background of the picture. Similarly, Lou's marriage is blissfully trouble free. In one contrived scene, Sam learns that Lou has been coming home late. Eleanor, playing the role of the cheated-upon spouse, tells Sam she knows where Lou is and that she's had enough. With Sam in the passenger's seat, assuming the worst, Eleanor drives to Lou's old neighborhood sandlot, where he is supervising a game between two teams of children.

Lou's baseball career is shown largely through montage and the scrapbooks of his accomplishments that Eleanor maintains. Cooper, who received an Oscar nomination for his portrayal, had little talent for baseball and was hampered by his inability to hit left-handed; the film was reversed (as was lettering on the uniforms) for action shots, and Cooper ran down the third baseline after a hit. A number of Yankees from the infamous Murderers' Row lineup play themselves, including Mark Koenig, Bill Dickey, and Babe Ruth. There is no indication of rivalry between Babe and Lou; young Lou is presented as idolizing the Babe, and as a rookie, awed by his presence. However, Sam Blake and reporter Hank Hanneman (Dan Duryea) carry on an intense rivalry, with Sam defending Lou's record against Hank's claims that Babe is the greater player.

One scene plays upon the famous tale of the Babe's hitting a home run for a sick child. A hospital visit to the bedside of young Billy (Gene Collins) is presented as a publicity stunt for Babe, who promises to hit a homer just for the boy; while Babe commands center stage for a bevy of reporters and photographers, Lou remains out of camera range, stepping forward to talk to Billy only after the press have retreated. Lou encourages Billy to walk, assuring him that trying hard enough will enable him to accomplish anything; Billy then asks Lou to hit *two* home runs for him, repeating the same encouraging words about "trying hard enough" when Lou balks at the tall order. Both Lou and the Babe produce the runs, and near the end of the film, Billy, now a young man (David Holt), appears outside of Yankee Stadium on Lou Gehrig Appreciation Day to thank Lou and to show him that he can indeed walk. In actuality, the Babe Ruth story has not been fully confirmed, and the addition of Lou Gehrig to the tale is pure fiction.

The film concludes with Lou's speech at Yankee Stadium, but the famous line "today I consider myself the luckiest man on the face of the earth" is placed at the end of the speech rather than at the beginning. Lou walks off the field between columns of his teammates and disappears through the grave-like door of the dugout into blackness.

Pride of the Yankees was released in the summer of 1942, a year after Gehrig's death and eight months after the Japanese attack on Pearl Harbor. Title cards at the beginning of the film cite Gehrig's "simplicity and modesty" as a model for young

Americans and connect his courage in confronting a fatal, debilitating disease with the "valor and fortitude that has been displayed by thousands of young Americans on far-flung fields of battle."

THE PRIZEFIGHTER AND THE LADY (1933)

DIRECTOR: W. S. Van Dyke. SCREENPLAY: John Lee Mahin, John Meehan. STORY: Frances Marion. PRODUCER: W. S. Van Dyke. CINEMATOGRAPHY: Lester White. EDITING: Robert J. Kern. ART DIRECTION: Fredric Hope, David Townsend.
CAST: Myrna Loy (Belle), Max Baer (Steve), Primo Carnera (Carnera), Jack Dempsey (Promoter), Otto Kruger (Willie Ryan).
RUNNING TIME: 102 minutes.
ACADEMY AWARD NOMINATION: Best Original Story.

A cocky boxer (played by real-life champion Max Baer) falls for a gangster's girlfriend.

THE PROGRAM (1993)

DIRECTOR: David S. Ward. SCREENPLAY: David S. Ward, Aaron Latham. PRODUCER: Samuel Goldwyn Jr. CINEMATOGRAPHY: Victor Hammer. EDITING: Kimberly Ray, Paul Seydor. MUSIC: Michael Colombier. PRODUCTION DESIGN: Albert Brenner. ART DIRECTION: Carol Winstead Wood. COSTUME DESIGN: Tom Bronson.
CAST: James Caan (Sam Winters), Halle Berry (Autumn Haley), Omar Epps (Darnell Jefferson), Craig Sheffer (Joe Kane), Kristy Swanson (Camille Shafer), Abraham Benrubi (Bud-Lite Kaminski).
RUNNING TIME: 112 minutes.
DVD: Touchstone Home Entertainment.

The Program is an uneven film that exposes the ugly side of college football while valorizing gifted athletes. James Caan, the ostensible lead, plays Sam Winters, a coach at "ESU" who has failed in two consecutive years to take his team to a bowl game. The boosters are upset, the university's endowment is suffering, and Sam's job is on the line.

Sam's strategy for the upcoming season is to recruit a talented tailback, Darnell Jefferson (Omar Epps). Darnell, an inner-city teen abandoned by first his father and then his mother, has been taken in by a community minister and has avoided being swallowed alive by the streets, but for Darnell college is little more than NFL training camp. His decision to attend ESU follows his introduction to an attractive young woman, Autumn Haley (Halle Berry), who has been recruited by the coach to show Darnell around campus.

Sam's other key players represent a variety of problems associated with "student athletes." Defensive standout Alvin Mack (Duane Davis) is barely literate but somehow maintains academic eligibility. Defensive hopeful Steve Lattimer (Andrew Bryniarski) has turned to steroids, gaining thirty-five pounds over the summer, in order to make the first team. Backup quarterback Bobby Collins (Jon Pennell) has a history of academic problems and has secretly begun dating the coach's daughter. Starting quarterback Joe Kane (Craig Sheffer), a much-hyped Heisman Trophy contender, is well on his way to becoming an alcoholic like his father and older brother; his recklessness borders on the suicidal. The only model player is Griffen, a premed student who is the starting tailback and Autumn's boyfriend. He is both Darnell's competitor and an unlikeable snob.

In spite of the players' problems, the season gets off to a solid start. Joe meets a girl, tennis player Camille Shafer (Kristy Swanson), who helps him keep his balance amidst mounting pressure to stay in competition for the Heisman. Darnell arranges for Autumn to be assigned as his tutor and under her influence begins studying in earnest; he persuades her to go out with him, and the two enjoy a casual date. When Darnell has the opportunity to take the field, he plays well. Alvin is on track to be a high NFL draft pick, and Steve has achieved his dream of making the first string.

Trouble is not long in coming. Sam's daughter, Louanne (Joey Adams), is caught taking a test for Bobby, and both students are expelled, leaving the team without a backup quarterback. Alvin suffers a career-ending injury. Steve, in a steroid-driven rage, attempts to rape a young woman at a party; the incident is covered up, and he is suspended for three games (allegedly out with a pulled hamstring) and ordered to clean up his act. Autumn introduces Darnell to her class-conscious father as her tutee rather than as someone she has been dating. Joe, the subject of a *Sports Illustrated* feature, begins drinking heavily and taking dangerous risks, at one point balancing on the rail of a railroad track as a train approaches. After losing a close game against a team whose quarterback is also in the running for the Heisman, Joe drinks too much at a bar, is involved in a fight, and is arrested while speeding away. Faced with a drunk-driving charge, he accepts a sentence of four weeks in rehab. Sam, who hates Bobby, must appeal to the university's gatekeepers to readmit the boy.

Without Joe and Alvin, the team struggles. Steve, having flushed his drugs, lacks the stamina to defend the line when it counts. In spite of two losses, the team is still in contention for a bowl invitation when Joe returns, now sober and feeling more in control of his life. He invites his father to attend the next game at which ESU will vie for the conference championship.

Because Joe's arm is still rusty, Sam alters his offensive strategy to rely more on the run. He shifts Griffen to fullback and Darnell to starting tailback. Steve has resumed steroid use and undergone a painful bladder cleansing procedure in order to pass his urine test. The big game contains few surprises as the score remains close until the final seconds. The resentful Griffen purposefully misses a key block, preventing Darnell from reaching the end zone, but in the end team spirit kicks in, and Griffen executes an outstanding block that allows Darnell to score the go-ahead touchdown. With the clock ticking down and the opposition threatening, Steve saves the day. When Sam congratulates him, the coach realizes his player is on drugs but says nothing. Joe's father has not attended the game, but he has watched it on television, an indication that his relationship with his son will improve. Alvin and his mother have also watched the televised game, a sad reminder that the young man's dreams have been destroyed, leaving him a semiliterate black man with a bad knee and no vocational skills.

After the game Darnell shows Autumn's father his latest test scores and win's the older man's respect. Meanwhile, Steve sits alone on the bench sobbing. The scene cuts to the coach, about to leave on his next recruiting mission.

The Program was panned by reviewers. Among the criticisms were that Darnell's success story clashes with the exposé of corruption and exploitation in college football; none of the characters expresses interest or concern in the fate of others; and no one's ethics have been challenged or changed. After his injury, Alvin is abandoned by his teammates, who do not visit him or discuss his fate among themselves. Similarly, Steve's drug use and Joe's drinking and risk taking fail to elicit concern for their well being. James Caan plays Sam Winters as if he is a man who has accepted that he has sold his soul. Bryniarski seems to have modeled his performance of Steve on a cartoon character. Sheffer, in spite of his acting abilities, looks like the thirtysomething actor he was at the time rather than a college junior, even a hard drinking one.

A scene was deleted from the film and the footage destroyed after the death of one teenager and serious injury to several others who imitated Joe's stunt of lying along the median strip of a highway.

PURELY BELTER (2000)

DIRECTOR: Mark Herman. SCREENPLAY: Mark Herman, based on the novel *The Season Ticket* by Jonathan Tulloch. PRODUCER: Elizabeth Karlsen. CINEMATOGRAPHY: Andy Collins. EDITING: Michael Ellis. MUSIC: Ian Broudie, Michael Gibbs. PRODUCTION DESIGN: Don Taylor. ART DIRECTION: Mark Kebby. COSTUME DESIGN: Jill Taylor.

CAST: Chris Beattie (Gerry McCarten), Greg McLane (Sewell), Charlie Hardwick (Mrs. McCarten), Roy Hudd (Mr. Sewell), Tim Healy (Mr. McCarten), Kevin Whately (Mr. Caird).

RUNNING TIME: 99 minutes.

Based on the novel *The Season Ticket* by Jonathan Tulloch, *Purely Belter* is a bittersweet comedy about two lads' desperate attempts to put together enough money for season tickets to Newcastle United's football (American soccer) matches. The film provides a diversion from the standard treatment of football hooligans and the English gang culture that has grown around U.K. football. Gerry McCarten (Chris Beattie) and Sewell (Greg McLane) are devoted fans, but they anticipate enjoying tea during the interval, not getting into fights. Football for them is an escape from the violence and despair of their homes.

Gerry lives with his mother (Charlie Hardwick), who is a heavy smoker with a serious cough; a sister, Clare (Tracy Whitwell); and Clare's baby. The McCartens move frequently to avoid Gerry's dad (Tim Healy), a vicious drunk who steals their money and pawns the furniture every time he tracks the family down. Another sister, Bridget (Kerry Ann Christiansen), is a heroin addict who has run away from home. Sewell's life is also sad. Abandoned by his parents, he has been raised by his grandfather (Roy Hudd), who is now elderly and showing signs of dementia. Sewell is in love, but the object of his affection, Gemma (Jody Baldwin), already has a boyfriend, referred to as "the Gorilla" because of his size and his personality.

Gerry and Sewell begin their fundraising with legitimate projects, babysitting for Clare and washing cars. A foray into the scrap metal business yields them a cuckoo clock from a dealer who lives "beyond the cash economy" and a dog that follows them home. Before long the two are scooping coins from fountains and using the baby as a prop for begging near train stations; they soon move on to larger scams. Sewell, wearing dark glasses, carrying a white cane, and keeping the dog (now called Rusty) on a lead, pretends to be blind. The two enter a shop separately, and while Gerry distracts the clerks by behaving suspiciously, Sewell shoplifts. Gerry then hawks the stolen goods at school, which he has promised a social worker to attend for two weeks in exchange for tickets to the Newcastle-Sunderland match. At school Gerry struggles with classes and a hostile physical education teacher; meanwhile, Sewell gets work planting bulbs. In a touching scene, when Gerry is asked to share a childhood memory, he describes going to a match with his dad, a story that later turns out to be Sewell's. After Gerry is humiliated by the phys ed teacher, who hangs him upside down, the two boys break into the teacher's house—they have burgled houses before—and scrawl "Bastard" upside down on a wall.

The next day, having completed his two weeks of schooling, Gerry collects the tickets, only to discover the match is being played in

Sunderland, not Newcastle. He and Sewell are greatly disappointed, but they travel into "enemy territory" and watch the game with restraint, lest they anger the local fans. It is the first match Gerry has attended, and Sewell tells the story, a verbatim repetition of Gerry's story, of attending a match with his father, making it obvious that Sewell has repeated his story often and that Gerry has made it his own.

After the match, the boys continue accumulating money in inventive ways. When the holiday season rolls around, they don paper crowns and carol for coins. Then Gerry's father tracks down the family, forces his way in, and steals Gerry's savings. Gerry waits until after Boxing Day to tell Sewell about their loss. To make matters worse, the television stations are airing a video of the two boys shoplifting, so they must now avoid the police. Gerry is convinced that to avoid being recognized, they must get rid of Rusty, who has also been caught on tape. However, Gerry can't bring himself to harm the dog and makes only a weak attempt at abandoning the animal by tethering it to a lamppost where Sewell will find him. The boys walk to a nearly deserted amusement park to contemplate their predicament, and there Gerry runs into Bridget, who is sleeping in a carousel chariot. She is on drugs and refuses to return home. Gerry offers to buy her something to eat, but while he is at a refreshment stand, she runs off. Gerry and Sewell sit on a curb with Rusty and eat the sandwiches.

Gerry and Sewell's notoriety amuses their friends, and Gemma, who has broken up with the Gorilla, agrees to keep Rusty while the boys maintain a low profile. She also begins dating Sewell. In spite of their efforts not to draw attention to themselves, the two boys dive into trouble again when they try to get an autograph from Alan Shearer, a Newcastle player who stares at them for a moment before turning away—apparently they look vaguely familiar to him, but he can't place their faces. Feeling snubbed, Gerry steals Alan's sports car, which is parked behind the stadium. The two go for a joy ride in the countryside and then skinny-dip at a childhood haunt. Afterward, as they warm themselves over a bonfire, Sewell admits that he never knew his father and that it was his grandfather who took him to the match that he recalls so fondly in his story. Both boys express the belief that a father shapes a son's identity, and they both are determined to be good fathers themselves; in fact, they were responsible and caring babysitters. This adventure signals an end to childhood for the friends. Sewell announces that Gemma is pregnant and that he is ready to be a good father. The football ticket project was just a game, he claims. However, their fortunes shift again, and the boys lose their grasp on maturity. Gemma tells Sewell she's returning to the Gorilla—who has found a steady job—because she needs a secure future. Shortly after, Gerry's mother learns she has cancer; for Gerry the potential loss and additional responsibility are frightening.

Gerry tracks down his father at a pub to tell him about the cancer, but his father is not interested. He continues to drink and takes his turn at karaoke, crooning "You Were Always on My Mind." Gerry starts sniffing inhalants, and Sewell tries to fight the Gorilla, getting battered in the process. Reunited, the boys determine to pull off one large heist, choosing their target based on what building they are in front of at the end of a song. It's a bank, and they charge in without a plan. The first thing that happens is that Gerry is recognized by a friend of his mother, and he pauses for a polite exchange before moving on to the teller. Gerry demands a thousand pounds, enough for the season tickets; the teller sets off an alarm and stalls Gerry. Sewell, who has wrapped his jacket around his arm, points his fist at the guard. A security gate closes, trapping the boys inside. The guard calls Sewell's bluff, and the boys end up in prison, where they are served tea.

A phone call from the hospital changes their circumstances. It is Gerry's father who has died. His mother has recovered enough to attend the funeral and laugh with Gerry and Clare at the service. A sympathetic judge sentences the boys to two hundred hours of community service. When football season resumes, the pair are delivering meals to elderly women, and have set their schedule so that they arrive at an apartment overlooking St. James Park at game time. The film closes with the boys perched on chairs on the balcony of a sweet little old lady, who fetches them tea.

The title means "grand" or "terrific" in the accent of northeast England. The accents are a bit troublesome at first for American viewers, but the acting is excellent and the characters so likeable that the hokey plot twists can be overlooked.

R

RACE THE SUN (1996)

DIRECTOR: Charles T. Kanganis. SCREENPLAY: Barry Morrow. PRODUCERS: Richard Heus, Barry Morrow. CINEMATOGRAPHY: David Burr. EDITING: Wendy Greene Bricmont. MUSIC: Graeme Revell. PRODUCTION DESIGN: Owen Paterson. ART DIRECTION: Richard Hobbs, Michelle, McGahey. COSTUME DESIGN: Margot Wilson.
CAST: Halle Berry (Sandra Beecher), Casey Affleck (Daniel Webster), Eliza Dushku (Cindy Johnson), Steve Zahn (Hans Kooiman), Kevin Tighe (Jack Fryman), James Belushi (Frank Machi).
RUNNING TIME: 100 minutes.
DVD: Sony Pictures.

Encouraged by their teacher and a mechanic, a handful of kids compete in an Australian race with the solar-powered car they built.

RACING STRIPES (2005)

DIRECTOR: Frederik Du Chau. SCREENPLAY: David Schmidt, Steven P. Wegner, Kirk De Micco, Frederik Du Chau. PRODUCERS: Broderick Johnson, Andrew A. Kosove, Edward L. McDonnell, Lloyd Phillips. CINEMATOGRAPHY: David Eggby. EDITING: Tom Finan. MUSIC: Mark Isham. PRODUCTION DESIGN: Wolf Kroeger. ART DIRECTION: Jonathan Hely-Hutchinson. COSTUME DESIGN: Jo Katsaras.
CAST: Hayden Panettiere (Channing Walsh), Bruce Greenwood (Nolan Walsh) Frankie Muniz (Stripes—voice), David Spade (Scuzz—voice), Mandy Moore (Sandy—voice).
RUNNING TIME: 102 minutes.
DVD: Warner Home Video.

In this live-action film with speaking animals, a zebra has dreams of becoming a champion racehorse.

RAD (1986)

DIRECTOR: Hal Needham. SCREENPLAY: Sam Bernard, Geoffrey Edwards. PRODUCER: Robert L. Levy. CINEMATOGRAPHY: Richard Leiterman. EDITING: Carl Kress. MUSIC: James Di Pasquale. PRODUCTION DESIGN: James Di Pasquale. ART DIRECTION: Shirley Inget. COSTUME DESIGN: Jerry Allen.
CAST: Bill Allen (Cru), Lori Loughlin (Christian), Talia Shire (Mrs. Jones), Ray Walston (Burton Timmer), Bart Conner (Bart Taylor).
RUNNING TIME: 91 minutes.
VHS: Sony Pictures.

In this film, a high schooler is more interested in competing in a BMX race than taking his SATs.

RADIO (2003)

DIRECTOR: Michael Tollin. SCREENPLAY: Mike Rich. PRODUCERS: Herbert W. Gains, Brian Robbins, Michael Tollin. CINEMATOGRAPHY: Don Burgess. EDITING: Chris Lebenzon, Harvey Rosenstock. MUSIC: James Horner. PRODUCTION DESIGN: Clay A. Griffith. ART DIRECTION: Thomas Minton. COSTUME DESIGN: Denise Wingate.
CAST: Cuba Gooding Jr. (Radio), Ed Harris (Coach Jones), Debra Winger (Linda), Alfre Woodard (Principal Daniels), S. Epatha Merkerson (Maggie), Brent Sexton (Honeycutt).
RUNNING TIME: 109 minutes.
DVD: Sony Pictures.

Radio is a sports drama inspired by the friendship between James Robert Kennedy, a developmentally disabled African American, and Harold Jones, a white athletic coach in Anderson, South Carolina.

As the film opens, James (Cuba Gooding Jr.), who is known as Radio, is pushing a grocery cart outside the fence of Hanna High School's football field. Inside the fence, Coach Jones (Ed Harris) is conducting a practice, stressing teamwork and discipline. The chain link fence represents a barrier, but a permeable one that allows visibility. Radio has drawn the attention of the coach, who observes that the young man frequently appears and watches practice from a distance. The players, however, fail to notice Radio's presence until he picks up a ball that has cleared the fence. The players shout for him to return the ball, but Radio, who collects found objects in his cart, regards the ball as one of his treasures. Jones has witnessed the incident but has not commented.

The next day at the field, Coach Jones sees Radio's cart, but not Radio. Several of his players, including star Johnny Clay (Riley Smith), are banging balls against a shed. When the coach approaches and asks what they are doing, they don't respond, but since they have stopped throwing the balls, a cry can be heard coming from inside. The coach discovers Radio, his wrists and hands bound with athletic tape. Once freed, he runs terrified from the field. Jones, with understated anger, tells his players to advise their parents that tomorrow's practice will "run a little long."

At school the next day Principal Daniels (Alfre Woodard) discusses the incident with Jones and places responsibility for resolving the situation quietly on the coach. He catches up with Radio at the edge of the school yard, where Radio has come to return the ball. Jones declines the ball, apologizes for the players' behavior, and asks Radio to come by practice, suggesting that the team could use his help.

Radio reappears outside the fence, where he watches the coach make the squad members who harassed him run suicide drills in full equipment. Radio also shows up for the Yellow Jackets' first game of the season, again watching from outside the fence. Afterward, Jones stops by the barbershop, where a number of the local men have gathered to discuss the game. This brief scene establishes the investment many residents have in high school football. The sport brings the community together and, as becomes evident later, functions as a medium through which the town tackles larger social issues.

The coach persists in his efforts to befriend Radio, eventually winning him over with offers of burgers and soft drinks. Soon Radio is attending practices and helping Coach Jones and his assistant, Honeycutt (Brent Sexton). Gradually, the players seem to accept his presence, and the fans cheer when he follows the team onto the field. However, the Yellow Jackets have lost three straight games, and the buzz at the barber shop, led by Johnny's father, Frank (Chris Mulkey), is that Radio has become a distraction.

Jones is also under some pressure at home from his self-sacrificing wife, Linda (Debra Winger), who expresses her concern that Jones spends too little time with their daughter Mary Helen, now a junior and a member of the cheerleading squad. Jones has missed a parent-teacher conference and has repeatedly been late to dinner. However, the coach has become absorbed in working with Radio, who is steadily developing stronger social skills and enough confidence to speak. He spends increasing amounts of time with the young man, and when the football season ends, Jones brings Radio into his classroom.

Radio's presence at the high school elicits complaints from Frank Clay, who applies pressure to the school board. However, Radio is gaining acceptance among the students, and Coach Jones has begun to teach him to read and write his name. On Christmas eve Radio joins the Joneses because his mother, a hospital worker, must report for duty over the holiday. There is a pile of presents for Radio from the Joneses and from people connected with the school. On Christmas day, Radio plays Santa, loading up his cart and distributing some of his gifts on porches of neighbors. However, his fun is interrupted by a rookie police officer who assumes Radio has stolen the cartload of gifts. Radio, being unable to explain himself, is handcuffed and hauled off to jail. When the two duty officers realize whom the rookie has arrested, they call the coach, and the misunderstanding is rectified: the rookie chauffeurs Radio around the community while he distributes the remainder of his gifts.

At school Radio serves as hall monitor, announces the day's menu, and helps with the basketball team, but there is still opposition to his presence. More trouble occurs when Johnny and several teammates trick Radio into entering the girls' locker room. Although pressured by the coach, Radio refuses to reveal Johnny as instigator. Principal Daniels's concern increases about allowing Radio to continue to attend school. In the midst of this controversy, Radio's mother dies suddenly of a heart attack. In his grief, Radio trashes the house and then hides in his room. Mary Helen and her father arrive and settle Radio until an older brother appears. On the drive home, the coach finally explains to Mary Helen the root of his concern for Radio: one morning, while he was on his paper route as a child, the coach discovered a boy about his age kept in a wire cage behind a house; Jones continued on his route without ever saying or doing anything and has felt guilty ever since.

Because of the locker room incident and Radio's furniture smashing, there is talk of placing Radio in an institution. His brother cannot care for him, and Frank Clay is determined to see Radio removed from the school. When Johnny returns to the team, he discovers that Radio has left him a gift—a transistor radio—and a "note," a piece of paper on which he has been practicing making Os. Johnny accepts the gift and gives Radio a friendly slap on the back.

Coach Jones learns that a town meeting has been called at the barber shop to discuss Radio's future. Principal Daniels presides. She is the only woman present until Jones enters with Linda and Mary Ellen. Jones gives an inspiring speech about how much everyone has learned from Radio about kindness and forgiveness. He also agrees that changes need to be made and announces he is resigning as coach to spend more time with his family.

The scene cuts to graduation, where Radio receives an honorary diploma. Principal Daniels announces that Radio may remain a junior at the school for as long as he likes, and Johnny gives Radio his athletic jacket. In a voice-over, Linda relates that after twenty-six years, Radio still helps with the football team and that Coach Jones has been inducted into the South Carolina Hall of Fame. Footage of James Robert Kennedy shows him cheering on the Hanna Yellow Jackets and assisting at practices.

RAGING BULL (1980)

DIRECTOR: Martin Scorsese. SCREENPLAY: Paul Schrader, Mardik Martin, Peter Savage, Joseph Carter, based on the book by Jake La Motta. PRODUCERS: Robert Chartoff, Irwin Winkler. CINEMATOGRAPHY: Michael Chapman. EDITING: Thelma Schoonmaker. SET DECORATION: Phil Abramson, Fred Weiler. COSTUME DESIGN: John Boxer, Richard Bruno.
CAST: Robert De Niro (Jake La Motta), Joe Pesci (Joey La Motta), Cathy Moriarty (Vickie La Motta), Nicholas Colasanto (Tommy Como), Frank Vincent (Salvy), Theresa Saldana (Lenore).
RUNNING TIME: 129 minutes.
ACADEMY AWARDS: Best Actor (De Niro), Best Editing. NOMINATIONS: Best Picture, Best Director, Best Supporting Actor (Pesci), Best Supporting Actress (Moriarty), Best Cinematography, Best Sound.
DVD: MGM.

Just as *The Godfather*, with Marlon Brando in the lead as Don Corleone, was Francis Coppola's breakthrough film, so *Raging Bull*, with Robert De Niro in the lead as professional boxer Jake La Motta, became the defining hit of Martin Scorsese's early career. However, *Raging Bull* did not define Scorsese in quite the way that *The Godfather* defined Coppola, who, unlike Scorsese, made two sequels to extend the popular success and profits of his Mafia epic. Scorsese moved more effectively to other varied projects, including *The Color of Money* (1986).

Scorsese came to the brutality of Jake La Motta after having filmed the brutality of the fictional Travis Bickel in *Taxi Driver*. Both characters were played by Robert De Niro. The screenplay for *Raging Bull*, started by Paul Schrader and completed by Mardik Martin, tells the story of Jake La Motta through flashbacks from the perspective of 1964; at the Barbizon Plaza Hotel in New York, a setting reviewer Vincent Canby described as "a peculiarly midcentury American purgatory," the fighter is preparing for a nightclub performance entitled "An Evening with Jake La Motta." In his *New York Times* review (November 14, 1980), Canby called *Raging Bull* Scorsese's "most ambitious film as well as his finest" but protested that the film could not "be conveniently classified as either a fight movie or a film biography," even though scrupulous attention was paid to "the factual details of Mr. La Motta's career" as he battled his way to the middleweight boxing championship by defeating Marcel Cerdan.

In his review, Chicago-based film critic Roger Ebert was more precise in describing the film: "*Raging Bull*, is not a film about boxing, but about a man with paralyzing jealousy and sexual insecurity, for whom being punished in the ring serves as con-

Robert De Niro as Jake La Motta in *Raging Bull*

fession, penance, and absolution. It is no accident that the screenplay never concerns itself with fight strategy. For Jake La Motta, what happens during a fight is controlled not by tactics, but by his fears and drives." Supporting De Niro's performance as an angry and jealous fighter propelled toward violence are Joe Pesci, playing Jake's younger brother Joey, and Cathy Moriarty, who plays Jake's second wife, Vickie. Both Moriarty and Pesci were nominated for supporting-actor Academy Awards, and De Niro won a Best Actor Oscar for his performance. Thelma Schoonmaker also won an Oscar for her editing, though *Raging Bull*, later to be regarded as the best picture of the 1980s by several polls of critics at the end of the decade, lost the Best Picture Academy Award to the more sentimental *Ordinary People*.

The first part of the film focuses on a series of bouts occurring between 1941 and 1947, when Jake is determined to do things "his way," to "make it on his own" without the assistance and control offered by Tommy Como (Nicholas Colasanto), the local mob boss who has the power to arrange title fights. Interspersed between the fights, most of which Jake wins, are other bouts, mostly with his wife, whom he soon divorces; "sparring sessions" with his brother Joey, whom he asks to hit him in the face; and "romantic" interludes with Vickie, who is just fifteen when he meets her. There is nothing to explain his rage, his sexual jealousy, his masochism, or his love/hate relationship with his brother. He and Sugar Ray Robinson (Johnny Barnes) fight three times by 1943, with Sugar Ray taking the first and third fights; Jake is making no progress toward a title bout. In 1945 he and Vickie marry, but their marriage only increases Jake's jealousy, so much so that when he is slated to fight Tony Janiro (Kevin Mahon), a handsome boxer who is a favorite with women, he somehow believes that destroying Tony's good looks will solve his sexual problems. In an ambiguous statement, he tells Tommy, "I don't know whether to fuck him or to fight him." He also has asked Joey to watch Vickie, who he feels is too friendly with Tommy and his henchman, Salvatore (Frank Vincent). In the Janiro-La Motta bout, Jake savagely attacks Tony's face, breaking his nose, and causing a ringsider to comment, "He ain't pretty no more."

Joey, more savvy than Jake, knows that Jake can't get a title shot without Tommy, but there is a price to pay for that assistance. Jake must do the flip flop, throw a fight to Billy Fox (Eddie Mustafa Muhammad), so that Tommy and his associates can clean up on bets. Despite his protestation that "I don't go down for nobody," Jake loses to Fox in a TKO (technical knockout) that is so obviously fixed that the New York State Board suspends Jake's license. However, boxing being what it is, Jake gets a title shot in 1949 with Marcel Cerdan (Louis Raftis), the current middleweight champion, and wins by a TKO. Rather than solving Jake's problems, being champion only compounds them. He turns on Joey, accusing him of withholding information about Vickie's infidelities and of having sex with her himself; he finally drives Vickie to falsely claim that she had sex with "all of them." Then, Jake attacks and beats Joey in front of his wife and children. Overweight, out of shape, and pathetic, he again takes on Sugar Ray, and this time the fight is stopped in the thirteenth round with Jake helpless on the ropes. As Joey watches the fight on the television in his home, he sees his brother approach Sugar Ray and brag, "You never got me down, Ray." This is schoolboy stuff.

Seven years later Jake, Vickie, and their three children are in Miami, where Jake has bought a nightclub named, appropriately, "Jake La Motta's." Here he entertains his customers with embarrassingly stupid jokes and intimidating putdowns besides serving alcohol to underage female drinkers who reciprocate with embraces. When the state's attorney and his wife, with their guests, visit his club, Jake drunkenly kisses the man's wife and spills drinks on the group. When a young woman is refused service because she doesn't look twenty-one, he tells her to prove her age to him: she later "proves" to be fourteen and claims that Jake "introduced" her to men. That act results in his conviction on a vice rap, and eventually he goes to prison. Thinking he can raise enough cash to buy off the police, Jake retrieves his championship belt from Vickie, who is divorcing him. He destroys the belt while prying out the jewels, which he intends to hock; however, the pawnbroker informs him that it is the belt, not the jewels, that has value. And that is one of Jake's problems: he has the pieces, but he does not have the picture. He lacks understanding. When Jake is incarcerated, he punches the walls and screams unconvincingly, "I'm not an animal."

In 1958 he is employed as an announcer and entertainer at the Markwell Hotel in New York City. Gross, coarse, insulting, and intimidating, he works the crowd before introducing Amber 48's, a stripper whom he dumps when he spots Joey across the street. Jake trails Joey, accosts him, embraces him, and tells him, "You're my brother." Joey responds by making vague promises about getting together later. By this time Jake is totally alone.

Yet the film ends eight years later, with precious little information about those eight years. Jake is at the Barbizon Plaza, getting ready to go on stage and rehearsing his monologue, which includes a recitation from *On The Waterfront*, a role immortalized by Marlon Brando. He quotes the lines "I coulda been a contender" and "It was you, Charlie, you shoulda looked out for me"—strange words for a person who was not only a contender but also a champion, and who not only failed to look out for his brother but also physically attacked him and falsely accused him of having slept with his wife. Before he leaves his dressing room, Jake throws punches at the mirror, repeating "I am the boss."

In showing the violence and brutality of the sport, Scorsese did not pull his punches, although he did decide to film the picture in black and white because he was reluctant to show so much blood in a color picture. Roger Ebert, who had done a stop-action analysis of the film with Thelma Schoonmaker at a master class at the University of Virginia, explains in his review of the film, "The fight scenes took Scorsese ten weeks to shoot instead of the planned two." The director also used "sponges concealed in the gloves and tiny tubes in the boxers' hair to deliver spurts and sprays of sweat and blood." As a result of this enhanced realism, La Motta "makes Rocky look tame" by comparison.

While it is difficult to argue with the technical virtuosity of the editing and the acting ability of the principals, notably De Niro, the film simply lacks wide appeal, not only with its original audiences, but also with later ones. It leaves a viewer with the same feeling one has after watching the talented Johnny Depp portray the dissolute Earl of Rochester in *The Libertine* (2005). And the Earl of Rochester, evil as he was, was a more complex and interesting character.

READY TO RUMBLE (2000)

DIRECTOR: Brian Robbins. SCREENPLAY: Steven Brill. PRODUCERS: Robert F. Newmyer, Jeffrey Silver. CINEMATOGRAPHY: Clark Mathis. EDITING: Ned Bastille, Cindy Mollo. MUSIC: George S. Clinton.

PRODUCTION DESIGN: Jaymes Hinkle. ART DIRECTION: Alan E. Muraoka. COSTUME DESIGN: Carol Ramsey.
CAST: David Arquette (Gordie Boggs), Scott Caan (Sean Dawkins), Oliver Platt (Jimmy King), Rose McGowan (Sasha), Martin Landau (Sal Bandini).
RUNNING TIME: 107 minutes.
DVD: Warner Home Video.

Several real-life wrestling stars appear in this comedy about a pair of fans who think the spectacle is real.

REBOUND (2005)

DIRECTOR: Steve Carr. SCREENPLAY: Jon Lucas, Scott Moore. STORY: William Wolff, Ed Decter, John J. Strauss. PRODUCER: Robert Simonds. CINEMATOGRAPHY: Glen MacPherson. EDITING: Craig Herring. MUSIC: Teddy Castellucci. PRODUCTION DESIGN: Jaymes Hinkle. ART DIRECTION: Bruce Crone. COSTUME DESIGN: Salvador Pérez Jr.
CAST: Martin Lawrence (Roy McCormick), Wendy Raquel Robinson (Jeanie Ellis), Horation Sanz (Mr. Newirth), Breckin Meyer (Tim Fink), Megan Mullally (Principal Walsh).
RUNNING TIME: 103 minutes.
DVD: 20th Century Fox.

A college basketball coach is demoted to coaching middle schoolers at his alma mater in this predictable film.

RED LINE 7000 (1966)

DIRECTOR: Howard Hawks. SCREENPLAY: George Kirgo. STORY: Howard Hawks. PRODUCER: Howard Hawks. CINEMATOGRAPHY: Milton R. Krasner. EDITING: Bill Brame, Stuart Gilmore. MUSIC: Nelson Riddle. ART DIRECTION: Arthur Lonergan, Hal Pereira. COSTUME DESIGN: Edith Head.
CAST: James Caan (Mike), Laura Devon (Julie), Gail Hire (Holly), Charlene Holt (Lindy), George Takei (Kato).
RUNNING TIME: 110 minutes.
VHS: Paramount Home Video.

This drama revolves around race car drivers and the women who love them.

REMEMBER THE TITANS (2000)

DIRECTOR: Boaz Yakin. SCREENPLAY: Gregory Allen Howard. PRODUCERS: Jerry Bruckheimer, Chad Oman. CINEMATOGRAPHY: Philippe Rousellot. EDITING: Michael Tronick. MUSIC: Trevor Rabin. PRODUCTION DESIGN: Deborah Evans. ART DIRECTION: Jonathan Short. COSTUME DESIGN: Judy L. Ruskin.
CAST: Denzel Washington (Herman Boone), Will Patton (Bill Yoast), Wood Harris (Julius Campbell), Ryan Hurst (Gerry Bertier), Donald Faison (Petey Jones), Craig Kirkwood (Jerry "Rev" Harris), Ethan Suplee (Louie Lastik), Kip Pardue (Ronnie Bass), Hayden Panettiere (Sheryl Yoast), Kate Bosworth (Emma Hoyt), Ryan Gosling (Alan Bosley).
RUNNING TIME: 113 minutes.
DVD: Walt Disney Video.

Based on events that occurred in 1971 after court-decreed integration, *Remember the Titans* focuses on the successful integration of the T. C. Williams High School football team in Alexandria, Virginia. Because all of the other coaches are white, public school officials have recruited an African American, Herman Boone (Denzel Washington), to replace head coach Bill Yoast (Will Patton). While hiring Boone will give the appearance of complying with the law and addressing the concerns of the black community, the school anticipates that Boone will fail to produce a winning team and Yoast, who is on the verge of being elected to the Football Hall of Fame in Virginia, can resume the position. But all does not go according to plan.

Yoast, who is supposed to move to another school, opts to stay on as defensive coordinator and assistant head coach so that his white players will not boycott the football team and lose their chances at getting football scholarships. Because they have different coaching philosophies (Boone is much harder on the players), the two coaches frequently argue, but they eventually come together. Their situation is paralleled by the interaction between the white All-American team captain, Gerry Bertier (Ryan Hurst), and the unofficial leader of the black players, Julius Campbell (Wood Harris).

As the film begins, there are race riots in Alexandria, and the white football players head for the fracas before Yoast can stop them. The situation appears to be hopeless, but the team's training camp at Gettysburg College will act as a kind of crucible in which black-white relationships will be resolved. To effect a reconciliation between the two groups, Coach Boone decrees that all defensive players ride on the same bus and eat at the same table, and all offensive players do likewise. He also makes blacks and whites room together and learn something about the opposite-race players. Gerry and Julius room together, fight, and distrust each other, but they eventually bond, just as their coaches do. The turning point at camp occurs at a Gettysburg battle site, where Boone compares their situation with the one between Union and Confederate soldiers, concluding that if they do not come together, they will also be destroyed. Aiding in the process are music and humor.

Although the team bonds, the first day of school demonstrates the amount of racial animosity that exists in the white student body; for example, Emma (Kate Bosworth), Gerry's girlfriend, will not shake Julius's hand when Gerry introduces them.

The first part of the season is full of downs and ups. A white father complains to Yoast after his son is replaced by a better (black) player. Boone accuses Yoast of coddling the black players and undermining his authority. When Ronnie (Kip Pardue) attempts to take some black teammates into a local bar, the bigoted bar owner throws them out. After Gerry refuses to leave his black teammates to go with Emma and Ray (Gerry's teammate, played by Burgess Jenkins), Emma dumps him. A rock is thrown through a window at Boone's house. A black player is attacked by some white students. When the assistant coach, Tyrell (Brett Rice), demonstrates his racism, Yoast and he quarrel, and Tyrell quits. Gerry and Julius call a team meeting to discuss problems. Louie (Ethan Suplee), a huge white player who has described himself as "trailer-park trash," unites the team (Ray remains a holdout) when he leads them in singing and dancing, and before the third game, the team creates a new entrance routine inspired by Louie's performance.

In this third game, the Titans, who are undefeated, take on a white team who call the black players "Sambo" and who are intent on injuring Julius, the quarterback. They succeed, but only because Ray deliberately misses a block. Ronnie, who has displayed a lack of confidence, takes Julius's place. When number 48 attempts to hurt him, Ronnie tells his teammates to let him through the line on the next play. As number 48 bears down on him, Ronnie deliberately throws the football at his head, taking him out of the game. In response to the opposing coach's call for a penalty, the referee asks, "On the quarterback?" Ronnie stars in the victory. After the game Gerry tells Boone he wants Ray off the team.

The coach agrees and instructs Gerry to break the news. Ray can't understand how Gerry will put the black players above their friendship.

A sign of changing times occurs when Julius, who is walking in Gerry's white neighborhood, is stopped by a white policeman in a patrol car. Fearing the worst, Julius is relieved when the officer simply congratulates him and the team on their success. When Julius arrives at Gerry's home, he hugs Gerry's mother, who had earlier complained about Gerry's friendships with the black players.

Yoast, who has already swallowed his pride, makes another sacrifice when he is told by football authorities that the Titans' next game against Tabor is fixed so that Boone will be fired, and he will be hired to become the head coach. Tabor's head coach tells television reporters that his players are adept at "knocking the chocolate out of people." When Yoast sees the officials making several bad calls against the Titans, he runs out on the field and threatens to go to the papers if the refs do not call a fair game. After the Titans win, Yoast is told, "You just lost yourself the Hall of Fame." The Tabor coach refuses to shake Boone's hand after the game. On the positive side, Emma tells Gerry that she will try to overcome her prejudice but that it will take her a little longer. Boone's neighbors, who were hostile when he first arrived, all turn out to cheer him after the Titans win in the regionals.

Tragedy strikes unexpectedly when Gerry's car is hit by a truck, and he is paralyzed from the waist down. When the nurse asks Julius to leave Gerry's room because only family are allowed to visit, Gerry claims Julius is his brother and points to the family resemblance. Later in the scene Gerry admits to Julius that he was afraid of him at first. Julius responds, "There is no black-white between us."

As the state championship approaches, the film moves toward a brighter future. Always upbeat, Gerry tells Yoast that he has been reading about the Olympics for handicapped people. Before the game, Louie hugs Coach Boone and informs him that he is "eligible," meaning that he has achieved the necessary grade point average to play college football. When Gerry's mother is given a standing ovation by the Titan fans, she and Julius's mother hug, and Emma shakes Julius's hand. Throughout the game, the team demonstrates how well they work together. Late in the fourth quarter, after a key block by Ronnie, Julius runs for the winning touchdown.

In a kind of epilogue that takes place at Gerry's funeral site, the narrator, Yoast's daughter Sheryl (Hayden Panettiere), informs the audience that Gerry won an Olympic medal in the shot put and died ten years after the accident. She also says that Boone and Yoast coached together for four more years and provides information about what happened to some of the players. The film ends fittingly with the team and coaches singing "Sha, na, na, na, Goodbye."

Although the film has been criticized by some reviewers as soft-pedaling the violence and racism of the period, *Remember the Titans* would not have received a PG rating and a large audience if it had included more violence, obscene language, and racial slurs. The script, by Gregory Allen Howard, who also wrote for *Ali* (2001) and *Glory Road* (2006), is tight and convincing, except for much of the footage involving Sheryl Yoast, an annoying child, and Boone's two daughters, who act as opposites, perhaps making a point about what is "feminine" and "white." The game footage, shot by Phillipe Rousselot, is excellent, and the tri-shot frame of practice sessions captures the intensity of the workouts taking place simultaneously all over the field. Washington and Patton turn in stellar performances.

THE REPLACEMENTS (2000)

DIRECTOR: Howard Deutch. SCREENPLAY: Vince McKewin. PRODUCER: Dylan Sellers. CINEMATOGRAPHY: Tak Fujimoto. EDITING: Seth Flaum, Bud S. Smith. MUSIC: John Debney. PRODUCTION DESIGN: Dan Bishop. ART DIRECTION: Gary Kosko. COSTUME DESIGN: Jill M. Ohanneson.
CAST: Gene Hackman (Jimmy McGinty), Keanu Reeves (Shane Falco), Brook Langton (Annabelle Farrell), Orlando Jones (Clifford Franklin), Jon Favreau (Danny Bateman), Jack Warden (Edward O'Neill), Rhys Ifans (Nigel Gruff).
RUNNING TIME: 118 minutes.
DVD: Warner Home Video.

During the 1987 football season the NFL players went on strike and were replaced by less highly talented athletes. The Washington Redskins, with replacement players, won three straight games, providing the inspiration for *The Replacements*. (In order to avoid conflict with the NFL, the film avoids specific reference to the NFL, renames the teams, and uses a contemporary setting.) Keanu Reeves stars as quarterback Shane Falco. Gene Hackman plays Jimmy McGinty, whom team owner Edward O'Neill (Jack Warden) asks to recruit and coach the replacement squad. Jimmy accepts the job but insists on having total control of his team.

Jimmy's list of men he wants for the team consists of a "dirty dozen" of misfits. His proposed roster includes Danny Bateman (Jon Favreau), a former SWAT team member; an ex-sumo wrestler; Nigel Gruff (Rhys Ifans), a skinny Welsh soccer player/kicker in debt to some gamblers; Brian Murphy (David Denman), a hearing-impaired wide receiver; the Jackson brothers (Faizon Love as Jamal and Michael Taliferro as Andre), who own and operate handguns; Clifford Franklin (Orlando Jones), a receiver who can't hold onto the ball; and Shane Falco, an All-American quarterback with an abbreviated NFL career. When Shane shows up late for practice, he parks his car in the space reserved for Eddie Martel (Brett Cullen), the starting quarterback for the Washington Sentinels. Eddie and his teammates, who call the replacements "scabs," turn Shane's truck over, precipitating a feud between the two quarterbacks.

Jimmy, who has faith in Shane, tells him he sees two men in him: "the man you are and the man you ought to be." In the first game, which the Sentinels lose to Detroit, Shane fumbles once, but his most serious mistake is changing the play Jimmy sent in at the end of the game. Instead of running with the ball, Shane hands it off to one of his backs, who fails to score. Jimmy comments, "Winners want the ball when the game is on the line." The team retires to the Endzone, a local bar, and is joined by the "real" Sentinels, led by Eddie. After the ensuing brawl, which Shane starts by coming to the aid of his deaf receiver, the replacements are jailed, while Eddie and his teammate go free. In the large holding tank the team comes together, singing "I Will Survive" and dancing the Electric Slide.

Shane has changed so much that Annabelle Farrell (Brooke Langton), the head cheerleader, who has recruited some lap dancers to act as the replacement cheerleaders, comments that he is not like the other football players she has known: "You care more about your teammates than yourself." She had earlier told Shane that she never dates football players, especially quarterbacks, but she changes her policy for him.

In the next game Annabelle's dancers distract the San Diego players with some of their routines, and the Sentinels come back to win, thanks to a sixty-five-yard field goal by Nigel, who smokes on the field. That night at the bar Annabelle owns, the local blue-collar clientele empathize with the replacements, who are, they say, "just like us." Eddie, however, wants to cross the picket line and rejoin the team for the Dallas game. Since the entire Dallas team has recrossed the line, owner Edward O'Neill insists that Jimmy, who wants to stick with Shane, start Eddie at quarterback. Jimmy's comment that Eddie has no heart proves to be true.

At the Endzone the night before the game, Shane tells his teammates about Eddie and is toasted as being a "great quarterback, leader, and friend." The next day he is back on his boat watching the Dallas game as Eddie fails to lead the Sentinels. Instead of encouraging his team, Eddie criticizes them, and the Sentinels trail 17–0 at the half. Eddie even threatens Jimmy. It's obvious that the Sentinels need "heart." Shane shows up in the locker room, and when Eddie protests, he is thrown out by Shane's loyal teammates. When the fans see Shane, they go wild, and the Sentinels mount a comeback. Jimmy tells Shane, "Do what you started, Shane." Trailing 17–14, the Sentinels are about to have Nigel kick a field goal when Nigel sees his gambling enemies in the stadium. To protect him, Shane, who is to hold the ball for the kick, runs with it instead and scores. Unfortunately, there is a penalty, nullifying the touchdown. On the last play of the game Shane, like a winner, wants the ball, which he passes to Brian for the winning touchdown. Edward, who was upset about Jimmy replacing Eddie with Shane, now acts as if it were his idea: "I knew it all along." Jimmy, who narrates, states that it was wonderful to be "part of something great," and the Sentinel replacements sing and dance to "I Will Survive" down on the field.

The film concerns trust, leadership, and confidence. Under Jimmy's tutelage Shane regains his self-confidence and leads his team of misfits to victory. The portrait of the striking players is negative, but the owners are also depicted unfavorably. The film makes it clear that the fans deserve better. Aside from the messages, mostly provided by Jimmy, the film also contains some pretty amusing sequences: Danny wiping out a cheerleading squad when he enters the field; the cheerleading misfits "reading" gestures; and the Jacksons destroying a car. Though the plot may sound familiar, the film is entertaining.

REQUIEM FOR A HEAVYWEIGHT (1962)

DIRECTOR: Ralph Nelson. SCREENPLAY: Rod Serling. PRODUCER: David Susskind. CINEMATOGRAPHY: Arthur J. Ornitz. EDITING: Carl Lerner. MUSIC: Laurence Rosenthal. PRODUCTION DESIGN: Burr Smidt. COSTUME DESIGN: John Boxer.

CAST: Anthony Quinn (Mountain Rivera), Jackie Gleason (Maish Rennick), Mickey Rooney (Army), Julie Harris (Grace Miller), Stanley Adams (Perelli), Val Avery (young fighter's promoter).

RUNNING TIME: 95 minutes. B&W.

DVD: Sony Pictures.

Requiem for a Heavyweight was originally a ninety-minute movie made for CBS television (1956) starring Jack Palance as Mountain McClintock. Both he and scriptwriter Rod Serling won Emmys for their work on the film, and Serling's script was used for the 1962 remake. In the remake Anthony Quinn plays the prizefighter, now named Mountain Rivera. Ralph Nelson directed both versions. The film concerns an over-the-hill boxer who, despite the possibility of blindness if his eyes are injured, agrees to become a wrestler in order to save his unscrupulous manager from death at the hands of the mob, to whom he owes money. He makes his decision despite the efforts of Grace Miller (Julie Harris), an unemployment counselor who sees the softer side of Mountain's nature and wants to find him a job where he can keep his dignity.

Maish Rennick (Jackie Gleason), Mountain's manager and longtime friend, has bet against Mountain in his bout with Cassius Clay. When Mountain goes seven rounds instead of the four Maish bet on, Maish owes Ma Greeny's (Madame Spivy) mob a lot of money. After being turned down by several of his acquaintances, Maish contacts Perelli (Stanley Adams), a wrestling promoter in league with Ma Greeny. If Mountain will dress and act like an Indian in a series of fixed wrestling matches, Maish's debt will be paid. To demonstrate the danger, Ma's henchmen corner Maish and give him a savage beating. By working on Mountain's friendship and the idea that Mountain is indebted to him, Maish hopes to persuade the reluctant Mountain to agree to the deal.

Meanwhile, Mountain, aided by his trainer, Army (Mickey Rooney), is trying to find employment to help Maish, whom he knows needs some money. When she interviews Mountain in her office, Grace sees that beneath the rugged looks, the half-articulate speech, and the lack of marketable skills, Mountain, who never threw a fight and was once ranked number five in the world, is a proud man with a kind heart. She visits him at a bar described by Maish as a "graveyard for retired boxers." Over a drink, she promises she will help him find a job. When he returns to his room, Mountain discovers that Maish has invited Perelli over to discuss the wrestling proposition. Although Maish senses that Mountain does not like the idea of being humiliated, he presses the idea before apparently giving in to Mountain's request that he not make him a "stumblebum." Grace calls with the news that Mountain has an interview with the owners of a summer camp, where he could work with children. However, Maish gets Mountain drunk so that he will not make the interview. Army arrives at the bar, calls Maish a jerk, and pleads with Mountain not to go to the interview drunk. Ignoring Army, Mountain meets his potential employer, behaves boorishly, and fails to secure the position.

In a last-ditch effort, Grace visits Mountain in his room and claims that he doesn't owe Maish anything. She asks, "Can't you see yourself as I see you?" Mountain can't; he says that he "belongs in dirty towns and locker rooms." It's clear that Grace is attracted to Mountain. When they kiss, she responds to him, but he is unable to control himself and forces himself on her. Afterward, in a confrontation with Maish, she says, "I wish it was something I could have given him." He replies that she should leave him alone: "You can put clothes on an ape, but he's still an ape."

The film ends with a showdown at the wrestling arena, where Mountain learns about the extent of Maish's debt and the danger he faces from Ma Greeny. He also learns that Maish had bet against him in the Clay bout. Mountain's response reflects his disillusionment: "You know, Maish, in all the dirty, crummy seventeen years I fought for you I wasn't ashamed of a single round. Not one single minute. Now you make me ashamed." Despite knowing about Maish's betrayal, Mountain dons the Indian garb, enters the ring, and, after an ominous pause, breaks into a war dance and begins a war whoop.

Although the fighting footage is confined to the relatively short Clay bout, this is a real sports film about what happens to someone who only knows how to fight and must, like the denizens of the "graveyard," confront the rest of his life. As the "requiem" of the title suggests, the heavyweight is dead, metaphorically if not physically. The film, shot in black and white, stresses the seamy side of the fight world and the grim future of the protagonist. By photographing the Clay fight from the point of view of the almost blinded Mountain, cinematographer Arthur Ornitz shows the extent of the damage to Mountain's eyes. The cameo appearances of such real boxers as Willie Pep, Barney Ross, and Jack Dempsey also add verisimilitude to the film.

RESURRECTING THE CHAMP (2007)

DIRECTOR: Rod Lurie. SCREENPLAY: Michael Bortman, Allison Burnett. PRODUCERS: Mark Frydman, Rod Lurie, Mike Medavoy, Bob Yari. CINEMATOGRAPHY: Adam Kane. EDITING: Sarah Boyd. MUSIC: Larry Groupé. PRODUCTION DESIGN: Ken Rempel. ART DIRECTION: Bill Ives. COSTUME DESIGN: Wendy Partridge.

CAST: Samuel L. Jackson (Champ), Josh Hartnett (Erik Kernan Jr.), Kathryn Morris (Joyce Kernan), Dakota Goyo (Teddy Kernan), Alan Alda (Ralph Metz), Rachel Nichols (Polly).

RUNNING TIME: 112 minutes.

DVD: 20th Century Fox.

A sportswriter believes that a homeless man he encounters is a former boxing champ.

REVERSAL (2001)

DIRECTOR: Alan Vint. SCREENPLAY: Jimi Petulla. PRODUCERS: Jimi Petulla, Albert Hasson. CINEMATOGRAPHY: William H. Molina. MUSIC: Jeff Danna. PRODUCTION DESIGN: Jory Adam. COSTUME DESIGN: Diane Collins.

CAST: Danny Mousetis (Leo Leone), Derrick Nelson (young Leo), Jimi Petulla (Coach Leone), Dawn Lafferty (Jessica).

RUNNING TIME: 104 minutes.

DVD: Vanguard Cinema.

This is a coming-of-age story about a teenager who has been following in the footsteps of his father, a former wrestling champion who has sacrificed nearly everything for his son.

RHUBARB (1951)

DIRECTOR: Arthur Lubin. SCREENPLAY: Francis M. Cockrell, Dorothy Davenport, David Stern, based on the novel by H. Allen Smith. PRODUCERS: William Perlberg, George Seaton. CINEMATOGRAPHY: Lionel Lindon. EDITING: Alma Macrorie. MUSIC: Van Cleave. PRODUCTION DESIGN: Henry Bumstead, Hal Pereira. COSTUME DESIGN: Edith Head.

CAST: Ray Milland (Eric Yeager), Jan Sterling (Polly Sickles), Gene Lockhart (Thaddeus J. Banner), William Frawley (Len Sickles), Elsie Holmes (Myra Banner), Taylor Holmes (P. Duncan Monk).

RUNNING TIME: 94 minutes. B&W.

DVD: Legend Films.

In this black-and-white comedy based on H. Allen Smith's novel, a feisty tomcat, Rhubarb (played by fourteen tabbies), inherits a fortune from Thaddeus Banner (Gene Lockhart), eccentric owner of the Brooklyn "Loons." Thaddeus, who claims to like artichokes because "they fight back," admires the spirit of the feral beast that steals golf balls coming within sight of his lair. After watching the cat send two guard dogs fleeing with tails between legs, Thaddeus decides that he must have the cat, which he calls "Rhubarb," a term used in the fifties to describe bench-emptying disputes on baseball diamonds. Rhubarb resists capture and domestication in a handful of staff-wounding, mansion-wrecking scenes, but takes quickly to Thaddeus Banner, who commemorates their "anniversary" each year with a photo and dies peacefully in bed with the albums nearby.

The aftermath of Thaddeus's death is far from peaceful once the terms of the will are revealed. Thaddeus's daughter, Myra (Elsie Holmes), wants to wrest control of her father's estate from Rhubarb's guardian, Eric Yeager (Ray Milland), who in turn must deal with a roster of men reluctant to play on a team owned by a cat. To make matters even worse, Yeager's fiancée, Polly Sickles (Jan Sterling in a rare comic role), sneezes uncontrollably in Rhubarb's presence.

Winning over the Loons, who have attempted a sick-out, is the simplest problem to solve. Eric, trading on the athletes' superstitious natures, tricks them into believing that the cat is a good luck charm. Immediately after he convinces two players to pet the cat, the team manager, Polly's father, Len (William Frawley), discovers the pair are owed bonuses. At the next game, against St. Louis, a player who rubs Rhubarb's head gets a hit, but a player who refuses trips over a row of bats. The Loons win after a minor disruption when Rhubarb decides to field a slow grounder and the St. Louis mascot, a dog, runs from the dugout in pursuit; the tables are rapidly reversed with Rhubarb chasing the dog.

Soon the Loons are on a winning streak and insist that the cat accompany them on their road trips, but Eric had planned to stay behind and marry Polly, who by this time has been diagnosed with an allergy specific to Rhubarb. Until whatever it is about the cat that triggers the allergic reaction is discovered, the wedding is on hold. Meanwhile, Myra is plotting to eliminate Rhubarb. When her attempt at catnapping fails, she sues, claiming that the real Rhubarb is dead.

In court Myra's attorney presents three exhibits: cats that look exactly like Rhubarb. When Rhubarb is placed in an identical cage, Eric must demonstrate that he can establish the identity of the rightful heir. What Myra doesn't know is that Polly's allergy isn't to cats in general, so after her physician testifies and the judge reminds Polly that she's sneezing under oath, she readily identifies Rhubarb. Case closed, and the Loons go on to win the pennant.

The Loons are facing a Manhattan team in the World Series, but the betting is running strongly in favor of the Loons, so much so that the mobsters backing the bookies are in trouble. The gangsters manage to nab the cat, and one of them, Pencil Louis (Richard Karlan), approaches Myra, offering to off the kitty for fifty thousand dollars. Myra, who is a primary suspect in the catnapping, needs time to raise the cash. Meanwhile, the Loons have dropped game 6 in the series, and Eric buys time by dropping dry ice over the stadium, causing rain and a postponement of the final game.

Polly, who has figured out that she's allergic to the late Thaddeus Banner's vicuna scarf, which now lines Rhubarb's cage, has been busy sniffing bookies. She finally locates the right one in a Manhattan funeral home. The bookie's confession leads Polly and Eric to a seedy hotel where Rhubarb is being held. While the thug who is supposed to be guarding him watches the ballgame on television, canny Rhubarb manages to escape. The chase is on with Eric, the police, and the gangsters following the cat, who, it turns out, is headed straight for the stadium, where a devoted fan has been bringing her own female feline fatale that has caught the eye of the team-owning tom. With the return of Rhubarb, the Loons win the series; the evildoers are arrested, and Eric and Polly at last can marry.

The movie ends on a humorous note, with Eric and Polly pushing a stroller through Central Park, accompanied by Rhubarb; his three "wives," identifiable by bows around their necks; and a pride of offspring. Rhubarb and family are quietly observed by a man on a park bench—actor

Paul Douglas, four times divorced and soon to be married to Jan Sterling, although the reference could be to Douglas's earlier film *A Letter to Three Wives* rather than to his marital record.

THE RINGER (2005)

DIRECTOR: Barry W. Blaustein. SCREENPLAY: Ricky Blitt. PRODUCERS: Bobby Farrelly, Peter Farrelly, John Jacobs, Bradley Thomas. CINEMATOGRAPHY: Mark Irwin. EDITING: George Folsey Jr. MUSIC: Mark Mothersbaugh. PRODUCTION DESIGN: Arlan Jay Vetter. ART DIRECTION: John Frick. COSTUME DESIGN: Lisa Jensen.
CAST: Johnny Knoxville (Steve Barker), Katherine Heigl (Lynn Sheridan), Brian Cox (Gary Barker), Geoffrey Arrend (Winston), Edward Barbanell (Billy), Jed Rees (Glen).
RUNNING TIME: 94 minutes.
DVD: 20th Century Fox.

In this comedy, a man poses as a mentally challenged adult to compete in the Special Olympics in order to make money. This surprisingly sweet film was endorsed by the Special Olympics.

RINGSIDE MAISIE (1941)

DIRECTOR: Edward L. Marin. SCREENPLAY: Mary C. McCall Jr., Wilson Collison. PRODUCER: J. Walter Ruben. CINEMATOGRAPHY: Charles Lawton. EDITING: Fredrick Y. Smith. MUSIC: David Snell. ART DIRECTION: Cedric Gibbons. COSTUME DESIGN: Robert Kalloch.
CAST: Ann Sothern (Maisie Rivier), Robert Sterling (Terry Dolan), George Murphy (Skeets Maguire), Margaret Moffat (Mrs. Doran), Nathalie Thompson (Cissy Reardon).
RUNNING TIME: 95 minutes.

A young woman falls for an undefeated boxer who hates to fight.

THE ROCKET: MAURICE RICHARD (2005)

DIRECTOR: Charles Biname. SCREENPLAY: Ken Scott. PRODUCERS: Denise Robert, Daniel Louis. CINEMATOGRAPHY: Pierre Gill. EDITING: Michel Arcand. MUSIC: Michel Cusson. PRODUCTION DESIGN: Michel Proulx. ART DIRECTION: Marc Ricard. COSTUME DESIGN: Francesca Chamberland.
CAST: Roy Dupuis (Maurice Richard), Stephen McHattie (Dick Irvin), Julie Le Breton (Lucille Richard), Rémy Girard (Tony Bergeron).
RUNNING TIME: 124 minutes.
DVD: Alliance (Universal).

This film is a biography of a Montreal Canadiens' hockey player who become the first man to score fifty goals in fifty games. This biopic won nine Genie Awards, the Canadian equivalent of the Oscar.

ROCKY (1976)

DIRECTOR: John G. Avildsen. SCREENPLAY: Sylvester Stallone. PRODUCERS: Robert Chartoff, Irwin Winkler. CINEMATOGRAPHY: James Crabe. EDITING: Scott Conrad, Richard Halsey. MUSIC: Bill Conti. PRODUCTION DESIGN: William Cassidy. ART DIRECTION: James H. Spencer.
CAST: Sylvester Stallone (Rocky Balboa), Talia Shire (Adrian), Burgess Meredith (Mickey), Burt Young (Paulie), Carl Weathers (Apollo Creed), Joe Spinell (Tony Gazzo).
RUNNING TIME: 119 minutes.
ACADEMY AWARDS: Best Picture, Best Director, Best Editing. NOMINATIONS: Best Actor (Stallone), Best Actress (Shire), Best Supporting Actor (Meredith), Best Supporting Actor (Young), Best Original Screenplay, Best Sound, Best Song ("Gonna Fly Now"; music by Bill Conti, lyrics by Carol Connors, Ayn Robbins).
DVD: MGM.

Rocky, the quintessential underdog boxing film, not only spawned sequels but also paved the way for underdog films in other sports. The rags-to-riches saga of the club brawler who proves his mettle in professional boxing also parallels the story of Sylvester Stallone, who penned the script and portrayed Rocky Balboa. Before his success with *Rocky*, Stallone had appeared in only a few mediocre films and had written *The Lords of Flatbush* (1974), a film in which his character foreshadows the Rocky persona. While Stallone did not win an Oscar for his screenplay, the film won Oscars for Best Picture, Best Director (John G. Avildsen), and Best Editing (Scott Conrad). In addition, Talia Shire (Adrianna or "Adrian") garnered Best Supporting Actress awards from the National Board of Review and the New York Film Critics. *Rocky* was not only a critical success, but also a financial blockbuster, raking in over $117 million.

Although the film begins with triumphant music, Rocky is initially depicted as a brawler whose victory in a small club fight nets him only $40.55; he is also employed as a "collector" for a loan shark, but he is a comparative failure at this job, getting only $130 on a $200 debt. Despite his rough exterior, Rocky is a softie, reluctant to hurt debtors and affectionate with pets. The latter trait helps him with his romantic interest, Adrian, who works in a pet store and seems almost as inarticulate as he is. Rocky is overdue for some introspection, as his intense glance in the mirror indicates, but he must endure some additional blows before he begins to rehabilitate himself. When he goes to the gym, Rocky finds that his locker has been given to someone else, a fighter who is, according to the trainer Mickey (Burgess Meredith), a contender, not a "tomato" like Rocky. Later when Rocky attempts to give a young woman some advice about her behavior, she tells him, "Screw you, creep." In a moment of self-revelation, Rocky asks himself, "Who are you to give advice?"

While Rocky is at a low point in his life, Apollo Creed (Carl Weathers), the current heavyweight champion, has his own problem: his scheduled opponent is hurt, and he needs a white contender to replace the injured man for a July 4 bout in Philadelphia. After consulting with his handlers and reviewing possible prospects, Apollo selects Rocky, the "Italian Stallion," a "novelty," a local underdog with ethnic backing. A reluctant Rocky (he respects Apollo's skill and believes he has no chance at the championship) agrees to the fight, which will pay him $150,000, and his rehabilitation begins. He signs Mickey on as his manager, gets Adrian's brother, Paulie (Burt Young), a job with the loan shark, convinces Adrian of his love, and begins a brutal training schedule for the fight just five weeks away. His daily runs through the neighborhood anchor him in South Philly and make him a local favorite, and when his pounding of sides of beef at the abattoir where Paulie works appears on local television, Apollo's handlers become concerned at the champ's nonchalant approach to the fight. In fact, Apollo's flamboyance and his Muhammad Ali–like poems stand in sharp contrast to Rocky's humble, serious demeanor. Rocky's training regimen, accompanied by Bill Conti's music, includes doing one-handed pushups; running with his dog, Butkus; sparring; and consuming six raw eggs daily—but it does not include "fooling around" because "women weaken the legs." Preparations are complete when Rocky raises his arms at the top of the steps to the Philadelphia Museum of Art and Conti's "Rocky" theme swells. That image of the triumphant Rocky is iconic.

Although Rocky finds himself on the cover of *Time* magazine, he retains his modest expectations. He says he can't defeat Apollo, but he thinks he can "go the distance," something no one has done. To underscore his status, Rocky appears at the fight wearing a robe with the name of Paulie's abattoir on the back. Apollo's entrance, on the other hand, is the height of hyperbole; he is dressed first as George Washington riding in a boat reenacting the historic crossing of the Delaware, and then he switches to Uncle Sam, declaring to Rocky, "I want you!"

Rocky demonstrates his skill and preparedness by knocking Apollo down in the first round, but for Apollo, the blow serves as a wake-up call. The two men battle to a split decision in Apollo's favor. In spite of the outcome, Rocky emerges a true winner: he has fulfilled his goal of going the distance; more importantly, he has taken control of his life and in the process fallen in love. The film ends with Rocky and Adrian embracing in the ring.

ROCKY BALBOA (2006)

DIRECTOR: Sylvester Stallone. SCREENPLAY: Sylvester Stallone. PRODUCERS: William Chartoff, Charles Winkler, David Winkler. CINEMATOGRAPHY: Clark Mathis. EDITING: Sean Albertson. MUSIC: Bill Conti. PRODUCTION DESIGN: Franco-Giacomo Carbone.

ART DIRECTION: Michael Atwell, Jesse Rosenthal. COSTUME DESIGN: Gretchen Patch.

CAST: Sylvester Stallone (Rocky Balboa), Burt Young (Paulie), Antonio Tarver (Mason "the Line" Dixon), Milo Ventimiglia (Robert Balboa), Tony Burton (Duke), Geraldine Hughes (Marie).

RUNNING TIME: 102 minutes.

DVD: Sony Pictures.

By making *Rocky Balboa*, not *Rocky VI*, Stallone signals a change of direction for his money-making protagonist. The intent seems to be saying goodbye to the old Rocky and letting a new Rocky emerge, one who can move on from his past. Although Adrian has died since the end of *Rocky V*, the Talia Shire character lives on through Rocky's daily visits to her grave and his memories and dreams about their past. Even Paulie (Burt Young), Adrian's brother, is tired of the graveyard visits and trips down "memory lane" to the razed ice rink where Rocky and Adrian had their first romantic moments. Paulie says to Rocky, "You're living backwards. I can't do this anymore."

As Rocky relives the past in his old neighborhood, the press bemoans the sad state of boxing, which urgently needs a "warrior with a passion." According to the press, Mason "the Line" Dixon (Antonio Tarver), the current champ, hasn't really faced a formidable opponent. What will bring Rocky out of retirement? A virtual boxing match on television between Rocky and Mason, which Rocky wins? Mason's trainer tells the champ he needs a challenge, needs to be tested, and undergo a "baptism under fire."

As in *Rocky V*, Rocky has problems with his son, Robert (Milo Ventimiglia), who doesn't visit his mother's grave and doesn't have time for him. When he goes to visit Robert in downtown Philadelphia, Rocky sees his son berated by his boss, who tells him, "I don't care who your father is." He does care because when he notices Rocky, he has the nerve to ask that a photo be taken of the "two old war horses." Rocky invites Robert to hold his birthday party at Adrian's Restaurant, which he owns, but Robert, who complains that his father "throws a big shadow," doesn't show up. Later, during the broadcast of the virtual bout, one of Robert's friends calls him "Baby Rocky," confirming the length of that shadow.

Meanwhile the audience gets to view a slice of Rocky's life. He shops at markets for food for the restaurant, stops to chat with folks, goes to the restaurant, where he takes off his Rocky jacket and dons a blazer before talking to customers. He provides food for Spider (Pedro Lovell), a down-on-his-luck former fighter who insists, over Rocky's objections, on working in exchange. Rocky also visits the Lucky Seven Tavern in the old neighborhood, where he meets an old acquaintance, Little Marie from *Rocky*, who in the original Rocky rejected his advice to "shape up." The two get along well, and after he straightens out a bum who insults Little Marie, he takes her home and meets her son, Steps. He offers Little Marie and Steps a card for a free meal at Adrian's and gives Steps a job. He also employs Little Marie as a hostess when his regular hostess quits after she gets pregnant.

However, Rocky is soon to leave his ordinary life. After he hears Mason's manager criticize him, Rocky decides he wants to fight again and applies for a license. The Pennsylvania Boxing Commission, understandably concerned about his "advanced" age and previous injuries, turns down his application, even though he passes all the physical exams. (The career-ending injuries from the previous films have disappeared.) The Boxing Commission is but a small monkey wrench in the machine, and Rocky arranges to meet Mason in a charity match in Las Vegas. Although Robert has opposed Rocky's desire to return to the ring and the two have quarreled, they reconcile, significantly at Adrian's grave, and Robert leaves his unfulfilling job to help Rocky train.

The fight itself allows both boxers to demonstrate their stamina and skill. Although Mason dominates at first, he breaks a bone in his hand, giving Rocky an edge. Neither man can take the other out, and, reminiscent of the original movie, this bout ends with Rocky's opponent winning a split decision. Rocky's career seems to have come full circle. Afterward, he visits Adrian's grave to announce, "We did it," and it seems that Rocky has moved forward through his efforts. He is no longer paralyzed by grief, and he has reestablished his closeness with his son.

ROCKY II (1979)

DIRECTOR: Sylvester Stallone. SCREENPLAY: Sylvester Stallone. PRODUCERS: Robert Chartoff, Irwin Winkler. CINEMATOGRAPHY: Bill Butler. EDITING: Stanford C. Allen, Janice Hampton. MUSIC: Bill Conti. ART DIRECTION: Richard Berger. COSTUME DESIGN: Sandra Berke, Tom Bronson.

CAST: Sylvester Stallone (Rocky Balboa), Talia Shire (Adrian), Burt Young (Paulie), Carl Weathers (Apollo Creed), Burgess Meredith (Mickey), Tony Burton (Duke), Joe Spinell (Tony Gazzo).

RUNNING TIME: 119 minutes.

DVD: MGM.

Rocky II begins where *Rocky* ends, with action from the fourteenth and fifteenth rounds of the championship fight, which Rocky (Sylvester Stallone) lost in a split decision to Apollo Creed (Carl Weathers). Both Apollo and Rocky declare that there will be no rematch, but both discover that they are as discontented as their audience with things as they stand at the end of their fight. Despite being a happily married man with a plump bank account, thanks in part to $300,000 in endorsements, Rocky seems unable to cope with his new-found success. Although he went the distance, he still has doubts about his performance. When he asks Apollo if he gave him his best, Apollo says he did, but Rocky is not satisfied.

Like too many professional fighters, Rocky makes bad financial decisions, squandering money on "stuff," like a flashy new car and a pricey collar for his dog, Butkus; he even buys a house without looking at the second floor. Acquaintances approach him, hoping to get him to invest in questionable ventures; he is saved from buying condominiums only because he confuses them with condoms, which he says he never uses. Hoping to capitalize on his fleeting fame, he signs on to do demeaning commercials, but he fails to perform outside the ring. He cannot read the cue cards for an after-shave ad, and the Rocky doll is noted chiefly for its ability to "take a terrific beating." Unfit for office jobs, he is reduced to asking Paulie (Burt Young) to get him a job at the meat-packing factory. Then, when the company is forced to reduce its workforce, Rocky, despite being a reliable employee, is let go because he lacks seniority. He hits bottom when he has to sell his car to Paulie, who asks him if he needs a "handout." Adrian (Talia Shire), now pregnant, goes back to work to help out with the dwindling family finances, a move that deeply troubles Rocky, who sees himself as the conventional breadwinner. Returning to the ring seems the only answer, but doctors have warned him against taking any further punishment, and Mickey (Burgess Meredith), after giving him an eye test, agrees. Rocky is reduced to helping out Mickey at the gym, where the fighters regard his apparent unwillingness to return to the ring as cowardice.

Apollo, meanwhile, seems bent on proving that Rocky's performance was a fluke, and, despite his handlers' warning that Rocky could be very dangerous, unleashes a public relations campaign to get Rocky to agree to a rematch. When Rocky refuses, even the young men on the South Philadelphia streets taunt him, and after Apollo speaks on television about Rocky running and hiding, Rocky begins to feel that he is becoming a "nobody." Adrian assures him that he does not have to prove anything to her, but Rocky tells her, "Don't ask me to stop being a man." Mickey, who has watched Apollo's verbal attacks, declares, "I think we ought to knock his block off."

Apollo and Rocky both train hard, but Mickey's training regimen is, as usual, unconventional: Rocky improves his footwork by chasing a chicken; he does squats while balancing logs on his shoulders. All this is captured in a two-minute montage that culminates with Rocky once again racing through the city streets and up the steps at the Philadelphia Museum of Art, but this time many Philadelphians trail him up the steps.

Once again, it is not the fight that is emphasized, but what the boxers bring to the ring. The fight sequence lasts only fourteen minutes. Exhausted, both men connect with punches and both go down, but Rocky, who is up at the count of nine, becomes the champion. After his victory, Rocky thanks God, declares that this is the greatest night he's ever had, except for the birth of his son, and then he also prays.

Rocky II brings underdog Rocky the victory he was denied in the original film, demonstrates what happens to fighters who achieve success but cannot handle their finances, and shows the triumph of humility, old-fashioned values, friendship, hard work, and religious faith.

***ROCKY III* (1982)**

DIRECTOR: Sylvester Stallone. SCREENPLAY: Sylvester Stallone. PRODUCERS: Irwin Winkler, Robert Chartoff. CINEMATOGRAPHY: Bill Butler. EDITING: Mark Warner, Don Zimmerman. MUSIC: Bill Conti. PRODUCTION DESIGN: William J. Cassidy. ART DIRECTION: Ron Foreman, J. Dennis Washington. COSTUME DESIGN: Tom Bronson.

CAST: Sylvester Stallone (Rocky Balboa), Talia Shire (Adrian), Burt Young (Paulie), Carl Weathers (Apollo Creed), Burgess Meredith (Mickey), Tony Burton (Duke), Mr. T (Clubber Lang), Hulk Hogan (Thunderlips).

RUNNING TIME: 99 minutes.

ACADEMY AWARD NOMINATION: Best Song ("Eye of the Tiger"; music and lyrics by Jim Peterik, Frankie Sullivan).

DVD: MGM.

Rocky III begins like *Rocky II*, with a reprise of the end of the previous Rocky installment. (The *Rocky* series in some ways resembles the old movie "serials.") Like its predecessor, the film concerns a postfight let down, this time not because of financial mismanagement, but because of Rocky's failure to keep his edge, what Apollo Creed (Carl Weathers) calls the "eye of the tiger." While Rocky (Sylvester Stallone) basks in his success, doing commercials for American Express, making guest appearances on *The Muppet Show*, and defending his title against some "stiffs," Mickey (Burgess Meredith) has hand-picked his opponents. Meanwhile, Clubber Lang (Mr. T of *The A-Team* fame) has been fighting his way to the top of the contender list. The crosscutting between Rocky and Clubber highlights the difference between the two fighters, one gentrified and community oriented (the grateful city of Philadelphia recognizes Rocky's charitable work with a sculpture), the other brutal and egotistical ("alone" is the word Clubber repeatedly uses). The juxtaposition of Rocky's possessions and Clubber's training regimen stresses Clubber's hunger and Rocky's complacency.

Like many good boxing films, the heart of *Rocky III* is not in the ring, but in personal relationships, in this case with Adrian (Talia Shire) and Paulie (Burt Young), his brother-in-law. In *Rocky* the romance between Rocky and Adrian is highlighted at a skating rink; in *Rocky III* it occurs in bed when Rocky coaxes the shy and reticent Adrian to sing a duet with him. With Paulie, the relationship remains as it was in the first two films. Paulie, as Rocky describes him, is a jealous, lazy bum who wants to coast on Rocky's success.

To emphasize the depths to which Rocky's fighting has descended, Stallone includes an exhibition match between Rocky and Thunderlips (Hulk Hogan), a gigantic professional wrestler who is billed as the "ultimate male." With the glowering Clubber in the audience, Rocky is manhandled, even getting thrown over the ropes before he comes back to hoist the nearly four-hundred-pound Thunderlips out of the ring to win a draw. The heavyweight championship is cheapened by the match, which is, as Thunderlips says, pure entertainment. After the fight, an "edgeless" Rocky asks Thunderlips to pose with him and his son for a picture.

At the dedication of his sculpture, Rocky suggests that it might be time to retire, but Clubber challenges him and calls him a coward. Although Rocky ignores Clubber's taunts, he cannot ignore Clubber's suggestive comments to Adrian and decides to take on the challenger. Truth time occurs when Mickey tells Rocky not to fight Clubber because he cannot win. According to Mickey, Rocky became "civilized" after winning the championship and is no longer "hungry." His title defenses have been scheduled to keep him winning and healthy, but Rocky responds by believing that Mickey has been "carrying" him. When Rocky tells Mickey, "I need this," Mickey relents and agrees to help him defend the title, but Rocky's training for the fight is totally inadequate. Surrounded by the press and distracted by fans, Rocky is training in a gym Mickey describes as a "zoo" and "a house of ill repute." Again there are intercuts of Clubber's serious training and Rocky's dancing, suggesting that Clubber is the more prepared fighter.

Before the fight begins, Mickey suffers a heart attack and has to remain in the dressing room, leaving Rocky on his own. Clubber then insults Apollo Creed. Rocky is knocked out in the third round and returns to the dressing room, where Mickey dies in his arms. Rocky clearly believes that he is responsible for Mickey's death and is distraught at Mickey's funeral. Since the film is only half over, a rematch is inevitable,

Rocky (Sylvester Stallone) takes on Clubber Lang (Mr. T) in *Rocky III*

and he has the indomitable Adrian by his side, plus help from an unlikely source, Apollo Creed, whom Rocky dethroned in *Rocky* II. Rocky and Apollo meet in Mickey's gym, where Apollo persuades Rocky to challenge Clubber. According to Apollo, Rocky needs to regain the eye of the tiger by going back to the beginning. Although he goes to California with Apollo, Rocky's training lacks the necessary intensity, partly because of his guilt over Mickey's death and partly because of Paulie's negative attitude, which is at odds with Apollo's training principles. Paulie wants to be at a "real gym," one without blacks, and he responds to Apollo's insistence that Rocky "dance" to improve his footwork and swim to develop his endurance by commenting that Rocky "can't train to no jungle music" and stating that Rocky "ain't no tuna." After the last sprint that he and Rocky run on the beach, Apollo finally has to concede that "it's all over." Enter Adrian, who, after hearing Rocky talk about his fear of losing what they have, gives him one of her trademark pep talks about not quitting. The following montage shows Rocky swimming, dancing, and beating Apollo in a sprint, all to the "jungle music" Paulie mocked.

The rematch is Rocky's resurrection. Stallone uses the upstretched arms of Rocky's sculpture and Clubber's prediction that he will "crucify" Rocky to suggest Rocky's Christ-like nature. Wearing red-white-and-blue boxing trunks like the ones favored by Apollo, Rocky wins the first round; takes a mauling and taunts Clubber into exhausting himself with wild swings in the second; and then in the third knocks out the tired champion. At the end of the fight Rocky and Adrian embrace, and Apollo reminds Rocky that he had promised him a "favor" after the victory. The favor is a sparring contest at Mickey's gym, and the film ends with a freeze frame as both fighters take a swing.

ROCKY IV (1985)

DIRECTOR: Sylvester Stallone. SCREENPLAY: Sylvester Stallone. PRODUCERS: Robert Chartoff, Irwin Winkler. CINEMATOGRAPHY: Bill Butler. EDITING: John W. Wheeler, Don Zimmerman. MUSIC: Vince DiCola. PRODUCTION DESIGN: Bill Kenney. ART DIRECTION: William Ladd Skinner. COSTUME DESIGN: Tom Bronson.
CAST: Sylvester Stallone (Rocky Balboa), Talia Shire (Adrian), Burt Young (Paulie), Carl Weathers (Apollo Creed), Tony Burton (Duke), Dolph Lundgren (Captain Ivan Drago), Brigitte Nielsen (Ludmilla).
RUNNING TIME: 91 minutes.
DVD: MGM.

After a montage sequence of the bout between Clubber Lang (Mr. T) and Rocky (Sylvester Stallone) in *Rocky III*, the audience sees two sets of boxing gloves, one decorated with the American flag, the other with the Russian flag, thereby establishing the focus of Rocky IV, a battle between America and Russia values. The film, which Stallone wrote and directed, is the most political of the Rocky films, and the "us-versus-them" theme prevails.

Early in the film the Russian boxing entourage—including Captain Ivan Drago (Dolph Lundgren), the world amateur boxing champ; his wife, Ludmilla (Brigitte Nielsen, Stallone's off-screen romance); and the propagandist/manager—come to the United States to propose an exhibition match between Ivan and Rocky. Rocky is not interested, but Apollo Creed (Carl Weathers) is intent on fighting Ivan. While Rocky can understand that he and Apollo have turned into "regular folks," Apollo claims that he and Rocky are "warriors" who cannot change. Even though Rocky is still in the limelight, Apollo believes that once "you're out of the ring, you're ancient history." Always the showman, Apollo misses the attention he once had and asks that Rocky stay in his corner. In Las Vegas it is Old Glory versus the Red Star in a match that Apollo insists means something. After some over-the-top prefight entertainment featuring James Brown singing "Living in America" in a performance that celebrates American values (but that unfortunately come across as being tawdry), the fight begins and ends quickly. Ivan gives Apollo a merciless beating, and Rocky wants to throw in the towel, but Apollo insists on continuing the fight, which ends with Apollo's death. Ivan's callous comment, "if he dies, he dies," motivates Rocky to agree to an exhibition match at Christmas in Moscow.

Realizing that there is no easy way out, Rocky, Paulie (Burt Young), and Duke, Rocky's new trainer (Tony Burton), travel to an isolated spot in Russia, where Rocky has all the equipment he has requested. As in other Rocky films, Paulie complains about the Spartan lifestyle and the lack of amenities, but Rocky has chosen his training regimen carefully. Stallone uses crosscutting to emphasize the difference between the two training styles and the cultural values they represent. The Russians' training headquarters stresses the "technology of human performance," complete with high-tech "strings" attached to Ivan so they can quantify their puppet's performance on machines. Rocky's "machines" consist of rocks and logs instead of weights; his running occurs on roads rather than indoor tracks; his inclines are mountains rather than treadmills; and he pulls sleds through snow instead of exercising on machines. While Ivan spars and takes performance drugs, Rocky, who has been joined by Adrian, chops down trees and saws logs. In effect, Ivan is the modern athlete, and Rocky is old-fashioned, exercising the resourcefulness and virtues of early American life, the kind of unaffected and homespun behavior that made America. To demonstrate American superiority, Stallone films Rocky escaping on foot from his two "chaperones" whose car cannot follow him as he runs through deep snow to the top of a mountain.

Before the fight Paulie, who has a love/envy relationship with Rocky in all the *Rocky* films, tells him that he wishes he were Rocky, who, he says, gives him respect. As usual, this rare admission is retracted after Paulie sees Ivan: "I take it all back."

The atmosphere at the arena adds to the us-versus-them theme, as the American television commentators describe the hostile crowd and observe that the mood "borders on hatred." Comparing the fight to the biblical battle between David and Goliath, they give Rocky little chance of winning the exhibition match. The Politburo officials sit smugly in their seats, anticipating Ivan's victory.

Rocky's strategy involves admitting "no pain," taking all that Ivan has, and winning by having more "heart." Mauled in the early rounds and knocked to the canvas, Rocky manages a comeback, bloodying Ivan and making him human, not a machine. As Rocky continues the fight, he begins to win the respect of the Russian audience, and by the eleventh round has them cheering for him. One Politburo official, concerned that Ivan will lose, makes his way to Ivan's corner before the fifteenth round and threatens the Russian fighter, who responds by grabbing him by the throat. Rocky knocks Ivan out before the end of the fight.

The conclusion is pure fantasy. The Russian audience cheers Rocky, and after one of the Russian politicians stands to applaud the American, the rest of the Politburo follow suit. In his victory speech, after the standard Rocky-Adrian embrace, Rocky talks about change, his change, the audience's change, and he concludes by saying, "If I can change and you can, everybody can change." One is reminded of Jake Barnes's remark in *The Sun Also Rises*, "Isn't it pretty to think so."

Although *Rocky IV* was the most financially successful of all the Rocky films, taking in over $300 million worldwide, and was at the time the most financially successful of all sports films, it did not do well with the critics. It did win seven RAZZIE Awards and the Marshall Trophy (for Meilleur Comédien—Best Comedian!) for Lundgren.

ROCKY V (1990)

DIRECTOR: John G. Avildsen. SCREENPLAY: Sylvester Stallone. PRODUCERS: Robert Chartoff, Irwin Winkler. CINEMATOGRAPHY: Steven Poster. EDITING: John G. Avildsen, Robert A. Ferretti, Michael N. Knue. MUSIC: Bill Conti. PRODUCTION DESIGN: William J. Cassidy. ART DIRECTION: William Durrell Jr.

CAST: Sylvester Stallone (Rocky Balboa), Talia Shire (Adrian), Burt Young (Paulie), Sage Stallone (Robert Balboa), Richard Gant (George W. Duke), Tony Burton (Duke).

RUNNING TIME: 104 minutes.

DVD: MGM.

Rocky Balboa (Sylvester Stallone) began as a street fighter in Philadelphia, punched his way to the top, became a contender, won the title, and then defended it through three sequels, risking brain damage in the Soviet Union. The Rock is back in *Rocky V*, punchier than ever, but this time he is more interested in talking than in trading punches. Doctors have advised that he needs to retire because of possible brain damage. If he fights again, someone might turn out his lights. Returning from Russia, he also learns that his accountant, with some "unwitting" assistance from Paulie (Burt Young) has swindled him out of his fortune. All that is left is the crummy gym, where he got his start.

So Rocky has to move back to the old neighborhood. His son, Robert (played by young Sage Stallone, who is quite good), has to go to an inner-city school and is short on both street smarts and survival skills. Rocky Jr. needs his dad to teach him how to protect himself, but Rocky Sr. is preoccupied training a street fighter from Oklahoma, another "great white hope," Tommy "Machine" Gunn (Tommy Morrison). Rocky needs to be a father to his own son, Robert, but seems intent on reprising the father-son relationship he had with Mickey: Rocky will be Mickey to Tommy's Rocky. Rocky remembers Mickey giving him one of his treasured possessions, one of Rocky Marciano's cufflinks. When Rocky gives the cufflink to Tommy, Robert resents it and drifts away from his father, who ignores him when he tries to tell him about how he beat up the bully who had stolen his coat. Under Rocky's training, Tommy wins bouts, then betrays the champ by returning the cufflink and shifting his allegiance to a flamboyant and sleazy fight promoter, George W. Duke (Richard Gant). As Tommy drives away from Rocky's house, Rocky tries desperately to convince him to resume the relationship, the one he had had with Mickey. He learns that he can't repeat the past and that Tommy is no Rocky.

Under George's management, Tommy gets his title shot and wins the belt, but the fans won't forgive him for deserting Rocky, and the press corps taunts him, pointing out that the chump he defeated was a champ by default. George advises him to challenge the brain-damaged Rocky to a title bout, and that's what this movie is all about. No state will license Rocky to fight, but George assures Tommy and Rocky that he can arrange a deal that will allow the bout to take place. When Rocky wisely turns down the challenge, Tommy invades Rocky's neighborhood, and in a neighborhood bar, surrounded by the press taunts Rocky, calling him yellow. So Rocky has to prove himself all over again, not in the ring this time, but on the streets of Philadelphia. Adrian (Talia Shire) tells Rocky over and over that he's a champ because of his heart, not because of his muscle. Since the younger Tommy is all muscle, Rocky finds the prospect of that final confrontation disheartening. As the final knock-down, drag-out begins, Bill Conti's familiar Rocky theme builds on the soundtrack. Could Rocky possibly get beat up while supported by this up-beat music? Or is the viewer to believe that this brutal assault could possibly mean the death of Rocky?

Rocky (Sylvester Stallone) is back in shape for *Rocky V*

Everything is a little off center here. Rocky talks like a punchy Palooka. Even his pronunciation of "cajones" is a little off. Rocky's brother-in-law Paulie (Burt Young) never remembers to shave and before the fight puts in an appearance as a drunken Santa Claus, shouting "Yo, Yo,

Yo!" Adrian is shriller than ever, and Stallone's screenplay is predictably maudlin. The smartest decision was to bring back director John G. Avildsen, the architect of *Rocky*'s initial success in 1976. Avildsen pumps up the audience for that final confrontation, which is emotionally more satisfying than all the other sequels combined. The movie lacks the kind of grit *Raging Bull* has, but it is surely a crowd-pleaser. At the end, Tommy is sullen and resentful, just waiting for the next installment as Stallone resists putting an end to the series.

ROLLERBALL (1975)

DIRECTOR: Norman Jewison. SCREENPLAY: William Harrison. PRODUCER: Norman Jewison. CINEMATOGRAPHY: Douglas Slocombe. EDITING: Anthony Gibbs. MUSIC: André Previn. PRODUCTION DESIGN: John Box. ART DIRECTION: Robert Laing. COSTUME DESIGN: Julie Harris.

CAST: James Caan (Jonathan E.), John Houseman (Bartholomew), Maud Adams (Ella), John Beck (Moonpie), Moses Gunn (Cletus), Pamela Hensley (Mackie), Burt Kwouk (Japanese doctor).

RUNNING TIME: 125 minutes.

DVD: MGM.

Directed by Norman Jewison and starring James Caan, *Rollerball* is a futuristic suspense film that, set in the twenty-first century, anticipates a world in which all information is stored electronically and multinational corporations have made national boundaries obsolete. Under corporate control there is no more poverty or disease, but comfort has come at the expense of independence. Power is maintained through manipulation of information, through availability of recreational drugs, and through globally televised rollerball, an extremely violent sport designed to demonstrate the futility of individual achievement while functioning as a social safety valve through which the masses vicariously express aggression.

Rollerball is played on an eighth-mile sloped track by teams of skaters and motorcyclists who score points by fielding a steel ball fired into a gutter at lethal speeds and, after circling the track twice, hurling the ball into a goal. Players wear spiked helmets and gloves that can be used to inflict injury on opponents. Although the game was intended by its creators to reinforce the idea of teamwork and mass conformity, it has produced a star player for the Houston team, Jonathan E. (Caan), whose popularity threatens the monopoly of power held by corporate executives.

The film opens with Bach's *Toccata and Fugue in D Mino*r playing as the camera takes the viewer into different areas of the sports arena, establishing distinctions between the executives and the fans, focusing on the studded leather gear of the players, and revealing an elaborate media center with thirty multivision cameras. As the music subsides, the crowd's chant of "Jonathan, Jonathan" intensifies. The game progresses rapidly: only enough of the competition is shown to provide a sense of how the sport is played and to highlight Jonathan's scoring skills; the camera shifts frequently to shots of the fans in a frenzy, the executives networking, and the media center broadcasting global coverage.

After the game Bartholomew (John Houseman), an executive in charge of the Houston team, informs the players that Jonathan is to be the subject of a documentary. However, the next day Jonathan learns that he is expected to announce his retirement at the end of the program. Bartholomew reminds Jonathan of the "social purpose" of rollerball and requests that he accept management decisions.

Jonathan travels to his ranch, where his current companion expresses her reluctance to leave at the end of six months, an arrangement that Jonathan insists on because he is still in love with his former wife, who either moved out because she felt neglected or was spirited off because an executive wanted her. Jonathan plays videos of his ex-wife on large-screen televisions, which dominate every room. Later in the evening, he discusses his situation with his trainer, Clete (Moses Gunn), a veteran of the game who remembers that there were three nations when he was a child. Jonathan asks Clete for help in determining what and who are behind the decision to remove him from the sport.

Clete and Jonathan visit a luxury center in search of information about the Corporate Wars in order to discover just who makes decisions now, but they learn that the "library" is merely a computer terminal with summaries of information. Jonathan decides to visit the computer center in Geneva; however, before he can do this, the rules of the game are changed, eliminating penalties and limiting substitutions.

Before the next match against Tokyo, Jonathan, his teammate Moonpie (John Beck), and other members of the Houston organization attend a party hosted by Bartholomew. Although the atmosphere is sedate, most of the partygoers appear to engage in casual sex and recreational drug use. The executive class objectifies the athletes, viewing them as sleek machines rather than as individuals. They are transfixed by the documentary when it is broadcast midway through the evening, attracted by Jonathan's personal achievement and by the violence of the footage. The party continues through the night, and at daybreak a small group of executives wander outside and amuse themselves by watching their female companions destroy a group of trees with an atomic pistol. The film cuts between scenes of the tree shooting and a final encounter between Bartholomew and Jonathan. Bartholomew again insists that Jonathan retire, and although Jonathan demands concessions, including seeing his wife again, he appears determined to continue with the team.

In Tokyo the Japanese team skates with military precision and is known to use martial arts techniques. With the suspension of penalties, the violence intensifies, and players tear off the helmets of downed opponents. Jonathan, temporarily sidelined while a cut is being treated, watches from the pit as Moonpie is set upon by three Tokyo players in an attack that leaves him brain dead. When Jonathan returns to the track, he seeks revenge and eliminates, perhaps permanently, the trio. At the hospital in Tokyo, Jonathan refuses to allow Moonpie to be euthanized and has him transported to Houston. Instead of returning immediately to his ranch, Jonathan travels to the computer center in Geneva, where he hopes to learn who controls the rules of rollerball and what happened during the corporate wars that ended national sovereignty. Although the librarian in charge, convincingly played by Sir Ralph Richardson, is cooperative, Zero, the mega computer, is not. Zero, which stores information via fluidity rather than electronically, is either careless—the entire thirteenth century has been lost—or subversive, systematically erasing history.

After Jonathan returns to his ranch, his ex-wife is sent by the executives to persuade him to honor their request, but he feels she has betrayed him, not because she now has a home and family with an executive, but because she is expressing the corporate point of view. She warns him that there will be yet another rule change, eliminating the time periods as well as the rules. In effect, if Jonathan plays in the final game against New York, he will be participating in a pure blood sport that will end when there is only one man left standing. Jonathan's response is to erase his videotapes of her and visit

Moonpie, now encased like Snow White in a glass chamber. Jonathan speculates that he will die playing rollerball while Moonpie lives on.

The locker-room scene before the final match contains no dialogue, no inspirational speeches by coach or star, only the ominous organ music. Jonathan skates into the arena wordlessly, and soon the slaughter begins. Jewison's depiction of violence is haunting. Instead of screams of agony, he uses the sound of a neck breaking. Instead of showing a gory body, he films a figure sliding down the slope of the track, leaving a smear of blood. When all but Jonathan and a New York motorcyclist remain on a track littered with flaming debris and fallen athletes, the final contest is over quickly, and Jonathan is the victor. Straddling the fallen rider, he holds the steel ball aloft, ready to smash it against the man's face. But he doesn't. Instead he uses the sphere to score the only goal of the game. His opponent remains inert, and as Jonathan circles the track in a victory lap, the fans chant, as they did in the beginning, "Jonathan, Jonathan." They are joined by the executives as the film ends with a close up of Caan's face.

Jewison intended the film, which is based on William Harrison's short story, "Roller Ball Murder," as a critical commentary on the escalation of violence in professional sports and among fans, particularly European soccer fans. In order to keep the film connected to contemporary audiences, he established a world that in many ways resembles that of the last quarter of the twentieth century. Characters wear conventional dress; interiors are sleek but not populated by robots—Jonathan's ranch features built-in appliances, including a tape player. The cylindrical building that houses the headquarters of the Energy Corporation is the BMW building in Munich. Much of the filming was completed in Munich, and German engineers redesigned a bicycle track from the 1972 Olympics to serve as the rollerball arena. The cast includes a large number of roller derby skaters and stuntmen in the roles of athletes; locals, including Asian students studying in Germany, were recruited to fill the seats of the arena. According to Jewison, both cast and extras became caught up in the game, with the cast engaging in play when the cameras weren't rolling; after the film was completed, a number of stuntmen expressed interest in forming a league but did not carry out the plan.

As a cautionary tale, the film has proved relevant in its depictions of computerization and corporate power, but its message about violence is largely overpowered by the attraction of rollerball as sport. *Rollerball* was successful at the box office, and a remake, also titled *Rollerball*, directed by John McTiernan (*Die Hard*, 1988; *Die Hard: With a Vengeance*, 1995) was released in 2002.

THE ROOKIE (2002)

DIRECTOR: John Lee Hancock. SCREENPLAY: Mike Rich. PRODUCERS: Mark Ciardi, Gordon Gray, Mark Johnson. CINEMATOGRAPHY: John Schwartzman. EDITING: Eric L. Beason. MUSIC: Carter Burwell. PRODUCTION DESIGN: Barry Robison. ART DIRECTION: Kevin Constant. COSTUME DESIGN: Bruce Finlayson.

CAST: Dennis Quaid (Jimmy Morris), Rachel Griffiths (Lorri Morris), Jay Hernandez (Joaquin "Wack" Campos), Beth Grant (Olline), Brian Cox (Jim Morris Sr.), Angus T. Jones (Hunter Morris).

RUNNING TIME: 127 minutes.

DVD: Walt Disney Video.

The Rookie is based on the career of pitcher Jimmy Morris, who made his major league debut with the Tampa Bay Devil Rays in 1999, when he was in his mid-thirties and had been away from the game for over a decade. While focusing on the theme of following one's dreams, the film also draws on father-son relationships.

Morris's father was a navy recruiter, and the family moved over a dozen times before settling in Big Lake, Texas, whose population was less than three thousand at the time the movie was made. As in many Texas towns, football is king, but according to the film's prologue, baseball was the sport of choice in the town's history. The film opens with a story of two nuns who invested in an oil well; when the investment failed to pay off, the two traveled to Big Lake to bless the site, praying to Saint Rita, Patron Saint of Impossible Dreams. The site failed to produce oil, so instead it was used as a baseball field by men hired to work the oil field.

Jimmy's story begins in the 1970s. His family is uprooted every few years because of his father's job. Jim Sr. (Brian Cox) is a stern military man who shows little interest in his son's passion for baseball. When a transfer means Jimmy won't be able to finish out a Little League season, his father refuses to allow him to stay behind for three weeks with a friend's family. When Jimmy visits his father at a military base after a game, the elder Morris barely acknowledges his presence, then announces another relocation, this time to Texas.

There is no baseball in Big Lake, and to add to Jimmy's disappointment, the box containing his baseball mitt has disappeared in the move. The local general store doesn't even stock baseball equipment, but the kindly owner offers to order what Jimmy needs and tells him the legend of the two nuns. Young Jimmy makes his way to the old ball field and scrapes the dirt from the rubber on the pitcher's mound; the scene transitions to the 1990s and adult Jimmy Morris (Dennis Quaid) scuffing the dirt from the rubber once again. After a disappointing stint in the minor leagues and a series of injuries, Jimmy finished college and is now teaching science at the local high school, where he also coaches the baseball team. The Big Lake Owls have yet to produce a winning season. There's little financial support since the football team receives most of the school's athletic budget. The baseball diamond is an expanse of dirt, thanks to seed-eating deer. The latter problem is resolved by scattering over the grass hair collected from the local barbershop, but the green turf doesn't improve the Owls' performance.

After a more-dismal-than-usual loss, Jimmy tries to inspire the team to pursue their dreams rather than give up, but one of the players challenges him, asking why he quit playing baseball. It's a difficult question for him. He has started throwing again, first at night to relax, then after practice with the team catcher. The catcher, who realizes that Jimmy loves pitching and that he can "lay in the heat," proposes a deal: if the Owls make it to the state championship, Jimmy will try out for a professional team. Later that night, as Jimmy is driving home, he comes upon a road sign that displays the speed of passing vehicles. He stops and positions himself to throw a few pitches in the range of the radar gun. His best effort registers only 76 mph, slower than when he was in the minors, but as he drives off, the sign flickers, and the lights actually read 96 mph. Convinced he hasn't a chance of restarting a professional career, he concentrates on helping the boys on the team achieve their potential and begins pitching during their batting practice. As a result of trying to connect with Jimmy's fastballs, the players become much stronger hitters and, sure enough, hold up their end of the deal. After winning the regional championship game, they give Jimmy the game ball and tell him it's his turn now.

Jimmy carries out his promise and goes to a tryout—with all three of his children in tow. Because he doesn't want to upset his wife, Lorri (Rachel Griffiths), who has stood by him through his early years of repeated injury and disappointment, Jimmy has not told her about the deal with the players. He has sworn his oldest child, Hunter (Angus T. Jones), the team batboy, to secrecy. At the tryouts, Jimmy has his hands full keeping the children content; when he is called on to pitch, he's in mid-diaper change. As he takes the mound, he draws a number of stares from the younger hopefuls, but once he throws a pitch, he stops traffic. After hurling a dozen balls at 98 mph, he's told to expect a phone call. The calls start coming before he even arrives home, and Lorri is the one who hears the messages. Although she accepts Jimmy's explanation for keeping the deal with the players to himself, she does not want him to play ball. Jimmy has a teaching/coaching offer from a Fort Worth high school that pays significantly more money than he makes at Big Lake or that he will make in the minor leagues, and the school provides more support for its baseball team. Furthermore, if he joins a team, he'll be out of town, leaving her to cope by herself with the children.

Uncertain of what he should do, Jimmy visits his father, even though the two have never fully reconciled. That Jimmy still calls his father "Sir" as if he were an enlisted man rather than a son indicates the distance between the two. Although Jim Sr. advises him that it's time for him to quit mulling over the situation and do what he's "meant to do," Jimmy leaves angry and hurt, believing that this is bad advice. Later that night, Lorri has a change of heart and encourages Jimmy to take advantage of this second chance. Soon Jimmy is in Orlando, playing with the Devil Rays' farm team.

In spite of pitching well, Jimmy finds life in the minor leagues tough. Fans jeer because of his age, and he has difficulty fitting in with his younger teammates. The long road trips by bus leave him exhausted. Back home, money is tight, and the children miss their daddy. Jimmy misses them as well, but when he's close to quitting, it is Lorri who convinces him to give it another two weeks. That turns out to be just enough time for him to get called up to the majors. He joins the Devil Rays on the road for a series against the Texas Rangers in Arlington. Back in Big Lake, the Owls are organizing a motorcade, so that it seems the entire town has traveled to the ballpark in Arlington to celebrate Jimmy's first game in "the Bigs."

Of course, Jimmy doesn't expect to play—he's just pitched the night before and hasn't slept—but with the Rays trailing and the relief pitcher in trouble, Jimmy is handed the ball to face Royce Clayton. In real life, it took Morris four pitches to retire Clayton, but in the film, Jimmy gets him out in three. His teammates offer warm congratulations, and in the locker room, the press is waiting. So is Jimmy's father. Jim Sr. expresses his pride in his son's achievement, and Jimmy gives him the ball he used to strike out Clayton. There are no hugs, but the moment is filled with emotion. As soon as Jim walks out, Lorri appears to escort him from the stadium, where, just outside, he finds nearly everyone he knows from Big Lake. The final scene returns to Big Lake High School, and the camera zooms in on the trophy case, featuring Morris's Devil Rays uniform and a photo of his school's championship team. The real Jimmy Morris played for two years before his old injuries forced him into retirement.

The plotlines of *The Rookie* are familiar ones in sports films—the underdog team that achieves the impossible, the veteran athlete who achieves the impossible, the community united in support of an athletic team—but the events depicted in the film actually occurred. The real Owls became so successful that they sometimes scored thirty runs against opponents; their improved performance had to be toned down for the movie to keep it believable. The family tension, also a frequent ingredient in the genre, adds depth to the main character, convincingly played by Quaid, whose other sports film credits include *Breaking Away* (1979), *Everybody's All American* (1988), *Any Given Sunday* (1999), and *The Express* (2008). *The Rookie* is the first feature film for director John Lee Hancock.

ROOKIE OF THE YEAR (1993)

DIRECTOR: Daniel Stern. SCREENPLAY: Sam Harper. PRODUCER: Robert Harper. CINEMATOGRAPHY: Jack N. Green. EDITING: Donn Cambern, Raja Gosnell. MUSIC: Bill Conti. PRODUCTION DESIGN: Steven Jordan. COSTUME DESIGN: Jay Hurley.

CAST: Thomas Ian Nicholas (Henry Rowengartner), Gary Busey (Chet "Rocket" Steadman), Albert Hall (Sal Martinella), Amy Morton (Mary Rowengartner), Dan Hedaya (Larry Fisher), Bruce Altman (Jack Bradfield), Eddie Bracken (Bob Carson), Daniel Stern (Phil Brickma).

RUNNING TIME: 103 minutes.

DVD: 20th Century Fox.

This fantasy film, like *It Happens Every Spring* (1949) and *Damn Yankees* (1958), allows a loyal baseball fan to play for a major league team. Unlike the earlier films, juiced baseballs and pacts with the devil are not required; furthermore, instead of being a grown man, the rookie is a little boy. (In *Great Baseball Films*, Rob Edelman calls the film an unofficial remake of the little-known *Roogie's Bump*, 1954, which also features a boy with a dynamite arm, although Roogie's talent is bestowed upon him by a ghost.)

When *Rookie of the Year* begins, it is opening day at Wrigley Field, and the announcer (John Candy in an uncredited role) is dreading another losing season. The Cubs' owner, Bob Carson (Eddie Bracken), needs sell-out crowds to retain the franchise, but the odds of increasing attendance are low. The veteran starting pitcher, Chet "the Rocket" Steadman (Gary Busey) has lost his arm, and the team's spirits are flagging.

At a Little League game, Henry Rowengartner (Thomas Ian Nicholas) runs into a fence chasing down a ball; then, his vision obscured by his hat, he throws the ball in the wrong direction. Back home, his mother, Mary (Amy Morton), suggests he should try pitching because his father—whose absence is yet to be explained—was a pitcher. Mary has been dating an overeager fellow, Jack Bradfield (Bruce Altman), whom Henry distrusts. Confirming Henry's concern that his mom's suitor is "moving too fast," Jack presents Mary with an extravagant necklace to celebrate their three-week anniversary and expects a passionate kiss in return. Mary turns her head, delivering a peck on the cheek and eluding Jack's embrace, indicating that she has her own reservations about the relationship.

Twelve-year-old Henry has his own romantic interest, Becky (Colombe Jacobsen-Dersine), who returns his smile in the school cafeteria. His friends Clark (Robert Gorman) and George (Patrick LaBrecque) tease him good-naturedly. Outside, his more malevolent classmates deride him about his performance in the outfield the previous day. One boy hits a fly ball in Henry's direction, and to impress Becky and the others, he charges after it, fails to notice another ball in the grass, and takes a spectacular spill, breaking his shoulder as well as his arm.

Four months later, when the cast comes off, Henry learns that the tendons in his right arm have fused, leaving him with a pistol-like recoil when he makes a throwing motion. He realizes the full effect at a Cubs' game he attends with Clark and George, who insist he return a foul ball that landed in the stands. He fires the ball back to the mound from high up in the bleachers, drawing the immediate attention of the desperate front office of the Cubs. Soon Henry is offered a contract. Jack assigns himself the role of Henry's manager and writes in a 10 percent commission.

For his first game, Henry's mother takes him to the players' entrance but no further. In the locker room the other Cubs eye him suspiciously, and Chet refuses him an autograph. Manager Sal Martinella (Albert Hall), who is skeptical about having a kid on his roster, hasn't bothered to learn Henry's last name. With Chet struggling in the ninth and the fans chanting "Put the kid in," Sal calls for Henry to close out the game. After giving up a home run on his first pitch and hitting a batter with his second, Henry hurls a wild pitch that leads to the base runner being thrown out. In spite of his disastrous performance, Henry has pulled out a save, and Chet is instructed to teach Henry how to pitch. At first, Chet resents the assignment, but Henry soon wins him over. With Chet's encouragement, Henry settles down on the mound and begins throwing strikes. After the game, Henry invites Clark and George onto the field, where they horse around, and Chet meets Mary, introducing a romantic complication for the grownups.

Henry's career goes into overdrive. On a road trip, he makes his first trip to the plate and, being so small that he affords no strike zone, walks. He taunts the opposing players, steals a base, and manages to score. On the mound he strikes out Pedro Guerrero, Bobby Bonilla, and Barry Bonds (themselves). He makes the cover of *Sports Illustrated* and lands a Pepsi commercial. However, his good fortune is about to change: Jack, unhappy about Mary's growing attraction to Chet Steadman, and worried about losing his seat on the gravy train, sets up a deal with Bob Carson's corrupt nephew, Larry Fisher (Dan Hedaya), to sell Henry to the Yankees.

On the home front, Henry's friends are hurt that he hasn't had time to work with them on a summer project, repairing a rowboat. Mary kicks Jack out after she learns about the contract with the Yankees, and Jack retaliates by telling Henry the truth about his father—that he was never a baseball player and that he walked out on Mary when he learned she was pregnant. However, Henry reveals that his grandmother told him the truth when he was in second grade and he has been going along with his mother's story to make her life easier. Meanwhile, Chet, who has been notified that his contract won't be renewed, advises Henry not to make baseball the center of his life.

Following Chet's advice, Henry opts out of a photo shoot and joins Clark and George, who are struggling to launch the boat. Henry helps them, and differences forgotten, the three boys cruise along the waterfront where Becky and two friends are sunbathing. The girls join the boys in the boat for an afternoon of innocent fun. Later, Henry talks with his mother about quitting baseball at the end of the season.

The next day, Henry meets with Mr. Carson to announce his decision and to question why he was being sold to the Yankees. Mr. Carson, however, knew nothing of his nephew's negotiations with the New York team. After demoting Larry to a hot dog vendor, Mr. Carson determines to sit in the stands instead of in the owner's box. When the first pitch is thrown in the game that will decide the division championship, Mr. Carson, Clark, George, and Mary are

Henry Rowengartner (Thomas Ian Nicholas) is *Rookie of the Year*

sitting together behind home plate, and it is Chet on the mound starting the final game of his career.

Inevitably, Chet's shoulder gives out, and Henry is sent in to save the game. He hurls strike after strike through the seventh and eighth innings, but on his way to the mound in the ninth, he fails to see the ball lying in the grass, and history repeats itself as Henry tumbles head over heels. Back on his feet, he quickly discovers that his throwing arm has been restored to normal. Suddenly, he is an ordinary twelve-year-old needing to orchestrate the most important three outs in the history of Wrigley Field. His warm up pitches bounce on their way to the plate. After the first batter walks, Henry calls in the infield with a plan. When the players return to their positions, the first baseman has the ball hidden in his glove, and he tags out the runner as soon as the man steps from the bag.

Henry walks the second batter intentionally, then dares him to steal, tossing the ball in the air. When the man finally breaks for second, Henry runs him down and tags him out. The third batter he faces is a snarling hitter, who makes solid contact, hitting two long fouls. In the stands, Mary whispers "floater," and Henry, who has looked toward her, receives the message. His underhand toss stays in the air—thanks to slow motion—so long that the batter's timing is thrown off, and when the ball finally drops, he misses.

In the last scene of the film, Chet is coaching Henry's Little League team, and Henry is back in the outfield, where he actually catches a fly as the camera zooms in on his championship ring. *Rookie of the Year* was a hit with fans, although reviews were mixed. Director Daniel Stern came under fire for casting himself in the role of an idiotic pitching coach; his performance is dreadful, and the character adds nothing to the story.

RUDY (1993)

DIRECTOR: David Anspaugh. SCREENPLAY: Angelo Pizzo. PRODUCERS: Robert N. Fried, Cary Woods. CINEMATOGRAPHY: Oliver Wood. EDITING: David Rosenbloom. MUSIC: Jerry Goldsmith. PRODUCTION DESIGN: Robb Wilson King. COSTUME DESIGN: Jane Anderson.

CAST: Sean Astin (Rudy Ruettiger), Jon Favreau (D-Bob), Ned Beatty (Daniel Ruettiger), Greta Lind (Mary), Scott Benjaminson (Frank Ruettiger), Charles S. Dutton (Fortune), Lili Taylor (Sherry).

RUNNING TIME: 114 minutes.

DVD: Sony Pictures.

Based on a true story, *Rudy* celebrates the determination of a young man of modest ability to achieve his dream. Rudy Ruettiger, an undersized athlete from a blue-collar family in Indiana, has grown up cheering for Notre Dame. In spite of average grades and an unimpressive record with his high school football team, he is intent on playing for Notre Dame.

The film opens by juxtaposing shots of a Notre Dame-Michigan football game, complete with marching bands, packed stadium, and lots of glitz, with a neighborhood game between two groups of boys all of whom are bigger and more athletic than Rudy, who they call a "spaz." The scene dramatizes how far Rudy is from realizing his dream. His working-class background provides another obstacle. The factory where his father and his brothers are employed offers a more realistic future. By the time he is in high school, his family, his girlfriend, and his teachers are united in their opinion that Rudy (now played by Sean Astin) should accept his destiny and forget about college. His brother Frank (Scott Benjaminson) is brutal in his assessment of Rudy's chances of escaping the factory. His civics teacher believes the only subject he could ace is daydreaming and prevents him from joining more academically gifted classmates on a bus trip to tour the Notre Dame campus.

Four years later Rudy seems to have taken that advice. He is working in the factory alongside his best friend, Pete (Christopher Reed), the only person who takes Rudy seriously. On Rudy's twenty-second birthday, Pete gives Rudy a Notre Dame jacket. When Pete is killed in an accident at the factory, Rudy is more determined than ever to attend college. He has saved up a thousand dollars, money that his girlfriend wants him to put toward a house so that the two can marry. In spite of pressure from the girlfriend and his father, who believes Notre Dame is "for smart, rich kids," Rudy boards a bus for South Bend.

When he reaches the campus, he is directed to Father Cavanaugh (Robert Prosky), who listens sympathetically, but tells him he will have to attend Holy Cross Junior College to improve his academic record before he applies to Notre Dame. Walking across the campus, Rudy is unable to resist entering the football stadium and walking onto the field. He is immediately ousted by the irate head groundskeeper, Fortune (Charles S. Dutton). As Rudy continues across campus, the wall that separates him from the field visually demonstrates the barriers he will have to overcome to achieve his dream.

After enrolling at Holy Cross, Rudy is almost penniless, but he has managed to befriend Fortune, who hires him to help out at the stadium and gives him an office key so that he can sleep there on a cot. In class he struggles, but he is aided in his studies by a teaching assistant, D-Bob (John Favreau). In return, Rudy has promised to introduce D-Bob to some girls. Since Rudy is nearly as socially inept as D-Bob, this is a challenging task; he succeeds when he finds a pretty girl playing matchmaker for a less attractive friend.

The partnership between Rudy and D-Bob pays off for both. D-Bob falls in love, and Rudy finally gets accepted at Notre Dame, but not before he makes a painful visit home, where he learns that his older brother John is now dating his former girlfriend and where he has yet another confrontation with Frank.

Back on campus, Rudy tries out for the football team. He's not good enough to make the roster, but the coach, Ara Parseghian (Jason Miller), is impressed by his effort and assigns him to the "scout team," the athletes who run the upcoming opposition's plays. After earning the respect of the regular squad, Rudy elicits a promise from Coach Parseghian that the following season he will be allowed to suit up for one game that his family will attend.

Unfortunately for Rudy, Parseghian is replaced by Dan Devine (Chelcie Ross), who is not aware of the promise. As the season nears its end, Rudy has yet to play and is ready to quit the team, feeling that his work has come to nothing. However, when he tells Fortune that he's giving up, Fortune confides that he had quit the team after warming the bench for two years, a decision he still regrets. He reminds Rudy that he has obtained a world-class education and counsels him to focus on proving himself to himself, not to others. Fortune, who has never watched a Notre Dame game, promises to attend when Rudy dresses for a game. Fortune's promise encourages Rudy to return to the practice field. There he is greeted with applause by teammates who have come to respect him.

Just before the last home game, the Notre Dame captain walks into Coach Devine's office and tells him that he wants Rudy to wear his uniform and take his place. The rest of the team follows suit. Devine gives in, and Rudy calls the folks at home, who show up, along with Fortune and D-Bob and date for the game against

Sean Astin as Rudy (center) makes the Notre Dame squad in *Rudy*

Georgia Tech. When Notre Dame gets a big lead late in the game, Devine sends all the seniors in except for Rudy. Soon a football player, then a fan, then a stadium erupt with cries of "Rudy! Rudy!" Devine agrees to put him in, but Notre Dame is on offense and Rudy plays only defense. To get him in the game, the players ignore Devine's play call and score, allowing Rudy on the field for the kickoff. He gets the tackle, stays in for the last play, gets another tackle, and is carried off by his teammates.

Rudy was written by Angelo Pizzo and directed by David Anspaugh, whose earlier *Hoosiers* (1986) was also set in Indiana. The two took liberties with the facts in order to heighten the drama. The family of the real Rudy Ruettiger was much more supportive of him: although his father didn't believe Rudy could make it to Notre Dame, he encouraged him to go to college; the celluloid older brother Frank is a total fabrication. An article by Richard Sandomir for the *New York Times* (October 10, 1993) reports that Coach Devine was displeased by his portrayal because he had readily agreed to let Rudy suit up; the scene in which the players arrive at his office to hand in their jerseys never occurred.

The movie was filmed on location. The Notre Dame administration permitted crews on campus after reading the script and determining it was motivating. Action scenes were shot by NFL Films.

RUN, FATBOY, RUN (2007)

DIRECTOR: David Schwimmer. SCREENPLAY: Michael Ian Black, Simon Pegg. PRODUCERS: Sarah Curtis, Robert Jones. CINEMATOGRAPHY: Richard Greatrex. EDITING: Michael Parker. MUSIC: Alex Wurman. PRODUCTION DESIGN: Sophie Becher. ART DIRECTION: Julia Castle. COSTUME DESIGN: Annie Hardinge.
CAST: Simon Pegg (Dennis Doyle), Thandie Newton (Libby Odell), Hank Azaria (Whit), Dylan Moran (Gordon).
RUNNING TIME: 100 minutes.
DVD: Warner Home Video.

With only days to prepare, an out-of-shape man enters a marathon to redeem himself to his son and ex-fiancée.

RUNNING (1979)

DIRECTOR: Steven Hilliard Stern. SCREENPLAY: Steven Hilliard Stern. PRODUCERS: Ronald I. Cohen, Robert M. Cooper. CINEMATOGRAPHY: Laszlo George. EDITING: Kurt Hirschler. MUSIC: André Gagnon. PRODUCTION DESIGN: Alfred Benson, Susan Longmire. COSTUME DESIGN: Linda Kemp.
CAST: Michael Douglas (Michael Andropolis), Susan Anspach (Janet), Lawrence Dane (Coach Walker), Eugene Levy (Ritchie Rosenberg).
RUNNING TIME: 102 minutes.

An unemployed man who has lost the respect of his family dreams of running in the Olympics.

RUNNING BRAVE (1983)

Director: D. S. Everett, Donald Shebib. Screenplay: Henry Bean, Shirl Hendryx. Producer: Ira Englander. Cinematography: François Protat. Editing: Peter Zinner. Music: Mike Post. Production Design: Carol Spier. Art Direction: Barbara Dunphy. Costume Design: Wendy Hudolin (Patridge).

Cast: Robby Benson (Billy Mills), Pat Hingle (Bill Easton), Claudia Cron (Pat Mills), Jeff McCracken (Dennis Riley), August Schellenberg (Billy's father), Graham Greene (Eddie Mills), Denis Lacroix (Frank Mills).

Running Time: 106 minutes.

DVD: Trinity Home Entertainment.

Running Brave is a biopic about American Olympic runner Billy Mills, who in 1964 won a gold medal in the 10,000-meter race and set an Olympic record. Mills, half Sioux and half Caucasian, is portrayed as a natural athlete whose talent promises him a way to escape the poverty of life on the reservation, but which places him in a hostile world. Running seems effortless for him, yet adjusting to a white world while maintaining cultural ties to friends and family proves to be his greatest challenge.

The film opens with Billy (Robby Benson) placing a comfortable first in a high school cross country championship. His finish is scrutinized by University of Kansas track coach Bill Easton (Pat Hingle), who expresses concern that Billy pulled up at the end of the race. Easton equates Billy's unwillingness to extend his already substantial lead to a lack of initiative. Easton, whose past experiences with Native American athletes have not been successful, perceives them as "quitters" and is reluctant to recruit Billy. But because Billy is half white and wants to attend college, Easton relents.

Billy's older brothers provide a different perspective on "quitting." Before Billy leaves for Kansas, Eddie (Graham Greene) describes another athlete from a neighboring tribe who won a football scholarship but dropped out of college and returned to the reservation because the university "wanted to make him white." Eddie, who possesses no outstanding skill that would provide entrance to the world of opportunity, has become an embittered cultural separatist. Frank (Denis Lacroix) is a talented artist, but in spite of his gifts and his desires, he has not been able to survive the discrimination of the white world. Frank has fallen into alcoholism and has served time in prison. Billy's father, who died when Billy was twelve (his mother died a few years earlier and is mentioned only briefly), believed that there was no future in staying on the reservation and helped prepare Billy for cultural assimilation by cutting his hair into a brush cut and encouraging him to pursue an education.

Although his father succeeded in steering Billy toward the larger world, Billy is not fully equipped to manage the hostility he encounters on the campus of the University of Kansas, where he is the only male Native American student. (The other Native American student, a woman whom he describes as "fat," is never shown.) Billy is shunned by the other athletes and harassed by campus security. The assistant coaches refer to him as "that Indian boy," and Coach Easton refuses to allow Billy to develop his preferred come-from-behind running style, which the coach believes fosters laziness. After some initial tension, Billy does bond with his roommate and fellow runner, Dennis Riley (Jeff McCracken), but this friendship does not lead to social acceptance, and Billy is denied admission to Dennis's fraternity.

When Billy begins dating a white woman, Pat (Claudia Cron), he starts to feel more comfortable at the university, but problems persist. Pat's parents disapprove of the relationship, a situation that she presents as a problem Billy must deal with rather than as something they must face together. On the track, Easton has Billy running in a large number of events. The coach's demands leave Billy exhausted, and his performance level begins to drop. A visit by Billy's brothers amplifies the tension Billy has been feeling. Eddie and Frank stay only a few minutes at Pat's parents' house, for the middle-class comfort of the home makes the pair feel inadequate. Frank, in awe of the furnishings, compares the interior to that of a pawn shop. Eddie is too uncomfortable to sit down, and when he stomps out, Frank follows, rejecting even the set of paints Billy has given him.

After losing his third race in a row and once again being deemed a quitter, Billy returns to the reservation, leaving behind Pat, a job opportunity with a campus booster, and his dreams of becoming an Olympic runner. He is immediately welcomed by his brothers. Eddie simply believes that Billy has finally seen the light and returned to his roots, where he belongs, but Frank, who once dreamed of going to Paris to study art, sees Billy's return as a defeat for them both. At a ritual dance, Billy joins the other members of the tribe, dancing and drumming; Frank gets drunk. The next day, Billy resumes running and rediscovers the joy he once felt in the sport. He has also discovered that he has become an important role model for children on the reservation and that his making an Olympic team would help restore pride and confidence to the community. Billy resolves to run in Tokyo and to take Frank with him, but when he arrives at Frank's place to share his plan, he finds Frank dead, an apparent suicide.

Although Pat has wired Billy asking him to return, he is too troubled to respond. Instead, he joins the Marines. The rigors of training help him to get into shape and to maintain his enthusiasm for running. With a clearer sense of direction and of acceptance, he is able to resume his relationship with Pat. They marry and Billy qualifies for the U.S. Olympic team. However, he is not the top American runner and has received little attention. Before the start of the 10,000-meter event, the coach directs his instructions to the others, and the announcer proclaims that Billy "is not considered a threat." But he proves to be a threat in the twenty-five-lap contest, staying with the leaders. As the athletes circle the track, the camera cuts to the spectators, where Pat is cheering Billy on and where Coach Easton is nervously watching his progress. After twenty laps Billy is running slightly ahead of Australian Ron Clarke and Tunisian Mohammad Gammoudi, but they close in, and in the final lap Billy is pushed and loses ground. While two American and Australian reporters hurl punches at one another in the press box, Billy shoots into overdrive, breasting the tape ahead of the field.

As the national anthem plays and Billy stands with his hand over his heart, Coach Easton brushes away a tear. After the award ceremony the coach approaches Billy to congratulate him. Easton, who has regained his composure, tells Billy it has been an honor to work with him. They shake hands and separate, but Billy runs after Easton to thank him. Easton offers a brief nod, then walks off. Back in Kansas, Billy and Pat are met by a large crowd at the train station. Dennis is there with members of his fraternity. As Billy rides in an open convertible through throngs of admirers, he spots a Sioux elder and makes meaningful eye contact. The film ends with the information that the real

Robby Benson as Billy Mills at the Tokyo Olympics in *Running Brave*

Billy Mills has become a successful executive and devotes time and energy to working with Native American children.

While *Running Brave* centers on Billy's internal conflict, the film offers an unflattering view of his coach, who instructs his athletes to push, trip, and punch competitors—without getting caught—and whose limitless devotion to the individual work ethic has the effect of depersonalizing the athletes. The final encounter between Billy and Easton is troubling in that Billy seems so willing to share credit for his success with a man who did little to help him develop his talent or adjust to the campus. Viewers may also find troubling the fact that a white actor was chosen to portray Mills, a decision most likely based on box office considerations, but one that also reflects limited opportunities for minority actors in 1983. The credits, too, are revealing of the time period. Coach Easton, who insists on being called "Coach," the title that reflects his authority, is never addressed by a first name, but his first name appears in the credits. Pat, whose key scenes occur in the early portion of the film, before she and Billy are married, is not assigned a maiden name and is listed as "Pat Mills." Billy is the only Native American given a surname. His family members are listed only by their first names, and the credits are segregated according to setting: Kansas, Tokyo, and the Reservation.

S

SAFE AT HOME! (1962)

DIRECTOR: Walter Doniger. SCREENPLAY: Robert Dillon, Tom Naud, Steven Ritch. PRODUCER: Tom Naud. CINEMATOGRAPHY: Irving Lippman. EDITING: Frank P. Keller. MUSIC: Van Alexander.

CAST: Mickey Mantle (himself), Roger Maris (himself), William Frawley (Bill Turner), Patricia Barry (Johanna Price), Don Collier (Ken Lawton), Bryan Russell (Hutch Lawton).

RUNNING TIME: 84 minutes.

DVD: Sony Pictures.

A Little League player claims his father is friends with Mickey Mantle and Roger Maris, and in desperation he heads to the Yankees' training camp in Florida to persude them to attend his Little League team's banquet.

SAINT RALPH (2005)

DIRECTOR: Michael McGowan. SCREENPLAY: Michael McGowan. PRODUCERS: Teza Lawrence, Andrea Mann, Seaton McLean, Mike Souther. CINEMATOGRAPHY: Rene Ohashi. EDITING: Susan Maggi. MUSIC: Andrew Lockington. PRODUCTION DESIGN: Matthew Davies. ART DIRECTION: Ken Watkins. COSTUME DESIGN: Anne Dixon.

CAST: Adam Butcher (Ralph Walker), Campbell Scott (Father George Hibbert), Jennifer Tilly (Nurse Alice), Gordon Pinsent (Father Fitzpatrick).

RUNNING TIME: 98 minutes.

DVD: Sony Pictures.

In this film, a young man believes that winning the 1954 Boston marathon will reverse a family tragedy.

THE SANDLOT (1993)

DIRECTOR: David M. Evans. SCREENPLAY: David M. Evans, Robert Gunter. PRODUCERS: Dale de la Torre, William S. Gilmore. CINEMATOGRAPHY: Anthony B. Richmond. EDITING: Michael A. Stevenson. MUSIC: David Newman. PRODUCTION DESIGN: Chester Kaczenski. ART DIRECTION: Marc Dabe. COSTUME DESIGN: Grania Preston.

CAST: Tom Guiry (Scotty Smalls), Mike Vitar (Benjamin Rodriguez), Patrick Renna (Ham Porter), Chauncey Leopardi (Michael "Squints" Palledorous), Marty York (Alan "Yeah-Yeah" McClennan), Brandon Adams (Kenny DeNunez), Karen Allen (Mom), Denis Leary (Bill), James Earl Jones (Mr. Mertle).

RUNNING TIME: 101 minutes.

DVD: 20th Century Fox.

This film offers a nostalgic look back at a group of young sandlot players in the 1960s. It was followed by direct-to-video sequels more than a decade later.

SCHOOL TIES (1992)

DIRECTOR: Robert Mandel. SCREENPLAY: Dick Wolf, Darryl Ponicsan. PRODUCERS: Stanley R. Jaffe, Sherry Lansing. CINEMATOGRAPHY: Freddie Francis. EDITING: Jacqueline Cambas, Gerald Greenberg. MUSIC: Maurice Jarre. PRODUCTION DESIGN: Jeannine Claudia Oppewall. ART DIRECTION: Steven Wolff. COSTUME DESIGN: Ann Roth.
CAST: Brendan Fraser (David Greene), Matt Damon (Dillon), Chris O'Donnell (Reece), Randall Batinkoff (Van Kelt), Andrew Lowery (Mack), Cole Hauser (Jack Connors), Ben Affleck (Chesty Smith).
RUNNING TIME: 106 minutes.
DVD: Paramount.

Anti-Semitism, exploitation, and abuse of authority are the themes of this gridiron movie set in 1955. The plot features a Jewish quarterback, David Greene (Brendan Fraser), who is offered a scholarship to an elite Episcopalian prep school, St. Matthew's, that is intent on defeating archrival St. Luke's. From the start, David realizes he must not reveal his Jewish heritage if he is to fit in.

The film introduces its major themes in a heavy-handed manner. Bigotry first presents itself in the form of hoodlums in the working-class neighborhood in Scranton, Pennsylvania, where the Greenes live. David joins his blond, blue-eyed high school teammates at a teen hangout and is enjoying himself when members of a motorcycle gang enter; one taunts David, calling him "sheeney bastard," and a fight breaks out. David's reliance on fisticuffs in response to hateful speech concerns his father (Ed Lauter), who fears his son will ruin his chances of a Harvard scholarship if David doesn't blend in at the prep school. The St. Matthew's coach, McDevitt (Kevin Tighe), offers a similar warning after first asking if David has special dietary needs. When David arrives at the dormitory and meets his roommate, Reece (Chris O'Donnell), and friends Dillon (Matt Damon), Mack (Andrew Lowery), and Van Kelt (Randall Batinkoff), almost immediately, one of them uses "jew" as a verb. That evening, as he gets ready for bed, David hides his Star of David in a bandage container.

In spite of the obvious socioeconomic differences between David and the others, he quickly gains respect by making fun of the pompous housemaster, Mr. Cleary (Zeljko Ivanek). Reece gives David a school tie and assumes responsibility for his orientation into the ways of St. Matt's, which include thrice-weekly chapel meetings. The only one of the boys who doesn't completely warm to David is Dillon, a running back who fears David will surpass him as the team's star. Dillon struggles to match the achievements of his older brother and the expectations of his father. In a reversal of stereotypical class envy, it is Dillon who wishes he came from a background like David's because he believes he would be praised for even the smallest achievement and forgiven even large mistakes. As the film progresses, Dillon is revealed to be as ugly an anti-Semite as the leader of the Scranton motorcycle pack.

The housemaster, who is also the French teacher, and the headmaster, Dr. Bartram (Peter Donat), are stereotypical abusers of authority. In the dormitory, Mr. Cleary refuses to allow the boys to listen to rock and roll, which he derides as "jungle" music; in the classroom, he so belittles Mack that the boy suffers a total psychological breakdown. Dr. Bartram, knowing that David is Jewish, criticizes him for playing in a Saturday game that coincides with Rosh Hashanah. (David is praying in the chapel after the game when Bartram confronts him about his faith.)

Nearly everywhere he turns, David encounters reminders that he is an out-

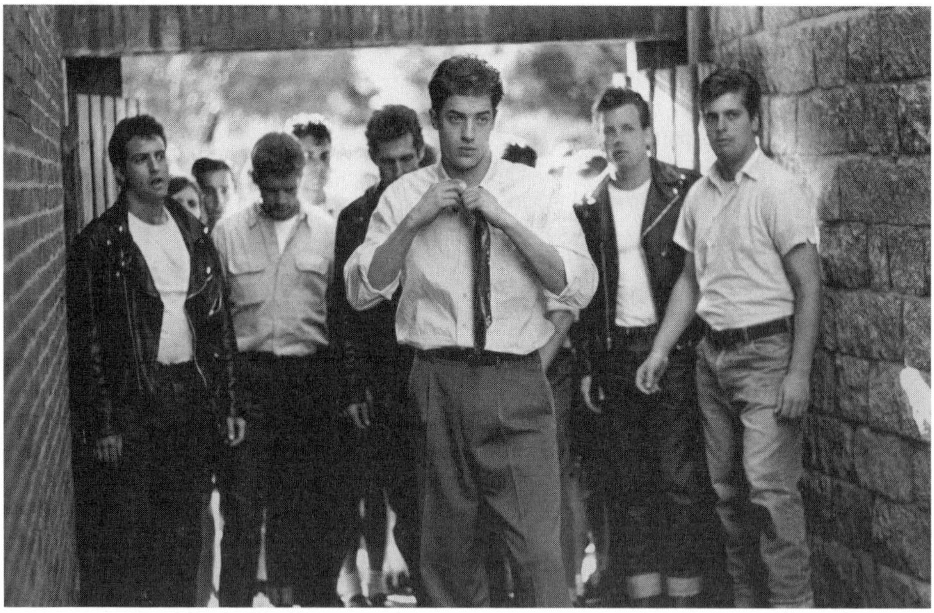

Brendan Fraser as David Greene in *School Ties*

sider. In the dining hall he waits tables as part of his financial package and must serve his friends and teammates, and he must bow his head with the others while the chaplain offers thanks in Jesus's name. At a school dance a chaperone places a balloon between a couple who are dancing too closely, instructing them to "make room for the Holy Ghost." In the locker room Dillon jokes about the "Hebes" at Harvard.

The conflict between Dillon and David intensifies after David proves his on-field mettle, drawing attention away from Dillon and attracting the attention of Sally Wheeler (Amy Locane), whom Dillon likes. Before the big game against archrival St. Luke's, Dillon's mother invites David to a postgame dinner at their club. In a pregame ceremony, Dillon's brother is inducted into the school's hall of fame, an honor that leaves Dillon desperate to emerge the hero of the St. Luke's contest. David does his best to assist, going so far as to ignore the coach's instructions and give Dillon the ball on a key set of downs. After Dillon fumbles, nearly causing a turnover, he pleads for another chance, but David, already in trouble with Coach McDevitt, must refuse. Instead of scoring the winning touchdown, Dillon throws a key block that allows David to carry the ball across the goal line. At dinner that evening, David enjoys the attention of Dillon's and Sally's families while Dillon broods. Not even praise from his father, who appreciates Dillon's role in the team's victory, ameliorates Dillon's gloom. Adding to Dillon's difficulty is his weak performance in history class. If he does not score a high mark on an upcoming exam, he will need to rely on family connections rather than his scholastic record for admission to an Ivy League school. When he overhears a club member referring to David as a *Jewish* quarterback recruited to deliver a winning season for St. Matt's, Dillon determines to reveal David's secret.

Dillon chooses his moment, telling an offensive joke in the communal shower and provoking David's anger. To David's surprise, he faces immediate rejection. His closest friends, Reece and Van Kelt, are hurt that he has concealed his Jewish heritage; Sally is embarrassed and concerned that her reputation has been tarnished. David's room is vandalized and a swastika scrawled on the wall beside his bed; he challenges whoever is responsible to meet him in the courtyard at night, but no one shows.

Meanwhile, all of the boys are preparing for exams. Dillon is also preparing crib notes. During the exam, David realizes that Dillon is cheating, but he does not report him. However, as the students leave the classroom, Dillon's crib notes slip from his pocket and fall to the floor, where they are found by the teacher. St. Matthew's prides itself on a student-devised and student-enforced honor code reflecting the principle that for the privileged, honor ranks above advancement (a principle that assumes honesty declines in proportion to wealth and social status). Because Dillon does not confess and David does not identify him as the cheater, the students themselves must determine who is responsible; otherwise, everyone in the class will fail. Some of the boys suspect David since they feel he deceived them by passing as a Christian. David confronts Dillon privately and asks him to accept responsibility for his actions; instead, Dillon claims to have seen David cheat. This act of treachery prompts David to tell the others the truth, but only Reece and Van Kelt believe him. When the others vote on the matter, they determine that David is the cheater. He agrees to uphold their honor code by lying to the headmaster, but when he appears before the administrators, he learns that Van Kelt also saw Dillon cheat and has turned him in. Although Van Kelt and David have also violated the code by not coming forward immediately, the headmaster waives their punishment. The film ends with David declaring that just as the school is using him to improve their athletic program, he will use them to get to Harvard.

There is not much football in *School Ties*, the emphasis falling on themes of classism, racism, and anti-Semitism. In spite of an excellent performance by Matt Damon, who brings depth to the privileged but troubled Dillon, characterizations are largely stereotypical. Adults of the upper classes and most of their offspring are irredeemably arrogant practitioners of all manner of discrimination, while the working classes, unless they are hoodlums, manifest a democratic ideal. Director Robert Mandel also wields a heavy hand with his scene setting. Streets are gridlocked with period vehicles. Every one of David's male friends in Scranton wears pegged jeans, a white T-shirt, and a cigarette behind an ear; the effect is that they look as if they've just arrived from a low-budget production of *West Side Story* and may break into song and dance at any moment. Minor characters display obvious attributes of the fifties; most noticeable is David's kid brother's Davy Crockett hat, which makes the boy appear as if there's a rodent sleeping on his head. This laughable display of props and costumes detracts from the seriousness of the subject matter. Viewers may believe that the film's portrayal of post–World War II/pre–civil rights movement prejudice is equally overdone.

THE SCOUT (1994)

DIRECTOR: Michael Ritchie. SCREENPLAY: Andrew Bergman, Albert Brooks, Monica Johnson, based on the article by Roger Angell. PRODUCERS: Andre E. Morgan, Albert S. Ruddy. CINEMATOGRAPHY: László Kovács. EDITING: Pembroke J. Herring, Don Zimmerman. MUSIC: Bill Conti. PRODUCTION DESIGN: Stephen Hendrickson. ART DIRECTION: Mike Okowita. COSTUME DESIGN: Luke Reichle.

CAST: Albert Brooks (Al Percolo), Brendan Fraser (Steve Nebraska), Dianne Wiest (Doctor Aaron), Anne Twomey (Jennifer), Lane Smith (Ron Wilson), Michael Rapaport (Tommy Lacy).
RUNNING TIME: 101 minutes.
DVD: 20th Century Fox.

This comedy/drama is about a desperate Yankees scout whose latest find is a wildly talented but also flaky phenom. The film features appearances by many broadcasters and baseball players, including Bob Costas, George Steinbrenner, Steve Garvey, Tim McCarver, Bret Saberhagen, Keith Hernandez, and Ozzie Smith.

SEABISCUIT (2003)

DIRECTOR: Gary Ross. SCREENPLAY: Gary Ross, based on the book by Laura Hillenbrand. PRODUCERS: Kathleen Kennedy, Frank Marshall, Gary Ross. CINEMATOGRAPHY: John Schwartzman. EDITING: William Goldenberg. MUSIC: Randy Newman. PRODUCTION DESIGN: Jeannine Claudia Oppewall. ART DIRECTION: Andrew Neskoromny. COSTUME DESIGN: Judianna Makovsky. Set Decoration: Leslie A. Pope.
CAST: Tobey Maguire (Red Pollard), Jeff Bridges (Charles Howard), Elizabeth Banks (Marcela Howard), Chris Cooper (Tom Smith), Gary Stevens (George Woolf), William H. Macy (Tick Tock McGlaughlin), Ed Lauter (Charles Strub, David McCullough (narrator).
RUNNING TIME: 141 minutes.
ACADEMY AWARD NOMINATIONS: Best Picture, Best Adapted Screenplay, Best Cinematography, Best Editing, Best Art Direction/Set Decoration, Best Costume Design, Best Sound Mixing.
DVD: Universal Studios.

This horse-racing movie has all the ingredients of Hollywood formula: the blue-collar worker who becomes a self-made millionaire but suffers a tragic loss; the eccentric loner who emerges from the edges of society to solve a problem; the talented young man who must overcome a near-fatal flaw or two in pursuing his goal; the rebellious athlete who must learn discipline. But *Seabiscuit* is not fiction; it is based on Laura Hillenbrand's nonfiction account of owner Charles Howard, trainer Tom Smith, jockey John "Red" Pollard, and Seabiscuit, grandson of Man o' War. Like the book, the film places the horse's story in an historical context and examines the lives of the principal players as well as providing an inside look at the racing industry during the Great Depression. Popular historian David McCullough narrates segments devoted to establishing the era, while fictitious reporter Tick Tock McGlaughlin (William H. Macy) reflects public response to Seabiscuit's career.

Seabiscuit takes its time getting to the races, devoting the first forty minutes to establishing characters and context. The film intercuts black-and-white footage of American life in the first three decades of the twentieth century with scenes depicting the changing lives of the three main characters. In 1910, Charles Howard (Jeff Bridges) is working as a bicycle mechanic, but within a few years he has established his own repair shop. Business is slow until a Stanley Steamer, a steam-powered motor car, breaks down in front of the shop, and Charles undertakes the repairs. After disassembling, then reassembling the engine, Charles is enchanted with the vehicle's potential, and before long, he's an extraordinarily successful car dealer who has developed an interest in automobile racing. Tragedy strikes when his young son, whom Charles has taught to drive, gets behind the wheel without adult supervision and is killed when the automobile collides with a logging truck on his father's property.

Charles's marriage dissolves soon after. Tom Smith (Chris Cooper) is depicted as a lone cowboy riding the range and lassoing horses and encountering barbed-wire fences with increasing frequency. Tom becomes a horse trainer, camping near stables, and generally keeping to himself. Red Pollard (Tobey Maguire) is the oldest child of a family hard hit by the Depression. Red has an affinity for horses that translates into money for his parents, who sell his services to a stable owner. He leads a hard life, riding for unscrupulous owners on circuits where lack of regulation compounds the dangers of the sport. In spite of his talent, Red loses races that appear within his grasp; to supplement his income, he takes up prizefighting, where he is no more successful. Later in the film, Red's inconsistency is explained—he is blind in one eye and sometimes just doesn't see another rider approaching or a punch coming.

The three men's lives intersect when Charles, having remarried a woman (Elizabeth Banks as Marcela) who enjoys riding, rediscovers both his love of horses and his love of racing. He sets out to buy a horse, but first searches for an expert to help him select an animal. Charles finds Tom, and Tom finds both Seabiscuit and Red. Seabiscuit has not lived up to his pedigree; he's undersized and is a lazy colt. At three years old, he is a training partner for more promising horses; his job is to lose races at the rate of two a week. But where others see a nearly worthless, bad-tempered animal, Tom Smith sees a champion. Tom also spots the potential in Red, a feisty rider who is a head taller than the average jockey. The men take Seabiscuit to the Charles ranch and let him run off the track. At first the horse is skittish, but responds to the introduction of another horse Tom brings in, and Red discovers just how astonishingly fast and competitive Seabiscuit is. Soon the horse is winning races and capturing the hearts of Americans, who seem to link Seabiscuit's fate to economic recovery. Because Seabiscuit has competed only on the West Coast, Charles wants to arrange a race against the East Coast champion, War Admiral, whose owner is reluctant to take on what he believes to be a decidedly inferior horse. Finally, Charles orchestrates enough public pressure to arrange a match race between the two horses at Pimlico in Baltimore, Maryland. To prepare, Seabiscuit requires some retraining. He must learn to break at the sound of a bell and to go for the lead rather than come from behind.

At the same time Red is preparing Seabiscuit for the race, he encounters a horse owner from his past who employed him when he desperately needed work. Red agrees to break a horse for the man. When the horse is startled by an engine, Red is thrown from the saddle. His foot catches in the stirrup, and he is dragged, severely breaking his leg. Charles, who has become a surrogate father to Red, is ready to cancel the contest, but Red asks him to call his friend and fellow jockey, George Woolf (Gary Stevens). George is a skilled rider, and with Red's advice is able to bring Seabiscuit to the finish line four lengths ahead of War Admiral. Red listens to the race on the radio from his hospital room.

Seabiscuit's story doesn't conclude with his victory at Pimlico. The horse continues to race until an injury seems to end his career. Back on Charles's ranch, Red and Seabiscuit limp along side by side until both improve enough for Red to hoist himself into the saddle. When the horse is fully recovered, Red wants to ride him in the Santa Anita Handicap, a race the two have never won. Although Red has constructed a brace to support his leg, his doctor is concerned that just the strain of riding could cause the bones to shatter. Charles, who still suffers the loss of his son, fears that Red could be killed if he falls during the race. But George and Marcela convince Charles to let Red ride, and the film ends with Seabiscuit's victory, one of the most remarkable comeback stories in the history of sports.

The film was a box office smash, earning seven Oscar nominations, including set design, costume design, sound mixing, cinematography, and editing. These nominations reflect the film's achievement in representing the historical era and the experience of horse racing. Former jockey Chris McCarron trained Toby Maguire to ride, and ten different horses played Seabiscuit. Some shots were filmed using equicisers, mechanical horses that were equipped with sculpted heads and mounted on a flatbed truck, but no special effects were used for the racing scenes.

SEMI-PRO (2008)

DIRECTOR: Kent Alterman. SCREENPLAY: Scott Armstrong. PRODUCER: Jimmy Miller. CINEMATOGRAPHY: Shane Hurlbut. EDITING: Debra Neil Fisher, Peter Teschner. MUSIC: Theodore Shapiro. PRODUCTION DESIGN: Clayton Hartley. ART DIRECTION: Jim Gloster, Virginia L. Randolph. COSTUME DESIGN: Susan Matheson.

CAST: Will Ferrell (Jackie Moon), Woody Harrelson (Monix), André Benjamin (Clarence), Maura Tierney (Lynn), Andrew Daly (Dick Pepperfield), Will Arnett (Lou Redwood), Andy Richter (Bobby Dee), David Koechner (commissioner), Rob Corddry (Kyle), Jackie Earle Haley (Dukes).

RUNNING TIME: 91 minutes.

DVD: New Line Home Video.

The merger of the American Basketball Association (ABA) and the National Basketball Association (NBA) would seem to be a topic that would appeal to basketball fans, and when comic Will Ferrell is added to the mix, the film ought to be a hit with critics and fans alike. However, *Semi-Pro* was not the successful movie it could have been. To say that the R-rated film richly deserves its rating is an understatement. The raunchy, obscenity-laced script limits the film's appeal. There is little real basketball footage, and the subplot, a reconciliation between point guard Monix (Woody Harrelson) and his former girlfriend, Lynn (Maura Tierney), is not developed.

Thanks to his one-hit success, "Love Me Sexy," played at every Tropics game, Jackie Moon (Ferrell), the owner, coach, and star player of the Flint Tropics (perhaps the only clean joke in the film), learns that the NBA will take four teams from the ABA to form a merged league. At a league meeting he persuades the other owners that the four teams should be the best in the league, not the ones with large markets that the NBA has already selected. The Tropics, with the league's worst record, need help, so Jackie trades the team's washing machine for Monix, a former member of the Boston Celtics. Monix accepts the trade because he wants to be reunited with Lynn, who is living with a lout who worships Jackie.

The games are treated farcically. The cheerleaders wear bikinis; the ref is Father Pat (Matt Walsh), complete with white collar; and the announcers, Dick Pepperfield (Andrew Daly) and Lou Redwood (Will Arnett), are foul-mouthed misogynists. The promotions are equally tasteless. One stunt, the floor-length, ten-thousand-dollar shot contest, backfires when Dukes (Jackie Earle Haley), a pothead whose condition perhaps enables him to make the shot, succeeds and is given a huge check that would bounce if a bank took it seriously. Perhaps to make a point about the role of violence in sports, Jackie's team and their opponents square off during a commercial break.

The Tropics' season turns around when the players ask Monix to be the coach, and he accepts the job of offensive and defensive coordinator, leaving Jackie as the nominal coach and choreographer (after all, basketball is entertainment). Thanks to the promotions, including a bogus Free Corn Dog Night and a featured wrestling match between Jackie and a trained bear (Randy), which escapes the ring, creating havoc, the Tropics manage to get their average attendance up. Monix's coaching leads to a string of wins, taking the team one game out of fourth place with a contest against the San Antonio Spurs approaching. Unfortunately, the NBA has insisted on the big-market teams, regardless of which four teams have the best records, so the game becomes meaningless.

When Clarence (André Benjamin, of the hip-hop group Outkast), the star of the team and a Julius Erving look-a-like, is traded to the Spurs so that he can make it to the NBA, the situation seems hopeless, but Monix tells the team that it's the last real game they're going to play and that they should do their best. Before a sold-out crowd, the Tropics trail the Spurs at the end of the half. Jackie, who has been knocked out by the Spurs' center, is in a coma in the dressing room when he has a dream. In that dream Jackie's deceased mother (Patti LaBelle!) appears with advice to use the "alley oop." Clarence, who can't bear to see his former teammates humiliated, leaves the Spurs' bench and dons a Tropics' uniform, despite threats by the Spurs' coach. In the second half the Tropics, using the alley-oop (after Father Pat is convinced it's legal), make a comeback. Having recovered from his coma, Jackie makes an elaborate, ritualized underhanded free throw and cuts the lead to one; Monix then scores the winning basket. In the wild postgame celebration a cannon fires confetti, and Father Pat is seen with a voluptuous cheerleader on his shoulders. Clarence is taken back by the Spurs, and the ABA commissioner promises Jackie a promotions job in the NBA, a promise he'll keep as long as he lives. Unfortunately, the missing bear reappears and then disappears with the commissioner. (Perhaps this is a reference to Shakespeare's "exit pursued by a bear" from *The Winter's Tale.* A year after filming, the same bear killed a trainer by biting his neck.) The last image is of Dukes with a check for $2,300 from Jackie and a promise for the rest.

SEMI-TOUGH (1977)

Director: Michael Ritchie. Screenplay: Walter Bernstein, based on the novel by Dan Jenkins. Producer: David Merrick. Cinematography: Charles Rosher Jr. Editing: Richard A. Harris. Music: Jerry Fielding. Production Design: Walter Scott Herndon. Costume Design: Theoni V. Aldredge.

Cast: Burt Reynolds (Billy Clyde Puckett), Kris Kristofferson (Shake Tiller), Jill Clayburgh (Barbara Jane), Robert Preston (Big Ed Bookman), Bert Convy (Friedrich Bismark), Lotte Lenya (Clara Pelf), Roger E. Mosley (Puddin Patterson), Richard Masur (Hooper), Carl Weathers (Dreamer Tatum).

Running Time: 108 minutes.

DVD: MGM.

Michael Ritchie's film, derived from Dan Jenkins's novel, concerns the football exploits, both on and off the field, of Billy Clyde Puckett (Burt Reynolds) and Shake Tiller (Kris Kristofferson), members of the Miami professional football team. *Semi-Tough* (the title refers not to football but to a wedding rehearsal) is a romantic comedy of Southern vintage that uses football as the source of its humor. What little game footage there is begins with an end-of-season contest and the subsequent playoff games. Most of the film takes place off the field where Billy and Shake compete for the affections of Barbara Jane (B.J., played by Jill Clayburgh), daughter of team owner Big Ed Bookman (Robert Preston). The film also lampoons various self-help theories and practitioners who bilk an insecure public.

As the film begins, B.J. is caught trying to dupe customs officials into buying her story about her expensive fur coat not having been purchased abroad. She introduces Billy and Shake to a book publisher she met on the plane; he wants to publish a book about professional football. The ensuing conversation between the publisher and Billy reveals the former's interest in collecting salacious information, albeit in a refined way, and the latter's ability to detect the publisher's hypocrisy. Trying to establish some bond with the football players, the publisher declares, "Intellectuals are the jocks of the mind," but Billy demolishes the publisher's pretention with a remark that would not pass today's standards for political correctness.

Back in the apartment they share with B.J., Shake and Billy discuss her, and Shake begins to use some of the jargon he learned from Friedrich Bismark (Bert Convy), the leader of a self-help movement known as B.E.A.T. (Dr. Bismark and his group are a parody of Werner Erhard and his est groups of the 1970s.) In an interesting reversal, Shake, not Billy, is featured in a photo shoot for an ad, and Big Ed is shown acting as a stereotypical team owner as he makes up a play that he insists his coach add to the playbook. After a plane trip to Green Bay, Wisconsin, where the team will face the Packers, it becomes clear that Shake and B.J. are romantically involved, and Billy is so jealous that he resorts to sleeping with Earline, an overweight woman he had earlier humiliated. To seduce Earline, Billy employs his own brand of popular psychology, double talk similar to that used by Bismark. Miami defeats Green Bay as a Gene Autry song airs in the background. (Autry's songs, some of them humorous accompaniment to the action, comprise much of the sound track.)

To attract B.J.'s attention, Billy tells her that he is writing a book on football, but he does not reveal that the book will be full of stories that will not reflect well on the game, including a tale about a teammate holding a young woman by her ankles and dangling her from the roof of Big Ed's home. Hooper (Richard Masur), Big Ed's assistant, raises objections; then Big Ed meets with Billy to tell him that he is "out of line," not metaphorically but physically. He suggests that Billy needs to be "pelfed," a term associated with a Dr. Pelf, who subjects Billy to a series of physical assaults masked as massage. (Dr. Pelf and her regimen may be modeled after an actual Dr. Rolfe, who had similar theories about balance, gravity, and alignment and whose trainees are known as "rolfers." Dr. Pelf, like Dr. Bismark, comes off as a quack.) This kind of satire about self-help theories is elaborated on when a television sports announcer interviews Billy and the Dallas captain, and the two argue about the relative merits of B.E.A.T. and "pyramid power," another bit of quackery.

Billy, of course, is only pretending to believe in the Bismark philosophy, and Shake, thanks to Billy's subtle undermining, is becoming concerned about B.J.'s inability to "get it." Obviously, B.J. is having second thoughts, as well, and she and Billy engage in conversations that suggest they belong together. After Miami defeats Dallas (former Green Bay Packer Paul Hornung is in the announcer's booth), the wedding between B.J. and Shake is scheduled to take place. The service is conducted by a traditional minister and Dr. Bismark, who begins with a jargon-ridden speech preceding the I do's, but Shake, who knows that B.J. does not share his desire to go to India for the honeymoon and who does not share her desire for children, says, "I don't." The present decision is fine for Bismark, but Big Ed knocks him out, and a melee follows in the church. At the end of the film B.J. and Billy are walking on the beach in their wedding clothes and playing liar's poker. To the sounds of "I'm Back in the Saddle Again," B.J. agrees to live with Billy in Hawaii. This is essentially a down-home version of *Jules and Jim.*

THE SET-UP (1949)

DIRECTOR: Robert Wise. SCREENPLAY: Art Cohn, based on the poem by Joseph Moncure March. PRODUCER: Richard Goldstone. CINEMATOGRAPHY: Milton R. Krasner. EDITING: Roland Gross. ART DIRECTION: Albert S. D'Agostino, Jack Okey.

CAST: Robert Ryan (Bill "Stoker" Thompson), Audrey Totter (Julie), George Tobias (Tiny), Alan Baxter (Little Boy), Wallace Ford (Gus), Percy Helton (Red), James Edwards (Luther Hawkins), Darryl Hickman (Shanley).

RUNNING TIME: 72 minutes. B&W.

DVD: Warner Home Video.

Directed by Robert Wise and starring Robert Ryan, *The Set-Up* is a distinctive film adapted from a long narrative poem by Joseph Moncure March. March's poem, intended to depict the racism of the era, features a black boxer, Pansy Jones, whose life parallels that of fighter Jack Johnson. March was upset that Wise's adaptation changed the race of the main character. Wise countered that his decision reflected the lack of black actors in Hollywood at the time; more likely, Hollywood feared a black actor would not hold the same box office appeal as a white one. As in *Body and Soul* (1947) and *Champion* (1949), the fight game is portrayed as a white domain.

Experienced collegiate boxer Robert Ryan plays an on-the-skids, middle-aged boxer, Bill "Stoker" Thompson, whose wife, Julie (Audrey Totter), wants him to retire. Julie refuses to watch him fight at Paradise City, a sleazy boxing arena. Unbeknownst to Stoker, his manager, Tiny (George Tobias), and his trainer, Red (Percy Helton), have accepted a fifty-dollar bribe to "fix" the fight since they figure Stoker doesn't have a chance of defeating his opponent, Tiger Nelson (Hal Fieberling), a much younger boxer who is on his way up, just as Stoker is on his way down. Surprisingly, however, Stoker realizes that he can beat the younger man and, ultimately, wins the fight. As a result, he is viciously attacked in an alley by the unforgiving gangsters who have paid for the fix. Actions have consequences.

The Set-Up is experimental in its structure in that it takes place in "real time." The film is seventy-two minutes long, exactly the number of minutes consumed by the action represented. When the action begins after the credits, it is 9:05 p.m.; the last clock the audience is shown at the end reads 10:16 p.m. The rest of the running time is reserved for the credits, superimposed over a fight sequence. One of the boxers in this montage is knocked to the floor just as "Directed by Robert Wise" completes the credits. Throughout the film the viewer is kept aware of time as Julie continually checks the time, and at one point, her image is reflected in the face of a clock.

The Set-Up is also tightly designed, limiting the action to a one-block area in a noirish neighborhood. On one corner is the Cozy Hotel, where Stoker and his wife live; diagonally across the street is the boxing arena, Paradise City. The main action occurs in the hotel room, the dressing room, and the ring of the arena; the subsidiary action takes place in a penny arcade (called "Dreamland") and in a bar next to the arena, where Stoker's manager and trainer accept the bribe. The film's unity of action focuses entirely upon the last fight of Stoker Thompson, an innocent man caught up in a corrupt world. He wins because of his courage, determination, and experience, and, ironically, because he knows how to absorb punishment.

Stoker is honest, self-sacrificing, and perseverant—a sort of American Everyman fighting in a moral allegory. Out to prove that he is still capable of fighting and winning, he gauges his opponent, then turns the match into a test of endurance. After taking a beating, the worst that his opponent can deliver, Stoker goes to work on the younger man, outlasting and finally defeating him. Slowly, as the crowd realizes what is happening, their allegiance shifts from the younger boxer to Stoker. But this is a fickle mob, and their allegiance ultimately means nothing.

Although Stoker wins by the rules of the conventional American success myth, he unwittingly has violated the code of the underworld. The characters of this moral allegory involve three sorts: the boxers; the fans who support and exploit them, paying to witness their pain and suffering; and the fixers, hoodlums led by a thug named Little Boy (Alan Baxter), who is a metaphoric foil to Stoker's "man." Little Boy is a coward who enjoys physical intimidation. The fight fans are nearly as repulsive as the hoodlums, a bloodlusting mob that changes its allegiances capriciously. Wise's criticism of the sport is evident in the way he concentrates on the ghoulish faces of those who seem to enjoy the gory spectacle, crosscutting between the fight, the handlers in the corner, and the fans. The point of view of the fight scenes keeps the theater audience ringside, as well.

In the end Stoker proves himself in the ring, but as a man of action brought by time and age to mature introspection and doubt, he only just begins to grasp the meaning of his existential victory. And this is where director Wise leaves him at 10:16 p.m., beaten and maimed on the street, but reunited with the woman he loves, surrounded by an ignorant mob of passersby. As an ambulance arrives, the camera withdraws in a long, departing crane shot, reversing the movement and direction of the film's open establishing shot—providing the perfect ending for a carefully planned and tightly structured and edited film.

Wise began as an editor who worked at RKO Pictures with Orson Welles on *Citizen Kane* (1941)—he cut the famous breakfast sequence showing the breakup of Charles Foster Kane's first marriage—and on *The Magnificent Ambersons* (1942). A few years later, Wise would go on to direct Paul Newman as Rocky Graziano in *Somebody Up There Likes Me* (1956). *The Set-Up* was prelude to that success.

SHAOLIN SOCCER (2001)

DIRECTOR: Stephen Chow. SCREENPLAY: Stephen Chow, Kan-Cheung Tsang. PRODUCER: Kwok-Fai Yeung. CINEMATOGRAPHY: Pak-Huen Kwen, Ting Wo Kwong. EDITING: Kit-Wai Kai. MUSIC: Jackie Chan, Lowell Lo, Raymond Wong. ART DIRECTION: Kim Hung Ho. COSTUME DESIGN: Yim Man Choy.
CAST: Stephen Chow (Might Steel Leg Sing), Wei Zhao (Mui), Yut Fei Wong (Iron Head), Man Tat Ng (Golden Leg Fung).
RUNNING TIME: 113 minutes.
DVD: Miramax.

In this Chinese film, a football (soccer) team employs martial arts to beat their opponents.

SHERGAR (1999)

DIRECTOR: Dennis C. Lewiston. SCREENPLAY: Dennis C. Lewiston. PRODUCERS: Jeff Geoffray, Walter Josten. CINEMATOG-

RAPHY: David Lewis. EDITING: Alan Strachan. MUSIC: John Scott. PRODUCTION DESIGN: Brian-Ackland Snow. ART DIRECTION: Roger Bowles. COSTUME DESIGN: Louise Stjernsward.
CAST: Andrew Connolly (Concannon), Tom Walsh (Kevin), Mickey Rourke (Gavin O'Rourke), Ian Holm (Joseph Maguire).
RUNNING TIME: 95 minutes.
DVD: Gaiam.

Though supposedly based on true events about a kidnapped Irish racehorse champion, this depiction is mostly fabricated.

SHE'S THE MAN (2006)

DIRECTOR: Andy Fickman. SCREENPLAY: Ewan Leslie, Karen McCullah Lutz, Kirsten Smith. PRODUCERS: Ewan Leslie, Lauren Shuler Donner. CINEMATOGRAPHY: Greg Gardiner. EDITING: Michael Jablow. MUSIC: Nathan Wang. PRODUCTION DESIGN: David J. Bomba. ART DIRECTION: John Burke, John R. Jensen. COSTUME DESIGN: Katia Stano.
CAST: Amanda Bynes (Viola), Laura Ramsey (Olivia), Channing Tatum (Duke), Vinnie Jones (Dinklage), David Cross (Gold), Julie Hagerty (Daphne).
RUNNING TIME: 105 minutes.
DVD: Dreamworks Video.

This soccer film bends it like Shakespeare in *Twelfth Night*—a young woman disguised as her twin brother falls in love with a man who is enamored of a woman who falls in love with the young woman disguised as her brother. *She's the Man* preserves the romantic triangle of the play and retains the names of the major characters, but any other resemblance is largely coincidental.

In the film, Cornwall and Illyria are rival prep schools. Twins Viola (Amanda Bynes) and Sebastian (James Kirk) have been attending Cornwall, where both play soccer; however Sebastian has been expelled for skipping school and is slated to attend Illyria after the summer break. Viola has also encountered difficulty at Cornwall: the girls' soccer team has been eliminated in a cost-cutting measure, and the school will not permit her to try out for the boys' team, of which her boyfriend, Justin (Robert Hoffman), is the captain. Both Justin and Viola's mother (Linda Boyd) would like to see her assume the trappings of femininity; mom has already been gown shopping in anticipation of an upcoming debutantes' ball. Meanwhile, Sebastian, who is more interested in writing music and performing with his band than in playing soccer, is scheming to attend a music festival in London during the first two weeks of classes at Illyria.

To prove to Justin that she can compete against the boys, Viola develops a scheme of her own. She tells her mother that she is going to spend the next two weeks at her father's house—the twins' parents are divorced; instead, she takes her brother's place at Illyria, a boarding school, after undergoing a transformation with the help of her friend Paul (Jonathan Sadowski), a stylist.

Viola/Sebastian's roommate at Illyria is the hunky Duke Orsino (Channing Tatum), star striker of the soccer team. Viola develops an instant crush, but Duke has his eye on the lovely Olivia (Laura Ramsey), Viola's lab partner, but Olivia is attracted to Viola/Sebastian. Viola, whose soccer skills aren't quite strong enough to get her onto the first string, agrees to intercede with Olivia on Duke's behalf in exchange for athletic coaching.

Making the starting lineup seems easier for Viola than establishing and maintaining her masquerade, and much of the film's humor rests on her efforts. When Duke notices she has packed a box of tampons in her luggage, she quickly explains she uses them to staunch nosebleeds; later in the film, she discovers Duke with a tampon stuffed up his nose—he confirms that they do the trick. To establish her chick-magnet creds, Viola recruits a few of her girlfriends from Cornwall to show up at Cesario's, a local teen hangout where she's meeting teammates; her friends file in separately and flirt with her. When Sebastian's girlfriend, Monique (Alexandra Breckenridge), arrives at Cesario's, Viola, who has never liked Monique, takes advantage of the situation to break up with her. At a Junior League Fair that her mother has helped organize, Viola arrives as Sebastian and performs several quick changes to keep the ruse going. As Viola, she works a shift at the kissing booth and draws Duke's attention. After she explains she's Sebastian's sister, the two enjoy a kiss, but their time together is interrupted by Justin, who starts a fight with Duke.

Back in their room, Viola/Sebastian encourages Duke to ask Viola out, but before he gears up the courage, Olivia, intending to make Sebastian jealous, begins flirting with Duke. Complicating the matter even further, Olivia suggests Viola/Sebastian join her and Duke at Cesario's; Olivia also recommends Viola/Sebastian invite Duke's homely lab partner, Eunice (Emily Perkins). When Viola/Sebastian and Eunice arrive, Duke and Olivia, who have found conversation awkward, are delighted. The date produces only one satisfactory outcome: since Eunice has been seen out with "Sebastian," she is suddenly considered desirable, and her social life improves immediately. Duke has yet to realize that Olivia is not the right girl for him, and Olivia is even more strongly convinced that she loves Sebastian.

The debutante ball is fast approaching, and Viola must participate in an orientation, requiring her to abandon her macho persona and display daintiness. In the ladies' lounge, Viola encounters Olivia and pries into the details of her relationship with Duke. To Viola's surprise, Olivia reveals that she is using Duke to make Sebastian jealous. Keeping a straight face, Viola advises her to tell everyone the truth. During their conversation, Monique has been eavesdropping. She emerges from a stall and confronts Olivia. The ensuing brawl is more intense than the parallel fight between Justin and Duke.

The masquerade begins to unravel when Sebastian returns a day early. Olivia greets him with a passionate kiss, much to the delight of the real Sebastian. But not to the delight of Duke, who has witnessed the exchange and believes he has been betrayed by his best friend. Duke kicks Viola/Sebastian out of their room, forcing Viola to bunk with Eunice. Sebastian enters his room while Duke is asleep. The next day is game day, but Viola has overslept. By the time she arrives at the stadium, Sebastian has taken her place. The twins' parents, sitting together in the stands, finally put their stories together and realize the children have been up to something.

Throughout, a minor villain, Malcolm (James Snyder), has also been suspicious of "Sebastian." After he and Principal Gold (David Cross) overhear Viola/Sebastian arguing on the phone with her mother about wearing heels, Malcolm begins looking into Sebastian's background. His investigation leads him to Monique, who knows Sebastian has been in London and who reveals that he has a twin sister. Having discovered the truth, the two convince Gold that Viola is impersonating Sebastian. They hurry to the stadium, where Gold calls a halt to the soccer match to expose Viola. However, the real Sebastian is on the field and willingly exposes himself, albeit off camera, making the foolish principal appear even more foolish.

At the half, Viola catches Sebastian's attention, and the twins quickly supply each other with missing information so that Sebastian understands Olivia's affection and Viola Duke's anger. The twins trade clothes, and Viola takes the field for the second half. Because Duke is still clueless and still angry, Viola finally confesses. And to prove she is a girl, pulls up her shirt (again off-camera). Duke remains hurt, but he supports Viola in her desire to play. And she does, over the objections of the Cornwall coach and her former boyfriend. Viola gets to score the winning goal against Justin on a shot set up by Duke, but at the game's end, Duke is not ready to forgive Viola. However, Sebastian has officially met Olivia, and the twins' parents appear close to reconciliation.

Viola has sent Duke an invitation to the ball, but he has not responded. In his stead, her escort is to be friend Paul; however, when the couple is announced, it is Duke, not Paul by Viola's side. Sebastian, of course, accompanies Olivia, and in the scene's only surprise, Monique turns up on Justin's arm. The closing footage is not of the dance, but of Viola playing soccer for Illyria.

Bynes's impersonation, which verges on the cartoonish most of the time, is never convincing, but it isn't supposed to be. Although the character excels at soccer and rejects high heels and ball gowns, there is nothing androgynous about her style. Much of the comedy turns on her difficulty maintaining her disguise. Viola's default position is traditionally "feminine." Viola's inadequacies are heightened by the physical contrast with her costar, Channing Tatum, whose mature, chiseled physique (Tatum was in his midtwenties when the movie was shot) is frequently on display. In spite of mixed reviews, *She's the Man* proved popular at the box office, and like other Shakespeare-inspired films, has drawn scholarly attention.

A SHOT AT GLORY (2001)

Director: Michael Corrente. Screenplay: Denis O'Neill. Producers: Rob Carliner, Michael Corrente, Robert Duvall. Cinematography: Alex Thomson. Editing: David Ray. Music: Mark Knopfler. Production Design: Andy Harris. Costume Design: Trisha Biggar.

Cast: Robert Duvall (Gordon McCloud), Michael Keaton (Peter Cameron), Andy Gray (commentator), Finlay MacDonald (Eric).

Running Time: 114 minutes.

DVD: Lions Gate.

A Scottish football (soccer) manager hopes his estranged son will help his team achieve success.

SIDE OUT (1990)

Director: Peter Israelson. Screenplay: David Thoreau. Producer: Gary Foster. Cinematography: Ron Garcia. Editing: Conrad Buff. Music: Jeff Lorber. Production Design: Dan Lomino. Art Direction: Bruce Crone. Costume Design: Marlene Stewart.

Cast: C. Thomas Howell (Monroe Clark), Peter Horton (Zack Barnes), Courtney Thorne-Smith (Samantha), Harley Jane Kozak (Kate Jacobs), Terry Kiser (Uncle Max).

Running Time: 100 minutes.

DVD: Sony Pictures.

A rookie beach volleyball player teams up with a former pro who teaches him the ropes.

SIT TIGHT (1931)

Director: Lloyd Bacon. Screenplay: Rex Taylor. Cinematography: William Rees. Editing: James Gibbon.

Cast: Joe E. Brown (Herbert "Jojo" Mullins), Winnie Lightner (Doctor Winnie O'Neil), Claudia Dell (Sally Dunlap), Paul Gregory (Tom Weston).

Running Time: 78 minutes.

DVD: Warner Bros. Archives.

This film is a wrestling comedy that was originally intended to be a musical, but most of the numbers were ultimately removed.

THE 6TH MAN (1997)

DIRECTOR: Randall Miller. SCREENPLAY: Christopher Reed, Cynthia Carle. PRODUCER: David Hoberman. CINEMATOGRAPHY: Michael Ozier. EDITING: Eric Sears. MUSIC: Marcus Miller. PRODUCTION DESIGN: Michael Bolton. ART DIRECTION: Eric Fraser. COSTUME DESIGN: Grania Preston.
CAST: Marlon Wayans (Kenny Tyler), Kadeem Hardison (Antoine Tyler), David Paymer (Coach Pederson), Michael Michele (R. C. St. John), Kevin Dunn (Mikulski).
RUNNING TIME: 107 minutes.
DVD: Walt Disney Video.

In this fantasy film, a dead basketball player haunts his brother and assists his old team on the court.

*61** (2001)

DIRECTOR: Billy Crystal. SCREENPLAY: Hank Steinberg. PRODUCER: Robert F. Colesberry. CINEMATOGRAPHY: Haskell Wexler. EDITING: Michael Jablow. MUSIC: Marc Shaiman. PRODUCTION DESIGN: Rusty Smith. ART DIRECTION: Denise Hudson. COSTUME DESIGN: Dan Moore.
CAST: Barry Pepper (Roger Maris), Thomas Jane (Mickey Mantle), Anthony Michael Hall (Whitey Ford), Richard Masur (Milt Kahn), Bruce McGill (Ralph Houk), Chris Bauer (Bob Cerv), Bob Gunton (Dan Topping), Donald Moffat (Ford Frick), Seymour Cassel (Sam Simon), Michael Nouri (Joe DiMaggio).
RUNNING TIME: 129 minutes.
EMMY AWARDS: Outstanding Casting for a Miniseries, Movie, or a Special; Outstanding Sound Editing. NOMINATIONS: Outstanding Made for Television Movie; Outstanding Directing for a Miniseries, Movie, or a Special; Outstanding Writing for a Miniseries or a Movie; Outstanding Lead Actor (Pepper); Outstanding Cinematography; Outstanding Single Camera Picture Editing; Outstanding Art Direction; Outstanding Single Camera Sound Mixing; Outstanding Makeup; Outstanding Hairstyling.
DVD: HBO Home Video.

Producer and director Billy Crystal has been a Yankees fan since he attended his first game with his father in 1956. He idolized Mickey Mantle, whom he finally met some twenty years later when they were both guests on Dinah Shore's talk show. Mantle and Crystal became close friends, and after the ballplayer's death in 1995, Crystal began planning a film based on his life. Unable to market his idea as a feature film, he turned to HBO, which had also been approached by writer Hank Steinberg about a Roger Maris biopic. Crystal and Steinberg joined forces to produce *61**, based on the 1961 homerun competition between Mantle and Maris to break Babe Ruth's single-season record. The result is a powerful drama that presents each character's strengths within a balanced framework. Crystal, who refers to Mantle as "Elvis in pinstripes," does not gloss over Mantle's weaknesses, and he reveals the inner turmoil of the reticent Maris, whom he calls "the most misunderstood" player in the game. Both the Mantle and Maris families cooperated with the filmmakers.

The body of the movie is presented as a flashback framed by Mark McGwire's quest to surpass Roger Maris's record. McGwire has just tied the record, and Maris's widow, Pat (Patricia Crowley), and children, now grown, are invited to attend the next game, but Pat suffers a spell of arrhythmia and must watch from her hospital bed. Although the film is not presented from her point of view, the television coverage she watches from the hospital frames the "M & M" story.

The flashback begins on opening day for the Yankees in 1961. The film introduces the major complications in the locker room rather than on the playing field. Mantle (Thomas Jane) is asked by manager Ralph Houk (Bruce McGill) to be a team leader, code for toning down his off-the-field partying. Maris (Barry Pepper), feeling badgered by reporters about going for Ruth's record, refuses to say anything print worthy. Press commentary that Maris, playing for the Yankees, won the 1960 Most Valuable Player Award even though his teammate Mantle was much more popular suggests tension between the two players. The early scenes also play up the differences in the two men's characters. Mantle punctuates his speech with obscenities, and his vulgar comments about women indicate he has a roving eye. In contrast, Maris is shown as a devoted family man, modest and wholesome; his only vice appears to be that he smokes, not an uncommon habit among athletes in the 1960s.

As the season gets underway, Mantle is hitting well, but Maris, concerned about his wife's pregnancy, is not, and the Yankees are losing. When the manager decides to change the batting order, placing Maris in the number three spot, ahead of Mantle instead of behind him, the press speculates that the move will create discord on the team. In fact, the switch works well; Maris begins hitting, Mantle continues, and the Yanks accumulate wins. Yet the New York fans, inflamed by the press, show no support for Maris, and when Mantle enters a brief slump, Maris is held responsible. The film does a good job of presenting the so-called feud between the two players as a media fabrication. While reporters and announcers talk of unfriendly rivalry, Mantle and Maris are not presented as antagonists, just as very different people. At first, encounters between the two are depicted only on the field, and without reaction shots, the audience has little information with which to assess media claims. The first real indication that the men are friendly occurs after Mantle goes on a drinking spree, plays badly the next day, and vents his frustration on the locker room furnishings. Maris joins teammates Whitey Ford (Anthony Michael Hall) and Bob Cerv (Chris Bauer) in retrieving the drunken Mantle and sobering him up. After the game Maris invites Mantle to move into the apartment in Queens that he shares with Cerv. Although Maris sets rules, including no women, Mantle agrees, and soon the three men are spending evenings watching sitcoms together.

Mantle quickly recovers from his slump. He and Maris begin swinging the bat so productively that both seem capable of reaching Ruth's record. For the press, this is a bitter rivalry, and the fans throw their support firmly behind Mantle. Maris cannot please the crowd no matter what: he is booed for a bunt that brings in a game-winning run; he is even booed by New York fans when he homers. Threatening letters arrive, and Maris's relationship with the press grows even worse. While the Mantle-Maris slugfest continues, both men deny that the record is important to them. Of course it is, but it's even more important to baseball commissioner Ford Frick (Donald Moffat), a former ally of the late Ruth and friend of his widow, Claire (Rene Taylor). Frick draws on the length of the season, expanded since Ruth played, to declare that any record not broken within 154 games will stand as a separate record.

Eventually Mantle and Maris have a dustup, but quickly recover. Mantle, having injured his forearm, grows impatient with Maris's admonishments to take care of himself as well as with his oversensitivity to the press. It seems that neither can follow the other's advice. Maris, struggling with hostile fans and reporters, breaks out in a rash and loses clumps of hair from stress. He smokes so much that, in a reversal of roles, Mantle cautions Maris about self-destructive behavior. Mantle's health problems worsen, and a hip abscess benches him; he'll watch Maris chase the record from a hospital bed.

Ironically, Mantle outlived Maris by a decade, a fact the film omits. *61** does follow the facts as Maris fails to get past number fifty-nine during game 154, playing in Baltimore against tailwinds from Hurricane Esther and knuckleballs from Hoyt Wilhelm (played by former L.A. Dodgers pitcher Tom Candiotti). When Maris does break the record during the final game of the regular season, only twenty-three thousand fans attend, but they do applaud. As the film draws to a close, Maris visits Mantle in the hospital; then the screen flashes forward to Pat Maris in the hospital watching Sammy Sosa congratulate Mark McGwire. In the stands of the movie, the fictional Maris family and a real grandson of Mickey Mantle add their applause.

Crystal and Steinberg aimed for verisimilitude. Steinberg completed extensive research before writing the screenplay, and Crystal transformed the old Detroit Tigers' stadium into a convincing reproduction of Yankee Stadium in 1961, right down to the color of paint on the seats. An upper tier and skyline were added digitally. Pepper and Jane were cast for their physical resemblances to their characters and worked with former pro Reggie Smith on capturing the stance and swing of the players. Sequences featuring right-handed actor Anthony Michael Hall as lefty Whitey Ford were reversed. The result is a realistic film that offers a sympathetic but balanced portrayal of both Maris and Mantle and that recaptures a competition unmarked by steroids.

SLAP SHOT (1977)

DIRECTOR: George Roy Hill. SCREENPLAY: Nancy Dowd. PRODUCERS: Stephen Friedman, Robert J. Wunsch. CINEMATOGRAPHY: Victor Kemper. EDITING: Dede Allen. ART DIRECTION: Henry Bumstead. COSTUME DESIGN: Tom Bronson.
CAST: Paul Newman (Reggie Dunlop), Michael Ontkean (Ned Braden), Strother Martin (Joe McGrath), Jennifer Warren (Francine Dunlop), Lindsay Crouse (Lily Braden), Jerry Houser (Dave "Killer" Carlson), Steve Carlson (Steve Hanson), David Hanson (Jack Hanson), Jeff Carlson (Jeff Hanson).
RUNNING TIME: 123 minutes.
DVD: Universal Studios.

Nancy Dowd, a Smith College graduate, originally planned to write a screenplay for a documentary based on the minor league ice hockey team the Johnstown Jets, but director George Roy Hill (*Butch Cassidy and the Sundance Kid*, 1969; *The Sting*, 1973) thought the script would work better as a feature-length comedy. He was probably right: *Slap Shot* has become a sports film classic that captures the attraction of the violence it satirizes.

Paul Newman stars as Reggie Dunlop, the aging player-coach of the Charlestown Chiefs, a minor league team with a losing record and a secret owner. When the Charlestown mill closes, putting ten thousand locals out of work, Reggie fears that the team is going to fold and that he will find himself unemployed. The team manager, Joe McGrath (Strother Martin), is selling off equipment to keep the team from folding and is looking for a new job. Reggie, who needs to start winning games if he's going to get another coaching offer, tries to energize the Chiefs by circulating a rumor that they are moving to Florida; he cons a reporter, Dickie Dunn (M. Emmet Walsh), into running a story to that effect.

The team does indeed win the next game, but only after Reggie taunts the goalie until he abandons his post, allowing the Chiefs an easy score. At the next game a fight breaks out between an opponent who baits Reggie about his age, and Chiefs' player Dave Carlson (Jerry Houser), who comes to Reggie's defense. The brouhaha proves so entertaining to the fans that Reggie decides to encourage violence on the ice in order to increase attendance. Dave embraces the plan, dubs himself "Killer," and starts wearing a vampire cape.

Reggie is aided in his endeavors by three new players, the Hanson brothers (hockey pros Jeff Carlson, Steve Carlson, and David Hanson), who are born rule breakers. When first seen, they are attacking a vending machine that swallowed their change without yielding a soda. The three wear horn-rimmed glasses, keep a brick in their locker and toys in their hotel room, cross themselves in unison before taking the ice, and play like madmen, tripping, high sticking, and slamming opponents into the boards. The aggressive play quadruples attendance ("Bring the kids," urges the radio announcer, promoting the matches as "family entertainment"), and a busload of boosters starts following the Chiefs to away games. Reggie continues to scheme, hiring an ambulance to circle the arena with sirens blaring and posting a bounty on an opposing player.

Not everyone is pleased with this turn of events. The team's top scorer, Ned Braden (Michael Ontkean), heralded as both Princeton graduate and U.S. citizen, refuses to "goon it up" on the ice. Ned is especially troubled by the direction the team has taken, and to make matters worse, his marriage is shaky. Lily Braden (Lindsay Crouse) is miserable being a hockey wife in a mill town and nags Ned to give up the game and accept a job offer from his father or his father-in-law. Ned refuses the offer and in a fit of desperation bursts into the arena broadcast booth to announce on the air that he plays hockey because he hates his father. Lily drowns her sorrows in a flask while Ned moves to a cabin in the woods. Reggie is having marriage problems as well. He is separated from his wife, Francine (Jennifer Warren), and although he still loves her, she makes it clear to him that she has moved on. Reggie recognizes that Lily and Ned are headed down the same path and convinces Lily to abandon her self-destructiveness. He introduces her to Francine, who restyles Lily's hair and offers advice from her own experience.

The Chiefs pull off a winning streak that Reggie is confident will draw interest in the club from a potential buyer. After blackmailing the manager into revealing the owner's identity, Reggie pays an unexpected visit to the McCambridge household, where he learns Anita McCambridge (Kathryn Walker), now a widow with children, is the club's owner. In spite of increased revenue, Anita plans to let the team fold, figuring to net a larger profit from the tax write-off than from a sale. She also informs Reggie that she doesn't allow her children to watch hockey because she believes children who witness violence will imitate the violence, a theory that seems to be supported in the very next scene in which a reporter interviews Dave about a child who has injured another while pretending to be Killer Carlson. Dave, though, points the finger at the home environment, and the darkly comic moment is a reminder that the violent circus the Chiefs have created is embraced enthusiastically by the community of Charlestown.

After Reggie leaves the owner, he drives to Ned's cabin. Ned elects to hide in the woods during Reggie's visit, so Reggie stands in the clearing, shouting that he wants the final game to be a clean one and asking him to rejoin the team. Getting no response, Reggie announces that Lily is staying with him. That evening in the locker room, Reggie confesses to the team that there is no Florida deal and asks them to honor the sport by playing "old-time hockey." Dave removes his cape, and the Hansons chant "old-time hockey." What the Chiefs do not know is that their opponents, the Syracuse Bulldogs, have beefed up their roster with a bevy of thugs, the fiercest being Ogie Oglethorpe (played by the writer's brother, Ned Dowd). As the Chiefs attempt to play with finesse, the Bulldogs flatten them. In the locker room between periods, the battered Chiefs learn from Joe that the NHL has sent scouts, an announcement that ends the team's resolve to play a clean game. They return to the ice in attack mode, and the match disintegrates into a free-for-all. Only Ned Braden refuses to participate. He remains on the bench a disgruntled observer until he spots Lily and Francine in the stands. Both women have dressed up for the occasion and are enjoying the spectacle.

In a moment of whacky inspiration, Ned skates onto the ice and, as the bloodbath continues around him, begins a striptease. The band breaks into appropriate accompaniment, and Ned keeps gliding around the arena until he's down to his protective cup. His act brings the fighting to a halt as the brawlers become aware of what he's doing. One of the Bulldogs insists that an official stop Ned's disgusting display, and when the official refuses, punches him. The official announces that the Bulldogs must forfeit the game and hands the trophy to Ned, who leads the Chiefs in a victory lap. The film ends with a parade honoring the team. Ned and Lily are reunited; Reggie and Francine are not, but Reggie remains hopeful. He has been offered a coaching job in Minnesota and envisions a bright future.

Slap Shot has been criticized for its crude language. The dialogue is peppered with obscenities; ethnic slurs are directed toward Canadian players; insults are often crudely sexist and homophobic. While Reggie plays upon the sensitivity of opponents about their masculinity through homophobic taunts, he also stoops to vulgarity when angry, as when he tells the Chief's owner that her young son "looks like a fag" and then continues to describe a scene of the boy in a few years engaged in homosexual activity. There is no humor in this attack, and it is immediately after that Reggie decides to abandon the dirty tricks and fisticuffs on ice. It is as if he has finally realized that he has gone too far. The serious moments in the script humanize the main characters, so that the film often rises above the level of cartoonish entertainment and locker-room laughs. The same cannot be said of the sequels.

SLAP SHOT 2: BREAKING THE ICE (2002)

Director: Steve Boyum. Screenplay: Broderick Miller. Producer: Ron French. Cinematography: Joel Ransom. Editing: Craig Bassett. Music: John Frizzell. Production Design: Jo-Ann Chorney. Art Direction: Don Macaulay. Costume Design: Patricia Flynn.

Cast: Stephen Baldwin (Sean Linden), Jessica Steen (Jessie Dage), Gary Busey (Richmond Claremont), David Hemmings (Martin Fox), David Paetkau (Gordie Miller), Callum Keith (Rennie Palmberg), Steve Carlson (Steve Hanson), David Hanson (Jack Hanson), Jeff Carlson (Jeff Hanson).

Running Time: 96 minutes.

DVD: Universal Studios.

Slap Shot 2, with a different director and writer, Steve Boyum and Broderick Miller, respectively (although Nancy Dowd gets a credit for characters), carries over little from the earlier film. The Hanson brothers put in appearances in the beginning and near the end, but Reggie Dunlop, Ned Braden, and the others are not even mentioned. The film opens with the Chiefs being sold to Richmond Claremont (Gary Busey), a media mogul promoting conservative "family values." Richmond is establishing a new hockey "league" consisting of the Omaha Icebreakers, a group of Ivy League graduates, and the renamed "Super" Chiefs, a modification designed to evoke images of a train rather than Native Americans, thus avoiding the sorts of objections Ted Turner faced when he acquired the Atlanta Braves. The "league" format is based on the Harlem Globetrotters/Washington Generals program of comedy, clowning, and trick shots; however, the Chiefs, whose role is to lose, take quite a pummeling. Richmond hires a Broadway choreographer to script the matches, and the teams rehearse rather than practice. The Hanson brothers are fired almost immediately.

The Chiefs' captain, Sean Linden (Stephen Baldwin), a player with a checkered past, convinces the others to sign on for the money, the publicity, and the promised opportunity that half of the matches will be real hockey. The team's new coach, Jessie Dage (Jessica Steen), is the granddaughter of a noted hockey player and hopes that being catapulted into the limelight with the Chiefs will lead to a coaching position with a professional men's team. After she proves her skating and shooting skills on the ice and demonstrates her knowledge of hockey lore, the men accept her as coach, and Sean develops a romantic interest that eventually becomes mutual. Richmond refuses to schedule legitimate games when the performances prove to be crowd-pleasers. Sean wavers between accepting bribes from Richmond to maintain cooperation within the ranks and encouraging the Chiefs to toss the script in favor of aggressive hockey. Jessie spends three-fourths of the film on the periphery.

The Chiefs get their revenge against Richmond and the Ice Breakers when Richmond's disgruntled attorney arranges a secret sale of the Chiefs to the Hanson brothers, who have just won a huge lottery. The brothers suit up and take on the Ice Breakers in the second period of a nationally televised match, much to the horror of Richmond and the executives from Better America, a conservative group of potential investors. The Chiefs win, the fans find "real hockey" more fun than staged hockey, and Sean and Jessie kiss.

Slap Shot 2 remains on the level of locker-room humor and keeps all of the characters two-dimensional. *Slap Shot 3: The Junior League*, featuring Leslie Niesen, was released straight to DVD. The Hansons end up coaching a junior league team that includes their alleged offspring. The film is intended for younger audiences and has been scrubbed of offensive language and inappropriate sexual references.

THE SLAUGHTER RULE (2002)

DIRECTORS: Alex Smith, Andrew J. Smith. SCREENPLAY: Alex Smith, Andrew J. Smith. PRODUCER: Gavin O'Connor, Gregory O'Connor, Michael A. Robinson, David O. Russell. CINEMATOGRAPHY: Eric Alan Edwards. EDITING: Brent White. MUSIC: Jay Farrar. PRODUCTION DESIGN: John Johnson. ART DIRECTION: Raymond Pumilia. COSTUME DESIGN: Kristin M. Burke.

CAST: Ryan Gosling (Roy Chutney), David Morse (Gideon Ferguson), Clea DuVall (Skyla Sisco), David Cale (Floyd).

RUNNING TIME: 112 minutes.

DVD: Sundance Channel Home Entertainment.

A suffering young man is recruited into playing for a rural football team by a coach who has troubles of his own.

THE SLUGGER'S WIFE (1985)

DIRECTOR: Hal Ashby. SCREENPLAY: Neil Simon. PRODUCER: Ray Stark. CINEMATOGRAPHY: Caleb Deschanel. EDITING: Don Brochu, George C. Villaseñor. MUSIC: Patrick Williams. PRODUCTION DESIGN: J. Michael Riva. ART DIRECTION: Rick Carter. COSTUME DESIGN: Ann Roth.
CAST: Michael O'Keefe (Darryl Palmer), Rebecca De Mornay (Debby Huston), Martin Ritt (Burly DeVito), Randy Quaid (Moose Granger), Cleavant Derricks (Manny Alvarado), Loudon Wainwright III (Gary), Lynn Whitfield (Tina Alvarado).
RUNNING TIME: 105 minutes.
DVD: Sony Pictures.

This uneven film from the mid-1980s is about an unlikely matchup between a mediocre outfielder and an aspiring singer. The collaboration of another unlikely matchup, writer Neil Simon (*California Suite*, 1976; *The Odd Couple*, 1965) and director Hal Ashby (*Being There*, 1979; *Shampoo*, 1975) resulted in disagreements over the script, which, in turn, led to Ashby's being fired when the film was in postproduction. The finished product is a disjointed movie that relies on montage to develop character and advance plot.

The Slugger's Wife opens with a potentially comic scene as Atlanta Braves outfielder Darryl Palmer (Michael O'Keefe) and two teammates are sitting in a nightclub with their dates. When Darryl turns his seductive charm on the woman to his left, he has mistakenly targeted his friend's date instead of his own. The friend's good-natured response provides an opportunity to extend the comedy and to reveal more about Darryl's character through his interactions with the others. Instead, both Darryl's attention and the camera's shift immediately to the club singer, whom Darryl has just noticed. He leaves the table and manages to get introduced to the singer, Debby Huston (Rebecca De Mornay), who barely pauses on her way backstage. Darryl appears soon after, intent on joining the small group in her dressing room, but she turns him away, literally pushing him out the door. Because the film fails to establish a comic tone, Darryl's actions seem disturbingly aggressive rather than charmingly boyish.

What comes next is a montage that cuts between shots of Darryl at the ballpark, Debby on stage singing Prince's "little red Corvette/ Baby, you're much too fast," and Darryl stalking Debby. This cycle ends only when Darryl causes a fender bender that damages Debby's car; Darryl is pleased to have made contact, at least metaphorically, and is happy to pay all expenses. Following the accident, Darryl reappears at the nightclub with his buddies Moose (Randy Quaid) and Manny (Cleavant Derricks). He has devised a plan to win a date with Debby by having the emcee announce that Darryl, whose batting average has dropped to .239, wants to wager that he can hit two home runs in the next day's game against the Astros; if he succeeds, he wins a dinner date with Debby, and if he doesn't, he'll donate a thousand dollars to her favorite charity. Debby accepts, confident that she'll earn a donation, and perhaps reluctant to alienate the cheering Atlanta audience. Darryl gets his home runs and his date.

The film jumps to a restaurant, where the couple is being served entrees. In what may have been intended as a slapstick routine, Darryl insists on returning Debby's dish before she's had a chance to taste it while she insists it is fine. Darryl grabs the plate and hands it to the waiter, Debby takes the plate back, and the whole business is repeated several times. Again, no context, comedic or otherwise, has been established to explain Darryl's behavior. Although after spilling his wine, he claims to be nervous, nothing in his demeanor reflects discom-

Michael O'Keefe (left), Randy Quaid (center), and Cleavant Derricks (right) in *The Slugger's Wife*

fort. He simply comes across as irrational and controlling. Nevertheless, Debby sees him again, and Darryl, whose hitting continues to improve, becomes convinced that her physical presence in the stands is responsible for his streak.

Debby rejects the role of good luck charm and seems determined to pursue her career, a pursuit that requires she go on her own road trips. Just before she leaves for a gig in Boston, Darryl protests that he wants to support her because she "won't be singing in clubs for the rest of [her] life." This line, coming from a struggling professional athlete, should carry some ironic twinge, but the film neglects to seize the moment. After a brief kiss and another montage cutting between ballpark and nightclub, Darryl and Debby are in bed, and she's wondering how she'll juggle career and relationship. Soon Darryl proposes. While Debby explains that she doesn't want to be a baseball wife, Darryl interrupts, repeating "Do you love me?" with the same insistence he displayed about returning her entrée on their first date, and the film jumps to the wedding.

Darryl's controlling behavior intensifies, and Debby transforms from an assertive, direct woman to a passive, deceptive one. Aboard the team plane, Darryl wakes Debby, who just wants to sleep, and demands she eat a roll he's had the flight attendant heat up; Darryl is so intent on playing the attentive husband that he is completely inconsiderate of her wishes. Unable to stand up to Darryl, who refuses to listen, Debby resorts to lying in order to gain time to rehearse her act. When she misses a game, Darryl plays poorly, then sulks at home. Not surprisingly, he returns home one evening to find she's packed her bags and left, pursuing an opportunity for a recording contract.

Darryl responds by getting drunk and creating havoc. After he sobers up and after the Braves' manager, Burly DeVito (Martin Ritt), advises him to give Debby some space, Darryl sets off in pursuit. When he finds her having breakfast at a diner with a fellow musician, Darryl slugs the guy, then throws chairs through the window.

At this point the movie attempts to shift into comic mode, and Burly devises a scheme to get Darryl out of his slump and return the team to the win column. Darryl's earlier streak not only has brought him within reach of Roger Maris's record of sixty-one home runs in a single season, but has also put the Braves in contention for the pennant. Burly's plan is to relieve Darryl's anxieties by getting him "drunk and laid." With the assistance of Manny and Moose, Burly reaches his first objective, but Darryl is simply too much in love with his estranged wife to commit adultery. Burly comes up with an even more ludicrous idea after Darryl is beaned during batting practice. While Darryl is recuperating in the hospital and suffering from blurred vision, Burly talks another singer into pretending to be Debby. The ruse never completely convinces Darryl, but even without Debby he manages to tie Maris's record and take the team to the final deciding game against the Astros.

Debby returns home just before the game and wants to talk. Again, Darryl doesn't want to listen, but this time he offers an explanation: if he doesn't know whether she's returning, then his performance during the game will be his own. Debby sees this as a sign that Darryl has matured. Darryl hits number sixty-two, and the game comes down to the bottom of the ninth with two outs and the Braves trailing by a run. Here, the script deviates from the expected. Darryl gets a hit, but not a homer, and the next batter, Moose, hits a long ball that is caught at the wall; the Braves lose the pennant. In a touching scene, Debby tells Darryl that she is willing to keep the door open but that for now she is pursuing her own dreams.

Even though it sidesteps a traditional Hollywood ending, the film remains unconvincing. Characterization is so shallow that Darryl comes across as more psychotic than sympathetic much of the time, and his newly subdued affect doesn't ring true. Debby never recaptures the sense of independence and confidence she displayed before she became involved with Darryl, in spite of her decision to follow her own dream.

One might expect from the title that the film is about a woman who is defined by her relationship to her husband and that there may be a political subtext. However, the conflict between Debby and Darryl plays out as one that is exclusively personal rather than as one that is representative of the seismic cultural shift brought on by the women's movement and the Equal Employment Opportunity Commission. *The Slugger's Wife* simply lacks a center, and hanging its fractured plotlines on a formulaic sports film structure doesn't win the game with a lone hit in the bottom of the ninth.

SOCCER DOG: THE MOVIE (1999)

DIRECTOR: Tony Giglio. SCREENPLAY: Daniel Forman. PRODUCERS: John H. Brister, Tony Giglio. CINEMATOGRAPHY: Christopher Duddy. EDITING: Alan Z. McCurdy. MUSIC: Victoria Dolceamore. PRODUCTION DESIGN: Nanette Vanderbilt. ART DIRECTION: Pamela Lansden. COSTUME DESIGN: Cynthia Hart.

CAST: James Marshall (Alden), Olivia d'Abo (Elena), Jeremy Foley (Clay), Sam McMurray (Coach Shaw).

RUNNING TIME: 98 minutes.

DVD: Sony Pictures.

This is another family film about an animal that displays exceptional skills, this time a dog that plays soccer.

SOMEBODY UP THERE LIKES ME (1956)

DIRECTOR: Robert Wise. SCREENPLAY: Ernest Lehman, based on the memoir by Rocky Graziano. PRODUCER: Charles Schnee. CINEMATOGRAPHY: Joseph Ruttenberg. EDITING: Albert Akst. MUSIC: Bronislau Kaper. ART DIRECTION: Malcolm Brown, Cedric Gibbons. SET DECORATION: Keogh Gleason, Edwin B. Willis.

CAST: Paul Newman (Rocky Graziano), Pier Angeli (Norma Skittish), Everett Sloane (Irving Cohen), Eileen Heckart (Rocky's mother), Sal Mineo (Romolo), Harold J. Stone (Nick Barbella).

RUNNING TIME: 113 minutes. B&W.

ACADEMY AWARDS: Best Art Direction/Set Decoration, Black-and-White; Best Cinematography, Black-and-White. NOMINATION: Best Editing.

DVD: Warner Home Video.

Middleweight boxing champion Rocky Graziano and veteran screenwriter Ernest Lehman collaborated in adapting Graziano's autobiography into a critically and financially successful biopic. When James Dean, who was originally slated to play Graziano, was unable to appear, Paul Newman, whose only previous film role was in *The Silver Chalice* (1954), replaced him and gave a sterling performance. To establish an authentic ring, the film begins with a Graziano quotation: "This is the way I remember it—definitely."

The first sequence shows Nick Barbella (Harold J. Stone) giving young Rocky (Terry Rangno) a boxing lesson in front of some of his drinking buddies. The lesson ends with Rocky getting a bloody nose, throwing the boxing gloves at his inebriated dad, and running out into the street, where two policemen try to capture him. When they fail, one comments, "Another greaseball on his way. In ten years he'll be at the death house at Sing Sing." That running episode segues into a shot of an older Rocky (Newman) also running from the police and being saved by his devoted mother (Eileen Heckart), who worries about his future. When his father confronts him, Rocky is more than a match for him physically and criticizes him.

As if to give credence to the police prediction, the next few scenes feature a series of criminal activities perpetrated by Rocky and his associates—stealing tires from a car, breaking into vending machines, fighting another gang—which results in Rocky and Romolo (Sal Mineo) being arrested. While Romolo escapes incarceration and is assigned to parental supervision, Rocky, whose father does not appear at the hearing, is sent to Mackinaw for an indeterminate sentence. Vowing not to be "broken," Rocky uses a cigarette to burn the hand of the warden, who then sends him to the reformatory. There on a work gang he knocks down a guard, takes his gun, and is prepared to shoot him before he is stopped by another inmate. At Riker's Island, his next stop, he does thirty days in the "hole" for more infractions. When his mother, whose mental derangement Rocky is partially responsible for, visits him, she tells him that he must reform or she will disown him. She says, "No one can help you but yourself." This theme pervades the film.

On January 6, 1942, Rocky completes his sentence, only to be drafted into the army, where he also refuses to take orders. When the military police arrest him, he assaults the captain in charge and goes AWOL. He returns to New York, where he attempts to contact Frankie Peppo (Robert Loggia), a hoodlum/fight promoter who will prove responsible for many of Rocky's later problems. At Stillman's Gym Rocky meets Irving Cohen (Everett Sloan), who becomes his manager and mentor. To earn some cash, Rocky spars with a promising fighter, whom he knocks out. While AWOL he has six fights, winning them all by knockouts. When the army catches up with him, Rocky receives a dishonorable discharge and is sentenced to a year at Leavenworth, where he learns to box and gets into prime condition. According to his coach, Rocky has one thing other boxers lack: hate.

When he is released, Rocky returns to fighting for Irving and revisits his parents. He learns that his mother blames herself for his father's failure because she made him give up his dreams of becoming a professional boxer, and he also meets his sister's friend, Norma Skittish (Pier Angeli). He initially keeps his distance, maintaining that "love is for the birds." Norma likes romantic movies and dislikes fighting, but Rocky says that boxing makes him feel "important." Eventually, she will come to understand that "it's all he's got" and will learn not to make the same mistake Rocky's mother made.

Although it is clear that he loves Norma, Rocky is reluctant to make a commitment. After the couple argue, they reconcile, but he misses an important fight and then must confess to the New York Boxing Commissioner that love was the reason. Rocky is so distracted by his relationship with Norma that Irving advises him to either get rid of her or marry her. According to his manager, the responsibility will be good for him, and after a delay in front of the courthouse, Norma finally nudges him past his excuses and into marriage. Rocky continues to fight and win, even though he is battered in the process. In a lighter sequence the audience sees a series of daughter Audrey's frightened reactions to the sight of her father's bandaged face.

After successive wins, Rocky gets his title shot at Tony Zale, the current middleweight champion, but he loses the fight. Before there can be a rematch, Rocky has a "tune-up" scheduled, but Frankie Peppo's reappearance threatens his future. Frankie wants Rocky to take $1 million to throw the fight or "someone" will expose Rocky's criminal past and dishonorable discharge. Rocky refuses, but when Frankie and some muscle appear at Stillman's, he is so concerned that he fakes a back injury to cancel the fight. When he returns from recuperating in Florida, District Attorney Hogan's men bring him in for questioning. They know about the proposed fix and want Rocky to identify the fixers. When he refuses, the commission revokes his license and cancels the fight between him and Tony.

Irving arranges for the bout to be rescheduled for Chicago, but Rocky is despondent about how his image has been shattered and his future ruined. Norma tells him, however, that he has to live with his past and own his behavior. He is not an "innocent bystander." Unable to face the truth, Rocky retreats to New York and his old haunts. He even tries to contact Frankie again. He runs into Romolo, who wants money for a gun and plans to open a bookie joint; Rocky tries to warn Romolo to change his ways, but fails to influence his former friend. When Rocky goes to the local candy store, Benny (Joseph Buloff), the philosopher/proprietor, offers him a rehash of Norma's comments. On his way to his parents' place, Rocky sees what his past has been and what it could be again as cops run in other greaseballs. Another confrontation with his father follows, but this time there is reconciliation between the two men. Rocky says, "It ain't over for me" and asks his father what he can do for him. "Be a champ," his father replies. Rocky returns to Chicago without talking to Frankie, brings Norma some ice cream from Bennie's (she's pregnant again), and prepares for the rematch.

The fight, broadcast by famous sports announcer Harry Wismer, goes Tony's way at first in what begins to look like a reenactment of the first bout. The camera cuts from the fight to the deserted streets in Rocky's neighborhood, then to the spectators—the fans at the fight, Norma, Rocky's parents watching on television, and bar patrons, among them Rocky's Leavenworth boxing coach. Though he has such serious cuts around his eyes that the referee says he would stop the fight if it were not the championship, Rocky perseveres, makes a comeback, and pummels Tony on the ropes until the referee calls the champ out. Almost immediately, the streets in Rocky's neighborhood come alive. The film segues into a parade with Rocky, Norma, his parents, and Irving waving to the fans. Rocky knows that his days as champ are numbered but insists that he has what he wants. He has been fortunate because "somebody up there likes me," the title song sung by Perry Como and written by Sammy Cahn.

Despite its storybook ending, one not palatable in a more cynical world, the film is excellent. Lehman was nominated for a Writer's Guild Award for the Best Written American Drama; Robert Wise was nominated by the Directors' Guild for Outstanding Directorial Achievement in Motion Pictures; and Joseph Ruttenberg won the Oscar for Best Cinematography. The editing for the film and the art direction also received Oscar nominations. Appearing in minor roles were actors who would go on to larger roles, including Sal Mineo, Robert Loggia, Steve McQueen, and Dean Jones.

SPACE JAM (1996)

Director: Joe Pytka. Screenplay: Leo Benvenuti, Steve Rudnick, Timothy Harris, Herschel Weingrod. Producers: Daniel Goldberg, Joe Medjuck, Ivan Reitman, Ron Tippe. Cinematography: Michael Chapman. Editing: Sheldon Kahn. Music: James Newton Howard. Production Design: Geoffrey Kirkland. Art Direction: David Klassen. Costume Design: Marlene Stewart.

Cast: Michael Jordan (himself), Billy West (Bugs Bunny, Elmer Fudd—voices), Wayne Knight (Stan Podolak), Theresa Randle (Juanita Jordan), Bill Murray (himself).

Running Time: 88 minutes.

DVD: Warner Home Video.

Michael Jordan is recruited into playing an intergalactic basketball game to save the earth, alongside Bugs Bunny, Daffy Duck, and other Warner Bros. animated icons. Several other basketball greats—including Larry Bird, Charles Barkley, and Patrick Ewing—also appear.

SPEED RACER (2008)

Directors: Andy Wachowski, Larry Wachowski. Screenplay: Andy Wachowski, Larry Wachowski, based on the Japanese animated television series. Producers: Grant Hill, Joel Silver, Andy Wachowski, Larry Wachowski. Cinematography: David Tattersall. Editing: Roger Barton, Zach Staenberg. Music: Michael Giacchino. Production Design: Owen Paterson. Art Direction: Hugo Bateup, Marco Bittner Rosser, Sebastian Krawinkel. Costume Design: Kym Barrett.

Cast: Emile Hirsch (Speed Racer), Christina Ricci (Trixie), John Goodman (Pops Racer), Susan Sarandon (Mom Racer), Paulie Litt (Spritle), Kick Curry (Sparky), Matthew Fox (Racer X).

Running Time: 135 minutes.

DVD: Warner Home Video.

A live-action film adapted from the Japanese cartoon series of the 1960s about a teen racer, his girlfriend, and his family.

SPEEDWAY (1968)

DIRECTOR: Norman Taurog. SCREENPLAY: Phillip Shuken. PRODUCER: Douglas Laurence. CINEMATOGRAPHY: Joseph Ruttenberg. EDITING: Richard Farrell. MUSIC: Jeff Alexander. ART DIRECTION: Leroy Coleman, George W. Davis.
CAST: Elvis Presley (Steve Grayson), Nancy Sinatra (Susan Jacks), Bill Bixby (Kenny Donford), Gale Gordon (R. W. Hepworth).
RUNNING TIME: 94 minutes.
DVD: Warner Home Video.

Between songs, Elvis plays a stock-car driver and Nancy Sinatra is an IRS agent on his tracks. Several real drivers, including Richard Petty and Cale Yarborough, appear in the film.

SPINOUT (1966)

DIRECTOR: Norman Taurog. SCREENPLAY: Theodore J. Flicker, George Kirgo. PRODUCER: Joe Pasternak. CINEMATOGRAPHY: Daniel L. Fapp. EDITING: Rita Roland. MUSIC: George Stoll. ART DIRECTION: Edward Carfagno, George W. Davis.
CAST: Elvis Presley (Mike McCoy), Shelley Fabares (Cynthia Foxhugh), Diane McBain (Diana St. Clair), Dodie Marshall (Susan), Deborah Walley (Les), Carl Betz (Howard Foxhugh).
RUNNING TIME: 90 minutes.
DVD: Warner Home Video.

Elvis alternates between singing and driving in this contrived film that failed to produce any hits for the King.

SPIRIT OF YOUTH (1938)

DIRECTOR: Harry L. Fraser. SCREENPLAY: Arthur Hoerl. PRODUCER: Lew Golder. CINEMATOGRAPHY: Robert Cline. EDITING: Carl Pierson. MUSIC: Elliot Carpenter, Clarence Muse. PRODUCTION DESIGN: Frank Paul Sylos.
CAST: Joe Louis (Joe Thomas), Clarence Muse (Frankie Walburn), Edna Mae Harris (Mary Bowdin), Mae Turner (Flora Bailey), Cleo Desmond (Nora Thomas), Mantan Moreland (Crickie Fitzgibbons), Jewel Smith (Duke Emerald).
RUNNING TIME: 66 minutes. B&W.
DVD: Echo Bridge Home Entertainment.

Joe Louis, world heavyweight boxing champion from 1937 to 1949, makes his acting debut as Joe Thomas, a boxer whose life and career path parallel those of Louis. *Spirit of Youth* was produced by Globe Pictures for African American theaters when racial segregation was legal in the South and common elsewhere in the country. The film was released a few months before Louis defended his title against the German Max Schmeling, to whom Louis had lost in 1936; with Hitler's rise to power and the threat of war in Europe, Americans of all races united in their support of Louis. Consequently, *Spirit of Youth* became one of the first crossover films and did well with white audiences in spite of concern that it would not be well received, especially in the South, because the Joe Thomas character is shown defeating white boxers.

The film opens in Birmingham, Alabama, in the 1920s in an African American neighborhood. Nora Thomas (Cleo Desmond) summons her children, Joe and Eleanor, inside to clean up. It is their father's birthday, and he is expected home from work shortly. However, when Mr. Thomas (Jess Lee Brooks) returns, it is on a stretcher. He has been injured on the job and left paralyzed. While the town doctor administers to Joe's father, Joe and the doctor's daughter Mary talk outside. Although he is still a boy, Joe is determined to work to help support the family.

Years pass rapidly, indicated by the turning of a calendar until it is 1932, and Joe is setting out for Michigan, where he believes there is more opportunity. Joe says goodbye to Mary (Edna Mae Harris), with whom he has remained close, and confides his desire "to get ahead and be somebody and do things for Momma and Poppa." At his first job as a dishwasher, he meets Crickie Fitzgibbons (Mantan Moreland), who becomes a good friend; Crickie manages to get them fired by breaking some dishes, but he has a knack for finding work. At their next job, shifting boxes, Crickie knocks over a container and is physically punished by a supervisor. Joe tries to intervene peaceably, but when the man swings at Joe, Joe's quick reflexes leave the man on the ground and both Joe and Crickie unemployed once more. Crickie, recognizing Joe's natural talent, approaches a fight promoter, Frankie Walburn (Clarence Muse). The promoter isn't interested at the time, but pays Crickie well for polishing his car. Crickie "invests" part of the money by taking Joe to a boxing match and encouraging him to become a fighter. Joe's father has just died, and his mother and sister (Marguerite Whitten) will be coming to live with him, so Joe has added motivation to pursue a profession that promises to be lucrative.

The scene shifts to the Chicago Golden Gloves tournament, which Joe wins after knocking out a succession of opponents. Celebrating with Crickie at the Bluebird Café (a setting that leads to a musical number), Joe meets the owner, Duke Emerald (Jewel Smith), and is reintroduced to Frankie Walburn, who wants to handle him. Before agreeing, Joe asks his mother for advice, and she gives him her blessing, provided he always fight fairly and honestly. Joe begins training in earnest. Duke appears during a session, bringing along Flora Bailey (Mae Turner), a performer from the club. Frankie tries to shoo Flora away, but it is clear that she and Joe are attracted to each other. Meanwhile, back at home, Mary has arrived for an extended visit. Joe is delighted to see her, but at this point, he regards her more as a family member than as a romantic interest.

Success comes early for Joe; undefeated, he is seen as a rising star. Duke has profited from betting on him and presents Flora with a bracelet. However, he does not appear to be courting Flora. In fact, he seems to encourage her growing relationship with Joe. As Joe spends more time at the Bluebird and with Flora, he neglects his training, and rumors spread that Duke is betting heavily against Joe in the upcoming bout. Frankie confronts Duke, but gains no confession from the club owner, who claims Joe as a good friend. Crickie, who is also concerned about Joe, talks with his mother, Eleanor, and Mary, who approaches Flora about Joe's training. Mary does not appear to be jealous when she talks with Flora, but afterward, she tells Frankie that she thinks Joe loves Flora. Mary packs her bags and leaves without saying goodbye to Joe.

Joe continues closing down the Bluebird with Flora. As Frankie and Crickie have feared, Joe loses his next fight. Later, Frankie takes Joe to a restaurant. One of Frankie's former fighters, now a broken-down drunkard, is at the bar. The man staggers over to their table and admits to Frankie that he destroyed his career by failing to train. Frankie hands him a few dollars, and the old boxer returns to the bar and buys drinks. Suddenly, Joe has lost his appetite; he goes back home, where his mother is waiting up for him. Joe returns to training. A montage of his workouts is layered with more peeling leaves from the calendar. Although Joe gets himself into prime physical condition, Frank and Flora note that he's lacking in spirit. Flora asks Joe about Mary, and Joe responds sadly that she has gone. Then he admits that he loves Mary.

On the night of Joe's match, he is fit, but dispirited. Recognizing that Joe misses Mary, Flora and Crickie drive off to retrieve Mary, who is listening to the fight on the radio. When they leave Mary's, round 3 is in progress, and Joe is fighting mechanically. As the group races through traffic, Joe barely holds up. In the ninth round he is knocked down and literally saved by the bell, which rings at the eight count. Joe is dragged to his corner. Crickie, who has just arrived, points out Mary sitting next to Flora in the crowd. Rejuvenated, Joe comes out swinging and knocks out his opponent. Flora slips discretely away, but Mary stays. At a banquet in Joe's honor, he tells the assembled group, "It's the little things you do day by day that count," and on that note, the film concludes.

Louis's acting is as mechanical as his fighting in the early rounds of his crucial match, perhaps because his character is so flat. As in the later biopic, *The Joe Louis Story* (1953), the boxer's success is credited to his adherence to a strong work ethic—natural talent alone is not enough.

SPLIT DECISIONS (1988)

DIRECTOR: David Drury. SCREENPLAY: David Fallon. PRODUCER: Joe Wizan. CINEMATOGRAPHY: Timothy Suhrstedt. EDITING: Jeff Freeman, Thomas Stanford, John W. Wheeler. MUSIC: Basil Poledouris. ART DIRECTION: Michael Z. Hanan. COSTUME DESIGN: Hilary Wright.

CAST: Gene Hackman (Dan McGuinn), Craig Sheffer (Eddie McGuinn), Jeff Fahey (Ray McGuinn), Jennifer Beals (Barbara Uribe), John McLiam (Pop McGuinn).

RUNNING TIME: 95 minutes.

DVD: Platinum Disc.

This drama is about three generations of boxers, including an estranged son who refuses to take a dive—with the usual consequences.

THE SQUARE RING (1952)

DIRECTORS: Basil Dearden, Michael Relph. SCREENPLAY: Robert Westerby, based on the play by Ralph W. Peterson. PRODUCERS: Basil Dearden, Michael Relph. CINEMATOGRAPHY: Gordon Dines, Otto Heller. EDITING: Peter Bezencenet. MUSIC: Dock Mathieson. ART DIRECTION: Jim Morahan. COSTUME DESIGN: Anthony Mendleson.

CAST: Jack Warner (Danny Felton), Robert Beatty (Jim "Kid" Curtis), Bill Owen (Happy Burns), Maxwell Reed (Rick Martell), Bill Travers (Rowdie Rawlings), Joan Collins (Frankie).

RUNNING TIME: 80 minutes.

DVD: StudioCanal (UK: PAL).

This British film is about a handful of boxers and how they chose to become fighters.

SQUEEZE PLAY (1979)

DIRECTOR: Lloyd Kaufman. SCREENPLAY: Charles Kaufman, Haim Pekelis. PRODUCERS: Michael Herz, Lloyd Kaufman. CINEMATOGRAPHY: Lloyd Kaufman. EDITING: George T. Norris. COSTUME DESIGN: Karen Galonough.

CAST: Jenni Hetrick (Samantha), Jim Harris (Wes), Diana Valentien (Maureen), Helen Campitelli (Jamie), Sonya Jennings (Max), Melissa Michaels (Mary Lou), Rick Giltin (Fred).

RUNNING TIME: 96 minutes.

DVD: Troma.

In this low-budget, low-standard comedy, an all-male softball team is challenged by a squad made up of their wives and girlfriends who are sick of being taken for granted.

STEALING HOME (1988)

DIRECTORS: Steven Kampmann, William Porter (Aldis). SCREENPLAY: Steven Kampmann, William Porter (Aldis). PRODUCERS:

Hank Moonjean, Thom Mount. CINEMATOGRAPHY: Bobby Byrne. EDITING: Antony Gibbs. MUSIC: David Foster. PRODUCTION DESIGN: Vaughan Edwards. COSTUME DESIGN: Robert de Mora.

CAST: Mark Harmon (Billy Wyatt), Jodie Foster (Katie Chandler), William McNamara (young Billy Wyatt), Blair Brown (Ginny Wyatt), Harold Ramis (Alan Appleby), Jonathan Silverman (young Alan Appleby).

RUNNING TIME: 98 minutes.

DVD: Warner Home Video.

After a former girlfriend commits suicide, a has-been baseball player recalls their times together.

STICK IT (2006)

DIRECTOR: Jessica Bendinger. SCREENPLAY: Jessica Bendinger. PRODUCER: Gail Lyon. CINEMATOGRAPHY: Daryn Okada. EDITING: Troy Takaki. MUSIC: Michael Simpson. PRODUCTION DESIGN: Bruce Curtis. COSTUME DESIGN: Carol Ramsey.

CAST: Jeff Bridges (Burt Vickerman), Missy Peregrym (Haley Graham), Vanessa Lengies (Joanne Charis), Nikki SooHoo (Wei Wei Wong), Maddy Curley (Mina Hoyt), Kellan Lutz (Frank), Jon Gries (Brice Graham), Polly Holliday (Judge Wiestrich), Julie Warner (Mrs. Charis).

RUNNING TIME: 103 minutes.

DVD: Touchstone / Disney.

Stick It covers the world of women's gymnastics, including ambitious moms, jealous contestants, and relationships between coaches and gymnasts. However, what emerges is not so much a critique of the sport as it is a good-natured though superficial introduction to problems that are swept away in less than two hours of viewing time.

The opening shots call to mind *The Lords of Dogtown* (2005), a film about renegade skateboarding, as three young people with bicycles and skateboards use the swimming pools in a housing development as their venue for daredevil stunts. When one of the three crashes through a window and does fourteen thousand dollars' worth of damages, alarms sound, the police arrive, and the one person they apprehend turns out to be a girl, Haley Graham (Missy Peregrym), who has made a habit of confronting authority. At her hearing the judge gives her a choice: she will have to do her juvie time at the rigorous Texas Military Academy or at the VGA (Vickerman Gymnastic Academy), which is run by Burt Vickerman (Jeff Bridges).

Haley, who has little choice, opts for VGA, where she gets a hostile reception from her fellow gymnasts, including the spoiled Joanne Charis (Vanessa Lengies), who is ready to sacrifice a real life for a shot at the Olympics. Initially, Burt seems like a tyrant, proclaiming, "This [the gymnastics academy] isn't the real world; it's my world." Defiant, Haley refuses to train, but Burt reminds her that jail is her alternative. Haley maintains that the sport is a "joke" and explains her past achievements are the result of her being, not talented, but "obedient," which she no longer wants to be. When she realizes that she has nowhere else to go and that nobody really cares what she does, she trains on her own, but she eventually admits that she "needs to control [her] tricks," that she needs to stop "popping her clutch," Burt's phrase for not exercising restraint, thereby risking injury. For the first meet, the IG Classic, Burt does not name her to the team. Her protests result in an in-house competition. She advises some of her teammates to take more risks, and predictably they do not score well. Joanne tells them that Haley is deliberately sabotaging them. Haley performs impressively and makes the team. Later, she explains to Burt that in the previous Olympics she walked off the junior team, thereby disqualifying them, because she learned another coach was involved with her mother and that her parents were divorcing.

At another hearing before her judge, Haley learns that Burt has written a letter in her defense, and she tells him, "I completely misjudged you." Haley decides to go out for the Olympic team, but she insists that Burt, an accomplished gymnast before being severely injured, work on the trampoline. He agrees, but is injured again. As the gymnasts gather around Burt, Joanne and her mother get into a spat. Joanne wants to go to the prom, but her mother rejects the idea because the tryouts are approaching. When Burt tries to intercede on Joanne's behalf, Joanne's mother (Julie Warner) turns on Burt, calling him a "has-been coach." Joanne stands up to her mother and demonstrates that she is not ready to give everything up for a chance at the Olympics.

At the tryouts Haley apologizes to Tricia Skilken (Tarah Paige), who failed to make the last Olympics because of Haley's actions. Tricia will have none of it. Then one of the gymnasts performs brilliantly, but is awarded a 9.5 instead of a perfect 10. When Burt asks the explanation for the deduction, he is told that part of his gymnast's bra was showing. What follows is a burlesque as Haley suggests that the gymnasts imagine the judges trying to do gymnastic stunts. An up-tight male judge does a fantasy performance that is amusing and fairly rhythmic, at least until he loses his trousers. Haley then challenges the judges and the vagaries of judges by deliberately exposing part of her bra and being disqualified. Other gymnasts follow suit, leaving no one for the judges to evaluate. The television announcers declare that the "athletes are sending a message to the judges" and that the meet has turned into a battle between the Old School ("competence") and the New School ("flash"). Finally, Haley gets her chance to compete in the floor exercise. Just before she begins, she wishes she had someone who cared about her. Burt steps up to be the one and is so emotional he can barely utter the words "I'm so proud to be your coach." He has become, in spite of himself, her surrogate father. The only thing in Haley's way is Tricia, who deliberately scratches, thereby forgiving Haley.

***STRANGERS ON A TRAIN* (1951)**

DIRECTOR: Alfred Hitchcock. SCREENPLAY: Raymond Chandler, Czenzi Ormonde, based on the novel by Patricia Highsmith. PRODUCER: Alfred Hitchcock. CINEMATOGRAPHY: Robert Burks. EDITING: William Ziegler. MUSIC: Dimitri Tiomkin. ART DIRECTION: Ted Haworth.

CAST: Robert Walker (Bruno Anthony), Farley Granger (Guy Haines), Ruth Roman (Anne Morton), Leo G. Carroll (Senator Morton), Patricia Hitchcock (Barbara Morton), Marion Lorne (Mrs. Anthony), Kasey Rogers (Miriam Joyce Haines), Jonathan Hale (Mr. Antony).

RUNNING TIME: 101 minutes. B&W.

ACADEMY AWARD NOMINATION: Best Cinematography, Black-and-White.

DVD: Warner Home Video.

In this Alfred Hitchcock thriller based on the Patricia Highsmith novel, a tennis player who works for a U.S. senator (Leo G. Carroll) finds his future in jeopardy when he crosses paths with a madman. Unlike Highsmith's portrayal, in which the hero succumbs to temptation and becomes as twisted as the villain by the book's conclusion, Hitchcock's treatment allows the main character, Guy Haines (Farley Granger), to remain sympathetic while the villain, Bruno Anthony (Robert Walker), is the embodiment of evil. Yet the film still maintains a close connection between the two characters, suggesting that virtue, reason, and order are more readily subverted than the appearances of a normal world would suggest.

Guy Haines's first encounter with Bruno Anthony appears to be a chance meeting as Guy takes a seat on a train across from Bruno, who quickly recognizes Guy and engages him in conversation. At first Bruno comes across as an obnoxious fan, one who has followed Guy's career closely and who is eager to confirm rumors that Guy is seeking a divorce from an unfaithful wife in order to marry Senator Morton's daughter. Although Guy is uncomfortable talking about his personal life, he is easily manipulated into revealing both that he is very angry with his wife and that he is on his way to visit her to persuade her to agree to a divorce.

Over lunch in Bruno's compartment, Bruno changes the topic to murder, claiming that everyone, at some point in their lives, would like to kill someone. As an example, he cites his desire to get rid of his wealthy father, who expects Bruno to work for a living; he also suggests that Guy would be happy if his wife were dead. Soon Bruno shares his plan for the perfect murder: two strangers meet on a train and agree to commit each other's murder. Since the murderer has no link to the victim and no obvious connection with the most likely suspect, the crimes will be unsolvable.

Realizing that Bruno is unbalanced, Guy makes a quick escape from his company and continues on to his meeting with Miriam (Laura Elliott), his estranged wife. At the music store where Miriam works, the two retreat to a sound-proof glass listening booth, where Miriam tells Guy that although she is pregnant with another man's child, she has decided against a divorce now that Guy has become a successful athlete and has a promising career in Washington. In the quarrel that follows, Guy grabs Miriam roughly, an action witnessed by others in the store. Afterward, he calls Anne Morton (Ruth Roman), the senator's daughter whom he loves, and, still in a rage, states he would like to strangle Miriam. Guy then continues to a tennis match in South Hampton, where he receives a telephone call from Bruno reminding him of the scheme, which he calls a "crisscross." Guy dismisses the call, but Bruno plans to carry out his end of the deal.

Bruno follows Miriam, who is with two young men, to an amusement park. Although Miriam soon becomes aware of Bruno's presence, she seems flattered by what she perceives as his interest and offers him encouraging smiles over the shoulders of her escorts. When Miriam and her friends take a boat through the Tunnel of Love to a small island, Bruno is right behind them, and as soon as Miriam is separated from her friends in the darkness, Bruno strangles her, taking with him her glasses.

Bruno catches up with Guy just before the police arrive to inform him of Miriam's death and question him about his alibi. Horrified by the crime, Guy first wants to report Bruno to the police, but Bruno convinces Guy that the two will be found equally guilty; consequently, Guy withholds the truth from the police and from the Morton family. But Guy is not successful in convincing the police of his innocence; he does not have a good alibi, and his manner suggests something amiss. A detective is assigned to watch him; meanwhile, Bruno stalks Guy, pressuring him to carry out his part of "the agreement." In one humorous scene at a tennis match, the camera turns to a shot of the crowd, where Bruno stands out as the lone person whose head is not turning from side to side, following the ball.

Tension returns quickly to the film in the next scene, where Bruno has managed an introduction to Anne Morton, and Guy discovers the two sitting at a table with mutual acquaintances. As Bruno speaks French with one of the acquaintances, Anne's flirtatious younger sister, Barbara (Patricia Hitchcock, the director's daughter), joins the group. When Bruno is introduced, he stares transfixed at Barbara, who wears glasses and bears a slight resemblance to Miriam. Bruno has a flashback to the murder, and it seems that Barbara has become a potential victim.

The next evening Bruno appears at a formal party thrown by the Mortons. He joins two middle-aged women and begins to discuss his favorite topic, murder. The two women soon become caught up in murderous fantasies, and one agrees to "lend" her neck to Bruno for a demonstration of strangulation. At that moment, Barbara appears, and Bruno begins to strangle the woman in earnest while staring at Barbara. His hold is broken only when someone screams. Bruno, conveniently, passes out. After another confrontation with Guy, Bruno leaves. At this point, Anne has figured that Bruno is responsible for Miriam's death. She confronts Guy, who confesses all and explains his current dilemma. The two devise separate plans to approach Bruno's parents, but both fail, and Bruno is enraged. He realizes that Guy will never fulfill what Bruno believes to be an obligation, so Bruno determines to frame Guy for Miriam's death by planting evidence at the crime scene—a monogrammed cigarette lighter that Guy carelessly left in Bruno's train compartment when they first met.

Guy must stop Bruno, but in order to avoid arousing the suspicion of the police, he can't miss his scheduled tennis match against Frank Reynolds at Forest Hills. Since Bruno is in Alexandria, Virginia, and the murder scene is close to New York, Guy plans to play quickly instead of maintaining his usual slow pace, defeat Reynolds in straight sets, and sneak off to the train station, arriving at the amusement park before Bruno.

In typically Hitchcockian fashion, suspense builds as the scene shifts between Guy's frenetic match and Bruno's progress. Assisted by Barbara, Guy makes his getaway with the police not far behind. He arrives at the amusement park shortly after Bruno, and a chase ensues with both Guy and the police in pursuit. When Bruno leaps onto the carousel, an officer shoots at him but hits the operator, who falls against the controls, sending the carousel into high gear. Bruno and Guy struggle as the carousel gains speed. In the midst of the pandemonium, a park worker crawls under the carousel to reach the controls, finally bringing the machine to a screeching halt. Guy—and all of the riders—are unhurt, but Bruno is crushed under the platform and dies with the incriminating lighter in his hand.

Strangers on a Train is dramatically filmed, using shadows and railings in scenes with Guy and Bruno to connect Guy's guilt to Bruno's crime. Parallel editing during the tennis match continues this theme of connection between good and evil. The carousel scene, which required that a technician actually crawl under the moving platform, exemplifies an innocent world spinning out of control.

For the tennis match, Granger, who had taken lessons from Don Budge, performed convincingly against the athlete Reynolds. Robert Walker's performance is considered the best of his career, but, sadly, he died before the film was released.

THE STRATTON STORY (1949)

DIRECTOR: Sam Wood. SCREENPLAY: Douglas Morrow, Guy Trosper. STORY: Douglas Morrow. PRODUCER: Jack Cummings. CINEMATOGRAPHY: Harold Rosson. EDITING: Ben Lewis. MUSIC: Adolph Deutsch. ART DIRECTION: Cedric Gibbons, Paul Groesse. COSTUME DESIGN: Helen Rose.

CAST: James Stewart (Monty Stratton), June Allyson (Ethel Stratton), Frank Morgan (Barney Wile), Agnes Moorehead (Monty's mother), Bill Williams (Eddie Dibson), Bruce Cowling (Ted Lyons), Cliff Clark (Josh Higgins).
RUNNING TIME: 106 minutes. B&W
ACADEMY AWARDS: Best Motion Picture Story.
DVD: MGM.

Sam Wood (*The Pride of the Yankees*, 1942) directed this biopic based on the life of pitcher Monty Stratton, whose major league career was halted when he lost a leg after a hunting accident. As with the earlier film about Lou Gehrig, Wood follows the theme of individual courage in the face of adversity. Jimmy Stewart stars as Stratton, and June Allyson as his supportive wife, Ethel.

The film takes place during the Great Depression and opens with a man climbing from a boxcar and tidying his suit. He is Barney Wile (Frank Morgan), a former catcher and something of a drifter, who rides the rails in search of promising young players. For Barney, whose references to "breaking training" when he was in the majors suggest a drinking problem in his past, this freelance scouting allows him to keep in contact with the sport he loves. When Barney spots Monty Stratton (Stewart) pitching a sandlot game, he is convinced he has located a "hot prospect."

Barney follows Monty to the farm where he lives with his mother (Agnes Moorehead), a stern, sensible woman who regards baseball as a waste of time. Monty needs little encouragement to develop his talent, but Mrs. Stratton is harder to convince. Barney offers to do chores over the next few months and coach Monty in exchange for room and board; it is the idea of completing needed repairs at the farm that wins Mrs. Stratton's consent. Throughout the fall and winter, Monty practices his pitching while Barney lends a hand, if not the most helpful one, with the chores. When spring arrives, the two men must next gain Mrs. Stratton's approval to travel to California to try out at the training camp. She expresses her disagreement with the plan, but yields to her son's wishes, giving him five dollars for the trip. When the two men arrive at the training camp, it becomes apparent that Barney has overestimated his influence, and the manager hesitates before allowing Monty to try out. Monty passively accepts the manager's initial refusal, but Barney persists until the manager gives in.

Stewart plays Monty as a modest and mild-mannered rube, yet the character has a strong moral sense as is evidenced when he meets his future wife on a blind date arranged by a teammate, Eddie Dibson (Bill Williams). When Eddie ignores his girlfriend, Dot (Mary Lawrence), because he finds Monty's date, Ethel (June Allyson), more attractive, Monty cuts the evening short, taking Ethel with him, not because he's jealous, but because he didn't want Dot to be hurt by Eddie's behavior. Once Ethel understands the reason for Monty's abrupt leave-taking, she recognizes that he is a very special person. They arrange a second date, and by the time Monty joins the White Sox in Chicago, they are married.

Monty's career trajectory is presented in a pattern typical of baseball films of the era: a training montage with a series of dissolves, a failed first chance in a major league game followed by a brief but successful stint in the minors, then a return to the majors and a performance that earns a starting position on the roster. Monty's first start is against the Yankees, whom he shuts out and against whom he drives in the winning run. After his first season, he and Ethel, now expecting, return to the farm.

The film jumps ahead to Monty's second season. He is on the mound when the telegram arrives telling him "It's a boy." Monty is the picture of calmness as he reads the news. Then he resumes his game, throwing a wild pitch and getting himself promptly pulled. The remainder of the season flashes by in press clippings and short takes. As Monty's celebrity increases, there's a hint of trouble—he's missing dinner and staying out evenings, telling Ethel he has press conferences, but Barney, who has been hired as a pitching coach, knows that Monty is up to something. The mystery is solved when, after returning to the farm, Monty asks Ethel to go out dancing and confesses that instead of doing interviews, he's been taking dance lessons. At four o'clock in the morning they finally leave the nightclub, conveniently located just down the road from the farm.

The turning point in this ideal relationship comes in the next scene, when Monty sets off with his dog and his rifle to go hunting. Tripping over a hedge, he shoots himself in the leg. Ethel, guided by the dog, locates the wounded Monty, who tells her he "shot the wrong rabbit." But Monty's wound is serious, requiring amputation above the knee, and afterward, he is unable to regain his positive outlook. For months, he refuses to wear his prosthesis. He ignores his fan mail and avoids well-wishers. It seems that not even his adoring family can restore his spirit. One evening Ethel confronts him, saying, "You lost your leg, but I lost you." After this encounter Monty begins to put his life back together. One day, while his wife and mother are out, the baby tries to walk, and Monty decides to show him how. Just as Monty learned to dance on the sly, he teaches himself to walk again in secret. Only when he has mastered the task does he reveal his progress to his family. Soon Ethel is pregnant again, and Monty is back practicing his pitching.

The following summer Barney and the Stratton family are invited to attend the All-Star Game. What none of them knows is that Monty has written asking to play. At the last minute, Monty gets a case of the jitters, but with Ethel's encouragement he takes the field. His first two batters hit his pitches, but fail to reach base thanks to expert fielding. Monty settles down and pitches well. In the top of the ninth inning, the opposing team decides to walk a strong hitter in order to get to Monty. The coach debates putting in a pinch hitter, but the team wants Monty to finish the game. So with the bases loaded and two out, Monty singles, driving in a run for the lead. With only three outs to go, the opposing team's coach instructs his players to bunt because Monty cannot field well; however, Monty manages to retire the side. The game is won, fans and family rejoice, and a voice-over announces that if one has courage, the possibilities are "limitless."

For scenes after the accident, Stewart was often filmed wearing a robe or an overcoat or standing beside a piece of furniture to hide his leg. To simulate walking with a prosthesis, he wore a brace. The film won an Oscar for its story. The real Monty Stratton made his comeback in an exhibition game, not the All-Star Game; he coached for the Chicago White Sox before returning to pitching with a minor league team.

STREET DREAMS (2009)

DIRECTOR: Chris Zamoscianyk. SCREENPLAY: Elisa Delson, Rob Dyrdek, Nino Scalia. PRODUCERS: Scott Mellini, Chris Zamoscianyk. CINEMATOGRAPHY: Jonathon E. Salzman. EDITING: Blake Harjes. PRODUCTION DESIGN: Lulu Stewart. COSTUME DESIGN: Jill Lucas.

CAST: Paul Rodriguez Jr. (Derreck Cabrera), Rob Dyrdek (Troy), Ryan Dunn (Cash), Ryan Sheckler (Eric), Terry Kennedy (Reese).

RUNNING TIME: 88 minutes.

A skateboarder's family and his girlfriend can't understand why he's so passionate about his sport.

STREETS OF GOLD (1986)

DIRECTOR: Joe Roth. SCREENPLAY: Dezsö Magyar, Heywood Gould. PRODUCERS: Joe Roth, Harry J. Ufland. CINEMATOGRAPHY: Arthur Albert. EDITING: Richard Chew. MUSIC: Jack Nitzsche. PRODUCTION DESIGN: Marcos Flaksman. ART DIRECTION: Bill Pollock. COSTUME DESIGN: Jeffrey Kurland.

CAST: Klaus Maria Brandauer (Alek Neuman), Adrian Pasdar (Jimmy Boyle), Wesley Snipes (Roland Jenkins), Ángela Molina (Elena), John Mahoney (Linnehan).

RUNNING TIME: 95 minutes.

VHS: Lions Gate.

Now in the United States, a former boxer from Russia takes two amateur fighters under his wing.

STROKER ACE (1983)

DIRECTOR: Hal Needham. SCREENPLAY: Hugh Wilson, Hal Needham, based on the novel *Stand on It* by Stroker Ace, William Neely, and Robert K. Ottum. PRODUCERS: Laurel Goodwin, Hank Moonjean. CINEMATOGRAPHY: Nick McLean. EDITING: William Gordean, Carl Kress. MUSIC: Al Capps. ART DIRECTION: Paul Peters. COSTUME DESIGN: Norman Salling.

CAST: Burt Reynolds (Stroker Ace), Loni Anderson (Pembrook Feeney), Ned Beatty (Clyde Torkle), Jim Nabors (Lugs Harvey), Parker Stevenson (Aubrey James).

RUNNING TIME: 96 minutes.

DVD: Warner Home Video.

Reynolds plays a race-car driver in this film that features several NASCAR drivers, including Dale Earnhardt, Terry Labonte, Kyle Petty, and Cale Yarborough.

SUGAR (2008)

DIRECTORS: Anna Boden, Ryan Fleck. SCREENPLAY: Anna Boden, Ryan Fleck. PRODUCERS: Paul S. Mezey, Jaime Patricof, Jeremy Kipp Walker. CINEMATOGRAPHY: Andrij Parekh. EDITING: Anna Boden. MUSIC: Michael Brook. PRODUCTION DESIGN: Beth Mickle. ART DIRECTION: Michael Ahern. COSTUME DESIGN: Erin Benach.

CAST: Algenis Perez Soto (Miguel "Sugar" Santos), Rayniel Rufino (Jorge Ramirez), Andre Holland (Brad Johnson), Ann Whitney (Helen Higgins), Ellary Porterfield (Anne Higgins), Jaime Tirelli (Osvaldo), Jose Rijo (Alvarez), Michael Gaston (Stu Sutton).

RUNNING TIME: 120 minutes.

DVD: Sony Pictures.

Filmmakers Ryan Fleck and Anna Boden decided to make a baseball film after they learned that nearly all of the major league teams operate training facilities in the Dominican Republic. However, *Sugar* is not a typical sports movie: it is unconcerned with victories or big plays; it avoids high drama and low comedy. Sugar, the title character, is a composite figure based on interviews with players from the major league academies. His story rings true.

The film opens in the Dominican Republic at a professional baseball academy operated by the fictitious Kansas City Knights, where young men are being prepared for major league careers in the United States. In addition to practice on the field, they attend language classes, where they learn enough English to understand umpires and to reassure coaches of their willingness to "try harder." The athletes live on-site and must follow curfews and training regimens. Miguel "Sugar" Santos (Algenis Perez Soto), so named because of a sweet tooth, is a pitcher who has drawn the attention of a scout. The scout has shown him how to grip a ball in order to throw a spike curve, and Sugar practices the grip during language lessons and in his bunk at night. Sometimes, he masters the pitch; other times he hits the batter.

A weekend visit home reveals the extent to which not only Sugar's family but also his entire village relies on American baseball. As he steps from the bus, Sugar is mobbed by a gang of boys eager for the scuffed baseballs he brings. His sister greets him by asking if he has received an offer yet, and even his girlfriend looks forward to him being sent to America. His mother, too, anxiously awaits news from the States. In the background a television is tuned to *American Idol.* The money Sugar has received from the academy has gone toward construction of a new house for the family; its completion depends on Sugar's being called up to the minor leagues. At a picnic Sugar's friends tease him about his chances; one of the group, who has returned to the Dominican Republic after being cut from an American farm team, now works selling cell phone chargers. When the scene shifts to Sugar's return to the academy, the camera pans a landscape of shabby houses, scrawny dogs in the streets, and a graveyard; then it turns to a pristine baseball diamond secure behind the gated entrance of the facility, where an unseen lecturer cautions against homesickness and reminds the players, "Everything depends on you."

When Sugar receives an offer, his agent demands and receives a standard cut of 40 percent. His entire neighborhood turns out to celebrate. One relative, an older man who played in the States, remembers those years as the best in his life. Sugar mistakes the man's gift of a pen—so that he will remember to write home—for a request for an autograph. Before he leaves home, Sugar spends some time working on a table he is making for his mother; Sugar has learned carpentry from his father, now dead, and he finds working with wood satisfying.

Sugar joins a group of Dominican players traveling to Phoenix, where Kansas City's spring training facility is located. Shortly after the young men make themselves at home in their hotel room, they are joined by another Dominican athlete, Jorge Ramirez (Rayniel Rufino), who has been in the United States for several months. He warns them about the minibars and pay-per-view movies in their rooms and teaches them to order breakfast in the dining room. They all eat French toast every morning because their English lessons, which included learning to sing "Take Me Out to the Ballgame," did not cover basic conversation off the diamond. When Sugar calls his girlfriend, he complains that American food is very sweet.

Sugar is one of seventy-five pitchers contending for fewer than fifty positions. During his first appearance on the mound, he nearly gives up a hit, but is saved by a quick infielder, Brad Johnson (Andre Holland). Unlike Sugar, who quit school when he was accepted at the Knights' academy, Brad, a dark-skinned Hispanic American, has a Stanford degree and a seven-figure contract. Brad helps Sugar improve his English and makes him feel more comfortable in America. When the coaches announce their selections, Brad, Sugar, and Jorge are sent to the Knights' Single-A team in Iowa.

Sugar is assigned to live with Helen (Ann Whitney) and Earl Higgins (Richard Bull), an older couple who know only a few words of Spanish and whose enthusiasm for the local baseball team parallels their devotion to Christianity. Sugar suffers their pitching advice, their prayers, and their meatloaf. He sits awkwardly between them at church and exchanges shy smiles with their granddaughter, Anne (Ellary Porterfield), who sings in the choir. He accepts Anne's invitation to attend a fellowship meeting. When he arrives for the meeting, he gives her the ball he threw for his first strikeout. Later, on the Higgins's porch swing, they kiss, but Anne quickly retreats, and Sugar abandons the fellowship meetings. A trip to a local night spot turns out badly when Sugar and Jorge dance with a pair of young white women. Several young white men start a fight, and all are thrown out.

On the baseball diamond Sugar performs well, but there are signs that trouble lies ahead. He is pulled in the sixth inning of a well-pitched game after Jorge makes a fielding error. Jorge, who is also struggling at the plate, has not had time to recover adequately from a knee injury. Soon Sugar injures his ankle on a routine play. When Jorge is released, Sugar realizes that he faces a similar fate. At the Higgins's he repairs a drawer and dries dishes. Helen and Earl have grown warmer, but his encounters with Anne remain stilted. After Brad is called up to a higher division team, Sugar is lonely. The arrival of fellow Dominican pitcher Salvador (Kelvin Leonarado Garcia) signals that Sugar is in danger of being replaced. To speed his recovery and improve his performance, Sugar ingests a sizeable dose of steroids, but by midgame, he loses his control, hits two consecutive batters, and watches, bewildered, as a bench-emptying brawl breaks out around him. At dinner that evening, he apologizes to the Higginses and bursts into tears.

Sugar is demoted from starting pitcher to reliever; Salvador is awarded his slot in the rotation. At the bus station before a road trip, Sugar slips off as the team bus is boarding and purchases a ticket for New York City, where Jorge has gone. On the trip he reads a book Brad has given him; his English has improved. In New York Sugar tries, unsuccessfully, to locate Jorge, but he finds employment at the diner where Jorge had worked. He befriends a Mexican cabinet maker, Osvaldo (Jaime Tirelli), who allows him to use his shop to make a table to replace the one he began in the Dominican Republic. When Sugar calls home, his mother insists he must return to the team, but by the time he contacts his agent, the season is over, management is displeased, and Sugar's visa has expired. Still, he remains in New York, even though he has nearly exhausted his savings. When he has no money left, Sugar appeals to Osvaldo, who invites him to stay with him and his wife. Osvaldo teaches Sugar to use a computer, and Sugar continues to work at the diner and to finish his table.

One day Sugar encounters Jorge and learns that his old friend has joined an amateur team. Jorge takes Sugar to a club, where, unlike their experience in Iowa, they enjoy themselves dancing and laughing among native Spanish speakers. Soon Sugar is able to send money back home; he tells his mother about the table and encourages her to get an e-mail account. He learns that his sister now has a job at the factory where his mother works and that his little brother is pitching. As she speaks, she looks out the window at her younger son, to whom she has transferred her hopes. Sugar is pitching again as well—at a ball field in Roberto Clemente State Park in the Bronx. His teammates face the camera and introduce themselves, naming the team that brought them to the United States. As he peers through the chain link fence of the park, Sugar seems pensive; then he turns back to look across the diamond and to his new friends sitting in the stands. This is not the life he had dreamed of, but for the moment he appears content.

Fleck and Boden began their research at Roberto Clemente State Park, which is named after the first Latino American player inducted into the Baseball Hall of Fame. Impressed by the strong sense of community surrounding the baseball games, the directors began asking players about their journeys from the academies. After developing the outlines of a story and a profile for Sugar, Fleck and Boden traveled to the Dominican Republic in search of a ballplayer to cast in the title role. Algenis Perez Soto was a shortstop with no prior acting experience, but the directors were impressed by how comfortable he appeared before the camera. Although he did need to work with a pitching coach and to "unlearn" English (being a significantly more fluent speaker than Sugar), his performance is utterly convincing. The film itself conveys such a sense of authenticity that it has been favorably compared to the basketball documentary *Hoop Dreams* (1994).

Sugar was nominated for an Independent Spirit Award and the Grand Jury Prize at Sundance in 2008. It was released as a feature film by Sony in 2009.

SUGAR AND SPICE (2003)

DIRECTOR: Francine McDougal. SCREENPLAY: Mandy Nelson. PRODUCER: Wendy Finerman. CINEMATOGRAPHY: Robert Brinkmann. EDITING: Sloane Klevin. MUSIC: Mark Mothersbaugh. PRODUCTION DESIGN: Jeff Knipp. ART DIRECTION: Maria Baker. COSTUME DESIGN: Wendy Chuck.
CAST: Marla Sokoloff (Lisa Janusch), Marley Shelton (Diane Weston), Melissa George (Cleo Miller), Mena Suvari (Kansas Hill), James Marsden (Jack Bartlett).
RUNNING TIME: 81 minutes.
DVD: New Line Cinema.

A high school cheerleading squad turns to crime when their captain gets pregnant by the school quarterback.

SUMMER CATCH (2001)

DIRECTOR: Michael Tollin. SCREENPLAY: Kevin Falls, John Gatins. PRODUCERS: Brian Robbins, Michael Tollin, Sam Weisman. CINEMATOGRAPHY: Tim Suhrstedt. EDITING: Harvey Rosenstock. MUSIC: George Fenton, Tarsha Vega. PRODUCTION DESIGN: John D. Kretschmer. COSTUME DESIGN: Juliet Polcsa.
CAST: Freddie Prinze Jr. (Ryan Dunne), Jessica Biel (Tenley Parrish), Matthew Lillard (Billy Brubaker), Fred Ward (Sean Dunne), Brian Dennehy (John Schiffner), Jason Gedrick (Mike Dunne).
RUNNING TIME: 108 minutes.
DVD: Warner Home Video.

This romantic drama is about a young baseball player whose dreams of making the big time are complicated by the woman who comes into his life.

SUNSET PARK (1996)

DIRECTOR: Steve Gomer. SCREENPLAY: Seth Zvi Rosenfeld, Kathleen McGhee-Anderson. PRODUCERS: Danny DeVito, Dan Paulson, Michael Shamberg. CINEMATOGRAPHY: Robbie Greenberg. EDITING: Arthur Coburn. MUSIC: Miles Goodman. PRODUCTION DESIGN: Victoria Paul. ART DIRECTION: Lee Mayman. COSTUME DESIGN: Carol Ramsey.
CAST: Rhea Perlman (Phyllis Saroka), Fredro Starr (Shorty), Carol Kane (Mona), Terrence Howard (Spaceman).
RUNNING TIME: 99 minutes.
DVD: Sony Pictures.

A white, female teacher coaches an all-black boys high school team to success.

SURFER, DUDE (2008)

DIRECTOR: S.R. Bindler. SCREENPLAY: S. R. Bindler, Mark Gustawes, Cory Van Dyke. PRODUCERS: Gus Gustawes, Mark Gustawes, Matthew McConaughey. CINEMATOGRAPHY: Elliot Davis. EDITING: Nancy Richardson. MUSIC: Blake Neely, Xavier Rudd. PRODUCTION DESIGN: T. K. Kirkpatrick. COSTUME DESIGN: Jon Pray.
CAST: Matthew McConaughey (Steve Addington), Woody Harrelson (Jack Mayweather), Scott Glenn (Alistair Greenbough).
RUNNING TIME: 85 minutes.
DVD: Starz / Anchor Bay.

In this comedy a surfer is tempted to sell out to a virtual reality company that wants to duplicate his skills.

T

TAKE DOWN (1979)

DIRECTOR: Kieth Merrill. SCREENPLAY: Eric Hendershot, Kieth Merrill. PRODUCER: Kieth Merrill. CINEMATOGRAPHY: Reed Smoot. EDITING: Richard Fetterman. MUSIC: Merrill B. Jenson. PRODUCTION DESIGN: Douglas G. Johnson.
CAST: Edward Herrmann (Ed Branish), Kathleen Lloyd (Jill Branish), Lorenzo Lamas (Nick Kilvitus), Maureen McCormack (Brooke Cooper), Stephen Furst (Randy Jensen).
RUNNING TIME: 107 minutes.
VHS: Unicorn Video.

A teacher who is forced to coach a wrestling team contends with a rebellious teenager.

TAKE ME OUT TO THE BALL GAME (1949)

DIRECTOR: Busby Berkeley. SCREENPLAY: Harry Tugend, George Wells. STORY: Gene Kelly, Stanley Donen. PRODUCER: Arthur Freed. CINEMATOGRAPHY: George Folsey. EDITING: Blanche Sewell. ART DIRECTION: Daniel B. Cathcart, Cedric Gibbons. COSTUME DESIGN: Helen Rose, Valles.
CAST: Frank Sinatra (Denny Ryan), Esther Williams (K. C. Higgins), Gene Kelly (Eddie O'Brien), Betty Garrett (Shirley Delwyn), Edward Arnold (Mr. Lorgan), Jules Munshin (Nat Goldberg).
RUNNING TIME: 93 minutes.
DVD: Warner Home Video.

Take Me Out to the Ball Game is a musical comedy starring Frank Sinatra and Gene Kelly as infielders who spend the off season performing a vaudeville act. Eddie O'Brien (Kelly) is more interested in chasing girls than in chasing grounders while Denny Ryan (Sinatra) would rather pursue the game than romance. Kelly created the story after teaming with Sinatra for *Anchors Away*; his idea was based on the baseball player–clown Al Schacht, who entertained fans between innings and performed on stage between seasons. The original treatment called for Leo Durocher (then a manager for the New York Giants) in the role of the team's first baseman and for Judy Garland as the team's owner, but Durocher was dropped in favor of Broadway performer Jules Munshin, and Garland, suffering from depression, was replaced with Esther Williams. These changes no doubt influenced the direction of the musical, resulting in less baseball on the part of the male leads and more athleticism on the part of the female. The plot is thin, resting on a tepid romantic triangle and a mobster's attempt to influence the outcome of a pennant race. Conflict is often resolved in musical numbers rather than through dialogue, resisting any dramatic impulse.

When the film opens, spring training has begun, but Eddie and Denny are still on tour with their vaudeville act. After their performance, Denny gets into a brief scuffle with a circus strong man. Denny's eagerness to put up his fists at the slightest provocation indicates his immaturity and introduces a running joke about his size and relative lack of physical prowess, for he is always knocked out cold with little force and before he has a chance to swing at his opponent. In keeping with his boyishness, Denny is shy around women and not quite ready for romance. Unlike Denny, Eddie fancies himself a playboy and keeps a multivolume set of address books. En route to training camp, Eddie flirts with young women on the train, and as soon as he and Denny arrive at the practice field, he begins boasting about his conquests while on the road in a song and dance number that ends with the two men pulling small American flags from their pockets.

The joyous reunion of the Wolves—Eddie and Denny's team—is interrupted by a telegram announcing the impending arrival of the team's new owner, K. C. Higgins (Williams), whom the players expect to be a man. This misunderstanding is not corrected until after Eddie has made a fool of himself by chatting her up in the lobby of the hotel where the Wolves are staying. Although the players are taken aback by K.C., their main fear is that she will prove meddlesome; once she demonstrates her knowledge of the sport, the men accept her involvement with the team. It is K.C.'s no-nonsense approach to baseball that troubles Eddie. Not only does she disapprove of the slapstick routine Eddie and Denny perform before games, but she insists that the men obey a strict curfew. For Eddie, an unrepentant rule breaker, K.C.'s business-like manner presents a challenge that keeps him at arm's length, but Denny has become smitten after watching K.C. field a ball.

Denny's shyness assures that his relationship with K.C. does not progress beyond friendliness, and his women troubles are compounded when he becomes the object of a fan's affection. The fan, Shirley Delwyn (Betty Garrett), pursues him aggressively. In a remarkable musical number, she corners him outside of the locker room after a game, then chases him up the bleachers, finally slinging him over her shoulder and carrying him off, albeit not far.

Following a road trip, presented in a montage of newspaper headlines and newsreel footage, the Wolves attend a clambake hosted by Shirley's boss, Mr. Lorgan (Edward Arnold), who owns a nightclub. As Shirley and Denny dance, she tries to talk him out of his infatuation with K.C. At the same time, Eddie asks K.C. about her feelings for Denny. When her response indicates fondness but not passion, Eddie asks for a kiss, and she complies. Romantic sparks fly, but they quickly turn to angry ones as K.C. discovers Eddie has kissed her to win a bet. Back at the hotel Denny, who has kissed Shirley, tells Eddie that he's over K.C. and that Shirley is his type—quiet and shy. But Eddie, thinking that he hasn't a chance with K.C. and unable to resist the opportunity to be surrounded by attractive young women, accepts an offer from Lorgan to play in a show featuring thirty chorus girls. The catch is that rehearsals are at night after the club closes, and Eddie must start immediately. What he doesn't know is that Lorgan has bet heavily against the Wolves and that the job offer is just a way of sidelining him as the season nears its end. Soon Eddie is exhausted by the late hours, and his play suffers. K.C. tries to woo him from his slump by rekindling the romance, then fires him when Lorgan appears and tells her about the rehearsals.

When Eddie figures out that he's been tricked by Mr. Lorgan, he plots to rejoin the team, showing up with a group of boys he's bribed to start a ruckus in the stands. Eddie's ploy works, to the horror of Lorgan, who instructs his thugs to make certain Eddie doesn't play. Shirley, overhearing Lorgan and fearing that Eddie will be killed, tells Denny to prevent Eddie from playing. Denny does this by beaning Eddie with a real baseball during their comedy routine. The thugs show up in the locker room pretending to be doctors and hit Eddie every time he starts to come around. Eddie is rescued when K.C. and Shirley burst into the locker room. Shirley reveals the true identity of the thugs, K.C. kisses Eddie, and thus revived, Eddie rushes after Denny to get revenge. Denny homers, inspired by the desire to put a safe distance between Eddie and himself. Not to be foiled, Eddie promptly homers in order to chase Denny around the bases. The men continue their chase after scoring the winning runs. The film ends with a final musical number in which the stars use their real names.

Directed by Busby Berkeley, *Take Me Out to the Ball Game* is primarily a vehicle for Kelly to display his talents. The plot seems to exist only to tie together the production numbers; the characters lack believability—and Kelly's O'Brien isn't even likeable. There are only a few shots of baseball playing, and none of Eddie, Denny, and Nat executing one of their famous double plays, but Kelly, Sinatra, and Munshin perform a rousing number in the hotel dining room. Although the film is set in the early 1900s—Teddy Roosevelt attends the opening game—the mood is late-1940s, complete with Esther Williams doing water ballet in a swimming costume quite similar to the one Betty Grable wore in those famous pin-up posters from World War II. The literal flag waving and the patriotic lyrics in many songs are part of a celebration of America that takes place against the backdrop of the national pastime.

TALENT FOR THE GAME (1991)

Director: Robert M. Young. Screenplay: David Himmelstein, Thomas Michael Donnelly, Larry Ferguson. Producer: Martin Elfand. Cinematography: Curtis Clark. Editing: Arthur Coburn. Music: David Newman. Production Design: Jeffrey Howard. Art Direction: Keith Brian Burns. Costume Design: Erica Edell Phillips.

Cast: Edward James Olmos (Virgil Sweet), Lorraine Bracco (Bobbie), Jeff Corbett (Sammy Bodeen), Jamey Sheridan (Tim Weaver), Terry Kinney (Gil Lawrence).

Running Time: 91 minutes.

DVD: Paramount.

A California Angels talent scout finds a Midwest phenom who lacks professional experience.

TALLADEGA NIGHTS: THE BALLAD OF RICKY BOBBY (2006)

Director: Adam McKay. Screenplay: Will Ferrell, Adam McKay. Producers: Judd Apatow, Jimmy Miller. Cinematography: Oliver Wood. Editing: Brent White. Music: Alex Wurman. Production Design: Clayton R. Hartley. Art Direction: Virginia Randolph. Costume Design: Susan Matheson.

Cast: Will Ferrell (Ricky Bobby), John C. Reilly (Cal), Michael Clarke Duncan (Lucius Washington), Jane Lynch (Lucy Bobby), Sacha Baron Cohen (Jean Girard), David Koechner (Hershell), Jack McBrayer (Glenn), Gary Cole (Reese Bobby).

Running Time: 108 minutes.

DVD: Columbia Pictures.

Will Ferrell's sports films, *Blades of Glory* (2007) and *Semi-Pro* (2008), have been satires, and *Talladega Nights* is no exception. Here the target is NASCAR; however, this time Ferrell has made a film that not only satirizes but also celebrates the sport. As Ricky Bobby, Ferrell dominates the NASCAR scene until he has an accident and is replaced atop the NASCAR standings by Jean Girard (Sacha Baron Cohen of *Borat* and *Bruno* fame), a gay Frenchman.

Clearly, the idea of NASCAR, the refuge for wannabe macho types, having as its spokesman a French homosexual undermines the image NASCAR has worked so hard to create. Ferrell also seems to be poking fun at buddy relationships when he and his sidekick Cal (John C. Reilly) split up after Ricky's accident, and Cal takes Ricky's wife, kids, and home, all the while insisting that the two have a friendship that surpasses all other ties.

The beginning of the film accounts for Ricky's success. His father is driving his pregnant wife to the hospital at breakneck speed when he stops on the proverbial dime at the hospital. The sudden stop causes Ricky to be expelled from his mother's womb. Ricky's father abandons his wife and baby son, turning up ten years later and offering the advice, "If you ain't first, you're last" and "It's the fastest who gets paid and laid." Ricky's father disappears again. Years later, after Ricky becomes a NASCAR star, he always leaves two tickets for his father at the box office, but they are never picked up. (After the sales people admire Ricky's thoughtfulness, they sell the tickets, thereby undercutting any idea about their decency.)

At Talladega, where Ricky has joined a pit crew, he gets his chance behind the wheel when the regular driver has to "take a whiz" and asks if anyone else wants to drive. Ricky does and finishes third. His rise to the top is rapid, especially when Cal also becomes a driver and helps Ricky win by doing the "shake and bake," "sling-shotting" Ricky past other drivers. Ricky's home life includes a wife with a "rack" and a 94 "ass rating," two sons named Walker and Texas Ranger, bad food, and a grandfather he insults. But Ricky is religious: he addresses "baby Jesus" in his lengthy and blasphemous before-meal prayers. The problem is that his satire of Southern values is so amusing that it's the humor, not the satire, that remains with the audience.

When Jean proclaims, "I came here to defeat you," Ricky is too egotistical to take the challenge seriously. During a physical altercation, Jean twists Ricky's arm and threatens to break it unless he says, "I love crepes." Since it's something "real men" don't do, Ricky refuses to admit even that he loves "really thin pancakes." With his broken arm, Ricky can't drive, so the owner of the car hires Jean to drive. After Jean introduces Ricky to his husband, Gregory (Andy Richter), Ricky's humiliation is almost complete. The proverbial last straw is Jean's promise to return to Paris if Ricky will kiss him on the lips. Irate, Ricky cuts off his cast and in the ensuing race totals his car, which catches on fire. Though he is uninjured, Ricky believes that he is on fire and strips to his underwear while calling out to "Jesus, Allah, Tom Cruise" for help. While he is in the hospital in catatonic shock, his wife, Carley (Leslie Bibb), demonstrates her love for him by asking the doctor to pull the plug. Later Ricky is suffering from psychosomatic paralysis so severe that Cal, the devoted friend, is about to smother him. When Ricky sticks a knife in his leg to show that his paralysis is real, Ricky screams in pain and recovers, but he does not regain his driving ability, maxing out at 26 mph. He is reconciled to Cal's impending marriage to Carley and moves in with his mother. Even his career as a pizza-delivery man is a failure. After losing his license, Ricky does deliveries by bus, then by bicycle, eventually delivering a pizza to his father, Reese Bobby (Gary Cole), who wants to help his son recover.

Reese's therapy requires Ricky to overcome his fear by driving with a cougar in the car, by driving blindfolded, and by driving to elude the police, who have been tipped off by Reese that Ricky is hauling cocaine (which turns out to be Lucky

Charms). After he passes the tests, Ricky, Susan (Amy Adams), his parents, and the two "rangers" celebrate at Applebee's; but when the celebration threatens to become sentimental, Reese acts so badly that he is thrown out of the restaurant. Ricky, however, does not return to the track until Susan, who has always loved him, gives him an inspirational talk culminating with "You're a man, aren't you?" When Ricky goes to see Jean, his opponent explains, "I came here for you to beat me." Just as God needs the devil and Diane Sawyer needs Katie Couric, so Jean Gerard needs Ricky. Before the race takes place, Reese, for the first time, picks up the tickets Ricky has left for him, but then sells the tickets.

In the race Ricky starts last in his car, which is sponsored by Julio's Thongs, but quickly moves up until he trails only the leaders, Jean and Cal. The owner of their cars, fearful of Ricky pulling an upset, orders Cal to take out Ricky, but Cal inexplicably refuses. Ricky and Jean are mano a mano when they collide, wrecking both cars. They get out of their cars and Ricky outsprints Jean to the finish line. Though Ricky's victory doesn't count, Jean concedes, and Ricky kisses him on the mouth—but refuses to shake his hand. Because Ricky and Jean were disqualified, Cal is the official winner of the race, but Carley, seeing where her future is, seeks reconciliation with Ricky. Despite the promise of her "pearls of delight," Ricky turns her down for Susan, who proves to have bigger "pearls." Reese states that he is proud of Ricky and concludes his speech with the suggestion that the whole family "get thrown out of Applebee's."

TA RA RUM PUM (2007)

DIRECTOR: Siddharth Anand. SCREENPLAY: Habib Faisal. PRODUCER: Aditya Chopra. CINEMATOGRAPHY: Binod Pradhan. MUSIC: Vishal-Shekhar, Salim Merchant. PRODUCTION DESIGN: ART DIRECTION: Christina Barth, Linda Jean Marlowe, Sharmishta Roy. COSTUME DESIGN: Surily Goel.

CAST: Saif Ali Khan (Rajveer "'RV" Singh), Rani Mukherjee (Radhika), Victor Banerjee (Subho Shekhar Rai Banerjee), Jaaved Jaaferi (Hariprasad Dhirubhai "Harry" Patel), Bharat Dabholkar (Billy Bhatia).

RUNNING TIME: 153 minutes.

DVD: Yash Raj Films.

This Indian film, set in the United States, is about a stock-car driver who must overcome his fears after a crash puts him in the hospital.

TEEN WOLF (1985)

DIRECTOR: Rod Daniel. SCREENPLAY: Joseph Loeb III, Matthew Weisman. PRODUCERS: Mark Levinson, Scott Rosenfelt. CINEMATOGRAPHY: Tim Suhrstedt. EDITING: Lois Freeman-Fox. MUSIC: Miles Goodman. PRODUCTION DESIGN: Chester Kaczenski. COSTUME DESIGN: Nancy G. Fox.

CAST: Michael J. Fox (Scott Howard), James Hampton (Harold Howard), Scott Paulin (Kirk Lolley), Susan Ursitti (Lisa Marconi), Jerry Levine (Rupert Stilinski).

RUNNING TIME: 91 minutes.

DVD: MGM.

A high school basketball player learns that he's a werewolf as well.

TENNIS, ANYONE? (2005)

DIRECTOR: Donal Logue. SCREENPLAY: Kirk Fox, Donal Logue. PRODUCERS: Donal Logue, Orian Williams. CINEMATOGRAPHY: Todd Kirschner. EDITING: Don Miller-Robinson, Jeffrey M. Werner. MUSIC: Don Miller-Robinson. PRODUCTION DESIGN: Chris Davis.

CAST: Donal Logue (Danny Macklin), Kirk Fox (Gary Morgan), Jason Isaacs

(Johnny Green), Kenneth Mitchell (Nick Allen), Stephen Dorff (T. C. Jackson), Paul Rudd (Lance Rockwood), Danny Trejo (Hector).
RUNNING TIME: 100 minutes.
DVD: Fireside Entertainment.

This comedy is about would-be Hollywood players who have enough celebrity status to play at charity tennis matches. The 1993 French Open doubles champion, Luke Jensen, plays Luke Dorkovich.

THAT'S MY BOY (1951)

DIRECTOR: Hal Walker. SCREENPLAY: Cy Howard. PRODUCER: Hal Wallis. CINEMATOGRAPHY: Lee Garmes. EDITING: Warren Low. MUSIC: Leigh Harline. ART DIRECTION: Franz Bachelin, Hal Pereira. COSTUME DESIGN: Edith Head.
CAST: Dean Martin (Bill Baker), Jerry Lewis (Junior Jackson), Marion Marshall (Terry Howard), Ruth Huseey (Ann Jackson), Polly Bergen (Betty Hunter).
RUNNING TIME: 104 minutes.
DVD: Paramount.

In this Lewis and Martin film, the former is pressured into playing football by his father and the latter is hired to coach him.

THERE'S ONLY ONE JIMMY GRIMBLE (2000)

DIRECTOR: John Hay. SCREENPLAY: Simon Mayle, Rik Carmichael, John Hay. PRODUCERS: Jeremy Bolt, Alison Jackson, Sarah Radclyffe. CINEMATOGRAPHY: John De Borman. EDITING: Oral Norrie Ottey. MUSIC: Simon Boswell, Alex James. PRODUCTION DESIGN: Michael Carlin. ART DIRECTION: Karen Wakefield. COSTUME DESIGN: Mary-Jane Reyner.
CAST: Lewis McKenzie (Jimmy Grimble), Gina McKee (Donna), Robert Carlyle (Eric Wirral), Ray Winstone (Harry).
RUNNING TIME: 106 minutes.
DVD: Pathe Distribution (UK: PAL).

In this British film, a hapless teenager's football (soccer) skills are transformed after he wears a pair of shoes once owned by a local superstar.

THIS SPORTING LIFE (1963)

DIRECTOR: Lindsay Anderson. SCREENPLAY: David Storey, based on his novel. PRODUCER: Karel Reisz. CINEMATOGRAPHY: Denys Coop. EDITING: Peter Taylor. MUSIC: Roberto Gerhard. ART DIRECTION: Alan Withy. COSTUME DESIGN: Sophie Devine.
CAST: Richard Harris (Frank Machin), Rachel Roberts (Mrs. Margaret Hammond), Alan Badel (Gerald Weaver), William Hartnell (Mr. Johnson), Colin Blakely (Maurice Braithwaite), Vanda Godsell (Mrs. Weaver), Anne Cunningham (Judith).
RUNNING TIME: 134 minutes. B&W.
ACADEMY AWARD NOMINATIONS: Best Actor (Harris), Best Supporting Actress (Roberts).
DVD: Criterion.

Based on the novel by David Storey, who also wrote the screenplay, and directed by Lindsay Anderson, *This Sporting Life* is an intense character study of an emotionally repressed man for whom rugby offers a brief hiatus from working in the coal mines of Yorkshire, but not the happiness he assumes will accompany his bit of local fame. Like the novel, the film is structured as a series of flashbacks. Although some reviewers found the structure confusing—the flashbacks themselves are not sequential—the violation in chronology underscores the absence of change in the lives of the main characters, whose essential natures appear socially determined.

Richard Harris stars as Frank Machin, a Yorkshire man who lets a room from a young widow, Margaret Hammond (Rachel Roberts), to whom he is strongly attracted, but who repeatedly rejects his affection. Mrs. Hammond keeps her late husband's boots by the hearth and polishes them every day, although she expresses no grief or devotion. She is barely tolerant of Frank, even after they begin an affair. When Frank first moved into Mrs. Hammond's, he was working in the mines and had not yet begun playing professionally.

The opening scenes of the film cut from the mine to the rugby field, outlining the boundaries of Frank's life. The mud of the rugby pitch mirrors the grime of the mines; the harsh physicality of labor in the pits translates to raw violence in the game. Throughout the film, game footage exploits the roughness of the sport to reflect the roughness of Frank's character. There is no emphasis here on big plays, underdogs, and comebacks; it doesn't matter who wins or who scores because Frank is destined to lose.

A visit to a dentist triggers the next set of flashbacks. After smashing his face during a game, Frank has half a dozen teeth extracted before continuing on to a Christmas party being thrown by the team owner, Mr. Weaver (Alan Badel). The anesthetic transports him to an earlier point in his relationship with Mrs. Hammond, who is still resisting emotional intimacy, then to his decision to try out for the local rugby team after he realizes that the athletes enjoy privileges and prestige that are not otherwise accessible to him. He persuades an older man, Mr. Johnson (William Hartnell), who serves as an unpaid talent scout for Mr. Weaver, to arrange a tryout for him. Frank asks Mrs. Hammond to come see him play in the tryout game, but she doesn't want to go and doesn't want to wish him luck. Frank performs well, managing to sneak in a punch that breaks an opponent's nose, and a small newspaper article suggests he'll make the team. Frank invites Mr. Johnson, whom he now calls "Dad," to Mrs. Hammond's for tea. When she returns home with her children, she is unhappy to find the fire stoked and a generous spread on the table. After Johnson leaves, Mrs. Hammond describes him as fawning over Frank. Frank, in turn, asks why she still polishes her late husband's boots.

The scene changes to Mr. Weaver's office, where Frank asks for and, after some gamesmanship, receives a thousand pounds for signing on. When Frank shows Mrs. Hammond the check, she responds bitterly that she received less when her husband died. Later, she appears outside of his door and asks if he'll be leaving now that he has money, but Frank intends to stay. Back in the dentist's surgery, Frank has just awakened, moaning, "She gives me bloody nothing." Riding from the dentist's in Weaver's car, Frank asks about a bag he has with presents for Mrs. Hammond's children. Then his mind wanders to an earlier point, when he arrived at her house with a new car that Mrs. Hammond said she would not ride in.

At the Christmas party Frank sequesters himself with a bottle. The alcohol and medication trigger more memories, and the film continues with flashbacks of his relationship with Mrs. Hammond and of his social life as a "star" player. Frank embarks on a traditional courtship, plying Mrs. Hammond with gifts about which she is at first ambivalent. There's a pleasant interlude in the country with the children during which she appears relaxed at times, but she is incapable of emotional connection, and their physical relationship is devoid of affection. Although Frank now finds himself pursued by other women, including Mrs. Weaver (Vanda Godsell), he refuses their offers, remaining faithful to someone who doesn't want him.

Frank leaves the Weavers' party, having retrieved his gifts from the car, and makes his way along a railroad track. Drunk and staggering, he drops the gifts and kneels to pick them up just as a train approaches. He survives only by chance: the train is running on a track parallel to the one he's on. When he finally reaches Mrs. Hammond's, he notices that her husband's boots have been returned to a cupboard. After she checks on the children, she agrees to go to Frank's bed.

Mrs. Hammond soon loses the holiday spirit. Frank's attentions have not escaped the notice of the neighbors, who are perhaps envious of the small luxuries he brings to the household. Mrs. Hammond suffers their disapproval. Nor does access to middle-class goods and services confer acceptance into the middle class. When Frank takes Mrs. Hammond to a fashionable restaurant, they are both so obviously uncomfortable that they draw attention to themselves, and Frank begins to act boorishly. Mrs. Hammond insists they leave, and as they do, they pass the Weavers, whose distaste for the pair is palpable.

Soon after, Mrs. Hammond and Frank begin quarreling violently. At the wedding of one of Frank's teammates, Mrs. Hammond tells Frank their relationship makes her feel shame, and he responds with a hard slap to the side of her face. A later fight escalates from shouting and furniture smashing to Frank's striking her again, then telling her he loves her. She spits in his face, and he leaves, vowing not to return. But at an unspecified later date, he does return, only to learn that she's been taken ill.

At the hospital, he's told that she's had a brain hemorrhage and lacks the will to live. Sitting by her side, Frank strokes her face and whispers reassurances, but she remains comatose. Frank notices a spider crawling on the wall and reaches to crush it. The spider descends toward the bed, and the film cuts to Mrs. Hammond's face. Blood trickles from her mouth. Realizing she is dead, Frank smashes the spider with his fist; as he storms from the room, he passes Mrs. Hammond's children in the corridor but does not acknowledge them. He returns to her house, forces the door, and gives in to his grief.

The film ends with a return to the rugby pitch. Frank, no longer a favored player and nearing the end of his brief career, gets slammed in the stomach, and the fans turn ugly. A drum thumps somewhere and play resumes.

This Sporting Life was a critical success, earning a Golden Palm nomination at Cannes for director Anderson and winning an acting award for Harris. Both Harris and Roberts were nominated for Oscars, and the film swept the British Academy of Film and Television Awards. Anderson, with Tony Richardson and Karel Reisz, is associated with the British New Wave, or Free Cinema, and *This Sporting Life* is considered one of the last of England's "kitchen sink" pictures—black-and-white films noted for harsh realism and attention to background detail. Anderson was also influenced by Eastern European filmmakers, such as Miloš Foreman, and by expressionism, as is evident in the hospital scene. For Harris, this was his first leading film role and is still considered one of his best screen performances. William Hartnell became the original Dr. Who of the British television series.

THRASHING (1986)

Director: David Winters. Screenplay: Paul Brown, Alan Sacks. Producer: Alan Sacks. Cinematography: Chuck Colwell. Editing: Lorenzo DeStefano, Nicholas C. Smith. Music: Barry Goldberg. Production Design: Catherine Hardwicke. Costume Design: Bernadette O'Brien.

CAST: Josh Brolin (Corey Webster), Robert Rusler (Tommy Hook), Pamela Gidley (Chrissy), Brooke McCarter (Tyler).
RUNNING TIME: 93 minutes.
DVD: MGM.

This film is about a rivalry between skateboarding gangs.

TIN CUP (1996)

DIRECTOR: Ron Shelton. SCREENPLAY: John Norville, Ron Shelton. PRODUCERS: Gary Foster, David Lester. CINEMATOGRAPHY: Russell Boyd. EDITING: Kimberly Ray, Paul Seydor. MUSIC: William Ross. PRODUCTION DESIGN: James Bissell. ART DIRECTION: Gae Buckley, Chris Burian-Mohr. COSTUME DESIGN: Carol Oditz.
CAST: Kevin Costner (Roy "Tin Cup" McAvoy), Rene Russo (Dr. Molly Griswald), Don Johnson (David Simms), Cheech Marin (Romeo Posar), Linda Hart (Doreen), Dennis Burkley (Earl), Rex Linn (Dewey), Lou Myers (Clint), Richard Lineback (Curt).
RUNNING TIME: 135 minutes.
DVD: Warner Home Video.

Perhaps hoping to repeat their earlier successful collaboration in *Bull Durham* (1988), writer-director Ron Shelton and actor Kevin Costner switched their focus from baseball to golf and made *Tin Cup*, which appeared the same year as *Happy Gilmore*, another golf film and one that it resembles in terms of its love triangle, if not its type of humor. *Tin Cup* features a contrast between two former University of Houston golfers who have gone their separate ways. Roy "Tin Cup" McAvoy (Costner) is the pro at a two-bit golf range in east Texas; David Simms (Don Johnson) is the successful Professional Golf Association (PGA) player who has yet to win a big tournament. The reason for their different fates lies in the way they approach the game. Roy "goes for broke," unable to resist taking chances that often lead to high scores; David, on the other hand, plays it safe, laying up before water hazards and making pars. One exchange illustrates the difference between the two: in response to Roy's comment "Thirteen years on the tour. You're still a pussy," David observes, "Thirteen years on the driving range. You still think this game is about your testosterone count."

Kevin Costner and Cheech Marin on the set of *Tin Cup*

Kevin Costner (left) gets advice from Cheech Marin (right) in *Tin Cup*

The conflict between the two rivals is highlighted when Dr. Molly Griswold (Rene Russo), a psychologist who has recently moved to the area, visits the driving range to take lessons with Roy. As his pals watch from the clubhouse, Roy strips her of all the special golfing apparatus she has purchased, as well as instructional manuals and tapes, and proceeds to blend instruction with a few romantic moves. There is some sexual banter, and Roy discovers that she is not only uptight, but that she is also David's girlfriend. The rivalry with David adds to the excitement of the chase. Roy thinks that if he is to win Molly's affections, he will have to impress her, so he decides to take a shot at the U.S. Open Championship. In order to have any chance at winning, Roy knows he will have to curb his risk taking and instead wait for the right opportunity to make his move. He explains his behavior as the result of "inner demons," which she chooses to interpret as "inner bullshit." At any rate, to get closer to Molly and improve his game, Roy asks her to be his therapist, and she agrees. When Roy visits her, he tells her about a "friend's problem" with a woman; and when Molly advises being honest, he tells her he's in love with her. Although she knows it isn't appropriate for her to date a patient, she is sufficiently interested in Roy to call her own therapist and ask for counseling. While there is some screen chemistry between the two and the dialogue is clever, the romance simply isn't up to *Bull Durham* standards, nor is Russo a Sarandon.

Two events demonstrate the contrast between the two golfers. David asks Roy to be his caddie at an event he is sponsoring, and even though Roy regards the request as an insult, he takes the job because he needs the money. In the tournament, David again lays up, much to Roy's disgust, before a water hazard; and when Roy states that he could have reached the green, an argument ensues. Roy bets some golfers about the shot and wins with a shot that clears the water and lands on the green. David then fires him as his caddie. Later the two quarrel about how far they can drive a golf ball; after Roy hits a ball far out in the driving range, David whacks his to the interstate, where it continues to bounce and roll out of sight. Slowly Molly learns that David's public persona is a front for his manipulative, vindictive, and snobbish behavior.

With the help of Molly and Romeo (Cheech Marin), his long-suffering caddie and friend, Roy manages to get his emotions fairly well in check. As Romeo points out, the answer to Roy's problems is focus. Roy qualifies for the U.S. Open but gets drunk before the first round and does not do well, shooting an 83. The next day he shoots a record 62 and is in contention. During the third round, however, his old nemesis reappears, and Roy rejects both Romeo's and television announcer Ken Venturi's advice about the right club to hit on a crucial hole. His testosterone perhaps leads him to under-club, and the mistake costs him. In the final round Roy and Peter Jacobsen are tied for the lead with David down by one stroke. At the eighteenth hole David lays up as usual, as does Jacobsen. If Roy takes the safe shot, he will probably be in a playoff with Jacobsen, but knowing that an eagle will not only win the tournament but also set a course record, he refuses to play conservatively. The gallery, other golfers, and the television commentators cannot believe he is taking the risk. His ball lands on the green, but then it slowly rolls away from the hole toward the water. By using the drop area, he can still salvage par, but he decides to hit his next ball from the same spot he hit from before. His next several balls also fail to reach the green. Finally, he has just one left, and if he loses it in the water, he will be disqualified. What to do? Molly's unlikely and totally zany response to the situation is to yell, "Let it rip." Apparently, she finally understands Roy and accepts his all-or-nothing behavior. He hits the next shot in the hole for a twelve, and everyone goes wild.

Roy has blown his chance for victory, but he comments, "I didn't come here to play for no second, Romeo . . . and Simms will always be second." Molly is fine with the result since his finish means that he will be able to play in other PGA events, and she herself has picked up several golfers as clients for her golf therapy practice. What happens in Roy and Molly's relationship is fairly typical of screwball romances: The apparently mismatched characters reconcile their opposing qualitiess as the practical person learns to take some chances, and the zany one learns some self-control.

TO PLEASE A LADY (1950)

DIRECTOR: Clarence Brown. SCREENPLAY: Marge Decker, Barré Lyndon. PRODUCER: Clarence Brown. CINEMATOGRAPHY: Harrold Rosson. EDITING: Robert Kern. MUSIC: Bronislau Kaper. ART DIRECTION: James Basevi, Cedric Gibbons. COSTUME DESIGN: Helen Rose.

CAST: Clark Gable (Mike Brannan), Barbara Stanwyck (Regina Forbes), Adolphe Menjou (Gregg), Roland Winters (Dwight Barrington), Will Geer (Jack Mackay).

RUNNING TIME: 91 minutes.

DVD: Warner Home Video.

This romantic drama is about a race-car driver and female reporter.

TOURNAMENT OF DREAMS (2007)

DIRECTOR: Don Abernathy. SCREENPLAY: Don Abernathy, Lisa King. PRODUCERS: Christopher Broughton, John Daly. CINEMATOGRAPHY: Joplin Wu. EDITING: David Lewis Smith. MUSIC: Christopher Broughton. PRODUCTION DESIGN: Jesse Benson. ART DIRECTION: Secha Breonni. COSTUME DESIGN: Safowa Bright-Asare.

CAST: Tony Todd (Isaiah Kennedy), The Game (Troy), Debbie Allen (Rhonda

Dillins), Shakira Bryant (Two Two), La Trice Harper (Kiwi), Keana Jackson (Boo Baby).
RUNNING TIME: 88 minutes.
DVD: Code Black Entertainment.

Tournament of Dreams is yet another sports film about a high school on the brink of losing a team in a round of bureaucratic downsizing, but this time it is a girls' basketball team at a predominantly black school that is in jeopardy. The film begins with a school board hearing with Principal Rhonda Dillins (Debbie Allen) under fire from board members who regard the girls' athletic program as a diversion from the school's mission and an unnecessary expense. After arguing that basketball provides an "expression of pride" for the players and gives them a "reason to succeed" in school, she wins a temporary reprieve for the Lady Cavaliers. The board allows the principal and the team one season in which to demonstrate that playing basketball will enhance academic performance.

The school's security guard, Darnel (Carl Lewis), approaches Isaiah Kennedy (Tony Todd) about coaching the Lady Cavs, whose current coach is the physical education teacher. Although Isaiah is reluctant to leave his current position as director of a recreation center, his daughter, Two Two (Shakira Bryant), easily talks him into accepting the job. Two Two is a talented athlete intent on becoming a Lady Cavalier. Isaiah cautions her that as her coach he must treat her like the other girls, and Two Two agrees. While this scene hints (erroneously) of tension developing between father and daughter, it points ironically to the needs of other players for their coach to become a father figure in their lives.

Writer-director Don Abernathy turns the film's attention to the importance of family and to the need for black men to assume responsibility as husbands, fathers, and role models. This sentiment is articulated most directly by the character Kiwi (La Trice Harper), whose mother has remarried a white physician. Her stepfather, Jim (Brian Patrick Clarke), is a good man who loves Kiwi's mother and wants very much to be a good father to Kiwi, but Kiwi wants and needs a "strong black man." Over the course of the movie, Kiwi will grow more accepting of Jim, but the film has made the point that he cannot completely fulfill her need for a "father" of her own race.

The other team members are not as fortunate as Kiwi. Shuga's (Robin Wilson) parents are divorcing because of her father's infidelities. Capricorn's (Joyful Drake) mother, apparently an addict, is a prostitute; her father is not mentioned. Neither Slick (Rae'Ven Kelly) nor Boo Baby (Keana Jackson) appears to have family. Slick, an aspiring rapper, lives in a garage, and Boo has sought a substitute family through gang affiliation.

All of the young women are gifted ballplayers, and Isaiah has little difficulty shaping them into a winning organization. He stresses teamwork, and the players comply without complaint: no one hogs the ball; no one showboats. When Capricorn lacks focus on the court, Isaiah gains her confidence, and she confides in him about her mother. His emotional support helps put her back on track. Isaiah talks firmly with Boo about the potential consequences of keeping company with West Side gang leader Troy (The Game) and influences her decision to choose the Lady Cavaliers over the West Side.

Boo has her West Side tattoo removed—by Kiwi's stepfather—and works to bring up her grades. However, Troy regards her choice as disloyalty and disrespect. He sends a female gangbanger armed with a semiautomatic handgun to change her mind. Boo refuses to return to the gang, and Shuga and Capricorn arrive in time to prevent Boo from being shot. But the violence has only been postponed.

After winning a semifinal match, the Cavaliers head off for a dance. Most of the players board the team bus, but Two Two persuades her father to let her drive his car. Boo slides into the passenger seat, but before Two Two can start the motor, Troy and his accomplice stage a drive-by, hitting Two Two. She dies instantly. Isaiah, who has been standing by the car, witnesses his daughter's murder. Boo, unharmed, cradles Two Two's body and sobs.

Blaming herself for the murder, Boo leaves Two Two's funeral, intent on taking her own life. However, Darnel has followed her and intercedes. Although she still carries her guilt, Boo wants to remain on the team. After a bit of drama the other players welcome her back and determine to win the championship in Two Two's memory.

Meanwhile, Isaiah understandably lacks the heart to continue coaching and announces his resignation. Darnel and Principal Dillins both encourage him to change his mind, but it is the Lady Cavaliers who convince him to return.

The championship game unfolds predictably. The Lady Cavs meet their fiercest rivals, the Pirates, whose cut-throat coach demands his players do whatever it takes to win. The film cuts between locker-room speeches to highlight contrasting philosophies of cooperation and teamwork versus aggressive self-centeredness. In the end, the Lady Cavs triumph, Two Two's number is retired, and the basketball program is saved.

Tournament of Dreams is a low-budget film that suffers from heavy-handedness. Many of the scenes among the teens take place on a playground, against a mural of wall-sized portraits of black male leaders. Martin Luther King's visage dwarfs the actors during dramatic moments. A film that wraps its plot around the fate of a girls' basketball team seems a strange venue for a message directed especially at a black male audience. The players' individual stories hold interest, but most are underdeveloped. A romantic subplot with Two Two and a male b-baller seems to serve the purpose of illustrating masculine irresponsibility in pressing for sex without considering the consequences. Slick, who has won a talent contest, is hoodwinked by a phony promoter and loses her savings; she also abandons the team, temporarily, but her absence fails to draw Isaiah's attention or to affect the team. And the starting point—to demonstrate that athletic participation improves academic performance—gets left in the dust. The team's salvation, coming on the heels of a gang killing, seems based on the team's winning record rather than on evidence of scholarly improvement and character development. At the end of the film, which contains the typical disclaimer that all events and characters portrayed are fictitious, the audience is told that Isaiah continued to coach, leading the Lady Cavs to four more championships. No follow-ups are provided on the futures of Boo, Slick, Kiwi, Shuga, and Capricorn.

TRADING HEARTS (1988)

DIRECTOR: Neil Leifer. SCREENPLAY: Frank Deford. PRODUCER: Josi W. Konski. CINEMATOGRAPHY: Karen Grossman. EDITING: Rick Shaine. MUSIC: Stanley Myers. PRODUCTION DESIGN: George Goodridge.

CAST: Raul Julia (Vinnie Iacona), Beverly D'Angelo (Donna Nottingham), Jenny Lewis (Yvonne Rhonda Nottingham), Paris Buckner (Robert Nottingham).

RUNNING TIME: 88 minutes.

VHS: Live / Artisan.

Sportswriter Frank Deford's romantic drama centers on a relationship between a has-been baseball player and a failed nightclub singer.

THE TRIPLETS OF BELLEVILLE (2003)

DIRECTOR: Sylvain Chomet. SCREENPLAY: Sylvain Chomet. PRODUCERS: Didier Brunner, Viviane Vanfleteren. EDITING: Dominique Brune, Chantal Colibert Brunner, Dominique Lefever. MUSIC: Benoît Charest. PRODUCTION DESIGN: Evgeni Tomov. ART DIRECTION: Thierry Million.
CAST (VOICES): Lina Boudreau, Béatrice Bonifassi, Michèle Caucheteux, Jean-Claude Donda, Mari-Lou Gauthier.
RUNNING TIME: 96 minutes.
ACADEMY AWARD NOMINATIONS: Best Animated Feature, Best Original Song ("Belleville Rendez-Vous"; music by Benoît Charest, lyrics by Sylvain Chomet).
DVD: Sony Pictures.

This animated French film is about a Tour de France cyclist who is kidnapped.

TRUE BLUE (1995)

DIRECTOR: Ferdinand Fairfax. SCREENPLAY: Rupert Walters, based on the book by Daniel Topolski and Patrick Robinson. PRODUCERS: Davina Belling, Clive Parsons. CINEMATOGRAPHY: Brian Tufano. EDITING: Les Healey. MUSIC: Stanislas Syrewicz. PRODUCTION DESIGN: Alison Riva. ART DIRECTION: Jane Tomblin. COSTUME DESIGN: Delphine Roche-Gordon.
CAST: Johan Leysen (Daniel Topolski), Dominic West (Donald MacDonald), Geraldine Somerville (Ruth MacDonald), Josh Lucas (Dan Warren).
RUNNING TIME: 118 minutes.

This film is based on the 1987 Oxford-Cambridge rowing race that was plagued with controversy.

TWO FOR THE MONEY (2005)

DIRECTOR: D. J. Caruso. SCREENPLAY: Dan Gilroy. PRODUCERS: Jay Cohen, James G. Robinson. CINEMATOGRAPHY: Conrad W. Hall. EDITING: Glen Scantlebury. MUSIC: Christophe Beck. PRODUCTION DESIGN: Tom Southwell. ART DIRECTION: William Heslup, Nicholas Lundy. COSTUME DESIGN: Marie-Sylvie Deveau.
CAST: Matthew McConaughey (Brandon Lang), Al Pacino (Walter Abrams), Rene Russo (Toni Morrow), Jeremy Piven (Jerry), Armand Assante (Novian).
RUNNING TIME: 122 minutes.
DVD: Universal Studios.

This film is about a former football player who uses his instincts to become a gambling promoter under the tutelage of a shady mentor.

TWO-LANE BLACKTOP (1971)

DIRECTOR: Monte Hellman. SCREENPLAY: Will Corry, Rudy Wurlitzer. PRODUCER: Michael S. Laughlin. CINEMATOGRAPHY: Jack Deerson. EDITING: Monte Hellman. COSTUME DESIGN: Richard Bruno.
CAST: James Taylor (Driver), Warren Oates (GTO), Laurie Bird (the girl), Dennis Wilson (Mechanic), David Drake (station attendant), Rudy Wurlitzer (hot rod driver), Harry Dean Stanton (hitchhiker).
RUNNING TIME: 102 minutes.
DVD: Criterion.

Musicians James Taylor and Dennis Wilson, who was the drummer for the Beach Boys, star in *Two-Lane Blacktop* as the unnamed Driver (Taylor) and Mechanic (Wilson) who live on the road in a '55 Chevy and support themselves by participating in illegal street races. Directed by Monte Hellman, the film opened to critical acclaim and was selected as *Esquire*'s movie of the year; although it bombed at the box office, it has a strong cult following and is often taught in film schools as an example of American New Wave cinema.

Before the opening credits Hellman establishes the counter-culture nature of the film as a drag race is broken up by police and a car chase ensues. The camera focuses on the Chevy rather than on the occupants, indicating the centrality of the automobile to the film. There is little dialogue, and the relationship between Driver and Mechanic is based on racing. Mechanic scouts out potential rivals at street meets, itemizing horsepower and torque as the two cruise rows of souped-up cars on display; Driver wastes few words in setting up a challenge. Typically, races are portrayed through sound, and the roar and hum of engines dominate these scenes. Although Driver and Mechanic win these contests, their interests lie in maintaining the car at peak performance rather than in wracking up victories; the races finance the journey, which in itself has no expressed purpose beyond its own continuation. In fact, the two young men are heading east on Route 66 from Needles, California, instead of traveling westward on the legendary road, the typical path followed by pursuers (such as Steinbeck's Joad family) of the American Dream.

One morning while Driver and Mechanic are eating at a diner, the camera draws attention to the parking lot, where a female hitchhiker, after looking over the vehicles, climbs into the back of the Chevy. Both Driver and Mechanic notice her when they return to the car, but neither acknowledges her presence, and they drive off in a silence that remains unbroken until they are back on the road and the girl asks about the car. She is willing to chat, but the men don't respond. Her attempts to attract the attention of Mechanic by massaging his shoulders are ignored; Mechanic is concentrating on listening to the engine, which he says isn't breathing right. In Santa Fe, New Mexico, the girl contributes to expenses by panhandling, and later that evening, they pick up an easy three hundred dollars racing a '38 Ford. That night they stay in a motel. Driver goes out drinking by himself. When he returns, he hears sounds of lovemaking coming from the room, so he remains outside, slumped with his back against the wall.

The fourth major character, referred to as GTO (Warren Oates), has also been following Route 66 eastward and has passed the Chevy on several occasions in his Orbit Orange muscle car. GTO picks up hitchhikers to keep him company. They provide an audience for his ever-changing life story and his pride in his machine, a showroom model with a 455-cubic-inch engine, 350 horsepower, and 500 foot pounds of torque. He complains to one passenger that the guys in the '55 Chevy have been shadowing him, a line that reveals GTO fabricates stories and manipulates reality; it also introduces a tension that fails to develop into a sustained rivalry or conflict.

The plot seems as if it will take off when the Pontiac and the Chevy end up at the same service station. After a halted conversation about cicadas with Driver, the girl walks across the pavement and gets into GTO's car. He tells her he won it shooting craps and has money he wants to spend. After looking over the Chevy, he challenges Driver and Mechanic. They offer to race for pink slips—that is, registration slips—and let GTO select the finishing point. GTO names Washington, D.C. When they set off, the girl has returned to the Chevy; she tries massaging Driver's shoulders, but he rejects the overture, turns off the radio—another distraction—and concentrates on driving. GTO, meanwhile, is singing along with his state-of-the art tape deck; he stops for another hitchhiker, this time a cowboy (Harry Dean Stanton) who makes a pass at him and, like the girl in the Chevy, is rejected. GTO attempts to ditch the cowboy by the side of the road, but it is raining and his passenger refuses to leave the car; they ride in silence to the next town, where GTO sends him off.

After both cars stop for burgers, GTO slips out, getting a head start on the Chevy, but he is soon pulled over for speeding. The Chevy stops as well, and Mechanic tells the officer that GTO has been driving recklessly, passing them on the right at 90 mph. Then the Chevy peels out, dividing the attention of the officer so that GTO can make his escape as well. When GTO catches up with the Chevy, he expresses irritation at their intervention, even though their actions saved him, at the very least, from an expensive ticket. Before a quarrel can develop, he is offered a hardboiled egg (already peeled), and GTO repays the gesture by sharing his stash of booze and pills. And because GTO is fatigued, they agree to a switch, so that Mechanic drives the Pontiac and GTO rides with Driver. Mechanic guns the Pontiac as they take off, but Driver easily leaves the Mechanic behind in a cloud of exhaust. GTO registers shock, but only briefly. He begins to tell Driver how his life fell apart, but Driver interrupts, saying that he's not interested; they continue into the night in silence.

In Oklahoma, the men stop at a garage that has not yet opened. The girl wanders off, and Driver takes the Chevy to find her, leaving Mechanic and GTO to get some sleep; GTO, who has continued to drink, passes out. When Driver locates the girl, she is once again hitchhiking, but she returns to the Chevy, and in the next scene she and Driver are physically intimate. By this point the men seem to have forgotten about the race. There is another near miss with the police. Mechanic maintains both cars, whose carburetors require constant attention. When the younger men run short of cash, GTO helps them con some locals into a race.

Later, the Chevy comes upon a bad accident which may have been caused by GTO. The driver and perhaps a passenger have been killed; two children were not harmed. A few days later, GTO stops for an elderly woman and her granddaughter, whose parents were killed a few days earlier "by a city car." GTO drops the pair off at a graveyard.

The cars make their way to yet another race track, where Driver casually mentions that after Washington, D.C., they may drive down to Florida. The girl's response is to grab her backpack and move to GTO's car. While Driver and Mechanic race a Corvette, GTO and the girl leave, and the race is once again on. GTO, who has invited the girl to ride with him several times, also mentions going to Florida after the race and relaxing on the beaches. He is willing to change his plans according to her whims, claiming that he will "go into orbit" if he is not "grounded" soon.

GTO stops at another burger stand, and Mechanic spots the car as the Chevy speeds past; he waits five miles before telling Driver, who then makes a U-turn. At the burger place, Driver and Mechanic join GTO and the girl at their table as if they had all planned to meet. Driver suggests they drive to Columbus for parts. While the men finish eating, the girl leaves the table. In the background she can be seen climbing behind a young man on a motorcycle; she abandons her backpack, which she can't carry on the bike. Driver and Mechanic arrange a race at a nearby airport. GTO leaves with a "see ya." He stops for a couple of soldiers, telling them he is on his way to New York and that he won his car in a pink slip race against a '55 Chevy. In the closing scene at the airport, Driver revs the engine, and the race starts, but in utter silence. The movie ends with the film apparently catching fire as it plays.

Two-Lane Blacktop was shot on location in sequence. Hellman, who is known for maintaining tight control over his work, would not allow the actors to see the entire script, providing them at the end of each day with just their lines for the next day's shooting. Like Miloš Forman, Hellman employs nonactors chosen for their natural attributes, and like Forman, he has discovered that amateurs, when given ample time to rehearse, will try to imitate their favorite actors and are often "directed" in their efforts by next of kin. Hellman also wanted his actors in a position similar to that of their characters, who are concerned only with the present moment, not the future. (James Taylor, whom Hellman sought for a screen test based on a billboard advertising Taylor's debut album, found this method of working deeply unsatisfying and went on strike until Hellman yielded and showed him the script; however, once Taylor was permitted to read it, he declined to do so.)

The characters stay consistently with the present moment throughout. Neither Driver nor Mechanic reveals anything about his past; the girl refers to family when she is panhandling and is clearly lying about her situation. GTO launches into a different story about his past every time he picks up a hitchhiker, but whether any of this is true cannot be established and seems not to matter. Nor do the characters show much of what they are thinking or feeling. The men's competition for the girl's companionship seems based on her unpredictability rather than on physical desire; she is merely more unpredictable than their race. She exhibits no interest whatsoever in any permanent connection. The characters exist in an emotional void, always moving, but never with direction.

U

UNDISPUTED (2002)

DIRECTOR: Walter Hill. SCREENPLAY: David Giler, Walter Hill. PRODUCERS: David Giler, Walter Hill, Brad Krevoy, Andrew Sugarman. CINEMATOGRAPHY: Lloyd Ahern II. EDITING: Freeman A. Davies, Phil Nordern. MUSIC: Stanley Clarke. PRODUCTION DESIGN: Maria Rebman Caso. ART DIRECTION: Michael D. Costello. COSTUME DESIGN: Barbara Inglehart.

CAST: Wesley Snipes (Monroe Hutchen), Ving Rhames (George "Iceman" Chambers), Peter Falk (Mendy Ripstein), Michael Rooker (A. J. Mercker), Jon Seda (Jesus "Chuy" Campos), Wes Studi (Mingo Pace).

RUNNING TIME: 94 minutes.

DVD: Miramax.

Convicted of murder, a prison boxer tests his skills against the world's champion, who has just begun to serve a sentence of his own. Three direct-to-video sequels followed.

THE UNKNOWN CYCLIST (1998)

DIRECTOR: Bernard Salzmann. SCREENPLAY: Matthew Carlisle, Betsy Pool, Howie Skora. PRODUCERS: Matthew Carlisle, Betsy Pool. CINEMATOGRAPHY: Mike Fash, Bernard Salzmann. EDITING: Irit Raz. MUSIC: Sydney Forest, Donald Markowitz. PRODUCTION DESIGN: W. Stewart Campbell. ART DIRECTION: Scott H. Campbell. COSTUME DESIGN: W. Stewart Campbell, Marcy Grace Froehlich.

CAST: Lea Thompson (Melissa Cavatelli), Vincent Spano (Frank Cavatelli), Danny Nucci (Gaetano Amador), Stephen Spinella (Doug Stein), Michael J. Pollard (Gabe Sinclair).

RUNNING TIME: 96 minutes.

At an AIDS bike-a-thon in California, friends and family of recently deceased man honor his last wishes.

V

VARSITY BLUES (1999)

DIRECTOR: Brian Robbins. SCREENPLAY: W. Peter Iliff. PRODUCERS: Tova Laiter, Brian Robbins, Michael Tollin. CINEMATOGRAPHY: Chuck Cohen. EDITING: Ned Bastille. MUSIC: Mark Isham. PRODUCTION DESIGN: Jaymes Hinkle. ART DIRECTION: Keith Donnelly. COSTUME DESIGN: Wendy Chuck.
CAST: James Van Der Beek (Jonathon Moxon), Jon Voight (Coach Kilmer), Paul Walker (Lance Harbor), Ron Lester (Billy Bob), Scott Caan (Charlie Tweeder), Ali Larter (Darcy Sears), Amy Smart (Jules Harbor).
RUNNING TIME: 106 minutes.
DVD: Paramount.

An unscrupulous high school football coach is forced to use his second string quarterback when the star player is injured.

VICTORY (1981)

DIRECTOR: John Huston. SCREENPLAY: Evan Jones, Yabo Yablonsky. STORY: Yabo Yablonsky, Djordie Milicevic, Jeff Maguire. PRODUCER: Freddie Fields. CINEMATOGRAPHY: Gerry Fisher. EDITING: Roberto Silvi. MUSIC: Bill Conti. PRODUCTION DESIGN: J. Dennis Washington. COSTUME DESIGN: Tom Bronson.
CAST: Sylvester Stallone (Hatch), Michael Caine (John Colby), Max von Sydow (Major von Steiner), Pelé (Luis Fernandez), Daniel Massey (Waldron), Carole Laure (Renée), Bobby Moore (Terry Brady).
RUNNING TIME: 116 minutes.
DVD: Warner Home Video.

In *Victory* a soccer match between World War II Allied prisoners of war and the German national soccer team provides the cover for a successful escape by the Allied players. The plot is similar to that of *The Great Escape* (1963), but despite having an excellent director (John Huston) and an extraordinary cast (Michael Caine, Max von Sydow, and Sylvester Stallone) with soccer stars Pelé and Bobby Moore, *Victory* lacks the intensity of the earlier movie.

Huston establishes the prison camp setting at Gensdorf and then films an unsuccessful escape attempt by "young Williams," who is shot to death as he tries to cut his way through barbed wire. Next we are introduced to John Colby (Michael Caine), a professional soccer player from England who will coach the Allied team, and Major von Steiner (Max von Sydow), a former member of the German soccer team, which at this point had never beaten an English team. Intent on finally defeating an English team, von Steiner offers Captain Colby enough concessions (better food, the use of regular soldiers in addition to officers, and the use of Polish and Czech players) to get him to agree to an exhibition match between the Germans and the Allies.

Another plotline involves Hatch (Stallone), an American who has hatched an escape plan. The escape committee approves his scheme and helps him secure the necessary documents and clothes for his attempt. Then, after the Germans announce that the soccer match will be staged in occupied Paris, the committee envisions a mass escape of the players. To pull off such a feat will require assistance from the French Resistance. Consequently, Hatch is appointed to get word to the French after his escape and then to allow himself to be recaptured in order to report back.

Hatch succeeds in escaping Gensdorf and traveling to Paris, where he meets Renée (Carole Laure) and the French Resistance, who propose an escape through the sewer system that runs beneath Colombe Stadium. When Hatch returns to Gensdorf, he is put in solitary confinement. Colby tries to secure his release by claiming he is needed as a trainer; however the Germans insist they will provide a trainer. Colby's follow-up ploy is to maintain that Hatch, an inept soccer player, is the backup goalie and is needed because the Allies' starting goalie, Tony (Kevin O'Callaghan), has a broken arm. Unfortunately for Tony, the Germans dispatch a physician to examine him, and he must allow his comrades to fracture the necessary bones.

The match at Colombe is played before fifty thousand French soccer fans who grow increasingly enthusiastic about the Allied players and their cause. Although the Germans have promised Colby a fair match, the referee has been instructed to ensure a German victory. The referee ignores the German team's rough tactics, which injure the Allied team's star player, Luis Fernandez (Pelé). While the game is played, the Resistance is busy making their way through the sewers. Huston crosscuts between the match and the Resistance efforts. At the half, during which the escape is to take place, the Germans lead 4–1.

After the Allied players enter their locker room, they find that the Resistance has broken through, providing them with the necessary escape route, but some of the players, led by Luis, want to finish the match first because they believe they can win. Reluctantly, Hatch agrees, and the Allies take the field for the second half. Cheered on by French fans screaming "Victoire," the Allies make an incredible comeback and apparently tie the score, but the referee disallows the goal. At this point Luis, who has a broken rib, insists on entering the game and scores the tying goal on an acrobatic backward kick.

After a questionable call by the referee, the Germans are allowed a point-blank penalty kick. As the audience sings the "Marseillaise," Hatch walks up to the German kicker, gives him the Rocky stare, returns to the goal, and stops the penalty kick, leaving the game tied at four. It is a tie, but it really is a win for the Allies, who are mobbed by fans. The Allies and fans then rush out of the gates, the players to freedom, and Hatch to Renée.

VISION QUEST (1985)

DIRECTOR: Harold Becker. SCREENPLAY: Darryl Ponicsan, based on the novel by Terry Davis. PRODUCERS: Peter Guber, Jon Peters. CINEMATOGRAPHY: Owen Roizman. EDITING: Maury Winetrobe. MUSIC: Tangerine Dream. PRODUCTION DESIGN: Bill Malley. COSTUME DESIGN: Susan Becker.

CAST: Matthew Modine (Louden Swain), Linda Fiorentino (Carla), Michael Schoeffling (Kuch), Ronny Cox (Louden's father), Harold Sylvester (Mr.

Tanneran), Charles Hallahan (Coach), Daphne Zuniga (Margie Epstein), Forest Whitaker (Balldozer).
RUNNING TIME: 105 minutes.
DVD: Warner Home Video.

Like many sports films featuring high school athletes, *Vision Quest* is also a coming-of-age story about sex and athletics. It features Louden Swain (Matthew Modine), a high-school senior who has had an impressive career wrestling at 190 pounds, but who now wants to drop two weight classes to take on Shute (Frank Jasper), a legendary "monster" in the 168-pound class, the "toughest weight class in the world." Louden, who has just turned eighteen, wants to "make his mark" during the year. He first must defeat his friend Kuch (Michael Schoeffling), number one at 178 pounds. Louden wins, but the two remain close and Kuch (who has invented a story about having Native American ancestry) wants to help Louden attain what Kuch terms his "vision quest," even though he's not exactly sure what the term means. Although the term, which is related to "finding your place in the circle," is never defined precisely, clearly there is a quest, and several people sense that Louden is on one.

In addition to having Kuch in his corner, Louden has help from an unexpected

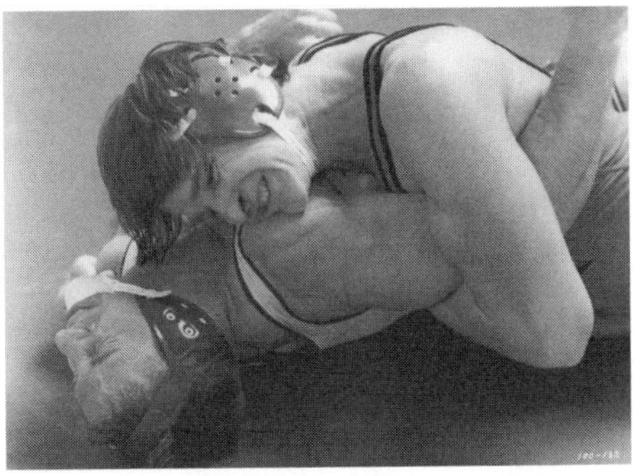

Matthew Modine as Louden Swain with Frank Jasper as his opponent, Shute, in *Vision Quest*

source, Carla (Linda Fiorentino), a twenty-one-year-old from New Jersey who is passing through but stays with Louden and his father (Ronny Cox) and who becomes another sort of quest for the virginal teen. Carla is an aspiring artist on her way to San Francisco, but she sees in Louden what others don't and helps him through a tough passage. Though he is in many ways a typical jock, he is also a talented writer. His English teacher, Mr. Tanneran (Harold Sylvester), helps him to develop his literary skills. Louden's response to Matthew Arnold's poem "Margaret" reveals him to have a sensitive side that is also reflected in the articles he writes for the school newspaper. He also battles hormones, discusses his nocturnal emissions, and eventually makes an unsuccessful pass at Carla, who deflates his passion, at least momentarily, when she says she thinks of him as a stepbrother.

Louden's attempts to lose weight worry his coach (Charles Hallahan), especially when he gets nosebleeds and loses by disqualification when the bleeding cannot be stopped. After that match and before his big match with Shute, Louden and Carla drive up into the Washington woods to see Louden's grandfather. Intimate talk around the campfire and the lantern light in the tent lead inevitably to sex. The next day Louden is not the self-assured man he may have hoped he'd be; he's still a kid concerned about performance. Clearly he sees his relationship with Carla progressing to another level, but she has more sense than he does and disappears before his match with Shute. She reappears when he is alone, tells him she didn't know how to say "goodbye," and adds that she "would do it again." "So would I," he responds. She watches him come from behind in his match with Shute and pin him, completing the quest. The film received mediocre reviews, but the performances of Modene and Fiorentino have drawn favorable mention.

W

THE WATERBOY (1998)

DIRECTOR: Frank Coraci. SCREENPLAY: Tim Herlihy, Adam Sandler. PRODUCER: Jack Giarraputo, Robert Simonds. CINEMATOGRAPHY: Steven Bernstein. EDITING: Tom Lewis. MUSIC: Alan Pasqua. PRODUCTION DESIGN: Perry Andelin Blake. ART DIRECTION: Alan Au. COSTUME DESIGN: Tom Bronson.

CAST: Adam Sandler (Bobby Boucher Jr.), Kathy Bates (Helen Boucher), Henry Winkler (Coach Klein), Fairuza Balk (Vicki Vallencourt).

RUNNING TIME: 90 minutes.

DVD: Walt Disney Video.

A slow-witted water boy is transformed into a football star when he shows he has skills to run and tackle.

WE ARE MARSHALL (2006)

DIRECTOR: McG. SCREENPLAY: Jamie Linden. STORY: Cory Helms, Jamie Linden. PRODUCER: Basil Iwanyk. CINEMATOGRAPHY: Shane Hurlbut. EDITING: Gregg London, Priscilla Nedd Friendly. MUSIC: Christophe Beck. PRODUCTION DESIGN: Tom Meyer. ART DIRECTION: Jonah Markowitz. COSTUME DESIGN: Danny Glicker.

CAST: Matthew McConaughey (Jack Lengyel), Matthew Fox (William "Red" Dawson), Anthony Mackie (Nate Ruffin), Ian McShane (Paul Griffen), David Strathairn (Donald Dedmon), Kate Mara (Annie Cantrell), January Jones (Carole Dawson), Kimberly Williams (Sandy Lengyel).

RUNNING TIME: 131 minutes.

DVD: Warner Home Video.

On November 14, 1970, a plane carrying seventy-five passengers, including thirty-seven members of the Marshall University football team, the head coach, five staff members, and twenty-two boosters, crashed, killing all aboard. *We Are Marshall* is a fictionalized account of the team's rebuilding in the aftermath of the crash.

The film opens with voice-over narration about the town of Huntington and the date and exact time that fountains are turned off. In fact, time itself seems to be suspended there. Footage of Marshall's last game before the accident is confined to the waning moments of the contest with the Thundering Herd trailing East Carolina. A desperation pass, with the ball spiraling in slow motion, goes incomplete, and Marshall loses. In his postgame talk, Coach Talley recognizes the players' efforts but declares that "winning is everything." In the course of the film, his words will undergo serious reexamination.

Following the accident, university president Donald Dedmon (David Strathairn), and the board of trustees plan to terminate the football program; but team member Nate Ruffin (Anthony Mackie), who was not on the flight because of an injured shoulder, spearheads a drive to unite Marshall students in support of the program's continuation. The students, chanting "We are Marshall," convince the president and trustees to change their minds. Not everyone, however, is able to support the decision. Nate's roommate and best friend, Tom (Brian Geraghty), will not or cannot return to the team because he suffers from survivor's guilt: he missed the plane ride because he overslept and believes that he should have been with his doomed teammates. Paul Griffen (Ian McShane), whose son starred on the team and was engaged to Annie Cantrell (Kate Mara), is tormented by the earlier loss of his wife as well as the death of his son. His hell-like life is suggested by repeated shots of him against a background of flames at the local steel mill. So profound is his grief that he refuses to take back the engagement ring his son had given his fiancée, thereby binding her to the past as well. The assistant coach, William "Red" Dawson (Matthew Fox), who was replaced on the flight by another coach, also has survivor's guilt and initially will not rejoin the coaching staff. His determination to rebuild his garage suggests his need to start anew. Although he finally accepts the job of assistant coach, he is so haunted by the past that during one game he hallucinates about his former coach and team.

Saving the football program is difficult, as the president discovers when he attempts to recruit a coach. He gets his man in Jack Lengyel (Matthew McConaughey), the coach at the College of Wooster, whose desire to help convinces the president he is the man for the job. With only three returning lettermen, Jack and his staff have trouble recruiting players, so he persuades the president to petition the NCAA to make an exception to the rule that freshmen cannot play. The president finally succeeds when he travels to Kansas City, gets drenched in a deluge, and approaches an official directly. Able to promise high school seniors that they can play the next year, Lengyel recruits some young talent, but, as one sportswriter points out, the team is about two years younger than most of its competition. Undeterred, Jack fills out his roster with athletes from other Marshall sports teams and with promising transfer students.

Once training gets under way, Jack realizes that he has the offensive linemen to make his favorite Power I formation work, and in a brainstorming session with the rest of the staff is convinced that the veer offense, played by in-state rival West Virginia University (WVU), may be the answer. He and Red, who can't believe that WVU will help them, approach Bobby Bowden, the WVU football coach, who surprises both Marshall coaches by granting them access to playbooks and films. Bowden says he is willing to help since the two teams do not play each other in the year, but the true extent of the gesture is revealed when Jack and Red see three WVU players' helmets adorned with a cross and an MU for Marshall.

Things improve as the team moves gingerly away from the past. At one point a new player walks into a dorm room, picks up a can of beer from a six-pack procured a year ago by a Marshall player who never got to drink it, and after a pause is joined by other players. Despite their improvement the Marshall squad is no match for Morehead State, their first opponent. Questions then surface about whether Marshall should have continued the program. As teammates begin to bicker and Nate, the captain, explodes in anger, Red suggests that continuing is bringing the worst, not the best, out in the players and in himself.

Paul worsens the situation by getting the board to fire President Dedmond. According to Paul, the town is "bleeding" and he is concerned about Annie's response to the continuation of the program. Dedmond, who knows better, tells him, "This is about the loss of your son," and adds that he needs to find the strength to heal himself.

Before playing Xavier, their first home game, there is "reflection time" as the cameras provide mid-shots of all the principals in the film: Annie looking at her ring; Paul grieving in his office; Nate trying to pretend that his injury will not prevent him from playing; Jack joining Red in church, where the winning-is-everything theme resurfaces. Jack says, "It's not true anymore, not now," and that keeping the game alive is paramount. Before the game, Jack takes his team to the memorial where six Marshall players are buried and links the past with the present and the future. He tells them that what will be remembered is not the score but "how you play today." Paul also has a change of heart. He visits Annie at Boone's Diner, takes her for a walk, and tells her to go to California, where she and his son had planned to go. When she protests that he will be alone, he tells her, "Grief is messy." He finally frees her by agreeing to take back the family engagement ring that she has been wearing.

Although Xavier's offense moves the ball, Marshall's defense holds on and the team goes into the half with a 3–0 lead. Nate, who has reinjured his shoulder and does not play the second half, assures Red that the team will retain its lead. With less than a minute to play, Marshall recovers the ball and drives for the goal line. The last play is almost a repeat of the pass thrown at the end of the East Carolina game. As the ball continues to spiral, the screen is filled with a montage of shots from the past, but finally the ball is caught, and Marshall wins. Jack presents the game ball for the Most Valuable Player to President Dedmond, and the crowd stays on the field celebrating for hours.

The last sequence focuses on Annie driving a Volkswagen Bug west, presumably to California. A voice-over provides information about the aftermath of the Xavier game: President Dedmond accepts the presidency of Radford University; Jack coaches another three years with a 9–36 record before becoming the athletic director at the U.S. Naval Academy; Red retires from coaching after the one season he promised Jack; and in 1984 Marshall completes its first winning season since the disaster. The team went on to win two NCAA AA championships. As Jack tells Red, "We play the game." Winning is important, but moving on and persevering have their own rewards.

WHEN SATURDAY COMES (1996)

Director: Maria Giese. Screenplay: James Daly, Maria Giese. Producers: James Daly, Christopher Lambert, Meir Teper. Cinematography: Grant Cameron, Gerry Fisher. Editing: George Akers. Music: Anne Dudley. Production Design: Hugo Luczyc-Wyhowski. Art Direction: Luana Hanson. Costume Design: Kate Carin.

Cast: Sean Bean (Jimmy Muir), Emily Lloyd (Annie Doherty), Pete Postlethwaite (Ken Jackson), Craig Kelly (Russell Muir), John McEnery (Joe Muir).

Running Time: 98 minutes.

DVD: IN2FILM (UK: PAL).

A hard-drinking football (soccer) player must prove to himself and others that he has the discipline to play on a professional team.

WHIP IT (2009)

Director: Drew Barrymoore. Screenplay: Shauna Cross, based on her novel. Producer: Barry Mendel. Cinematog-

RAPHY: Robert Yeoman. EDITING: Dylan Tichenor. MUSIC: The Section Quartet. PRODUCTION DESIGN: Kevin Kavanaugh. COSTUME DESIGN: Catherine Marie Thomas.
CAST: Ellen Page (Bliss Cavendar), Drew Barrymore (Smashley Simpson), Kristen Wiig (Maggie Mayhem), Marcia Gay Harden (Brooke Cavendar), Juliette Lewis (Iron Maven), Jimmy Fallon (Hot Tub Johnny), Alia Shawkat (Pash).
RUNNING TIME: 111 minutes.
DVD: 20th Century Fox.

Drew Barrymore makes her directorial debut in this coming-of-age story starring Ellen Page as Bliss Cavendar, a restless seventeen-year-old looking for a way out of her claustrophobic hometown and an alternative to her mother's obsession with beauty pageants. Barrymore, who also plays a minor character, roller derby skater Smashley Simpson, keeps the tone light in spite of the dramatic potential of the plotlines.

The Cavendars are a blue-collar family living in a small town outside of Austin, Texas. Like most of the men in the community, Bliss's father, Earl (Daniel Stern), depends on a local factory for employment and spends as much time as he can manage watching football on television. Bliss waitresses after school at the Oink Joint, a diner known for its giant barbeque sandwich, the Squealer (free if consumed within three minutes), and for the enormous plastic pig on the roof. Bliss is a competent but unenthusiastic server earning little from tips. Her mother, Brooke (Marcia Gay Harden), is a former beauty queen who regrets not having capitalized on her youthful triumph. Although she shares a loving relationship with Earl, the film suggests that marriage and family came too soon. Now she works as a mail carrier and devotes her spare time to grooming Bliss for a more promising future. However, Bliss approaches the pageants rebelliously, as is evident in the opening scene, where she adds blue streaks to her hair just before going onstage in a local contest. She stands out among the other contestants not only because of her daring "do," but also because of her original response to the question "With whom would you want to have dinner?" Bliss selects Amelia Earhart, whose courage and sense of adventure she admires.

Soon Bliss discovers heroes closer to home. While on a shopping trip to Austin, she encounters a group of skaters distributing flyers for the upcoming women's roller derby season. She convinces her best friend, Pash (Alia Shawkat), to accompany her to an exhibition match. Dressed in their school colors and carrying pennants, the girls drive to Austin under the pretense of attending a football game. At the venue, the appropriately named Warehouse, Bliss and Pash become caught up in the excitement.

Roller derby is a contact sport skated on an oval track. One skater from each team, the "jammer," scores a point for each member of the opposing team she passes. Skaters can block, throw hip-checks, and "whip" the jammer ahead. The league portrayed in the film, like most in the United States, is a grassroots organization with all-female teams. Skaters often affect a punk style and skate under witty track names. An emcee provides colorful commentary. Generally, the scene is good-naturedly irreverent. Rivalries between teams and among players are part of the entertainment, but the sport is known for fostering camaraderie among the participants, who often practice and socialize together no matter what their team affiliations.

This is the world Bliss wants to inhabit. Her invitation comes after the exhibition match when she approaches some of the skaters and announces they have become her heroes. One of the women, Maggie Mayhem (Kristen Wiig), challenges her to try out for the league, hence becoming her own hero. The next week, Bliss boards the

Bingo Bus—a converted school bus that transports senior citizens to Austin for nightly bingo sessions—and travels to the Warehouse. At the tryout, she discovers that she is quite the speedster. She qualifies for the league, joining the Hurl Scouts, a team with a losing record but a sincere coach (Andrew Wilson as Razor).

After telling her parents that she is taking an SAT prep course in the evenings, Bliss travels regularly on the Bingo Bus. Skating as Babe Ruthless, she develops into an effective jammer and helps spirit the Hurl Scouts to a winning season. After the matches, she and Pash party with the other skaters at emcee Hot Tub Johnny's (Jimmy Fallon), where Bliss meets a musician (Landon Pigg as Oliver) and falls in love. However, in accomplishing all of this, she has woven an incredibly complex web of deception, which unravels quickly when the police and fire marshals raid the Warehouse and Pash is arrested. The Cavendars learn that Bliss has not been preparing for the SAT or working extra shifts and that on the night of the raid, she was not having a sleepover at Pash's. What's more, Bliss's derby rival, Iron Maven (Juliette Lewis) of the Holy Rollers, has discovered that Bliss is not twenty-two, as she claimed, but underage and an insurance liability—she will need parental permission to continue with roller derby.

Bliss's parents are angry that she has lied to them, and Bliss is angry that her mother is pushing her toward the Miss Bluebonnet Pageant. Pash blames Bliss for the trouble she is in, and the two quarrel. On the heels of all of this disruption, Oliver and his band leave on a month-long tour. Bliss moves in with Maggie, a single parent who understands Brooke's position as well as Bliss's. When Bliss checks Oliver's band's website and discovers a photo of him with another girl, a girl wearing a T-shirt Bliss had given him, she returns home and makes an awkward peace with her mother. Then she apologizes to Pash.

Although the Hurl Scouts have made it to the season-ending championship, the final is scheduled for the same evening as the Miss Bluebonnet Pageant, which Bliss has elected to enter. She is in her dressing room, wearing the custom gown her mother has ordered and applying makeup when her father and the Hurl Scouts arrive. Earl, having watched a video of Bliss thoroughly enjoying herself as Babe Ruthless, has determined to take matters into his own hands. Bliss lends her gown to another contestant and leaves with her father and the team.

Oliver shows up just before the tournament begins and offers excuses for not returning calls and explanations about the girl in the photo. Bliss kisses his cheek before slapping him soundly; it seems doubtful that she will resume the relationship. Once the championship is underway, the contest falls into a predictably close match. As Bliss and Maven compete as jammers, Bliss makes a spectacular jump and scores a respectable number of points, but not enough to win. Still, Razor and the Hurl Scouts are ecstatic, and Brooke has joined the cheering crowd. The mother-daughter reconciliation is completed serendipitously when Brooke discovers the statement Bliss had prepared for the Miss Bluebonnet Pageant: Bliss has described Brooke as the person she most admires and has credited the importance of her mother's faith in her in helping her to mature.

In spite of a flabby structure that fails to build toward dramatic moments, even in a closely fought championship match, *Whip It* is an enjoyable film that received largely favorable reviews. The acting is strong. Page and Harden maintain a tension that makes the mother-daughter relationship ring true. Barrymore avoids turning Brooke, as well as rival skater Iron Maven, into two-dimensional villains; her skaters are interesting characters rather than the caricatures they could easily have become. The action sequences showcase the skills of the skaters and their enjoyment of the sport. To prepare themselves for roller derby action, the actors attended an intense three-week camp, and they did most of their own skating. Barrymore's character, Smashley, takes a number of spills, but she gets right back up again and keeps skating, having fun in spite of the odd scrape. Barrymore's film is a lot like her character.

WHITE MEN CAN'T JUMP (1992)

DIRECTOR: Ron Shelton. SCREENPLAY: Ron Shelton. PRODUCERS: David Lester, Don Miller. CINEMATOGRAPHY: Russell Boyd. EDITING: Kimberly Ray, Paul Seydor. PRODUCTION DESIGN: J. Dennis Washington. ART DIRECTION: Roger Fortune. COSTUME DESIGN: Francine Jamison-Tanchuck.

CAST: Wesley Snipes (Sidney Deane), Woody Harrelson (Billy Hoyle), Rosie Perez (Gloria Clemente), Cylk Cozart (Robert), Tyra Ferrell (Rhonda), Kadeem Hardison (Junior), Ernest Harden Jr. (George).

RUNNING TIME: 115 minutes.

DVD: 20th Century Fox.

Directed by Ron Shelton, *White Men Can't Jump* is a variation on the buddy film, combining the art of the con and the art of street basketball. Woody Harrelson stars as Billy Hoyle, a hustler who turns stereotypes about white basketball players to his advantage on playground courts in the black neighborhoods of Los Angeles. Hoyle joins forces with Sidney Deane (Wesley Snipes), a black player living with his family in a crime-ridden apartment complex. Sidney is being pressured by his wife, Rhonda (Tyra Ferrell), to acquire the means to move to a safer neighborhood. Billy needs to produce quick cash to pay off a gambling debt.

The film opens at Venice Beach, where among the skateboarders and body builders, Billy Hoyle has paused to listen to a trio of older men singing "Just a Closer Walk with Thee." Billy taps an accompanying rhythm on his ball. After the song, he moves to the basketball court and lounges on the sidelines, now using the ball for a pillow. Nearby, Sidney is trash-talking his opponents in a pickup game. When a man drops out, Billy is the only available replacement. He joins Sidney's opponents and makes a quick impression, not by shooting, but by passing off strategically. Assuming that Billy can't shoot well and needing to raise another twenty dollars, Sidney challenges him to a free throw contest. Billy, who has become the main target of Sidney's wit, turns the tables, winning the match when his taunts about losing twice in a row to a "white chump" throw Sidney off his mark.

Billy returns to his motel room, where his girlfriend, Gloria (Rosie Perez), greets him by asking how much money he has lost. It is revealed that he owes seven thousand dollars to loan sharks, the Stucci brothers (Eloy Casados and Frank Rossi), from whom he and Gloria are running. Gloria, who is obsessed with becoming a contestant on *Jeopardy*, spends her days studying an almanac and sneaking sips of Stolichnaya. A knock on the door throws them into a panic, but the visitor is not the Stuccis, but Sidney, who has an offer for Billy.

Soon the two are running a successful con: Sidney arrives at a playground and makes himself known with a flamboyant verbal display directed at a confident-looking pair of players. He challenges them to a game of two-on-two, handicapping himself by allowing them to select his partner. Billy is always at a distance but highly visible and carrying his basketball, and he is always the only white person present. He is

Wesley Snipes and Woody Harrelson as con artists Sidney Deane and Billy Hoyle in *White Men Can't Jump*; Harrelson and Snipes in action

always appointed Sidney's partner, and the two always win.

In spite of their success, they have not made enough money to resolve their problems. Rhonda wants to buy a house, but Sidney can't swing the down payment yet. The Stuccis are threatening Billy. Consequently, on their next con, when their opponents want to raise the stakes, Sidney and Billy bet their entire bankroll. And lose. Sidney, it turns out, is having a bad day. Billy fears Gloria will leave him when she learns he has lost everything; instead she tells him that he has been hustled and that she is going to retrieve their money. Gloria boards a bus headed for the Crenshaw district, with Billy in pursuit, complaining that she's not playing by the rules. Gloria ignores him. They find Sidney in his living room, watching basketball with friends. Gloria and Rhonda go into the kitchen to talk, leaving the men to what is about to become fisticuffs until the game on television gets interesting and the men's attention is immediately diverted to the screen. By the time the women have devised a plan, the men have bonded in front of the television.

Rhonda has agreed to return a portion of the money so that Billy and Sidney can enter a tournament with a five-thousand-dollar prize. The two men team up once again, but their verbal sparring takes on a hostile edge. In spite of their arguing, they win the tournament. On the way home, they continue to squabble. Billy insists he can dunk a basketball; Sidney counters, "White men can't jump." Determined to prove himself, Billy wagers his share of the prize money. And loses.

For Billy, matters quickly worsen. Gloria leaves him; the Stucci brothers find him. He has a week in which to produce what he owes. With no pride left to swallow, Billy asks Sidney for help. A friend of Sidney's who works security for a production company can get Gloria into the *Jeopardy* studio. But in Billy and Sidney's world, favors don't come for free: Billy must earn the favor by sinking a long basket; if he misses, Sidney will lose his car. Billy points at the hoop in the manner of Babe Ruth, and in the next frame, Gloria is a contestant on the show. She wins a fortune. Afterward, Billy serenades her, and once again, they kiss and make up.

Billy has promised to reform, to quit the hustle and get a real job. Saying she trusts him, Gloria gives him two thousand dollars to buy the clothing and accessories he needs for interviews. However, Billy's intentions to go straight are derailed when Sidney's apartment is robbed and his money stolen. Sidney wants Billy to partner with him again for another contest with a good payoff for the winners. Billy explains the situation to Gloria, but she is not sympathetic. Faced with a choice between keeping his promise to Gloria and repaying his debt to Sidney, Billy opts for the latter. He has convinced himself that he will win and that Gloria will forgive him.

In "the Game" Billy and Sidney face two legendary street players, Eddie "the King" Faroo (Louis Price) and Duck Johnson (Freeman Williams). The score remains close, but Billy sinks the winning basket on an alley-oop. Not only has Billy won, but he has dunked the ball. He has also lost Gloria. Sidney's response is to fault Billy for not listening to her. Shortly after Sidney leaves, the Italians appear for their cash. The scene cuts to a very dead-looking Billy being photographed in an abandoned lot by the brothers. But the scene is staged, and Billy is unharmed. The Stuccis explain they must maintain their image. The film ends where it began in Venice Beach with the trio humming in the background. Billy is talking to Sidney about using him as a job reference, and the two walk off together, deep in disagreement abut Jimi Hendricks.

Like Shelton's earlier film, *Bull Durham* (1988), *White Men Can't Jump* is characterized by fast-paced, witty dialogue. Sidney's on-court chatter and his snipes at Billy play off clichéd street talk without relying on coarseness and without adhering to political correctness. Instead of colorblindness, Shelton foregrounds race and maintains a comic tension without sacrificing character. To this end, he is aided by first-rate performances from Snipes, Harrelson, and Perez.

WHITE PALMS [FEHÉR TENYÉR] (2006)

DIRECTOR: Szabolcs Hajdu. SCREENPLAY: Szabolcs Hajdu. PRODUCERS: Ivan Angelusz, Mathieu Kassovitz, Gábor Kovács, Ági Pataki, Péter Reich. CINEMATOGRAPHY: András Nagy. EDITING: Péter Politzer. MUSIC: Ferenc Darvas. PRODUCTION DESIGN: Mónika Esztán. ART DIRECTION: Szilvia Ritter. COSTUME DESIGN: Krisztina Berzsenyi.

CAST: Zoltán Miklós Hajdu (Miklós Dongó), Orion Radies (Miklós at age ten), Silas Radies (Miklós at age thirteen), Gheorghe Dinica (Puma), Kyle Shewfelt (Kyle Manjak), Oana Pellea (Miklós's mother), Andor Lukáts (Miklós's father).

RUNNING TIME: 100 minutes.

DVD: Strand Releasing.

White Palms is a stunning semiautobiographical/biographical film written and directed by Szabolcs Hajdu and starring his brother Zoltán Miklós. Both brothers trained as gymnasts in Hungary during the 1980s, and Zoltán continued with a career in the sport before joining Cirque du Soleil as an acrobat. The title refers to the powdered chalk gymnasts use on their hands to improve grip.

Hajdu develops the story of Miklós Dongó (Zoltán Miklós Hajdu) through a series of flashbacks moving between Calgary, Alberta, in the first years of the twenty-first century and Budapest, Hungary, in the 1980s. The film opens with

Miklós, now in his thirties, arriving in Calgary to start a job coaching young gymnasts. That he will need to adjust to a new culture becomes quickly apparent as he runs afoul of a city ordinance requiring smokers to stay at a distance from public buildings. His introduction to the Canadian gymnasium leads to the first flashback of his own childhood, training in Hungary under a sadistic coach known as Puma (Romanian star Gheorghe Dinica). Puma carries a sword and uses the flat side of the blade to punish the young athletes for minor infractions. Ten-year-old Miklós (Orion Radies), one of Puma's most promising prospects, is subject to intense pressure and suffers regularly from his coach's discipline, while his parents, consumed with pride in his talent, ignore the evidence of abuse.

As a coach, Miklós has no positive role models from his past on whom to draw, so he is ill-prepared to handle Western children. It is not long before he encounters trouble on the job when he strikes a disobedient boy. Enraged parents call for him to be fired; instead, his employer assigns him to work solely with a talented but difficult teenager, Kyle Manjak, played by Canadian Olympic medalist Kyle Shewfelt. Kyle's behavior ranges from unresponsiveness to surliness, leaving Miklós frustrated. Flashbacks reveal that Miklós exhibited a defiant streak, dodging practice and smoking cigarettes, but his actions seemed a direct response to his treatment by the adults in his life. In contrast, there appears to be no reason for Kyle's rebelliousness.

A breakthrough finally occurs when Miklós arrives at the gym early and begins working out. After Kyle observes his coach's skills, the teenager's competitiveness kicks in, and he starts to practice. Soon the gulf has been bridged, and the two maintain a rigorous schedule. By the 2002 Hungarian World Championship, Miklós is both Kyle's coach and his competitor in the vault. At this point the film crosscuts between the present competition and a flashback to thirteen-year-old Miklós (Silas Radies), who has fled Puma and joined a circus as a trapeze artist. Tension builds as Miklós, tied with Kyle going into the final vault, must execute a nearly perfect performance to medal, and young Miklós on the trapeze must complete a dangerous move without a net. As the climactic moments merge, Adult Miklós nearly slips dismounting the horse, and thirteen-year-old Miklós misses his catcher at the circus. Kyle wins the competition, and young Miklós is rushed from the circus tent on a stretcher.

After the competition, which Miklós's camera-wielding parents have attended, Kyle, transformed into a polite and personable young man, learns that Miklós has left the arena to talk with some circus people. The scene shifts to Las Vegas, a year later, where Miklós, now performing with Cirque du Soleil, is getting ready for rehearsal. The film concludes with a behind-the-scenes look at the high-tech aerial routines. As the circus orchestra plays, the screen goes dark, and the credits roll.

White Palms is a visually exciting film, one that relies on body language rather than dialogue to move the story. All of the athletes are played by real gymnasts—including excellent work by the Radies brothers—who express themselves largely through movement. Thematically, Miklós's quietness reflects his silencing as a child, when his parents refused to believe his complaints about Puma. However, the film is far from silent. Miklós listens to English language tapes when he drives, a reminder of his outsider status in western Canada. An excellent score by Ferenc Darvas provides a backdrop for many scenes, while the squeaking of gymnastic equipment, the thudding of a trampoline, and the roar of traffic signal transitions to flashbacks. Architectural cues connect scenes as well as foreshadow young Miklós's dramatic fall near the end of the film. Miklós frequently looks up at high rise apartment buildings and skyscrapers or gazes down from their roofs. As a child in Hungary, he is nearly hit by a Christmas tree blown or thrown from an upper deck of a high rise; in a parallel, almost dreamlike sequence, when he is cutting practice, he hears a thud behind him and turns to discover Puma lying on the pavement as if he has jumped; it is a trick, and the coach seizes the boy's leg and drags him back to the gymnasium. Hajdu uses blue and brown tones in the sequences depicting Hungary in the 1980s and brighter light for later scenes in Calgary and Las Vegas. *White Palms* received special mention at the Karlovy Vary International Film Festival and the Czech Ministry of Culture Award at the Zlin International Film Festival.

WHO'S YOUR CADDY? (2007)

DIRECTOR: Don Michael Paul. SCREENPLAY: Don Michael Paul, Bradley Allenstein, Robert Henny. PRODUCERS: Christopher Eberts, Tracey E. Edmonds, Kia Jam, Arnold Rifkin. CINEMATOGRAPHY: Thomas Callaway. EDITING: Vanick Moradian, Scott Mosier. MUSIC: Jon Lee. PRODUCTION DESIGN: Paul Luther Jackson. ART DIRECTION: Chester Maxwell. COSTUME DESIGN: Jayme Bohn.

CAST: Antwan Andre "Big Boi" Patton (C-Note), Jeffrey Jones (Richard Cummings), Tamala Jones (Shannon), Sherri Shepherd (Lady G), Faizon Love (Big Large), Garrett Morris (Reverend).

RUNNING TIME: 93 minutes.

DVD: Weinstein Company.

In this crude and predictable film, a rapper has intentions of joining a snobbish country club.

WILDCATS (1986)

DIRECTOR: Michael Ritchie. SCREENPLAY: Ezra Sacks. PRODUCER: Anthea Sylbert. CINEMATOGRAPHY: Douglas E. Thorin. EDITING: Richard A. Harris. MUSIC: James Newton Howard. PRODUCTION DESIGN: Boris Leven. ART DIRECTION: Stephen Myles Berger.

CAST: Goldie Hawn (Molly McGrath), Swoosie Kurtz (Verna McGrath), Robyn Lively (Alice Needham), Brandy Gold (Marian Needham), James Keach (Frank Needham), Jan Hooks (Stephanie Needham), Bruce McGill (Dan Darwell), Mykelti Williamson (Levander "Bird" Williams), Wesley Snipes (Trumaine), Woody Harrelson (Krushinski).

RUNNING TIME: 106 minutes.

DVD: Warner Home Video.

Directed by Michael Ritchie (*Bad News Bears*, 1976) *Wildcats* is a comedy designed to challenge stereotypes about gender and sports, particularly about football, traditionally a man's domain, with women's roles confined to those of cheerleaders, long-suffering girlfriends, and wives who must have the game explained to them. The movie, however, is both preachy and superficial in its attempt to level the playing field. Goldie Hawn stars as Molly McGrath, a single parent and the coach of a girls' track team at a suburban school who wants to coach football.

The film begins with childhood photos of Molly playing football with the boys and then posing in a football uniform, much to the patronizing amusement of Dan Darwell (Bruce McGill), coach of the Prescott High School football team and director of athletics for the school system. Molly wants to put her extensive football knowledge to use as the coach of Prescott's JV (junior varsity) football team. Her principal doesn't object, but she also needs Dan's approval; she suggests that they get together for a game of racquetball and dinner. Although she beats him, he ridicules the request but tells her he'll think about it. When she and the principal meet the next day, she is told that Dan has already filled the position with a male home economics teacher, who displays his lack of football knowledge in a question-and-answer session. It culminates with Molly asking the teacher if he knows how to get "penetration," a double entendre embarrassing to both the principal and the home economics teacher. Dan then explains to Molly that there is another reason she can't have the job: he wants her to coach the varsity football team at Central High School, an inner-city school with a losing record. When she goes to see Ben Edwards (Nipsey Russell), the principal of Central, Molly intends to turn the job down, but by insinuating that she will never get another chance at coaching football if she does not take the position, Edwards convinces her to accept it.

Initially, the raunchy, misogynistic team resists accepting her as their coach. One player smokes, another passes gas in her direction, and one says she has a "cute ass." While some of the players won't listen to her, some do; and in a scrimmage her players show up the holdouts. After the players are humiliated, one deliberately knocks her down and several others trash her office, breaking her treasured watch in the process. The next day she challenges them: they will run laps around the track, and if she quits before they do, she will resign; if she wins, they will stop being jerks. Having run two marathons, Molly outdistances all of them.

At the next practice Molly brings music to the field, and the players get in shape as she exercises with them; however, the team loses its first game 31–12 to the Jackson Cougars. The team does succeed in stealing the Cougars' mascot, a goat, and when Principal Edwards suspects the players of the theft, Molly covers for them and returns the goat.

Without a passing quarterback, the team has dismal prospects, and when Krushinski (Woody Harrelson), the current quarterback, suggests that they need Levander "Bird" Williams (Mykelti Williamson), last year's quarterback, Molly decides to get him to play. Principal Edwards thinks that Bird is a hopeless case. In fact, Bird is a supplier who works for a thug named Maurice. But Molly is undeterred. When Molly finds Bird, he cons her into taking him and two friends to "retrieve" some goods; the arrival of the police prompts Molly and Bird to hide in a Dumpster, where the two strike a deal—she won't reveal their whereabouts, and he will join the team. With Bird at the helm, Central wins the next game.

At the victory party Molly has to confront problems on the home front. Her daughters, Alice (Robyn Lively) and Marian (Brandy Gold), feel that Molly is neglecting them (Alice is disturbed because she hasn't succeeded in angering her mother by dying her hair red!), and the party gets a little out of hand. When Frank (James Keach), Molly's ex-husband, arrives with his wife, Stephanie (Jan Hooks), he is appalled at what is going on. In a fit of anger he turns around and hits Principal Edwards. Then he apologizes by saying, "I thought you were one of them" (meaning, presumably, "blacks") and hears Edwards say, "I am one of them." From this point on Frank attempts to get Molly to stop coaching or risk losing custody of their two daughters. He even arranges a deal whereby the girls can attend a prestigious prep school in exchange for Molly teaching "jazzercise" to the Chatham students. Dan, meanwhile, is furious at Molly's success. He tells her she is "the joke of Chicago," and tries to get some Central players ruled academically ineligible, but Edwards thwarts the attempt.

At another victory party Molly's situation worsens. Alice drinks some spiked punch and is taken home by Trumaine (Wesley Snipes) and his girlfriend, who are on the couch when Frank and Stephanie arrive. Molly and Finch (Tab Thacker), one of the players, arrive at about the same time, and there is a confrontation that ends with Frank insulting Finch, who punches Frank. Frank then succeeds in getting a hearing about his request for custody. At the hearing Frank accuses Molly of letting her coaching interfere with her parenting, and when her team arrives to be character witnesses, their unruly behavior does Molly more harm than good. Molly is forced to agree to resign effective after the season.

The championship pits the dispirited Central squad against Dan's Prescott team, which manhandles them. Urged on by Dan, the Prescott team plays dirty football, and Dan taunts Molly. At the half Molly chides the team for quitting, but they remind her that she quit on them. Molly races up to the stands and asks Frank to allow her to continue coaching for the sake of the team and for her daughters, whom she fears will regard her as a quitter. Frank relents, even agreeing, despite Stephanie's protests, to cheer for Central. A rejuvenated Central team ties the score, but the oversized Finch, whose mercenary nature outweighs team loyalty, volunteers to help Dan if he is paid. Dan insults him, and an angry Finch returns to the Central team. When Prescott lines up to kick the winning field goal, Finch persuades Molly to put him in, and he blocks the attempted kick. A Central player picks up the loose ball and scores the winning touchdown. After the game Dan refuses to shake Molly's hand and insults Finch again, but Finch picks him up, forces him to shake Molly's hand, and drops him in the mud when Molly tells him to put him down.

Chicago critic Roger Ebert summed up the plot when he stated that Molly's coaching is a "gimmick, not the subject" of the film. Even reviewers who were more positive in their assessment noted the predictability of the script, and the story, with its dogmatic approach to sexism, ignores issues of race and class. The film has not aged well.

WIMBLEDON (2004)

DIRECTOR: Richard Loncraine. SCREENPLAY: Adam Brooks, Jennifer Flackett, Mark Levin. PRODUCERS: Tim Bevan, Liza Chasin, Eric Fellner, Mary Richards. CINEMATOGRAPHY: Darius Khondji. EDITING: Humphrey Dixon. MUSIC: Edward Shearmur. PRODUCTION DESIGN: Brian Morris. ART DIRECTION: Tony Halton, John King. COSTUME DESIGN: Louise Stjernsward.

CAST: Kirsten Dunst (Lizzie Bradbury), Paul Bettany (Peter Colt), Jon Favreau (Ron Roth), Sam Neill (Dennis Bradbury), Bernard Hill (Peter's father), James McAvoy (Carl Colt), John McEnroe (himself), Chris Evert (herself), Mary Carillo (herself), John Barrett (himself).

RUNNING TIME: 98 minutes.

DVD: Universal Studios.

Peter Colt (Paul Bettany), a thirty-two-year-old English tennis player, has received a wildcard entry into Wimbledon, but England has little hope that he will succeed in the tournament. His ranking has slipped from 11th to 119th, and he has decided to leave the tour following the tournament for a position at a country club. As Peter explains, winning at the professional level generally requires that one enjoy strong family support and possess a hunger for success, and he has neither: his parents (played by Eleanor Bron and Bernard Hill) are absorbed in their own matters; his brother, Carl (James McAvoy), enjoys placing wagers against him; and family money has left him with no financial motive to drive him toward fulfilling his potential.

However, Peter's life and his game change when he meets Lizzie Bradbury (Kirsten Dunst), a young American tennis diva with a protective father and an intense desire to win. Their first encounter occurs at the posh Dorchester Hotel, where they are mistakenly booked into the same suite. Predictably, Peter arrives at the room to find Lizzie in the shower, but her reaction is one of pure amusement. Later, she seeks him out on the practice courts, and the two begin an earnest flirtation that leads to their first date. Although Lizzie is the aggressor in the early phase of the courtship, she also cautions Peter that she needs to "keep it light" so that the relationship doesn't interfere with her game. It's one thing, she tells him, on which she and her father agree.

Although Lizzie cruises through the early rounds of the tournament, her footwork is off and she's not serving well. Peter's game, however, continues to improve. Soon he hears from his agent, Ron (Jon Favreau), an American who, in spite of his good nature, represents the business side of contemporary sports. The agent invites Peter to a gala event hosted by a tournament sponsor, an invitation indicative of Peter's enhanced marketability. At the party, Peter catches up with Lizzie, much to the concern of her father (Sam Neill) and her former beau, Jake Hammond (Austin Nichols), one of the top-ranked players. When Jake insults Lizzie, Peter throws a well-executed punch that leaves Jake on the floor. Lizzie and Peter flee the gala, dashing through a throng of reporters to Peter's car, which they drive to a seaside resort where Peter's parents keep a flat.

This romantic interlude allows the two to discuss their own fears of commitments, which they attribute to their parents' relationships: Lizzie's parents are divorced, and Peter's father is now living in a tree house on the family estate. Peter tells Lizzie he plans to retire after the tournament; she does not try to convince him otherwise, but she does insist that he keep on winning. In the morning, Lizzie's father arrives to retrieve her, and to Peter's dismay, she agrees to a recess from the relationship for the remainder of the fortnight.

Without Lizzie courtside to cheer him on, Peter plays horridly; he wins his quarterfinals match only after his opponent sprains his ankle, and even then, Peter struggles to outperform the nearly immobile player. Peter's agent, recognizing the source of the problem, tells Peter where Lizzie is staying, and that night Peter climbs a trellis, sneaks into her room, and persuades her to let him stay. The next morning, he slips out early without disturbing her. Although Peter's intentions are to let her rest up for her match, Lizzie feels used and abandoned when she wakes up alone.

The players' performances follow the pattern dictated by their relationship: Peter is at the top of his game; Lizzie is distracted. Following his victory and her defeat, the two quarrel, and Lizzie prepares to leave England. Meanwhile, Peter's successes at Wimbledon have magically reunited his family. His parents, drawn together during the semifinals, have patched up their relationship, and even Carl is showing signs of fraternal affection. Over a family dinner Peter invites his family to attend what he insists will be his last match.

Meanwhile, at the airport, Lizzie and her father are waiting for their flight to board when Lizzie catches a pre-match interview with Peter, who offers a public apology for letting Lizzie down. Realizing that he truly does love her, Lizzie starts off on a mad rush to Wimbledon. Back at Centre Court, Peter is about to face Lizzie's ex, Jake Hammond, and although Peter is determined to prove himself, he cannot handle Jake's 144 mph serves. Down two sets and a break, Peter is on the verge of making a quick and embarrassing exit when a sudden shift in the weather causes a rain delay. Then he discovers Lizzie in the locker room; she tells him she loves him and offers a few key tips on reading Hammond's serve. Peter survives the third set, fights off a championship point in the fourth, and serves out the match, securing the title for England and Lizzie for himself. As the film ends, viewers are informed that Lizzie continued her career to win three Grand Slam titles while Peter now coaches children, including their own two.

Wimbledon was filmed at Wimbledon, and some scenes were shot during the 2003 tournament. Most of the tennis action is achieved through computer generated images. Although Peter's and Lizzie's opponents were portrayed by professional athletes (most notably Murphy Jenson as Ivan Dragomir), Bettany and Dunst, who were coached by Pat Cash, performed only the motions; the balls were added digitally. Still, the special effects are not entirely convincing. Product placement throughout the movie serves to remind the viewer of the commercialization of the sport as does the characterization of Ron, the American agent who is portrayed as acting always in the interests of profiteering. Interestingly, *Wimbledon* is dedicated to Mark McCormack, the founder of IMG (International Management Group) and the major force behind contemporary sports management and marketing strategies.

WIND **(1992)**

DIRECTOR: Carroll Ballard. SCREENPLAY: Rudy Wurlitzer, Mac Gudgeon. STORY: Jeff Benjamin, Roger Vaughan, Kimball Livingston. PRODUCERS: Tom Luddy, Mata Yamamoto. CINEMATOGRAPHY: John Toll. EDITING: Michael Chandler. MUSIC: Basil Poledouris. PRODUCTION DESIGN: Laurence Eastwood. COSTUME DESIGN: Marit Allen.

CAST: Matthew Modine (Will Parker), Jennifer Grey (Kate Bass), Cliff Robertson (Morgan Weld), Jack Thompson (Jack Neville), Stellan Skarsgård (Joe Heiser).

RUNNING TIME: 126 minutes.

DVD: Sony Pictures.

In this film, yacht racers try to win back America's Cup.

WINNERS TAKE ALL **(1987)**

DIRECTOR: Fritz Kiersch. SCREENPLAY: Ed Turner. STORY: Christopher W. Knight, Tom Tatum. PRODUCERS: Christopher W. Knight, Tom Tatum. CINEMATOGRAPHY: Fred Murphy. EDITING: Lorenzo DeStefano. MUSIC: Doug Timm. PRODUCTION DESIGN: Steven P. Sardanis. COSTUME DESIGN: Darryl Levine.

CAST: Don Michael Paul (Rick Melon), Kathleen York (Judy McCormick), Robert Krantz (Billy Robinson), Deborah Richter (Cindy Wickes).

RUNNING TIME: 66 minutes.

DVD: MGM.

Former friends compete in a high-stakes motocross competition.

WINNER TAKE ALL **(1932)**

DIRECTOR: Roy Del Ruth. SCREENPLAY: Robert Lord, Wilson Mizner, based on the story "133 at 3" by Gerald Beaumont. PRODUCER: Roy Del Ruth. CINEMATOGRAPHY: Robert Kurrle. EDITING: Thomas Pratt. PRODUCTION DESIGN: ART DIRECTION: Robert Haas. COSTUME DESIGN: Orry-Kelly.

CAST: James Cagney (Jimmy Kane), Virginia Bruce (Joan Gibson), Marian Nixon (Peggy Harmon), Guy Kibbee (Pop Slavin).

RUNNING TIME: 68 minutes.

Two women fight for the attention of an arrogant prizefighter.

WINNING (1969)

DIRECTOR: James Goldstone. SCREENPLAY: Howard Rodman. PRODUCER: John Foreman. CINEMATOGRAPHY: Richard Moore. EDITING: Edward A. Biery, Richard C. Meyer. MUSIC: Dave Grusin. ART DIRECTION: Alexander Golitzen, John J. Lloyd. COSTUME DESIGN: Edith Head.

CAST: Paul Newman (Frank Capua), Joanne Woodward (Elora), Robert Wagner (Lou Erding), Richard Thomas (Charley), Clu Gulager (Larry).

RUNNING TIME: 123 minutes.

DVD: Universal Studios.

This critically acclaimed drama starring Paul Newman and Joanne Woodward is an unusual racing film in that the sport takes a back seat to romance, unlike *Le Mans* (1971) and *Grand Prix* (1966) from the same era. As the movie opens, the camera focuses on a close-up of a dandelion, then pans slowly to the face of a white-haired man lying in the field, squinting against the sun. From the man's point of view, the audience catches glimpses of a multigenerational group picnicking. A humming in the background intensifies until it becomes the unmistakable whine of an engine, and the scene jumps to a race track. Frank Capua (Newman) avoids a crash to defeat friend and rival Lou Erding (Robert Wagner).

Later that night, Frank leaves his victory celebration and walks down a nearly deserted street, past a car rental agency, where the woman behind the counter is just about to close. Because she is attractive, Frank backtracks and knocks on the glass. He asks to rent a car, but the clerk, Elora (Woodward), refuses because he is drunk. Frank suggests she drive. She does—all the way to the coast, leaving behind, temporarily, a teenaged son, Charley (Richard Thomas). Elora's ex-husband left when Charley was three; now she and her son live with her mother. Her decision to travel with Frank to his next race, like her decision to marry, is based on loneliness and desire and prefigures trouble ahead.

When Elora can no longer postpone returning home to her son and her job, Frank proposes by suggesting that Charley come to California for the wedding. Charley and Frank bond immediately and Frank asks to adopt him. At first, Elora is happy with their domestic arrangement, but once Frank rejoins the racing circuit, she becomes bored. Although Frank is articulate in person, he is not a good telephone conversationalist, and his awkwardness contributes to Elora's frustration. Meanwhile, Frank is experiencing his own frustration at the track. Both he and Lou are driving cars owned by Leo Crawford (David Sheiner), but Frank has been finishing behind Lou and is worried about qualifying for the upcoming Indianapolis 500.

By the time Elora decides to join Frank on the circuit, he is focused on regaining his edge. After a dinner with Lou and Frank, Elora insists on seeing a movie while Frank insists on returning to work. Elora declares she will go to the movie alone; when she leaves the restaurant, Lou follows. After a week of living in a motel and doing needlepoint, Elora is desperate for a diversion. She pleads with Frank to take Sunday off for a picnic, but he refuses. When he returns that night, he is too tired for romance, falling asleep in her arms.

At the track, Leo's mechanic convinces Frank to leave early and rest. At the motel, he finds Elora and Lou in bed together. In a sequence without dialogue, Frank closes the bedroom door, leaving only after an extended, silent pause to sit outside in his car. Lou dresses and departs wordlessly as Elora weeps. Then Frank returns to the room, throws the keys on the bed, and kicks open the door to the bathroom, where Elora has wrapped herself in a towel. Frank packs and leaves the room, still silent. He hits his head getting into his car, the only physical injury in a situation ripe to erupt in violence. The film cuts to the roar of engines and the time trials, where Lou has just set a track record and Frank's car has sputtered out. During his next trial, Lou blows the engine, and Leo gives Frank's car to Lou. Frank can race only if the damaged engine can be repaired in time. In the midst of this, Charley arrives in an attempt to affect a reconciliation between Frank and Elora, but the parents are not cooperating. Charley announces that he wants to live with Frank and that he will stay for the race.

Frank qualifies and will start in the seventeenth position; Lou has earned the pole slot. Charley spends the evening at the race track with Frank, and the two drink champagne, something Charley has not yet tried. Charley overdoes it. When Frank returns him to his mother's motel, she and Frank exchange their first on-screen remarks since the adultery: Elora shouts at Frank that Charley is drunk; Frank responds, "He's with me," words that indicate Frank will honor Charley's wishes.

On the day of the race Charley and his mother sit together in the stands. An accident occurs at the start. Neither Lou nor Frank is involved, but Frank is obviously shaken. The scene serves the purpose of allowing Charley once again to demonstrate his love for Frank by running into the restricted area to make certain Frank is all right; it also shows Elora's concern. As the race continues, Lou takes the lead and begins lapping the slower vehicles; Frank has moved up into fifth place. A showdown between Lou and Frank doesn't occur. In keeping with his character, Lou pours on as much speed as he can, pursing records as well as victory, and once again he blows the engine. Ultimately, Frank wins the 500. Lou offers congratulations and an apology, declaring him the winner. Frank responds with a right to Lou's jaw. At the motel Frank discovers Elora and Charley have already checked out.

Instead of traveling to the next race on the circuit, Frank travels home to convince Elora to give their marriage another chance. The scene ends with a tableau of dramatic tension. Frank has thrown his luggage onto the front porch. Elora, who has just returned from shopping, stands in the driveway clutching the grocery bags. Yet there is no doubt that this is a happy ending and that the man in the opening scene is an older Frank enjoying his family, which has now added a generation.

Winning is a winning film. The four principal actors turn in excellent performances, aided by a script that balances drama and wit. The plot steers clear of clichés, right down to the big win and reconciliation. Visually, *Winning* is an interesting film, using a combination of jump cuts and dissolves that connects the tranquility of the first scene with the closing tableau.

THE WINNING TEAM (1952)

DIRECTOR: Lewis Seiler. SCREENPLAY: Ted Sherdeman, Seeleg Lester, Merwin Gerard. PRODUCER: Bryan Foy. CINEMATOGRAPHY: Sidney Hickox. EDITING: Alan Crosland Jr. MUSIC: David Buttolph. ART DIRECTION: Douglas Bacon.

CAST: Ronald Reagan (Grover Cleveland Alexander), Doris Day (Aimee Alexander), Frank Lovejoy (Rogers Hornsby), Eve Miller (Margaret Killefer), Russ Tamblyn (Willie Alexander).

RUNNING TIME: 98 minutes.

DVD: Warner Home Video.

This is a biographical film about baseball player Grover Cleveland Alexander and his wife's efforts to help him overcome alcoholism.

WITHOUT LIMITS (1998)

DIRECTOR: Robert Towne. SCREENPLAY: Robert Towne, Kenny Moore. PRODUCERS: Tom Cruise, Paula Wagner. CINEMATOGRAPHY: Conrad L. Hall. EDITING: Charles Ireland, Robert K. Lampert, Claire Simpson. MUSIC: Randy Miller. PRODUCTION DESIGN: William Creber. ART DIRECTION: William J. Durell. COSTUME DESIGN: Grania Preston.

CAST: Billy Crudup (Steve Prefontaine), Donald Sutherland (Bill Bowerman), Monica Potter (Mary Marckx), Jeremy Sisto (Frank Shorter), Matthew Lillard (Roscoe Devine), Dean Norris (Bill Dellinger), Billy Burke (Kenny Moore), Judith Ivey (Barbara Bowerman).

RUNNING TIME: 117 minutes.

DVD: Warner Home Video.

Like *Prefontaine* (1997), *Without Limits* is a biopic about the athletic career of Steve Prefontaine, America's best long-distance runner in the 1970s. The film focuses on the relationship between Prefontaine, played by Billy Crudup, and his coach and mentor, Bill Bowerman, played by veteran actor Donald Sutherland. Steve's girlfriend, Mary Marckx (Monica Potter), serves primarily as a sounding board for Steve, who speaks of his motivation and his self-confidence. So intense is he about his competiveness that she tells him that he has made her "feel too much" and she can't handle it. At the University of Oregon , where a number of young women wear sneakers Steve has been given by his sponsors, he is known as something of a Cassanova.

As does the earlier film, *Without Limits* devotes footage to Steve's childhood, but scriptwriters Kenny Moore and Robert Towne (Towne also directed the film), stress the Prefontaine family's blue-collar status. Steve's father is a millworker, and Steve is tormented by bigger, taller kids who subject him to ethnic slurs. His flight from them is intercut with footage of him running at the Oregon high school championships. Heavily recruited, Steve chooses Oregon even though the letter from Coach Bowerman, which he has been expecting for months, arrives just before the beginning of the academic year.

Steve and the coach meet at the first practice, where Bowerman proclaims track a team sport rather than an individual one. The two clash immediately over strategy: Bowerman, describing running as craft, advocates that runners conserve energy for the final segment of a race; for "Pre," running is an art that requires an all-out effort from start to finish—anything else is "chickenshit."

At the Olympic trials Steve reluctantly follows Bowerman's advice. There, he sets a new American record in the 5,000 meters. However, during the Olympics, the race starts at a slow pace; Steve stays with the pack and works his way into the lead, only to find that he lacks the kick required to win. He places fourth.

Dispirited, he returns to Oregon, where Mary offers encouragement and Bowerman expresses pride in his performance. Pre asks if he can work out with the team, although his eligibility has expired. At the informal "Restoration Event" meet, his fans cheer him on to victory, and he decides to train for the Montreal Olympics. He sets a three-mile record wearing Bowerman's shoes (the eventual Nike shoe).

While driving to see Mary, Steve is killed in an auto accident. At the memorial service, Bowerman, who also serves as narrator of the film, delivers a eulogy as long as Steve's record. Bowerman also admits that Steve taught him he was wrong about running. The race "is a work of art," and Steve, he proclaims, was an artist.

Moore, who was a member of the 1972 Olympic team, also collaborated with Robert Towne on *Personal Best* (1982). Crudup trained with *Personal Best* star Patrice Donnelly and received accolades for his imitation of Prefontaine's running style. *Without Limits* is generally considered a more successful film than *Prefontaine* on the strength of the relationship between runner and coach and the performances of Crudup and Sutherland.

WONDROUS OBLIVION (2003)

DIRECTOR: Paul Morrison. SCREENPLAY: Paul Morrison. PRODUCER: Jonny Persey. CINEMATOGRAPHY: Nina Kellgren. EDITING: David Freeman. MUSIC: Ilona Sekacz. PRODUCTION DESIGN: Eve Stewart. COSTUME DESIGN: Anushia Nieradzik.
CAST: Sam Smith (David Wiseman), Delroy Lindo (Dennis Samuel), Stanley Townsend (Victor), Emily Woof (Ruth Wiseman).
RUNNING TIME: 106 minutes.
DVD: Palm Pictures.

In 1960s London, a young Jewish boy who loves cricket is thrilled when his new neighbors from Jamaica set up a cricket net in their garden.

THE WORLD'S FASTEST INDIAN (2005)

DIRECTOR: Roger Donaldson. SCREENPLAY: Roger Donaldson. PRODUCERS: Roger Donaldson, Gary Hannam. CINEMATOGRAPHY: David Gribble. EDITING: John Gilbert. MUSIC: J. Peter Robinson. PRODUCTION DESIGN: Robert Gillies, J. Dennis Washington. ART DIRECTION: Roger Guise, Mark Hofeling. COSTUME DESIGN: Nancy Cavallaro, Jane Holland.
CAST: Anthony Hopkins (Burt Munro), Diane Ladd (Ada), Paul Rodriguez (Fernando), Tessa Mitchell (Sarah), Aaron Murphy (Thomas), Bruce Greenwood (Jerry).
RUNNING TIME: 127 minutes.
DVD: Magnolia.

The Indian of the title is not a person, but a motorcycle: an Indian Scout manufactured in Massachusetts in 1920 and purchased in New Zealand by twenty-one-year-old Burt Munro, who spent nearly half a century customizing the bike, casting his own parts in old tins, hand-carving rods from a tractor axle, and constructing an aerodynamic racing shell. Munro became a legendary hero Down Under, setting world records in the sixties (when he was in his sixties), and was the subject of a 1970s documentary, *Offerings to the God of Speed*, directed by fellow New Zealander Roger Donaldson. Thirty-five years later, Donaldson directed *The World's Fastest Indian*, a biopic based on the life of Munro, who died in 1978.

The film begins in the early 1960s. Burt (Anthony Hopkins) is introduced as an eccentric senior citizen who lives alone, putters about in his shed, and dreams of motorcycle racing. He rises early, urinates on a lemon tree in the yard (a ritual started by his twin brother, who died when they were children), and revs his motorcycle, disturbing the neighbors. The boy next door, Thomas (Aaron Murphy), likes to hang around the workshop and watch Burt build engine parts from odd bits.

For Burt's birthday, his friends throw a party and hold a raffle to raise money for a trip to the salt flats at Bonneville, Utah, where Burt plans to set a world's record with the Indian. His party is crashed by a motorcycle gang of young toughs who challenge him to a race on the beach. At the appointed time, Burt and a small entourage appear. He needs a push to start his machine, but once he gets into second gear, he quickly overtakes the field, only to spill on a turn. Neither Burt nor the Indian is harmed, but he is now out a hundred dollars, leaving him with little more than half of what he needs for his journey.

His plans are further complicated when he suffers a spell of angina and is diagnosed with arteriosclerosis. But as Burt sees it, the wallet is half full, and he is still on his feet. He mortgages his property, sets the lawn on fire to placate the neighbors' complaints about the height of his grass, and leaves Thomas in charge of feeding the chickens and peeing on the lemon tree. The motorcycle blokes show up to make a donation toward his expenses and escort him to the dock, where he has booked passage in return for working in the galley. Although Burt is much older than his shipmates and lectures them on the dangers of smoking, the younger men accept his company. After an interview with a puzzled customs officer who doesn't understand what Burt means about coming to America to set a record with his Indian, Burt discovers another officer who is a motorcycle enthusiast, and a six months' visa is granted immediately. The Indian, in spite of being stowed on its side under a ton of cargo, comes through the sea voyage without a scratch, and another potential difficulty fails to materialize.

Much of the film follows Burt's journey from Los Angeles, his point of entry into the United States, to Bonneville. The story continues in the pattern of presenting a potential problem, then resolving it simply and quickly. Whatever the situation, it is Burt's ability to get on with strangers that buoys him along. Although he does have a testy encounter with a greedy cab driver who drops him off at a motel that rents rooms by the hour, Burt easily befriends the night manager, Tina (Chris Williams), and displays nonchalance when Tina turns out to be a transvestite. Next, Burt charms a used car dealer, applying his mechanical skills to several autos on the lot, and uses the dealer's garage to construct a trailer for the motorcycle. After some unnecessary silliness about driving on the other side of the road, Burt heads off with the Indian in tow.

There are a few mishaps along the way, but each time, he finds willing assistance. When his trailer loses a wheel, a Native American comes to his aid, puts him up for the night, and gives him an alternative remedy for enlarged prostate. Burt continues, having fashioned a runner from a tree limb to replace the damaged trailer wheel, until he comes upon a farm yard filled with rusting machinery. The widow who runs the farm (Diane Ladd) helps repair the trailer, then offers to share her bed, an arrangement agreeable to both. After leaving the farm, Burt sleeps in his car; a highway patrol officer shoos him from a shoulder near a curve, but doesn't ticket him. At a roadhouse, the regulars eye him suspiciously and don't warm to his antismoking lecture; however, the barkeep notices Burt doesn't seem to feel well—in fact, he's had another spell of angina—and offers directions to the nearest hospital, directions that Burt ignores, pushing on through the desert heat. His final encounter of the trip is with a hitchhiking young soldier on leave between tours in Vietnam. The soldier tells Burt that he's certain the war will end soon because of the effectiveness of the defoliant Agent Orange in eradicating dense growth where the Viet Cong hide. Burt's ready concurrence with the soldier's prediction is in keeping with his generally cheery outlook, but given the duration of the war in Vietnam and the damage Agent Orange caused to those, including U.S. soldiers, exposed to the chemical, this discussion seems out of place in a feel-good film.

Burt arrives at the salt flats in time to watch the sun set and wakes to watch it rise. The first person he encounters is Jim (Christopher Lawford), a well-respected racer whose reputation and influence save the day when Burt runs afoul of officialdom. Not only has he failed to preregister, but his Indian fails to meet any of the safety standards—its tires are inadequate, its brakes useless, and it lacks insulation and a parachute. Jim persuades the officials to allow Burt to share some of Jim's track time, and once they realize that Burt is determined to run with or without official consent, they offer a compromise: a "handling run" during which they will follow him in their vehicles. Of course, the officials doubt that the Indian will do much over the 55 mph upper limit of the original engine. And of course, Burt leaves them far behind once he gets into third gear and creates such an impression that he is granted an official run.

However, Burt has not been happy with the outing. The Indian starts shaking at high speeds, becoming difficult to control, and heat from the exhaust endangers his legs.

To improve stability, he manufactures a lead brick from old car batteries and places it in the front of the Indian's shell to shift the "center of pressure." He tests the bike on a highway in Nevada, where there are no speed limits, and once again attracts the attention of a police officer, who clocks the Indian at around 130 mph and suggests Burt take it easy.

On the day of the run, Burt tries wrapping his legs in asbestos, but the wrappings are too thick, and he must discard one of the wraps in order to fit into the shell. He has also abandoned the lead brick. Just before he takes off, Burt pops a triglyceride for himself and drops another one in the gas tank for "the old girl."

The climactic run takes up little time. The film cuts between shots of Burt and shots of the officials' speed guns. As Burt moves closer to the 200 mph mark, smoke curls around his unprotected pants leg, and the wind rips his goggles from his face, yet he keeps going until the trembling machine goes into a skid, sliding on its side. The engine stops, and Burt rolls out of the shell, a fierce burn visible on his leg. Lying on his back on the salt flats, he laughs in triumph. The scene ends with Burt still on his back and no longer moving and jumps to a young boy peeing on a lemon tree, suggesting that Burt is badly injured or dying and envisioning his long-dead twin. But the boy is Thomas back in New Zealand, where friends and neighbors have gathered to welcome Burt home. Just before the closing credits, viewers are informed that Burt returned several times to Bonneville and that his 1967 record (183.586 mph) still stands. The real Burt Munro achieved an unofficial speed of 206 mph with his Indian.

The film has won a number of awards in New Zealand and Australia, but its reception in the United States has been less enthusiastic. Hopkins's performance received generally favorable reviews.

THE WORLD'S GREATEST ATHLETE (1973)

DIRECTOR: Robert Scheerer. SCREENPLAY: Gerald Gardner, Dee Caruso. PRODUCER: Bill Walsh. CINEMATOGRAPHY: Frank Phillips. EDITING: Cotton Warburton. MUSIC: Marvin Hamlisch. ART DIRECTION: John B. Manbridge, Walter Tyler. COSTUME DESIGN: Chuck Keehne, Emily Sundby.

CAST: John Amos (Coach Sam Archer), Jan-Michael Vincent (Nanu), Tim Conway (Milo Jackson), Roscoe Lee Browne (Gazenga), Dayle Haddon (Jane).

RUNNING TIME: 93 minutes.

DVD: Walt Disney Home Entertainment.

A college coach travels to Africa and discovers a phenom who can turn around his school's ailing athletic program. Announcers Frank Gifford, Jim McKay, and Howard Cosell appear as themselves.

THE WRESTLER (1974)

DIRECTOR: James A. Westman. SCREENPLAY: Eugene Gump. PRODUCER: W. R. Frank. CINEMATOGRAPHY: Gil Hubbs. MUSIC: William Castleman, William Loose.

CAST: Ed Asner (Frank Bass), Elaine Giftos (Debbie), Verne Gagne (Mike Bullard), Billy Robinson (Billy Taylor).

Running Time: 95 minutes.
DVD: Echo Bridge Home Entertainment.

This low-budget film is about a pro wrestling promoter who tries to legitimize the sport. The film features pro wrestling superstars Lord James Blears, Billy Graham, Dick Murdoch, Dusty Rhodes, and Vince McMahon.

THE WRESTLER (2008)

Director: Darren Aronofsky. Screenplay: Robert D. Siegel. Producers: Darren Aronofsky, Scott Franklin. Cinematography: Maryse Alberti. Editing: Andrew Weisblum. Music: Clint Mansell. Production Design: Tim Grimes. Art Direction: Matthew Munn. Costume Design: Amy Westcott.
Cast: Mickey Rourke (Randy "the Ram" Robinson), Marisa Tomei (Cassidy), Evan Rachel Wood (Stephanie), Mark Margolis (Lenny), Todd Barry (Wayne), Wass Stevens (Nick Volpe), Judah Friedlander (Scott Brumberg).
Running Time: 109 minutes.
Academy Award Nominations: Best Actor (Rourke), Best Supporting Actress (Tomei).
DVD: Fox Searchlight.

Mickey Rourke was nominated for an Academy Award for his portrayal of Randy "the Ram" Robinson, a professional wrestler who reached the top of his career in the 1980s. Twenty-some years later, the Ram is wrestling in school gymnasiums; his day job, unloading trucks at a supermarket, barely keeps him in performance-enhancing drugs. At the beginning of the film, Randy is sleeping in his van because he can't make the rent on his slot in a trailer park; he has an action figure of himself on the dashboard and vanity license plates.

In spite of the fading career and lack of money, Randy appears to be a cheerful, gentle man who enjoys people; he takes time for old fans and young children in the trailer park; he offers advice and encouragement to opponents trying to work their way up the card. Early in the film, opportunity smiles. Randy has a romantic interest—a lap dancer who doesn't date clients, but really likes him—and a promoter wants to arrange a twentieth-anniversary rematch of his career-topping contest against a grappler known as "the Ayatollah." In preparation, Randy visits a tanning salon and a beauty parlor to have his roots touched up. But with the rematch several months in the future, Randy needs to broaden his audience. He agrees to a Combat Zone bout that involves the wrestlers' battering each other with common household items. In a humorous scene, Randy shops at a discount store for cheaply made cooking utensils that will break and bend upon contact with a body part. Randy's opponent, the Butcher, draws laughs as well when he asks Randy about stapling, but there is nothing comic about the scene once the match is underway and the Butcher staples a five-dollar bill to his own forehead. From there on, the blood flows freely.

After the match, Randy collapses in the dressing room. When he comes to, he has undergone a coronary bypass, and his surgeon tells him he can't return to the ring. Once he is released from the hospital, Randy asks his supervisor at the grocery for extra work and finds himself assigned as a deli clerk, where his nametag, based on his real name, reads "Robin." Randy takes the new job in stride, and his personality shines through. After work, he visits the bar where Cassidy (Marisa Tomei) dances and explains why he hasn't been around. She advises him to get in touch with his estranged daughter, advice that he follows, but the encounter does not go smoothly. When Randy returns to the bar with his report, Cassidy suggests he try again, this time going to his daughter armed with a gift, and she volunteers to take him shopping. The next day at a consignment store, Randy picks out a gaudy jacket, and Cassidy selects a pea coat; Randy buys both. Afterward, they have a beer, and Cassidy repeats mantra-like that she doesn't date clients. Still, Randy holds out hope. He has given her the Ram action figure for her young son.

Randy's second meeting with his daughter, Stephanie (Evan Rachel Wood), is more successful than the first. She puts on the pea coat, they both laugh at the shiny jacket, and the two go to Coney Island, which is largely shut down for the winter. They recall some pleasant times from the past, and Stephanie agrees to meet him for dinner the next week. But when the next week rolls around, Randy sabotages himself. First, he is recognized at the deli by a fan and is humiliated by the exposure. "Robin" slams his hand into a meat slicer before running out. At the bar, Cassidy rejects him. At another bar, Randy finds a woman who doesn't; the two snort coke and have sex. Randy wakes up in a strange place, realizing that he has missed his dinner date. He hurries to Stephanie's house, where he finds her enraged. There are, she tells him, no more chances.

Randy determines to go ahead with his match against the Ayatollah. In contrast to his earlier preparations, this time Randy applies tan-in-a-can and dyes his own hair; his primping, once amusing, now underscores both how far he has fallen and how difficult it is for him to admit it. Just before the match, Cassidy shows up to tell Randy that she has quit her job and that she thinks they have a future together. But for Randy, it is too late. His fans are the only family he has, he tells her. As Randy makes his grand entrance, his cape seems shroud-like, encasing him in a past that he cannot reactivate. Standing in the center of the ring, Randy gives an impassioned speech reiterating his feelings about the fans. The match, which has been preplanned, tires Randy, who struggles to carry out his part of the act. Finally, as the Ayatollah waits on the canvas, Randy climbs onto the top rung for his signature move, the Ram Bam. The frame freezes on his outstretched figure flying in midair. How he lands is left to speculation.

Rourke, who was a boxer before he studied at the Actor's Studio in New York and who quit acting to return to the ring in 1991, has said in interviews that he feels he has lived the character. He trained for two months for the role and completed many of his own stunts. Although his boxing experience provided him with the scarred physique of a wrestler, it did not prepare him for the very different styles of the two activities: in boxing one attempts to conceal one's moves from an opponent, but in wrestling, the moves are telegraphed.

The film has been praised by professional wrestlers for its portrayal of the sport, both in front of the fans and behind the scenes. Although moves are choreographed and outcomes predetermined, the execution of the moves—not to mention the pain—is real. *The Wrestler* demonstrates the reality of the pain and the camaraderie of the participants, but it also weighs in on the question of how one's occupation influences one's sense of identity. For Randy and for Cassidy, who both rent out their bodies, albeit in different ways, this question is enormously significant. The main obstacle to their romance seems to lie in their very different answers.

Y

YESTERDAY'S HERO (1979)

DIRECTOR: Neil Leifer. SCREENPLAY: Jackie Collins. PRODUCERS: Oscar Lerman, Ken Regan. CINEMATOGRAPHY: Brian West. EDITING: Antony Gibbs. MUSIC: Stanley Myers. PRODUCTION DESIGN: Keith Wilson.
CAST: Ian McShane (Rod Turner), Suzanne Somers (Cloudy Martin), Adam Faith (Jake Marsh), Paul Nicholas (Clint Simon).
RUNNING TIME: 95 minutes.
VHS: Cinema Group Home Video.

From widely panned novelist Jackie Collins comes this romantic drama about an alcoholic soccer player and a rock star played by Suzanne Somers.

YOUNGBLOOD (1986)

DIRECTOR: Peter Markle. SCREENPLAY: Peter Markle, John Whitman. PRODUCERS: Peter Bart, Peter Markle, Patrick Wells. CINEMATOGRAPHY: Mark Irwin. EDITING: Jack Hofstra, Stephen E. Rivkin. ART DIRECTION: Alicia Keywan. COSTUME DESIGN: Eileen Kennedy.
CAST: Rob Lowe (Dean Youngblood), Cynthia Gibb (Jessie Chadwick), Patrick Swayze (Derek Sutton), Ed Lauter (Murray Chadwick).
RUNNING TIME: 110 minutes.
DVD: MGM.

A young hockey player falls for the daughter of his coach.

APPENDIX A: FILMS BY SPORT

Arm Wrestling

Over the Top (1987)

Australian Rules Football

Australian Rules (2002)
The Club (1980)

Auto Racing

The Big Wheel (1949)
Bobby Deerfield (1977)
Cars (2006)
The Crowd Roars (1932)
Days of Thunder (1990)
Death Race (2008)
Death Race 2000 (1975)
Driven (2000)
Fireball 500 (1966)
Genevieve (1953)
Grand Prix (1966)
The Great Race (1965)
Heart Like a Wheel (1983)
Hell on Wheels (1967)
Herbie: Fully Loaded (2005)
Herbie Goes Bananas (1980)
Herbie Goes to Monte Carlo (1977)
Herbie Rides Again (1974)
Indianapolis Speedway (1939)
The Last American Hero (1971)
A Man and a Woman (1967)
Le Mans (1971)
The Love Bug (1968)
Race the Sun (1996)
Red Line 7000 (1966)
Speed Racer (2008)
Speedway (1968)
Spinout (1966)
Stroker Ace (1983)
Ta Ra Rum Pum (2007)
Talladega Nights: The Ballad of Ricky Bobby (2006)
To Please a Lady (1950)
Two-Lane Blacktop (1971)
Winning (1969)

Baseball

Alibi Ike (1935)
Amazing Grace and Chuck (1987)
American Pastime (2007)
Angels in the Outfield (1951)
Angels in the Outfield (1994)
The Babe (1992)
The Babe Ruth Story (1948)
The Bad News Bears (1976)
The Bad News Bears (2005)
The Bad News Bears Go to Japan (1978)
The Bad News Bears in Breaking Training (1977)
Bang the Drum Slowly (1973)
The Benchwarmers (2006)
The Bingo Long Traveling All-Stars and Motor Kings (1976)
Blue in the Face (1995)
Blue Skies Again (1983)
Brewster's Millions (1983)
Bull Durham (1988)
Chasing 3000 (2010)
Cobb (1994)
Damn Yankees (1958)

Ed (1996)
Eight Men Out (1988)
Elmer, the Great (1933)
Everyone's Hero (2006)
The Fan (1996)
Fear Strikes Out (1957)
Fever Pitch (2005) [U.S.]
Field of Dreams (1989)
The Final Season (2007)
Fireman, Save My Child (1932)
For Love of the Game (1999)
Game 6 (2006)
Hardball (2001)
It Happens Every Spring (1949)
The Jackie Robinson Story (1950)
The Kid from Left Field (1953)
Kill the Umpire (1950)
A League of Their Own (1992)
Little Big League (1994)
Major League (1989)
Major League: Back to the Minors (1998)
Major League II (1994)
Mickey (2004)
Mr. Baseball (1992)
Mr. Destiny (1990)
Mr. 3000 (2004)
The Natural (1984)
Night Game (1989)
Pastime (1991)
The Pride of St. Louis (1952)
Pride of the Yankees (1942)
Rhubarb (1951)
The Rookie (2002)
Rookie of the Year (1993)
Safe at Home! (1962)
The Sandlot (1993)
The Scout (1994)
*61** (2001)
The Slugger's Wife (1985)
Stealing Home (1988)
The Stratton Story (1949)
Sugar (2008)
Summer Catch (2001)
Take Me Out to the Ball Game (1949)
Talent for the Game (1991)
Trading Hearts (1988)
The Winning Team (1952)

Basketball
Above the Rim (1994)
Air Bud (1997)
The Air Up There (1994)
Basketball Diaries (1995)
Blue Chips (1994)
Celtic Pride (1996)
Coach (1978)
Coach Carter (2005)
Crossover (2006)
Dribbles (2007)
Eddie (1996)
Fast Break (1979)
Finding Forrester (2000)
The Fish That Saved Pittsburgh (1977)
Forget Paris (1995)
Full-Court Miracle (2003)
Glory Road (2006)
He Got Game (1998)
Home of the Giants (2007)
Hoosiers (1986)
Juwanna Mann (2002)
Like Mike (2002)
Love and Basketball (2000)
O (2001)
One on One (1977)
Pistol: The Birth of a Legend (1991)
Rebound (2005)
Semi-Pro (2008)
The 6th Man (1997)
Space Jam (1996)
Sunset Park (1996)
Teen Wolf (1985)
Tournament of Dreams (2007)
White Men Can't Jump (1992)

Bobsledding
Cool Runnings (1993)

Bowling
The Big Lebowski (1998)
Dreamer (1979)
Kingpin (1996)

Boxing
Against the Ropes (2004)
Ali (2001)

Annapolis (2006)
Battling Butler (1926)
Body and Soul (1947)
The Boxer (1997)
Carman: The Champion (2001)
The Champ (1932)
The Champ (1979)
Champion (1949)
Cinderella Man (2005)
City for Conquest (1940)
City Lights (1931)
The Crowd Roars (1938)
Dans Les Cordes (2007)
Diggstown (1992)
Fat City (1972)
Gentleman Jim (1942)
Girlfight (2000)
Gladiator (1992)
Golden Boy (1939)
The Greatest (1977)
The Great White Hope (1970)
The Great White Hype (1996)
The Hammer (2007)
The Harder They Fall (1956)
Hard Times (1975)
Here Comes Mr. Jordan (1941)
The Hurricane (1999)
Let's Do It Again (1975)
The Main Event (1979)
Million Dollar Baby (2004)
Movie Movie (1978)
Penitentiary (1979)
Penitentiary II (1982)
Penitentiary III (1987)
Play It to the Bone (1999)
The Power of One (1992)
The Prizefighter and the Lady (1933)
Raging Bull (1980)
Requiem for a Heavyweight (1962)
Resurrecting the Champ (2007)
Ringside Maisie (1941)
Rocky (1976)
Rocky Balboa (2006)
Rocky II (1979)
Rocky III (1982)
Rocky IV (1985)
Rocky V (1990)
The Set-Up (1949)
Somebody Up There Likes Me (1956)
Spirit of Youth (1938)
Split Decisions (1988)
The Square Ring (1952)
Streets of Gold (1986)
Undisputed (2002)
Winner Take All (1932)

Cheerleading
Bring It On (2000)
Fired Up! (2009)
Sugar and Spice (2003)

Cricket
The Final Test (1953)
Lagaan: Once Upon a Time in India (2001)
Playing Away (1987)
Wondrous Oblivion (2003)

Curling
Men with Brooms (2002)

Cycling
The Amateur (1999)
American Flyers (1985)
BMX Bandits (1983)
Breaking Away (1979)
The Flying Scotsman (2006)
Rad (1986)
The Triplets of Belleville (2003)
The Unknown Cyclist (1998)

Dodgeball
Dodgeball (1995)
Dodgeball: A True Underdog Story (2004)

Fencing
By the Sword (1991)

Fictional Sports
BASEketball (1998)
Rollerball (1975)

Field Hockey
Chak De! India (2007)

Football

Air Bud: Golden Receiver (1998)
All the Right Moves (1983)
Any Given Sunday (1999)
The Bear (1984)
Best of Times (1986)
Big Fan (2009)
Black Sunday (1977)
The Blind Side (2009)
Brian's Song (1971)
The Comebacks (2007)
Everybody's All American (1988)
The Express (2008)
Facing the Giants (2006)
The Freshman (1925)
Friday Night Lights (2004)
Full Ride (2002)
The Game Plan (2007)
Gridiron Gang (2006)
Gus (1976)
Heaven Can Wait (1978)
Hometown Legend (2002)
Horse Feathers (1932)
Invincible (2006)
Jerry Maguire (1996)
Johnny Be Good (1988)
Knute Rockne: All American (1940)
The Last Boy Scout (1991)
Leatherheads (2008)
Little Giants (1994)
The Longest Yard (1974)
The Longest Yard (2005)
The Longshots (2008)
Lucas (1986)
Necessary Roughness (1991)
North Dallas Forty (1979)
Paper Lion (1968)
The Program (1993)
Radio (2003)
Remember the Titans (2000)
The Replacements (2000)
Rudy (1993)
School Ties (1992)
Semi-Tough (1977)
The Slaughter Rule (2002)
That's My Boy (1951)
Two for the Money (2005)
Varsity Blues (1999)
The Waterboy (1998)
We Are Marshall (2006)
Wildcats (1986)

Golf

Bobby Jones: Strokes of Genius (2004)
Caddyshack (1980)
Caddyshack II (1988)
Follow the Sun (1951)
A Gentleman's Game (2002)
The Greatest Game Ever Played (2005)
Happy Gilmore (1996)
The Legend of Bagger Vance (2000)
The Man with the Perfect Swing (1995)
Tin Cup (1996)
Who's Your Caddy? (2007)

Gymnastics

American Anthem (1986)
Peaceful Warrior (2006)
Stick It (2006)
White Palms (2006)

Horse Racing

The Black Stallion (1979)
The Black Stallion Returns (1983)
Boots Malone (1952)
A Day at the Races (1937)
The Derby Stallion (2005)
Dreamer: Inspired by a True Story (2005)
The Galloping Major (1951)
International Velvet (1978)
Just My Luck (1957)
Lightning, the White Stallion (1986)
National Velvet (1944)
Phar Lap (1983)
Racing Stripes (2005)
Seabiscuit (2003)
Shergar (1999)

Ice Hockey

D2: Mighty Ducks (1994)
D3: Mighty Ducks (1996)
Les Boys (1997)

The Love Guru (2008)
The Mighty Ducks (1992)
Miracle (2004)
MVP: Most Valuable Primate (2000)
Mystery, Alaska (1999)
The Rocket: Maurice Richard (2005)
Slap Shot (1977)
Slap Shot 2: Breaking the Ice (2002)
Youngblood (1986)

Ice Skating
Blades of Glory (2007)
The Cutting Edge (1992)
Ice Castles (1978)
Ice Princess (2005)

Martial Arts
Enter the Dragon (1973)
The Karate Kid (1984)
The Karate Kid (2010)
The Karate Kid, Part III (1989)
The Karate Kid II (1986)
The Next Karate Kid (1994)

Motorcycle Racing
Winners Take All (1987)
The World's Fastest Indian (2005)

Multiple Sports
College (1927) [Baseball, Sculling, Track and Field]
Million Dollar Legs (1932) [Olympic Events]
Pat and Mike (1952) [Golf and Tennis]

Pool
The Color of Money (1986)
The Hustler (1961)
Poolhall Junkies (2002)

Rodeo
8 Seconds (1994)
Junior Bonner (1972)

Roller Derby
Kansas City Bomber (1972)
Whip It (2009)

Rowing
Oxford Blues (1984)
True Blue (1995)

Rugby
Forever Strong (2008)
Invictus (2009)
This Sporting Life (1963)

Sailing
Wind (1992)

Skateboarding
Gleaming the Cube (1989)
Lords of Dogtown (2005)
MVP2: Most Vertical Primate (2001)
Street Dreams (2009)

Skiing
Downhill Racer (1969)

Snowboarding
Out Cold (2001)

Soccer
The Arsenal Stadium Mystery (1939)
Bend it Like Beckham (2002)
The Big Green (1995)
The Damned United (2009)
Fever Pitch (1996) [U.K.]
Goal! The Dream Begins (2005)
Goal! II: Living the Dream (2006)
Goal! III (2009)
The Goalie's Anxiety at the Penalty Kick (1971)
Gracie (2007)
The Great Game (1930)
The Great Game (1953)
The Great Match (2006)
Gregory's Girl (1981)
Her Best Move (2007)
Kicking & Screaming (2005)
Ladybugs (1992)
Looking for Eric (2009)
Mean Machine (2001)
Mike Bassett: England Manager (2001)

The Miracle of Bern (2003)
Offside (2006)
Purely Belter (2000)
Shaolin Soccer (2001)
She's the Man (2006)
A Shot at Glory (2000)
Soccer Dog: The Movie (1999)
There's Only One Jimmy Grimble (2000)
Victory (1981)
When Saturday Comes (1996)
Yesterday's Hero (1979)

Softball
Beer League (2006)
Squeeze Play (1979)

Special Olympics
The Ringer (2005)

Surfing
Big Wednesday (1978)
Blue Crush (2002)
In God's Hands (1998)
North Shore (1987)
Point Break (1991)
Surfer, Dude (2008)

Swimming
On a Clear Day (2005)
Pride (2007)

Table Tennis
Balls of Fury (2007)
Ping Pong Playa (2007)

Tennis
The Break (1995)
Match Point (2005)
Nobody's Perfect (1990)
Players (1979)
Strangers on a Train (1951)
Tennis, Anyone? (2005)
Wimbledon (2004)

Track and Field
Across the Tracks (1991)
Chariots of Fire (1981)
Jim Thorpe: All American (1951)
The Loneliness of the Long Distance Runner (1962)
Personal Best (1982)
Prefontaine (1997)
Run, Fatboy, Run (2007)
Running (1979)
Running Brave (1983)
Saint Ralph (2005)
Without Limits (1998)
The World's Greatest Athlete (1973)

Volleyball
All You've Got (2006)
The Iron Ladies (2000)
The Iron Ladies 2 (2003)
Side Out (1990)

Wrestling
. . . All the Marbles (1981)
Body Slam (1986)
Grunt! The Wrestling Movie (1985)
Nacho Libre (2006)
Night and the City (1950)
No Holds Barred (1989)
Paradise Alley (1978)
Ready to Rumble (2000)
Reversal (2001)
Sit Tight (1931)
Take Down (1979)
Vision Quest (1985)
The Wrestler (1974)
The Wrestler (2008)

APPENDIX B: CHRONOLOGICAL TITLE LIST

1925, *The Freshman*
1926, *Battling Butler*
1927, *College*
1930, *The Great Game*
1931, *City Lights*
1931, *Sit Tight*
1932, *The Champ*
1932, *The Crowd Roars*
1932, *Fireman, Save My Child*
1932, *Horse Feathers*
1932, *Million Dollar Legs*
1932, *Winner Take All*
1933, *Elmer, the Great*
1933, *The Prizefighter and the Lady*
1935, *Alibi Ike*
1937, *A Day at the Races*
1938, *The Crowd Roars*
1938, *Spirit of Youth*
1939, *The Arsenal Stadium Mystery*
1939, *Golden Boy*
1939, *Indianapolis Speedway*
1940, *City for Conquest*
1940, *Knute Rockne: All American*
1941, *Here Comes Mr. Jordan*
1941, *Ringside Maisie*
1942, *Gentleman Jim*
1942, *Pride of the Yankees*
1944, *National Velvet*
1947, *Body and Soul*
1948, *The Babe Ruth Story*
1949, *The Big Wheel*
1949, *Champion*
1949, *It Happens Every Spring*
1949, *The Set-Up*
1949, *The Stratton Story*
1949, *Take Me Out to the Ballgame*
1950, *The Jackie Robinson Story*
1950, *Kill the Umpire*
1950, *Night and the City*
1950, *To Please a Lady*
1951, *Angels in the Outfield*
1951, *Follow the Sun*
1951, *The Galloping Major*
1951, *Jim Thorpe: All American*
1951, *Rhubarb*
1951, *Strangers on a Train*
1951, *That's My Boy*
1952, *Boots Malone*
1952, *Pat and Mike*
1952, *The Pride of St. Louis*
1952, *The Square Ring*
1952, *The Winning Team*
1953, *The Final Test*
1953, *Genevieve*
1953, *The Great Game*
1953, *The Kid from Left Field*
1956, *The Harder They Fall*
1956, *Somebody Up There Likes Me*
1957, *Fear Strikes Out*
1957, *Just My Luck*
1958, *Damn Yankees*
1961, *The Hustler*
1962, *The Iron Maiden*
1962, *The Loneliness of the Long Distance Runner*
1962, *Requiem for a Heavyweight*

1962, *Safe at Home!*
1963, *This Sporting Life*
1965, *The Great Race*
1966, *Fireball 500*
1966, *Grand Prix*
1966, *Red Line 7000*
1966, *Spinout*
1967, *Hell on Wheels*
1967, *A Man and a Woman*
1968, *The Love Bug*
1968, *Paper Lion*
1968, *Speedway*
1969, *Downhill Racer*
1969, *Winning*
1970, *The Great White Hope*
1971, *Brian's Song*
1971, *The Goalie's Anxiety at the Penalty Kick*
1971, *The Last American Hero*
1971, *Le Mans*
1971, *Two-Lane Blacktop*
1972, *Fat City*
1972, *Junior Bonner*
1972, *Kansas City Bomber*
1973, *Bang the Drum Slowly*
1973, *Enter the Dragon*
1973, *The World's Greatest Athlete*
1974, *Herbie Rides Again*
1974, *The Longest Yard*
1974, *The Wrestler*
1975, *Death Race 2000*
1975, *Hard Times*
1975, *Let's Do It Again*
1975, *Rollerball*
1976, *The Bad News Bears*
1976, *The Bingo Long Traveling All-Stars and Motor Kings*
1976, *Gus*
1976, *Rocky*
1977, *The Bad News Bears in Breaking Training*
1977, *Black Sunday*
1977, *Bobby Deerfield*
1977, *The Fish That Saved Pittsburgh*
1977, *The Greatest*
1977, *Herbie Goes to Monte Carlo*
1977, *One on One*
1977, *Semi-Tough*
1977, *Slap Shot*
1978, *The Bad News Bears Go to Japan*
1978, *Big Wednesday*
1978, *Coach*
1978, *Heaven Can Wait*
1978, *Ice Castles*
1978, *International Velvet*
1978, *Movie Movie*
1978, *Paradise Alley*
1979, *The Black Stallion*
1979, *Breaking Away*
1979, *The Champ*
1979, *Dreamer*
1979, *Fast Break*
1979, *The Main Event*
1979, *North Dallas Forty*
1979, *Penitentiary*
1979, *Players*
1979, *Rocky II*
1979, *Running*
1979, *Squeeze Play*
1979, *Take Down*
1979, *Yesterday's Hero*
1980, *Caddyshack*
1980, *The Club*
1980, *Herbie Goes Bananas*
1980, *Raging Bull*
1981, *. . . All the Marbles*
1981, *Chariots of Fire*
1981, *Gregory's Girl*
1981, *Victory*
1982, *Penitentiary II*
1982, *Personal Best*
1982, *Rocky III*
1983, *All the Right Moves*
1983, *The Black Stallion Returns*
1983, *Blue Skies Again*
1983, *BMX Bandits*
1983, *Brewster's Millions*
1983, *Heart Like a Wheel*
1983, *Phar Lap*
1983, *Running Brave*
1983, *Stroker Ace*
1984, *The Bear*
1984, *The Karate Kid*

1984, *The Natural*
1984, *Oxford Blues*
1985, *American Flyers*
1985, *Grunt! The Wrestling Movie*
1985, *Rocky IV*
1985, *The Slugger's Wife*
1985, *Teen Wolf*
1985, *Vision Quest*
1986, *American Anthem*
1986, *The Best of Times*
1986, *Body Slam*
1986, *The Color of Money*
1986, *Hoosiers*
1986, *The Karate Kid II*
1986, *Lightning, the White Stallion*
1986, *Lucas*
1986, *Rad*
1986, *Streets of Gold*
1986, *Wildcats*
1986, *Youngblood*
1987, *Amazing Grace and Chuck*
1987, *North Shore*
1987, *Over the Top*
1987, *Penitentiary III*
1987, *Playing Away*
1987, *Winners Take All*
1988, *Bull Durham*
1988, *Caddyshack II*
1988, *Eight Men Out*
1988, *Everybody's All-American*
1988, *Johnny Be Good*
1988, *Split Decisions*
1988, *Stealing Home*
1988, *Trading Hearts*
1989, *Field of Dreams*
1989, *Gleaming the Cube*
1989, *The Karate Kid, Part III*
1989, *Major League*
1989, *Night Game*
1989, *No Holds Barred*
1990, *Days of Thunder*
1990, *Mr. Destiny*
1990, *Nobody's Perfect*
1990, *Rocky V*
1990, *Side Out*
1991, *Across the Tracks*
1991, *By the Sword*
1991, *The Last Boy Scout*
1991, *Necessary Roughness*
1991, *Pastime*
1991, *Pistol: The Birth of a Legend*
1991, *Point Break*
1991, *Talent for the Game*
1992, *The Babe*
1992, *The Cutting Edge*
1992, *Diggstown*
1992, *Gladiator*
1992, *Ladybugs*
1992, *A League of Their Own*
1992, *The Mighty Ducks*
1992, *Mr. Baseball*
1992, *The Power of One*
1992, *School Ties*
1992, *Wind*
1992, *White Men Can't Jump*
1993, *Cool Runnings*
1993, *The Program*
1993, *Rookie of the Year*
1993, *Rudy*
1993, *The Sandlot*
1994, *Above the Rim*
1994, *The Air Up There*
1994, *Angels in the Outfield*
1994, *Blue Chips*
1994, *Cobb*
1994, *D2: The Mighty Ducks*
1994, *8 Seconds*
1994, *Little Big League*
1994, *Little Giants*
1994, *Major League II*
1994, *The Next Karate Kid*
1994, *The Scout*
1995, *Basketball Diaries*
1995, *The Big Green*
1995, *Blue in the Face*
1995, *The Break*
1995, *Dodgeball*
1995, *Forget Paris*
1995, *The Man with the Perfect Swing*
1995, *True Blue*
1996, *Celtic Pride*
1996, *D3: The Mighty Ducks*

1996, *Ed*
1996, *Eddie*
1996, *The Fan*
1996, *Fever Pitch* [U.K.]
1996, *The Great White Hype*
1996, *Happy Gilmore*
1996, *Jerry Maguire*
1996, *Kingpin*
1996, *Race the Sun*
1996, *Space Jam*
1996, *Sunset Park*
1996, *Tin Cup*
1996, *When Saturday Comes*
1997, *Air Bud*
1997, *The Boxer*
1997, *Les Boys*
1997, *Prefontaine*
1997, *The 6th Man*
1998, *Air Bud: Golden Receiver*
1998, *BASEketball*
1998, *The Big Lebowski*
1998, *He Got Game*
1998, *In God's Hands*
1998, *Major League: Back to the Minors*
1998, *The Unknown Cyclist*
1998, *The Waterboy*
1998, *Without Limits*
1999, *The Amateur*
1999, *Any Given Sunday*
1999, *For Love of the Game*
1999, *The Hurricane*
1999, *Mystery, Alaska*
1999, *Play It to the Bone*
1999, *Shergar*
1999, *Soccer Dog: The Movie*
1999, *Varsity Blues*
2000, *Bring It On*
2000, *Driven*
2000, *Finding Forrester*
2000, *Girlfight*
2000, *The Iron Ladies*
2000, *The Legend of Bagger Vance*
2000, *Love and Basketball*
2000, *MVP: Most Valuable Primate*
2000, *Purely Belter*
2000, *Ready to Rumble*
2000, *Remember the Titans*
2000, *The Replacements*
2000, *A Shot at Glory*
2000, *There's Only One Jimmy Grimble*
2001, *Ali*
2001, *Carman: The Champion*
2001, *Hardball*
2001, *Lagaan: Once Upon a Time in India*
2001, *Mean Machine*
2001, *Mike Bassett: England Manager*
2001, *MVP2: Most Vertical Primate*
2001, *O*
2001, *Out Cold*
2001, *Reversal*
2001, *Shaolin Soccer*
2001, *61**
2001, *Summer Catch*
2002, *Australian Rules*
2002, *Bend it Like Beckham*
2002, *Blue Crush*
2002, *Full Ride*
2002, *A Gentleman's Game*
2002, *Hometown Legend*
2002, *Juwanna Mann*
2002, *Like Mike*
2002, *Men with Brooms*
2002, *Poolhall Junkies*
2002, *The Rookie*
2002, *Slap Shot 2: Breaking the Ice*
2002, *The Slaughter Rule*
2002, *Undisputed*
2003, *Full-Court Miracle*
2003, *The Iron Ladies 2*
2003, *The Miracle of Bern*
2003, *Radio*
2003, *Seabiscuit*
2003, *Sugar and Spice*
2003, *The Triplets of Belleville*
2003, *Wondrous Oblivion*
2004, *Against the Ropes*
2004, *Bobby Jones: Strokes of Genius*
2004, *Dodgeball: A True Underdog Story*
2004, *Friday Night Lights*
2004, *Mickey*
2004, *Million Dollar Baby*
2004, *Miracle*

2004, *Mr. 3000*
2004, *Wimbledon*
2005, *Bad News Bears*
2005, *Cinderella Man*
2005, *Coach Carter*
2005, *The Derby Stallion*
2005, *Dreamer: Inspired by a True Story*
2005, *Fever Pitch* [U.S.]
2005, *Goal! The Dream Begins*
2005, *The Greatest Game Ever Played*
2005, *Herbie: Fully Loaded*
2005, *Ice Princess*
2005, *Kicking & Screaming*
2005, *The Longest Yard*
2005, *Lords of Dogtown*
2005, *Match Point*
2005, *On a Clear Day*
2005, *Racing Stripes*
2005, *Rebound*
2005, *The Ringer*
2005, *The Rocket: Maurice Richard*
2005, *Saint Ralph*
2005, *Tennis, Anyone?*
2005, *Two for the Money*
2005, *The World's Fastest Indian*
2006, *All You've Got*
2006, *Annapolis*
2006, *Beer League*
2006, *The Benchwarmers*
2006, *Cars*
2006, *Crossover*
2006, *Everyone's Hero*
2006, *Facing the Giants*
2006, *The Flying Scotsman*
2006, *Game 6*
2006, *Glory Road*
2006, *Goal! II: Living the Dream*
2006, *The Great Match*
2006, *Gridiron Gang*
2006, *Invincible*
2006, *Nacho Libre*
2006, *Offside*
2006, *Peaceful Warrior*
2006, *Rocky Balboa*
2006, *She's the Man*
2006, *Stick It*
2006, *Talladega Nights: The Ballad of Ricky Bobby*
2006, *We Are Marshall*
2006, *White Palms*
2007, *American Pastime*
2007, *Balls of Fury*
2007, *Blades of Glory*
2007, *Chak De! India*
2007, *The Comebacks*
2007, *Dans les Cordes*
2007, *Dribbles*
2007, *The Final Season*
2007, *The Game Plan*
2007, *Gracie*
2007, *The Hammer*
2007, *Her Best Move*
2007, *Home of the Giants*
2007, *Ping Pong Playa*
2007, *Pride*
2007, *Resurrecting the Champ*
2007, *Run, Fatboy, Run*
2007, *Ta Ra Rum Pum*
2007, *Tournament of Dreams*
2007, *Who's Your Caddy?*
2008, *Death Race*
2008, *The Express*
2008, *Forever Strong*
2008, *Leatherheads*
2008, *The Long Shots*
2008, *The Love Guru*
2008, *Semi-Pro*
2008, *Speed Racer*
2008, *Sugar*
2008, *Surfer, Dude*
2008, *The Wrestler*
2009, *Big Fan*
2009, *The Blind Side*
2009, *The Damned United*
2009, *Fired Up!*
2009, *Goal! III*
2009, *Invictus*
2009, *Looking for Eric*
2009, *Street Dreams*
2009, *Whip It*
2010, *Chasing 3000*
2010, *The Karate Kid*

APPENDIX C: MOVIES MADE FOR TELEVISION OR DIRECT TO VIDEO

Auto Racing

The Challengers (TV: CBS, 1970)
The Circuit (TV: ABC Family, 2008)
Death Racers (V, 2008)
Finish Line (TV: Spike, 2008)
The Love Bug (TV: ABC, 1997)
Right on Track (TV: Disney Channel, 2003)
Silent Victory: The Kitty O'Neil Story (TV: CBS, 1979)
3: The Dale Earnhardt Story (TV: ESPN, 2004)

Baseball

Air Bud: Seventh Inning Fetch (V, 2002)
Amos (TV: CBS, 1985)
Angels in the Infield (TV: ABC, 2000)
Aunt Mary (TV: CBS, 1979)
Babe Ruth (TV: NBC, 1991)
Bleacher Bums (TV: Showtime, 2002)
The Comeback Kid (TV: ABC, 1980)
The Comrades of Summer (TV: HBO, 1992)
Cooperstown (TV: TNT, 1993)
The Court-Martial of Jackie Robinson (TV: TNT, 1990)
Don't Look Back (TV: ABC, 1981)
Eddie's Million Dollar Cook-Off (TV: Disney, 2003)
Finding Buck McHenry (TV: Showtime, 2000)
Frankie & Hazel (TV: Showtime, 2000)
Hustle (TV: HBO, 2004)
It's Good to be Alive (TV: CBS, 1974)
Joe Torre: Curveballs along the Way (TV: Showtime, 1997)
The Kid from Left Field (TV: NBC, 1979)
Long Gone (TV: HBO, 1987)
A Love Affair: Eleanor and Lou Gehrig (TV: NBC, 1978)
The Man from Left Field (TV: CBS, 1993)
Million Dollar Infield (TV: CBS, 1982)
Murder at the World Series (TV: ABC, 1977)
One in a Million: The Ron LeFlore Story (TV: CBS, 1978)
Past the Bleachers (TV: ABC, 1992)
Perfect Game (V, 2000)
The Sandlot 2 (V, 2005)
The Sandlot 3 (V, 2007)
Soul of the Game (TV: HBO, 1996)
Tiger Town (TV: Disney, 1983)
A Winner Never Quits (TV: ABC, 1986)
The Winning Season (TV: TNT, 2004)

Basketball

Annie O (TV: Showtime, 1996)
Bad as I Wanna Be: The Dennis Rodman Story (TV: ABC, 1996)
Double Teamed (TV: Disney, 2002)
Edge of America (TV: Showtime, 2005)
Final Shot: The Hank Gathers Story (TV: Syndicated, 1992)
Full-Court Miracle (TV: Disney, 2003)
The Harlem Globetrotters on Gilligan's Island (TV: NBC, 1981)
Like Mike 2 (V, 2006)
The Luck of the Irish (TV: Disney, 2001)

Michael Jordan: An American Hero (TV: FOX Family, 1990)
A Mother's Courage: The Mary Thomas Story (TV: ABC, 1989)
Never Give Up: The Jimmy V Story (TV: CBS, 1996)
One Special Victory (TV: NBC, 1991)
Passing Glory (TV: TNT, 1999)
Rebound: The Legend of Earl "the Goat" Manigault (TV: HBO, 1996)
The Red Sneakers (TV: Showtime, 2002)
A Season on the Brink (TV: ESPN, 2002)
Slam Dunk Ernest (V, 1995)
That Championship Season (TV: Showtime, 1999)

Bowling

Alley Cats Strike! (TV: Disney, 2000)

Boxing

Ali: An American Hero (TV: FOX, 2000)
Dempsey (TV: CBS, 1983)
Flesh and Blood (TV: CBS, 1979)
Goldie and the Boxer (TV: NBC, 1979)
Goldie and the Boxer Go to Hollywood (TV: NBC, 1981)
Heart of a Champion: The Ray Mancini Story (TV: CBS, 1985)
Joe and Max (TV: Starz!, 2002)
Jump In! (TV: Disney Channel, 2007)
Marciano (TV: ABC, 1979)
Muhammad Ali: King of the World (TV: ABC, 2000)
Percy and Thunder (TV: TNT, 1993)
Ring of Passion (TV: NBC, 1978)
Terrible Joe Moran (TV: CBS, 1984)
Tyson (TV: HBO, 1995)
Undefeated (TV: HBO, 2003)
Undisputed II: Last Man Standing (V, 2006)
Undisputed III: Redemption (V, 2010)

Cheerleading

Bring It On Again (V, 2004)
Bring It On: All or Nothing (V, 2006)
Bring It On: Fight to the Finish (V, 2009)
Bring It On: In It to Win It (V, 2007)
Gotta Kick It Up! (V, 2002)
The Positively True Adventures of the Alleged Texas Cheerleader-Murdering Mom (TV: HBO, 1993)
Willing to Kill: The Texas Cheerleader Story (TV: ABC, 1992)

Football

Angels in the Endzone (TV: ABC, 1997)
Backfield in Motion (TV: ABC, 1991)
Brian's Song (TV: ABC, 1971)
Brian's Song (TV: ABC, 2001)
Coach of the Year (TV: NBC, 1980)
Code Breakers (TV: ESPN, 2005)
The Comeback (TV: CBS, 1989)
The Dallas Cowboys Cheerleaders (TV: ABC, 1979)
The Dallas Cowboys Cheerleaders II (TV: ABC, 1980)
Fighting Back (TV: ABC, 1980)
Footsteps (TV: CBS, 1972)
Frankenstein: The College Years (TV: FOX, 1991)
The Garbage Picking Field Goal Kicking Philadelphia Phenomenon (TV: ABC, 1998)
Glory Days (TV: CBS, 1988)
Grambling's White Tiger (TV: NBC, 1981)
The Halfback of Notre Dame (TV: Showtime, 1996)
The Junction Boys (TV: ESPN, 2002)
Monday Night Mayhem (TV: TNT, 2002)
The O.J. Simpson Story (TV: FOX, 1995)
The Oklahoma City Dolls (TV: ABC, 1981)
Pigs vs. Freaks (TV: NBC, 1984)
The Quarterback Princess (TV: CBS, 1983)
Quiet Victory: The Charlie Wedemeyer Story (TV: CBS, 1988)
Rise and Walk: The Dennis Byrd Story (TV: FOX, 1998)
The Second String (TV, 2002)
Something for Joey (TV: CBS, 1977)
The Sophisticated Gents (NBC: 1981)
The Sports Pages (TV: Showtime, 2001)

Superdome (TV: ABC, 1978)
A Triumph of the Heart: The Ricky Bell Story (TV: CBS, 1991)
Weapons of Mass Distraction (TV: HBO, 1997)

Golf

Babe (TV: CBS, 1975)
Dead Solid Perfect (TV: HBO, 1988)
Miracle on the 17th Green (TV: CBS, 1999)
The Tiger Woods Story (TV: Showtime, 1998)

Horse Racing

Derby (TV: ABC, 1995)
Ruffian (TV: ABC, 2007)

Ice Hockey

The Boy Who Drank Too Much (TV: CBS, 1980)
The Deadliest Season (TV: CBS, 1977)
Go Figure (TV: Disney, 2005)
Gross Misconduct (TV: Canadian Television, 1993)
H-E-Double Hockey Sticks (TV: ABC, 1999)
Miracle on Ice (TV: ABC, 1981)
Net Worth (TV: Canadian Television, 1995)
Trapped in a Purple Haze (TV: ABC, 2000)

Ice Skating

A Brother's Promise: The Dan Jansen Story (TV: CBS, 1996)
Champions: A Love Story (TV: CBS, 1979)
The Cutting Edge: Going for the Gold (V, 2006)
The Cutting Edge 3: Chasing the Dream (TV: ABC Family, 2008)
Go Figure (TV: Disney Channel, 2005)
My Sergei (TV: CBS, 1998)
A Promise Kept: The Oksana Baiul Story (TV: CBS, 1994)
Ronnie & Julie (TV: Showtime, 1997)
Tonya & Nancy: The Inside Story (TV: NBC, 1994)

Olympics

The First Olympics: Athens 1896 (TV: NBC, 1984)
The 500-Pound Jerk (TV: CBS, 1973)
The Golden Moment: An Olympic Love Story (TV: CBS, 1980)
King of the Olympics: The Lives and Loves of Avery Brundage (TV: Syndicated, 1988)
Nadia (TV: Syndicated, 1984)
Perfect Body (TV: NBC, 1997)
Special Olympics (TV: CBS, 1978)
Top of the Hill (TV: Syndicated, 1980)
21 Hours at Munich (TV: ABC, 1976)

Pool

Kiss Shot (TV: CBS, 1989)

Rodeo

Cowboy Up (V, 2000)
Goldenrod (TV: CBS, 1977)
Rodeo Girl (TV: CBS, 1980)
Still Holding On: The Legacy of Cadillac Jack (1998)

Snowboarding

MXP: Most Xtreme Primate (V, 2004)

Soccer

Air Bud 3: World Pup (V, 2000)

Surfing

Johnny Tsunami (TV: Disney, 1999)

Swimming

Breaking the Surface: The Greg Louganis Story (TV: USA, 1997)

Tennis

Balls Out: Gary the Tennis Coach (V, 2009)
Little Mo (TV: NBC, 1978)
Second Serve (TV: CBS, 1986)
When Billie Beat Bobby (TV: ABC, 2001)

Track and Field

Dying to Be Perfect: The Ellen Hart Peña Story (TV: ABC, 1996)
Finish Line (TV: TNT, 1988)

Four Minutes (TV: ESPN, 2005)
The Jericho Mile (TV: ABC, 1979)
The Jesse Owens Story (TV: Syndicated, 1984)
The Loneliest Runner (TV: NBC, 1976)
The Loretta Claiborne Story (TV: ABC, 2000)
Marathon (TV: CBS, 1980)
The Miracle of Kathy Miller (TV: CBS, 1981)
Run for the Dream: The Gail Devers Story (TV: Showtime, 1996)
See How She Runs (TV: CBS, 1978)
A Shining Season (TV: CBS, 1979)
The Terry Fox Story (TV: HBO, 1983)
Wilma (TV: NBC, 1978)

Volleyball

Air Bud: Spikes Back (V, 2003)
All You've Got (TV: MTV, 2006)
Beach Kings (V, 2008)

Wrestling

Going to the Mat (TV: Disney, 2004)
The Jesse Ventura Story (TV: NBC, 1999)
Mad Bull (TV: CBS, 1977)

APPENDIX D: MOVIES INSPIRED BY OR BASED UPON ACTUAL EVENTS

Made-for-television films are followed by the film's subject matter, if not already indicated by the title. For all other films, see main entry for more information.

Auto Racing

Heart Like a Wheel (1983)
The Last American Hero (1971)
Silent Victory: The Kitty O'Neil Story (TV: CBS, 1979); deaf driver Kitty O'Neil

Baseball

American Pastime (2007)
Aunt Mary (TV: CBS, 1979); Baltimore handicapped woman who coached thousands of boys and girls
The Babe (1992)
Babe Ruth (TV: NBC, 1991)
The Babe Ruth Story (1948)
Chasing 3000 (2010)
Cobb (1994)
The Court-Martial of Jackie Robinson (TV: TNT, 1990)
Eight Men Out (1988)
Fear Strikes Out (1957)
The Final Season (2007)
Hardball (2001)
Hustle (TV: HBO, 2004); Pete Rose
It's Good to Be Alive (TV: CBS, 1974); Roy Campanella
The Jackie Robinson Story (1950)
Joe Torre: Curveballs along the Way (TV: Showtime, 1997); Yankees manager
A Love Affair: Eleanor and Lou Gehrig (TV: NBC, 1978)
One in a Million: The Ron LeFlore Story (TV: CBS, 1978); former inmate turned pro baseball player
The Pride of St. Louis (1952)
Pride of the Yankees (1942)
The Rookie (2002)
*61** (2001)
Soul of the Game (TV: HBO, 1996); Satchel Paige and Josh Gibson
The Stratton Story (1949)
A Winner Never Quits (TV: ABC, 1986); one-armed baseball player Pete Gray
The Winning Team (1952)

Basketball

Bad as I Wanna Be: The Dennis Rodman Story (TV: ABC, 1996)
Basketball Diaries (1995)
Final Shot: The Hank Gathers Story (TV: Syndicated, 1992); college basketball star with a heart condition
Full-Court Miracle (2003)
Glory Road (2006)
Michael Jordan: An American Hero (TV: FOX Family, 1990)
A Mother's Courage: The Mary Thomas Story (TV: ABC, 1989); Isiah Thomas
Never Give Up: The Jimmy V Story (TV: CBS, 1996); coach Jimmy Valvano
One Special Victory (TV: NBC, 1991); coach of a mentally handicapped basketball team

Pistol: The Birth of a Legend (1991)
Rebound: The Legend of Earl "the Goat" Manigault (TV: HBO, 1996)
A Season on the Brink (TV: ESPN, 2002); Bobby Knight

Bobsledding

Cool Runnings (1993)

Boxing

Against the Ropes (2004)
Ali (2001)
Ali: An American Hero (TV: FOX, 2000)
Cinderella Man (2005)
Dempsey (TV: CBS, 1983); Jack Dempsey
Gentleman Jim (1942)
The Greatest (1977)
The Great White Hope (1970)
Heart of a Champion: The Ray Mancini Story (TV: CBS, 1985)
The Hurricane (1999)
Joe and Max (TV: Starz!, 2002); Joe Louis and Max Schmeling
Marciano (TV: ABC, 1979); Rocky Marciano
Muhammad Ali: King of the World (TV, 2000)
Raging Bull (1980)
Resurrecting the Champ (2007)
Ring of Passion (TV, 1978); Joe Louis and Max Schmeling
Somebody Up There Likes Me (1956)
Tyson (TV: HBO, 1995)

Cheerleading

The Positively True Adventures of the Alleged Texas Cheerleader-Murdering Mom (TV: HBO, 1993)
Willing to Kill: The Texas Cheerleader Story (TV: ABC, 1992)

Cycling

The Flying Scotsman (2007)

Football

The Bear (1984)
The Blind Side (2009)
Brian's Song (TV: ABC, 1971 and 2001); Brian Piccolo and Gale Sayers
Code Breakers (TV: ESPN, 2005); 1951 cheating scandal at West Point that involved players
The Express (2008)
Friday Night Lights (2004)
Grambling's White Tiger (TV: NBC, 1981); James Gregory, only white athlete at Grambling
Gridiron Gang (2006)
Invincible (2006)
Jim Thorpe: All American (1951)
The Junction Boys (TV: ESPN, 2002); Coach Paul "Bear" Bryant's first year at Texas A&M
Knute Rockne: All American (1940)
The Long Shots (2008)
Monday Night Mayhem (TV: TNT, 2002); ABC's *Monday Night Football*
The O.J. Simpson Story (TV: FOX, 1995)
Paper Lion (1968)
The Quarterback Princess (TV: CBS, 1983); Tami Maida, female junior varsity football player
Quiet Victory: The Charlie Wedemeyer Story (TV: CBS, 1988); football player/coach who had Lou Gehrig's disease
Radio (2003)
Remember the Titans (2000)
Rise and Walk: The Dennis Byrd Story (TV: FOX, 1994)
Rudy (1993)
Something for Joey (TV: CBS, 1977); John Cappelletti and his leukemia-stricken brother
A Triumph of the Heart: The Ricky Bell Story (TV: CBS, 1991); pro football player with heart condition
We Are Marshall (2006)

Golf

Babe (TV: CBS, 1975); Babe Didrikson
Bobby Jones: Strokes of Genius (2004)
Follow the Sun (1951)
The Greatest Game Ever Played (2005)

The Tiger Woods Story (TV: Showtime, 1998)

Gymnastics
Peaceful Warrior (2006)

Horse Racing
Dreamer: Inspired by a True Story (2005)
Phar Lap (1983)
Ruffian (TV: ABC, 2007); champion horse of the 1970s
Seabiscuit (2003)
Shergar (1999)

Ice Hockey
Miracle (2004)
Miracle on Ice (TV: ABC, 1981); 1980 U.S. Olympic hockey team
The Rocket: Maurice Richard (2005)

Ice Skating
A Brother's Promise: The Dan Jansen Story (TV, 1996)
My Sergei (TV: CBS, 1998); figure skaters Sergei Grinkov and Ekaterina Gordeeva
A Promise Kept: The Oksana Baiul Story (TV: CBS, 1994); figure skating champion
Tonya & Nancy: The Inside Story (TV: NBC, 1994); Tonya Harding and Nancy Kerrigan

Motorcycle Racing
The World's Fastest Indian (2005)

Olympics
The First Olympics: Athens 1896 (TV: NBC, 1984)
King of the Olympics: The Lives and Loves of Avery Brundage (TV: Syndicated, 1988); president of the International Olympic Committee
Nadia (TV: Syndicated, 1984); Nadia Comaneci
21 Hours at Munich (TV: ABC, 1976); murder of Israeli athletes at 1972 Olympics

Rodeo
8 Seconds (1994)

Rowing
True Blue (1996)

Rugby
Invictus (2009)

Skateboarding
Lords of Dogtown (2005)

Snowboarding
Out Cold (2001)

Soccer
The Damned United (2009)
Fever Pitch [U.K.] (1996)
The Game of Their Lives (2005)

Surfing
Big Wednesday (1978)

Swimming
Breaking the Surface: The Greg Louganis Story (TV: USA, 1997); Olympic diver
Pride (2007)

Tennis
Little Mo (TV: NBC, 1978); Grand Slam winner Maureen Connolly
Second Serve (TV: CBS, 1986); transsexual Renee Richards (Richard Radley)
When Billie Beat Bobby (TV: ABC, 2001); Billie Jean King and Bobby Riggs

Track and Field
Chariots of Fire (1981)
Dying to Be Perfect: The Ellen Hart Peña Story (TV: ABC, 1996); runner who suffered from bulimia
The Jesse Owens Story (TV: Syndicated, 1984)
The Miracle of Kathy Miller (TV: CBS, 1981); athlete who persevered after being hit by a car

Prefontaine (1997)
Run for the Dream: The Gail Devers Story (TV: Showtime, 1996); Olympic champion
Running Brave (1983)
A Shining Season (TV: CBS, 1979); John Baker, cancer-stricken coach of winning girls' team
The Terry Fox Story (TV: HBO, 1983); one-legged athlete with cancer who walked across Canada
Wilma (TV: NBC, 1978); Olympic track star Wilma Rudolph
Without Limits (1998)

Volleyball
The Iron Ladies (2000)
The Iron Ladies 2 (2003)

Wrestling
The Jesse Ventura Story (TV: NBC, 1999)

APPENDIX E: SPORTS DOCUMENTARIES

There have been numerous documentaries produced for television on network, PBS, and cable stations, HBO chief among these. Bud Greenspan has produced several films on the Olympics and Warren Miller has helmed dozens of films on extreme skiing. While the list below is far from complete, it does include key films on selected sports.

Auto Racing

Afternoon of a Champion (1972)
Chasing the Horizon (2006)
Dale (2007)
La Carrera Panamericana (1992)
Love the Beast (2009)
NASCAR 3D: The IMAX Experience (2004)
The Quick and the Dead (1975)
Super Speedway (1997)
Truth in 24 (2008)

Baseball

The Ball Game (1988)
Baseball (1994)
Dummy Hoy: A Deaf Hero (2007)
The Life and Times of Hank Greenberg (1998)
Signs of the Time (2008)
Touching the Game: The Story of the Cape Cod Baseball League (2004)

Basketball

Hoop Dreams (1994)
More Than a Game (2009)
Quantum Hoops (2007)
The Year of the Yao (2004)

Bodybuilding

Pumping Iron (1977)

Bowling

Strikes and Spares (1934) [Academy Award nominee: Best Short Subject, Novelty]

Boxing

Legendary Champions (1968)
On the Ropes (1999)
Tyson (2009)
Unforgivable Blackness (2004)
When We Were Kings (1996)

Cycling

Gila Cyclophilia (2009)
Hell on Wheels (2004)
Klunkerz (2006)
Overcoming (2005)
Road to Paris (2001)
A Sunday in Hell (1976)

Football

Gridiron Gang (1993)

Motorbike Racing

Dust to Glory (2005)
The Last Game (2002)

Olympics

The Olympiad (1938)
Various Bud Greenspan films

Rugby (Wheelchair)

Murderball (2005)

Soccer

Dare to Dream: The Story of the U.S. Women's Soccer Team (2007)

The Game of Their Lives (2002)

Hero: The Official Film of the 1986 FIFA World Cup (1987)

Maradona (2008)

Once in a Lifetime: The Extraordinary Story of the New York Cosmos (2006)

One Night in Turin (2010)

The Other Final (2003)

Pelé Forever (2004)

Real: The Movie (2005)

Skateboarding

Dogtown and Z-Boys (2001)

Under the Influence (2005)

Skiing

The Edge of Never (2009)

Steep (2007)

Various Warren Miller films

Ski Jumping

The Great Ecstasy of the Sculptor Steiner (1974)

Snowboarding

First Descent (2005)

Surfing

Endless Summer (1964)

Endless Summer 2 (1994)

Riding Giants (2004)

Step into Liquid (2003)

Surf Ninjas (1993)

Tennis

Unstrung (2007)

Wrestling

Beyond the Mat (2000)

Hitman Hart (1998)

APPENDIX F: ESPY AWARDS FOR BEST SPORTS MOVIE

Winners are in boldface type.

2010

Big Fan
The Blind Side
The Damned United
Invictus
The Karate Kid

2009

The Express
Sugar
The Wrestler

2008

The Game Plan
Leatherheads
Resurrecting the Champ
Semi-Pro

2007

Invincible
Talladega Nights: The Legend of Ricky Bobby
Pride
We Are Marshall

2006

Dreamer: Inspired by a True Story
Four Minutes
Glory Road
The Greatest Game Ever Played

2005

Cinderella Man
Coach Carter
Friday Night Lights
Million Dollar Baby

2004

Bobby Jones: Strokes of Genius
Dodgeball: A True Underdog Story
Miracle
Radio
Seabiscuit

2003

Bend It Like Beckham
A Gentleman's Game
The Junction Boys
Like Mike
Poolhall Junkies

2002

Ali
Joe and Max (TV)
Monday Night Mayhem (TV)
The Rookie
*61** (TV)

BIBLIOGRAPHY

Abrahams, Peter. *The Fan.* New York: Warner Books, 1995.

Ali, Muhammad, with Richard Durham. *The Greatest: My Own Story.* New York: Random House, 1975.

Allen, Maury. *Roger Maris: A Man for All Seasons.* New York: Donald I. Fine, 1986.

Angell, Roger. "Scout." *New Yorker*, www.newyorker.com/archive/1976/08/16/1976_08_16_034_TNY_CARDS_000321182.

Ardolino, Frank. "Ceremonies of Innocence and Experience in *Bull Durham, Field of Dreams,* and *Eight Men Out.*" *Journal of Popular Film and Television* 18, no. 2 (Summer 1990): 43–51.

Asinof, Eliot. *Eight Men Out.* New York: Henry Holt, 1963.

Bagnold, Enid. *National Velvet.* New York: Avon Books, 1935.

Baker, Aaron. *Contesting Identities: Sports in American Film.* Champaign: University of Illinois Press, 2003.

Baker, Aaron, and Todd Boyd, eds. *Out of Bounds: Sports, Media, and the Politics of Identity.* Bloomington: Indiana University Press, 1997.

Beaumont, Gerald. "133 at 3." *Redbook,* March 1921, 61.

Bergan, Ronald. *Sports in the Movies.* New York: Proteus Books, 1982.

Bernardi, Daniel, ed. *Classic Hollywood, Classic Whiteness.* Minneapolis: University of Minnesota Press, 2001.

Bissinger, H. G. *Friday Night Lights: A Town, a Team, and a Dream.* Cambridge, Mass.: De Capo Press, 2000.

Boggs, Carl, and Tom Pollard. *A World in Chaos: Social Crisis and the Rise of Postmodern Cinema.* Lanham, Md.: Rowman & Littlefield, 2003.

Bogle, Donald. *Toms, Coons, Mulattoes, Mammies, & Bucks.* New York: Continuum International, 2003.

Bowerman, William J. *Jogging.* New York: Grosset & Dunlap, 1967.

Brashler, William. *The Bingo Long Traveling All-Stars and Motor Kings.* New York: Harper & Row, 1973.

Briley, Ron, Michael K. Schoenecke, and Deborah A. Carmichael, eds. *All-Stars & Movie Stars: Sports in Film & History.* Lexington: University Press of Kentucky, 2008.

Britton, Andrew. "Blissing Out: The Politics of Reaganite Entertainment." *Movie* 31/32 (1986): 1–42.

Browne, Lois. *Girls of Summer: The Real Story of the All-American Girls Professional Baseball League.* New York: Viking, 1973.

Canby, Vincent. "Robert De Niro in *Raging Bull.*" *New York Times,* http://movies.nytimes.com/movie/review?res=9C06E6D71238F937A25752C1A966948260.

Carlin, John. *Playing the Enemy: Nelson Mandela and the Game That Made a Nation.* New York: Penguin, 2008.

Carroll, Jim. *The Basketball Diaries.* New York: Penguin, 1995.

Carter, Rubin "Hurricane." *The 16th Round.* New York: Penguin Global, 1991.

Cashmore, Ellis. *Making Sense of Sports.* 3rd ed. New York: Routledge, 2000.

Chalton, Sam, and Terry Swinton. *Lazarus and the Hurricane* (rev. ed.). New York: St. Martin's Griffin, 2000.

Childs, James. "Interview with John Hancock." *Literature/Film Quarterly* 3, no. 2 (1975): 109–16.

Coakley, Jay. *Sport in Society: Issues and Controversies.* St. Louis: Times Mirror, 1998.

Cobb, Ty, with Al Stump. *My Life in Baseball: The True Record.* New York: Doubleday, 1961.

Connelly, Marie Katheryn. *Martin Scorsese: An Analysis of His Feature Films, with a Filmography of His Entire Directorial Career.* Jefferson, N.C.: McFarland, 1993.

Cooper, Caroline M. "*Field of Dreams*: A Favorite of President Clinton, but a Typical Reaganite Film?" *Literature/Film Quarterly* 23, no. 3 (1995): 163–68.

Corbett, James J. *The Roar of the Crowd: The True Tale of the Rise and Fall of a Champion.* London: Phoenix House, 1925.

Courtenay, Bryce. *The Power of One.* New York: Random House, 1989.

Coyle, Daniel. *Hardball: A Season in the Projects.* New York: HarperCollins, 1995.

Creamer, Robert. *Babe: The Legend Comes to Life.* New York: Simon & Schuster, 1974.

Cross, Shauna. *Whip It.* Harrisonburg, Va.: R.R. Donnelley & Sons, 2007.

Deford, Frank. *Everybody's All-American.* New York: Viking Press, 1981.

Diawara, Manthia, ed. *Black American Cinema.* New York: Routledge, 1993.

Dickerson, Gary E. *The Cinema of Baseball: Images of America, 1929–1989.* Westport, Conn.: Meckler Publishing, 1991.

Dougan, Andy. *Martin Scorsese: Close Up.* New York: Thunder's Mouth Press, 1997.

Ebert, Roger. Review of *Raging Bull.Chicago Sun-Times,* http://rogerebert.suntimes.com/apps/pbcs.dll/article?AID=/19980510/REVIEWS08/401010354/1023.

———. Review of *Power of One. Chicago Sun-Times,* http://rogerebert.suntimes.com/apps/pbcs.dll/article?AID=/19920327/REVIEWS/203270302/1023.

———. Review of *Wildcats. Chicago Sun-Times,* http://rogerebert.suntimes.com/apps/pbcs.dll/article?AID=/19860214/REVIEWS/602140303/1023.

Edelman, Rob. *The Great Baseball Films: From "Right Off the Bat" to "A League of Their Own."* Secaucus, N.J.: Carol Publishing Group, 1994.

Erickson, Hal. *The Baseball Filmography: 1915 through 2001.* Jefferson, N.C.: McFarland, 2002.

Frommer, Harvey. *Rickey and Robinson: The Men Who Broke Baseball's Color Line.* New York: Macmillan, 1987.

Frost, Mark. *The Greatest Game Ever Played: Harry Vardon, Francis Ouimet, and the Birth of Modern Golf.* New York: Hyperion, 2002.

Gallagher, Robert. *The Express: The Ernie Davis Story.* New York: Random House, 1999.

Gent, Peter. *North Dallas Forty.* New York: Ballantine, 1984.

George, Nelson. *Elevating the Game: Black Men and Basketball.* New York: HarperCollins, 1992.

Gilmore, Al-Tony. *Bad Nigger: The National Impact of Jack Johnson.* Port Washington, N.Y.: Kennikat Press, 1975.

Good, Howard. *Diamonds in the Dark: America, Baseball, and the Movies.* Lanham, Md.: Scarecrow Press, 1997.

Graziano, Rocky. *Somebody Up There Likes Me: The Story of My Life until Today.* New York: Simon & Schuster, 1955.

Grieveson, Lee. *Policing Cinema: Movies and Censorship in Early Twentieth-Century America.* Berkeley: University of California Press, 2004.

Griffith, James. "Say It Ain't So: *The Natural.*" *Literature/Film Quarterly* 19, no. 3 (1991): 157–61.

Grindon, Leger. "Body and Soul: The Structure of Meaning in the Boxing Film Genre." *Cinema Journal* 35 (1996): 54–69.

Hall, Oakley. *The Downhill Racer*. New York: Viking, 1962.

Harris, Mark. *"Bang the Drum Slowly," by Henry Wiggen: Certain of His Enthusiasms Restrained by Mark Harris*. New York: Alfred A. Knopf, 1956.

Harrison, William. "Roller Ball Murder." In *Roller Ball Murder and Other Stories*. London: Robson Books, 1975.

Hemmeter, Gail Carnicelli, and Thomas Hemmeter. "The Word Made Flesh: Language in *Raging Bull*." *Literature/Film Quarterly* 14, no. 2 (1986): 101–5.

Highsmith, Patricia. *Strangers on a Train*. New York: W. W. Norton, 1950.

Hill, John. *Sex, Class and Realism: British Cinema 1956–1963*. London: British Film Institute, 1986.

Hillenbrand, Laura. *Seabiscuit: An American Legend*. New York: Random House, 2002.

Internet Movie Database [website]. www.imdb.com.

Jacobson, Harlan. "Shot in the Dark: Born Again Baseball." *Film Comment* 25, no. 3 (May/June 1989): 78–79.

Jenkins, Dan. *Semi-Tough*. New York: Atheneum, 1972.

Kael, Pauline. "After Innocence." *New Yorker*, www.newyorker.com/archive/1973/10/01/1973_10_01_113_TNY_CARDS_000310058.

Kandel, Aben. *City for Conquest*. New York: Harlequin Books, 1949.

Kempley, Rita. Review of *The Great White Hype*. *Washington Post*, www.washingtonpost.com/wp-srv/style/longterm/movies/videos/greatwhitehype.htm.

———. Review of *The Power of One*. *Washington Post*, www.washingtonpost.com/wp-srv/style/longterm/movies/videos/thepowerofonepg-13kempley_a0a2ab.htm.

Kersh, Gerald. *Night and the City*. New York: Simon & Schuster, 1946.

Keyser, Michael. *A French Kiss with Death: Steve McQueen and the Making of "Le Mans": The Man, the Race, the Cars, the Movie*. Cambridge, Mass.: Bentley Publishers, 1999.

King, C. Richard, and David J. Leonard, eds. *Visual Economies of/in Motion: Sport and Film*. New York: Peter Lang, 2006.

Kinsella, W. P. *Shoeless Joe*. Boston: Houghton Mifflin, 1982.

La Motta, Jake, with Joseph Carter and Peter Savage. *Raging Bull: My Story*. Englewood Cliffs, N.J.: Prentice-Hall, 1970.

Lardner, Ring. *How to Write Short Stories (with Samples)*. New York: Charles Scribner's Sons, 1924.

Leab, Daniel. "The Blue Collar Ethnic in Bicentennial America." In *American History/American Film: Interpreting the Hollywood Image*, edited by John O'Connor and Martin Jackson, 257–72. New York: Ungar, 1979.

Lee, Spike, with Ralph Wiley. *Best Seat in the House: A Basketball Memoir*. New York: Random House, 1997.

Lewis, Michael M. *The Blind Side*. New York: W. W. Norton, 2006.

Librach, Ronald S. "The Last Temptation in *Mean Streets* and *Raging Bull*." *Literature/Film Quarterly* 20, no. 1 (1992): 14–24.

Lindner, Katharina. "Fighting for Subjectivity: Articulations of Physicality in *Girlfight*." *Journal of International Women's Studies* 10, no. 3 (March 2009): 4–17.

Malamud, Bernard. *The Natural*. New York: Harcourt, Brace, 1952.

Maltin, Leonard. *Leonard Maltin's Movie Guide, 2010 Edition*. New York: New American Library, 2009.

Manchel, Frank. *Great Sports Movies*. New York: Franklin Watts, 1980.

Mantle, Mickey, with Herb Gluck. *The Mick*. Garden City, N.Y.: Doubleday, 1985.

Maslin, Janet. "Float like a Butterball, Hit like a Flea." *New York Times*, www.nytimes.com/library/filmarchive/great_white_hype.html.

McCallum, John D. *The Tiger Wore Spikes: An Informal Biography of Ty Cobb*. New York: A. S. Barnes, 1956.

McCrisken, Trevor, and Andrew Pepper. *American History and Contemporary Hollywood Film*. Edinburgh, Scotland: Edinburgh University Press, 2005.

McKernan, Luke. "Sport and the First Films." In *Cinema: The Beginnings and the Future*, edited by Christopher Williams, 107–16. London: University of Westminster Press, 1996.

Millman, Dan. *Way of the Peaceful Warrior: A Book That Changes Lives*. 20th Anniversary Edition. Novato, Calif.: New World Library, 2000.

Moes, Daniel. *Keaton: The Silent Features Close Up*. Berkeley: University of California Press, 1977.

Nadal, Alan. *Flatlining on the Field of Dreams: Cultural Narrative in the Films of President Reagan's America*. New Brunswick, N.J.: Rutgers University Press, 1997.

Naison, Mark. "Sports and the American Empire." *Radical American* 6 (July/August 1972): 95–120.

Neely, William, and Robert K. Ottum. *Stand on It: A Novel by Stroker Ace*. New York: Random House, 1974.

Nixon, Howard. *Sports and the American Dream*. New York: Leisure Press, 1984.

Obree, Graeme. *Flying Scotsman: Cycling to Triumph through My Darkest Hours*. Boulder, Colo.: VeloPress, 2005.

O'Hehir, Andrew. "Beyond the Multiplex." *Salon*, www.salon.com/entertainment/movies/review/2007/03/22/btm.

Peckham, Tony. "Writers on Writing." *Script* magazine, November/ December 2009: 58–63.

Penner, Allen R. "Human Dignity and Social Anarchy: Sillitoe's 'The Loneliness of the Long Distance Runner.'" *Contemporary Literature* 10 (1969): 253–65.

Peterson, Ralph W. *The Square Ring*. London: Barker, 1954.

Peterson, Robert. *Only the Ball Was White*. Englewood Cliffs, N.J.: Prentice-Hall, 1970.

Piersall, Jim, and Al Hirshberg. *Fear Strikes Out: The Jim Piersall Story*. Philadelphia: Curtis Publishing, 1955.

Pittman, L. Monique. "Dressing the Girl/Playing the Boys: *Twelfth Night* Learns Soccer on the Set of *She's the Man*." *Literature/Film Quarterly* 36, no. 2 (2008): 122–36.

Plimpton, George. *Paper Lion: Confessions of a Last-String Quarterback*. 40th Anniversary Edition. Guilford, Conn.: Lyons Press, 2003.

Poulton, Emma, and Martin Roderick, eds. *Sport in Films*. New York: Routledge, 2008.

Pressfield, Steven. *The Legend of Bagger Vance: A Novel of Golf and the Game of Life*. New York: HarperCollins, 1999.

Reilly, Adam. *Harold Lloyd: The King of Daredevil Comedy*. New York: Collier Books, 1975.

Review of *The Great White Hype*. *Variety*, www.variety.com/review/VE1117791373.html?categoryid=31&cs=1.

Roberts, Randy, and James Olson. *Winning Is the Only Thing: Sports in America Since 1945*. Baltimore: Johns Hopkins University Press, 1989.

Rollins, Janet Buck. "Novel into Film: *The Loneliness of the Long Distance Runner*." *Literature/Film Quarterly* 9, no. 3 (1981): 172–88.

Romano, Frederick V. *The Boxing Filmography: American Features, 1920–2003*. Jefferson, N.C.: McFarland, 2004.

Rotten Tomatoes [website]. www.rottentomatoes.com.

Rowe, David. *Sport, Culture and the Media*. 2nd ed. Berkshire, England: Open University Press, 2004.

Ruth, Babe, as told to Robert Considine. *The Babe Ruth Story*. New York: Dutton, 1948.

Salsinger, H. G. "Which Was Greatest: Ty Cobb or Babe Ruth?" Baseball Register Column. *Sporting News*, 1951.

Sandomir, Richard. "His 15 Minutes of Fame Took Only 17 Seconds." *New York Times*, www.nytimes.com/1993/10/10/movies/his-15-minutes-of-fame-took-only-17-seconds.html?scp=2&sq=richard+sandomir&st=nyt&pagewanted.

Sayers, Gayle, with Al Silverman. *I Am Third*. New York: Bantam Books, 1972.

Schaap, Jeremy. *Cinderella Man: James Braddock, Max Baer, and the Greatest Upset in Boxing History*. New York: Houghton Mifflin, 2005.

Scott, A. O. "Final Score: Future 1, Past 0." *New York Times*, http://movies.nytimes.

com/2009/12/11/movies/11invictus.html?scp=1&sq=%22invictus%22&st=cse.

Shaara, Michael. *For Love of the Game*. New York: Ballantine Books, 1999.

Shakespeare, William. *Othello*. Ed. Barbara M. Mowat and Paul Werstine. Washington, D.C.: Folger Shakespeare Library, 1993.

Sillitoe, Alan."The Loneliness of the Long-Distance Runner." In *The Loneliness of the Long-Distance Runner*, 7–55. New York: Alfred A. Knopf, 1968.

Smith, H. Allen. *Rhubarb*. New York: Doubleday, 1946.

Sobchack, Vivian. "Baseball in the Post-American Cinema." In *Out of Bounds: Sports, Media and the Politics of Identity*, ed. Aaron Baker and Todd Boyd, 186. Bloomington: Indiana University Press, 1997.

Sperber, Murray. *Shake Down the Thunder: The Creation of Notre Dame Football*. New York: Henry Holt, 1993.

Storey, David. *This Sporting Life*. New York: Macmillan, 1960.

Stump, Al. *Cobb: The Life and Times of the Meanest Man Who Ever Played Baseball*. Chapel Hill, N.C.: Algonquin Books, 1994.

Swindell, Larry. *Body and Soul: The Story of John Garfield*. New York: William Morrow, 1975.

Tevis, Walter. *The Color of Money*. New York: Thunder's Mouth Press, 1984.

———. *The Hustler*. New York: Thunder's Mouth Press, 1959.

Thompson, David, and Ian Christie. *Scorsese on Scorsese*. London: Faber and Faber, 1989.

Toole, F. X. *Million Dollar Baby: Stories from the Corner*. New York: HarperCollins, 2005.

Topolski, Daniel, and Patrick Robinson. *True Blue*. Toronto: Doubleday, 1989.

Truffaut, Francois. *Hitchcock*. New York: Simon & Schuster, 1985.

Tudor, Deborah V. *Hollywood's Vision of Team Sports: Heroes, Race, and Gender*. New York: Garland Publishing, 1997.

Tulloch, Jonathon. *The Season Ticket*. London: Jonathan Cape, 2000.

Turchi, Peter. "Roy Hobbs's Corrected Stance: An Adaptation of *The Natural*." *Literature/Film Quarterly* 19, no. 3 (1991): 150–56.

Turner Classic Movies [website]. www.tcm.com.

Wagenheim, Kal. *Babe Ruth: His Life and Legend*. Maplewood, N.J.: Waterfront, 1990.

Wallop, Douglass. *The Year the Yankees Lost the Pennant*. New York: W. W. Norton, 2004.

Weisman, Stephen R. "Japanese Buy Studio, and Coaching Starts." *New York Times*, www.nytimes.com/1991/11/20/movies/japanese-buy-studio-and-coaching-starts.html?scp=1&sq=Weisman.+Steven+R.&st=nyt&pagewanted=print.

Williams, Randy. *Sports Cinema 100 Movies: The Best of Hollywood's Athletic Heroes, Losers, Myths, and Misfits*. Pompton Plains, N.J.: Limelight Editions, 2006.

Wolfe, Tom. "The Last American Hero." *Esquire*, www.esquire.com/features/life-of-junior-johnson-tom-wolfe-0365.

Wulf, Stefe. "Field of Dames." *Sports Illustrated* 76, no. 26 (1992): 4.

Zucker, Harvey, and Lawrence Babich. *Sports Films: A Complete Reference*. Jefferson, N.C.: McFarland, 1987.

INDEX

Aaron, Quinton: *The Blind Side,* 60–63
Abbott, George: *Damn Yankees,* 121–23
Above the Rim, 1–4
Abraham, F. Murray: *Finding Forrester,* 168–70
Abrol, Tanya: *Chak De! India,* 87–90
Ackland, Joss: *The Mighty Ducks,* 312–15
Across the Tracks, 4–5
Adams, Stanley: *Requiem for a Heavyweight,* 383–85
Against the Ropes, 5–6
Air Bud, 6
Air Bud: Golden Receiver, 7
The Air Up There, 7
Albert, Eddie: *The Longest Yard* (1974), 290–92
Albright, Lola: *Champion,* 91–94
Aldrich, Robert: *The Longest Yard* (1974), 290–92
Alexander, Grover Cleveland: *The Winning Team,* 487
Alexander, Jane: *The Great White Hope,* 207–9
Ali, 7–10
Ali, Muhammad: *Ali,* 7–10; *The Greatest,* 200–202
Alibi Ike, 10
Allen, Debbie: *Tournament of Dreams,* 461–63
Allen, Ray: *He Got Game,* 224–27
Allen, Woody: *Match Point,* 307–9
Allison, June: *The Stratton Story,* 444–46
Allodi, James: *Men with Brooms,* 310–12
...All the Marbles, 10
All the Right Moves, 10–12
All You've Got, 12
Altman, Bruce: *Rookie of the Year,* 402–5
Alvarado, Trini: *The Babe,* 24–26
The Amateur, 12
Amazing Grace and Chuck, 12
American Anthem, 12–13
American Flyers, 13–16
American Pastime, 16
America's Cup: *Wind,* 485
Amin, Shimit: *Chak De! India,* 87–90
Amos, John: *American Flyers,* 13–16
Anaheim Angels: *Angels in the Outfield* (1994), 18–20
Anconina, Richard: *Dans les Cordes (On the Ropes),* 123–24
Andersen, Elga: *Le Mans,* 285–87
Anderson, James: *The Freshman,* 178–81
Anderson, Lindsay: *This Sporting Life,* 456–58
Andoh, Adjoa: *Invictus,* 245–47
Angarano, Michael: *The Final Season,* 166–68; *Lords of Dogtown,* 294–97
Angel, Vanessa: *Kingpin,* 266–68
Angeli, Pier: *Somebody Up There Likes Me,* 435–37
Angels in the Outfield (1951), 16–18
Angels in the Outfield (1994), 18–20
animal movies: *Air Bud,* 6; *Air Bud: Golden Receiver,* 7; *MVP: Most Valuable Primate,* 326; *MVP 2: Most Vertical Primate,* 326; *Soccer Dog: The Movie,* 434. *See also* horse racing
animated movies: *Everyone's Hero,* 147–49; *Space Jam,* 437; *The Triplets of Belleville,* 464
Annapolis, 20
Ann-Margaret: *Any Given Sunday,* 20–23
Anspaugh, David: *Rudy,* 405–7

Any Given Sunday, 20–23
Apatow, Judd: *Celtic Pride,* 84–87
arm wrestling: *Over the Top,* 346–47
Arnett, Will: *Blades of Glory,* 58–60; *Semi-Pro,* 418–19
Arnold, Edward: *Take Me Out to the Ball Game,* 451–53
Arnold, Tom: *The Final Season,* 166–68; *Pride,* 363–65
The Arsenal Stadium Mystery, 23
Ashby, Hal: *The Slugger's Wife,* 432–34
Astin, Mackenzie: *The Final Season,* 166–68
Astin, Sean: *The Final Season,* 166–68; *Rudy,* 405–7
Auster, Paul: *Blue in the Face,* 65–66
Australian football: *Australian Rules,* 23; *The Club,* 102
Australian Rules, 23
auto racing: *The Big Wheel,* 53; *Bobby Deerfield,* 67; *Cars,* 84; *The Crowd Roars,* 115; *Days of Thunder,* 127–29; *Death Race,* 129–30; *Death Race 2000,* 130; *Driven,* 138; *Fireball 500,* 170–71; *Genevieve,* 185–86; *Grand Prix,* 198–200; *Heart Like a Wheel,* 220–22; *Hell on Wheels,* 227; *Herbie: Fully Loaded,* 227; *Herbie Goes Bananas,* 227; *Herbie Goes to Monte Carlo,* 227–28; *Herbie Rides Again,* 228; *Indianapolis Speedway,* 244; *The Last American Hero,* 274–76; *Le Mans,* 285–87; *The Love Bug,* 299; *A Man and a Woman,* 306; *To Please a Lady,* 461; *Race the Sun,* 373; *Red Line 7000,* 379; *Speed Racer,* 437; *Speedway,* 437; *Spinout,* 438; *Stroker Ace,* 447; *Talladega Nights: The Ballad of Ricky Bobby,* 453–55; *Ta Ra Rum Pum,* 455; *Two-Lane Blacktop,* 464–67; *Winning,* 486–87
Avildsen, John G.: *The Karate Kid* (1984), 263–64; *The Power of One,* 359–61; *Rocky,* 387–89; *Rocky V,* 395–97
awards, ESPY, 517
Axton, Hoyt: *Heart Like a Wheel,* 220–22
Aykroyd, Dan: *Celtic Pride,* 84–87
Azaria, Hank: *Dodgeball: A True Underdog Story,* 131–35; *Mystery, Alaska,* 326–28
The Babe, 24–26
The Babe Ruth Story, 26
Badel, Alan: *This Sporting Life,* 456–58
Badham, John: *American Flyers,* 13–16; *The Bingo Long Travelling All-Stars and Motor Kings,* 53–56
The Bad News Bears (1976), 26–28
The Bad News Bears (2005), 28–29
The Bad News Bears Go to Japan, 29–30
The Bad News Bears in Breaking Training, 30–32
Baer, Max: *The Prizefighter and the Lady,* 368
Baffico, James A.: *All the Right Moves,* 10–12
Bagnold, Enid: *National Velvet,* 329–32
Bailey, David: *Above the Rim,* 1–4
Baio, Jimmy: *The Bad News Bears in Breaking Training,* 30–32
Baker, Ray: *Everybody's All-American,* 145–47
Bakula, Scott: *Major League: Back to the Minors,* 304
Baldwin, Stephen: *Slap Shot 2: Breaking the Ice,* 430–31
Balls of Fury, 32–33
Baltimore Orioles: *The Babe,* 24–26
Baltimore Ravens: *The Blind Side,* 60–63
Bang the Drum Slowly, 33–35
Banks, Elizabeth: *Invincible,* 247–49; *Seabiscuit,* 416–18
Barkin, Ellen: *The Fan,* 152–56
Barnes, Chris: *The Bad News Bears* (1976), 26–28; *The Bad News Bears Go to Japan,* 29–30; *The Bad News Bears in Breaking Training,* 30–32
Barrie, Barbara: *Breaking Away,* 72–75
Barrymore, Drew: *Fever Pitch* (2005), 160–62; *Whip It,* 474–77
baseball: *Alibi Ike,* 10; *Amazing Grace and Chuck,* 12; *American Pastime,* 16; *Angels in the Outfield* (1951), 16–18; *Angels in the Outfield* (1994), 18–20; *The Babe,* 24–26; *The Babe Ruth Story,* 26; *The Bad News Bears* (1976), 26–28; *The Bad News Bears* (2005), 28–29; *The Bad News Bears Go to Japan,* 29–30; *The Bad News Bears in Breaking Training,* 30–32; *Bang the*

Drum Slowly, 33–35; Base*ketball,* 35; *The Benchwarmers,* 40–41; *The Bingo Long Travelling All-Stars and Motor Kings,* 53–56; *Blue in the Face,* 65–66; *Blue Skies Again,* 66; *Brewster's Millions,* 75; *Bull Durham,* 78–81; *Chasing 3000,* 97; *Cobb,* 104–8; *Damn Yankees,* 121–23; *Ed,* 139; *Eight Men Out,* 141–43; *Elmer, the Great,* 144; *Everyone's Hero,* 147–49; *The Fan,* 152–56; *Fear Strikes Out,* 156–58; *Fever Pitch* (2005), 160–62; *Field of Dreams,* 162–66; *The Final Season,* 166–68; *Fireman, Save My Child,* 171; *For Love of the Game,* 174–78; *Game* 6, 185; *Hardball,* 218; *It Happens Every Spring,* 249–51; *The Jackie Robinson Story,* 252–53; *The Kid from Left Field,* 265–66; *Kill the Umpire,* 266; *A League of Their Own,* 276–79; *Little Big League,* 288; *Major League,* 302–4; *Major League: Back to the Minors,* 304; *Major League II,* 305–6; *Mickey,* 312; *Mr. Baseball,* 323–25; *Mr. Destiny,* 325–26; *Mr. 3000,* 326; *The Natural,* 332–35; *Night Game,* 337–38; *Pastime,* 348–50; *The Pride of St. Louis,* 365; *Pride of the Yankees,* 365–68; *Rhubarb,* 385–87; *The Rookie,* 399–402; *Rookie of the Year,* 402–5; *Safe at Home!,* 412; *The Sandlot,* 412; *The Scout,* 415–16; *61*,* 426–28; *The Slugger's Wife,* 432–34; *Stealing Home,* 440–41; *The Stratton Story,* 444–46; *Sugar,* 447–50; *Summer Catch,* 450; *Take Me Out to the Ball Game,* 451–53; *Talent for the Game,* 453; *Trading Hearts,* 463–64; *The Winning Team,* 487

Base*ketball,* 35

basketball: *Above the Rim,* 1–4; *Air Bud,* 6; *The Air Up There,* 7; *Basketball Diaries,* 36–38; *Blue Chips,* 63–65; *Celtic Pride,* 84–87; *Coach,* 102; *Coach Carter,* 102–4; *Crossover,* 115; *Dribbles,* 138; *Eddie,* 139–41; *Fast Break,* 156; *Finding Forrester,* 168–70; *The Fish That Saved Pittsburgh,* 171; *Forget Paris,* 178; *Full-Court Miracle,* 182–84; *Glory Road,* 191–92; *He Got Game,* 224–27; *Home of the Giants,* 231; *Hoosiers,* 231–34; *Juwanna Mann,* 261; *Like Mike,* 287; *Love and Basketball,* 297–99; *O,* 341–43; *One on One,* 346; *Pistol: The Birth of a Legend,* 357; *Rebound,* 379; *Semi-Pro,* 418–19; *The 6th Man,* 426; *Space Jam,* 437; *Sunset Park,* 450; *Teen Wolf,* 455; *Tournament of Dreams,* 461–63; *White Men Can't Jump,* 477–79

Basketball Diaries, 36–38

Bateman, Jason: *Dodgeball: A True Underdog Story,* 131–35

Bates, Kathy: *The Blind Side,* 60–63

Batinkoff, Randall: *School Ties,* 413–15

Battling Butler, 38–40

Bauer, Chris: *61*,* 426–28

Baxter, Alan: *The Set-Up,* 421–22

Bay, Frances: *Happy Gilmore,* 216–18

The Bear, 40

Beattie, Chris: *Purely Belter,* 370–72

Beatty, Ned: *He Got Game,* 224–27; *The Last American Hero,* 274–76

Beatty, Warren: *Heaven Can Wait,* 222–24

Beck, John: *Rollerball,* 397–99

Becker, Kuno: *Goal! The Dream Begins,* 192–95; *Goal! II: Living the Dream,* 195; *Goal! III,* 195

Bedelia, Bonnie: *Heart Like a Wheel,* 220–22

Bedford, Brian: *Grand Prix,* 198–200

Beer League, 40

Beery, Wallace: *The Champ* (1932), 90–91

The Benchwarmers, 40–41

Bendinger, Jessica: *Bring It On,* 77–78

Bend It Like Beckham, 41–42

Benedict, Brooks: *The Freshman,* 178–81

Benjamin, André: *Semi-Pro,* 418–19

Benjaminson, Scott: *Rudy,* 405–7

Bennett, Bruce: *Angels in the Outfield* (1951), 16–18

Benson, Robby: *Ice Castles,* 240–42; *Running Brave,* 408–11

Bentt, Michael: *Ali,* 7–10

Bercovici, Luca: *American Flyers,* 13–16

Berenger, Tom: *Major League,* 302–4; *Major League II,* 305–6

Berg, Peter: *Great White Hype,* 209–11

Berkoff, Stephen: *The Flying Scotsman*, 171–74
Bernsen, Corbin: *Great White Hype*, 209–11; *Major League*, 302–4; *Major League: Back to the Minors*, 304; *Major League II*, 305–6
Berry, Halle: *The Program*, 368–70
The Best of Times, 42–46
Bettany, Paul: *Wimbledon*, 483–85
Bickford, Charles: *Jim Thorpe: All American*, 256–58
Bierko, Craig: *Cinderella Man*, 97–99
Big Fan, 46
The Big Green, 46
The Big Lebowski, 46–50
Big Wednesday, 50–53
The Big Wheel, 53
The Bingo Long Travelling All-Stars and Motor Kings, 53–56
Bird, Laurie: *Two-Lane Blacktop*, 464–67
Birdwell, Russell: *Jim Thorpe: All American*, 256–58
Bissinger, H. G.: *Friday Night Lights*, 181–82
Black, Lucas: *Friday Night Lights*, 181–82
The Black Stallion, 56–57
The Black Stallion Returns, 57–58
Black Sunday, 58
Blackthorne, Paul: *Lagaan: Once Upon a Time in India*, 271–74
Blackwood, Vas: *Mean Machine*, 309–10
Blades of Glory, 58–60
Blakely, Susan: *Over the Top*, 346–47
The Blind Side, 60–63
Blue Chips, 63–65
Blue Crush, 65
Blue in the Face, 65–66
Blue Skies Again, 66
Blumas, Trevor: *Ice Princess*, 242–44
Blunt, Emily: *The Bad News Bears* (1976), 26–28; *The Bad News Bears in Breaking Training*, 30–32
Blye, Margaret: *Hard Times*, 219–20
BMX Bandits, 66
Bobby Deerfield, 67
Bobby Jones: Strokes of Genius, 67
bobsledding: *Cool Runnings*, 113–15
Boden, Anna: *Sugar*, 447–50
Body and Soul, 67–69
Body Slam, 69
Bogart, Humphrey: *The Harder They Fall*, 218–19
Bolam, James: *The Loneliness of the Long-Distance Runner*, 288–90
Bolin, Shannon: *Damn Yankees*, 121–23
Bond, Ward: *Gentleman Jim*, 186–87
bookies: *Just My Luck*, 261
Boothe, Powers: *The Final Season*, 166–68
Boots Malone, 69
Borgnine, Ernest: *The Greatest*, 200–202
Boston Braves: *The Babe*, 24–26
Boston Celtics: *Celtic Pride*, 84–87
Boston marathon: *Saint Ralph*, 412
Boston Red Sox: *The Babe*, 24–26; *The Babe Ruth Story*, 26; *Fear Strikes Out*, 156–58; *Fever Pitch* (2005), 160–62; *Game 6*, 185
Bosworth, Kate: *Remember the Titans*, 379–82
Bowen, Julie: *Happy Gilmore*, 216–18
bowling: *The Big Lebowski*, 46–50; *Dreamer*, 137; *Kingpin*, 266–68
The Boxer, 69–72
boxing: *Ali*, 7–10; *Annapolis*, 20; *Battling Butler*, 38–40; *Body and Soul*, 67–69; *The Boxer*, 69–72; *Carman: The Champion*, 83–84; *The Champ* (1932), 90–91; *The Champ* (1979), 91; *Champion*, 91–94; *Cinderella Man*, 97–99; *City for Conquest*, 99–100; *City Lights*, 100–102; *The Crowd Roars*, 115; *Dans les Cordes (On the Ropes)*, 123–24; *Diggstown*, 130; *Fat City*, 156; *Gentleman Jim*, 186–87; *Girlfight*, 187–90; *Gladiator*, 190; *Golden Boy*, 195–98; *The Greatest*, 200–202; *The Great White Hope*, 207–9; *Great White Hype*, 209–11; *The Hammer*, 216; *The Harder They Fall*, 218–19; *Hard Times*, 219–20; *Here Comes Mr. Jordan*, 228–31; *The Hurricane*, 237; *Let's Do It Again*, 287; *The Main Event*, 300–302; *Million Dollar Baby*, 315–17; *Movie Movie*, 322–23; *Penitentiary*, 352–53; *Penitentiary II*, 353; *Penitentiary III*, 353; *Play It to the Bone*, 358; *The Power of One*, 359–61; *The Prizefighter and the*

Lady, 368; *Raging Bull*, 376–78; *Requiem for a Heavyweight*, 383–85; *Resurrecting the Champ*, 385; *Ringside Maisie*, 387; *Rocky*, 387–89; *Rocky Balboa*, 389–90; *Rocky II*, 390–91; *Rocky III*, 391–93; *Rocky IV*, 394–95; *Rocky V*, 395–97; *Against the Ropes*, 5–6; *The Set-Up*, 421–22; *Somebody Up There Likes Me*, 435–37; *Spirit of Youth*, 438–40; *Split Decisions*, 440; *The Square Ring*, 440; *Streets of Gold*, 447; *Undisputed*, 468; *Winner Take All*, 485–86
Boxleitner, Bruce: *The Babe*, 24–26
Boyd, Billy: *The Flying Scotsman*, 171–74
Boyum, Steve: *Slap Shot 2: Breaking the Ice*, 430–31
Bracco, Lorraine: *Basketball Diaries*, 36–38
Bracken, Eddie: *Rookie of the Year*, 402–5
Bradford, Jesse: *Bring It On*, 77–78
Brashler, William: *The Bingo Long Travelling All-Stars and Motor Kings*, 53–56
The Break, 72
Breaking Away, 72–75
Brennan, Walter: *Pride of the Yankees*, 365–68
Brewster's Millions, 75
Brian's Song, 75–77
Bridges, Beau: *Heart Like a Wheel*, 220–22
Bridges, Jeff: *The Big Lebowski*, 46–50; *The Last American Hero*, 274–76; *Seabiscuit*, 416–18; *Stick It*, 441–42
Brimley, Wilford: *The Natural*, 332–35
Bring It On, 77–78
Brison, Sam: *The Bingo Long Travelling All-Stars and Motor Kings*, 53–56
Broadbent, Jim: *The Damned United*, 118–21
Bronson, Charles: *Hard Times*, 219–20
Brooklyn Dodgers: *Blue in the Face*, 65–66; *The Jackie Robinson Story*, 252–53
Brooks, Hazel: *Body and Soul*, 67–69
Brown, Clarence: *Angels in the Outfield* (1951), 16–18; *National Velvet*, 329–32
Brown, Dwier: *The Cutting Edge*, 115–17
Brown, Joe E.: *Alibi Ike*, 10; *Elmer, the Great*, 144; *Fireman, Save My Child*, 171
Brown, Jophery C.: *The Bingo Long Travelling All-Stars and Motor Kings*, 53–56
Brown, Rob: *The Express*, 149–51; *Finding Forrester*, 168–70
Brown, Russ: *Damn Yankees*, 121–23
Bryant, Paul "Bear": *The Bear*, 40
Buchanan, Robert: *Gregory's Girl*, 212–13
Buchman, Sidney: *Here Comes Mr. Jordan*, 228–31
Bull Durham, 78–81
Bullock, Sandra: *The Blind Side*, 60–63
bull riding: *8 Seconds*, 143–44
Bunnage, Avis: *The Loneliness of the Long-Distance Runner*, 288–90
Burton, Tony: *Rocky IV*, 394–95; *Rocky V*, 395–97
Buscemi, Steve: *The Big Lebowski*, 46–50
Busey, Gary: *Big Wednesday*, 50–53; *The Last American Hero*, 274–76; *Rookie of the Year*, 402–5; *Slap Shot 2: Breaking the Ice*, 430–31
Busfield, Timothy: *Field of Dreams*, 162–66
Bynes, Amanda: *She's the Man*, 423–25
By the Sword, 81

Caan, James: *Brian's Song*, 75–77; *The Program*, 368–70; *Rollerball*, 397–99
Caddyshack, 82–83
Caddyshack II, 83
Cagney, James: *City for Conquest*, 99–100; *The Crowd Roars*, 115
Caine, Michael: *Victory*, 469–70
Calderon, Paul: *Girlfight*, 187–90
California Angels: *Talent for the Game*, 453
Calleia, Joseph: *Golden Boy*, 195–98
Campbell, Nicholas: *Cinderella Man*, 97–99
Candy, John: *Cool Runnings*, 113–15
Cannon, Dyan: *Heaven Can Wait*, 222–24
Capri, Ahna: *Enter the Dragon*, 144–45
Carafotes, Paul: *All the Right Moves*, 10–12
Carlin, John: *Invictus*, 245–47
Carlson, Jeff: *Slap Shot*, 428–30; *Slap Shot 2: Breaking the Ice*, 430–31
Carlson, Steve: *Slap Shot*, 428–30; *Slap Shot 2: Breaking the Ice*, 430–31
Carman: The Champion, 83–84
Carr, Lamont: *Full-Court Miracle*, 182–84
Carroll, Jim: *Basketball Diaries*, 36–38

Carroll, Leo G.: *Strangers on a Train*, 442–44
Cars, 84
Carson, Jack: *Gentleman Jim*, 186–87
Carter, Rubin "Hurricane": *The Hurricane*, 237
Cattrall, Kim: *Ice Princess*, 242–44
Cavagnaro, Gary Lee: *The Bad News Bears* (1976), 26–28
Celtic Pride, 84–87
Chadha, Gurinder: *Bend It Like Beckham*, 41–42
Chak De! India, 87–90
The Champ (1932), 90–91
The Champ (1979), 91
Champion (1949), 91–94
The Champion (1915), 101
Chan, Jackie: *The Karate Kid* (2010), 264–65
Chaplin, Charlie: *City Lights*, 100–102
Chariots of Fire, 94–97
Charleson, Ian: *Chariots of Fire*, 94–97
Chase, Chevy: *Caddyshack*, 82–83; *Caddyshack II*, 83
Chasing 3000, 97
Chatman, Glenndon: *Love and Basketball*, 297–99
cheerleading: *Bring It On*, 77–78; *Fired Up!*, 171; *Sugar and Spice*, 450
Cherrill, Virginia: *City Lights*, 100–102
Chicago Bears: *Brian's Song*, 75–77
Chicago Cubs: *The Pride of St. Louis*, 365
Chicago White Sox: *Eight Men Out*, 141–43; *Field of Dreams*, 162–66
Ching, William: *Pat and Mike*, 350–52
Chong, Rae Dawn: *American Flyers*, 13–16
Christian-themed films: *Facing the Giants*, 152; *Hometown Legend*, 231
Christie, Julie: *Heaven Can Wait*, 222–24
Christopher, Dennis: *Breaking Away*, 72–75; *Chariots of Fire*, 94–97
Cinderella Man, 97–99
City for Conquest, 99–100
City Lights, 100–102
Clarkson, Patricia: *Miracle*, 320–22
Clayburgh, Jill: *Semi-Tough*, 419–21
Clemente, Roberto: *Chasing 3000*, 97
Cleveland Indians: *Major League*, 302–4; *Major League II*, 305–6
Clooney, George: *Leatherheads*, 279–82
Close, Glenn: *The Natural*, 332–35
Clough, Brian: *The Damned United*, 118–21
The Club, 102
Clyde, Andy: *Million Dollar Legs*, 317–20
Coach, 102
Coach Carter, 102–4
Cobb, 104–8
Cobb, Lee J.: *Golden Boy*, 195–98
Cobbs, Bill: *The Color of Money*, 109–12
Coburn, James: *Hard Times*, 219–20
Cochran, Steve: *Jim Thorpe: All American*, 256–58
Coen, Ethan: *The Big Lebowski*, 46–50
Coen, Joel: *The Big Lebowski*, 46–50
Cohen, Sacha Baron: *Talladega Nights: The Ballad of Ricky Bobby*, 453–55
Colasanto, Nicholas: *Raging Bull*, 376–78
Cole, Gary: *Dodgeball: A True Underdog Story*, 131–35
Coleman, Dabney: *Downhill Racer*, 135–37
College, 40, 108–9
Collins, Jackie: *Yesterday's Hero*, 494
The Color of Money, 109–12, 239
The Comebacks, 112–13
Connery, Sean: *Finding Forrester*, 168–70
Conrad, Michael: *The Longest Yard* (1974), 290–92
Conrad, William: *Body and Soul*, 67–69
Considine, Paddy: *Cinderella Man*, 97–99
Convy, Bert: *Semi-Tough*, 419–21
Conway, Kevin: *Invincible*, 247–49
Cook, Rachel Leigh: *The Final Season*, 166–68
Cool Runnings, 113–15
Cooper, Chris: *Seabiscuit*, 416–18
Cooper, Gary: *Pride of the Yankees*, 365–68
Cooper, Jackie: *The Champ* (1932), 90–91
Corbett, James J.: *Gentleman Jim*, 186–87
Corcoran, Donna: *Angels in the Outfield* (1951), 16–18
Cornwall, Anne: *College*, 108–9
Costner, Kevin: *American Flyers*, 13–16; *Bull Durham*, 78–81; *Field of Dreams*, 162–66;

For Love of the Game, 174–78; *Tin Cup*, 459–61
Courtenay, Bryce: *The Power of One*, 359–61
Courtenay, Tom: *The Loneliness of the Long-Distance Runner*, 288–90
Cousy, Bob: *Blue Chips*, 63–65
Cox, Brian: *The Boxer*, 69–72; *The Flying Scotsman*, 171–74; *For Love of the Game*, 174–78; *Match Point*, 307–9; *The Rookie*, 399–402
Cox, Ronny: *Vision Quest*, 470–71
Craven, Frank: *City for Conquest*, 99–100
Craven, Matt: *The Longshots*, 292–94
crew: *College*, 40, 108–9
cricket: *The Final Test*, 168; *Lagaan: Once Upon a Time in India*, 271–74; *Playing Away*, 358; *Wondrous Oblivion*, 489
Crisp, Donald: *City for Conquest*, 99–100; *Knute Rockne: All American*, 268–70; *National Velvet*, 329–32
Cromwell, James: *The Babe*, 24–26
Cron, Claudia: *Running Brave*, 408–11
Cross, Ben: *Chariots of Fire*, 94–97
Cross, David: *She's the Man*, 423–25
Crossover, 115
Crouse, Lindsay: *Slap Shot*, 428–30
The Crowd Roars, 115, 244
Crowe, Cameron: *Jerry Maguire*, 253–56
Crowe, Russell: *Cinderella Man*, 97–99; *Mystery, Alaska*, 326–28
Crudup, Billy: *Without Limits*, 488–89
Cruise, Tom: *All the Right Moves*, 10–12; *The Color of Money*, 109–12; *Days of Thunder*, 127–29; *Jerry Maguire*, 253–56
Crystal, Billy: *Forget Paris*, 178; *61**, 426–28
Cukor, George: *Pat and Mike*, 350–52
curling: *Men with Brooms*, 310–12
Curtis, Tony: *The Bad News Bears Go to Japan*, 29–30
Cusack, Ann: *A League of Their Own*, 276–79
Cusack, John: *Eight Men Out*, 141–43; *Ice Princess*, 242–44
The Cutting Edge, 115–17
cycling: *The Amateur*, 12; *American Flyers*, 13–16; *BMX Bandits*, 66; *Breaking Away*, 72–75; *The Flying Scotsman*, 171–74; *Rad*, 373; *The Triplets of Belleville*, 464; *The Unknown Cyclist*, 468

Daly, Andrew: *Semi-Pro*, 418–19
The Damned United, 118–21
Damn Yankees, 121–23
Damon, Matt: *Invictus*, 245–47; *The Legend of Bagger Vance*, 282–85; *School Ties*, 413–15
Dangerfield, Rodney: *Caddyshack*, 82–83; *Ladybugs*, 271
Dans les Cordes (On the Ropes), 123–24
Danza, Tony: *Angels in the Outfield* (1994), 18–20
D'Arbanville, Patti: *Big Wednesday*, 50–53
D'Arcy, Jake: *Gregory's Girl*, 212–13
David, Keith: *Blue in the Face*, 65–66
Davies, Valentine: *It Happens Every Spring*, 249–51
Davis, Brad: *Chariots of Fire*, 94–97
Davis, Ernie: *The Express*, 149–51
Davis, Geena: *A League of Their Own*, 276–79
Davis, Mac: *North Dallas Forty*, 338–40
Davis, Milton, Jr.: *Angels in the Outfield* (1994), 18–20
Dawson, Rico: *The Bingo Long Travelling All-Stars and Motor Kings*, 53–56
A Day at the Races, 124–27
Day, John: *Champion*, 91–94
Day, Otis: *The Bingo Long Travelling All-Stars and Motor Kings*, 53–56
Days of Thunder, 127–29
Dean, Dizzy: *The Pride of St. Louis*, 365
Death Race, 129–30
Death Race 2000, 130
DeCerchio, Tom: *Celtic Pride*, 84–87
Dee, Ruby: *The Jackie Robinson Story*, 252–53
Deford, Frank: *Trading Hearts*, 463–64
DelBuono, Brett: *Balls of Fury*, 32–33
DeLillo, Don: *Game 6*, 185
Del Toro, Benicio: *The Fan*, 152–56
De Medeiros, Maria: *Dans les Cordes (On the Ropes)*, 123–24
De Mornay, Rebecca: *Lords of Dogtown*, 294–97; *The Slugger's Wife*, 432–34

Demsey, Patrick: *Miracle,* 320–22
De Niro, Robert: *Bang the Drum Slowly,* 33–35; *The Fan,* 152–56; *Raging Bull,* 376–78
The Derby Stallion, 130
Derricks, Cleavant: *The Slugger's Wife,* 432–34
Deschanel, Caleb: *The Black Stallion,* 56–57
Desmond, Cleo: *Spirit of Youth,* 438–40
Detroit Lions: *Paper Lion,* 348
Devane, William: *The Bad News Bears in Breaking Training,* 30–32
Devine, Aidan: *Against the Ropes,* 5–6
Dewhurst, Colleen: *Ice Castles,* 240–42
Diaz, Cameron: *Any Given Sunday,* 20–23
DiCaprio, Leonardo: *Basketball Diaries,* 36–38
Dickens, Kim: *The Blind Side,* 60–63
Diggstown, 130
Dillane, Stephen: *Goal! The Dream Begins,* 192–95; *Goal! II: Living the Dream,* 195; *The Greatest Game Ever Played,* 202–5
Dinica, Gheorghe: *White Palms,* 479–81
"direct to video" movies, 507–10
The Dirty Dozen, 213
documentaries, 515–16
dodgeball: *Dodgeball,* 130–31; *Dodgeball: A True Underdog Story,* 131–35
Dodgeball, 130–31
Dodgeball: A True Underdog Story, 131–35
Donnelly, Patrice: *Personal Best,* 353–55
Dooley, Paul: *Breaking Away,* 72–75
Dorff, Stephen: *The Power of One,* 359–61
Dorrell, Artie: *Body and Soul,* 67–69
Dotrice, Roy: *The Cutting Edge,* 115–17
Doug, Doug E.: *Cool Runnings,* 113–15
Douglas, Kirk: *Champion,* 91–94
Douglas, Paul: *Angels in the Outfield* (1951), 16–18; *It Happens Every Spring,* 249–51
Douglas, Santiago: *Girlfight,* 187–90
Dowd, Nancy: *Slap Shot,* 428–30; *Slap Shot 2: Breaking the Ice,* 430–31
Downhill Racer, 135–37
Doyle-Murray, Brian: *Caddyshack,* 82–83
Dreamer, 137
Dreamer: Inspired by a True Story, 137–38
Dribbles, 138
Driven, 138
Dumbrille, Douglass: *A Day at the Races,* 124–27
Dumont, Margaret: *A Day at the Races,* 124–27
Dunst, Kirsten: *Bring It On,* 77–78; *Wimbledon,* 483–85
Duryea, Dan: *Pride of the Yankees,* 365–68
Dushku, Eliza: *Bring It On,* 77–78
Dutton, Charles S.: *Against the Ropes,* 5–6; *Rudy,* 405–7
Duvall, Robert: *Days of Thunder,* 127–29; *The Natural,* 332–35
D2: The Mighty Ducks, 138
D3: The Mighty Ducks, 138

Eastwood, Clint: *Invictus,* 245–47; *Million Dollar Baby,* 315–17
Eckhart, Aaron: *Any Given Sunday,* 20–23
Ed, 139
Eddie, 139–41
Eight Men Out, 141–43
8 Seconds, 143–44
Eldard, Ron: *Mystery, Alaska,* 326–28
Elise, Kimberly: *Pride,* 363–65
Elliott, David: *Ali,* 7–10
Ellis, Jim: *Pride,* 363–65
Elmer, the Great, 144
Elwes, Cary: *Days of Thunder,* 127–29
Emery, John: *Here Comes Mr. Jordan,* 228–31
Emmerich, Noah: *Miracle,* 320–22
Enter the Dragon, 144–45
Epps, Omar: *Love and Basketball,* 297–99; *Major League II,* 305–6; *The Program,* 368–70; *Against the Ropes,* 5–6
Ermey, R. Lee: *Prefontaine,* 361–63
ESPY awards, 517
Estevez, Emilio: *D2: The Mighty Ducks,* 138; *D3: The Mighty Ducks,* 138; *The Mighty Ducks,* 312–15
Everybody's All-American, 145–47
Everyone's Hero, 147–49
The Express, 149–51

Fabares, Shelley: *Brian's Song,* 75–77
Facing the Giants, 152

Fallon, Jimmy: *Fever Pitch* (2005), 160–62; *Whip It*, 474–77
The Fan, 152–56
Fan, Roger: *Ping Pong Playa*, 355–57
Farina, Dennis: *Eddie*, 139–41
Farmani, Golnaz: *Offside*, 343–45
Farrell, Nicholas: *Chariots of Fire*, 94–97
Fast Break, 156
Fat City, 156
Favreau, Jon: *The Replacements*, 382–83; *Rudy*, 405–7; *Wimbledon*, 483–85
Fear Strikes Out, 156–58
fencing: *By the Sword*, 81
Ferrell, Tyra: *White Men Can't Jump*, 477–79
Ferrell, Will: *Blades of Glory*, 58–60; *Semi-Pro*, 418–19; *Talladega Nights: The Ballad of Ricky Bobby*, 453–55
Fever Pitch (1996), 159–60
Fever Pitch (2005), 160–62
fictional sports: *Rollerball*, 397–99
field hockey: *Chak De! India*, 87–90
Field of Dreams, 162–66
Fields, W. C.: *Million Dollar Legs*, 317–20
The Final Season, 166–68
The Final Test, 168
Finding Forrester, 168–70
Fine, Budd: *Battling Butler*, 38–40
Fiorentino, Linda: *Vision Quest*, 470–71
Fireball 500, 170–71
Fired Up!, 171
Fireman, Save My Child, 171
Firth, Colin: *Fever Pitch* (1996), 159–60
Fischer, Jenna: *Blades of Glory*, 58–60
The Fish That Saved Pittsburgh, 171
Fleck, Ryan: *Sugar*, 447–50
Fleming, Susan: *Million Dollar Legs*, 317–20
Fluellen, Joel: *The Great White Hope*, 207–9
The Flying Scotsman, 171–74
Flynn, Errol: *Gentleman Jim*, 186–87
Fogler, Dan: *Balls of Fury*, 32–33
Follow the Sun, 174
football: *Air Bud: Golden Receiver*, 7; *All the Right Moves*, 10–12; *Any Given Sunday*, 20–23; *The Bear*, 40; *The Best of Times*, 42–46; *Big Fan*, 46; *Black Sunday*, 58; *The Blind Side*, 60–63; *Brian's Song*, 75–77; *The Comebacks*, 112–13; *Everybody's All-American*, 145–47; *The Express*, 149–51; *Facing the Giants*, 152; *The Freshman*, 178–81; *Friday Night Lights*, 181–82; *Full Ride*, 184; *The Game Plan*, 185; *Gridiron Gang*, 213–14; *Gus*, 215; *Heaven Can Wait*, 222–24; *Hometown Legend*, 231; *Horse Feathers*, 234–37; *Invincible*, 247–49; *Jerry Maguire*, 253–56; *Johnny Be Good*, 259; *Knute Rockne: All American*, 268–70; *The Last Boy Scout*, 276; *Leatherheads*, 279–82; *Little Giants*, 288; *The Longest Yard* (1974), 290–92; *The Longest Yard* (2005), 292; *The Longshots*, 292–94; *Lucas*, 299; *Necessary Roughness*, 335; *North Dallas Forty*, 338–40; *Paper Lion*, 348; *The Program*, 368–70; *Radio*, 374–76; *Remember the Titans*, 379–82; *The Replacements*, 382–83; *Rudy*, 405–7; *School Ties*, 413–15; *Semi-Tough*, 419–21; *The Slaughter Rule*, 431; *That's My Boy*, 456; *Two for the Money*, 464; *Varsity Blues*, 469; *The Waterboy*, 472; *We Are Marshall*, 472–74; *Wildcats*, 481–83
Forever Strong, 178
Forget Paris, 178
For Love of the Game, 174–78
Forsyth, Bill: *Gregory's Girl*, 212–13
Foster, Phil: *Bang the Drum Slowly*, 33–35
Fox, Matthew: *We Are Marshall*, 472–74
Fox, Michael J.: *Blue in the Face*, 65–66
Fox, Rick: *Eddie*, 139–41
Foxx, Jamie: *Ali*, 7–10; *Any Given Sunday*, 20–23; *Great White Hype*, 209–11
Frankenheimer, John: *Grand Prix*, 198–200
Fraser, Brendan: *School Ties*, 413–15
Fraser, Laura: *The Flying Scotsman*, 171–74
Frawley, William: *Rhubarb*, 385–87
Freeman, Morgan: *Invictus*, 245–47; *Million Dollar Baby*, 315–17; *The Power of One*, 359–61
The Freshman, 178–81
Fricker, Brenda: *Angels in the Outfield* (1994), 18–20
Friday Night Lights, 181–82

Friel, Anna: *Goal! The Dream Begins,* 192–95; *Goal! II: Living the Dream,* 195
Frost, Mark: *The Greatest Game Ever Played,* 202–5
Full-Court Miracle, 182–84
Full Ride, 184

The Galloping Major, 185
gambling: *Hardball,* 218; *Two for the Money,* 464
The Game Plan, 185
Game 6, 185
Gammon, James: *Major League II,* 305–6
Gant, Richard: *Rocky V,* 395–97
Gardenia, Vincent: *Bang the Drum Slowly,* 33–35
Garfield, John: *Body and Soul,* 67–69
Garner, James: *Grand Prix,* 198–200
Garrett, Betty: *Take Me Out to the Ball Game,* 451–53
Garr, Teri: *The Black Stallion,* 56–57
Gartner, James: *Glory Road,* 191–92
Gaye, Nona: *Ali,* 7–10
Gazzara, Ben: *The Big Lebowski,* 46–50
Gbewonyo, Nana: *Coach Carter,* 102–4
Gehrig, Lou: *Pride of the Yankees,* 365–68
Gemmell, Ruth: *Fever Pitch* (1996), 159–60
Genevieve, 185–86
Gentleman Jim, 186–87
A Gentleman's Game, 187
Gerety, Peter: *Leatherheads,* 279–82
Gerstad, Harry: *Champion,* 91–94
Giamatti, Paul: *Cinderella Man,* 97–99
Gielgud, Sir John: *Chariots of Fire,* 94–97; *The Power of One,* 359–61
Gilbert, Lou: *The Great White Hope,* 207–9
Girlfight, 187–90
girls' soccer: *Bend It Like Beckham,* 41–42
Gladiator, 190
Glaser, Paul Michael: *The Cutting Edge,* 115–17
Gleaming the Cube, 190–91
Gleason, Jackie: *The Hustler,* 237–39; *Requiem for a Heavyweight,* 383–85
Gleason, James: *Here Comes Mr. Jordan,* 228–31
Glenn, Scott: *Personal Best,* 353–55
Glory Road, 191–92
Glover, Bruce: *Hard Times,* 219–20
Glover, Danny: *Angels in the Outfield* (1994), 18–20
Goal! The Dream Begins, 192–95
Goal! II: Living the Dream, 195
Goal! III, 195
The Goalie's Anxiety at the Penalty Kick, 195
Godsell, Vanda: *This Sporting Life,* 456–58
Gold, Brandy: *Wildcats,* 481–83
Goldberg, Whoopi: *Eddie,* 139–41; *Everyone's Hero,* 147–49
Goldblum, Jeff: *Great White Hype,* 209–11
Golden Boy, 195–98
golf: *Bobby Jones: Strokes of Genius,* 67; *Caddyshack,* 82–83; *Caddyshack II,* 83; *Follow the Sun,* 174; *A Gentleman's Game,* 187; *The Greatest Game Ever Played,* 202–5; *Happy Gilmore,* 216–18; *The Legend of Bagger Vance,* 282–85; *The Man with the Perfect Swing,* 306–7; *Tin Cup,* 459–61; *Who's Your Caddy?,* 481
Gonzalez, Rick: *Coach Carter,* 102–4
Goode, Matthew: *Match Point,* 307–9
Gooding, Cuba, Jr.: *Gladiator,* 190; *Jerry Maguire,* 253–56; *Radio,* 374–76
Goodman, John: *The Babe,* 24–26; *The Big Lebowski,* 46–50; *Everybody's All-American,* 145–47
Goodwin, Harold: *College,* 108–9
Gordon, Josh: *Blades of Glory,* 58–60
Gordon, Ruth: *Pat and Mike,* 350–52
Gordon-Levitt, Joseph: *Angels in the Outfield* (1994), 18–20
Gracie, 198
Grand Prix, 198–200
Granger, Farley: *Strangers on a Train,* 442–44
Grant, David: *American Flyers,* 13–16
Graziano, Rocky: *Somebody Up There Likes Me,* 435–37
The Greatest, 200–202
The Greatest Game Ever Played, 202–5
The Great Game (1930), 205
The Great Game (1953), 205
The Great Match, 205–7
The Great Race, 207
The Great White Hope, 207–9

Great White Hype, 209–11
Greene, Graham: *Running Brave*, 408–11
Gregory's Girl, 212–13
Gretsch, Joel: *The Legend of Bagger Vance*, 282–85
Grey, Jennifer: *American Flyers*, 13–16
Gridiron Gang, 213–14
Griffiths, Rachel: *The Rookie*, 399–402
Grodin, Charles: *Heaven Can Wait*, 222–24
Grogan, Clare: *Gregory's Girl*, 212–13
Gross, Paul: *Men with Brooms*, 310–12
Grunt! The Wrestling Movie, 214
Guilfoyle, Paul: *Celtic Pride*, 84–87
Gunn, Moses: *Rollerball*, 397–99
Gus, 215
gymnastics: *American Anthem*, 12–13; *Peaceful Warrior*, 352; *Stick It*, 441–42; *White Palms*, 479–81

Hackman, Gene: *Downhill Racer*, 135–37; *Hoosiers*, 231–34; *The Replacements*, 382–83
Hajdu, Szabolcs: *White Palms*, 479–81
Hale, Alan: *Gentleman Jim*, 186–87
Haley, Jackie Earle: *The Bad News Bears* (1976), 26–28; *The Bad News Bears Go to Japan*, 29–30; *The Bad News Bears in Breaking Training*, 30–32; *Breaking Away*, 72–75; *Semi-Pro*, 418–19
Hall, Albert: *Rookie of the Year*, 402–5
Hall, Alexander: *Here Comes Mr. Jordan*, 228–31
Hall, Anthony Michael: *61**, 426–28
Hallahan, Charles: *Vision Quest*, 470–71
Hamilton, Hale: *The Champ* (1932), 90–91
Hamilton, Murray: *The Hustler*, 237–39
Hamlin, Harry: *Movie Movie*, 322–23
The Hammer, 216
Hampton, James: *The Longest Yard* (1974), 290–92
Hancock, John Lee: *The Blind Side*, 60–63
Hanks, Tom: *A League of Their Own*, 276–79
Hanson, David: *Slap Shot*, 428–30; *Slap Shot 2: Breaking the Ice*, 430–31
Hanukkah stories: *Full-Court Miracle*, 182–84
Happy Gilmore, 216–18
Hardball, 218
Harden, Marcia Gay: *The Bad News Bears* (2005), 28–29; *Whip It*, 474–77
The Harder They Fall, 218–19
Hard Times, 219–20
Hardwick, Charlie: *Purely Belter*, 370–72
Harmon, Pat: *The Freshman*, 178–81
Harper, Frank: *Bend It Like Beckham*, 41–42
Harper, La Trice: *Tournament of Dreams*, 461–63
Harrelson, Woody: *Kingpin*, 266–68; *Semi-Pro*, 418–19; *White Men Can't Jump*, 477–79; *Wildcats*, 481–83
Harrington, Joseph: *The Freshman*, 178–81
Harris, Ed: *Radio*, 374–76
Harris, Edna Mae: *Spirit of Youth*, 438–40
Harris, Julie: *Requiem for a Heavyweight*, 383–85
Harris, Mark: *Bang the Drum Slowly*, 33–35
Harris, Richard: *This Sporting Life*, 456–58
Harris, Wood: *Above the Rim*, 1–4; *Remember the Titans*, 379–82
Harris, Zelda: *He Got Game*, 224–27
Harrison, William: *Rollerball*, 397–99
Hartnell, William: *This Sporting Life*, 456–58
Hartnett, Josh: *O*, 341–43
Havers, Nigel: *Chariots of Fire*, 94–97
Hawkins, Darius: *Above the Rim*, 1–4
Hawn, Goldie: *Wildcats*, 481–83
Hayes, Helen: *Herbie Rides Again*, 228
Haysbert, Dennis: *Love and Basketball*, 297–99; *Major League*, 302–4; *Major League: Back to the Minors*, 304; *Major League II*, 305–6; *Mr. Baseball*, 323–25
Healy, Tim: *Purely Belter*, 370–72
Heart Like a Wheel, 220–22
Heaven Can Wait, 222–24, 228, 231
Heckart, Eileen: *Somebody Up There Likes Me*, 435–37
Hedaya, Dan: *Rookie of the Year*, 402–5
Heder, Jon: *Blades of Glory*, 58–60
Hedlund, Garrett: *Friday Night Lights*, 181–82
He Got Game, 224–27
Heisman Trophy: *The Express*, 149–51
Heller, Randee: *The Karate Kid* (1984), 263–64
Hellman, Monte: *Two-Lane Blacktop*, 464–67

Hell on Wheels, 227
Helton, Percy: *The Set-Up,* 421–22
Hemingway, Mariel: *Personal Best,* 353–55
Hemmings, David: *Mean Machine,* 309–10
Hendra, Tony: *Great White Hype,* 209–11
Henry, Buck: *Heaven Can Wait,* 222–24
Henson, Darrin Dewitt: *The Express,* 149–51
Henson, Elden: *The Mighty Ducks,* 312–15
Hepburn, Dee: *Gregory's Girl,* 212–13
Hepburn, Katharine: *Pat and Mike,* 350–52
Her Best Move, 227
Herbie: Fully Loaded, 227
Herbie Goes Bananas, 227
Herbie Goes to Monte Carlo, 227–28
Herbie Rides Again, 228
Here Comes Mr. Jordan, 223, 228–31
Hernandez, Juan: *Against the Ropes,* 5–6
Hershey, Barbara: *Hoosiers,* 231–34; *The Natural,* 332–35
Heston, Charlton: *Any Given Sunday,* 20–23
Hill, Bernard: *Wimbledon,* 483–85
Hill, George Roy: *Slap Shot,* 428–30
Hill, Walter: *Hard Times,* 219–20
Hillenbrand, Laura: *Seabiscuit,* 416–18
Hiller, Arthur: *The Babe,* 24–26
Hingle, Pat: *Running Brave,* 408–11
Hirsch, Emile: *Lords of Dogtown,* 294–97
Hitchcock, Alfred: *Strangers on a Train,* 442–44
Hitchcock, Patricia: *Strangers on a Train,* 442–44
Hoffman, Gaby: *Field of Dreams,* 162–66
Hoffman, Philip Seymour: *The Big Lebowski,* 46–50
Hogan, Ben: *Follow the Sun,* 174
Hogan, Hulk: *Rocky III,* 391–93
Holden, William: *Golden Boy,* 195–98
Holland, Andre: *Sugar,* 447–50
Holmes, Elsie: *Rhubarb,* 385–87
Home of the Giants, 231
Hometown Legend, 231
Hong, James: *Balls of Fury,* 32–33
Hooks, Jan: *Wildcats,* 481–83
Hoosiers, 225, 231–34
Hopkins, Anthony: *The World's Fastest Indian,* 489–91
Hopper, Dennis: *Hoosiers,* 231–34
Horse Feathers, 234–37
horse racing: *The Black Stallion,* 56–57; *The Black Stallion Returns,* 57–58; *Boots Malone,* 69; *A Day at the Races,* 124–27; *The Derby Stallion,* 130; *Dreamer: Inspired by a True Story,* 137–38; *The Galloping Major,* 185; *International Velvet,* 244–45; *Just My Luck,* 261; *Lightning, the White Stallion,* 287; *National Velvet,* 329–32; *Phar Lap,* 355; *Racing Stripes,* 373; *Seabiscuit,* 416–18; *Shergar,* 422–23
Horton, Edward Everett: *Here Comes Mr. Jordan,* 228–31
Houseman, John: *Rollerball,* 397–99
Houser, Jerry: *Slap Shot,* 428–30
Howard, Gregory Allen: *Remember the Titans,* 379–82
Howard, Ron: *Cinderella Man,* 97–99
Howard, Terrence: *Pride,* 363–65
Howe, James Wong: *Body and Soul,* 67–69
Huddleston, David: *The Big Lebowski,* 46–50
Hudlin, Reginald: *Great White Hype,* 209–11
Hudson, Hugh: *Chariots of Fire,* 94–97
Huffman, David: *Ice Castles,* 240–42
Hunt, Bonnie: *Jerry Maguire,* 253–56
Hunter, Tab: *Damn Yankees,* 121–23
The Hurricane, 237
Hurst, Ryan: *Remember the Titans,* 379–82
The Hustler, 109–10, 112, 237–39
Huston, John: *Victory,* 469–70
Hutton, Timothy: *Everybody's All-American,* 145–47

Ice Castles, 240–42
Ice Cube: *The Longshots,* 292–94
ice hockey: *D2: The Mighty Ducks,* 138; *D3: The Mighty Ducks,* 138; *Les Boys,* 287; *The Love Guru,* 299; *The Mighty Ducks,* 312–15; *Miracle,* 320–22; *MVP: Most Valuable Primate,* 326; *Mystery, Alaska,* 326–28; *The Rocket: Maurice Richard,* 387; *Slap Shot,* 428–30; *Slap Shot 2: Breaking the Ice,* 430–31; *Youngblood,* 494
Ice Princess, 242–44
ice skating: *Blades of Glory,* 58–60; *The Cutting Edge,* 115–17; *Ice Castles,* 240–42; *Ice Princess,* 242–44

Ifans, Rhys: *The Replacements,* 382–83
illnesses: *Bang the Drum Slowly,* 33–35; *Brian's Song,* 75–77
Indianapolis Speedway, 244
In God's Hands, 244
International Velvet, 244–45
Invictus, 245–47
Invincible, 247–49
Irani, Shayesteh: *Offside,* 343–45
Ireland, Jill: *Hard Times,* 219–20
The Iron Ladies, 249
The Iron Ladies 2, 249
It Happens Every Spring, 249–51

The Jackie Robinson Story, 252–53
Jackson, Joshua: *The Mighty Ducks,* 312–15
Jackson, Keana: *Tournament of Dreams,* 461–63
Jackson, Samuel L.: *Coach Carter,* 102–4; *Great White Hype,* 209–11
James, Clifton: *The Bad News Bears in Breaking Training,* 30–32; *Eight Men Out,* 141–43
James, Walter: *Battling Butler,* 38–40
Jane, Thomas: *61*,* 426–28
Jarmusch, Jim: *Blue in the Face,* 65–66
Jenkins, Dan: *Semi-Tough,* 419–21
Jenkins, Jackie: *National Velvet,* 329–32
Jensen, Luke: *Tennis, Anyone?,* 455–56
Jerry Maguire, 253–56
Jewison, Norman: *Rollerball,* 397–99
Jim Thorpe: All American, 256–58
Johansson, Scarlett: *Match Point,* 307–9
Johnny Be Good, 259
Johnson, Ben: *Angels in the Outfield* (1994), 18–20; *Junior Bonner,* 259–61
Johnson, Doi: *American Flyers,* 13–16
Johnson, Don: *Tin Cup,* 459–61
Johnson, Dwayne: *Gridiron Gang,* 213–14
Johnson, Junior: *The Last American Hero,* 274–76
Johnson, Lamont: *The Last American Hero,* 274–76
Johnson, Lynn-Holly: *Ice Castles,* 240–42
Johnson, Rita: *Here Comes Mr. Jordan,* 228–31
Jones, Allan: *A Day at the Races,* 124–27
Jones, James Earl: *The Bingo Long Travelling All-Stars and Motor Kings,* 53–56; *Field of Dreams,* 162–66; *The Greatest,* 200–202; *The Great White Hope,* 207–9
Jones, Jill Marie: *The Longshots,* 292–94
Jones, Julian Lewis: *Invictus,* 245–47
Jones, Orlando: *The Replacements,* 382–83
Jones, Richard T.: *Full-Court Miracle,* 182–84
Jones, Tommy Lee: *Cobb,* 104–8
Jones, Vinnie: *Mean Machine,* 309–10
Jordan, Michael: *Like Mike,* 287; *Space Jam,* 437
Junior Bonner, 259–61
Just My Luck, 261
Juwanna Mann, 261

Kaaya, Brad: *O,* 341–43
Kallen, Jackie: *Against the Ropes,* 5–6
Kallianiotes, Helena: *Kansas City Bomber,* 262–63
Kanin, Garson: *Pat and Mike,* 350–52
Kansas City Bomber, 262–63
The Karate Kid (1984), 263–64
The Karate Kid (2010), 264–65
The Karate Kid II, 265
The Karate Kid, Part III, 265
Katt, William: *Big Wednesday,* 50–53
Katzin, Lee: *Le Mans,* 285–87
Kazan, Elia: *City for Conquest,* 99–100
Keach, James: *Wildcats,* 481–83
Keaton, Buster: *Battling Butler,* 38–40; *College,* 108–9
Keegan, Andrew: *O,* 341–43
Keitel, Harvey: *Blue in the Face,* 65–66
Kelley, David E.: *Mystery, Alaska,* 326–28
Kelly, David: *Mean Machine,* 309–10
Kelly, Gene: *Take Me Out to the Ball Game,* 451–53
Kelly, Jim: *Enter the Dragon,* 144–45
Kelly, Moira: *The Cutting Edge,* 115–17
Kennedy, Arthur: *Champion,* 91–94; *City for Conquest,* 99–100
Kerr, Schin A. S.: *Glory Road,* 191–92
Kersh, Gerald: *Night and the City,* 336–37
Keyes, Evelyn: *Here Comes Mr. Jordan,* 228–31
Kgorogo, Tony: *Invictus,* 245–47
Khan, Aamir: *Lagaan: Once Upon a Time in India,* 271–74
Khan, Shahrukh: *Chak De! India,* 87–90

Kharbanda, Kulbhushan: *Lagaan: Once Upon a Time in India,* 271–74
Kher, Anupam: *Bend It Like Beckham,* 41–42
Kicking & Screaming, 265
The Kid from Left Field, 265–66
Kidman, Nicole: *Days of Thunder,* 127–29
Kill the Umpire, 266
King, Mabel: *The Bingo Long Travelling All-Stars and Motor Kings,* 53–56
King, Regina: *Jerry Maguire,* 253–56
Kinnear, Greg: *The Bad News Bears* (2005), 28–29; *Invincible,* 247–49
Kingpin, 266–68
Kirby, Bruno: *Basketball Diaries,* 36–38
Kittles, Tory: *Against the Ropes,* 5–6
Kling, Heidi: *The Mighty Ducks,* 312–15
Knight, Ted: *Caddyshack,* 82–83
Knightley, Keira: *Bend It Like Beckham,* 41–42
Knoxville, Johnny: *Lords of Dogtown,* 294–97
Knute Rockne: All American, 268–70
Kotcheff, Ted: *North Dallas Forty,* 338–40
Koteas, Elias: *The Greatest Game Ever Played,* 202–5
Kove, Martin: *The Karate Kid* (1984), 263–64; *The Karate Kid II,* 265; *The Karate Kid, Part III,* 265
Kraft, Sammi Kane: *The Bad News Bears* (2005), 28–29
Kramer, Stanley: *Champion,* 91–94
Krasinski, John: *Leatherheads,* 279–82
Kriege, Alice: *Chariots of Fire,* 94–97
Kristofferson, Kris: *Semi-Tough,* 419–21
Kurtz, Swoosie: *Wildcats,* 481–83
Kusama, Karyn: *Girlfight,* 187–90

LaBeouf, Shia: *The Greatest Game Ever Played,* 202–5
Lacroix, Denis: *Running Brave,* 408–11
Ladd, Diane: *The World's Fastest Indian,* 489–91
Ladybugs, 271
Lagaan: Once Upon a Time in India, 271–74
La Motta, Jake: *Raging Bull,* 376–78
Lancaster, Burt: *Field of Dreams,* 162–66; *Jim Thorpe: All American,* 256–58
Lancaster, William: *The Bad News Bears* (1976), 26–28; *The Bad News Bears Go to Japan,* 29–30
Landau, David: *Horse Feathers,* 234–37
Lange, Jessica: *Everybody's All-American,* 145–47
Langella, Frank: *Eddie,* 139–41
Langton, Brooke: *The Replacements,* 382–83
Lansbury, Angela: *National Velvet,* 329–32
The Last American Hero, 274–76
The Last Boy Scout, 276
Lathan, Sanaa: *Love and Basketball,* 297–99
Laure, Carole: *Victory,* 469–70
Laurie, Piper: *The Hustler,* 237–39
Lauter, Ed: *The Last American Hero,* 274–76; *The Longest Yard* (1974), 290–92
A League of Their Own, 276–79
Leatherheads, 279–82
Leavitt, Charles: *The Express,* 149–51
Ledger, Heath: *Lords of Dogtown,* 294–97
Lee, Bruce: *Enter the Dragon,* 144–45
Lee, Canada: *Body and Soul,* 67–69
Lee, Spike: *He Got Game,* 224–27
The Legend of Bagger Vance, 282–85
Leguizamo, John: *The Fan,* 152–56
Lehman, Ernest: *Somebody Up There Likes Me,* 435–37
Leigh, Janet: *Angels in the Outfield* (1951), 16–18
Le Mans, 285–87
Lemmon, Jack: *The Great Race,* 207; *The Legend of Bagger Vance,* 282–85
Lengies, Vanessa: *Stick It,* 441–42
Lennon, Thomas: *Balls of Fury,* 32–33
Lerner, Michael: *Eight Men Out,* 141–43
Les Boys, 287
Leto, Jared: *Prefontaine,* 361–63
Let's Do It Again, 287
Levene, Sam: *Golden Boy,* 195–98
Levinson, Barry: *The Natural,* 332–35
Lewis, Jerry: *That's My Boy,* 456
Lewis, Juliette: *Whip It,* 474–77
Lewis, Michael: *The Blind Side,* 60–63
Lewis, Rawle D.: *Cool Runnings,* 113–15
Lightning, the White Stallion, 287

Like Mike, 287
Linklater, Rick: *The Bad News Bears* (2005), 28–29
Linz, Alex D.: *Full-Court Miracle*, 182–84
Liotta, Ray: *Field of Dreams*, 162–66
Lipnicki, Jonathan: *Jerry Maguire*, 253–56
Little Big League, 288
Little Giants, 288
Little League: *Amazing Grace and Chuck*, 12; *The Bad News Bears* (1976), 26–28; *The Bad News Bears* (2005), 28–29; *The Bad News Bears Go to Japan*, 29–30; *The Bad News Bears in Breaking Training*, 30–32; *The Benchwarmers*, 40–41; *Safe at Home!*, 412
Lively, Robyn: *Wildcats*, 481–83
LL Cool J: *Any Given Sunday*, 20–23
Lloyd, Christopher: *Angels in the Outfield* (1994), 18–20
Lloyd, Harold: *The Freshman*, 178–81
Locane, Amy: *Prefontaine*, 361–63
Lockhart, Gene: *Rhubarb*, 385–87
Loggia, Robert: *Over the Top*, 346–47
Lohan, Lindsay: *Herbie: Fully Loaded*, 227
The Loneliness of the Long-Distance Runner, 288–90
Long, Justin: *Dodgeball: A True Underdog Story*, 131–35
The Longest Yard (1974), 213, 214, 290–92, 309, 310
The Longest Yard (2005), 213, 214, 292
The Longshots, 292–94
Looking for Eric, 294
Lopez, George: *Balls of Fury*, 32–33
Lords of Dogtown, 294–97
Louis, Joe: *Spirit of Youth*, 438–40
Louisiana State University: *Everybody's All-American*, 145–47
Love and Basketball, 297–99
The Love Bug, 299
The Love Guru, 299
Lovitz, Jon: *Great White Hype*, 209–11; *A League of Their Own*, 276–79
Lowery, Andrew: *School Ties*, 413–15
Lucas, 299
Lucas, Josh: *Glory Road*, 191–92
Luke, Derek: *Friday Night Lights*, 181–82; *Glory Road*, 191–92
Lumbly, Carl: *Everybody's All-American*, 145–47
Lundgren, Dolph: *Rocky IV*, 394–95
Lupino, Ida: *Junior Bonner*, 259–61

Mac, Bernie: *Above the Rim*, 1–4; *Pride*, 363–65
Macchio, Ralph: *The Karate Kid* (1984), 263–64; *The Karate Kid II*, 265; *The Karate Kid, Part III*, 265
Mackie, Anthony: *We Are Marshall*, 472–74
Macy, William H.: *Everyone's Hero*, 147–49; *Seabiscuit*, 416–18
Madigan, Amy: *Field of Dreams*, 162–66
Madonna: *Blue in the Face*, 65–66; *A League of Their Own*, 276–79
Maguire, Tobey: *Seabiscuit*, 416–18
Mahoney, John: *Eight Men Out*, 141–43
Mahr, Jay: *Jerry Maguire*, 253–56
The Main Event, 300–302
Major League, 302–4
Major League: Back to the Minors, 304
Major League II, 305–6
Malamud, Bernard: *The Natural*, 332–35
Malco, Romany: *Blades of Glory*, 58–60
Malden, Karl: *Fear Strikes Out*, 156–58
Malone, Jena: *For Love of the Game*, 174–78
Malvade, Vidya: *Chak De! India*, 87–90
Mamoulian, Rouben: *Golden Boy*, 195–98
A Man and a Woman, 306
Mandel, Robert: *School Ties*, 413–15
Mankiewicz, Joseph: *Million Dollar Legs*, 317–20
Mann, Michael: *Ali*, 7–10
Mantle, Mickey: *61**, 426–28
The Man with the Perfect Swing, 306–7
Mara, Kate: *We Are Marshall*, 472–74
Maravich, Pete: *Pistol: The Birth of a Legend*, 357
March, Joseph Moncure: *The Set-Up*, 421–22
Marin, Cheech: *Great White Hype*, 209–11; *Tin Cup*, 459–61
Marion, Frances: *The Champ* (1932), 90–91

Maris, Roger: *61**, 426–28
Marshall, Garry: *A League of Their Own*, 276–79
Marshall, Penny: *A League of Their Own*, 276–79
Marshall University: *We Are Marshall*, 472–74
martial arts: *Enter the Dragon*, 144–45; *The Karate Kid* (1984), 263–64; *The Karate Kid* (2010), 264–65; *The Karate Kid, Part III*, 265; *The Karate Kid II*, 265; *The Next Karate Kid*, 335–36
Martin, Dean: *That's My Boy*, 456
Martin, Duane: *Above the Rim*, 1–4
Martin, Mardik: *Raging Bull*, 376–78
Martin, Strother: *Hard Times*, 219–20; *Slap Shot*, 428–30
Marx, Chico: *A Day at the Races*, 124–27; *Horse Feathers*, 234–37
Marx, Groucho: *A Day at the Races*, 124–27; *Horse Feathers*, 234–37
Marx, Harpo: *A Day at the Races*, 124–27; *Horse Feathers*, 234–37
Marx, Zeppo: *Horse Feathers*, 234–37
Mason, James: *Heaven Can Wait*, 222–24
Mastrantonio, Mary Elizabeth: *The Color of Money*, 109–12
Masur, Richard: *Semi-Tough*, 419–21
Match Point, 307–9
Matthau, Walter: *The Bad News Bears* (1976), 26–28
Maxwell, Marilyn: *Champion*, 91–94
Mazurki, Mike: *Night and the City*, 336–37
McAvoy, James: *Wimbledon*, 483–85
McCarthy, Kevin: *Kansas City Bomber*, 262–63
McConaughey, Matthew: *We Are Marshall*, 472–74
McCormick, Mary: *Mystery, Alaska*, 326–28
McCormick, Myron: *The Hustler*, 237–39
McCracken, Jeff: *Running Brave*, 408–11
McCullough, David: *Seabiscuit*, 416–18
McDonald, Christopher: *Happy Gilmore*, 216–18
McDonald, Francis: *Battling Butler*, 38–40
McDonnell, Mary: *Blue Chips*, 63–65
McGill, Bruce: *Cinderella Man*, 97–99; *The Legend of Bagger Vance*, 282–85; *61**, 426–28; *Wildcats*, 481–83
McGillis, Kelly: *The Babe*, 24–26
McGinley, Ted: *Major League: Back to the Minors*, 304
McGraw, Tim: *The Blind Side*, 60–63; *Friday Night Lights*, 181–82
McGuigan, Barry: *The Boxer*, 69–72
McGuire, Michael: *Hard Times*, 219–20
McGwire, Mark: *61**, 426–28
McLane, Greg: *Purely Belter*, 370–72
McQueen, Steve: *Junior Bonner*, 259–61; *Le Mans*, 285–87
McShane, Ian: *We Are Marshall*, 472–74
McSorley, Gerald: *The Boxer*, 69–72
Meaney, Colm: *The Damned United*, 118–21
Mean Machine, 309–10
Mendenhall, David: *Over the Top*, 346–47
Menjou, Adolph: *Golden Boy*, 195–98
Men with Brooms, 310–12
Meredith, Burgess: *Rocky*, 387–89; *Rocky II*, 390–91; *Rocky III*, 391–93
Meyers, Jonathan Rhys: *Bend It Like Beckham*, 41–42; *Match Point*, 307–9
Michele, Michael: *Ali*, 7–10
Mickey, 312
Mifune, Toshiro: *Grand Prix*, 198–200
The Mighty Ducks, 312–15
Mike Bassett: England Manager, 315
Miklós, Zoltán: *White Palms*, 479–81
Milland, Ray: *It Happens Every Spring*, 249–51; *Rhubarb*, 385–87
Miller, Broderick: *Slap Shot 2: Breaking the Ice*, 430–31
Miller, Jonny Lee: *The Flying Scotsman*, 171–74
Miller, Omar Benson: *The Express*, 149–51
Miller, Seton: *Here Comes Mr. Jordan*, 228–31
Million Dollar Baby, 315–17
Million Dollar Legs, 317–20
Mills, Billy: *Running Brave*, 408–11
Mineo, Sal: *Somebody Up There Likes Me*, 435–37
Miracle, 320–22
The Miracle of Bern, 322

Mobarak-Shahi, Sima: *Offside*, 343–45
Modine, Matthew: *Any Given Sunday*, 20–23; *Vision Quest*, 470–71
Moffat, Donald: *The Best of Times*, 42–46; *61**, 426–28
Mofokeng, Patrick: *Invictus*, 245–47
Montand, Yves: *Grand Prix*, 198–200
Montgomery, Robert: *Here Comes Mr. Jordan*, 228–31
Moore, Bobby: *Victory*, 469–70
Moore, Dickie: *Million Dollar Legs*, 317–20
Moorehead, Agnes: *The Stratton Story*, 444–46
Moore, Julianne: *The Big Lebowski*, 46–50
Moore, Kenny: *Personal Best*, 353–55; *Without Limits*, 488–89
Moore, Norma: *Fear Strikes Out*, 156–58
Moreland, Mantan: *Spirit of Youth*, 438–40
Morgan, Debbi: *Love and Basketball*, 297–99
Morgan, Peter: *The Damned United*, 118–21
Moriarty, Cathy: *Raging Bull*, 376–78
Moriarty, Michael: *Bang the Drum Slowly*, 33–35
Morita, Pat: *The Karate Kid* (1984), 263–64; *The Karate Kid II*, 265; *The Karate Kid, Part III*, 265; *The Next Karate Kid*, 335–36
Morris, Jimmy: *The Rookie*, 399–402
Morrow, Vic: *The Bad News Bears* (1976), 26–28
Mortimer, Emily: *Match Point*, 307–9
Morton, Amy: *Rookie of the Year*, 402–5
motorcycle racing: *Winners Take All*, 485; *The World's Fastest Indian*, 489–91
Movie Movie, 322–23
Mr. Baseball, 323–25
Mr. Destiny, 325–26
Mr. 3000, 326
Mueller-Stahl, Armin: *The Power of One*, 359–61
Muhammad, Herbert: *The Greatest*, 200–202
Muldowney, Shirley: *Heart Like a Wheel*, 220–22
Mulligan, Robert: *Fear Strikes Out*, 156–58
Mulroney, Dermot: *Angels in the Outfield* (1994), 18–20
Munro, Burt: *The World's Fastest Indian*, 489–91
Munshin, Jules: *Take Me Out to the Ball Game*, 451–53
Murphy, Aaron: *The World's Fastest Indian*, 489–91
Murray, Bill: *Kingpin*, 266–68
Muse, Clarence: *The Black Stallion*, 56–57; *Spirit of Youth*, 438–40
MVP: Most Valuable Primate, 326
MVP 2: Most Vertical Primate, 326
Mystery, Alaska, 326–28

Nacho Libre, 329
Nagra, Parminder: *Bend It Like Beckham*, 41–42
National Velvet, 245, 329–32
The Natural, 332–35
Necessary Roughness, 335
Negro baseball leagues: *The Bingo Long Travelling All-Stars and Motor Kings*, 53–56
Neill, Sam: *Wimbledon*, 483–85
Nelson, Craig T.: *All the Right Moves*, 10–12; *Blades of Glory*, 58–60
Nelson, Ralph: *Requiem for a Heavyweight*, 383–85
Newman, Paul: *The Color of Money*, 109–12; *The Hustler*, 237–39; *Slap Shot*, 428–30; *Somebody Up There Likes Me*, 435–37; *U.S. Steel Hour*, 35; *Winning*, 486–87
New York Giants: *Big Fan*, 46
New York Knicks: *Eddie*, 139–41
New York Yankees: *The Babe*, 24–26; *The Babe Ruth Story*, 26; *Damn Yankees*, 121–23; *Everyone's Hero*, 147–49; *Pride of the Yankees*, 365–68; *The Scout*, 415–16; *61**, 426–28
The Next Karate Kid, 335–36
Nicholas, Thomas Ian: *Rookie of the Year*, 402–5
Nielsen, Brigitte: *Rocky IV*, 394–95
Nielsen, Leslie: *Men with Brooms*, 310–12
Night and the City, 336–37
Night Game, 337–38
Nivola, Alessandro: *Goal! The Dream Begins*, 192–95
Nobody's Perfect, 338

No Holds Barred, 338
Nolte, Nick: *Blue Chips,* 63–65; *North Dallas Forty,* 338–40
North Dallas Forty, 338–40
North Shore, 340
Nouri, Michael: *Finding Forrester,* 168–70
Nunns, Bill: *He Got Game,* 224–27

O, 341–43
Oakie, Jack: *Million Dollar Legs,* 317–20
Oates, Warren: *Two-Lane Blacktop,* 464–67
Obree, Graeme: *The Flying Scotsman,* 171–74
O'Brien, Pat: *Indianapolis Speedway,* 244; *Knute Rockne: All American,* 268–70
O'Connell, Jerry: *Jerry Maguire,* 253–56
Odet, Clifford: *Golden Boy,* 195–98
O'Donnell, Chris: *School Ties,* 413–15
O'Donnell, Rosie: *A League of Their Own,* 276–79
Offside, 343–45
O'Grady, Gail: *Celtic Pride,* 84–87
Oher, Michael: *The Blind Side,* 60–63
O'Keefe, Michael: *Caddyshack,* 82–83; *The Slugger's Wife,* 432–34
Olivares, Geraldo: *The Great Match,* 205–7
Olympic games: *Chariots of Fire,* 94–97; *Cool Runnings,* 113–15; *The Cutting Edge,* 115–17; *The Hammer,* 216; *Ice Princess,* 242–44; *Million Dollar Legs,* 317–20; *Miracle,* 320–22; *Peaceful Warrior,* 352; *Personal Best,* 353–55; *Prefontaine,* 361–63; *Running,* 407–8; *Running Brave,* 408–11; *Without Limits,* 488–89
On a Clear Day, 345
O'Neal, Ryan: *The Main Event,* 300–302
O'Neal, Shaquille: *Blue Chips,* 63–65
O'Neal, Tatum: *The Bad News Bears* (1976), 26–28
O'Neil, Sally: *Battling Butler,* 38–40
O'Neill, Ed: *Blue Chips,* 63–65
One on One, 346
Ontkean, Michael: *Slap Shot,* 428–30
O'Quinn, Terry: *The Cutting Edge,* 115–17
O'Sullivan, Maureen: *A Day at the Races,* 124–27
Oswalt, Patton: *Balls of Fury,* 32–33
Out Cold, 346
Outerbridge, Peter: *Men with Brooms,* 310–12
Over the Top, 346–47
Oxford Blues, 347

Pacino, Al: *Any Given Sunday,* 20–23; *Bobby Deerfield,* 67
Page, Ellen: *Whip It,* 474–77
Page, Gale: *Knute Rockne: All American,* 268–70
Palance, Holly: *The Best of Times,* 42–46
Palmer, Keke: *The Longshots,* 292–94
Palmer, Lilli: *Body and Soul,* 67–69
Panahi, Jafar: *Offside,* 343–45
Panettiere, Hayden: *Ice Princess,* 242–44; *Remember the Titans,* 379–82
Panjabi, Archie: *Bend It Like Beckham,* 41–42
Papathanassiou, Vangelis: *Chariots of Fire,* 94–97
Paper Lion, 348
Paquin, Anna: *Finding Forrester,* 168–70
Paradise Alley, 348
Pardue, Kip: *Remember the Titans,* 379–82
Parker, Molly: *Men with Brooms,* 310–12
Pastime, 348–50
Pat and Mike, 350–52
Patton, Will: *Remember the Titans,* 379–82
Paxton, Bill: *The Greatest Game Ever Played,* 202–5
Paxton, James: *The Greatest Game Ever Played,* 202–5
Payne, John: *Indianapolis Speedway,* 244
Peace, David: *The Damned United,* 118–21
Peaceful Warrior, 352
Peckham, Tony: *Invictus,* 245–47
Peckinpah, Sam: *Junior Bonner,* 259–61
Pelé: *Victory,* 469–70
Penitentiary, 352–53
Penitentiary II, 353
Penitentiary III, 353
Penn, Chris: *All the Right Moves,* 10–12
Peralta, Stacy: *Lords of Dogtown,* 294–97
Peregrym, Missy: *Stick It,* 441–42
Perez, Rosie: *White Men Can't Jump,* 477–79
Perkins, Anthony: *Fear Strikes Out,* 156–58
Perrine, Valerie: *The Last American Hero,* 274–76

Persian Gulf War: *The Big Lebowski*, 46–50
Personal Best, 353–55, 488–89
Pesci, Joe: *Raging Bull*, 376–78
Peters, Bernadette: *The Longest Yard* (1974), 290–92
Peters, Jean: *It Happens Every Spring*, 249–51
Petty, Lori: *A League of Their Own*, 276–79
Pevney, Joseph: *Body and Soul*, 67–69
Phar Lap, 355
Phifer, Mekhi: *O*, 341–43
Philadelphia Eagles: *Invincible*, 247–49
Phoenix, Rain: *O*, 341–43
Piazza, Ben: *The Bad News Bears* (1976), 26–28
Piersall, Jim: *Fear Strikes Out*, 156–58
Ping-Pong: *Balls of Fury*, 32–33; *Ping Pong Playa*, 355–57
Ping Pong Playa, 355–57
Pinkins, Tonya: *Above the Rim*, 1–4
Pistol: The Birth of a Legend, 357
Pittsburgh Pirates: *Angels in the Outfield* (1951), 16–18
Pizzo, Angelo: *Rudy*, 405–7
Plank, Scott: *Pastime*, 348–50
Players, 358
Playing Away, 358
Play It to the Bone, 358
Plimpton, George: *Paper Lion*, 348
Plummer, Glenn: *Pastime*, 348–50
Poehler, Amy: *Blades of Glory*, 58–60
Point Break, 358
Poitier, Sidney: *Let's Do It Again*, 287
Polonsky, Abraham: *Body and Soul*, 67–69
pool: *The Color of Money*, 109–12; *The Hustler*, 237–39; *Poolhall Junkies*, 358–59
Poolhall Junkies, 358–59
Porter, Sean: *Gridiron Gang*, 213–14
Porterfield, Ellary: *Sugar*, 447–50
Potter, Monica: *Without Limits*, 488–89
The Power of One, 359–61
Pratt, Kyla: *Love and Basketball*, 297–99
Prefontaine, 361–63
Prefontaine, Steve: *Without Limits*, 488–89
Presley, Elvis: *Speedway*, 437; *Spinout*, 438
Preston, Kelly: *Jerry Maguire*, 253–56; *For Love of the Game*, 174–78
Preston, Robert: *Junior Bonner*, 259–61; *Semi-Tough*, 419–21
Price, Paige Lyn: *All the Right Moves*, 10–12
Pride, 363–65
The Pride of St. Louis, 365
Pride of the Yankees, 365–68
Priestly, Tom: *Above the Rim*, 1–4
Prince-Bythewood, Gina: *Love and Basketball*, 297–99
prisoners of war: *Victory*, 469–70
The Prizefighter and the Lady, 368
The Program, 368–70
Pryce, Jonathan: *Leatherheads*, 279–82
Pryor, Richard: *The Bingo Long Travelling All-Stars and Motor Kings*, 53–56
Purcell, Lee: *Big Wednesday*, 50–53
Purely Belter, 370–72

Q, Maggie: *Balls of Fury*, 32–33
Quaid, Dennis: *Any Given Sunday*, 20–23; *Breaking Away*, 72–75; *Everybody's All-American*, 145–47; *The Express*, 149–51; *The Rookie*, 399–402
Quaid, Randy: *Days of Thunder*, 127–29; *Kingpin*, 266–68; *The Slugger's Wife*, 432–34
Quinn, Anthony: *City for Conquest*, 99–100; *Requiem for a Heavyweight*, 383–85
Quinn, J. C.: *The Babe*, 24–26

Race the Sun, 373
racing. *See* auto racing; cycling; horse racing; motorcycle racing
Racing Stripes, 373
Rad, 373
Radies, Orion: *White Palms*, 479–81
Radio, 374–76
Raging Bull, 376–78
Rains, Claude: *Here Comes Mr. Jordan*, 228–31
Ralston, Jobyna: *The Freshman*, 178–81
Ramis, Harold: *Caddyshack*, 82–83
Ramsey, Laura: *She's the Man*, 423–25
Rasuk, Victor: *Lords of Dogtown*, 294–97
Rattian, Terrence: *The Final Test*, 168
Rauch, Siegfried: *Le Mans*, 285–87
Rawat, Chitrashi: *Chak De! India*, 87–90

Ray, Aldo: *Pat and Mike,* 350–52
Read, James: *Eight Men Out,* 141–43
Ready to Rumble, 378–79
Reagan, Ronald: *Knute Rockne: All American,* 268–70
Rebound, 379
Redford, Robert: *Downhill Racer,* 135–37; *The Legend of Bagger Vance,* 282–85; *The Natural,* 332–35
Redgrave, Michael: *The Loneliness of the Long-Distance Runner,* 288–90
Red Line 7000, 379
Reed, Lou: *Blue in the Face,* 65–66
Reed, Nikki: *Lords of Dogtown,* 294–97
Reed, Pamela: *The Best of Times,* 42–46
Rees, Jed: *Men with Brooms,* 310–12
Reeve, Christopher: *Everyone's Hero,* 147–49
Reeves, Keanu: *The Replacements,* 382–83
Reid, Tara: *The Big Lebowski,* 46–50
Reilly, John C.: *For Love of the Game,* 174–78; *Talladega Nights: The Ballad of Ricky Bobby,* 453–55
Reiner, Rob: *Everyone's Hero,* 147–49
Remember the Titans, 379–82
Reno, Kelly: *The Black Stallion,* 56–57
The Replacements, 382–83
Requiem for a Heavyweight, 383–85
Resurrecting the Champ, 385
Revere, Anne: *Body and Soul,* 67–69; *National Velvet,* 329–32
Reversal, 385
Reynolds, Burt: *The Longest Yard* (1974), 290–92; *Mystery, Alaska,* 326–28; *Semi-Tough,* 419–21; *Stroker Ace,* 447
Rhubarb, 385–87
Rhymes, Busta: *Finding Forrester,* 168–70
Rhys-Davies, John: *Great White Hype,* 209–11
Rich, Irene: *The Champ* (1932), 90–91
Ri'chard, Robert: *Coach Carter,* 102–4
Richard-Serrano, Magaly: *Dans les Cordes (On the Ropes),* 123–24
Richardson, Tony: *The Loneliness of the Long-Distance Runner,* 288–90
Richter, Andy: *Talladega Nights: The Ballad of Ricky Bobby,* 453–55
The Ringer, 387
Ringside Maisie, 387
Ritchie, Michael: *The Bad News Bears* (1976), 26–28; *The Bad News Bears Go to Japan,* 29–30; *Downhill Racer,* 135–37; *Semi-Tough,* 419–21; *Wildcats,* 481–83
Ritt, Martin: *The Slugger's Wife,* 432–34
Robbins, Marty: *Hell on Wheels,* 227
Robbins, Tim: *Bull Durham,* 78–81
Roberts, Rachel: *This Sporting Life,* 456–58
Robinson, Jackie: *The Jackie Robinson Story,* 252–53
Robinson, John: *Lords of Dogtown,* 294–97
Robinson, Leon: *Above the Rim,* 1–4; *Cool Runnings,* 113–15
Robinson, Randy ("The Ram"): *The Wrestler* (2008), 492–93
Rochon, Lela: *Any Given Sunday,* 20–23
The Rocket: Maurice Richard, 387
Rockne, Knute: *Knute Rockne: All American,* 268–70
Rocky, 248, 249, 387–89
Rocky Balboa, 389–90
Rocky II, 390–91
Rocky III, 391–93
Rocky IV, 394–95
Rocky V, 395–97
rodeo: *8 Seconds,* 143–44; *Junior Bonner,* 259–61
Rodriguez, Michelle: *Girlfight,* 187–90
Rollerball, 397–99
roller derby: *Kansas City Bomber,* 262–63; *Whip It,* 474–77
Roman, Ruth: *Champion,* 91–94; *Strangers on a Train,* 442–44
Rooker, Michael: *Days of Thunder,* 127–29
The Rookie, 399–402
Rookie of the Year, 402–5
Rooney, Mickey: *The Big Wheel,* 53; *The Black Stallion,* 56–57; *National Velvet,* 329–32; *Requiem for a Heavyweight,* 383–85
Root, Stephen: *Dodgeball: A True Underdog Story,* 131–35; *Leatherheads,* 279–82
Roseanne: *Blue in the Face,* 65–66
Ross, Ted: *The Bingo Long Travelling All-Stars and Motor Kings,* 53–56
Ross, Chelcie: *Hoosiers,* 231–34

Rossen, Robert: *Body and Soul,* 67–69
Rossi, Leo: *Heart Like a Wheel,* 220–22
Rourke, Mickey: *The Wrestler* (2008), 492–93
Rousselot, Phillipe: *Remember the Titans,* 379–82
rowing: *College,* 40, 108–9; *Oxford Blues,* 347; *True Blue,* 464
Rudy, 405–7
rugby: *Forever Strong,* 178; *Invictus,* 245–47; *This Sporting Life,* 456–58
Rule, Janice: *American Flyers,* 13–16
Ruman, Sig: *A Day at the Races,* 124–27
Run, Fatboy, Run, 207
Running, 407–8
Running Brave, 408–11
Russ, William: *Pastime,* 348–50
Russell, Kurt: *The Best of Times,* 42–46; *Miracle,* 320–22
Russell, Nipsy: *Wildcats,* 481–83
Russo, Rene: *Major League,* 302–4; *Tin Cup,* 459–61
Ruth, Babe: *The Babe,* 24–26; *The Babe Ruth Story,* 26; *Everyone's Hero,* 147–49; *Pride of the Yankees,* 365–68
Ryan, Meg: *Against the Ropes,* 5–6
Ryan, Robert: *The Set-Up,* 421–22

Sackler, Howard: *The Great White Hope,* 207–9
Sadeqi, Ayda: *Offside,* 343–45
Safe at Home!, 412
Sahni, Jaideep: *Chak De! India,* 87–90
sailing: *Wind,* 485
Saint, Eva Marie: *Grand Prix,* 198–200
Saint Ralph, 412
Sale, Robert: *Ali,* 7–10
Salley, John: *Eddie,* 139–41
Sand, Paul: *The Main Event,* 300–302
Sanders, Jay O.: *Angels in the Outfield* (1994), 18–20
Sandler, Adam: *Happy Gilmore,* 216–18; *The Longest Yard* (2005), 292
The Sandlot, 412
San Francisco Giants: *The Fan,* 152–56
Santiago, Ray: *Girlfight,* 187–90
Sarandon, Susan: *Bull Durham,* 78–81
Saxon, John: *Enter the Dragon,* 144–45
Sayles, John: *Eight Men Out,* 141–43; *Girlfight,* 187–90
Schoeffling, Michael: *Vision Quest,* 470–71
School Ties, 413–15
Schrader, Paul: *Raging Bull,* 376–78
Schram, Bitty: *A League of Their Own,* 276–79
Schroder, Rick: *The Champ* (1979), 91
Scorsese, Martin: *The Color of Money,* 109–12; *Raging Bull,* 376–78
Scott, George C.: *The Hustler,* 237–39
Scott, Tony: *Days of Thunder,* 127–29
The Scout, 415–16
Seabiscuit, 416–18
Segall, Harry: *Here Comes Mr. Jordan,* 228–31
Selleck, Tom: *Mr. Baseball,* 323–25
Semi-Pro, 418–19
Semi-Tough, 419–21
Serling, Rod: *Requiem for a Heavyweight,* 383–85
The Set-Up, 421–22
Sexton, Brent: *Radio,* 374–76
Shaara, Michael: *For Love of the Game,* 174–78
Shakespeare adaptations: *O,* 341–43; *She's the Man,* 423–25
Shakur, Tupac: *Above the Rim,* 1–4
Shalhoub, Tony: *Against the Ropes,* 5–6
Shaolin Soccer, 422
Shaver, Helen: *The Color of Money,* 109–12
Shawkat, Alia: *Whip It,* 474–77
Shaw, Stan: *The Bingo Long Travelling All-Stars and Motor Kings,* 53–56
Sheen, Charlie: *Eight Men Out,* 141–43; *Major League,* 302–4; *Major League II,* 305–6
Sheen, Martin: *O,* 341–43
Sheen, Michael: *The Damned United,* 118–21
Sheffer, Craig: *The Program,* 368–70
Shelley, Rachael: *Lagaan: Once Upon a Time in India,* 271–74
Shelton, Ron: *Bull Durham,* 78–81; *Great White Hype,* 209–11; *Tin Cup,* 459–61; *White Men Can't Jump,* 477–79
Shergar, 422–23
Sheridan, Ann: *City for Conquest,* 99–100
Sheridan, Jim: *The Boxer,* 69–72
She's the Man, 423–25
Shih, Kien: *Enter the Dragon,* 144–45

Shioya, Toshi: *Mr. Baseball*, 323–25
Shire, Talia: *Rocky*, 387–89; *Rocky II*, 390–91; *Rocky III*, 391–93; *Rocky V*, 395–97
A Shot at Glory, 425
Shue, Elisabeth: *Gracie*, 198; *The Karate Kid* (1984), 263–64
Side Out, 425
silent films: *Battling Butler*, 38–40; *City Lights*, 100–102; *College*, 108–9; *The Freshman*, 178–81
Sillitoe, Alan: *The Loneliness of the Long-Distance Runner*, 288–90
Silver, Ron: *Ali*, 7–10
Simmons, J. K.: *For Love of the Game*, 174–78
Simon, Neil: *The Slugger's Wife*, 432–34
Sinatra, Frank: *Take Me Out to the Ball Game*, 451–53
Sinatra, Nancy: *Speedway*, 438
Sinclair, John Gordon: *Gregory's Girl*, 212–13
Singh, Gracy: *Lagaan: Once Upon a Time in India*, 271–74
Sit Tight, 425–26
The 6th Man, 426
*61**, 426–28
skateboarding: *Gleaming the Cube*, 190–91; *Lords of Dogtown*, 294–97; *MVP 2: Most Vertical Primate*, 326; *Street Dreams*, 446–47
Skerritt, Tom: *Ice Castles*, 240–42
skiing: *Downhill Racer*, 135–37
Skolnick, Barry: *Mean Machine*, 309–10
Slap Shot, 428–30
Slap Shot 2: Breaking the Ice, 430–31
Slap Shot 3: The Junior League, 431
The Slaughter Rule, 431
Sloan, Everett: *Somebody Up There Likes Me*, 435–37
The Slugger's Wife, 432–34
Smith, Adrian: *The Flying Scotsman*, 171–74
Smith, Alexis: *Gentleman Jim*, 186–87
Smith, H. Allen: *Rhubarb*, 385–87
Smith, Jada Pinkett: *Ali*, 7–10
Smith, Jaden: *The Karate Kid* (2010), 264–65
Smith, Jewel: *Spirit of Youth*, 438–40
Smith, Lane: *The Mighty Ducks*, 312–15
Smith, Tasha: *The Longshots*, 292–94
Smith, Will: *Ali*, 7–10; *The Legend of Bagger Vance*, 282–85
Smith, William: *The Last American Hero*, 274–76
Snipes, Wesley: *The Fan*, 152–56; *Major League*, 302–4; *White Men Can't Jump*, 477–79; *Wildcats*, 481–83
snowboarding: *Out Cold*, 346
soccer: *The Arsenal Stadium Mystery*, 23; *Bend It Like Beckham*, 41–42; *The Big Green*, 46; *The Damned United*, 118–21; *Fever Pitch* (1996), 159–60; *Goal! The Dream Begins*, 192–95; *Goal! II: Living the Dream*, 195; *Goal! III*, 195; *The Goalie's Anxiety at the Penalty Kick*, 195; *Gracie*, 198; *The Great Game* (1930), 205; *The Great Game* (1953), 205; *The Great Match*, 205–7; *Gregory's Girl*, 212–13; *Her Best Move*, 227; *Kicking & Screaming*, 265; *Ladybugs*, 271; *Looking for Eric*, 294; *Mean Machine*, 309–10; *Mike Bassett: England Manager*, 315; *The Miracle of Bern*, 322; *Offside*, 343–45; *Purely Belter*, 370–72; *Shaolin Soccer*, 422; *She's the Man*, 423–25; *A Shot at Glory*, 425; *Soccer Dog: Movie*, 434; *There's Only One Jimmy Grimble*, 456; *Victory*, 469–70; *When Saturday Comes*, 474; *Yesterday's Hero*, 494
Soccer Dog: The Movie, 434
softball: *Beer League*, 40; *Squeeze Play*, 440
Sokolinski, Stéphanie: *Dans les Cordes (On the Ropes)*, 123–24
Sokol, Marilyn: *Basketball Diaries*, 36–38
Somebody Up There Likes Me, 435–37
Somers, Suzanne: *Yesterday's Hero*, 494
Sorvino, Mira: *Blue in the Face*, 65–66
Soto, Algenis Perez: *Sugar*, 447–50
Space Jam, 437
Spall, Timothy: *The Damned United*, 118–21
Sparv, Camilla: *Downhill Racer*, 135–37
Special Olympics: *The Ringer*, 387
Speck, Will: *Blades of Glory*, 58–60
Speed Racer, 437
Speedway, 438
Spinout, 438
Spirit of Youth, 438–40

Split Decisions, 440
The Square Ring, 440
Squeeze Play, 440
St. Louis Cardinals: *The Pride of St. Louis*, 365
Stallone, Sylvester: *Over the Top*, 346–47; *Rocky*, 387–89; *Rocky Balboa*, 389–90; *Rocky II*, 390–91; *Rocky III*, 391–93; *Rocky IV*, 394–95; *Rocky V*, 395–97; *Victory*, 469–70
Stanton, Harry Dean: *Two-Lane Blacktop*, 464–67
Stanwyck, Barbara: *Golden Boy*, 195–98
Stapleton, Jean: *Damn Yankees*, 121–23
Statham, Jason: *Death Race*, 129–30; *Mean Machine*, 309–10
Stealing Home, 440–41
Steen, Jessica: *Slap Shot 2: Breaking the Ice*, 430–31
Steinberg, Hank: *61**, 426–28
Sterling, Jan: *Rhubarb*, 385–87
Stern, Daniel: *Breaking Away*, 72–75; *Celtic Pride*, 84–87; *Rookie of the Year*, 402–5
Stevens, Gary: *Seabiscuit*, 416–18
Stevenson, Juliet: *Bend It Like Beckham*, 41–42
Stewart, Jimmy: *The Stratton Story*, 444–46
Stewart, Paul: *Champion*, 91–94
Stick It, 441–42
Stiles, Julia: *O*, 341–43
Stiller, Ben: *Dodgeball: A True Underdog Story*, 131–35
Stone, Lindsay: *Bring It On*, 77–78
Stone, Oliver: *Any Given Sunday*, 20–23
Stott, Ken: *The Boxer*, 69–72
Strangers on a Train, 442–44
Strathairn, David: *Eight Men Out*, 141–43; *We Are Marshall*, 472–74
The Stratton Story, 444–46
Street Dreams, 446–47
Streets of Gold, 447
Streisand, Barbra: *The Main Event*, 300–302
Stroker Ace, 447
Strong, Mark: *Fever Pitch* (1996), 159–60
Stump, Al: *Cobb*, 104–8
Sturgis, John: *Le Mans*, 285–87
Sugar, 447–50
Sugar and Spice, 450
Summer Catch, 450
Sunset Park, 450
Super Bowl: *Black Sunday*, 58
Suplee, Ethan: *Remember the Titans*, 379–82
Surfer, Dude, 450
surfing: *Big Wednesday*, 50–53; *Blue Crush*, 65; *In God's Hands*, 244; *North Shore*, 340; *Point Break*, 358; *Surfer, Dude*, 450
Sutherland, Donald: *Without Limits*, 488–89
Swank, Hilary: *Million Dollar Baby*, 315–17; *The Next Karate Kid*, 335–36
Swanson, Kristy: *The Program*, 368–70
Sweeney, D. B.: *The Cutting Edge*, 115–17; *Eight Men Out*, 141–43
swimming: *On a Clear Day*, 345; *Pride*, 363–65
Sylvester, Harold: *Vision Quest*, 470–71
Syracuse University: *The Express*, 149–51
Szpindel, Louise: *Dans les Cordes (On the Ropes)*, 123–24

T, Mr.: *Rocky III*, 391–93
table tennis: *Balls of Fury*, 32–33; *Ping Pong Playa*, 355–57
Takakura, Ken: *Mr. Baseball*, 323–25
Takanashi, Aya: *Mr. Baseball*, 323–25
Take Down, 451
Take Me Out to the Ball Game, 451–53
Talent for the Game, 453
Talladega Nights: The Ballad of Ricky Bobby, 453–55
Tampa Bay Devil Rays: *The Rookie*, 399–402
Ta Ra Rum Pum, 455
Tarver, Antonio: *Rocky Balboa*, 389–90
Tatum, Channing: *She's the Man*, 423–25
Taylor, Christine: *Dodgeball: A True Underdog Story*, 131–35
Taylor, Elizabeth: *National Velvet*, 329–32
Taylor, James: *Two-Lane Blacktop*, 464–67
Taylor, Lawrence: *Any Given Sunday*, 20–23
Teen Wolf, 455
television movies, 507–10
tennis: *The Break*, 72; *Match Point*, 307–9; *Players*, 358; *Strangers on a Train*, 442–44; *Tennis, Anyone?*, 455–56; *Wimbledon*, 483–85
Tennis, Anyone?, 455–56
terrorism: *Black Sunday*, 58

Tesich, Steve: *American Flyers,* 13–16; *Breaking Away,* 72–75
Tevis, Walter: *The Hustler,* 237–39
Texas Western University: *Glory Road,* 191–92
Thalberg, Irving: *A Day at the Races,* 124–27
That's My Boy, 456
Thaxter, Phyllis: *Jim Thorpe: All American,* 256–58
There's Only One Jimmy Grimble, 456
Theron, Charlize: *The Legend of Bagger Vance,* 282–85
This Sporting Life, 456–58
Thomas, Richard: *Winning,* 486–87
Thompson, Lea: *All the Right Moves,* 10–12
Thomson, R. H.: *Full-Court Miracle,* 182–84
Thornton, Billy Bob: *The Bad News Bears* (2005), 28–29; *Friday Night Lights,* 181–82
Thorpe, Jim: *Jim Thorpe: All American,* 256–58
Thrashing, 458–59
Tierney, Gene: *Night and the City,* 336–37
Tierney, Maura: *Semi-Pro,* 418–19
Tin Cup, 459–61
Tintori, John: *Eight Men Out,* 141–43
Tirelli, Jaime: *Girlfight,* 187–90; *Sugar,* 447–50
Tobias, George: *The Set-Up,* 421–22
Todd, Thelma: *Horse Feathers,* 234–37
Todd, Tony: *Tournament of Dreams,* 461–63
Tomei, Marisa: *The Wrestler* (2008), 492–93
Tomlin, Lily: *Blue in the Face,* 65–66
Toney, James: *Ali,* 7–10; *Against the Ropes,* 5–6
To Please a Lady, 461
Torn, Rip: *Dodgeball: A True Underdog Story,* 131–35
Toronto Maple Leafs: *The Love Guru,* 299
Totter, Audrey: *The Set-Up,* 421–22
Tournament of Dreams, 461–63
Towne, Robert: *Personal Best,* 353–55; *Without Limits,* 488–89
Trachtenberg, Michelle: *Ice Princess,* 242–44
track and field: *Across the Tracks,* 4–5; *Chariots of Fire,* 94–97; *Jim Thorpe: All American,* 256–58; *The Loneliness of the Long-Distance Runner,* 288–90; *Personal Best,* 353–55; *Prefontaine,* 361–63; *Run, Fatboy, Run,* 207; *Running,* 207–408; *Running Brave,* 408–11; *Saint Ralph,* 412; *Without Limits,* 488–89; *The World's Greatest Athlete,* 491
Tracy, Spencer: *Pat and Mike,* 350–52
Trading Hearts, 463–64
Trintignant, Jean-Louis: *A Man and a Woman,* 306
The Triplets of Belleville, 464
True Blue, 464
Tsai, Jimmy: *Ping Pong Playa,* 355–57
Tudyk, Alan: *Dodgeball: A True Underdog Story,* 131–35
Tulloch, Jonathan: *Purely Belter,* 370–72
Turner, Mae: *Spirit of Youth,* 438–40
Turturro, John: *The Big Lebowski,* 46–50; *The Color of Money,* 109–12; *He Got Game,* 224–27
Two for the Money, 464
Two-Lane Blacktop, 464–67
Tyler, Aisha: *Balls of Fury,* 32–33

Uecker, Bob: *Major League,* 302–4; *Major League: Back to the Minors,* 304; *Major League II,* 305–6
Undisputed, 468
Union, Gabrielle: *Bring It On,* 77–78
University of Notre Dame: *Knute Rockne: All American,* 268–70; *Rudy,* 405–7
University of Southern California: *Love and Basketball,* 297–99
The Unknown Cyclist, 468
U.S. Steel Hour, 35

Van Patten, Joyce: *The Bad News Bears* (1976), 26–28
Van Patten, Vincent: *The Break,* 72
Van Peebles, Mario: *Ali,* 7–10
Van Sant, Gus: *Finding Forrester,* 168–70
Varsity Blues, 469
Vaughn, Vince: *Dodgeball: A True Underdog Story,* 131–35
Ventimiglia, Milo: *Rocky Balboa,* 389–90
Verdon, Gwen: *Damn Yankees,* 121–23
Victory, 469–70
video, direct to, 507–10
Vidor, King: *The Champ* (1932), 90–91
Vincent, Frank: *Raging Bull,* 376–78

Vincent, Jan Michael: *Big Wednesday*, 50–53
Vision Quest, 470–71
Vogler, Karl Michael: *Downhill Racer*, 135–37
Voight, Jon: *Ali*, 7–10; *The Champ* (1979), 91; *Glory Road*, 191–92
volleyball: *All You've Got*, 12; *The Iron Ladies*, 249; *The Iron Ladies 2*, 249; *Side Out*, 425
von Sydow, Max: *Victory*, 469–70

Wagner, Robert: *Winning*, 486–87
Wahlberg, Mark: *Basketball Diaries*, 36–38; *Invincible*, 247–49
Walker, Joseph: *Here Comes Mr. Jordan*, 228–31
Walker, Robert: *Strangers on a Train*, 442–44
Walsh, J. T.: *Blue Chips*, 63–65
Walsh, M. Emmet: *The Best of Times*, 42–46
Walston, Ray: *Damn Yankees*, 121–23
Walter, Jessica: *Grand Prix*, 198–200
Wang, Wayne: *Blue in the Face*, 65–66
Ward, David: *Major League*, 302–4
Warden, Jack: *Brian's Song*, 75–77; *Heaven Can Wait*, 222–24; *The Replacements*, 382–83
Warner, Julie: *Stick It*, 441–42
Warren, Jennifer: *Ice Castles*, 240–42; *Slap Shot*, 428–30
Washington, Denzel: *He Got Game*, 224–27; *Remember the Titans*, 379–82
Washington, Kerry: *Against the Ropes*, 5–6
Washington Redskins: *The Replacements*, 382–83
Washington Senators: *Damn Yankees*, 121–23
The Waterboy, 472
Watson, Emily: *The Boxer*, 69–72
Watson, Minor: *The Jackie Robinson Story*, 252–53
Wayans, Damon: *Celtic Pride*, 84–87; *Great White Hype*, 209–11
Wayans, Marlon: *Above the Rim*, 1–4
We Are Marshall, 472–74
Weathers, Carl: *Happy Gilmore*, 216–18; *Rocky*, 387–89; *Rocky II*, 390–91; *Rocky III*, 391–93; *Rocky IV*, 394–95
Webber, Robert: *The Great White Hope*, 207–9
Welch, Raquel: *Kansas City Bomber*, 262–63
When Saturday Comes, 474
Whip It, 474–77
White Men Can't Jump, 477–79
White Palms, 479–81
Whitmore, James: *Angels in the Outfield* (1951), 16–18
Whitney, Ann: *Sugar*, 447–50
Whitton, Margaret: *The Best of Times*, 42–46; *Major League*, 302–4
Who's Your Caddy?, 481
Widmark, Richard: *Night and the City*, 336–37
Wiig, Kristen: *Whip It*, 474–77
Wild, 485
Wildcats, 481–83
Williams, Adam: *Fear Strikes Out*, 156–58
Williams, Bill: *The Stratton Story*, 444–46
Williams, Billy Dee: *The Bingo Long Travelling All-Stars and Motor Kings*, 53–56; *Brian's Song*, 75–77
Williams, Esther: *Take Me Out to the Ball Game*, 451–53
Williams, Robin: *The Best of Times*, 42–46; *Everyone's Hero*, 147–49
Williamson, Mykelti: *Wildcats*, 481–83
Willingham, Noble: *Pastime*, 348–50
Willis, Bruce: *The Last Boy Scout*, 276
Wilson, Dennis: *Two-Lane Blacktop*, 464–67
Wimbledon, 483–85
Wind, 485
Winger, Debra: *Radio*, 374–76
Winners Take All, 485
Winner Take All, 485–86
Winning, 486–87
The Winning Team, 487
Wise, Robert: *The Set-Up*, 421–22; *Somebody Up There Likes Me*, 435–37
Withers, Googie: *Night and the City*, 336–37
Without Limits, 488–89
Wolfe, Tom: *The Last American Hero*, 274–76
women's boxing: *Dans les Cordes (On the Ropes)*, 123–24; *Girlfight*, 187–90; *Million Dollar Baby*, 315–17
Wondrous Oblivion, 489
Wood, Evan Rachel: *The Wrestler* (2008), 492–93
Wood, Sam: *A Day at the Races*, 124–27; *The Stratton Story*, 444–46
Woodard, Alfre: *Blue Chips*, 63–65; *Radio*, 374–76

Woods, James: *Any Given Sunday*, 20–23
Woodward, Joanne: *Winning*, 486–87
Wooley, Sheb: *Hoosiers*, 231–34
The World's Fastest Indian, 489–91
The World's Greatest Athlete, 491
World War II: *American Pastime*, 16; *Victory*, 469–70
The Wrestler (1974), 491–92
The Wrestler (2008), 492–93
wrestling: *...All the Marbles*, 10; *Body Slam*, 69; *Grunt! The Wrestling Movie*, 214; *Nacho Libre*, 329; *Night and the City*, 336–37; *No Holds Barred*, 338; *Paradise Alley*, 348; *Ready to Rumble*, 378–79; *Reversal*, 385; *Sit Tight*, 425–26; *Take Down*, 451; *Vision Quest*, 470–71; *The Wrestler* (1974), 491–92; *The Wrestler* (2008), 492–93
Wright, Teresa: *Pride of the Yankees*, 365–68
Wuhl, Robert: *Blue Chips*, 63–65; *Cobb*, 104–8
Wynn, Keenan: *Angels in the Outfield* (1951), 16–18

Yablans, Frank: *North Dallas Forty*, 338–40
Yates, Peter: *Breaking Away*, 72–75
Yesterday's Hero, 494
Yoba, Malik: *Cool Runnings*, 113–15
Young, Burt: *Rocky*, 387–89; *Rocky Balboa*, 389–90; *Rocky II*, 390–91; *Rocky III*, 391–93; *Rocky IV*, 394–95; *Rocky V*, 395–97
Youngblood, 494
Yu, Jessica: *Ping Pong Playa*, 355–57

Zabihi, Mahnaz: *Offside*, 343–45
Zabka, William: *The Karate Kid* (1984), 263–64
Zellweger, Renée: *Cinderella Man*, 97–99; *Jerry Maguire*, 253–56; *Leatherheads*, 279–82
Zumwalt, Rick: *Over the Top*, 346–47

ABOUT THE AUTHORS

K Edgington is an associate professor of English at Towson University in Baltimore, Maryland, where she teaches writing in the undergraduate and graduate programs. She has published articles on film, television, and popular culture and is a frequent contributor to the Magill Book Reviews series. Since 1998, she has served on the editorial board of BrickHouse Books, Maryland's oldest continually operating small press. She holds a Ph.D. in Literary Studies from the American University, Washington, D.C.

Thomas L. Erskine, professor emeritus of English, Salisbury University (Maryland), was educated at Bowdoin College, the University of Kansas (M.A.), and Emory University (Ph.D.). Having served as department chair and academic dean at Salisbury University, he founded the periodical *Literature/Film Quarterly* in 1973. Among other book projects, he coedited *Video Versions: Film Adaptations of Plays on Video* (2000) with Jim Welsh and has lived in retirement in Portland, Maine, since 2002.

Consulting editor **James M. Welsh**, professor emeritus of English at Salisbury University (Maryland), was educated at Indiana University, Bloomington, and at the University of Kansas (M.A. and Ph.D.). He was cofounding editor with Tom Erskine of *Literature/Film Quarterly* in 1973, which he then edited for thirty-three years. He coedited *The Encyclopedia of Orson Welles* with Chuck Berg and Tom Erskine (2003) and now serves in retirement as consulting editor for Scarecrow Press.